1/25

ON THE FRONT LINE

'Marie Colvin was the most courageous journalist I ever knew, and a wonderful reporter and writer.'

JON SNOW, presenter of Channel 4 News

'Marie was an extraordinary figure in the life of *The Sunday Times*, driven by a passion to cover wars in the conviction that what she did mattered. She believed profoundly that reporting could curtail the excesses of brutal regimes and make the international community take notice.' JOHN WITHEROW, Editor of *The Sunday Times*

'To the many who read her dispatches, Marie was one of the great foreign correspondents of her age, known to plunge to the point of deepest conflict and remain there for longer than anyone else. Her byline picture would gaze seriously out of the pages of this paper. But although she was, of course, serious, brave, clever and phenomenally daring, those weren't the qualities that made her such a great friend. Marie was the most feminine of women, the girliest of girls.' ALEX SHULMAN, Editor of British *Vogue*

'She was a brave and tireless reporter and an inspiration to women in her profession.' DAVID CAMERON, Prime Minister

'It was such fun and such a privilege being Marie's friend because she was at once the fearless, committed, globally distinguished war correspondent, and at the same time a total girl's girl. She really cared about her friends. She was kind. She made time for us, she listened, she cheered us up and let us cheer her up. And she would always laugh – especially at herself.' HELEN FIELDING, author

'She was brave, magnificent, tenacious.'

ANDREW NEIL, presenter and former Editor of *The Sunday Times*

'Marie Colvin embodied the highest values of journalism through-out her long and distinguished career as a foreign correspondent for *The Sunday Times*. For years she shone a light on stories that others could not and placed herself in the most dangerous envi-ronments to do so.'   WILLIAM HAGUE, Foreign Secretary

'She was passionate, funny and deeply caring. Marie was a lioness – she seemed to be indestructible, she was indomitable.'
CHRISTIANE AMANPOUR, journalist for ABC News

'The journalistic community have lost one of their finest and their most fearless. Marie Colvin was not only a brave and tireless reporter across many continents and in many difficult situations, she was also an inspiration to women in her profession.'
ED MILIBAND, Labour leader

'She was a wonderful combination of combat fatigues and elegance. She used to get very cross with me because I said when we first met her she was wearing camouflage, and she absolutely denied this. Her dress sense was incredible. I bet Marie was wearing the most wonderful underwear when she died.'
JANE BONHAM CARTER, Liberal Democrat politician

'She was not interested in the politics, strategy or weaponry; only the effects on the people she regarded as innocents. "These are people who have no voice," she said.'
ROY GREENSLADE, *Guardian* journalist

'Exceptionally warm, intelligent, enthusiastic and funny, a person instantly likeable, who made friends wherever she went. She had great physical presence with her good looks and animated features, so when I recall her features now, five days after her death, it is her smiles and laughter that come first to mind.'
PATRICK COCKBURN, *Independent* journalist

'She was generous and funny and knew precisely the risks she was running. For decades, she has been a ubiquitous presence in the war zones of the world and her reports in *The Times* were admired in the close-knit world of foreign correspondents for their scrupulous and straightforward eloquence.'

DAVID REMNICK, *New Yorker* journalist

'We were all, as a people, better for her. At a time when journalists are being examined as never before, it's time to acknowledge someone who made a difference, a moral difference, to our country and our lives. That was Marie.'

BILL NEELY, International Editor of ITV News

'She was a real nuts and bolts journalist who would get down and work hard to get the story. She'll be sadly missed and this is a great tragedy.'   JEREMY BOWEN, BBC Middle East Editor

'She often wrote about the quiet bravery of the civilians. Telling the story wasn't her job. It was the life she lived. She had guts and glamour, brave and beautiful. She had a wicked laugh, she had a great sense of camaraderie in the field.'

LYSE DOUCET, BBC journalist and presenter

On the Front Line

The Collected Journalism
of Marie Colvin

Harper
Press

Harper*Press*
An imprint of HarperCollins*Publishers*
1 London Bridge Street
London SE1 9GF
www.harpercollins.co.uk

Published by Harper*Press* in 2012

A catalogue record for this book
is available from the British Library

ISBN 978-0-00-748796-7

Typeset in Minion and Photina by
G&M Designs Limited, Raunds, Northamptonshire
Printed and bound in the United States of America by LSC Communications

Find out more about HarperCollins and the environment at
www.harpercollins.co.uk/green

18 19 20 21 22 LSC 20 19 18 17

A portion of the proceeds from the sale of this book
goes to the Marie Colvin Memorial Fund

The Colvin family has established a memorial fund in honour
of Marie. The fund will direct donations to charitable and
educational organisations that reflect Marie's lifelong dedication
to humanitarian aid, human rights, journalism and education.

We thank you for sharing this information with others
who may be interested.

Donations may be made payable to:

The Marie Colvin Fund at LICF
1864 Muttontown Road
Syosset, N.Y. 11791

More information on the Marie Colvin Memorial Fund,
and online payment options are available at:
www.mariecolvin.org

Marie at a university party during her time at Yale, New Haven, CT.

Marie on the beach, Cyprus, 1987.

Marie with her mother Rosemarie Colvin, at her wedding
to Juan Carlos Gumucio in London.

Marie with nieces Michelle Colvin, right, and Justine Colvin,
Oyster Bay, 2004.

Marie sailing near Zakynthos, 2007.
Photograph by Richard Flaye.

Simply: there's no way to cover war properly without risk. Covering a war means going into places torn by chaos, destruction, death and pain, and trying to bear witness to that. I care about the experience of those most directly affected by war, those asked to fight and those who are just trying to survive.

Going to these places, finding out what is happening, is the only way to get at the truth. Despite all the videos you see on television, what's on the ground has remained remarkably the same for the past 100 years. Craters. Burnt houses. Women weeping for sons and daughters. Suffering. In my profession, there is no chance of unemployment. The real difficulty is having enough faith in humanity to believe that someone will care.

MARIE COLVIN

The Sunday Times, 21 October 2001,
'Bravery is not being afraid to be afraid'

CONTENTS

FOREWORD   xix
by Cat Colvin

PART ONE

IRAN–IRAQ WAR

Basra – blitzed and battered, but not beaten – 25 January 1987   3

Black banners of death fly over Baghdad – 25 January 1987   5

Wine and lipstick lay Iran's ghost to rest – 29 October 1989   7

MIDDLE EAST

Soviet settlers jolted by the promised land – 11 February 1990   10

Love sours for Romeo and Juliet of the West Bank – 1 April 1990   14

Desperately seeking answers in the Arafat slipstream – 5 June 1990   17

Home alone in Palestine – 19 September 1993   21

Arafat thrives amid cut and thrust of peace – 9 January 1994   24

LIBYA 1992–93

Frightened Libyans await the next blow – 19 April 1992   28

Adie's minder cracks up – 26 April 1992   31

Lockerbie drama turns to farce – 3 October 1993   32

GULF WAR

Under fire – 27 January 1991   34
Ghosts of war stalk Basra's empty streets – 23 August 1992   48
Critics are silenced as Saddam rebuilds Iraq – 4 October 1992   52
Shadow of evil – 22 January 1995   56
Blood feud at the heart of darkness – 8 September 1996   64

MIDDLE EAST

The Hawk who downed a dove – 12 November 1995   72
Israel's peace hopes wither – 2 June 1996   83
Israeli bulldozers rev up for showdown in Jerusalem
    – 16 March 1997   88
Arafat encircled in battle for Jerusalem – 6 April 1997   91

KOSOVO

The centuries of conflict over a sacred heartland – 8 March 1998   94
Kosovo's silent houses of the dead – 15 March 1998   95
Kosovo guerrillas fight Serb shells with bullets – 25 April 1999   100
Massacre in a spring meadow – 2 May 1999   104
Letter from … Kosare – 4 June 1999   113
The neighbour who burned with hate – 20 June 1999   118
British detectives on trail of men behind massacres – 27 June 1999   125
The enemy within – 15 August 1999   131

CHECHNYA

Wrath of Moscow leaves no place for Chechens to hide
    – 19 December 1999   137
Escape from Chechnya to a trial by ice – 2 January 2000   142

EAST TIMOR

Trapped by the terror squads in city of death – 12 September 1999   149
Courage knows no gender – 10 October 1999   160

PART TWO

ETHIOPIA
Horror of Ethiopia's living dead – 9 April 2000   167

ZIMBABWE
Rape is new weapon of Mugabe's terror – 28 May 2000   172
Hunzvi's surgery is turned into a torture centre – 14 May 2000   176

SIERRA LEONE
Drug-crazed warriors of the jungle – 3 September 2000   178
How the hi-tech army fell back on law of the jungle and won
    – 17 September 2000   182

SRI LANKA
Fighting Tigers talk of peace deal – 15 April 2001   189
'The shot hit me. Blood poured from my eye – I felt a
    profound sadness that I was going to die' – 22 April 2001   193
Fighting back – 15 July 2001   201
Bravery is not being afraid to be afraid – 21 October 2001   211

MIDDLE EAST
A bitter taste for vengeance – 7 April 2002   215
Jenin: the bloody truth – 21 April 2002   224
Two terrible deaths tell story of the Palestinian predicament
    – 21 July 2002   233

GUANTANAMO
Mindless torture? No, smart thinking – 27 January 2002   238

IRAQ

One call from the great dictator and another day of designer
torture began in prison – 4 August 2002   243
Why the great dictator thinks he can still win – 2 March 2003   249
Hunt for Saddam & Son, the murderous duo most wanted
– 23 March 2003   253
Target Saddam – 21 December 2003   256
Iraq – 7 March 2004   265
Face to face with death in a 'pacified' Iraqi town
– 29 October 2006   272
The butcher of Baghdad awaits his death sentence
– 5 November 2006   276
'I watched Saddam die' – 31 December 2006   279
Sunni sheikhs turn their sights from US forces to Al-Qaeda
– 9 September 2007   283
I felt a new terror on Basra's streets – 16 December 2007   290
Saddam's victims left to suffer as henchmen prosper
– 3 February 2008   299

MIDDLE EAST

Gaza's mourners plan 'spectacular' revenge – 28 March 2004   305
Into the underworld – 17 July 2005   310
Bulldozer Sharon wins through, but bigger battles may lie ahead
– 21 August 2005   320
Fear and defiance in the battered city – 16 July 2006   326
Birth, death and destruction on Lebanon's road to hell
– 30 July 2006   330
Gaza's deadly guardians – 30 September 2007   334

IRAN

Iran split as fun-hungry young spurn rigged poll
– 15 February 2004   347
Despair and fear among the Tehran dancing classes
– 26 June 2005   351

EGYPT

Mubarak lights a democratic flame – 4 September 2005 353

KOSOVO

How one careless phone call ended Radovan Karadzic's liberty
   – 27 July 2008 357

PART THREE

MIDDLE EAST

Bloodied Gaza set for the endgame – 11 January 2009 369
Beyond the violence, a solution is on the table – 11 January 2009 378
Netanyahu stokes fears to take poll lead – 8 February 2009 382
Israel's secret war – 15 January 2012 385

IRAQ

War-weary Iraqi voters catch election fever despite attacks
   – 6 March 2010 390
US departure from Iraq opens the door for Al-Qaeda
   – 22 August 2010 394
Terror returns to stricken Fallujah – 29 August 2010 399
Battered Kurds attempt to cling on to city of oil
   – 5 September 2010 403

AFGHANISTAN

Corrupt, untrained, underpaid, illiterate – 6 December 2009 406
Hamid Karzai fails Taliban who gave up arms – 31 January 2010 410
Swift and bloody – 9 May 2010 413
Afghans find pride in hunt for Taliban – 4 July 2010 419

IRAN

Anger at Mahmoud Ahmadinejad's election – 14 June 2009 422
Clashes show depth of fury – 21 June 2009 425

EGYPT

Flames and fighting flood along the Nile – 30 January 2011   434
Raging mob bays for Mubarak's head – 30 January 2011   438
I ran for my life from a crazed, cursing mob – 6 February 2011   441
Egypt's bloody road to reform – 6 February 2011   444
The kids triumph with Facebook and flyers – 13 February 2011   450
Feral mobs and fanatics rule Terror Square – 27 November 2011   457

LIBYA

'I'll still be running Libya when my foes have retired,'
    insists Gadaffi – 6 March 2011   463
Siege falters as loyalists defect to side of rebel 'rats' – 15 May 2011   467
'We had our orders: rape all the sisters' – 22 May 2011   471
Professor leads adopted sons into battle – 29 May 2011   476
Mad Dog and me – 28 August 2011   478
Killing rooms plot bloody retreat of troops loyal to Tyrant Jr
    – 4 September 2011   488
Toxic tyrant's chemical cavern – 11 September 2011   491
Desert storm flushes Gadaffi from oasis of dictator chic
    – 25 September 2011   494
Brutal retribution – 23 October 2011   500
Libya keeps silence over vampire dictator's grave
    – 30 October 2011   510

SYRIA

'Bombs fell like rain. You could only pray' – 5 February 2012   514
A vet is only hope for Syrian wounded – 19 February 2012   518
Final dispatch from Homs, the battered city – 19 February 2012   519

MARIE COLVIN: THE LAST ASSIGNMENT   529
by Jon Swain – 26 February 2012

'REPORTS OF MY SURVIVAL MAY BE EXAGGERATED'   539
by Alan Jenkins

FOREWORD

To me, a world without Marie is unimaginable. I am just now beginning to experience this shadow of a place, and for the first time there is no Marie to give me comfort or guide me through. Marie had so many friends and colleagues who loved her so deeply, and countless admirers who were awed by her courage as a journalist. While I mourn together with those who loved her and take enormous pride in Marie's accomplishments, my tribute is to my big sister and lost soulmate.

I try to force thoughts of her broken body out of my mind with memories of our time together – the wild adventures and late-night talks, her offbeat advice and unique view of the world. Most of all, I try to recapture the love with which she so totally and constantly enveloped me for as long as I can remember. She was my greatest admirer, my unwavering ally, my fiercest defender. To have someone as brilliant and amazing as Marie offer such love, support and admiration to me is a gift I will always treasure and desperately miss.

Marie was always my hero and to her I was perfection. She claimed me as her own when I was just a toddler, and in her eyes, I could do no wrong. She opened a big, beautiful world to me, full of laughter, excitement and adventure. My earliest memories of Marie are the bedtime stories she used to tell me, like 'postage stamp kisses' – my favourite. Marie would lie in my bed and tell me about some faraway place, with vivid descriptions of the sprawling cities, dusty back roads, flowering countrysides or lush jungles. She told me of the customs, languages and dress of the people who lived there, and what they like to do for fun. She told elaborate stories of queens and medicine women, and the beautiful clothes they wore. I learned from her how people danced in the streets of Rio at Carnival and ran with the bulls in Spain. She opened a world of adventure to me, and we explored it together. Each night, when the story was over, she would plaster me with postage stamp kisses to send me off to explore some new place in my dreams.

As we got older, Marie included me in her life in ways that were extraordinary, in retrospect. She took me with her everywhere, and dressed me to her (not my mother's) liking. We sailed all over Long Island as kids, and later in the Chesapeake Bay and the Florida Keys. We went on protest marches and hung out in the park singing to guitar music during her high school years. I tagged along with her to long classroom lectures and wild parties at Yale. She taught me the lyrics to her favourite songs by Joni Mitchell, Bonnie Raitt and Patsy Cline, and often had me sing them for her friends at parties (Marie could never carry a tune). Marie inspired me to explore the world with an open heart and mind, from backpacking through Europe at seventeen (with a luxurious stop in Paris to visit Marie) through the birth of my daughter in Santiago, Chile, nearly twenty years later.

On my last trip to London, my daughter, now 13, was still young enough to appreciate bedtime stories, and I told her that Aunt Marie was the greatest master storyteller of all time. I remembered the beautiful, exciting world she had created for me as a girl, and was thrilled for Justine to share my experience. Not long after Marie went up to Justine's bedroom, I began to hear loud bangs, crashes and shouts. I went upstairs to find Marie throwing her hands in the air and leaping around the room delivering a full warzone soundtrack for her story, as Justine listened wide-eyed and intent from her bed, resplendent in the gorgeous new pyjamas Aunt Marie had given her. The stories had changed, but in Justine's eyes I saw the same fascination I had felt as a girl basking in Marie's attention.

Marie really was the greatest master storyteller of all time, there is no doubt. She could have written novels, poems or plays and enraptured the world with the gift of her written and spoken words. But Marie chose to devote her gift to bringing the attention of the world to the innocent victims of war. Even as her reporting grew so much more dangerous and intense, and the damage to her body and soul became manifest, she never forgot how to capture the imagination of a young girl, and she never stopped believing in the importance of a little girl's dream. I hope and believe that Marie will continue to inspire young women everywhere, not only as they read about her dedication and talent, but as they dream of the difference just one little girl can make in this world.

Cat Colvin
March 2012

PART ONE

Marie in Amman, Jordan, 1991.
Photograph by Simon Townsley.

Iran–Iraq War

Basra – blitzed and battered, but not beaten

25 January 1987

Marie Colvin sends the first front-line report from inside Basra, Iraq's besieged city.

In Basra, they say the day belongs to Iraq; the night to Iran. Iraq's second city is under siege, and Iranian shells slammed into houses for the seventeenth successive day yesterday.

Two missiles hit residential areas on Friday. Long bursts of automatic fire and the sound of close fighting intermittently carry across the Shatt al-Arab waterway that flows past Basra's corniche to the Gulf.

During the day the Iranian shells fall only about once an hour. But at nightfall the shelling begins in earnest, perhaps because the Iranians are using it to cover troop movements.

The streets remain deserted and only military cars and trucks dare venture out. The shells seem to fall at random throughout the city, crashing into homes, businesses and shops. People here believe that if the Iranians cannot take Basra, they will at least make it uninhabitable.

Although thousands have fled, many remain cowering in homes behind sandbags, piled high to window tops, leaving only cracks to let in daylight and air. Basra has taken on the semblance of a giant military camp, but it has not emptied.

The train I arrived in from Baghdad consisted of 20 coaches filled with soldiers heading to the front. The few women aboard wore the black of mourning.

I took a bus which arrived at 8.30am at Saad Square in the heart of Basra. The shelling began at 8.45am. The few pedestrians on the street started hurrying for cover.

One man stopped and gave me sound advice. 'It's not a good idea to walk around Basra when they are shelling,' he said. 'You're very exposed here.'

The Ashrar neighbourhood is one of the heaviest hit in the city. A nearby hotel had its windows blown out and an air conditioner hung from one screw in a window. Branches from trees and masonry littered the streets. On a road leading into the square there was a large crater with a dead horse lying next to it.

In front of the Sheraton Hotel on the Corniche burned-out cars are scattered along the street. All the windows in the building have been shattered and the empty swimming pool is filled with shrapnel from a shell that blew apart a taverna.

While I was there, another shell slammed into the hotel, but did not explode. The building shuddered. An hour later a shell landed nearby on Al-Watani Street, the main street through the city centre which is lined with stores and night clubs which were thriving only three weeks ago.

I took refuge in a basement with a businessman who had been sleeping behind his desk for 16 hours. He gave a depressing view of the city's chances. 'I think this is how Germany must have felt in the last days of the Second World War,' he said. 'People are just waiting. It's not that they think the Iranians will take Basra, but maybe they will make it impossible for us to live here.'

The western part of the city has escaped heavy shelling, and there shops are still open and people are on the streets. Even at night soldiers stand outside at corner restaurants eating kebabs.

But everywhere there are tales of tragedy. One soldier was crying as he described how three friends had gone out to telephone home when the bombardment appeared to ease on Wednesday. All three were killed by a shell.

The hospitals are overwhelmed. Members of the Popular Army, the militia that handles logistics for the regular army, make daily rounds asking for blood donations and the sick are being moved out of hospitals to make room for soldiers.

Last week, with doctors exhausted by the influx of wounded soldiers, engineers were called to the hospital to help with amputations.

At about 9 on the evening of my arrival the incoming fire became more frequent. The Iraqis sent up huge pink flares that hung suspended over the Shatt for 10 minutes. It was night time, and night time in Basra belongs to Iran.

Black banners of death fly over Baghdad

25 January 1987

After more than two weeks of fighting, the Iranian offensive which began on 9 January appears to have established a bridgehead of about 40 square miles, according to military analysts here. The Iranian front lines are about six miles east of Basra, writes Marie Colvin in Baghdad.

Iranian troops have infiltrated at night, adding incrementally to their occupied ground. But they have not been able to breach the first main defence line between them and their target of Basra, on the east side of the Shatt al Arab waterway which, farther south, forms the border between the two countries.

Iraq has not launched a counter-offensive on the ground, the only way it could drive the Iranians out of the marshes. Iraqi officials insist this is a deliberate strategy. Iraq's acting prime minister,

Taha Yassin Ramadan, in an interview with *The Sunday Times*, said: 'We could easily repulse the Iranians but such an operation would be at the expense of losing the opportunity to kill as many of them as possible. Oddly enough they keep up their influx into this killing zone.'

Both states have about 1 million men under arms. But Iran, with its population of 45m, can afford more casualties. It relies on 'human waves' of young volunteers, who have been promised heaven if they are killed, to overwhelm the enemy's initial defences, before sending in the revolutionary guards.

Iraq, with its smaller population of 14 million, cannot afford the huge casualties such tactics entail.

As the Americans realised in Vietnam, a ground counter-offensive would prove costly in Iraqi lives and would be politically unacceptable at home. So the Iraqis in this battle, as before, have stood back and used their superiority in arms to shell the Iranian positions.

The Iranian show of muscle is potentially frightening because of Ayatollah Khomeini's vow that he will spread his brand of Shi'ite fundamentalism to the Gulf, beyond Iraq. Kuwait is the next state in line and the sound of the fighting in southern Iraq can be heard late at night in its capital, where the summit will be held. But Iraq goes into the summit holding a strong hand. Other Islamic states are known to resent the fact that Iran has completely ignored Iraq's peace initiatives. Iran has said it will not end the war until the regime of President Saddam Hussein is ousted, while Iraq would settle for peace and a return to international borders. Iran has also lost its claim to be a pure revolutionary state because of the recent revelations that it bought arms from 'Great Satan' America and 'Little Satan' Israel.

Wine and lipstick lay Iran's ghost to rest

29 October 1989

It might have been Manhattan. Guests sipped Scotch or wine and grumbled about the government. The last visitors dined on pot luck from the fridge and took a late-night tour of the wine cellar.

But this was Tehran. The host bought his Scotch on the black market for about 600,000 rials a bottle, or £372. The 'cellar' was a backyard shed hiding huge bottles of wine brewed from a Boots kit. Tame peacocks preened on the lawn and someone quietly smoked opium.

Iran has changed under its new president, Hojatolisalam Hashemi Rafsanjani. Most well-to-do Iranians have made their peace with the regime, and the mullahs need their skills. Their lifestyle is tolerated so long as it stays behind the villa walls in wealthy, tree-shaded northern Tehran.

Although women must still cover their heads in public, a new Tehran 'look' has replaced the voluminous chador. Trendy women wear stove-pipe jeans and high heels under three-quarter-length black raincoats and cover their heads with flowered scarves. Lipstick and black eyeliner have returned.

The feeling of relaxation can be deceptive. A group of West Germans had to be rescued by their ambassador a few weeks ago after a local revolutionary committee broke up their late-night party. Three other foreigners sentenced to 90 lashes for having affairs with local women had to be spirited out of the country.

But among Iranians, even former royalists have come round to Rafsanjani as the alternative to radical clerics and renewed revolutionary turmoil. 'He's a mullah but he's the only hope for Iran,' said a wealthy doctor.

Having squared the rich, Rafsanjani faces a new and much more serious threat. Tehran's poor southern suburbs, home to the 'oppressed' in whose name Ayatollah Khomeini proclaimed revolution in 1979, are seething.

Wages are low, prices mount daily, and housing is hard to find. Hopes raised by Rafsanjani's election in August are fading fast. The discontent is dangerous. The poor feel they have as much claim to the revolution as the mullahs. Their street protests drove out the shah, and they could do it again.

Anger is openly expressed. Ismail, 34, a shoemaker in the Shahpur bazaar in southern Tehran, was one of Khomeini's foot soldiers.

'Everyone around here went out in the streets,' he recalls. 'Even the six-year-olds. They promised us everything. They said it was Allah's land and we would get some of it.'

Ten years later, Ismail pays 40,000 of his 60,000-rial monthly wage (£37) to rent one ground-floor room in which he, his wife and three children eat, sleep and receive visitors. The home is meticulously clean but shabby and cramped.

The family's energy goes into finding food. Subsidies should make staples such as sugar, rice and cooking oil cheap. But Ismail's wife cannot remember the last time the government distributed rice in their neighbourhood.

A black market mafia controls food distribution and locals say government officials take bribes. Corruption goes beyond the bazaar. A surgeon said middle-men received state money for drugs but provided cheaper, often toxic, substitutes and pocketed the difference.

Despite the privations, Rafsanjani still enjoys tremendous goodwill among the poor as well as the rich. But Iran's future will be determined by whether he can overcome radicals in the regime who oppose both his desire to open Iran to the West and to give more freedom to private businessmen at home.

To secure his position he has been quietly dismantling revolutionary committees, set up to enforce Khomeini's line, and sending their members back to their own jobs.

He also seems to get support from an unexpected source. Khomeini's daughter, Fatima, said last week she was considering running for parliament in elections due in December. She is intelligent and more astute than her ambitious brother, Ahmed.

She said Rafsanjani's policies 'followed the Imam's mind', and she can cite Khomeini's name with more authority than any radical.

Rumours abound of struggles in the leadership. The strangest concerns a mysterious shipment of gold allegedly linked to radicals trying to finance their own projects.

One night earlier this month national television showed film of two lorries loaded with 10 tonnes of gold ingots, worth $120 million, allegedly captured near the border with Pakistan. Three days later the government announced the bars were in base metal painted gold. Nevertheless the entire smuggled shipment went to the central bank. Ominous graffiti reads: Khar Khodefi 'You can't fool us here'.

The unsettled climate comes at a time when Rafsanjani is trying to find an accommodation with the United States so that he can convince foreign investors their money will be secure in Iran. But the situation is stalemated. President George Bush wants Rafsanjani to show good faith by securing the release of hostages in Lebanon. Rafsanjani told western correspondents last week that Iran needed a western gesture of good faith first.

There is so little contact between them that a friendly embassy sends facsimiles of the *Tehran Times*'s leaders to Washington every day because Americans for a while believed the regime was planting messages for the administration in the newspaper's editorial page.

Middle East

Soviet settlers jolted by the promised land

ARIEL, WEST BANK

11 February 1990

Dmitri Rafalovsky had just arrived off a flight from the flatlands of the Ukraine. Now he stood in Ariel, a small town in the occupied West Bank of Israel, and stared at the starkly beautiful view.

In the distance he could see picturesque villages with stone houses wedged among unfamiliar hills. Everything looked peaceful in the promised land.

But what he and his wife, Elizabeth, did not know when they arrived here last week was that they had abandoned the Soviet Union with its anti-Semitism and threat of pogroms for a land where the villages they were now looking at housed Palestinian Arabs in revolt against their Israeli masters.

The shock was considerable. 'What do you mean, this is the West Bank? Oh my God, don't tell my wife!' he said. Rafalovsky, 55, knew only too well the dangers; Soviet television had been full of the violence for over a year, although all seemed quiet now. 'It doesn't look that dangerous,' he muttered, doubtfully.

The Rafalovskys are a tiny part of a mass emigration of Jews from the Soviet Union which is changing the demographic map of Israel. Fearful of the changes at home, and witnessing growing signs of hostility and violence, they are flooding into Israel.

The surge has been relentless. Last year 13,000 entered; in January this year 4,500 arrived; in the first week of February no fewer than 1,300 came in.

Because there are no direct flights from the Soviet Union, charter planes are arriving almost daily from East European capitals carrying the latest victims of the diaspora.

The numbers coming in are now so great that the predictions last year of 100,000 look inadequate. Some observers expect between 500,000 and 1m will enter Israel over the next few years, changing for ever a country of just 4m inhabitants.

Rafalovsky, like many of the Soviet Jews who disembarked last week, has only a vague notion of Israel. All he knew was that he wanted to leave the Soviet Union and, with the door to the United States closed, an Israeli visa was the only quick way out.

He was still vague about how he had arrived in Ariel. 'We were at Ben Gurion airport in the reception office, and the man from Ariel told me it was a small town in the mountains with not many people. He showed me on the map and said, "See, it is in the middle of Israel." I said it sounded like the place for me.'

It was only dawning on him now that he had arrived in the midst of a controversy equal to anything in the Soviet Union.

Soviet Jews are meant to be able to settle where they like, and there are clear Israeli government denials that they are being encouraged into the occupied territories.

Everyone knows, especially the United States, Israel's most generous benefactor, that immigration into these lands could jeopardise the already delicate Middle East peace process.

Despite the risks, it became evident last week that the government is concealing how many Soviet Jews are settling there. Figures released on Friday said only 63 had settled in the West Bank. In Ariel alone, however, an estimated 150 people have arrived in the past four months.

It has been a difficult choice for the Rafalovskys. Despite the intifada, they saw advantages in their new West Bank home. Their two-bedroom house is larger than their Kiev apartment, and they have brought their 17-year-old son, Vadim, and Elizabeth's elderly mother.

They have also been overwhelmed by their welcome. Neighbours have taken them shopping and have invited them to dinner. They have received a government grant for monthly rent, food and Hebrew lessons. Their first days are spent in a daze at the amount of food in the shops and the fact they are in a Jewish state.

Above all, they have escaped anti-Semitism. 'I have lived with anti-Semitism all my life. I am accustomed to it. But my son is very intelligent and he should have a chance,' said Rafalovsky.

Nobody underestimates how tough it is for these immigrants to start afresh. Few speak Hebrew. They arrive with only their luggage and $140, the maximum they are allowed to take out of the Soviet Union.

In turn they have triggered euphoria among the normally cynical Israelis, who have agonised about criticism over their treatment of Palestinians. 'This has made us feel special again. Israelis suddenly feel desired. It's the same feeling we had after the 1967 war,' said Gad Benari, a spokesman for the Jewish Agency, which handles the immigration.

But the immigrants do face a problem over their Jewishness. Under Israeli law, all Jews have a right to return to their homeland. This influx, however, is very different from the rush of Soviet 'refuseniks' in the 1970s.

They were committed Zionists who had waited in virtual internal exile for exit visas, spending the years studying Hebrew. Few of the new arrivals are religious. Many have never been to a synagogue and are the children of mixed marriages, which will raise problems with the orthodox Jews.

But for now, the benefits outweigh the problems. Most Soviet Jews feel satisfied because they have enough money to live, an apartment and work, however menial.

For most it is enough to escape the Soviet Union. There, Jews are being blamed for the failures of the economy and the uncertainty of the political situation. 'What I can't believe is that any of my Jewish friends stayed behind,' says Victor Savitsky, an engineer who arrived with his wife and their tiny daughter.

Others talk of being barred from universities by anti-Semitism and of the virulently anti-Semitic organisation, Pamyat, which has been holding rallies in cities.

The desire to leave the Soviet Union is now so great that an estimated 12,000 Soviet Jews cannot get seats on planes. The Israelis are trying to persuade the Moscow authorities to allow direct flights to Israel, but for now most immigrants come through Bucharest or Budapest. The Savitskys waited four months before they could buy a plane ticket.

Desperation has bred daring. One couple, Mark and Louisa Puzis, drove their Lada from the Ukraine with their two-month-old baby in the back, trading vodka in exchange for petrol.

Israel is just coming to terms with the magnitude of the problem. The system of absorption is showing signs of falling apart. Reception centres are full and the government budget is overspent.

Critics say the government has been slow to deal with an emerging crisis. Resources in Israel are scarce. There is high unemployment and 20% inflation. 'We should be treating this like a war situation,' said Michael Kleiner, head of the Absorption Committee at the Knesset, Israel's parliament.

He is trying to convince the government to cut red tape and provide money. He has proposed that Israel should stop all development for two years and put that money towards absorbing the new immigrants.

'Responsible people won't even make estimates on how many will arrive or how much money we will need,' said Kleiner. 'Teddy Kollech [mayor of Jerusalem] has been waiting for 20 years to finish a soccer stadium for Jerusalem. He can certainly wait another two years.'

Love sours for Romeo and Juliet of the West Bank: Avi Marek and Abir Mattar

JERUSALEM

1 April 1990

The script would probably have been rejected by even the most schmaltzy Hollywood producer. Abir, a 19-year-old Palestinian beauty who has gone home to her West Bank village to stay with her mother, meets Avi, a dashingly handsome Israeli officer who spots her when he careers by in his jeep. They go together like humous and pitta bread and talk of marriage.

If the film were ever made, love would no doubt conquer the differences of race, politics and religion. But in the harsh world of the occupied territories, life is more complicated.

Last week, the star-crossed lovers were both outcasts from their communities. Avi was suspended pending the outcome of a military investigation into his breach of the regulations forbidding fraternisation with Palestinians. Abir was hiding in a Palestinian hotel.

The story of Avi Marek and Abir Mattar is a rare glimpse of the human dramas hidden beneath the conventional rocks and riots image of the intifada. Marek is a 30-year-old Israeli captain whose infantry unit is stationed in Beit Jalla, a mostly Christian village that has virtually closed down during the three years of the Palestinian uprising.

Home life held few joys. He had married a much older woman, Rivka, less than a year ago and lived in her flat in a sterile apartment block in the settlement of Gilo outside Jerusalem. But it was better than his own neighbourhood, Shmuel Hanavi, a poor suburb of Jerusalem populated mostly by Sephardic Jews, immigrants from Arab countries.

Marek, who speaks Arabic, by all accounts fell at first sight for Mattar, who was educated in a convent school in Bethlehem and used to babysit for tourist families.

Mattar says it was mutual. In her hotel room last week, she looked at herself in the mirror and smiled when she said: 'Yes, I love him. We met for the first time eight months ago; we have been happy ever since.'

Sitting looking out on a view of a west Jerusalem street, the Jewish side of the divided city, she reflects on how circumscribed her life has become. She cooks meals on a gas burner in the room and feels out of place among package-trip tourists who fill the lobby. She is also three months pregnant with Marek's baby.

But Mattar says her life has always been difficult. Her father drank and gambled until her mother kicked him out, and she married at 16 to a man who already had a wife and five children. When he was imprisoned she returned home to Beit Jalla with a child.

Marek began his courtship by calling to her from his army jeep as she walked to a friend's house. Soon her mother, Nina, noticed she was out all night every night.

'When I asked,' she said, 'Abir replied that it was none of my business. Then I noticed an army jeep would stop outside and beep. The jeep seemed to be around all the time.'

Nina worried that her daughter's relationship would bring unwanted attention. The Mattar family was already ostracised. Nina's lifestyle is hardly suited to a traditional Arab village. Last week she dressed to greet visitors in leopard-print stretch pants and a black lace top.

Nina went out to work when her husband left, something that is not done in traditional Arab culture, and had a series of boyfriends before remarrying. 'I'm not a virgin,' she said, chain-smoking as she looked out at the village of sun-splashed stone homes. 'I've always had a boyfriend. That doesn't make me a whore like everyone in this town says. Look at my apartment, if I was a whore I would have made some money. I've only one bed and not even a proper bathroom.'

She also collaborated with the Israeli occupying forces. Left with seven children and spurned by her neighbours, she says she felt few loyalties. The police gave her 200 shekels (about £70) every time she passed them information. She stopped when the intifada began.

Before that, such activities meant ostracism. Now, with young teenagers controlling the streets and talking of purifying the Palestinian community, they are life-threatening. About 200 Palestinians have been killed for collaboration or prostitution.

But although Nina warned her daughter she was endangering the family, there was little a mother could do. 'Their love was burning. Avi was crazy about her and she lost her head.' The young couple would return together in broad daylight after nights of passion in Marek's jeep and Mattar would bring him coffee before he returned to his unit.

The family began to receive threats and Marek made things worse. He and his unit began picking up local teenagers and beating them. Nina says she thinks he was trying to show off to her daughter.

Desperate, Nina complained to the police and sent word to Marek's Israeli wife. The police ignored her but his wife came down and staked out the house in the Arab village. When Marek and Mattar returned, she ran out into the street with a kitchen knife. Mattar made off in his jeep but the story was too public to be kept quiet.

The military suspended Marek. Mattar found a mongrel dog hanging in the family toilet, dead, its head in the water. She quickly left town. Publicity about the case has made it the gossip of Israelis as well as Palestinians.

Mattar says she and Marek plan to marry after they both divorce. She says she will convert to Judaism. 'I can't go back to live among the Arabs,' she said. But she is worried that Marek's return to Israel may change him. He has been heavily criticised in the Hebrew press.

Marek now faces a military tribunal to explain the liaison. His defence is that he was only fraternising with Mattar in a patriotic endeavour to recruit her as a spy. At the moment observers are not betting on a happy ending to the tale.

Desperately seeking answers in the Arafat slipstream: Yasser Arafat

5 June 1990

The Times

When people know you have spent a year making a film about Yasser Arafat, the question they ask most often is 'Were you ever afraid?' At times I felt frustrated, angry, despairing and very tired, but not afraid. In his manner, Arafat is one of the less threatening people you are likely to meet.

Making a documentary of him takes endurance, not courage. We had flown into Tunis for a scheduled interview to begin our filming. But Arafat was in Baghdad. The film opens with a Tunis to Baghdad telephone call. It is 2am and Arafat seems to think the only way we can get a connection in Baghdad in time to meet him is to find a boat to Paris. We agree instead to fly separately to China where he is due for a state visit, then fly back together in his borrowed Iraqi jet.

This scene must cause great pain to BBC accountants. But at the time it seemed the ideal trip. We would film behind the scenes in an exotic location while the terrorist-turned-statesman wheeled and dealed, then have him as a captive interviewee for the hours it took to fly back to the Middle East. The latter was the most alluring. Arafat grows bored in interviews and will often stand up, unclip his microphone and thank you as he walks out.

But the Chinese Foreign Ministry called Arafat while we were somewhere over Pakistan and said: 'We cannot receive you, the students are causing trouble.' We headed back to Tunis, arriving in

Marie with Yasser Arafat, *c.*1994.

time to board his borrowed Iraqi jet and set off to the summit in
Casablanca. But the China trip did pay off. Arafat takes everything
personally. Had we decided not to go it would have signalled a lack
of commitment, however well-founded our misgivings.

When we finally caught up with him, he owed us one. We were
instantly famous in PLO ranks as the crew that had gone to Peking
to see the 'Old Man' and been stood up. Everyone had a similar
tale; this time it was not Arafat's fault, but it usually is. People
around him, a travelling entourage that is both family and staff,
began helping with tips on the etiquette of living alongside him.
One of my journal entries notes a word of advice from a senior
aide: 'When I break your foot, you have gone wrong.'

Arafat's schedule is exhausting and it wears down everyone
around him. Half the hotels in Tunis seem to be filled with people
waiting to see Arafat. Fighters with blood rivalries meet in the
lobby of the Hilton and turn their backs. Arafat maintains his own

rigid personal organisation within the chaos around him. Days are for seeing to problems such as parents seeking university tuition for their children. Serious business takes place at night, dating from the time the PLO was an underground organisation. Meetings begin about 9pm and rarely end before 3am. Everyone is expected to be at Arafat's call.

He never tells anyone, even close aides, his schedule in advance for security reasons. When you fly with him you do not know your destination until you take off. Asking a simple question at breakfast such as 'What are you doing today?' brings startled stares from aides and silence from Arafat.

The PLO is Arafat's life and he expects the same commitment from everyone around him. He accepts planes and villas from Arab leaders, but remains a nomad and just out of their control. All his villas look the same – sterile, furnished with a print or two of Jerusalem, a television, some nondescript sofas and a desk. The head of the Palestinian government travels in four suitcases: one for his uniforms, one for his fax machine, one for 'in' and 'out' faxes and one for a blanket to curl up in for cat naps.

His obsessive precision can be maddening. He arranges his keffiyeh headdress meticulously every day in the same way. It must hang down his shoulder in the shape of the map of Palestine. He empties his machinegun pistol precisely as his jet takes off, carefully lining up the bullets on his tray. He marks every single fax sent to the PLO with a felt-tip red pen. But doubts begin to set in when one spends a lot of time around him. Does Arafat really have to read every single fax? Does he have to control every disbursement of funds, the purchase of an office desk in Singapore? It is Jimmy Carter as PLO leader.

Arafat is up on every detail of running the organisation, but never takes time to review policy, listen to advice or plan ahead. The PLO is run from moment to moment from Arafat's head. The main criticism one hears in the ranks of the PLO is of this autocratic style. Arafat brooks no criticism and, as a result, many educated and independent Palestinians have opted out.

Now, when he desperately needs good advice on the workings of the western world as he tries to convince it that he is sincere in his current drive for a peaceful settlement with Israel, few around him know its ways. He himself is unsophisticated about the West, not surprisingly, as he spent most of his youth organising a resistance movement and has been banned from most of it for his adult life.

So why do Palestinians follow this unlikely leader? In person, Arafat is warm and inspires devotion. Palestinians who disagree with his views respect his devotion to the cause. He has always managed to compromise and lead by finding the highest common denominator within the fractious Palestinian movement. Arafat has no political ideology. He wants one thing: to liberate the homeland of his people. He has become more than a leader. For most Palestinians he is a symbol of their aspirations.

Arafat today is a desperate man. He is 60, has no heirs, and wants to achieve something tangible before he dies. In renouncing terrorism and recognising Israel in 1988, he played his best card and cannot understand why he has not received more support from the United States in convincing Israel to make a similar concession.

Arafat is now flying around even more obsessively than when we were filming, trying to stave off attacks from radicals within his own organisation and from Arab states who say he has given everything in return for nothing. Arafat is hoping to convince enough people to stay with him, hoping to keep the organisation together long enough, hoping to stay alive long enough, so that he can one day land his own plane in Palestine.

Home alone in Palestine: Suha Arafat

19 September 1993

When Yasser Arafat went to Washington, his wife stayed in Tunis. But she wasn't hiding away. Marie Colvin profiles the determined Mrs Arafat.

Suha was never going to have it easy. She faced an entrenched PLO bureaucracy where proximity to Arafat meant power. But there was little they could do: by all accounts it was a love match. For the historic peace deal last week, Yasser Arafat wore a uniform, a keffi-yeh that caught the slight breeze like a jib sail, and the designer stubble it might be said he pioneered. His wife Suha wore red. But while he was standing on the White House's South Lawn, the PLO leader's 29-year-old, French-educated wife was sitting at home in the couple's whitewashed villa in Tunis, while the wives of Bill Clinton and Yitzhak Rabin were escorted to their seats on the South Lawn.

Arafat would no doubt have liked her to attend, but his advisers counselled him that bringing along his chic young wife would set Palestinian conservatives and radicals alike clucking away that he was treating the signing of the Palestinian–Israeli peace accord as a social event. They shuddered at the imagined sniping: Palestinians are dying in Gaza and she is parading herself in the White House.

So the Arafats were foiled. Well, not quite. She snapped on her gold earrings, donned her favourite Paris couture suit, a tasteful scarlet number decorated with jewelled buttons, and invited the CNN correspondent Richard Blystone to come and watch the ceremony *chez elle*. Blystone brought along a satellite dish and broadcast Suha's thoughts and plans live to the television audience of several million watching the historic ceremony.

Standing on the mosaic portico of the marital home, she told Blystone how she was happy 'to stay with my people in Tunis to share with them this great historical moment'.

She spoke of her future role as the first lady of Palestine in echoes of Hillary Clinton. 'I think I have to assume great responsibilities. I must concentrate on health care for the casualties of the intifada and for all the Palestinians all over the world, to compensate for their long years of suffering.'

The public relations coup epitomised her deft manoeuvring since Arafat, a confirmed bachelor who for years had vowed he was 'married to Palestine', shocked the Palestinian community in July 1991 by wedding a pretty blonde less than half his age.

She recalls first hearing of her future husband when she was four years old and 'hiding in fear' in her family's basement in Nablus as Israeli soldiers searched the West Bank city for a resistance leader named Arafat. In 1988, because of her fluent French and the long association of her mother Raymonda with the PLO (she founded the first Palestinian news agency in the occupied territories), Suha was asked to help out during an Arafat visit to Paris where she was living after finishing her education at the Sorbonne.

Within weeks Arafat asked her to come to Tunis as his personal assistant. Soon she was flying around the world with him and had supplanted his long-time secretary, Um Nasr. When he married Suha, there was a hair-pulling cat-fight between the two women at Arafat's office. Um Nasr, a forty-something woman who had dedicated her life to the revolution, felt that she would make a much better wife.

Much of the resentment of Suha seems inspired not by anything she has done but rather by what she is. She is neither a traditional Arab wife in a culture that is still very conservative, nor is she the politicised revolutionary that many assumed Arafat would choose were he ever to wed. She likes French fashion and perfumes and visits Paris to stock up. Her upper-class trappings rankle among Palestinians more than the difference in age or religion (she is a Greek Orthodox Christian, he a Sunni Muslim).

For years Arafat's nomadic existence and paucity of possessions had been a symbol of his refugee people; now Palestinians had a first lady who said: 'It's so difficult to take all of the luggage and go all over.'

But Suha is no bimbo. She comes from a prominent Palestinian family; her father is a wealthy banker and likes to talk of how her ancestors lived in a crusader castle. She is trying to carve out a middle role, somewhere between being a traditional wife and a public figure in her own right.

She recently took along a film crew with her to visit a Palestinian orphanage in Tunis to publicise their plight. Arafat has symbolically adopted all the children, most of whose parents are considered martyrs of the Palestinian cause. And she has founded a society to care for Palestinian children.

But unlike Hillary Clinton, who seems to tolerate Bill's presence only because it gives her the power to implement her own programmes, Suha genuinely seems to adore Arafat. She pours him tea in the morning and nags him to rest. His schedule is less erratic these days, although he still maintains his nocturnal habits, often meeting with other PLO officials until three or four in the morning.

'She is suffering with me,' Arafat said last week during his Washington visit. 'I am working 18-hour days.'

But she has given the PLO leader the chance to think of a home as well as a homeland.

Arafat thrives amid cut and thrust of peace

MIDDLE EAST

9 January 1994

For a man who was supposed to be going mad under the gruelling pressure of negotiations with Israel, Yasser Arafat, the Palestine Liberation Organisation leader, was in an extraordinarily good mood last week.

He opened a meeting of Palestinian engineers in Tunis, joking that if his political career did not work out he could always join their ranks and resume his former profession. He met for three days with a delegation of disgruntled Palestinians from the occupied territories.

He dispatched Farouq Qadoomi, the PLO foreign minister, to try to patch things up with King Hussein of Jordan. He met an all-party group of British MPs and a Gaza businessman with plans to build a floating port.

He also delivered a New Year's Day address from his Tunis head-quarters to a carphone in Yarmouk Square in Gaza; and he persuaded the executive committee, his cabinet, to stand firm in the latest contretemps with Israel over talks on the implementation of their peace accord. All the while, faxes and telephone calls flew back and forth between Arafat, his representative in Cairo, and Israel to resolve the deadlock in negotiations.

It was all in a week's work. Arafat has changed very little in his last three decades as a Palestinian leader, much less in the three months since the peace agreement was signed in Washington. But at 64, he has been rejuvenated by Israel's recognition of the PLO, working more hours than ever before, impatient with constraints. On New Year's Eve he paused only for a piece of celebratory cake before signing his first working paper of the year at five minutes past midnight.

Arafat wants the peace accord to go ahead and he is twisting arms, using financial pressure, threatening those who do not agree with him and playing off internal rivalries for all that he is worth. He even bangs the table in meetings of the executive committee, and, heaven forbid, has been known to shout.

He is acting like a leader; yet this behaviour has led to charges that his style of governing is undermining the peace process and even to absurd reports that he is mentally unstable.

Perhaps this is because he has actually done something he has been criticised for not doing during his entire leadership of the Palestinian movement. It has long been the conventional wisdom that Arafat is incapable of taking the bold steps required of a leader, insisting instead on securing the consensus of even the most radical PLO faction.

When he signed the peace accord with Israel last September, Arafat took a bold and dangerous step for the first time, leaving behind anyone whom he could not convince to join him. He felt Yitzhak Rabin, the Israeli prime minister, was offering the best deal possible and that if he waited to bring along every fractious member of the PLO, that handshake on the White House lawn would still be merely a dream. In his view, those who are now accusing him of being autocratic are the same people who previously lambasted him for failing to take the initiative.

The second criticism that has lately been floated is that Arafat's style of leadership has opened serious divisions in the PLO and that this threatens the peace process. Israel has tried to play on these divisions, making it clear for example that it would prefer to deal with Abu Mazen, the senior PLO official who signed the peace accord in Washington.

This is a serious misinterpretation of what is going on inside the PLO. In its decades of scrutiny of its enemy, Israel may have missed the forest for the trees. Although the Israeli intelligence services can identify which individual Palestinian mounted such-and-such an operation, they do not appear able to explain to their government how the PLO works.

In fact, titles mean little. Power is based on shifting internal alliances, party membership, past history, and money. Arafat is the unquestioned leader because he works the system best and because he rises above all of them as the lasting symbol of Palestinian nationalism.

Even Arafat's most vocal opponents have not called for his replacement; they know there is nobody else who can keep the organisation united behind this peace accord. There is criticism in the PLO ranks, but this reflects the changes in Palestinian politics rather than any change in Arafat.

For years, there have been divisions along ideological lines, from the Marxist left to the Islamicists on the right. That is all irrelevant today. The divisions are now social and economic, and Arafat is having to juggle them, conducting the peace talks while he tries to put together a reliable and competent team for his new government.

He has to balance the demands of returning guerrillas and wealthy Palestinian businessmen who have made their money in the diaspora and who now want to run the economy of the new Palestinian entity; between Palestinian technicians who have worked in the West and loyal political appointees who are afraid there will be no place for them; between Palestinians inside the occupied territories, who feel they have borne the brunt of the occupation, and those returning, who feel they have sacrificed normal lives for the revolution.

The entire situation is in flux; nobody knows what his future will be, so everyone has a word for or against any move Arafat makes. But it is self-defeating for Israel to search for chinks at the top of the PLO.

There is a danger of misinterpreting events. Last week a delegation, headed by Haidar Abdel-Shafi, a soft-spoken Gaza doctor who led the PLO negotiating team in Washington, came to Tunis with a petition signed by 118 Palestinians. The visit was seen outside the PLO as an attack that could break Arafat; in fact, he had invited the delegation to discuss criticism of the way he has been proceeding with the implemention of the accord.

They talked for three days. They did not get all they wanted but Arafat agreed that Abdel-Shafi should head a 'national debate' on the future of the Palestinian entity. As he left, Abdel-Shafi said: 'Arafat is monopolising power but we cannot blame Abu Ammar [Arafat] when no members of the executive committee stand up to insist on sharing this power.'

Arafat talks openly about criticism: 'We are now facing a new era, and in this new era no doubt we can expect hesitation, criticism, worries, misunderstandings. I am not leading a herd of sheep.'

Rabin complains that dealing with Arafat is like dealing in a 'Middle East bazaar'. Why is he surprised? Arafat is trying through any means to get the best he can out of what Palestinians see as a pretty bad deal. Arafat faced severe criticism for making too many compromises when he signed the peace agreement. Now that he has refused to compromise further, his support is growing daily.

The PLO leader is difficult to deal with. That is why he has survived. He has managed to slip through the grasp of every Arab state trying to control him – Jordan, Syria, Egypt, to name just a few. He survived in 1970 when the Jordanian king turned his army against the Palestinian guerrillas in Black September, and in 1982 when Israel turned its might against him in Lebanon.

Rabin, when he shook Arafat's hand in Washington, seemed to be acknowledging that no matter how much he despised Arafat, the PLO leader was the only possible partner for peace. Since then, the Israeli prime minister has conducted peace negotiations not as if he was dealing with a partner but with an enemy that must be controlled and contained to the most minute detail. The last Israeli negotiating document stipulated that there should be opaque glass between the partitions at crossing points.

In making such details the focus of negotiations, and in seeking to divide and conquer, Israel has lost sight of what it agreed to do

in Washington – make peace with the PLO, led by Arafat, for better
or for worse. Rabin should begin dealing again with Arafat as a
partner in peace. And the judgement of Arafat should be left to
when it really matters, when he enters his homeland and heads the
government.

Rabin last week told his cabinet: 'We will let them sweat.' Who?
The PLO?

'Look at me,' said Arafat on Friday night. 'I'm not sweating.'

Libya

Frightened Libyans await the
next blow: sanctions

TRIPOLI

19 April 1992

The omens had been bad all week. Colonel Muammar Gadaffi lay tucked
up in bed with tonsillitis, UN sanctions had closed off the country and
Russian military advisers haggled for suitcases in the souk before
making a break for the border. When the chill Hamsin wind blew in off
the desert it seemed that even the weather was conspiring against the
Libyan leader.

Out on the streets, Libyans felt anxious, vulnerable and isolated.
While the sanctions imposed last week caused inconvenience not
hardship, they were a severe psychological blow. Once again the
Libyan people felt trapped in confrontation with the West. They
are dreading the next turn of the screw. Oil sanctions? Another air
strike?

The disgruntled middle-class expresses resentment only in private. At a dinner party in Tripoli last week guests lamented how Libya's wealth had been frittered away, siphoned off to military and revolutionary movements all over the world.

'We are only 4m Libyans and we export 1m barrels of oil a day,' a businessman said. 'We could be like Saudi Arabia. Instead look at us.'

His expansive wave of disgust took in the shabby clothes of his countrymen, the dirty hospitals where patients often sleep two to a bed and the vast, grimy supermarkets like the Souk al Jumaa that stand empty or display rows of plastic candelabra from Romania.

Such anger is, of course, impotent because Gadaffi brooks no opposition. After rumblings of discontent, he has reinstated his 'revolutionary committees', the young shock troops that were stood down three years ago after an outcry over their 'excesses'.

The escalating tension evoked memories of the weeks leading up to the American bombing of Tripoli and Benghazi in 1986, during which at least 70 civilians, including Gadaffi's adopted daughter, were killed. On television, announcers condemn George Bush as 'unjust' and read telegrams of support. 'The crusaders think they can humiliate these people, the Libyan people, but they are mistaken,' raged one Muslim preacher in a televised sermon. 'We will bend our heads only to Allah.'

The appeals may be the same but there is a key difference. Gone is the fury of the organised daily demonstrations; one protest in Tripoli's Green Square drew only about 50 young men who danced to Algerian rai music before drifting away in good humour.

Gadaffi was chastened by the bombing and has so far forsworn the revolutionary rhetoric of 1986. As he lay on his sickbed, he was no doubt pondering the dilemma of whether to surrender the two Libyan intelligence agents accused of planting the bomb that exploded aboard a Pan Am jet over Lockerbie three years ago, killing 270 people.

Although his old friend Yasser Arafat, the PLO leader, returned to Tripoli saying 'I must stand by Libya and my brother Gadaffi', solidarity is in short supply. The Soviet Union, Gadaffi's long-time backer, is no more and Arab leaders refused landing permission to the planes he sent out in defiance of the UN sanctions.

It is no easy choice. Should Gadaffi surrender the accused men unconditionally, they may implicate more senior Libyan officials and prompt further demands. 'If you hand them over, you are lost,' one Arab envoy advised him last week. 'The Americans will come back with a list of 100 names, then the name of Abdelsalam Jalloud [Gadaffi's second-in-command], then your name.'

Jalloud, a rough-spoken major and Gadaffi's close comrade since they seized power with a gang of young officers in 1969, is said to be arguing fiercely against surrendering the two suspects, both members of his tribe.

For many Libyans, fed up with 22 years of revolution and crisis, the new openness of Gadaffi's own brand of perestroika now appears under threat. Should Gadaffi play a wrong move in his poker game his people are unlikely to forgive him, even though few think the West's demands are just.

His low-key response suggests that he has been seeking a compromise behind the scenes to have sanctions against air travel, diplomats and arms lifted. He does not wish to repeat the mistake of Saddam Hussein, and knows that taking foreign workers as a 'human shield' would only unleash a violent reaction.

But Libyans are disillusioned. Today only the revolutionary committee apparatchiks believe the new sign on the road to the airport: 'We are all Muammar Gadaffis.'

Adie's minder cracks up: Saleh

TRIPOLI

26 April 1992

Saleh is a broken man, his health uncertain, his job insecure. But his plight has little to do with the political pressures on the beleaguered Libyan regime that employs him. Recovering from a nervous break-down, Saleh sums up his woes in two words: Kate Adie.

Assigned as a government 'minder' to the roving doyenne of the BBC, Saleh looks back on it all from his sickbed with the horror of a man plucked from the deck of a sinking ship in shark-infested waters. 'Oh dear,' he moaned. 'Kate Adie has been very bad for my health. I have very tender nerves.'

Adie, a veteran of Tiananmen Square, Tripoli and the Gulf, succeeded where sanctions had failed: she had brought the government to its knees.

The extent of the Libyan anguish emerged last week in an extraordinary telex to the BBC, in which Tripoli bemoaned the pugnacious temperament of Adie and pleaded for her to be withdrawn.

'All our attempts to obtain a common and satisfactory solution were gone with the wind,' lamented the telex. 'We are demanding never ever send Kate Adie to Libya whatever the reasons are.'

By that stage, Saleh was at his wits end. Wandering into the lobby of the Bab al-Bahar hotel, he fainted. Coming round, he muttered, 'If you ask me to choose Kate Adie or prison I would not hesitate to choose the prison.'

Grimacing as he relived their last encounter, in a crowded hotel lobby, Saleh said: 'She said she should be filming demonstrations. I told her there were no demonstrations or clashes. But she insisted we find some.'

Deploying ruthless hyperbole, Adie said Libya was treating the foreign press 'in a manner that had gone out of fashion with Stalin'.

Saleh respectfully suggested Adie should leave. But that was like waving a red flag at a bull. 'If you are throwing me out it will be very bad for your country,' she stormed.

Saleh went on: 'I felt shy, so small, like an ant. I am from a good family but she was treating me as if I was a slave or an illegal boy [bastard]. But because of her age I am not allowed to shout or attack her. I must treat her like a mother or a grandmother.'

His next step was to assign an underling to Adie. The colleague was soon on the phone. 'He was calling me all the time and begging me to release him. He said, "Saleh what have you done to me?"'

The ministry adopted new tactics. The BBC was banned from filming, as were other television crews. But Adie soon found her way round that. 'Kate Adie said I had to choose between going to the souk [market] with her or have her shout at me. I took her to the souk,' recalls Omar, the replacement minder.

As a last resort, the information ministry hosted 'a farewell dinner' in which, it was hoped, Adie would get the message. The next day, to their horror, officials received intelligence that she had embarked upon another embroidery square, her favourite method of whiling away time.

In the end, she left on Thursday. 'We have sanctions,' said one official, 'but even worse is Kate Adie.'

Lockerbie drama turns to farce

3 October 1993

Although Muammar Gadaffi, the Libyan leader, is on the brink at last of surrendering the two men suspected of the Lockerbie bombing, justice is far from being done.

After one of the biggest international investigations ever mounted, the expenditure of more than £12 million of British taxpayers' money, and interviews with 16,000 witnesses in 53 countries, most of the evidence indicates that those who made the decision to bomb Pan Am flight 103 will be nowhere near the court.

Libyan sources said yesterday that, under threat of increased United Nations sanctions, Gadaffi had decided to hand over the suspects for trial in Scotland.

Few who have investigated the case think these men, Abdel Baset al-Megrahi and Al Amin Khalifa Fhimah, initiated or planned the operation.* They are low-level intelligence operatives. One is obviously slow-witted. They are accused of smuggling a suitcase bomb aboard a plane from Malta to Frankfurt, where it was loaded aboard the Pan Am flight that exploded over Lockerbie, killing 270 people, at Christmas 1988.

Critics say the American and British governments have ignored evidence that the attack was ordered and paid for by Iran, in retaliation for America shooting down an Iranian jet, and that Iran contracted out the bombing to Ahmed Jibril's PFLP-GC, a radical Palestinian faction based in Damascus, with Syrian connivance.

According to a well-documented line of investigation, Jibril only turned to Libya for help in completing the operation after his own men were arrested by German police. Neither Washington nor London wanted to alienate the Syrian and Iranian leaderships at the time of the investigation, which coincided with the Gulf War.

Relatives of the victims are enraged. 'It's like trying the hit man and ignoring the person who paid him to pull the trigger,' said Susan Cohen, whose daughter, 20, was killed. 'Nobody thinks that these two guys sat in a café and decided to bomb an aeroplane.'

Even the conviction of the Libyans is by no means certain. Prosecutors fear they may have insufficient evidence. No witness,

---

* Al Amin Khalifa Fhimah was found not guilty and acquitted of 270 counts of murder, conspiracy to murder and a breach of the Aviation Security Act 1982 by a panel of three Scottish judges sitting in a special court at Camp Zeist, Netherlands.

fingerprint or any other forensic evidence links either of them directly to the explosion.

None the less, all the might of the British and American governments has been brought to bear on Gadaffi through the UN to surrender the men, and Libyan sources said yesterday that he had finally been convinced that neither country would accept any compromise.

Travel and diplomatic sanctions were imposed last year, and on Friday the UN security council tabled a draft resolution imposing further sanctions if Gadaffi does not surrender. Apparently at the request of Boutros Boutros-Ghali, the UN secretary-general, the vote has been delayed to give Gadaffi time to declare his intentions. The denouement could come this week.

Gadaffi has been assured that the pair will get a fair trial in Scotland, where the stringency of evidence laws would give them the best chance of acquittal. He has also been promised that they would not be interrogated by MI6 or any other security agency. Security sources see this as an important concession because the men cannot be forced to reveal any Libyan secrets.

The British have even told the Libyans that Scottish cells are 'very comfortable' and that the men will be taught English – a puzzler for Libyan negotiators, who thought the Scots spoke Scottish. The farce continues.

Gulf War

Under fire

27 January 1991

Hussein stood alone in the carpet souk on the eastern bank of the Tigris, fingering his ivory worry-beads and gazing at the huge sun setting behind the Ottoman tenements on the far side of the river. The dying sunlight washed his dishdasha robe a wintry red.

The market square of the souk usually bustled at this time of the early evening as people stopped to gossip or do last-minute shopping on the way home from work. But it was 15 January, the United Nations' deadline for Iraq's withdrawal from Kuwait. Baghdad was silent and edgy. The souk was deserted.

Hussein greeted me with far more warmth than our acquaintance merited. I had visited him on and off in his shop over the past five months, using the excuse of fingering a Kurdish bangle, or looking at a carpet, to pick up the rumours and rhythms of daily life in Baghdad. For him, it had been an excuse for a rare talk with a foreigner, something that for an Iraqi is akin to a visit to the confessional.

Now, in this chance encounter, we seemed the only people left in the capital. We walked to his shop under the vaulted roof of the souk. Inside, there was none of the usual salesmanship or the ritual cup of sugared tea. 'Would you like a whisky?' he asked, and picked up a half-full bottle of Whyte & Mackay. He poured us two tea glasses full.

Amid the clutter of piled up carpets, silver necklaces, antique frames, heavy Kurdish belts and, beside the ubiquitous picture of Saddam Hussein, a likeness of President John F Kennedy beaten into a copper plate we discussed whether he should stay in Baghdad or take his family to a place safe from American bombs, as other merchants had.

Tareq, who owned the House of Antiquities across the street, had taken his wife and sons to Kurdistan in northern Iraq. 'The Americans like the Kurds, they won't bomb them,' he had said.

Hussein agonised. Baghdad was home; perhaps thieves would come to the empty souk and steal his carpets; but there was no business anyway because everybody was hoarding their money.

We drank another tea glass of whisky, standing up, too edgy to sit down. His wife, five children aged two to 12, younger brother and mother were at home waiting. His children had their school exams on the 20th; if they missed them, it would mean losing a year of school. 'But perhaps it is better that they lose a year than that they lose their lives,' he said.

Darkness was falling and we walked out of the shop. He said: 'If you have any problems you can come to my house. Really.' For an Iraqi, it was an enormous act of faith. A visit by a foreigner in this tightly controlled society meant a follow-up visit by the security police. But these were extraordinary times. It was a way of saying we were not enemies. I drove back to the Rashid hotel through dark and deserted streets.

Baghdad is normally a bustling city. Although its glorious antiquity was long ago buried under drab concrete, its spirit was irrepressible, even at the height of the first war in the Gulf, when taxis returning from the front with coffins on their roofs raced among the fierce traffic on its highways. To see the city now was chilling.

Many middle-class families had closed their homes and left to stay with relatives in the country after the failure of the talks in Geneva between Tariq Aziz, the foreign minister, and James Baker, the American secretary of state. Others held out, fiddling for good news between the BBC, Voice of America and the pan-Arab station, Monte Carlo.

They had heard the ominous tone in Saddam's speech on Friday to an Islamic conference in Baghdad. They had heard Joe Wilson, the American chargé d'affaires, dramatically announce as he left on Saturday: 'This is the last flight out.' They knew most western diplomats had left with him.

But even illiterate taxi drivers held an irrational faith that Javier Perez de Cuellar, the United Nations secretary-general, might be able to avert war when he arrived to see Saddam at the weekend. 'Maybe Saddam will leave Kuwait,' the taxi driver said as he drove me to Perez de Cuellar's news conference at the airport. When the secretary-general said 'only God knows' if there would be a war, it was the last straw. Iraqis knew Saddam was ready to take on the world.

Everybody was jumpy. We lost our way leaving the airport and when we drove up to a checkpoint to ask a soldier for directions, there was an audible click as he flipped the safety catch off his AK-47 and walked up to the car with the barrel pointed through the window.

There were many poignant moments in those days overshadowed by the deadline. The most striking thing perhaps, to somebody who had been visiting Iraq on and off since the crisis began, was the sudden openness of the usually careful and closed Iraqis.

This is a society that usually keeps its head down and offers no political opinions. Most dissidents are dead or in exile. The tiny middle class would, in general, be glad to see Saddam's regime fall; but the merchants did well out of the war against Iran and reached an accommodation with those in power. The urban poor, who have enjoyed cheap, and even free, housing and subsidised food under Saddam, are compliant to his will. The long war against Iran united society and now I found that his stand against the world was filling many Iraqis with pride as well as fear.

After seeing Hussein in the souk hours before the deadline expired, I went into the Al-wiyah club with Falah, an Iraqi businessman. It is a former British club now frequented by Iraq's elite, a place of contrasts. A huge Saddam portrait greets arrivals in the club car park, but members still leave their own private bottles of whisky behind the bar, their names printed on them, in the old British club tradition. We were the only customers, but there was still food, some salads and chicken.

Falah spoke over dinner about statistics, trying to put on a brave face that Iraq would somehow continue. He had been helping as a consultant to the government in what he called 'food security' since the crisis began. He had managed to cut sugar consumption by 60% by closing down ice-cream and confectionery shops; Iraq was now making its own liquid sugar from dates. Farmers had had to kill most of Iraq's chickens because of the shortage of grain, but cows had been switched to grass and still gave milk. Wheat was a problem; Iraq produced 4 million tons annually and consumed 6.5 million but increased subsidies for farmers would make up much of the shortage. Meanwhile, rationing filled the gap: his office had made charts of human consumption, added 20% and produced rationing amounts and distributed coupons.

Such statistics are usually impossible to come by; but I had barely the energy to commit them to memory (you don't take notes in public in Iraq). Falah relaxed, dropped his beloved subject and lapsed into tales of his childhood.

The club was significant to him and to the current situation. He had come here first as a young and proud university student, the first Arab of his generation to visit it, brought by a British professor as a reward for being number one in his class. 'You realise for us this is much more than a war between Iraq and America. For us, even for the Arabs who are not with Saddam, it is a struggle for our dignity. The West has humiliated us and we see Saddam as a leader who has finally stood up to the West and said we want our dignity.'

On the way home, I went by the French embassy where André Jenier, the last western diplomat in Baghdad, was preparing to leave in proper French style. He had laid out the embassy's last French cheeses, pâtés and salamis and served champagne until midnight, when he and his few remaining staff clambered into their cars and drove through the night to the Jordanian border.

At the Hotel Palestine, previously the Meridian but now run-down and shabby after a change from French to Iraqi ownership at the start of the economic embargo five months ago, I stopped at a 'challenge the deadline' celebration, an Iraqi version of an end-of-the-world party.

Kadum Al-Sahir, a popular singer, was on the floor amid a group of men who danced and waved Iraqi flags. But most of the rest of the hall was filled with sombre beer drinkers, sitting at their tables without much enthusiasm. Most were government recruits; the only guests who seemed to have paid the 20 dinar ($35) entry price were 10 Palestinians who had come in a delegation from Jordan to show solidarity with Iraq. A wedding party had been recruited to build up the numbers.

I went to bed in my room at the Rashid hotel and waited for the worst.

The Americans had announced that the deadline would fall at midnight New York time, 8am local time next day, Wednesday the 16th. When I woke, a heavy fog had settled across the flat city. For a moment, looking out of the hotel window, unable to see anything but white mist obscuring the skyline, I thought perhaps the attack had come and I had slept through it.

Downstairs, among the government 'minders' who watched the comings and goings of the few of the 40 or so journalists left at the Rashid hotel, there was premature euphoria. 'You see, I told you there would not be war,' said Karim, one of the men from the information ministry.

Baghdad thought otherwise. Driving around town, I saw only a few knots of men in quiet discussions. Rashid Street, the main thoroughfare, lined with colonnaded mock-Ottoman buildings from the 1930s, was usually packed with cars. Instead, it was a wide deserted avenue at 9am.

Windows were taped over against bombs for the first time. The Mandarin restaurant on Karada Street, once Baghdad's busiest fast-food joint but closed for months because of a ban on serving meals, had its wide windows taped in large Xs. At the Shorjah souk, Baghdad's most popular market because of its cheap clothing, household items and canned goods, only four of the 200 stores had opened. One man, hanging up flannel robes from the ceiling of his shop, said: 'We will open for an hour. If it stays like this, we will close.' Schools had opened, but with few teachers and fewer students they quickly closed for the day.

There was no sign of backing off by Saddam. The headline of the government newspaper, *Al-Jumhuriya*, said: 'We shall never compromise on Iraqi and Arab rights.' Midday television news showed perhaps the unluckiest people in the world that day: 177 former prisoners of war descending from an Iraqi Airways flight to Baghdad after years of captivity in Iran.

Sources were fast disappearing. I telephoned the foreign ministry to try to see Nizar Hamdoun, the under-secretary. But the ministry's number had changed and its officials had moved to a new location. The last time I had seen Hamdoun, he was sitting in his office, morosely watching CNN television. 'I feel like I'm watching a bad fiction movie,' he had said.

During his tenure as Iraqi ambassador to Washington, Hamdoun had been the architect of the Iraqi–American rapprochement of the 1980s. He still felt Iraq could be America's best ally in the Middle East. It was the only local power able to enforce stability in the region under Bush's new world order; it had oil America needed; it was a potentially wealthy market; and it would guarantee American interests. But by 16 January 1991, policy was long out of the hands of thoughtful diplomats such as Hamdoun.

At the ministry of information that evening, the receptionist at the office of Naji Hadithi, the director-general, was watching cartoons. Inside, Hadithi and I watched a film showing Saddam visiting troops in Kuwait. The president looked confident as he had in every appearance that week, although rather awkward as he sat wrapped in a huge greatcoat with troops who looked terrified by his presence. He asked them oddly personal questions. 'Have you had your dinner?' he said to one. A long pause ... 'Is this place warm?' he said to another.

Hadithi switched to CNN and we watched a demonstration of allied fire control in Dhahran, where Saudi, American and British forces are based. A lieutenant-commander was interviewed, saying his men were prepared. Hadithi commented: 'The only thing missing from this is reality.'

He meant on the allied side. It was a cherished belief of many Iraqis I spoke to, even those who were desperate to avoid war, that if it came to a battle, Iraqi soldiers, hardened in the war against Iran, would defeat their better armed but inexperienced enemy.

As Wednesday evening drew on, Marlin Fitzwater, Bush's spokesman, caused the first real worry among the foreign press corps. He said any journalists in Baghdad were in danger and should leave immediately. All American print reporters had left on the 14th, but the American television networks remained. Now they started getting prearranged signals from Pentagon sources that an attack was imminent.

Larry Doyle of CBS received the message: 'Your family is fine but your children have colds.' Doyle, a veteran journalist who reported on the Vietnam war, put down the phone and said simply: 'Shit.'

A delegation of journalists hurried to Hadithi's office. Some wanted to move out of the Rashid hotel, located in central Baghdad near most of the ministries and the presidential palace, all obvious targets for attack. But Hadithi said: 'We are still here. Our ministry is a dangerous place and yet we did not evacuate.'

John Simpson of BBC Television said in his understated manner: 'The Americans have 2,000lb bombs which could make things extremely unpleasant.'

Latis Jassim, the information minister, arrived and reassured us. 'You are safe. This is a commitment on our part. We are willing and eager to offer you the necessary services so that you can report the facts as you see them. But at no time will communications fail completely.'

It was midnight. We went back to the hotel. The attack could come at any moment. Nobody knew how bad it might be. We waited.

I took a small bag down to the bomb shelter below the hotel, just in case. Already women and children were huddled along the walls wrapped in blankets. Somehow the warning had swept through the hotel.

The lights in the shelter flickered. I had to see what was happening. I turned and started up the steps but was met by a flood of panicked people coming down the stairs, women with crying children, Sudanese waiters still in uniform, an Iranian delegation staying at the hotel.

At entrance-hall level, I could hear booms from outside. Upstairs, from the fifth-floor BBC office, we saw out of the window a spectacular display of tracer fire shooting across the sky. Tracers spewed up as if from a Roman candle. Others shot across the sky

as if following an unseen and unheard enemy. White flashes illuminated the tops of buildings on which, during the last five
months, we had watched the crews of anti-aircraft guns shelter first
from the August sun and lately from January's rain and cold.

Strange video game noises filled the air. The staccato thud-thud-
thud of heavy artillery sounded. Bob Simpson of BBC Radio had
a microphone out of the open window and leaned on his elbows
on the windowsill as he calmly described the spectacular display.
Down the hall, a CBS cameraman knelt on the floor, his camera
out of the window, and filmed through a down-tilted eye scope.

Huge yellow flashes appeared on the horizon. Something to the
right thudded and the impact threw me back across the room.
Smoke rose from the building. There could no longer be any suspicion that it was a false alarm or jittery anti-aircraft gunners. It was
2.35am Iraqi time and Baghdad was under attack.

Doyle, spotting the flashes on the horizon, narrated for those of
us less knowledgeable about armaments. 'Those are the big boys,
the cute 2,000lb bombs,' he said. 'Unfortunately I've been through
this before. They are just pounding the hell out of that place.'

The bombing appeared to be about 20 miles off, probably at the
Rashid military complex. The attack slackened off, then started
again at 3.35am. The city, which had remained lit up, went
completely black. The anti-aircraft fire stopped and started again
in almost 15-minute intervals, sometimes directed above our hotel,
filling the skies but seeming to have little effect.

About 4.25am, hotel security guards came into the room and
tried to drag us downstairs to the shelter. They settled for taping
over the emergency light that had gone on when the hotel lights
failed. From below, during a lull, an earnest ABC reporter yelled
up: 'What are your departure plans?' Somebody yelled down: 'Up
in the air at the moment.'

I wandered back to my room at 6am as dawn broke and the
attack appeared to have stopped. A man I had never seen before
was asleep in my bed still wearing large boots. I went down the hall
and took a nap on the floor of the BBC office.

Morning came cold and misty again when I woke at 7.30am. After the drama of the night, it was strange to see the city skyline unchanged. Smoke from a fire behind the hotel drifted through the hallways. But little damage was visible from the hotel room. We clustered around to hear Baghdad radio for the first communiqué of the war. 'This is communiqué number one. The mother of battles has begun. President Bush will regret this attack. Victory is near.' The voice announced the immediate call-up of reserve soldiers born in 1954, 1955 and 1956. The radio returned to martial music.

My driver had disappeared. He was born in 1955 and had been worrying about the call-up for the last month. 'War is very bad,' he had said to me. 'I fought eight years in the war with Iran. No wife, no children. Now maybe I have to go to Kuwait.' His fears had been realised.

I grabbed a taxi on the street and drove around the city. The first evidence of attack was at the international post and telecommunications building. It had been hit by at least four missiles that had left gaping holes and dangling wires. Chunks of building and glass littered the streets, but no surrounding buildings suffered damage more than broken windows.

A bit further on, the Ba'ath party headquarters had taken a direct hit in the roof. Again, no surrounding buildings were touched. On Abunawas Street, across the river from the presidential palace, a car tilted crazily into a 30-foot crater already filled with water. But, other than that, there seemed to be almost no damage to civilian targets.

Anti-aircraft guns sounded again at 9am and 10am. Soldiers in uniform lined the roads at bus stations trying to flag down cabs or cars to head south to register with their units. The few families that had left it too late to leave stood, suitcases and children in hand, trying to do the same.

At 10.30am I was standing in front of the ministry of information, now deserted despite the minister's brave words just hours earlier, as a thud sounded and a mushroom of smoke went up from the defence ministry about half a mile away. Two more thuds shook the building. Neither a plane had been visible nor an engine heard. Anti-aircraft fire went up but it was too late.

Driving by the ministry – an old Ottoman building still marked the Abbassid Palace on tourist maps and so secret that a government official once told me it was a museum – I could see flames in the central section. A wing had been flattened as if by a giant fist.

The reaction from soldiers in the barracks across the street from the defence ministry was as surprising as the suddenness of the attack. They stood standing and watching the fire as if it was a show unconnected to them. Nobody seemed to be in much of a hurry to put it out. Like the foreign ministry, the defence department must have transferred its operations elsewhere in the days before the deadline.

As I drove around town, the calm and lack of panic were impressive. Orderly lines formed for bread and cars queued for petrol. It was a far cry from the day after the bombing of the Libyan city of Tripoli, when Libyans crashed their cars into each other trying to flee, the government disappeared and rumours that Colonel Gadaffi had been overthrown filled the capital.

Baghdad's militiamen had appeared overnight to keep order. In the Amriyah area, a civilian neighbourhood, six teenagers dressed in jeans and jackets walked along the streets with Kalashnikov assault rifles casually slung over their shoulders. A man in a cheap suit and a keffiyeh Arab headdress manned an anti-aircraft gun placed in the bed of a Nissan pick-up truck at a crossroads. But there were no new checkpoints, nor was there hostility towards foreigners.

Saddam came on Baghdad radio at 12.40 in the afternoon, speaking in calm and confident tone: 'At 2.30am the great duel started. The valiant sons of Iraq, your brothers, sons and fathers, confronted the invaders. Damn King Fahd, the traitor of Mecca, damn the invaders, damn these criminals. We shall win. The dawn will break and they will be damned.'

My taxi driver, taking me back to the hotel, said he was not at the front because he had a piece of shrapnel still in his head from the Iran war. It hurt when the weather got cold. Like most Iraqis that day, he appeared worried but unfazed. 'I did not think we should have taken Kuwait,' he said. 'I don't agree with this. But the Americans should not come to Iraq. Iraqi soldiers will fight for Iraq and for Saddam. We have fought for eight years against Iran and they cannot frighten us.'

This was the mood of Baghdad under fire. An Iraqi businessman explained to me why people were so calm. Listening for weeks to the propaganda from Washington, they had expected Armageddon. Now that the bombing had come at last and they had survived, he said, their attitude was: 'Well, if that's it, we can take it.'

People had even begun to listen for the first time to Iraqi radio, and to believe its propaganda, because they felt that the BBC and Voice of America had lied about allied successes against the air force and missile sites in the first attack.

In addition, the government maintained at least a semblance of control. The city was without water or electricity, and the streets began to smell of sewage and cordite. But soldiers directed traffic in place of traffic lights, papers continued to publish daily, and the television news appeared every night at the same time, with its usual announcer, and on the same television studio set.

Only a few shops opened; and prices were astonishing: I saw a bottle of whisky, a packet of cigarettes and three Mars bars bought for 147 dinars, the equivalent of $441 at the official rate and equal to three-quarters of the monthly salary of a middle-ranking government official.

But in the poor neighbourhoods such as Saddam City, where more people had remained because they had no way of escape, and which the regime regards as its centres of support, government lorries distributed bread under normal ration regulations.

Anti-aircraft fire erupted sporadically during the day. Tracer fire, the thud of guns and falling bombs filled the night, but there were few civilian casualties.

There were makeshift shelters to be found almost anywhere in the city. Driving back to the hotel, I ducked into Baghdad Hotel when anti-aircraft guns went off at the nearby presidential palace. The discotheque had been turned into a bomb shelter and guests were handed candles at the door. People were worried but there was still an air of unreality. 'Palestine seems closer than it has for 40 years,' said a Palestinian businessman also sheltering inside.

Baghdad's survival and the news that Saddam had launched Scud rockets at Israel had many Palestinians and their Iraqi supporters still believing that he would achieve his goal of somehow freeing Palestinian land from Israel.

As the sun set on Friday, I watched two orbs of light streak low across the city skyline, just missing the rooftops, and smash into the Dora oil refinery. A huge ball of fire erupted and smoke drifted back over Baghdad.

Bombing continued sporadically that night and at dawn the refinery had only three instead of four chimneys. The 20-storey communications tower which had lost its top three storeys to an unseen missile on Friday, as if to an invisible hand, had completely disappeared from the skyline by Saturday morning.

On Saturday afternoon, I was gazing idly from a fifth-floor window across the Zawra zoo park opposite the hotel when I suddenly realised that a cruise missile was heading above the trees straight for us. It seemed to be white. I could see its little fins. There was no smoke trail coming from it.

I thought it was going to hit the hotel, and I yelled out. But it turned right and skirted the building, as if following a street map, and hit the old parliament building about half a mile away, sending up a white pall of smoke.

Another cruise landed even closer, disappearing with a deafening crash into breeze-block staff quarters next to the hotel. The huts burst into flames and shrapnel showered the lawn and swimming pool. Glass from broken windows littered the hotel lobby as hotel workers dragged an electronic circuit board into the air-raid shelter, dancing around it, ululating and shouting that they had downed an American plane.

It was a relentless afternoon attack. At least two more missiles hit the Dora refinery again, sparking a fire that lit Baghdad with a beautiful rose glow late into the night.

Conditions at the Rashid hotel were becoming primitive. Electricity remained off and journalists worked at night by candle-light. Sanitation had broken down, toilets could not flush, and we had been washing in the swimming pool.

The officials minding us had had enough. They had stayed in the shelter for days and had not seen their families nor been able to contact them by telephone. They were worried about our safety and about the detail of what we were reporting. We were ordered to leave.

On Saturday night, as I packed and sat up late with other journalists discussing our departure, a Palestinian friend stopped by to say farewell. An articulate, educated man, he was trying to explain why so much of the Arab world had come out in support of Saddam despite his invasion of Kuwait and oppressive policies at home.

'You must understand that if Saddam goes, no Westerner will be safe walking down an Arab street. I will pick up a machinegun and fight the Americans. A year ago I would have told you I hated Saddam and his regime. But he has become a symbol for us. Saddam is the result of the humiliation of the war of 1967 and of all the humiliations we have suffered from the West. If we let you destroy Saddam now, you will destroy all of us Arabs again.' He added: 'It is a question of dignity. Saddam came along with his rockets and stood up to you and we said, "Why not?"'

I rose at 5am to the incongruous sounds of a cock crowing and another barrage of anti-aircraft fire, this time a light and sparkling scattering of shots of tracer into the air. The government newspaper headline read: 'Hussein rockets answer the call of Palestine. The road to Jerusalem is open.' Uniting under attack behind Saddam, people might even believe this hyperbole.

Downstairs the taxi drivers demanded the exorbitant sum of $3,000 a car to the Jordanian border, because a convoy of cars that had left on Saturday had been bombed near the town of Rutba in the western desert.

We drove out of Baghdad on the deserted highway, past military camps on the city's perimeter that appeared surprisingly intact, with anti-aircraft guns still manned on mounds along their boundaries. Government army lorries trundled south towing anti-aircraft guns, but there was little other traffic. The journey through flat, unbroken rocky desert was uneventful. Iraqi guards stamped exit visas into our passports at the desolate border station of Trebeil. Among the shabby breeze-block buildings we left behind the stacks of abandoned cheap luggage from earlier refugees and drove across the no man's land into Jordan.

Ghosts of war stalk Basra's empty streets

SOUTHERN IRAQ

23 August 1992

The fat singer in the smoky gloom of the Eastern Nights Club in Basra was just getting into her stride when the lights went up. The laughter at a table of rich merchants died instantly.

An unsmiling officer in khaki swept through the beads hanging across the door followed by eight soldiers, who fanned out between tables draped in red velvet and dotted with bottles of Scotch. The customers froze. They knew that last month Saddam Hussein executed 42 merchants for profiteering.

The officer scanned the room, but he had no interest in the traders or the soldier sitting with a buxom prostitute. His eyes fell on a table of eight young men.

Two soldiers moved forward, ordering the men to their feet with the flick of a Kalashnikov. The officer pulled out battered papers.

The first passed and was motioned to sit; the second was led away.

'Oh, he didn't even have time to change his clothes,' lamented Ishar, a young prostitute. A second glance told the story: the arrested man still wore his olive army trousers under a white shirt and maroon jacket. He was a deserter. Four more of his companions were led away.

As the soldiers left, there was a moment of silence. Then the manager strode to the dance floor and, with a grandiose flourish, restarted the band and the singer. The lights dimmed and laughter flooded the room again – the forced laughter of relief.

Basra, capital of the south and home to Iraq's Shi'ite majority, is a city under siege. Whereas Baghdad has been largely rebuilt since the Gulf War, Basra still bears the scars of allied bombing and the rebellion that saw officials of the ruling Ba'ath party slaughtered in the streets and government buildings and hospitals looted and torched.

Today, fear of Iranian infiltrators, army deserters and fugitive rebels empties the city's streets after 9pm. Food is scarce and expensive. The factories, port and oil plants are closed; its hospitals desperately short of medicine and filled with malnourished babies.

Fifty life-sized statues of dead heroes of the Iran–Iraq war line the corniche on the Shatt al-Arab, their arms pointing across the water towards the old Iranian foe. Locals, fearful of the enemy within, joke that they should point in every direction.

The man charged with keeping order in Basra is Brigadier General Latif Omoud, a governor who sits behind a desk with 10 telephones. It is impressive, but unconvincing.

The city's telecommunications have not been restored since the end of the Gulf War 18 months ago, and a line has to be installed to each number he wants to call. 'The pink telephone is for my girlfriend,' he joked.

Dressed in a neatly pressed uniform and with his hands manicured, Omoud appears unbowed by the calamitous state of the city he took over after Iraqi forces crushed the Shi'ite rebellion in March last year.

He has not been amused, however, by the news that Britain, France and the United States were preparing to enforce an air exclusion zone south of the 32nd parallel to protect the Shi'ites in the southern marshlands from destruction by Saddam.

Any Iraqi plane or helicopter that flies will risk being shot down. Since Basra is 100 miles south of the 32nd parallel, Omoud was angry and perplexed. The general, who sees himself on the front line with Iran, claims to have quelled the 'security problem' in Basra.

But the road south from al-Amarah to Basra remains a no-go zone at night; checkpoints are attacked, soldiers killed and civilians robbed. It will get much worse, said Omoud, if the allied plan is enforced.

'We have arrested many infiltrators in Basra,' he said. 'They come from Iran to commit acts of sabotage. We should be allowed to fly our planes and helicopters to counter the Iranian menace.'

He made no apology for the attacks on the marshes, insisting they were a haven for rebels and Iranian agents. The West, Omoud said, was short-sighted: 'The Iranians are still interested in export-ing their revolution.'

Then the governor was off, speeding away in his armoured white Mercedes followed by a jeep with a mounted machinegun and two cars full of soldiers. Behind him, sweltering in the 53°C heat, brick-layers continued rebuilding his governor's garrison, which had been gutted during the rebellion.

The real picture in the south is difficult to piece together in a tightly controlled nation of nervous people. But it is clear that the government has won the upper hand in the war with the 30,000 rebels in the Hawaiza marshes, a 6,000-square-mile swampland of waterways and reed banks.

The attacks against insurgents in the marshes, according to diplomats in Baghdad and interviews in Basra and al-Amarah, began around 21 July. There is little doubt they were brutal. Diplomats believe that Iraq used helicopter gunships and artillery against the marsh Arabs but has not sent in ground troops because of the treacherous terrain.

The rebels had little chance. Besieged, they were killed or forced to flee or surrender. Many civilian marsh dwellers also died. The season favoured the army; in July and August the marshes dry up, making operations easier. One source said 9,000 rebels had surrendered or been captured.

The few townspeople in al-Amarah willing to talk say the roads are too dangerous to travel at night. At the Saddam Hussein general hospital, Dr Ayad Abdul Aziz said there had been constant attacks on civilians and soldiers in the area near the marshes.

But operations by the Iraqi army seem to have ended. The military appears to be in defensive positions. Nightly on Iraqi national television, captured rebels make their confessions.

One Iraqi, a PoW from the Iraq–Iran war, claimed he had been forced to fight for Iran: 'It was decided to start a sabotage campaign. I received verbal instructions to go on a fact-finding mission in Iraq. We needed information on the security status. I carried false identification, money and a pistol.'

He said he met rebels who had plentiful supplies of explosives and weapons, and sent back information to Iran. The interviewees show extraordinary calm while making their confessions; it is widely assumed they are executed afterwards.

'Of course they are calm,' said one Iraqi viewer last week. 'They know it is the end of their lives.'

Critics are silenced as Saddam rebuilds Iraq

BAGHDAD

4 October 1992

Arc lights on the roof of the National Conference Palace shone through the night and into the pink dawn last week as construction workers hammered and welded round the clock to repair the bombed building. It might have been an unremarkable scene in a city recovering from 43 consecutive days of air attack, except for one thing: it was the last important building to be restored.

Little more than 18 months after the Gulf War ceasefire, you have to scour the back streets of Baghdad for any sign of the heavy bombing it underwent. Iraqi engineers have repaired all but one of the bridges destroyed during the hostilities and rebuilt the 14-storey central telephone exchange on the bank of the Tigris, bombed so often that by the end of the conflict it was just a concrete shell with steel and wires curling from the windows. Gutted ministries have been reconstructed, rubble removed.

The main power plant, which was lit almost nightly by flashes from explosions, is working at 90% of its pre-war capacity. Soon after the bombing ended, an engineer at the plant said it would take at least two years to get it working again; but there was not one blackout during the blazing hot summer, when Baghdadis ran their air-conditioning at full blast.

The list of achievements goes on. Oil production is back to about 800,000 barrels a day, although United Nations sanctions prohibit Iraq from selling its petroleum abroad. Restored refineries supply more than enough petrol and heating oil for Iraq's domestic needs and exports to Jordan. Iraqi experts say they could now pump 2 million barrels a day.

The six-lane highway from Baghdad to the Jordanian border, littered with craters from nightly raids, is now a smoothly surfaced superhighway. Three weeks ago the evening news showed Saddam Hussein congratulating workers for finishing repairs on the presidential palace.

In fact, much of the current construction in Baghdad is of new buildings. Enormous villas are sprouting in the wealthy Mansour district, financed by war profits. Newspapers report the progress of the Third River project, the construction of a 350-mile canal that will drain the rising water in the Tigris-Euphrates basin to reclaim land.

Yesterday, Saddam announced that construction would resume, using Iraqi designs and expertise, of an enormous petrochemical complex which the war forced foreign companies to abandon. When finished, it will be the largest in the Middle East.

What happened? Just 18 months ago, Saddam sat in a window-less bunker, wrapped in a heavy woollen greatcoat because there was no heat and in dim light because even the president had to rely on a diesel-fuelled generator for electricity. Outside, his country lay in ruins. The electricity grid was destroyed. Sewerage and water systems, telephones, even traffic lights did not work. His oil refineries were reduced to tangled machinery and holed tanks. He had just been kicked out of Kuwait, his army was in disarray, a rebellion raged in 14 of his 18 provinces, and much of his air force was parked on the territory of his enemy, Iran.

Since then, Iraq has been rebuilt without money from oil exports, without the teams of foreign experts that once staffed the military and civilian industries, without the $4 billion of assets frozen in overseas banks, and under strict sanctions that ban the import of spare parts or construction materials.

The key to the revival is Saddam. According to those around him, he did not even falter in the face of devastation so massive that allied leaders believed his downfall to be inevitable. Saddam never, ever, gives up, they say. This mentality was a liability during the Gulf crisis, when he refused to leave Kuwait, but it was crucial to the rebuilding of Iraq. He went from the Mother of all Battles to the Mother of all Reconstructions without missing a beat.

Saddam emerged unrepentant from his bunker and ready to rebuild. The 53-year-old president knows his people well. He needed to remove the daily reminders of the war, and his responsibility for it. 'I don't want to see any war damage in the capital,' an Iraqi official quoted him as saying. In a dictatorship as absolute as Iraq, such an order concentrates the mind. Construction crews began working 24 hours a day, even on Saturday, the Muslim Sabbath.

Saddam was fortunate in the resources he commanded. When UN sanctions were imposed in August 1990, Iraq had two years' supply of spare parts in storage. There were millions of dollars in overseas slush funds, which his brother, Barzan al-Tikriti, Iraqi representative to the UN in Geneva, used to buy spare parts that were smuggled in through Jordan. Perhaps most important, Iraq is home to the best educated and disciplined people in the Arab world. He had no need for foreign technical expertise.

Saddam identified himself with the reconstruction effort. News programmes regularly broadcast East-European-style footage of him inspecting repaired factories.

A special Order of the President was created to reward those who excelled in the rebuilding effort, and the annual conference of the ruling Ba'ath party was named the Jihad (Holy War) of Reconstruction Congress.

Nothing proved too insignificant for Saddam's attention. During a nationally televised meeting, he advised education officials to 'give special attention to sanitary facilities for students. The student who cannot go to the bathroom all day because it is dirty cannot concentrate.'

There has been no let-up in the momentum. Saddam warned his ministers last month: 'From now on, those government officials who fail in their responsibilities will be considered as being involved in economic sabotage. Stringent measures will be taken against them, similar to the strict measures taken against the traitors who were involved in profiteering and monopoly.' It was an undisguised reference to the 42 merchants executed in July for profiteering.

The success of the reconstruction has won Saddam the admiration of his greatest critics. Ordinary Iraqis, who love their bridges and modern buildings the way Europeans love their nation's art treasures or scenic vistas, are proud that Iraq has rebuilt its infrastructure quickly, and without outside help.

The country still has serious problems, though. Inflation has wrecked the economy, with prices spiralling higher almost daily – last week rice sold for 8½ dinars ($25) a kilo, a spare tyre for 2,000 dinars. The country's future wealth is mortgaged to old debts and war reparation. On Friday, the UN security council voted to seize $1 billion of Iraq's frozen assets to pay for UN operations.

But the dissatisfaction of Iraqis with their financial lot is irrelevant. Along with his bridges, Saddam has reconstructed his formidable security apparatus. The army has been restored to 40% of its pre-war capacity, with about 400,000 troops under arms; the ubiquitous Mukhabarat security men are back on the streets. The south is under undeclared martial law; generals have replaced civilians as governors in every southern province.

Saddam's success has also undermined Washington's attempts to persuade Iraqis to oppose the regime. I heard again and again in Baghdad, albeit in hushed tones, that Saddam and Bush had a secret deal: why else would the allied forces have stood by as the Republican Guard crushed the rebels?

In case anyone in Baghdad needed a reminder that Saddam's rule has been restored as surely as his capital, they need only look to the shore of the Tigris in the exclusive Adamiya district of Baghdad. An enormous building, designed on the lines of a Sumerian palace, has begun to emerge from its scaffolding. It is a new presidential palace.

Shadow of evil

IRAQ

22 January 1995

Latif Yahia spat in the mirror when he saw himself for the first time after being forced to undergo plastic surgery. But it was too late. He now looked exactly like Uday Hussein, the eldest son of the Iraqi president.

He spent the next four years as Uday's double, a time he now refers to as 'years of blood'. He was trapped at the heart of one of the most secretive, paranoid and brutal regimes on earth, learning its secrets while treading a tightrope between the pampered privileges of the inner circle and the terror of knowing that he could be shot at any moment.

Yahia has now spoken for the first time about how he was tortured into taking on the role, how he was turned physically and mentally into a terrible imitation of Saddam's murderous and licentious son, how he eventually escaped, and how he is now trying to exorcise the evil persona that entered him.

He has also revealed that Saddam, like Stalin and Churchill, has his own series of doubles, who are forced to undertake potentially dangerous public appearances. The present 'Saddam' replaced one who was assassinated in an attempt on the dictator's life.

Yahia attended public parties and football matches in his assumed role and posed with soldiers at the Kuwaiti front so that Uday would face no danger but the Iraqi people would believe Saddam had sent his son to serve in the Mother of all Battles. Yahia survived nine assassination attempts.

Only once did he give thanks for his hated new identity. When Yahia finally fled Iraq, soldiers manning checkpoints leaped out of the way and saluted as he sped north in his Oldsmobile, also a double for one of Uday's cars.

He came to think of himself as a monster. The man he had to impersonate is feared as much as his father in Iraq. He is a spoilt, brutal playboy who flies into uncontrollable rages when crossed and whose violent excesses are covered up by the security forces.

Uday even fell out with his father when he beat to death Saddam's favourite retainer in a drunken rage in 1988 and was briefly exiled to Geneva. Father and son now appear to be reconciled; last year, Iraqi exiles reported that Saddam had executed three senior military officers after they suggested Uday was not up to the job of defence minister that his father wanted to give him.

Since the Gulf War, Uday has tried to make his image more serious by founding *Babil* newspaper and a radio and television station that broadcasts popular western entertainment. But Yahia witnessed the sinister private activities of Saddam's son, which he said included earning millions of pounds from black-market deals in whisky, cigarettes and food while normal Iraqis suffered under international sanctions, and entertaining friends with torture videos shot in his father's prisons.

Yahia's story is fascinating, not just as the tale of a man pushed to unbelievable psychological limits, but also because it gives a remarkable insight into the most secretive of worlds, the life of Saddam Hussein and his family.

Now in Vienna as a political exile, the 30-year-old refugee is trying to recover his lost identity. It is disconcerting to meet him. He still looks exactly like Uday, still dresses in the same sharp European suits the dictator's son favours, sports the same heavy gold jewellery and black Ray-Ban sunglasses. He smokes a Cuban cigar with the same motions and has the same beard that distinguishes Uday from other Iraqis, who have only moustaches.

He is soft-spoken and polite, but old habits die hard. Taking out a cigar, he holds it until somebody lights it, even though the retainers that swarmed around him in his old role as Uday are long gone. He has, however, stopped beating his wife: the violent streak he picked up from his double now sickens him.

Yahia wants to destroy Uday, but he has not changed his appearance because he has no other identity, a dilemma that would have fascinated Sigmund Freud, who lived in the same Vienna street where Yahia's hideout is.

Yahia's case is like none Freud ever came across. He grew up in Baghdad, the son of a wealthy Kurdish merchant, and attended the exclusive Baghdad High School for Boys. Uday was in the same class and the two boys resembled each other. 'But I did not welcome looking similar,' he said. 'Uday had very bad manners with people even then.'

After graduating from Baghdad University in 1986 with a law degree, he went off to fight in the Iran–Iraq war, like most young Iraqi males. He was a first lieutenant serving in a forward reconnaissance unit in September 1987 when he received a presidential order to report to Baghdad.

Uday welcomed him in an ornate salon in the presidential palace. There was chit-chat about their schooldays and polite questions about his family before Uday came to the point. 'Do you want to be a son of Saddam?' he asked. Wary, Yahia answered: 'We are all sons of Saddam.'

'Well, I would like you to be a real son of Saddam, working with me. I don't want you as protection but as my double.'

Yahia recalled: 'I was afraid. I knew this was a government of criminals. So I asked him what would happen if I agreed, and what would happen if I refused. Uday told me that if I agreed, "all that you dream will happen". He said I would have money, servants, houses, women. If I refused, he said, "We will remain friends".'

Uday left him alone, desperately trying to think up an excuse. When he returned, Yahia had formulated what he thought was a diplomatic way out. 'All Iraqis want to serve the president,' he said. 'I am serving my president as a soldier and I would not like to be more than that.'

Uday's eyes reddened in rage; he tore the military epaulettes from Yahia's shoulders and called in security officers. Yahia was blindfolded, driven for an hour in a car (later he would realise he had only been driven around the presidential grounds), and imprisoned in a tiny cell that was painted entirely blood-red.

'I suffered every kind of torture,' Yahia recalled. He said he was beaten with a cable, hanged from the ceiling by his hands, fed only bread or rice and water at different times of day so that he would become disorientated. He was told that if he continued to refuse, he would spend the rest of his life in the cell. After a week, he cracked.

Four days later he signed papers promising he would act as Uday's double and reveal nothing about his activities. The contract ended with a warning: any violation and the penalty was death by hanging. Two weeks later, surgery began at the Ibn Sina hospital in the palace complex. Dentists removed his front teeth and replaced them with teeth like Uday's; doctors cut a cleft into his chin.

'I hated myself,' he said. 'All my family and friends hated Saddam; so looking like his son, I was disgusted with myself.'

He began his 'special education': 16 hours a day watching videos of Uday walk, dance, drive, talk, get in and out of cars, light cigars, drink Scotch. A trainer would then take him through each movement over and over 20, 30, 40 times, day after day until he got it right.

'I never drank before, or smoked, or danced. I was very correct with people,' Yahia said. 'I had to learn to drink Dimple (Uday's brand of whisky), smoke cigars and talk differently. And I had to learn to be rude with people, like him.' He also learned intelligence and sabotage techniques, and was taught to check under cars before getting into them.

After six months of intensive training, Yahia made his first public appearance as his double at a football match at the People's Stadium, where he was surrounded by people who knew the president's son. With a trainer by his elbow every moment, even driving the black Mercedes 500SL that was Uday's favourite car, Yahia passed muster. He remembers thinking when he arrived back at the sumptuous villa Uday had given him: 'Latif Yahia doesn't exist any more.'

Four lost years followed. Yahia appeared as Uday and travelled with him to London, Geneva and Paris. Whenever Uday wanted a suit – he preferred Christian Dior and Yves St Laurent – he bought two: one for himself, one for Yahia. Uday owned more than 100 luxury cars, and selected them daily to match the colour of his suit.

Outside Baghdad, Yahia would travel in a security convoy as Uday, sometimes with as many as 72 bodyguards. By the time of the Gulf War, Saddam had so much confidence in Yahia that he used him in a cruel confidence trick against his own people. Every Iraqi remembers the visit by Uday to troops on the Kuwaiti front; in fact it was Yahia, sent there with a television crew to counteract truthful reports that Saddam's family had fled to safety outside Iraq.

During the years of their 'partnership', Uday gave him only one rule: 'Don't touch my girls.' At one point, Uday sent him to prison for 21 days because a girlfriend of Uday's became angry with Yahia, and told the president's son that he had tried to seduce her. When he was released, his double gave him a Mercedes by way of apology.

Uday often beat his guards, so in public Yahia would have to do the same. He had to learn to curse people; now, in an embarrassed voice, he repeats Uday's favourites. 'I would have to say "Your mother is a whore" and things like that,' Yahia said.

Gradually his public life merged with his private; he is ashamed to admit that he began to beat his wife, Bushra. 'I would kill Uday if I saw him again,' Yahia said. 'I would cut his body into small pieces and feed it to dogs. He made out of me a criminal like himself.'

Yahia was at a party on the river Tigris given for Suzanne Mubarak, the wife of the Egyptian president, when Uday committed one of his worst outrages. Uday hated Kamel Hanna, his father's favourite retainer, for serving as the go-between for Saddam's mistress, Samira Shahbandar, wife of the president of Iraq Airways. When Hanna failed to invite Uday to the Mubarak reception, he threw a party nearby out of spite; hearing shots at midnight, he crashed drunkenly into Hanna's celebration.

Uday saw Hanna firing into the air, Yahia recalled, and ordered him to stop shooting. 'I only take orders from the president,' Hanna replied. The night degenerated into violent chaos. Uday cut Hanna's neck and beat him, then downed pills at the thought of his father's anger. Both were taken to hospital, where Uday met Saddam waiting for word of his aide.

'Saddam grabbed Uday by the shirt and said: "If Kamel dies, you die",' Yahia said. Hanna died that night, but Uday's mother intervened to save her son. Yahia worried that he would be executed instead of Uday, but there had been too many witnesses.

Life was not all misery. Yahia had three villas, six luxury cars, all the money he wanted, beautiful women in droves. 'But I was always afraid,' he said. 'I was afraid Uday would kill me. I was afraid of being killed instead of Uday. Nine times I suffered assassination attempts.'

The attempts to kill him were sometimes by family members outraged that Uday had dishonoured their women, sometimes by political opponents. Once, he recalled, an outraged man burst into Uday's office at the Special Olympic Committee, which he headed, claiming he had raped his young daughter. The father said he had killed his daughter because of the dishonour and wanted satisfaction from Uday.

'Uday pulled out his pistol and shot him on the spot,' Yahia recalled. 'I sat in his office, six metres away. I was not shocked. I had seen it before. I knew I could do nothing.'

Yahia described a permanent atmosphere of fear in the presidential palace. Even those closest to Saddam refrained from speaking openly; everyone was afraid that they would be reported as disloyal, and the penalty was death.

He said Qusay, Saddam's younger son, who now heads the presidential intelligence agency, was the Iraqi president's favourite and heir apparent. 'Uday never called his father "dad",' Yahia said. 'Even in private he addressed him as "your excellency".'

One of the few people with whom Yahia could relax was Saddam's double, Fawaz al-Emari. He was the second man trained to impersonate the Iraqi president; his predecessor was killed posing as Saddam in 1984.

Emari had undergone far more extensive surgery than Yahia. His face had been entirely remodelled in Yugoslavia, and Russian doctors in Baghdad had operated on his vocal cords so he would speak exactly like Saddam. 'Sometimes when I met him, for a moment I would be afraid, thinking he was Saddam. And we were good friends,' said Yahia.

He and Emari would practise target-shooting together in the palace grounds, which included a swimming pool, cinema, theatre, hospital and sports centre. 'We spoke about general matters, but never about what we really felt or our activities. We were both too afraid one would betray the other,' he said.

Both doubles had to undergo weekly medical examinations. Doctors at the presidential palace would check that they were still the same weight as their masters, that their health was good, and that their surgery work remained sufficient for impersonation.

Saddam's double remains in the palace to this day, a virtual prisoner of his identity. 'Fawaz had a much more difficult life than me,' Yahia said. 'At least Uday went out all the time to restaurants, parties and discos, so I could. Saddam never did these things so Fawaz never could. He could not even go outside and walk on a street looking like Saddam; he would have been killed. He was banned from ever leaving the palace except when he was working.'

Work meant big formal occasions, including a hugely publicised swim by 'Saddam' in the Tigris on 26 July 1992. The swim was staged to prove that the president was alive and in good spirits despite the devastation of the Gulf War. In fact, he was afraid to appear in public and exposed his double to danger instead.

Yahia made the decision to flee almost a year after the allies liberated Kuwait in February 1991. His relationship with Uday had become increasingly tense.

'We were at a party at the Rasheed hotel,' Yahia recalled. 'Uday was invited by the president to receive four medals for his role in the Mother of all Battles. I joked, "You are not worth receiving these: I was in Kuwait instead of you." Uday said there was no difference, but he was not happy with me.'

The danger sign came the next night at another party, when Uday's 'love-broker', who procured girls for the president's son, upbraided Yahia for refusing to sell him a car. Then Uday also turned on Yahia.

The master apparently sensed that his double was going to make a break for freedom and decided to stop him. As Yahia stepped from a lift into the lobby of the Babylon hotel in Baghdad the next morning, Uday suddenly appeared and shot him. The bullet hit him high in the chest, missing vital organs.

Bleeding heavily, he says, he managed to get to his car and drive north towards the UN-protected safe haven in Kurdistan. To his surprise, Iraqi guards had not been alerted. 'At every checkpoint, nobody stopped me, they just waved me through. I would see them saluting in my (rear-view) mirror.'

Yahia has the scars to support his story: a round wound in the top of his right chest, an exit hole out the back. As he approached Kurdistan, he needed urgent medical treatment and feared the reception he would get from the Kurds. 'I could not go directly to Kurdistan. If the Kurds saw me, they would think I was Uday and kill me. So I abandoned my car in the woods, and went to a friend's house. I am from a Kurdish family, so they helped me.'

Through the Kurdish underground, he reached the American operations headquarters in the Kurdish town of Zakho. The Americans, wary at first, flew in four intelligence officers to debrief him. His wife, who had gone into hiding, was helped out by the same Kurdish underground, and their baby daughter was smuggled to Jordan by friends.

With the help of the Americans, he was granted political asylum in Vienna where many Iraqis live. But an import-export company he set up has failed to prosper and, because of Vienna's close connections with Baghdad, the city has a high number of Iraqi government representatives. Any one of them, he fears, might be a potential assassin.

His anxiety heightened last September when he received a letter from the Iraqi embassy saying he had been granted an amnesty and should return to Baghdad. The message came on his personal fax machine, even though he is living in hiding and gives the number only to close personal friends.

Yahia is afraid to send his daughter, Tamara, now five, to school in case his whereabouts can be traced through her. He keeps his wife, daughter and Omar, their 18-month son, with him even at the office.

Most of all, he finds it difficult to recover any sense of himself. 'Uday stole my life, my future, my identity,' he said. His wife agrees. Watching videos of Yahia posing as Uday in Baghdad, she shivered when she saw the man on the screen roughly grab a tissue proffered by an aide.

'He changed so much in his manners,' she said. 'Before, he was a normal person, but after he was tough and violent. He would hit me or kick me, and many times I thought of getting divorced. But I know now he is trying very hard to recover himself.'

Blood feud at the heart of darkness

8 September 1996

Terrible deaths in the family of Saddam Hussein illlustrate the brutality of a tyrant still powerful enough to shake the world. Marie Colvin reports from Oman.

In the glistening marble and gilt palace of Hashemiya, high on a hilltop overlooking the Jordanian capital, Ali Kamel, nine, spent many hours of his exile drawing brightly coloured pictures for his grandfather. Ali never learnt why he was living in this strange place. He was too young to be told his family had fled there in terror of the grandfather he loved: Saddam Hussein.

Hussein Kamel, Ali's father, had been the Iraqi tyrant's closest adviser. He had risen from lowly bodyguard to head of military procurement, and had been put in charge of rebuilding his country after the Gulf War. Kamel even married Saddam's favourite daughter, Ragda. But he fell out with the dictator's son, Uday, a thug who had repeatedly killed on impulse.

In August last year, Kamel was in such fear of his life that he took Ragda, Ali and his two daughters across the barren Iraqi desert to seek safety in Jordan. Other members of the family accompanied him in a fleet of black Mercedes.

There was a brother, Saddam Kamel, who had been responsible for the dictator's personal security. His wife Rana, Saddam's second daughter, came too, clutching their three children. A second brother followed, with a sister, her husband and their five children.

The family's terrible fate, details of which are disclosed here for the first time, gives a chilling insight into the methods used by Saddam to retain power despite isolation from the world and hatred at home.

The defection of so many family members was a devastating blow to the tyrant. In the days that followed he retaliated: scores of Kamel's relatives and followers disappeared. For months afterwards Saddam plotted his revenge with the cunning and lethal aggression that was so much in evidence again last week in his latest challenge to the international order.

Kamel's family settled comfortably at first into the luxury of the palace provided for them by King Hussein of Jordan. Stuffed with Persian carpets and other finery, it provided them with a secure home behind the shelter of tall, white stone walls.

Ali took lessons from a private tutor. Although the boy did not excel in his academic work, it did not take him long to work out that all was not well with his parents. Kamel had expected to be seen by the world as the potential successor to Saddam. But he had too much blood on his own hands. The Americans came only to pump him for information about the Iraqi military establishment. Even the Iraqi opposition shunned him.

Early in February, Ali often saw his father walking in the palace garden despite the cold and rain, speaking on his cellular telephone. Hussein Kamel had become so disillusioned with exile that he had begun discreet negotiations to return to Baghdad.

It was part of Saddam's game plan that he responded by making strenuous demands. Not only would Kamel be obliged to return millions of dollars he had hidden in a German bank; he would also have to provide a detailed written account of everything he had told his western interrogators, a lengthy process for a man who was barely literate.

His departure was precipitated by the growing impatience of his hosts with public statements in which he criticised the king. On the first day of the Muslim feast of Eid, he was visited by Prince Talal of Jordan, who told him he was 'free to go', the unspoken message being that he had outstayed his welcome.

Kamel strapped a pistol to his hip, drove to the home of the Iraqi ambassador and sat in animated discussion with him in the reception hall. Then they went to the embassy and telephoned Baghdad.

Once he was sure that Kamel had fulfilled the conditions set for his return, Saddam sent a video of himself, in which he promised he had forgiven his son-in-law. 'Come during the feast,' he said. 'The family will be together.' He implored him to bring all his relatives back with him. A written amnesty followed from the Iraqi leadership council.

Kamel made his decision abruptly. 'We are going home,' he announced to a family gathering. Ragda and Rana, suddenly frightened, began crying. At the last moment, Ragda telephoned her mother, seeking reassurance. But the phone was answered by Uday, who, in his latest outrage, had shot an uncle in the leg in an argument over an Italian car that he wanted to add to his collection of classics.

Ragda begged her brother to tell her the truth: would they be safe if they came home? '*Habibti* [Arabic for my love], I give you my word,' he said.

Hours before he left, Kamel telephoned one of his few friends to say goodbye. The man, a fellow Iraqi, was appalled. 'You know you are going to your death,' he said. Kamel bragged that he had obtained personal assurances from Saddam. 'To this day, I don't know why he trusted Saddam,' the friend said last week. 'He was one of them. He should have known.'

Arriving at the border, the returning defectors were greeted by a smiling Uday in sunglasses and suit. The men were separated from their wives and children. Kamel would never see Ragda and Ali again.

With his brothers, he was taken to one of Saddam's presidential palaces, where they were rigorously questioned about their experiences in Jordan and their contacts with western representatives and opponents of the Iraqi regime. After three days, they were released and went to the home of Taher Abdel Kadr, a cousin. Here, they were joined by two sisters and the women's children. But their relief and jubilation were short-lived. Within 48 hours, they learnt from a statement broadcast on television that their wives had denounced them as traitors and had been granted divorces.

As dawn filtered through the windows of their villa on 20 February, a cousin who still worked at the presidential palace woke them with the news that they had been betrayed. He brought weapons. Grimly, the Kamels prepared for their assassins as the children slept on.

Their killing was a family affair. While army vehicles and police cars blocked off the neighbourhood, an armed gang led by Uday and Qusay Hussein, Saddam's second son, surrounded the house. Uday and Qusay were accompanied inside by the former husband of one of Kamel's sisters. He showed his loyalty to Saddam by opening the firing on his family's house.

The attack, carried out with assault weapons, was ferocious. Although Kamel's men fired back, they were swiftly overwhelmed.

Some of the family were killed in the initial onslaught; others when the armed men entered the house. They included Kamel's elderly father, all the women and at least five young children, gunned down in their nightclothes.

Outside in a parked Mercedes sat Ali Hassan Al-Majeed, a cousin of Saddam's who had earned the nickname 'The Hammer of the Kurds' after gassing villages in northern Iraq with chemical weapons in 1989. Al-Majeed was on a mobile phone, describing each step of the assault to Saddam as it happened.

'We have 17 bodies,' he said. The only member of the family who was missing was Kamel himself. Saddam barked: 'I want his body.'

As bulldozers were brought in to destroy the house, Kamel, naked to the waist, wounded and bleeding, burst from a hiding place inside and appeared at a door brandishing his personal pistol and a machinegun.

He had barely fired a shot before he was riddled with bullets. When the gunfire ceased, Al-Majeed walked up to the body and emptied his pistol into it. He dragged Kamel by one foot through the sand, yelling to his men and to neighbours cowering behind closed doors: 'Come and see the fate of a traitor.' The bulldozers moved in and the house was razed.

The massacre was a vivid reminder to the people of the ruthless-ness of the regime under which they live. If Saddam was willing to eliminate close and even innocent members of his own family in such a fashion, there was no limit to what he could do to them.

During the summer, however, came two further reminders of the apparent futility of resistance. In June a member of the presi-dential bodyguard fired shots at Saddam and was executed. Less than a month later, according to western diplomats and Iraqi exiles, a rebel group of Iraqi officers planned to kill Saddam by bombing a presidential palace from a plane that was to have taken off from Rasheed airport in Baghdad.

The conspiracy was discovered and hundreds of members of Saddam's armed forces were arrested. Between 1 and 3 August, 120 of the officers were executed.

Iraqis have grown used to atrocities since Saddam came to prominence. His first known political act was an attempt in 1959 to gun down Abdel-Karim Qassem, then the Iraqi leader. When he became president 20 years later, he began by accusing 21 senior members of the leadership of treason. He formed a firing squad with his remaining colleagues, and together they shot all the condemned men.

In the years that followed, his people learned to voice their opposition only to close friends and family. Criticism of Saddam is punishable by death, and the security services are ubiquitous. Iraqi couples do not even speak in front of their own children for fear they might innocently repeat something and bring down the wrath of the regime.

The long series of confrontations into which Saddam has led Iraq has made life immensely difficult in a country whose citizens should be as pampered as those of Saudi Arabia. Iraq, unlike most Arab states, has both oil and water. Two huge rivers, the Tigris and Euphrates, nourish the land, and before the imposition of United Nations sanctions following the invasion of Kuwait in August 1990, Iraq earned $10 billion a year by lifting 3m barrels of oil a day.

Much of the money was spent on creating not comfort, but the largest army in the Middle East. Within a year of taking power, Saddam ordered the invasion of Iran, starting a bitter war that lasted for eight years and left 1 million people dead.

The attack on Kuwait was another miscalculation. The 43 days of allied bombing, supported by Arab countries afraid of his might, destroyed not only military sites but roads, bridges, oil refineries, communications, sewage facilities and the rest of an extensive infrastructure built by oil revenues.

Last week's conflict, in which Iraqi support for one group of Kurds against another provoked two waves of bombardment with American cruise missiles, was by no means the first test of the allies' resolve since the Gulf War. But after previous confrontations, Saddam has simply waited out his enemies. Those close to him say he is proud to have outlasted in office both George Bush and Margaret Thatcher, who led the coalition against him in 1990.

The few who have risen in revolt have been crushed, but his inner circle has tightened around him and now consists almost solely of relatives from Tikrit, his home town.

According to Arab dignitaries who have visited Saddam, he has become so paranoid about his security since the Gulf War that he maintains 250 safe homes. The staff in each house prepares dinner every night as if he is to arrive; nobody knows where he will sleep until he shows up at the door.

The Kamel clan was not the first to betray him. Last June he was shaken by a coup attempt led by the powerful Dulaimi clan from his Sunni heartland that had been a pillar of his armed forces. Provoked by the torture and death of a clan member accused of involvement in a previous coup attempt, General Turki al-Dulaimi led his troops in a bold but suicidal march on Baghdad. The rebels were defeated in a day.

It has not escaped the attention of most Iraqis that while the latest confrontation has occurred less than six years after the Gulf War, the reaction around the world this time has been quite different. America's use of missiles was backed wholeheartedly only by Britain, Canada and Germany. Although he lost a few isolated radar and anti-aircraft batteries, Saddam succeeded in dividing the coalition that had been ranged against him.

The main reason for the change was the nature of Saddam's offensive. He did not roll his army across an international border and occupy another country, but sent a limited force of tanks and infantry into Arbil, a Kurdish city 12 miles inside the Kurdish 'safe haven' patrolled by allied jets.

He was also invited in by the Kurdish faction that represents the majority of Kurds, the Kurdish Democratic party (KDP). Other Middle Eastern countries saw the American intervention as a blatantly inconsistent piece of interference in an internal problem. The United States had not objected when Turkey sent 35,000 troops into northern Iraq last year to attack bases of rebellious

Kurds; nor when Iran sent 3,000 troops across the border into northern Iraq last month.

Turkey and Saudi Arabia, among the countries that are the closest allies in the Middle East, refused Washington permission to launch strikes from their soil. The Arab League, for once in agreement, denounced the attacks on Iraq.

Just as striking, the first criticism of the American bombing came from a Gulf newspaper, condemning the action and saying that all Arabs should oppose it 'as a matter of honour'. It was the first time since the Gulf War that any paper in the region used the word 'brothers' to refer to Iraqis.

France was critical and Britain was unable to get a resolution denouncing the Iraqi incursion through the UN security council following strong opposition from Russia. By the end of the week, Saddam's tanks were still dug in in northern Iraq and the allied coalition was in tatters.

For now, Saddam may have little choice but to accept the establishment of a security zone inside its territory by Turkey, which says this is needed to fight Kurds battling for independence from Ankara. He should not be expected to be quiescent forever, however. He has every prospect of increasing his power and has a lot of grudges to settle. Those who know Saddam say the one certainty is that he never forgets and never forgives.

For the ordinary Iraqi, life seems likely to get harder. While the so-called 'war rich' who have profited from the black market in Baghdad continue to work on new palaces, most people are worried about food prices driven to new peaks by the crisis.

Privations, large and small, continued last week. People had to shower at 4am because electricity cuts meant there was no water during daytime. In a hospital in Baghdad, surgeons who no longer had paediatric surgical equipment operated on children with adult-sized instruments. 'It is butchery,' one doctor agonised.

Saddam's offensive put into limbo a UN-negotiated deal that would have enabled him to sell oil for food. There now seems little hope of relief in the near future.

Life is more comfortable but barely less bleak for Saddam's two daughters and their six young children. They were not in the villa where Kamel and his other relatives were killed, but face a dark future.

The two young widows were forced to move into the house of their mother's sister, where they are virtual prisoners. They cannot go out. Their children were taken away and they have been told they may never see them again. Sources in Baghdad said Rana, who was close to her husband Saddam Kamel, tried to kill herself and had to be hospitalised.

Ali, his sisters and cousins are living a sequestered life in Tikrit, Saddam Hussein's birthplace. Ali may still be drawing pictures for his grandfather in vain. He and the other children are being raised to know that their parents were traitors.

Middle East

The Hawk who downed a dove: assassination of Yitzhak Rabin

12 November 1995

Marie Colvin and Jon Swain

Her name was Nava, and she was everything that Yigal Amir, a rather serious student at the religious university of Bar Ilan, wanted. Amir, his friends say, was an arrogant man, lonely and aloof, who had never had a girlfriend before because no girl had been good enough.

He began pursuing her as soon as they met in the spring of 1994. 'She was rich, pretty, clever, pure and religious. She had it all,' said a fellow student. They dated for five months. 'They never broke the limits of what is permissible between a religious pair, but there was a huge commitment.' So intense was the relationship, they planned to marry.

Then, in January this year, she abruptly left him for his best friend, Shmuel Rosenblum. Amir was stunned. 'The talk on campus was that her parents had disapproved of her marrying him because he was poor and of Yemeni extraction,' the friend said. A month later Nava married her new boyfriend.

Amir changed. He had always been fiercely nationalist, with a deep religious belief that God's holy land had to be zealously guarded by the Jews. He was utterly opposed to Yitzhak Rabin, the prime minister, and his policy of trading land for peace with the Palestinians.

Now he became outrageous, outspoken and dangerous. The extremist, angered and rejected, had tipped over into a potential assassin. 'I think that not only political views caused the murder, but also his feeling of disappointment in his personal life,' the friend said. 'Suddenly we heard him talking about the duty to kill Rabin.'

A fellow student, Shmulik, recalled: 'His arguments were always based on the Torah [the body of Jewish sacred writings and traditions].' Amir would tell his friends that, since Rabin had given up parts of the land of Israel, it was a mitzvah (positive obligation) to kill him.

Eight days ago, on a Saturday night in Tel Aviv, he walked up to Rabin, pumped two exploding bullets into him, and discharged that obligation.

In the weeks before, Amir was on such a public rampage that it now seems astonishing that he was able to get near the prime minister with a gun in his hand and a clear line of fire. All last week, stunned Israelis asked why nobody had been watching him.

Amir had made no secret of his deadly intentions. He was a member of an extremist Jewish group that denounced Rabin for treason; he was dragged away by security guards for heckling Rabin at meetings; before he succeeded last Saturday, he had already made two unsuccessful assassination runs. Weren't the groups of fundamentalist Jews who vowed to stop the peace process at all costs under any kind of surveillance?

The murder raised other, more profound questions. Nobody had believed a Jew would ever kill a Jew; despite the venomous rhetoric that had followed Rabin's peace treaty with Yasser Arafat, the Palestinian leader, nobody believed that taboo would be broken. So what was this nation of Jews if the land had become more important than an individual's life?

The shock and incomprehension deepened as Israelis learned more details about the killer in their midst. Amir grew up in the heart of Israel, the Tel Aviv suburbs, and served in an elite brigade of the army. His background might have given him something of a chip on his shoulder; he was a Sephardi, an Israeli descended from Jews who came from Arab lands, rather than an Ashkenazi, the elite of Israel who came from Europe and founded the state. But he had done well.

Born in 1970, the second of eight children, he was raised in a two-room house by his father, Shlomo, a scribe who supplemented his income with the ritual slaughter of chickens, and his mother, Geula, a large, warm woman who supported the family with a creche in the back garden. They had come to Israel in the 1950s from the Yemen.

Religion played a strong role in Amir's life from the beginning, first at Wolfson, a school run by the ultra-orthodox Aguda movement and dominated by Ashkenazis. He was out of place as a dark-skinned Sephardi, but he surpassed everyone in his work.

When most of his fellow religious students opted out of armed service, allowed for those pursuing religious studies, he joined the elite Golani brigade while continuing to study the Torah at the fiercely nationalist Yeshiva Kerem De'Yavne institute.

In October 1993, a month after Rabin signed the agreement with Arafat in Washington to hand over land occupied by Israel in the 1967 war in return for peace, Amir entered Bar Ilan University. There, too, he was unable to forget his Sephardic background.

Although he was a top student in the most difficult of Israeli studies – a triple course of law, computer and Torah studies – he always felt a misfit. When Nava left him, he felt it even more keenly: she was Ashkenazi.

As his politics became more virulent, he spent most of his time in the Institute of Advanced Torah Studies and in fierce religious and political debates. He began organising student demonstrations, obtained a gun licence and bought a short-barrelled Beretta 9mm, the gun he shot Rabin with. He wore it ostentatiously, tucked in his left trouser hip pocket, the handle protruding over his belt.

Somehow, though, he escaped the attention of Shin Bet, the Israeli version of MI5, even when he joined Eyal, a violently anti-Arab group operating in the West Bank and a venomous agitator against the Rabin government. He became a friend of its founder, Avishai Raviv, who was under surveillance and had been arrested. Still Amir went unnoticed.

In the final weeks he was a publicly angry young man who was hiding nothing. The incidents mounted. On 30 September, he went with other Bar Ilan students to Hebron, where about 20 Jewish families live at the heart of a city of 100,000 Arabs. There they went on a tour with a settler, Maisha Meishcan, a man who defiantly walks the streets with a cowboy hat on his head and an Uzi on his shoulder, and visited the site of a 1929 pogrom against Jews.

There, Meishcan revealed last week, Amir 'beat up' two Christian women pacifists, dragging them 20 yards, before police arrived. Two of the group were arrested but Amir slipped away.

A week later he was stopped and his identity details taken by police at a demonstration outside the home of a right-wing Israeli minister who had revealed his support for Rabin over the second phase of the peace agreement. There were other demonstrations. He was twice arrested and released.

On 23 October, Bar Ilan reopened. The last time fellow students remember seeing him was on 2 November, the Thursday before the assassination, at a computer class. He arranged with a friend for a lift to the university that Sunday. He never went.

On the evening of 4 November, at 5:45, Amir locked himself in his family's garden shed and loaded his Beretta. This time his plan would work.

He had made his first attempt to murder the prime minister months earlier, in June, but at the last minute Rabin had failed to show up at a ceremony at Yad Vashem, the holocaust memorial in Jerusalem. Thwarted, he tried again in early September, when Rabin was opening a new road in Herzliya, near Amir's home. He joined right-wing demonstrators against the premier, gun in pocket, and got close before security 'closed like a clam' around the prime minister.

Now Amir loaded his gun with special hollow-point bullets prepared by his brother, Haggai, 27. In the previous weeks, while Amir was demonstrating, Haggai had painstakingly drilled holes in the heads of about 20 bullets, filling the tiny space with mercury. Ordinary bullets pass cleanly through a target, but hollow-points flatten like a mushroom on impact, bounding around in the body and ripping apart flesh and bone. Amir was now ready.

He walked out of the shed, past the family car and took a bus to the Kings of Israel Square in Tel Aviv, where more than 100,000 Israelis had gathered for a demonstration in support of the peace process. It was the largest rally in Israel since 1982, when Israelis protested against their country's invasion of Lebanon. Rabin was on stage and in a more ebullient mood than anyone could remember.

Out of the public eye, the security operation was under way to protect the prime minister. Its code name: Operation Sunrise. The special techniques for protecting VIPs in Israel are so straightforward that they can be written on one side of a sheet of paper.

But on the night of Rabin's murder, the much-vaunted organisation was preoccupied. Evidence is emerging of recent infighting that may have weakened Shin Bet's morale, upset its discipline and damaged its capabilities in the crucial weeks leading up to the assassination.

The trouble began six months ago when a new head of Shin Bet was appointed amid vociferous praise in the Israeli intelligence community. The fact that this man, who cannot be identified under Israeli censorship laws, spoke only broken Arabic was considered of minor importance; he had other vital qualifications, principally his expert knowledge of Jewish extremist organisations.

While at university in the 1970s he had written a thesis on Jewish fringe groups and how to deal with them from a legal point of view. Here was the man to carry Shin Bet into the new era of the peace process between Israel and the Palestinians.

But when Yaakov Perry, the outgoing head of Shin Bet, who was a close friend of Rabin's, chose him as his heir, the result was devastating. Six section heads resigned when they realised their way to the top was blocked by the appointment, creating a serious vacuum within the organisation.

Even during Perry's last years as director-general, signs of unease within Shin Bet had become discernible. Part of these were about Perry himself, who was nicknamed the 'trumpeter' for his taste for boisterous parties and wild music. There were two commissions of inquiry into Shin Bet's activities during Perry's tenure. But Rabin, in keeping with his customary loyalty to his friends, overlooked the reports against him.

In the words of a leading Israeli security specialist, Shin Bet had grown 'complacent, sloppy and corrupt'. In common with many other bodies in Israel, a malaise had set in, derived from the deep divisions in Israeli society, the lack of a common goal and the pursuit of peace amid continuing terror.

None the less, it knew that an assassination was in the wind. Three weeks earlier, the heads of Shin Bet summoned leaders of the Jewish settler movement to meetings in Tel Aviv where they were urged to help build a profile of a potential assassin. They refused, saying that as leaders of their communities their involvement with the security services was inappropriate.

They assured Shin Bet that it was highly unlikely that a settler would assassinate a Jewish leader anyway. It would be better, they warned, for the security service to concentrate its energies on the Israeli heartland – the suburbs of Tel Aviv, for example.

They were right, and the view is that the new head of Shin Bet, as an expert on Jewish extremists, should have evaluated their advice better, and followed it. Like Britain's naval guns guarding the fortress of Singapore in 1941, Shin Bet was pointing the wrong way last Saturday night.

The plain fact is that everyone knew the prime minister was in danger that night. In the days leading up to the peace demonstration, the intelligence services had publicised their fears of an attack, perhaps by sniper fire or a car bomb. The assumption was that it would come from Palestinian extremists.

There was extra surveillance around the square, with more than 1,000 policemen on duty, snipers crouched on rooftops and checks on hundreds of apartments.

Even so, Rabin failed to take the most elementary precaution of wearing a bullet-proof vest. One Israeli security expert last week laid some of the blame for this on the chummy relationship between the prime minister and the man in charge of VIP security, Colonel Benny Lahav (since resigned) of Shin Bet. It meant that Lahav could not exercise his authority. 'Had I been in charge,' the expert said, 'I would have told the prime minister that either he wore a bullet-proof vest or I would, that I could not protect him without it. Such a firm stand would have got through to Rabin.'

Error was compounded by error. Shin Bet's rules require the prime minister to be in a 'sterile zone' at all times, surrounded by a minimum of three Shin Bet bodyguards, preferably six. Last Saturday there were only two near him as he took his place on the stage with Shimon Peres.

By that time a vital breach in security had already taken place. The original plan had been for Rabin to arrive at a nearby municipal building and go to the rally via a basement door through a secure area not open to the public.

Instead, the premier's car was parked next to the stage and he climbed to it up an open flight of stairs. 'I don't know why the change was made, but it cost Rabin his life. Under the original plan, he would not have been exposed to the public at all,' said a security official.

Just after 8pm, Rabin took the microphone to address the cheering crowd. 'Allow me to say that I am excited. I was a military man for 27 years. I fought as long as there was no chance for peace. I believe there is now a chance for peace that must be taken.'

Surprisingly, since he was awkward in public and usually fled after speaking, he stayed with Peres and other Israeli personalities to sing the Song of Peace, an anthem that was banned in Israel when it was released in 1969. Nobody had ever seen Rabin sing in public. It was a sign of his joy that after all the criticism of his policies he felt that the unprecedented numbers at the rally validated his decisions.

Then, 15 minutes before Rabin took his fatal walk down the stairs from the podium, two more security lapses gave Amir his chance. Shin Bet should have been guarding the car parking area beneath the stage. They were not. When an officer noticed that this area had not been secured, he ordered police to do so. By then, Amir was already inside, explaining to the police that he was a VIP driver called up for extra duties. Nobody challenged his story. As he waited behind a barrier for the right moment to strike, the Beretta lay hidden in his clothes.

By now, the Shin Bet officer in charge had reason to be distracted. Over his radio he received a tip-off that a shooting was imminent. 'The tension was immense, and he wanted to get Rabin off the stage as fast as possible. But he was convinced that the main threat was from Palestinians,' said a security official.

At the end of the demonstration, Rabin came down the stairs to his car, failing to make sure the bodyguards were around him. Another blunder. The police unit in the parking area had not received a message that Rabin was arriving, so no safe channel was formed. 'We let down our guard,' said the security official. 'We felt that the rally had passed peaceably and that we had done our job.'

At 9.44, as Rabin was getting into his armoured Cadillac, Amir stepped forward. From 5 feet away he drew his pistol and fired.

Ingeniously, he shouted to the police that it was 'only an exercise' and he was firing blanks. They believed him.

Rabin's bodyguard, hit in the shoulder, knew otherwise. He bundled the prime minister, a bullet in his stomach, another in his back, into the car and they sped off. At the hospital, there was the final blunder: nobody was ready to receive them. In the confusion nobody had radioed ahead. The chief surgeon, summoned to an emergency on a badly wounded man, found he was treating the dying prime minister.

One top Jewish counter-terrorist expert said of the colossal foul-up: 'It is beyond negligence of the most simple basic procedures. Rabin was abandoned.'

Amir told security officials who surrounded him immediately after the killing, the gun still in his hand: 'God told me to do it. I have no regrets.' The fact that he believed he had a religious mandate shocked Israelis.

So did the crass statements by supporters. One student at Bar Ilan sent a message on the Internet: 'Happy holiday everyone. The witch is dead; the wicked witch is dead.' The West Bank settlement of Maale Amos hung out a sign: 'We are all Yigal Amir.'

'I am very happy that the dictator Rabin is dead,' said Aryeh Bar Yosef, a resident of Kiryat Arba, a radical settlement outside Hebron, which has made a shrine of the grave of Baruch Goldstein, who gunned down 29 Palestinians at the Hebron mosque last year.

'I hope that the Nazi Arafat and his friend Peres will die like Rabin. Rabin, the head of the traitors, got what he deserved. Praise be to God. Yigal Amir redeemed us from the terrible situation we were in.'

Such statements have forced Israelis to face the dark netherworld of Jewish extremist groups. Eyal follows the teachings of Meir Kahane, a Brooklyn-based rabbi who moved to Israel and founded the extremist Kach movement.

Kahane was assassinated five years ago – eerily, on exactly the same day as Rabin – while making a speech in New York and his movement was outlawed last year by the Israeli government after

Goldstein's massacre. With Kach banned, groups such as Eyal, with the same ideology and many of the same members, have become increasingly active.

Even more disturbing for Israelis is the realisation that these groups flourish among young people from comfortable, ordinary homes. When police searched the Amir family house and the kindergarten run by his mother they found a cache of ammunition and explosives. Car tyres that were used as swings for children were packed with explosives. One of those arrested as part of the alleged conspiracy to kill Rabin, Ohad Skornik, is the son of Yehuda Skornik, an eminent surgeon at Ichilov hospital, where Rabin died. It has made parents all over Israel wonder what their children are up to.

Last week, the issue confronting Israel was the allegation of a conspiracy to kill Rabin. There is no doubt Amir was a member of an extreme right-wing group that considered Rabin a traitor.

Eyal, founded in 1991 by Raviv, good-looking, arrogant and, like Amir, a student at Bar Ilan, is fanatical, albeit in an immature way. Members are given a Hebrew code word, and go through a dramatic swearing-in ceremony at the graveside of Avraham Stern, the leader of the Stern Gang terror group that fought the British mandate.

It is believed to take orders from Baruch Marzel, a Boston-born settler based in Hebron who is a former member of Kach but resigned when it became illegal. Last week, he would not support the killing, but blamed Rabin for his own death. 'When you force people underground, when you shut their mouths, their hands work and you have violence. There will be more, I am sure. Israel is heading to civil war.'

Before last Saturday, though, Eyal was 'known for words rather than actions', said one security official. That is indeed what Raviv said when he denied all knowledge of Amir's plans to kill Rabin. 'Yes, he was very close to us, but we knew nothing of his intentions,' Raviv said after his arrest. 'I am in complete shock. The guy ruined his life. We knew he said that Rabin must be killed but he didn't speak more than anyone else here. We all shouted all kinds of things at demonstrations.'

In fact, Raviv was shouting those very things the night of Rabin's assassination, with a few dozen right-wingers who staged a counter-demonstration in a side street at the peace rally in Kings of Israel Square. Amir was seen to join them briefly, then leave after talking to Raviv.

Was there a conspiracy? A total of six people are now in police custody, charged with complicity in the killing. All are religious men in their twenties.

Along with Amir, his brother Haggai, Skornik and Raviv, police also have in custody two other students, Dror Hadani and Michael Epstein. All deny any connection.*

The signs are that Amir acted alone on the day. He took a bus to the rally and later told investigators: 'I never believed it would be so easy.' Investigators believe Amir would have aborted his plan had the opportunity not been there. 'He didn't know he was going to do it until he pulled the trigger,' said one.

But while he may have acted alone on that night, police believe the others helped him procure weapons, and did not report the possibility of his plans to police. 'We think there was a connection between a group of persons … who established a form of organisa-tion to assassinate the prime minister and other political persons based on their ideology to try to prevent the peace process,' Moshe Shahal, the police minister, said.

All week, mourners visited Rabin's grave side at Mount Herzl ceme-tery and his widow's home, leaving flowers, candles in makeshift cans or just a handwritten note. Tonight, at the end of seven days of mourn-ing, hundreds of thousands, the largest crowd ever seen in Israel, are expected to gather at the Kings of Israel Square in Tel Aviv for a cere-mony renaming the plaza where Rabin died in his honour.

---

* Haggai Amir and Dror Hadani were convicted of conspiring to assassinate Rabin, conspiring to carry out attacks against Arabs, illegal weapon production and illegal weapon possession. Michael Epstein and Ohad Skornik were not prosecuted.
Avishai Raviv was acquitted of charges that he failed to prevent the assassination of Rabin.

Peres, the acting prime minister, will try to move on. He plans to push forward the peace process, which he helped broker and which cost Rabin his life. It will be a difficult task. Rabin, a gruff old soldier, was trusted by Israelis to look out for their security. Peres's language is visionary, but he lacks his predecessor's credibility.

The process is too far advanced, however, to be easily derailed. Arafat has ruled Gaza for more than a year and, starting this week with the Israeli withdrawal from the West Bank town of Jenin, will take over the West Bank in a phased process that will culminate in elections in January. The hard decisions have been pushed through. Rabin's death may help move along the peace process that he came to reluctantly but once converted pursued like one of his military campaigns. A poll released on Friday showed the proportion of Israelis supporting the peace process had risen by 31%.

And the outrage Israelis feel at the assassination of Rabin by a Jewish fundamentalist may win Peres support from those who now see the right as tainted because it provided fertile soil for such an extremist as Amir. With the death of Yitzhak Rabin, Israelis may no longer see a peacemaker as a defeatist, but as a hero.

Israel's peace hopes wither: Netanyahu victory gives voice to the hardliners

2 June 1996

Marie Colvin, Gaza; Andy Goldberg, Tel Aviv

It was a mournful gathering. Meeting for lunch in Gaza yesterday, Palestinian politicians mulled over the results of Israel's election with an air of grieving relatives at a wake. The surprise election of Binyamin Netanyahu as prime minister, they grimly concurred, could prove a mortal blow to peace. Even the menu seemed to symbolise their worst fears. They were eating roast dove.

The Likud leader, they recalled, had vowed his first act would be to close Orient House, the Palestinians' diplomatic outpost in Jerusalem.

What is more, he plans to ignore Shimon Peres's promise to withdraw Israeli troops from the West Bank city of Hebron, which was to be the next step on the road to a permanent peace. 'We feel the Israelis have voted against peace,' sighed Um Jihad, a Palestinian minister. 'There are difficult days for us ahead.'

The shock at the rise of Netanyahu was not limited to the Palestinian camp. President Bill Clinton congratulated him, as did Peres, his defeated rival and Labour leader. Yet they were stunned. Clinton had urged Israelis to vote for peace, in a thinly disguised endorsement of Peres.

Another worried man was Yasser Arafat, the Palestinian leader. He had stayed awake until 7am on Thursday after the previous day's voting. He watched the returns on television in anxious disbelief. Netanyahu won the vote by just one percentage point. Yesterday an adviser said the Palestinian leader was 'in a state of shock'. Israel's political status quo had been turned on its head.

The man responsible relaxed yesterday with his wife and children at their home in Jerusalem. Within hours of his victory he had begun to look as if he had been a prime minister all his life. He waved regally to a crowd before stepping into a chauffeur-driven Cadillac for a trip to the Wailing Wall, where he slipped a thank you note to God into a crack. To the delight of cameramen, he ruffled the blond locks of his two young sons as they arrived home.

He has never even held a cabinet post and at 46 is a beginner by contrast with Peres, who had counted on five decades of experience and a Nobel prize for peace to secure him victory. Yet Netanyahu espouses an old idea: Israel's paramount need, he believes, is for strong government that can provide security for Jews. He has consequently ruled out an Israeli withdrawal from the Golan Heights, effectively scuttling any chance of a peace deal with Syria. He has promised to resume Jewish settlement in the West Bank and said he would send the army and Shin Bet, the Israeli intelligence service, back into what is now autonomous territory patrolled by Palestinian soldiers.

By contrast, Peres seems to have believed he was leading a nation converted to peace, satisfied with a booming industry and improved economy. It was a fatal miscalculation. A wave of suicide bombings by Hamas extremists in which dozens of people were killed left the country feeling pessimistic about Peres's vision of a new and peaceful Middle East.

Supporters of Peres made pilgrimages to the grave of Yitzhak Rabin, the prime minister who was assassinated in November by Yigal Amir, a right-wing student. One left a note saying 'Sorry, friend', a melancholy echo of Clinton's 'Goodbye, friend' uttered at Rabin's funeral.

Netanyahu had been unrelenting in his opposition to Rabin, who led his country into the historic peace agreement with the Palestinians in 1993. Netanyahu would stand among the corpses left by an Islamic fundamentalist attack aimed at stopping the peace process, blame the government for the deaths and call for the revocation of the Oslo accord. He turned a blind eye to posters at Likud rallies depicting Rabin in Nazi uniform. Rabin's widow, Leah, refused to shake Netanyahu's hand at his funeral and was said to be in despair at Likud's victory.

Rabin's death had left Peres with a seemingly unassailable 26-point lead. But ironically, it was Peres's attempt to 'get tough' that led to his downfall. With his approval, Israel's security services used a booby-trapped mobile phone to assassinate Yehia Ayyash, a Hamas bomber revered by the Islamic fundamentalist group. Israel hailed the death as a glorious blow against terrorism: but then Hamas struck, killing 63 people in revenge suicide bombings. Peres's lead was wiped out overnight.

Sensing the newly subdued mood in Israel, Netanyahu restrained his accusations and let the bloody scenes on television do the talking. He moved to capture the political centre, refining his position on the Oslo accord from outright rejection to acceptance of the agreement as a fait accompli that needed revision.

And, in what would be the deciding factor in the campaign, the worldly Netanyahu wooed the ultra-orthodox vote, 10% of the electorate. Netanyahu took to wearing a skullcap and adopted the phrase 'with God's help'. He persuaded the rabbis that Likud's belief in Eretz Israel or the greater Israel that includes the biblical land of the Jews was preferable to Labour's commitment to territorial compromise.

One of the most dramatic moments of Netanyahu's campaign came with his endorsement by Rabbi Yitzhak Kadurie, a 106-year-old mystic, 36 hours before polling. Every Israeli newspaper and television station showed pictures of the frail rabbi, his hands resting on the head of a reverential Netanyahu, saying: 'Bibi, Bibi, Bibi, may God grant that next week you will be premier.' More than 90% of the ultra-orthodox community voted for Netanyahu. This tipped the election.

Netanyahu was also helped by the disastrous Labour campaign. While Likud was stealing Labour's message of peace, Labour tried to dress up as Likud. Peres bombed southern Lebanon to hit Hezbollah, the Islamic fundamentalist group, but everyone saw it as an election ploy. The operation backfired when Israeli artillery fire killed 100 Lebanese civilians in a United Nations camp at Qana, losing Peres some of the Israeli Arab support.

In a final blow, Likud mounted a scare campaign that touched on racist themes. Posters proclaimed 'Netanyahu is good for the Jews' and warned them that Peres was the candidate of the Arabs.

But Netanyahu still might not have won had Peres not practically given the election away. While a brash and confident Netanyahu pressed ahead, Peres was advised to ignore him and act like a statesman. It is a role that has never worked for him. He has lost every election campaign he has waged, including two earlier runs for prime minister. He could not shake off his image of a loser. The contrast between the two could not have been more noticeable when the results were announced on Friday night. A jubilant Netanyahu greeted crowds as he entered his home in what was an old Arab neighbourhood before 1967, shouting they should welcome 'a new Israel of peace and security'.

Peres spent the day in seclusion in his 12th-floor apartment in a luxurious suburb of Tel Aviv. He emerged briefly, looking exhausted and speaking in a flat voice. 'This was not a choice between two parties,' he told waiting reporters. 'It was a choice between two different ways. We shall remain loyal to our way.' But at 72, he can do little to implement his vision. There will be no more elections.

This week will see the first steps towards Netanyahu's 'new Israel'. The West and Israel's Arab neighbours are hoping Netanyahu will be more pragmatic than his campaign rhetoric suggested.

But there are few early signs of moderation. He owes enormous debts to right-wing nationalist and ultra-orthodox religious parties, which themselves won unprecedented numbers of seats in the Knesset. To put together a governing coalition Netanyahu will have to give the right-wing and religious parties ministries and a say in policy.

The lineup for his cabinet includes retired generals Ariel Sharon, the former defence minister who launched the 1982 Lebanon war, tipped for the finance portfolio, and Rafael Eitan, candidate for the Ministry of Domestic Security (police), who as Sharon's chief of staff enforcing the siege of Beirut announced the Arabs were 'trapped like drugged bugs in a bottle'. Netanyahu's new Israel is likely to bear little resemblance to the vision many have had in their sights in the past three years.

Israeli bulldozers rev up for showdown in Jerusalem

JERUSALEM

16 March 1997

Sasson Shem-Tov drives a black Jaguar and wears sunglasses whatever the weather. He does not usually take much interest in politics. But this week he finds himself in the middle of a dispute between Israel and the Arabs that risks bathing his country in blood.

Shem-Tov is about to order his bulldozers into Arab east Jerusalem to help build a Jewish settlement that the Palestinians have vowed to stop by any means. Even America, which is usually supportive of Israel, has denounced its plan to build 6,500 homes for Jews on a hill within sight of the church spires of Bethlehem. On Thursday the United Nations general assembly called for construction to stop.

Yasser Arafat was so angry that he twice refused to take calls from Binyamin Netanyahu, the Israeli prime minister. It is not only the settlement plans that have provoked Arab ire: Netanyahu recently announced that the first step of a three-phase withdrawal from rural areas of the West Bank, mandated under the Oslo accords, would include only a fraction of the territory Palestinians expected. The prime minister then ordered the closure of four Palestinian offices in Jerusalem, a move whose legality is being debated.

King Hussein of Jordan sent a bitter letter charging that the Israeli prime minister was 'dragging the peace process to the edge of the abyss'. When a Jordanian gunman opened fire on Israeli schoolgirls on Thursday, killing seven of them, commentators in both countries suggested he had been angered by Netanyahu's intransigence and insinuations.

Shem-Tov, a wealthy Israeli construction magnate, is unperturbed. 'We are going in next week,' he said over his car telephone. His yellow bulldozers were already in place near Har Homa, the pine-covered hill Israel seized from Jordan in the 1967 war, which he has been contracted to clear for the new homes. To him, it is just business. But for the right-wing Israeli government, the settlement means much more.

If built, Har Homa will close the last gap in a half-moon of Jewish settlements constructed on hilltops around the outer edges of Arab east Jerusalem. By encircling the Arab area with these self-contained Jewish townships, right-wing Israelis want to create 'facts on the ground' to ensure they will never have to cede an inch of Jerusalem to the Palestinians, who claim east Jerusalem as their capital.

Under the Oslo accord, the final status of Jerusalem is supposed to be decided in talks scheduled to conclude in 1999, but Palestinians argue that there will not be much to talk about if Israel keeps building. Netanyahu showed no sign of backing down. 'I am building Har Homa this week and nothing is going to stop me,' he said in an interview. The Israeli cabinet on Friday reaffirmed his decision, and government sources said the bulldozers are likely to move in tomorrow.

The army will no doubt be called in to keep back protesters, who have vowed to lie down in front of Shem-Tov's machines. Palestinian leaders have pledged that the demonstrations will be peaceful, but emotions are running so high among Palestinians that they are widely expected to explode into violence. 'The minute the bulldozers go in I think only God knows the consequences of what will happen,' said Saeb Erekat, a Palestinian minister involved in the Israeli–Palestinian negotiations.

Yesterday Arafat made a last-ditch effort to thwart Netanyahu diplomatically. Amid Israeli condemnations, he gathered American, European and Arab sponsors of the peace process to an emergency conference at his seaside headquarters in Gaza to seek their help in stopping the Har Homa settlement and putting the peace process back on track.

Although the Americans used their veto in the United Nations vote, they showed their opposition to the settlement plans by sending Edward Abington, the American consul in Jerusalem, to the talks, despite a direct Israeli request that Washington should boycott the meeting. The Palestinian president is making no secret of his anger. 'The situation is really serious,' Arafat told envoys to yesterday's meeting. 'We are facing a plan to destroy the peace process.'

The conference in Gaza is not expected to make any difference on the ground. Arafat called the meeting to send a signal to Netanyahu that he is not alone; the governments who sent envoys wanted to reassure Arafat of support, which they hoped would head off an explosion of Palestinian violence.

The threat of bloodshed is no secret. Under the codename Thornbush, Israeli army units with tanks have been practising manoeuvres to re-enter cities on the West Bank controlled by Arafat's Palestinian authority, in case Palestinians fight to stop the building at Har Homa. Israeli intelligence sources said yesterday that the army wanted to be better prepared than it was in September, when 60 Palestinians and 15 Israeli soldiers were killed in clashes after Netanyahu's decision to open a tunnel in Jerusalem.

Given the reluctance on both sides to fight, there is still a good chance violence can be avoided. Crises have come and gone since Netanyahu's government took over from Labour in May, and generally he has compromised.

Nor is Arafat in a strong position. His army is no match for the Israeli forces. If he had to fight, the peace process that would finally win a homeland for Palestinians would be shown up as a failure. He would then be vulnerable to Islamic extremists.

Netanyahu needs the support of the ultra-right-wing parties in his coalition government. But he may well have miscalculated the strength of anger his moves have inspired among Palestinians. The test of that will come when the bulldozers close in on Har Homa.

Arafat encircled in battle for Jerusalem

6 April 1997

In his first interview with a foreign journalist since the latest Middle East crisis erupted, the Palestinian leader tells Marie Colvin in Gaza why the new Israeli township must be stopped.

It was an odd spectacle: Yasser Arafat marched briskly around his modest office, arms swinging, eyes fixed on the carpet. He might have been deep in thought. But the diminutive Palestinian leader calls his compulsive pacing 'speed walking', a form of daily exercise that seems a perfect metaphor for his political predicament: he has little room for manoeuvre.

Sweating in the heavy military jacket he wears in all seasons, he marched round and round on Friday, skirting the conference table and ignoring the breathtaking view from his windows of the sparkling Mediterranean sea. After half an hour's wear of the dull, grey carpet, he sat down, mopped his forehead with a yellow Kleenex and turned his attention to a visiting reporter.

On his desk were reports of yet another day of violent Palestinian protests in the West Bank against the decision by Binyamin Netanyahu, the Israeli prime minister, to build a new Jewish settlement in Arab east Jerusalem.

'I am asking Netanyahu to understand exactly the sensitivity of the question of Jerusalem,' Arafat said, swivelling his chair to face the sea, then turning it abruptly back again. 'I am astonished at how he does not understand it. Or perhaps he understands it but insists on challenging the Palestinians, Arabs, Christians and Muslims.'

On the eve of Netanyahu's summit with President Bill Clinton tomorrow, Arafat knows he has no alternative but to continue the Israeli–Palestinian peace process. Yet if he accepts the new Jewish township he will lose any credibility among his own people.

From the Israeli side, Arafat is faced with overwhelming force and an intransigent prime minister. The Americans, meanwhile, are pressuring him to halt street protests. They also want him to arrest extremists who have dispatched three suicide bombers to attack Israel since the bulldozers began clearing the way for homes to be built for 30,000 Jews on a pine-covered hill known as Har Homa to the Israelis and Jebel Abu Ghneim to the Palestinians.

An Arab League decision last week to sever Arab ties with Israel gave Arafat some support for what he calls 'the battle for Jerusalem'. But the backing of other Arab countries has been largely rhetorical. Thus Arafat feels very much alone as he marches in his headquarters by the sea.

For his part Netanyahu, say those who know him, believes that if he can force Arafat to accept the new settlement, the Palestinians will 'lower their expectations' in future peace talks. Yet Arafat, already under attack for conceding too much to the Israelis in the Oslo agreements, cannot give up any more if he is to survive as leader.

'Netanyahu must stop this settlement on Jebel Abu Ghneim,' he insisted, adding that this was a condition for Palestinians returning to the peace talks. 'Netanyahu must return to the honest and accurate implementation of the peace process. Nothing less.'

Arafat says he has 'no contact' with Netanyahu these days. He has ordered his security chiefs to stop sharing intelligence information with their Israeli counterparts. Netanyahu's generals have warned that this is dangerous. Since Arafat took over Gaza and the West Bank cities, shared information from Palestinian security forces has prevented several planned attacks against Israeli targets.

But the Palestinian leader has lost faith in any idea that Netanyahu can be a partner in the peace process. Instead, he sees him as dangerously dependent for his political survival on the support of religious and ultra-right-wing parties who believe in Eretz Israel, or greater Israel.

'I am sorry to say Netanyahu is following the ideology of the (Jewish) fanatic groups,' said Arafat. 'He must remember he is committed to Oslo, which was signed by the previous Israeli governments, or we will be at a real impasse.'

For a few moments, Arafat stared through his heavy black-framed glasses into the middle distance, as if trying to see the way ahead. There was none. 'We are at a real impasse now,' he sighed.

One possible hope is American mediation. 'The peace process now needs the attention of the American administration – especially President Clinton,' the Palestinian leader said. 'The agreement was signed under his supervision. This is not a bilateral agreement. It is an international agreement.'

Arafat has not yet received an invitation from Washington to take part in a meeting with the Israelis. But some analysts believe the Americans are trying to work out a deal. Sources in Washington say the Clinton administration is trying to piece together a compromise that would include delaying the settlement, rather than definitively stopping it, while simultaneously speeding up the schedule for final negotiations.

At the moment, however, the Americans, who have generally supported Netanyahu's position that the Palestinians must stop their protests before peace talks can resume, seem intent on winning concessions from Arafat.

Last week Madeleine Albright, the secretary of state, telephoned Arafat twice to seek his approval for three-way talks. She urged him to try to calm the violence in the West Bank, arrest Islamic extremists and resume security co-operation with the Israelis.

In one lengthy telephone call, Arafat explained that as Netanyahu had ignited the crisis with his 'violent' action of sending in bulldozers, she should be asking the Israelis, not him, for concessions. He could not return to security co-operation before the political negotiations resumed.

'Let's not get into a discussion of which came first, the chicken or the egg,' Albright responded. To which Arafat replied, cryptically: 'But we have to remember that in the end there is the hen and there is the egg.' The response of the new secretary of state is not recorded.

Kosovo

The centuries of conflict over a sacred heartland

8 March 1998

Like earlier Balkan wars, the battle in Kosovo, the impoverished southern province of former Yugoslavia, has its roots in history. For the Serbs the region is the sacred heartland of their long-lost medieval state. For the ethnic Albanians who make up 90% of its population, it has been home for centuries.

The rise of virulent Serbian nationalism was the trigger for the current conflict. In the Yugoslavia of Josip Broz Tito, the former communist leader, Kosovo, although extremely poor, enjoyed a degree of formal autonomy within Serbia.

Under Slobodan Milosevic, the bullet-headed Serbian nationalist, everything changed. In 1989, two years after he came to power as Serbian Communist party leader, he visited Kosovo and proclaimed himself the protector of local Serbs claiming to be the victims of discrimination. He rescinded Kosovo's autonomous status later that year.

The province is seen as the spiritual home of the Serbian nation: in 1389, at Kosovo Polje, the Serbs lost a battle with Turkish troops that consigned them to 500 years of rule by the Ottoman empire.

Milosevic's initiative to reclaim Kosovo prompted riots in 1989 and 1990. He sent tanks against the protesters and their leaders fled or were killed.

The ethnic Albanians have never given up their demand for independence. They have ignored the state network, setting up a 'parallel society' of schools and hospitals. The driving force behind the policy of passive resistance has been Ibrahim Rugova, known as the 'Gandhi of the Balkans' – a quiet intellectual who is president of the self-styled republic of Kosovo.

The present violence appears to have been provoked by younger, more militant Kosovans who feel frustrated at Rugova's failure to win concessions for them. The Kosovo Liberation Army, an armed guerrilla group, emerged 18 months ago, claiming responsibility for the killings of Serbian policemen and informers. It appears to be funded by Kosovan emigrés in Germany and Switzerland.

By last month the attacks had grown so lethal that the Serbian police withdrew from much of the Drenica region, a stronghold of separatists northwest of Pristina, the capital. Milosevic responded last week by ordering troops to raze villages there.

The fear now is that fighting in Kosovo, which was largely unaffected by the conflicts that engulfed Croatia and Bosnia in the early 1990s, may lead to a wider Balkan war. This could drag in Albania and Macedonia, which has its own ethnic Albanian population. Turkey is sympathetic to fellow Muslims in Kosovo, while Greece could be drawn in on the side of the Orthodox Serbs.

Kosovo's silent houses of the dead

PREKAZ

15 March 1998

All 11-year-old Basorta Jashari knew was that the artillery shells had stopped crashing into her house. For hours, the noise had been unbearable.

As she hugged herself tightly beneath the table her mother used to prepare bread, the ceiling had collapsed and the walls had appeared to explode. Now it was the silence that was terrifying. Choking on smoke and dust, she screamed for her mother.

Weeping as she crawled through the rubble, she found her sisters, Lirie, 10, Fatima, 8, and seven-year-old Blerina. She tried to shake them awake and was covered in blood by the time she realised they were dead.

Then Basorta saw her brothers: Selvete, 20, Afeti, 17, Besim, 14, and Blerin, 12. They had always seemed so strong. Now, all were dead.

Finally, there was her mother, Ferida, whose dark shiny hair and beautiful voice Basorta had cherished, lying with her limbs protruding at impossible angles. She would never again respond to her daughter's cry of 'nene' (mummy).

Basorta climbed through a hole in the wall and ran round the house, shouting: 'Anybody … is anybody still alive?' When nobody answered, she crawled back under the table.

The pause in the shelling was all too brief. Basorta would spend the night and the next day alone, with her family dead all around her, as the Serbs' rockets came again and again, smashing into the whitewashed house with red-tiled roof that had once been home.

A bright, happy pupil at school, Basorta was the sole survivor of an attack that can now be revealed as nothing less than a calculated, cold-blooded massacre.

The house in Prekaz, a village in a pastoral landscape of neatly tilled fields and rolling hills, had sheltered 22 members of the families of two brothers, Hamza Jashari, Basorta's father, and Adem Jashari, her uncle – ethnic Albanians in Kosovo, the southernmost province of what remains of Serb-ruled Yugoslavia.

Their deaths were no accident of war. I pieced together the horror last week from the account Basorta – now in hiding in the nearby town of Srbica – gave to relatives who managed to escape from other homes in Prekaz. I saw the gaping holes in the roofs and walls of the three Jashari homes in the compound – one for

Basorta's grandparents and one each for Hamza and Adem – and the brown pockmarks left by close-range machinegun fire on the walls.

In the muddy farmyard lay strewn the detritus of domestic life: a little boy's shredded sports bag, postcards from relatives in Germany and a satellite dish dented by bullets. The nose cones and tailfins of two rockets were scattered amid the debris.

Yesterday all that moved in the compound that once teemed with children were two black and white cows and a flock of chickens pecking at the rubble. On the other side of the dirt road that runs in front of the compound were 51 fresh graves with mounds of dark earth and wooden crosses.

These were the final resting places of the Jasharis who died in the house, four relatives who were killed nearby and neighbours who got in the way of the Serbian forces.

There is little doubt that the Jashari brothers were connected to the Kosovo Liberation Army (KLA), a militant force that emerged last November dedicated to fighting for the interests of the ethnic Albanians who make up 90% of Kosovo's population.

They had grown impatient with the policies of the mainstream Kosovo Democratic League. The league advocates passive resistance to the strong-arm tactics of Slobodan Milosevic, the nationalist Serbian president of Yugoslavia, who revoked the province's autonomous status 10 years ago.

However, this was not the killing of suspected terrorists in a firefight, nor the ambush of dangerous outlaws. It was a military assault on three family homes without warning: on men, women and children asleep in their beds.

The Serbian offensive in the Drenica valley, a region of farming villages that is the stronghold of Albanian resistance, began on 28 February, the day after four Serbian policemen were killed in an ambush as they chased KLA guerrillas. The Serbs moved first against the village of Llaushe, killing 24 Albanians. Then they prepared to attack Prekaz, where the Jasharis were the principal family.

Jetish Durmishi, a bus driver, was alerted to danger when a friend telephoned from his home near the local police station in Mitrovica with the warning that a convoy of buses full of Serbian police was moving towards Prekaz.

Durmishi escaped to the woods, leaving his family behind; in the past the Serbs had targeted only men. He saw what happened from the woods above the Jashari compound.

'Within minutes it seemed, the police came and the village was surrounded by a cordon of Serbs,' Durmishi said. 'They were standing about half a yard apart all along the road and up across the hills.'

The artillery fire came at 6am from a Serbian base above Prekaz. There was no warning. The first to die were the Agas, members of a gypsy family who panicked and tried to flee their house.

The mother, a small boy and a girl were gunned down in their garden. The next victim was Nazmi Jashari, who ran a kiosk in Prekaz selling cigarettes and sundries and lived opposite the main family compound.

He tried to carry his elderly mother, Naile, out of the back door, and was shot in front of her. The signal was clear. Anyone seen leaving their home would be a target for Serbian snipers.

The extended Jashari family gathered in what they thought would be the safest room, which had a new brick wall. But they were trapped: they faced gunfire if they came out or bombing if they remained inside. Soon, the shells were coming through the roof, then the walls. Basorta's last memory of her family is that her uncle, Adem, was singing Albanian folk songs above the noise to keep up their spirits. She remembers the moment he stopped singing. Then, for 36 hours, there was only the sound of the bombs.

When they thought everybody inside was dead, the police entered the house, throwing grenades into several rooms ahead of them. One officer stood guard while another sprayed the bodies with bullets.

Perhaps they had had their fill of killing when they found Basorta cowering. Perhaps they thought she was too young to accuse them. Or perhaps they could not look a terrified schoolgirl in the eye and shoot her. But she is the reason the truth can be told.

'I tried to pretend I was dead,' she said to her uncle Hilmi. 'But one of the soldiers put his hand on my chest and he felt I was alive.'

Still dressed in her red shirt and black trousers, by now covered with blood, she had to step over the bodies of her family to leave the room, surrounded by Serbs. She was taken to the military base nearby and interrogated for three hours.

Basorta believed her only chance was to lie. She denied that she was a Jashari, claiming her father was abroad and she was merely a guest in the compound. 'They asked about my father and about Uncle Adem,' she said. 'I told them nothing, nothing.'

The Serbs dumped her on a road in Srbica and she ran to the home of a school friend. Yesterday, shocked and finding it increasingly difficult to speak, she was being moved from house to house for protection.

Unbeknown to Basorta, the bodies of her father, mother, uncle, aunt and all her cousins were lined up by the police at a bus depot in Mitrovica last week.

When nobody from the family turned up to identify them and friends tried to insist on post-mortem examinations, the Serbs dumped them in the graveyard they had dug opposite the remains of their house, leaving the coffins poking through the earth. The surviving villagers came back in the night to finish the job with respect.

All that was left of Basorta's family was a pile of numbered black bin bags at the bus station, each filled with the bloody clothing they had been wearing when they died.

Kosovo guerrillas fight Serb shells with bullets

25 April 1999

Marie Colvin, the first reporter to enter Kosovo from Albania, is with a KLA unit fighting to open supply lines. She braved sniper fire and shelling to send this report.

At night, the foothills of Kosovo are silent except for the sporadic sound of gunfire. The silence makes them even more terrifying to walk through. Serbian snipers are in the woods but we do not know where they are. The anticipation of a shot at any moment is unnerving. Nobody speaks.

There are no civilians left in these woods or villages. It is dark and cold and when the shooting starts the crossfire can be petrifying. Bullets slam into trees.

I walked in single file on Friday night with a KLA special forces unit advancing towards the distant lights of the city of Djakovica. The Serbs were 500 metres away.

We walked through a village of six houses. All the red roofs had been holed by shells and half of one house was a pile of rubble. First the Serbs had driven out the ethnic Albanian farmers, then the KLA had driven out the Serbs. There is little for the families to return to.

Our goal was a gully in the forest overlooking Serbian positions in the village of Batusa. It was cold and wet and I slipped off a log when I was trying to cross a stream. A soldier held me up with the butt of his Kalashnikov.

Camp for the night was in camouflaged tarpaulins strung over branches. A pile of sleeping bags stashed earlier was sodden with the cold rain that had fallen all day and into the night. It is difficult to sleep in a flak jacket on a slope; it is like being an upended turtle with a detached shell. I keep slipping down the slope.

A patrol set out into the darkness and the night was broken intermittently by gunfire: single shots, automatic weapons fire and the crack of snipers' rifles resounding off the hills. At 1am there was a long exchange of fire. Shells boomed intermittently though none landed close. One man in a returning patrol said he had killed a Serb, but nothing is sure here.

The watch came in for breakfast and a soldier passed round packets of cigarettes, bread and tins of sardines. This unit travels light. We overheard the Serbs on the radio asking to go back to their bunkers.

Every night has been like this for the past two months for this unit on the front line of the KLA offensive. The last weeks have been the worst. The Serbs have not attacked on foot; they have just shelled. Their tanks and artillery are beyond the hills. Two shells landed during breakfast.

It is heartbreaking for these men to hear Nato planes fly overhead on their way to Belgrade and Novi Sad. Everyone asks me when Nato will start bombing Serbian tanks and artillery and when the Apache helicopters will arrive.

The men in this special forces unit are different from the raw recruits one sees in most of the KLA camps. They have been fighting together for a year and seem like the units seen in old war movies.

There is 'Doc', who looks after communications as well as the wounded and to whom most of the men turn in time of crisis. Their commander was killed by a sniper 10 days ago. Another soldier, Morina, remembers his village and how the old men wept when he left. Another refuses to get out of bed, saying he cares more about the cold than the Serbs.

Few have heard from their families for months. They accept that there will be no news until the Serbs leave.

The KLA holds a small but strategic foothold in Kosovo at this point. The group I am with has so far penetrated about 8 kilometres from Kosare, a Serbian border post captured by the KLA just over two weeks ago.

Kosare is in a small cleft between the mountains and the KLA holds the mountains, including a towering, snow-bound peak where KLA soldiers sleep in 3 foot of snow. They will dominate the valley as soon as they take Batusa, the next target.

The KLA is trying to meet up with other units inside Kosovo who have been besieged and are running low on food and ammunition. They can hear that the Serbs are low on food and ammunition and constantly requesting to go back to their bunkers. The spirits among the units are rising.

There is still a big question of whether any of these units will be able to join up with the inside forces because of the superior armaments of the Serbs. They have tanks and artillery and the KLA is fighting with Kalashnikovs and a few modern Nato-issue guns; but their spirit and courage are extraordinary.

On the first day when the KLA fought its way into Kosare, the Serbs replied with a welter of shells; now shells fall three or four times a day. Shards of broken flowerpots cover two unexploded shells in a concrete courtyard outside the former Yugoslav barracks – now KLA headquarters in Kosovo – and there are six shellholes in its red-brick facade.

When the sun came out for a moment on Friday, I took a bowl of bread and soup outside for my lunch. Within minutes there was a whistle of a shell, which burst 100 metres away. As I moved inside, another whistled down.

In between shells, the men waited to go on their 24-hour shifts at the front, smoking, sleeping, talking about home. The uniforms are from Switzerland, Germany and America – all bought by the KLA recruits on their way to war. One man wears a black jacket that says 'Let's go!' on the sleeve. Most have good boots but some set off to battle in black rubber wellingtons.

Those returning from patrol collapse onto iron bunk beds still in their clothes. The beds are warm from those who have left to replace them.

It is a barracks with no comfort. The windows have been blown out by shellfire. Off-duty soldiers cook on wood-burning stoves, heating up big pots of stew from tins left behind by the Serbs. There is no electricity. There is a generator but the base commander thinks it makes too much noise so it goes unused. At night those who cannot sleep stand in the halls lit by a fire and talk of home – never of war.

Coffee, cigarettes and sometimes bread arrive by donkey from Albania. Soldiers cluster around to greet them. Days are spent cleaning out the barracks. A sodden pile of detritus from Serbs is in the courtyard – fatigues, sweaters, playing cards, empty soft-drinks bottles and letters. Soldiers amuse themselves by looking through photographs of Serbs in uniforms with their girlfriends.

Last week they passed around one letter that horrified even these people who are used to news of Serbian attrocities. It was written by a Serbian doctor, Bojan Mihailovic, to his son at the front. It closed by saying: 'When you come back home, can you bring me the body of one dead Albanian so that I can cut its neck.' The letter went on to say love from 'Jasna, mother Anka and grand-mother Milica'.

From the front line overlooking Batusa yesterday, a landscape that would under normal circumstances be a lovely valley of red roofs, farmhouses and green fields instead looked empty and dangerous. We could see through binoculars that Djakovica, in the distance, had been burnt and shelled. Only Serbs were left.

All the ethnic Albanians fled or were bused out. All the villages I have walked through are empty. Many of the men with me know these villages. There is almost nothing left behind in them. Whatever was not stolen has been smashed or broken.

On two days last week the Serbs fired shells that emitted white smoke. It seemed to be some kind of chemical. Those who breathed it suffer red eyes, an inability to breathe, small pupils and disorientation. Doctors do not know what it is. A few gas masks have now arrived.

The spirit of the men here is extraordinary. Many are young and have no experience. Most have families in Kosovo and are constantly worried about mothers, fathers, children, sisters and brothers.

There is Burim, 19, an architectural student, who after being expelled from Kosovo by the Serbs joined the KLA as soon as he crossed the border.

Angel left his restaurant in Sweden and told his mother he was going to find a wife in Albania. 'I am not a soldier and I have no experience, but I have come to Kosovo with all my heart,' he said.

Pren left his friends and family in Zurich without a word because he feared they would try to stop him.

All are very young. It is somehow more heartbreaking that some of these men will die with the end of Serbian occupation in sight.

Massacre in a spring meadow: war in Europe

2 May 1999

In a war of numerous atrocities Marie Colvin talks to over 100 witnesses of the most horrifying slaughter Kosovo has endured.

Seven-year-old Egzon Zyberi interrupted adult conversations late last week with a childish monotone. 'Long live Milosevic!' he chanted. 'Kosovo is Serbian!'

The little boy in orange trousers seemed to want an explanation, his brown eyes darting about for a reaction.

They were strange words to hear from a young Kosovan refugee but everyone around him knew what had happened.

They were what Serbs in uniforms and black masks had made Egzon, his brothers and cousins shout as the children watched their fathers and grandfather being dragged away to a killing field at the village of Meja in southwestern Kosovo on Tuesday morning.

'I didn't feel well to say this,' Egzon muttered to a translator, when asked what had happened at Meja.

Egzon's 40-year-old father, Dani, his 30-year-old uncle, Skandar, and his 65-year-old grandfather, Burim, were all pulled out of a refugee convoy by the Serbs. Arbur Hajosaj, a 16-year-old boy they had picked up on the road with his grandmother, was also taken.

They appear to have been some of the many victims of what is emerging as the worst Serbian atrocity of the war in Kosovo.

The women and children last saw them being escorted into a field in the centre of Meja where lines of men already sat in the open under the barrels of what they described as hundreds of Serbian gunmen. Then the Serbian forces on a narrow road shouted at the family to move, move, move. There was no chance to say goodbye.

None of the women knew how to drive a tractor so a 12-year-old neighbour jumped into the seat. 'He kept bumping into the other tractors,' said Egzon, perking up at something he could talk about. 'He didn't even know how to drive.'

Egzon and what remains of the Zyberi family now live in a tent in a muddy field outside the city of Kukes in northern Albania. Snow-capped peaks tower over them. Their tent shelters Egzon's mother, grandmother and two aunts, his three small brothers and his two little cousins, one only two months old.

In a corner, weeping silently, is Fawze Hajosaj, the elderly woman who lost her grandson to the Serbs. The Zyberi family does not know her; but she has nobody else so they have taken her in.

The Zyberis are far from alone in their affliction. They are in a camp, run by Médecins sans Frontières which shelters most of the families who arrived last week from the latest wave of Serbian ethnic cleansing around the city of Djakovica.

Women wash clothes in brightly coloured plastic basins, children play in the dirt, a few old men gather in little clusters. But in row after row of dark green tents there are no fathers. Family after family tells the same story and it always ends with Meja.

Yesterday the Zyberi women were still hoping their men had somehow escaped the Serbs. They had not been told that other families who passed through Meja after them had seen a pile of bodies in the field in the centre of the village. 'There has certainly been a mass killing,' confirmed the United Nations High Commissioner for Refugees (UNHCR).

Estimates of the total dead ranged yesterday from 200 to more than 1,000. Whichever proves correct, the Serbian forces are now killing on a scale that matches their bloodlust in the Bosnian and Croatian wars. In Bosnia, they reached a peak of savagery shortly before their strategic position began to deteriorate.

The trigger that turned Meja into a killing field may have been the assassination there of a senior Serbian officer and several of his bodyguards by the Kosovo Liberation Army (KLA) about 10 days ago. Shortly afterwards, a renewed wave of ethnic cleansing began in the area.

The Zyberi family had already been 'cleansed' once from its farmland around a remote village called Molic.

A month ago, under pressure from the Serbs, Nushe Zyberi, the grandmother and matriarch of the family, took her husband, her two sons and their families to live with her sister's family in the village of Dobros. They hoped to sit out the Serbian offensive there and return to their farm instead of ending up homeless in Albania or Macedonia.

There was no work and little food. The only shops open in nearby Djakovica were Serbian and the owners had started refusing to sell food – even bread and milk – to ethnic Albanians.

Last Monday night, the adults and children went to sleep as usual crowded together in blankets on the floor. Tuesday morning dawned cold and rainy. While the children slept, the adults rose early. The women started a wood fire and began baking bread.

At 6am gunfire sounded throughout the village. The children awoke, crying and frightened. Dobros had been surrounded by what seemed to the Zyberis like hundreds of Serbs with tanks.

Soldiers were firing into the air. Others were shouting at the villagers to leave their homes: 'Go to Nato if you like them so much. Go to Albania, this is not your home, this is Serbia.'

The time had arrived at last to submit to Serbia's systematic programme to 'cleanse' Kosovo of its 1.2 million ethnic Albanians. The men moved quickly. Dani and Skandar hitched their two tractors to metal carts and the families piled in. Their wives, young children, mother and father went into one cart, driven by Skandar; their mother's sister and her family were in the second, with Dani at the wheel.

There was no time to take clothes or supplies. They grabbed some blankets to wrap the frightened children in and tacked a plastic sheet over the carts to protect them from the rain, before heading for Albania. They had only been on the road for a few minutes when the farmhouse burst into flames behind them, torched by the Serbs who were rampaging through the village.

Similar scenes were taking place in other villages around Djakovica, once a lovely city of white stone houses but now an armed Serbian encampment, and the road towards the border was becoming clogged with tractors, trailers and their human cargo. Serbian soldiers and police with tanks and armoured personnel carriers lined the route.

At Meja, a hitherto insignificant village on the route, Serbian soldiers and paramilitaries began stopping the convoy. The Zyberi family reached Meja at about 8am. They saw Serbian soldiers walking down the convoy, pulling men from tractors and beating and kicking some of them by the roadside. There was nowhere to turn off and escape.

Skandar Zyberi twice ignored Serbian demands to get off his tractor; then they hauled him off by his sleeve. Describing the scene later, his wife Sheribone, 28, wept and cuddled their two-month-old daughter, Ezuntina.

Skandar's brother and father were ordered out of the cart at gunpoint by Serbs wearing black masks. 'The children started crying and yelling "daddy, daddy" but the Serbs laughed,' said

Nushe, who watched in horror as her husband and two grown-up sons were led away.

'Then they made the children say the Serbian things, terrible things. The children were so frightened.'

The last the family saw of the three men was their backs as they walked at gunpoint into the field where several hundred men were sitting surrounded by armed Serbs. With his hands clasped on his lap, Egzon apes the way they sat.

Another member of the family, Aphrodite Zyberi, 19, said the Serbs had shouted: 'You killed seven of us; we will kill 700 of you.' In Yugoslavia during the Second World War, the Nazis killed 100 people in retribution for every German slain by partisans.

Family after family reaching the refugee camp outside Kukes last week was interviewed separately yet described the same scene at the same place. Males aged from 16 to 60-plus had been forced from their families into the meadow at Meja. Serbs had shouted and beaten anyone who did not move quickly enough.

Xhamal Rama, a 58-year-old farmer, a neighbour of the Zyberis in Dubros, had held out for as long as he could at home; but at 9am he had also piled his wife and 10 children into a cart and had driven off on his tractor. His brother and family followed. 'The Serbs were firing their guns and setting fire to the houses,' he said. 'They had masks and some had red handkerchiefs. They ordered us to leave and we could do nothing.'

Reaching Meja after the Zyberis, he found the Serbs behaving like 'beasts'. Three of his nephews were hauled off his brother's trac- tor and taken to the field, where about 250 men were being made to show the Serbian three-finger sign and shout, 'Long live Serbia.'

Zek, 55, another farmer, who would not give his full name, had bruises on his arm and said he had been beaten by the Serbs for shouting, 'Leave him alone', when they took his 16-year-old nephew. Zek looked far older than his years, which may have saved his own life.

A slight, frail woman called Birami described how Serbs had arrived early on Tuesday at her village, Dalasaj, shooting and shouting that they would kill anyone who did not leave in five minutes.

Her husband, Alban, had piled their four children and their parents into his tractor-drawn cart and departed. As houses went up in flames behind them, Alban balanced Blerim, his blonde, five-year-old son, on his knee.

On reaching Meja, said Birami, they were confronted by masked Serbian paramilitaries or soldiers; she was not sure which.

Ordered off his tractor, Alban handed her Blerim and walked away into the meadow to join the other men. She could not drive and a neighbour had to take the wheel.

Another of the families caught in this terrible exodus had already been in a fleeing convoy a little more than two weeks ago but had been attacked from the sky.

'A tractor in front of us burst into flames,' recalled Fana, the mother of the family, who had seen too much to reveal her full name. People had been burnt in front of her eyes. Other people had jumped from their tractors off a bridge and drowned.

Nato later admitted it had mistakenly bombed the convoy but – like all the refugees – Fana and her family would not say a word against Nato. They insisted the plane must have been Serbian.

After that incident, they had camped in a ruined house in a village called Dalas. At 7am on Tuesday, they said, Dalas was surrounded by Serbs, some wearing black balaclavas, shooting in the air. The family took to the tractor again – and, again, the houses went up in flames behind them.

'Serbs with guns and tanks stopped us at the village of Meja,' Fana said. 'They took my nephews and my son, he was only 16. We began to cry and scream but we could do nothing because they had guns. They were pushed to the ground and then made to walk into the field where other men were sitting.'

Her youngest son, 12-year-old Vilsan, began driving the tractor. 'I couldn't see for my tears,' Vilsan said quietly as the family replayed the scene at the refugee camp.

'They knocked my father down on the ground and beat him with their guns. But we had to drive because the Serbian soldiers said move immediately. I was afraid to look back.'

Vilsan is now the oldest male in the family. Two young women, the wives of Fana's nephews, sat crying near him surrounded by young children. They had only the clothes they were wearing.

Several miles after Meja, the family had been stopped by other Serbian soldiers and robbed of all their money, DM700. Another family, the Salihus, had travelled from the village of Ramizi on foot after Serbs forced them to leave at 5am. They reached Meja at dusk on Tuesday.

'We were so afraid,' said Rucka Salihu, 23. 'I saw dead bodies in a field in the middle of Meja. I was too frightened to look for long. I could only see that they were lying across each other on their stomachs, in this pasture near some bushes. Hundreds of them. Maybe 200.'

She crossed her hands, one over the other, to show how she saw the bodies lying. She said other men were sitting in the meadow, still alive and under Serbian guard.

Serbian soldiers pulled her uncle, Niman Salihu, 50, and a neighbour off the road into the meadow. Two soldiers then spotted Rucka's brother, Kiytim, 18, who is small and dark and looks young for his age. 'Two Serbian soldiers shouted to me to put down my bag and stop,' said Kiytim. 'The bag was full of bread. Then my sisters began weeping and surrounded me and I was so afraid I was sick.

'One of the Serbian soldiers, the older one, shouted at me again but the other one said, "Oh, let him go, he's too young", and we kept walking and I was surrounded by my family and they just let me go. My sisters' tears saved me.'

He cannot forget the sight of the meadow in Meja. 'There were bodies in the field. A pile of bodies. I was too scared to make any accurate count. I tried not to look for long because the Serbs would notice me.'

After five minutes of walking, the Salihu family heard a burst of gunfire that went on for about 10 minutes.

The first news of the massacre at Meja came in the hours after the refugees started crossing into Albania at the Morina border post under a full moon late on Tuesday night.

Nobody expected them, as the Serbs had closed the border days earlier. The only aid agency to meet them was Action Hunger whose workers began dispensing hot tea in the chilly air. UNHCR officials raced to the border.

In all, 47 tractors hauling carts full of women and children and a few elderly men reached Albania that night. The first arrivals looked merely anxious.

By the time the last tractor rolled across the border, the road down to the refugee camp at Kukes was a trail of misery. Their faces etched with horror, the last to arrive could barely speak.

More refugees from Djakovica poured across the border all week, with 10,000 arriving on Friday alone.

Madeleine Albright, the American secretary of state, has announced that the events at Meja will be investigated as a possible war crime. But no international outrage comforts the families who had to leave their men in Meja. 'I feel like I want to die,' said Safeta Zyberi, Egzon's mother.

THE MACEDONIAN BUSINESSMAN

Petrovski Gupco runs an import/export company in Skopje.

'I can no longer see a future in Macedonia for me or my children. We were lucky to avoid the war, but it will go on around us for many more years. You cannot look for serious investment. When you have poor neighbours, you cannot expect your economy to grow. Albania is the poorest country in Europe. The Serbian economy is destroyed.

'I am seriously considering leaving, to live in a normal country, maybe to Singapore. If these refugees stay in Macedonia, no one will be happy. They cost money. The UN and Nato help out, but it also costs our government. We have 200,000 unemployed and now we have the same number of refugees. We have excellent relations with the Albanians who have lived in Macedonia for generations.

'I have visited the refugee camps. The conditions are very poor. I feel sorry for them. But there is a background to this. This century, when Serbs began to rule Macedonia, they started to kill Albanians. When Bulgarians took Macedonia in World War Two, they killed Albanians. After the war, Albanians killed the Macedonians. But I do not approve of Milosevic. Only a madman would.'

THE TEENAGER

Arta Abizi, 15, a refugee with a family in Kumanovo, Macedonia.

'When we were forced to leave our home in Pristina by the Serbs, I just cried. Not only because we were frightened, but for the things I had to leave behind. I left my photographs that told my whole life's story from when I was three. I left my rings, my earrings, my nice socks. Emin, my brother, who is nearly 12, had to leave his parrot.

'We tried to go to the border but we were turned back to Presovo, a Serbian town near the Kosovan border. The soldiers made us walk back in a line along the tracks. We had to sleep in the open but we could not light a fire because they told us Nato would shoot us. The nights were so cold. When we finally got to the border, we spent six nights in no-man's land. I did not sleep one night. I was frozen and it was so very dirty that I was afraid to sleep.

'Since I came here I have started going to school in Kumanovo. People from the school invited me to come to class, because I was a refugee. I hate being a refugee; you have nothing and everything is so uncertain. I don't want to stay here. Every day, all day, all I think is what am I doing here?'

Letter from ... Kosare

4 June 1999

The Times Literary Supplement

The Kosare Barracks of the Kosovo Liberation Army was never much to look at. The fight to capture it from the Serbs had been fierce. Six shell-holes pierced one red-brick wall and there was a hole in the roof. When the wind blew at night, glass fell from the shattered windows. It looked lonely. To get there, you had to walk down a narrow path from Albania, across a barbed wire fence that used to be the international border, past a deserted farmhouse now half tumbled into stones and the corpses of four horses in a grassy field pitted with craters of black soil. Everyone said the border minefield had been cleared, but everyone stayed on the narrow winding path which bore the comforting footprints of those who had walked that way before.

The barracks stood alone in a narrow valley between mountains covered with scrub oak. No one ever sat outside in the spring sun; the Serbs might see you and fire off a shell. There was no electricity. The Serbs were on the next hill and the commander thought the noise of the generator might attract their attention, although since they had lived there first and clearly knew where it was, that really didn't make too much sense. But there were always bean stews cooking in cauldrons over wood-fired stoves, and there was always someone to talk to at night when you couldn't sleep.

When I heard Nato had bombed the KLA barracks at Kosare, it was those late-night conversations I thought of. They never started out as war conversations. Someone would come out of the sleeping rooms that were crowded with bunk-beds and Kalashnikovs hanging over the metal bedsteads and pour some oil in a tin pot or whatever he could find, dip in a rag until it was soaked, light the cloth and then a cigarette. It would draw the other non-sleepers and we would stand around, offering each other cigarettes, smoking. There was always the boom of artillery in the background, but no one talked about it – it wasn't close enough to worry about – and we had learned you only really had to worry when you heard a whistle that meant an incoming shell was close, and then there was not much you could do except dive for the ground. It was from Kosare Barracks that KLA units walked out at night, in single file, up into the mountains to fight the Serbs, to push them back. The gains and losses were unspectacular but dependable: a mile a week, a comrade killed when he was shot trying to lob a grenade into a Serb bunker. Kosare Barracks, for all its discomforts, was somewhere safe before you had to walk out and try again.

The talk would always start with families, now lost in Kosovo. We were in Kosovo, of course, the young men talking at night were proud that they had fought and captured this small piece of their homeland, but the Serb army was between us and where their families lived. The only villages we saw were those we walked through late at night, remaining silent in honour and in awe of the bombed and destroyed homes and the absence of people.

Perhaps in all barracks in a war there is a camaraderie that – intensified by the ever-present possibility of sudden death – thrives on deep and immediate intimacy, that removes the need for formalities, and that, once established, is only broken by death. One night in the hole lit by the flicker of an oil fire, Xhavit said it was his son's sixth birthday, and showed us pictures of his boy and two older daughters. He was a big beefy man and had been working in Switzerland, sending home money when the war started. He hadn't seen his family for four months and now he didn't know if his son had turned six or was dead. He was a sniper. He didn't even need to say why he was there; everyone in the barracks had reached a point where years of Serb oppression meant they were ready when the time came to pick up a gun. Burim, who had left his restaurant and his girlfriend in Spain, where he had lived for fourteen years, would tell us again about how he found his sister in the mountains. He had not seen her in all that time, but had found her lying exhausted on the ground with her three children, the nephews and nieces he had never met. He had taken his sister and her children to a refugee camp in Kukes in Northern Albania and returned to join his fellow KLA guerrillas. He told us this story every night in the barracks, as if by telling it he would somehow understand how that miracle could happen.

Standing in the oil-lit hallway, everyone knew when the next patrol was due to return, but never talked about it. When the returning KLA soldiers walked in, tired and wet after three days in the mountains, the group around the fire would line up and solemnly, ceremoniously, embrace the arriving men and, anxiously but without saying it, never asking, look to see if anyone who had walked out of Kosare three nights ago had not come back.

Eventually, the talk would always turn to Nato. The KLA soldiers, young men who had grown up quickly or at least tried to seem as if they had, were proud that they were now allied with Nato; when they said it, it was as if they stood a bit straighter, looked a bit taller. They were fighting for their country and it had to turn out okay because Nato, the West, the Americans and the British, those countries where people had unimaginable choices, unimaginable freedoms, were on their side. They would always talk about Nato with awe in their voices. They liked to joke that Nato was the KLA air force. And yes, they would always ask when the Apaches were coming.

The Apaches, of course, are helicopters. That was important because the KLA are fighting with light weapons. Some had bought themselves expensive kit in Europe, but mostly they all carried battered Chinese copies of Russian Kalashnikovs or even just single-round hunting rifles. They were trying to fight their way across Serb lines, but they faced three emplacements of artillery and tanks – at Batusha, Mount Plahnik and Morine. Against all odds, they had captured not just Kosare Barracks, but fought their way ten kilometres into Serb-held Kosovo, and taken the mountains for another ten kilometres horizontally along the front (Kosare Barracks is at the centre), carving out a foothold of almost

100 square kilometres. Testimony to the continued fighting came to Kosare every day when KLA soldiers carried back injured comrades, and put them on donkeys for the journey up the narrow path to Albania, where they would be put on carts pulled by tractors and, it was hoped, arrive at a hospital two hours away.

Nato could break this stalemate, could destroy those tanks and artillery in hours. If the KLA rushed those positions head on, however, with no weapons other than Kalashnikovs, they would lose hundreds of men. Nato did not strike. There was news of bridges bombed, oil refineries hit, electricity grids destroyed, but never those artillery guns or tanks. The positions of the Serb heavy weapons were no secret. KLA commanders would call Astrit Huskaj, the KLA–American liaison officer in Kukes, give him the co-ordinates of the Serb positions and the KLA positions so that there could be no mistakes. Everyone at Kosare Barracks believed that one day, soon, Nato would take out those Serb tanks and guns blocking their offensive. They all heard the BBC reporting on the reluctance of Nato to send ground troops, but for these KLA men that made no sense. Tell them, they would say to me, an American working for a British newspaper ('so you must know them'), tell them just arm us and we will go in. We need weapons against tanks, not much more. Our families are there. Our homes are there. We can fight, we have to.

That was before Nato bombed the Kosare Barracks and killed seven of these young men, men I knew, although no one has bothered to list the names of the dead. It was a small place. There is no doubt it was a mistake. The KLA has been anxious to say they understand mistakes can happen and Nato must continue bombing, because it is the only way to end the reign of their enemy, Slobodan Milosevic. Since returning from Kosovo, I have heard all the reservations about arming the KLA, but none has really made sense when I thought of the young men I met and with whom I travelled into the mountains. There was Ramis, very proud that a British journalist was with his unit, a village boy whose family was only about ten miles away in the village of Ratkovac, if they were still alive. We could see the lights of Djakovica, the nearest city, at night, and the fires of the houses the Serbs were burning. He would point to where his village was and tell me it was dark because people slept early, but neither of us believed that. He told me about how the old men in the village had cried when he left and how he told them not to worry: his generation would free Kosovo. There was Ghani, a young philosophy student who would never talk seriously but made a bet with everyone else in the unit that he could eat eight hamburgers and drink two pints of beer when they arrived in Pristina, Kosovo's capital. Doc, laconic, bespectacled, who held the unit together after their commander was shot in the head and killed by a Serb sniper. Doc never talked about bravery; no one did. He had had to travel outside Kosovo for education because Albanians cannot become doctors under the Serbs.

'You don't understand freedom,' he said one day, during a lull in fighting, sitting in a freezing mountain bivouac: 'you can't. You grow up with freedom, you've never thought about it. I picked up a gun because there is no way we can live under the Serbs any more. This will be over soon. The West understands that.'

I'm not sure how any of these young men feel now that the planes we saw flying overhead every day and that were supposed to destroy the artillery and tanks between them and their villages and families have instead bombed their barracks. I'm not sure whether they are still alive. I do think anyone who met them would also feel it is hypocritical for a Nato spokesman to get up on television every day and talk about the success of hundreds of warplane sorties, and for diplomats to brief journalists that Nato is doing all it can to defeat Milosevic, and not to help the only people who are fighting his troops and paramilitaries every day and are willing to die doing it. There was no talk in the Kosare Barracks about zero tolerance for returning body bags. They saw too many.

The neighbour who
burned with hate

DJAKOVICA

20 June 1999

**Bozhidar Dogancic was a loser who for the duration of the war had the
power to decide whether his neighbours lived or died at the hands of the
Serb paramilitaries, reports Marie Colvin in Djakovica.**

In Djakovica, a quaint, cobbled town that used to be home to many
of Kosovo's leading writers, artists and intellectuals, Bozhidar
Dogancic was a nobody.

He lived near the bus station in a concrete, single-storey house
with peeling paint and dirty curtains. His front windows looked
out on to a dank garden of earth and weeds, darkened by unkempt
trees that hid the property from passers-by.

Dogancic, known in his neighbourhood as Bozho, liked to sit on
his porch and drink slivovitz from half-gallon bottles, shouting,
singing and talking with friends. What he enjoyed talking about
most of all was how much he hated Albanians.

The day before Nato troops entered Kosovo last weekend,
Dogancic dumped all the food from his refrigerator into a rotting
heap on his living room floor. He could not take it with him and
he did not want to leave it for his neighbours. They were Albanians
and Dogancic was a Serb.

Dogancic, 65, left Kosovo, knowing he could never return. There
was too much blood on his hands.

In almost any other country, he would have remained
nothing more than a resentful loser. Neighbours regarded him
as something of a bully and avoided him. He rarely troubled
them except when his noisy drinking sessions kept them awake at
night.

But this was Kosovo and for 10 years, since Slobodan Milosevic rose to high office with passionate promises to protect the Serbs of Kosovo, Dogancic had also exercised power.

Milosevic rode a wave of Serbian nationalism that led to a decade of war in the Balkans. Dogancic did the same thing, on a smaller scale, in his little district of Djakovica. His power over Albanians enabled him to exact intoxicating revenge for slights, imagined and real.

The son of a saddler, Dogancic grew up in Djakovica's tiny minority community of Serbs and worked for local government. His job was to patrol the forests to stop people felling trees illegally. He was a handsome youth and married a pretty local girl, Radmilla. They had four children.

Albanians, who made up 90% of Kosovo's population, dominated senior positions in the government at that time and ran most of the businesses. Many had big houses and sent their sons abroad for education and work. Dogancic lived in squalor with little money and few prospects. Everything changed when Milosevic rescinded Kosovo's autonomy in 1990 and Albanians were kicked out of their jobs. Dogancic had what were considered the right opinions. He told anyone who would listen that Albanians should be deported from Kosovo. After all, he would say, they had Albania, didn't they?

His mentors were two pairs of brothers from similarly inauspicious backgrounds. Momcilo and Sava Stanovic, and their first cousins, Milan and Jokica Stanovic, are infamous among ethnic Albanians in Djakovica.

There was little education among them; Milan was a sheep farmer, Momcilo a building inspector's clerk. Under Milosevic's regime, however, they were able to establish a semi-autonomous dictatorship. Jokica Stanovic, who had friends in Milosevic's circle, was appointed mayor by Belgrade in 1991. He made Milan his police chief.

Momcilo, his cousin, became a local minister in charge of government property, including state factories. He gave Dogancic, the lowly forest patrol man, the job of director in a brick and tile plant.

In 1996 Momcilo took over as mayor when Jokica became a deputy in the Yugoslav senate. He built several Serbian Orthodox churches and soon became a priest. But his religious beliefs did not stop him from intensifying repression of Djakovica's ethnic Albanians.

He built up a private police force and was under investigation by the Organisation for Security and Co-operation in Europe for suspected war crimes when it became obvious that Nato was about to launch its airstrikes and the OSCE pulled out.

While Milan arranged for the deportation of countless local Albanians from Djakovica, Momcilo directed squads of special police and paramilitaries into the town. The separatist Kosovo Liberation Army had waged guerrilla warfare against these forces in the surrounding area since early this year. The hatred between them was fierce.

Djakovica, with its thuggish Serbian leadership, ruthless para-militaries and poorly defended Albanian community, was about to became a microcosm of Kosovo as it was torn apart. Dogancic would exercise the power he held in his community to devastat-ingly lethal effect.

The local Albanians had been growing increasingly fearful of Dogancic for years. He walked around with a pistol in his belt. Serbian police and members of the security forces in civilian clothes came in and out of his house. Whenever he had an argu-ment in his part of town, the neighbour concerned would be taken into the local police station and beaten.

The danger in the rise of such a man is evident now in the devastation that surrounds his house. The homes of all his Albanian neighbours – mechanics, shopkeepers, barbers – are blackened ruins with overgrown gardens. No more than a cher-ished rose bush still blooms here and there.

Dogancic has gone, but there is no jubilation at his departure. His neighbours paid too high a price for living next door. Last week, as the first of them returned to begin clearing out their homes, they spat his name with fury and contempt.

The Serbs started burning Djakovica on 24 March, the night Nato began bombing. About 100 high street shops were looted and then torched. The homes of professional men and anyone who had had contact with international organisations were set alight.

For the first few days, people were killed one at a time. Izat Hima, Djakovica's most prominent ethnic Albanian doctor, was shot dead on his doorstep. Paramilitaries cut the throat of Kujtim Dula, a lawyer who had defended political prisoners, in front of his wife.

But as the bombing went on, the Serbs launched a systematic campaign to murder the Albanians who remained in the town and to empty the surrounding villages.

Dogancic would walk through the streets pointing out houses to long-haired men in dark camouflage uniforms with black cowboy hats characteristic of the so-called Frenki's Boys, a paramilitary group that reports to Frenki Simatovic, Milosevic's state security chief.

'The paramilitaries didn't know the neighbourhood,' said Xhavet Beqa, a heavily built man who got his wife and four children out to Albania but stayed in Djakovica, slipping back to his district through Serbian patrols. 'They needed Bozho to tell them where to go. He told them who was in hiding.'

Beqa said Dogancic, his wife Radmilla and their eldest son, Nebojsha, a 26-year-old policeman, had stood in the middle of his street, arms folded, as they watched Beqa's three houses burn. The paramilitaries surrounded Dogancic, he said, joking and congratulating themselves on a job well done. Radmilla also had a pistol.

After choosing which houses should be the first to burn, Dogancic asserted his authority over the fate of people. He meted out virtual death sentences, simply by identifying places of concealment.

Beqa led me through the overgrown back garden of the building opposite his home to a cellar where Dogancic had pointed out the hiding place of the Vesja family. They were poor and frightened and did not want to risk fleeing to Albania. Twenty-four people were hiding in the basement when Dogancic and the paramilitaries arrived.

Five men ran; they had been taken in by the Vesjas and had no relatives to worry about. Lurzim Vesja, a shopkeeper, stayed with his family.

Scorched bed springs and a child's partly burnt boot are all that is left to testify to their presence in the shelter. Nineteen men, women and children, including Lurzim, were led to a row of garages behind the house. The paramilitaries shot them in one of the garages and set fire to the row. Nobody escaped. They were people Dogancic would have seen every day.

Few traces of the massacre remain. There are bullet holes in the scorched grey walls and shells on the overgrown garden in front. The bodies lay untouched for two days. Beqa and other men from the neighbourhood who were too afraid to give their names – 'I know we are free now, but you can't know how deep the fear is in us' – saw them that night, a charred huddle.

Finally, gypsies pulled up with a tractor and cart and hauled the bodies away for burial in the Djakovica cemetery under wooden markers with numbers and a date. 'I saw them put the bodies in the cart,' Beqa said. 'I couldn't believe how small they were.'

If you have ever seen a charred body, you know he was telling the truth. The human body, when burnt, is reduced to an almost childlike size. It is a horrible piece of knowledge that comes with reporting from Kosovo. In house after house, village after village, I have seen those bodies, so small that it seems they must be those of children, yet they are not.

Dogancic's reign of terror did not end with the Vesja family. Around the corner, amid the burnt-out skeletons of other houses, is the home of the family of Skandar Dylatahus, a barber. In front of the walled garden is a jar of pickles and a silver-plated tray. This family also tried to hide rather than risk their men on the road to Albania.

Dogancic knew they had stayed. Nobody in the neighbourhood understands how, because they had laid in supplies and never gone out. But paramilitaries directed by Dogancic found 17 people in the basement of the two-storey home.

This time they were more merciful. They told 10 women and children to leave, saying: 'Go to Albania, that is your home.' They lined seven men up in the garden and shot them, then put their bodies back in the basement and torched the house. Dogancic stood in the road, again staring into the flames.

Today Djakovica looks like Dresden at the end of the Second World War. Beautiful old buildings in the centre and big mansions in the suburbs have been reduced to blackened shells. On the main street, every shop is without its roof. In the old bazaar, where traders sold cloth, books, bric-a-brac and tiny cups of coffee, there are only charred walls.

The cemetery contains 238 new graves, each marked with a flat wooden stake. A name, or sometimes just a date and number, is written in marker or pencil. Semi-literate gypsies did the burying, so most of the names are misspelt. Next to the graves are two large areas of disturbed earth, each covering about 20 yards by 50. About 1,500 men are missing in Djakovica – the highest number of any town in Kosovo – and many are no doubt dead.

In the countryside within a few miles' radius, the atrocities committed by Frenki's Boys and other paramilitary groups with the aid of local agents such as Dogancic are no less in evidence.

In the village of Celin, to the west, Serbian forces from Djakovica set up on three hills on 25 March, the first day after the Nato bombing began, and started firing artillery at 8am. Several thousand villagers hoping to escape to Albania made for another hill less than two miles away. There, they were surrounded by 'Frenkis' who demanded jewellery and cash.

The first to die was Agim Ramadani, 23, a student who was accused of being in the KLA, told to run for his life and shot in front of his mother when he did so.

The villagers were goaded for most of the day. A Serb named Banzic Novica from nearby Opterusa recognised Hait Bytyqi, 35; they had worked together in a factory. 'Hait, come here,' Novica yelled. 'I'm going to show you I'm your God. Give me 1,000 deutschmarks [£330].' Bytyqi's father collected the money from people standing around in terror, but Novica shot the top of his head off anyway. Bytyqi was the father of a young son and daughter.

Finally the men were separated from the women. Some lived; some died. Twenty-one are buried at one spot, eight lie in a shallow grave covered with daisies and thistles at another. Altogether there are 86 graves.

In Meja to the south, where more than 100 people are thought to have been shot in a single incident, I followed a smell to the bodies of three men, dressed in the rough suits of peasants, lying under the bushes. Many others are said to have been removed from a mass grave.

Momcilo Stanovic, the mayor of Djakovica, fled from his flat on the day of Nato's arrival. He was in a small police car with no escort.

Stanovic left behind rooms full of dark wooden furniture, oriental carpets and marble. Every cabinet is filled with foreign liquors. At the door is a bucket of empty beer bottles. From the two terraces where he drank, Stanovic would have seen Djakovica burning.

The flat is now inhabited by Skandar Dubruna, 62, a bearded, bespectacled intellectual whose family was active in the party of Ibrahim Rugova, the moderate ethnic Albanian leader. Dubruna and his wife Shyretta have painted their Albanian name on the door so that nobody attacks them by mistake.

'He burnt down our house,' Dubruna said. 'So I came and took his house.'

It will probably matter little to Stanovic. He moved his family to the palatial villa he had built in Montenegro a month before the bombing campaign, and will no doubt join them there.

As for Dogancic, he and his family escaped with their belongings piled high on their Yugo car. They are unlikely to taste power again. But the enduring horror of Djakovica is that Dogancic was not alone. There were many like him: little men whose brief rise to unrestrained authority led to the destruction of a town and a society.

British detectives on trail of men behind massacres

27 June 1999

Marie Colvin in Bela Crkva reveals how Serbs mowed down fleeing families.

A pile of clothes on the bank of the River Belaja tells you who died here. There is a child's pair of black rubber boots, size 28; another little pair of bright red rubber boots, size 35; tiny blue-and-green pyjama bottoms, with a bullet hole in the left leg; a baby's bottle, half-filled with what looks like apple juice; and a hand-knitted, sage green woman's vest, unravelling around two bullet holes.

Five yards from the pile of clothes is a mound of dark earth that covers 14 bodies. British war crimes investigators are due to arrive at this scene, near the village of Bela Crkva, today. They will dig up the bodies, bag the clothes and sift the earth for the copper-coloured 7.62-calibre bullets – Kalashnikov issue.

They will also walk upstream to the graves of 65 men who were shot in cold blood after being forced to strip to their underclothes: husbands, fathers, neighbours of the women and children in the riverside grave. The evidence will go to the international criminal tribunal for the former Yugoslavia at the Hague.

The deaths are listed in the tribunal's indictment of Slobodan Milosevic, the Yugoslav president and commander-in-chief

responsible for those who killed 79 men, women and children of
Bela Crkva on the night of 25 March.

The language of the indictment is matter-of-fact. The dead
women in that riverside grave are listed as 'Spahiu, FNU (first
name unknown), wife of Xhemal' and 'Zhuniqi, FNU, wife of
Clirim'. There are four listings of 'Spahiu, FNU, daughter of
Xhemal'. But the villagers who survived knew these people, and
guarded their graves last week, waiting for the British team.

'Zhuniqi, FNU, wife of Clirim' was Lumniya Zhuniqi, 35, who
fled into the cold night with her husband, 40, and their five children, desperate to hide them from the Serbian forces that had
surrounded the village at 4am and from the tank shells that had
begun crashing into its terracotta tile roofs at 5.30am.

Sabri Popaj, a neighbour, found the Zhuniqis trying to cross the
river to what they thought would be safety. Popaj was hiding from
the Serbs but he heard children crying. 'I carried one of Lumniya's
babies across, a little boy, maybe two years old, and she and Clirim
helped the others. I handed the boy up to her where she stood on
the bank.'

Also with Lumniya was her grandfather, Qamil Spahiu, 77, his
daughter-in-law and her five children. Popaj left them hiding
under the lip of the bank and fled across a field. 'We thought they
would kill the men, but not women and children,' he said. He heard
machinegun fire soon afterwards. About 20 Serbs dressed in
camouflage uniforms with white bandannas around their arms
stood on the bank and fired down at the cowering families. Popaj
crawled back half an hour later.

'Lumniya was spread out over her children. She was trying to
hide them from the bullets. Heads were burst open. I walked a few
metres and sat down and smoked a cigarette. I couldn't think
anything.'

He did not know it, but the two-year-old boy had survived
under Lumniya's body. Another villager found the child, and hid
him in blankets. A woman from the village took him with her own
children to Albania.

The Spahiu and Zhuniqi families were killed at 6.30am. The 20 Serbian soldiers – probably paramilitaries – continued walking upriver. About half a mile away, they found several hundred villagers hiding near a narrow railway bridge.

The Serbs stood on the bridge and fired into the air, shouting for the villagers to move into a field. Men, women and children emerged. It was 9am, cold and foggy.

Isuf Zhuniqi, a small, wiry man with the weathered skin of a farmer and now a bullet scar in his shoulder, is another survivor. With the other men of the village, he was separated from his family: his wife Nuriya, 37, and his four children. His four-year-old son Adnan ran after him, screaming in terror, and Serbian soldiers took the boy and bashed his head against the track.

While Popaj was hiding near the bodies of the slain families, his wife Fedayia, 35, and two sons, Shendet, 17, and Agon, 14, his only children, were forced into the field; Agon was torn from his mother's arms. She screamed that he was just a child, but he was big for his age: he liked boxing and worked on his physique.

The women and children were kept in a field on one side of the river; about 50 or 60 men were forced to cross to the other. 'The river was so cold. We were all frozen,' Zhuniqi said.

'The Serbs pointed their guns at us and said, "Take off your clothes." They went through our pockets and took any money. Then they told us to put our clothes back on.'

The Serbs told Sabri Popaj's son Shendet to lie down with his hands behind his head. Nobody knows why he was singled out. Nesim Popaj, 43, Sabri's brother and the local doctor, tried to talk to the commander, saying: 'This is not right, what you are doing.' The commander ordered him out of the group, shouted: 'F*** your mother,' and shot him.

He turned and shot Shendet in the head. Then the Serbs opened fire on the group with Kalashnikovs. Men fell wounded and dead on the field as they fled towards the river.

'I was in the water. The shooting was everywhere. Dead bodies fell on me,' Isuf Zhuniqi recalled. 'The Serbs came down the riverbank and shot anyone who was moving with automatic pistols. I thought I was dead.'

After 20 minutes in the freezing water, he heard the Serbs leave. Around him were bodies without arms, heads split open, blood in the water. He knew all the men. Somehow he made his way to the nearby village of Zrze, where the women had taken refuge. 'Everyone is dead,' he told his wife. 'Everyone.'

Sabri Popaj returned to the river that night with his wife. He found Shendet on the riverbank. The body of his younger boy, Agon, was in the water.

The couple buried their sons and Popaj's two brothers on the bank, with their names on a slip of paper in a soft drink bottle to mark the spot. Thirty other men are buried next to the four Popajs, all with soft drink bottles and their names. The rest lie further along in the fields beside the river.

This weekend, Popaj is alone in his burnt-out house. A wooden cradle painted in blue with white flowers stands on the porch. He carries photographs of his sons in a small bag, and a handwritten list with the names of the bodies in the graves in his pocket.

As we left the place where he had buried his boys, he found a hypodermic needle the Serbs had left behind and placed it carefully in a shoe lost by one of the slain men.

He was waiting for the international war crimes investigators and justice.

Milosevic and four of his inner circle have been indicted on three counts of crimes against humanity and one of 'violation of the laws or customs of war'.

The indictment lists seven 'incidents of mass killings' – the murders of several hundred Kosovars at Bela Crvka, four other villages and the town of Djakovica, in southern Kosovo. Too many crimes were committed, too many thousands killed, to list them all.

British and American investigators have begun compiling evidence to help prosecutors prove the charges in court. The British team started work in a house in Velika Krusa, where 40 men had been herded together on 25 March, then shot, covered with straw and burnt.

Clive Donner, a big, beefy detective with 27 years' experience in Scotland Yard, is not easily shocked, but he was appalled by what he saw. The bodies had decomposed into each other because the men had tried to flee the gunfire and died in a heap. Scavenging dogs had dragged off limbs. 'I'm from the anti-terrorist squad, and I've never seen anything as bad as this,' Donner said.

The team's report to the Hague will explain what happened in Velika Krusa. 'There is "stratification" at the site,' said Dave Halliday, the team's fire expert. 'That tells you something. The first layer is bodies. On top of the bodies is broken glass, then the bullets, then straw. Roof tiles are the final layer. That tells you that the men were there first, the killers broke the windows, fired the bullets through the windows, and laid the straw on top after the men were shot.'

Their colleagues from the FBI are up the road in Djakovica. They have roped off a single-storey white house, scorched by flames. Xhamal Caka, 68, slumps nearby with a school photograph of granddaughters whose bones lie among the broken roof tiles.

Dalina, 13, sits in the front row, a tall brunette wearing a yellow T-shirt; Delvina, 8, a little blonde stands in the second row in her red-and-white striped top, her chin tilted upwards a little as if she is trying to look taller. Diona was two on 2 April, the day Serbs in uniform shot her and her sisters.

Caka is filled with regret. Valbona Caka, his daughter-in-law, the girls and his 10-year-old grandson Dren spent 2 April in his house. They went next door to hide in a basement when the Serbs began shooting.

'I keep seeing them and wishing I had stopped them. But we didn't think the Serbs would kill women and children.'

His son Ali, the children's father, thought the same. He was hiding elsewhere when his family was killed. Shortly after 1am, he heard Dren shouting in terror. Dren was on the other side of a garden wall and could not climb over. He had been shot in the arm.

The boy had seen what no 10-year-old should see after Serbian police had fired through the windows of his hiding place. 'Dren remembered who was shot first and he remembered exactly one by one who was shot after that,' Caka recalled. 'He escaped when the Serbs started a fire.'

Twenty people died in that house on Milos Gilic Street, 19 of them women and children. Their names are listed in the Hague indictment.

Apart from Milosevic, the war crimes tribunal has indicted Colonel-General Drogoljub Ojdanic, the chief of staff of the Yugoslav army; Vlajko Stojiljkovic, the Serbian minister of internal affairs, whose police went into the villages with paramilitaries to deport and kill; Milan Milutinovic, the president of Serbia;* and Nikola Sainovic, Milosevic's deputy prime minister responsible for Kosovo. A second indictment is expected, of men in lower ranks.

Investigators are documenting not only the work of the killers but their chain of command. Major-General Vladmir Lazarevic is one of those likely to feature in further indictments; he commanded the Third Army, known as the Pristina Corps, which deployed in Kosovo.

It would have been his men who surrounded the village of Bela Crkva, shelled the red-roofed houses and gave protection to the interior ministry police or paramilitaries who went in and did the killing. Most of the men who pulled the triggers and killed Shendet and Agon Popaj, and Dalina, Delvina and Diona Caka, will probably go unpunished. There are too many of them.

But Sabri Popaj will greet the British investigators today with his piece of paper listing those killed in Bela Crkva and where they are buried.

Popaj's grieving wife left for Canada last month, and his mission is the only thing he cares about now. 'I think justice may help,' he said as he stood on the riverbank where he had hidden his dead son's jacket in the weeds to give to the investigators. 'I don't have the words for anything else.'

---

* Milan Milutinovic was acquitted on charges of war crimes.

The enemy within

15 August 1999

With Serbs now the target of revenge ethnic cleansing and British troops caught in the crossfire, Kosovo has all the ingredients to become a Balkan Northern Ireland, writes Marie Colvin in Pristina.

Godsa Draza was the darling of the Royal Hussars. When all the other Serbs of the village of Donje Ljupce fled, including her two sons, the 78-year-old grandmother decided to hold her ground. She remained in her cottage, as she had throughout the Nato bombings, tending her two pigs and a scattering of chickens and weeding her vegetable garden.

The Hussars, based in nearby Podujevo, visited her once or twice a day, never at the same time, to show her Albanian neighbours that she had protection. She would brew cups of thick, sweet Turkish coffee. The soldiers laughingly called their visits the 'granny beat', but they admired her courage.

When the Royal Hussars arrived last Wednesday, there was no answer to their knock. They went around the back.

Her two withered feet were sticking up out of a pile of hay that had been dumped on the rubbish tip at the bottom of her garden. Some time on Tuesday night, Draza had been shot in her bed, shot again at the back door of her house, dragged down the garden and hidden. None of her neighbours admitted hearing or seeing anything unusual.

'The boys were pretty cut up. They had become very attached to her,' said Captain Tom Mallinson of the Royal Hussars. 'She meant no harm to anyone.'

It was not a good week to be a lonely old Serbian woman in Kosovo, one of the diehard matriarchs who have stayed behind to tend the animals, hoping that their families will some day come back.

On Thursday, Mica Stolic stood in her garden in the village of Gornje Brnjka, weeping and wringing her hands as military investigators sifted through the smashed furniture and appliances inside her farmhouse.

Stolic was lucky. At 5.30am, Irish Guards patrolling the village in a Warrior had heard shooting. They arrived at the scene in minutes and chased two Volkswagen Golfs along the winding dirt road at high speed. When a man in the back seat started firing at them, the commander remained cool. Rather than responding with his cannon or machinegun, which would have obliterated the car, he fired back with a rifle.

Four ethnic Albanian men, two of them wounded, were captured when the cars slewed to a halt; a fifth man was arrested later that day when he sought treatment for a wound at Pristina hospital.

The cycle of ethnic hatred has turned in Kosovo. About 100 houses along the dirt road through the village of Zhiti, 25 miles south of Pristina, have the Serbian symbol painted in white on their courtyard gates – a cross with four backward Cs into the four right angles.

During the Nato bombing, the sign protected the Serbian farmers from marauding Serbian paramilitaries who drove out their Kosovar neighbours. They survived the war unscathed, but last week the Serbian families of Zhiti had had enough. Four of their men had been shot dead in the eight weeks since the war's end.

The Zhiti Serbs were escorted to the border by their supposed protectors, the 82nd Airborne, American troops serving with Kfor [Kosovo Force]. Their homes were looted and burnt in their wake, the crosses that once ensured survival now inviting destruction. All that remained of Zhiti's Serbian community were burnt and roofless homes, their courtyards littered with cooking pots, charred window boxes and blackened geraniums.

An Albanian farmer prised a charred window frame from a house as a dozen Albanian youths with bicycles and a football occupied the street. 'We are very happy the Serbs have left. Very happy. But of course it was not us who burnt their homes,' said one.

During the war, the Serbian army and paramilitary forces drove into exile three-quarters of the ethnic Albanian population of Kosovo – 800,000 men, women and children – and laid waste their homes. Almost every surviving Kosovar has lost a father, brother, child or cousin; almost every village has a mass grave; 1,500 men are still missing.

Even the most moderate Kosovar shrugs off the thought that not all Serbs are guilty, insisting: 'We were targeted because we were Albanians.' The Balkan creed is familiar and unforgiving: an eye for an eye, a tooth for a tooth.

In this cauldron, two parallel forces are trying to shore up the idealistic policy that Kosovo must remain a mixed Albanian-Serbian entity. Kfor, the international army, is charged with enforcing law and order, which has in recent weeks come down to protecting the 50,000 Serbs who remain. Unmik, the United Nations Mission in Kosovo, led by Bernard Kouchner, the flamboyant former French health minister, is responsible for civil administration, which is almost non-existent. Kouchner is on his summer holiday.

The violence last week seemed to indicate that the euphoric welcome given to Nato troops had worn out and Kosovo was spiralling out of control. Given the increased number of attacks on Kfor troops and nightly incidents of intimidation against the dwindling Serbian community, can the peace be kept in such a scarred and divided population? Is this another Northern Ireland in the making, another example of a community turning on its liberators?

Major-General Andrew Ridgeway, chief of staff to General Sir Mike Jackson, the head of Kfor, and his replacement while Jackson is in Britain for a working holiday, says Kfor cannot protect every Serb. But he insists that his troops have a hold on the situation.

'Multi-ethnicity is not a concept on everyone's lips in the Balkans,' Ridgeway said over dinner in a tent at Kfor headquarters.

He is an informal sort of general: dinner was chicken pie and vegetables, and staff officers pitched up on the benches around the picnic table at will. The red wine was the only touch that distinguished his table from others, as he joked with noisy soldiers holding a going-away party nearby. But he is very serious and well-experienced from a term in Bosnia, where he believes serious mistakes were made.

'We're just looking for tolerance, for Serbs and Albanians to live together in some areas without killing each other,' Ridgeway said. 'But, of course, forcing people into that creates tensions.'

Despite the murder of Draza and the daily scuffles with French Kfor forces in the divided city of Mitrovica, statistics support Ridgeway's words. On Friday night the only incident reported in Pristina was a brick thrown through the window of a Serbian home. 'Must mean the buggers have run out of grenades,' joked the British soldier first on the scene.

The number of murders in Kosovo has steadily fallen, from 33 in week one after Kfor's arrival to 18 in week eight. Given that almost 600,000 Albanians have returned in the interval, the figures are even more striking. Arson, almost non-existent in week one, jumped to 187 incidents in mid-July, when Kosovar Albanians returned to their destroyed villages and avenged themselves on Serbian property, but fell again to 75 in week eight.

Who is attacking the Serbs? It is not as simple as it seems. The Kosovo Liberation Army (KLA) is most often blamed because it is the most obvious opposition force. Yet every authority in Kosovo – from Ridgeway to Bishop Artemije, the spiritual leader of the Serbs – rejects the theory that the KLA leadership is ordering the attacks.

'The chaps behind these attacks have nothing to do with the KLA,' Ridgeway said. 'The leadership does not condone them. Most of it seems to be organised crime. That is not to say that there are not some KLA radicals who are as keen to drive out the Serbs as we are to keep them. There are certainly some who believe they are the victors and to the victors belong the spoils.'

In the British sector, the men of 'Britfor' say they have been increasingly successful. 'We're beginning to get good intelligence and arrest a lot of these people,' Ridgeway said. .

In a 24-hour period last week, 11 of 15 ethnic Albanians arrested in Pristina carried KLA cards. None, however, was on the official list of the KLA that Kfor has put together.

The problem is that the KLA is a mixed bag. During the war regulars were joined by overseas recruits, villagers, students. Now, everyone in Kosovo claims to have fought.

Kfor and UN investigations have shown that while crimes in the villages are almost certainly revenge attacks, most of the crimes against Serbs in the cities are committed by criminals using a 'political' cover.

'If a gang knows Serbs are living in an apartment, they go and intimidate them. They know they sound even more frightening if they say they are KLA,' said Bill Okula, a former American police officer now serving with the UN police, who are due to take over eventually from Kfor.

'They either chase them out or buy a DM100,000 flat for DM1,000. It's straightforward crime for gain. No politics there.'

Much of the anti-Serbian violence is committed by a group called the BIA. Since the return of Nato troops, BIA has been scrawled on city walls alongside KLA graffiti. Kosovan sources say the BIA comprises young former fighters. The initials stand for Bahria, Ilyir and Agron, three Albanian youths from Pristina who joined the KLA and were killed.

'Ilyir and Agron were killed before the war, and Bahria died fighting with the KLA during the war,' one Kosovan source said. 'They are revered by the boys of Pristina because most of the fighting was done by the people from the villages and these were city boys. They are famous here.'

Although the BIA no longer has connections with the KLA, the sources doubt that members are unknown to the leadership; but stopping their activities is another matter.

According to an undertaking signed with Jackson by Hashem Thaci, the prime minister of the self-styled KLA-led 'transitional government', the KLA must disband as a military group by 19 September. Thaci is in negotiations with Kfor over the KLA's continued existence. Getting into a war with young radicals is not something he needs at a time when he must convince his followers to lay down their arms and take up politics.

The belief in Pristina is that if the transitional date of 19 September is met, the tensions will lessen. Kfor proposes that Thaci and his leadership should become a political party, while their fighters could become an unarmed 'Rescue and Protection Corps'. That would allow them to remain militarised but not as an army.

As the bargaining continues, the remnants of the Serbian community are terrified. Artemije, holed up in the Serbian Orthodox monastery of Gracanica near Pristina, says that unless anti-Serbian violence is stopped, the community will disappear.

'I try to persuade people to stay in their homes. I tell them that as long as we are here Kosovo will be ours. It can never be only Serbian, but at least it will not be only Albanian,' said the bishop, a small rotund figure with a wispy grey beard, dressed in a black robe and turban.

His cloistered receiving room is a dissonant mix of ancient and modern: faded icons adorn the walls and priests who enter kiss his hand, while in the background two black-robed priests tap away at computers. British soldiers guard the gate of the monastery.

He is desperate. 'I have only words,' Artemije said. 'Every grenade is saying something else. The international community cannot sit by while they [the Albanians] finish the ethnic cleansing of Serbs.'

Chechnya

Wrath of Moscow leaves no place for Chechens to hide

19 December 1999

Pinned down by fire, Marie Colvin shares the anguish of the Chechen rebels.

Everyone in Chechnya travels at night. In mud-smeared 4x4 vehicles on dirt roads pitted with pot holes and bomb craters, the Chechen rebels head to the front to fight, or back to the mountains to rest.

Convoys of refugees, many in Ladas, drift by carrying families too scared to leave on roads that are bombed all day and often at night. They are even more scared to stay.

Fires started by the bombs burn on mountain ridges. The planes are bombing villages and roads indiscriminately and most of the victims are civilians, judging by those being treated in the few hospitals still functioning. There is no way of predicting when the planes will come.

I spent 12 hours yesterday pinned down in a field by a road south of Grozny. The planes, evil machines with the sun glinting off their sleek silver bodies, circled again and again. They trailed thunder, dropping bombs that whined as loudly as high-speed trains as they fell.

The car I was travelling in was blasted by shrapnel, its windows blown out. The quiet field where I took refuge, with only bracken and beech trees denuded by the winter for cover, felt like a death trap.

It takes no imagination to understand the fear of civilians who have to endure this day after day and who must decide whether to flee and face a day's drive on the open road, or take their chances in a basement.

Alkayez and his wife, Taus, have tried three times to escape along the supposed 'safe corridor' established by the Russians to Ingushetia. They are now living in a cave with four young children, not far from the ruins of their home in Vashenkali.

Outside is their car which has been hit by a missile. A woman and a man were killed in the explosion and were buried beside the road, but nobody knows their names.

The cave measures about 10 yards by 20 yards. One bed, where the whole family sleeps, lies on the rocky dirt floor and there is a crudely built brick wood stove. A bag of potatoes, a sack of onions and some flour they took from home are piled by the walls.

Family life is lit by two oil lamps that burn all day. Taus, 41, says they have no desire to leave the cave; they panic even to hear the engine of a passing car.

Three-year-old Kazishet, with blonde curls to her shoulders, sits in her mother's lap, chewing on a dummy. Eight bombs were counted on Thursday during my visit. 'The children are facing death with all the bombing,' their mother said. 'They bomb the village day and night.'

The few hospitals offer only primitive care to those injured on the roads. In Shattoi, a town of single-storey houses that has been bombed so often that it looks like a miniature Dresden, the hospital has somehow survived intact. But there are no windows and it has no electricity. Inside it is so cold that you can see your breath.

Two rooms are filled with the injured. There is one doctor and, according to one of the patients, 'he is only good for changing bandages'.

On one bed, lying on his back, is a frail, middle-aged man with a bloody towel wrapped around his head. Each breath is loud and laboured. His name is Khoja Khamoratov; he was on his way to his cousin's funeral in Tetoy when his car was bombed near Dai village by a Russian plane.

His brother, the driver, was killed instantly. The top of Khoja's skull was blown off and there is no treatment for him here. His face is still streaked with dried blood. 'We don't know what to do with him,' said the doctor.

In the other room is 15-year-old Timur Patirov, who has his arm in a sling. He was travelling in a Lada near Gote with his brother and cousin, trying to escape Ingushetia, when Russian tanks opened fire on them.

Heider Kaurnukoy, his sister, is holding the hand of her unconscious brother, Arby, 44. Half his foot has been amputated after their house in Khalkiloy was struck by a 1,000-pound bomb.

'How could we have believed they would hit our house?' she said. 'When I came to my senses my brother was lying in a pool of blood. He loves children. I want the world to feel ashamed of what has happened. The world is doing nothing while we are being slaughtered.'

The view from the mountain looking over the plains stretching from the village of Komsomolskaya to Grozny in the distance makes one wonder how a pilot can bomb in the way the Russian pilots have.

From the mountains, Komsomolskaya looks as it must from the cockpit of a plane – a place of white roofs, dirt streets and barn yards of cows and chickens. Smoke rises from the few chimneys, yet pilots dive on this village day and night. All last week Russian artillery crashed into homes.

The inhabitants of the village are no different from villagers anywhere. It is no military base. The victims are the old, the poor and women and children. Any sons who may be fighting with the rebels are not here.

The worst hit so far have been the Zakriyev family. They are too poor to have a basement. Dakov, the 51-year-old father, works as a labourer on building sites and their house is made of mud and straw bricks.

Last week the family was asleep on the floor of the front room when a missile crashed into the house and exploded. Adem, Dakov's 18-year-old son, died instantly.

'I was knocked out,' said Virlant, 39, his mother. 'The crying of the children woke me.' The youngest of her four surviving children, two-year-old Medina, is now a very quiet child who clings constantly to her.

The family buried Adem just before dawn because, they say, the Russians have been bombing funerals. Komsomolskaya is a village in shock.

In Grozny itself, it is difficult to see how the Chechen fighters can hold out indefinitely. They are faced with overwhelming numbers of Russian troops and the constant threat of helicopters and artillery.

However, for all the Russian superiority in numbers and weaponry, there could yet be a repeat of 1996 when the Russians last captured Grozny, only to lose it soon afterwards.

This is fighting country, with mountains that are almost impenetrable and studded with rebel strongholds. I stayed at one such base last week – a camp in which fighters recuperate after time at the front. The mountains were bombed daily but nothing changed in the rebels' grim, craggy faces.

General Hussein Isabayev is the base commander. There is a concern for individual fighters in the Chechen army that is rarely seen elsewhere. Each commander is required to build a resting post, just as he builds bomb shelters on the front lines. 'We don't have many people, so each one is precious to us,' said Isabayev.

Like most of his peers he pays for his unit's expenses – food, guns and ammunition – and most of the men are related to him or come from his clan.

Conditions are primitive: the house he occupies is built from flat stones hewn from the mountains and there is one long bed on a raised platform where at any time between five and 20 fighters are sleeping or resting and watching television.

Sometimes there is the odd sight of some young rebels watching a Russian pop video while more devout fighters kneel on the bed in prayer, leaning towards Mecca.

The atmosphere is sometimes excessively relaxed: when I curled up to sleep one night I pulled out from under me some annoyingly lumpy objects, only to find they were two hand grenades.

Isabayev's wife is known as the 'deputy commander'. She constantly brews up tea and cooks meals from big chunks of slaughtered wild goat that hang from the rafters outside.

A poster of Dzhokar Dudayev, the Chechen president killed in 1996, hangs on the wall next to a collection of weapons, including Kalashnikovs, a 1920s hunting rifle and a shoulder grenade launcher. Ammunition is stashed under the bed.

The soldiers have no doubt about their cause. Turpal Ali, 35 and a nephew of Dudayev, is in a special regiment known as Duki. He has not worked since the 1994–96 war, when a piece of shrapnel pierced his neck and cut a nerve, disabling his left hand. Before that he was a director of a trading company.

He has a bearded, thin face and speaks with a soft voice. 'I wouldn't be able to look into my friends' eyes if I didn't stand in a line of fighters,' he said, explaining his return to uniform.

Isabayev is a father figure to the young men here and has a tendency to philosophise. 'The trouble with the Russians is that they did not understand the psychology of the Chechens,' he said.

'They thought that by bombing and striking, they could divide our nation. These strikes will not do anything. They imagine that these people in occupied villages are theirs. That is not true. The villages are on our land. Every bit of this land is ours, every piece of soil. In every bush lurks an enemy to Russia.'

The final assault on Grozny began on Wednesday evening, when a column of Russian armoured tanks and transports drove in from the Khankala area to the east. Brigadier General Aslandek, leading the defence of the city, claimed that his troops were holding their positions.

Aslandek, 36, another veteran of the 1994–96 war, is seen by Chechens as a master strategist. Reached by radio yesterday, he sounded calm but said the fighting had been 'terrible'.

The Russians had attacked from Khankala every day, co-ordinating simultaneous advances from the north and the northwest.

The events of Wednesday night had raised Chechen morale, however. The first Russian column to penetrate the city centre had been destroyed, an armoured car had been captured and many Russians had been killed with rocket-propelled grenades and machineguns.

'We did not stop to calculate how many corpses were lying on the ground,' Aslandek said.

Escape from Chechnya to a trial by ice

2 January 2000

As Russian paratroopers cut off her last line of retreat, Marie Colvin was forced to flee with Chechen help by the only route left open: a range of 12,000-foot mountains.

The two moonlit gravestones were the only signs of humanity in the mountain range that stretched far around us. Magomet Amin Katayev, our guide, sat in their shadows and seemed to find comfort from them.

A small wiry Chechen who has spent his life on these slopes, Magomet had agreed to lead me and Dmitry Beliakov, a Russian photographer working for *The Sunday Times*, across these mountains from Chechnya to safety in Georgia. We had jackets and boots but little else for a trek across the 12,600-foot peaks.

The journey began four days before Christmas. It continued for eight increasingly desperate days, ending in rescue by helicopter last week from a snow-bound field in Georgia.

It was a trip that was not supposed to be necessary. I had been smuggled into the country from Georgia on 10 December in a four-wheel-drive vehicle to report first-hand from the towns and

Marie reporting from Chechnya, 1999.
Photograph by Dmitry Beliakov.

villages under bombardment. I had planned to leave by road. But then Russian paratroopers seized Melkhist, an ancient centre known as the Dead City, taking control of the only road to Georgia. They shot at any vehicles that tried to pass. I was trapped.

If we travelled a day north, we would reach the so-called safe corridor into Ingushetia set up by the Russians. But I knew that road and was not going back to it. On the way in, Russian fighter planes had attacked and destroyed the vehicle I was travelling in and had returned again and again, firing missiles into the field where I had taken refuge under a stunted beech tree. The pilots tried to scare us into making a run for it so that we would be easy targets. It was torture to listen to the babble of a stream in the silence after each attack, only to hear the returning roar of the jets.

I had also met refugees who had reached the 'safe corridor' only to be attacked from the sky. They had taken refuge with their injured in caves, or in the dark, unheated ruins that passed for hospitals, where the few doctors left could only stop the bleeding.

The alternative route, east over the border to Dagestan, was blocked by fighting. Sitting in a mountain hideout, we agreed that a trek over the peaks was preferable to being hunted from the skies.

For hours on the day we hoped to set out, Tuesday 21 December, planes attacked the slopes nearby with rockets that set brush and trees on fire in great arcs of flame. We left our hideout just after sunset. As we reached the gravestones, where Magomet said a friend would meet us, the dark ridge above us began glowing orange. One of the fires was burning our way. 'It will take 15 minutes to cross this field,' Magomet said. I asked why we were sitting there. 'We are waiting for my friend.' There did not seem much point in arguing.

Valed, Magomet's friend, showed up before the fire reached us. Unlike our laconic guide – who was dressed in a sheepskin coat, jeans and lightweight climbing boots – Valed was in full combat camouflage gear with a Kalashnikov over his shoulder. He told us about his ambition to join the Foreign Legion.

Valed said he would escort us until there was no more danger from kidnappers and smugglers. That was the first we had heard of them, but to Valed the perils seemed as commonplace as a weather report. He kept up a stream of patter, walking ramrod straight and talking about how he needed training missions like this. Dmitry and I struggled behind the silent Magomet.

Within an hour we were zigzagging up a mountain on a 6-inch-wide path covered in snow and ice. I was carrying a pack with a satellite telephone and a computer, and wearing a flak jacket. I felt every ounce.

I tried to time my breath to my strides, but it was impossible. I struggled to breathe and the air kept getting thinner. Magomet paced silently in front. I looked down to the spectacular depths below us and the snow-covered slopes across the gorge, then thought better of this and kept my eyes on the path. I regretted every cigarette I had ever smoked – and I had smoked a lot in the past few days: cheap Russian tobacco that gave some respite from the bombs and the decisions. Without a word, Magomet took Dmitry's camera bag and Valed shouldered my rucksack.

We stopped at a spring where, like all those we would come across, a tin cup had been left on a stone. Valed took off his shoes and socks and washed his feet in the freezing water, then knelt to pray while I collapsed and tried to breathe.

'Normal?' asked Magomet.

'Normal,' seemed the only response. I would find out during the next days that 'normal' was Magomet's way of indicating anything from 'okay' to 'will you survive?' – and that 'normal' to a Chechen and to me were two different things.

The path was ghostly grey in the moonlight and seemed deserted. But it was alive. Three human shapes appeared along it and Magomet and Valed stiffened. The meeting was like one between suspicious dogs. Both parties circled each other, speaking quietly, until some obscure test was passed and grins broke out and all five embraced.

Some agreement to travel together had been reached. The newcomers – Leche, Mussa and Omar – took our baggage and one of them put on my flak jacket. I was sure we would be bombed as soon as I relinquished it, but I was beyond caring about anything except the relief from the weight on my back. I was thirstier than I can ever remember being and scooped up handfuls of snow to suck. I thought of the Chechen refugees who had fled along this route.

About midnight, after almost six hours of walking, we reached the top of a peak, where a roofless stone hut provided shelter from the wind. Magomet lit a fire and said we would eat. I lay on a bed of woven saplings covered with damp sheepskins and fell asleep. When I awoke, the Chechens were breaking out bread and opening tins of salty Russian stewed beef. I drank a cup of hot water but could not eat anything.

Magomet insisted we get going. The path took us towards another mountain that looked so close in the moonlight that it seemed hyper-real, a dark shape lined with white veins of snow. It was a moment of pure beauty, but when we reached the bottom of the slope it turned out that one of the white veins was the path we would have to climb up.

Dmitry sat down and said he could not continue. 'Leave me here. Someone will find my body.' I sympathised but we had to get over the mountain before dawn or the Russian planes would find us. Magomet sat down beside Dmitry and quietly talked him out of suicide.

We walked up the slope, looking down thousands of feet into a gorge that one slip would take us into. Magomet hauled me by the hand to the last summit. I slept for an hour sitting against a stone in the snow until Magomet woke us at dawn with a warning that we were still in Chechnya and would have to move.

We slid and walked down the mountainside, but the way forward over a mountain river was blocked. The river had frozen into a stream of silver ice, 30 feet across. This was pure ice with no footholds and a drop of about 1,000 feet. We detoured back up the slope, then down across fields towards another river and another path. Suddenly, two Russian fighter planes flew overhead. We froze.

It was a discouraging day. Travelling up the next river, I stepped in the wrong spot and plunged through the ice up to the hip into the raging torrent below. Our three fellow travellers went ahead but returned to say they had reached the head of this half-frozen river and could not find a pass over the mountain. They declared that they were going back because 'we cannot see any chance for success in this mission'.

We had now been walking for 24 hours. As night fell, Magomet lit a fire on the ice of the frozen river and then set off on his own. He returned at about 10pm and told us he had found the pass. He said the departure of Leche, Mussa and Omar should not concern us. They were young town boys, wannabe weapon smugglers out to make some fast money, and had decided that this route was too difficult.

I remembered Leche hauling me up 200 yards of an almost vertical slope and reflected on the Chechen meaning of 'town boys'.

Without my noticing, Valed had also gone – replaced by another Chechen, Murad, who was walking to Tblisi, the Georgian capital, to buy a weapon.

The next 12 hours were passed in a daze, one foot in front of the other, up and over another mountain. The air was so thin that I could not fill my lungs, and the wind was so strong that several times I was almost blown off the mountainside. Just before dawn we reached a snow-covered field amid the peaks. It looked like the top of the world. Dmitry could not walk, so Magomet placed him on a small tree and hauled him across.

There was a pile of stones ahead – the Georgian border. Two shots rang out. We dived into the snow and another two shots sounded. It seemed unfair that here, yards from the border, we would die. Magomet began shouting in Chechen and the shots stopped. We crossed the border. But we had not yet reached safety. We could not find Giveri, the Georgian village that was our goal.

I had been dreaming of coffee and a bed. Magomet said Giveri would have been deserted anyway as it was winter. Despair, for the first time, set in. I fell asleep on an exposed bluff, impervious to the wind and cold. When I awoke, Magomet had found an abandoned shepherd's hut.

It was Christmas. The symbolism of spending it in a shepherd's hut seemed a better omen than the graves at the start of our trek. I got a call out over the satellite phone to *The Sunday Times* foreign desk to say that we had crossed the border, and I also managed to reach Georgian contacts in Tblisi who had promised to pick us up by helicopter. There were no roads here and it was the only way out. The helicopter was promised for 11am the next day.

We foraged through the hut and found some flour, which we boiled up with melted snow into a gluey porridge. We took it in turns to stoke the fire, working in four-hour shifts.

Christmas turned out to be a time of disappointments and broken promises, however. Timor, one of the Georgians who was supposed to be organising the helicopter, kept promising and not appearing. The battery on my satellite phone was running out. We were marooned.

For the next two days we lived in the shepherd's hut on flour and water. I supplemented the porridge once with wild onions. They tasted horrible but they would give us some vitamins. Magomet gave me a pistol loaded with nine bullets – telling me not to shoot a wild animal until it was 10 metres away but to shoot a man the moment one appeared – and set off to find a way forward.

After his return, we walked down a river valley into Georgia. Magomet said that in the Caucasus, people built their villages along the rivers and we might find some inhabitants. He was right: we found Giveri, a collection of dark stone houses. All were open and unlocked but had been abandoned for the winter. We found a house with beds, a stove, some more flour and a can of peas.

Using the last power in the satellite phone battery, I made my final, brief call to Sean Ryan, foreign editor of *The Sunday Times*. Could he take over and try to get a helicopter here?

In fact, Ryan was already in touch with Georgy Gvasaliya, a Georgian general who was helping to provide the helicopter. The general had painted him a false rosy picture: Dmitry and I were being cared for in a village with traditional Caucasian hospitality, downing great stews and sleeping in warm sheepskins, he said.

On 28 December, a storm set in and we were down to the last of our flour. We decided to try to walk out. According to the map, about 30 kilometres down the river was a town and a road. I fried up the last of the flour into five flatbreads and we set out along the valley. After walking for five hours, we found another shepherd's hut and spent the night in the cold, eating half our bread.

The dawn was clear and cold. The storm had passed but left about 1ft of snow. In a village along the river we heard a dog barking and found an elderly couple, Bartanz and Elizabetha Kacunkubev, too poor to leave for the winter.

They took us into their tiny stone house, where a portrait of Stalin looked down from the wall, and gave us fried potatoes, preserved cabbage and a shot of vodka each. Bartanz then drew a map, showing us how to get to another village, Omala, which he said had a radio and was only 5 kilometres away.

Setting out for it, we walked until an hour before dark, when we heard a helicopter. We waved madly. The helicopter ducked its nose and landed below us in a field. The Georgian general had let us down but *The Sunday Times* had sent my colleague Jon Swain to Tblisi. He had gone to the American embassy and told them a US citizen was missing in the mountains on the frontier. I was never happier to have an American passport.

I walked down the slope to be greeted by an Ernest Hemingway figure with a white beard and blue snow jacket, who said: 'Jack Hariman, American embassy. Are we glad to find you …'

He told us Omala was much further away than the old couple had said. We would have spent another cold night on a mountainside with no shelter. Instead, the helicopter lifted off, whirling over the frozen landscape of snow and dark fir trees towards Tblisi.

East Timor

Trapped by the terror squads in city of death

DILI

12 September 1999

Marie Colvin is one of three foreign journalists who stayed behind in Dili after hundreds of colleagues withdrew in response to warnings that their lives were at risk. Her broadcasts on the BBC, CNN and Sky enabled a worldwide audience to follow events in the United Nations compound where 80 staff and 1,000 refugees sheltered from militia attacks. Colvin, 43, an American citizen, has been a *Sunday Times* foreign correspondent since 1986 when she witnessed the American bombing of Tripoli. She has covered several Middle East conflicts and remained in Baghdad throughout the bombing of Iraq during the Gulf War in 1991. Earlier this year, braving snipers and shelling, she became the first journalist to enter Kosovo from Albania with KLA guerrillas after the airstrikes had begun. Yesterday she said she was astonished that all her male colleagues had left the compound as the danger intensified, commenting drily: 'They don't make men like they used to.'

The first sound of trouble was the screams of two little old ladies who slashed themselves on the razor coils topping the walls of the United Nations compound, desperate to enter.

Militiamen were in the UN car park next door to the compound, firing in the air, terrifying the refugees in an overflow camp outside and the 1,000 slightly luckier ones who were inside the walls.

The militia had just seen most of the UN staff being evacuated, leaving behind a small and vulnerable group of UN officials, a host of refugees, and three foreign journalists – myself among them.

The swaggering militiamen wanted a UN car and they walked up to the blue iron bars of the compound and demanded one. They carried a grenade. Indonesian soldiers on the perimeter were supposed to provide security, but they stood back as more militia poured in.

General Razaz, the dashing Bangladeshi commander of the UN's unarmed military mission, arrived with his bamboo walking stick. The militia fired off more rounds.

The commander of the Indonesian guards said he was under orders not to shoot at them. 'Give them a vehicle and we can solve this. What's the problem?' he asked. To emphasise the point, the militia began smashing windscreens and looting UN vehicles. Two Indonesian soldiers helped them.

It was proof, if needed, of what everyone has known all along: 'The military and militia are two sides of the same face,' as a

UN liaison officer said. For all the denials of the military, UN analysts believed that many of the militia are moonlighting soldiers.

Surrounded by 'defenders' who are in league with their besiegers, the remaining occupants of the UN compound were still holding out yesterday after a week of terror. UN officials insisted they would not leave the refugees to die. They pointed out that the Timorese had voted for independence in a UN-sponsored election and the UN had promised to stay and protect them through to the transition. Yet Dili was in ruins. There were now 200,000 displaced people in the country.

The UN was helpless. The least its officials could do was to save the comparatively few refugees who had reached the sanctuary of their compound.

The siege of the UN compound began last Monday, a day when Dili was a city in hiding. No cars moved on the streets except military vehicles and the motorbikes and vans of the militia. Buildings had begun burning overnight and the militia had rampaged through the residential neighbourhoods, shooting wildly, threatening death to anyone they met.

Foreigners were fleeing. Several cars of election observers, driving to the airport with their local staff, were pursued by two militiamen on a motorcycle. The pillion passenger started firing and one driver managed to force the motorcycle off the road. When the convoy fled to a nearby police station, the militiamen walked in the door.

Gillian Flies, of the East Timor Observer Mission, said the police forced the delegation to sign a statement admitting dangerous driving and speeding, to say they had not been fired at and to pay the militiamen for damage to the motorbike.

Monday was also the day when the East Timorese found there was no limit to what their Indonesian enemies would do. About 1,000 refugees woke at dawn in the International Red Cross compound. Sleepy children played amid the piles of bedding, suitcases and plastic carry-alls that held the few possessions their parents had been able to carry to what they had thought would be a safe refuge in the walled rear courtyard.

These refugees had come to the Red Cross because they believed it offered international protection, like an embassy. But they were wrong. At 11.30am soldiers in camouflage uniforms and wild-eyed militia dressed in T-shirts, the black shirts of the Aitarek (Thorn) militia and bandannas poured into the compound. They fired into the air, shouting curses and commands.

I was in the Turismo hotel next door. A cacophony of screams and shouts sounded from the Red Cross compound. Dodging patrols of soldiers running through the hotel with guns pointed forward, I reached a balcony and looked down on a terrifying scene. Women rolled on the ground of the compound in terror, clutching children. A soldier stood in the centre, pointing his assault rifle at a woman and shouting and gesturing at her as she held her hands over her head. Other women scrambled for their children and were kicked or hit with rifle butts. Militiamen roamed around the courtyard, shouting and firing in the air.

It was all over in about half an hour. Women, children and men were marched at gunpoint into the street, while international Red Cross staff were driven away to the airport to be evacuated to Darwin.

The deserted courtyard was strewn with food, blankets and overturned cooking pots. The silence was broken only by the crowing of a rooster. While police stood around the walls, a militiaman smashed open suitcases and searched piles of refugee possessions. He paused to look for identification when he found an East Timorese independence banner, and took the banner and a wallet with him. In another suitcase he found a woman's beaded purse and pawed through the jewellery inside, pocketing a string of pearls. His search completed, he walked out to where the refugees were being held at gunpoint.

About 200 people, mostly men, were separated from the 1,000 who had been in the compound and were marched east down the beach, in the direction of the huge statue of Christ on the cliffs overlooking the city. There has been no news of these men since. Their families were allowed back into the compound to collect their belongings. Weeping women bundled cooking pots and clothes into blankets and fled.

Down the corniche from the Red Cross, a simultaneous attack had taken place on the refugees in the seafront compound of Bishop Ximenes Belo – a co-ordination which gives the lie to Jakarta's attempt to blame the violence on militias who had run amok. At the Turismo hotel, soldiers tried to find the journalists who had witnessed the brutality. They banged on doors but nobody opened them.

John McCarthy, the Australian ambassador to Jakarta, came to the rescue, arriving with consulate cars and his defence attaché. On the way, his clearly marked diplomatic vehicle had come under fire and he was angry. We were not allowed to collect our bags. 'What do you want, your life or your clothes?' the ambassador shouted at one journalist before we were driven to the walled UN compound in a former teacher-training college in the Matadoro neighbourhood.

The situation was hardly better there. Militiamen invaded the refugee encampment outside, shooting automatic fire almost at the refugees' heels as they fled. Men and women threw themselves over the walls into the compound, slashing themselves badly on the coils of razor wire that had protected the UN personnel. Children were caught in the wire. The UN clinic treated 50 people for cuts.

Refugees streamed in steadily on Tuesday with tales of terror. Sister Esmeralda, an elfin nun in a grey habit and gold spectacles, led 800 people to safety from her convent. The nun, just 4ft tall, held a Bible in her tiny hands as she softly described how a commander of the Aitarek militia jumped over the wall, yelling: 'Out, out, out. You are going to Polda [the police compound].'

'He was like in a horror movie. The people were crying: "They will kill us, madre." I say to the people: "Calm. Stop crying. We will go to the United Nations." They looked at me: "Who is she? She is so small."

'I organised the people and said: "We will not go running." I lined them up and told the people: "Silence." We came out like you see in television and we walked toward the Aitarek and Brimop [army unit] in front of the convent and I led the people through them and they parted for me. I led the way to the United Nations.'

One of the luckiest to make it there was Aida Ramos Horta de Assis, the sister of Jose Ramos Horta, co-winner of the Nobel peace prize with Belo and a hate figure for the forces roaming the streets. This tiny woman in shorts and flip-flops knew she was a target and had fled to a relative's home with her five children before the announcement of the referendum result.

On Monday night the military had surrounded the house, yelling and banging, but a neighbour said nobody was home. Aida said she heard them talking about killing and needed to hear no more. She fled at dawn but had to leave her husband behind. 'He said to me, "Don't wait for me, save the children".'

By late Tuesday the compound was filling up. The dwindling number of UN staff occupied two-storey houses with tin roofs. Refugees slept on concrete pathways and patches of ground if they could not find a space in the open-air conference hall.

In the morning the tiled floor of the conference hall was cleared and scrubbed down by its temporary occupants. Women washed their children's little frilly dresses and baby clothes and hung them on the barbed wire.

Columns of smoke rose from the city, just below the compound. Night-time brought a spectacular view of fires leaping hundreds of feet into the air. The UN transport compound had been torched and the militia were driving the streets in UN vans.

We heard that there were 200,000 refugees and that many were being forced to Indonesian-controlled West Timor, by boat or overland. More than 10,000 people were being held at the Dili police compound and refugees with missing relatives were terrified of what would happen to them. Rumours of mass executions circulated.

Word came that the Aitarek had ordered: 'No white faces will be seen on the streets.' Journalists were executed here in 1975, so it was a warning to be taken seriously. McCarthy advised all the journalists to evacuate and many took him up on the offer. They were driven out with some UN staff, lying in the backs of open lorries, surrounded by Indonesian soldiers.

An American officer briefed a convoy setting out to the airport to rescue a group of terrified UN staff workers, all local Timorese, who had arrived from a UN outpost in Bacao. The convoy was in danger, as the militias and army were targeting UN workers. Ten had been reported killed already. 'Pack them in,' said the officer as the rescue column headed out. 'The good news is they're all small.'

The convoy returned with a weeping group who said militiamen had overrun their Bacao outpost that morning, the first attack on a UN compound. There was shooting all around the compound, breaking windows and doors.

They had fled to a church next to the UN post, but many were left behind when a UN convoy headed for the local airport. Those that made it were promised they would be flown to Darwin, but at the airport the Indonesians allowed only international staff to continue.

Manuel, 40, who did not want to give his full name, last saw his wife, Maria, 42, a UN interpreter, hiding in the St Anthony church in Bacao. His seven children, aged from one year old to 20, are missing in Dili, where they were staying with his sister while he and Maria worked for the UN during the election campaign.

Numbers still grew in the UN compound. Food stocks dwindled and fuel for the pump that drew water from the well was running low. UN security men were more confident by Wednesday morning, despite the continued gunfire. They had been told that the local Indonesian troops guarding the UN compound had been replaced by Kostrad, an elite force with no connections to the local militia. 'I looked into their eyes and I saw commitment,' said Alan Mills, the Australian commander of the UN civilian police.

The confidence proved ill-founded. Guarded by two trucks of the new soldiers, a convoy set out for the UN warehouse near the port to pick up supplies. They were ambushed by 50 militiamen while the guards stood and watched.

'As soon as we opened the warehouse door and started loading boxes of water, the militia opened fire,' said Ronnie Wahl, a Norwegian driver in the convoy. 'They tried to smash the windshields with machetes, clubs and sticks.'

The convoy drove off, leaving the doors of the warehouse open for potential looters.

This disaster left things desperate in the compound which was by then a sanctuary for about 2,000 refugees, plus the 208 international staff and 63 local staff, many with their families. There were only 400 ready-to-eat meals and enough rice for one more day. The Australians, who had decided to evacuate, offered a bottle of whisky, packets of biscuits and six bright yellow tennis balls.

That night, the mood in the compound darkened. The gunfire was relentless and for the first time a bullet was fired into the compound. It swished through a tree and hit a UN car about 10 feet from where I was talking to Brian Kelly, a lanky UN information officer from Ireland. 'Heavy leaves here,' Kelly said, rolling his eyes.

The security men examined the car and went quickly to the office of Ian Martin, the UN mission head. Children walked around holding hands, oblivious to the crisis atmosphere that was developing.

'You look around at these kids and it's hard not to get emotionally involved,' said Michael Holworth, a police officer with the UN who comes from Sussex. 'Luckily I'm used to it from police work – but not on this scale, of course.'

There was a nervous twitter in the camp as I walked through, giving out the Australians' yellow tennis balls. Everyone knew that the UN was preparing to evacuate.

Was the UN really going to leave all these people behind? Privately, Kelly confirmed that it was, but we were not to report this. Clearly deeply upset, Kelly kept a calm exterior and said local UN staff would be evacuated with their families.

Refugees began asking what was happening. 'Just tell me the truth and I will tell the people calmly. We cannot have panic,' said Dr Nilton Tilman, a softly spoken Timorese doctor who had emerged as a leader in the camp. 'They know they will die if the UN leaves, but I will try to calm them. Just tell me the truth.'

People were already panicking. Babies squalled. An exhausted and tearful local UN worker stayed awake all night for fear that the UN would sneak out while she was sleeping. Another, Angelita Buak, who worked for the UN for five days during the election as a voter identification officer, was not on the list to be saved. She was threatened by the militia and had to move house during the election to stay safe, but only full-time staff were being evacuated. Tiny, scared and clutching a Bible with a coloured picture of Jesus on its cover, she begged to use my satellite phone and called her sister in Australia.

'Sister, sister, save me,' she howled into the phone in Tetum, the Timor language. 'Sister, they will kill us. We are going to die. You must do something tonight, now.'

Her howls drew everyone and spread terror. People started trying to leave the compound through the back, climbing under a coil of barbed wire and up a stone culvert. The escape route then passed through large boulders and up a steep hillside. Everybody was silent, even the smallest child. A little boy fell between two boulders and his mouth opened in a silent scream.

Firing broke out as soldiers camped outside noticed what was happening. The refugees were forced to stop. Teresa DeGama, 19, was halfway up the hill with her family when the shooting started. Terrified, she left them and ran back down again. Now she stood alone, staring blankly at the wire, holding the sack of rice that was to have been her family's only food for the coming weeks in the hills.

At midnight, Sister Esmeralda asked if she could use the satellite telephone to call her mother superior in Rome, surrounded by seven other nuns in dove grey robes and head-dresses, all with tissues to their eyes. Over the phone, she said in Latin, 'We are ready to die but what about the people we brought to this place? There are many women and children.'

She listened to the answer, hung up and embraced me. Her head came to my waist. She wept, but then she straightened and said, 'God is strong.' She and her seven sisters marched out into the night.

There were other forces at work. UN staff started signing a petition saying they did not want to leave and would remain whatever the security situation. 'The refugees – we can't leave them,' said a jolly, middle-aged American woman who ran the now non-existent supply operation. 'My government tried to order me home but I told them I work for the United Nations. Stuff 'em.'

At 1.15am, Kelly arrived with another statement. The evacuation would be postponed for 24 hours. Local staff and families would be evacuated as well. And a solution would be found for the refugees.

On Thursday morning I slipped out of the compound. The Aitarek militia ruled the roads, driving by on motorcycles or in vans with assault weapons pointing out of the windows. One Aitarek with a machete told me not to continue, it was dangerous. He pulled his finger across his throat to illustrate what he meant.

Two soldiers pulled up in their truck and invited me to meet their commander, a lieutenant, who turned out to be articulate and professional. 'We came here for a civic action,' he said. 'We have failed. We have failed to win the hearts and minds of the Timorese people.'

I told him I was trying to get to my hotel, where I had had to leave all my baggage. 'I know you are a reporter,' he said. 'No matter. Have some breakfast and I will drive you. My orders are to protect foreigners.'

Over noodles and an omelette, my first hot meal in days, we talked about his ambition to go to West Point, the American military academy. His orders not to fire on the militia clearly grated.

We drove through a devastated city in his pickup truck with four soldiers in the back for protection.

It was an apocalyptic vision. Hundreds of militia roamed the streets, some walking, some riding three to a motorcycle with one carrying looted goods, the second an assault rifle, the third driving. It was a frenzy of looting. The post office was still burning, but most of the other buildings were burnt-out skeletons. Gunfire sounded nearby.

The lieutenant drove grimly. There were no civilians or cars on the streets. It was as if the barbarians had taken over. One motorcycle passed us, the militiaman on the back waving his pistol at us and smiling maniacally, showing no fear of the army vehicle or its occupants.

The police compound was the centre of their activity; militia families waited under trees, loot piled high next to them in boxes and bags, while militia drove in and out depositing their latest gains. The Turismo, my hotel, had been looted but not burnt. Oddly, the militia had taken all my underwear but left behind my flak jacket.

Early the next morning the evacuation of most UN staff from their compound began at last. Many had debated all night whether to get on the plane.

At 5am, 120 UN staff, 160 local staff and their families and 23 journalists got on the trucks heading to the airport, sitting in the back surrounded by Indonesian soldiers. Those staying behind watched sombrely.

'Goddamn way to run an international mission – going out on my belly like a dog,' complained one Australian policeman who had wanted to stay behind.

Courage knows no gender

10 October 1999

Award-winning war reporter Marie Colvin, who has roughed it in Kosovo and East Timor, argues that women don't have to use feminine wiles to win the battle for stories.

Do women report wars differently from men? The question used to make me bristle. It irritated me to think that I would be judged as a woman war correspondent rather than as a writer, taking the same risks and covering the same story as my male colleagues.

My feelings were hardly new. 'Feminists nark me,' wrote Martha Gellhorn, one of the great war correspondents of the century. 'I think they've done a terrible disservice to women, branding us as "women's writers". Nobody says men writers; before, we were all simply writers.'

I have been covering wars for 13 years now, ever since the Americans bombed Libya in 1986. In those days war reporting was very much a man's world. It seemed important to blend in and the only way to do that was to be 'one of the boys'. Now, roughly a quarter of the correspondents covering any conflict will be female.

The image of the glamorous female correspondent, weighed down by mascara, fluttering her eyelashes and showing a bit of leg, is as dated as a 1950s *Life* magazine spread, if it ever was true. Yet Ann Leslie, foreign correspondent of the *Daily Mail*, has just revived the myth in a book, *Secrets of the Press*. Acting the 'harmless bird brain', 'chirruping' about cooking and 'twittering' about babies, helps to land the scoops, she argues.

I have only to think of myself in Kosovo and East Timor to laugh.

In March I walked over the Albanian mountains into Kosovo with a unit of the Kosovo Liberation Army. The war was being reported second-hand from videos and briefings in Nato headquarters and from tales told by fleeing refugees. I wanted to see what was happening at first hand. That doesn't seem to me a very male or female notion, just a commitment to what all journalists should be doing – trying to find out the truth for ourselves.

The idea that I was glamorous would have seemed pretty comical to the guerrillas who took me in. I walked and slept in the same clothes for days. I had to carry my own gear and, as far as I was concerned, a satellite phone was heavy enough. A change of clothes just wasn't a priority. I was quickly covered with mud up to my knees. On the one day that the sun came out, I took off my flak jacket. I was so smelly, I quickly put it back on. Even I couldn't stand the odour. And when you are huddled in a cold gully under shellfire with 12 men, fear is as great an equaliser as dirt.

My decision to stay in the United Nations compound in East Timor incited a lot of comment, because the three journalists who refused to leave were women (the other two were Dutch reporters). Again, there was little glamour involved. I was sleeping rough, mostly on the ground, and was once again short of clothes. I had been forced to leave my hotel when it was overrun by angry Indonesian soldiers and militiamen and, in my haste, I escaped with only a computer and satellite phone.

It underestimates men to say they are suckers for women who behave like sex kittens on the battle front. There are very few soldiers on a front line who wouldn't take up the offer of a drink or a flirt with a woman correspondent – not least because there is not a great deal of female companionship around. But that doesn't mean the femme fatale will land the story – she may get a drink at the price of enduring a really boring hour or two. Most likely, she will then be considered a lightweight and the object of her wiles, if he has a big story, will give it to somebody he considers a serious journalist. Men aren't fools all of the time.

That said, there are differences. I don't have to dab Chanel under my ears or play dumb for it to be easier for me to get through a checkpoint manned by surly militiamen with automatic weapons. They do react differently to me simply because of my sex. They feel less threatened by a woman, and however crazed they are, some vestigial feeling of protectiveness towards the 'weaker sex' means they are more likely to help, or at least less likely to hurt.

This happened in East Timor, when I was trying to walk into the centre of Dili and was accosted by a militiaman with a machete, who drew his hand across his neck as a warning of what would happen to me if I continued on my way. An Indonesian officer rescued me, and drove me around the burning city.

I also think that gender can work in men's favour. Male reporters can play on the boys' club mentality, swapping dirty jokes with soldiers, or discussing the merits of different weapons. I've never been interested in types of guns, just what the people firing them mean to do.

There are other differences which are more difficult to pinpoint. Women, I think, tend to try harder to understand what is really happening to people on the ground. They are less inclined to settle for writing an analysis of a situation and leaving it at that. I think of Maggie O'Kane of the *Guardian*, who covered Bosnia and most recently the East Timor conflict with fearlessness; her war reporting is marked by vivid observation and tireless interviewing. This is a huge generalisation, and by no means always true, but writing about the 'big picture' seems to carry a certain prestige that, to me, often misses the point of journalism.

I remember talking to a male colleague after writing a story about a man whose wife and five young children had been executed by the Serbs. It didn't seem enough for me to simply report on his loss. I sat for hours with him, by their grave on a river bank, staring at a bloody and bullet-ridden romper suit, listening to his memories and his guilt.

My colleague mused that he simply would not have stopped. 'There would have been other things to do that day, a briefing, whatever, more important or not. I would have written down his details and moved on.'

Why? That's hard to work out. From experience I know men think differently from women, but since I've never been able to figure out their behaviour in other walks of life, I find it just as impossible to explain why they think differently in wars. Again, Gellhorn said it best describing her 40 years of reporting wars. 'Beware of the Big Picture,' she wrote. 'The Big Picture always exists. And I seem to have spent my life observing how desperately the Big Picture affects the "little people" who did not devise it and have no control over it.'

There is probably a darker side to all this. Fewer women than men become foreign correspondents, and even fewer cover wars. Those of us who do are probably more driven than most, simply because it is harder to succeed. Maybe we feel the need to test ourselves more, to see how much we can take and survive. Bravery is personal.

But it is wrong to say that women are inevitably more sensitive. Since my return from East Timor, people have said to me that I must have stayed in the UN compound after my male colleagues had left because I felt more strongly about the women and children who would have been slaughtered had the UN evacuated it.

I felt proud that my reporting contributed to the reversal of the UN's decision to pull out. I embarrassed the decision-makers and that felt good because it saved lives. It is rare to see such a direct result in journalism. I was moved by the children, who greeted me with 'Hello, Mister' as I walked through the compound. But for me, it was a moral decision, made passionately but not out of sentimentality. I simply felt it would have been wrong for the UN to have promised these people protection and then to have abandoned them to certain death. It would have been a betrayal. I can't believe that is a judgment that has a gender.

PART TWO

Marie at the entrance to a smuggler's tunnel in Gaza, 2005.
Photograph by Seamus Murphy.

Ethiopia

Horror of Ethiopia's living dead

9 April 2000

Five months ago, Miyir Mohammed thought he was a well-off little boy. His father had 40 cattle and 50 sheep and goats, and was middle-class by the standards of southern Ethiopia. Miyir helped to herd the smaller animals.

I never got to meet him. Miyir, 4, died of hunger on Friday morning as I drove into his camp. Hours later, his father was still waving flies away from his tiny body, which was wrapped in his mother's headscarf. It looked far too festive for such a tragic thing as the death of a child.

There was little joy in Miyir's last days. His family's livestock began dying as the drought in Ethiopia moved into its third year. For months Miyir's parents, Hassan and Safia, and their five children drove their herd for hundreds of kilometres, criss-crossing the Nogup region in search of pasture, hoping that somewhere it would rain. It never did.

Sometimes the boys would haul up a sheep or a goat and help it to walk, but the animals always died anyway. There was simply nothing for them to eat.

Two months ago Hassan and Safia gave up their nomadic life when the last animal died. The herd had been their life: it provided milk and meat, which they sold when they needed anything from town.

The family walked to Danan, a village where they had heard there was some food. They walked for four days, resting at midday when the temperature passed 40°C.

A donkey carrying their belongings died and they had to leave behind everything except plastic water containers. The parents could carry only the younger children. 'We came here with nothing, nothing,' said Safia as she gazed down at her son's body.

In Danan, Hassan and Safia had no money and no way to earn it. They built a small dome shelter on the edge of the village, piling straw mats and grass on top of a structure made from branches. By last week, 6,300 nomads were living in a makeshift refugee camp, all of them in similar straits.

The Mohammed family lived for a while on one meal a day: porridge made from wheat distributed by the government. Then the children began to die.

Fadoma, 12, their eldest girl, died two months ago. Two weeks ago it was one-year-old Mohammed. Finally the couple lost Miyir. He had slipped in and out of consciousness for two weeks, able to eat only water and sugar.

There is a doctor at the local clinic – which is two rooms in a building erected as a school – but they had no money to pay for the oral rehydration salts and intravenous dextrose that might have saved Miyir.

In death, his face is peaceful but painful to look at: chocolate-coloured skin is pulled tight over sharp cheekbones. His neck is so thin that his hairless head looks far too big for his body. His tiny shoulder blades almost cut the skin of his back. His eyes are half-open. It is the face of famine.

Safia is so stricken that she cannot cry. She tells her story in the monotone of shock. Her six-year-old daughter, Amran, is ill; only her son Noor, 9, is still healthy, although he is very thin. The children cannot live on the food that the government distributes, Safia says. It is only wheat, which they have never eaten before.

'Miyir could not digest this wheat,' she said. 'We were used to eating meat and milk, and sorghum that we bought from selling our animals.'

In the afternoon, Safia washed Miyir's body in the red dust outside their hut and wrapped him in a white shroud. Hassan and some male relatives built a wooden stretcher to carry him 2 kilometres to a cemetery that is expanding on the outskirts of Danan.

They buried him in a double grave with a four-year-old boy he had never met – Abdi Baalul, who also died from hunger on Friday. The two families dragged the leafless branches of an acacia bush over the grave.

New arrivals who pass this place need no signpost to know they have reached Danan. Before the first hut comes into view, rows of desiccated carcasses appear along either side of the dirt road – big packages of hide-covered bones for cows, small ones for sheep and goats.

The population of Danan, the epicentre of Ethiopia's famine, has swollen to 10,000 with the coming of starving nomads. Their stories are heartbreaking.

A year ago Fadoma Sultan had four children and a husband, 30 cattle and 200 sheep and goats. A year ago her husband died; six months ago she lost the last of her livestock. She was destitute.

Fadoma, a tiny woman with fine features, hardly seems strong enough for the trials she has endured, but she decided to walk to Danan where she had heard there was food. The family walked for five days.

Fadoma carried her youngest child, Trishi, an 18-month-old girl, and some water. Her eldest child, Mohammed, who would be six now, died on the road and she had to bury him in the dirt with nothing to mark his grave.

There was food in Danan but that was no guarantee of survival. In their six months at the camp, Fadoma and her remaining three children ate one porridge meal a day. Last Wednesday Trishi died, too.

'She could not swallow,' Fadoma said. 'She had diarrhoea and stomach problems for a long time, but I could not find her soft food or milk. She could not digest this wheat.'

Her two remaining children cling to her blue and yellow robe. Oba is five and Derq is four, but they are so thin that it is almost impossible to tell which is a boy and which a girl. 'They are not healthy, but they are living,' Fadoma said.

There is death in the camp every day, but the most terrible sight is of those who are clearly about to die. They can be saved with so little – the right food, the right drugs – but there are not enough of either and so they will die.

They seem resigned to it. Their eyes are blank and there is no expression in their faces. They no longer wave away the flies on their faces. They wave away food, weakly. The families of those who are dying have seen the look before. Osman Hashi Ahmed is one of the desperate ones. He insists that I come to his hut to see his daughter and leads me at marching pace, the tail of his white turban waving behind him.

Four-year-old Nasteho is lying on the dirt floor fanned by Fatimo, her mother. She tries to pour water into Nasteho's mouth but the little girl lets it run down her cheek.

Nasteho is skeletally thin. She has a big head, tiny neck and arms and her legs are so narrow that they are just little sticks. Ahmed carried her to the clinic on Thursday but the doctors had nothing to treat her with. He thinks Nasteho is going to die and he can tell by my silence that I also think so.

Ahmed is one of those who knows the face of death. Five days ago he washed the body of his two-year-old daughter, Shukri, in front of this same hut. Shukri joined her sisters, Fordoza, 5, and Nasri, 6, in Danan's cemetery.

This is a proud man who, with his 60 cows, 100 sheep and goats, was wealthy. He now has to watch his family die one by one in the camp where he brought them for refuge.

I cannot help his daughter but he has two more children and a plea. 'We have prayed for Allah's help, but we need assistance. Tell the other nations they must send us food and medicine or we will all die.'

Danan provides a glimpse into the depth of the horror of a famine that could grip much of Ethiopia. This is not like the 1984–85 famine when 1 million people died in a disaster that Band Aid drew to everyone's attention. So far, enough food relief has dribbled in to keep the strong alive. But the situation is more desperate by the day.

Wheat was delivered to Danan in March, enough for 4.5 kilos per person. The April delivery is said to be 'in the pipeline', but it is late and there is no sign of it.

Much more desperately needed are supplementary rations: a high-energy mix of cereal, skimmed milk and vitamins which is needed by the young and elderly alike.

At first glance there appear to be a lot of people in Danan who are skinny but look healthy enough. Then you realise that there are no old people and few toddlers.

American aid has pledged 480,000 tons, but the next delivery is of only 85,000 tons and not until 15 April. According to Oxfam, the European Union has provided little more than half the food it promised last year. It has pledged only 50,000 tons and says this could take up to nine months to deliver. The distances are vast and the roads are poor. A huge airlift is urgently needed. But some donors are wary of sending food to a country whose government is·spending millions fighting a border war with Eritrea.

Britain has halved its aid to Ethiopia from £39.3 million to £19 million because of fears that renewal of war with Eritrea would stop the money reaching projects designed to tackle poverty.

Some 230 trucks that were previously used for relief have now been sent to the front line.

Still, there is a chance in the first year of the new century to stop a disaster before it happens. The politics of aid distribution mean little to children such as Miyir. But food means everything.

Zimbabwe

Rape is new weapon of
Mugabe's terror

MUREWA

28 May 2000

The manicured lawns and bright red poinsettia shrubs of St Paul's
Catholic mission school in Murewa, 50 miles northeast of Harare, made
it seem a safe haven in the eyes of Tabitha, a 16-year-old cook. That was
before she became the victim of a campaign of systematic rape and
violence by the thugs terrorising Zimbabwe's countryside on behalf of
President Robert Mugabe's Zanu-PF party.

A tiny, delicate teenager, too young to vote in next month's elections, Tabitha has no understanding of the brutal politics behind
the attack on her as she walked to nearby shops with her friend
Florence. She simply sits on a couch, wraps a white woollen shawl
tightly around her body and talks in a quiet monotone about the
day that ended her hitherto happy life.

'I have lost my virginity and I want only death,' she said.

St Paul's mission became a target for Zanu-PF activists after
they entered the school and found T-shirts signifying support for
the opposition Movement for Democratic Change (MDC). They
beat up two teachers and accused the school of disseminating
MDC propaganda. The teachers were stooges, they said, for white
imperialists who would destroy Zimbabwe.

Until their arrival, Tabitha had loved her job at the mission. She
earned money for her family of subsistence farmers, and could sit
and gossip with other young girls between preparing meals.

One afternoon earlier this month she finished cooking lunch, put on her new blue dress and strolled out of the compound with Florence, also 16. The two girls chatted as they walked down the dirt road that leads from St Paul's to the nearby Musami shoping centre to buy meat for the following day's meal.

Tabitha was proud to be trusted with the mission's money. It was like play-acting for the role of wife and mother she dreamt of for her future. She had no fears: Murewa is a village of traditional round brick houses with thatched roofs, where people instinctively look out for each other.

The girls might have felt differently had they paid more attention to national politics. The ruling Zanu-PF is facing its first real challenge since independence 20 years ago. Its reaction to the emergency of the MDC has been to bus young supporters and war veterans into villages across the country.

They have been unleashed in an attempt to cow communities into voting for Zanu-PF. In Murewa, the party enforcers had taken over the local Shavanhwoye nightclub, just a grassy slope away from the shopping centre.

It was dusk when two men wearing Elections 2000 Zanu-PF T-shirts approached Tabitha and Florence, and prevented them from passing. The men carried newly cut switches. The girls turned and ran.

They did not get far. More Zanu-PF men came running out of the fields and chased the girls down 'like animals', Tabitha said. 'They tore off my dress and I had only my panties left. I was screaming, "Mother, mother, save me," but nobody came.'

Two men dragged Tabitha behind the nightclub, threw her to the ground and covered her face with a Forward with the Land Zanu-PF banner. One held her arms while the other raped her, then they switched positions.

'I felt a huge pain between my legs,' she said. 'I thought I was looking at my death.'

Covered in blood, Tabitha was left to crawl away. Her screams finally brought a local shopkeeper. He took her to a hospital in the

St Paul's compound, where she stayed for three days. Florence was found by the side of the road, badly beaten about the head, back and arms.

Physical and psychological pain are not the only traumas faced by rape victims such as Tabitha, who is now stricken with nightmares. One in four Zimbabweans is HIV-positive, so there is a chance that she may have been infected with the Aids virus.

Two white women who were raped by war veterans on a farm near Harare last month flew abroad for treatment with a cocktail of drugs to stave off potential infection. Tabitha is a poor black girl and does not even have the money for a blood test.

'They told me at the hospital that, if I start feeling ill in some months, I should come back,' she said.

Cruel though it was, Tabitha's ordeal is virtually routine today in the rural areas of Zimbabwe. Few such incidents are reported: the police are either allied with the perpetrators or seem powerless to stop them.

The deaths of four farmers focused international attention on the plight of whites in the build-up to voting on 24–25 June, but most of those falling prey to Zanu-PF's campaign of terror are black. The violence is about politics, not race or even land.

'There is what I would call a low-intensity war going on in the rural areas,' said Tony Reeler, of the Zimbabwe Human Rights Organisation. He estimates that 6,000 men, women and children have fled the rural violence for refuge in the capital.

Tabitha is one of at least eight women to have been raped in her small village alone. All the victims say their attackers came from the Zanu-PF encampment.

Fideline, 33, a tall, handsome mother of two, with high cheekbones and almond-shaped brown eyes, said she felt luckier than some. Now hiding with relatives in Harare, she showed three knife slashes the war veterans had left on her skull and a horrific 6in wound on her breast where she was beaten with barbed wire.

She was left unconscious on the side of the road after she and her friend Gladys, 33, were attacked by a group of about 30

Zanu-PF men as they walked home from Good Friday services at St Paul's church. Gladys suffered most. She was dragged into a field and raped by four men. She still cannot walk, Fideline says.

'The shopkeeper who found me thought I was dead,' she said last week. 'I remember as they beat me, I thought, "Now I am going to die."'

The reign of terror shows no sign of abating. Many parents in Murewa have sent their children to the city for safety. Those left behind have no protection from the Zanu-PF raiding parties.

The one home where they found an MDC T-shirt was burnt to the ground. The party enforcers go from door to door, accusing people of being MDC supporters, seemingly at random.

Eveline, 16, and her 18-year-old sister Susan were forced from their home by intruders who found her washing the breakfast dishes before going to school. The girls were marched through the village as the Zanu-PF men forced more and more young women onto the street. 'They told us if we ran away, they would catch us and we would not go home any more,' Eveline said.

The raiding party eventually gathered a group of about 30 girls and marched them to the village of Ngomamowa, where they arrived in the late afternoon.

Eveline, a pretty, chubby teenager, can barely utter the words to explain what happened. She speaks almost in a whisper, picking at her hands as she talks.

She and Susan were forced to cook sadza, a maize porridge, and elephant meat for their captors. Then they sang party songs and danced for hours.

During the night, the so-called war veterans took some of the girls into a local grain mill and raped them on the concrete floor. 'I don't know how many were raped. Many,' Eveline said.

She and Susan were released in the morning. Others were held for days.

There appears to be no stopping the excesses of what Zanu-PF calls its election campaign. Anyone who believes Mugabe's promise of free and fair elections should spend a day in Murewa.

Hunzvi's surgery is turned into a
torture centre: Africa in crisis

14 May 2000

It is an evil inversion of the oath sworn by every doctor. In Harare, men can walk when they pass through the door of the surgery of Dr Chenjerai 'Hitler' Hunzvi, the physician who has led the war veterans occupying farms throughout Zimbabwe. But they leave so bruised and battered that they can barely move.

Hunzvi's surgery in the Budiriro neighbourhood of the capital looks innocent enough at first glance. It is a single-storey concrete building with a tin roof, painted a pale blue and emblazoned with 'Dr C Hunzvi, Surgery' in block capitals across the front.

But merely stopping in the road outside draws an angry swarm of menacing men through the front gate, who try to prevent the car from leaving when they see a white face. This former place of healing has become a torture centre.

A week and a half ago, about 50 men calling themselves war veterans moved into Hunzvi's surgery compound and began sending out gangs to kidnap local residents they suspected of supporting the opposition.

Once through the doctor's gates, their victims were subjected to hours of beatings and sadistic abuse. Their move into Harare was evidence that the violent campaign to intimidate people into voting for President Robert Mugabe's Zanu-PF party had widened from the farms to the cities, the stronghold of the Movement for Democratic Change (MDC), the main opposition party.

A man who can be identified only as Emanuel was forced into the centre on Thursday. When I met him in the casualty ward of Harare hospital, he wore a detached blue hood to try to hide his injuries. His left cheekbone was swollen and his left eye blood-red.

He could barely hear because the 'war veterans' had boxed his ears so ferociously. His back was a mass of bruises and welts that went all the way down his thighs. The welts on his buttocks were bleeding.

He wouldn't show me the worst of his injuries and I didn't want to look. His captors had tied a rubber strip tight around the tip of his penis and kept it bound for the 13 hours that they held him in the surgery, preventing him from urinating.

Emanuel's sin was to buy a membership card for the MDC, the party that hopes to challenge Zanu-PF in elections due by August. 'About 12 of them picked me up near my friend's shop at about noon,' Emanuel, 28, said. 'I had no chance. They said you are MDC and drove me to Hunzvi's surgery.'

Two other men were already on the floor, naked and bruised. His ordeal began at once.

'They beat me with electric cables and wooden poles like table legs,' he said. 'They kept shouting, tell us the names of your MDC members. I kept telling them I am just a simple man, I am not participating in the party, but they didn't care.'

The Zanu-PF thugs based in Hunzvi's surgery are terrorising the neighbourhood. Residents call the surgery 'the concentration camp'. They named three other men who had been abducted, taken to the surgery and beaten, and said many more had suffered the same fate.

Hunzvi toured the country last week in a government helicopter with a delegation of white farmers, claiming to be seeking an end to the occupation of farms that has provoked weeks of violence.

On Friday, just hours after Emanuel was released from Hunzvi's surgery, the physician turned politician sat to Mugabe's left at a negotiating session with white farmers to resolve Zimbabwe's crisis. Three white farmers have been killed by his followers.

Mugabe, say those who have met him in recent weeks, turned on the farmers not so much because he wanted their land but because he was furious that they were helping finance the MDC, led by Morgan Tsvangirai, the trade union leader.

Sierra Leone

Drug-crazed warriors
of the jungle

FREETOWN

3 September 2000

It is hard to talk to Junior Savage. He has sewn the front half of a rat's pelt to the baseball cap that is pulled down low over his forehead, so the beady eyes of the dead rodent stare at you as a human voice talks from somewhere below. The tail and another bit of the pelt hang off the back of the cap – every once in a while he turns it around and then you look into the dead, flat eyes of a young West Side Boy.

The young men who captured 11 British soldiers are members of Junior's gang. Embittered by years in the bush and lack of recognition, they are maddened by constant drink and drug use – and by the knowledge that they are not going anywhere.

It is that volatile state of mind that is most dangerous to the British major and five non-commissioned officers from the Royal Irish Regiment still being held by the West Side Boys in their jungle base last night. The servicemen were seized just over a week ago, together with five other soldiers, when they apparently took a wrong turning in the jungle.

In another time and place, Junior might not have turned out to be a bad guy. He speaks softly, his chin almost on his chest, the rat eyes staring out from above the peak of his baseball cap.

His tone does not change when he talks about the drug he was given before military operations. It is called brown-brown and is probably a cocaine derivative.

'They put this white powder in a big bowl and they squeezed lime juice over it to make it liquid. Then they injected us.' Asked who 'they' are, he says: 'My colleagues.'

Did he ever have any doubts about taking the drug? 'No one among us can say no. And when you get the injections, you are feeling good. Death is in front of you and you don't feel her. If anyone gives you any order, you do it.'

Junior has just come out of the Occra hills, where about 500 of his fellow West Side Boys live in tin-roofed shacks in the jungle about 50 miles east of the Freetown peninsula.

The story he has brought with him does not bode well for the Britons still being held – much less for this beautiful and war-ravaged country.

Most Sierra Leoneans view the soldiers – part of a contingent of 220 sent to train government troops – as their saviours. They are appalled that troops they believed to be invincible could be seized by a gang of young bandits like Junior.

Ironically, the West Side Boys actually fought under the direction of British soldiers in May in the battle against the Revolutionary United Front rebels. The British, who they respected, gave them rifles and ammunition during the fight to protect Freetown. But several months ago, the West Side Boys reverted to banditry. The soldiers they have taken hostage have become merely a means of getting what they want.

The West Side Boys evolved out of the Armed Forces Revolutionary Council (AFRC), a group that overthrew what was seen as the country's then corrupt government and took power in 1997. Nigerian-led Ecomog troops forced the AFRC out of power in 1998. Then, with the return to power of President Kabbah, AFRC members such as Junior, together with thousands of other rebels, fled into the bush.

'Sometimes we were sitting there and crying, asking "Why are we here?"', he recalls. The long march was made through the jungle with no food and no medicines against malaria and other diseases.

The rebels came under the leadership of a man Junior knows as Commander Bomblast, born as Papeh Kamara in Freetown.

The self-styled Commander Bomblast was the disillusioned son of a Sierra Leonean sergeant who, after 40 years' service, was kicked out of the army and as a thank-you was given only a bundle of corrugated iron, used here for roofing.

Bomblast, of whom there is no known photograph, has long been a hero of the rebels here. He has only come to world attention because he is now in Pademba Road central prison and his release is the key demand of the West Side Boys, who are holding the British hostages.

He earned his name from his fighting stance. 'When we would fight, Bomblast would hold two RPGs [rocket-propelled grenades], one on either hip, and fire both at the same time,' Junior said. 'Any other man would have been blown backwards from the recoil.'

There is little likelihood of an early release for Bomblast, who is held with Foday Sankoh, the rebel leader, awaiting an international tribunal under United Nations auspices.

Human Rights Watch, the international organisation, has catalogued a file of offences committed by men under Bomblast's command that would constitute war crimes. These include rape, destruction of property and summary executions, and most date back to the January 1999 attack on Freetown by the West Side Boys.

Bomblast was actually put in prison because of a gun battle with a rival commander over a four-wheel-drive vehicle in May, coincidentally on the day when Robin Cook, the foreign secretary, arrived to review British troops. Security was high and both men and their supporters were carted off to jail.

British military sources here are still unable to explain how an experienced Royal Irish Regiment unit could have fallen into the hands of drunken, drugged and demoralised young men like Junior.

The unit of 11 British soldiers – accompanied by a Sierra Leonean officer – had travelled to Masiaka, about 40 miles east of

Freetown, on 25 August. They lunched with a Jordanian UN unit and were travelling back to the capital when they turned off on a side road heading to Foradugo – a known base of the West Side Boys.

Kai Kai, the president's spokesman, said he did not know why they were on that road but believed the British soldiers had been surrounded by armed children, as young as 11 and 12, and decided to surrender without a fight rather than hurt the youngsters.

'My information is that they were surrounded by the child soldiers, 11- and 12-year-olds who have been abducted and made soldiers of the West Side Boys,' he said.

'How would it have looked if you saw on your television screens the bodies of these little tiny children and were told that they had been killed by British soldiers who were defending themselves?

'I think the British had no choice when they were faced with these children.'

British military sources in Sierra Leone agree with the government that Bomblast should not be released in exchange for the six remaining hostages. The danger now is that the West Side Boys' demands have escalated.

Last week, speaking on a British military satellite phone that was traded for the release of the five junior soldiers, the rebels increased their demands to say that they wanted Bomblast's release but also required the dissolution of the government of President Kabbah and the formation of a power-sharing administration that would include leaders of the West Side Boys.

Tony Camp, a British military spokesman here, said he had spoken on the phone to a British captive on Friday but there was no contact yesterday.

Negotiations, meanwhile, have been continuing in a roundabout way. The British high commission representative has been meeting relatives of the West Side Boys in an attempt to convey messages to secure the soldiers' release.

This volatile group seems daily to change its demands. The crisis may ultimately be resolved more easily, though, than the escalating demands would indicate. When I left Junior, he asked me for money to pay for a pair of shoes to replace his plastic flip-flops. In return, he agreed that he would attend church today.

How the hi-tech army fell back on law of the jungle and won

17 September 2000

Marie Colvin, James Clark and Peter Conradi

The first Chinook C-47 flew low over the jungle as the African sun started to rise. There was just enough light for the pilot to see where he was going – but not enough for his helicopter to be seen – as he swooped towards Rokel Creek in the heavily wooded Occra Hills of Sierra Leone.

His target was a camp sprawling over both banks of the muddy creek, where six British soldiers had been held in sweltering heat for more than two weeks by heavily armed members of the rebel militia that called itself the West Side Boys.

On board the Chinook and four other helicopters that followed were more than 120 paratroopers and members of the Special Air Service (SAS) trained in hostage rescue. Their mission: to recover the six members of the 1st Battalion, Royal Irish Regiment and, if possible, to capture Foday Kallay, the rebels' 24-year-old leader.

Operation Barras, co-ordinated from Permanent Joint Headquarters, the army's nerve centre almost 2,700 miles away in Northwood, northwest London, had received the green light from Tony Blair four days earlier. Within 20 minutes of the first landing last Sunday, the British hostages were being flown to safety, their 16-day ordeal over. Within hours, at least 25 of the West Side Boys had been killed and Kallay was on his way to jail.

For the military planners it was a textbook operation, worthy of study for years to come and marred only by the death of Brad

Tinnion, a 26-year-old member of the SAS snatch squad, who was shot as he jumped from his helicopter.

'You cannot resolve a situation like this with a laser-guided bomb from 30,000 feet,' said Brigadier Andrew Stewart, who monitored the operation from Northwood. 'As a purely military operation, it knocks the lifting of the Iranian embassy siege into a cocked hat.'

Few of the hostages would have dared envisage such an outcome during the dark days after they fell into the West Side Boys' hands on 25 August. At one point, they were subjected to a mock execution at a place known as the dead zone, because so many of the West Side Boys' enemies had been shot there.

Eleven members of the Royal Irish – five of whom were subsequently released – had been returning to their Benguema base after visiting a Jordanian peacekeeping battalion in Masiaka, east of Freetown, when Major Alan Marshall, their commander, turned sharp right off the main road, down a narrow red dirt road that led for seven miles to the West Side Boys' camp at Magbeni.

Marshall thought there were only a few rebels there. He was wrong. His men were overwhelmed, he was beaten and all were taken across the creek in dugouts with outboard motors to Gberi Bana, Kallay's headquarters on the north bank.

There they were stripped of their uniforms and searched. Kallay personally stuffed possessions ranging from watches to spare clothes into a bag, putting their rings on his fingers and admiring the glitter of the gold. He later put on a spare British uniform as he swaggered around the camp, and used one of the three British Land Rovers to check on his followers.

Kallay visited his captives every day, repeatedly demanding to know why they had driven to his camp. 'Explain your mission or I will shoot you,' he would say.

Several days after their capture, Kallay hyped himself up with cocaine and decided he had had enough. The six soldiers were taken to the dead zone and placed in front of wooden poles that had been hammered into the ground about a yard apart.

Their hands were secured behind the poles with cuffs twisted out of twine. The bodyguards lined up, stony-faced, pointing their weapons at the captives, awaiting the order to shoot.

As the rest of the Britons fell silent, Marshall tried to reason with the rebel leader, who, maddened by cocaine, was shouting: 'I will kill you! I will kill you!'

'Even when he was tied to the stake, the major continued to speak to Kallay,' said the rebel leader's chief bodyguard, who styled himself Corporal Blood. 'He was very cool. He told Kallay, "We just came to see you, to tell you to forget fighting. We did not come with any bad intentions. If you kill us, it will not be for any reason."'

Then, after half an hour of threats, Kallay relented and ordered the men to be returned to their hut in the main camp. He gave no reason.

Unbeknown to the rebels or their captives, Kallay's increasingly erratic behaviour was being monitored by a handful of SAS men who spent a week in the jungle before the rescue.

While the British Army continued to negotiate with Kallay in the hope of a peaceful resolution, the SAS's task was to supply intelligence that would facilitate any eventual rescue mission.

Working in pairs, they lay in shallow trenches, just below eye-line, dressed in 'ghillie suits' – a type of overall to which they attach twigs, leaves and branches picked up from local vegetation as camouflage. Eating carefully packed rations, and urinating into bottles, they used night-vision, thermal and infrared scopes to provide commanders in Northwood with information so detailed that a replica of the West Side Boys' camp was built for training purposes.

The mango swamps along the creek in which they were hidden are heavily wooded. Anyone concealed there would have faced water snakes in the river and the danger of being given away by curious monkeys.

On 6 September, 'H hour' was set for 6.16am local time on Sunday – 7.16am in London. Three of the giant Chinook C-47s and two smaller Lynx craft took part in a two-pronged assault. One group of Paras was assigned to destroy the positions held by the rebels at Magbeni, on the south bank of the creek. This was intended to give the helicopter heading for Gberi Bana camp, on the north bank, the chance to land without taking fire from two sides.

Captain Danny Matthews, aide-de-camp to the commander, Major Matthew Lowe, was apprehensive as his Chinook came in to land. At 22, Matthews had already had one tour of duty in Sierra Leone and been a platoon commander in Kosovo. This time, the risks were far greater.

'We knew the West Side Boys had lots of equipment, mortars, rifles, machineguns and heavy machineguns,' he said. 'There is obviously no set format and obviously that plays on your mind – not being able to predict your enemy's intentions or reactions.'

The West Side Boys had little more than a minute from the moment they heard the clatter of the helicopters to prepare to defend themselves.

From their camouflaged positions, as close as 180 feet from the camp, the SAS men could see the rebels take up their firing positions. They sent a snap radio message back to Northwood warning that the landing would be made under fire. The first target was the hut in which the hostages were being held. As the Chinook touched down in the centre of the village, it came under fire from West Side Boys shooting from a captured Land Rover.

The helicopter responded with machinegun fire. The SAS men in the jungle opened up, causing panic among the rebels by firing from behind positions they had thought were safe.

The West Side Boys retaliated with British-made general purpose machineguns and Kalashnikov AK-47 assault rifles. Heavy fire also came from Magbeni, where the rebels had heavy-calibre machineguns and a double-barrelled anti-aircraft gun. But they were no match for the British.

'We never experienced anything like this,' said Blood. 'We saw the soldiers coming down to the ground. I fired my RPG [rocket-propelled grenade] two times, but both times the helicopter balanced [swerved] and I missed.'

As the battle raged, SAS men came sprinting towards the hut where their colleagues had reported the hostages to be, firing bursts from their 5.56mm Canadian assault rifles and hurling grenades. 'It was all about speed,' said one British-based special forces officer. 'They had to be in and out very quickly.'

The assault was brutal: the government claimed last week that 25 of the West Side Boys were killed. One source close to the operation said the death toll would prove higher. 'If you followed every blood trail into the jungle you might well be able to quadruple that figure.'

Inside the hut, the SAS found Marshall, his men and a Sierra Leonean liaison officer who had been captured with them.

On the south bank, meanwhile, a Chinook loaded with Paras had landed in front of a swamp, leaving Matthews and his fellow soldiers to wade up to their midriffs for at least 10 minutes, each man weighed down by as much as 60 pounds of kit. They then had to hack their way through 150ft of jungle.

The platoon successfully took its first objective – a crumbling one storey-building – but came under heavy fire as it approached a second. A mortar bomb exploded in front of the men, injuring seven, who might have been killed had it not sunk so deep into soft ground. The wounded included Lowe, who went down with shrapnel wounds to his legs. 'The OC [Lowe] called me up and told me I was to take over command of the company,' Matthews said.

As another Chinook braved enemy fire to pick up the wounded, Matthews sent his three platoons in different directions to secure the area and retrieve the British vehicles. A Lynx helicopter touched down at speed to the north to collect the hostages.

It was an audacious piece of flying, but Tinnion, a new recruit to the SAS, was shot from behind shortly after getting out of the helicopter.

The bullet passed through his body and out through his shoulder. Under heavy fire, his colleagues treated him as well as they could. He died shortly after reaching medics aboard Royal Fleet Auxiliary Ship *Sir Percivale*, off the coast near Freetown.

The mood in headquarters in Northwood changed dramatically: 'Within 20 minutes of the go, we knew all the hostages were safe and away from the scene, but within a minute of that we knew Tinnion had been hit and looked unlikely to survive,' said Stewart.

The carnage the SAS left behind them was considerable. 'There were many corpses and wounded people lying on the ground moaning,' said Unisa Sesay, 16, one of the West Side Boys' child soldiers, who reached the base just after the British had left.

'One commander was standing and his friend was trying to remove a fragment from his shoulder. The rest of the people were on the ground.'

Another soldier, who gave his name as Cyrus and his age as 17, said they had been told the wounded would be shot and thrown into the river because there were no medical supplies. Both boys said they saw too many corpses, and were too shocked, to count. The dead included a 14-year-old boy soldier and one Sierra Leonean hostage who panicked and ran into the firefight.

General Sir Charles Guthrie, the chief of the defence staff, had been booked three months earlier to be interviewed that morning on BBC1's *Breakfast with Frost*. At about 9.20am, Major Tom Thornycroft whispered to Guthrie in the wings of the studio confirmation that all the hostages were safe. Guthrie then broke the first news to the nation that an operation was under way in West Africa.

The prime minister, who had spent the weekend at Chequers approving the last details of the plan, had already received a call from Guthrie informing him of the success. Blair returned to London and made a statement to television cameras in Downing Street.

Kallay, meanwhile, had been captured at his hut and flown by British helicopter to JordBat2 [second Jordanian Battalion] on the Freetown–Masiaka highway. He was hustled into the base, his hands secured behind his back with white plastic cuffs, his oversized Calvin Klein T-shirt flapping almost down to his knees.

He was stripped naked and searched. Then British soldiers threw him to the ground and exploded in anger. A large black boot was placed on his back and another on his legs, pinning Kallay to the ground, face down. He peered around, not responding to shouts from soldiers who had spotted the rings Kallay stole from the British hostages.

One soldier with a heavy Irish accent shouted, 'You f****** f***, stealing f****** soldiers' rings' as his colleague, one by one, twisted and pulled until all the rings were back in British hands. Kallay grimaced in pain, but did not let out a single cry.

The operation terrified the West Side Boys. More than 50 have surrendered since the raid. But defectors revealed that a hard core had regrouped at a base inland from Gberi Bani.

In London, jubilation was tinged with sorrow at the death of Tinnion, who had served with distinction in 29 Commando Royal Artillery. The army believes he was almost certainly killed by a round, believed to be of 7.62mm calibre, from a self-loading rifle (SLR) of the type provided by Britain to pro-government forces in Sierra Leone. The West Side Boys' militia supported the Freetown government until a few months ago.

On Friday, as Marshall faced the prospect of disciplinary action after taking the blame for his men's capture, Tinnion's parents and girlfriend were at his graveside after he was buried with full military honours at his regiment's base in Hereford.

Anna Homsi, his girlfriend, who is seven months pregnant, described him as 'the man of my dreams'. She added: 'We are obviously deeply shocked and devastated by Brad's death, but enormously proud he died doing the job he loved.'

Under army rules, neither Homsi nor the unborn child would be eligible for Tinnion's pension or other money. However, the Ministry of Defence is preparing to make an exception. One SAS officer said: 'Because of the level of danger the lads face, the wives need to know somehow that there is security for the family there if it all goes wrong. It's in the regiment's interests as well as the blokes' and their families.'

Sri Lanka

Fighting Tigers talk of peace deal

15 April 2001

Marie Colvin, the first foreign journalist to visit Tamil-held Sri Lanka since 1995, reports from Mallawi.

Conciliatory words do not come easy to Thamilthevlan, the second-in-command of the Tamil Tigers. His walking stick is a legacy of the three times he was shot in battle since joining the founding ranks of one of the most ruthless guerrilla movements in the world.

For the first time in 18 years of armed struggle that has cost 60,000 lives, however, he claims the group is now ready to settle for an autonomous homeland rather than continue fighting for an independent state in northern Sri Lanka.

His message, direct from Velupillai Prabhakaran, the reclusive Tamil leader, is far removed from the uncompromising rhetoric long the signature tune of the Liberation Tigers of Tamil Eelam (LTTE).

'There must be a political solution,' Thamilthevlan told *The Sunday Times* last week. 'The name is immaterial. Federation, confederation, northeast council, autonomous region, we can accept any of these solutions as long as we are guaranteed our equal rights, our dignity and justice. We don't want a lifestyle decided by Buddhist monks in Colombo.'

The decision does not appear to spring from military weakness. Last April the Tamil Tigers overran a huge Sri Lankan military complex to capture Elephant Pass, the neck of land that controls access to the Jaffna peninsula, their heartland. They swept the army out of Vanni, the four northern Tamil provinces on the mainland,

and today control more than 50% of the ancestral land they claim as their own.

Rather, the LTTE decision to enter the diplomatic water appears to come from a realisation that even while they cannot be defeated militarily, neither can they win on the battlefield. They are increasingly isolated and not just politically: the Vanni region is ringed by the army and navy and under an economic siege. Journalists are banned by the Sri Lankan government from entering.

Travelling to Tamil Tiger headquarters in Mallawi was an education in the LTTE networks. I left Vavuniya, the northernmost town controlled by the government, in a car with civilian LTTE sympathisers who held army passes and told me to say that I was going to 'Kanthaudaiyarpuvarsankulam' at checkpoints. Fortunately, nobody asked.

Fed by a family of farmers, I slept on the floor of a school near Mannar on the west coast, sitting up late into the night with the principal, hearing how government oppression of the Tamils had turned him from a moderate to a militant. 'I don't want this war,' he said. 'But I can't see any other way to win our rights.'

At dawn, 10 Tamil Tiger fighters arrived dressed in bits of camouflage and flip-flops. All were armed with automatic weapons and grenades. Nobody seemed concerned that we were in government territory.

We rode by tractor through a ruined cashew plantation, until the dirt road became too narrow and the jungle too dense.

The thick foliage overhead turned into a green tunnel; the air was so thick with humidity that my arm felt as if it was furred when I swung it.

Scouts ranged ahead across open fields, checked for Sri Lankan army soldiers, then motioned us in single file across at 10-yard intervals – if one of us were unfortunate enough to step on a mine, at least nobody else would be hurt by the blast.

By sunset another obstacle lay across our path: a river. Following the lead of my Tiger guides, I waded tentatively through the water as the level swiftly rose to my chest.

By 9pm we crossed the main road between army territory and the Tamil Tiger area, and on to the group's headquarters in Mallawi. The sense of relief was overwhelming.

En route the guerrillas had told me their stories. Most of those in the patrol were village boys and all were from families living as refugees. They are fanatically loyal to Prabhakaran, who they speak of reverentially as 'national leader'. He sounds a strict master. Tamil Tigers cannot smoke or drink alcohol and must remain celibate until they are allowed to marry; women at 24, men at 28. They receive no wages.

All Tigers, even those in the political wing, wear cyanide capsules around their necks – they know they will be tortured if captured and are ready to die rather than reveal information. This is not paranoia. The American State Department reported last year that 'torture continues with relative impunity'.

Until the 1970s the Tamil protest movement eschewed violence. The LTTE emerged in 1983, when Sinhalese mobs turned on the Tamils, slaughtering hundreds with machetes and burning tyre necklaces and sending thousands fleeing north.

The youth turned to Prabhakaran's advocacy of armed resistance and secession. The LTTE's ruthless reputation comes from the Black Tigers, an elite suicide unit. They have bombed government buildings, assassinated a president and killed Rajiv Gandhi, the Indian leader who sent a taskforce to Sri Lanka in 1987.

Although the government claims the Tamil Tigers intimidate civilians, there is evidence of extensive popular support in the areas they control. 'The Tamils would be all dead, shot up, without these Tigers,' said Father Xavier, a parish priest. 'My parishioners want an end to war, but they say to me, "We have lost our lives, our properties, our land, we need a settlement that guarantees us our rights so that we don't have to go through all this again".'

The government has alienated Tamil hearts and minds. Ministers in Colombo deny that there is an economic embargo on the Vanni, the Tamil area on the mainland, while checkpoints on the internal border enforce a ban on items ranging from fuel, cement, and plastic sheeting to instant noodles and vegetable oil. Even sanitary towels are not allowed; they can presumably be used to dress wounds.

The Vanni region, which covers 2,000 square miles, has no mains electricity or telephone service; its roads have deteriorated to potholed dirt tracks. Most people travel by bicycle because of the fuel shortage.

The embargo has created a huge but unreported humanitarian disaster for the 500,000 civilians who live here, more than half of them internal refugees. The majority live below the national poverty line of about £12 a month.

Colombo prohibits international aid agencies distributing food. International aid agencies estimate that 40% of the children in the Vanni are undernourished or malnourished.

Pushiparani, a teacher, 52, has been displaced seven times after she fled Jaffna with her six children when the army captured the city five years ago. This is fertile recruiting ground for the Tamil Tigers. One of her sons died in battle and a daughter now serves as a Sea Tiger.

In Killinochchi town, a thriving commercial centre of 300,000 until it was bombarded by the Sri Lankan army in 1996, classes are held in the bombed-out shells of school buildings; hospitals are chronically short of surgical supplies.

'Last week one of my cardiac patients walked into the jungle leaving behind a note that said: "I have suffered enough. Suicide",' one doctor said. 'I had no medicine to give him. I feel helpless.'

A unilateral ceasefire declared by the Tamil Tigers on Christmas Eve, and renewed every month, is due to expire on 24 April. The group said this weekend that the ceasefire would be renewed to give Norwegian mediators more time.

After two weeks in the Tamil-held area, I set out southwards late in the evening. Government lines lay a 24-hour walk away; my Tiger guides promised to lead me back across them under cover of darkness. The river lay beyond.

'The shot hit me. Blood poured from my eye – I felt a profound sadness that I was going to die'

22 April 2001

Last Monday, award-winning reporter Marie Colvin was attacked as she returned from a rare interview with Tamil Tiger leaders in Sri Lanka. From her hospital bed in New York she writes about her escape.

It was the most difficult decision of my life. I was lying in an open field with a clump of tall weeds on a slight rise for cover. The moon had not yet risen and the night was pitch black. Every five minutes or so a flare, fired from the nearby Sri Lankan army base, seemed to expose every blade of grass. Advancing soldiers intermittently raked the field with automatic weapons fire. They had to be as scared as I was.

I just wanted to lie still and wait for it all to go away. I thought I would not mind lying here for hours. I noticed little things. One of my trouser legs had come up to my knee and that meant my white calf might draw attention in the dark.

There were three options. I could crawl away. But if one soldier had night-vision goggles – didn't even the poorest armies these days? I would be the only moving object on the field and would be shot.

If I was not spotted, I would still be alone in the jungle with no shoes. If I lay here until the soldiers stumbled on me, they would shoot first. If I shouted and identified myself as a journalist they might shoot anyway. There was no fourth option.

It was 10pm, on the forward defence line of the Sri Lankan army at Parayanlankulam, about 3½ miles from the Madhu road junction. I thought of how I came to be here. There didn't seem to be any one moment when it all went wrong.

A week earlier I had secretly entered the Vanni, a 2,000-mile area of northern Sri Lanka that has been the refuge of the rebel Tamil

Tigers since the government captured the Jaffna peninsula in 1995. The Sri Lankan government bans journalists from travelling there.

The ban meant journalists could not talk to the leadership of the Liberation Tigers for Tamil Eelam (LTTE), even though the government was involved in negotiations with them through a Norwegian envoy to begin peace talks. The only news of the problems with those negotiations came from the government.

More important, the ban prevented any reporting on the plight of the 500,000 Tamil civilians, 340,000 of them refugees, bottled up in the Vanni suffering under an economic embargo that the government denied existed.

I had travelled through villages in the Vanni and found an unreported humanitarian crisis – people starving, international aid agencies banned from distributing food, no mains electricity, no telephone service, few medicines, no fuel for cars, water pumps or lighting.

I had filed the story and had been trying to leave the Vanni to return to the government-controlled south for three days. This involved walking 30 miles a night through jungle and the knee-deep water and mud of marsh and rice paddies – only to end up sleeping on the same straw mat, on the same dirt floor, in the same mud hut. Even the bugs were starting to look familiar.

Each night I tried to leave, guided by local Tamils. But each time they decided it would be too risky to cross army lines. On Sunday night we came within 50 yards of the border between the two sides. The leader studied the army post we were supposed to slip past. Suddenly, he made a somersaulting motion with his hands and started walking back.

There was no argument; we used hand signals and observed silence until several miles from the army line.

'My mistake,' he said. 'Military alert. Too dangerous.' I watched my guides' tireless brown feet, clad only in black rubber flip-flops, pad unceasingly ahead of me until we reached the base house near the Catholic church at Madhu, home to 10,000 refugees living in tents and huts. At dawn I collapsed into sleep.

Monday night was meant to be third time lucky. As the sun slipped below the horizon, I sat with my guides under a banyan tree, looking out over a silvery lake, waiting for dark in a rare moment of peace and beauty.

We were a motley group. The civilians with me were dressed in a collection of shorts and sarongs. An emaciated old man carried a string shopping bag with two bottles of Pepsi, our only drink. A teenager kept trying the little English that he had learnt in St Patrick's college in Jaffna before the army overran the town and killed his father.

'Tonight, you will be in my father's house sipping milky tea,' the leader of the group said. He was the only one who was armed; he carried an old rifle to protect us from wild boar or elephants. 'We are going a way that is safe and secure.'

The plan was to reach his family's house in the government-controlled area that night. The Tamils would return before dawn and I would get the morning bus to Vavuniya. I had a last cigarette as the sun went down; there would be no smoking, talking or even coughing as we walked the next seven miles to sanctuary.

We trekked single file along narrow jungle trails, sometimes pushing our way through thickets of thorn trees; we waded waist-deep round the edges of a lake, eyeing the lights of an army base on its far edge. They are dotted along the Mannar–Vavuniya road that marks the border we would have to cross. At about 8pm, we crept through dark scrub about half a mile from the road, then waited crouching in a marsh – letting the mosquitoes bite because slapping could alert a soldier – while the group's leader scouted ahead.

I took off my shoes to walk more quietly. At a signal from the leader we followed him to the road. Half-crouched, we negotiated our way through barbed wire on both sides of the road and seemed safely across.

We were running through the last dark field for the line of jungle ahead when the silence was broken by the thunder of automatic weapons fire about 100 yards to the right.

I dived down and began crawling, belly on the ground, for some cover. For a few minutes, someone was crawling on top of me – protection or panic, I don't know. Then I was alone, behind weeds.

A tree was 10 yards away, but it seemed too far. The shooting went on and on. Flashes and light came from an army post nobody had seen.

The shooting stopped and dark and quiet descended. There had not been a sound from my side. I could not tell where anyone was. The only sound was the occasional bellow of a cow which had been hit.

I had a few mad moments of thinking it was over, I had survived. But I knew this was not true. We had been spotted. The army would think this was a Tamil Tiger patrol and would come after us. They would be scared and trigger-happy.

The reputation of the two forces is that the army has superior manpower and weapons, the rebels superior manoeuvrability and commitment. The advantage was to the army this night. I was lying in a field with a decision to make: run for it, lie still or shout.

I lay there for half an hour under the penetrating glare of the flares. I turned my face to the earth when one came drifting down directly above me, worried that my white skin would reveal my hiding place.

Bursts of gunfire began across the road about half a mile away. The search and destroy patrols had come out. I heard soldiers on the road, talking and laughing. One fired a burst from an automatic weapon that scythed down the weeds in front of me and left me covered in green shoots.

If I didn't yell now, they would stumble on me and shoot. I began to shout.

'Journalist! Journalist! American! USA!'

A soldier sighted on the sound and fired. This army was not taking prisoners.

The shot hit me with an impact that stunned me with pain, noise and a sense of defeat. I thought I had been shot in the eye.

Blood was pouring from my eye and mouth onto the dirt. I felt a profound sadness that I was going to die.

Then I thought it was taking an awful long time to die if I was really shot in the head (it was actually shrapnel), so I started yelling again. 'English! Anyone speak English?'

There were more shots, but they seemed half-hearted, and lots of hysterical shouting from the soldiers. This was bad. They were as scared as I was. I did not really care because it seemed that I would die anyway, so I just kept shouting.

Searching for a word that non-English speakers might recognise, I fixed on doctor and shouted over and over that I needed one. Finally a voice screamed in English: 'Stand up, stand up.' He fired a few more shots for emphasis.

I stood up slowly, hands in the air, saying, 'Don't shoot, American,' and whatever else I could think of just so that they would keep hearing a foreign voice.

'Take off your jacket,' came the voice. I dropped my blue jacket and stood straight up, hands in the air. Blood poured down my face so I could not see much. Someone yelled, 'Walk to the road.' I stumbled forward.

Every time I fell, feeling faint, they would shout hysterically, afraid that I was pulling some trick, and I would struggle up again. I made it up the incline to the road and was shoved to the ground, flat on my back and kicked by shouting soldiers. A bright light shone in my face. I could not see any of my captors.

I am not sure how long I lay there on my back. I was searched for weapons, then told to walk at gunpoint, prodded by the weapons. The soldiers live in fear of women suicide bombers carrying explosives underneath their clothing.

The LTTE has a ruthless reputation as a result of the activities of the Black Tigers, an elite unit for suicide missions, who have bombed government buildings, assassinated a president and killed Rajiv Gandhi, the Indian leader.

I thought the soldiers were taking me somewhere to shoot me. I remember thinking that they were all scared and that I should act scared and vulnerable. I reached the limit. I could not walk any more and fell, telling them to get a doctor. They relented and put my arms round the shoulders of two men. But they pummelled me again when my hand fell and a soldier shouted that I was going for his grenade.

The nightmare seemed endless. We reached some lighted space outdoors and I was thrown on the ground on my back. A bright light again was in my face and questions shouted in Sinhalese and broken English. Someone ripped open my shirt and pulled it off. They shouted for my weapons. I kept saying, 'Journalist, I need a doctor.'

An officer, or someone in authority, came on the scene and the questions changed into an interrogation: 'Where did you get your training? How many people were with you? Where is your vehicle? Ah, you say you are American but you have no vehicle?'

Things were calming down and my sense of the ridiculous returned. If I had a vehicle, why would I be lying in a field on a dark night?

'Admit that you came to kill us,' he said. 'At least admit that your side fired grenades first. This is true, is it not?'

I said, 'No sir, there was no fire until your soldiers shot at us.'

Then began an endless series of journeys. I was put in the back of a truck and driven, bouncing over potholes, hyperventilating because I could not seem to breathe. I thought it was shock; later, I found that my lungs had been bruised by the shock of the grenade and were filling with fluid.

Someone kind was in the truck. He kept telling me in English: 'We are taking you for medical treatment, you are going to be okay.' I fixed on his voice, and he held my head up so that I could breathe.

At the first hospital I was taken to, the military hospital in Vavuniya, shrapnel was taken out of my head, shoulders and chest. I realised I could not see out of my left eye and I think the doctors panicked the soldiers into some sanity.

I was put in the back of another truck and driven for an hour to Army Victory hospital in Anuradhapura, where an x-ray revealed shrapnel in my eye. A truck took me to a third hospital, the Anuradhapura general hospital. I was never out of army custody.

The doctors seemed scared for me and I asked one to call the American embassy. But an army surgeon kept insisting that they should operate immediately.

'You are going to lose your eye anyway. I can operate now,' he said. I fended him off, but he would appear again, sharpening his imaginary knives, asking to operate.

Telephone calls were being made. It seemed that my request to be taken to Colombo was going to more senior people. At one point I heard a conversation in English. A soldier was saying, 'No, she cannot come to the phone. What is your message?'

I heard him trying to pronounce the name of Steve Holgate, the personable public affairs officer of the American embassy. I shouted: 'Give me the phone.' I had a huge sense of relief that someone knew where I was.

At dawn, someone in the Sri Lankan army hierarchy relented. I was put aboard a military helicopter and flown to Colombo. At the eye hospital, I was shoved on a stretcher against a wall in the crowded emergency room surrounded by hostile soldiers.

Miraculously, Holgate showed up moments later, clipboard in hand, and simply told the soldiers he was taking me into the custody of the American embassy. It was like the moment in a classic Wild West movie when the quiet guy faces down the armed and dangerous gang. I was safe.

Why do I cover wars? I have been asked this often in the past week. It is a difficult question to answer. I did not set out to be a war correspondent. It has always seemed to me that what I write about is humanity in extremis, pushed to the unendurable, and that it is important to tell people what really happens in wars – declared and undeclared.

War has changed remarkably little over the centuries. Do not believe the nice clean videos where Gameboy jets hit Nintendo tanks framed in a satisfying and sanitary 'X'. War is not clean. War is about those who are killed, limbs severed, dirt and rock and flesh torn alike by hot metal. It is terror. It is mothers, fathers, sons and daughters bereft and inconsolable. It is about traumatised children.

My job is to bear witness. I have never been interested in knowing what make of plane had just bombed a village or whether the artillery that fired at it was 120mm or 155mm.

War is also about propaganda. Both sides try to obscure the truth. Foreign journalists arriving in Sri Lanka are told in a government handout that parents in the rebel area keep their children home from school because the Tamil Tigers are recruiting them for service. But the parents told me they keep their children at home because they are hungry and faint in the classroom and do not have money for school supplies.

The Sri Lankan government reacted with anger to my presence in the Tamil-held area of the Vanni. It made no apologies for what had happened to me. I had no permission to go there, the government said, therefore I must have had a 'secret agenda'.

I had no secret agenda. I had a journalist's agenda. I went to the rebel-held areas because talking to the Tamil Tigers and writing about a previously unreported humanitarian crisis are important issues.

I am not going to hang up my flak jacket as a result of this incident. I have been flown to New York, where doctors are going to operate on my injured eye in about a week's time. They have told me it is unlikely I will regain much use of it as a piece of shrapnel went straight through the middle. All I can hope for is a bit of peripheral vision.

Friends have been telephoning to point out how many famous people are blind in one eye. They seem to do fine with only one eye, so I'm not worried. But what I want most, as soon as I get out of hospital, is a vodka martini and a cigarette.

GRATITUDE FROM TAMILS WORLDWIDE

Sri Lanka, April 2001

Colvin was the first foreign reporter in six years to enter Sri Lanka's dangerous northern Vanni region where the Tamil Tigers are waging a civil war against government forces. She went to interview the leaders and was ambushed while trying to walk out of the area last Monday. After reports of Colvin's ordeal last week *The Sunday Times* received many letters from Tamils all over the world offering their support.

This one was typical:

'We Tamils are so proud about your brave foreign correspondent Marie Colvin ...We [are] all aware of the risk she undertook and we appreciate her visit to [the] Vanni area of north Sri Lanka for bringing the news to the outside world. We are deeply concerned about her health and wish her to get well soon. Thank you.'

Signed Elan Ramalingham, Carleton University, Ottawa, Canada.

Fighting back

15 July 2001

Marie Colvin, who was blinded in one eye three months ago while reporting the Sri Lanka conflict, reveals the lingering physical and psychological scars of the ordeal – and describes her new life as 'the lady with the pirate patch'.

Lying on the operating table in New York, sleepy but still awake and very nervous, I could hear the two surgeons chatting as they began cutting into my left eye.

'That lens has to go,' said one.

A tiny pulling feeling. The 'buckle' they were sewing into my eye seemed to be causing problems. More tiny pulling sensations. I started feeling claustrophobic under the green mask that covered my good eye but left the injured one exposed to their blades.

I knew what was going on because I had opted to go under the knife with a local anaesthetic. I'd been warned the operation was likely to take so long that recovery from a general anaesthetic would be uncomfortable.

The surgeons weren't sure what they would find when they went in. A 6mm piece of shrapnel had blasted through my eye, entering the front right side and tearing out through the retina that lines the eye, detaching it completely. The tiny missile had taken some of my iris with it and lodged against my optic nerve. I had been warned the prognosis was not good.

'How are you doing in there?' asked Dr Stanley Chang, the eye surgeon who had invented some of the microsurgery equipment he was using to operate on me.

'Stop the whale music,' I managed to croak. Whale music was playing in the operating room, and I suppose it was meant to calm me down in a new age sort of way, but I've always found it incredibly irritating. Something Brazilian came on. They got on with cutting.

From their conversation, I could tell that blood was the main problem. The shrapnel had caused extensive haemorrhaging in the eye and blood had pooled behind the retina. To reattach the retina and save the eye, the blood needed to be scraped out, bit by microscopic bit, so as not to damage the retina further.

Scrape, scrape, scrape; I was now about four hours into the operation.

The days before the surgery had been full of dread.

I had been exhausted but hopeful the night I arrived in New York by air medivac from Sri Lanka. It was late on 19 April, three days after soldiers fired the grenade that injured me. My mother and my sister Cat were waiting for me at Columbia Presbyterian hospital. So was Chang.

He examined my eye and then sat with me in his darkened office to give me a verdict I had not expected. He said he would try to save the eye, but didn't think the chances were good with such a traumatic injury.

I appreciated his honesty – he is a quiet-spoken man whose manner inspires unquestioning confidence – but it hadn't occurred to me my injured eye might have to come out. I went to sleep in tears, the first time I had cried since being shot. I think it was because it only hit me then that my life would never be the same.

In the next few days, I wrote myself questions to ask the doctor in a pre-op examination. Rereading them last week, I relived my fears.

'Are you saying that I may wake up from the operation with only one eye?' I wrote. It was a new and very strange world. 'You were talking about shrinkage of the eye. How does that happen?' Although I knew I had probably lost my sight, the idea of my eye being removed was unbearable.

The worst part of the operation came towards the end. Chang tried again and again to reattach the retina, but couldn't do it. I remember at one point hearing him saying with grim determination: 'We are going to attach this retina,' in a voice that made it clear he was not going to give up.

Five hours into the operation, the pulling in my eye became unbearable and I asked for more anaesthetic. Finally, Chang succeeded and silicone oil was placed into my eye to keep the retina in place. The operation had taken five and a half hours.

Claustrophobia overwhelmed me and I tried to pull the head covering off. A nurse calmed me, took it off and wheeled me into recovery.

The ordeal had just begun, however. Nurses were under orders to lay me on my stomach to keep the retina and oil in place in the eye. Waves of nausea and pain engulfed me. Every bump of the bed knifed into me as I was wheeled to my room. It was a reaction to the anaesthetic.

I lost any sense of politeness, yelling at the nurses to please give me something to stop the pain. It's an impossible position, having to lie on your stomach and keep your head down, when all you want to do is vomit and have the pain go away.

The next three days passed in a haze. I remember thinking I want this eye out, regretting ever agreeing to surgery to save it, just wanting the pain to go away.

Chang was unexpectedly poetic when I saw him to hear his verdict on my operation. 'Your retina was like a morning glory folded in on itself,' he said, making a slow, clenching motion with his hand to illustrate the floral image. 'A morning glory full of blood.'

The good news was that I would keep my eye. I had lost the perception of light and dark; that was depressing. But I would keep the eye, blind as it now was.

The other good news was that there was no evidence yet of 'sympathetic ophthalmia', a condition which can blind the second eye once one is injured.

On the fourth day, I went to a rented service flat in New York City to recuperate. My eye was covered in a bulky white bandage. I presented a bizarre spectacle to the curious, because I had to walk looking at the ground to keep the retina and oil in place.

I was still under doctor's orders to lie on my stomach for a week. This seemed torture just to think of. But there was one thing I had to do before getting into bed.

I smoked a couple of cigarettes and went into the bathroom. I took off the bandage and looked up into the mirror for the first time.

No flower comparisons came to mind. The pain made my eye feel like the enemy. The eye itself looked even worse.

It was swollen to the size of a peach, bright red, with a thin line – like that little indentation that peaches have across their middles – the only evidence that the two lids had ever opened or would ever open again.

I went and lay on my stomach, my head off the foot of the bed, looking face down through a weird contraption that seemed like an inverted and padded toilet seat. With one eye, I examined the carpet.

Recuperation is not always restful. Friends sent books and flowers, and one provided the most thoughtful, if daunting, of gifts, a box of 84 tapes entitled *Great Minds of the Western Intellectual Tradition*. I thought I might make up for all those university lectures I skipped.

My former husband, Patrick Bishop, with whom I'd been reunited about a year ago, flew from London and turned out to be a pretty good nurse, squeezing into my swollen eye endless drops of steroid and antibiotic drugs.

My mother sent home-cooked comfort food. The most successful was meatloaf, which Patrick, being British, had only seen on *The Simpsons* cartoon show.

With nothing to distract it, my mind began playing endless reruns of what had happened to me. I didn't feel the need to consult Freud; my subconscious was clearly seeking an outcome it liked better. The pain of being shot was not the focus of my nightmares, but that didn't make them much more bearable.

I had been wounded trying to leave the northern, Tamil area of Sri Lanka and re-enter the government-controlled south at the end of an assignment to visit the Tamil Tigers, the LTTE.

Leaving LTTE territory was not a simple matter of hitching a ride. For the past six years, the government in Colombo has banned journalists from the area, hoping to hide the catastrophic humanitarian crisis engulfing 500,000 Tamil civilians bottled up behind a siege line of army bases. I had to cross this line clandestinely.

For three nights my guides led me from a hut at Madhu, a shrine to the Virgin Mary and home to 10,000 refugees in tents and wood shelters, to the army lines. We padded along jungle paths, sloshed through abandoned rice paddies and waded waist-deep through lakes surrounded by banyan trees.

As I lay face-down in the New York apartment, I remembered cascades of white butterflies in shafts of sunlight that penetrated the emerald foliage. The air had been filled with the cries of peacocks, which sounded more like deranged cats, and we came across the spoor of elephant.

For two nights the guides decided it was too dangerous to cross. The third night, 16 April, after we had squatted for hours in a rice paddy, bitten by mosquitoes I couldn't swat for fear the noise would be heard, the lead guide waved us quietly forwards.

Ahead lay ditches, a road and a deep expanse of open ground. In the distance was the jungle. I took my shoes off; one of the things I had learnt was how difficult it is to walk in water wearing shoes. A young man grabbed my hand to haul me more quickly between the two barbed wire fences that lined the road, whispering 'bang, bang' to himself. I wasn't the only one who was frightened.

As we ran, stooped low, towards the safety of the jungle, a rolling flash erupted from the right. Sri Lankan soldiers in a forward listening post had opened fire. I crawled on my belly as long as the gunfire lasted, frantically, as if I could somehow escape. Flares went up, arcing high into the sky and falling slowly, turning night to day. I was trapped in a field, behind a clump of weeds, alone. And that's where the nightmares always begin.

My mind has recorded in exact detail what happened next, except that the tape is slowed down and spools endlessly. Soldiers are coming for me in the night, and I have to make a decision. They come forward inexorably, endlessly.

In reality, I think I only lay in the field for about half an hour. Finally, aware that if they stumbled on me they would shoot me, I shouted 'journalist'. They fired a grenade at the sound of my voice. Shrapnel hit me with a shocking impact of pain and noise.

Usually that wakes me up, but sometimes the dream continues and I am walking forward – as I did that night when I figured out I wasn't going to die, and I kept yelling, and someone speaking English told me to stand up, and I went on walking and falling down at times from weakness and shock and loss of blood. Only, in the dream, I am being shot at each time I fall, and I can feel what it is like to be shot across the chest.

The dream now has flashes of the horrific injuries I have seen in other wars – an old man lying in a basement in Chechnya, the back of his head blown off by a rocket fired from a Russian plane, somehow still rasping out breath until he died. A body I found under a bush in Kosovo, his chest riven by bullets, still wearing the worn wool suit of a peasant who has dressed up for the day. The knowledge of the fragility of the human body never leaves you once you have seen how easily flesh can be rent by hot flying bits of metal. What shocked me after the operation was my sheer exhaustion. I asked Chang what was wrong. 'Let's recap,' he said. 'You've been hit by a grenade in Sri Lanka. You've travelled halfway across the world, not to mention the trauma. You have just undergone a 5½-hour operation, and we're not even taking into account what is going on in that stubborn head of yours. And you ask me why you're tired?'

The first time I went out alone on the street with my new pirate-patch look, I couldn't cope. I had left my bag of clothes – along with my computer and satellite phone – behind at the scene in Sri Lanka, and I thought it would be a simple matter to buy some more.

I like shopping, but I had got only two steps into Barney's department store before I just had to get out again. People were coming at me. I couldn't trust the steps.

People on the street glanced at my eye patch and looked away, but the doorman at my apartment block asked: 'What the heck happened to you?' American friends said they loved the patch but wanted to see what was behind it.

On a week's recuperative holiday on the Ligurian coast, I was told by Italian men that the patch was very sexy. Back in London, I find that friends are surprised I don't appear worse. People in the street still glance away, but children ask me why I am dressed as a pirate, which is delightful.

Everyone professes to like the patch. A designer friend offered to make me a party patch with rhinestones for evening wear; and even the Prince of Wales pronounced it 'very fetching' when I was introduced to him at a reception.

I have become very fond of my patch. At home I usually take it off; but when I see myself in the mirror without it – rarely, as I am not a great looker in mirrors – I am taken aback. What I see doesn't look like me. So I put the patch back on as it makes it clear to my mind what has happened to me.

In some ways it is harder to cope with the frustrating tiredness. I used to be so energetic. Now I have to have a nap after lunch like a little child. I also can't drive, which is fine as I have always hated driving in London. But the Underground is also out, as I don't trust myself on the escalators. I now know what 'blind-sided' means.

Ridiculously, I can't even light a cigarette – I'm always lighting them in the middle or waving the flame two inches from the end – and I'm learning again to pour a glass of wine without missing.

At the back of my mind all the time is the fear for my good eye and the phenomenon of sympathetic ophthalmia. As I understand it, the auto-immune system can react to the injury and operation in one eye by attacking the other. At Moorfields hospital two weeks ago, I was assured there was no sign of this. But I discovered that the retina in the injured eye had become detached again. This isn't unusual, but it was depressing.

Next month, I'll go to New York to consult Chang about another operation. It's a toss-up, of course, as further surgery could increase the danger to the good eye.

I have been asked if my trip to Sri Lanka was worth it. One blunt BBC reporter last week argued in an interview, not unkindly: 'Some people would say it was stupid, Marie.' Was it? That's a hard question to answer.

Certainly, Sri Lanka is a forgotten conflict. Some 60,000 people have died since the country exploded in civil war in 1983, a loss barely noticed except by their families. The public message for the Sri Lankan government that I was given by the Tamil Tiger leadership was barely noticed, either. They said they were willing to negotiate for autonomy rather than the independence they had sought for 18 years. After I left, they ended a four-month unilateral ceasefire, saying the government had refused to reciprocate. Fighting has resumed. On a smaller scale, however, the trip did seem to me worthwhile. I may be exhausted and haunted, but not all the images that flash back to me evoke dread. I remember a government agent in a town in the Vanni – the region controlled by the LTTE – who put his neck on the line just to give me information. He received me late at night in his office, very formal but resolute. He put a suit on and asked me not to reveal his name for fear of retaliation from the very government that paid his salary.

He had facts and figures of the type that make on-the-ground reporting worthwhile. I wanted to resolve two contradictory stories: the government in Colombo claimed to be distributing food to Tamil civilians on the same monthly basis as the rest of the country, yet in village after village people told me they received little. Many were painfully thin.

This government agent explained. He said he notified Colombo monthly that 36,400 families in his district (about 140,000 people) qualified for food aid. They sent him food for 8,900 families (about 35,000 people), claiming he had inflated his figures.

'So I hold the first shipment, and divide up what I have to distribute every two months,' he said. 'There is no basis for this misery.'

Not everyone was as easily persuaded that I was worth talking to. Father Xavier, the Roman Catholic priest of Mallawi, was garrulous, opinionated and angry. He told me he had given up on the West: nobody cared about the plight of the Tamils, why should he waste his time talking to me. So what if I was the first journalist to come to the Vanni in six years? Western television cameras went to famines in Africa every year. They sent back pictures from Kosovo of Serbian killings. What about here?

When he calmed down, he served me sweet tea and we talked about his parishioners. He said people were tired of the war, mostly, but that it had its own dynamic.

'People tell me they feel they have suffered so much, it is not worth ending the war to return to the same situation,' he said. 'They have lost their homes, their land, their sons and daughters. The only way to end the war is for the Tamils to have their self-determination.' The government siege had turned people to the Tamil Tigers. 'I know you in the West say they are terrorists,' he said. 'Here, they are the only people that have protected us Tamils from being chopped up.'

Weeks after my operation, a letter arrived wrapped in brown paper. It had been smuggled out somehow by Father Xavier – no doubt at great risk, there being in the Vanni no electricity, few cars, much less any postal service.

'I was sorry to hear of your injuries,' he wrote. 'You are remembered here as a brave and honest person.' It meant a lot to me.

A surprising amount of mail arrived from Sri Lanka during my weeks of recuperation. Messages from Tamils were mostly sympathetic. None was under the impression that I supported their cause, but they sent heart-rending appreciations for providing the first report on their homeland in years.

The Sinhalese majority was divided. A man wrote from Colombo: 'I am not a Tamil, but if there were more journalists reporting the truth as you did, this war would be over in 24 hours.'

Others were less kind. One of the more printable Sinhalese critics – a woman claiming to be a doctor – wrote: 'If you sleep with dogs, you wake up with bugs.'

So, was I stupid? Stupid I would feel writing a column about the dinner party I went to last night. Equally, I'd rather be in that middle ground between a desk job and getting shot, no offence to desk jobs.

You can only describe what I do as 'stupid' if you agree wars shouldn't be covered by journalists, or think they should be reported by way of government press conferences. If journalists are to report on what really happens in war, on the atrocities and pain and death, they are going to face risks.

For my part, the next war I cover, I'll be more awed than ever by the quiet bravery of civilians who endure far more than I ever will. They must stay where they are; I can come home to London.

Bravery is not being afraid to be afraid

21 October 2001

Marie Colvin, Woman of the Year, defined in her acceptance speech the complex nature of courage.

Receiving the Woman of the Year award is a great honour – not least because I got to meet Ellen MacArthur, who's done the only thing I ever really wanted to do – sail round the world. And also Pam Warren, whose experience embodies the concept of the award: bravery.

This is a tough time to be a war correspondent (let alone a grounded one, as I am, for medical reasons). The need for front-line, objective reporting has never been clearer. We are engaged in a war that will affect us all, yet know almost nothing about events on one side.

Marie reporting from the mountains of Chechnya, 1999.
Photograph by Dmitry Beliakov.

There are no western journalists in Taliban-held Afghanistan.

Equally, the risks of going and getting that information has been made clear by the experience of Yvonne Ridley, who could have paid with her life. What level of risk should we take? What is bravery, and what is bravado?

I, too, almost didn't make it. In April I was hit by shrapnel from a grenade fired by the Sri Lankan army. I had gone to the northern Tamil area to report on the plight of 500,000 people under government siege. There was no medicine, little food, an unreported war that had left 340,000 of them refugees. The government had not allowed journalists into the area for six years. I entered illegally, and lost the sight of my eye. Worth the risk? Brutal question – one I've thought about a lot. I did think so at the time, and have to say I do now.

Simply: there's no way to cover war properly without risk. Covering a war means going into places torn by chaos, destruction, death and pain, and trying to bear witness to that. Not so much as to what kind of toys are being used – I've never been able to figure out if that is a MiG or a Tornado shooting at me, or 105mm or 155mm artillery. I care about the experience of those most directly affected by war, those asked to fight and those who are just trying to survive.

Despite all the videos you see on television from Pentagon or Nato briefings, what's on the ground has remained remarkably the same for the past 100 years. Craters. Burnt houses. Women weeping for sons and daughters. Suffering. In my profession, there is no chance of unemployment.

There is no easy way to cover a war. In Chechnya, the war could not be reported from the Russian side, so I travelled into Chechnya from Georgia to report on the indiscriminate bombing of civilians. I stayed with Muslim fighters in the mountains: as I walked in to their base, little more than a one-room hut with a 20-foot bed for everyone, the commander put his devout Muslim fighters at ease by saying: 'There is no woman here, only a journalist.'

I went from village to village. I remember an old man, lying in a basement, his skull cracked and brains leaking out and somehow he was still breathing. His wife sat next to him holding his hand. She knew he would die: there were no doctors, no medicine, the Russian planes would come again soon, but she wanted to be there to his last breath. That's bravery.

One of the rules I have in covering war is: don't be afraid to be afraid – perhaps more important for a woman because you are often with men trying to prove they're macho and watching you for signs of cowardice. In Chechnya, I was pinned down in a snowy field as Russian planes came back, over and over, bombing the field. After hours of this, a Chechen fighter lit a fire, saying with great bravado that impressed his fellow rebels: 'It is better to die warm than to live cold.' I said: 'Put the fire out, you idiot.' They all thought me a coward. I thought I'd rather survive.

My strongest memory of East Timor is walking through the besieged United Nations compound and being stared at, with fear, by all the women and children who were camping on the ground under palm trees. They knew that, if I stayed, they had a chance to live. If I left, they would die. I was a kind of human shield.

The compound was besieged by militiamen wielding machetes and guns, and likely to be overrun at any moment. The UN decided to evacuate, leaving 1,500 women and children behind. Except for two Dutchwomen, my journalist colleagues made the decision to get out on the last flight. I decided to stay – and had the most irritating conversation with my foreign editor. 'What do you mean everyone's left and you're staying?' he asked.

'Don't know. I'm staying.'

'Well, why have all the men left?'

In exasperation, I said: 'I guess they don't make men like they used to.' To his great credit, and my embarrassment, he printed that comment in the paper. It's been tough getting dates ever since.

I stayed, and reported to anyone I could over my satellite phone – CNN, BBC, Australian television – that the UN evacuation was a death sentence for these women and children. Women barred from entering the compound threw their babies over the walls, into barbed wire, to save them from the militia. Three days later, the UN reversed its decision and evacuated all 1,500 women and children. That risk was certainly worth it.

The war in Afghanistan worries me. Let me make clear, I am not from the 'yes, but' brigade. I despise what Osama Bin Laden stands for. I despise the ways of the Taliban. But this war is being fought in our names, and it is our business. Explaining something, trying to help people to understand it, does not mean support. I wish there was reporting from both sides – at the least, it keeps governments and generals honest. In the words of Martha Gellhorn, one of the bravest war correspondents of her generation: 'Never believe governments, not any of them, not a word they say; keep an untrusting eye on all they do.'

I worry when I hear phrases from the Pentagon that American missiles destroyed the 'command and control centre' at Kandahar airport. I was there – there's a mud building and a guy with a phone that can take only incoming calls.

Going to these places, finding out what is happening, is the only way to get at the truth. It is not perfect, it is a rough draft of history. But historians can come later. You see such huge injustices happening and, as a reporter, you have the chance to tell people about that.

To me, bravery is not something gigantic and definitive. I don't go into a war thinking I have to prove myself brave: that would be about me and that would be bravado. Bravery is secondary. When you are covering a war, you have to be 'brave' over and over again because it means going to places where you could be killed, and where people are being killed, and putting one foot in front of the other – however afraid you are.

The point is to try to report as truthfully as you know how, about what you see and make that part of the record. You can't get that information in a war without going to a place where people are being shot and they are shooting at you. The real difficulty is having enough faith in humanity to believe that someone will care.

Middle East

A bitter taste for vengeance

RAMALLAH

7 April 2002

Marie Colvin, Uzi Mahnaimi, Tel Aviv; Tony Allen-Mills, Washington; Peter Conradi and Tom Walker, London

Behind its campaign to crush militant Palestinian factions, Israel has embarked upon a brutal conflict that has escalated into all-out war. As the death toll mounts, Marie Colvin reports from Ramallah on the human impact of the political posturing.

Soraida Abu Gharbieh probably died because she believed that Israeli soldiers would not shoot civilians. She was born in America and had idealistic views. But as her husband drove her around the corner to her father's house, she was shot in the head and killed. When he pried their 10-month-old son from her arms, the baby was chuckling. He thought it was a game.

Last week Soraida was buried in a mass grave in the car park of Ramallah hospital. The city was under curfew, her family could not retrieve her body and the mortuary was overflowing with the dead. Soraida's husband remembers the last word that she spoke – his name, Murad – as she keeled forward, her body around the chubby boy in her lap.

The family's crime was to be frightened. When Israeli tanks began shelling buildings on the first night of the incursion nine days ago, Soraida thought they should go to her father's house because it was larger and lower down the hill.

'We were sleeping when we heard the explosions,' Murad said. 'The drive to my father-in-law's is only 200 metres. The soldiers began shooting at the car and I stopped. They were five metres away. Then came a rain of bullets.'

Murad was hit in the shoulder and neck; he remembers the soldiers walked up to the car, looked in and laughed.

He struggled out, carrying tiny Muhsin, then fell and began screaming for help. Neighbours who tried to reach him were raked with gunfire. Farhan Saleh, his father-in-law, finally dragged him into the house. They found Soraida the next day, slumped in the front seat.

The silver Renault Clio is still there, its windows shattered by bullets, dried blood staining the steering wheel and her seat. 'She was the smartest of my children,' said Saleh, who brought his family back to Ramallah after 24 years in America because he was afraid of the crime and drugs in Washington DC. 'And she thought her baby was the smartest, best baby in the whole world.'

The Abu Gharbieh family was not alone in mourning last week. By Friday night 27 people had been killed in the city. Buried in the car park next to Soraida was Wadeed Safran, a grandmother in her fifties.

She had been shot dead by an Israeli sniper as she walked from Ramallah hospital on her cane. She had broken the curfew because the cast on her leg had become too painful to bear. 'She was nothing, nothing, no danger to the Israelis,' said Dr Ahmed Haleem.

Across the West Bank there were similar stories of heartbreak and despair as Israeli forces rolled into all the cities they had withdrawn from in the mid 1990s – Ramallah, Qalqilya, Jenin, Bethlehem, Nablus and finally Hebron.

In Bethlehem, the siege of the Church of the Nativity entered its fifth day yesterday as an estimated 200 Palestinian fighters continued to seek refuge in the ancient building. The stand-off began on Tuesday as Israeli soldiers chased local militiamen into Manger Square. By Tuesday afternoon, panicked and exhausted, the Palestinians shot the lock off a door of the church and in so doing dragged the Arab–Israeli fighting into one of the most sacred shrines of Christianity, the birthplace of Christ.

The cloister was quickly surrounded by Israeli tanks and snipers, ensnaring not only the resistance fighters but also the monks and nuns of the three religious orders who live and work inside the compound.

The religious community suffered its first victim at dawn on Thursday when Samir Salman, a Palestinian Christian, walked into the open from his nearby house to ring the church bells, as he had done for 30 years. He was shot dead and his body was left where he fell, in the middle of Manger Square.

More violence followed when the Israeli artillery reportedly struck a metal gate to the rear of the basilica. Convinced that an Israeli offensive was imminent, a few Palestinian militiamen tried to break out of the basilica but a heavy gun battle ensued, sending a clear message to those remaining inside that there would be no escape, only surrender.

The Pope sent a fax appealing for those trapped inside to trust in prayer. Israel pledged not to storm the church, but those inside were still not safe. Yesterday morning Father Ibrahim Faltas, the church's Franciscan superior, was shot at as he tried to open a window. Food ran low. 'We haven't got much left,' said Sister Lisetta Vingi, 69, a Roman Catholic nun. 'We try to give a piece of bread to everyone. But we won't be able to hold out much longer.'

Elsewhere across the region the casualties mounted as Israel continued its occupation of every West Bank city except Jericho. In Jenin, tanks and armoured personnel carriers tried to enter the narrow alleys of the refugee camp on Friday night, protected by Apache helicopters. A local journalist filming the incursion was shot dead; residents said ambulances were prevented from entering the area so nobody knew how many were killed or wounded. Other reports said that the town's Al-Razi hospital was hit by gunfire and vital supplies of water and oxygen had been damaged.

If the Israeli offensive was designed to wear down the will and capability of local fighters, then it has had little success so far. In the face of mounting opposition, Palestinians have learnt new tactics of resistance. When Israeli soldiers tried to enter the house of a wanted man in Jenin, Islamic militants lying in wait exploded a bomb in the house. Wounded Israeli soldiers were ferried out by helicopter. Residents of the nearby refugee camps are also said to have been equipped with explosive belts and hand grenades, with one Palestinian woman blowing herself up yesterday when Israeli troops approached her door.

In Nablus, an Israeli tank appeared to have been targeted by a home-made bomb, while fierce street fighting led to the death of at least a dozen militants as support for the fighters mounted.

In the words of one resident: 'I am 32, but I'm more radical than Arafat. My nephew is 15 and more radical than me. We are all with the resistance now. What choice do we have?'

Another Palestinian fighter said that many had been inspired by Arafat's telephone interviews from his besieged compound in Ramallah. 'We have seen that Abu Amar [the familiar name that Palestinians use for Arafat] is standing steadfast. We are standing steadfast for this reason. We don't need orders.'

He added that the divided militia factions had now combined – gunmen from Fatah, Hamas and Islamic Jihad (see below) were fighting side by side.

Whether he intended it or not, the military operation launched by Ariel Sharon, the Israeli prime minister, has progressed from an incursion into all-out war.

Demonstrators poured into the streets of Arab capitals. Thousands protested in Jordan and Egypt, the two countries that have ties with Israel.

'Sharon's actions are threatening the whole region,' said Marwan Muasher, the Jordanian foreign minister, who headed for Washington with a letter of appeal for President George W Bush from King Abdullah. Even Israelis, largely supportive of Sharon's operation, began to wonder if he had an exit strategy.

By Thursday the Americans had begun to rethink their hands-off approach. A week after the tanks had rolled into Ramallah,

Bush announced that he was sending Colin Powell, his secretary of state, to the Middle East.

Bush criticised Arafat, saying the desperate situation that the Palestinian leader found himself in 'was of his own creation', but for the first time he demanded that the Israelis make political concessions, anathema to Sharon, who has insisted that there must be a ceasefire before any peace negotiations can resume.

The Israeli leader has refused to listen to western diplomats, who believe no ceasefire can be brokered unless Arafat can offer his people political gains.

Arafat, despite the criticism, was heartened by the Bush speech. 'He told me that he understood Bush is under heavy pressure,' said a senior adviser trapped in the compound. 'Contrary to news reports, Arafat thought the Bush speech was very positive.'

He said Arafat had focused on the concrete issues in the speech: Bush's request for the Israelis to withdraw from the West Bank cities, stop the expansion of Jewish settlements in the occupied Palestinian territories and seek a solution that would see the creation of a Palestinian state alongside Israel.

Bush repeated his demands yesterday, calling on Israel to 'withdraw without delay' from Palestinian territory. Sharon responded by saying Israel was aware of the Americans' wish for a quick end to the military offensive. In a statement, his office said: 'Israel will make every effort to accelerate Operation Defensive Wall.'

Israel has shown little inclination to bow to American pressure. On Friday Israeli soldiers fired on journalists who were trying to report on the arrival of General Anthony Zinni, the American envoy, in Ramallah. Sharon also refused to allow Zinni to meet a delegation of senior Palestinians, appointed to follow up his meeting with Arafat. Palestinians feared that Powell's predicted arrival towards the end of this week would be too late, with the Israelis stepping up their action before the diplomatic mission arrives. A repeated call by Powell yesterday that Israel should begin an immediate withdrawal appeared to have fallen on deaf ears.

'The partial pullback will not take place this week,' said one Israeli military source. 'We are not driving a speedboat that can be easily diverted. We are like a big ship which takes some time to turn around.'

Others suspect more sinister motives. Along with destroying the 'infrastructure of terror', Sharon's army has been busy systematically dismantling the Palestinian Authority civilian infrastructure built up since the mid-1990s. Such a wholesale operation will take time. Shaul Mofaz, the Israeli chief of staff, said last week that his army needed 'four full weeks to complete the operation, and four more weeks to establish security'.

Late on Tuesday, tanks and helicopters began shelling the headquarters of the Preventive Security Force, the Palestinian MI5, on the edge of the industrial zone. If the aim of the Israelis was to catch terrorists, it was a bizarre choice of targets. The PSF, armed and trained by the US Central Intelligence Agency, was the only force carrying out the Israeli demands and arresting known militants, often to the anger of the local population.

Other Israeli attacks in Ramallah struck directly at government buildings. During a brief curfew on Friday, Naim Abu Hummus, the Palestinian education minister, visited the shattered remains of his former headquarters.

Israeli soldiers had gone from room to room destroying as they went. 'At each room, they threw me in first,' said the caretaker. 'I was their human shield, even though I told them there is nobody here.'

Smashed computers and ceiling tiles littered the floors alongside trampled pages of high school results. The ministry safe hung open, scorched by blast marks. The ministry accountant said 40,000 shekels (£5,800) was missing.

'I am sick,' Abu Hummus said. 'Our education ministry is sacred to us. If they want to search, I understand. But this is not the way to search. What can I tell our future generation about peace when they see this?'

Across a square, the building of the Palestinian Legislative Council was a similar scene of destruction. Both departments had been set up with millions of dollars from Europe, Japan and the World Bank. By the time the troops withdraw there may well be no government left to run the West Bank.

Sharon's plan may be to weaken or remove Arafat and return to the situation a decade ago when an Israeli military administration ran the occupied territories. No Palestinian, however critical of Arafat, thought this could succeed, but now many are wondering whether Sharon may have gone too far down the line to stop.

Even as the heavy fighting subsided, Palestinian families were struggling to come to terms with what had befallen them.

Near the Greek Orthodox church in central Ramallah, the Ziadi family was yesterday still holding a vigil for Majd, their 19-year-old son, taken by Israeli soldiers on Tuesday night with his father and the other men of the building, rounded up as house-to-house searches continued.

'The soldiers came and started shouting, "You are Hamas, you are Hamas"', recalled a neighbour. 'We told them, "No, we are Christian", but they would not listen.'

Mohamed Ziadi, Majd's father, was also taken but later released. Forty-eight years old and bespectacled, he was still in shock yesterday. The Israelis forced everyone from their building, then separated the men from the women and children. All the men were made to walk to the Israeli headquarters, their hands on their heads, in front of a tank that herded them through the streets.

When they were blindfolded and taken by bus to a nearby settlement for questioning, the soldiers' behaviour turned sadistic. 'One soldier called a friend in Tel Aviv on his mobile phone and said: "Listen to this."

'He held out the phone and began to beat one of us. The man screamed in pain. Then the soldier came back to his mobile phone and asked his friend, "Did you hear that?" He was laughing.'

Ziadi was kicked in the stomach and beaten. After questioning, he was released and walked three miles back to his house in the rain. Majd is still missing.

The family insists he is no militant; his room, now littered with the clothes and debris of smashed wardrobes from the Israeli search, seems to bear this out. There are no pictures of the martyrs that normally adorn the walls of militants.

As Powell prepares for his tour of surrounding Arab countries, rallying support to drive a peace plan forward, such tales of Israeli brutality will do little to aid America's cause. Well-meaning missions and verbal posturing do not count for much in a region where the common language is violence.

As one normally moderate Israeli put it last week: 'We gave these guys all the chances in the world to live in peace with us. They rejected every possible proposal, one after another, and started a war against us. They asked for a war and they got a war, so they should not complain now.' It is one of the many tragedies of the past fortnight that such views are no longer the exception.

THE PALESTINIAN MILITANTS

HAMAS

Founded in 1987 during the early days of the first Palestinian uprising, this Islamic resistance movement was centred on the mosques of Gaza, where funding from Saudi Arabia enabled it to provide welfare services for the local population. It later gave rise to a more militant faction whose long-term goal is the destruction of Israel and the creation of an Islamic state. It was a Hamas attack on a hotel in Netanya two weeks ago that prompted the recent incursions, but the group now enjoys even greater popularity among the Palestinian population than Arafat's own party.

PALESTINIAN ISLAMIC JIHAD

Although sharing much of the ideology of Hamas, Islamic Jihad is even more militant in its aims, pressing for the immediate over-throw of Israel. Following the assassination of the group's former leader, Dr Fathi Shikaki, by Mossad agents in 1995, it experienced a brief decline but the second intifada has given it fresh impetus and attacks have been stepped up with funding from Iran. Although its hardline approach is only supported by a minority of Palestinians centred on Gaza, its small size and independence make it a difficult group for Arafat to control.

HEZBOLLAH

A fundamentalist Shi'ite organisation that was established in 1982 in response to the Israeli invasion of Lebanon. Although primarily concentrating on military targets across the Israeli border, it carried out the bombing of the Israeli embassy in Buenos Aires in 1992, causing hundreds of casualties and it is also said to have helped arm Palestinians by smuggling weapons through Jordan. Although attacks were scaled down following the withdrawal of Israeli troops from Lebanon two years ago, cross-border fighting increased in the past week, fuelling concerns that Hezbollah is preparing for a wider war in the Middle East with backing from Iran.

AL-AQSA MARTYRS BRIGADES

A new group directly linked to Yasser Arafat's Fatah movement through its Tanzim military wing, the brigades are behind the majority of recent shootings and suicide attacks against Israelis. Well-equipped and ruthless in its tactics, its aims are purely secular, hoping to pressure Israel into greater concessions over the creation of a Palestinian state. Tanzim's leader, Marwan Baghouti, tops Sharon's most wanted list.

PFLP

The Popular Front for the Liberation of Palestine was once the prime organisation linked to hijackings and terror attacks against Jewish targets around the world, but its secular Marxist ideals led to dwindling support during recent uprisings. However, it was

responsible for the assassination of the Israeli tourist minister last
October, after its own leader was killed by an Israeli missile attack
on Ramallah. Its followers have recently carried out a number of
suicide bombings.

Jenin: the bloody truth

21 April 2002

**Was it a massacre? Marie Colvin in the ruins of the refugee camp found
cold comfort for propagandists on either side.**

The first medical teams allowed into the Jenin refugee camp last
week followed the chickens. Human senses were overwhelmed by
the devastation and the stench of death, but the birds were not
distracted. They were hungry. Two rusty-coloured fowl pecking
away at a bundle in the street drew a Red Cross team to the remains
of Jamal Sabagh.

He wasn't really recognisable to an untrained eye. His body had
been lying there for more than a week. The Israeli army had banned
ambulances from the camp for 11 days, and neighbours were too
terrified to go to him.

Tank tracks led to his body, over it and onwards through the
mud. What had once been a young man was rotting flesh mingled
with shredded clothing, mashed into the earth. One foot was all
that looked human.

Sabagh was no fighter, his brother and friends say. He was 28
and a father of three. His wife and children had fled on the first day
of the Israeli invasion, Wednesday 3 April, but he stayed because
he was diabetic and was too ill to run away. He was also afraid he
would be mistaken for a fighter.

Two days later, he left his house when the Israelis yelled over
megaphones that they were going to blow it up. He walked, directed

by soldiers in armoured personnel carriers, with other men to Seha Street at the centre of the camp, carrying his bag of medicines. He joined the crowd. Soldiers yelled at him to take off his shirt, then his trousers. He clung to his bag of medicine as he tried to unbuckle his belt, and he was slow. The soldiers shot him, friends say.

Medical workers shooed away the chickens, wrapped Sabagh's remains in a rug, then lifted them into the back of a small open-bed truck. It drove off, past burned and shell-holed buildings, looking like a medieval plague wagon.

Across the narrow street was a forlorn pile of men's jeans, polyester tracksuit tops and cheap shoes – left by those who had got their clothes off in time, to prove they had no bombs strapped to their bodies, and had been taken to the Israeli army base at the nearby village of Salem.

As the rescue teams spread out over Jenin camp last week, after the Israeli army claimed victory in its battle against several hundred armed Palestinian radicals, it was clear something cataclysmic had occurred.

Instead of the Hawamish neighbourhood – previously a jumble of mismatched cinderblock homes – a vista lay open to the hills beyond.

Stunned and dusty in this new world, returning Palestinians wandered around a moonscape the size of two football pitches. It was littered with the detritus of human life – blankets, a little girl's tartan skirt, a child's orange boxing glove, shoes, a musical keyboard. Women in hijab headscarves dug at the crushed rubble with buckets and bare hands. Five-year-old Ahmed Hindi cried: 'I want to go home.' He didn't know he was standing on it.

Images of this man-made earthquake zone have flashed around the world as evidence that the Israeli prime minister, Ariel Sharon, is responsible for another war crime in Jenin on a par with the massacre of Palestinians in the Chatila and Sabra refugee camps in Beirut 20 years ago.

Israel has responded that the devastation was the consequence of a pitched battle against entrenched terrorists.

What really happened? Tragedy doesn't necessarily breed truth. The propaganda war had begun before the white dust settled over Jenin.

Rafi Laderman, a personable Israeli reserve major, emerged from the battlefield and made the rounds of the media in his rumpled green uniform. His clear plastic spectacles signalled his real job as a marketing consultant.

Laderman insisted that all the buildings in the refugee camp had been destroyed by explosive booby traps set by the terrorists, or levelled by Israeli bulldozers because they 'presented additional engineering difficulties' that could endanger civilians. He himself had stopped the fighting to lead Palestinian civilians to safety.

All that seemed disingenuous. Equally unlikely were Palestinian claims that the Israelis had killed 500 Palestinians in cold blood, most civilians, and buried them in mass graves under the rubble after running them over with tanks. Israel said about 70 had been killed.

Terje Roed-Larsen, the United Nations envoy to the Middle East, cut through the propaganda by stating the obvious: 'No military operation can justify this scale of destruction. Whatever the purpose was, the effect is collective punishment of a whole society.'

He and his family received telephone death threats from Israeli callers for his pains.

Under pressure from many sides – including the United States, Britain, the United Nations and the European Union – Israel has agreed to a UN fact-finding mission. The trouble with such missions, however, is that they become bogged down by obfuscation while evidence goes cold.

To get an objective idea of what happened in Jenin requires an almost forensic investigation, weeding out lies and half-truths and the rumours that a stunned and terrified population has come to believe are true. By doing so, I have come to conclusions that are unlikely to satisfy the propagandists of either side.

Jenin was bound to be a prime target for the Israeli military backlash after a Palestinian suicide bomber killed 28 Israelis as they sat down to dinner in Netanya on Passover eve three weeks ago.

There has been a refugee camp in Jenin since the foundation of Israel in 1948 when Palestinians fled there from the Haifa area. The first residents worried only for their next rations and fretted impotently as their rich orange groves in Haifa were rebranded Jaffa oranges by Israel and exported around the world.

Since then, Jenin has become a stronghold of radical Palestinian nationalism with a population of 11,000 refugees. The Israeli defence force (IDF) believes half the suicide bombers who have struck Israel in the past year were trained in the Jenin refugee camp.

When the Israelis invaded Ramallah on 29 March, in retaliation for the suicide bombings, radicals in Jenin knew they would be next. Sources there said local leaders of Hamas, Islamic Jihad and Fatah, including its militant Tanzim and Al-Aqsa Martyrs Brigades offshoots, organised small fighting cells that included members from each group.

At 2am on Wednesday 3 April, five days after the invasion of Ramallah, Merkava tanks and armoured personnel carriers rumbled through Jenin and headed for the refugee camp on the edge of the city.

The Namal brigade and commandos entered from the west; the Golani brigade from the south; and the Fifth Brigade, a unit of reserve troops called up from their day jobs, went in under the command of Laderman.

The odds were far from equal. The Israelis had tanks, armoured personnel carriers and rocket-firing helicopter gunships. Its soldiers were in full battle gear with bulletproof vests, helmets and M-16s. Against them was a guerrilla force of several hundred men armed with Kalashnikovs and home-made bombs called *kuwa* – Arabic for elbow – manufactured from pieces of plumbing.

The two sides faced each other in a camp about 2½ miles long by ½ mile wide. In this tiny battlefield the radicals not only resisted the might of the Israeli army longer than the combined Arab armies did in the 1967 six-day war, but turned themselves and their militant cause into the stuff of instant Palestinian legend.

'The fighting was the fiercest urban house-to-house fighting Israel has seen in 30 years,' said Laderman.

The narrow dirt alleys provided perfect ambush hides for Palestinians who grew up in this maze. The Israelis tried to keep off the streets, progressing from house to house by breaking through the walls with explosives and hammers.

On the first night of the invasion, Israeli soldiers blew out the yellow metal door of Ismael Khatib's home in the Hawamish district and hauled him out to act as a human shield as they knocked on his neighbours' doors.

As they did so, two gunmen across the alley opened fire. Hugging Khatib in front of him with his left arm, an Israeli soldier balanced his M-16 on Khatib's right shoulder and fired back wildly.

Kuwa bombs were hurled by Palestinians. Khatib threw himself on the ground and crawled away, only to circle around and climb in his back window. 'I felt like I died and came alive again,' he says.

The next day another Israeli patrol crashed through the wall into his living room. They stayed, keeping him, his wife and children hostage in a room.

A far more serious ambush sealed the Hawamish area's fate. By Monday 8 April, most of the surviving gunmen had been forced into this neighbourhood. Early next day, 16 reservists of the Fifth Brigade moved into an alley in Hawamish, searching for a house to use as a lookout post. Their leader, Major Oded Golomb, set charges to blow the door.

As he did so, a Palestinian bomb exploded and gunmen began firing from the opposite roof. Thirteen Israelis were killed.

Israel's retribution was swift. Armoured bulldozers, two-storey behemoths as impregnable as a tank, began knocking down houses in Hawamish. Hurriya Kreini was in her home with her family when an Israeli bulldozer began destroying the house without warning. She and her husband managed to push their children out of a window before the house tumbled down.

By Thursday 11 April, Hawamish had disappeared. That was the day the Israeli operation officially ended, but hours after the Israelis announced that the last 35 fighters had surrendered (they ran out of ammunition) I stood in a village called Borqin looking down into the camp. The sound of heavy machinegun fire still rose from the valley. Helicopter gunships shot bursts of heavy-calibre bullets. Explosions sounded and white puffs rose above the camp.

The Israelis let in the outside world slowly and grudgingly. The camp was finally opened to international aid agencies on 14 April, but journalists were barred. Until only two days ago, Israeli soldiers shot at journalists they spotted trying to slip through the olive groves that slope up from the camp, or along a back dirt road.

The obstruction fuelled speculation that the Israelis were trying to hide something. There were mass graves, some said; bodies had been hauled off in refrigerated trucks; others swore hundreds of bodies were under the bulldozed homes.

Israelis bridled. 'Our mission was to penetrate into Jenin area and dismantle the terrorist infrastructure and we did that,' insisted the ubiquitous Laderman. 'I have a five-year-old daughter and now I feel I can let her out in the playground.'

I eventually gained access last Tuesday, walking in with as open a mind as I could muster.

Late in the day, when all was quiet, I was walking past the Jenin hospital. Nearby, women and children were slowly making their way back to temporary lodgings after a day trying to find their homes and relatives. An armoured personnel carrier pulled up at the end of the street behind us. The Palestinians took no notice – until the soldier in the turret opened fire straight down the street with his machinegun.

I dived for shelter. Children cried in terror. The soldier initially fired over our heads, but now bullets flashed by at chest height. The screams turned to moans as the APC headed towards us down the street.

It rolled into sight, stopped the gunfire and swivelled the huge barrel to point directly at us. Then the soldier waved his hand in anger, yelling: 'Go, go.' I think he just wanted everyone off the streets.

If I was now convinced by claims Israelis opened fire indiscriminately on civilians, weighing up the truth of other allegations would be much more difficult. Even what can seem obvious is not necessarily true.

From a house hit by a missile in the centre of what the Palestinians now call their own Ground Zero, rescue workers pulled human remains that people said were of a small child. They lay on a rug and seemed indeed very small to the eye. But when I found a doctor, he was dubious.

'This person has been reduced; I think in a fire,' the doctor said. 'See that bone?' He poked around and found a large thigh bone. Not a child.

When I tracked down the owner of the house, he said that four fighters had been holed up in his house firing on the Israelis when a missile hit it.

Scores of interviews in the camp did show consistency, however. Story after story – from people who had not yet met one another since they fled – indicated the Israelis had used Palestinians as human shields and had taken families hostage to protect their makeshift posts set up in their houses.

In a house overlooking Hawamish, the Sabagh family were sweeping out after having Israeli soldiers there for eight days. Trying to scrub off Hebrew slogans, Jamili Sabagh, 52, said the family were held in a tiny room upstairs.

'They gave us no food, no water. The room they put us in was too small for 13 people. They fed our dog to torment us, and not the children,' she said. 'Our home was a garbage heap when they left.'

It is one of the few on the block untouched by missile strikes, a sign that it was indeed used as a post by the Israelis.

Ismahan Stati is a pretty, shy university student. Israeli soldiers came to her house on the third day and blew open the door, she said.

'They took me as a hostage,' she said. 'They were afraid.'

They knocked on a nearby house, and when nobody answered they blew open the door with a grenade fired from a gun. In fact, Afaf Dusuqi, 52, had been slow coming to the door and was killed instantly by the shrapnel.

Afaf's mother held her body, covered in blood, and screamed for an ambulance but the soldiers fired into the house to drive her back. 'I was shaking with fear,' Stati recalled.

Outside the Dusuqi house, there is still blood on the concrete stoop, and there is a 6in hole in the yellow door where the lock used to be.

Afaf's body stayed in the house for five days until the family could smuggle it to the cemetery for burial in a hurried mass grave. I found her name scrawled on a stone where she will lie until her family can give her a proper burial. Doctors at the Razi hospital have her death certificate.

There is a bizarre twist to this story. A rumour began that Stati was a suicide bomber. The story started, her family believes, when a neighbour saw her standing in the group of soldiers, heard an explosion and ducked, then looked again to see the body of a woman.

The rumour is still around the camp, illustrating why every fact must be tracked down here.

Stories of cold-blooded executions were told to me in detail but could not be substantiated. A woman said she saw 'with my own eyes' the execution of eight Hamas members and a 16-year-old boy who was the son of one of the men but had nothing to do with politics.

It sounded difficult to believe of the IDF, but she had a name. In the end, I found the true story; an awful tale, but not a cold-blooded assassination.

Fathi Chalabi, a bird-like elderly man, showed me where the Israelis had blown a hole in his door to enter his home at night. About 30 soldiers had forced their way in and separated out Chalabi, his son Wada'a, 32, and another man, Abed Sa'adi, 27, in the courtyard.

'They told us to face the wall and take off our shirts,' Chalabi said. 'They were looking for suicide bombers. But we were not. My son was the caretaker at school. He was one month from getting his university degree.'

It was dark, and as Wada'a picked up his shirt, the Israelis spotted an elastic bandage he wore for back pain. Someone shouted in Hebrew.

Chalabi remembers the officer's name was Gabi. They opened fire, hitting the two younger men, who fell on Chalabi.

The last he remembers is some kind of argument between the soldiers. Then they shone lights on the bodies and he played dead. 'I was covered in Wada'a's blood,' he said. The Israelis left up the alleyway. Dark dried bloodstains still marked the concrete when Chalabi spoke to me.

Equally callous was the shooting of Omar Nayel, a shop owner. 'I was in my house looking out, trying to see what was happening,' said Fathi Abu Aita, a neighbour. 'I saw him walk across his courtyard, I think going to the loo.' Two shots rang out and he fell. Nayel's body lay in the garden for days.

My conclusion after interviewing scores of refugees is that there is no evidence Israeli troops entered the camp aiming to 'massacre' Palestinian civilians. But in many cases they shot first and did not take much care to find out if the target was a civilian or not.

Under the fourth Geneva convention, they are required to protect the civilian population, and wilful killing of a civilian is a potential war crime.

I am also certain that numerous Palestinians were held hostage in their homes while Israeli troops used the building as a base or a firing post, and that others were taken door to door as a human shield, sometimes thrown into rooms ahead of Israeli troops.

Both are violations of international law, which protects civilians in wartime.

As for the bulldozing of the Hawamish area, this seems to have been out of a combination of fear and revenge rather than premeditated.

I asked Laderman how he felt now. He said he was satisfied that the 'nest of snakes' has been snuffed out. As for the new generation of suicide bombers the military operation has probably created, he said: 'They would have become suicide terrorists anyway.'

Two terrible deaths tell story of the Palestinian predicament: last assignment for a local hero

21 July 2002

A young Palestinian man was killed last week in Jenin. Few noticed: he was not that different from ambitious young men anywhere in the world. He wrote, took photographs and ran his own newsletter about the heritage of his city until the mayor closed it down.

His name was Imad Abu Zahra and his greatest challenge was trying to be a journalist in the West Bank under Israeli occupation.

The Committee to Protect Journalists (CPJ), based in New York, has this year listed the West Bank and Gaza as the world's most dangerous places for reporters to work because of Israeli gunfire – all the more so for Palestinian journalists, who lack even the nebulous protection of an international organisation.

On a hot and sunny day last week a gunner on an Israeli tank shot Imad in the leg as he photographed an armoured vehicle that had run into an electricity pole in the central square of Jenin.

According to the Red Crescent charity in Jenin, he bled to death because Israeli soldiers halted the ambulance that was trying to reach him. The Israeli Defence Force (IDF) disputes the account.

Whatever the facts, they do not begin to convey the loss. Imad was my translator earlier this year as I tried to unravel the reality of an Israeli army attack on the Jenin refugee camp in pursuit of armed militants.

The invasion left a neighbourhood flattened by army bulldozers amid charges – unfounded, as it turned out – that there had been a massacre.

Imad – a burly single man of 34 who dressed like a public schoolboy and was self-conscious about his premature balding – was indefatigable in his desire to discover what had happened. He could not bear propaganda. If someone tried to sell him a line, he would listen politely and dismiss the tainted testimony.

He could also be infuriating. Something of a local hero for his independent reporting, he would stop and talk to everyone as we walked through the camp – a handshake here, a hug and condolences for someone in distress there, a conversation with a young man who wanted to know about his video camera. It took an unnervingly long time to get anywhere.

'I know we need to work, but I can't walk past people who have just lost everything,' Imad said.

In an interview with a father who had seen his two sons shot in front of him, Imad gently questioned him over and over again, never losing his patience when the distraught old man kept losing his train of thought. He meticulously photographed and videoed the destruction for his own purposes of documentation; nobody would buy most of his pictures.

Imad belonged to no political group. The mayor had thrown him in prison for criticising him in his newsletter; he called the Palestinian Authority a 'bunch of crooks', although he respected Yasser Arafat; most of the Islamic militants, he said, did not even know their Koran.

He was, above all, an unaffiliated Palestinian nationalist. In 1987 he had been a student leader during the first intifada (uprising), led by teenagers throwing stones. He attended two terms of Bir Zeit University, but had to stop going when the Israelis made travel between West Bank cities impossible and the university was closed for most of the time anyway.

In the new intifada that began 22 months ago, he felt his best role would be to get at the truth of what was happening.

The tragedy of his death is heightened by its senselessness. Israelis feel besieged by suicide bombers – justifiably, since 236 people have been killed in such attacks aimed at civilians. But Imad's friends say that is no excuse for opening fire on an innocent Palestinian journalist, or any other civilian.

The IDF command denies this is happening. I know there is unprovoked firing on civilians because I survived a similar situation with Imad.

We were walking out of the Jenin camp in the late afternoon, on a street filled with women and children returning to temporary shelter in the city after seeing their destroyed homes for the first time.

I heard the grinding gears of a tank pulling around the corner, and then the terrifying sound of the machinegun on its turret firing a fusillade of bullets in our direction. There was no provocation, no attack.

I had a flak jacket marked in yellow tape with foot-high letters 'TV', identifying me as a journalist – in theory in any language – as did Imad. It made no difference. The soldier who was firing was about 20 yards away with a clear line of sight.

There was very little shelter on a street lined with closed shops. We threw ourselves behind a low concrete wall as bullets streamed past at chest height. Women screamed; a little boy sobbing with fear clung to my legs. A man across the street opened the door of his house and yelled for us to run to him for refuge but there was no way of crossing.

That night I realised how brave Imad was. The tank rolled down the street to our hiding place. The turret swivelled to point directly at us. We were silent, except for the little boy, who sobbed more loudly and hid his eyes. Then the turret popped up, and a soldier yelled: 'Go, go.' The women and children huddled around us, hoping the jackets identifying us as journalists would protect them.

Dusk was closing in as I reached the flat where I would sleep. I was shaking and all I could think of was getting inside. The group of about 15 women and children who had been following begged us to walk them home across town. A burst of gunfire and the grinding movement of a tank sounded again on the next street. I could not do it.

I had been hit by a grenade a year earlier, and that day I had seemed to feel what it would be like to be struck by a bullet. Imad, however, walked on with them. He told me the next day that the journey had taken him five hours, and he had been shot at twice.

He knew he was taking too many chances. When I told him he had to be more careful, he said: 'I'm from Jenin. I'm a journalist. I have the right to walk on my streets. Don't worry …'

The IDF's account of his death is that the armoured vehicle that had run into a pole was attacked by a Palestinian mob throwing fire bombs and firing at the accompanying tank. The tank returned fire in self-defence.

The story is contradicted by eyewitnesses and by pictures taken by Sayeed Dahla, a Palestinian photographer who was with Imad and who was also shot. The photographs show the armoured vehicle marooned on an empty street. There is no mob. There is not even a person in the photograph.

'The Israelis are lying,' Sayeed says. 'Everyone had fled when the tanks came into the centre of Jenin. People were terrified. They left their shops open and their cars on the street and ran.

'Imad and I were alone on the street when the tank opened fire at us. I told him to be careful of that tank, but he just said, "This is a good photo". Then they shot us.'

Sayeed points out that both men were wearing jackets – his said 'Press', Imad's 'TV'. A boy removed Imad's jacket when he was struggling to breathe after being shot.

Btselem, an Israeli human rights group that monitors the actions of the IDF with the help of former Israeli soldiers, claims that hundreds of unlawful killings of Palestinians should be investigated. But few actually are.

Of 25 IDF investigations opened in the past 22 months, six were closed without a result; others have yet to be completed. Only three have resulted in disciplinary action.

'The army hardly ever opens investigations into cases of unlawful killing,' says Lior Yavne, Btselem's spokesman. 'The army is basically conducting a policy of impunity. Soldiers realise they can do anything they want and they will not face problems. They know nobody is monitoring their behaviour.'

Yavne points to what he regards as the important difference between now and his time in the army between 1991 and 1995. 'Before this intifada every shooting death was investigated. The commanders have now decided we are in an armed conflict short of war, but that means they don't have to open an investigation in case of death.'

Even when they do, Yavne claims, the investigators – military police – rely on the word of the soldiers who did the shooting and their unit commander.

Forty Palestinians are reported to have been killed since 20 June, when tanks rolled into West Bank cities. Btselem says that at least 20 of the dead were unarmed civilians.

The CPJ has taken up Imad's case, but is not optimistic. Sixteen journalists have been wounded by Israeli fire, two of them fatally, since September 2000. 'In none of the cases has the IDF taken responsibility,' says Ann Cooper, the CPJ's director.

'I don't think there is a deliberate policy to kill journalists, but certainly this year we did see the IDF using major force to keep journalists out of areas where they did not want that story covered – they didn't want eyewitnesses.'

The last photograph of Imad, taken by his friend Sayeed, shows him sitting in the street pressing his hand into a huge wound in his right thigh.

His trousers are soaked red, and his grey polo shirt is splattered with blood. His sunglasses hang from his neck and his eyes look way too old for his age. He is quiet, perhaps the first time I saw him not talking.

A number of organisations have called, offering help to his dependants. His family have turned them down, saying their boy would rather have had justice.

Guantanamo

Mindless torture? No, smart thinking

27 January 2002

The treatment of captives in Cuba has provoked outrage, but it is sending a powerful message: don't mess with the US. Marie Colvin reports.

It is difficult these days being essentially liberal-minded and American. As someone who has spent years covering insalubrious and ignored parts of the world, trying to illuminate the aspirations of people struggling under poverty and oppression, I have grown used to incomprehension or antagonism.

It's a lot worse this time round. To disagree with the chorus of condemnation of the American detention of 158 Al-Qaeda and Taliban prisoners at Camp X-Ray in Guantanamo Bay is to face a firing squad of criticism, insults and, maybe worse, the disappointment of people one respects. The left, in particular, has cribbed from George Bush Jr: you are with us or against us.

The anger at the American treatment of arguably the most committed terrorists in the world has united many on the left and right in Britain. Columnists wring their wordsmith hands; the Americans have 'lost the moral high ground'. Tony Blair, the prime minister, is a 'poodle' for not condemning the conditions in this tropical prison.

Nobody writing this has been there. Those from the International Red Cross and the British Foreign Office who have inspected the camp reported that the prisoners' main concern was not their harsh conditions but how to contact their families.

It is, then, Osama Bin Laden's second success, after the bombing of the World Trade Center, the Pentagon and the death of almost

3,000 people, to be responsible for this disintegration of the western consensus that we face a common enemy.

In Britain the media used to be filled with moving stories of the 76 Brits who had lost their lives in the attacks. Now, suddenly, we are told it is the Al-Qaeda fighters who deserve our sympathy. So what has changed?

The outpouring of condemnation of American action in Guantanamo Bay comes from photographs released by the Pentagon last weekend of prisoners kneeling in Day-Glo orange suits, bizarre blacked-out ski goggles, ear mufflers and blue masks. Inhumane, the commentators cried; sensory deprivation, torture.

Torture? I have seen the victims of torture. They are crippled because the soles of their feet have been beaten so badly. They have burns all over their bodies. They are missing fingernails, limbs, ears. They are traumatised because their women and children have been raped in front of them.

The prisoners pictured in Guantanamo were in a state that moved the human heart: complete vulnerability. But what was really happening? These were not young naive Pakistanis unwittingly caught up in a war. These, if you believe the Pentagon, were the 'hardest of the hard': Al-Qaeda members who had trained in suicide bombings.

If the Americans were guilty of anything, it was of not making clear the context in which the photographs were taken. Now it has emerged that the captives on view had just got off a transport plane and were waiting to be registered. Their restraints were a temporary measure.

The Americans, worried that the captives could see or hear their colleagues and plot an attack during the flight, cut off those means of communication. They manacled their hands and feet to prevent movement. In the camp, the goggles, mufflers and masks are off. They are manacled only when they are out of their cells to exercise. They spend most of their time in 8 x 6 foot cells under roofs with chain-link walls. Not comfortable, but conditions in a Texan jail are probably worse.

Why the precautions? One prisoner has already vowed to kill an American before he leaves Camp X-Ray.

Yet despite these clarifications, the images continued to provoke outrage. One British newspaper movingly described Taliban prisoners in Afghan jails being tortured under the new regime, including an elderly man who was beaten to death. It added that these abuses 'pale into insignificance before the cynical acrobatics that George W Bush's administration has gone through to strip these prisoners of their most basic rights'.

The *New Statesman* decried the fact that the Americans were 'denying them insect repellent'. This, among other charges, led the magazine to conclude that the Americans had 'dropped all pretensions to be a defender of human rights and a source of moral authority'.

Back in the White House, such protestations were initially brushed aside by Donald Rumsfeld, the defence secretary, as 'the questions, allegations and breathless reports' of people he described as 'either uninformed, misinformed or poorly informed'.

In public he stuck to his verbal guns. For all the liberal simpering, America was playing hardball. The captives were not prisoners of war, they were 'unlawful combatants'; the Geneva convention protecting prisoners' rights would apply only in so far as it suited the American investigators, eager to continue their questioning of the captives that the convention rules would prohibit.

Behind the scenes, though, resolve was wavering. In a leaked document revealed by *The Washington Times* yesterday, it has emerged that for all of Rumsfeld's macho posturing on the media podium, an internal conflict was taking place. Unnerved by the tide of opprobrium against America's treatment of the prisoners, Colin Powell, the secretary of state, has urged the president to reconsider the classification of the captives.

The request, revealed in a memo from White House counsel Alberto Gonzales to the president and forwarded to the most senior figures of his war cabinet, outlines the legal issues involved, reminding the president of Powell's original request. 'Specifically he has asked that you conclude that GPW [Geneva Convention II on the treatment of prisoners of war] does apply to both Al Qaeda and Taliban fighters,' he writes.

Such a stance pits Powell against the vast majority of Bush's national security team, shattering the carefully honed image of a united front in the war council.

Gonzales advises the president that 'the arguments for reconsideration and reversal are unpersuasive', but even so the issues will now be debated at a National Security Council meeting tomorrow. Rumsfeld is also due to visit Guantanamo shortly to witness the conditions first hand and to allay the continuing fears that whatever the circumstances of the captives themselves, the handling of the incident has been a public relations disaster for the White House.

For in Britain and the rest of Europe, the Cuban issue is not just about the 158 prisoners, it is about uneasy feelings over a resurgent America. The Bush administration has declared war on terrorism and shows every sign of following through with what will be a long fight.

The Central Intelligence Agency has been given expanded powers, including the right to assassinate a 'terrorist' on executive order. The Americans are making up the rules as they are confronted with a new world containing new threats, and that makes everyone uneasy. And it should.

Yet how to fight an organisation present in 40 countries, with sleeper cells in most of the West, that abides by none of our rules?

Knee-jerk condemnation may not be the answer, comes the response from some unlikely quarters at home and abroad.

In Britain the vast majority of the public feel little sympathy for the captives. 'The treatment of prisoners in Camp X-Ray is an issue for the liberal elite, of which I confess I am one,' said Chris Huhne, Liberal Democrat MEP. 'Most Europeans relate to the opinions in the US.'

Polls here certainly bear out Huhne's opinion. *The Mirror* has been running an emotive campaign questioning the detentions.

One front page headline read 'Stop it'. Its readers thought differently. Despite the campaign, 91% of readers thought the conditions at Guantanamo were fine. In a poll on Radio 4 last Friday of perhaps a more liberal audience, 61% of those questioned thought the same.

Interestingly, the place where there has been almost no debate is the Middle East, original home to most of the detainees. Reports in the Arab press say there are at least 10 Saudis in Camp X-Ray, yet the Saudi government has made no representations.

'The Arab governments hate these people,' said Bari Atwan, editor of the independent London-based *Al-Quds Al-Arabi*. 'They want the Americans to execute them. Most of them are charged with crimes in their home countries and if they were sent back they would be charged in one day, tried on the second in secret and executed on the third. Try to send them home, they will apply for asylum at that camp.'

There is a dark side to the silence in the Middle East, of course. 'Nobody in the Middle East will complain,' said Khairallah Khairallah, a respected Lebanese commentator based in London. 'They know their own jail cells are even smaller, with no light. What's this about too much light? Nobody wants these people. Nobody wants to admit they are the products of our society.'

Unlike the reaction in America, in the Middle East the response to the offending photograph has been so strong that some have accused the Americans of deliberately leaking it in a 'dark ops' plan to deter terrorists.

Wittingly or not, it has succeeded. 'In the Middle East, people say the picture is the other face of America,' said Khairallah. 'Nobody will stand up to America now. They know if they do they will get a "shower" from Donald Rumsfeld.'

If it was planned, it goes back to the statements of Bin Laden gloating over the weakness of America. In one interview he talked about the lesson he had learnt in Somalia, when the American forces withdrew after 18 soldiers were killed in a debacle dramatised in the new film *Black Hawk Down*.

'Our boys were shocked by the low morale of the American soldier and they realised the American soldier was just a paper tiger,' Bin Laden said.

'After a few blows, America ... rushed out of Somalia in shame and disgrace, dragging the bodies of its soldiers. America stopped calling itself world leader and master of the new world order.'

That statement has been believed across the Middle East since the failed Somalia operation: Americans quailed at the first sign of violence.

If you were a Muslim and died in a martyrdom operation you went directly to paradise and your own 70 virgins. Even if you got caught at least you got your televised day in court and a chance to broadcast your cause to the world. For such men, the images of Guantanamo have been a salutary lesson.

Americans react differently when their country is attacked. The photographs show would-be extremists that there is no glory, just Day-Glo overalls, mosquitoes and anonymity. In the war against terrorism, that is as significant as any victory on the battlefield.

Iraq

One call from the great dictator and another day of designer torture began in prison

4 August 2002

When Saddam took power he stamped out all opposition. Marie Colvin talks to a man who endured his brutality.

It was not just the torture. It was the morning telephone call. Every day the duty officer at Abu Ghreib prison in Baghdad would call for instructions on the 'programme' for the 33 men isolated in one wing. When it was Saddam Hussein on the phone, the officer would stand to attention. Beating on the back today? Yes, sir.

Four times a day, the prisoners were taken from their cells and tortured. The methods varied – whipped with cables, battered with wooden beams, barbecued alive. No questions were ever asked, no information was ever sought. This was sadism Saddam-style – systematic and with extraordinary personal involvement and attention to detail.

The prisoners had started out as a group of 54 senior military men and civilian officials in the leadership of the Iraqi regime alongside Saddam before he seized the presidency more than two decades ago. They were all men who had been close to him, all men who, his spies had told him, were strong enough to oppose his bid for control.

Twenty-one were executed within a week of their arrest, another 14 during 3½ years of imprisonment. Only 19 survived. They went home to their families as living skeletons.

One of these men, who now lives in exile in Europe, has decided to tell their horrific story for the first time in the hope that it will inspire Iraqis to fight Saddam.

This survivor, who wants to be known as Mohammed, has taken 19 years to summon the courage to give the first insider's account of the barbaric methods Saddam used to consolidate absolute power.

In Iraq in the late 1970s, Saddam was vice-president but increasingly became more powerful than Ahmed Hassan al-Bakr, the elderly head of state.

Other members of the ruling Revolutionary Command Council (RCC) whispered to each other that there was 'something fishy' about Saddam, Mohammed remembered. Those close to him and his family were being given powerful positions at home while strong military officers were being sent abroad to far-off diplomatic posts.

Saddam was not too powerful to be criticised to his face. 'In those days we could say to him, "You are wrong", and we did,' Mohammed said. 'But he was a very good actor.

'Once, when I said to him, "You are behaving like a corrupt businessman, accumulating money and palaces", Saddam invited me out to the country.

'We had a barbecue in a small house with two rooms. He was warm and generous. "See," Saddam said, "this is the reality. I am a simple man." Of course, later he built a palace on that same spot.'

On 12 July 1979, Saddam made his move. He called a secret meeting of Ba'ath officials and said there had been a coup plot against him. He also said the president wanted to resign for health reasons.

The charges were false – there had been no conspiracy – but Saddam had an extensive network of spies and security agents to build his case.

The arrests began. Most of the detainees were members of the ruling RCC. Saleh al-Saidi, a powerful colonel who had jokingly referred to Saddam as 'Al Capone', was arrested at his command centre in western Iraq. Shukri Sabri al-Hadithi, ambassador to Morocco, was arrested and his cousin Murtada, a foreign minister, was also seized.

The prisoners did not take their arrests seriously – until all 54 were taken to the offices of the Mukhabarat, the intelligence agency. They were beaten, questioned perfunctorily and taken into a hallway. 'We were put facing the wall,' said Mohammed. 'Then we were told to turn and our sentences were pronounced. There was no trial.'

Twenty-one were sentenced to death. Thirty-three received sentences of one to 15 years.

After a week they were led into the hall again. 'They told Noori Hamoodi Ahmed [a senior government official] to sit on a chair under a spiral staircase. One man shot him with a Kalashnikov. There was blood all over the walls.'

An hour later Ismail al-Najar, another senior bureaucrat, was put on the chair and the others watched as 15 rounds were fired into him.

On 8 August a further 19 were executed. By then, those sentenced to imprisonment had been taken to a wing of Abu Ghreib – where the torture began.

'On day one, I was taken four times to be beaten on the back,' said Mohammed. 'This was 30 to 80 strokes each time. On day two, I was beaten chest and face. You have to realise we were beaten with thick cables with metal in the middle. Every hit you bleed.

'Day three, on the head. Day four, we were told "put your legs out of the cell" and beaten. We weren't taken out of our cells; maybe the guards were tired.

'All of us found the beating on the legs most painful. When they finished, they made us march in our cells with our bleeding legs. I couldn't believe I was still standing. I thought to myself, "God gave humans amazing resilience."' On day five they were told to stick their hands out of their cells, which were hit on both sides. On day six they were beaten on the back again.

Between torture sessions, each prisoner was told to sit on the floor in the corner of his cell in silence. Anyone who disobeyed was beaten. 'There were days when I wanted to die, but there was no means to commit suicide,' said Mohammed.

The military men tapped to each other in Morse code, making futile plans to overwhelm the guards. They asked each other to take care of their families if they died. They lost track of time.

'We only knew if it was hot or cold,' Mohammed said. 'In the summer they would make us lie under four black blankets. In winter we slept on the floor with no cover.'

The torture grew more sadistic. 'Once they asked me, "What are you thinking?", and when I said "I am thinking of a good meal", they said I was lying and beat me.'

Prisoners were forced to pull hair from each other's beards. They were made to bark like dogs. They were told to sing a song, and if they did not know the words they were beaten.

Small things that had brought Mohammed joy now became horrors: 'When I heard the songs of the birds in the morning, I thought only that now the torture will resume.'

He remembers the day when they were all beaten with wooden beams and a blow knocked out a piece of Abdel al-Qubaisi's skull. It bounced off a prison wall.

'It was a triangular piece from the lower right of his skull,' Mohammed said. 'Two of us put it back in, sort of fitted it as best we could, and wrapped his head with a dirty cloth. He lost his mind for two weeks.'

When al-Qubaisi, deputy commander of the Ba'ath party, regained his senses, the guards resumed torturing him.

On another day Ahmed Wahed Maedi, a prominent colonel, was brought a shirt and trousers, cleaned up and taken away. He came back mentally disturbed but later told a horrific story.

He had been taken, all cleaned up, to see Barzan al-Tikriti, Saddam's half-brother and head of the Mukhabarat. Barzan, whom he knew, had asked about his family and given him a glass of orange juice. After 15 minutes he was taken to a room with no furniture, only a carpet in the middle of the room. Guards put cuffs on his hands and legs.

'They brought my fiancée,' he told Mohammed in a monotone. 'A man came in half-naked. By his accent he was from Tikrit [Saddam's home village]. He started tearing off her clothes. She was screaming and naked. I couldn't do anything so I put my face to the wall and started hitting my head on the wall.'

They forced him around to watch his fiancée being raped. 'She was panicking, choking, fighting and then she was speechless.'

After the rape they brought her an orange juice which looked identical to the one Maedi had been given by Barzan. It was poisoned: she died in 15 minutes. The naked man kicked her to make sure she was dead, kicked Maedi and left.

Then the killings started. The prisoners were herded naked into a basement room where the guards chased and beat them with huge beams of wood.

'We were climbing over each other and trying to use our friends' bodies as shields. Everyone had bones broken. My collarbone shattered,' Mohammed said.

A doctor came with a white coat and stethoscope. Anyone who was injured was to put his hand out through the cell doors. Murtada al-Hadithi, who had been a foreign minister, was told: 'You will be treated first out of respect for your position.'

He was taken away.

'When Murtada came back, he told us the doctor had given him a tablet. He knelt to pray, then he started screaming and collapsed. It was late afternoon. He died at midnight. His cellmates yelled to the guards, but they were told to "sleep with him and shut up".

'The rest of us thought, "He is very lucky". We wished we could follow him.'

A month later, two more were killed. 'They were taken downstairs and given tablets that killed them immediately. They left their bodies and we could smell them after some days. It was hot. The guards thought it was funny. They would yell to the bodies, "Hey, why don't you answer me, you think you are so special?"' Hamid al-Dulaimi, a colonel from a powerful tribe who had been exiled to Nigeria as ambassador before he was called home, suffered the worst fate. 'He was aggressive and Saddam disliked him.'

Dulaimi was tied to a ladder in his cell. Guards then lit timbers under his feet and watched while they burnt, making jokes about a barbecue.

'He screamed for 10 minutes, then he stopped. We did not understand why. All his skin and fat and tendons burnt off. They stopped the fire when his legs were half gone.'

One by one they were killed off. Riad al-Qadoo, a lieutenant-colonel, was made to dance in the centre of a circle of guards while they beat him to death. Mohamed Sabri al-Hadithi, who had been ambassador to Kuwait, died the same way. But the torture did not end there.

Al-Saidi, who had joked about Saddam and Al Capone, was the 14th and last to be killed. He was beaten to death in July 1982.

In 1983 the survivors were released to house arrest and discovered that their families had been sent fake confessions of treason. None recovered fully. Their property had been confiscated and their movements were restricted.

Mohammed escaped in 1991 after the Gulf War. He said he wanted to speak now in the hope that decent Iraqis, both in the regime and outside, would hear the story for the first time and would be encouraged to work against Saddam.

Why the great dictator thinks he can still win: Saddam's mind

2 March 2003

To the outside world it seems astounding that Saddam Hussein has not taken the opportunity to survive. The closer war looms, the more it is a racing certainty that the Iraqi leader will die, buried in the rubble of his bunker, shot through the head with the one bullet he says he keeps for himself, or hanged by a vengeful mob while trying to flee.

Why won't he just cough up his weapons of mass destruction, add the documentation the United Nations wants, and in one swoop defuse the American-led campaign to oust him? Or, if he can't bring himself to do that, why not step down, hand over to an ally, and leave a disappointed Washington pretty much forced to call the war off? Why commit suicide?

Because that's not how he sees it. Looking out at the world through Saddam's eyes, the perspective is fairly distorted. Some of that view even Tony Blair might envy.

No one disagrees in cabinet, for example; the last time a minister begged to differ, the Iraqi leader took him next door and shot him. So no one tells him uncomfortable truths.

There appears no shortage of love and loyalty. When Saddam

met a group of civil administrators last week, they chanted with joy
and pledged to be a 'sword in his hand'. And these were the men
who deal with things such as pensions, not sarin gas.

But in a country ruled by fear the reality is very different. Saddam
is a master of manipulation and self-delusion. In a rambling three-
hour television interview with the American television star Dan
Rather last week, he spoke in lofty terms of Iraq as a beacon of
freedom, peace and humanity; this from a man who has invaded
two of his neighbours and driven 4m of his countrymen into exile.

He also explained why Iraq had really won the war in 1991 (it
was George Bush Sr who asked for a ceasefire, not him), and that
he could never go into exile because that would mean betraying
the Iraqi people.

If Saddam's view of home is distorted, the perspective gets even
further from the truth when he looks beyond his borders. It should
be no surprise that international politics are not his forte. This is a
man to whom no one speaks anything he doesn't want to hear and
who has travelled out of Iraq only once since taking power in 1979.

That trip would not have given him much insight into world
diplomacy – it was to Cuba, where he and Fidel Castro spent most
of their meeting discussing their bad backs. Castro sent Saddam to
his favourite osteopath.

Those who know him say this lack of understanding of international intricacies is the key to his belief that he can survive a
confrontation with America. So far, they say, Saddam believes he is
winning on the diplomatic front.

From his perspective, just by sitting in Baghdad he has wreaked
havoc among his enemies. He looks out and sees an increasingly
divided Europe, with Britain taking the lead in supporting an
American-led military strike, backed by Spain and Italy, while
France and Germany remain opposed to any war, and the smaller
countries are torn between.

He can then see Nato facing one of the greatest tests of its unity
since it was founded 54 years ago. It has been riven by a dispute in
which France, Belgium and Germany blocked the alliance from

making preparations to defend Turkey in case it was attacked by Iraq.

Saddam may also smile with satisfaction at the bitter rows between the US and France and Germany. He will have noted the mutiny of Labour MPs against Blair last week, the most serious since Labour took power.

All that before he even looks to the United Nations Security Council, where Britain and America are pushing for a second resolution, against virulent opposition from France, Russia and China, which say weapons inspections in Iraq should continue.

'Saddam is encouraged, he feels he is on stronger ground,' said Abdel Bari Atwan, the editor of *Al-Quds Al-Arabi*, an independent Arabic newspaper based in London.

'He is loving creating divisions in the western world. He feels he is definitely in a better position now.'

Saddam still thinks he can make a deal. He is like a grudging trader in the souk, conceding inch by inch, unembarrassed about reversing himself.

In the interview with Rather, he insisted he would not destroy the Al-Samoud missile system, as ordered by Hans Blix, the chief UN weapons inspector, because it has a range of more than the 150 kilometres limit set by the United Nations. It seemed a showdown was in the making.

A day after the interview was aired, Iraq had announced it would start destroying the missile system by yesterday's deadline. Crisis averted, as ever at the last moment.

That is the other key to Saddam's belief that he can survive as leader of Iraq. He will spin out every deadline, play for time. He believes if he can hold off the American–British invasion long enough, it will be the heat of summer and all will be put off until next year. By then, something else will come up.

It's not a very graceful strategy, but nor is it, yet, a failure. With 200,000 American troops in the Gulf backed by 40,000 British forces, the ultimate outcome should not be in doubt – but Saddam doesn't seem to have learnt from his earlier miscalculations.

Ghassan Charbel, the assistant editor of the newspaper *Al Hayat*, last week recalled the countdown to war in 1991 after Saddam's invasion of Kuwait. The Yemeni foreign minister was in Baghdad on 16 January, trying to persuade Saddam to pull out of Kuwait and avert conflict. 'Saddam told him: "We will eat the Americans", and sent him home,' Charbel recalled. The next day, the American bombing campaign began.

Saddam did finally agree to withdraw, giving his offer to Yevgeny Primakov, the Arabic-speaking former Russian foreign minister who is an old friend from his stint as ambassador to Iraq. Almost at the same time that Primakov conveyed the last-minute offer, allied troops invaded Kuwait from Saudi Arabia.

Beyond misreading international politics, another thing that makes Saddam unlikely to surrender power is his megalomania. He really believes he is heir to Nebuchadnezzar, the king of Babylon who captured Jerusalem in 586BC, and Saladin, who evicted the crusaders from Jerusalem in 1187. 'He has a deep, mystical relation with Iraq,' said Charbel, who has researched the Iraqi leader for years.

Saddam is not completely relying on his gamble that the Americans will not invade, however. Sources in Baghdad said that in the past month, however confident he may appear, Saddam has started preparing for a possible war.

He has already given orders to his generals on what to do in case of invasion, so that he cannot be found by monitoring his communications. Trenches are being dug around Baghdad and the speculation in the intelligence community is that they will be filled with oil and ignited to obscure the view of troops and from planes, although they will not affect smart bombs.

Like Saddam's other hero, Joseph Stalin, the Russian dictator (Saddam has read all his biographies and can recite long passages from Stalin's speeches), he seems to be planning for a siege. Iraqi sources said he knew he could not win outright, but if he could hold out long enough – and enough civilian casualties appeared on television screens around the world – the United Nations might step in to halt the war.

There is one last scenario. He told a friend, now in exile, he would never be taken alive. 'In my pistol, I will guard one bullet,' the friend quoted Saddam as saying. 'It is for me. I will never be in the hands of the Americans.'

Hunt for Saddam & Son, the murderous duo most wanted: Uday the unstable

23 March 2003

In the early days of Saddam Hussein's presidency, Iraqi magazines carried *Hello!*-style profiles of their new ruling family. There were stories about the president working late, then returning home to help the children with their homework. Saddam and his first wife Sajida were pictured in idyllic settings with their brood – Uday, the elder son, his brother Qusay and the girls, Ragda, Rana and Hala – swimming, picnicking or shopping for clothes.

The reality was that already the children, especially the boys, had grown demanding and imperious. With their father as an example, they considered themselves to be above the law.

Saddam was proud of his elder son and one day took the four-year-old Uday, whom he called his 'cub', out for a treat. Some doting fathers take their sons to the office; Saddam took Uday to watch dissidents being tortured in the cells of a Baghdad prison.

While it was clear that Uday had inherited Saddam's brutal tendencies, at first he showed little sign of his father's drive. After university he was content to swan around Baghdad in his collection of smart cars, adding to his reputation as a playboy and dabbling in business. He hired a woman to jump naked out of a mountain of pilau rice at a party; girls he lusted after risked the health of their male relatives if they refused to submit.

In 1984 Saddam went to a school picnic for his youngest daughter, Hala, where he met Samira Shahbandar, the daughter of Hala's teacher. A beautiful woman from an old Baghdad merchant family, she became Saddam's official mistress and later his second wife.

The liaison infuriated Uday, who believed his mother Sajida had been wronged. Uday could not challenge his father, but on a warm October night in 1988 he snapped.

Kamel Hanna Jejjo, Saddam's favourite retainer and his intermediary to Samira, attended a party for Suzanne Mubarak, wife of the Egyptian president, on an island in the Tigris. Jejjo began shooting off volleys from an automatic rifle – nothing out of the ordinary in Baghdad, but the noise annoyed Uday, who was holding his own party nearby.

After Jejjo ignored Uday's message to stop, the president's son muscled his way into the party, hit Jejjo with a stick and stamped on his back until his spine broke. Jejjo died in hospital that night.

Saddam threatened to execute Uday, then jailed him for three days after Sajida intervened. Uday was sent to Geneva, into the care of an uncle, Barzan. The exile lasted a month until he pulled a knife on a Swiss policeman and was deported home.

'Uday was never the same after he killed Jejjo,' said Ahmed Allawi, a civil engineer who was in Uday's university class. 'Before, he was arrogant and did what he wanted, but after that he was out of control. It was like he went mad.'

The next subject of Uday's wrath was Hussein Kamel el-Majeed, husband to Saddam's daughter Ragda. He had organised Iraq's clandestine overseas procurement network for programmes of biological, chemical and nuclear warfare. After the first Gulf war he had also crushed Shi'ite rebel leaders. But in 1995 Hussein Kamel's relationship with Uday, who was once more back in Saddam's favour, reached crisis point.

During an argument with a cousin, Uday shot his uncle Watban in the leg. Hussein Kamel saw the writing on the wall: nobody was safe from this homicidal 'cub'. That night he packed Raghad and their four children into a Mercedes and fled to Jordan.

With him went his brother Saddam Kamel, Rana and their three children. Saddam Hussein was shaken and humiliated and burnt Uday's fleet of luxury cars.

But Hussein Kamel became disillusioned with his exile. Saddam promised him all had been forgiven, but when he was met at the border by a smiling Uday wearing sunglasses and a sharp suit, he must have known that it was all over.

Within four days Hussein and Saddam Kamel were dead, murdered in their home with other family members by Uday and his gunmen.

As Uday's behaviour became more and more unpredictable, Qusay began to emerge as an increasingly powerful figure. Saddam gave him sensitive jobs in the security forces that had never been offered to, or perhaps had never been desired by, the flashier Uday.

Rumours of Uday's extremes seemed impossible to credit until the arrival in exile of Latif Yahia, who had been forced to undergo plastic surgery by Uday because he wanted a double. Yahia described Uday's private world. Torture videos were weekly entertainment and he had his own torture cells in the basement of the Olympic headquarters.

When Uday was shot in an assassination attempt in 1996, Saddam had little sympathy. But he gave him control of a 30,000-strong militia and a place on the National Security Council, a central body of the regime.

Now, however, there are rumours from Baghdad that in the current conflict the notoriously unstable Uday has been placed under house arrest to prevent him revealing any information to the enemy.

Target Saddam: life on the run

21 December 2003

Marie Colvin in Baghdad; Tony Allen-Mills in Washington

**When Saddam Hussein was pulled from his tiny bolthole he had with
him a briefcase full of papers. Marie Colvin in Baghdad and Tony Allen-
Mills in Washington unravel his eight months in hiding.**

In the end it all came down to a hole in the ground and a battered
green briefcase. The new Nebuchadnezzar, the man who had
rebuilt Babylon to his own glory, crouched on a bin bag in the
damp earth as his enemies closed in. But he still had his empire.
There it was in his briefcase: documents, hand-written reports –
the proof he needed that he was still in power, still in control, still
killing, still able to make men tremble at the sound of his name.

'I am Saddam Hussein, the president of Iraq,' he insisted as
American soldiers pulled him from his rat hole. The smelly, shag-
gily bearded figure had made the blinkered blunder of a megalo-
maniac, however.

In the eight months since the collapse of his government, he had
successfully commanded a phantom regime from hiding. His
briefcase held copious evidence of a resistance movement run on
the lines of a Ba'athist totalitarian state with himself at the top. It
contained hundreds of key names – and now all of them were in
American hands.

Intelligence sources who revealed its contents last week said they
were amazed both by the unexpected extent of Saddam's involvement in the resistance and by his folly in keeping this detailed
dossier with him. Does Osama Bin Laden walk around with the
name and function of his every military commander in his shoulder bag? Did Martin McGuinness?

Saddam's biggest mistake, however, may have been to believe the
reports in his green briefcase. As ever, he was being lied to by his

acolytes. The 'battle reports' they couriered to him said what he wanted to hear: that the resistance was defeating the American army. Did he dream that he would soon be restored to power?

As the Ba'athist resistance network is now rolled up by the Americans and their Iraqi allies, thanks to the briefcase, it is possible to reconstruct Saddam's life on the run since the tanks entered Baghdad.

This is also the story of how the Americans tracked down the dictator, overcoming their own initial mistakes and finally using logic, deduction and the help of anti-Saddam Iraqis to pinpoint his lair.

The potted palm looked strangely familiar to Nada Yunis, a 36-year-old Iraqi businesswoman. She suddenly realised as she watched Saddam in a television propaganda broadcast that he was sitting in her living room.

It was 6 April. After a fortnight of uncertainty about the Iraqi dictator's whereabouts as American troops closed in on Baghdad, Yunis's sighting provided the first clear evidence that he had survived a 'decapitation strike' at the start of the US invasion.

Yunis's furnished house in the elite Mansur district of Baghdad was rented by a senior member of the Republican Guard.

As she watched the latest pictures of Saddam talking to senior aides, she recognised the orange curtains. They were sitting on her dining room chairs. The palm stood where she had left it.

It was as close as anyone would come to identifying Saddam's precise location.

Next day a CIA informant claimed to have spotted the elusive president entering another Mansur compound only half a mile from Yunis's home. Within 45 minutes a US Air Force B-1 bomber demolished the compound with four precision-guided bunker-busting 'smart' bombs.

'Just in case he didn't die before, let's have him die again,' joked a US intelligence official.

Of course, he did not die at all. It would take eight frustrating months and one of the world's most expensive manhunts to track him down to a hole in the ground.

Having failed to seize Osama Bin Laden in Afghanistan, the American intelligence officials were in little doubt how difficult it would be to find Saddam, however advanced their technology.

They had some of the world's most sophisticated surveillance tools on hand. The pride of the Pentagon's monitoring 'platforms' is the RC-135 Rivet Joint aircraft, a converted Boeing 707 loaded with antennae for picking up electronic communications.

Flying high over Iraq for up to 10 hours, the RC-135 could pick up signals up to 230 miles away and pinpoint the source of the conversation to within one to three nautical miles.

Further data was provided by spy satellites codenamed Micron and Trumpet. Micron is permanently positioned 22,300 miles above the Middle East and transmits signals to a British monitoring base at Menwith in Yorkshire. Trumpet flies in an elliptical orbit and is configured to monitor mobile phone calls.

Suspect intercepts were instantly compared to computerised profiles of Saddam's voice.

To the massive eavesdropping effort were added drones that scanned potential hiding spots with thermal probes, hoping to detect body movement underground; the radar in Apache attack helicopters, originally designed to target moving tanks, was also used to monitor unusual traffic patterns, such as fast-moving convoys.

It was a technically formidable operation that got US forces nowhere.

Time and again special forces were sent into action in the Sunni triangle between Baghdad and Saddam's stronghold, Tikrit. Somehow the fugitive ex-dictator always seemed to have moved on.

When his sons Uday and Qusay were killed in early July there was a surge of fresh leads from local Iraqi informants. But still no sign of Saddam.

Col James Hickey, commander of the US 4th infantry battalion based at an old Iraqi military compound in Tikrit, was in charge of the hunt. Looking out from his terrace over the River Tigris last

August, as a junior officer at his shoulder shot doves at dusk, Hickey said: 'There is a high probability that this old man is in my area of operations. I'm ready. If he's here, he's got a problem.'

He added: 'If he's here we'll get him. I think it will be sooner rather than later.'

It proved to be a long time later, but Hickey was correct. Saddam was on his patch.

Ad Dawr, a village of nondescript concrete homes, palm trees and sunflower fields beside the Tigris, was the scene of one of the great moments in Saddam's mythology. He boasted that after trying to assassinate Iraq's President Abdel Karim Al-Qassem in 1959, he fled by swimming the river to Ad Dawr, where he holed up to recover from a bullet in the leg.

Only minor elements of the story are true, but Ad Dawr – in the heart of the Sunni triangle – resonated with Saddam. He spent his unhappy, violent childhood in another nearby village, Awja, which he is said to hate. Ad Dawr was safer.

Sure enough, this is where he was found skulking in his hole near a squalid hut last weekend. So far, so predictable. Why was he not found earlier? The reason is that for several months his actions – and those of his protectors – were far less predictable.

Appearances are deceptive. His last hiding place looked as if this man of many palaces had hit bottom – the egg shells on the floor of his tin-roofed shanty kitchen, the few T-shirts and socks still in their plastic wraps. If these are all indications of a life with no baggage, they equally indicate a life with a well-organised support system. Somebody brought him those T-shirts and socks and his eggs and Mars bars.

Nor would he necessarily have felt uncomfortable in simple surroundings. As president, he preferred to spend his nights in small, secure houses in the grounds of his palaces. Identical presidential meals were prepared simultaneously at palaces and houses alike. In his world, it was better that no one knew where he ate or spent the night. In effect, he had lived on the run for years before he vanished from view last April.

There is strong evidence that he remained initially in Baghdad as the Americans took over. Those who admit to giving him shelter there live in sumptuous villas with walled gardens. He would have had little hardship.

In one Baghdad house a woman who admitted that her family had sheltered Saddam for a night showed off the butt of a cigar he had smoked under her roof. 'I will always treasure this,' she said.

In another, the owner revealed that Saddam had given him £2,800 for just one night. A high price for a bed and breakfast?

'No, it was a gift,' he said, smiling. Saddam had brought his own breakfast; he refused even to take tea, albeit politely – no doubt a vestige of the days when he had a taster in every home.

Outside Baghdad conditions were less luxurious. Mud-brick huts are the norm for much of the country. It is believed that he rotated between about 20 such huts once he left the capital for the Sunni triangle.

Iraqi and American sources believe that – realising movement itself would attract detection – he lay low at each place for a few weeks, occasionally travelling in a small, battered car to meet resistance commanders.

The documents in his briefcase show that the resistance members were all approved by the military bureau of Saddam's Ba'ath party, an organisation so ruthlessly intrusive that it investigated army officers' fiancées and promoted men who turned in their own brothers for execution.

One of the documents reveals a 'talent spotting' committee of eight senior officers who recommended former officers, all Sunnis, who had skills the resistance needed.

'Someone would [then] come to your door, and say the president sent us and he needs you to co-operate,' revealed an Iraqi working with the Pentagon to translate the documents into actionable information. Nobody declined.

The resistance had a standard hierarchical military structure.

Baghdad was divided into two sectors, each headed by a former top officer. Under each of these men were four senior officers, then 13 cells each also headed by an officer.

The money and authority for operations came from Saddam. At least five men from Baghdad were able to contact him directly for orders and to deliver information and money, but the cell leaders had the authority to make their own decisions on specific attacks.

'Saddam's strategy was to embarrass and humiliate Americans,' said an Iraqi source who has seen the documents.

'The people working for him had choice of target, within the outline of attacking American soldiers, international organisations, the Iraqi police – any target that would embarrass the Americans. That was the goal. If you, as a cell leader, believed you had the capability, you were authorised to go ahead.'

The operational reports submitted to Saddam sound, in the words of an American military source, 'like a son reporting to his parents'.

This was no guerrilla army running on faith, however. All the reports in the briefcase make clear that the resistance leaders were jockeying for favour and expected money for their successful attacks. Their reports were highly exaggerated. In one, a cell leader reported that his group had killed 200 American soldiers, clearly an exaggeration. He was still paid.

As the number of resistance attacks increased and America's post-war death toll surpassed its wartime total, Hickey's senior officers at Tikrit watched the hunt for Saddam unfold on highly detailed digital maps projected onto wall-mounted computer panels.

Using special antennae mounted on every tank, Humvee and Bradley fighting vehicle, commanders had a pinpoint view of all operations under way across the Tikrit region. Unmanned flying drones beamed back video pictures of target locations.

There were 12 raids after tip-offs. In one, troops raced to a farm-house where they found furniture covered with thick dust in the front room. The back bedroom, however, was newly cleaned. There were pristine Italian suits (favoured by Saddam) in a wardrobe. Bottles of men's cologne and shampoo were on the night table. These were not the luxuries of the average farmer, but the suits' owner was nowhere to be found.

Saddam's lifestyle would soon get tougher, however. The US was about to change its tactics.

Until late summer the Americans were preoccupied with rounding up what Hickey called 'high-value targets', the 55 most wanted members of the old regime and their bodyguards. Then they realised Saddam was with lower-level but highly trusted relatives.

The work that led to him through this tribal network was distinctly low-tech. A pair of junior intelligence specialists used coloured pencils and paper to disentangle Saddam's family tree.

Lt Angela Santana, 31, and Corporal Harold Engstrom, 36, compiled a chart that analysed Saddam's links to the six main tribes of the Sunni triangle – the Husseins, al-Douris, Hadouthis, Masliyats, Hassans and Harimyths.

Santana and Engstrom were members of the 104th Military Intelligence Battalion in Tikrit. She was an executive secretary before joining the army; he a schoolteacher.

It took weeks of legwork before the chart began to take shape. From an initial pool of 9,000 names gleaned from military databases, detainee interrogations and Iraqi informers, Santana and Engstrom steadily zeroed in on the inner tribal circles believed to be close to Saddam.

Their work was initially too slow for the Pentagon. The US military occupation was looking increasingly ragged. Infighting broke out between rival intelligence agencies, seriously hampering the flow of data to US special forces.

By early November General John Abizaid, commander of troops in the region, had decided to disband the separate special operations task forces that were hunting for Saddam.

In their place came a new highly classified commando group known as Task Force 121. Assembled from elite special forces such as the US Army's Delta Force, Navy SEALS and CIA paramilitary operatives, the task force was given the mission of 'neutralising' by capture or assassination any remaining Ba'athist leadership figures. Saddam was HVT-1 – High Value Target number one.

A former CIA station chief declared: 'We have to resuscitate Iraqi intelligence, holding our nose, and have Delta and agency shooters break down doors and take [the Saddam loyalists] out.'

This new task force fared little better than its predecessor. Donald Rumsfeld, the US defence secretary, was becoming increasingly perturbed. 'The fact he's alive is unhelpful,' he said last month.

When Rumsfeld travelled to Iraq to pay a pre-Christmas visit to troops, he was openly amazed that so much American time and money had failed to capture Saddam.

'I'm dumbfounded when I think about it,' he told Major General Raymond Odierno, the 4th infantry's commander.

'The chances of us using that kind of money to find somebody – to figure out how to develop a network and produce the information that would do it – I mean, that ought to be do-able.'

The Americans' problem lay in a shortage of intelligence and linguists to sort through the data that poured in from informants. Things began to change after they brought in the Information Collection Programme (ICP), which is run by the Iraqi National Congress in co-operation with the Pentagon.

In exile, the ICP had helped defectors leave Iraq. It is now operating out of headquarters in Baghdad. Its information and analyses proved accurate.

'We passed their information to units on the ground, and it was solid,' said an American military source.

Santana and Engstrom's detective work identified a close associate of Saddam whose name kept popping up in intelligence reports. He was originally believed to be one of the former dictator's bodyguards, but his significance increased as the two intelligence officers added more information to their chart.

Hickey described him last week as a member of a 'very important family' based in Tikrit, and as 'a middle-aged man with a very large waistline'. He has not been named but has been identified as

a former senior officer in Saddam's elite Special Security
Organisation.

Three times in early December Hickey's troops tried to capture
this man. Each time they missed him, but seized relatives and other
individuals who added a little more information to Santana and
Engstrom's chart.

Finally, on Friday 12 December, a Special Forces raid on a house
in Baghdad netted the 'fat man'.

'When I heard this source was captured I knew we were onto
something,' Santana said. 'We had someone who was very close to
Saddam talking, so there was a great chance we would find him
that night.'

It took only four hours for the captive to spill the beans. He
revealed that Saddam was on a farm on the Tigris, and that the
soldiers should look for 'an underground facility'.

The farm belongs to Qais Naqim, an apparently insignificant
former clerk in the presidential office who had retired because of
heart disease some years ago. That he had escaped the attention of
American or Iraqi investigators, yet provided Saddam's ultimate
bolthole, proves how difficult the hunt had been.

At Naqim's farm Hickey's troops had their rendezvous with
history. The underground facility turned out to be a T-shaped hole
barely wide enough for Saddam to wriggle into, but wide enough
for him to put his hands up in surrender.

Saddam had a gun but did not use it. Few of his resistance
commanders appear to have been any braver.

The ICP and Americans are now going on nightly raids together
to round up Saddam's network in Baghdad. None of the commanders has put up a fight. All have been found with large amounts of
money at their disposal, a key indication of involvement in the
resistance, because senior army officers' official salaries are blocked.
In one house, £38,000 was found, in another £45,000.

'At first they deny everything,' said an Iraqi source involved in
the debriefings. 'They say they were just sitting at home, that they
only joined the Ba'ath party because they had to under Saddam.

They were angels! Then, in a few days, they start implicating their colleagues.'

An American military source described the joint raids with the ICP as a 'good combination'.

'They blend in to the neighbourhood, and know the people. We have the expertise in interrogation,' said the source.

Saddam's network is being rolled up in a targeted, meticulous manner. There are none of the mass neighbourhood searches that angered Iraqi civilians earlier in the year.

One night last week a senior Iraqi officer – who had been identified from Saddam's briefcase dossier – drove with an ICP and American team to point out the villa of a resistance colleague. He was given a balaclava to hide his face.

Photos of the house were taken, a GPS location punched in, and plans for an arrest began. The following night the target was seized.

Not everyone believes this is really happening, however. Diehards say Saddam is free. Awja, his home town, is gripped by the rumour about a little girl who was walking in the street crying last week.

A black BMW pulled up and the man inside asked: 'Why are you crying?' She said she was crying because her president was captured. He laughed, and she recognised the laugh. It was Saddam. He gave her money for sweets, and said: 'Stop crying, go to school, and be sure I will never be captured.'

Iraq: the mind behind the horror

7 March 2004

Marie Colvin, Mitchell Prothero in Baghdad; Richard Woods,
Tony Allen-Mills and Nick Fielding

More than 200 Shi'ite worshippers were slaughtered by suicide bombers in Iraq last week. America blames an ally of Osama Bin Laden who, it says, is trying to foment civil war.

Inside the administrative Green Zone, the one small area of Baghdad that is comparatively secure and peaceful, officials were preparing on Friday to mark a new dawn for Iraq. An interim constitution leading to democratic elections was ready for signing: good news after a week that had left the country scarred by religious terrorism on an unprecedented scale.

Television cameras and reporters were on hand. A slogan in Arabic – 'We all participate in a new Iraq' – hung over a table on which fountain pens were laid out. But at the last moment the representatives of Iraq's 15 million Shi'ite community, which was still mourning its dead, refused to sign.

Officials played down the debacle but in private Paul Bremer, head of the Coalition Provisional Authority, was furious. Almost one year on from the invasion, Iraq's volatile mix of Shi'ite and Sunni Muslims, Kurds, Turkomen and other factions are refusing to play the parts that Washington has written for them.

Is it all going to blow up in George W Bush's face during this American presidential election year? Is civil war imminent? After last week such fears cannot be dismissed.

On Tuesday, hundreds of thousands of Shi'ites had gathered in Baghdad and the religious city of Karbala for the festival of Ashura when a series of suicide bombs ripped through the crowds, killing and maiming pilgrims on the holiest day of the Shi'ite year. About 200 died and hundreds more were wounded.

The atrocities were part of a pattern of anti-Shi'ite attacks stretching from northern Iraq across to Pakistan, where terrorists machinegunned crowds in Quetta killing at least 40 people.

The Americans immediately blamed Abu Musab al-Zarqawi, a notorious Jordanian-born terrorist with a bounty of $10 million (about £5.4 million) on his head and links to Al-Qaeda. Such foreigners were trying to foment civil war in Iraq, the Americans claimed, adding that Grand Ayatollah Ali al-Sistani, the main Shi'ite leader, was staying commendably calm.

Al-Zarqawi may well have a hand in attacks in Iraq and he is a useful bogeyman for the Americans to target. But he is not the only problem.

In a mosque in Baghdad last week, Sheikh Moyad al-Baydhani warned of Sunni–Shi'ite tensions and anger against the American occupiers. Al-Baydhani is a follower of another Shi'ite leader, Moqtada al-Sadr, who is a radical willing to urge violence.

'We will wait for permission from [al-Sistani] before we go forward with any violence,' said al-Baydhani. 'But we are ready to fight the Americans for failing to protect Iraq and the Shi'ites.'

Another atrocity, or a change of heart by al-Sistani, could tip the balance. The Arab world fears the worst.

'Iraq is now facing a grim future,' said Abdel Bari Atwan, editor of *Al-Quds*, the well-informed Arabic newspaper based in London.

'Most people in the south, the Shi'ites, now believe the United States cannot guarantee even the basic necessities of life, such as electricity and fuel, let alone security.'

The split between Sunni and Shi'ite Muslims goes back 1,300 years to a battle near Karbala between rival claimants to lead the Muslim caliphate. In the bloodshed, Imam Hussein, a grandson of the prophet Muhammad and a Shi'ite leader, was killed.

Sunni and Shi'ite sects diverged and have followed different customs ever since.

For extremists, antipathy runs deep. Like Osama Bin Laden, al-Zarqawi is not just a Sunni but also a Wahhabi, a fervent believer in fundamentalist Islam. Wahhabis hold that Shi'ites are infidels.

Al-Zarqawi is believed to have been jailed in Jordan in the early 1990s for militant activities. After he was released, he was suspected of plotting to blow up bridges and hotels during millennium celebrations.

He fled to Afghanistan where he set up training camps for militants. Although linked to Al-Qaeda, he kept his distance.

When the Taliban regime was collapsing, al-Zarqawi was badly injured in Kabul, losing a leg, but escaped into Iran and moved on to Iraq where he was treated in hospital. He has since been linked to Ansar al-Islam, a fundamentalist group in the north of Iraq, and also to terrorist cells in Europe.

'Al-Zarqawi is developing a global profile similar to that of Osama Bin Laden,' said MJ Gohel, an international terrorism expert at the Asia-Pacific Foundation. 'In our view he is likely to be the catalyst for creating a system in Europe and the Middle East for providing new recruits for global terror attacks.'

According to American intelligence, al-Zarqawi met Mohammed Ibrahim Makawi, an Al-Qaeda commander, in eastern Iran in February last year as America and Britain prepared to invade Iraq.

In early January this year, al-Zarqawi is believed to have met Hassan Ghul, another Bin Laden emissary. Days later Ghul was captured in the Kurdish border area. According to US intelligence, he was carrying a letter from al-Zarqawi outlining his Iraqi operations.

The letter identifies the Shi'ites as the key to destabilising Iraq, because 'targeting their religious, political and military symbols will make them show their rage against the Sunnis and bare their inner vengeance'.

Whether or not the letter is genuine, the anti-Shi'ite strategy ascribed to al-Zarqawi is an obvious one for a Sunni terrorist seeking to create turmoil in Iraq.

The Shi'ites were oppressed under Saddam Hussein. Last year, in the final weeks of his regime, he had 15 Shi'ites executed in Karbala for trying to celebrate Ashura.

The festival falls on the 10th day of the first month of the new Islamic year. This year was the first for decades that Iraqi Shi'ites could freely celebrate.

Hordes poured into Karbala, beating their chests and ritually cutting their heads. The first bomb exploded in the courtyard of the main shrine. As pilgrims ran for their lives, according to some witnesses, two suicide bombers blew themselves up by the exits. 'It was planned to inflict the maximum number of casualties,' said Khalil Shakir, a guard at the main gate.

More bombs followed. Hassan Hadio, a 22-year-old Shi'ite, saw a man run into a throng of pilgrims and explode. The bomber's head flew 25 yards through the air. As the crowds fled in panic there were more explosions.

The local hospital was overwhelmed by the dead as volunteers offered to donate blood. Ali Hussein, its deputy director, said: 'I don't need people to give blood; I need people to carry bodies.'

In Baghdad there was further carnage when bombs exploded at the shrine of Kazimiya and other Shi'ite sites. In Basra, police officers found a car packed with explosives at a petrol station near the path of a Shi'ite procession. Four suspected terrorists, including two wearing explosive belts, were arrested. In Kirkuk, in northern Iraq, another bomb was defused.

What was remarkable, after such bloodshed, was the reaction of the Shi'ites. If this was an attempt to make them 'bare their inner vengeance', it failed. There was anger – much of it targeted at American troops – but no violence. Can this restraint last?

The fact is that most members of Iraq's Shi'ite and Sunni communities rubbed along peaceably enough under Saddam's yoke and are not blood enemies. Iraq's almost daily violence is the work of a minority of Sunni forces – mostly former Ba'ath party members embittered at the overthrow of Saddam – augmented by foreign Arabs pursuing their own 'jihad'.

The Shi'ites have assassinated former Saddam officials whom they blamed for anti-Shi'ite atrocities, but they have left alone the majority of Sunni, who were not part of Saddam's regime. That restraint has been largely down to al-Sistani, who has been the guiding hand behind Shi'ite political strategy and tactics.

He has refused to meet Bremer, but called for co-operation with the Americans as long as they made it clear that they would be leaving Iraq. He has insisted that the future of the country must be decided by elections, calculating that this would lead to the Shi'ites, who make up 60% of the population, commanding the majority share of power.

His influence was clearly at work last week: restraint in the face of brutal terrorist provocation, followed by the politically devastating boycott of Bremer's showpiece constitutional ceremony.

The danger is that more radical elements in al-Sistani's constituency – such as al-Sadr – are advocating violent confrontation. Some observers fear that last week's violence will reduce al-Sistani's influence and promote the power of the radicals.

'The building blocks of civil war are being put into place,' said Gareth Stansfield, an associate fellow at the Royal Institute of International Affairs in London. 'Three big issues are coming together all at once. The Sunni desire to hold on to power, the Shi'ite resurgence and Kurdish nationalism.'

As the bombs caused mayhem in Iraq last Tuesday, Senator John Kerry was clinching the Democratic nomination for the next American presidential election. He is ready to make Iraq a key issue in his coming battle with Bush.

On Wednesday General John Abizaid, America's top military commander in the Middle East, appeared in Washington to give senators and congressmen an unusually candid appraisal of the situation in Iraq. Although Abizaid said he was 'optimistic' that civil war would not break out between Sunni and Shi'ite Muslims, he warned that the Iraqi security forces still lacked the training to replace American troops.

Even if the coalition does manage to hand over sovereignty as planned at the end of June, many American troops will have to stay in the country. Last week Sir Jeremy Greenstock, the senior British representative in Iraq, said that British troops would have to remain for 'at least another two years, maybe more'.

Any big losses of American forces would revive Democratic accusations that Bush blundered into Baghdad without thought for the consequences. On the other hand, Kerry could be badly undermined if coalition moves towards Iraqi democracy make progress.

For all the carnage and failure to find weapons of mass destruction, most Americans still believe that Bush was right to go to war against Saddam. The big question mark is the unquantifiable threat of further violence between Sunnis and Shi'ites or against American forces.

Alarmists play on the Sunni–Shi'ite divide, but it is more complex. In the main cities, Shi'ites and Sunnis intermarry, go into business together and live side by side. In other areas tribal, family and class ties are as important as religion and have so far ensured that neither Sunni nor Shi'ite populations have become unified blocs.

The danger is that more atrocities will cause both communities to retreat into religious allegiances for safety.

In Baghdad yesterday, Bremer was still in intense talks with Iraqi leaders, trying to secure agreement for the interim constitution. Officials hoped that it would be signed this week. But as Greenstock warned, the days in the run-up to the handover of sovereignty in June are likely to be 'bloody'.

THE RELIGIOUS DIVIDE HAMPERING A NATIONAL REBIRTH

Under Saddam Hussein the Sunni Muslim minority dominated the Shi'ite majority for decades. There are about 20 million Arabs in Iraq, of whom about 75% are Shi'ite and 25% are Sunni.

After the first Gulf war, a Shi'ite uprising in the south of the country was brutally suppressed by Saddam. They now see the chance of dominating any freely elected government.

The Sunni minority are concentrated north of Baghdad, along the Tigris and Euphrates rivers. Beyond them in the northeast there are up to 5 million Kurds, who want their own autonomous region.

The dispute over the interim constitution last week centred on a clause that would have given the Kurds considerable power in deciding the long-term future of the country. Though the Shi'ites and Kurds are separated geographically and have no territorial disputes, the Shi'ites refused to allow the minority such power.

Other minorities include Turkomans, Iranians and Arab Christians.

Face to face with death in a 'pacified' Iraqi town

BAGHDAD

29 October 2006

A few months ago Saab al Bour was a showpiece town where Americans were building schools and fixing the water and electricity supplies. Even the Shi'ites and Sunnis rubbed along.

The dusty settlement of sand-coloured brick buildings six miles northwest of Baghdad is now a ghost town, shorn of its residents by Iraq's relentless sectarian wars. They took to the road when mortars, 15–20 a day, started crashing into the town, fired by Sunni extremists targeting the Shi'ites.

Sunni neighbour turned on Shi'ite neighbour in a struggle that eventually drove out 90% of the original population of 30,000.

Before I set out for Saab al Bour yesterday, I had been assured that it had been 'pacified'. Our two UH-60 helicopters flew low out of Baghdad's fortified green zone, swooping over the capital, its once-crowded arteries devoid of traffic.

We banked over flat stretches of baked earth and a few patches of green and came in low to a wasteland in the middle of the town, guided by grey smoke rising from two armoured cars that had been sent ahead to secure the landing. This did not look like a pacified town.

American soldiers in desert camouflage uniforms leapt out of the helicopters to set up a perimeter, 6ft apart, around us. Crouching, M16s perched on their shoulders pointing out in a circle, they eyed the mud and sand brick houses suspiciously. Only a mangy yellow dog moved.

Within half an hour of my arrival Apache helicopter gunships filled the sky, firing on insurgents just the other side of a canal with loud blasts of their cannons.

In the town's police station, sandbagged and covered with camouflage netting, Lieutenant-Colonel Dave Thompson sat with two members of the local council. The police were supposed to be there to brief us, but they had been called to an 'incident'. Later one policeman told me the incident was an attack on their commander's home and they had rushed to help.

This is just a microcosm of the problems besetting Iraq. The town of Saab al Bour had been quiet when the American army, backed up by Iraqi soldiers, was based there. It sits on the edge of Anbar province, a Sunni stronghold. Shortly after the soldiers handed over to the Iraqi police at the end of last month, the fighting began.

Khaled Lateef, a councillor who stayed throughout, said the mortars were fired by Sunni extremists from across the canal, aimed mostly at the Shi'ite areas.

The police were outgunned by the insurgents. The Iraqi and American armies had to move back to pick up where they had left off. Thompson tried to be upbeat: 'We're down to one mortar a day,' he said. 'We're back to rebuilding.'

Every time one tiny corner of Iraq is fixed, another chunk falls apart. Take Yarmouk, a wealthy Baghdad neighbourhood famed for its manicured gardens, fashionable boutiques and spacious villas. Living just a mile from the American troops in the green zone, residents have until recently felt far removed from Iraq's sectarian violence.

They were wrong. A district that for decades was 70% Sunni and 30% Shi'ite, where members of the two different strands of Islam lived side by side, mingled and even married, has been 'cleansed' of 90% of its Shi'ite residents. Their choice was to leave or die.

A doctor forced out of Yarmouk by Sunnis described the thugs' methods. 'They kidnapped my son,' he said. 'They broke his nose, then they raised a pick-up truck on a jack, turned the truck on and put his legs under the spinning tyres. All the skin was torn off.' After payment of £10,500, he got his son back. The 20-year-old university student wore shoes last week for the first time in months.

'I hired security guards but they fired an RPG [rocket-propelled grenade] at my house. I couldn't stand it any more. We left Yarmouk.'

Yarmouk is a shocking example of Iraq's sectarian strife because the Sunni–Shi'ite violence is usually portrayed as a cancer confined to slums run by radical militias. But this area was home to an educated elite who played tennis at the club and went abroad for the summer.

The slaughter consuming Sunni and Shi'ite Muslims in roughly equal measure may appear like anarchy from afar, but a closer look reveals a sinister plot. Starting in the west of the city, Sunni militants have seized district after district, creating their own zone that extends into the heart of Baghdad.

The Shi'ites are not innocent. Since the explosion at a Shi'ite mosque in Samarra in February, their militias have exacted vicious revenge. The morgue classifies victims according to their injuries; if a victim has been beheaded, he is a Shi'ite killed by Sunnis. If he has been killed by a power drill to the head, he is a Sunni murdered by Shi'ites. Most victims have been tortured. Bodies are dumped by the roadside and lie there for hours.

Nouri al-Maliki, the prime minister, vowed last week – not for the first time – to clamp down on the militias. He has made scant progress, partly because he depends on a political party allied to a Shi'ite militia. The US Operation Together Forward launched in August to pacify Baghdad has failed dismally.

While the Shi'ites are fired by blind vengeance, the Sunnis appear to have a plan.

They are trying to split Baghdad in half in advance of a proposal to carve Iraq into three federal regions.

Most of the country divides easily. The north is mainly Kurdish, the south Shi'ite, and the central desert region Sunni. Baghdad, too mixed to divide without a massive population transfer, is the sticking point in this plan.

But look at the changing map of Baghdad today. From the western suburb of Abu Ghraib, neighbourhoods have fallen under the control of Sunni radicals, their Shi'ite residents sent fleeing, their homes abandoned or taken by Sunni families, their businesses bombed, shuttered or reopened under Sunni ownership. Baghdad is on its way to becoming two cities, the west Sunni, the east and north Shi'ite.

The militias conducting this ethnic cleansing have a deadly system, described by an Iraqi intelligence officer and former residents of Yarmouk. First they terrorise the area, shooting children selling ice or black-market petrol on the street. Then they go for the shops and businesses.

It worked in Yarmouk. The Amari bakery was run by three brothers; two were killed and one injured. He fled. The bakery is now the Ahmed bakery, run by a Sunni. Abu Allah, also a Shi'ite, ran the grocery. He was shot and survived, but fled Yarmouk.

In the third stage, the Sunni militants go after the police, attacking checkpoints until they pull out. Then they target Shi'ite residents. 'You wake up to a bullet in your garden. Or a note saying leave this area in 36 hours. After all the killings, you pack up and go,' said another former resident, who knew of eight people killed near his home.

The Shi'ite houses and shops are considered 'ramim', Arabic for spoils of war, and handed to Sunni families.

There is a police station in Yarmouk but the police are holed up inside, powerless to intervene, because the insurgents are better armed. The best way to bribe a policeman these days is with bullets; they stop expensive cars and where once they demanded money, they now want ammunition. Last week 18 policemen were killed in a Sunni ambush in Khan Bani Sa'ad, 20 miles north of Baghdad, because they had run out of bullets.

Two police officers from the Yarmouk precinct described their predicament. One was a Shi'ite married to a Sunni, the other a Sunni married to a Shi'ite. One had been shot seven times on his doorstep; the other had his car blown up.

When the Sunni officer's in-laws came to stay, he woke to find a note wrapped around a bullet. It read: 'There are Shi'ite in your house. Your future is this bullet if they do not leave.' They left.

There are some signs of social resistance. On Thursday in Mansour, which borders Yarmouk, 3,000 people, mostly families, gathered at the Hunting Club to celebrate Eid, the end of Ramadan. The skirts were low on the girls' hips, there was barely a hijab in sight, and Abir the DJ spun western and Arabic discs.

'This is our way of fighting the terrorists who are trying to destroy life in Iraq,' said Hasanain Mualla, the manager.

And then there is the bravest ice-cream seller in Baghdad, a Sunni. When Sunni militants demanded he close because there had been no ice cream in the time of the prophet Muhammad, he told them: 'I'll stop selling ice cream when you ride up on camels to threaten me. There were no BMWs in the time of prophet Muhammad either.'

The butcher of Baghdad awaits
his death sentence

BAGHDAD

5 November 2006

In 24 years of tyrannical rule, Saddam Hussein brought death to millions in three wars, torture to the countless pitiful souls incarcerated in his dungeons and isolation from much of the world to the once-proud country that he cowed.

Today Iraqis expect to see the leader who terrorised them condemned to face a hangman's noose for just one of his many crimes – the execution of 148 Shi'ite men from the village of Dujail, 40 miles north of Baghdad, in retaliation for an attempt on his life there in 1982, when he had been in power for only three years.

The country is braced for the verdict amid fears that the dictator's Sunni supporters will mount revenge attacks on Shi'ite areas.

In a clear echo of the mood of most Iraqis, Nouri al-Maliki, the prime minister, said yesterday that he hoped Saddam would be given 'what he deserves' when the verdict is handed down.

If, as expected, Saddam is convicted of crimes against humanity and stands in the dock to hear his sentence, I will watch with that particular attention that comes from fascination and disgust. I have reported on the misery that he has inflicted on his country-men for more than 20 years, from the ill-judged invasion of Iran that left more than a million dead, to his equally disastrous foray into Kuwait, which left his nation in ruins.

He has cast a dark shadow of evil over every moment I have spent in Iraq – a man who had personally tortured some of his victims and even walked his young sons through his prisons to witness the barbarity.

Today's case dates back 24 years to an ambush in which 10 gunmen fired at his convoy. In revenge, the surviving villagers testified, Saddam had hundreds of them arrested and tortured. As well as the 148 executed, a further 399 men, women and children were consigned to a desert camp.

The survivors say they relish the prospect of Saddam suffering the same punishment that he meted out to so many others. He ordered myriad death sentences for crimes as petty as insulting him or his sons, Qusay and Uday, sometimes in remarks conveyed to the authorities by teachers overhearing their pupils' accounts of conversations at home. Nowhere was safe in Saddam's Iraq.

The chief judge is due to read out a 200-page verdict on Saddam and seven co-defendants. Also facing possible death sentences will be Barzan al-Tikriti, his half-brother and intelligence chief, and Taha Yassin Ramadan, the former vice-president.

It will be the culmination of a bitterly divisive case that began in October last year in a crowded and chaotic courtroom where Saddam and the others heard shocking testimony from their seats in a heavily guarded 'cage'.

A Dujail woman who was 16 in 1982 testified that she had been hung by her wrists, then by her ankles. She was tortured with electric shocks, beaten with cables and forced to watch her family being killed, she said. The court was told that by the time the hangman received a list of 148 men to be executed, 46 had already died under torture.

Saddam's cold disregard was emphasised when he intimated that he had no reason to recall Dujail's destruction or the deaths of men, women and children. 'It's not as if Saddam Hussein did not have [other] work to do,' he told the judge.

His contempt for the villagers reflected his attitude to far bloodier campaigns against the Kurds in the north and Shi'ites in the south. In his 1988 campaign against the Kurds, he unleashed his army on northern Iraq and killed 100,000, including 5,000 in the village of Halabja, where chemical weapons rained down death.

In 1991, after the Americans drove Saddam out of Kuwait, he killed a similar number of Shi'ites in the south, mowing them down with helicopter gunships when they dared to rise up against him.

Saddam and his cousin, Ali Hassan al-Majeed, known as Chemical Ali for his role in the poison gas attack, both face the charge of genocide for the Kurdish campaign in a separate trial.

The dictator's complete lack of remorse is striking. He seemed genuinely puzzled when confronted by testimony of torture and killing. 'Where's the crime?' he asked the judge, arguing that such reprisals were only to be expected against traitors.

The 55-week trial was meant to mark the start of Iraq's Nuremberg – the exposure of an evil regime. Instead, dogged by delays and interruptions, it has veered between tragedy and farce.

Saddam harangued the judges, insisted that he was still the president of Iraq and told the court to 'go to hell'. Two judges were changed: one resigned and a second was forced to step down after saying that Saddam had never been a dictator. Three defence lawyers were murdered.

Amnesty International has been among the strongest critics of the trial, arguing that it was 'a deeply flawed process'. American officials in Baghdad were relieved that it had not collapsed. 'A verdict on Saddam is what we wanted and at last that's what we're getting,' said one.

Saddam's case will automatically go for review to an appellate chamber, Iraq's highest court. If it upholds the outcome, he will face the gallows 30 days later.

Saddam's death could go a long way towards curbing the insurgency that is tearing Iraq apart. Most of the Sunni militants are former members of his Ba'ath party, fighting to win back the power they have lost. They still harbour the faint hope that he will lead them again.

The crime he will never answer for is the ruination of the lives of millions of Iraqis who survived the wars and repression, but are still condemned to lives of chaos and despair.

'I watched Saddam die'

31 December 2006

The knock on the door came just before 6am. Saddam Hussein's executioners were disguised with black balaclavas.

He spent his last minutes yesterday in the sordid bowels of Iraqi military intelligence headquarters, once home to his own torturers and killers.

Just as the dawn call to prayer was beginning over the city, he was led, shambling in leg irons, to the scaffold to pay the price for his crimes against the Iraqi people.

'We took him to the gallows room and he looked like he wondered what was going on,' said Mowaffak al-Rubaie, the Iraqi government's national security adviser, who saw him die. 'He looked at the gallows not believing what was going to happen.'

As the world reacted with mixed jubilation and condemnation to the hanging, Rubaie revealed that the deposed dictator muttered as he was taken to his death: 'Do not be afraid; it is where we all go.'

Rubaie was among the 15 people in the ill-lit room that was Saddam's last sight on earth. The former Iraqi dictator showed no remorse, said Rubaie, speaking by telephone from Baghdad.

'He was respected throughout before and after the execution. We followed rigorously international and Islamic standards.'

After the dramas of Friday night, when Iraqi officials said Saddam's death was imminent but his lawyers tried to stay his execution with an appeal to a United States court, his fate was set early yesterday.

Nouri al-Maliki, the Iraqi prime minister, had signed the death warrant before going to celebrate his son's wedding, and the presidential council had endorsed it.

The American jailers who had custody of Saddam were ordered to surrender him to the Iraqi government. They offered him tranquillisers but Saddam refused. 'We received physical custody of Saddam Hussein around 5.30am from the coalition forces, and we took over and he became ours,' said Rubaie.

As US troops stood guard outside, Saddam was first led to a sparse and unheated holding room in the bowels of the headquarters of Iraqi military intelligence. It would not have been lost on him that his own security forces had tortured and killed many people in the same grim building. Saddam was left for about half an hour to contemplate his fate. Iraqi law provides that a condemned man be allowed a final cigarette and a meal before his execution.

'He was handcuffed and we took him and sat him down,' said Rubaie. 'There was a judge, a deputy general, deputy minister of justice, deputy minister of interior, a couple of other ministers, myself and a doctor.' After formalities they took him through 'a huge file' of documents detailing his trial.

'The judge took him through the conviction. He was silent until he saw a video camera, and then began shouting slogans such as "God is great". He started his rhetoric: "Long live Islam, down with

Persia", down with this and that. He started shouting his head off.'
Rubaie made a last gesture of mercy. 'His handcuffs were a little
tight, and hurt him, and I instructed the guards to loosen them.'

The formalities over, the four masked executioners stepped
forward, taking his hat and scarf. Short, tubby and dressed in
leather jackets, they looked more like Al-Qaeda killers in an
amateur terrorist video than those responsible for carrying out the
sentence of death on a former head of state. Even though Saddam
had shrunk in stature since the days of his pomp, he towered over
them.

He had dressed for death in clothes sewn by his personal Turkish
tailor: black trousers, shined black shoes, a starched white shirt,
black pullover and a black wool overcoat that protected him
against the deep chill of his remaining minutes in the execution
suite. His hair was dyed his signature black, but he had heavy bags
under his eyes.

In sight of a new hemp noose hanging from the ceiling of the
dank room, the executioners removed his handcuffs to tie his
hands behind his back. As he stood close to the trapdoor one
wrapped Saddam's black scarf around his neck to shield it from
rope burns.

When they went to put the black hood over his head, he
mumbled: 'That won't be necessary.' The noose was slipped over
his head.

He stood looking almost bewildered, and an executioner
awkwardly tightened the knot of the noose on the left side of his
neck.

Even on the brink of death Saddam had not forgotten the video
camera. Just before he dropped through a trapdoor on a platform
surrounded by red railing, he shouted the Muslim profession of
faith, 'God is great and Muhammad is his prophet' and 'Palestine
is Arab'.

'He was standing with the rope round his neck,' said Rubaie.
'The executioner started reading verses from the Koran, "There is
no God but Allah and Muhammad is his messenger". He repeated

it twice and [Saddam] went down in no time.' The hangman pulled a lever, and Saddam dropped silently about 3 feet through a metal trapdoor. It was 6.10am. Rubaie said he died instantly. 'It was so, so quick, totally painless and there was no movement after that.'

Sami al-Askari, who represented the prime minister at the hanging, said he 'heard his neck snap'. A video appearing later on Arabic websites showed Saddam dangling on the rope, his neck apparently broken.

Saddam hung from the rope for about 10 minutes, watched by the audience of about 15 people who could see him dangling under the platform. A doctor checked that his heart had stopped, then one of the executioners untied him. There was blood on the rope. The executioners put him in a white body bag and took photographs as proof for diehard loyalists that Saddam was dead. Iraqi television broadcast a still photograph of the last image of the dictator, his neck at an unnatural angle, sticking out of the white shroud.

Munir Haddad, an Iraqi appeals court judge, also witnessed the execution. He said afterwards: 'One of the guards present asked Saddam Hussein whether he was afraid of dying. Saddam said, "Why would I? I spent my whole life fighting the infidels and the intruders."

'Another guard asked him, "Why did you destroy Iraq, and destroy us? You starved us, and you allowed the Americans to occupy us." His reply was, "I destroyed the invaders and ... I destroyed the enemies of Iraq, and I turned Iraq from poverty into wealth."

'Saddam was normal and in full control. He said, "This is my end. I started my life as a fighter and as a political militant. So death does not frighten me."

'He said, "We're going to heaven, and our enemies will rot in hell."

'When he was taken to the gallows, the guards tried to put a hood on his head, but he refused. Then he recited verses from the Koran. Some of the guards started to taunt him.'

The guards chanted the name of the Shi'ite firebrand cleric Moqtada al-Sadr. 'Who is Moqtada?' Saddam sneered.

'A cleric who was present asked Saddam to recite some spiritual words,' Haddad said. 'Saddam did so, but with sarcasm. These were his last words, and then the cord tightened around his neck and he dropped to his death.'

Sunni sheikhs turn their sights from US forces to Al-Qaeda

9 September 2007

Former insurgents queue to take money and promise to back the coalition in a military volte-face. Marie Colvin reports from Jurf as Sakhr, Iraq.

Four months ago the scene would have been unthinkable. Captain Henry Moltz of the 501st Parachute Infantry Regiment led a small group of men up the deserted street to a single-storey municipal building of mellow ochre brick that had been cracked by mortar blasts during months of ruinous fighting with Sunni insurgents.

At the entrance he was greeted with a kiss by Sheikh Sabah al-Janabi, a leading member of the tribe that had spearheaded many of the pitiless Sunni attacks on American forces in and around the little town of Jurf as Sakhr, 25 miles south of Baghdad.

As Moltz, 28, ducked out of the sun into the sparsely furnished interior last Thursday, a second sheikh was waiting for him with another kiss and a look of eager expectation. Moltz swiftly put him at his ease. 'Sheikh, we have the first payment,' he declared.

An aide pulled from his knapsack a thick, heavy wad of used notes tied with rubber bands, and placed it on a table. Then came another, and another, until the table was piled high with 19 bundles of 2.5 million dinars – each worth $38,000 (£19,000) in all.

Moltz looked the second sheikh, Taleb al-Janabi, in the eye. 'If you keep to your contract and keep fighting the enemy, we owe you the balance,' he said.

The balance is $189,000 (£93,000), to be paid over three months if the sheikh sticks to his side of the bargain and drives out the largely foreign fighters of Al-Qaeda in Iraq who have set up camp in date palm groves along the banks of the Euphrates in Ruwiya, to the west.

Taleb nodded acknowledgment of the deal. The bricks of cash were bundled into a plastic bag and he sat on a sagging sofa, cradling the money contentedly in the lap of his grey dishdasha.

Now it was the turn of a third sheikh, Hamid al-Janabi, to step up to the battered table, where three documents had been pinned down against the breeze of a fan by a coffee cup, a mobile phone and a handheld radio.

As he signed them in green ink, it was possible to make out three blue dots on the back of his hand – a traditional tattoo denoting membership of a Sunni tribe that had been allied to Al-Qaeda and had helped to make life hell for the Americans in a fertile strip of land that became one of the most perilous in Iraq.

More bricks of dinars worth just over $30,000 (£15,000) were handed over, the downpayment on an agreement worth $181,600 (£90,000). According to the United States government purchase order-invoice voucher that Hamid signed, he had undertaken to supply 'cops' to the quantity of 'one (force)'. His contract required him to provide 160 tribesmen to fight insurgents in Farisiya, to the northwest, and prevent them from attacking American troops.

The 'cops', who will earn the hefty local rate of $370 (£180) a month, have been fingerprinted and retina-scanned and will carry US identity cards. They have already set up checkpoints and clashed with Al-Qaeda fighters whom they supported before switching sides to the Americans.

One of the younger members of Moltz's A Company acknowledged that he found it hard to grasp such a rapid shifting of alliances.

'I'm not sure about this,' he said. 'Two months ago, these guys were shooting at us. Now we're supposed to be friends. It's kind of hard when you know that guy blew up your buddy.'

Moltz, a Texan who has lost three close comrades in the attacks of the past year, said simply: 'They used to want to kill me, now they want to sign a contract with me. It's hard to get your head around but it is working.'

Taleb and Hamid were the latest recruits to a programme that could prove pivotal in some areas to the prospects for the American 'troop surge' under General David Petraeus, the US commander in Iraq.

When Petraeus appears before Congress tomorrow to deliver his report on the progress of the surge since troop numbers rose from 130,000 in February to 160,000 in June, he will be able to point to several startling successes in parts of Iraq where violence has abated.

Although fighting continues to exact a grim toll of American soldiers and Iraqi civilians alike in towns and cities where it is hard to see hope, the recruitment of enemy sheikhs to the coalition cause has made officers such as Moltz optimistic for the first time in four years of brutal insurgency.

The initiative is being run under the euphemistic title of 'concerned citizens programme'. 'We thought of calling it the ex-terrorist programme but that didn't fly,' one officer joked.

In the area where Moltz's A Company operates, the number of improvised explosive devices (IEDs) detonated against American troops fell from 30 in May to none in August. Nobody is saying the problems have gone away. However, the policy of allying US forces with Sunni insurgents to confront Al-Qaeda has proved so effective to the west of Baghdad in Anbar province – where Falluja and Ramadi used to be the terrorist strongholds – that President George W Bush described it as one of the safest parts of Iraq during a flying visit last week.

Four American soldiers nevertheless died in combat operations in Anbar last Thursday – a reminder, if any were needed, that after so much war, any peace remains fragile. American deaths in Iraq have now passed 3,760 and the number of Iraqi civilians killed last month alone was officially put at 1,773. Independent estimates of civilian deaths go as high as 2,800.

Some critics also worry that the deals with Sunni sheikhs might ultimately turn them into warlords, even if the stated aim is for their private armies to be absorbed into the Iraqi security forces as soon as possible.

However, the agreements signed in Jurf as Sakhr, Babil province, after a year of intensive fighting seem to point to a way forward, both in protecting American soldiers from attack and in crushing Al-Qaeda.

In the past year the Americans based in Babil have endured one of the most relentlessly ferocious onslaughts seen by any US forces in Iraq. They found themselves on a Sunni–Shi'ite faultline that runs to the south of Baghdad's suburbs, and became targets for Iraqi militants on both sides of the religious divide even before Al-Qaeda arrived to compound the misery.

The trouble went back to 2003, when the Iraqi army was disbanded after the fall of Saddam Hussein. Members of the Janabi clan, many of whom had been elite soldiers, returned home bitter at their loss of power to the Shi'ite majority.

They formed the backbone of the Sunni insurgency in the province, establishing makeshift bases among the groves of the Euphrates and its canals.

But this predominantly Sunni area also contains the Shi'ite towns of Iskandariya and Musayyib, where the Mahdi Army holds sway.

The Mahdi militias rose up in a bloodthirsty quest for vengeance after the Shi'ite Askariya shrine at Samarra was bombed in February 2006. They attacked seven Sunni mosques in Babil and then turned their anger on American troops.

US losses were heavy – 51 American soldiers have died in Babil in the past 10 months – and Moltz's A Company faced the grinding daily certainty of an attack.

Mortars and rockets rained down on its Jurf as Sakhr compound, little more than a collection of shipping containers with five camp beds each where the men snatched what sleep they could behind concrete walls.

Whenever they left their outpost, they knew there was every chance of coming under attack, whether from snipers or roadside bombs. 'It was crazy,' said Captain Kevin McDaniel, a platoon leader. 'On one patrol in December, we hit three IEDs and an ambush.'

On that particular patrol, McDaniel and his men were driving north up the Euphrates when the lead vehicle was hit by by the first improvised explosive device. 'The second one was really big,' McDaniel said. 'They had dug a tunnel under the road and placed a ridiculous amount of explosive there. It blew the front off a Humvee. The crater was up to my chin and 12 feet wide.'

When he followed the detonating wire into a field to investigate, gunmen opened up from behind the palms. 'We fired off more than 1,000 rounds and called in Apache helicopters,' he said. 'On the way back we hit a third IED. I couldn't believe it.'

A series of disasters befell the men in rapid succession. Staff Sergeant Christopher Brerard, a company favourite, was killed when insurgents detonated explosives hidden beneath a roof where he was keeping watch. 'You felt if it could happen to him, it could happen to anyone,' McDaniel said.

Another member of the company lost both legs to an IED, and a third who was wounded in the head has had nine brain operations and might never recover.

The outpost was mortared on Thanksgiving evening; the company's Christmas dinner was blown up; and at one point a lorry pulled up to the blast wall and gunmen who jumped out started blasting away at a watchtower.

Nobody was hurt in the latter incidents but morale hit rock bottom. The company rarely saw the enemy and there seemed no prospect of a let-up in the cycle of violence. The beginning of the troop surge in February went virtually unremarked in Jurf as

Sakhr. Many in the company were questioning the point of being there.

When Sunni tribesmen started coming to parley, the troops' suspicion was understandable.

Why the sheikhs' sudden change of heart? Several reasons have been given. Al-Qaeda followers who were initially honoured as allies, who led the resistance from the front and paid well, had outstayed their welcome. Many of the foreigners tried to enforce the strict rules of the Wahhabi strand of Islam: locals were tortured for 'un-Islamic' behaviour – punished for smoking, drinking and possessing photographs and films.

The tipping point seems to have come when Al-Qaeda fighters began forcibly taking sheikhs' daughters for their wives, perverting a tribal tradition of forging alliances through marriage.

'It was a harsh, tyrannical regime,' said Lieutenant-Colonel Val Keaveny, a commander who was in Anbar when its Sunni tribes came to the Americans to talk about changing their allegiance. 'Iraqis simply don't want to live like that.'

In the Jurf as Sakhr area, the Sunnis' dissatisfaction coincided with Petraeus's surge strategy.

In Baghdad the surge brought boots on the ground; in the Babil area, it meant more airpower. Fierce air assaults were launched on insurgent hideouts up the Euphrates valley.

Moltz found that he was able to call for helicopter cover. Logistics improved. The objectives were extended from pacifying the area to preventing insurgents from using one of Babil's main roads to transport weapons and car bombs to Baghdad.

The Sunni sheikhs were getting worried. 'They saw we were not going anywhere, and they risked losing everything as the Shi'ites gained power,' said Major Rick Williams, 45, who hosted the first talks. His expertise on tribal politics is derived in part from his Cherokee Indian ancestry. Colleagues call him 'the sheikh dude'.

'They thought they should get some power while it was still possible or they would be hung out to dry,' Williams said. 'They are in the end responsible for the wellbeing of their tribe.'

Williams called both Sunni and Shi'ite leaders to talks, but only the Sunnis turned up. The negotiations started badly. The Sunnis insisted that the Americans remove Nouri al-Maliki, the Shi'ite prime minister. Otherwise, they said, they would stage a coup.

Discussions became serious in July with the involvement of Fadl al-Janabi, an engineer at the local power plant. A colonel came across him carrying the body of his sister, who had been killed by a mortar, down a road and gave him a lift to the hospital. Later he came to the Americans and said: 'I have 300 guys who want to come with you.'

The discussions ended with a vote among the tribe that was orchestrated by Sheikh Sabah al-Janabi, who has become Moltz's point man in persuading others to switch to the Americans' side.

In August, Moltz began signing contracts with the sheikhs lined up by Sabah. The documents set out in detail what the Americans expect for their money, from the deployment of patrols to the elimination of anyone who attacks their soldiers.

US forces will not go on operations with their new Sunni allies but will support them with firepower or helicopters if necessary. The model is spreading. Deals have also been done with insurgents in Diyala province, north of Baghdad, which Al-Qaeda once proclaimed part of the 'Islamic Caliphate of Iraq'. Today, 25 tribes in the area have men on the US payroll and Al-Qaeda is on the run.

In the Amariya district of western Baghdad, a Sunni leader known as Abu Abed has received 50 fighters and weapons from sheikhs in Anbar, and is fighting with a militia to eject Al-Qaeda.

As for Jurf as Sakhr, the town is slowly being restored to life. The Americans are moving quickly to rebuild, reflecting another component of Petraeus's strategy to bring order to war-torn areas wherever possible.

There are plans to remove the piles of concrete rubble that were once shops or homes. Teenagers have been hired to clear the streets of rubbish. Moltz and Sabah walked round with an engineer last week, working out what needs to be done.

'There is no doubt that he [Sabah] was one of the bad guys,' Moltz said. 'It's not easy doing business with someone who may have been responsible for some of the operations against us. But this area is secure now.'

Sabah is circumspect about his former role in attacks on American soldiers and it has never been discussed openly with his new allies. 'I know some people were fighting the coalition forces,' he said cautiously, 'but now is the time for peace.'

Moltz is hoping to build a new police station, start a medical clinic and renovate the municipal offices. 'Every time in the past I've talked about the town, a bomb would follow within 24 hours,' Moltz said. 'This time, nothing. That leads me to one of two conclusions. Either we have killed all of the enemy, or they [Sabah and his friends] were the enemy.'

He shook his head and made for the exit, only to find no fewer than seven sheikhs blocking his way. Nervously fingering their robes, they asked to discuss getting their men into the new American force. 'We're very happy to work with you,' Moltz said. 'Talk to Sheikh Sabah.'

I felt a new terror on Basra's streets

BASRA

16 December 2007

Islamic militias are waging a brutal campaign for control in Iraq's second city as British troops give way to local forces today, reports Marie Colvin in Basra.

There are two photographs in every police file. One is a long shot of a woman's discarded body, the other a close-up of her last expression.

All the women fell foul of the unwritten rules of the new Basra – they dressed wrongly, they left the home to work, or perhaps they were merely rumoured to have a boyfriend.

Forty-eight manila files have been opened in the past six months. Not one case has been solved. The bare number cannot begin to conjure the horror of these deaths at the hands of Islamic extremists who have the port city in a tightening grip of fear.

In one folder at the Basra police station, the young woman in the autopsy photograph seems to be straining upward in agony, her eyes popping in terror. She is 'female unknown identity, found in Hayer Hussein neighbourhood, behind the electric station. 24/8/2007'.

In another, a woman's nose has been crushed. Trails of blood run from her closed right eye like lines of tears. She is 'female unknown identity, found in Al-Mishraq al-Jaid neighbourhood, behind the car dealer. 7/11/2007'.

Their autopsies revealed painful deaths. One woman found in 'a red dress' had a 9mm bullet wound in her left hand, three in her right hand, three in her right upper arm, and three in her back. Two of the women were beheaded, one with a saw.

Residents say police have not been investigating. 'Everyone knows the militias are doing this, but the police live in fear of them. We all do,' said a middle-aged businessman who was too afraid to give his name.

The walls of Basra would be a good place to start looking for the killers. One graffito on a wall bordering the main Al-Dijari road reads: 'We warn all women of Basra, especially those who are not wearing abbaya [a long, loose black cloak worn over everyday clothes], that we will kill you.' It is signed in the name of an offshoot of the Mahdi Army, the strongest militia in Basra.

It is not just women who live in fear. Professionals such as engineers, doctors and scientists have been dragged from their homes and murdered.

Yet last week Gordon Brown responded angrily in the House of Commons when challenged over the security situation in Basra.

'Iraq is now a democracy,' the prime minister said. 'Millions of people have voted. When I went to Basra, only two days ago, I found that there had been a 90% fall in violence over the past few months. We are now able to hand over Basra to provincial Iraqi control … This is Iraqis taking control over their own security.'

But what kind of security will the British be passing on to local forces in a ceremony at Basra's international airport today? Will David Miliband, the foreign secretary, who is flying in to represent the government at the formalities, genuinely be able to remark upon a job well done? Or are the Basrawis being delivered into the hands of the militias?

The phone rang on the walnut desk of Major-General Jalil Khalaf's office at midnight. He is the new police commander of Basra and had just been telling me about his determination to stop the killing spree.

The call sent him into agitated overdrive. He picked up another receiver and started barking orders: 'Put checkpoints around the area. Seal it. Quickly. Quickly. The car is white model Crown. All checkpoints, arrest all cars of that description.'

Half an hour earlier, a young Christian woman had been kidnapped in the Kharj neighbourhood, and he feared the worst.

Khalaf, a dapper dresser in a sharply tailored black suit with matching waistcoat, arrived in mid-June and appears to be the first commander to start taking any action. Brown's figures suggest it is taking effect.

'I have reopened all 48 women's files and started investigating them,' he said.

'They are also slashing their faces for wearing make-up. These groups declare "We are religious", but this is not religion.'

He believes the true death toll is higher. Families have buried their dead rather than face what is considered a loss of honour, whether the victim is blameless or not.

He has sent a 100-page report back to the national government in Baghdad, detailing Basra's problems. They differ from those in Baghdad, which had descended into fighting between Sunni and

Shi'ite factions before the American 'surge' policy of increasing troop numbers brought some semblance of order this autumn.

Basra's 2m residents are almost all Shi'ite – the fighting is among the main three parties that represent this branch of Islam who are vying for wealth and power.

The stakes are high. Basra, through Umm Qasr just to the east, is the country's only port and the outlet for most of Iraq's oil, of which the province has the country's greatest reserves. Most of the nation's imports come across its docks too.

It should be a wealthy city, but to drive around reveals the extent of its deterioration. The whole place stinks. The governor, a member of Fadila, the region's third most powerful militia, couldn't fix the sewage pipes, so he diverted them into the Ashar river.

The city is mostly low concrete buildings, many crumbling, and whole neighbourhoods are inhabited by squatters who have thrown up illegal and badly built brick or shanty houses. There are daily cuts in electricity and water supplies.

The only civic project that seems to be going well is the provision of new pavements with red tiles. This despite the fact that the city's roads are pitted with potholes. Strange until one learns that the province's governor has just opened a tile factory.

Khalaf's efforts to bring order to the city have given him black bags under his eyes. He describes a world in which the police and the political parties and militias are separate and competing forces. So far the militias are winning.

'The problems are like an interlocking chain,' he said. 'The militias control the ports, which earns them huge sums of money. That money they use to fund their own activities.

'Second, borders,' he continued. 'There is a 280-kilometre border between us [and Iran].

'Smugglers cross the borders with guns and weapons and these go to the militias. We don't have enough guards or the sophisticated equipment you need to stop them. You could smuggle a tank across that border if you wanted.'

The militias are exporting oil products and animals, too, he said.

His efforts to stop them and weed the militias out of his own force have not gone unnoticed. So far he has survived seven assassination attempts. Many of his bodyguards have been killed. He believes most of the attempts came from within his own force.

'I will enter the *Guinness Book of Records* for assassination attempts,' he said.

The root of the problem, Khalaf believes, was the misguided manner in which the British set up the security forces, particularly the police.

'They relied on the political parties and allowed them to nominate people for positions in the police,' he said. 'Of course, the parties nominated their own members.'

Khalaf's personal stock-taking revealed huge quantities of police communications equipment had been delivered directly from police warehouses to the militias, and 1,000 cars had disappeared.

'They were cars with police insignia painted on the side!' he said, exasperated.

Khalaf also found he was paying 3,500 members of the force, at the cost of millions to the Iraqi national treasury, who were actually serving with the militias. They didn't even bother to show up for work.

His report to the government detailed 28 militias or their offshoots. 'All of them have weapons, all are well-trained,' he said. 'They have RPGs [rocket-propelled grenades], many rifles, bombs, mortars. Their weapons are stronger than ours.'

So worried was he for my safety at the end of my interview that he gave me four trucks of soldiers as an escort to the building I was staying in, and his personal Koran for extra safety. I was already forced to travel under cover of traditional abbaya for fear of identification as a westerner.

The level of lawlessness is striking even during a short visit to Basra. On my first day, a male relative of the family I was staying with was kidnapped driving into Basra. A series of desperate calls began to try to find him. It has become a well-established ritual.

The next day, waiting in the anteroom of Major-General Farid Mohan, commander of the army in Basra, I asked the man next to me if he was okay. He had two black eyes and lumps on his bald head.

It turned out he was the leader of the first ministry of finance delegation to visit Basra in five months. He had been kidnapped and tortured. Mohan had negotiated his release hours earlier.

Iyad Ahmed sat slumped forward in the grey dishdasha (robe) and leather sandals that he had on when he was kidnapped from his room at the Qusr Al-Sultan, the best hotel in Basra. He had arrived 20 days earlier to investigate the ports and borders.

'When I was kidnapped, I was investigating the theft of 653 new cars stolen from the international free zone in the middle of the afternoon. The thieves killed the guard at the gate as they drove the cars out.'

Following the trail, the ministry team found that 90 of the cars had been used in assassinations, and 35 in suicide bomb attacks.

Ahmed thinks he was targeted when he started investigating free zone officials for what he believed was their involvement in the car hijacking. The free zone is said to be controlled by the Badr organisation, the Islamic party controlled by Abdul Aziz Hakim, the second most powerful Islamic party in Basra.

'I was threatened,' said Ahmed in an outraged voice. 'A Mr Falah, the senior man, told me, "See what we will do to you today".'

About 11.30 that evening eight new 4x4s full of gunmen stormed into the hotel.

'They dragged me out of my room in just this,' he said slapping his dirty robe. 'I was shouting, "I am a government employee". I thought at first they were after the two women working on my team.'

He was blindfolded, driven to what he believes was a farm because of the noises and tortured for 24 hours. 'They beat me all over, they kicked me, and they hung me by my wrists for three hours.'

Mohan secured his release by promising the kidnappers a 'gift' if they gave him Ahmed. It is a mark of the hypocrisy of some Islamic extremists that because the Koran forbids them from extorting money they pretend that their ransom for a kidnapping is a 'gift'.

Ahmed vowed to keep working, although rather fearfully. 'These militias are bigger than the government,' he said.

The government of Nouri al-Maliki, the prime minister, appears finally to have acknowledged the problem in Basra, but it is unclear if it has the will to wrest the city from the grip of the Islamic parties and their thugs.

'The government is trying to support the forces in Basra,' said Ali Dabbagh, its spokesman. 'We're not trying to hide the fact that there is a threat in Basra, but we think most of the threat is coming from organised criminal gangs who are hiding behind the slogans of JAM [local shorthand for the Mahdi Army].'

He pointed out that 15,000 police had been fired from forces across Iraq because they were engaging in criminal activity or belonged to a militia.

He said that another part of the problem in Basra was that there was a 'political struggle – [Islamic] parties are fighting each other'. He said, however, that he thought today would witness 'a smooth transfer of power to Iraqi security forces.

'They are capable of dealing with Basra and we can ask the Iraqi security forces or multinational forces to intervene if there is a problem.'

Yet it is hard for the Baghdad government to move against the religious militias because it is itself led by Shi'ite religious parties. In the cauldron of Iraqi politics, being seen to attack one's coreligionists is not a good idea.

The Mahdi Army is in theory observing a six-month ceasefire, which it announced in late August. Huge murals of Moqtada and his father Mohammed Sadiq al-Sadr line the main roads, rather like larger-than-life portraits of Saddam Hussein did when he was president.

The Sadr office in Basra is a rival centre of power to the official government. Pick-up trucks, new Toyotas, even two police cars are parked outside the gates of the compound. Inside the activities are not just military. There are departments for welfare and even a tribunal run on sharia principles.

I met Sheikh Ali As-Sayeedi, one of their leaders, in his office, furnished with stuffed faux-Louis XIV furniture, korans and kitsch plastic ivy.

Many leaders used to declaim openly that their ambition was to take power in the city. But now that the British troops are leaving and Iraqis are taking over, they are more cautious in their language.

Sayeedi, however, insisted that the Mahdi Army had driven British forces from Basra and that they would not give up fighting until the US-led coalition left Iraq.

'It is a good next step for Iraqis to take back their sovereignty in Basra,' said Sayeedi. 'We believe all forces should leave the country. We don't respect any agreement with these forces.

'Our people are freedom fighters not militias.

'Our programme is to help the Iraqi people and make everyone happy in Basra.'

Why then, I asked him, is everyone in Basra blaming the Mahdi Army for the violence in the streets?

'People here support us,' he insisted, leaning forward and visibly angering.

'Criminals do crime and then say that they are the Jaish al-Mahdi [the Arabic term for the militia] to appear stronger.'

It is not hard to find the signs of muscle-flexing on the streets, however. On Friday, the Muslim day of prayer, Mahdi checkpoints closed down the city's main roads for their new custom of busing in hundreds of followers to pray in the middle of the main arteries.

Traffic snarled as drivers wove through dirty side roads to get around the jams.

As prayers broke up, men wearing the black turbans of the Mahdi Army strolled away, machineguns slung casually over their shoulders.

The British gave up the battle for control of the streets of Basra months ago. In September they withdrew from Basra Palace, their base for four years, to the airport.

They say they expect the transition to be smooth. The Iraqis have been policing themselves for four months without calling for help. The British insist the handover is no defeat but the next step in the nationwide transition to Iraqi control.

'The formal handover allows them to deliver Iraqi solutions in an Iraqi way,' said Major-General Graham Binns, the commanding officer for British forces in Basra province. 'The way forward is to have the Iraqis take the next step.'

He insisted the British were not cutting and running. They will remain at the airport, reducing to 2,500 by next spring. The Basra government can call on them for support that ranges from surveillance to re-entry.

Binns confessed to regrets. 'I was more of an idealist when I arrived and perhaps too ambitious,' he said. 'I didn't think it would end this way.

'I'm proud of the way we built up the Iraqi security forces, but we were unable to meet the aspirations of the Iraqi people. I would like to have done better.'

Tomorrow the Iraqi police and army will mark their first day of independent control of Basra with a military parade at Basra Palace.

Last Thursday, Iraqi army guards lounged in sociable groups at the massive arch that leads into the compound on the Shatt al-Arab waterway. Three drank tea together, their weapons leaning against the concrete blast wall installed by the departed British.

They seemed unworried, unlike the civilians outside the walls of the new army headquarters. They certainly didn't look like soldiers ready to take on the well-armed militias.

Few in Basra would say that the British have met their goal, 'to establish the security necessary for the development of political institutions and for economic reconstruction'.

An opinion poll published today suggests that 70% of Basrawis believe security will improve after the British have left – mostly because they have been removed as a target – but every one I spoke to said this was their number one worry.

'I must look over my shoulder every minute when I am on the street,' said Rula, a 36-year-old mother of four who has refused to quit journalism despite threats. 'I look hard at the face of my daughter before I leave for work. Someone might cut my throat and I will not come home again.'

Fears that the militias will begin an all-out battle for Basra or that the city will descend into chaos are unlikely to materialise. The factions will no doubt clash as they jockey for power, but they have carved out their lucrative spheres of influence and have too much to lose to go to war.

Iran will play a key role in the future of Basra. Tehran has more influence here than anywhere else in Iraq. The mullahs fund all the Shi'ite groups rather like a wealthy donor hedging his political bets.

Essentially, the political players are happy with their lot. It is the rest of the people in Basra who will suffer, most likely for years to come.

'I went to university because I had dreams for my future,' said 18-year-old Nayla. 'Now I only go to classes twice a week because I am so afraid to leave the house. I have no future.'

Saddam's victims left to suffer as henchmen prosper

HILLA

3 February 2008

Forlorn mounds of sun-bleached clothes stretch across the barren field. Traces of the people who died wearing them – a washed-out vertebra near a small canvas shoe, a jawbone by a faded lavender dress – reveal

that they mark the shallow graves of 1,200 of Saddam Hussein's unidentified victims.

Little else except a lingering stench marks the bleak burial site that
lies up a muddy track in Mahawil, a farming village just outside the
Shi'ite southern Iraqi city of Hilla. Even the weeds have not grown
back.

Up to 15,000 men, women and children are believed to have
been shot and buried here when Saddam unleashed the elite
Republican Guard on his rebellious people in 1991, just days after
he promised the United Nations that he would 'end all military
action'. He had lost his war in Kuwait; he would win this one.

An estimated 100,000 Shi'ites and Kurds died as the Republican
Guard tanks rolled northwards in a murderous onslaught on those
who had risen up against him.

The vengeful Iraqi troops struck hard in Hilla which, like most
of the Shi'ite south, had been seized by an angry population
following encouragement from the first President George Bush to
rebel against Saddam. American help never came.

Hilla lists 4,800 families who lost a member.

When American-led troops invaded in 2003, the city was buoyed
by the knowledge that President George W Bush and Tony Blair
had cited Saddam's massacres as part of their justification for war.

Many were impoverished because they had lost their breadwinner or had suffered as Saddam cracked down on the region. They
thought their lives would be transformed when the Americans and
a nascent Iraqi government pledged to give them compensation
and help.

Paul Bremer, the American diplomat who ruled Iraq as head of
the new Coalition Provisional Authority, told a press conference in
May 2004 that the CPA would pay $25 million to compensate
Saddam's victims. A press release announced the formation of a
task force to distribute the money.

Less than a year later, the Iraqi government's assurances of help
were enshrined in draft legislation. It promised a monthly pension,

cancellation of debts, help with home loans and provision of land to 'the victims of mass graves'.

Yet today, most of the families who uncovered relatives in the Mahawil field are still living in desperate poverty.

Their anger is compounded by the fact that all but the most senior members of Saddam's ruling Ba'ath party, mostly Sunnis who victimised them, have either returned to their jobs after an initial purge, or are collecting government pensions.

Sadiya Saleh, a 67-year-old widow who found her daughter, Halda Aboud, 34, and her grandson, Mohammed Aboud, 12, in the mass grave, was left in a wheelchair after Iraqi soldiers kicked and beat her as she tried to save her son.

Surviving on handouts from relatives and sales of sunflower seeds, she is one of the many still waiting for the promised compensation for appalling suffering at the hands of their own government.

'Soldiers came to my house looking for guns. I told them we are poor, we have no weapons,' said Saleh, dressed in the traditional black abbaya robe, last week. 'My daughter was in my house because she used to visit me once a month. They dragged her out with her son. He was only 12. They were screaming.'

Saleh threw herself on top of her own son Nasir, who was the same age as his cousin. Her voice breaks as she continues. 'They punched me and kicked me in the back until they got me off him and took him away.' The beating left her crippled.

Nasir returned traumatised two days later. He did not speak of what had happened for 12 years. Formerly a bright, happy boy who loved football, he never went back to school or played with his friends again. Only when the news came that Saddam's regime had fallen did he break his silence.

Saleh gathers her abbaya closer as she tells his story. 'Nasir told me that every night a group was taken out and never came back,' she said. One night, Halda, Mohammed and Nasir were driven to the field in Mahawil and shoved into the night, blindfolded and with their wrists tied. The soldiers opened fire.

'Nasir said they all fell and he was covered with blood but not shot,' Saleh said.

'Dirt fell on top of him but not too much. After a while he crawled out and hid in the trees.' After Nasir told his story, Saleh went to the field.

It was a chaotic, desperate scene, as I recall from seeing it myself. I remember walking over the hill to a vision from hell.

In the blazing heat, a yellow mechanical digger was gouging a huge trench, gently dumping dirt and bundles of bones wrapped in cloth.

Men dug with shovels and their bare hands. Others separated the bodies and laid them out gently on blankets, placing recognisable objects on top – a watch here, a small gold necklace on a pile topped by a skull. The smell was overpowering.

A loudspeaker broadcast a name when an identity card was found. Thousands of men and women walked past the rows of bodies, some throwing themselves on a dirty jumble of rags and bones they recognised. Others trudged by with their dead wrapped in plastic bags.

Saleh recognised Halda's body by her clothes, a grey dress over brown trousers and a brown scarf. 'I knew her clothes. I bought them for her,' she said. Next to her daughter were the bones of her grandson.

She now relies on Ayat, a nine-year-old granddaughter, to push her decrepit wheelchair and clean for her. She has not been able to afford heating gas for a fortnight, despite the bitterly cold Iraq winter.

Ayat sits on the arm of her chair, wearing a woolly hat and scarf and embroidered jeans, solemnly listening to the story. Her only smile comes when her grandmother says that 'she is such a help to me'. The 500,000-dinar (£200) monthly payment now being mooted by the government would change everything but there is little sign it will be paid soon.

Saleh's sense of injustice is intensified by the relative comfort enjoyed by former members of the Ba'ath party, which Saddam built into his personal fiefdom during three decades of power. 'The Ba'athists have their land, their houses and their cars,' Saleh said bitterly. 'We have nothing.'

Shalah Jabar, 62, would be one of the targets of her anger should she meet him. He worked as an accountant in the government fabric factory in Hilla and rose through the ranks in the Ba'ath party.

Bremer's first decree expelled all Ba'athists from public jobs. As the insurgency took hold in 2004, fuelled by Sunni bitterness at their treatment, the decree was watered down.

Teachers, who generally held lower ranks in the party, were allowed to return to their jobs. Jabar and others of similar rank could apply for pensions. He now receives £200 a month, along with what he earns from rent on his grandfather's farm. He makes no apologies.

'I joined the Ba'ath party out of a sense of patriotism in 1976,' he said last week. Many of his rank, called district officers, spied on their fellow residents, but he insisted that he had merely given lectures and organised cultural events.

Asked why he had stayed in the party as it turned into an instrument of Saddam's oppression, he replied: 'I wished to continue my studies. I could only do that if I was in the party.'

There is no doubt that it was almost impossible to get ahead in Saddam's Iraq without joining his party. But this is small solace to Saddam's victims.

On a wall outside the government-run Martyrs Memorial Foundation in Hilla, a handwritten sign reads, 'Ba'athists not welcome'. Inside the ramshackle office, there is no electricity. Men in shabby suits and women in black abbayas queue to fill out the forms that the government requires for a job or compensation.

Few have been helped, admits Hussein Jabar, the 32-year-old director, who lost a nephew and two uncles in the mass grave. He is angry with the Americans who, he says, should help since they are the occupying power. He also chides the Shi'ite-led Iraqi government.

'Our young government has forgotten many things and this mass grave is one of them,' said Jabar in his unlit office. He said he had given plots of land to 534 families, although he is aware they have no money to build homes.

'The families have already been caused too much pain by the deaths of their relatives. I hope we can give them something,' he said.

Story after story is told as if it is fresh. Najia Aziz, now in her sixties, saw Iraqi soldiers shove her 20-year-old son Mazen Yousef into a car as he walked to a friend's house. He had just returned from serving in Kuwait.

'I ran to the car, begging and screaming at them to release him. I kept running after the car,' she said.

She never gave up hope, going from prison to prison, asking for him for years. 'I almost didn't go to the grave. I was telling myself, "He didn't do anything. He won't be there",' she recalled. She did not know that Saddam regarded the returning soldiers as suspect because so few fought.

Aziz identified her son's bones through the army leave permit still in the pocket of his jeans. A friend who had been with him in prison told her he had been so badly beaten before he was shot that he couldn't open his eyes. 'My spirit left with him that day,' she said.

There are fears that the desperation and injustice felt in Hilla and among other families who lost relatives to Saddam's brutality could provoke renewed sectarian fighting unless the government acts on its promises.

The Mahdi army, the radical Shi'ite militia responsible for attacks on allied forces, has been boosted by their rage. Many of its recruits from Hilla, who had relatives buried in the mass grave, joined because they felt their plight was being ignored.

The unclaimed bones in the field are as neglected as the living. After a few months of lying exposed, dirt was spread over them and clothes and personal items were left on top of the shallow graves for those still looking for their loved ones. There is little chance of that now.

Every year on the anniversary of the March 1991 uprising, Hilla residents travel to the site and stage a demonstration calling for a memorial to honour the dead.

Even that small plea has been ignored. They will be there again next month.

REBELS CRUSHED

After Saddam Hussein's crushing 1991 defeat in Kuwait, rebellions broke out in Kurdish areas of northern Iraq and among Shi'ites in the south.

The rebels seized 14 of Iraq's 18 provinces. Many expected American support. It never materialised.

Instead, Saddam regrouped and brutally suppressed the uprisings. Up to 100,000 died.

Middle East

Gaza's mourners plan 'spectacular' revenge: War on Terror

GAZA CITY

28 March 2004

The huge kitchens at Hamas's chosen catering company worked non-stop last week.

By tradition, the families of the latest 'martyrs' had to feed the hundreds who sat at new marquees put up for the mourning period. Taxis and battered cars were loaded up at Eastern Catering with foil-covered platters of rice and lamb, and sped off to the vigils of the bereaved.

Last Friday the martyrdom industry was in full swing. Under a green awning in the courtyard of the El-Amrain family home, men sat stoically on white plastic chairs as little boys with green Hamas headbands raced about in play, twirling child-sized Hamas flags bought for the occasion.

A nearby minaret broadcast the sermon of the local imam, who promised that every shaheed, or martyr, would be granted automatic passage to heaven for 70 members of his family as well as his own 72 virgins in paradise.

The preacher thanked God for giving martyrdom to Sheikh Ahmed Yassin, the spiritual leader of Hamas, the militant Islamic group he founded in 1987. It was said that the 67-year-old Yassin had long craved martyrdom, lamenting that because he was paralysed, 'martyrdom had to come to him'.

On Monday it did – in the form of an Israeli missile that struck after bodyguards pushed his wheelchair out of a mosque at the end of early morning prayers. Anger and emotion at his assassination sent support for Hamas, which had already grown during 3½ years of intifada, soaring.

After the imam on the minaret finished his sermon, everyone at the El-Amrain family's mourning tent dug their white plastic spoons into their lamb platters.

They were there for Hamman El-Amrain, 26, who was one of seven brothers, all Hamas members.

Like thousands of boys in Gaza, Hamman had joined Hamas's youth group, aged 12.

Five years later he graduated to Izzedine al-Qassam brigades, its military wing.

He died on Wednesday after being shot by an Israeli tank he was trying to hit with a 'betar', a rocket grenade that Hamas manufactures locally.

There was little doubt among the men at the mourning tent that more martyrs would soon join Hamman. Hamas leaders have vowed vengeance. 'Martyrdom is one of our strongest assets,' said Mohamed El-Amrain, 29, Hamman's brother and a ranking Hamas member who sits on a committee that hands out cheques to the families of verified martyrs.

Bloodthirsty threats are common after Israel kills Hamas officials, but last week in Gaza there was growing evidence to support the Israeli fears that emptied streets and cafés in Jerusalem and Tel Aviv alike.

Mohamed El-Amrain warned that Hamas was planning a 'spectacular' attack. He said he expected the near future would see a continuation of smaller incidents such as a failed Hamas raid on Thursday night on the Gush Katif settlement, where two Hamas gunmen tried to swim ashore. Both were shot dead. The revenge for Yassin, however, would be different.

'We will strike the Israelis in a totally new way, where they will not expect us,' El-Amrain said. 'This will be a revenge that shows them we can hit them anywhere and that we will never stop.'

There was agreement with his words even among Palestinians who oppose such attacks. 'Hamas has to act against the Israelis and avenge Sheikh Yassin, or they will lose respect on the street,' said Saeb al-Ajez, a general in the Palestinian Authority (PA) government forces in Gaza.

He is in the unenviable position of being responsible for stopping Palestinian attacks on Israelis, under the terms of an agreement with Israel. His own population views that agreement as moribund and his efforts as betrayal.

'For Hamas's credibility, their answer has to be in a dramatic and different way,' al-Ajez said.

He believed they might try to assassinate Israeli ministers, a suspicion borne out by the recent appearance on a Hamas website of a 'most wanted' pack of cards depicting the Israeli government, headed by Ariel Sharon, the prime minister, on the joker card.

Al-Ajez, whose hair has gone grey and who dresses in starched khaki uniforms, says Hamas is now far more popular in Gaza than the Palestinian Authority, which is dominated by Yasser Arafat's secular group, Fatah.

'To the population now, Hamas is the valiant resistance,' the general said. 'My soldiers at the checkpoints feel in such a difficult position. They are supposed to prevent Hamas from attacking Israel, but at the same time Israel attacks them. The door is closing on our fingers.'

The assassination of Yassin has left open the possibility that the fundamentalist Hamas could turn in a more radical direction. Yassin, although an implacable foe of Israel, had in recent years moderated Hamas's insistence that it would fight on for a Palestinian state that included Israel proper as well as the West Bank and Gaza.

He had adopted the position that Hamas would settle for a state on the West Bank and Gaza, although not as a final resolution – the next generation would be free to fight on.

Abdel Aziz al-Rantissi, a paediatrician who replaced Yassin as Hamas leader in Gaza last week, has taken a far more radical stand. He has been implacable in insisting that Hamas will settle for nothing less than every inch of former Palestinian land, and that military struggle – not negotiation – is the way forward.

Last week, however, some Palestinian observers said that al-Rantissi might moderate his position now that he had the top job in concert with Khaled Masha'al, Hamas's political leader, based in Damascus.

Strains between the authority and Hamas could come to a head if Sharon goes ahead with a plan to withdraw unilaterally from Gaza. Last week Israeli commentators said the killing of Yassin and promised assassinations of other Hamas leaders indicated that Sharon intended to proceed, but that he wanted to decapitate the group first. This would prevent any possibility of Hamas taking over from the Palestinian Authority in Gaza and turning it into 'Hamas land' on Israel's southern border.

The authority and Hamas are in talks to try to avert civil war. Ziad Abu Amr, an independent member of the Palestinian parliament who is on the committee that negotiates with the Islamic forces, said Hamas was insisting on power-sharing in the event of an Israeli pull-out from Gaza.

'Hamas wants to be a partner. It doesn't want to be excluded after Israeli withdrawal,' Abu Amr said. 'So far Arafat doesn't accept any partnership with Hamas. But if we don't succeed in persuading Arafat to accept power-sharing, we are going to face civil strife.'

More young men lined up for death last week, and most of them seemed far more committed than 16-year-old Hussam Abdu, whose photograph went round the world last week after he was stopped at an Israeli checkpoint with a suicide bomber's vest and decided he wanted to live.

Asked by Israeli interrogators why he had agreed to undertake the mission, he replied: 'It's because people don't like me.' He said he had been teased at school and wanted to be a 'hero'. The services of 72 virgins in paradise had been an additional incentive, he acknowledged.

At another mourning tent in Gaza on Friday, a further line of silent men in white plastic chairs sat with the family of Ishaq Nasar, 19, a Hamas 'frogman' killed trying to swim ashore at the Jewish settlement in Gaza on Thursday.

Abu Osama Nasar, 17, seemed strangely joyful as he described how his brother, now in paradise, had told him he planned to avenge Yassin's death. Abu Osama was raring to join him. He had always wanted to be a suicide bomber, he said, but his parents had told him to wait until he grew up. Now that he was 17, he had put his name down.

Over and over, the teenager acted out, with obscene enthusiasm, the motions of his chest blowing up. There was no way, he said, that Palestinian Authority forces could stop Hamas from continuing to fight.

'If the PA wants to stop the resistance, they will fail,' Abu Osama said. 'They are a failed leadership. If they try to come here, we will cut their necks.'

There is unlikely to be any shortage of business in the foresee-able future for the Eastern Catering company. Yesterday, children at Yassin's grave watered wilting carnations in the rectangle of rocks and cinderblocks that marked the outline of his resting place. All agreed that they would like to be Hamas martyrs when they grew up.

A seven-year-old Palestinian boy was shot and killed as he stood at the window of his home in a refugee camp in the West Bank city of Nablus yesterday. The Israeli military blamed stray Palestinian gunfire.

Into the underworld

17 July 2005

Beneath the Israeli–Egyptian border is a secret world: a network of narrow tunnels, through which Palestinians smuggle weapons – and even wives – into the Gaza Strip. But these 'snake holes' also carry the risk of disaster and death. Marie Colvin enters the subterranean labyrinth.

Nadr Keshta was 18 and his attractive young neighbour had caught his eye. He started hanging about on street corners, trying to catch sight of her as she walked home from school in her blue-and-grey uniform. For weeks she ignored him. When she finally waved back to his wink, it was her signal that she returned his interest. Without ever exchanging a word, they considered themselves 'engaged'. That was where their story, as told by his younger brother Mohamed, led into the subterranean world of the 'tunnel people' of Rafah, the southernmost city in the Gaza Strip. He needed money now, to build a house for his bride and, truth be told, to show off a bit – buying a new gun was first on his list. For young men in Rafah, a gun is street cred; it's cool, like having the latest pair of trainers.

Nadr was earning a pittance on his father's farm. Gaza has been locked down by the Israeli army since the armed Palestinian intifada began in September 2000. There are no jobs for young men, because Gaza can no longer export the fruit and vegetables that were the staples of its economy – tomatoes that used to sell for $20 a crate are down to $3 in the local market. Only a few men have permission to enter Israel for work.

Nadr turned to the only paying job in Rafah: digging tunnels under the Israeli-Egyptian border. I had heard rumours of tunnels for years, but never really believed them, because there is nothing but white sand that runs through your fingers. How could you have a tunnel network in this flimsy sand? My scepticism was buttressed by knowledge of Israel's defences: the army has erected an 8 foot wall that plunges invisibly many more feet underground along the Rafah side of the Philadelphi road – a dirt stretch patrolled by armoured Israeli Jeeps that parallels the Egyptian border – to stop tunnellers. Then there are explosions every night in Rafah, set off arbitrarily by Israeli engineers in the hope that they might collapse an undiscovered tunnel.

But a chance conversation resulted in my living in Rafah for a week with the 'tunnel people'. It was like discovering a lost tribe in a city I had been visiting for 15 years. I found an extraordinary, secret tunnel culture known only to a few Palestinians. The tunnel people told me they originally smuggled in contraband drugs, women, cigarettes (5 shekels in Egypt, 12 shekels in Gaza), and even the python that still slithers around in the Rafah zoo, and the ostrich that escaped during the May 2004 Israeli incursion, to the great glee of Rafah kids, who rode bareback on the big bird until the zookeepers recaptured him. Since the second intifada began five years ago, however, the tunnellers have mostly smuggled weapons.

The profits are huge. A Kalashnikov sells for $200 on the Egyptian side, but fetches $2,000 on the Gaza black market. A good night's delivery is 1,200 Kalashnikovs – a profit of more than $2 million. Bullets – 50 cents in Egypt, $8 wholesale in Gaza – are even more profitable. A standard one-night delivery returns a profit of $750,000. The tunnels are financed by wealthy families – locals call them the 'snakeheads' – who run the tunnels as businesses. They rent the passage to anyone who pays $10,000 for one night's use – a gun dealer, Hamas or Islamic Jihad, the militant Islamic fundamentalist groups, or a man who can't get his wife legally into Gaza. Cash is the currency, not politics, patriotism or sentimentality.

They rent, build or buy a house, even an entire farm, just to disguise a tunnel's 'eye', as they call the entrance. The gun dealers are their biggest clients. 'We call them blood dealers,' said Abu Sibah, 36, the bearded head of a rogue Palestinian militia in Al-Bureij refugee camp north of Rafah, outside a car mechanics' shop where he had stored his latest shipment of Kalashnikovs and a rocket-propelled grenade (RPG). 'But there is nothing to do about them. We depend on the tunnels for guns.' He was particularly proud of the shiny black Belgian revolver in his belt – at $3,000, a special order. It was to this world that Nadr Keshta turned for the money to marry.

His relatives were in the tunnel business and he heard a 'big project' was about to start. He signed on with a group of eight young men, all relatives. In the tunnels there is a hierarchy: those not related to the patron work for $100 a day as diggers, while those who are relatives get a share of the profit in return for their labour, a much better deal. When the tunnel is finished they are entitled to a percentage on every load that passes through it.

Israel has made endless efforts to stop the tunnellers; apart from explosives, bulldozers have chopped away at Rafah's unlovely blocks of concrete houses that used to sprawl right up to the border fence. But all that has done is make the digging longer and more arduous. Tunnels now have to extend about 880 yards to span the bulldozed divide. Keshta expected to make $20,000 as his share of the tunnel's first load, and then a continuing profit as long as it remained undiscovered. In Gaza, that was enough to build a house and have some left over for his new gun and a wedding reception. But disaster struck.

At the start, the new project ran smoothly following well-rehearsed procedures. Keshta and his fellow diggers began excavating a shaft from a back bedroom of a three-storey house. The tunnel was financed by Hisham al-Sha'ir – the al-Sha'irs are known as Gaza's premier tunnelling family.

An al-Sha'ir grandmother had died there and the house was empty. The tunnel 'eye' was concealed by four marble floor tiles. They dug a narrow shaft, barely wider than their bodies, 40 feet down through 'hard sand' – red sand that is impacted and solid – until they reached a layer of soft sand. The tunnellers of Gaza are self-taught geologists; their grandfathers discovered that a 'hard sand' stratum runs under Rafah to varying depths.

They dig through it until they hit the soft sand below – the layer of hard sand becomes their ceiling. They are hunted by both the Israelis and the Palestinian Authority (PA).

Keshta and the other young diggers lived day and night in the house, so that their comings and goings would not arouse suspicion. They hid the telltale sand in other rooms. But unbeknown to them, the explosives that the Israelis periodically set off had weakened the hard-sand ceiling. Three days of unexpected rain weakened it further, and the tunnel collapsed on Keshta and his two cousins, Nidal al-Sha'ir and Sufiyan al-Sha'ir.

The three were trapped. Other diggers heard Nadr yelling over the intercom that goes through every tunnel: 'Help us, help us, help us to live.' The three entombed teenagers began chanting 'There is no God but Allah, and Muhammad is his prophet,' the phrase that Muslims intone in times of crisis.

The tunnel financier raced to the scene and began digging with a bulldozer along the tunnel's path, but nobody knew the boys' location. Friends and relatives gathered at the intercom in the back bedroom.

'There is no air, it is too dark, we are feeling like we are in a grave,' Nadr's brother, Mohamed, heard him shout. 'I was sure then that they would die,' Mohamed said, remembering his sense of helplessness. For nine hours, the cousins were heard praying aloud and pleading for rescue. The Palestinians dug on their side of the Philadelphi wall and the Israelis began digging on theirs after a desperate relative broke the tunnel code of secrecy and drew the Israel Defence Forces (IDF) a map of the tunnel's path.

Nadr Keshta's illicit fiancée heard of the disaster, but she could not come even just to hear his voice: her parents would have been furious if they had known of her relationship with a boy they had not approved. She would have been considered to have dishonoured the family. Juliet, who doesn't want her real name used, was despondent. She had no idea her Nadr had gone down the tunnels. 'Why did he do this? I wanted him, not money!' she cried in secret. But she had to hide her distress from her family. After nine hours of solid digging, an Israeli bulldozer accidentally cut the intercom wire and there was silence on the line that connected the three cousins to the world above.

Keshta and his cousins had made the mistake of young men the world over: succumbing to the lure of the big score. But the price in Rafah's tunnels is higher than elsewhere. However vast the sums to be made in the tunnel business, it is not easy money. Death stalks this subterranean world – the horrific slow death of suffocation below the surface. The day before I arrived in Rafah, a teenager had been electrocuted in a tunnel and his body dumped where he, but not the tunnel 'eye', would be found. Families who receive the bloated bodies of their tunnel dead take a little consolation from the fact that tunnellers who die digging are considered *shaheed* – martyrs to the Palestinian cause – even if they mostly die in the pursuit of profit. In Rafah, the culture of the martyr is as pervasive as guns.

Yousef and Ahmed Keshta, 24 and 31, run the most popular barber's shop in Rafah, the Shaheed Salon – the Martyrs' Salon. The walls are plastered with photographs and posters of late former customers. Instead of shampoos and conditioners, the shelves of mirrored cabinets are lined with keepsakes from the dead: a string of worry beads left by Mahmoud al-Sha'ir the day before he was killed; a toy gun from their youngest customer to die in a tunnel. Their most popular hairstyles are the side-buzzed marine cut – modelled on that of the American marines seen on the news, even though most young Gazans are vaguely anti-American – and the French cut, so called because it resembles a mushroom when done properly. I asked a bearded Martyrs' Salon customer, who sat with a white bib in front of a mirror, if it was not disconcerting to be stared at from all sides by the dead. He looked at me as if I came from a different planet. 'Of course not. I remember them all: most are relatives, neighbours, friends – it is my duty to remember them.' There are more realistic voices, but they don't drown out the siren call of money.

Israeli tanks rolled into Rafah in May 2004 after five Israeli soldiers died when Palestinians fired an RPG at an armoured personnel carrier. IDF tanks and bulldozers destroyed another entire block of homes. Ibrahim Keshta knocked holes through his walls to get his family out. 'It used to be a big neighbourhood here. Now there are only dogs,' he said as he brought a tray of glasses of sweet tea and sat cross-legged on the floor of his half-ruined house to talk. 'You die alone here.'

Looking down through windows emptied of glass by tank shells, Ibrahim's view is of a mound of rubble – all that remains of a small tin-roofed house custom-built to hide the 'eye' of the tunnel where his younger brother Mohamed died. A baby fig tree grows above the barely visible sunken path of sand that is the only trace of the destroyed tunnel beneath.

Ibrahim blames a 'snakehead' for luring his brother underground. 'He told my brother, "Join my crew and you will have nice expensive guns, a nice house, you can marry,"' he says, waving his arms around with lingering outrage, shooing away his three small children, who return moments later to listen and giggle.

After hundreds of yards of digging and one day away from punching through in Egypt, on his first tunnel job, the roof collapsed above Mohamed and his boss. Both died.

In Ibrahim's neighbourhood alone, locals reckon there are about 20 tunnels in various stages of destruction or excavation. Down the street from Ibrahim's ruin is the rubble of a house destroyed because the owner had financed one of the most famous tunnels in Rafah: the one commissioned by Yasser Arafat, then president of the Palestinian Authority, to smuggle in 50 tonnes of weapons from Iran aboard the freighter *Karine A*, which the Israelis captured in the Red Sea. Arafat denied any connection, but the trace was clear: the PA had commissioned the $100 million cargo of rockets, missiles, mortars and sniper rifles. When I went to the site of the destroyed house, a white baby donkey lay basking in the sand at the foot of all that was left: a mound of dirt and concrete slabs. After my visit, the PA found the 'eye' of another tunnel dug to connect to the main one – right underneath where the baby donkey had been tethered by a rope invisible to the casual observer.

More terrifying than the spectre of sudden death is the psychological trauma of spending months underground in a space 2 foot wide by 2 foot 4 inches tall.

A 770-yard tunnel can take six months to finish. When tunnellers lowered me by rope down a shaft that began in a little girl's bedroom with posters of cuddly animals on the walls, I was gripped by panicky claustrophobia. The so-called 'safe' hard-sand walls trickled away on my head as I passed into the depths; the sand crumbled each time I scrabbled for footing on the way down; the walls closed in, and the bare bulbs did little to alleviate the darkness or the fear that the whole thing might cave in on top of me at any moment.

'To do this work, you have to throw your heart away,' says Ayed (not his real name), who at 28 is considered a veteran digger. So comfortable with his work has Ayed become that he sleeps in tunnels. He has a muscular, wiry body and spade-like callused fingers. He brews coffee up top, and takes a flask down with him and thinks nothing of staying underground for days. As I would learn, each tunneller has his own methods. Unlike the tunnel that I went down, where hard sand formed the walls of the shaft, Ayed's entry shaft is lined with metal plates specially welded for the job. As boss, he checks the tunnel's progress with a compass every 10–15 yards; after 20 yards he installs a bespoke engine that hauls back nine 'boats' containing pails of sand. Two tunnellers work at the face, Ayed digging and the other loading the pails. Two work at the foot of the shaft unloading the buckets, then buzz when the buckets are empty, and the forward crew starts the engine to haul them back.

If the sand gets soft on the horizontal he is digging, Ayed either installs supports or just tunnels lower to make sure he has a hard-sand ceiling. He is nostalgic about the time he worked in a well-financed tunnel where the owner installed air conditioning.

At 55 yards, he brings in a vacuum cleaner and hooks it up to a hose to draw in air. It is gospel in Gaza that Israel has banned the import of vacuum cleaners. By the time the tunnel reaches 55 yards there are three systems operating: a specially engineered motor-and-pulley system to get the pails of sand to the mouth of the tunnel; an intercom on a separate wire to connect him to the top; and a third wire that brings in electricity to power the bare bulbs that line the tunnel.

Ayed can judge the distance by experience; nine buckets of sand equals one yard. A typical day is 10–11 hours of digging, 10–15 yards of progress.

Every tunnel is measured meticulously: 2 feet wide, 2 feet 4 inches high. Wider than that, and experience shows collapse is likely.

There is black humour, much as in any other dangerous profession. Ayed laughs as he recalls the time he put up a pipe to see where he was going, and it came up in the living room of a house and he could hear a mother yelling at her child. He traced the location and paid the family for their silence. As in gold-prospecting, all tunnellers dream of the big score.

'Even when we have no tunnel, we meet – and what do we talk about?' said Ayed. 'We talk about houses we have spotted that might be good for a tunnel; if anyone has heard of a tunnel deal going down.'

Their hero is Salman al-Sha'ir, now 85, the grandfather of all the tunnellers. He was called in whenever a tunnel had a problem and could always solve it. Famously (at least in tunnel lore), he once single-handedly dug a tunnel to Egypt when his son was caught on the Egyptian side, and rescued him. Salman's tunnel career ended when Israeli commandos snatched him from his farm; he now languishes in an Israeli prison.

Ayed's experience on the Egyptian side – punching out the other 'eye' – gives an incredible insight into how this strange underworld connects to a larger network of international arms dealers. Over the years he has been working, he has seen the provenance and quality of weapons change. Guns used to come from Egypt and Yemen; now the great bulk come from Darfur in Sudan, where civil war is raging. The dealers have migrated there and sell weapons by the tonne to the Bedouin who live on the mountainous border and are subject to no law. The Sudan connection is well known in Gaza, but Israel's military intelligence, usually among the best-informed in the world, still lists Egypt and Yemen as the main provenances for the guns used against them.

Ayed told an extraordinary tale of the time he was stranded in Egypt. As tunnel boss, he was responsible for the diggers, all relatives of the tunnel patron, so he could not leave them behind without risking a blood feud. When they punched through on the tunnel into the Egyptian side, the army had been tipped off and started firing. Ayed got everyone and the shipment down into the tunnel but was too late to escape himself. He fled with the Bedouin suppliers into the mountains, then watched them take delivery of tonnes of weapons from dealers in Darfur. 'I stayed with the Bedouin for 12 days until I found a tunnel to go back to Rafah,' Ayed said.

'In the mountains, the Bedouin are heavily armed; they even have anti-aircraft weapons. The Egyptian army can't go there.' Abu Sihab, of the rogue militia in Al-Bureij, says: 'The good guns we are getting now are from Darfur. The bullets from Darfur are shit – I always check them and they are bad.'

There are exceptions, probably as common as the Las Vegas gambler who gives up after his big score. The only tunneller I met who had given up described tunnelling as addictive. 'It takes a special kind of person,' he said. He would only talk to me in secret; we met in the middle of a field of 3 foot-high corn and sat on the ground. Even then, he was nervous. He treated his 10-month digging as a high-risk investment; he got shares in return for labour and earned $45,000. Unlike any other tunneller, he never went back.

He now has a house and is looking for a wife. He is the exception.

Tunnellers such as Ayed live for the next tunnel; he says there are always shipments waiting with the Bedouin in Egypt; anyone who can get a tunnel across is assured of business.

Ayed has been buried three times, but never as disastrously as Keshta and his cousins. 'Only my head was free,' he said. 'It only took me two hours to dig myself out, and then I went back to digging.'

Neither his wife nor his family knew he was working on a tunnel; he told them he was working in construction in Gaza City and that it was difficult to come back at night because of the Israeli checkpoints that cut Palestinian Gaza into three sectors. When he did go home, he showered first and walked a circuitous path back.

Nadr never got to marry his Juliet or buy his 'cool' gun; the Israelis found him, still alive, in the collapsed tunnel. The photo of his miraculous rescue is on the wall of the Martyrs' Salon, but he is now in an Israeli prison with a lengthy sentence to serve; his secret fiancée has vowed to wait, but their life is essentially over.

For Ayed, given the number of tunnels being dug, and the Israeli explosives, his experience may not be enough; the chances are the night will come when he won't be showering and walking home ever again. Ayed and I discuss how many tunnellers have died, and he tells me he will leave the tunnel business for a steady job. But when I ask him what he dreams about, his eyes light up and he says: 'I dream of building a tunnel all for myself. I'll wait for this "hot" time [pressure from Israel and the PA] to pass. Now I have my own connections on the Egyptian side.' I point out the odds are against him. Even after the Israelis withdraw from Gaza soon, the PA's hunt will continue. He says with a big smile: 'No one will stop the tunnels. I'll teach my children.'

Bulldozer Sharon wins through, but bigger battles may lie ahead

NEVE DEKALIM

21 August 2005

Marie Colvin, Aviram Zino, Uzi Mahnaimi and Hala Jaber

Most of the teenagers had been awake all night at the three gates of Neve Dekalim when, just before dawn, they caught the first sight of the Israeli soldiers who had come to evacuate the largest Jewish settlement in Gaza. They roused themselves into a linked-arm barricade and began singing psalms.

By 8am the sun was beating down and the teenagers, mostly infiltrators from Israel and West Bank settlements, were joined by long-time residents who were actually the ones being moved out.

One young couple wheeled a pushcart with twin toddler girls with blonde ponytails to the front line. Teenage boys sporting what have become the settlers' characteristic orange T-shirts darted forward with sharpened screwdrivers to puncture the tyres of the army buses.

Despite such initial signs of youthful bravado, by yesterday Neve Dekalim's 2,500 residents had gone – barring a few left behind to ease the handover – as had some 85% of the 8,500 other people who until last weekend had lived in 21 settlements built in the midst of Gaza's 1.3 million Palestinians.

When the process resumes today after a break for the Sabbath, Israeli forces hope to clear the remaining settlements of Netzarim and Elei Sinai in northern Gaza and Katif, Atzmona and Slav in the Gush Katif bloc, before turning their attention to four isolated settlements in the West Bank. Once the bulldozers have destroyed the houses, the Palestinians are expected to move onto the land by October.

Some of the last settlers may yet put up resistance, however, especially in the Sanur and Homesh settlements, built on territory in the West Bank that religious Jews regard as part of Eretz, or biblical, Israel. And, in a further bizarre twist, youths from Neve Dekalim were last night frantically text messaging each other to gather this morning at the gates of their settlement, which they believed would be lightly guarded, to retake their now empty homes.

Militant Palestinian groups, too, could cause problems despite attempts by Mahmoud Abbas, the Palestinian president, to keep a lid on violence. Yesterday dozens of Hamas gunmen took over Gaza City's central square, threatening further attacks.

I spent the week with the Jashis, a Yemeni Jewish family. Avi, the father who had never lifted a hand in the home, was in charge of the packing. Naomi, his wife, shouted at him not to touch her things because she was not leaving, cooked ever bigger meals, and washed ever more laundry – even though her five children and husband had lived and slept in the same clothes for days.

On the night the army arrived I went out on a resistance operation with one of their sons, Adiel, 21, and other young 'commandos' as they set out to implement a plot they had cooked up since Ariel Sharon, the Israeli prime minister, announced the evacuation. Their plan was to short out the entire electricity grid to stop the soldiers. Rubi Braun, 19, led us down secret shortcuts to pick up fellow plotters.

Our raid swiftly turned to farce. First, Adiel shouted abuse at a passing army patrol – not the best move for undercover saboteurs – and broke down in tears. The 'commando' team retired to the Jashi family's veranda to make him tea to soothe his nerves. Then it turned out nobody had brought any tools, obliging the boys to disperse to their parents' homes to find some.

It was 3am, after another break for tea and hugs, when our group finally reached the electricity box. They poured their parents' barbecue accelerant onto newspaper, stuffed it into the box and lit a match.

The paper flared and fizzled out and that was it. Everyone appeared hugely relieved and went home, but not before swearing a solemn oath that they would return to Gaza.

Walking home in the moonlight, they passed the settler girls who had arrived from the West Bank in support, now sitting on the kerb in their orange T-shirts, no longer shouting abuse at the soldiers but in quiet one-to-one conversations.

When the army surrounded the synagogue at Neve Dekalim at 10am that day, its loudspeakers rang with Sharon's voice. They were playing a recording made six months ago in which the prime minister, once the settlers' champion, had reminded soldiers they had the right to refuse any order that interfered with their personal beliefs. There could have been no more dramatic demonstration of the volte face the pull-out represented for Sharon.

Inside the compound of the main synagogue, the teenage boys and girls finally separated after three days into same-sex groups, the girls into the Sephardic synagogue, the boys across the court-yard to the Ashkenazi synagogue.

The army also split up: male soldiers into the synagogue where the boys had holed up, female soldiers to the synagogue where the girls had gone.

As Neta Balban, an Israeli major, announced they would have to leave, the girls shouted her down with religious songs. They went on for more than 12 hours until the last were finally talked into leaving. Dehydrated and distraught, they were put on a bus to Ashkelon.

Late that night the soldiers came for the Jashi family. Avi cried quietly in the corner. Naomi was hanging up another batch of laundry and had the makings of chocolate cake on the kitchen table. She shouted and cried, was put on the bus out, ran back to kiss her house and was put on the bus again.

But she returned, scampering like a child a quarter her age to give her house a last kiss. Her sons sobbed as they finally corralled her into the bus.

On Friday night, in a hotel in Jerusalem for her first Sabbath outside Neve Dekalim and the first in 20 years that she had not cooked, Naomi sat bewildered at a picnic table, picking like a small bird at the donated fish.

'Where will I live? My boys can be ruined by this city,' she muttered. 'I am not feeling stable; this is not a good life.'

So what really happened last week? What was theatre and what was real? If the army had really wanted – and despite the threats posed by the 8,000 settlers of Gush Katif and 7,000 more infiltrators – it could have evacuated the settlements in 24 hours. Instead the troops listened to lectures from everyone from rabbis to 10-year-old girls on democracy and religion, and stood stone-faced as they were accused of being as bad as the Nazis.

Not one soldier dared to challenge the absurdity of such comparisons and point out to settlers they were being moved three miles, with their families, to inside the borders of a nation ready to receive them sympathetically and compensate them for their monetary, if not spiritual, losses.

For Sharon, like the rest of Israel watching the harrowing scenes on television, there should be cause for quiet satisfaction this weekend. Some 59% of people questioned in a poll for the *Yedioth Ahronoth* newspaper backed the pull-out; 89% said the security forces had handled it well.

For many members of his right-wing Likud party, however, Sharon remains guilty of the worst betrayal. Binyamin Netanyahu, his main rival, has called for an emergency party conference at which he is expected to challenge him for the leadership.

The polls give Netanyahu a 20% lead over Sharon among the 140,000 Likud members, many of whom are angry about the Gaza withdrawal and out for revenge. Sharon's position is complicated by the pressure from America to follow up the withdrawal with other concrete actions, almost all of them anathema to his rank and file.

Abbas, too, who has announced that long-delayed Palestinian elections will be held on 25 January, is under pressure from the militants – as yesterday's show of strength by Hamas demonstrated.

Both Hamas and Islamic Jihad, another militant group, have hailed Israel's withdrawal from the Gaza Strip as the victorious outcome of their military attacks. Although agreeing to maintain a ceasefire to allow an orderly Israeli pull-out, they have vowed to target the 235,000 Jewish settlers still in the West Bank and the 180,000 living in and around Arab east Jerusalem.

'The battle is not over,' said Osama Hamdan, Hamas's representative in Beirut. 'Negotiations alone failed to achieve such results; it was only the second intifada and the armed resistance that made this possible.'

There are other questions, too, linked to the ultimate economic viability of Gaza and its 1.3 million Palestinians, most of them impoverished. Palestinian sources say the crucial issue to be hammered out with the Israelis over the next few weeks is guaranteeing Gaza unfettered access to the outside world.

The Israelis have been insisting they should have a presence at the crossing to Egypt from Gaza. The Palestinians have refused, but say they will accept monitors from a third party, such as the European Union.

With unemployment running at an estimated 70%, the World Bank has warned that the withdrawal from Gaza could go badly wrong unless the Israeli government relaxes border controls to allow imports of necessities and exports of vegetables and fruit.

'Only when the people of Gaza can make stable contracts and import-export controls are relaxed will their economic situation get better,' said a source in the International Crisis Group, 'and that is the only security for Israel.'

Sharon may be loath to give in to any further pressure from the Americans, let alone from the Palestinians. Those who know him say he has now consolidated the boundaries of Israel to what he considers defensible.

The question now will not be how to move Sharon, because historically he moves only how and when he wants, but rather how he wants history to view him. At 77, this old warrior may be as difficult to predict as the people he leads.

MON 15 AUG

8,500 settlers in 21 settlements across Gaza are given leaflets telling them they have to leave by the following night.

TUE 16 AUG

First three settlements – Dugit, Rafiah Yam, and Pe'at Sadeh – are cleared, with little resistance.

WED 17 AUG

Settlers weep amid growing demonstrations in Netzer Hazani and Ganei Tal. A female soldier is stabbed and protesters set up barricades.

THURS 18 AUG

Settlers in Netzer Hazani throw paint and stones at soldiers before hiding in synagogue.

FRI 19 AUG

Bulldozers move in to Kerem Atzmona, while protesters in Kfar Darom try to blind soldiers with mirrors and pour sugar into petrol tanks.

SAT 20 AUG

Operation suspended for the Sabbath.

Five settlements in Gaza – Netzarim, Eli Sinai, Katif, Atzmona and Slav – and four in the West Bank – Ganim, Kadim, Sa-Nur, and Homesh – remain to be cleared.

Fear and defiance in the battered city: Beirut

16 July 2006

Marie Colvin and Uzi Mahnaimi

It was with the first sip of her morning coffee that Kokhi Hatan saw the Israeli tank explode before her eyes. 'The tank had moved only a few metres into a firing position when it was blown to bits by a huge mine,' she said.

The drama she watched from her back garden in the Galilee border village of Shtulah last Wednesday, as Hezbollah gunmen ambushed an Israeli patrol on the road running along the frontier with Lebanon, was the trigger for the worst crisis in the region for two decades.

Sources in Hezbollah, the radical Islamic organisation that runs a state-within-a-state in Lebanon, say the attack was five months in the planning.

The purpose was to seize hostages and hold them to ransom for prisoners in Israel.

The Hezbollah assault unit had clearly done their reconnaissance. After infiltrating overnight they smashed Israeli CCTV cameras that monitor the border and hid in a peach orchard to wait for two Israeli armoured 'Hummers' to begin a daily 9am patrol.

The border area had been mostly quiet since May 2000, when Israeli forces withdrew from southern Lebanon. Now the Hatans, an Israeli Kurdish family, watched in horror.

'They waited in the best location,' said Assaf, Kokhi Hatan's husband, pointing to a curve in the patrol road through his fields.

The two Hummers were hit by rocket-propelled grenades and went up in flames. Three soldiers were killed outright and two taken prisoner by the Hezbollah unit, which crossed back into Lebanon before a nearby Israeli base even knew what was happening.

The attack made clear how well-trained and equipped Hezbollah has become with the help of Iran, its main backer, since the Israeli withdrawal from south Lebanon. It has built outposts along the border, in some places only a hundred yards from the Israelis.

As Israeli reinforcements scrambled, Hezbollah units inside Lebanon began a harassing barrage. Mortars crashed with a sickening sound close to the Hatans' back garden as soldiers with megaphones urged villagers to take cover.

About 500 feet above, two Israeli Cobra assault helicopters fired missiles to stop the Hezbollah mortars. Every five seconds they released a puff of hot metal balloons to divert Hezbollah anti-aircraft rockets.

By the end of the fight, eight Israelis were dead including the tank crew, killed as they came to the rescue.

In the chaos it was 10.30am before the Israeli military realised that two soldiers – Ehud Goldwasser, 31, and Eldad Regev, 26 – had been captured. It was another 15 minutes before the military secretary to Ehud Olmert, the Israeli prime minister, passed him a note: two soldiers were confirmed abducted by Hezbollah.

Olmert could not believe what he was reading, Israeli sources said. He had been in an emotional meeting with the distressed parents of Gilad Shalit, 19, the Israeli soldier abducted in Gaza on 25 June. They had just been pressing him to order an immediate exchange of prisoners to free their son.

Now he was embroiled in a second crisis involving captured soldiers, unheard of in modern Israeli history. He called General Dan Halutz, the chief of staff, and said, 'Danny, try to find the soldiers.'

Then he had to tell Shalit's unhappy parents: 'I'm sorry. I'll do my best to bring back your son, but as you can see I can't give in to the terrorists' demands to release thousands of prisoners.'

Olmert, elected only four months ago, knew that the crisis could decide his fate.

Unlike his predecessor, Ariel Sharon, Olmert has no military career to bolster his authority.

Already two weeks into a massive military assault on Gaza in reaction to Shalit's abduction by Palestinians, Olmert ordered the opening of a second front. By midday Israel had launched a full-scale operation on its northern border.

Israeli sources said that the first air force sorties were aimed at 50 buildings where Hezbollah is thought to hide long-range Iranian-made rockets. Planes attacked 150 targets within 24 hours, dropping hundreds of tonnes of explosives.

As the confrontation grew Hezbollah rockets poured into northern Israel on an unprecedented scale – as many as 200 in the first 48 hours, according to the Israelis – and hitting as far south as Haifa, Israel's third city, for the first time.

The Israeli response rapidly escalated into an all-out attempt to cripple Hezbollah. Israel destroyed bridges across Lebanon, power stations, roads and glass-fronted business centres in Beirut. It bombed the international airport, sent warships to enforce a naval blockade and hit the highway to Damascus, the main overland route out of the country. All the fragile Lebanese government could do was appeal for a ceasefire.

'Our aim is to smash the Hezbollah,' said a military source, 'but if the rocket attacks do not stop, we'll consider sending in ground troops.'

Israel was gripped by the drama. Everyone serves in the army and knows someone in uniform. There is a tradition of 'never leaving a single soldier behind'. As a result, while the Arab world fulminated that the capture of 'only' three soldiers had caused the killing of scores of civilians, and the European Union criticised Israel's 'disproportionate response', no Israeli questioned the military onslaught to rescue three soldiers.

It was a catastrophe for Beirut, which had been in the final stages of recovery from many years of civil war, expecting a bumper crop of tourists. Now it is a city under siege.

By far the heaviest toll from the bombing has been borne by civilians. Most of the dead – 96 according to the latest count yesterday – have been civilians, hospital staff said.

In Bir al-Abed, Hezbollah's south Beirut heartland and home of its leader, Sheikh Hassan Nasrallah, downed wires snaked across streets littered with bomb damage and young men scurried for cover as Israeli planes appeared overhead for the fourth day running.

Usually in Bir al-Abed, a teeming suburb of tenements and shops, a stranger cannot walk the crowded streets more than a few yards without being stopped and questioned threateningly by Hezbollah militants. Now the streets were deserted and the young men asked their questions in a near frenzy.

'Okay, come, see, the Israelis are killing us!' Then, 'Planes, I can see them, hear that!' Bombs or missiles hit targets nearby with three loud crumps.

The ferocity of the Israeli attacks took Hezbollah by surprise. On the front line, its leaders appear nervous but resolute. It may have miscalculated the response to its raid but it was not backing down. 'If you want open war, we will give you open war,' Nasrallah said to Israel in a television address in Beirut on Friday after Israeli missiles struck his house.

Dramatically, he introduced video footage of an attack on an Israeli gunboat, saying, 'Now in the middle of the sea, facing Beirut, the Israeli warship that has attacked the infrastructure, people's homes and civilians – look at it burning.'

Israel confirmed that a ship had been hit. Four Israeli sailors were reported missing.

Celebratory gunfire erupted around the city, including, it appeared, from the Lebanese army as tracer fire from anti-aircraft guns arced overhead.

Although Hezbollah is unpopular in Christian east Beirut, it retains broad support because it is seen as having forced the Israeli withdrawal from southern Lebanon in 2000. The question now is whether this crisis will increase support or eventually rebound against it.

The fragile political situation in Lebanon has become dangerously fluid. Both Iran, Israel's arch-enemy, and Syria – the former occupying power and another Hezbollah sponsor – are manoeuvring for advantage. And Beirutis are dreading the return of their violent past.

'We are so depressed,' said Layal al-Arab, 22, a nurse. 'Two days ago we had everything, shopping and beautiful cafés. Now everything is damaged – including ourselves.'

Birth, death and destruction on Lebanon's road to hell

30 July 2006

Marie Colvin sees the innocents caught up in retreat from besieged village.

Three hours after she gave birth to a boy named Attar, 27-year-old Abir Feras started walking. Her home had been destroyed by an Israeli airstrike and when the next barrage blew in the windows of the hospital where she should have been resting, she feared that all her family would die unless they left.

First she took the intravenous drip out of her arm. Then she wrapped the newborn in a blanket as her husband Mohammed gathered her three other young children together.

With the scream of Israeli jets overhead, they began the nine-mile trek from Bint Jbeil, a southern Lebanese village besieged by the Israeli army, to the town of Tibnin, where 1,600 desperate men, women and children had taken refuge in another hospital.

They had to walk because no cars could be driven on the cratered road.

'I was breathing so hard I was dizzy and in so much pain,' Feras said when she reached the hospital, a stopping place for the poor, the old and the infirm, many of whom had been trapped in their villages under an onslaught for the past two weeks.

The last stretch of the road to Tibnin rises up a steep hill with no shelter from the sun, and families clutching white pieces of cloth to show that they are not fighters are weeping, shaking and barely able to speak by the time they arrive.

Feras carried her baby for four hours until she reached the fragile safety of the hospital as more jets roared down in dives, terrifying everyone inside, and surveillance drones swarmed overhead like angry wasps.

Last Thursday four-day-old Attar lay on a mat in the basement of the hospital, writhing and grimacing, apparently from pains in the stomach.

The basement was lit only by candles on the floor because the electricity had been cut off. The bread and beans that the adults were given every day were of no use to Attar. 'I have no milk for him,' Feras said, gesturing to her breast.

'I think I was too frightened. We are getting milk from every person who can help us, but every day it is different milk. There is no Nido [formula milk for babies].'

The hospital at Tibnin is a milestone on the road from hell. When they reach it, the shattered but relieved villagers look as if they are falling into the safety of a battlefield fox hole. They bring heart-stopping stories from a devastated hinterland.

Sometimes they strain to be heard against the background noise of huge bombs landing nearby. Everyone cringes and children scream.

A little girl called Hibba ran around the hospital courtyard, picking geraniums until her father dragged her inside when the planes came closer. He was feeling guilty. Hibba had a cut under her eye because when an Israeli bomb fell near her family as they were walking to Tibnin, her father threw her to the ground for protection. The family survived but she was wounded by a stone on the ground.

There is only one doctor in the hospital and he is angry. Nabil Harkus earned his degree in Bulgaria, worked in Europe for 10 years and then came home to Tyre, the main southern Lebanese city.

He volunteered to serve at Tibnin hospital and in another time he would have ended a long day with a cold beer. But when I arrived, he pounced on me as the only foreigner, denouncing Israel, the West and what people in Lebanon see as the destruction of their country.

After an argument Harkus apologised, saying: 'I lost my control but who can see this and not scream?'

What Harkus sees is a daily stream of misery. He chainsmokes at night in his bed just off the emergency room, where he gets no sleep and has lived in the same bright blue hospital scrubs for a week.

'I see injured civilians and they're only the poor people who have no money to run away,' he said yesterday. 'Only the poor people die. I am a doctor but I have to wrap the dead people for their coffins.'

Nobody in this hospital refuge sleeps until 6am, when the bombing subsides.

Children run through hallways that are dark in daytime because there is no power.

They are shooed back only when they try to run outside; their parents sit shell-shocked along the walls and others are ready when the drones overhead might target a gathering.

Everyone here knows that two Israeli missiles hit two Red Cross ambulances last week and one precision-guided bomb scored a direct hit on a United Nations post, killing four UN officers. They had been calling headquarters for six hours to liaise with the Israeli army, which was well aware of their co-ordinates.

They were in a border post founded in 1948 and took shelter in the bunker that was constructed to survive the 155mm artillery normally used by the Israelis.

According to the UN, the bomb that hit the officers in their shelter was designed for exactly what it did: it crushed the building on top of them and left no chance that anyone would survive.

The atmosphere at the hospital is febrile. On Friday Arbid Malek, a 38-year-old professor of mathematics who had come to southern Lebanon on holiday to visit his family, arrived at the hospital, having spent 16 days under bombardment.

Beside him was Latifa Baraqat, 45, who has eight children. When I met her she was in the hospital basement, living in a room measuring 10 foot by 5 foot. There, lying on a pallet, were her 10-month-old twins Ali and Mohammed.

Baraqat was dressed in a black robe and gold hijab and this was the first time she had seen a distinct difference in the twins' personalities. Ali, whom she cradled as we spoke, never cried, even though there were huge explosions outside. Mohammed erupted in screams.

This family, like so many others, had come from Bint Jbeil. Baraqat had held out there for 15 days and served a last meal of bread and the slices of cheese that they kept for the other children.

Baraqat said they had fled from house to house until Israeli helicopters hovered above the building next door to them and rocketed it nine times. They then decided to walk to Tibnin.

'We were surrounded by missiles. They were hitting everywhere – we only decided to walk because we were staying for so many days in a basement and we had no more food or water for the children,' she said.

Later in the day a desperate family group of 13 people came from the village of Aitaroun, near Bint Jbeil.

One woman, 7½ months pregnant with her first child, collapsed in the emergency room still wearing her pink pyjamas, the only thing she had managed to leave her house with.

Her husband Mohammed, 27, a labourer, sat next to her, his hands on her belly because they were so worried that the walk had damaged their baby.

'He's kicking and kicking so much – I am in a lot of pain,' she said. It had taken them six hours to walk from Aitaroun because she kept having to sit down and rest.

Her mother wept beside her: they had left a sister behind and nobody knew where she was.

Gaza's deadly guardians

30 September 2007

A radical Islamist state has emerged from the smoking ruins of Gaza, threatening a new war with nearby Israel. Marie Colvin ventures into the lair of the Hamas extremists imposing their hardline doctrine on Palestinians trapped there.

Hamas wants you to believe it has created a benevolent sanctuary where once chaos reigned. At the beginning of the journey into Gaza it's easy to believe that things are better.

There is no longer a Palestinian immigration desk after the long walk from the air-conditioned Erez terminal on the Israeli side, past concrete blast walls, and down a dusty track in the furnace heat. But further down the road, Hamas gunmen have taken over the checkpoints. They are polite and well turned out in blue camouflage trousers, clean black T-shirts, shiny black boots.

Once hostile, they now smile at returning foreigners who fled after the kidnapping of Alan Johnston, the BBC reporter, and the savage bloodletting between the Palestinian National Authority (PNA) forces and Hamas in June that left the fundamentalist party in absolute power.

So does everyone else in Gaza. It's like hearing the first songbird of spring. The welcome starts in the taxi. 'Gaza is safe now. We have security, praise be to God,' says Munir, my driver for years, who always in the past shook his head and moaned about how terrible everything was.

It's the same at the Al Deira hotel, mostly empty, where once aid workers, diplomats, journalists and sophisticated Gazans mixed on the terrace overlooking the Mediterranean. 'Everything is safe now. You are welcome,' says Amir at the front desk.

For the first time on a trip to Gaza, I was stopped going the wrong way down a one-way street, by one of the young Hamas volunteers in yellow vests now standing up to drivers in a culture that considers a red light to be a mere suggestion to slow down.

The rubbish still smells, but now it is piled neatly in the streets. Families stroll late at night. Gone is the gunfire that used to punctuate days and nights and often escalated into street battles that left innocents dead on the pavements.

Then you start talking to people in private.

Young men show you bruised limbs and welts on their feet; every girl wears a hijab head covering and, for the first time, women wear niqab Saudi-style face coverings that reveal only the eyes. And people whisper.

Welcome to Hamastan.

Ahmed Al-Naba'at, 24, sits in his courtyard in an oversized Barcelona shirt. He looks too young to be the father of the three young children who toddle barefoot round the tiny dirt courtyard.

His feet still hurt. Hamas came for him at 2am.

About 30 armed men, their faces masked but wearing the black uniforms and badges of the Izzedine al-Qassam Brigade, the military wing of Hamas, had surrounded the house. They covered his eyes and took him away in a car.

'They took me somewhere, I don't know, a room,' Naba'at says. He has high cheekbones and the near-black skin of his Sudanese ancestry. 'They were screaming and beating me, punching me, slapping me on the face,' he says. 'Then they tied my legs together and started falaka' – a traditional Arabic torture where the soles of the feet are beaten with sticks. 'I relaxed.'

He sees the surprise in my face. 'I thought they were going to kill me,' he explains. 'When I realised it's just falaka, I thought, okay, it's just torture.'

Qassam dumped him near his home, hours later. It took him half an hour to walk what usually takes two minutes. 'You were lucky,' interjects his unsympathetic father, who is sitting against a courtyard wall. 'Most of the people they beat, they throw them unconscious in the street and they are not found until the morning.'

His crime? Earlier that night at a party for a friend's wedding, Naba'at had danced and played a song popular in Gaza – an over-romanticised ballad to Samih al-Madhoun, a Fatah commander executed by Hamas during the fighting. Hamas cameramen had filmed as Madhoun was dragged down the street amid spitting crowds, shot in the stomach, beaten and shot some more. It was shown on Hamas television that night.

The overblown ballad of his death 'Your blood is not for free Samih/You left behind an earthquake/We will not forget you Samih' is such a Gazan hit that many young people have it on their mobile phones. Hamas, predictably, is furious. Three of Al-Naba'at's friends who had danced at the wedding were also beaten.

Al-Naba'at, who left school at 14 and worked as a farm labourer and painter, has little recourse. He is too afraid to sleep at home any more. His father is clearly exasperated like many of the older generation, he thinks his sons should shut up. He points to another son, 17-year-old Mustafa. Hamas came after him when he burnt a Hamas flag: they arrested his father and twin brother until he gave himself up.

Hamas is not just going after the poor. Azil Akhras is a sophisticated 24-year-old woman with heavily kohled eyes, thick, flowing black hair and rouged lips, comfortable in her jeans and tight red shirt. Life used to be shopping, going out maybe to Roots, a popular Gaza nightclub even though it now serves only soft drinks and going to the beach. Her life changed dramatically three months ago when Hamas took over Gaza.

'Now, I cover my head when I go in a car. Hamas is at the checkpoints. Last week, they stopped a girl who was not covered and they beat her brother when he tried to protect her.'

She and her sister must be careful; they are alone. Their father, a former government health minister, has fled Gaza to escape Hamas. He has holed up in Ramallah, the West Bank capital, and is unable to return.

It's not just shopping trips she misses. A university graduate, Akhras had wanted to sit her master's degree; she wanted to travel. 'I had an idea, I wanted to be famous in history. Maybe a journalist,' she says. 'Now, there's no chance, I can't even go outside.' She resents Hamas's repression. 'If I decide to cover [my head], it will be for my God, not some Qassam soldier.'

Gazans are living in a climate of fear. The place is eerily serene, not only because of the presence of disciplined Hamas security forces on the streets but, as in all successful police states, because everyone has started policing themselves, afraid of the consequences of stepping over a line not defined in formal law.

Hamas took power after five days of vicious, internecine fighting with the security forces of the PNA, who mostly belong to the rival Fatah organisation co-founded by Yasser Arafat, the late president.

Tension had escalated into clashes between the secular Fatah, who governed for a decade and whose members stack the civil service and security forces, and Hamas, after the religious party won national elections in March 2006.

The differences were exacerbated by Gaza's isolation. The international community cut funds to the Palestinian government after the Hamas election victory. Israel blocked the millions in tax revenue it was supposed to pass on for imports, and closed the borders intermittently. The economy went into freefall.

A national unity government formed in February failed to end the confrontation. But the speed of the coup in Gaza was shocking.

Hamas fielded only about 7,000 members of the Executive Force, its police force, which was backed by the Izzedine al-Qassam Brigade, the military wing of the party, against the 70,000-strong government forces loyal to Mahmoud Abbas, the Palestinian president.

There are many reasons for the swift collapse: the government security forces hadn't been paid for 18 months and were demoralised by the corruption of their own leaders. Their commanders fled, and many foot soldiers found that their guns were locked in storage. Hamas was better armed, better trained, and fought with the single-mindedness of those with a cause.

It was the worst ever clash among Palestinians: 110 died, and the population is still shocked by the brother-on-brother nature of the battle. Today there is a deadlock, and essentially two Palestinian governments. Abbas fired the Hamas-led coalition government and named a new emergency cabinet, but its powers run only in the West Bank. Hamas ministers refused to step down.

By Palestinian law, the government must be renewed by the parliament, but Hamas dominates the legislature and, anyway, it lacks a quorum: about one third of its members are in Israeli jails for belonging to Hamas.

The evidence of the ferocity of the fighting can be seen across Gaza city. The headquarters of the Preventive Security Service, the PNA's main security force, was the last stronghold. Now occupied by the Executive Force, there are gaping holes in the walls from bullets and rockets.

Abbas's presidential house is guarded by Hamas police who brew tea under new posters of Hamas members killed in the fighting. They shake their heads at the marble floors and luxurious furnishings, contrasting it with the home of Ismail Haniya, the Hamas prime minister, who lives in the al-Shati refugee camp.

At the Muntada, the Palestinian version of the White House, Hamas fighters stroll the corridors, and dust gathers on Abbas's rosewood desk, where Arafat once sat.

Hamas is extending its control. Nobody is safe if the example of Ashraf Juma, one of their more articulate opponents, is anything to go by. Juma is a senior member of Fatah, who refused to leave his home or office in Rafah, Gaza's southernmost city on Egypt's border. He is one of the most popular politicians in Gaza: when Hamas won the election, sweeping Gaza, he was one of the few elected from the Fatah list.

He was leader of the al-Aqsa hawks during the first intifada (uprising), and hands out money from his own pocket to the needy of both Fatah and Hamas (these days it's from his brother's, a wealthy businessman). His latest project is to find £5,000 for school uniforms for poor children.

None of it was any protection from Hamas. It began on the internet. Juma was criticised on the official Hamas website for supposedly sending Abbas the names of people whose salaries should be cut because they were Hamas members. Then critical leaflets were distributed in the local mosque. 'Someone called from Hamas and said, "Leave your office. This is a preparation for an attack on you,"' he says, sitting at home in a white short-sleeved shirt, dark trousers and sandals.

The next day, as he and his office staff finished evening prayers, blue police cars pulled up, disgorging men in the uniform of the Executive Force. They also wore black masks.

As he opened the door, he saw his secretary, Osama, trying to fend them off with a table. The gunmen began screaming and shot Osama in the thigh. They started beating him in the hallway before running off. 'You were my sons. I served you,' he shouted after them.

Juma shakes his balding head, and describes how the situation turned almost farcical. As word spread that he had been attacked, hundreds of people poured into Shifa hospital and packed the emergency room and courtyard.

'There were so many people, the doctors couldn't work properly. Look, they put stitches in wrong,' he says, ducking his head to show newly healed scars. The crowds carried him out of the hospital before the doctors had finished, afraid that Hamas would return, and grabbed Osama from the operating room before his broken hand and gunshot wound were treated.

They almost killed their hero. Juma fell unconscious, Osama writhed in pain. Hundreds poured into the streets, denouncing the Executive Force. A doctor finally came and treated both of them at home.

It was a night of terror for many. Ismael, 29, an English teacher for the United Nations Relief and Works Agency, sits in the front room of the house he had just painted for a marriage that now will never happen.

'My last hours before they came were happy,' recalls Ismael, who doesn't want his last name used because Hamas threatened to kill him if he told the story.

'I had just gotten engaged and I spent from 7.30pm to 11pm talking with my friends about what we would do for the celebrations,' he says.

Suddenly, his house was surrounded by armed men in black with Qassam Brigade emblems. 'One tried to hit me with a stick, and I said, "What are you doing? I have done nothing."'

They took him first to the Sayed Sayel Executive Force post. 'They put me against a wall and started shouting, "Have you been to a demonstration?"' he says. 'They became hysterical, shouting, "You have been making riots here," beating me with sticks, metal bars, stones.'

His ordeal had just begun. 'They said, "What about the orphans?"' Ismael supports two orphans, Allah, who is nine and needs an eye operation, and Dina, who is 11, while trying to get them medical help through an American charity. Hamas said he should have no contact with foreigners.

They beat Ismael for an hour and a half, moving him at one point during the night to Idara Madaneh, the civil administration building in Jabaliya camp. He was blindfolded, but two young teenagers who had been taken in ran to him, screaming 'Teacher! Teacher!', probably recognising him from school.

'Then Hamas started beating me on the arm I was using to try to protect the children,' he says.

He was finally released at 4am with a warning not to talk, and not to go to a hospital. A doctor friend came round and treated him secretly.

Photographs from the June beating show welts on his back, ferocious bruises on his left arm, and a swollen right arm and elbow. He won't show me his legs out of modesty, but says they were black, and his knees are still not right.

But that was not the worst. His fiancée's family heard of the incident and believed he was a political activist against Hamas, which would endanger her future. Her father revoked his permission to marry and he has not spoken to his fiancée, a fellow teacher, since then. 'My sister tells me she is crying and crying,' Ismael says.

Can't they marry when things calm down? 'No chance. This is our tradition.' For the first time in a long story, he brushes away a tear.

'Most of the educated people here feel they are living in a country that doesn't belong to them,' he says when he recovers.

Hamas is not triumphalist in its takeover, as was the first prophet of militant Islam, Ayatollah Khomeini, who immediately set himself up against the West and all who didn't want to follow his unforgiving brand of Islam.

But then he had oil, 50 million people, an army, air force and navy, and control of his own borders. Hamas is isolated and depends on international aid, with little but farming, fishing and a hostile neighbour that controls its borders, sea and skies.

This heavily armed statelet is squeezed between Israel's southern border and Egypt's northern border, separated by a chunk of Israel from the West Bank, the bigger, richer other half of the Palestinian 'state'.

The West Bank is still occupied by Israeli soldiers and Jewish settlers: they withdrew from Gaza two years ago, but still control the borders and ban all air and sea traffic, except for tiny wooden fishing boats allowed to go out six miles.

Since the Hamas takeover in June, Israel has not opened the main crossing points for even a day, and the economy has collapsed. The United Nations Relief and Works Agency (UNRWA) estimates unemployment at 80% among the 1.4 million inhabitants. There are no exports; a trickle of food bought by private Palestinian merchants from their Israeli counterparts is allowed across at the tiny Sufa crossing. It must be one of the strangest commercial dealings in the world. The Israeli army moves in pallets from about 100 trucks a day, shooting at anyone who approaches before they withdraw behind the fence; then there is a bizarre Mad Max-style race by forklifts to get the merchandise left in the no-man's-land.

In three months, an estimated 70,000 jobs have been lost in the construction industry alone. UNRWA has had to stop £47 million in projects funded by donors; apartments for those whose homes were destroyed by Israeli fire, oxidation projects for Gaza's overflowing sewage-treatment plants. Everyone is desperate. 'This place is a powder keg waiting to explode,' said John Ging, UNRWA's Gaza director.

Instead of the open defiance of Khomeini's Iran, Hamas has developed a parallel system: show a reasonable face to the world in the hope of ending Gaza's isolation, while enforcing the unforgiving law of the state of Hamastan at home.

Ismail Haniya, the silver-haired Hamas prime minister, could be a poster boy for moderate Islam. When I see him, he is sitting with Arab journalists, and gently lecturing them like the professor he once was. Aware he stands little chance with the West, he is seeking Arab support.

He tells them that negotiations are possible under certain conditions with Mahmoud Abbas, who is welcome to come back to Gaza. No women will be forced to wear the hijab – that is a personal choice. Well, of course there can be no negotiations with Israel, although that could happen if they recognise Palestinian rights.

There is duplicity even in the detail, however: Haniya may say that women are free not to cover their heads, but before I go to his office an aide calls to tell me to be sure to wear a headscarf.

And recognising Palestinian rights is Hamas-speak for 'We want all of the land of mandate Palestine, from the Mediterranean to the Jordan River,' a maximalist position that ignores the fact that most Palestinians have moved on from 1948 to accept the existence of Israel, and would settle for a two-state solution. Negotiations are moribund, but Fatah-led governments have signed agreements with Israel recognising the reality that two states is the only solution.

Haniya may be the smooth-talking Hamas frontman but he lacks real power. A former professor of religion, he was a compromise choice fielded by Khaled Mesha'al, the exiled Hamas leader based in Damascus. 'When we were negotiating, whenever a difficult point came up, Haniya had to leave the room to call Mesha'al,' one of Abbas's top lieutenants said.

The real power lies with Mahmoud Zahar, who is in the strange position of being a foreign minister who can't travel from Gaza (Israel has closed the borders even to government officials).

A militant once expelled by Israel, he was expected to be prime minister after the Hamas victory, but Mesha'al apparently considered him too radical, and more of a threat than Haniya.

Sitting on a couch in the foreign ministry damaged in an Israeli bombing, he is scathing about Abbas. '[He] committed big crimes against the law, against human interest.' Zahar is dressed in a light-grey safari suit, his beard neatly trimmed, his shoes polished. He exudes confidence and scorns any need for Hamas to reach out for a compromise. 'Abbas is acting as an agent of America and Israel.'

The power that stretches beyond his title peeps out. 'We have information that Fatah are organising themselves into cells,' he says. 'We will find them and we will crush them.'

There is no sense of urgency in finding a solution to the desperate need of the average Gazan with a large family and no work.

'We are not in a hurry. Palestinians are used to being under siege. I believe sooner or later the West will change its mind,' he says calmly.

Again, during the interview, his power beyond that of the average diplomat is revealed when he takes a phone call about the siege of the powerful Dagmoush clan, the kidnappers of Alan Johnston, the BBC journalist. Earlier in the week the clan killed two Hamas policemen.

'Tell them that by 10pm we will go in if they have not agreed. We will enter their houses one by one.'

Across town that very siege is under way. Hamas has again surrounded the Dagmoush neighbourhood as they did to get Johnston back. They have cut off the water and electricity.

Few in Gaza have any sympathy for the Dagmoushes. One of the leaders of the clan and Johnston's main kidnapper, Mumtaz Dagmoush spouts extremist Al-Qaeda rhetoric, but his so-called Army of Islam has about 20 members and is better known for theft, gun smuggling and kidnapping. Fatah let Gaza's powerful families run wild, sometimes using them against Hamas.

Hamas has taken them on. Breaking the Dagmoushes is crucial to consolidating power.

The discipline of Hamas on the front line of the siege of the concrete-block houses in the neighbourhood is in contrast to Fatah's members who won't talk until they get word from a commander over the walkie-talkie. Once allowed to talk, Abu Yehia, the local commander, doesn't have much to say. 'We are imposing law and order. This is our duty. Islam tells us that.'

Hamas is demanding that the Dagmoushes surrender the guilty members of the family, and give back stolen weapons.

That night, the family does surrender, led by Mumtaz Dagmoush. He is double the size of the average Gazan, tall, broad-shouldered, with a shaggy dark beard and wild hair. He and his entourage screech their pick-up trucks into the Preventive Security compound, jump out waving guns and, seeing me, starts waving his M16, shouting: 'Get this journalist out of here!' With both sides jostling and shoving, for moments it seems there will be a shoot-out.

Dagmoush finally hands over bags of guns, then marches with his bodyguard into the darkened police headquarters and starts pounding on the commander's door, shouting: 'I gave you my weapons, let me in there.'

The M16 is in the air again, 50 men all shoving with guns and elbows, and shouting.

Eventually, he calms down and half an hour later is talking to Abu Dahab, the Hamas commander.

Dagmoush tells me, 'We've just had an English guest staying with us for a while,' referring to Alan Johnston, the kidnapped journalist. I asked him why he kidnaps, and if his activities other than kidnapping will be affected under Hamas. He shrugs: 'Business is business,' he says.

Now that Hamas has solidified power, they are putting in place their system of keeping it. One part of this is a new 'ladies unit', reminiscent of the one in Iran where fierce, make-up-free women drag other women out of cars and away for re-education. Ominously, Hamas have failed so far to set up a court system, so cases are being heard by an Islamic judge.

The one thriving industry is the arms industry.

I visit a Qassam area leader in Yibne camp in southern Gaza who has been 'cooking' for three days making the explosive mixture that goes in the rockets they fire into Israel.

He takes me to one of the many armouries they have and shows me the extraordinary range of weapons they manufacture locally, mostly in underground factories. What they can't make, they smuggle through tunnels from Egypt.

The armoury is in a small, concrete block house, indistinguish-able from its neighbours in the squalid maze of the camp. The home-made weapons I see include foot-wide land mines, tank-busting missiles, guns, rocket-propelled grenades, all stored amid the clutter of a bedroom with flowers on the shelf above the bed and a teddy bear lying belly-up on the floor.

He is nervous while we are there – the Israelis target such places if they get information from collaborators – but he opens up when we go to another house for tea, although he won't give his name. He is unconcerned about his outside image, and this is the true voice of Hamas.

'Of course we will create an Islamic state. This is called for in the Holy Koran,' he says. What would that mean, I ask him.

Well, for one, sharia law. 'For a murder, death, not this life sentence there is now. A thief should have his hand cut off. An adulteress must be stoned,' he says, in a chillingly nonchalant voice.

'There is no possibility of recognising Israel,' he says. 'All the land is ours. We are taught this by our leaders and they will never compromise.'

His certitude comes from how Hamas recruits. It gets them young; my informant started at 14. Only when he proved himself 'mentally and spiritually' was he allowed to join Qassam and receive military training.

And not all girls are like Azil Akhras. Gehad Nehan, 19, is studying law at the Hamas-dominated Islamic University in Gaza. She wears glasses, a hijab, and is covered in a navy-blue robe down to her thick black shoes. 'Hamas has taken over the police stations and now the life is good.'

She insists women are equal, but as she talks, a different reality is revealed. At the university, she says, 'the boys say woman is weak, her work must be in the home. I say this is wrong.'

Even getting to study was a struggle. 'My father hits me and he punishes me and says I should not go to the university. It's difficult.'

But despite having described Hamastan as virtually a perfect state, she has the yearning of all here to leave. 'I want to travel all over the world and see people and how they live.'

Those who have already travelled are the most angry at Hamas.

One restaurant owner begins by extolling Hamas for improving security. He sits at a banquette in his eatery in a yellow polo shirt. Christmas streamers still hang from the ceiling, and Whitney Houston is on the soundtrack.

'And they cancelled all family connections,' he adds. 'Before, if someone was connected to the government, they could eat and just not pay.

'But they are not the future for the Palestinian people,' he insists. 'We need a government that can deal with the international community.' Despite growing dissatisfaction such as his, there is little sign that the green flags of Hamastan will be coming down any time soon.

Iran

Iran split as fun-hungry young spurn rigged poll

TEHRAN

15 February 2004

They call themselves the Third Generation. Twenty-five years after Ayatollah Khomeini returned from exile, the grandchildren of his Islamic revolution are angry that conservatives have blocked their hopes of reform by engineering almost certain victory in elections this week. What they will do about it is probably the most important question for the future of Iran.

They are a powerful force by sheer weight of numbers: an estimated two out of three Iranians are under the age of 30. Most of them are more likely to turn to the internet for guidance than the mosque. They do not agree with Khomeini's edict: 'There is no fun in Islam.'

Perhaps the most prominent of the new generation is Zahra Eshraghi, Khomeini's granddaughter. Despite her credentials, she was among more than 2,000 reformist candidates that the Guardian Council, a 12-man unelected conservative body that vets candidates for their adherence to Islamic law, banned from standing in the elections.

She is soft-spoken but blunt in her outrage. 'There is no defence for their actions,' Eshraghi said yesterday. 'What they did was illegal. Now I cannot defend the government any longer.'

The result of the ban was that half of the parliament resigned. A boycott of the election has been called by the reform parties, including one led by Eshraghi's husband, Muhammad Reza Khatami, a sitting MP who was also barred from standing and who is the brother of Muhammad Khatami, the president.

Eshraghi, 40, could not be further from the image of the stern, turbaned Khomeini.

Like most younger Iranians, she loves fashion and dresses in a thigh-length shaved fur coat with fur cuffs and high-heeled suede boots. She throws a long black chador, the covering for women that is law in Iran, over the ensemble when a man enters her office.

She laughs easily but is stern in her denunciations, calling her famous ancestor into the fray. 'If he was alive, it would never have come to this. I think the conservatives have set us back 300 to 400 years,' she said.

Last Friday, the traditional day for prayers, teenagers out of sight of their elders at the resort village of Darband, in the mountains above Tehran, stretched the concept of the chador beyond recognition.

One teenage girl made do with a hip-length leather jacket and a skirt, her scarf pushed back to reveal blonde streaks in her dark hair. Boys in reflective sunglasses and tracksuits chatted and laughed with girls at open-air restaurants.

Nobody seemed worried about the clerics' mandatory separation of the sexes.

However, this cheery scene concealed confusion, disillusionment and anger. A gaggle of fashionably dressed girls curled up on one banquette, discussing whether to boycott the parliamentary election this Friday. One had taken an informal poll at her university; nine out of 10 were planning to stay away from the polls.

'I'm not going to vote,' said Somayeh, a 23-year-old business administration university student. 'How can we vote when there is no choice? This is not a democratic vote.'

It is a far cry from the parliamentary election in 2000, when 80% of Iran's 22 million voters selected the reformists. During their four-year term they tried and failed to loosen the strict Islamic guidelines and to rein in the power of the unelected conservatives who control the judiciary, intelligence and security and discipline the press.

The reformists did not get a single piece of important legislation into law. The Guardian Council, which checks whether proposed legislation complies with sharia (Islamic law), vetoed them all. In this election the conservatives ended any pretence of democracy.

Campaigning began on Thursday, a day after celebrations of the 25th anniversary of Khomeini taking power. These were far more muted than in previous years, with pamphlets being handed out on the streets. The government's biggest challenge will be getting enough people to the polls; a low turnout would be an embarrassment in a country where more than 50% routinely vote.

Predicting what will happen after Friday's ballot is difficult. There are two Irans. On the day when the teenagers were enjoying spring temperatures in the mountains, hundreds attended prayers at the University of Tehran led by Ayatollah Khamenei, the supreme religious leader and Khomeini's successor. He told a crowd of women in all-enveloping chadors and men in baggy suits that their enemies were trying to undermine the elections. It was clear he meant the reform candidates.

Watching was 25-year-old Hamide Mostafavi, a computer student with three children.

'He [Khamenei] is perfect,' she said. 'I can't see any problem with him.'

Asked what he thought about the banned MPs, Ali Rabbani

Nejad, a hefty cleric in robes and a white turban, said: 'They are spies.'

So far there is no sign that the majority of the Third Generation will do more than boycott the elections, undermining the legitimacy of the expected conservative government.

Active resistance will certainly not come from the 'first generation' – the peers of Khomeini – nor from the fathers and mothers who lived through the revolution and fear a return of the violence of the early years of the regime.

After the banning of the elected reformists, however, there is a nascent movement among the young for what is being called phase two of the reform movement. They are taking an increasingly vocal stand, a risky business in a country that jails outspoken journalists and writers.

Most had been committed to reconciling Islam and democracy, but now say the fact that unelected conservatives could overrule majority opinion has shown that to be impossible.

'We believed we could achieve change gradually, within the democratic institutions. Now we have lost all hope of that,' said Omid Memarian, a 26-year-old journalist who moved to a non-governmental organisation after the youth magazine that employed him was closed down for being un-Islamic.

'I couldn't believe it when I heard that they banned all the reform people,' Memarian said. 'I have voted in every election since I was 16, but I'm not going to vote in this one. I'm not going to take part in their theatre.'

He added: 'You can use my name – I don't care if I go to prison.'

Memarian said the conservatives had allowed a small measure of social freedom to depoliticise the younger generation so that it would be easier for them to hang on to power.

Many students are loath to take to the streets – partly because when they last did so they were attacked by regime thugs; and partly because they believe that the reform party failed to live up to their expectations. Disillusionment has bred apathy among many.

'President Khatami says the right things, but he is no hero,' Memarian said.

He and others who support change in Iran believe that the reform movement must go back to basics and organise grassroots opposition among students, non-governmental and women's organisations.

'The strategy of the reform people was to reform from inside, through law building,' said Hamid Jalaiepour, a professor at the University of Tehran and former editor of several closed reformist newspapers. He was banned from standing in the last election and served a prison sentence. He has another court date three days after the election. 'Now we want an Islamic republic without special rights for the clergy.'

There are fears among more liberal Iranians about what will happen next. 'It is possible the conservatives will try to ban everything after the election,' said Eshraghi – strange words from the granddaughter of the man who founded the Islamic Republic of Iran.

Despair and fear among the Tehran dancing classes

26 June 2005

At a dinner last week I sat with a young Iranian friend who was weeping openly by the end of our Indian tandoori, writes Marie Colvin.

He faced an impossible choice: he loved his country and wanted to stay to work within the system but had just spent two months in prison without charge, apparently over something carried on his mildly critical internet website. He had been beaten for hours each day.

He was crying at the memory of his head being smashed against the concrete wall of a prison cell for four hours one day and because he felt a coward. Mostly he was crying because, as he put it: 'I just can't take even one more minute in prison,' and he felt he should be stronger and stand up for his belief in reform.

All he could think was that if Mahmoud Ahmadinejad were elected they would come for him the next day.

I told him to go. At the time, I thought he was being paranoid. Ahmadinejad, the mayor who looks and sounds like a throwback to bygone revolutionary days, seemed such a long shot.

In fact my young friend was prescient. At the age of 28 he foresaw better than I who would be the next president.

At noon the next day he boarded a bus to Turkey. He was not even sure whether he would be allowed to cross.

Others had tried, only to find themselves listed at the border as 'people not allowed to leave the country'.

Unlike most of his generation, he had dedicated his few adult years to trying to build what he called civic society – trying to reach out to the less educated, the less privileged. He held workshops about 'understanding democracy' and 'women's rights in Islam'. 'They didn't want to hear about human rights,' he complained. 'We never reached them. It's our big failure.'

It was impossible to underestimate the depth of fear, panic and incomprehension among Iran's wealthier and more liberal youth yesterday. One young woman told me: 'I fainted when I woke up and heard the news.'

The young had pushed the boundaries of earlier restrictions to the point that they didn't seem especially harsh any more. They drank alcohol at weekend parties, danced at ecstasy raves in underground car parks and had serial relationships in a country where, officially, contact between the sexes is illegal unless you are married or brother and sister.

Girls wore make-up that in the early days of the revolution would have earned them an 'acid facial', and hijab scarves were pushed so far back they would be fashionable in Paris.

A member of Iran's most successful rapper band – illegal, of course – had confidently told me: 'It's not as bad as it seems. We have got so many fans they'll never stop us.' When I called him yesterday the bravado was gone. He said he was going to keep his head down and 'see what happens'.

Some ripples of concern were already felt by a rich young crowd, few of whom had bothered to vote, at a glitzy party in northern Tehran on Friday.

Roxanne, standing by her pool in a clinging white mini-dress said: 'I'm going to have to leave this country. It's not going to be a place I want to live any more. Our country has been hijacked.'

A young disillusioned reform party researcher said: 'We are still going to get where we want. It's inevitable. The only difference is that whereas under [Ali Akbar Hashemi] Rafsanjani we would have got there slowly and peacefully, now there will be bloodshed.'

When I said goodbye to my idealistic friend on the eve of his bus ride, he made a simple but proud gesture: he solemnly shook my hand in full view of everyone in the restaurant. He could have been arrested. 'You are no coward,' I thought.

He made it across the border.

Egypt

Mubarak lights a democratic flame

CAIRO

4 September 2005

There could not have been more of a contrast on the campaign trail last week.

Hosni Mubarak, who after four terms is facing his first multi-candidate presidential election, read his speech to a partisan crowd from behind a cordon of twitchy security men. At an opposition rally, his main rival called for change and was hoisted on the shoulders of ecstatic young men.

The 77-year-old Mubarak, wearing a light grey suit and a white shirt open at the collar – his one concession to the young technocrats on his campaign who are trying to soften his image – arrived in the town of Zagaziq hours late for 10,000 supporters sitting in the stifling heat of a huge tent.

He promised reform, 4.5 million jobs and land redistribution, all music to the ears of the audience, mostly peasants. But it was unclear how much they understood of the promised new era of democracy.

They interrupted his speech with chants of 'Nam, Mubarak' (Yes, Mubarak), recalling the system by which presidents have been elected since King Farouk was overthrown by a revolution in 1952. Parliament nominates a president, always the incumbent, and he submits to a yes-or-no referendum. Mubarak has won four of those.

This year is different. After an unprecedented wave of dissent in the past year, and pressure from America, Mubarak agreed to a constitutional amendment allowing opposition parties to contest the presidency.

Nine candidates, all but two of them obscure – including an elderly fortune teller – are running against the Egyptian president.

Mubarak allowed only 19 days of campaigning, ending today. Egyptians go to the polls on Wednesday when Mubarak will seek to extend his 24 years in the presidency by another six-year term. He is almost certain to win.

Earlier this year Egypt's conversion to multi-party democracy, elections in Iraq and the mass protests that drove Syrian forces out of Lebanon appeared to herald profound change across the Middle East. There was talk of an 'Arab spring'.

However, democracy seems to be having some teething troubles in Egypt: eligible Egyptians who did not have a voter's card when the election was announced in January have not been allowed to sign up; the estimated 4 million Egyptians living abroad cannot vote; a demand by President George W Bush for international monitors has been rejected, and local groups which had asked to observe the polls have been refused.

Nor does Mubarak's praetorian guard appear to have been briefed on press freedom.

Confronted by a press corps making its way to collar officials before his speech, one nervous guard complained: 'Do you all have to go? Can't you just send one person and he will tell you the important things?'

The election coverage of the state-owned media has been heavily weighted in favour of Mubarak, although the independent newspapers have been anything but sycophantic – they have called the president corrupt, decrepit and dictatorial and attacked Gamal, his son and political heir.

Egypt's strongest opposition movement, the Muslim Brotherhood, is banned and does not even appear on the ballot. That said, the election has stirred those in Egypt who have been able to follow it. For the first time in a country ruled by emergency law since Mubarak came to power after the assassination of Anwar Sadat in 1981, they have been able to listen to criticism of the president without being imprisoned for it.

Many have seen Mubarak – his hair dyed black but looking surprisingly vigorous for his years – in the flesh for the first time. He used to remain aloof in his office. When candidates such as Ayman Nour, head of the liberal El-Ghad party, started touring the country, Mubarak's advisers said that he had better get out there as well.

It has not been the most comfortable experience for the former fighter pilot.

After a few trips to face sweating citizens, Mubarak is said to have told a friend: 'It is as if I own my house and now I have to bid for it at auction.'

Mubarak has some formidable supporters, however. Yousef Boutros-Ghali, his finance minister and nephew of the former United Nations secretary-general, does not mince words. Educated in America and with a doctorate in economics, he traces the main issues of the campaign – poverty and corruption – back to the economy he is trying to reform.

'We had a medieval tax system. It's taken four years but I've reformed it, top tax 20%, lowest 10%. We've had a surge in tax receipts. Our customs law was the most obscure and confusing in the world – I went at it with an axe.'

Boutros-Ghali believes the groundwork has been laid for democracy and that international intervention has nothing to do with it. 'Democratic elections do not come from the foreign press or foreign intervention,' he said in an interview.

'If democracy is not home-grown, it will not last. The test is not if this is a perfect democratic election – it is: have we let the genie out of the bottle? I think we have. Irreversibly.'

Nour boldly challenges the gradual approach of Mubarak and Boutros-Ghali. At 41, he is of a less patient generation and by nature a grandstander. His campaign has been chaotic. A bus was scheduled to take journalists to a rally in Port Said at 4pm on Thursday. At 5pm Nour was still sitting in his apartment in a bedraggled suit and a bright orange tie that is the symbol of his campaign, in tribute to the Ukrainian people's revolution.

'People are thirsty for change,' he said. 'We've found that one of the problems is that they can't quite believe it will happen. But I believe we've broken the barrier of silence.'

Nour finally left Cairo at 8pm, arriving just before 11pm. An enthusiastic crowd was waiting and there were no security guards. People pushed up to the podium, rapt and sweating.

He has his finger on the pulse of the dissatisfaction in Egypt, where 25% unemployment has decimated the hopes of the younger generation. Young men cheered when he focused on the lack of jobs. When he talked about the desperate conditions of a nearby slum, nobody stopped a young woman who jumped on stage to bare an arm, shouting that mice had bitten it in her slum house.

Many had come just for the show of free speech. 'Arab spring? I haven't seen enough democracy to know which season we are in,' Nour said. He will not win and fears what will happen after the election.

Mubarak is expected to name a vice-president, perhaps two. More controversially, there are indications he could manoeuvre Gamal into the leadership of the NDP ruling party, which would set him up for the succession.

While this is a far from perfect democratic election, the genie may well be out of the bottle.

Kosovo

How one careless phone call ended Radovan Karadzic's liberty

27 July 2008

Marie Colvin and Andrew Wander

A careless phone call brought Radovan Karadzic's colourful life on the run to an abrupt end, write Marie Colvin and Andrew Wander in Belgrade.

As the long-haired, bearded man who had become known as the local eccentric walked out of the Leotar supermarket in a suburb of Belgrade nine days ago, he unexpectedly turned back to the checkout girls.

'I want to say goodbye,' he said. 'I'm going on vacation. I need a rest, I've been working a lot.' He could not know how prescient his words were.

Radovan Karadzic, 63, wartime leader of the Bosnian Serbs and one of the most wanted men in the world, had only a few hours of freedom left after almost 13 years on the run.

Sofia Kaluderovic, 44, at the checkout, rang up the usual purchases for the man she believed was Dragan Dabic, a new age doctor: yoghurt, specially ordered cherries, the nationalist newspaper *Pravda* and a bottle of Bear's Blood, a cheap Serbian red wine.

As he left the shop, he cut his usual distinctive figure, dressed in a black T-shirt and trousers, sandals, his long white hair bound with an elastic band into a top knot and his face buried beneath an enormous white beard and oversize glasses.

In retrospect, Uros, the shop's owner, realised that his customer may have found comfort in the shop's name, Leotar – a famous mountain in the Serbian part of Bosnia that Karadzic ran as president of the self-styled Srpska Republic.

'He was a real gentleman,' Uros said, remembering his jokes and generous tips. 'If I'd known who he really was, I would never have charged for anything. I will die sorry that I didn't recognise him.'

Karadzic's disguise was effective right up until the moment he was caught. He boarded the 73 bus from the stop around the corner, carrying a bag containing a laptop, two mobile phones, clothes including swimming trunks, and Euro 600 (£472) in cash.

His plan to leave Belgrade apparently spurred Serbia's security services into action. They had been watching him for a month and did not want to take the chance of him slipping away.

As the bus passed the Teloptic factory in an industrial part of town, a group of men in civilian clothes boarded and asked if they could talk to Karadzic. He refused. They showed him their badges, told him that they knew who he was, blindfolded and handcuffed him. He went quietly. It was a surprisingly pedestrian end to an extraordinary life on the run.

Karadzic had been a wanted man since 1996, when international arrest warrants were issued for him and Ratko Mladic, the army general who was his partner in the slaughter and 'ethnic cleansing' in the 1992–5 Bosnian war that left an estimated 200,000 dead.

Karadzic's lawyer filed an appeal against his extradition from Serbia just before the deadline at 8pm on Friday, but the former leader is expected to be flown this week to the United Nations tribunal at the Hague to stand trial on charges including genocide. He faces life imprisonment.

In Belgrade there was a muted reaction to the arrest of the one-time Serbian hero. Had he been arrested a decade ago, nationalist Serbs would have poured onto the streets in violent fury, but last week the protests came mainly in the form of disgruntled youths.

Serbs attributed the lack of an outcry to the length of time that had elapsed since the end of the war. Equally, it may just have been that everyone was stunned at the revelation of Karadzic's life on the run. They had expected something more like a dramatic shootout on a mountain.

No one knew quite how to react when it emerged that he had been selling 'human quantum energy' diviners on the internet from a flat in surburban Belgrade, speaking at conferences for alternative health and maintaining an intimate friendship with a rather good-looking younger woman.

The breakthrough in the hunt for Karadzic came last month from a single telephone call. A Serbian security source said that the call, from Karadzic's mobile phone, was his 'fatal error'.

For years, Serbian and international security services, including Britain's GCHQ eavesdropping centre, had tapped the telephones of his family, relatives and friends and routinely raided their homes and took them in for questioning as part of a campaign to locate Europe's most wanted man. That would have been no secret to Karadzic, who had a $5 million bounty on his head.

He appears, however, to have become complacent after years in his new skin. At some time in June, according to two Serbian security sources, a telephone call from a mobile number in Belgrade was monitored on the tapped line of one of his relatives. The number was traced to a Dr Dragan David Dabic, living in a small rented apartment in New Belgrade.

Serbian security agents monitored Dabic, following him on his walks in downtown Belgrade and stops at coffee shops and cinemas, visits to his favourite local, the Madhouse, where he would pick up and play the gusle, the traditional Serbian string instrument, and monitoring his telephone calls. It is unclear when they realised that Dabic was in fact Karadzic. 'I think he started to believe himself that he was not Radovan Karadzic,' said Bruno Vekaric, the senior adviser of the war crimes prosecutor in Belgrade. 'We've been following him for a long time.' Pressed, he agreed it was 'about a month'.

Having decided that he could be arrested without posing a security threat and sure he was their man, they decided to act.

'We believed he was moving home,' Vekaric said.

Bozo Prelevic is the former Serbian police minister who served in the first government after the fall of Slobodan Milosevic, the Serbian president who died in prison during his trial at the Hague. Prelevic believes that Karadzic's success was his downfall.

'He started to believe that he would never be arrested,' said Prelevic, who is still close to Serbian security forces. 'He had become overconfident, speaking at conferences. Karadzic could not live without an audience. Calling that relative was his fatal error.'

It may not have proved so had there not been a change in the Serbian government three weeks ago. After elections in May, Boris Tadic, the president, was able to form a new pro-western government with its sights set on membership of the European Union. Key to that prospect was the EU's insistence that war criminals would have to be apprehended. It can be no coincidence also that Karadzic's arrest came the day after an ally of Tadic's was installed as head of the state security service.

Indeed, in a more favourable political climate in Bosnia, near the ski resort of Pale above Sarajevo which is still a stronghold of

Bosnian Serb nationalism, Karadzic had been able to live openly even after his international arrest warrant had been issued.

Last week, friends and former supporters in the picturesque town said that everyone in Pale knew where Karadzic lived until the beginning of 2000 – except Nato it seems. Its green jeeps carrying troops who were searching for him routinely drove by his not-so-secret safe house, where he was often joined by his wife Ljiljana.

'In the early days there were 40 security people around him,' recalled Milovan Bjelica, a leader in Karadzic's Serbian Democratic party, last week. 'Up until late 1999 it was normal to see him. If I wanted to talk to him about something, he would send a car to pick me up. We would sit and discuss things. We would eat dried fruit and nuts and drink coffee.'

Karadzic's former house, a three-storey, wood-fronted chalet set back from a dirt road behind tall pine trees, was deserted last week. Broken windows let in the slanting rain and pine cones littered the stairs to the french windows on the ground floor, but it must once have been a luxurious residence. Karadzic and Ljiljana also spent time in a small white house outside Pale that they still own.

Bjelica does not think Nato was really interested in capturing Karadzic. 'They believed it would endanger their own forces,' he said, a view endorsed by regional experts at the time.

He insists that he did not see Karadzic after he left Pale in early 2000. He said the rumours were that the former Serbian leader was hiding in remote mountain villages, monasteries or even caves.

'But Radovan was not a country man,' Bjelica said. 'He needed the city, so I never believed these stories. I thought he was in Russia, or maybe Argentina.'

It was a renewed initiative by international forces that forced Karadzic to abandon Pale. Yet he still managed to see his family. Letters seized by Nato forces during a raid on the marital home as late as December 2002 reveal clandestine visits from Ljiljana while he was on the run. 'Now summer is practically here, everybody is going somewhere, so it would not be a problem [to meet],' said one missive.

Later, presumably after they had met and done more than hold hands, he jokes about his wife feeling unwell: 'If I was younger, I would hope you were pregnant.'

It is not certain precisely when he moved to Serbia, but it was after Vojislav Kostunica, the hardline president, was elected. It soon became clear that the government was opposed to returning alleged Serbian war criminals to the Hague.

'Karadzic realised he had a better chance of hiding in a forest of people in the big city than in a forest of trees,' said Goran Petrovic, former head of the Serbian intelligence agency. 'He said goodbye to the people he knew and came to Belgrade alone. In Belgrade there were people who knew who he was, but they were less than five [in number].'

The first time he showed up as Dabic, the full-blown new age character, was in 2005. Mina Minic, an alternative healer from Belgrade, recalled last week an unusual visitor to the large house he shares with three generations of his family.

'He [Karadzic] came to my house and brought flowers to my wife,' Minic said. 'He kissed her hand and asked for me to become his teacher. I remember he was so tall, dressed like he was from a monastery.'

Minic explains that after taking a five-day course in 'human quantum energy', a student is awarded a military-style 'rank' based on their talent for the subject. Karadzic was given the rank of general.

He threw himself into the role. His articles in *Healthy Life*, a Serbian alternative medicine magazine, show a man who was fluent in new age thinking. 'It is widely believed our senses and mind can recognise only 1% of whatever exists around us. Three per cent we understand with our hearts. All that remains is shrouded in secrecy, out of the reach of our five senses; however, it is within our reach in the extrasensory manner,' he wrote in one article.

Minic's teaching helped to form the cornerstone of Karadzic's new identity. 'Dragan Dabic' rented a small flat on the third floor of a block in Belgrade, decorated with a gaudy glass lampshade and a vase of dried flowers by the window.

Last week Karadzic's books were still piled on shelves and papers were strewn across a desk next to a fax machine and office desk lamp. On a rail in front of the door hung coats and suits.

Karadzic was a regular customer in the Madhouse bar, where he drank red wine and listened to traditional Serbian music, sitting at a banquette where he could look at the portraits above the bar – of himself and Mladic.

He ate at the Arkidiye, a smart café-restaurant nearby. He always sat at the same table, in a screened booth in the corner of the restaurant, where he would eat cheap, simple meals of *prebranac* (dried beans) or *topli obrok* (a fish meal).

'He had great charisma,' said the restaurant manager Ziza Stevo. 'He was always alone and was not a man you could chat with. I had the impression that he was always fasting. He seemed much taller than Karadzic.'

The revelation that has transfixed Serbia is that while supposedly on the run he enjoyed a close bond with Mila Cicak, an attractive 53-year-old divorcee who lives in an apartment with her university-age son in the Zemun neighbourhood of Belgrade.

Certainly her association with alternative medicine is working; she looks a decade younger than her years. Cicak is coy about how they met and denies allegations in Serbian newspapers that they were having an affair. Kosa Maksimovic, a neighbour who knows Cicak well enough to have lent her money in the past, said Cicak had told her that she went to Dabic for treatment for migraines.

Last week, sitting on a stool in her tiny flat, Cicak looked exhausted from the week's events. 'Of course I didn't know who he was. Who could know that?' she said. 'You can't imagine how I feel.'

She admits she bought into the strange world of alternative therapy. 'I had read about quantum energy, so I knew that Dr Dabic was a great expert. He told me he was working with an autistic child, so I asked to meet the child and work with him. That's how our co-operation began.'

She says she last saw him on the Friday morning before he was arrested: 'We went together to visit the autistic child. He said he needed to travel, that he was going away for two weeks.'

Cicak denies having an affair with Karadzic, but their relationship was clearly close. 'They always came together and they would hold hands,' said Tanya, a secretary at *Healthy Life*. 'I thought they were husband and wife.'

Whatever the truth of their relationship, there was no contact last week as the family of Karadzic took over.

Dragan Karadzic arrived at the empty apartment in Belgrade on Thursday to collect his uncle's belongings. Accompanied by two thick-set men wearing baseball caps and leather jackets, he was intercepted by police as he entered the flat.

They demanded to see written permission but, after a heated discussion, they accompanied Dragan into the apartment, allowing him to leave with a pair of battered trainers, a black tracksuit, two dictionaries and some vitamins.

After an angry tirade and threats against journalists, Dragan revealed that his uncle was fasting and needed the vitamins, before racing off in a muddy black Mercedes estate car.

This weekend Karadzic was in a Belgrade prison cell with a barred window in the door. He was refusing prison food, but eating hazelnuts and walnuts brought by Luca, his brother, and reading newspapers that all pictured him on their front pages. It is already an outdated image – he has yet again changed his appearance, demanding to be allowed to shave and cut his hair.

This week will be one of recovery from shock in Serbia and legal manoeuvres that will most likely see Karadzic in a new role: that of prisoner in the Hague.

The UN high representative in Sarajevo has denied permission for Ljiljana or his children, Sasa and Sonja, to travel to Belgrade to visit him.

Intelligence agencies are now engaged in the process of piecing together Karadzic's movements. Attention will turn to Dragan Karadzic, who this weekend told a Serbian newspaper that he had been the only person helping his uncle over the past six years as he hid from justice.

There were clearly some near-misses with the authorities along the way. Yesterday Austrian police said anti-terror units had found a man who looked exactly like Dabic while searching an apartment in Vienna for a murder suspect last year. The man was not connected to the killing and was released without being finger-printed. Meanwhile, an Austrian newspaper reported that Karadzic had worked in Vienna as a 'miracle healer' in 2006, seeing patients in the homes of Serbians living there.

In Serbia, the government has vowed to move on and focus on capturing Mladic, the next most wanted man in Europe. Serbian sources say that will be a different odyssey. The general behind the Srebrenica massacre is never alone and is surrounded by armed bodyguards willing to fight to the death rather than give up their leader.

Rumours that Mladic had given up Karadzic to save himself were just that.

Petrovic said: 'Arresting Karadzic was not a big risk. To catch Mladic would be different. Mladic's bodyguards have orders to kill him rather than let him be captured. Karadzic was a doctor. Mladic is a crazy military man.'

Karadzic's home for the foreseeable future is already waiting. At the detention centre at the Hague they have prepared an en-suite cell, about 18 metres square, with a television, facilities to cook Balkan specialities with fellow war criminals and a ping-pong table.

If he is to represent himself in court, as he has promised to do, Karadzic will also need one more thing: the bearded guru of human quantum theory could soon be swapping his tomes on alternative health for law books.

PART THREE

Marie with Billy Smith, the cat she rescued
from the streets of Jerusalem.

Middle East

Bloodied Gaza set for the endgame

GAZA

11 January 2009

Marie Colvin, Sara Hashash; Uzi Mahnaimi in Tel Aviv;
Sarah Baxter in Washington

In the emergency room of Al Shifa hospital in Gaza City, Dr Raed al-Arayni was entering his twelfth day of nonstop work and was preparing for yet another operation when his worst nightmare came true.

The bloodied little boy being carried into the room by a neighbour was screaming at him. 'Baba, baba [daddy, daddy],' the child cried.

'I did not recognise my own child because of his injuries,' recalled Arayni. 'For a few seconds I couldn't move, my knees became weak. I could barely stand at the sight of my child halfway between life and death.'

Running over he realised that both his sons – Hathifa, 7, and Abdul Rahman, 5 – were lying in his emergency room, severely wounded.

Tears streaming down his face, Arayni began working feverishly on Hathifa, who had the worst injuries. A chunk of shrapnel had pierced his chest, his right leg was broken and blood poured from his wounds.

A colleague began treating Abdul Rahman. The nerves in his broken left arm had been severed and he had no feeling in his hand. They were able to stabilise the two boys.

'I just thank God my children didn't arrive to me in bits and pieces, missing body parts as the women and children I see arriving daily,' said Arayni, standing by Hathifa's bedside, his face showing the exhaustion of almost two weeks of back-to-back operations. The slight, bearded surgeon had not returned home for 12 days, grabbing a nap or a meal at the hospital when he could.

When the Israelis launched a massive attack against Hamas, the Islamic extremist group that rules Gaza, to stop it launching rockets against Israel's southern cities, he had moved his family from their home in Jabaliya, a crowded refugee camp just north of Gaza City. They took refuge with a relative in the more central Fakhura district, believing they would be safer.

The surgeon pushed aside the thought of his own children as the wounded poured in, sometimes so many that the operating floors were slick with blood. Injured men, women and children were piled in the corridors and surgeons commandeered the recovery room.

On Tuesday Um Mustafa, his wife, and their boys had gone up on the roof of the building, desperate for some fresh air after almost a week inside while Israeli jets screamed overhead and missiles, tank and artillery rounds pounded the coastal strip day and night.

The boys had been playing for about an hour when Um Mustafa sent them downstairs for a bottle of water. Moments later a huge explosion rocked the building, followed by a second. Two missiles had slammed into the girls' primary school next door run by the United Nations Relief and Works Agency, where Gazans fleeing the fighting had been given refuge. Some 40 people, many of them women and children, were killed.

A controversy still rages over the strike on the school, one of three bombed by the Israelis within 24 hours. Israel claimed militants had fired mortars from near the school. UN officials insisted their security guards kept militants out of their compounds and that they had even given the Israeli military the GPS coordinates for their 23 schools, refuge for some 15,000 Gazans, to avert such a tragedy.

As soon as Hathifa and Abdul Rahman were stabilised, Arayni went back to operating on the casualties from the school bombing. As he left their room on Friday, leaving the boys in the care of their weeping mother, Abdul Rahman woke from a feverish sleep and began calling out for his father.

'I want my daddy. Where is he? Is he hurt?' he cried. His older brother, the shrapnel still in his chest because it is too dangerous to remove, reassured him. 'No, he's treating other kids who got hurt like us,' Hathifa said.

By the standards of the past fortnight in Gaza, the Arayni boys were lucky. At the last count 830 Palestinians had been killed and some 3,000 wounded, according to health officials in Gaza. The Hamas-run health ministry said at least a third were children.

Israeli troops were dug in on the outskirts of Gaza City and hunkered down in Palestinian homes they had seized. Hamas's security forces had been driven from the streets, but struck back in hit-and-run attacks from tunnels, sniped from rooftops and continued to launch rockets into Israel.

Northern Gaza was a wasteland. Whole blocks of the concrete apartment buildings and small homes of the refugee camps of Jabaliya, Beit Hanoun and Beit Lahiya were devastated, hit by missiles or demolished by military bulldozers.

Aid officials warned of a humanitarian disaster. The UN said two thirds of Gazans were without electricity and half had no water. Food and medical supplies were running low.

On Wednesday Israel relented slightly, announcing it would stop firing between the hours of 1pm and 4pm to allow aid agencies to deliver supplies.

Nevertheless, it showed no sign of ending its operations any time soon. From Israel's perspective it is fighting a crucial battle, backed by near-unanimous popular support, against an enemy committed to its ultimate destruction and which has continued to target its citizens in the south.

There was more evidence of that yesterday as at least 10 Hamas rockets were fired at Israeli targets. One hit a block of flats in the city of Ashkelon, wounding two people.

'Israel has acted, is acting and will act only according to its considerations, the security needs of its citizens and its right to self-defence,' Tzipi Livni, the foreign minister and the ruling Kadima party's candidate for prime minister, said on Friday.

How close is Israel to achieving its goals? What has the blood-shed achieved and is there any sign of it stopping? Israel launched Operation Cast Lead on 27 December, little more than a week after Hamas refused to renew a six-month truce that had largely held and resumed its rocket attacks on southern Israel.

The operation's aims were to stop Hamas's rocket launches into southern Israeli cities and end the smuggling of weapons through tunnels under Gaza's southern border with Egypt.

Israeli intelligence repeatedly warned that Hamas was stockpiling increasingly sophisticated long-range Grad rockets, manufactured in China but passed to Hamas by Iran, along with its homemade Qassam rockets. Israel believed that unless it acted soon, Hamas's ability to strike would present a grave danger.

That prediction proved accurate. As soon as the Israeli missiles began landing in Gaza, Hamas launched rockets that reached further than before, hitting the cities of Ashkelon, Ashdod and Beersheba.

Last week a Grad rocket landed on Gedera, a town 28 miles from Gaza and less than a mile from the Israeli air force base at Tel Nof, where nuclear weapons are believed to be stored.

The wider strategic aim of the operation is the need to confront Iranian-sponsored bellicosity. The supply of Grad rockets to Hamas followed Tehran's sponsorship of Hezbollah, the Lebanese-based Shi'ite militant group which had fired rockets at Israel's northern cities and fought a war with Israel in the summer of 2006.

The threat of a nuclear-armed Iran, the rising power in the region, is foremost in Israel's thoughts. Last week in Washington, Sallai Meridor, Israel's ambassador to the United States, warned in an interview that Iran would have enough enriched uranium this year to manufacture a nuclear bomb.

If Israel is to address such a threat militarily in the future, it will need to have subdued the immediate threats on its borders. The timing of the attack on Gaza was also influenced by the Israeli general election, due on 10 February. As rockets terrorised southern Israel, the ruling coalition, led by Kadima, was increasingly open to accusations of being soft on defence and trailed the right-wing Likud party, led by Binyamin Netanyahu, in the polls.

The arithmetic of Israeli politics is fiendishly complicated, but the effect of the Gaza operation is revealed in the fortunes of the Labour party headed by Ehud Barak, the defence minister. Two weeks ago, before the attack, it was struggling in third or fourth place in the polls with only nine or 10 expected parliamentary seats (out of 120) after the elections. After a week of operations that figure had risen to 16 seats.

Likud is still leading the race with an expected 32 seats and Kadima is likely to win 27 or so seats, but the centre-left block is closing fast.

A decisive victory over Hamas may pull the rug from under the right-wing bloc and possibly allow a Barak–Livni coalition. But if Hamas can claim victory, it will strengthen Likud and its allies and Israel will probably get Netanyahu as its next prime minister.

There could be no doubt that Israel had the upper hand after two weeks of fighting, but the operation, which Barak described as one of 'shock and awe', had reached a difficult point by this weekend.

Israeli pundits all agreed that the government needed a 'clear win', such as an assurance of quiet on the southern front, to withdraw with any semblance of victory and to justify the high price of international opprobrium.

That was not even on the horizon. On Friday, Palestinian sources said Hamas's weapons caches had been decimated and scores of the tunnels it used to import weapons had been destroyed in the bombings. But with its leadership hiding in underground bunkers or holding talks in Egypt, and only about 400 of its 15,000 officers and foot soldiers killed, the organisation was largely intact.

For Israelis this provided two starkly different choices. One was to declare victory and withdraw, either unilaterally or with a semblance of a ceasefire brokered by the international community.

The other was to implement 'stage three' of Operation Cast Lead, following the initial bombing and subsequent ground assault, and continue into the crowded neighbourhoods of Gaza City and refugee camps. Here Hamas has created a virtual under-ground city of tunnels and the warren of alleys and narrow streets make it far more difficult for Israeli forces to manoeuvre.

Ehud Olmert, the outgoing prime minister, was said to be advocating going even further and aiming to topple Hamas. The organisation had won elections in 2006 and 18 months ago ousted Fatah, led by Mahmoud Abbas, the moderate president who runs the rival Palestinian Authority, from Gaza.

Avigdor Ben-Gal, a decorated and influential retired Israeli general, said this weekend: 'We need to conquer the Gaza Strip and put the Hamas military and political leaders on a French ship to leave Gaza for good, just as we did with [the former Palestinian leader Yasser] Arafat in Beirut 1982. We've already conquered a bigger Arab city than Gaza [namely, Beirut], our army is trained and fit for the mission. The politicians should give the order.'

Some Fatah officials have even privately expressed the hope that Israel would rout Hamas, so stung were they by being forced out of Gaza.

Expanding the incursion would carry high risks. So far the Israeli population has supported the operation: a poll on Friday showed 91% of Israelis in favour. But that could change dramatically if casualties start piling up, as they did when an operation was launched against Hezbollah in Lebanon in 2006 to stem the flow of missiles on Israel's northern cities. Israel did not then secure the crushing victory to which its people were accustomed.

For Hamas, however battered, the equation is far simpler. All it has to do to declare victory is survive. The leadership is certain to reap the kudos from having stood up to the most powerful army in the Middle East without jets, tanks or sophisticated weaponry.

Hamas appeared to be regrouping after, incredibly, being shocked at the original Israeli attack. This was despite the tanks that had been massing on its borders for days and Israel's public warnings that it would not tolerate rockets being launched on its soil.

'Hamas actually believed that firing rockets into Israel would force it to open the Rafah crossing [into Egypt],' said a senior Palestinian who has negotiated with them.

'They were shocked at the massive Israeli response. They are very naive.'

However, Izzedine al-Qassam, Hamas's military wing, was said still to have high morale and other extremist groups in Gaza were fighting side by side with Hamas.

Whatever the Israelis decide to do – and there were reports that leaflets had been dropped on Gaza yesterday warning the residents to expect a dramatic escalation in hostilities – they have to do it quickly.

Israeli soldiers stationed on lines at the edge of Gaza City were increasingly becoming sitting targets. The thousands of reservists who had been called up finished a week's training on Friday and could not be kept in the camps indefinitely; they have civilian jobs and families at home.

In addition, the Israeli government was well aware that international pressure was building, fuelled by horrific images that have emerged from Gaza despite Israel's refusal to allow foreign journalists to enter the coastal strip.

International diplomatic efforts to end the conflict were grinding slowly forward. Both Israel and Hamas rejected a UN security council resolution that had called for an 'immediate ceasefire'. Olmert called the resolution 'unworkable' and Hamas rejected the resolution on the grounds that it had not been consulted.

Crucially, the Americans, Israel's superpower sponsor, abstained from the vote, preferring to back an Egyptian-brokered ceasefire. These efforts appeared to be moving ahead. General Amos Gilad, a senior Israeli official, visited Cairo last week and will do so again today, and a Hamas delegation, both from Gaza and its Damascus-based politburo, travelled to Cairo yesterday.

A senior Palestinian source who had seen the proposal said it contained four points and put Egypt as the sole broker between the two sides.

The first point, he said, called for an agreement between both 'factions' on an immediate ceasefire; the second point was the opening of the Gaza border crossings to allow humanitarian aid and 'Egypt to continue its efforts'; the third point was a vague provision for an international element, presumably to monitor the border; and the fourth point provided for Egypt to oversee talks between Hamas and Fatah to end their bitter dispute and form a united leadership.

Despite fighting talk from Hamas members, those dealing with them say that although they are still insisting they will not stop fighting until the Rafah crossing into Egypt is open – their key demand and their own litmus test of a real victory – they want a ceasefire.

In the longer term, both Israelis and moderate Palestinians realise that the only way forward is a political solution. Israel would love to see Abbas retake power in Gaza. Should he replace Hamas on the back of an Israeli invasion, however, he would be perceived as an Israeli stooge.

'There is no eliminating Hamas. They are part of the Palestinian people whether we like it or not,' said Ghassan Shaqa'a, a senior Palestinian politician and an adviser to Abbas. 'You have to talk to them.'

Everyone is waiting for the US presidency of Barack Obama, who will be sworn in on 20 January. Despite the economic crisis, sources in his administration said that he knew he would have to engage in the Middle East crisis, although he was hoping that there would be a ceasefire by the time he took office.

'God knows he will have enough on his plate, but he has to work from day one on this or the only options left will be bad ones,' said Martin Indyk, a Middle East adviser to Hillary Clinton, the incoming secretary of state.

Indyk, the author of a new book, *Innocent Abroad*, based on his experience as an American ambassador to Israel, reiterated the US policy that the only solution was a two-state solution, with some special provision for Jerusalem, the city holy to Jews, Muslims and Christians.

Obama indicated last week that he could open contacts with Hamas, a first for an American president.

He is likely to begin a complicated three-way chess game involving talks with Syria and contacts of some sort with Iran. A diplomatic breakthrough with Syria could isolate Iran, a bonus in the campaign to stop it from going nuclear, and encourage other Arab states to come to the negotiating table.

'Obama won't be able to do it alone,' Indyk said. 'He'll need leaders in the region like Anwar Sadat [the late Egyptian president and the first Arab leader to make peace with Israel in the 1970s]. The president will need to be ready to grab the moment when it arises.'

For the citizens of Gaza it cannot come too soon. Of all the suffering among Gazan civilians, few endured worse than the Samouni clan. Last week four young boys from the extended family were rescued after three days of being trapped in a home with the bodies of their mothers and relatives.

Their emaciated condition horrified aid workers who had spent days trying to get permission from the Israelis to rescue them.

Their ordeal began last Sunday, shortly after Israel invaded. Troops ordered families to gather in one large house while they searched the Zeitoun neighbourhood. On Monday morning, with about 90 men, women and children inside, three Israeli missiles slammed into the house, according to the survivors.

Sixteen were killed in the strike – seven women, six children including a baby found curled up under its dead mother's arm, and three men. Ahmed Samouni, 15, told his tale from his hospital bed, a tube snaking out of his nose and his hands still black with blood and grime.

'Some of their heads were exploded,' he said, still shaking from the experience. 'The door was open. A chicken came in and started to eat the brains from their heads. I pulled off the chicken, crawled to the door and closed it with my feet.'

Down the hall are his brother Yaqub, 10, and cousin Abdullah, 8, so badly wounded that they can barely speak. Another cousin is in intensive care.

Yesterday more horrors visited Gaza. Eight members of a family, including two women and two children, were killed in Jabaliya when an Israeli tank shell hit them as they sat out in their garden to bask in the unseasonable winter sun.

The neighbour who took them to hospital did so in the boot of his car because their bodies were mangled together.

Amid all the uncertainty about Israel's intentions and the search for a ceasefire, human tragedy seems to be the only thing guaranteed.

Beyond the violence, a solution is on the table

11 January 2009

The ferocious fighting in Gaza between Israel and Hamas, the militant group, might seem to make the prospect of peace between Israelis and Palestinians more distant than ever. Stand back from the spasm of violence, however, and the two sides are closer than the fighting might suggest.

Polls show consistently that the majority on both sides agree that the solution to their conflict must be two states side by side: an Israeli state with a Jewish majority and a Palestinian state. No doubt they would be edgy, suspicious neighbours and any agreement would be grudging on both sides but the acceptance of the concept has taken root.

On the main issues there is now more agreement than division on how these states could look and function.

TERRITORY

The Palestinians have long insisted that Israel must withdraw to the borders recognised by the United Nations before the 1967 war when Israel seized the West Bank from Jordan and Gaza from Egypt.

The negotiations are now down to detail that might seem pedantic elsewhere.

The latest idea is of a 'land swap', whereby Israel would keep the four main settlements in the West Bank that have been built over the 1967 line and have grown into virtual cities, such as Ma'ale Adumim, essentially a suburb of Jerusalem.

In return for recognising that reality on the ground, the Palestinians would be compensated with land from within the borders of Israel proper. Maps have been drawn which would cede areas of the southern Negev desert to a Palestinian state.

The two sides are now only percentage points apart. Ehud Olmert, the outgoing Israeli prime minister, has offered the Palestinians 93% of the area of the West Bank. Mahmoud Abbas, the Palestinian president, has said he could cede 2% but no more, according to Palestinian sources.

Israel has said that it would uproot 70 of the 120 settlements on the West Bank, home to about 60,000 settlers. But 440,000 people would stay.

JERUSALEM

Both sides claim the city as their capital and it remains a hugely contentious issue. However, the Israelis have accepted that no deal can be made that does not offer the Palestinians some part of Arab East Jerusalem. There are various ideas for an international component for the sites holy to Jews, Muslims and Christians in the Old City.

LINKING PALESTINIAN LANDS

The Palestinians insist their state must be contiguous, so there are various solutions that would connect Gaza on the Mediterranean in the south to the West Bank, which lies to the north. They range from a tunnel that would cost billions of dollars (preferred by Israeli security), to a bridge, to a heavily guarded road that would go from Gaza to the West Bank city of Hebron.

REFUGEES

Millions of Palestinian refugees, who left what was then the British mandate of Palestine during the 1948 war, are scattered far and wide.

They want to come home, but most of those homes are in what is now Israel and their return would overwhelm and end the idea of a Jewish state. The outlines of a solution would be to allow refugees the right to return only to the West Bank and Gaza. Those relinquishing claims to their ancestral homes would be given compensation.

SECURITY

Israel wants to be sure that once it cedes control of territory, rockets will not start coming over the border, as they have from Hamas in Gaza. One proposal is for an international force in the West

Bank. The Palestinians have requested a multinational force led by the Americans.

It is also worth noting that the Israeli use of Gaza as proof that rockets would come from the West Bank is somewhat disingenuous. While Israeli soldiers did pull out of Gaza in 2005, Israel retained control of the borders, air and sea; and for the past 18 months, since Hamas took power, it has maintained a virtual siege which destroyed the economy and radicalised many living in the coastal strip.

ELECTIONS

There is no doubt that the violence, now in its third week, has set back the chances of any peace negotiations. And getting them onto a track that could realistically result in a settlement is made more difficult by the weakness of both governments.

In Israel, Olmert faces corruption charges and stepped down as his party's candidate for leadership, leaving Tzipi Livni, the foreign minister, as the candidate for the centrist Kadima party which is now in power. Lacking military credentials, she is vulnerable to a challenge from Binyamin Netanyahu, the hardline Likud candidate, who was ahead in the polls last week for the 10 February election.

Abbas is also weakened by the fact that his writ runs only in the West Bank since Hamas's violent coup in Gaza in 2007.

For any settlement with the Palestinians to succeed, there would first have to be unity between Fatah and Hamas, which rejects the existence of Israel, or the election of a Fatah-dominated government. Elections are due next year.

Netanyahu stokes fears to take poll lead

8 February 2009

Israel's right-wing hawk is striking a chord with election voters who mistrust peace with Palestinians.

His silver hair blowing in a chill wind, Binyamin Netanyahu, the right-wing front-runner in Israel's general election, was eager to reassure a crowd of Jewish settlers in the West Bank last Friday: victory this week for his Likud party would mean no Palestinian state on their land.

'The election on Tuesday will be about one issue – whether this place will remain in our hands or will be handed over to Hamas [the Islamic extremist group] and Iran,' he roared to adoring supporters in Beit Aryeh, a small settlement.

If Palestinian militants were in control, rockets would rain down on Israel's international airport only 15 miles away, he warned.

Netanyahu, 59, has won his lead in the opinion polls by repeatedly articulating the anxieties of voters like the inhabitants of Beit Aryeh, whose settlement is built on land won by Israel in the 1967 war. It would therefore be returned to Palestinian rule under the peace agreement envisaged by the United States.

Despite the global financial crisis, Israel's politicians have largely ignored the economy on the campaign trail. This election is about how to deal with the Palestinians.

Coming just six weeks after Israel's invasion of Gaza to stop Hamas rocket attacks, it has seen the right making large gains as a result of Israeli fears of the Palestinian threat.

The latest poll in the *Haaretz* newspaper predicts that right-wing parties led by the hawkish Likud will win 66 seats in the

120-member Knesset, Israel's parliament, with 54 going to Kadima, the governing centrist party, and smaller parties on the left.

Kadima, led by Tzipi Livni, 50, the foreign minister, is closing the gap with a predicted 25 seats to Likud's 27, but commentators say the trend is clear. 'A wind from the right is blowing through the country,' said Shlomo Yerushalmi, an analyst on Israeli television.

Netanyahu, who was prime minister from 1996 to 1999, was not spelling out the details of his plans publicly and refused Livni's challenge to a debate. In briefings, however, the Likud leader – who grew up partly in America – has disclosed that he would spurn any US attempt to negotiate the creation of a Palestinian state in the West Bank and Gaza.

'We will not withdraw from one inch. Every inch we leave would go to Iran,' Netanyahu said, referring to the financial and military support that the Tehran regime gives Hamas. The Islamic extremist group controls Gaza and has a growing presence in the West Bank.

Under Netanyahu's plan, Palestinians would not have a sovereign state but self-governing, non-contiguous 'population centres'. He also proposes an 'economic peace' that would improve living conditions for Palestinians in the hope that this would help moderate opinion to prevail.

Gideon Levy, a *Haaretz* columnist, expressed a common view when he called the plan 'a mix of condescension and dehumanisation', but it strikes a chord with those voters who distrust the idea of making peace in the face of a growing Palestinian radicalism.

A Likud government would annihilate Hamas, Netanyahu claimed, a goal seen as unrealistic even by the Israeli intelligence establishment.

Netanyahu's election would be a setback for the administration of President Barack Obama, who vowed to push for Middle East peace 'from day one' and appointed George Mitchell, the former Northern Ireland envoy, as his representative in the region.

The resurgence of the right is exemplified by the startling rise of Avigdor Lieberman, 50, the Russian-born leader of Yisrael Beiteinu (Israel Our Home), once considered to be a fringe party.

The one-time Moldovan nightclub bouncer and former aide to Netanyahu rose to third place in the polls last week and is predicted to gain 18 seats, more than the Labour party.

Lieberman, who relishes his hardline reputation, has called for all Israeli Arab citizens to swear a loyalty oath to the Jewish state or lose their citizenship. He also proposes to transfer many Arab Israelis to Palestinian rule by redrawing Israel's borders.

'I think Lieberman will be the big kingmaker in this election,' said Michael Barak, an Israeli pollster.

In the complex world of Israeli politics, Lieberman's surge has helped the centrist Livni by siphoning votes away from Netanyahu.

Their supporters could hardly be more different. While Netanyahu stood on that West Bank hill surrounded by dour men in suits, Livni held a rally at which she belted out, karaoke-style, 'Non, je ne regrette rien' (No regrets), the signature tune of Edith Piaf, the French singer. The show starred Dana International, Israel's trans-gender Eurovision winner.

Livni's speech echoed the themes of Obama's campaign in the United States.

'We are going to do it,' she told the ecstatic crowd of women in tight, low-slung jeans and men in T-shirts. 'Don't vote from fear or despair. The easiest thing to do is to paint the future as black.'

Livni, a lawyer and former agent for Mossad, Israel's overseas intelligence agency, entered the Knesset only 10 years ago. As foreign minister she has led negotiations with the Palestinians for the past year, but she has also been short on details during her campaign, fearing that her backing for a separate Palestinian state would alienate many voters.

Whoever wins the popular vote on Tuesday will still have to form a coalition government. The smaller parties seem certain to hold the larger parties to ransom in pursuit of their special interests. Alliances in Israel can be bizarre and by Friday Livni was saying she would consider taking Lieberman into a coalition led by her.

Netanyahu's dream coalition would include Labour, once Israel's leading party but now in fourth place despite being led by Ehud

Barak, Israel's most decorated soldier and the present defence minister.

All the pollsters were making cautionary noises last week, with up to a third of the 5.2 million voters still undecided. Few people were prepared to predict which of the two starkly opposing options for bringing peace to Israel and its neighbours would win the day.

Israel's secret war

15 January 2012

Marie Colvin and Uzi Mahnaimi

In the desperate race to stop Iran developing nuclear weapons, shadowy forces are assassinating its top scientists.

Early in Tehran's grey wintry morning last Wednesday, Mustafa Ahmadi Roshan, a young scientist in Iran's controversial nuclear programme, got dressed at his home in the northern suburbs. The events of this last hour of his life could have come out of a spy film.

Small groups of Israeli agents were watching key points in the Iranian capital. Their target was Roshan. They would be dead themselves if they were caught.

For Israel it was a classic assassination mission. 'What is seen in espionage films as a simple operation is a result of hard work, many months of intelligence gathering and a well trained team,' said a source who released details, impossible to verify, to *The Sunday Times*.

'There is zero tolerance for mistakes. By nature, every failure not only risks the neck of the agents but also risks turning into an international scandal.'

Since its foundation in 1948, Israel has used assassination as a national weapon, striking targets abroad ranging from Palestinians who killed Israeli athletes at the 1972 Olympic Games in Munich, to enemies on the streets of Amman and a Hamas leader in a Dubai hotel room in 2010.

Now Iran is the target. In the past two years assassins have attacked five scientists in the state nuclear programme, killing four of them. Mossad, the Israeli external intelligence agency, is widely believed to be responsible.

The murder of civilians divides Iran's critics – and Israel's. Some find it repugnant, others see them as casualties in an undeclared war that is greatly preferable to the alternative of full-scale conflict.

One Israeli source claimed the killings were a precursor to a military strike, not merely an alternative, to make it more difficult for Iran to rebuild facilities if they are bombed.

Last week Iran defiantly announced it was enriching uranium at a new site, Fordow, built under a mountain near the holy city of Qom to protect it from aerial attack. The assassins were ready. As Roshan, 32, prepared to leave home, he was monitored from a makeshift control room in a safe house nearby.

Israeli agents were also watching the entrance to Iranian intelligence headquarters in the city centre. Suddenly they noticed a number of cars and people running; then they saw police rushing into the nearby streets. Another agent monitoring radio traffic between the Tehran police and security forces confirmed unusual activity. Had the operation been exposed?

In 1997 two agents of Caesarea, Mossad's top hit squad, had bungled an attempt to kill a Palestinian leader in Jordan and were arrested before they could flee, triggering a diplomatic crisis.

Jordan is relatively friendly to Israel. Iran is its bitterest enemy. There was no point in hesitation. If the agents had been rumbled, they would never escape anyway. The mission commander decided to go ahead.

Just before 8am on Wednesday, Reza Qashqai, Roshan's bodyguard and driver, arrived. Qashqai knew the risks. He checked under the silver Peugeot 405, a state-issue car, and looked beneath the bonnet before slipping into the driver's seat to wait for the scientist.

The house was in the Cheezar neighbourhood of northern Tehran, a village overtaken by the sprawl of the capital but still home to quiet traditional families who supported the regime.

Roshan got into the car, ready for a long day as deputy head of the Natanz uranium enrichment site, where he supervised procurement.

It was two years almost to the day since the murder of Masud Ali Mohammadi, an expert in quantum physics at Tehran University, who had been one of Roshan's mentors at the Iranian nuclear programme. Mohammadi, 50, was the first victim of the wave of assassinations.

Iran claims that its nuclear programme is for peaceful purposes, but the West accuses Tehran of working to develop a nuclear bomb.

Europe and America have led an unsuccessful diplomatic effort, based on sanctions, to try to stop the research. Israeli hawks, knowing their nation would be the target of an Iranian bomb, talk of a bold pre-emptive strike from the air that, Washington fears, would lead to war. So the reality is a secret campaign against soft targets such as the Mohammadis and Roshans fulfilling the mullahs' ambition for an Islamic nuclear weapon.

Roshan, a chemist, was one of the young scientists in the programme. He was not the most brilliant but was trusted by an increasingly paranoid regime because he came from a traditional religious family and had remained loyal while many of his fellow students had objected to the restraints of the Islamic regime. He had been talent-spotted at the Sharif technical university, where he joined the Basij, a fearsome militia controlled by the Iranian Revolutionary Guards.

Soon after graduation he married and was recruited to the Iranian nuclear programme to work at Natanz, Iran's main uranium enrichment complex. Colleagues said that like any new father he was transformed when he talked about his young son.

As the clock ticked towards 8am, an Israeli spotter reported via a secure text that Roshan was being driven from his home. Qashqai was at the wheel, a crucial detail because the bodyguard would be slower to respond if he was driving.

The assassins' commander took the final decision. 'Go,' he told agents who were standing by with a motorcycle in a hidden garage. They left immediately, weaving through the gridlocked streets of rush-hour Tehran.

In the five attacks on nuclear scientists, the hit squad has used a motorbike every time. The motorcyclist is ubiquitous in the capital's traffic jams, often wearing a surgical mask for protection against the heavy pollution and able to move close to the target between the lines of stationary cars without attracting attention.

Wednesday's team were familiar with the streets, the hallmark of a successful operation. They speeded up to reach Gol Nabi Street, which Roshan always passed on his way to work.

At 8.20am they spotted the Peugeot. The masked figure on the pillion seat made a quick check that Roshan was the passenger, then attached a magnetic bomb to the car. The motorbike sped away. The plastic explosive had been shaped to deliver its full force at the passenger. Nine seconds later it exploded. The scientist was killed instantly. Qashqai, badly injured, died in hospital.

After the bombing, onlookers milled about watching Roshan's car being hauled away under a cover of blue plastic and taking photographs on their mobile phones. At his funeral on Friday hundreds of regime supporters swore revenge.

'Two targets were always in Mustafa's mind,' Reza Najafi, a friend, said. 'To fight Israel and to become a shaheed [martyr]. He achieved both his targets.'

America denied having any connection with the assassinations last week.

'We were not involved in any way with regards to the assassination that took place there,' said Leon Panetta, the defence secretary. But he did say enigmatically that he had 'some idea' of who was.

The Foreign Office also said Britain had 'no involvement whatsoever' in the deaths of the scientists.

Most experts in the field have few doubts: the assassinations have all the hallmarks of Israeli operations.

Israel did not comment but Lieutenant-General Benny Gantz, chief of the general staff, told a parliamentary committee that this year would be 'critical' for Iran because of 'things that happen to it unnaturally'. Certainly the events of the past two years have been 'unnatural'.

The first assassination victim, Mohammadi, one of the leading lights of the nuclear programme, was killed by a bomb on a parked motorcycle as he walked from his house to his car. Then came more deaths.

In November 2010 motorcycles pulled alongside two cars in different parts of Tehran and then sped away. Bombs attached to the cars killed Majid Shahriari and injured Fereydoun Abbasi-Davani, both nuclear scientists. Davani was named head of the Iranian atomic programme when he recovered.

Target number four was Dariush Rezaeinejad, an electronics expert responsible for high-voltage switches, a dual-use item that can be used in nuclear warheads. He was shot in Tehran by gunmen on motorcycles.

There has also been a series of mysterious explosions. Last November a blast hit a military base used by the Revolutionary Guards, killing General Hassan Tehrani Moghaddam, head of Iran's ballistic missile programme.

The most effective strike, however, was not deadly. The Stuxnet worm, a cyberweapon, attacked and disabled the centrifuges crucial to Iran's programme of enriching uranium. It has been speculated that both Israel and the United States were involved.

The nuclear programme has also suffered from a CIA operation that infiltrated sabotaged parts into some of Iran's black market supply lines.

In December the United States made it illegal for an American company to deal with a foreign bank used by the Iranian petro-chemical industry. The European Union has advanced a scheduled meeting to 23 January to consider further sanctions.

The worry now is how Iran will react. The regime may begin to feel as if it cannot protect its own. Sanctions are beginning to bite and the economy is in freefall.

Tehran has threatened to close the Strait of Hormuz, the narrow mouth of the Gulf through which 17 million barrels of oil pass daily; Washington has made it clear this is a 'red line' that would result in military action, western diplomats said last week.

President Barack Obama telephoned Binyamin Netanyahu, the Israeli prime minister, after the latest killing; according to one Israeli source, Obama urged restraint but Netanyahu refused. The United States is thought to have stepped up safeguards at American facilities in the region.

Diplomats believe there is still a chance of luring Tehran back into nuclear talks that could avert a showdown. 'We don't consider an escalation to war an inevitability and we are pursuing a strategy of actions designed to avert conflict. We still think they can succeed,' a western diplomat said.

Iraq

War-weary Iraqi voters catch election fever despite attacks

BAGHDAD

6 March 2010

A country brought to the brink of anarchy by sectarian violence is emerging as a vibrant democracy, despite Al-Qaeda's suicide bombings.

The purple ink on his right index finger was important to Ali Obeid. He held up a shaking hand from his hospital bed to show he had voted before a suicide bomber stepped on to the bus taking his army unit back to base on the eve of today's parliamentary elections.

Obeid, 50, a father of four, was supposed to be on duty today with 200,000 of Iraq's security forces to protect the polling stations. That is why he was voting on Thursday. At least 17 people died when suicide bombers struck two army units and a market.

'They haven't said yet whether they'll have to amputate,' Obeid said, his large brown eyes welling as he stared down at feet wrapped in bloodied gauze.

Still wearing his camouflage uniform, Obeid insisted his enthusiasm for the election was undimmed. He wanted his three daughters and son to have chances he never had.

'The government we need is one that will give us that security to live in peace,' he said. Obeid's ordeal began as a sandstorm obscured the Baghdad sun. A badly dressed man described by the soldiers as 'ugly' blew himself up when the soldiers tried to stop him.

Al-Qaeda in Iraq had vowed to do all it could to stop the election. The bombings seemed to be an attempt to frighten would-be voters into staying at home. But in the emergency room at the Al-Kharkh hospital, the soldiers' eyes flashed with anger and pride, mingled with tears for those who had lost lives or limbs.

'The message we want to give to this bomber, and to the people who sent him, is that we are challenging you,' said Shaheed Salem, 36, who had four gauze patches on his back to cover shrapnel wounds. As he was wheeled into X-ray, Salem, a father of six with a pregnant wife, said he saw the election as a watershed. 'I will protect all the Iraqis who want to vote in this election,' he insisted. 'This determines our fate.'

The theme was repeated fervently last week. While Iraq has been slipping from the headlines amid a diminishing body count, most Iraqis have quietly embraced democracy.

Even the followers of Moqtada al-Sadr, the founder of the Shi'ite Mahdi army, who once vowed not to lay down arms until foreign troops had left Iraq, took to the airwaves to deliver rhetoric, not rounds.

Some 19m Iraqis are going to the polls to choose from among 6,200 candidates vying for 325 seats in parliament in the second general election since the American-led invasion ousted Saddam Hussein in 2003. Turnout is expected to be up to 60%.

The campaign has been a rollicking free-for-all. There are no laws to restrict how much parties spend or where they get their money from. Money for some Shi'ite candidates is said to have come from Iran, while Saudis are supposed to have funnelled cash to hardline Sunnis.

Every street is festooned with placards. In one, a female candidate glows beatifically in a pink suit; in another, an elderly cleric kisses a skull symbolising Saddam's victims. Many are shaking fists.

'They look like maniacs to westerners, but we Iraqis see them as passionate about their ideas,' an earnest university linguist tried to explain.

Every night on the myriad television channels, candidates have shouted, hectored and lectured. Channel-hopping Iraqis have watched them all, mesmerised by this new phenomenon. I met a cleric who turned up smoking a Cohiba cigar, and another candidate who gave a telephone interview to a Tehran station with a glass of whisky in his hand. Every campaign must feed the crowds who attend rallies. There have been so many that the price of lamb has soared from $11 (£7) to $15 per kilo.

One of the main differences compared with the 2005 election is a relative lack of sectarian rhetoric. Among those driven from their homes during the violence of 2006–7, which left tens of thousands dead, the desire is not for revenge, but for security.

'I'm voting for a secular candidate,' said Hekmet Jawad, 42, a Shi'ite engineer from a northern village who now lives as a squatter in an abandoned building in Baghdad, home to 16 refugees including nine children. His brother Qadhum was taken off a bus in 2006 and shot by gunmen who spared Sunni and Christians.

Yet despite his grievances, he insists that a secular candidate can serve the country best.

'We don't need more religion. We need jobs. Families need food for their children.' Three main groups are competing for the vote today. Favoured to win most seats is Nouri al-Maliki, the prime minister, who leads the State of Law coalition, comprised of secular Shi'ite and Sunni groups.

Maliki is running on his record of improving security. Following a series of Al-Qaeda bombs, his lead has slipped. The election appears to be closer than expected.

In second place is Ayad Allawi, a secular Shi'ite politician and former prime minister who heads the Iraqiya bloc.

Allawi, a one-time favourite of British security forces, has locked up a good chunk of the Sunni vote as well as attracting Shi'ite support. He has benefited from controversy over the banning of hundreds of Sunni candidates because they had once been members of Saddam's Ba'ath party.

The third bloc is the Iraqi National Alliance. This includes the Islamic Supreme Council of Iraq (ISCI), led by Ammar al-Hakim, and other well-known politicians such as Ibrahim al-Jaafari, the former prime minister, and Ahmed Chalabi, a former minister.

Although they are running under a religious banner, they have also set out a nationalistic agenda. 'The next government of Iraq will be a coalition,' said Humam Hamoudi, a senior ISCI cleric. 'We need all the main components of the political spectrum.' It is an acceptance that Iraqis went to the brink, and do not want to go back. 'Moderate Shi'ism sells well in this climate,' said one diplomat.

The election is seen in America as a test of President Barack Obama, who campaigned on his opposition to the Iraq war. Obama has promised to withdraw all combat troops this summer, with a complete exit by the end of 2011.

Some fear wrangling over the formation of the new government could lead to further violence, putting this timetable in doubt. The resolve of Obeid and his fellow soldiers may be tested sooner than they wish.

US departure from Iraq opens the door for Al-Qaeda

22 August 2010

Wrangling Iraqi politicians have left the fragile Middle East state with no leadership. As America leaves, terrorists are ready to pounce.

The Stryker vehicles trundled across the border in the dark, lumbering under the weight of their armour like giant armadillos. Jubilant young Americans shouted out to camera crews, overjoyed to be leaving Iraq alive.

'We're going home! We won. It's over, America,' one soldier yelled, incoherent with emotion as he crossed the border into Kuwait in the last combat brigade to leave Iraq after seven and a half years of war.

They had travelled 360 miles, moving only at night to avoid attacks and the 50°C daytime temperatures. They left behind a country frustrated at its lack of a government nearly six months after elections, and shaken by almost daily attacks, including a huge suicide bomb in central Baghdad last week, that many fear could presage a resumption of insurgency.

The Stryker brigade, officially 4th Infantry, 2nd Brigade, is nick-named after its ungainly vehicles, developed during the war to counter lethal roadside attacks by improvised explosive devices (IEDs). It passed clusters of shuttered shops, endless vistas of hard yellow desert and the odd rusted skeleton of a bombed truck, a landscape almost the same as when it came up the highway as a conquering army in March 2003.

Officially, Stryker soldiers were the last brigade combat team to leave Iraq as part of the US withdrawal from 170,000 troops to 50,000 by 1 September, a deadline set by President Barack Obama.

Major-General Terry Wolff, commander of the Baghdad and Anbar provinces and on his third tour of Iraq, last week remembered his own drive in the opposite direction as a young colonel leading the 2nd Armored Cavalry Regiment to destroy Saddam Hussein's regime.

'In 2003 we could not even have imagined where we are today,' said Wolff, 53, sitting in an office surrounded by maps and charts of tribal leaders of Anbar, in the sprawling Camp Liberty outside Baghdad. Mistakes were made, Wolff admits, which meant the removal of the tyrannical Saddam turned into a seven-year occupation, but he has no time for what he believes should be left to the historians. He has a job to do: get the Iraqi army ready for the real withdrawal next year.

The 50,000 American soldiers that are remaining behind will be rebranded as 'advise and assist brigades'. When they cross the border on New Year's Eve next year, the Iraqis will be on their own. 'That's when we kick off the training wheels,' said one US officer.

Wolff says he believes the training wheels are already off. He is, metaphorically, in the position of every worried dad, hovering protectively over a determined and pedalling youngster, murmuring encouragement, sometimes shouting in worry.

Unlike on his first tour, he has learnt an 'amazing' amount about the country, liaises daily with his Iraqi counterpart in Baghdad Operations Centre, and believes the Iraqi military can 'step up to the plate'.

'We've built an Iraq "good enough",' Wolff said. 'I could have built them an American system, but then they're not going to use that.'

Yesterday, the American army stood at 52,000, with 2,000 scheduled to leave by 31 August. The cost of the war so far: $736 billion from the American treasury, with billions more to come this year;

4,416 American lives; 179 British lives; and the lives of at least 100,000 Iraqi civilians and security forces.

The efficiency of that force was not on display in Baghdad last week. On Tuesday 1,000 young men, mostly Shi'ites from poor families, were waiting in Maidan Square in Baghdad to sign up for the army. Unemployment is at 30%, and as high as 75% for young, uneducated men from poorer families. Some had been queuing for days.

Just after 7am, an officer came out. 'The officer started taking our identity cards, and suddenly I was hurled into the air,' said Marwan Ramthan, 18, from New Baghdad, a poor Shi'ite neighbourhood.

He lay on his back in Medical City hospital, four tubes coming out of his battered body. His mother, Ghazia Farhan, 52, wept at his bedside as she said she had to send him for work because, with seven children and a disabled husband, the family needed the money.

'Other places you have to pay bribes to get a job, but we heard the army was giving jobs for free,' she said.

In all, the bomber killed 61 young men and injured more than 100. The explosive, packed with nails, had been tied to his legs so that he could pass a 'pat down' inspection. Security officials said they believed the young bomber was sent by Iraqi insurgents, a mixture of Al-Qaeda and the mostly Sunni Ba'athists embittered that they lost power with Saddam's overthrow. They want to undermine the government, hoping – in a dream that seems increasingly quixotic – to return to power.

Iraqis placed the blame on their politicians, who five months after the March election have yet to form a government. 'The politicians are bickering while we are dying,' screamed one man, sweat and blood mingling on his shirt as he shouldered a coffin on to a taxi.

'Curses on the father of [Nouri] Maliki!' shrieked an elderly woman in an abbaya, a black robe worn by traditional women, denouncing the serving prime minister, a Shi'ite who should have been her natural political ally. 'Curses on the father of Dawa [Maliki's original party]!'

The anger at politicians was widespread. The bomb and a wave of assassinations of police, municipal officials and judges last week has created an air of apprehension.

Iraqis take it personally because they have individually stood up to the terrorist threat. In March they braved Al-Qaeda warnings to vote in their second parliamentary election. But no party won enough seats to form a government.

Abu Ahmed, 39, who works at Baghdad's ancient book market, said: 'People are shocked. They were so happy to vote, but they found that the politicians did nothing. Nothing!'

Iraqis fear a return of the sectarian violence that erupted in a similar political vacuum in 2006–7 after it took five months to form a government after June 2005 elections.

The current wrangling is Byzantine. Until last week, Ayad Allawi, a former prime minister whose Iraqiya party won 91 seats, was negotiating with Maliki's State of Law party, lying second with 89 seats.

It was to be a marriage of convenience between Allawi, a Shi'ite whose party won by attracting the votes of Sunnis who felt disenfranchised by the Shi'ite government, and Maliki, the increasingly authoritarian Shi'ite prime minister who has clung to power with American support.

Both Maliki and Allawi insist they should be prime minister. Allawi upped the stakes at the weekend, saying he would no longer consider Maliki a partner and turning to negotiations with his Shi'ite rivals.

In an interview, Allawi threw down the gauntlet, offering to negotiate with the leaders of the insurgency. 'We need to get the insurgents back into the system,' Allawi told me, echoing a strategy being considered in Afghanistan. 'I would negotiate with the top-level leaders as long as they lay down their arms and say they will obey the rules of this country.'

His remarks will infuriate Maliki's camp, who see the insurgents as remnants of the Saddam regime.

The Islamic Supreme Council of Iraq, one of the main Shi'ite
parties, refused to enter any coalition headed by Maliki, despite
threats from Iran to withdraw funding. 'We believe in the rule of
law,' said Hamam al-Hamoudi, a senior council official and key
negotiator. 'If Maliki returns as prime minister, we risk returning
to the one-party rule and intimidation we experienced under
Saddam.'

Hoshyar Zebari, the foreign minister, said meddling by regional
powers had been a huge problem. Iran, he said, had been manoeuvring for a Shi'ite government, while Turkey and the Sunni Arab
states had lined up behind Allawi.

Leila Khafaji, 59, a two-term member of parliament who is
involved in the council's political negotiations, said leading Iraqi
politicians had let down their voters in their refusal to find a
compromise.

Khafaji is a vivid reminder of the need for a democratic solution. As a 23-year-old with a degree in engineering, Khafaji was
imprisoned and tortured by Saddam's intelligence service after
refusing to join the Ba'ath party. She was arrested, blindfolded,
thrown down stairs, kicked and slapped in prison. 'I found myself
hanging from the ceiling,' she said last week of her months of
torture.

Eventually sentenced to death, she served 10 years for being a
threat to national security, before escaping into exile in Canada.
She returned when Saddam fell, and her anger is now turned on
her fellow politicians.

'We the politicians are helping the insurgents,' she said last week.
'The politicians are acting in their own interests, not the interests
of the people we should be serving. People are now saying it was
better under Saddam!'

For the Iraqis, the crisis may be just beginning; for the Americans,
the sense of relief at the draw-down is palpable. Outside the
concrete blast walls of Camp Liberty, the enemy is gathering for a
final push. The Iraqi army is in its cross hairs.

Terror returns to stricken Fallujah

29 August 2010

In the Iraqi city, Marie Colvin finds Al-Qaeda are striking back with a renewed intensity and recruiting a younger generation.

Just down the street from Faisal's Takeaway in Fallujah, an explosion shattered the sweltering morning heat last week, igniting an Iraqi army Humvee on the corner and a police car.

A suicide bomber had driven into the stationary vehicles, killing a policeman. His colleagues heaved bloodied and burnt victims into cars and rushed them to hospital.

Within the hour another police officer had been killed by a 'sticky bomb' attached to his car and detonated as he set off for work. A third bomb blew up at a policeman's house but he was not at home.

The attacks were part of a ferocious onslaught by Al-Qaeda in Iraq on 13 cities, just 24 hours after the departure of the last American combat troops from the country they had occupied since 2003. More than 60 died in the bombings and hundreds were injured.

As I drove through Fallujah the next day, shopkeepers were sweeping glass from the pavement to restore some semblance of normality. But there was no hiding the fact that the insurgents had returned in force to the former Al-Qaeda stronghold and scene of the most devastating American attack of the seven-year war.

'Everyone is worried,' said Sami Sultan, 23, clearing debris from the front of his perfume shop. 'Security has been deteriorating for the last three months.'

Despite the US blitz that destroyed 60% of the city's buildings in 2004, Al-Qaeda was not driven out until 2006, when Sunni tribes formed the Sons of Iraq militia. Its members fought with the Americans and turned the war in Washington's favour.

Last week members of the Sons of Iraq huddled in hot little rooms, lamenting the miserable turn their fortunes had taken since they joined forces with the 'surge' troops of General David Petraeus, the US commander.

Angry and disillusioned, they claimed they had been all but discarded by the Iraqi and American governments, which had promised them jobs and a place in the country's future.

Many had not been paid for two months, they said. They believed their job prospects in the security forces and ministries had diminished because they were out of favour with the Shi'ite dominated government of Nouri al-Maliki, the prime minister.

Major General Mudhir al-Mawla, the official responsible for integrating the 52,000 Sons of Iraq, confirmed yesterday that the process had been frozen for a year. Worse still, the militia has been increasingly targeted by a resurgent Al-Qaeda, particularly in the towns and cities of Anbar province, including Fallujah. Here Al-Qaeda is offering young men $200 (£129) a time to take part in attacks – a huge sum in a city with few jobs.

Leaders of the Sons of Iraq believe some of their members are so desperate that they are accepting cash to turn a blind eye to Al-Qaeda's activities, or even to join the insurgency that they had risked their lives to put down. They can earn about $400 a month to do so, compared with their militia salary of $250.

'When we were fighting Al-Qaeda in 2006, the majority were foreigners,' said Sheikh Hamid al-Hashim, head of the city council. 'Now we are finding 70% are Fallujah natives.'

The return of Al-Qaeda to Fallujah and the degree of support it is attracting from young men enraged by the devastation that still surrounds them have disturbing implications for Iraq as a whole.

The situation highlights not only the divisions between Sunnis and Shi'ites but also the dangers of the politicians' failure on both sides to form a government almost six months after a keenly fought general election.

All eyes will be on President Barack Obama this Tuesday, when he marks the combat troops' withdrawal with a speech. It will no doubt avoid the triumphalism of President George W Bush's ill-judged declaration of 'mission accomplished' in 2003.

Rightly so. The latest surge in violence has intensified concerns that Iraq's forces are not up to securing the country, with less than 18 months to go before the departure of the final 50,000 US troops who have stayed on to assist and advise. Last week's bombings were seen by many in Fallujah as a sign of more trouble to come.

'There is a clear message,' said Sheikh Hamid al-Hayes, a local leader of the Sons of Iraq who knows his enemy well: assassination attempts have left him with a scar from a bullet that passed through the left of his chest, and a missing finger on his right hand.

'They are saying: we exist, and we can strike where we want, when we want. Imagine what we can do when the Americans leave.'

My journey to Fallujah was fraught with anxiety. Until 20 months ago only residents carrying a biometric card were allowed into the city. Now a visitor can enter if a Fallujah resident vouches for them but I had been told of arbitrary exclusions. I pulled on a black hijab (headscarf) and abaya (black robe); women dressed traditionally are rarely searched.

The four-lane highway from Baghdad to Fallujah and on to the Jordanian border was once the best in Iraq. During last week's 30-mile drive I had to cross to the opposite carriageway in six places where the road had been blown up.

A member of the Sons of Iraq met me just outside Fallujah and arranged for a police escort past a long queue of vehicles at a checkpoint into the city.

Soon we were driving at nerve-jangling speed down the main street – to reduce the risk of kidnap, my escorts said. As far as we knew I was the only westerner in town.

Every building flying by seemed to be marked by the fighting: heavy weapons had pierced walls and missile-sized holes deformed apartment buildings where people had hung out blankets to shield themselves from the searing sun. There was little visible evidence of the $190m in reconstruction money that the Americans have poured in.

The police station was protected by two tiers of blast walls. About 20 cars that had been mangled in explosions were heaped in a courtyard.

Brigadier General Mahmoud al-Essawi, the police commander, sat behind his walnut desk, gold damask curtains blocking out the light. He looked exhausted.

'It is true. We are experiencing an increase in violence,' said Essawi, dressed in a camouflage uniform; he received his 10th death threat last week. 'We attribute it to the political negotiations that have been going on so long and we have no government.'

Essawi has been in charge of 4,000 officers since 2008, when he won reinstatement after being purged as a former colonel in Saddam's security apparatus. He has posts available for Sons of Iraq but the government will not approve them.

The militia's resentment of both the US and the Iraqi governments over the failure to integrate them into the security forces was a growing concern, he confirmed.

Hayes keeps a photograph of his brother with Bush on his mantelpiece but says his men have been betrayed. 'We have accomplished what the Americans and the Iraqi army failed to do,' he said, a wide leather belt with a Beretta pistol strapped over his green polo shirt. 'We defeated Al-Qaeda, but the leaders who fought them are sitting in cafés with no jobs and they aren't being paid a penny.'

Al-Qaeda's new tactics have made the position more complex. The group has alternated between brutal attacks and offers of forgiveness as well as wages if the militiamen switch sides and take up arms against the US and Baghdad.

'I'm not sure that many are being paid to join Al-Qaeda, but I am sure they are accepting money to turn the other way when there is an Al-Qaeda operation,' said Hashim, resplendent in a white dishdasha, white flowing headdress and black robe.

'They are saying: why should I fight when I am receiving nothing, despite all the promises?'

Battered Kurds attempt to cling on to city of oil

5 September 2010

Insurgents are trying to drive out Kurdish families before a census that could transform their future by deciding who will profit from oil wealth.

The desperate call came through to the mobile phone of Brigadier Sarhed Qadr, Kirkuk central's police commander, at midday last week. One of his officers was under fire in his own home in the centre of this disputed city in northern Iraq.

Qadr, a former Kurdish resistance fighter, mimicked firing an AK-47 assault rifle as he recalled what happened. 'In al-Riyadh district just two days ago, four of these insurgents attacked the home of one of my men,' said the 40-year-old commander, dressed in an impeccable navy blue uniform with three silver stars and an eagle on his shoulder.

'He was fighting back with his gun, but by the time we reached him his three-year-old son was dead and his wife was injured.'

The onslaught was the latest in an escalating series of attacks as tensions increase between Kirkuk's Kurdish, Arab and Turkoman populations in the run-up to a census on 24 October.

The census will determine whether the Kurds make up the largest ethnic bloc in the city. It is important because the Kirkuk region possesses 13% of Iraq's gigantic oil reserves and generates $27 million a day in revenues. If Kurds prove to be in the majority, this will boost the efforts of the semi-autonomous Kurdish region's government to claim the oil for its own treasury.

Qadr believes security in Kirkuk will deteriorate as Sunni Arab insurgent groups, including Al-Qaeda, intensify attacks on Kurds before the census. He recently fought a pitched battle against an Al-Qaeda unit, killing two and arresting two others.

The captives admitted 30 attacks in the city and said they had been told to speed up operations in the past six months. 'They told us the police are working for the infidels so they are fair targets,' Qadr said.

The commander has survived several assassination attempts. A few months ago insurgents fired a 120mm rocket at his convoy, wounding two of his bodyguards with shrapnel.

Seven improvised explosive devices have exploded on the road as he was passing. 'These are the sacrifices we have to make,' he said. Since the fall of Saddam Hussein in 2003, 280 police had been killed in Kirkuk, he said.

The census, the first to be held in Kurdish regions of Iraq since 1987, has reopened bitter divisions created when Saddam strengthened his grip on the city with a campaign of ethnic cleansing, driving out Kurds and trucking in Arabs.

A sign of how vicious the fight over the city has become is that Izzat Ibrahim al-Douri, Saddam's former vice-president and the last wanted member of his regime still at large, is financing a new insurgent group, Nakshabandiya, active only in the Kirkuk area. Police say it aims to frighten away Kurds and ensure Kirkuk stays in the Arab-ruled part of Iraq.

Iraqi security forces have dismissed recent reports that Douri is dead or incapacitated. They say he is well funded and is thought to have moved from his former base in Syria to a Gulf country from which he masterminds his campaign.

'The coming census is not the only problem,' Qadr said. 'The violence is increased because the Americans are withdrawing and we don't have a government yet that can make decisions.'

Iraq's politics have been paralysed since elections in March failed to give any party a decisive victory. American combat troops withdrew last week, leaving fewer than 50,000 behind to assist and advise Iraqi forces. Because of the ethnic tensions, Kirkuk is one area where they are expected to stay until the final withdrawal on 31 December 2011.

The census is so controversial that local councillors are insisting three census takers call at every door – one Kurd, one Arab and one Turkoman. Given that every Iraqi will be required to stay at home for the one or two days of the census, the operation appears to be hugely unwieldy.

No one knows how many Kurds or Arabs live in the city. Many Kurds who were displaced by Saddam have returned.

'Saddam flattened our area in 1988,' said Hussein Sharif, 38. 'We lived for the summer in a valley; then we had to go to Irbil when it got so cold. We left behind all our sheep and cows.'

After years working as a labourer in Irbil, he dismantled his house and rebuilt it in a barren area that is officially part of Kirkuk's cemetery. Thousands of Kurds have joined him.

Sharif, who runs a small shop that sells everything from soap to carrots, says he cannot take his wife and four children back to the district Saddam levelled. 'There are no services, no water, no electricity,' he said.

Officials in Kirkuk insist the census will not be derailed by the violence. 'We will do all we can to make it a success, because it is important for the future planning of the city,' said Abdul Rahman Mustafa, Kirkuk's governor. The armed guards and blast walls protecting his office are testimony to just how difficult that may be.

Afghanistan

Corrupt, untrained, underpaid, illiterate: the forces waiting to take over

KABUL

6 December 2009

The Afghan police chief sat shivering at his desk, his hands in the pockets of his wool coat, as he tried to answer questions about his men. Police station three is in one of central Kabul's better districts but it had had no electricity for days. It was colder inside than out.

Lieutenant-Colonel Amanullah, the acting chief, was having a tough time satisfying his American 'mentors', young soldiers from Camp Phoenix. They were, in fact, being quite gentle, but the facts about his station kept eluding him.

How many of his men had been trained, asked Staff Sergeant Jimmie Stokely, 30. 'Ninety per cent studied, but I don't know how many passed,' replied Amanullah, sinking a bit in his chair.

He answered a question about staffing by saying he had 105 men on active duty. His personnel manager interjected. The station had '16 officers, 44 sergeants and 98 soldiers'. Were they all on duty? That was unclear. Amanullah slumped further down.

Did he still have 13 checkpoints? At that point Amanullah took a mobile phone call and practically ran out of the room, saying a fight had broken out. He turned the meeting over to Shamsullah Habibzani, the deputy, who sat rigidly erect.

Did police district three still have 13 checkpoints? He would get back to the Americans on that.

Not a piece of paper appeared during the meeting, and the ancient computer on the desk remained dark without power. 'I have to go to the internet café to file my reports,' Habibzani, 25, said sadly.

The Afghan police and army are at the forefront of the strategy announced by President Barack Obama last week, which called for a 'surge' of 30,000 new US troops in the country.

Nearly a brigade of the newcomers – 3,000–4,000 troops – would be trainers, and much of the rest would work with or mentor Afghan security forces. Obama proclaimed that the surge would mean that 'more Afghans can get into the fight'.

Within 18 months, the Afghan army is scheduled to grow from 97,000 to 134,000, and the police force to double. From July 2011, Afghan forces will take gradual control of their own territory and the Americans will begin withdrawing.

At least that is the theory. Last week, however, in visits to the Afghan security forces, a woeful picture emerged of the reality on the ground. The model endorsed by Obama could well work, but to do so, there will have to be an acknowledgement of just how threadbare the forces are, and measures taken to reverse the neglect and ignorance that has caused the problem.

Lieutenant-Colonel Todd Goehler is the head of a 12-man training team that since July has been mentoring Charlie kandak – Afghan for battalion – in Kabul's capital division.

Goehler, a 24-year veteran of the special forces, described a disastrous situation that differed dramatically from the official projections. 'They have been putting Band-Aids on this for a while,' he said.

On paper, Charlie kandak is one of six battalions in the brigade covering the 14 districts of Kabul and outlying areas. In reality, he revealed, only one other exists. Two kandaks are only at 30% capacity and are consequently not deployable. The final two are still 'in the training pipeline'.

Decrepit Russian barracks at Kabul international airport have been earmarked for their arrival. The buildings lack running water and all the electrical fittings have been stripped. At any given moment, 20% to 30% of the 600 soldiers on Charlie kandak's roster are absent without leave. In the Afghan army, a soldier can be missing for up to 60 days before any action – other than the suspension of his pay – is taken.

Illiteracy is high: 70% of inventory receipts are signed with a thumbprint. This engenders corruption because a soldier who cannot read has no idea what he has just confirmed receipt of.

Compounding the difficulties, senior commanders had so little understanding of the mentoring process that they were undermining the programme by breaking up teams that worked well together to plug holes elsewhere. 'They're ripping apart our teams,' said Goehler. 'They [the Afghans] would be much further ahead if they had solid mentoring teams, the right people with the right experience.'

Nevertheless, Charlie kandak has started to fall into some kind of shape. When Goehler's team took over, its colonel refused to leave the base; officers had no idea of logistics, the need to brief for missions, or the inventory and supply process.

On a trip last week to Farzeh, a tiny village in the mountains northwest of Kabul, the difficulties of the transfer to Afghan control were obvious – and so was an image of how it could succeed.

The Americans are anxious that Afghans accept their national security forces, which is felt to be as much a part of the transition process as getting them up to speed technically. So Goehler's team put together humanitarian aid parcels, planned the trip to impoverished Farzeh, then put Charlie kandak in the lead to make the delivery while they followed.

The Afghans were enthusiastic, revving their Humvees like drag racers. 'They drive like a 14-year-old boy joyriding in the spare family car he grabbed when the parents went out,' said one American mentor in exasperation.

Once they reached Farzeh, Colonel Rahmatsha Qimati, commander of Charlie kandak, took the lead. He told the gathered elders: 'You can call us any time, day or night. We know Farzeh is very poor, so we have brought 50 parcels of food and clothing.' Afghan soldiers handed them out to the elders, who complained a bit about the paucity of supplies but seemed happy to have been remembered.

While offering the prospect of hope, this was an isolated example: the army remains in poor shape. However, it is a well-oiled machine compared with what could be seen of the Afghan police force last week. Station three should have had some of the best policemen in the city. The neighbourhood is home to more than 30 foreign companies, a university and two ministries.

Habibzani, the deputy, spelt out the problems. He had graduated from the Kabul police academy, but he could barely support his family of five on an officer's salary of $200 (£120) a month.

The $120 paid to the lowest ranks meant the force attracted those who had no other possibilities – and needed the three meals a day that come with the job – but also meant they felt no guilt about demanding bribes.

A key aspect of the US strategy is to make working for the state more attractive than taking the Taliban's shilling. Yet there was no sign of the wage increase to $165 that the government had announced. Meanwhile, the Taliban pay $220 a month.

Habibzani said 90% of the police could not read or write. Abdullah Fattah, a police trainer standing with him in the gloom of the hallway as black cables dangled uselessly from the ceiling, said police received five months' training. 'They start from such a low level. I need five years,' he said. 'With all the attention of the international community, maybe three years minimum.'

Corruption is rife, and many police are addicted to drugs. There is some evidence that Hamid Karzai, the president inaugurated last month amid allegations of fraud in the election and corruption in his government, has got the message.

'I can confirm we have this cancer of corruption in the police but very soon we will start cleaning it out,' said General Haider Basir, deputy at the interior ministry, which is responsible for the police. Biometric prints have been taken of 25,000 police so that if they moonlight for the Taliban, they might be caught.

But Basir set official standards fairly low. 'To be a policeman, it is necessary to be healthy and not addicted to drugs,' he said. 'They don't need to read and write.'

Hamid Karzai fails Taliban who gave up arms

PUL-I-ALAM, LOGAR PROVINCE

31 January 2010

Marie Colvin and Miles Amoore

The room the Taliban commander Mullah Mohammad now calls home, after bringing his 21 fighters to join the Afghan government's reintegration programme earlier this month, is barely more comfortable than the mountain redoubt he left.

He sits on a thin mat and leans against the wall, his skin dark and weathered, facing the battered Kalashnikovs and a vintage Russian mortar launcher he surrendered in return for promises of money, jobs and land for him and his men.

Instead, the peace and reconciliation commission (known as PTS, its acronym in Dari), set up by the president, Hamid Karzai, in 2005, handed them letters guaranteeing free passage. And nothing else. Mohammad, 48, is stunned and speaks slowly.

'We were fighting all day, and we had nothing to show for it,' he said. 'I began thinking, "Why are we killing our Afghan brothers?"'

Like many mid-level Taliban commanders, he is a conservative tribal Pashtun, not an extremist ideologue. He is the perfect candidate for the government's reintegration programme, which will be absorbed into the bigger and better-funded reintegration council announced by Karzai at last week's London conference. Donors there pledged $140 million (£90 million) towards a $500 million fund to pay the Taliban to lay down their arms.

'They [the PTS] told us they'll protect us, and that we would have the chance to have jobs. Now we have nothing,' Mohammad says.

The drive to Pul-i-Alam, the capital of Logar province, most of which is controlled by the Taliban, was fraught.

The former Taliban commanders I went to meet there had fought in the Haqqani organisation, led by Jalaluddin Haqqani, a 60-year-old warlord who battled the Soviets.

He is said to be ailing and has ceded control of his military wing to his son Sirajuddin Haqqani, a militant in his early forties responsible for a deadly escalation in the Afghan war.

Haqqani is based in north Waziristan, just across the Pakistani border, but most of his attacks are inside Afghanistan. He has boasted that he sent down this same highway the suicide bombers and gunmen who attacked Kabul ministries, shops and a hotel earlier this month, on the day Karzai swore in his new cabinet.

His other great coup was to prime a Jordanian double agent to kill seven CIA agents inside an American base last month.

Last year, Haqqani set up flying checkpoints on this highway to Logar, which is hated by American troops because the Taliban constantly seed the route with improvised explosive devices.

Huddled in the back seat of a car, I was swathed in a brown wool blanket, and instructed to pretend I was asleep if we were stopped at a checkpoint. I was happy it was snowing and the windows were steamed up. Nobody could see inside.

An hour outside town, I called the PTS and it sent an armed escort. Several of its officials have been killed on this road. In Pul-i-Alam, I was bundled into its compound by armed men, keen that nobody should see a foreigner.

The Taliban commanders in Logar gave an insight into the gulf between the promises at last week's conference and the harsh reality on the ground.

Few in London appeared to recall that Karzai set up the PTS five years ago, although it has been poorly funded so far.

Two former Taliban commanders joined Mullah Mohammad. Moulana Saheb Said Ajan, a senior Taliban figure, was angry. 'I brought 40 fighters to the PTS,' he said. 'I told my men: "Other countries are making planes and computers. Why are we freezing in the mountains? We should be building our country."'

Ajan changed sides after falling out with Haqqani's 'Pakistan Taliban', so called because they allegedly receive money from Pakistan's intelligence service, the ISI. He said many more would join if the money was there and they felt safe.

As a commander, Ajan was not paid a salary, although foot soldiers are paid about $200 a month, considerably more than the Afghan police.

'I told the leaders what I needed, and they sent it,' Ajan said. 'They always paid immediately.' He said he received 200,000–500,000 Pakistani rupees (£1,500–£3,700) every month, either smuggled from Dubai, or in bags of cash that would fill the back of pick-up trucks from Pakistan. Ajan decided to take the PTS offer after he was ordered to carry out a raid he disagreed with. 'We were on top of the mountain and Haqqani's people ordered us to the district office here in Pul-i-Alam, to destroy a United Nations vehicle to make them leave,' he said. 'I'm 28 years old. I just didn't want to do this any more.'

He sent tribal elders to check out the PTS and they came back with assurances of money, jobs and security for his family and fighters. 'I'm now living on the floor of this office,' Ajan said dejectedly. 'The Taliban are now dropping letters through our doors, saying if we don't return they'll kill us.'

The success of the reintegration programme is crucial to any transition to Afghan rule. It would take hardened fighters off the battlefield and into the army and police force, which Nato wants to increase to 400,000 men by 2015. But for the system to work, the money must reach the fighters and not be siphoned off.

Ajan's story also illustrates the differences between commanders on the ground and the Taliban leadership, which will have to be part of a political solution if there is to be any lasting peace. 'I strongly believe we need to reach the Taliban leaders,' said Najibullah Mojadidi, the elder son of the PTS chairman and a member of Karzai's national security committee.

'As long as they're not convinced, they'll always have people in Afghanistan prepared to continue the fighting.'

Swift and bloody: the Taliban's revenge

9 May 2010

Marie Colvin, Christina Lamb, Washington

Rebels have returned to terrorise a former stronghold with shootings and beatings, raising doubts about America's ability to secure Kandahar.

The sniper's aim was merciless. Lieutenant Brandon Barrett was shovelling sand into bags to fortify his post in the Helmand town of Marjah when a Taliban gunman slotted a bullet between armoured vehicles pulled around for protection, hitting him in the chest.

Although the sun was setting and the fierce heat of the day had softened, it was still hot and Barrett and Lance-Corporal Marcus Lounello had taken off their flak jackets as they worked.

The sniper's second bullet hit Lounello in the chest.

The call came in to the US marines' forward operating base (FOB) Marjah at 6pm last Wednesday: 'Two down, gunshot wounds to the chest, non-responsive.'

Barrett, 27 and unmarried, from Indiana, was dead before the medical team reached them. Lounello, 21, lost a kidney, his spleen and part of his diaphragm but will survive.

'It's surreal,' Captain Tony Zinni, Barrett's commanding officer in the 1st Battalion, 6th Marine Regiment, said yesterday outside his tented office on a barren base. 'I keep expecting him to walk around the corner, big smile on his face.'

Barrett had been running a post that checked traffic coming in and out of Marjah, a former Taliban stronghold that was taken by the marines and their Afghan allies with an overwhelming show of force in February. A small, wiry officer, he was a favourite at FOB Marjah at the centre of the market town.

Zinni held his emotions in check as he described his last visit to Barrett's post. 'It was a really boring duty but he was good about it,' Zinni said, smiling at the memory.

Some elders arrived and Barrett had chatted to them. 'I said where the hell did you learn Pashto,' Zinni recalled. Barrett had been visiting the neighbourhood's elders, trying to win them round, learning words and phrases.

Zinni thinks the lieutenant was targeted and it makes him angry. 'Everyone in the block knew him, knew he was the officer,' the captain said. Barrett had 60 days left in Afghanistan. His was the first death in Marjah for the battalion's weapons company.

That night Zinni gathered Barrett's platoon for what he said had been one of his toughest moments in his 10 years in the Marine Corps. One of the men still had blood on his trousers.

The 41 soldiers had been together since they were at Camp Lejeune in North Carolina, where Barrett held weekend parties at his beach house. He would dress up as a penguin with aviator sunglasses and a cigar to make people laugh. There were only tears last week. 'I don't even know what to say to you. Our loss is so great,' Zinni said. 'But I do know that Barrett would have wanted us to make a success of this mission.'

Last week was the worst in living memory for weapons company, the first unit to enter Marjah on D-Day, 13 February.

Hours before the sniper killed Barrett, another 13-man squad in the company had been walking down a dusty street in the fierce morning heat, spread out on either side of the road so that only one of them would die if anyone stepped on an improvised explosive device (IED), when an insurgent jumped out from behind a building 40 yards ahead and fired three shots.

One bullet hit Lance-Corporal Matthew Hunter, the point man, in the stomach, just below his flak jacket. The second skidded around the armoured vest of a lucky Lance-Corporal Kyle Schneider, leaving him uninjured. Hunter, known in the squad for his 60 socks, which he would wear for two days and then discard, was seriously injured but survived.

On Thursday a member of the elite Afghan National Civil Order Police, which works side by side with the marines, was also shot and killed. The unidentified officer had arrived at FOB Marjah only two days earlier, determined to get his men out of the check-points and onto the streets.

Marjah was supposed to be safe. When 5,000 marines and their Afghan national army partners rolled in to oust the Taliban who had ruled the town for almost three years, the fighting lasted just two weeks.

'If you go to Marjah today, you will find a city that is free of the Taliban, that has schools that are open, a marketplace, a bazaar,' Major-General Richard Mills, commander of the US Marine Corps in Afghanistan, said just last month.

Marjah has indeed improved. The idea was to set up 'security bubbles', to get the economy and normal life going inside them in the hope that at some point the locals would throw in their lot with the government. Major David Fennell, a civil affairs officer for the marines, explained that his men had moved as soon as the fighting eased.

'We decided to get in there immediately and spend money. To use money as a weapon system,' Fennell said. He started a project paying $5 (£3.40) a day to clean the canals. Only a few nervous locals turned up on the first day, but when cash started to flow, 1,000 workers soon came on board, defying Taliban threats.

Contractors are now engaged in what the marines call 'quick impact projects' – bridges, wells, mosque restorations, anything that shows tangible improvement.

Last week hundreds flocked to the unpainted concrete villa that is the district government's headquarters, a building said to have been commandeered from a local drug lord.

Some farmers received cash in hand for destroying their poppy crop. Others pushed new wheelbarrows full of cheaply purchased mung beans, alfalfa seeds and huge 50-kilo (110-pound) bags of fertiliser. Further down, the stalls of the once shuttered Loy Chareh bazaar lined the street with wooden crates spilling okra, tomatoes, chilli peppers, mint, watermelon.

All that progress is threatened by the Taliban 'surge'. There were always fears that they would re-emerge, bolstered by poppy taxes levied from farmers. But nobody expected their return to be so swift and bloody.

My first night in Marjah had left little doubt that the Taliban were back. On Tuesday I walked out of FOB Marjah with a weapons company squad charged with 'rolling up' an IED-maker called Izra, or 'signature' in Pashto, probably a nom de guerre.

Izra was thought to be sleeping in a small local mosque. There was no moon and it was pitch black. After 20 minutes a light glowed on a rooftop, a suspicious sight in an area where there is no electricity and everyone sleeps during the hours of darkness.

The flashlight followed our progress. Corporal Josh Hurst, the squad leader, realised we had been spotted by the Taliban when his point man saw four men slipping through the tree line. Hurst motioned the squad down a path to a field of dry furrows and mud channels. I realised why I was slipping and sliding while the marines remained sure-footed – they all had night-vision goggles.

I slid noisily into a canal that I had not noticed. Lance-Corporal Tim Ryan hauled me out by the scruff of my flak jacket. Dogs barked. I was terrified that we were walking into an ambush.

After three hours we found the mosque, but Hurst decided to move on because of the danger. 'It just kept getting worse and worse and worse,' Hurst said with good humour when we were back on base.

The strength of the Taliban's presence is gradually becoming clearer. One of their targets is Wafa Aghasheran, a contractor for the marines who builds bridges and wells. He sat cross-legged in his cream-coloured shalwar kameez and dark wool vest last week recalling how Hazrat Gull, 19, his young business partner, had been killed by the Taliban several weeks ago.

'They pulled up on a motorcycle at our project, asked who is the contractor and shot him in the head,' Aghasheran said. 'I ran to the bridge and found him. His head was in the canal. All our workers had run away.'

More recently two motorcycles carrying four Taliban converged on Aghasheran's truck and pointed Kalashnikovs at the driver. They broke both the driver's arms with the butts of their guns and set fire to the vehicle. Their aim was to stop anyone from working with the Afghan government and marines.

They then put up a letter to Aghasheran in the local mosque saying: 'Stop your business or we will kill you and your family.' He smiled and said that he could not afford to stop: at 42, he has three wives and 18 children.

The Taliban are growing bolder. A man in his early twenties known only as Sharitulla was at home about two weeks ago when the Taliban came knocking in broad daylight. When he refused their demand for taxes, they took him out to the desert and beat him to death. His body was left on the doorstep of his elderly father.

While they may not want the Taliban back, many of Marjah's people are reluctant to commit themselves to the administration that has replaced them. 'The local residents don't trust we will provide security,' said Naimatullah, the acting district governor of Marjah, in a late-night interview.

'They are taking a wait-and-see attitude to the government,' he said, fingering black worry beads. 'The people are worried that the Taliban will return and punish them for supporting the government.'

The offensive in which Marjah was captured was the largest in Afghanistan since 2001, when the Taliban regime was driven out

by US-supported Afghan warlords after the September 11 attacks
on America.

After that victory, Afghanistan was largely neglected as America
and Britain became bogged down in the war in Iraq. Only last year
did attention shift back. Heavy-handed military operations that
killed civilians helped the Taliban to re-establish support and
organise a virulent insurgency.

General David Petraeus, who came up with the idea of the
'surge' that quelled the violence in Iraq, has tailored his theory to
Afghanistan at a pivotal moment in the nine-year war. The Obama
administration is deploying 30,000 new troops to Afghanistan as
part of a shift to a counter-insurgency strategy.

Until recently Marjah was seen as a success story that could
serve as a template for an expected operation against the Taliban
in Kandahar, the birthplace of the Taliban.

'In many ways [the Marjah operation] is a model for the future:
an Afghan-led operation supported by the coalition, deeply
engaged with the people,' General Stanley McChrystal, leader of
Nato and American forces, said.

Yet worries are growing in the Pentagon that if thousands of
marines and Afghan security forces cannot entirely defeat the
Taliban in Marjah, a town of only 50,000, securing the far larger
prize of Kandahar may be an even greater struggle than has been
foreseen.

This week Hamid Karzai, the Afghan president, flies to
Washington for a meeting with President Barack Obama. The two
men know that success in Kandahar will be crucial both to persuading the Taliban to the negotiating table and to enabling Nato forces
to leave.

Yet after Marjah, McChrystal is playing down expectations. Last
week he warned that it could be the end of the year before any
progress is seen.

Afghans find pride in hunt for Taliban

LASHKAR GAH

4 July 2010

Recent raids have shown that well-trained and motivated local troops in Afghanistan are backing Nato's new counter-insurgency plan.

It was the Afghan soldiers who uncovered the cache. Squatting on the dirt floor of a mud-walled house, they found a plastic bag filled with black gunpowder, two yards of detonator cord and a detonator beneath a pile of carpets.

The find was the culmination of a joint raid by a squad of soldiers from the Queen's Royal Lancers and their Afghan partners. As they had suspected, this was a Taliban safe house.

To reach the compound had required a long, slow walk across sun-baked fields behind Lieutenant Will Pope as he swept a Vallon mine detector back and forth, looking for buried improvised explosive devices. Twice he identified suspicious metal and we crouched with our backs turned in case there was an explosion.

By the time we arrived at the compound across the river from Lashkar Gah, Helmand's provincial capital, the soldiers were sweating but determined to be polite. Troops have stopped kicking in doors under the counter-insurgency strategy put in place by Nato's American commanders.

The Afghan soldiers knocked on the huge wooden door and asked to see the elder of the household. They had received reports that a Taliban commander was leaving weapons there overnight.

Inside, women shrieked. An elderly man who came to the door tried to bar the soldiers, saying the women and children were too upset. 'Well, I'm sorry for that,' said Lieutenant Rob Campbell, 28. 'Please put your women in a separate room and we will wait. But we are here to search the compound and we will do so.'

As we waited, Ahmed, the unit's interpreter, started talking to some sullen teenagers watching us across an alley. There were no smiles.

'These two say they will not shake the hand of Isaf [the American-led Nato force in Afghanistan],' Ahmed said. 'They won't give me their father's name. I think we should search their compound.'

Accompanying the squad was Captain Malcolm Dalzel-Job, who was there to map 'human terrain'. He carries a gun, but in the new world of counter-insurgency it is more important to know who lives where, and where their sympathies lie.

Campbell and 'DJ', as Dalzel-Job is known, decided to follow the Afghan's advice and diverted the unit to the next-door compound where the teenagers lived. This was where the gunpowder and detonator were found.

Every patrol by British soldiers now takes members of the Afghan security forces. 'We've stepped beyond the fight against the Taliban,' said Lieutenant-Colonel Lincoln Jopp, commander of Task Force Lashkar Gah. 'We're partnering the Afghan security forces. Any patrol without them, we are 50 per cent less effective.'

In Lashkar Gah there is growing hope that the new emphasis on 'partnering' brings a prospect of turning the country over to the Afghans.

British officials acknowledge that training the army and police is not enough, however: there must also be a parallel track that includes negotiations with the Taliban.

In Lashkar Gah the British Army no longer focuses on chasing Taliban suspects and killing them, thereby creating even more enemies.

In a show of confidence, Jopp walked through a farmers' bazaar, removing his helmet and body armour. The moment might have been staged but the local merchants clearly knew him. The interaction was real.

Rather than ask about the Taliban, he concentrated on everyday concerns, asking how many hours of electricity they had, how much rent they were paying and what the new police were like. Men crowded in to listen and chat, nodding when a bystander said the police had got much better recently. 'They are not robbing us any more,' said one.

Police training has made an enormous advance. A patrol with the Afghan National Police in Kabul last year was dispiriting and dangerous. Few could read, recruits were high on drugs and they demanded bribes at checkpoints.

The change was evident at a recent graduation ceremony at the police academy in Helmand. Graduates stood to attention in clean blue-grey uniforms and polished black boots.

Mohammad Daoud, 26, a former member of the Taliban, could not stop smiling. He had worked for the insurgents in Uruzgan province before fleeing to Lashkar Gah with his family. 'I'm comfortable in myself now,' he said. 'When I came here, I couldn't read. Now, I can write my name and my father's name.'

Lieutenant-Colonel Andy Hadfield, who mentors the police at the Helmand Training Academy, admitted that when he was assigned he was disappointed: he would have preferred to be out commanding his battalion. Like Jopp and the other British officers, he has since been converted to the idea that partnering the Afghan security forces is the way ahead.

'Go back to your communities and be their guardians. Be courageous and honest and proud to say, "I serve Afghanistan",' he said at the graduation ceremony for 94 new officers.

Fears persist that the new strategy may be too little too late. But as the men marched forward to receive their certificates, their pride was evident. One could almost believe they might be the vanguard of an Afghanistan that, while not a democracy as we know it, could achieve the new, more realistic goal of sustainable stability.

'For Afghanistan!' each man cried, as he held up his certificate in the sun.

Iran

Anger at Mahmoud Ahmadinejad's election

14 June 2009

The motorcycle police came from behind. They fired stun grenades that exploded as I was walking among thousands of demonstrators on Tehran's central boulevard, talking to two young women about their anger at what they called the 'theft' of the Iranian election.

Tempers ran high. Protesters jostling shoulder to shoulder filled the road and pavements, punching the air with their fists and shouting, 'Down with the dictator', and, 'Be ashamed and give us back Iran.'

They were convinced their candidate in the presidential election, Mir Hossein Mousavi, a former prime minister, had been cheated of victory by the government of President Mahmoud Ahmadinejad.

The election had been hard fought – Mousavi and Ahmadinejad were the frontrunners in a field of four – and an evidently tight race had been predicted to go to a second round this Friday.

It was an emotionally charged campaign. Mousavi's supporters, many of them young men and women, nearly shut down the city last week with all-night street campaigning, dancing until dawn as they handed out campaign leaflets.

Such a spectacle had never been seen in a conservative city where women are legally obliged to wear the hijab (headscarf) and an overcoat, and the sexes are not allowed to mix unless married or related.

Rallies for both candidates drew tens of thousands of fervent supporters.

Just as they had all week, yesterday's demonstrators waved green ribbons and banners and wore green T-shirts signalling their support for Mousavi.

'The election was stolen,' Safoor Nayafi, 26, shouted over the din of the march, clutching her black hijab at her chin. 'We are marching to the ministry of interior to get our stolen votes back.' She was just telling me she had a master's degree in science when her voice was drowned out by the roar of motorcycles from behind us and along the sides of the road.

They were riot police, dressed in camouflage uniforms, wearing black flak jackets and black helmets with their menacing visors pulled down.

They fired several grenades, scattering the crowd. Women screamed and fell to the ground; men leapt onto the pavements, then ran back to drag the fallen out of the road. Shop owners pulled scared bystanders inside and slammed down their metal grates.

It took only seconds to realise they were stun grenades, fired into the air to scatter the marchers, but they were terrifying seconds.

An acrid smell hung in the air as young men started shouting and running forward after the riot police. They were from a special unit trained to put down protests and named after Hassan Nasrallah, the Lebanese Hezbollah leader. Confronting them seemed a brave, but foolish, gesture.

About 50 yards ahead of us, at the junction of Vali-asr Street and a square called Saei Park, there was a skirmish, with motorcycles roaring and fired-up young men yelling, 'Allahu akbar' (God is great).

Smoke rose from the scene as the crowd cleared. Two riot police motorcycles lay burning in the middle of the junction, flames leaping from their metal carcasses and smoke rising into the overcast sky. A loud cheer went up from the crowd.

The demonstrators were not seasoned fighters. Tehran residents told me they had never seen such a crowd – young men and women, intellectuals, workers.

One elderly woman came up to me, screaming: 'We hate this government. It's my generation's fault to have let them come in 1979 [when the shah was ousted]. These children are doing what we were not brave enough to do.'

The riot police returned with much roaring of engines and more wielding of stun grenades, but the marchers stubbornly regrouped and the stand-off continued.

Walking back to my hotel, I saw burning dustbins surrounded by riot police swinging their batons at bystanders – they had clearly been set alight by protesters. A colleague said he had counted four more burnt-out police motorcycles and seen dozens of riot police beating people in the street.

Clashes continued into the night and there were reports of one person being killed.

No one knew what to expect next. I asked one of the march's leaders, sweating in his black T-shirt and green wristband, if the protests would turn into a fully fledged revolution.

'I don't know,' he said. 'This is new to us.'

The first protest had begun at about 4am, as Mousavi supporters, who had stayed up all night to wait for the results, converged on the ministry of interior, the department in charge of the poll, in the centre of the city. They were beaten back by riot police, who seemed to have been expecting them.

Later in the morning, I visited Mousavi's headquarters in a five-storey building on a residential street. The riot police had already been there.

A guard in the lobby of the building told me they had stormed in about three hours earlier, firing tear-gas canisters and shouting that they had seen a suspect flee into the building. They beat people with batons, the guard said, and Mousavi had ordered the head-quarters to be closed to stop any more violence.

The disappointment at Mousavi's defeat quickly turned to anger as people absorbed the scale of Ahmadinejad's victory.

Polls in Iran are unreliable, but every unofficial sampling had indicated a close race. The outpouring of support for Mousavi in

Tehran could have been deceptive as Ahmadinejad's supporters are mostly the rural poor and urban working class, but the gap between the two candidates caused Iranian analysts and voters alike to suspect that something was amiss.

Mousavi was ensconced with advisers last night, but said he would challenge the result: 'I will not surrender to this dangerous charade.'

He called on his supporters to remain calm until he decided his course of action. Few seemed to be listening, however. Another demonstration was planned in central Tehran for late last night.

Ayatollah Ali Khamenei, Iran's supreme leader, said the election result should stand. 'Other honourable candidates must refrain from any kind of provocative and distrustful words or deeds,' he said on state radio.

News of the clashes travelled only by word of mouth; state-run television was still showing film of queues of voters on Friday. The texting network that Mousavi's supporters had used to organise their campaign was blocked.

Even before yesterday's riots, it was clear many ordinary people felt they had been cheated. 'Almost everybody I know voted for Mousavi but Ahmadinejad is being declared the winner. The government announcement is nothing but widespread fraud. It is very, very disappointing. I'll never again vote in Iran,' said Nasser Amiri, a Tehran hospital clerk.

Clashes show depth of fury

TEHRAN

21 June 2009

Yesterday's open defiance of the supreme leader was astonishing and shows how fast events are moving in Iran.

The two men cradled the woman as she collapsed backwards onto the street, a pool of blood at her feet. The men pressed their hands onto a bullet wound in her neck as her hands fell limp above her shoulders.

Within seconds, her eyes rolled sideways and her pale features were obscured by haemorrhaging from her nose and mouth. Her would-be rescuers shrieked in panic. There was nothing they could do to save her.

The scene, captured on a number of mobile phones, unfolded yesterday in Tehran as protesters fought running battles with riot police and militia on the streets of the Iranian capital.

Another video showed hundreds of people milling about in a street with fires burning in the road. Some were collecting rocks. A helicopter buzzed overhead.

At least five shots were heard and soon after a group of men raced through the crowd carrying a man by his arms and legs. His head was lolling. He was laid on the ground and a crowd gathered. A large bloodstain filled the centre of his white shirt. He lay still and appeared to be dead.

Yet more footage emerged of young men throwing stones at riot police. A number shouted 'Death to Khamenei!', underlining the seriousness of the protests. As supreme leader, Ayatollah Ali Khamenei traditionally occupies an untouchable position in Iranian society.

There was also video of a member of the security forces who had been knocked off his motorbike. A black-clad woman tried to protect him as a number of people, many of them wearing suits, kicked and punched him. A motorbike was on fire a few feet away.

Last night these videos revealed the extent of the defiance of the regime that has sprung from last week's disputed presidential election. Yesterday tens of thousands of supporters of Mir Hossein Mousavi, who claim Mahmoud Ahmadinejad, the incumbent, stole victory in the election, poured on to the streets again. They were confronted with water cannon, tear gas and targeted gunfire.

The largest crowd gathered near the University of Tehran, after evading a riot police cordon which had tried to disperse them. Soon a volley of 20–30 shots rang out – which state television later claimed were warning shots – and the group broke up into roaming knots of protesters. Street battles then erupted as they took the fight to police with rocks.

As night fell it was unclear how many people had been killed or injured in the clashes. What was certain was that Iran was entering uncharted territory.

On Friday, Khamenei had said opposition leaders would 'be held accountable for all the violence, bloodshed and looting' if they encouraged more rallies. It was a clear threat to Mousavi and his supporters.

'It must be determined at the ballot box what the people want and what they don't want, not on the streets,' Khamenei told the thousands gathered for Friday prayers at the University of Tehran. He threw down the gauntlet. 'If the things I have said now are not observed, I will be back here talking in a far more serious tone.'

His seriousness was apparent yesterday with the crackdown on the protesters. Nevertheless, the popular will, represented by the crowds' willingness to risk their safety by taking to the streets yesterday, appeared undimmed. The Islamic Republic of Iran was facing the worst crisis in its 30-year history.

What gave so many ordinary citizens the courage to take to the streets in numbers not seen since Ayatollah Khomeini overthrew the Shah in 1979? Where was this heading? Will yesterday's events presage a brutal crackdown, or are they just a pause in an extraordinary display of 'people power'?

Artemis, a 41-year-old Tehrani woman, is the proud holder of a law degree, but one who has never been allowed to work. She was clear about why she joined the million-plus men, women and children who took to the streets of Tehran last Monday.

'People want freedom and justice,' she said. 'They stole the vote. No one in his right mind believes this result.'

She said she had been afraid to voice criticism before. 'The neighbours listen to you, and people go to prison just for what they say, or what they write. But this is contagious. What you are seeing, all these people, this comes from 30 years of oppression and now we have had enough.'

Gathering in Revolution Square in the summer sun, they walked miles to Freedom Square. Nobody believed the election result, which gave Ahmadinejad more than 60% of the vote in what was expected to be a knife-edge contest, and the sense of anger and betrayal was palpable. 'Where is my vote?' asked placards held aloft. People walked with determination, emboldened by their sense of injustice.

Shouts of 'Down with the dictator!' and 'Death to the Taliban in Kabul and Tehran!' – echoes of the 1979 chant 'Death to the Shah!' – filled the air. Green ribbons, banners and wristbands adorned the marchers.

Mousavi's supporters had been ridiculed by supporters of the regime as merely the wealthy young crowd from the northern, tree-shaded neighbourhoods of Tehran. Last Monday, however, saw the old and the young, designer-clad groups of young women side by side with workers in worn clothes and government clerks in suits.

A young woman with a matching Burberry scarf and handbag walked between an elderly man and woman, a hand in each of theirs as they stared in wonderment. A middle-aged man in a suit walked carrying his briefcase, grey balding head held high.

'Look at all the white hairs here,' pointed out Siamak, a 28-year-old mechanical engineer. 'All of Tehran is here. I think Khamenei will not sleep tonight.'

They passed down the boulevard for hours.

'I was afraid to speak at all before. I thought we were a tiny minority,' said Mona, a 24-year-old software designer in the over-sized designer sunglasses favoured by Tehran's fashionable young women, and a tight red 'manteau', the overcoat that gives a scant nod to the law that women must cover their heads and bodies in public. 'But now I feel we are the majority. I am not afraid any more. For me, fear is over.'

That afternoon Mousavi appeared in Freedom Square for the first time since he had heard in the early hours of last Saturday that Ahmadinejad had won the presidency.

He had been a grey, uncharismatic figure during the campaign, buoyed in the polls mostly by his wife, Zahra Rahna-vard, a scholar and artist with a mischievous sense of humour. She set the tone by holding his hand in public on the campaign trail, endearing the couple to the younger generation.

Now he stood in Freedom Square on the top of a car, dressed in a blue-and-white striped shirt, shouting defiance over a handheld loudspeaker. 'We want respect. We will reclaim our rights,' he promised a cheering crowd. 'We fight on!'

There was tragedy to come that night. As the demonstration wound down, youths wandered home in the darkened streets. The riot police and Basiji volunteer militia had disappeared in the face of such numbers during the day, but they returned with a vengeance.

A swarm of Basiji riding two to a motorcycle attacked one group of youths walking back to the university. 'We tried to run, but they caught us,' said Shabab, 24, a computer science student in jeans and a T-shirt, a green ribbon on his wrist and a huge bandage on the back of his head.

'They were bastards,' he said, pulling a bloodied sweatshirt out of his rucksack. 'When they saw I was bleeding they beat me even more.'

Other students attacked a Basiji headquarters north of Freedom Square with Molotov cocktails and stones. The reply was devastating – gunmen from inside the building fired a fusillade of bullets, killing seven and wounding 26.

They were not the first deaths of the new era in Iran. The students had attacked the Basiji building because their dormitories had been raided before dawn that morning. Basiji crashed through the doors of sleeping undergraduates, ransacking bedrooms and destroying the books in the library. Five students died in the raid.

The violence was not all on one side. During Thursday's protest, I saw a crowd of men and women descend on a Basiji who tore down a poster of Mousavi. They beat and kicked him viciously while others on the march yelled: 'Don't hit him! Don't beat the Basiji!' He was eventually allowed to limp away.

The sight of hijab-wearing teenage girls walking away sweating from punching him as hard as they could was just as disconcerting as the sight of the girls partying all night in the heady days before the vote.

The parallels with 1979 cannot have been lost on the regime, nor Mousavi, who served as prime minister under Khomeini from 1981 to 1989.

The uprising against the Shah spiralled ever higher on a cycle of funerals and deaths.

Demonstrators would take to the streets to mourn fellow protesters shot by the Shah's security forces, suffer losses themselves, and take to the streets again for the new victims.

By Thursday last week, the cycle appeared to be repeating itself. As news of the deaths filtered out slowly on Tuesday and Wednesday, anger grew.

Even members of the national football team, including the captain, Mehdi Mahdavikia, wore green wristbands during a World Cup qualifying match against South Korea, which was shown on state-run television, to signal their support of the protests.

Impromptu shrines were set up around the city. A new march was planned for Thursday: this time the mood was different.

Earlier in the week the rallies had been rumbustious affairs; now they were silent in commemoration of the dead so as not to give the authorities any excuse to attack. Any marchers trying to start a chorus of 'Down with the dictator!' were quickly shushed.

Shunning the bright colours of earlier protests, most women now wore black hijabs and black clothing. One marcher said black had a deep emotional effect as well.

'The colour black is changing the mood,' he said. 'People are preparing for more militant confrontations.'

As much as the millions of people on Tehran's streets last week appeared to be a revolution in the making, aimed at overthrowing the government, in reality they had been allowed to continue because they were playing out a struggle for the future of the Islamic Republic, not its overthrow.

Behind the unprecedented scenes in public, a vicious internecine political battle was unfolding. Khamenei, who has almost unlimited power as supreme leader, with control of the armed forces, media and foreign relations, has abandoned the traditional role of the office, which is to remain above the fray. He has openly taken the side of Ahmadinejad in wanting to retain the unyielding regime of social restrictions and uncompromising international policies.

On the other side, Mousavi is backed by Hashemi Rafsanjani, the wealthy former president who is regarded as the second-most powerful man in Iran. He was defeated by Ahmadinejad in 2005 in an election that was also clouded by allegations of fraud, but heads the Assembly of Experts, a clerical body that is responsible for supervising the supreme leader.

In many ways, Ahmadinejad and Mousavi are the face of the struggle between Rafsanjani and Khamenei.

Rafsanjani's antagonism towards Ahmadinejad was inflamed when the president accused his two sons of corruption during a national television debate. He funded Mousavi's campaign from behind the scenes.

The support of Rafsanjani, whose reputation is of a wily, shrewd diplomat, for Mousavi comes from a shared view of Iran's future. Both believe that the days of Iran's unforgiving revolution are over and that the regime should relax the strict Islamic rules on social behaviour and moderate foreign policy to end Iran's isolation in the world.

'Mousavi believes in evolution, not revolution,' said Sadegh Kharazi, a senior Mousavi adviser.

He described Mousavi's potential foreign policy. 'Mousavi believes in reducing the tension internationally and

confidence-building that could result in a normalisation of relations,' Kharazi said.

He spoke openly of the most sensitive areas in Iranian international policy, relations with the United States and Iran's nuclear
programme. 'If President Obama understands Iran policy and Iran
society, there is a good chance that Mr Mousavi can make a bridge
between the US and Iran.'

On the contentious nuclear issue, neither Mousavi nor
Ahmadinejad would survive politically if they abandoned Iran's
uranium enrichment programme, which the West fears is aimed at
manufacturing a nuclear bomb despite Iran's denials. Mousavi has,
however, made clear he would be open to negotiations to find a
solution.

The reformist view of the world differs markedly from the one
Khamenei made clear in his Friday speech. Both he and
Ahmadinejad have blamed the street protests on 'foreign
intervention'.

'The aggressive powers of the western world showed their true
faces finally, and they are the faces of wolves,' said Khamenei.

'Not only in the United States, but in "dark-hearted" England.'
The hall resounded with chants of 'Death to America! Death to
England! Death to Israel!'

Khamenei also made no secret of whom he supported on Friday.
Praising Rafsanjani for his role in the Islamic revolution, he
concluded: 'There have been differences of opinion between Mr
Ahmadinejad and Mr Hashemi about issues related to foreign
policy, the nuclear issue and some cultural issues. This is natural,
but I personally approve Mr Ahmadinejad's decisions more.'

By putting himself so firmly behind Ahmadinejad, Khamenei is
taking a gamble. Pitting the authority of the state against the
marchers, rather than acknowledging their complaints, forces
them to make a stand on the authority of the revolutionary government. This could have dangerous consequences for the regime,
something that not even Rafsanjani and Mousavi would happily
countenance.

Yesterday's bloodshed will polarise the situation.

One of the placards at a demonstration by Basiji and Ahmadinejad supporters after prayers on Friday read: 'O leader, point the direction and we will run that way,' suggesting they will do whatever the authorities tell them to do.

There are questions, however, about whether the Revolutionary Guard, who were not involved in yesterday's shootings but are waiting in the wings, would fire on the protesters. They are charged with defending the revolution, not the supreme leader, and some guards are loyal to Rafsanjani.

'I will not be able to fire on these people,' said a young off-duty Revolutionary Guard as he watched a march pass by last week. 'Maybe some of us will, but I won't.'

The simple fact of yesterday's demonstrations was remarkable. The protesters had directly disobeyed the supreme leader – which just last week would have been an unthinkable act.

Mousavi himself yesterday further upped the ante, saying that he was 'ready for martyrdom'. In a letter to the country's legislative body he insisted that the election result be annulled, claiming that it that been 'rigged' months in advance. He also called for a national strike if he were to be arrested.

'We will only accept new elections,' a senior adviser to Mousavi said. 'Our representatives are the people on the street.

'Mousavi himself has told me he has had a good life and it is coming to an end. He is willing to fight to the death for justice in this election.

'What you see today is like a medieval confrontation. We are witnessing what happened in Europe with the emergence of John Calvin versus the Catholic Church. At the moment his supporters believe he can continue the reformation.'

How strong their faith will be in the face of a crackdown by the regime will become apparent in the coming days and weeks.

Egypt

Flames and fighting flood along the Nile

CAIRO

30 January 2011

Even after Tunisia's revolt, the rage engulfing Egypt has taken the world by surprise, leaving it trembling at the outcome.

It all began, ironically, on the annual Police Day, when the Egyptian regime calls on its people to honour its widely despised police force.

For the third year running, a group of young Egyptians had posted a notice on Facebook calling for a protest to mark the day. They wanted to highlight police abuse.

Little had happened on the previous two occasions. But this year, Police Day fell just 11 days after street protests in Tunis forced Zine Ben Ali, the Tunisian president, to flee to Saudi Arabia.

The chain of events that led to his exile had started with the suicide of Mohamed Bouazizi, a young fruit vendor who set himself alight in protest at police seizing his cart. Now the Middle East was trembling with anticipation – who would fall next?

In macabre emulation of Bouazizi, several young Egyptian men had already set themselves on fire to protest against poverty, unemployment and the humiliation that comes from not having enough money to get married.

Besides, Egypt already had its own martyr – Khalid Saeed, 28, whose fate has come to symbolise state injustice. Last year he was hauled out of an internet café in Alexandria and beaten to death by the police in full view of people on the street after he accused officers of taking part in a drugs deal.

To begin with, the calls for protest came from Egypt's disaffected youth. One of the internet sites calling for a mass turnout on Police Day was called 'We are all Khalid Saeed'. It had a huge number of hits.

If Saeed was the martyr, Tunisia was the catalyst. The Facebook call to arms struck a chord.

'Without Tunisia, there would have been the same 100 to 200 protesters, tops, surrounded by twice as many police,' a western diplomat in Cairo said last week. 'Tunisia charged the atmosphere with the sense of possibility.'

The Jasmine Revolution in Tunisia convulsed just one small country but it echoed across the Arab world – and nowhere louder than in Egypt.

It is hard to grasp the sheer size and weight of Egypt in the Arab identity: with 80m people, it is the most populous nation, the fount of classical Arabic, an ancient centre of Sunni Muslim learning and a fertile source of newspapers, books, music, films and soap operas adored from Casablanca to the Gulf.

Yet an undercurrent of terrorism lurks on the fringes of Egyptian civilisation. Ayman al-Zawahiri, Osama Bin Laden's right-hand man who helped to plan the September 11 attacks, was born in Cairo. Terrorists killed 58 western tourists at Luxor in 1997 and at least 88 people died, including 11 British tourists, in a bomb attack at the Sharm el Sheikh resort in 2005.

Egypt embodies the woes of other Arab nations – economic deprivation, an oppressive political system, a super-wealthy elite and a family that has ruled for decades.

Its armed forces, once the most powerful in the region, consume billions in American aid but 30 years of peace with Israel have left them indolent and riddled with corruption. They do, however, command patriotic prestige, an asset that could now become crucial.

So the warning signs were there. But none of President Hosni Mubarak's generals or secret policemen seems to have expected the torrent of events last week.

On Tuesday thousands of mostly young men poured into the streets, taking the government by surprise and overwhelming the security forces, who broke ranks and ran.

On Wednesday the authorities outlawed public gatherings and detained hundreds of demonstrators and political activists. The protesters held their nerve. Skirmishes ignited in the afternoon, with riot police chasing people to clear streets, beating some with bamboo staves and lengths of rubber hose.

In the northern city of Suez protesters set fire to a provincial government office and a fire station. Satellite television relayed images to a restive Arab world. At that point, governments and markets around the globe took notice, because Suez commands the strategic canal that carries trade between Europe and the booming economies of the Far East.

Thursday was tense but quiet, except for a bizarre protest in Cairo by lawyers who started throwing rocks from inside the neo-classical building of their union at riot police on the streets outside.

In fact, the eerie calm of Thursday was just the sound of people regrouping, via Facebook, Twitter and mobile phone messages. They called for a Day of Rage on Friday, the Muslim holy day.

After prayers, the word went out to head for Tahrir Square at the heart of old Cairo, which had become the centre of the protests.

Few details were on Facebook, as it had become clear the authorities were monitoring the site. But, as it turned out, few details were needed.

As crowds spilled out of the mosques they scorned the anodyne sermons they had heard as proof that the clerics were in the pay of the government. 'We must express our opinion as individual human beings without bloodshed or destruction of property,' the speaker at the Fat'h mosque said, telling the faithful that the leader should 'be your guide'.

The time had passed for that. The anger of the crowds was directed at Mubarak personally – his rigged elections, the corruption of his circle and his ceaseless grip on power.

'Mubarak must go!' they chanted. Rasha El Sayed, 36, said: 'There are no jobs, and the prices are so high we cannot afford bread. The women are becoming spinsters and the men are sitting at home doing nothing.'

Within half an hour the police started firing tear gas. Only a few brave young men stood their ground, throwing rocks and at one point hurling a tear-gas grenade back towards the police.

After that, protests swelled like the Nile in flood.

Buildings burned, cars were set ablaze, clouds of tear gas hung in the air and gunshots punctuated the chants of protest in towns and cities across the country.

By midnight on Friday, when a haggard Mubarak went on television to say he had listened to his people and sacked his government, pledging to make things better, Egypt was in flames.

The wind of change in the Arab world – long predicted by both Bin Laden and George W Bush – had come. So important is Egypt in the region that the future of the whole Middle East could now be forged on the streets of Cairo and Suez.

Western governments and Islamic revolutionaries from Tehran to Peshawar are holding their breath this weekend. There appear to be three possible outcomes: a transition to democracy; a new dictatorship, perhaps led by a general around whom the old guard would coalesce; or an Islamic state.

However, nowhere has technology combined with peaceful protest beaten a truly ruthless regime, as the Burmese could testify.

From Tehran there came predictions that Muslim fundamentalists would triumph in Tunis and Cairo, as they did over the liberal and leftist factions in the Iranian revolution.

As Washington hopes for an acceptable strongman to emerge, foreboding in Israel may be mixed with a feeling that it might have been better to make peace with a moderate Palestinian state, as Mubarak urged, before the deluge.

Seen from Cairo, it may not be as bad as that. The rich seam of Egyptian political life has included Muslim activists for a century or more.

The government tried last week to portray the demonstrations as the work of the Muslim Brotherhood. It arrested senior Brotherhood members, including Essam Elaryan, the public face of the movement.

In reality, a new political force has emerged: tens of thousands of mostly young people, joined by middle-aged housewives and government clerks. Islam is part of it – but not all of it.

The tide of protest has come so fast that even potential leaders such as Mohamed ElBaradei, the former head of the International Atomic Energy Agency who returned home last week, were caught by surprise.

'Frankly, I didn't think the people were ready,' he said last week in a telephone interview. But they were – and now the world must be ready, too.

Raging mob bays for Mubarak's head

CAIRO

30 January 2011

Demonstrators and police clash in Cairo as officers fire rubber bullets and tear gas while youths attack party HQ and ministries.

The young man was distraught. Ahmed Yassin thought he had proved his mettle by protesting against the government he works for even though he knew it would endanger his job. Then he found himself carrying a dying woman to an ambulance.

'It was a peaceful demonstration,' said Yassin, 28, who works in the oil ministry and felt strongly enough to defy his ministry's ban on joining the protests. 'The police started shooting tear gas. There was a young woman. She fell and I was helping her up, trying to carry her, when a tear-gas canister hit her in the head,' he added, still shocked. 'Her brain came out.'

Yassin, dressed in the black designer jeans and sports jacket of Egypt's middle class, said he and others hauled her to an ambulance. The medics said she was severely injured, but Yassin knew she had died in his arms.

As he spoke, other young men ran past, their faces flushed, their eyes and noses streaming with tears and mucus. 'Mubarak must go! The people want the regime to fall!' others chanted, calling for the end of Hosni Mubarak, the Egyptian president.

Yassin's shock and anger were reflected across Cairo on Friday at the height of a 'Day of Rage' that cast Egypt into confrontation and uncertainty.

'I am a member of the NDP [the ruling National Democratic party],' said Yassin, pulling out his party card. 'But I cannot be quiet. I feel the injustice in my country. We feel humiliated every day.'

Across Cairo there were scenes not seen in living memory. At the October 6 bridge that spans the Nile, young men stumbled down the stairs, their eyes and noses streaming. They had been battling riot police dressed in black who had helmets and riot shields and batons. The police had lined up on the bridge to stop them from exiting onto the road that passed the headquarters of the NDP.

The fighting erupted after midday prayers, with the youths building up numbers and charging the police, only to retreat when officers regrouped and fired tear gas, or charged with their batons and lengths of yellow rubber hose.

The tear gas hit the young men but one canister landed in a passing boat. A soldier aimed so badly that his commanding officer came up from behind and smashed him over the head with a baton.

Thuggish men in jeans and leather jackets – probably secret police, as they passed through the riot police lines – lined up with batons, one with an iron bar. They launched into the crowd, beating everyone they could reach.

The crowd cheered as other protesters toppled a hut used by traffic police and set it ablaze.

In retaliation, the tear gas came in salvos, one after another – choking fumes that stung eyes, nose and throat.

As the crowd threatened to overwhelm the police, there came a barrage of rubber bullets. A police boat launched tear gas canisters from the river that, leaving graceful arcs of acrid grey smoke, sped into the ranks of protesters.

Similar clashes occurred across the capital and were reported in Alexandria, Suez and other Egyptian cities.

The numbers of protesters grew, and the police became increasingly beleaguered. At one point, on a street off Tahrir Square in central Cairo, they appeared to run out of tear gas and started throwing stones at the demonstrators.

By evening, the feared police had fled the streets, routed by the sheer numbers pouring off Qasar al-Nil bridge to seize their goal, Tahrir Square.

But then a strange dynamic developed as the army roared onto the streets for the first time in armoured personnel carriers. They were welcomed with cheers by the demonstrators, who consider the police an arm of the regime, while the soldiers are seen as the 'sons of the nation'.

By midnight, the headquarters of the NDP party were burning, the information ministry was surrounded and fires blazed across Cairo, mostly cars that had been set alight.

The thump of tear gas rounds continued until well past midnight, as did the intermittent crack of live bullets. The big question was whether the army would fire on the crowds. By yesterday, they appeared to have fired into the air instead of at protesters.

The demonstrators ignored the curfews declared by the government and a televised address in which Mubarak announced that he was sacking his cabinet. As they returned to the streets again yesterday, central Cairo resounded to the crump of tear gas rounds being fired.

A huge pillar of black and grey smoke was still rising from the NDP headquarters when dawn broke. The square – tahrir means 'freedom' in Arabic – was littered with rocks, shattered glass, iron bars and charred police cars.

In another day of chaos, two mummies were destroyed in an attack on the Egyptian Museum, which has the world's largest collection of Pharaonic antiquities. Thousands of protesters gathered to storm the interior ministry, the hated co-ordinator of the police, and shots were fired. In the mayhem, it was claimed that at least three people had been killed and their bodies carried through the crowd. It was not clear whether live ammunition or rubber bullets had been fired.

Two police stations were later set on fire, in addition to 17 that had been torched in the capital the previous night.

The army, however, continued to be greeted warmly. In the winter sunshine two tanks were parked on each road entering Tahrir Square. At one, a crowd gathered around the soldiers. 'We are so proud of you. You stopped those sons of bitches of the police from attacking us,' said Ahmed Hussein, a businessman, to a young lieutenant.

Another man said: 'You have finally come to save us from police, we need you to save us from the regime. We do not want just the cabinet to go – we want Mubarak out.'

It seemed that Mubarak's party could soon suffer the same fate as its burnt-out headquarters.

I ran for my life from a crazed, cursing mob

6 February 2011

While speaking to a family whose son had been shot, Marie Colvin found herself in one of the most threatening situations in her career.

The mob had gathered in the alley below the apartment as I spoke to a family whose son had been shot during the anti-government demonstrations.

I had no idea I would soon be running for my life.

Mohamed Salah's father broke into tears, weeping silently, as he told me that friends had carried his body to the door of the house.

It was a heartrending interview. It is always difficult to intrude on a family's grief, but I had been invited by his brother because the family were angry that Mohamed had been killed by the police and they had no recourse to justice.

As I talked to Mohamed's mother and wife, the men in the family grew agitated. They asked for my press card and the national identity card of Madiha Qassem, my translator. They ran up and down the stairs, talking in worried tones.

'People' downstairs in the alley needed to see our identity documents, they said. No problem, don't worry, they said. What we didn't know was that word had gone out through the poor neighbourhood of Embaba in Cairo that a foreigner was in its midst.

It would soon become clear how dangerous was this new Egypt. I am used to threats in Afghanistan, Iraq and other countries in the Middle East, but Egypt has always been a country populated by people friendly to foreigners. Madiha, who has worked in journalism for decades, had no qualms about visiting the Embaba neighbourhood.

But the country has changed. State-owned television has broadcast the poisonous and constant theme that foreigners in Egypt are behind the political unrest that has caused the country to grind to a halt.

I was isolated. My car had been guided to the apartment by a family friend on a motorcycle, and then I had walked the rest of the way because Mohamed's family lived in a ramshackle building on a dirt-floored alley.

By the time I had finished my interviews, the mob below the apartment were beyond reasoning. Even though I was wearing a hijab, or headscarf, I had been spotted and, unknown to me, the word had gone through the alleys that a 'foreign woman' was in the neighbourhood.

I walked down the narrow, unlit stairway to a frightening scene. About 100 men had gathered, shoving each other, shouting that I was a spy, or maybe worked for the hated Al-Jazeera television station. Some had knives shoved in the waists of their trousers.

The men of the family formed a circle around Madiha and me to protect us and try to get us out of the alley.

It was a terrifying moment. In a mob, there is no individual responsibility and these people were working themselves into a frenzy. The men shouted and cursed. The few women in the crowd spat in anger.

Mohamed's brothers and father panicked. They threw us in to the tiny shop of a friend, who locked the metal grille gates against the crowd that was now baying for blood.

The young wife of the store owner spoke no English, but she held my arm and pulled me to the shadows at the back of the shop. There was no back door.

Men came in and out of the darkened shop, allowed one by one through the metal gate, hearing our case and shouting, as Madiha bravely and calmly explained that we were journalists.

A tall, burly young man in a striped sweater took away my press card and Madiha's identity card. The crowd outside pressed against the metal grille.

I called *The Sunday Times* foreign desk to say I was besieged in a neighbourhood called Embaba, but there was little more I could do. In Egypt these days, you cannot call the police; they are either confined to barracks or too frightened or corrupt to be of any use.

Mohamed's brothers had gone to get my driver to move the car as close as he could to the shop; he could not get to the door because the alley was too narrow.

As the anger of the crowd ebbed and flowed, they decided we should make a break for safety. It was a wise decision. Any push by the crowd would have broken through the metal door. A Molotov cocktail tossed in there would have been impossible to escape.

They bustled us through the crowd to the car, and then jumped in on top of us. The crowd pounded on the car, and the windows.

At one point, the angry young man in the striped sweater hauled a policeman into the car. He wanted to arrest us.

Mohamed's family kicked the policeman out of the car, refusing his demand to arrest us. He cursed me and Madiha as 'you bitches'.

My luck was that nobody knew what to do with us – chaos reigned outside and within the car. The first sign of authority was an army checkpoint.

The crazed men, and Mohamed's brothers, agreed to turn me over to the soldiers. A calm, articulate officer shooed everyone away, checked my press card, and said: 'Go to your hotel. It is very dangerous on the streets now.'

Egypt's bloody road to reform

CAIRO

6 February 2011

Marie Colvin and Uzi Mahnaimi

Change seems certain, but while President Hosni Mubarak clings to power there are many innocent victims of the tumult along the Nile.

Mohamed Salah did everything he could to make a success of his life. Despite coming from a Cairo slum, he managed to graduate from high school – a success normally confined to children of the wealthy and members of Egypt's ruling party.

He won a job at the Conrad hotel as a housekeeper, an enviable achievement in a country where 40% of the people live on less than £1 a day. When tourism waned because of the world economic depression and he was fired, he took out a loan to buy a rickshaw and worked late every night, earning a few pence on each trip. He toiled all the harder after his first child was born three months ago.

Like many in Cairo, however, Salah had had enough by the time anti-government protests broke out nearly two weeks ago. Unfortunately for him, so had the police.

Last Wednesday, as pitched battles broke out in Tahrir Square, the centre of the rebellion, Salah was in a crowd that gathered outside the police station in the Imbaba district, a few miles north down the Nile.

A police officer named Mohamed Mktar climbed on top of the building and, in full view, shot an automatic weapon into the crowd. Salah, 25, was struck in the chest.

'They brought his body to my door,' his father said a few hours later. 'I laid him on this bed. I sent for a doctor because I would not believe he was dead.'

The government of President Hosni Mubarak is trying to portray the protests as provoked by foreigners and the middle classes. Salah, however, came from the poorest of the poor. His parents' home is on a dirt alley that smells of sewage. Live chickens lie around, tethered by their ankles. Daylight barely filters through the dilapidated buildings.

Hayam, Salah's 25-year-old wife, sat in her in-laws' house, distraught in a black hijab and abaya. Her infant son, dressed in a lime-green bodysuit, jiggled on her lap.

'Our last conversation was at breakfast,' she said. 'Mohamed said we had to be serious now, and find a way to educate our son. He wanted our boy to have a future that we did not have.'

Salah embodied a popular revolution unlike anything Egypt's class-restricted society has seen. In Tahrir Square, well-dressed doctors mixed last week with bearded members of the Muslim Brotherhood, and women in full-length robes were side by side with glamorous figures in Gucci sunglasses and miniskirts.

Death was indiscriminate. Dr Ahmed Kamal, who was in the square again yesterday, said his room mate at Al-Azhar University, a famous centre of Islamic learning in Cairo, had been shot dead on Thursday morning. 'We are too tired of lies, poverty, corruption

and dictatorship,' said Kamal. 'We are here for our principles. We
will not go home until Mubarak leaves.'

Yesterday, the 12th day of the demonstrations, was quiet
although protesters still chanted: 'Go now, go now.'

The army had reinforced the perimeters of the square. Soldiers
wore flak jackets for the first time and stopped supporters of
Mubarak from approaching. After the high drama and vicious
fighting of the week, however, there was a feeling of stalemate in
the square. Who could force Mubarak to quit if he refused to relin-
quish office?

Holed up with his family in the heavily guarded presidential
palace at Heliopolis, eight miles from the square, Mubarak just
seemed to become more stubborn each time a foreign leader – led
by Barack Obama and David Cameron – publicly urged him to
begin the process of surrendering power. At 82, he was fed up and
would love to quit, he told an American television interviewer, but
not yet. That would have to wait until elections in September.

America, his paymaster, seemed to have lost all influence.
Mubarak sent away his old friend Frank Wisner – dispatched to
Cairo by Obama with a message that it was time to let go – with a
flea in his ear.

Admiral Mike Mullen, chairman of the US joint chiefs of staff,
said on Friday: 'There is a lot of uncertainty out there, and I would
just caution against doing anything until we really understand
what's going on.'

Wisner muddied the waters further yesterday by saying Mubarak
should stay on to steer political changes.

Effectively, however, Mubarak has already quit. Although the
demonstrators have not achieved their aim of throwing him from
office, the way Egypt is being run now is very different from the
way it was only 10 days ago. Behind the scenes, a military triumvirate has taken over – reflecting the army's long-standing role as the
true power in Egypt.

The new vice-president, Omar Suleiman, a retired general,
stands at the apex of a pyramid with the prime minister, Ahmed

Shafiq, also a retired general, and the defence minister, Field Marshal Mohamed Tantawi, operating below him. They are already known as 'the junta' by some Egyptians.

Yesterday, Mubarak attended a meeting with the finance minister to discuss the grim economic situation, which has deteriorated because of the riots – more than 1 million tourists have fled.

However, a source close to him said: 'This is one big show. The president is now a figurehead, not by any means in a position to take decisions, which are being taken by the triumvirate. The three meet every night, taking decisions and then, updating the president.'

Their public posture has been non-confrontational. Suleiman has been on television, saying political transition takes time and urging the opposition to negotiate. Shafiq publicly apologised for the violence; and Tantawi went to Tahrir Square to see things for himself. The army stepped up security for the anti-government demonstrators soon afterwards.

Tantawi was in the square again yesterday with Amr Moussa, the secretary-general of the Arab League, and was greeted with applause and whistles of support.

Suleiman became vice-president last weekend, as the government was overhauled after the interior ministry's riot police had clashed murderously with protesters. However, he has long been close to the apex of power as Mubarak's 'brain' – his intelligence chief, fixer and strategist.

Diplomats saw him as the perfect foil for the president, who is a non-intellectual former fighter pilot. Mubarak regards himself as 'tough, strong and fair', according to a US diplomatic cable released by WikiLeaks, while Suleiman shows the feline political skills of an Egyptian Peter Mandelson.

Suleiman prefers to work from his old intelligence services HQ, arriving every day at 8am sharp for a briefing. He is in control of the intelligence apparatus, although a new intelligence minister has stepped in. Hundreds of his men have been mixed up among the demonstrators in Cairo, Alexandria and Suez, and they have sometimes been beaten up if exposed.

Their main role, however, has not been to act as *agents provocateurs* but to report back to headquarters so that Suleiman stays up to date with the public mood.

His strategy last week was to let the anger in Tahrir Square wear itself out while a number of sacked ministers – including the former head of the interior ministry – were placed under judicial investigation and the military stood by to intervene if the trouble spread really dangerously.

At 10am every day, a giant Russian-made Mi-8 helicopter painted in creamy desert colours started circling around central Cairo. According to an officer on the ground, it was not on a reconnaissance mission but carrying a force of 20 elite commandos, waiting for instructions to land if events got out of control. The flights are set to continue.

'So far what we've seen was a stroll along the Nile river bank,' said the officer. 'If things go out of control, special forces with more choppers are standing by in a nearby airbase.'

While the defence minister, Tantawi, and his chief of staff, General Sami Enan, look after security, the prime minister, Shafiq, is busy with running the non-emergency parts of the state.

'Of Egypt's 84 million people, less than 10% are being directly involved in the demonstrations,' said a local politician. 'People still need to be taken care of.'

Banks and shops have been closed, and long lines of cars were waiting outside petrol stations yesterday. 'I'm not interested with Mubarak or not Mubarak,' said Saide, a taxi driver. 'I have 13 children to feed and the government should make sure there is enough fuel.'

All operations are coordinated to maintain a crisis 'road map', as Suleiman calls it. The timeline extends seven months into the future, with Mubarak nominally remaining in charge. 'It will take two months to alter the constitution,' Suleiman said on television, and then 'five months to prepare for general elections'.

Will this road map survive? The Egyptian army has bolstered its good standing among the population by its handling of the crisis, so a peaceful resolution to the street rebellion is not impossible.

Mubarak signalled last week that he would lift the emergency law, in place for 30 years, that bans opposition parties from running for presidency or parliament. The opposition was yesterday organising a committee for talks with the government that would have been unprecedented just a week ago.

The president remains the stumbling block to formal negotiations, however, as so many lives have been lost by demonstrators demanding that he should go.

The members of the triumvirate, who consider him a father figure, are personally reluctant to humiliate him by forcing him out – as well as arguing that it would be politically destabilising – but they are looking for a way of putting him more obviously in the back seat.

'He is stubborn and wants to keep the [presidential] chair for his own legacy,' said one source close to the regime. 'But he is also afraid that he could lose everything.'

He and his family are said to fear that if he stepped down he could be prosecuted, either for the corruption that has meant he and his family have amassed a fortune, or by victims of his repressive police and army.

Egyptian sources said they believed that Mubarak could save face by agreeing to an internal exile in Sharm el-Sheikh, the resort on the Sinai peninsula where he has a villa on the sea.

One of the leading members of the opposition, Mohamed ElBaradei, the former head of the International Atomic Energy Agency, signalled that there might be room for compromise. He said: 'I'm for a safe exit for President Mubarak. We're going to turn the page; we can pardon the past.'

Who will take over?

The man tipped to succeed Hosni Mubarak, if only in the short term, is his new vice-president, Omar Suleiman, 74. Born into a poor family, Suleiman rose through the army and fought in the 1967 and 1973 wars against Israel. He joined military intelligence and Mubarak made him its head in 1993, with the organisation earning a reputation for the brutal suppression of Mubarak's political opponents, including the use of torture. On a 1995 visit to Ethiopia Suleiman insisted he and Mubarak take an armoured car, which saved them in an assassination attempt.

The kids triumph with Facebook and flyers

13 February 2011

Marie Colvin and Hala Jaber

Egypt's inspirational youth were galvanised when their leader wept on TV. Then they had to reach the low-tech masses by any means necessary.

Tahrir Square, the focus of the world, resembled a city fair. Hundreds of thousands of Egyptians chanted and danced; men with 'dignity' painted on their foreheads pounded drums; young women handed out sweets; children bounced on their parents' shoulders.

They had all come to witness the final act of Egypt's 'people power' revolution. President Hosni Mubarak, 82, was scheduled to speak, and television and radio were reporting that he was stepping down. They thought it was all over.

Finally, at 10.45pm, nearly three hours late, the old man's basso tones boomed through loudspeakers. The crowd began muttering in disbelief. Mubarak wasn't quitting. He was 'adamant to continue to shoulder my responsibility to protect the constitution and safeguard the interests of the people'.

'Donkey,' someone shouted as the square erupted in fury.

That was Thursday. On Friday, it really would be all over, but the crowds didn't know it yet. Perhaps a million spilt out of Tahrir Square into the streets and onto the steps of parliament, demanding Mubarak's resignation. Thousands marched to the television centre and the presidential palace.

Marie in Tahrir Square, Egypt.
Photograph by Ivor Prickett.

At midday, the faithful in the square – including soldiers who had dismounted from their tanks and armoured cars – knelt for noon prayers. At the same moment, Mubarak and his family secretly boarded a helicopter from his palace to the airport, where the presidential plane waited to take them into internal exile at the Sinai resort of Sharm el-Sheikh.

Only a few figures in the highest reaches of his regime knew that one of the most momentous events in modern Middle Eastern history was taking place. As the afternoon drew on, the demonstrators in the square grew shriller in their demands.

Shortly after dusk fell, the long and inscrutable face of Vice-President Omar Suleiman, Egypt's Mr Fix-it, appeared on television screens. Because of the 'very difficult circumstances Egypt is going through', he announced, Hosni Mubarak had resigned.

Power had been handed to the armed forces. 'May God help everyone,' the retired general added briskly.

Tahrir Square exploded. Weeping soldiers standing on their tanks grasped hands with demonstrators. The whole city came out to celebrate. Alexandria, Suez and other towns stayed up all night.

Far away in Washington, a relieved President Barack Obama, who had been tripped up repeatedly in his attempts to manage the Egyptian crisis, compared it to the fall of the Berlin Wall.

The manner of Mubarak's departure raised many questions. What happened last week to bring Egypt's 18-day revolt to such a bumpy ending?

The catalyst was a young man called Wael Ghonim, a local Google executive who had set up the Facebook site that attracted demonstrators to the first anti-government rally on 25 January. He had then been arrested by the secret police.

At the beginning of last week, after days of tumultuous demonstrations, Cairo seemed to be slipping back into routine. There were still large crowds in Tahrir Square, but people were answering the government's calls to return to work while it started negotiations with opposition groups. Had Mubarak regained the initiative?

Then Ghonim emerged from detention. On an independent Egyptian television station – in an interview that illustrated how far the regime's grip over the news media had collapsed – he spoke of his ordeal at being grabbed off the street and held incommunicado for 12 days.

When the interviewer flashed images of young men who had died in the protests, most of them wearing T-shirts and jeans, Ghonim was visibly struck by how similar they looked to himself. They were his tribe. He broke down in tears, watched by a nation that no longer tuned into pro-Mubarak state television.

'I am telling all the mothers and fathers who lost their kids, it was not us who killed them, it was all the people hanging on to their power,' Ghonim said, weeping. The crowds in Tahrir Square swelled and talked of little else.

Ghonim had become the voice of the revolution. He represented the element in the revolt that Mubarak found so hard to grapple with, intellectually or physically: the social media generation.

Mohamed Taman, 34, one of the organisers of the protests, explained: 'We started with a Facebook invitation on a site set up by Ghonim.'

The site was named in honour of a young man beaten to death by police on a street, in plain view of passers-by, because he refused to show his identity card. The Facebook crowd chose national Police Day, 25 January, for their first – illegal – demonstration against abuse of power.

'We didn't have a plan other than to protest,' said Taman. 'We started with 300, and step by step we thought on our feet, and by the end of the day our 300 was 15,000.'

Another of the organisers, Ahmed Maher, 30, had been at a conference in Doha with Ghonim. 'We used the internet to co-ordinate, and also to study revolutions around the world,' said Maher. Knowing that Facebook would not reach Cairo's working class, they also distributed leaflets in poor neighbourhoods.

On the day, he was surprised by their success: 'The police were shocked. Actually, we were shocked.'

The Tahrir Square protesters refused to attend the talks early last week between Suleiman and other opposition groups, including the outlawed Muslim Brotherhood – the first meeting of the government and 'brothers' in almost 60 years.

Mubarak seemed to believe that if he could talk round his long-time opponents, they could talk some sense into the 'kids'. What the regime should have noticed was that – unlike Egypt's 30% illiterate minority – most of the 'kids' running the show were in their late twenties or early thirties, and connected to a cybercommunity whose freedoms they wanted to share.

The protest leaders remained firm: they would not negotiate until Mubarak had left office. Until then, they would remain in the square – where, behind a huge screen made of sewn-together sheets, they gathered to discuss tactics in the office of the Safir

Travel agency, which had been smashed and destroyed in an attack by Mubarak's thugs. Next door, the wrecked Pizza Express was the food bank.

As they plotted, support for the revolution grew wider, reaching into all levels of Egyptian society.

'What our youth have done is a dream,' said Abdel Hakim Nasser, 56, the youngest son of Egypt's late, still revered, President Nasser, who overthrew the monarchy in 1952.

Sitting in the plush office of his construction company in Heliopolis, not far from the presidential palace, he looked the model of upper-class Egypt, but he spoke words unimaginable just two weeks ago.

'Under Mubarak, people have lived in fear, and the establishment has no values except for bribery, favouritism and corruption. This is not what my father risked his life for. Mubarak should resign.'

The same sentiment had reached the highest levels of the military, who see themselves as the guardians of Nasser's revolution. The army had notably fraternised with protesters on the streets, and – urged on by Washington – it moved reluctantly towards the logical consequence of this behaviour: the ousting of the president. But how?

For nearly three weeks the military leadership had been torn between the regime and the protesters, without giving a hint as to whether they would dump Mubarak – one of their own, a former air force commander and hero of the 1973 Arab–Israeli war – and seize control for the first time in nearly 60 years.

As the protests increased in mid-week, however, and Mubarak alienated himself through his 'stubbornness and arrogance' from the one institution that any leader needs to lead or run a country – the military – the mood in the high command finally turned against him, said a senior Egyptian source with first-hand knowledge of the developments.

'The rage and mood in the country dramatically changed as of [Wednesday], when the protests spread not only to main cities across the country but to small towns, villages and nearly every part of Egypt,' the source said. 'Egypt was boiling. The situation on the ground was dangerous and would have erupted in a bad way for everyone concerned.'

As the demonstrators turned out in ever greater numbers and Mubarak made one minor concession after another, growing ever weaker but refusing to go, the Supreme Council of the Armed Forces announced that it was in 'permanent session' – meaning it was on a war footing.

Senior military officials told Mubarak that if he did not leave, the country would enter a state of civil uprising that could eventually split the army itself, according to the source.

It is reported that late on Wednesday, CIA and Pentagon officials – in close touch with the Egyptian generals, who rely on $1.3 billion (£800 million) a year in US military aid – learnt that Mubarak was to be deprived of most of his powers and reduced to a figurehead or step down altogether.

The White House shied from publicly demanding the departure of its former ally, but after Mubarak failed to announce his resignation on Thursday, Obama finally acknowledged that the balancing act was over, and that the protesters had to win. 'The Egyptian people have been told that there was a transition of authority,' Obama said, 'but it is not yet clear that this transition is immediate, meaningful or sufficient.'

When, a day later, Mubarak stepped down, the White House was able to congratulate itself that it had at least ended up on the right side of history. Yet Washington was also faced with the cruel reality that its influence was minimal. For, in the end, it was the Egyptians who applied the coup de grâce.

After his defiant speech on Thursday, a series of senior army and intelligence officers pressed Mubarak to go throughout the night and into the morning. The entire leadership of the military, security services, general intelligence and military intelligence painted a stark picture for him of the reality on the ground.

He was told that Egypt was on the verge of entering a civil insurrection that would bring it to a complete standstill. The entire country would stop functioning and be on the streets. Transport, education, finance, day-to-day business – the whole nation would come to a standstill, plunging it into extremely dangerous waters.

'The picture was depressing and stark, and worsened by the warning that such an eventuality could split the army or force it to confront the people,' said the senior source familiar with the transition of power.

'Even Suleiman explained the dangers to Mubarak,' the source said, adding that the former vice-president and head of intelligence was still working closely with the armed forces and was involved in all the decisions and preparations from behind the scenes.

In the strange hours between Mubarak's flight from Cairo at noon on Friday and the announcement of his resignation, there were clues that the fin de régime had come. Demonstrators who reached his Cairo palace were confronted by razor wire, tanks and armed soldiers. The crowds shouted, sang and waved banners, calling on the army to join them. The soldiers, members of the presidential guard, threw sweets and biscuits to the crowd. The crowd threw them back.

As dusk drew in, the military's resolve weakened. They reached through the razor wire and grasped posters of demonstrators killed in earlier protests and with great reverence laid them on their tanks.

State television was disintegrating, too. The shouts from the crowd demonstrating outside its headquarters became so loud they could be heard on air.

A young woman presenter collapsed on screen, practically weeping. 'We are in chaos here,' she said. 'I am so sorry. We have been telling you things that are not true. Now we can tell the truth.'

A state television reporter went down to the crowd and stuck a microphone through the barbed wire barricade to broadcast – for the first time – what the protests were all about.

Yesterday, the elation of the moment continued. But reality was beginning to set in. The psychological victory was clear. Egypt was no longer a rusting old machine. Overnight it had regained the role of the most important country in the Middle East, its revolution being watched by other Arab populations and their authoritarian governments.

The crowds occupied Tahrir Square late into the night, vowing to return next Friday, if necessary. The young opposition leaders had not received an answer to their demands for the lifting of the state of emergency and the introduction of an electoral programme – although since they had sent it by email, they joked, they were unsure the military had received it.

Feral mobs and fanatics rule Terror Square

CAIRO

27 November 2011

The mood in Egypt's divided 'second revolution' is far darker as brutal police crackdowns put looming elections in jeopardy.

There was a painful sting in the air from lingering tear gas as dusk fell on Tahrir Square and the crowd became more menacing. Once a scene of altruism, idealism and hope, the square that had become the symbol of Egypt's revolution was now divided and unforgiving in the run-up to the parliamentary elections scheduled to begin tomorrow.

Protesters had returned to Tahrir Square in their tens of thousands last week to demand that the ruling military leadership step down, reviving the mass protests of the revolution that forced President Hosni Mubarak to resign in February.

Back then the atmosphere had been festive and communal. Doctors and nurses worked round the clock as volunteers and everyone who came to join the crowds brought food or handed out sweets. Foreigners, especially journalists, were welcomed into the makeshift tent camps and musicians played newly written revolutionary songs to entertain the crowds.

Last week, in what Egyptians were calling the 'second revolution', the atmosphere was darker and violence seethed beneath the surface. Unlike the earlier Tahrir occupation, this time the square – actually a roundabout in central Cairo just off the Nile corniche – had been divided into encampments according to political affiliation.

There were suspicious glances at strangers. It was frightening, especially for a lone woman. I was caught in a tidal wave of young men running from tear gas and shotgun pellets launched from one side of the square. I was already feeling vulnerable, having been gassed in an earlier attack by military police against people throwing stones at the interior ministry in anger at the killing of at least 42 protesters.

Tear gas had often been used in the early days of the revolution. But whereas last time the crowds in the square had gone out of their way to help, journalists have now become targets. I was groped by men who were supposed to be fleeing in fear, unable to see even who was grabbing me and unable to flee because I was hemmed in by a leaderless mob.

In my mind was the attack the day before on Caroline Sinz, a reporter for French television, who was covering the events in Tahrir Square when she was surrounded by teenagers, beaten and assaulted, and then dragged off by adults, stripped and sexually assaulted for almost an hour, an experience, she said, that 'amounted to a rape'.

There is nowhere to turn. During the January 25 revolution the activists had organised the volunteers into groups who divided the tasks, from cleaning to distributing food to keeping order.

Last week men who tried to help Sinz were beaten back. The police were no help. Mona Eltahawy, an Egyptian-American blogger and columnist, was grabbed by riot police, dragged by her hair, beaten so badly that they broke both her arms and sexually assaulted by the military police. 'I lost track of how many hands went down my pants,' she said.

The riot police arrested thousands of protesters and held them without charge. One of the main complaints fuelling the violence was that the interim military government had gradually returned to the ways of the Mubarak regime, arresting awkward civilians on trumped-up charges.

Hossam Bahgat, of the Egyptian Initiative for Personal Rights, said 12,000 civilians had been brought before military courts since February.

'It is terrible but they are doing our work,' said Bahgat, a lawyer. 'The more they abuse the rights of people, the more they reveal their true face.' Tahrir Square is now a political minefield. I escaped the melee of fleeing young men, only to tumble into the area of tents dubbed 'Tahriristan', where the banner of the extreme Salafist movement flew from a lamppost.

Men with the thick black beards that denote pious Muslims sat on blankets engaged in intense conversations about Islam. One handed out pamphlets entitled *How to be a Good Muslim*.

They all eyed me suspiciously and started gathering around me, muttering 'she's a spy' and insisting I showed them my passport. An interrogation began. 'Where are you from? What are you doing here?' If they had not been so menacing it would have been comical. Spying on what – on who is donating the sweet potatoes to be roasted?

Liberals are still to be found in the square, although in lesser numbers, roughing it in tents with Facebook addresses stencilled on their sides. Their discussions last week were still about how to install democracy in a country that has experienced only military rule since 1952 and debates raged about the endless new parties emerging on the liberal end of the political spectrum.

They were heavily outnumbered by the Islamic groups, who were organised and disciplined, and the thousands of poor, uneducated Egyptians and thugs, some remnants of the Mubarak regime's semi-official muscle, who had come for no reason other than that they relished heaving stones at the police.

Pickpockets were rife in the crowd and even patients who lay overcome by tear gas in the square's makeshift clinics woke up missing their wallets, watches and jewellery.

The change in mood reflected a fundamental darkening of the revolution that had been founded 10 months ago on a wave of bravery and hope for the future, of young men and women standing up to a dictatorship and, against impossible odds, overthrowing the despot. The revolutionaries, having decapitated the monster, did what they thought was best for Egypt and deferred to the military, which was supposed to stay in power for six months before handing over to a civilian government.

Now, with parliamentary elections due to begin, the protesters are demanding that the Supreme Council of the Armed Forces step down immediately. They want the resignation of Field Marshal Mohamed Hussein Tantawi, the council's head and a former defence minister under Mubarak.

Their resolve was deepened last week when Tantawi appointed, as a political concession, Kamal Ganzouri, a 78-year-old former prime minister, to lead the transition to civilian power. The young who had created the revolution felt they were being betrayed.

'We will not let them hijack our revolution,' said Ali Sultan, a 28-year-old lawyer who had been arrested by the military. 'I am staying in the square for as long as it takes for them [the military] to leave. The Egyptian revolution will continue until Egypt is under civilian rule.'

The violence ebbed yesterday, partly as a result of a 7 foot wall erected between the protest camp and the interior ministry, which had been a target all week because of the brutality of the police crackdown.

Volunteers distributed free food and donated medicines were brought in to makeshift tent clinics which last week were overwhelmed by the victims of tear gas, rubber bullets and live ammunition. Much of the anger at the ruling military came because they were seen as allowing the interior police to act so brutally against a peaceful protest.

No one had predicted such a violent and sudden 'second revolution'. Instead, the country had been gearing up for peaceful elections. But there was growing anger at the ruling military council, particularly when it published a draft of what it envisioned as a new constitution that put the military above the civilian government and proclaimed there would be no oversight of its budget. The document was withdrawn after protests but the damage had been done.

Ironically, it was a crackdown by the military police last weekend against about 100 protesters who were camped out in Tahrir Square that had re-energised the protesters.

Egyptians from all walks of life rushed to the square in solidarity with those attacked. Every time police and soldiers attacked the protesters their numbers grew, until on Friday more than 100,000 had reclaimed the square.

Anger at the military rulers came pouring out. Critics noted that the military was growing comfortable with its expanding power and attributed that to its desire to maintain its immunity from scrutiny and a status that has for decades given it membership of special clubs, access to exclusive seaside resorts and control over billions of dollars in assets and the levers of political power.

Tantawi used a televised speech last week to dismiss the protesters calling for his resignation but it was unclear if he could cling on to office.

'We are the ones who should be appointing a prime minister, not Tantawi,' said Ahmed Naguib, one of the activists who organised the January 25 revolution via Facebook and is now an independent candidate for a Cairo district.

The elections will still go ahead, although yesterday there was a growing move to boycott them. Naguib, who was staying in a tent, said he no longer wanted to participate in an election that, under this military regime, appeared to have reverted to Mubarak's ways and would result only in a 'sick parliament'. Naguib said he would not leave the square until Tantawi resigned.

The Muslim Brotherhood was the unheard voice in the melee, mainly because it wants the elections to go ahead. The Freedom and Justice party, the brotherhood's political wing, is the most organised party and is expected to garner a substantial slice of the parliamentary vote, which will take place in three stages over the next six weeks. The brotherhood has kept its members out of Tahrir Square, although some are there unofficially.

The protesters received a boost from Washington as the White House called on Friday for 'the full transfer of power to a civilian government ... as soon as possible'. The Americans have a good deal of leverage as they donate an annual $1.3 billion in aid to Egypt, money that is even more important now that the economy is in freefall.

By Friday night fevered meetings of the leaders of a loosely organised coalition of political parties, protest leaders and charismatic stars of the January 25 revolution had called for an interim civilian government, which they termed the National Salvation Front, to take over immediately from the military.

To head the new civilian leadership they nominated Mohamed ElBaradei, former head of the International Atomic Energy Agency, Abdel Moneim Abul Fatouh, a former leader of the Muslim Brotherhood, and Hamdeen Sabahy, a left-wing politician. All three are presidential candidates.

'Tantawi should step down and the military should go back to the barracks,' Fatouh told me yesterday. He added, however, that he was opposed to postponing the vote.

'We need immediate elections and the drafting of a new constitution,' he said. 'In fact, I would move the presidential election forward. The future of Egypt can only be secured by a civilian government.'

Amid all the political manoeuvring there was nostalgia in the square for what had seemed to be a revolution, paid for at the price of 800 lives, that could only lead to a better future.

'This is our fault,' said Naguib, meaning the fault of Egypt, as he helped me out of the Islamic encampment but into the path of scampering feral boys he had to chase away. 'We failed to educate them.'

Libya

'I'll still be running Libya when my foes have retired,' insists Gadaffi

6 March 2011

Under-fire Libyan leader sends strong message of defiance to world leaders after managing to cling to power against the odds last week.

The more confidence that Muammar Gadaffi radiated in his ability to hold on to power last week, the more his opponents had to fear.

Scores of young men who felt able to protest a few days earlier when he had looked vulnerable found themselves arrested in night-time raids by the Libyan leader's secret police. Parents have not been told where their sons are held.

'We were all in our beds sleeping when the secret police broke through our door,' said Ali, a mechanical engineer, whose sons, aged 17 and 19, were taken at night with other young men from the Tajura district in eastern Tripoli.

He described how a convoy of dozens of pick-up trucks and 4x4s had swarmed into his street at 1am. His teenagers had been blindfolded and led into the darkness.

'We do not know what prison they are in,' he said. 'We hear they are probably with the intelligence force.'

Secret police raided homes in Tajura and Fashloom almost nightly last week, residents said. Both working-class areas have been hotbeds of rebellion. After Friday prayers nine days ago, five people were shot and killed in Tajura and two in Fashloom.

'There is a great feeling of terror,' said another Tajura resident, a 57-year-old builder. 'Anyone speaking up knows that he will be carted off to prison or worse.' He said police appeared to be using photographs and videos, some from YouTube, to identify men involved in earlier protests.

Last week's arrests appeared to be aimed at stopping another violent demonstration after Friday prayers. If so, the clampdown partially succeeded. There were far fewer protesters – only about 300 – but they still took to the streets. After prayers at the Murad Agha mosque, where men spilled out on to the court-yard to pray, demonstrators marched to a nearby roundabout and chanted 'down, down, Gadaffi', and 'the people want the regime to go'.

Half an hour later black vehicles pulled up and police began firing tear gas into the crowd. Acrid fumes filled the street. Some protesters fled, while others tried to throw the tear gas canisters back at the police.

When protesters began throwing rocks the police fired salvo after salvo of rubber bullets into the crowd and everyone scattered, believing they were being attacked with live rounds as they had been before. The last few were chased off with bullets which police appeared to fire into the air. Residents reported about 40 arrests afterwards.

There is little doubt that Gadaffi's writ still runs in Tripoli, as he went to great pains to demonstrate last week. He exuded bullish optimism in spite of the rebels controlling almost half his cities and world leaders calling on him to step down. A belly laugh burst from him when I asked if he would leave his country. 'Does anybody leave his own homeland?' he said. 'Why should I leave Libya?' He retained the veneer of self-assurance throughout an interview with *The Sunday Times*, BBC and America's ABC.

More laughter punctuated his answers, reinforcing the image that he was still very much in control, despite a rebellion that began last month when his security forces fired on a funeral procession.

Gadaffi, 70, his hair dyed jet black, was speaking as Libya's revolt began to look dramatically different from earlier rebellions in Tunisia and Egypt, where the regimes' leaders stepped down in the face of largely peaceful protests. The rebels who now control eastern Libya seized machineguns, rocket-propelled grenade launchers and even anti-aircraft guns from arms depots.

Gadaffi's message that he was determined to fight on began with his choice of venue for our interview. We met in a fish restaurant with floor-to-ceiling windows that looked out over the sparkling blue water of Tripoli harbour.

It was chosen to put paid to rumours that he had fled Libya and to show that he had no fears about travelling anywhere in his capital.

It was a stunning departure from his usual routine. Gadaffi lives hidden behind the walls of the Bab al-Aziziya army barracks in Tripoli and rarely sits in a room with an outside view, unless it is his desert tent.

His choice of transport conveyed the same message. He arrived dressed in a brown turban and flowing ankle-length robe in a white BMW and walked up the steps to the restaurant. Again it was a far cry from his usual tight security. Normally, his guards race ahead of him, tripping over each other in their zeal.

His show of being in control of the city continued throughout the week. On Thursday he delivered a two-hour speech to the faithful before driving away in a vehicle that looked like a Noddy car.

There were indications that Tripoli is nowhere near as relaxed as Gadaffi made out. Along the main corniche, only smashed glass remains in the frames that once held pictures of the Libyan leader.

In the poorer suburbs of Tajura and Fashloom, graffiti saying 'Down, down, Gadaffi' had been painted over with black paint.

Tajura police station was a burnt-out shell. Sporadic shots rang out at night.

Gadaffi's clampdown appeared to have terrified many Tripoli residents. In Tajura, where little more than a week ago men waiting for the funeral of a demonstrator had openly denounced Gadaffi, people were too afraid to speak.

'I'm sorry, we're afraid. I apologise,' said a man who last week was happy to give reporters his name.

Gadaffi seemed coherent when I spoke to him. He denied that his forces had bombed civilian areas, the chief reason for a United Nations security council resolution that warned of crimes against humanity and imposed sanctions.

'It was media agencies that said such things,' Gadaffi claimed. 'The UN should send a fact-finding mission and then they can take such a decision.'

He insisted that the rebellion was fomented by Al-Qaeda, which had drugged Libyan youths to make them enlist.

He grew emotional when I asked what he thought of David Cameron's move to freeze his family's assets and strip them of their diplomatic immunity.

'I challenge Cameron and everybody else if he can bring one dinar that belongs to me in any foreign bank,' he said, raising his voice. 'I have a tent. I don't like money like him. I'll put my two fingers in their eyes if I have any accounts, whether it is inside or outside Libya,' he added, making a stabbing motion with his fingers.

He had one final message for western leaders: 'Today's presidents who say I should go, I say to you that you will serve out your terms and then you will retire – but I will still be leader of the revolution.'

Siege falters as loyalists defect to side of rebel 'rats'

MISRATA

15 May 2011

Deserters from Gadaffi's army say they were tricked or forced into fighting and are now siding with the rebels.

Two months ago, Naji Mabrouk went proudly to war in the belief that he was fighting for his country. Six weeks later, disillusioned, angry and depressed, he waved down a rebel pick-up truck and defected to his former opponents defending the besieged city of Misrata.

Mabrouk, 29, who had served 10 years in the marines, had believed his commanding officers when they told him that Al-Qaeda and foreign troops had seized Libyan cities.

Why wouldn't he? He had watched Colonel Muammar Gadaffi, the Libyan leader, say the same thing on state television and call for his armed forces to defeat the 'rats'.

But after the fall of Benghazi and the east to the rebels, his faith was destroyed. His naval unit was sent to join loyalist forces that had recaptured Zawiya, a city to the west of Tripoli, the capital.

'There was no Al-Qaeda there,' said Mabrouk, one of 102 prisoners of war being held in a school in Misrata last week, awaiting a decision on whether he could be trusted sufficiently to join the rebels' ranks.

'One of us recognised the body of a man we killed in Zawiya as his friend. Another was a marine. He's now buried in the square, as a martyr.' Mabrouk said he had carried on fighting because prison or worse awaited deserters.

On the eve of his last mission, an attack on Misrata from the sea, Khamis Gadaffi, the leader's son and commander of his own elite brigade, addressed the troops on the beach. 'You're fighting for the freedom of Libya,' Gadaffi said. 'Go into Misrata and push the rats out,' he boomed, before driving off with an escort of 200 soldiers in pick-up trucks armed with anti-aircraft guns.

As Mabrouk's unit waited to launch its skiffs, he told his commanding officer: 'Those rats had better not be Libyans.' Mabrouk said his officer replied: 'Anyone who refuses to fight, I will kill.'

After Grad rockets rained down on the port for an hour, Mabrouk said, a 12-boat attack was launched. His boat steered towards a beach, where he and his comrades hid for the night. In the morning, he flagged down the rebels' truck and surrendered his Kalashnikov assault rifle and four hand grenades.

He does not consider himself a traitor. Like many rank and file troops in Gadaffi's army, he symbolises its weakness in the face of determined revolt. He joined the armed forces straight from school because his family needed the money. Now he wants to take on the regime. 'Gadaffi has taken our money and given us nothing but lies,' he said bitterly.

Many loyalist soldiers who have fought in earlier battles no longer have any faith in the party line. They now know the rebels are fellow Libyans, not drugged Al-Qaeda fighters or foreigners, and the cities, far from being abandoned, are home to families like their own.

A series of interviews last week with soldiers who had deserted or surrendered revealed a deeply demoralised force. One battle group of 40 men surrendered en masse rather than battle on. Many men said they had been tricked or bribed to come to the front line in Misrata, where the fighting has been intense for the past month as Gadaffi has attempted to crush the only rebel-held city in the west of the country.

The former loyalists are being held in a disused school, where they cook their own meals. Omar Shariani, 29, had left the army years ago but was recalled when the rebellion erupted in February. He was sceptical of the regime's claims about Al-Qaeda and had seen police attack unarmed protesters in Tripoli's Tajura district.

He said he had no choice but to obey orders and was sent to Misrata with 30 other men. He was given a Kalashnikov and a pick-up truck armed with a 14.5mm anti-aircraft gun mounted on the back, a weapon favoured by both sides.

As soon as he spotted an opportunity, he said, he escaped and surrendered, taking with him Ali Masoud, 18. 'I took Ali with me because he had no shoes, no weapon and he was so scared of all the gunfire that he couldn't move,' he said.

'I want to tell all of the soldiers who are still fighting for Gadaffi that this man is destroying our country,' he added. 'Do not fight for this man.'

Other members of Gadaffi's forces were also pressed into battle. Mohamed al-Hawat, 25, was in his fourth year at university when he was ordered to take part in a pro-Gadaffi demonstration or he would not be allowed to graduate. He said he was taken by bus to Dafniya on the western outskirts of Misrata. He was issued with a gun and given 45 minutes' instruction. There was no need to worry, he was told: the weapon was just for his protection.

When he was issued with a uniform, it was explained this was so that government soldiers could tell him apart from the rebels. By the time he was put on a lorry to Misrata, the penny had dropped. 'We were all upset,' he said. 'I came for a civilian demonstration, and I found myself in this miserable situation. And I'd told my family I'd be gone a day or two.'

He finally heeded the call of rebels who yelled to him: 'Come to us! We're from Misrata; we're Libyan just like you.'

Last week Gadaffi's forces suffered setbacks in Misrata that far exceeded the impact of deserters leaving their ranks. On the western front, rebels fought desperately to drive his forces back so that their Grad rockets and artillery could no longer reach the city centre.

It was a front that changed hour by hour. When on Thursday I drove from the coastal road towards what had been a relatively secure area the day before, bullets whizzed past and mortars landed in the next field. I jumped out of the car to seek the safety of a low sandbank. The bullets whipped by, sounding like angry hornets. The road had turned into a free fire zone.

At the front, 500 yards ahead, about 100 rebels held a line to which they had fallen back overnight. They called for support and ammunition over a radio. It could have been a scene from the First World War. Rebels lined up, squatting with their backs to a sand berm, the butts of their Kalashnikovs in the sand, ready to go over the top.

Reinforcements roared to the scene in pick-up trucks with metal plates welded to them as makeshift armour. My translator grabbed a Kalashnikov and raced forward, joining rebel troops who advanced shouting, 'Allahu akbar' (God is greatest), only to be beaten back by the loyalists' barrages. Yet late in the day the government forces simply gave up and retreated.

'We're attacking them from three sides,' said Abdel Latif Soweili, the rebels' commander and grandson of a hero of the fight against the pre-war Italian occupation of Libya. 'Yesterday we couldn't get to them. They had families in front of them. They were using the women and children as a human shield.'

By the weekend Gadaffi's lines had been pushed back in the west, yard by yard, out of range of the city.

The biggest rebel victory of the week came on the city's southern border. Loyalists had dug in at the airport and the air academy next door for almost two months, lobbing rockets and tank shells into the city.

Finally last week the rebels tried a plan that had been successful last month on Tripoli Street, the city's main boulevard, where Gadaffi's troops had hidden in high buildings, using them for snipers and as vantage points from which to mortar the city. Unable to force them out by frontal attacks, the rebels cut their supply lines by building barricades of sand and blocking roads.

At the airport they used the same tactics. Gadaffi's forces finally broke under intense fire, leaving behind tanks, cars and lorries and abandoning their dead. The rebels buried them in graves with numbers on the headstones.

Last week loyalist forces attempted another seaborne assault on the port. It failed after HMS *Liverpool*, a Royal Navy Type 42 destroyer, silenced Gadaffi's shore batteries with its 4.5-inch gun.

Yesterday in Misrata, shortages of food and medical supplies were growing. Cooking gas was nowhere to be found, and electricity was cut as generators ran out of diesel because shelling had set the port's storage tanks on fire. Petrol queues were half a mile long.

Families are living on tinned tuna; no fresh vegetables or fruit have crossed the siege lines. There are long queues for bread. Morale among the rebel fighters and civilians remains high, though.

Mabrouk, the marine deserter, said he would continue agitating to join their ranks despite the daily losses and deprivations of the siege. 'We've had enough,' he said. 'We all want to be rats now.'

'We had our orders: rape all the sisters'

MISRATA

22 May 2011

Colonel Gadaffi's forces are accused of violating at least 1,000 women trapped by fighting in the front-line city of Misrata.

The young Libyan soldier showed almost no emotion as he described how his unit had raped four sisters, the youngest about 16, after breaking into a home in the besieged port of Misrata.

'My officer sent three of us up to the roof to guard the house while they tied up the father and mother and took the girls to two rooms, two each to a room,' said Walid Abu Bakr, 17.

'My two officers and the others raped the girls first,' he recalled in a monotone, still dressed in the camouflage uniform he was wearing when he surrendered 12 days ago.

'They were playing music. They called me down and ordered me to rape one of the girls.'

Abu Bakr, from Traghen, a poor southern town, claimed he had been given hashish and was not responsible.

'She did not move much when I raped her,' he said, admitting the girl had already been gang-raped. 'She said in a low voice, "There is Allah. He is watching you." I said, "Yes, Allah is watching me."'

Abu Bakr seemed to regard himself as a victim, however. He said he had become his family's breadwinner after his father left his sick mother and his siblings.

He joined the army when he was offered 200,000 dinars (£100,000), payable on victory for Colonel Muammar Gadaffi, the Libyan leader, he said.

But he had received only a week's training at Yarmouk camp in Tripoli before being sent to Misrata as part of a militia attached to the elite Khamis brigade, named after Gadaffi's youngest son. Their mission was simple. 'We were just told to kill,' Abu Bakr said.

The teenager said he did not keep track of how many times the four girls in the house had been raped. The soldiers in his unit had stolen 12,000 dinars and jewellery from the family, but he had not received a penny, he said.

When rebel forces began closing in on the airport road, the officers sent the family to Zlitan, the next town controlled by Gadaffi's troops, and left, ordering Abu Bakr and eight others to guard the house. They never returned.

'The rebels surrounded us, and we threw away our guns and surrendered.'

Abu Bakr, who is now held in a Misrata school with other former Gadaffi soldiers while the rebels decide what to do with them, said he had decided to speak about the rapes after talking to an Islamic cleric.

Misrata officials said the ruthless assaults by Abu Bakr and his unit had been repeated across the city. Gadaffi's soldiers, they said, had engaged in an orgy of rapes that mirrored their destruction of the city's homes and buildings.

Nothing would have prepared the women of Misrata, or their families, for the ferocity of the onslaught that occurred when they were trapped amid the fighting, mostly in districts that were controlled by Gadaffi's forces for two months.

The brutality emerged only when the rebels broke through loyalist lines and chased Gadaffi's troops beyond the city limits. In their wake, they found horror stories.

Doctors at Hekma hospital found that some of Gadaffi's soldiers had recorded video footage of rapes on their mobile phones. 'They made the girls identify themselves to the camera and show their faces. Then they raped them,' one doctor said. The phones were found on loyalists who had been wounded or killed.

'In one of the videos, there's a woman. She's moaning, "Oh no, no, the sixth one, God help me,"' said one doctor.

A video seen by *The Sunday Times* showed a group of Gadaffi's soldiers in camouflage uniform breaking down a door and confronting a frightened family – a man, a woman, five girls whose ages ranged from about five to early 20s, and a boy aged about 7. The soldiers, shouting and waving their guns, stripped the four older girls in front of the family and took them into the next room, where they raped them. The girls cried for mercy, calling on Allah. A soldier at one point yells: 'Gadaffi is our Allah.' The video was found on the phone of a loyalist soldier.

A Filipina nurse said her best friends had fled to Tunisia after their four daughters and 13-year-old son were raped repeatedly after the family was trapped in their flat on Tripoli Street, the scene of some of the heaviest fighting in Misrata.

'I spoke to their mother,' the nurse said. 'She said the boy was terrible. She said, "Don't even ask about my girls."'

The stories emerging from Misrata mirrored the earlier charges of Iman al-Obeidi, 28, who burst into a Tripoli hotel in March claiming to have been gang-raped by Gadaffi loyalists.

So horrified is Misrata by its rapes that young rebel soldiers have offered to marry the victims, who face ostracism in this deeply traditional society.

'The rebels feel guilty that they did not arrive in time to save these families from Gadaffi's men,' said Dr Ismael Fortia, an obstetrician who estimates that up to 1,000 women may have been raped.

Hardly any of those attacked have come forward because a raped woman is regarded as virtually unmarriageable if she is single, or a shame to her family if she is married.

Doctors and psychologists in Misrata have banded together to help. They will check victims for sexually transmitted diseases and offer abortions.

One of their concerns is that unless they are treated, the women may commit suicide rather than live with their memories.

'The images of their rape will go around and around in their heads, like an endless nightmare, unless they receive counselling and help,' said Dr Mustafa Shigmani.

The terrible revelation comes as Misrata's rebels fight on three fronts around the city, loyalists try almost daily to mine the port and explosions reverberate day and night.

Last week there were faint signs that the regime might be faltering under increased Nato bombing and political pressure.

Safia Gadaffi, the Libyan leader's wife, and Aisha, 35, his daughter, were said to have left the country for Tunisia, although his spokesman denied it. Shukri Ghanem, the oil minister, was reported to have defected.

Gadaffi's regime proffered a Russian-brokered deal under which they would withdraw their troops from the cities if the rebels did the same, and if Nato stopped bombing. The rebels refused, but the mere existence of such an offer from Tripoli suggested that the regime might be apprehensive.

'Time is working against Gadaffi,' said Barack Obama last week in a speech on the Middle East. 'The opposition has organised a legitimate and credible interim council.'

Although Obama's statement stopped short of official recognition, it was the furthest Washington has gone towards acknowledging the council as the country's leadership.

The people of Misrata have suffered the greatest toll in the Libyan conflict, largely because their city has been so bitterly contested by Gadaffi. It is the only population centre in the west of the country that is under rebel control.

In districts newly liberated by the rebels, residents described a reign of terror under Gadaffi's soldiers.

'The soldiers ordered our family out of the house while they searched,' said Fatima, 47, of the Zreig neighbourhood. 'They said they were looking for weapons, but they took our money, our jewellery, everything they could carry while we waited for three hours.'

Families were forced to fly the green flag of the regime. Foot patrols raided homes at all hours. 'They would shoot up the television if you were watching anything other than the state channel,' said Fawzi Damir, 21.

Men disappeared. 'They caught my husband and two of my sons,' said Fatima. The men would usually flee if they spotted loyalists on their street, but two weeks ago they had been taken unawares early in the morning. One son escaped by hiding under her bed.

City officials have said more than 1,000 men, women and children have disappeared.

Some residents took to the streets last week to celebrate an end to the shelling of the city centre. They waved flags and shouted with joy.

They were the lucky ones. One of the unforgivable legacies of Gadaffi is that many of the women of Misrata will never again emerge from their homes and think only of the beautiful sunshine.

Professor leads adopted sons into battle

29 May 2011

A university dean and his loyal students are battling to hold the rebel front line as Gadaffi's shells rain down daily.

A university professor turned rebel commander on Misrata's most fiercely contested front line was wrestling last week with a dilemma far beyond that of most military leaders. He felt a deep personal responsibility for his fighters because most were students who had followed him into battle.

'It is difficult for me because I believe we must fight for our country and I know freedom comes at a price,' said Ali Kerzab, 42, who, until three months ago, was Dean of the Department of Education at Misrata University.

'But most of these boys are students, and I want them to have a future,' said Kerzab, a slim, wiry figure in a makeshift uniform of khaki shirt and dark green jacket and trousers, as he walked behind a sand berm protecting the company from loyalist guns.

'They are enthusiastic and they don't think.'

Kerzab and his 150-strong Abu Bakr Sadiq katiba, or militia company, yesterday marked their second week in Dafniya on the western front, 19 miles from the centre of the besieged port of Misrata. The city is the only rebel-held enclave in the government-controlled west.

The rebels have pushed back the forces of Muammar Gadaffi, the Libyan leader, far enough for his rockets to be out of range of the city centre but their new lines are being pounded daily.

The open farmland of the new front is very different terrain from the buildings and alleyways of the city where they used their local knowledge to drive out Gadaffi's troops.

Last week, Grad rockets whistled malevolently as they arced over the concrete farmhouse and row of small shops Kerzab had chosen as a temporary camp on the road to Tripoli, the rebels' ultimate goal.

One Grad landed in a nearby field, setting fire to dried wheat and filling the air with an acrid scent. A salvo of Grads fired in quick succession from a multiple rocket-launcher landed on the tree line, sending up six columns of black smoke.

Kerzab's katiba has seen six men killed in two months and 30 injured in the past two weeks, a huge cost for a close-knit company. The last death, on 2 May, was of Kerzab's brother, Hussain, 46.

Kerzab was one of just 10 local men who launched an initial assault on Gadaffi's forces on 23 February. His students later joined in, along with drivers, shopkeepers and engineers from his neighbourhood.

'He is like a father to me,' said Salem Shavish, 23, who studied English with Kerzab.

'We all feel Gadaffi took our lives,' said Shavish. 'We see America, the UK and the Emirates and we say, "We have oil, why are we always suffering?"'

So close are members of the katiba that Rabia Mustafa al-Gneidi, 19, another student, has written in careful calligraphy on his Toyota the names of the six men killed since the rebellion against Gadaffi began on 18 February, sparked by troops firing on peaceful protesters.

Gneidi said he and other students felt they had a new life ahead of them.

'I can say what I want,' he said. 'Before, the secret police were always present, and you could go to prison just for saying something bad about Gadaffi, even just to your friends.'

Kerzab is focused largely on the students' survival. 'I worry for each one of them,' he said before racing off in a pick-up truck through an olive grove to retrieve a wayward group who had surged ahead and seemed about to be surrounded by loyalists.

But as the carnage mounted last week, the rebel soldiers in Kerzab's company and their comrades on the front line began to chafe at the high command in Misrata, which ordered them to remain in the same positions on the road to Zlitan, the next town, 100 miles east of Tripoli.

The military council decided the rebel force should halt its advance until Zlitan, a town of 110,000 inhabitants where 1,000 of Gadaffi's troops hold sway, rises up of its own volition.

According to Ibraham Bet-Almal, a member of the city's military council, Misrata's rebels have supplied Kalashnikovs and FN assault rifles to Zlitan's rebel representatives. They meet secretly at night in olive groves, and last week 70 Zlitan rebels came for training with the men of Misrata.

'Our target is Tripoli, not Zlitan,' said Kerzab, who attends military meetings in Misrata when he can leave the front. 'If we impose our will on Zlitan, they will fight us. So we tell them, "We are going to Tripoli, let us go together".'

Mad Dog and me

28 August 2011

Marie Colvin, who has known Gadaffi for 25 years, offers an insight into the mind of Libya's fallen tyrant.

When I saw the looted chaos of the Bab al-Aziziya compound in the centre of Tripoli after its capture by rebels last week, I had a flashback to a night quarter of a century ago – the first time I met Muammar Gadaffi.

In April 1986 I was driven through the empty, dark streets of the city to what was then his stronghold. The tall gates of Bab al-Aziziya swung open and I passed several tanks hidden in the shadows. I remember thinking I would not be leaving without the permission of the Libyan leader.

I was nervous. Gadaffi was in a tense stand-off with Ronald Reagan, the American president, who had called him 'the mad dog of the Middle East' for sponsoring anti-western terrorism, including a nightclub bomb attack that month against American military personnel in Berlin. The US Sixth Fleet was off the coast. Superpower vengeance was expected at any moment.

Gadaffi had given no interviews to the scores of journalists in Tripoli. I was an American citizen, working at the time for United Press International, a US news agency. Why had I, a young female reporter, been awakened at 3am and told that 'the leader' had summoned me?

I didn't know it at the time, but this was classic Gadaffi. He kept no set hours and summoned people. His whim had to be implemented immediately. You had only to see how quickly his aides scurried when he issued a command to know that his rule was based on fear.

My car was met by several beautiful young women in tight camouflage uniforms, high heels and make-up with pistols at their hips. They glared at me, led me underground down several staircases and left me alone in a room with a large desk and a sofa.

The door opened. In walked Gadaffi, dressed in a red silk collarless shirt, white silk pyjama trousers and lizard skin slip-ons. Over it all he wore a gold cape. He turned, locked the door, put the key in his pocket and said, 'I am Gadaffi.'

I remember saying to myself, 'No kidding.' But I think I was just stunned.

It was a weird interview. I kept turning on the tape recorder and he kept turning it off, putting his hand on my knee and saying he was tired and wanted to talk about something else. He seemed isolated. At one point I asked a not particularly clever question, something like, 'How are you feeling now that President Reagan is about to bomb you?'

'Who told you that?' he demanded. Missing my chance to be considered a journalist with highly placed sources, I said: 'I heard it on the BBC.' Gadaffi leapt up, crossed the room and switched on a radio tuned to the World Service.

It was clear that he lived in a bubble of his own making. Libya was at the centre of an international crisis, yet he was sitting alone in his bunker, relying on the radio for news. The isolation could only have been enhanced by his obsession with the security he found underground.

We now know that the tunnels under the compound were more than just a secret way in and out. There was a whole world of living quarters where I must have interviewed him years ago, never knowing I was in a tiny corner of a secret complex.

The famous bedouin tent where he met dignitaries, including Tony Blair for the 2004 handshake, was one of the many props of his personal theatre. He played the bedouin sheikh but he never really lived there. He felt safe only in his burrow.

His paranoid obsession with safety underground became even more clear last week when I entered the house of Moatassim Gadaffi, one of his sons and the national security adviser. Neighbours in the Ben Ashour district said Gadaffi senior had built the house about nine years ago, then given it to Moatassim.

Inside it was decorated in terrible taste, with mud-coloured leather furniture, dark brown modern paintings and an ostentatious, black-and-white swirled marble floor. But down three staircases was an underground world. Much larger living quarters sprawled beneath the manicured gardens, complete with a fully-equipped operating theatre, an x-ray machine and a medical clinic. Armoured doors, painted green, punctuated the wide hallways, with instructions on how to release the lock if trapped by rubble.

'For four years workers were sending out trucks of dirt and no building appeared,' said Dr Ashraf al-Khadeiri, who lived across from the compound's 30 foot walls. 'For four years, an enigma. We thought, maybe he is walking in the ground under us. Now we know.' Khadeiri was the first outsider to enter the underground home after Moatassim fled last week.

During the crisis of April 1986 I interviewed Gadaffi several times, always summoned at the last moment in the early hours, always meeting him underground. I never saw anyone besides drivers and guards. There was no sound from outside.

The interviews were increasingly strange. I arrived for one to find that a bodyguard had laid out petite green shoes for me to wear. It was Gadaffi's favourite colour: he had changed Libya's flag to a flat green banner and he had renamed Tripoli's central square Green Square. But green shoes for an interviewer?

Late on Friday 11 April, he summoned me again and seemed in a more serious mood. He told me he had decided to 'include all of southern Europe in a Libyan counterattack plan'.

Gadaffi painstakingly went over a communiqué with me, changing several words in a statement typed by his office and explaining exactly what he meant. He was anxious to hear what I thought the Reagan administration might do, and he pressed me for information from Washington. He told me: 'I think Reagan must be mad.'

On the night of 15 April the Americans attacked. The use of Stealth F-117 aircraft was vetoed at the last minute – it would have been the first time the top-secret planes were used in anger – and a squadron of F-111s flew from American bases in Britain to hit the compound and other targets.

I called the private number Gadaffi had given me to find out whether he had survived. An aide answered and hung up.

Several weeks later Gadaffi ended a long period of speculation that he had been killed by emerging to make one of his characteristic rambling speeches. He said Reagan was the problem, the American people loved Gadaffi, and to prove it he distorted the content of my phone call – which had been to find out if he was alive – to say that 'an American woman had called and tried to warn me'. I was grateful he did not use my name.

Three years later I was in Tripoli again. It was a month after the Lockerbie bombing, which had not yet been definitively pinned on Libya.

American and British intelligence had identified a chemical weapons plant at Rabta, 60 miles south of the capital. US fighters patrolling the Mediterranean shot down two Libyan planes that had intercepted them. Gadaffi put human shields into Rabta, but this time no bombers came.

I saw him from a different perspective when I accompanied Yasser Arafat, the Palestinian leader, on a visit to Libya. On the plane, Arafat worked through a mass of papers, always with his green pen. Without a break in stride after landing, he climbed into the limousine that whisked him to the hotel Gadaffi had assigned to him. When Gadaffi had still not seen him after 12 hours, Arafat took it as an insult.

He sent me in his convoy back to the airport. It was a feint. The call immediately came that the Libyan leader wanted to see Arafat, so my driver drove me at 100mph to join him at Gadaffi's headquarters.

Gadaffi, in his finest robes, greeted Arafat then turned and noticed me. 'Mary,' he asked (he has never been able to pronounce my name), 'what are you doing here?' It was as if I had wandered in off the street.

'She's with me,' Arafat said proudly, as though we were at a London film premiere. He then went on to lie outrageously about the state of my nose, which at the time was on the wrong side of my face.

Arafat told Gadaffi the Israelis had broken it. The truth was that Palestinian demonstrators had thrown a rock through the window of my car when I was posing as a Jewish settler on a reporting assignment.

Sometimes our encounters were even more surreal. When Madeleine Albright was Bill Clinton's secretary of state, more than a decade after the bombing of Bab al-Aziziya, Gadaffi asked me at the end of an interview if I could get a message to her.

I thought I had a journalistic coup: the mad dog of the Middle East bidding for peace with Washington. Instead, he told me he loved 'Madeleine'. He watched her every appearance on television, and he was annoyed that sometimes the cameras did not show her full face. The fact that, in her sixties, she was five years older than him and no longer a beauty seemed of no importance. Could I get her special phone number for him, preferably for the phone next to her bed? Would I also communicate to her that if she felt the same as he did, she should wear green in her next television appearance?

Albright appears to have been replaced since by a younger edition. An album of cut-out photographs of Condoleezza Rice, George W Bush's national security adviser and secretary of state, was found in one of Gadaffi's underground salons last week. In 2007 he told an interviewer on Al Jazeera television how much he liked her: 'Leezza, Leezza, Leezza – I love her very much. I admire her and am proud of her because she's a black woman of African origin.'

For years, he seemed to be starring in his own movie. I never saw him in the same outfit twice. He was a bedouin tribesman, a colonel and a self-styled revolutionary. He was an Arab and an African, a nationalist and a socialist, a Muslim, a poet and a would-be 'philosopher king' and he had outfits for every role. His military uniforms had more medals than a Latin American generalissimo, and yet he had never fought a war until this year.

Beneath the ludicrous military caps his eyes were dark; they never revealed any emotion other than a canniness, as if a reptile within was always plotting. For his own people he was, in their words, 'the leader'. He preferred 'supreme guide' and fancied himself their mentor, patriarch and uncle.

It was the people, though, who felt the vicious side of his character, and where the lack of pity in those eyes mattered most. He was feared and hated. He would stop at nothing to maintain power.

Gadaffi made much of his birth in 1942 into an illiterate bedouin family in the desert near Sirte, the coastal town where his diehard supporters have been fighting their final battle. But his world view seems to have been shaped during his schooldays by revolutionary upheavals in the Arab world, principally Colonel Gamal Abdel Nasser's seizure of power in Egypt.

He joined the army as the path out of poverty and seized power in 1969 in a coup similar to Nasser's: the virtually bloodless unseating of a weak king by young officers from whom Gadaffi emerged as the most prominent and then dictator.

For a while he was fairly normal. I once thumbed through an old photo album put together by one of his former confidants, which showed Gadaffi on a building site in a pork-pie hat and shorts, looking at an architect's drawing. 'He was always a little strange, but he was easy with us, like a normal person. He changed greatly,' the friend said.

He posed as a tribesman who wanted only the simple life, but Libya under Gadaffi degenerated into a corrupt state that enriched his family and hangers on. He made himself colonel, then abolished all military ranks above that. Despite all his talk of rule by the people for the people, it soon became clear there was only one colonel in Libya – and only one voice, among 6m, that really mattered.

Increasingly unchallenged, he gradually created an unreal world in Libya that mirrored his own fascinations. Grandiose projects never worked. All that remains of his $20 billion man-made river are oversized pipes scattered by the sides of roads or standing bizarrely at the centre of roundabouts in mute testimony to his folly.

He could afford it. Libya had valuable oil on the doorstep of European markets. Until the events of this year it was earning about $47 billion a year from exports – and Gadaffi used the wealth and influence it brought to keep potential enemies at bay and the country under firm control.

Much of the oil wealth was squandered, stolen or embezzled. Gadaffi and his six sons, increasingly important props for his one-man regime, became immensely rich.

He was an impossible interviewee in many ways. When I last talked to him during this year's uprising, I asked who was giving the army orders. He looked puzzled and said, 'But there is no army in Libya!' This at a time that Libyan soldiers were shooting unarmed demonstrators in the streets of Benghazi, Misrata and Tripoli.

He said he would not have to step down as he held no government position, and chided me for not understanding the Libyan
system of rule. In 1977, he had invented the 'jamahiriya' or state of
the masses, in which the nation is supposedly governed by the
people through local councils. In reality, it was a parallel power
base that he, his relatives and tribal allies controlled.

His ego knew no bounds. He fancied himself a philosopher,
setting out his ideas in a 'green book' filled with banalities such as,
'A man is male, and a woman is female'. Every Libyan school child
had to study the pocket-sized tome.

The green book was based on his 'third universal theory', which,
an aide once told me admiringly, Gadaffi came up with after lying
in a darkened room for weeks with a blanket over his head. When
Tony Blair's new Labour announced the 'third way', Gadaffi claimed
it vindicated his theory and even threatened to sue for
plagiarism.

Libya's population was small in comparison with countries such
as Egypt, but despite its riches its people struggled and infrastructure fell apart. It was impossible to imagine Libya as a wealthy oil
country. Streets were potholed, cheap brick housing lined the
highways.

Libyans went abroad for good healthcare, the wealthy to Europe
or America, the middle class next door to Tunisia and only the
poor attended Libyan hospitals. Education was among the worst
in the Arab world. Gadaffi banned the study of English, pointedly
keeping his people isolated from the wider world.

For Gadaffi, the great disappointment was that he never graduated to the bigger stage. He was desperate for international recognition. No matter how much he jumped up and down like a child,
the great powers did not consider Libya important enough – stra-
tegically or militarily – to worry too much about him, at least at
first. So he took to violence to get attention. He made Libya into an
isolated, pariah state by spending millions backing anti-western
terrorist groups, part of his revolutionary mission to change the
world.

His support was as indiscriminate as it was lavish. He funded and armed the Provisional IRA, but when Ulster Protestant paramilitaries came begging, he gave them money too. His largesse went to the Red Brigades in Italy, and Eta in Spain, to Shining Path in Peru and the Sword of Islam in the Philippines.

European capitals were bombed. Assassination squads were sent around the world, targeting Libyan dissidents whom Gadaffi labelled 'stray dogs'. There was no escape; one exile was gunned down at his grocery store in west London.

But it was when Gadaffi turned his murderous attentions directly to the United States, sending agents to bomb the nightclub in Berlin packed with American servicemen in 1986, that Washington and its allies drew the line.

He was not even very good with his few misguided supporters. He put on an Alice in Wonderland 'victory party' after the 1986 US bombing of Libya. Western peaceniks watched from stands erected in the ruins of Bab al-Aziziya as cute children marched by with examples of their hobbies. Then came the Libyan boy scouts carrying live chickens and a few live rabbits.

They appeared to be showing how well they cared for animals – until they suddenly threw them to the ground, disembowelled them with their bare hands and ate chunks of the still-quivering flesh. The peaceniks ran from the stands, screaming.

Gadaffi seemed ever more eccentric. After another interview, I went back to my hotel to be awakened in the middle of the night by a knock at the door. Standing in the doorway were a tall woman and a short Libyan man. She was wearing a full nurse's uniform, complete with hat. Her little companion came up to her hip.

He announced that Gadaffi had thought I looked tired in the interview and had sent his personal nurse. She pulled out what looked to my sleepy eyes like the largest hypodermic needle I had ever seen, and said: 'I Bulgarian. I take blood?'

I said no, I was exhausted, she could do that tomorrow. It was never healthy to give an outright refusal in Gadaffi's Libya. She insisted – 'Just a little blood' – obviously under strict orders. I said:

'Okay, but I know myself and if you take my blood I will definitely be too tired to interview the leader tomorrow.' They conferred, and we agreed she could come by in the afternoon.

I decided to catch the first plane out of Tripoli – to anywhere. But when I went downstairs to check out, I found that reception was under orders to keep my passport.

Luckily, Arafat was in town again and was seeing Gadaffi. Members of Force 17, Arafat's elite bodyguard, had decided to have a coffee in the hotel while they waited for him. When they walked into the lobby, they saw me in distress.

They asked what was the matter, and wrested my passport back after a fierce argument. Driving me to the airport, they saw me safely on to the plane.

The next time I went to Libya I was nervous; but Gadaffi started the interview by practically slapping his leg and laughing: 'Remember the time I tried to take your blood?'

The Lockerbie bombing in 1988 succeeded in winning the attention Gadaffi craved, but it led to tougher international sanctions and ostracism.

Libya was cast into outer darkness for more than a decade. Then came the 9/11 attacks in 2001 and with them, an opportunity. The Americans' subsequent overthrow of Saddam Hussein in 2003 spooked Gadaffi.

In a spectacular volte-face, the Libyan leader came over to the West. Oil companies returned to the desert. His comeback was crowned in 2009 by his first address to the UN general assembly.

He admitted no fault for the terrors of the past, and oppression at home continued. The Libyans were never fooled. As younger generations across the Arab world rose in search of their rights this year, young Libyans decided to fight too.

His rehabilitation has, with hindsight, been rescinded by Europe and America over the past six months as his army has ruthlessly killed civilians to defend his regime. If captured he will now face an international indictment for war crimes. Or will the Libyans mete out their own justice?

'My people love me,' he said in the last interview I had with him
this year.

Did he really believe that? I looked into his eyes, trying to read
him, and saw not a spark of duplicity showing. Yet he must have
known his world was crumbling.

He chose the site of the interview cannily, appearing for the only
time I met him above ground – in a fish restaurant of all places. It
was puzzling until I realised the backdrop to the huge windows
was Tripoli's distinctive port, which would counter rumours that
he had fled the country.

Where is he now? The streets I drove through to Bab al-Aziziya
25 years ago are littered with spent bullet cases, broken glass and
burnt cars. The walls are daubed with cartoon caricatures of
Gadaffi with exaggerated permed hair. The Libyan leader is on the
run, with a bounty of $2 million on his head. But he remains a
showman. Will his exit be as dramatic as his entrance that night
when he told me: 'I am Gadaffi'?

Killing rooms plot bloody retreat
of troops loyal to Tyrant Jr

4 September 2011

**Libya's civilian death toll rises as Khamis Gadaffi's withdrawing forces
continue their murderous brutality in makeshift prisons.**

The four men murdered in a trailer must have felt they were on the
verge of freedom after months in a makeshift prison on an abandoned construction site. Instead, troops led by Khamis Gadaffi, the
Libyan leader's youngest son, shot them in a final act of revenge
before fleeing as rebel forces rolled in to Tripoli.

The men, one of them a doctor from Misrata, had been held with
about 80 other prisoners in the southern suburb of Qasr al-Ghashir.

Local residents only learnt of their plight on 24 August when they found emaciated strangers wandering around their farms.

They had no idea that Bab al-Aziziya, the Tripoli headquarters of Muammar Gadaffi, had fallen the day before after a fierce battle with rebel troops.

'The poor guys – some of them were injured, some had bare feet,' said Amr Ghinewa, 42, a farmer. 'I shouted at them, "Who are you?" We knew the soldiers were living there, but we did not know about the prisoners.'

The men begged for help for two prisoners who had been shot but were still alive. Ghinewa said an ambulance raced the wounded men to hospital, but they died.

He found a harrowing scene at the construction site, which had been used by the Khamis brigade as an unofficial barracks. The men had been imprisoned in cinderblock cells in a metal-sided storage hangar that was stiflingly hot and had no electricity or water. Last week, tangled blankets and discarded jeans were all that remained in the 10 x 4 foot cells.

In the killing room, a small bedroom with two single beds in a temporary building, dried blood remained on the carpet and floor. A mobile phone video taken by the resident who found them documented the full horror. A balding man, said to be Dr Ali Durati, from Misrata, lay in a grey T-shirt slumped against one bed, blood dripping down the side of his head. His family said he had been driving an ambulance with an emergency case when he was captured at a Gadaffi checkpoint. Another body lay in a corner at the end of the bed.

Two more men, one in a red Puma T-shirt and a second in a T-shirt and navy blue tracksuit bottoms, lay together, slumped against a mattress upended by the wall, both shot in the chest. Thirteen spent casings from AK-47 bullets littered the floor.

The identity of their killers was clear. Stacks of badges from the 32nd Brigade, run by Khamis, along with receipts documenting the delivery of 10 flak jackets, other military hardware and food, were abandoned.

Scenes such as this, showing the murderous brutality of withdrawing Gadaffi forces, brought home the ordeal the Libyan revolution has become for many civilians and rebel fighters.

At the Khamis brigade's Yarmouk barracks, huge craters and burnt, flattened buildings mark the Nato bombings that began in February. The troops seem to have retreated to civilian buildings and left behind a small warehouse littered with the charred corpses of at least 50 prisoners.

Construction sites, abandoned when the war began, seem to have been their preferred next stop. They were perfect places to hide, with ready-made living quarters, office equipment, coffee makers and a civilian veneer to fool Nato planes.

At the New Palace Construction Company in southern Tripoli, stores of weapons have been left behind, some burnt by the Khamis brigade as they retreated. Last week, rebels picked through the barrels of 106mm cannon and Kalashnikovs, loading what they salvaged on to pick-up trucks heading for Sirte, Gadaffi's home town.

They left to local residents their more gruesome finds. The body of one man lay on the floor of a cramped office in a temporary building, shot several times in the chest and stashed under a mattress.

Another four men who had been executed were lined up along the wall of a warehouse, blindfolded. 'It was horrible,' said Mohammed Haddar, a 42-year-old neighbour. 'The bodies had been raked by bullets.'

All four were from Misrata, he said. He recognised one: a doctor aged about 60 who had made a forced television confession. The others were younger.

Other prisons were scenes of inhumanity.

'I cannot show you my body,' said Ibrahim al-Aghi, 46, an engineer thrown in to the infamous Abu Salim jail for organising a network of opposition cells in Tripoli.

His face still swollen and his eyes red, he said he was beaten daily and, when he refused to talk, hung from a tree and beaten with cables and pipes by passing prison guards. They threw sea water into his wounds to revive him when he passed out.

In Ain Zahra, jail to hundreds of political prisoners liberated last week, rebel soldiers still paced the narrow, dark corridors, singing 'Allahu akbar' (God is greatest), trying to persuade prisoners they believed were held in underground cells that they were saviours, not Gadaffi's men.

'We were beaten from the moment we were arrested at the border crossing,' said Alla'a Abdullah, 40, who had been held there with his two brothers since February. 'I was hit on the head with a gun, wood and cables.'

He said guards would come on shift drunk and take prisoners out of their cells to beat them. Others dressed prisoners as women and raped them. It was difficult to doubt his story; on one walkway four new bras lay abandoned, two purple and two red. Abdullah lost 3½ stone in prison.

As the rebel forces liberated more neighbourhoods, the National Transitional Council (NTC), the acting government, sought to bring security to the capital. Tripoli is awash with guns, and much of the city is still without water or reliable electricity. The euphoria of victory is fragile, as so far the only security is enforced by neighbourhood watch checkpoints manned by untrained youths, some as young as 12.

The NTC said it would move to Tripoli this week.

Toxic tyrant's chemical cavern

AL-AJAYLAT

11 September 2011

Chilling new evidence of the brutality of Colonel Gadaffi has emerged among the trampled uniforms at a military base in Libya.

At first sight, the abandoned military base in western Libya appeared to be empty. Army trucks had been left with their doors gaping open in a flat wasteland of red sand and sparse desert grasses.

There were no bodies to be seen in the camp outside Al-Ajaylat, 50 miles west of Tripoli – just uniforms that lay crumpled by the sides of the dirt roadways, as if the soldiers who were stationed here had stripped and fled.

The first warehouse we came to, however, was full – crammed with thousands of wooden crates and boxes piled up to the tin ceiling of a football-pitch-sized cavern. And the contents spilling on to the concrete floor revealed that this was a chemical and biological warfare facility.

I opened some green metal tins in the crates to find black rubber-rimmed gas masks, wrapped in clear plastic. Other crates contained yellow rubber 'NBC' suits with grey boots attached – protection against nuclear, biological and chemical weapons. Cardboard boxes of spare filters marked 'Made in Iran' rose to the roof.

In another warehouse were hundreds of flame-throwers with spare fuel canisters, napalm, detonators for explosives, crates of assault rifles, thousands of anti-personnel and anti-tank mines and countless boxed vials of atropine, an antidote to nerve gas.

The most worrying discovery was in a corner of a third warehouse. A dark, malodorous liquid leaked out of metal barrels. I held my breath, then tentatively snatched a mouthful of air, thinking of the gas masks in the first warehouse – should I get one? There was no telling what was in the barrels other than that it was corrosive; one was holed from inside. Cleared of dust, the label revealed only a skull and crossbones and the word 'poisonous' in Cyrillic script.

Outside, ambulances had been left at skewed angles, including one that seemed to have crashed into a eucalyptus tree. Their interiors were observation chambers designed to test victims of exposure to radiation or chemicals.

Military experts who viewed the contents of the warehouses said they believed that the equipment had defensive and offensive purposes. 'An army uses this stuff to protect its troops from an attack by the enemy, or to protect its troops when they are launching an attack,' a British military expert said.

'The equipment would be imperative in both defensive actions and offensive actions.'

Much of the material in the warehouses was outdated but there was evidence that Colonel Muammar Gadaffi, the fugitive Libyan leader ousted by the rebels last month, had not forgotten his stash.

Documents found in a single-storey office building near the camp entrance revealed that the Libyan defence ministry ordered that 2,000 Czech gas masks and 2,000 chemical protection suits be sent on 26 July from the base to Al-Jufrah, a town in the south still under Gadaffi's control.

Another document recorded shipments to Sirte – Gadaffi's home town on the coast, which was besieged last week by rebel forces – between April and June, including 7,500 gas masks, decontamination powder and liquid, napalm and flame-throwers.

The discovery increased fears that a cornered Gadaffi might be tempted to resort to unconventional weapons, although most observers believe he no longer has the capability to launch them.

From the start of its military intervention in Libya, Nato has set up early warning systems against such a contingency, according to Noman Benotman, a senior analyst at the Quilliam Foundation, a London think tank.

Benotman, the former head of an anti-Gadaffi Islamist insurgent group, said the dictator's next move, as the rebel forces close in, was hard to predict. 'Now there are no rules, no red lines,' he said.

The Pentagon and an international monitoring organisation have indicated that Gadaffi's remaining stockpiles are secure, but it is known that more than nine tons of mustard gas remains in Libya. Some of it may be in bases still controlled by Gadaffi loyalists.

There is less of it than there would have been just a few years ago. Gadaffi agreed to dismantle his weapons of mass destruction in 2003 in return for a rapprochement with the West. To demonstrate his commitment, he ordered that 3,300 bombs that could have been used to drop chemical weapons be bulldozed. But the stockpiles of mustard gas have taken longer to eliminate.

An American embassy cable in November 2009, released by WikiLeaks, suggested that Libya was acting more slowly than it had agreed in the hope of securing greater rewards for its co-operation. As a result, 9½ tons of the poison gas was still in Libya when the uprising against Gadaffi began in February, according to the Organisation for the Prohibition of Chemical Weapons, a body that works closely with the United Nations.

The spread of weapons through Libya has become a significant concern. Mortar shells, mines and even missiles have been abandoned by Gadaffi's fleeing forces at sites the rebels have failed to secure.

Desert storm flushes Gadaffi from oasis of dictator chic

JUFRA

25 September 2011

Our reporter joins a convoy rolling south in search of the colonel – and drives into a ferocious ambush from Gadaffi's protectors.

The shattering of the calm of an empty road in the desert of southern Libya was astonishingly quick. An explosion burst on the rocks near a convoy of anti-Gadaffi forces, sending up a spray of sand with a deafening boom that echoed off the mountains around us.

Bullets zipped by with the buzz of hornets, making tiny puffs in the dust when they hit.

Flashes of light bursting in the red bluffs rising 100 yards from the road revealed the gunmen's positions, but the only sound I could hear was the roar of return fire.

We had left Tripoli in pursuit of Muammar Gadaffi, the fugitive Libyan leader. Now, despite an agreement with the elders of the desert town of Sukna, we were being ambushed by Gadaffi's protectors just outside the town.

Another rocket-propelled grenade (RPG) hit the side of the road and my car skewed to a halt. Abduladiem Majdub, one of the convoy's commanders, thrust a Beretta pistol at me from the front seat and shouted: 'Take this. If they overrun us, can you use it?'

I nodded and jumped out, running doubled-over to avoid bullets, and threw myself down behind a sand dune. Then I decided it was too low and crawled to a rock. I had a pistol, a notebook and a pen.

My main goal was to avoid distracting the fighters who might think they had to protect me. This was a fight for survival. They regrouped and fired 14.5mm anti-aircraft shells horizontally into the mountains, then launched four Grad missiles.

One fighter was hit in the arm and carried off by his comrades before I could see his face. Then the firing from across a moon-scape of rocks stopped and the anti-Gadaffi forces raced towards the source.

I followed them to a small camp under a thorn tree. A green army jacket lay abandoned next to tin tea pots, cans of sardines and tomato paste, seven onions and two packs of pasta. About 50 yards further on, new RPGs lay glinting in the sun at the rim of a gulley. A large machinegun stood on its spindly legs with a rope of heavy-calibre bullets threaded through its barrel. Kalashnikov rifles lay nearby in neat stacks.

Our attackers had evidently dropped everything and run for their lives from the 150 fighters in our convoy.

The men, from Tripoli and Gharyan, in northwest Libya, had been thrown together at the last minute from four 'katibas', or brigades, when a tip came into the capital that Gadaffi was holed up in one of his farmhouses in the south.

These men had driven into enemy territory – the Sahara, where tribes and towns stood loyal to the dictator born to a Bedouin herder. Three ambulances joined the convoy.

At 10am on Tuesday we stopped at a sign saying 'Welcome to Jufra', the central region south of Sirte. The rebels fired off guns to make sure they were working, or just to entertain themselves, and a falling bullet struck me on the shoulder, stinging like a bee.

Later that day we headed up a narrow road through an oasis where a spotter claimed to have seen Gadaffi at a farmhouse. The Gadaffi hunters, pointing Kalashnikovs out of the car windows, twitched at the only sign of movement, a gazelle leaping away among the trees.

This place was a far cry from the dusty roads and cinderblock homes we had passed on the 500-mile journey south from Tripoli. We passed a man-made lake, then came to a long drive leading to a walled compound. The men erupted out of their trucks, guns at the ready, and raced through a gate in the wall, fanning out to search low, modern buildings gleaming white in the setting sun.

The huge swimming pool was empty. 'He is not here,' said Majdub, the 39-year-old organiser of the convoy, before collapsing exhausted on one of the dictator's comfortable beds. 'He is running every day. This is his home. Choose a bedroom.'

The compound contained twin houses – one for Gadaffi, the other for Safia, his wife – each with buttermilk-coloured sofas and prints of desert scenes on the walls. Smaller houses in the compound were for guards and workers.

Abubudellah Hamruni, a second commander of the convoy, drove off without even getting out of his car. He was still nursing a leg shattered during the uprising by a large-calibre bullet and now pinned by an external steel frame.

Frustrated to find Gadaffi not at home, Hamruni began another hunt, for the gazelles he had seen in the date palms. He shot five for dinner, a minor but satisfying victory: the dictator allowed no one but family to hunt his game.

I slept under the stars on an Oriental carpet dragged out of the house. Documents found in one of the outbuildings showed that Gadaffi spent a small fortune on these homes and gardens, although he visited only a few times a year.

A rebel who had never seen a flush lavatory marvelled at a huge marble bathroom. 'Look at this five-star place,' said Ibrahim Gashir, 26, a dental assistant turned fighter. 'He had everything and we had nothing.'

By morning, new intelligence had arrived that Gadaffi was in a second house, one they had not known about, 50 miles to the south.

The route took us through Sukna, the first big town in the Jufra region. The convoy stopped at a checkpoint as four of the town's elders emerged. Elsewhere in Libya, at Bani Walid and Sirte – where heavy fighting was reported yesterday – the anti-Gadaffi forces had tried to negotiate their way in. But this convoy, hot on their quarry's trail, was in a hurry.

The elders, dressed in white robes, listened nervously to guarantees that if Sukna surrendered, nobody would be hurt. Hamruni and Majdub, the convoy's leaders, assured them that water and electricity, which had been cut off three months earlier, would be restored.

'I think it will be OK,' Hamruni said as he watched them return down the road to Sukna. 'I made it clear if they break their word, their city is finished.'

Meanwhile, the rebels took prisoners from cars coming out of the town. A former soldier who would not speak was driven into the desert and made to run at speed in the hot sun, guns trained on his back. He suddenly became helpful.

It was late afternoon when the elders returned and sat in a tent with the convoy's leaders.

'I have brought the message to Sukna and we have an agreement that you can enter peacefully,' said Mohamed Bashir Ibrahim, 67. 'We can guarantee our families will stay in their homes, but we cannot guarantee any of the Gadaffi forces will not attack you.'

Hamruni replied: 'You take care of your families, we will take care of the [military].'

It soon became clear that the agreement had not been unanimous. The convoy ventured down a dirt road just outside town to check the flanks and drove right into the ambush.

Moving on afterwards, the rebels discovered Sukna's secret. Green-painted crates, some of them 20ft long and piled 6ft high, lined a so-called 'valley of the dam' for mile after mile close by. It was the most extensive weapons store anyone had seen.

There were rocket launchers and missiles, anti-aircraft guns, rocket-propelled grenades and innumerable assault rifles and machineguns. Gadaffi's forces had apparently gambled that Nato would not risk bombing this place for fear of fracturing the large concrete dam looming over the valley.

Suddenly word came through that Sukna had surrendered. In the central square, men were celebrating, sweating in the heat and waving red, black and green flags. Gadaffi posters and flags were scattered on the ground.

'Freedom! We can taste it! Finally, we are with the rest of our Libya,' shouted a man who reached into the car to shake everyone's hand. Was he genuine? Was anyone?

Night fell as we drove down another deserted road from which we could see huge fires burning in the hills. Gadaffi's army had launched missiles on the next town, called Hun, razing houses on the outskirts. Nonetheless, the convoy was driving into a final spasm of resistance.

In the end, only a few hardliners were prepared to fight the men Hamruni and Majdub sent in to free the town. We found the inhabitants tired after months of deprivation.

Atik Mohamed, 62, who described himself as a retired army

officer, met the convoy in Hun's central square, where men were firing off guns and waving flags.

'We are happy to see you,' Mohamed said. 'We have been cooking with wood, like our grandparents.'

Young men described more arduous ordeals. Hamza Taweela, 26, said the security forces had ruled with impunity in the last month. He had been arrested returning from a meal during Ramadan, the holy month.

'They fired in the air over us, then threw us on the ground and handcuffed us and blindfolded us,' said Taweela, an engineer. 'They took us to the station and beat us on our backs.'

He never knew what he was accused of. 'They kept telling me I was a rat [Gadaffi's word for rebel]', he said. 'They made us chant, 'God, Muammar [Gadaffi], Libya, it's enough'.'

Another captive, General Sa'ad Suweidi, from Sebha, who had been second-in-command in Hun, said: 'At first, we did not believe that the rebels had captured the towns on the coast.

'My forces here were huge. I had 40,000 men. We didn't think they could ever defeat us,' he said, still wearing his uniform as he sat in the back seat of a Toyota from the convoy. 'But my men – they began slipping away ... I thought the rebels would cut my throat.'

The taking of the two towns meant that the road was now clear to the second Gadaffi house – a white villa with a marble fountain. This was far more ostentatious than the oasis farmhouse, reflecting the 'dictator chic' of the Gadaffi family's homes in Tripoli, with gold-framed mirrors and faux Louis XVI furniture on plush carpets and an enormous king-sized bed in an ornate bedroom.

The house had been used recently: in the kitchen, a box of dates had been chopped open. Cold tea stood in tin pots. But Gadaffi was not in residence and the steam was going out of the chase. The consolation was the capture of tons of weapons and the chance to fire into the sky for hours.

The taking of Sukna and Hun was also celebrated in Tripoli by the new government. With the Jufra region taken, Gadaffi's possible hiding places had diminished. This weekend fresh intelligence came that he might be heading for a second country, en route to a third.

'I am disappointed, of course I wanted to catch him,' said Majdub. 'Maybe someone else will. The point is, we will find him and he will face justice.'

Brutal retribution

23 October 2011

Marie Colvin, John Cantlie, John Follain, Michael Smith,
James Foley, Hala Jaber and Sara Hashash

He called his enemies rats. Yet it was Muammar Gadaffi who was cornered in a sewer pipe, his cruel dictatorship of Libya ending in ignominy and death.

There was always something weird about Sirte, a slice of faux Beverly Hills in the middle of nowhere. Many houses were opulent, with 60-inch plasma television sets on the walls and multi-car garages. The roads were neat and the hedgerows perfectly trimmed, walls whitewashed and the shopfronts new. Everything was clean, almost sterile, unlike the rest of Libya with its crazy old cars, dirt, corner shops and cafés.

Hated by his own people, Colonel Muammar Gadaffi had turned to Africans to inhabit this city of his dreams. Posters around the ring road proclaimed that 'Arab space and African space are one' and 'Africa is progress'. Gadaffi hosted an Organisation of African Unity summit there and proposed it as the capital of a pan-African union.

It was just a grimy coastal village when he was born nearby in 1942; and it is now once again a ruin, destroyed street by whitewashed street in the dictator's last stand, which culminated on

Thursday in the world's first YouTube lynching of a tyrant, a lethal happy-slapping of global significance.

The many mobile phone videos posted on the internet tell the final story: the groggy, bleeding despot about to succumb to the howling mob around him. So do the bodies – nearly 100 of them scattered among the debris of his escape convoy on the western highway out of Sirte and in surrounding fields. Burnt, blown up, chopped up by gunfire, shot in the head, most are black Africans. One was decapitated, his dreadlocked head next to his body. They were loyal in extremis to Sirte's notorious son.

The frustrating paradox of the grisly filmed images is that they are inconclusive. Who fired the fatal shot that left Gadaffi with a bullet in his brain? Journalists have flooded into Sirte and other coastal cities to try to winnow truth from the many contradictory claims made by the men caught up in that last moment of frenzy – and by rival factions within the rebel forces.

None accepts the official version that the deposed Libyan leader was shot in crossfire as he was taken alive from the scene by ambulance – any more than they bothered even to register the Nato bromide that the air attack that halted Gadaffi's escape was ordered because his convoy threatened the civilian population. But what did happen?

One clue came yesterday from a rebel commander who confessed anonymously to a Reuters news agency reporter: 'We wanted to keep him alive, but the young guys – things went out of control.'

Though few knew it at the time, the net began closing on Gadaffi on 16 September when rebels pushed into Sirte from the west of the city. For three days they met fierce resistance as regime loyalists massed against them.

Venturing up to the front line, John Cantlie, a photo-journalist who contributes to *The Sunday Times*, found a nightmarish scene. The rebels would reverse up the main street in their gun trucks and let rip, but at about 5pm each day the loyalists moved their best men to the front and the rebel casualties would soar.

Foreign photographers and reporters took to calling that time 'death o'clock'. After three days, with 60 dead and 500 wounded, the rebels pulled back to tend their wounds and reconsider.

Despite the fierceness of the resistance, none thought Gadaffi himself was hiding in the city. Everyone suspected that his fifth son, Mutassim, was leading the resistance in Sirte. His name was heard on radio transmissions.

'We hear them on the radio saying Mutassim this, Mutassim that,' said Mustafa Jalil, the commander of the rebel katiba (brigade), at the time. 'I am sure he is inside. But as for Gadaffi? Who knows. He is like a mouse, a rat. He has run and hidden underground somewhere far away.'

When rebels twice raided the western outskirts of Sirte they arrested groups of Mauritanian immigrants, young men with no passports and no ID.

'These are fighters for Gadaffi!' said one rebel as they conducted basic questioning. 'These men all say they work on the same farm, yet they know nothing about farming and three of them admit to owning a Kalashnikov.'

Yet British military sources said the colonel was believed to have fled to a third country after the fall of Tripoli in August. Western diplomats thought he was on the run in the vast desert of southern Libya, bribing locals to give him refuge. Fierce armed resistance in Bani Walid, a desert town that is home to tribes loyal to Gadaffi, strengthened suspicions that he was hiding there. Sirte, by contrast, seemed too obvious a place to hide.

Two weeks ago, Cantlie was again caught up in the chaos of Sirte at the end of a day's fighting. He had hitched a ride in a pick-up truck inching through a jam of cars and gun-laden vehicles when a rebel clinging to the side yelled: 'Gadaffi! Big hair! Here!'

The rebel gestured to illustrate Gadaffi's long hair – but suddenly the truck hit the splintered casing of a missile, bursting two tyres. 'We need new car. Please get out,' said one of the rebels. What about Gadaffi? 'It is our mistake, he is not here.'

But he was. It is now known that Gadaffi had made Sirte a fortress over the years and stockpiled weapons and ammunition in houses in the city and in the desert outside – where the rebels found some of them.

'Gadaffi knows Nato will hit his bunkers, so he tells his soldiers to empty the bunkers and spread the weapons across the desert so they are safe,' one rebel said. 'It makes life easier for us!'

Details of Gadaffi's weeks in Sirte came from Mansour Daou, one of his top aides, who was caught with him on Thursday but survived thanks to the intervention of Taieb Mohammed Imbais, a rebel brigade leader. Imbais told *Le Figaro*, the French newspaper: 'Daou told me that Gadaffi had sought refuge in Sirte when Tripoli fell, in August.

'He thought he was safe in his tribe. Then when the siege started, it got harder. Gadaffi lived in private homes which had been abandoned. He changed house every day to avoid betrayals and the Nato bombings. He was very discreet. Gadaffi didn't command the battles.

'It was Mutassim who gave the orders. On Wednesday it became untenable. The rebels were very close and Mutassim was hit by a bullet in the foot. He told me he had then taken all the petrol there was left and that they had tried to flee.'

The endgame had come quickly. At the beginning of October, Mutassim's defences were still secure despite suicidal onslaughts by rebel brigades from Misrata, the city between Sirte and Tripoli that took the heaviest pounding from Gadaffi's forces in the early months of the civil war.

From the top of the Sirte hotel, held by rebels, the brave or foolhardy could look out as sniper bullets and rockets whistled all around. The rebels to the east were pinned down. So were rebels to the south. It seemed like a stalemate could last until the end of the year. And still nobody had a clue that Gadaffi was in the city.

It all changed after a Nato bombing assault on 8 October, when the ground did not stop shaking all night. Next morning the rebels pushed forwards expecting the usual fierce resistance. There was none.

In the space of 36 hours rebels surged into the city from the south and east and met at an intersection just south of District Two, a middle-class neighbourhood of spacious houses in the western part of Sirte. District Two was flooded in knee-deep water, perhaps from a bomb or perhaps deliberately. It was to become Sirte's final stand.

For four days the Misratan rebels flattened the area with everything they had, bringing their tanks and heavy guns into the city and blazing away at every building standing between their own positions and the sea.

More and more Gadaffi fighters surrendered, finally conceding the hopelessness of the situation as their city was demolished around them.

Gadaffi, who sometimes styled himself 'king of kings', appears to have spent his final nights in the one-storey home of a loyalist. Hanging on one of the walls inside yesterday was a signed photograph of the dictator in naval uniform. A neighbour said: 'We knew he stayed there. His guards would sleep outside.'

Piles of new army green uniforms littered the floor of one sitting room, along with mattresses for about a dozen men.

Early on Thursday at another house in District Two, Jibril Abu Sharaf, one of the surviving defenders, was preparing breakfast. 'I was cooking for the other guys when all of a sudden they came in and said, "Come on, we're leaving",' he told Reuters later while in custody. 'I got in a civilian car and joined the end of the convoy. We tried to escape along the coast road. But we came under heavy fire so we tried another way.'

Nato planes, including RAF Tornados, had spotted the breakout. Colonel Thierry Burkhard, a spokesman for the French defence ministry, takes up the story: 'There was a presence over Sirte. We were notified about a convoy with heavy armament.'

An American Predator drone fired the first missile. 'Then a patrol made up of one Mirage 2000D and one Mirage F1CR

attacked the convoy. Both were from the base at La Sude in Crete.
I believe they left the base at dawn,' Burkhard said.

'The Mirage 2000D dropped a 250 kilogramme, laser-guided
GBU bomb on the convoy. The F1CR monitored the situation. We
were not aiming at Gadaffi's vehicle because we didn't even know
he was in the convoy. We only found out afterwards that he was
there. We don't know whether he was injured by the Nato strikes.'

According to Nato sources, the convoy contained at least 75
vehicles, suggesting it was about half a mile long. It is a mystery
how so many had been hidden in District Two, an area only about
1,000 yards by 500, and had survived the rebel shelling.

The huge convoy – with Gadaffi was at its centre – dashed west
out of the city at about 8am and tried to break through rebel lines.
The Predator strike destroyed 11 vehicles, burning many of the
occupants alive. Jibril recalled: 'Then the only thing I saw was dead
bodies all around, dust and debris. It went dark.'

The convoy split up and Gadaffi's core group of about 20 vehicles was heading southwest at high speed on the main highway.
There are few roads in the area; they were easily spotted and hit by
the Mirage's bomb. Gadaffi survived the huge blast with Mansour
Daou and Abu-Bakr Yunis Jabr, minister of defence in the old
regime, and a handful of others. They appear to have staggered
through a line of trees beside the highway and taken refuge in a
concrete drainage culvert beneath it.

'I was with Gadaffi and Yunis and about four volunteer soldiers,'
Daou said. Wounded in the back by the shell blast, he passed out
and did not witness the final scenes of the 42-year dictatorship.

At first. Ahmed Al-Ghazal and his rebel team drove right by. 'We
didn't see anyone under the road, so we drove past them,' Ghazal
said. 'We only stopped when someone from a sand berm that was
next to the culvert started shooting at us.'

Ghazal, a slight 21-year-old who ran a kitchen supply shop in
Misrata before the war, was with other members of the Gheran
brigade in a 'technical', a pick-up truck with an anti-aircraft gun in
the back. They leapt out and – unable to bear down with their

heavy gun – fought back with Kalashnikovs. The fighting was suddenly fierce.

One of the enemy fighters dressed in civilian clothes began screaming, 'My leg is broken, I can't help "sayeedi". I can't help the leader.'

Sayeedi is an Arabic word for the respected one. Ghazal and his men thought it must be a senior military officer or one of Gadaffi's regime officials. 'It didn't even occur to us that there would be any Gadaffi there, much less Muammar Gadaffi,' he said.

'Suddenly, Gadaffi was in front of me, half in the tunnel, half out of the tunnel,' Ghazal said. 'I threw away my Kalashnikov and jumped on him. I thought maybe he will disappear or something. I was so shocked I was looking at Gadaffi in person for the first time in my life.'

Omar Shaibani, the 37-year-old businessman turned soldier who leads the Ghiran militia, said that although Gadaffi was heavily armed when his militiamen dragged him out of the culvert, he did not fire a shot despite his calls for Libyans to fight to the death for their leader.

The most striking of his guns was a gold pistol. 'This gold pistol, his private weapon, was in his waistband, fully loaded,' Shaibani said last night. It was inscribed 'Muammar Gadaffi', and on one side had an engraving of his green flag, and in Arabic script the saying, 'The sun never sets on the revolution.'

Shaibani said: 'The fact that Gadaffi had all these weapons, and he didn't shoot means to me that Gadaffi was scared.' He did not know who had killed him: 'Everyone was firing. Our young men were hysterical. I don't know who killed him, but I am not sorry.'

The Libyan peacock, renowned around the world for his colourful and bizarre uniforms, had been transformed into a ragged and bloodied wreck, mumbling incoherently.

The rebels surrounded Gadaffi, and men started slapping him. They were joined by crowds of other rebel fighters, some of them nearly hysterical. Many took out their mobile phones and, as they had done so often in their peaceful lives before this war, began to record what was happening.

This jumbled footage and the confused recollections of those who were present form the raw evidence of what happened next. It is plain that the rebels immediately divided between those who wanted to shoot him on the spot and those who wanted to save him for interrogation.

Shouts of 'Keep him alive! Keep him alive' and 'ya kalb' [you dog!] can be heard through the commotion as Gadaffi is jostled by a throng of men, six or seven holding his arms either side of him.

He has blood on his head and appears to fall to the ground; the men drag him up. Some shout: 'Misrata, Misrata, Allahu akbar [God is greatest], ya kalb!' Gunshots and machinegun fire are heard ringing out in the background.

Even in his confused state, Gadaffi must have realised there was no real likelihood of mercy. One of the rebels put Gadaffi on the bonnet of a yellow Toyota pick-up and started driving it around to show the fighters who they had captured. Gadaffi slid forward, off the bonnet.

A video shows him in a blood-soaked shirt and bloodied face leaning up against it, restrained by fighters. Then he is lying on it in his bloodied khaki uniform, with three men around him holding him down.

They then push him off the bonnet towards another car, as he shouts and struggles against them, waving his arms about and clearly alive. In another video, men make barking noises at him and call him 'shafshoofa' [frizzy-haired one]. Some start pulling the locks of curly black hair, which shows an inch of white at the roots as he has been unable to dye it on the run.

He looks around him confused and disorientated. He wipes his forehead with his hand, looks at his hand and sees blood and extends the bloody palm out to the men surrounding him as if to say: 'Look what you've done to me.' He is wearing his gold wedding ring. A young rebel holding up a heeled black boot with a zip to the camera shouts 'Muammar's boot! His boot! Victory! This is victory!'

Gadaffi himself appears to be saying: 'What is going on? What is going on? What are you doing?' And then he says: 'Haram alay-kum, haram alaykum!' This translates as: 'You should be ashamed of yourselves!' He then adds: 'Don't you know what is haram [forbidden by Islam]?'

In the fourth video that can be deciphered, he is dead. Fighters roll his body over on the pavement. He is naked to the waist with a pool of blood under his head, his arms raised above his head. The body is then paraded through the streets on top of a vehicle surrounded by a large crowd chanting: 'The blood of the martyrs will not go in vain.' What was not clear was how he had been killed.

In Benghazi, the eastern city where the revolt began in February, a young fighter called Sanad Sadek al-Ouraybi was being hailed as a hero yesterday for firing the fatal shot.

Sanad, who said he was in Sirte searching for his missing brother, claimed he was with Misratan rebels when they stumbled on Gadaffi by mistake. He insisted that the colonel was not hauled out of a drainhole but was found walking incognito among a group of women and children.

'I called out his name not believing it could be him,' Sanad said, 'and Gadaffi turned on hearing his name. As he tried to reach for a pistol from his pocket we jumped him and I started slapping and beating him.'

According to Sanad, he managed to get Gadaffi into an ambulance to take him to Benghazi. The Misratan militia intervened, and a firefight broke out for possession of the prisoner. When the Misratans got the upper hand, Sanad said, he shot Gadaffi in the head rather than surrender him alive.

While this account did not ring true to reporters who had investigated Gadaffi's death – not least because there were no women or children in any of the video images of Gadaffi's capture – it illustrates the deadly tensions between eastern and western Libya, and it gives some plausibility to the official Libyan account that Gadaffi died in crossfire during a firefight while being transported in the ambulance.

What seems to have happened, according to another video, is that after Gadaffi had been pulled off the bonnet of the pick-up truck, he was dragged towards a car and then pulled down by his hair.

There are shouts of 'Keep him alive!' and then a man gives out a high-pitched hysterical scream. Gadaffi then goes out of view and gunshots ring out. Some accounts say Gadaffi died in the ambulance. But its driver, Ali Jaghdoun, told Reuters that Gadaffi was dead when he picked him up and drove him to Misrata. 'I didn't try to revive him because he was already dead,' he said.

The dictator's body – and the corpse of his son Mutassim, who was filmed smoking in captivity before apparently being executed – were on show in Misrata yesterday.

In a macabre scene, thousands of people lined up to view the remains of their former leader laid out in a refrigerated room in a market on the outskirts of the city.

The line stretched, several deep, for at least half a mile. Some brought their children.

As evening shadows drew in, two little girls, dressed in their finest dresses and holding their father's hand, skipped as they left.

Gadaffi lay on a single flowered mattress, a plastic sheet under his head where there was a pool of blood. In death, he was still distinctive.

He had clearly shaved on the morning of his flight from Sirte, preserving his strange preference for a moustache, small line of beard under his lower lip.

His face was bent towards the left, covering the bullet hole in his left temple, and his nose had clearly been broken.

His chest was bare, marred by blood smears and holes that might have been bullet wounds; his left side was misshapen with a strange lop-sided swelling.

The scene was surreal. Young men knelt down by his head in the bright light, making the V for victory sign, and smiling, as if he was a big game trophy brought down in the wild.

Somehow, in death he looked smaller, shrunken. His thin shanks and feet stretched below khaki trousers pushed up to just below the knee, their stretch waist bloodied by his wounds.

The fear he had inspired seemed far away from this pale, inert figure.

Many had come to see just that. 'I drove from Tripoli to see him,' said Ahmed al-Nuda. 'I wanted to make sure it was Gadaffi. The man who has made our life hell for 42 years. It is him. Thank you God.'

Libya keeps silence over vampire dictator's grave

MISRATA

30 October 2011

The fighters who ritually buried the dictator in an unmarked grave have sworn to keep the site secret – but are there clues to the whereabouts?

The spectre of Muammar Gadaffi still looms large over the country he terrorised for four decades. Last week a handful of rebels drove into the desert in the dark of the night and lowered his cheap pine coffin into a waist-deep grave they had dug themselves. Then they went silent.

No one would reveal the grave's location. The representatives of Libya's new government had scattered stones to keep wild dogs from digging up his body, but otherwise left unmarked the desolate site in the scrub desert that rolls south of Misrata for hundreds of miles.

Gadaffi's body may have been buried, but Libyans have not yet exorcised the larger-than-life power he wielded and the fear he inspired.

Several of the grave diggers were commanders with whom I had endured missile and mortar fire during the months of Misrata's siege. We had become comrades in the way that the extremes of war create intimate bonds. I had seen their brothers die; they had seen I would not run. They had vowed: 'Anything you need. Anything.'

Last week that changed. 'You were with us in our dark hours,' said Salahdine Badi, the commander of Misrata's katibas, or militias, who was twice wounded in the war. 'I will do anything for you, but I cannot talk about the grave. I cannot betray my country.'

Everyone at the grave, he said, had sworn on the Koran not to reveal its location. Badi explained they did not want supporters to turn it into a shrine or those who reviled Gadaffi to desecrate the site.

Their hushed tones revealed that the reason went far deeper. The way they buried him resonated with ritualistic practice that might suit a vampire. Reports said he was buried at dawn, but everyone there said it was during the early hours of Tuesday, next to Mutassim, his 35-year-old son, and Abu-Bakr Yunis Jabr, 59, his defence chief.

As with all Muslims, Gadaffi's body was washed and wrapped in a white sheet. Then they accompanied him into the desert. 'We each shovelled the dirt ourselves,' said Badi. He could even count the shovels – seven.

Ibrahim Beitelmal, the head of Misrata's military council, who held briefings during the siege in the dark because there was no electricity, also refused to disclose the grave's location. 'Nobody should ever know where we buried him,' he said.

Everyone in Misrata knows everyone else's business and rumours are a favourite pastime. 'My father said it is the first time in memory that Misrata keeps a secret,' said Faruq Ben Ahmeida, 36, a rebel fighter.

At one point a commander considered blindfolding me and taking me to the grave, but then reneged. 'No, the experts will recognise the soil. Maybe in a year, when he is just bones,' he said.

Abdel Rahman Abdel Hamid, the dictator's 43-year-old nephew, now a prisoner, read a Koranic verse over the grave that night while Huneish Nasr, 58, his driver of 30 years, stood quietly. The burns on his bandaged hands had been sustained when Nato missiles ripped through the dictator's convoy as he tried to escape Sirte, his birthplace.

The two men had been forced to keep their heads down during the drive from their cells so they would be unable to identify the location. 'We couldn't see anything,' said Abdel Hamid. 'It was too dark.'

There were sufficient hints, however, that I could narrow down the location to the south of Misrata, in the scrub desert where rebels battled Gadaffi's soldiers.

Libyans have many names for the 'desert' and last week I discovered why when I resolved to follow the clues and try to find the graves.

The desert I wanted was the *hammada*, which translates as 'the stony desert with the red soil and scrubby grass'.

The hammada of Misrata stretches for hundreds of square miles. I consulted a hunter, rented a 4x4 and spent hours travelling over rock, scrub and rolling sand berms, into natural wadis and walking the likeliest locations.

The search yielded tyre tracks that turned out to belong to hunters, stones balanced on top of each other in formations that were obscure markers to all but their builders and beautiful empty vistas. Gazelle and rabbit tracks meandered everywhere; no one moved except for the rare shepherd tending a flock of sheep. The hammada kept the secret of the graves.

The burial was the final indignity for Gadaffi. He died brutalised, stabbed and shot by a mob of blood-crazed rebels he had called 'rats'.

The marks of his sordid death were visible to all as he lay bare-chested in a meat refrigerator on the edge of Misrata. Several onlookers said they had come to see 'that he was really just a man'.

Libya's new government last week began trying to unravel the secrets taken to the grave by Gadaffi, who gave almost all his orders verbally, leaving behind few documents. The interrogators' main goal is to find the billions that he stole from the country he treated 'like a family farm', said one official.

Efforts this week will focus on interrogating members of Gadaffi's inner circle who had been caught when fleeing Sirte, their last stand.

Officials said Abdel Hamid was 'still acting like a Gadaffi' despite having attended his uncle's funeral.

'He doesn't seem to realise the seriousness of his situation,' said Beitelmal, who is questioning him.

'He is a spoilt young man,' said Beitelmal, who defected from Gadaffi's forces to join the rebels and is disdainful that Abdel Hamid, a captain, had no military training but gained his rank because of his uncle. 'He asks for grape juice or milk. He wants his "top-of-the-line Audi" back. Tonight he asked me for the key to his cell!'

Abdel Hamid, when interviewed in the military headquarters, was sallow but healthy and complained about his prison clothes – a navy blue uniform from the local electric company. He said he believed his uncle 'went down fighting to the last'.

Claiming he was against the war, he spoke of Gadaffi admiringly but said he had no idea where the money went, despite living far beyond the means of an army officer.

The death of the dictator triggered rapid changes last week. Nato is to end its seven-month mission tomorrow. At its height, Nato fielded more than 200 aircraft over Libya and some 20 ships off the coast.

Their reach was devastating. Britain flew more than 3,000 out of 26,000 sorties; nearly 6,000 targets were bombed, including 1,600 military facilities, bases and bunkers. By this weekend British forces were already heading home.

The most dramatic immediate result was the 'declaration of liberation', which began a week of celebrations and a political process to lead to elections in 20 months.

Politicians in the national transitional council are in negotiations over the new government. It will be formed within two weeks and will move to Tripoli from Benghazi, where the rebellion began on 17 February.

While it begins to look to its future, the nascent country is still nervous about threats from beyond its borders. Saif al-Islam Gadaffi, the dictator's son who was once seen as a reformer but who adopted his father's fight-to-the-death attitude, is still at large. He was said to be trying to negotiate a surrender to the International Criminal Court, the war crimes tribunal in the Hague.

His lawyer, reached in Algeria by *The Sunday Times*, said he believed he would win his case and wanted a guarantee that if he was acquitted of charges of killing unarmed protesters he would be freed and not deported to Libya. 'He believes he is innocent and has been organising his case for months,' the lawyer said, asking to remain anonymous.

The former rebels fear his supporters could still wreak havoc. Last week Badi said he planned to head south with his men to defend the southern border. 'We have to organise safety for the country,' he said.

Syria

'Bombs fell like rain. You could only pray'

5 February 2012

Marie Colvin, Peter Kellier and Annasofie Flamand in Beirut;
Hugh Macleod and Sara Hashash

As the Syrian opposition steps up its attacks on the regime, a stand-off in the city of Homs claims more than 200 lives.

The fighting in Syria spiralled yesterday into the worst violence since protesters began their uprising against the regime of President Bashar al-Assad almost a year ago. More than 200 men, women and children were killed in Homs, a northern city that has become the centre of the opposition, rebel sources said.

Wounded civilians sprawled bleeding in a makeshift clinic at a mosque in the Khalidiya district, which appeared to have borne the brunt of mortars and tank shells fired by government forces.

Independent journalists have been banned from the area but desperate inhabitants got the information out in brief, fearful telephone calls. 'We have just buried 50 martyrs,' said Abu Jihad, an opposition activist. 'We've had to build a new graveyard for them because the old one was full.'

He said the residents had named the new burial site Maqebrat Al-Shohadaa, or 'graveyard of the martyrs'.

The attack on Homs came at a critical moment, hours before the United Nations security council met in New York to consider endorsing Arab League demands for Assad to step down and transfer power to his vice-president. Thirteen countries including Britain and the United States supported the resolution but it was vetoed by Russia and China.

An anti-government activist from Homs who asked to be identified only as Muhammad gave a graphic account of the build-up to the onslaught.

He said an armed opposition group, which he thought was a unit of the rebels' Free Syrian Army (FSA), attacked a checkpoint in Khalidiya and kidnapped 17 soldiers. At roughly the same time, he said, another armed opposition group struck at a Syrian air force security base in the area. Shortly after that, the army responded by attacking the opposition in Khalidiya.

'The sudden escalation was on both sides,' he said. 'There were victims on both sides, but the bombing was indiscriminate.'

Separate accounts spoke of four apartment blocks being largely destroyed in the bombardment and dozens of bodies being pulled from the rubble.

Residents of Homs described a night of terror. 'It was like a machinegun shooting randomly, only much, much heavier,' said Omar Shakir. 'The bombs fell like rain. You didn't know where they would fall. You could only pray.'

Shakir said his best friend, Madher Tayyara, 23, a civil engineering student and volunteer medic, had died in his home after being hit by shrapnel in his chest and head.

Several hospitals treating the dead and dying were raided by security forces, according to activists' reports gathered by Avaaz, a human rights group, which described the humanitarian situation as 'appalling'.

Small field hospitals set up to treat injured protesters were overwhelmed with hundreds of injured, according to activists. They accused security forces of preventing medical supplies from reaching the wounded and warned that many of up to 1,000 injured would die because there was no way to treat them.

Another witness, Waleed Fares, said that when the shelling began at around 10pm on Friday most residents stayed indoors. Then an enormous crashing sound prompted many to run outside where they saw the first two apartment blocks collapse.

Two further buildings, each with around 30 flats, had subsequently been devastated, with others partially destroyed.

As he tried to dig out the bodies of the dead and injured, Fares heard more shells exploding from the rooftops as the cry of 'God is great' rang out from minarets.

'There were children crying, women screaming, standing in their nightclothes because they had not had time to dress,' said Fares. 'We took the bodies and the injured to a nearby park. I counted around 40 bodies from the building collapse. The injuries were appalling: people missing limbs, people crushed so badly you couldn't recognise them, people pierced by metal.'

According to Fares, three bombs fell on the park, killing around 30 people, including his friend Omar Zarour, who left his home to help rescue those trapped.

Government sources said the army had reacted strongly to the kidnapping of its soldiers, in part because it has been losing increasing numbers of young men who do not want to fight their own people.

Residents described intolerable conditions in Homs. 'We're building a hospital in one of the houses but there's little medicine,' said one. 'We're afraid the army will come back.'

A 19-year-old boy who has spoken to *The Sunday Times* from Khalidiya over the past few weeks said residents had been living with little food, and heating oil had become prohibitively expensive.

'For much of the day, the electricity is cut,' he said. 'People are so poor that burglars broke into the local school and stole the windows.'

Sources in Homs and other predominantly Sunni cities warned that the regime appeared to be arming the minority Alawite community, to which the Assad family belongs.

There are growing fears of a civil war, with the FSA not only controlling parts of Homs, but also fighting in Damascus, the capital.

An FSA spokesman said it had lost 27 soldiers in the past four days and claimed the death toll from the shelling in Homs exceeded 350.

'We capture soldiers to show how weak the regime is,' said Abu Ali, an FSA commander. 'Their soldiers fight for one person: Bashar.'

A vet is only hope for Syrian wounded

HOMS

19 February 2012

Wounded civilians arriving at a makeshift clinic in the Syrian city of Homs are relying on a vet to save their lives because there is no doctor to treat them.

I found the vet struggling to treat patients who had been injured by shelling and sniper fire in the district of Baba Amr, a besieged enclave where 28,000 people are trapped by relentless bombardment. He was using his knowledge of sheep anatomy to treat life-threatening wounds in the sitting room of a house.

One of his patients, a 32-year-old mobile phone repairman named Mohammed Mohammed, had been shot in the back by a sniper. The bullet had come to rest in his chest. Fear filled Mohammed's eyes as the vet stuck a tube into his chest to siphon off blood and relieve pressure on his heart.

Another patient, Zaccharia Mutlaq, a carpenter aged 26, had a thigh wound and a broken foot from shell fire. The vet said his priority was to keep the man's wounds clean.

Neither the vet nor his location can be identified. Three so-called field clinics in Baba Amr, an opposition stronghold, have been destroyed by the Syrian army since the siege began 15 days ago.

Mohammed and Mutlaq were injured after going into a house that had exploded to find a mother decapitated, a father ripped apart by shrapnel and the couple's two daughters dead or dying.

The men's plight reflects the desperation of the civilians cowering in basements or scurrying from house to house to avoid shelling by the forces of President Bashar al-Assad as troops build up around Homs for a possible ground offensive.

Final dispatch from Homs, the battered city

19 February 2012

Marie Colvin was the only British journalist reporting from inside the besieged Syrian enclave of Baba Amr. This is her final report.

SYRIA, 2012

They call it the widows' basement. Crammed amid makeshift beds and scattered belongings are frightened women and children trapped in the horror of Homs, the Syrian city shaken by two weeks of relentless bombardment.

Among the 300 huddling in this wood factory cellar in the besieged district of Baba Amr is 20-year-old Noor, who lost her husband and her home to the shells and rockets.

'Our house was hit by a rocket so 17 of us were staying in one room,' she recalls as Mimi, her three-year-old daughter, and Mohamed, her five-year-old son, cling to her abaya.

'We had had nothing but sugar and water for two days and my husband went to try to find food.' It was the last time she saw Maziad, 30, who had worked in a mobile phone repair shop. 'He was torn to pieces by a mortar shell.'

For Noor, it was a double tragedy. Adnan, her 27-year-old brother, was killed at Maziad's side.

Everyone in the cellar has a similar story of hardship or death. The refuge was chosen because it is one of the few basements in Baba Amr. Foam mattresses are piled against the walls and the children have not seen the light of day since the siege began on 4 February. Most families fled their homes with only the clothes on their backs.

The city is running perilously short of supplies and the only food here is rice, tea and some tins of tuna delivered by a local sheikh who looted them from a bombed-out supermarket.

A baby born in the basement last week looked as shellshocked as her mother, Fatima, 19, who fled there when her family's single-storey house was obliterated. 'We survived by a miracle,' she whispers. Fatima is so traumatised that she cannot breast-feed, so the baby has been fed only sugar and water; there is no formula milk.

Fatima may or may not be a widow. Her husband, a shepherd, was in the countryside when the siege started with a ferocious barrage and she has heard no word of him since.

The widows' basement reflects the ordeal of 28,000 men, women and children clinging to existence in Baba Amr, a district of low concrete-block homes surrounded on all sides by Syrian forces. The army is launching Katyusha rockets, mortar shells and tank rounds at random.

Snipers on the rooftops of al-Ba'ath University and other high buildings surrounding Baba Amr shoot any civilian who comes into their sights. Residents were felled in droves in the first days of the siege but have now learnt where the snipers are and run across junctions where they know they can be seen. Few cars are left on the streets.

Almost every building is pock-marked after tank rounds punched through concrete walls or rockets blasted gaping holes in upper floors. The building I was staying in lost its upper floor to a rocket last Wednesday. On some streets whole buildings have collapsed – all there is to see are shredded clothes, broken pots and the shattered furniture of families destroyed.

It is a city of the cold and hungry, echoing to exploding shells and bursts of gunfire. There are no telephones and the electricity has been cut off. Few homes have diesel for the tin stoves they rely on for heat in the coldest winter that anyone can remember. Freezing rain fills potholes and snow drifts in through windows empty of glass. No shops are open, so families are sharing what they have with relatives and neighbours. Many of the dead and injured are those who risked foraging for food.

Fearing the snipers' merciless eyes, families resorted last week to throwing bread across rooftops, or breaking through communal walls to pass unseen.

The Syrians have dug a huge trench around most of the district, and let virtually nobody in or out. The army is pursuing a brutal campaign to quell the resistance of Homs, Hama and other cities that have risen up against Bashar al-Assad, the Syrian president, whose family has been in power for 42 years.

In Baba Amr, the Free Syrian Army (FSA), the armed face of opposition to Assad, have virtually unanimous support from civilians who see them as their defenders. It is an unequal battle: the tanks and heavy weaponry of Assad's troops against the Kalashnikovs of the FSA.

About 5,000 Syrian soldiers are believed to be on the outskirts of Baba Amr, and the FSA received reports yesterday that they were preparing a ground assault. The residents dread the outcome.

'We live in fear the FSA will leave the city,' said Hamida, 43, hiding with her children and her sister's family in an empty ground-floor apartment after their house was bombed. 'There will be a massacre.'

On the lips of everyone was the question: 'Why have we been abandoned by the world?'

Ban Ki-moon, the secretary-general of the United Nations, said last week: 'We see neighbourhoods shelled indiscriminately, hospitals used as torture centres, children as young as 10 years old killed and abused. We see almost certainly crimes against humanity.' Yet the international community has not come to the aid of the innocent caught in this hell.

Abdel Majid, 20, who was helping to rescue the wounded from bombed buildings, made a simple plea. 'Please tell the world they must help us,' he said, shaking, with haunted eyes. 'Just stop the bombing. Please, just stop the shelling.'

The journey across the countryside from the Lebanese border to Homs would be idyllic in better times. The villages are nondescript clusters of concrete buildings on dirt tracks but the lanes are lined with cypresses and poplar trees and wind through orchards of apricot and apple trees.

These days, however, there is an edge of fear on any journey through this area. Most of this land is essentially what its residents call 'Syria hurra', or free Syria, patrolled by the FSA.

Nevertheless, Assad's army has checkpoints on the main roads and troops stationed in schools, hospitals and factories. They are heavily armed and backed by tanks and artillery.

So a drive to Homs is a bone-rattling struggle down dirt roads, criss-crossing fields. Men cluster by fires at unofficial FSA check-points, eyeing any vehicle suspiciously. As night falls, flashlights waved by unseen figures signal that the way ahead is clear.

Each travelling FSA car has a local shepherd or farmer aboard to help navigate the countryside; the Syrian army may have the power, but the locals know every track of their fields.

I entered Homs on a smugglers' route, which I promised not to reveal, climbing over walls in the dark and slipping into muddy trenches. Arriving in the darkened city in the early hours, I was met by a welcoming party keen for foreign journalists to reveal the city's plight to the world. So desperate were they that they bundled me into an open truck and drove at speed with the headlights on, everyone standing in the back shouting 'Allahu akbar' – God is the greatest. Inevitably, the Syrian army opened fire.

When everyone had calmed down I was driven in a small car, its lights off, along dark empty streets, the danger palpable. As we passed an open stretch of road, a Syrian army unit fired on the car again with machineguns and launched a rocket-propelled grenade. We sped into a row of abandoned buildings for cover.

The scale of human tragedy in the city is immense. The inhabitants are living in terror. Almost every family seems to have suffered the death or injury of a loved one.

Khaled Abu Salah, an activist who took part in the first demonstrations against Assad in Homs last March, sat on the floor of an office, his hand broken and bandages covering shrapnel wounds to his leg and shoulder.

A 25-year-old university student, who risked his life filming videos of the slaughter of Baba Amr residents, he narrowly escaped when he tried to get two men wounded by mortar fire to a make-shift clinic.

He and three friends had just taken the wounded to the clinic, which was staffed by a doctor and a dentist, and stepped away from the door when 'a shell landed right at the entrance', he recalled last week.

'My three friends died immediately.' The two men they had helped were also killed.

Abu Ammar, 48, a taxi driver, went out to look for bread at 8am one day last week. He, his wife and their adopted daughter had taken refuge with two elderly sisters after their home was hit by shells.

'When I returned the house was obliterated,' he said, looking at all that remained of the one-storey building. Only a few pieces of wall still stood. In the ruins a woman's red blouse was visible; bottles of home-made pickled vegetables were somehow unscathed. 'Dr Ali', a dentist working as a doctor, said one of the women from the house had arrived at the clinic alive, but both legs had been amputated and she died.

The clinic is merely a first-floor apartment donated by the kindly owner. It still has out-of-place domestic touches: plasma pouches hang from a wooden coat hanger and above the patients a colourful children's mobile hangs from the ceiling.

The shelling last Friday was the most intense yet and the wounded were rushed to the clinic in the backs of cars by family members.

Ali the dentist was cutting the clothes off 24-year-old Ahmed al-Irini on one of the clinic's two operating tables. Shrapnel had gashed huge bloody chunks out of Irini's thighs. Blood poured out as Ali used tweezers to draw a piece of metal from beneath his left eye.

Irini's legs spasmed and he died on the table. His brother-in-law, who had brought him in, began weeping. 'We were playing cards when a missile hit our house,' he said through his tears. Irini was taken out to the makeshift mortuary in a former back bedroom, naked but for a black plastic bag covering his genitals.

There was no let-up. Khaled Abu Kamali died before the doctor could get his clothes off. He had been hit by shrapnel in the chest while at home.

Salah, 26, was peppered with shrapnel in his chest and the left of his back. There was no anaesthetic, but he talked as Ali inserted a metal pipe into his back to release the pressure of the blood building up in his chest.

Helping tend the wounded was Um Ammar, a 45-year-old mother of seven, who had offered to be a nurse after a neighbour's house was shelled. She wore filthy plastic gloves and was crying. 'I'm obliged to endure this, because all children brought here are my children,' she said. 'But it is so hard.'

Akhmed Mohammed, a military doctor who defected from Assad's army, shouted: 'Where are the human rights? Do we have none? Where are the United Nations?'

There were only two beds in the clinic for convalescing. One was taken by Akhmed Khaled, who had been injured, he said, when a shell hit a mosque as he was about to leave prayers. His right testicle had had to be removed with only paracetamol to dull the pain.

He denounced the Assad regime's claim that the rebels were Islamic extremists and said: 'We ask all people who believe in God – Christians, Jews, Muslims to help us!'

If the injured try to flee Baba Amr, they first have to be carried on foot. Then they are transferred to motorbikes and the lucky ones are smuggled to safety. The worst injured do not make it.

Though Syrian officials prohibit anyone from leaving, some escapees manage to bribe their way out. I met refugees in villages around Homs. Newlywed Miriam, 32, said she and her husband had decided to leave when they heard that three families had been killed and the women raped by the Shabiha militia, a brutal force led by Assad's younger brother, Maher.

'We were practically walking on body parts as we walked under shelling overhead,' she said. Somehow they made it unscathed. She had given an official her wedding ring in order to be smuggled out to safety.

Abdul Majid, a computer science student at university, was still shaking hours after arriving in a village outside Homs. He had stayed behind alone in Baba Amr. 'I had to help the old people because only the young can get out,' said Majid, 20, wearing a leather jacket and jeans. He left when his entire street fled after every house was hit.

'I went to an army checkpoint that I was told was not too bad. I gave them a packet of cigarettes, two bags of tea and 500 Syrian pounds. They told me to run.'

Blasts of Kalashnikov fire rang out above his head until he reached the tree line. He said the soldiers were only pretending to try to shoot him to protect themselves, but his haunted eyes showed he was not entirely sure.

If the Syrian military rolls into Baba Amr, the FSA will have little chance against its tanks, superior weaponry and numbers. They will, however, fight ferociously to defend their families because they know a massacre is likely to follow any failure, if the past actions of the Assad regime are anything to go by.

The FSA partly relies on defections from Assad's army because it does not accept civilians into its ranks, though they perform roles such as monitoring troop movements and transporting supplies. But it has become harder for soldiers to defect in the past month.

Abu Sayeed, 46, a major-general who defected six months ago, said every Syrian military unit was now assigned a member of the Mukhabarat, the feared intelligence service, who have orders to execute any soldier refusing an order to shoot or who tries to defect.

The army, like the country, may well be about to divide along sectarian lines. Most of the officers are members of the Alawite sect, the minority Shi'ite clan to which the Assad family belongs, while foot soldiers are Sunni.

The coming test for the army will be if its ranks hold if ordered to kill increasing numbers of their brethren.

The swathe of the country that stretches east from the Lebanon border and includes Homs is Sunni; in the villages there they say that officers ordering attacks are Alawites fighting for the Assad family, not their country.

The morale of Assad's army, despite its superiority, is said to be low as it is poorly paid and supplied, although this information comes mostly from defectors. 'The first thing we did when we attacked the house was race to the refrigerator,' said a defector.

Thousands of soldiers would be needed to retake the southern countryside. Hafez al-Assad, Bashar's father and former president, crushed his problems with Islamic fundamentalists in 1982 by shelling the city of Hama into ruins and killing at least 10,000 men, women and children. So far his son appears to have calculated that a similar act would be a step too far for his remaining allies of Russia, China and Iran.

For now it is a violent and deadly standoff. The FSA is not about to win and its supplies of ammunition are dwindling.

The only real hope of success for Assad's opponents is if the international community comes to their aid, as Nato did against Muammar Gadaffi in Libya. So far this seems unlikely to happen in Syria.

Observers see a negotiated solution as perhaps a long shot, but the best way out of this impasse. Though neither side appears ready to negotiate, there are serious efforts behind the scenes to persuade Russia to pull Assad into talks.

As international diplomats dither, the desperation in Baba Amr grows. The despair was expressed by Hamida, 30, hiding in a downstairs flat with her sister and their 13 children after two missiles hit their home. Three little girls, aged 16 months to six years, sleep on one thin, torn mattress on the floor; three others share a second. Ahmed, 16, her sister's eldest child, was killed by a missile when he went to try to find bread.

'The kids are screaming all the time,' Hamida said. 'I feel so helpless.' She began weeping. 'We feel so abandoned. They've given Bashar al-Assad the green light to kill us.'

LOYALTIES OF 'DESERT ROSE' TESTED

Asma, the British-born wife of President Bashar al-Assad, may well be feeling a sense of divided loyalty as the violence continues in the Syrian city of Homs. Her family are from the area, which has been a focal point for many of the recent protests against her husband's regime and the Syrian army's brutal response.

Despite growing up in Acton, west London, Asma visited her family's home in Homs every year throughout her childhood. She is also a Sunni Muslim, unlike her husband, who comes from the country's minority Shi'ite community.

Asma, 36, has been criticised for displaying an 'ostrich attitude', keeping a low profile as the conflict has intensified. She has refused to comment on the way her husband's regime has used tanks and other lethal means to crush protesters. In an email sent earlier this month, her office merely said: 'The first lady's very busy agenda is still focused on supporting the various charities she has long been involved with as well as rural development and supporting the President as needed.'

The daughter of a consultant cardiologist and a retired diplomat, Asma was born in London. She attended a Church of England state school in Acton and gained a BSc in computer science and a diploma in French literature from King's College London.

She went on to work for Deutsche Bank and married Assad in Syria in 2000. Now a mother of three, she was once described by *Vogue* as a 'rose in the desert'. In Homs, the beleaguered people may now take a different view.

MARIE COLVIN:
THE LAST ASSIGNMENT

26 February 2012

Jon Swain

She braved the dangers of Syria to tell the truth about its horrors. Jon Swain reveals the story of how his friend and colleague paid the ultimate price.

Inside the makeshift 'media centre' in Baba Amr, the journalists had retreated to the ground floor. It was an ordinary building, chosen because the narrow streets and surrounding structures offered some protection from the rockets and shells.

The top floor had been hit by the Syrian forces besieging the district, part of the city of Homs, but the others had largely escaped – so far.

On the ground floor Marie Colvin was asleep in a room on her own last Wednesday morning when the lethal rain of explosives resumed. An American who had worked as a foreign correspondent for *The Sunday Times* for 25 years, Marie was used to war zones and was expert in the ways of the Middle East.

The streets were littered with rubble, many houses wrecked, nowhere was safe. Yet the media centre was her temporary home and, true to local custom, Marie had left her shoes in the hall.

It was a gesture that would cost her life.

Also in the building were Paul Conroy, a *Sunday Times* photographer; Javier Espinosa, a Spanish journalist; Edith Bouvier and William Daniels, a French couple; and Rémi Ochlik, an award-winning French photographer. They were in the care of seven Syrian activists.

'Two rockets hit near the house,' said Abu Haneen, one of the activists reached last week. 'Then a third.' The explosion ripped through an upper room. Part of the floor caved in, crashing onto the journalists below. 'Dust was everywhere. Everyone was terrified.'

Believing the building was being targeted and more rockets were likely, Haneen shouted at the others to get out. Grabbing their belongings, the journalists gathered in the main room trying to formulate a plan.

It was the safest part of the building, towards the front side that had not been hit before. Earlier damage to the media centre had come from another direction, striking the back. This time the Syrians had changed their angle of fire.

Marie and the others knew they had to get to the safety of another building. But first she needed her shoes. She made a dash for the entrance hall. At that moment Hussein, another of the activists, heard a distant 'puff' – the sound of a rocket leaving its launcher.

It was early this month that Marie decided she had to go to Syria. The uprising against President Bashar Assad's regime was gathering force and the backlash was becoming more violent. The Syrian government was trying to hide its brutality by keeping journalists out. Marie felt the truth needed to be told.

When the Syrians obfuscated over a visa, she flew to Beirut, the capital of Lebanon, on 7 February, planning to find her own way across the border. She stayed one night at Le Bristol, but moved to the Gefinor Rotana hotel, which was more to her taste and where other contacts were based. Even as she prepared for the horrors of Homs, Marie, whose life flitted between combat kit and cocktail dresses, had certain standards.

In an email on Friday 10 February, she explained her hopes and motives to Sara Hashash, a friend and young journalist in Cairo. 'The overall picture I have been told about is that Homs is ringed by the army and tanks, and the army is stopping anyone from entering and leaving. I may have found a way in …

'The people inside, and the surrounding villages, fear they are about to be overrun … So, no pressure then.' She wanted to help before it was too late.

Other journalists had previously sneaked in to Syria across the border with Lebanon, but Marie had identified the area that seemed hardest hit as Assad's crackdown intensified. In an email the following day to Sean Ryan, foreign editor of *The Sunday Times*, she outlined the situation in Homs: 'Heavy shelling again … Trying to get more detail, seems it is mostly in Baba Amr and Ishaat neighbourhoods, the main strongholds of the FSA [Free Syrian Army]'.

Although parts of Syria are largely hostile to Assad, his forces still have checkpoints everywhere. Getting in would require the help of Syrian activists opposed to Assad.

Marie's years of covering the Middle East had brought her numerous contacts in the region, from high-ranking politicians to well connected fixers. The latter were what she needed now. Later that afternoon she sent another email: 'I am meeting Syrian "transporter" (read smuggler) tonight. The fixer came earlier today, and reading between the lines, it increasingly looks like tonight's meeting will not be actual transport but a discussion of logistics, inspection of gear (ie no flak jackets or helmets, can you fit three on a motorbike, yes, if it is that or walk).'

Her plans delayed, she had time to catch up with old friends in the field and swap the latest local intel. In Beirut she dined with with Neil MacFarquhar of *The New York Times*, revealing her concerns about the looming trip across the border. 'I cannot remember any story where the security situation was potentially this bad, except maybe Chechnya,' she told him.

She dined, too, with Lindsey Hilsum, international editor of Channel 4. Last week Hilsum recalled: 'I told Marie that I would not sneak across the border into Homs because it was too dangerous. She said she was going to have a go anyway. She felt it was important. "Anyway, it's what we do," she said.'

Days later Marie slipped over the border and was guided by activists through back roads and fields into Homs. It was dark and dangerous, cold and wet; the final leg of her journey into the besieged neighbourhood of Baba Amr she promised to keep secret to protect the smugglers.

Although she knew certain types of communication were risky, late on Thursday 16 February, she contacted Ryan: 'This is a secure line so I am taking advantage to send you a quick message to say I have arrived safely at the heart of Baba Amr. The journey was eventful to say the least. Pretty much every kind of danger, cold, wet and muddy, but we made it! We are in what seems to be the one place in the city that has electricity. There is a lot of shelling, and snipers during the day.'

Conroy, a photographer who had worked extensively with Marie in Libya last year, had also been smuggled in.

The only way to get communications out was via satellite. Marie had decided to use a Thuraya satphone as little as possible because its calls could easily be intercepted and its location identified. Instead, she was mainly sending messages via Skype, which is harder to track, on another system.

To do so, however, she was making use of equipment at the makeshift media centre set up in Baba Amr where the activists had been uploading videos to the internet. The centre had already come under fire and internet security, Marie suspected, 'was out the window'. Whether the Syrians were already targeting the site deliberately or not, it was inevitably at risk as Assad's troops bombarded the district.

Early on Friday 17 February, Marie sent another message to Ryan: 'Cupla [sic] technical things. Forget that number I sent you, it was knocked out when the top floor of building I am in was hit yesterday.'

The top floor was badly damaged, but the activists kept operating from the other two. Marie continued: 'Heavy shelling this morning. I counted 45 shells in 7 minutes nearby. When it lets up I will try to get out to the field clinic.'

That day she braved the snipers to interview locals huddled in houses and basements and to visit a makeshift clinic treating the wounded. The scenes she witnessed were grim.

In an email to a young friend, Lucy Fisher, she admitted her fears, writing: 'I did have a few moments when I thought, What am I doing?' Then she added: 'Story incredibly important though. Mx.'

That night she was smuggled out of Baba Amr and the next day, from a safer location, she filed a searing account of what she had seen. It appeared across two pages of *The Sunday Times* last weekend and could leave no one in any doubt of the indiscriminate violence being meted out by the Syrian army.

Marie, however, was never one to give up on a story. Last Sunday she spoke to Ryan and they discussed her next move. Should she go to another area, he asked. Hama, he suggested, another city about 30 miles north. Marie thought Baba Amr remained the epicentre. The residents were terrified they would be slaughtered if the Syrian army forced its way in.

Then last Tuesday another email dropped into Ryan's inbox. 'I am in Baba Amr, the shelling started at 6.30am.' She had gone back.

For all Marie's glamour and impressive connections, she remained down to earth, a defender of the oppressed and the wronged. The next part of her message to Ryan made clear why she was risking her life by returning to Baba Amr.

'It is sickening that the Syrian regime is allowed to keep doing this,' she wrote. 'There was a shocking scene at the apartment clinic today. A baby boy lay on a head scarf, naked, his little tummy heaving as he tried to breathe. The doctor said "we can do nothing for him". He had been hit by shrapnel in his left side. They had to just let him die as his mother wept.'

She knew that in a voraciously competitive media there was a risk that she might be regarded as repeating her earlier report.

Determined that the world should not ignore Syria, she added: 'I feel strongly that we have to include these stories of the suffering of civilians to get the point across.'

Supplies of water and electricity were short. The shelling was wreaking havoc. Two cars driven by activists had been hit that day, she had emailed, one destroyed.

Growing increasingly concerned for her safety, Ryan responded: 'I'm alarmed to read what happened to the two cars ... the first [question] is whether it's safe to move at all.'

The three of them, Marie, Conroy and Ryan, discussed the situation over Skype. Marie wanted to stay, arguing that it was an important story and she was the only British newspaper journalist there to tell it.

Shortly afterwards Conroy, unknown to Marie, sent a further email to Ryan, expressing his reservations. 'The situation here is extreme,' wrote Conroy, a former soldier who had served in the Royal Artillery. 'The shelling is only getting worse and expect it to continue ... I suspect that Marie's high profile due to this week's material in paper and TV interviews also compromises our safety.'

He added: 'As I am sure you are aware Marie can be tricky to convince once she has the bit between her teeth.'

Ryan responded with an email sent to both of them. They should all speak in the morning about getting out of Baba Amr at the first opportunity, he said.

Instead, Marie had a message to get out first, a message for the world about the truth of Baba Amr. In links to the BBC, Channel 4 News and to CNN, the US news network, she described the misery she was witnessing. She told the CNN presenter Anderson Cooper how she had watched the baby die. 'It is a complete and utter lie they're only going after terrorists. The Syrian army is simply shelling a city of cold, starving civilians,' she said.

David Remnick, editor of *The New Yorker*, saw her CNN broadcast and noted the next day: 'There was cool but profound rage in her voice.'

After her report in *The Sunday Times* a couple of days earlier, Marie's broadcasts rammed home the point: atrocities were being committed. Assad and his generals could no longer conceal the horrors of their three-week assault on Baba Amr.

A Facebook group of fellow journalists sent Marie a message applauding her courage for being in Homs. One of them thought she had already left the battered city and expressed relief that she was safe.

'I think the reports of my survival may be exaggerated,' Colvin responded. 'I'm in Baba Amr. Sickening, trying to understand how the world can stand by and I should be hardened by now.'

She told *The Sunday Times* that she wanted to stay one more day, saying in an email to Ryan sent at 10.36pm on Tuesday that she wanted to go back to the clinic the following morning. 'We would stay as long as possible; once inside we are pretty safe,' she said.

Her message included a wry afterthought: 'I have spent tonight gathering stories from some FSA guys from the front. Everyone I meet invites me to the front, what is it with me?'

Trouble and Marie had often gone together, but this time she had decided there was no point risking a visit to the front line: 'It is a line of destroyed buildings. I don't see the point in going, nor Paul, especially after the discussions you and I had [about the risk].'

Ryan messaged back: 'But I still think you should be ready to leave Wednesday night if conditions deteriorate and a ground offensive is coming.'

One more day and they would be out. That was the plan.

All the journalists were sleeping when, early the next morning, the shelling erupted again. After the broadcasts had Assad ordered the troublesome critics silenced? It was clear foreign journalists had got into Baba Amr – and the Syrians are known to be able to locate satellite transmissions. The means to target the journalists were there, but no one can be sure whether they were used.

For the first time the Syrian forces started firing at the media centre from a new direction. As explosions shook the building and the ceiling fell in, the journalists gathered their belongings.

Marie was not the only one who had left shoes in the hall. Espinosa, 47, a reporter with the Spanish daily *El Mundo*, grabbed his and raced back inside, crouching in a corridor on the far side of the living room wall with Daniels.

As Marie ran to the entrance to get her footwear, another rocket landed at the front of the building, a few yards away. The blast killed her and Ochlik instantly, rubble falling on their bodies in the hallway.

Espinosa and Daniels, sheltered by a wall inside, escaped almost unscathed. Conroy and Bouvier, in the living room near the hall, were hit by the blast and shrapnel.

Bouvier was the most seriously wounded, with multiple fractures to her leg. Conroy tried to stanch blood pouring from his leg. An activist tried to help him up. 'No, leave me here. Save yourself,' Conroy replied.

'They are words I will never forget,' the activist said later.

Espinosa helped up a wounded activist and fled the house through a haze of dust and smoke. Such was the chaos and confusion that he unwittingly stepped on the bodies as he went.

'This for me was the most horrible thing. I stepped on their bodies. I didn't know it was them,' he said.

As Williams stepped over them to leave, he slapped Ochlik's face to see if he was alive. There was no response and he moved on.

The journalists and activists struggled into a house opposite the media centre and the shelling continued. They managed, with the help of a car, to get the wounded to a field clinic.

For several hours no one dared to recover the bodies of the dead. Later, when the bombardment and gunfire eased, two of the activists ran back into the media centre where Marie and Ochlik lay and wrapped them in a shroud.

As soon as the deaths were confirmed, tributes poured in from politicians, friends and colleagues around the world. In Britain,

David Cameron said: 'This is a desperately sad reminder of the risks that journalists take to inform the world of what is happening and the dreadful events in Syria.'

In France, President Nicolas Sarkozy said the deaths of Colvin and Ochlik amounted to 'murder'. He urged that those responsible be found and held accountable.

For Peter Bouckaert, the emergencies director of Human Rights Watch, the killing of the journalists was a crime whether or not they had been deliberately targeted. 'There are two possibilities,' he said. 'Either it was a targeted attack on the building and it was a crime, or the journalists were the victims of the same kind of criminal attacks that have killed hundreds in Homs, which is also a crime.'

On Wednesday evening friends and journalists who had worked with Marie gathered at the Frontline club in London of which she was a founder member. There were tears but also much laughter as they celebrated her extraordinary life and listened to Jon Snow pay a closing tribute on Channel 4 News. 'She was a one-off and one of the most courageous of our age,' Snow said.

From New York, Marie's mother, Rosemarie, said: 'She was totally, totally committed to what she did and the importance of telling the story and writing it and getting it out to the world. That was her life.'

For Conroy and the other survivors the ordeal continued. Trapped inside Baba Amr, they were patched up by the activists as best they could. Bouvier needed urgent specialist treatment; Conroy, although suffering three large wounds to his leg, appeared calm in a video he posted to the internet, saying that 'any assistance would be welcome'.

Activists from a few miles away set out to smuggle medical supplies to them by crossing through an area controlled by the Syrian army. They never arrived. A search party later found seven of them shot dead, their hands tied behind their backs. Medical supplies were strewn in the street around them. There was no trace of two other members of the team, one a foreign paramedic.

When one opportunity for the walking wounded to escape did arise, Conroy refused to go. He did not wish to leave behind Bouvier or Marie's body.

From London to Beirut and Damascus, desperate talks went on to try to secure a ceasefire or any means of allowing in rescuers and medical help. When members of the Red Crescent aid service finally made their way to the wounded on Friday, Conroy again refused to accompany them, apparently fearing a trap and that he might be handed over to the forces of Assad.

Attempts to bring out the wounded and the bodies continued yesterday. Ambulances from the Red Crescent made their way through Homs, seeking to extract both civilians and the journalists.

Syria's conflict remains far from over. After diplomats and politicians from numerous countries failed to agree any firm action at a conference in Tunisia on Friday, there is little solution in sight to the clashes between Assad's regime and the popular opposition to it.

As the killing went on Haneen, who had pulled Marie's body from the rubble, expressed growing despair. 'We cannot count the ones that die in the shelling and are buried under rubble. No one knows of them,' he said.

'We are all waiting for our turn to die. Every evening we tell each other: thank God for your safety. Another day has passed and we have not been killed.'

But sadly, not for Marie.

'REPORTS OF MY SURVIVAL MAY BE EXAGGERATED'

(Marie Colvin, 20 February 2012)

The poet Alan Jenkins was a friend of Marie's and wrote this poem as a tribute to her.

> How can you be lying there?
>   Immodestly, among the rubble
> When we want you to be here
>   In some other kind of trouble –
>
> Luffing up, in irons, perhaps,
>   Just downstream from the Dove,
> Lost in South London, without maps,
>   Or capsized in love.
>
> What's keeping you? A kind of dare?
>   Come back and tell us how you stayed
> One step ahead, how you gave fear
>   The slip, how you were not afraid –
>
> As we are. Look – here's my idea.
>   Come back – this time, for good.
> Leave your flak jacket and your gear
>   In that burnt-out neighbourhood,

And fly home, via Paris. You'll be met.
   I'll buy a bottle from the corner store,
Like old times. You can have a cigarette.
   Marie, get up off that bloodstained floor!

             * * *

   Tonight you threw your thin brown arm
Around my shoulders, and you said
   (There was this unearthly calm)
'Can't you take in that I am dead?

   Learn to expect the unexpected turn
Of the tide, the unmarked reef,
   The rock that should be off the stern
On which we come to grief?

   The lies, the ignorance and hate –
The bigger picture? No safe mooring there,
   In Chechnya or Chiswick Eyot.
Those nights I drank my way out of despair,

   And filling ashtrays filed the copy
You would read – or not read – with
   A brackish taste and your first coffee
Contending on your tongue; while Billy Smith,

   My street cat rescued from Jerusalem,
Barged in, shouting, from his wars. . . .
   As many lives as his – and now I've used them.
I wish I'd made it back to yours.'

            Alan Jenkins

Marie photographed by Patrick Bishop.
This was her favourite photograph of herself.

Marie, sailing off the coast of Turkey on the
boat of Richard Flaye, her boyfriend.
Photograph by Maryam d'Abo.

MW00756750

Also by Robert A. Caro

The Power Broker:
Robert Moses and the Fall of New York
(1974)

The Years of Lyndon Johnson:

The Path to Power
(1982)

Means of Ascent
(1990)

Master of the Senate
(2002)

THE PASSAGE
OF POWER

THE YEARS OF
LYNDON
JOHNSON

———— ★ ★ ★ ★ ————

THE

PASSAGE

OF POWER

Robert A. Caro

Alfred A. Knopf   New York   2012

THIS IS A BORZOI BOOK
PUBLISHED BY ALFRED A. KNOPF

Copyright © 2012 by Robert A. Caro, Inc.

All rights reserved. Published in the United States by Alfred A. Knopf,
a division of Random House, Inc., New York, and in Canada
by Random House of Canada Limited, Toronto.

www.aaknopf.com

Knopf, Borzoi Books, and the colophon are registered trademarks
of Random House, Inc.

A portion of this work was previously published in *The New Yorker.*

Cataloging-in-Publication Data is on file with the Library of Congress

ISBN 978-0-679-40507-8

Jacket design by R. D. Scudellari, adapted by Carol Devine Carson

Manufactured in the United States of America
Published May 1, 2012
Reprinted Two Times
Fourth Printing, May 2012

For Ina

and

For Chase and Carla

and

For Barry, Shana and Jesse

With love

Contents

Introduction: "What the hell's the presidency for?"   ix

PART I   JOHNSON VS. KENNEDY: 1960

1   The Prediction   3

2   The Rich Man's Son   27

3   Forging Chains   54

4   The Back Stairs   109

5   The "LBJ Special"   144

PART II   "RUFUS CORNPONE"

6   "Power Is Where Power Goes"   159

7   Genuine Warmth   176

8   "Cut"   199

9   Gestures and Tactics   251

10   The Protégé   275

PART III   DALLAS

11   The Cubicle   307

12   Taking Charge   319

PART IV   TAKING COMMAND

13   Aboard Air Force One   339

14   Three Encounters   373

15   The Drums   378

PART V   TO BECOME A PRESIDENT

16   EOB 274   391
17   The Warren Commission   437
18   The Southern Strategy   452
19   "Old Harry"   466
20   "The Johnsons in Johnson City"   484
21   Serenity   503
22   "Old Harry" II   552
23   In the Books of Law   558
24   Defeating Despair   571
25   Hammer Blows   587
26   Long Enough   598

     Debts, Sources, Notes   607
     Index   693

PHOTOGRAPHS   *follow pages 202 and 426*

INTRODUCTION

"What the hell's the presidency for?"

AIR FORCE ONE, the President's plane, is divided, behind the crew's cockpit, into three compartments. In the first of them, just behind the cockpit, women sat weeping and Secret Service agents were trying to hold back tears ("You've heard of strong men crying; well, we had it there that day," recalls a reporter) as the pilot lifted the big jet off the Dallas runway in a climb so steep that to a man standing on the ground it seemed "almost vertical," leveled off for a few minutes, and then, warned that there were tornadoes between him and Washington, put the plane into another climb to get above them. In the rear compartment the widow, her suit stained with blood, was sitting next to the coffin of the dead President. And in the center compartment was the new President.

Lyndon Johnson hadn't been aboard Air Force One on the trip down to Texas. He had long since given up asking John F. Kennedy if he could accompany him on the presidential plane when they were flying to the same destination ("You don't mean to say that Mr. Johnson is again insisting on riding with me?" Kennedy had once asked his secretary in an exasperated tone), as he had given up on all his attempts to obtain some measure of recognition, or at least dignity, as Vice President. Once, as Senate Majority Leader, he had been a mighty figure—"the second most powerful man in the country"—but that seemed a long time ago now. Although initially he had been favored to win the Democratic nomination for President, he had been outmaneuvered by the younger man, and, having accepted the vice presidency, had, in that post, become not just powerless but a figure of ridicule. The gibe ("Whatever became of Lyndon Johnson?") that had started over Georgetown dinner tables was now in headlines over articles about his predicament. He himself was worried about whether or not he would be retained on the 1964 Democratic ticket, and was convinced that whether he was or not, his dreams of becoming President one day were over. He had advised more than one aide whom he would have wanted with him were he to run for or become President to leave his staff. "My future is behind me," he told one member of his staff. "Go," he said to another. "I'm finished." But he was on Air Force One now.

IN PART, this book is the story of the five years—from late 1958, when Johnson began campaigning for the presidency, to November 22, 1963—before that flight from Dallas to Washington: a story of how a man who all his life had yearned for the presidency failed in his great chance to attain that goal, of how, to a large degree because of aspects of his character that crippled him in his efforts to attain it, he allowed the prize for which he had planned and schemed and worked (worked with a tirelessness that made an ally say "I never thought it was *possible* for anyone to work that hard") to be snatched away from him. It is a story of not only failure but humiliation, of how, after he had lost the presidential nomination in 1960, he had taken a gamble—giving up the Senate leadership to accept the vice presidential nomination—because he felt that was his only remaining chance to achieve his goal, and of what followed after he became Vice President. Although Kennedy might not have won in 1960 without his presence on the ticket and his old-fashioned, whistle-stop campaigning—a fact that Kennedy himself privately acknowledged—he received no credit for that. "Power is where power goes," he had boasted in explaining why he had traded in the Senate leadership: he would be able, through his political gifts, to transform the traditionally powerless vice presidency. But when, not long after the election, he had made two attempts—one with the Senate, one with Kennedy himself—to grab powers no previous Vice President had enjoyed, both were carried out in ways so clumsy and embarrassing that it was obvious that not his old skills but only desperation was behind them. And during the three years since Kennedy had turned aside, with contemptuous ease, Johnson's attempt to maneuver him into ceding a portion of presidential power, Vice President Johnson had become among Kennedy's White House aides the object of dislike and distrust, and of derision embodied in the mocking nicknames by which they often referred to him: "Uncle Cornpone" or "Rufus Cornpone." These nicknames, and a hundred other slights, make this part of the book also a story about what being without power can mean in a city in which power is the name of the game; in a city as cruel as Washington. That part of the story—the five-year part—had ended when Kennedy's aide Kenneth O'Donnell had walked into the cubicle in Dallas' Parkland Hospital in which Lyndon Johnson, standing all but motionless against a wall, had been waiting for long minutes for definitive word on the President's fate. Seeing the stricken "face of Kenny O'Donnell who loved him so much," I knew, Lady Bird Johnson was to say, even before O'Donnell said, "He's gone."

And in part this book is the story of a period that began during that flight, for it was on Air Force One, after he had sworn the oath of office with Jacqueline

Kennedy standing beside him in a sweltering, dimly lit cabin, its window shades closed to foil would-be assassins, that his first presidential decisions were made: that the transition between the Kennedy Administration and that of Lyndon Baines Johnson began.

THAT STORY—the transition story, a story just seven weeks long: its end came, as will be seen, on January 8, 1964—is a story of a period in Lyndon Johnson's life very unlike that of the preceding five years.

Although seven times previously in the history of the American republic a presidential transition had come about not through election but through death, the death of a President in office, and in three of those seven instances, death had come by assassination rather than through natural causes, the Johnson transition took place in circumstances that made it in some ways different from—and in some ways more difficult than—any of its predecessors. The very jolt of the news was different. As the first assassination to take place in the age of television, it was the first an entire nation learned about almost at the same moment: by the time Air Force One touched down in Washington, after a flight of two hours and six minutes, 92 percent of the American people had heard the news, which crossed the country, *Newsweek* said, "like a shock wave." Tens of millions of Americans saw the coffin, escorted by Jacqueline and Robert Kennedy, descend from the plane on an hydraulic lift. And hard on the first shock came others. Forty minutes into Air Force One's flight, it was announced that a Dallas policeman had been shot, and, a few minutes later, that a twenty-four-year-old man had been arrested for questioning, and a half hour later that he was "a definitive suspect in the assassination," and on the heels of Lee Harvey Oswald's name came rumors that seemed to link him to both Cuba and the Soviet Union. With America barely a year past the Cuban Missile Crisis, the fears that had accompanied the realization in October, 1962, that the country was on the very brink of a nuclear confrontation with those two countries were still fresh in America's mind. And then, two days later, the assassin was assassinated—on live television. The shadowy figure lunging onto the screen from the right; glimpses of a pistol; "He's been shot! He's been shot! Lee Harvey Oswald has been shot!" "For one moment of total horror," the *New York Times* said, "nothing could quite compare with the killing of . . . Oswald . . . before the live cameras of the National Broadcasting Company." Concern that John F. Kennedy's assassination was the work not of a lone gunman but of a conspiracy escalated—as did concern about where (in Russia? in Cuba?) the conspiracy might have originated. "Lyndon Johnson's ascent to the presidency," says presidential historian Henry Graff, "came at the most traumatic moment in American political history." And the assassination's impact was magnified by television during the next three days, days of funeral ceremonies for the dead President unrivaled in American history for their pageantry and poignance. During the day of the assassination and the three days following, television in the average American home was tuned to the Kennedy funeral ceremonies for almost eight hours a day. The events in modern American history most comparable in their impact on the public, social scientists found, were Pearl Harbor and Franklin Roosevelt's death, but, the scientists also found that because these events had occurred before the television age, they were not in fact comparable. The pervasiveness as well as the immediacy of television coverage—"There were times during those days when *a majority of all Americans* were apparently looking at the same events and hearing the same words . . . participating together . . . in a great national event," the scientists concluded; "Nothing like this on such a scale had ever occurred before"—made the assassination and the ceremonies following it an event "probably without parallel in history."

Adding to the difficulties was the attitude toward the new President among many—most, in fact—of the late President's advisers, the men on whom Johnson would have to rely for advice and for the operation of the government. So smoothed over have their feelings been during the intervening decades that in recollections today they bear little resemblance to reality, which was that at the time Lyndon Johnson stepped into office, these men not only disliked and despised him—held him in contempt remarkable in its depth and intensity—but were aware also of what they considered indications of how President Kennedy himself had felt about him, feelings also not at all like those that have come down to us in history; it was a matter of common knowledge around the White House, for instance, that although the Vice President was a member of the group (ExComm, it was called) convened to advise John Kennedy during the Cuban Missile Crisis, the Vice President had been excluded from the meeting at which the final decision about the American response had been made. And there was yet another circumstance that made this transition unique in American history. The murdered President had a brother, who hated the new President—as the new President hated *him*. This book is therefore also the story of Lyndon Johnson and Robert Kennedy— one of the great blood feuds in American political history. It was a feud that arose out of something visceral, something deep within both men—those who witnessed their first face-to-face encounter, in the Senate cafeteria in 1953, when Robert Kennedy was only a young Senate staffer and Lyndon Johnson was the mighty Majority Leader, would never forget it—and over the years, it had only intensified: Lyndon Johnson never forgot or forgave, could never, until he died, stop talking about, Robert Kennedy's visits to his hotel room during the 1960 Democratic convention to try to force him off the ticket. Possessing during his brother's presidency the power to humiliate Johnson, Bobby Kennedy had taken many opportunities to do so. And now, in a single instant, in the crack of a Dallas gunshot, their positions had been reversed, tables turned completely, and Lyndon Johnson had the power to repay the favor—which he soon began to do. Adding still another element to the feud was a factor that seemed likely to make the transition especially problematical. During the final year before the assassination, it had become apparent that the brother had set his sights on becoming President himself one day, perhaps on succeeding John Kennedy after his presidency was over. Should he decide now to mount a challenge to Johnson, he might have on his side, in addition to the Kennedy name and aura, and the sympathy engendered by the assassination, the support of most of his brother's White House staff and Cabinet, as well as of political leaders across the country who had been members of the Kennedy camp since 1960. While ordinarily a sitting President could easily turn back any challenge to his renomination from within his party, this would be no ordinary challenge, particularly if, with November, 1964, so close upon him— Jack Kennedy's death was also the first death of a President to have occurred so late in his term; the "challenge of assuming office and then running for election in the same first year" made Johnson's transition "unprecedented" in American history, says presidential historian Richard Neustadt—the new President should prove unable to quickly unify the Democratic Party behind him. Years later, during his retirement, Johnson would speak of "the thing I feared from the first day of my presidency": an announcement by Robert Kennedy of "his intention to reclaim the throne in memory of his brother."

Were these not enough complications to imperil a transition? There was yet another: scandal, scandal on the grand scale.

A pair of scandals on that scale had been looming over the Vice President for months and were both coming to a head on the morning of November 22. One, involving Johnson's protégé Bobby Baker (known in Washington as "Little Lyndon"), had during the weeks before the assassination become a sensational cover story in national magazines. Baker was later to say that if he had talked, Johnson "might have incurred a mortal wound by these revelations. . . . They could have driven him from office," but he hadn't talked yet. Nor had any of his associates, and as a result the Vice President had not been directly implicated. But on the morning of November 22, at the very time that the motorcade was carrying Kennedy and Johnson through Dallas, back in Washington, that had been about to change. And at the same time, the other scandal—potentially even larger in scope—was escalating to a new stage in New York, in a conference at the offices of *Life* magazine, where a team of nine reporters had been working for weeks on a series of articles, with the working title of "Lyndon Johnson's Money." Editors were dividing up areas for final investigation, and trying to decide whether to run the first article in the next week's issue, which would shortly go to press, when suddenly, all over *Life*'s newsroom, phones began ringing frantically, and a secretary ran into the office shouting the news.

And finally—and most significantly—there was the situation on Capitol Hill.

For all John F. Kennedy's remarkable ability—his eloquence on the podium, whether for a speech or a press conference—to inspire a nation, to rally it to its better, most humane, aspirations, and for all his triumphs in dealing with the rest of the world—the Peace Corps, the Nuclear Test Ban Treaty, the Cuban Missile Crisis—few of his domestic goals that required legislation had been turned into reality, and at the time of his death, every major Administration bill that was before Congress was stalled, even the two bills that in 1963 the young President had lumped together as his "first priority": a civil rights bill and a tax reduction bill vital not only to expansion of the economy but to liberal aims, since economic expansion, and the resultant increase in tax revenues, were necessary if government was to fund new social welfare programs. The coalition blocking his bills—the southern Democrat-Republican coalition, the conservative coalition, that had ruled Capitol Hill for a quarter of a century—in November, 1963, was ruling Capitol Hill still. During the last week or two before the President's trip to Texas, in fact, the stalemate in Congress—the press had taken to calling it a "logjam"—had escalated to new, historic levels; both the bills were stalled, caught in a logjam that on the day John F. Kennedy died gave no signs of breaking up.

But the story of Lyndon Johnson's transition is a story not only of difficulties he faced but how he surmounted them.

He not only broke the congressional logjam, he broke it up fast, and he broke it up on civil rights.

Civil rights had always crystallized liberals' doubts about Lyndon Johnson. What they knew about him—besides his southern roots and accent, the "magnolia drawl" that raised the hackles on liberal necks—was his southern record, a twenty-year record that had begun with his arrival in Congress in 1937 and lasted through 1956, on civil rights: a perfect 100 percent record of voting against every civil rights bill that had ever made it to the floor, even bills aimed at ending lynching, and a record, moreover, as a southern strategist, protégé of the chieftain of the mighty Southern Caucus, Richard Brevard Russell, who had helped Russell ensure that most civil rights bills never made it to the floor. In 1957, in a dramatic reversal of that record, Majority Leader Johnson had rammed through the first civil rights bill to pass Congress since 1875. Significant though that breakthrough was, however, and though he passed another civil rights bill in 1960, liberal antagonism toward him had been softened scarcely at all since the bills were weak, only meagre advances toward social justice, and because his championing of them was regarded by most liberals as mere political opportunism: an attempt to lessen northern opposition to his presidential candidacy.

But although the cliché says that power always corrupts, what is seldom said, but what is equally true, is that power always *reveals*. When a man is climbing, trying to persuade others to give him power, concealment is necessary: to hide traits that might make others reluctant to give him power, to hide also what he wants to do with that power; if men recognized the traits or realized the aims, they might refuse to give him what he wants. But as a man obtains more power, camouflage is less necessary. The curtain begins to rise. The revealing begins. When Lyndon Johnson had accumulated enough power to do something—a small something—for civil rights in the Senate, he had done it, inadequate though it may have been. Now, suddenly, he had a lot more power, and it didn't take him long to reveal at least part of what he wanted to do with it. On the evening of November 26, the advisers gathered around the dining room table in his home to draft the speech he was to deliver the following day to a joint session of Congress were arguing about the amount of emphasis to be given to civil rights in that speech, his first major address as President. As Johnson sat silently listening, most of these advisers were warning that he must not emphasize the subject because it would antagonize the southerners who controlled Congress, and whose support he would need for the rest of his presidency—and because a civil rights bill had no chance of passage anyway. And then, in the early hours of the morning, as one of those advisers recalls, "one of the wise, practical people around the table" told him to his face that a President shouldn't spend his time and power on lost causes, no matter how worthy those causes might be.

"Well, what the hell's the presidency for?" Lyndon Johnson replied.

IN HIS SPEECH the next day, sympathy for the martyred President was enlisted to advance the cause, as was America's desire for continuity, for stability, for reassurance that the government was holding to a firm course despite the loss of the man who had sat at its head. Invoking Kennedy's name, he said that "No words are strong enough to express our determination to continue the forward thrust of America that he began," that "This is our challenge . . . to continue on our course," and that "no memorial oration or eulogy could more eloquently honor President Kennedy's memory than the earliest possible passage of the civil rights bill for which he fought so long. We have talked long enough in this country about equal rights. We have talked for one hundred years or more. It is time now to write the next chapter, and to write it in the books of law."

Writing it into these books would require more than sympathy, always a highly fungible emotion in politics anyway, and, as will be seen, one that had no influence whatsoever on the southern committee chairmen who ruled Congress. Strategy was necessary, too, a strategy on the grand scale, and, as will be seen, Johnson had one, a brilliant overview of a means of getting a civil rights bill passed, that he had urged on Kennedy, only to be ignored. As he had demonstrated in the Senate, moreover, it was not only strategy but tactics of which he was a master. Identifying and throwing his weight behind a seldom-used procedural lever—perhaps the only lever that could have worked—within a month after he had taken office he had broken the civil rights bill free of the congressional logjam. The bill wouldn't be passed until 1964. It would be passed then only after a half year of struggle (whose heroes included not only liberal congressmen and senators, but the men, women and children who marched and protested, and who, many of them, were beaten and tortured—and, some of them, murdered—on the streets of the South. But it was a struggle whose strategy and day-by-day tactics were laid out and directed by him, and by the end of that first month it was at least on the road to passage.

By the end of that month, the tax cut bill was also on the road to passage. And by the end of that month, by the time he left Washington for a Christmas vacation on his Texas ranch, he had won another victory, on a third bill—

defeating a seemingly innocuous measure, involving the sale of wheat to Russia, that would have curtailed the President's authority in foreign affairs. Grasping the instant he heard about the bill that it had been introduced because conservatives, emboldened by their victories over Kennedy, were confident that they could defeat a President—that, as he put it, "They've got the bit in their teeth," and thought they "could bully me" the way they believed they had bullied Kennedy— he decided in that instant that the way to yank out the bit was to make the bill a test of strength with Congress, and to win the test. A simple majority wasn't going to be enough to teach Congress a lesson. "I hope that [bill] gets *murdered*," he snarled, and, sitting in the Oval Office, he kept telephoning senator after senator, cajoling, bullying, threatening, charming, long after he had the majority, to make the vote overwhelming enough to ensure the lesson was clear. The vote *was* overwhelming, and when, a week later, conservatives attempted a maneuver that would have overturned it, Johnson had a maneuver of his own ready. His tactic was so risky that congressional leaders warned him not to use it; he used it—and murdered the bill once and for all. "At that moment the power of the federal government began flowing back to the White House," he was to say—and boastful though that statement might be, it was true. To watch Lyndon Johnson deal with Congress during the transition—to watch him break the unbreakable conservative coalition—is to see a President fighting not merely with passion and determination but with something more: with a particular talent, a talent for winning the passage of legislation (in this case legislation that would write into the books of law a measure of justice for millions of people to whom justice had been too long denied) that was more than talent, that was a gift, and a very rare one. To watch Lyndon Johnson during the transition is to see political genius in action.

He handled all the problems—the Kennedy men's antipathy, the Kennedy brother's hatred, the rumors over the assassination that, had they not been defused, might have escalated into international crisis—with the same sureness of touch. If the story of the five years is a story of failure, the story of the seven weeks is a story of what rose out of failure: triumph. So on one level, the biographical level, the recounting of the life of Lyndon Baines Johnson, the two stories in this book are really one story: a narrative with a single, sweeping arc. It rises from the depths of a man's life, a period in which utterly without power he stands naked to his enemies, a period in which a man who dreads above all else what he calls "humiliation" suffers what he dreads day after day. It sweeps up to the heights of that life, as he is catapulted in an instant, in a gunshot, into the power he had always wanted—and he proceeds to demonstrate, almost in the instant he attains that power, how much he is capable of accomplishing with it.

IF IT IS to succeed in its purposes, however, this book must explore another level as well.

This is the fourth in a series of volumes that I call *The Years of Lyndon Johnson* because it attempts to portray not only his life but his years: the era in which he lived, rose to the presidency and finally abandoned the presidency—America in the middle decades of the twentieth century, in other words. It tries most particularly to focus on and examine a specific, determinative aspect of that era—political power; to explore, through the life of its protagonist, the acquisition and use of various forms of that power during that half century of American history, and to ascertain also the fundamental realities of that power; to learn what lay, beneath power's trappings, at power's core.

The transition period covered in this book is particularly well suited to that purpose, for a way to gain insight into the most fundamental realities of any form of power is to observe it during its moments of deepest crisis, during its most intense struggles, when, under maximum stress, its every resource must be brought to bear—with the undiluted pragmatism born of absolute necessity—if the challenges facing it are to be met. It is at such moments that every one of those resources, every component of that power, is not only visible but, being used to its utmost, can be observed in all its facets. In trying to understand presidential power, one would find that the transition of 1963—the seven-week-long passage of power between John Fitzgerald Kennedy and Lyndon Baines Johnson—is one of those moments. Because of the difficult—in some ways unique—challenges facing the incoming chief executive, it was a moment in which the use of presidential power to the limits of its practical, pragmatic possibilities was necessary if the transition was to be successful. Johnson used that power to those limits. To watch him deal with Congress, deal with the Kennedys, confront a dozen other challenges for which there was no precedent—for which he had to create his own precedents—is to watch a President, in very difficult circumstances, triumph over them, and it is therefore a means of gaining new insight into some fundamental realities about the pragmatic potential in the American presidency.

AND ABOUT POTENTIAL beyond the pragmatic.

Brief though the transition period was, during it Lyndon Johnson not only rescued his predecessor's programs but launched one of his own. Barely into his second month in office he seized on a concept that had just begun to surface—a suggestion, a gleam in the eyes of a few members of the Kennedy Administration, that the late President had endorsed in theory but had done almost nothing to push forward—seized on it the moment a Kennedy adviser mentioned it to him, seized on it with such passion ("so spontaneous . . . instinctive and intuitive and uncalculated") that the adviser knew in that moment that he had been very wrong about Lyndon Johnson. Enlarging it far beyond anything previously envisioned, he pushed it forward, prodded his advisers into bringing their imagination to bear on it, and, in the second major speech of his presidency, the State of the Union address he delivered to Congress on January 8, 1964, announced it, and it was a program whose title, however hyperbolic, made clear that he viewed it—this crude, coarse, ruthless, often cruel man, who all his life had made a mantra of pragmatism ("It's not the job of a politician to go around saying principled things")—as nothing less than a crusade. It was a crusade for a noble end. The speech made clear on whose behalf the crusade would be launched. "Unfortunately, many Americans live on the outskirts of hope—some because of their poverty, and some because of their color, and all too many because of both," he said in that State of the Union address. "Our task is to help replace their despair with opportunity. This administration today, here and now, declares unconditional war on poverty in America." The speech made clear also the weapons he was going to deploy in the crusade, and the enemies—ancient enemies, hitherto invincible, whom he named by name—that he intended the crusade to conquer. "Our chief weapons . . . will be better schools, and better health, and better homes, and better training, and better job opportunities to help more Americans, especially young Americans, escape from squalor and misery and unemployment," he said. And the speech announced also the crusade's goal, which was revolutionary: "not only to relieve the symptom of poverty, but to cure it and, above all, to prevent it." By the time Lyndon Johnson stepped down from the dais after that speech, it was apparent that the program to which he was committing his still-infant Administration was one whose purpose was to right, on a vast scale, vast wrongs, to use to an extent rare in history a great nation's wealth to ameliorate the harshness of life for a portion of its citizens (a substantial portion: one-fifth of America's 150 million citizens in 1964 was 30 million people) too often overlooked by government in the past. It was clear that it was a program whose aim was to launch America on a course toward social justice that, were it to be completed, would result in nothing less than a society's transformation. If, as Martin Luther King Jr. had said, "The arc of the moral universe is long, but it bends toward justice," during the two centuries since the United States of America had come into existence, the arc had bent slowly indeed. During those transition weeks (and, in fact, during the following years, as Lyndon Johnson widened the War on Poverty by introducing legislation on a dozen fronts to transform not just low-income America but the nation as a whole into "the Great Society") one can see the new President trying to bend it faster. That State of the Union speech—delivered forty-seven days, just short of seven weeks, after the assassination of John Kennedy—marked the moment when Lyndon Johnson, moving beyond a continuation of Kennedy's policies, made the presidency fully his own, so it is therefore the event that signifies the end of the transition, the moment when the passage of power from Kennedy to Johnson is completed. And to see Lyndon Johnson take hold of presidential power, and so quickly begin to use it for ends so monumental is to see, with unusual clarity, the immensity of the potential an American President possesses to effect transformative change in the nation he leads.

LITTLE OF THAT potential—those possibilities—was to be realized. This book is not the story of Lyndon Johnson's five-year presidency as a whole, but only of its brief first phase, and the longer story will not be a triumphant one. His presidency would, as I have written, be marked by victories: his great personal victory, his election, in November, 1964, to the presidency in his own right by what was then, and, as of this writing almost half a century later, is still, the greatest popular majority ever won by a candidate for the American presidency, and his great legislative victories. Taken as a whole, the bills passed between the beginning of 1964 and the end of 1968 make the Johnson presidency one which saw the legislative realization of many of the noblest aspirations of the liberal spirit in America. Not only the two great civil rights measures but Medicare and Medicaid, and the sixty separate education laws, including the Act that created Head Start—however inadequately thought through and in some cases flawed and contradictory some of these measures might have been, due to the haste with which he pushed them through, they were laws of which liberals had dreamed for decades, laws that embodied government's responsibility to fulfill what Johnson's father, the Populist legislator, believed was the highest duty of government: to help people caught in "the tentacles of circumstance."

Yet victories would not, as I have written, be the only hallmarks that would make the presidency of Lyndon Johnson vivid in history. Civil rights, the War on Poverty, Medicare, Head Start—but Vietnam. Vietnam and the credibility gap. The loss of trust in the presidency, of belief in what the President was saying, escalated under Richard Nixon, Johnson's successor, but it began under Johnson.

And there were other casualties. The cost of the Vietnam War had to be borne by the same national treasury that was funding the War on Poverty, and the implications of that fact for liberal dreams would be devastating. Monumental as were some of the achievements of Lyndon Johnson's Administration, they were as nothing beside the dreams he had enunciated in that first State of the Union speech. Although there would be many reasons that the poverty war was lost, one of the main reasons was the Asian war.

THE TRANSITION PERIOD on which we are concentrating in this volume contains the seeds of all that was to follow. Few as they were, the decisions that Lyndon Johnson made about Vietnam during these seven weeks (he was, as will be seen, making every effort to keep them few, to tamp down Vietnam as a political issue until after the November, 1964, election) nonetheless display the secrecy and deceit that were to play such a large role in making Vietnam—and Johnson's presidency—a tragic drama. But the story of Lyndon Johnson during the opening, transition, weeks of his presidency is a triumphant story, one in which it is possible to glimpse the full possibilities of presidential power—of that power exercised by a master in the use of power—in a way that is visible at only a few times in American history.

Part I

JOHNSON
vs.
KENNEDY
1960

1

The Prediction

WHEN HE WAS YOUNG—seventeen and eighteen years old—Lyndon Johnson worked on a road gang that was building a highway (an unpaved highway: roads in the isolated, impoverished Texas Hill Country weren't paved in the 1920s) between Johnson City and Austin.

With little mechanical equipment available, the road was being built almost entirely by hand, and his job, when he wasn't half of a pick-and-shovel team with Ben Crider, a burly friend—six years older—from Johnson City, was "driving" a "fresno," a heavy two-handled metal scoop with a sharpened front edge, that was pulled by four mules. Standing behind the scoop, between its handles, as the mules strained forward to force the scoop through the hard Hill Country caliche soil, he would push as they pulled. Since he needed a hand for each handle, the reins were tied together and wrapped around his back, so for this work—hard even for older men; for a tall, skinny, awkward teenager, it was, the other men recall, "backbreaking labor," "too heavy" for Lyndon—Lyndon Johnson was, really, in harness with the mules. But at lunch hour each day, as the gang sat eating—in summer in whatever shade they could find as protection from the blazing Hill Country sun, in winter huddled around a fire (it would get so cold, Crider recalls, that "you had to build a fire to thaw your hands before you could handle a pick and shovel . . . build us a fire and thaw and work all day")— Lyndon would, in the words of another member of the gang, "talk big" to the older men. "He had big ideas. . . . He wanted to do something big with his life." And he was quite specific about what he wanted to do: "I'm going to be President of the United States one day," he predicted.

Poverty and backbreaking work—clearing cedar on other men's farms for two dollars a day, or chopping and picking cotton: on your hands and knees all day beneath that searing sun—were woven deep in the fabric of Lyndon Johnson's youth, as were humiliation and fear: he was coming home at night to a house to which other Johnson City families brought charity in the form of cooked dishes because there was no money in that house to buy food; to a house on which, moreover, his family was having such difficulty paying the taxes and mortgage that they were afraid it might not be theirs much longer. But woven into it also was that prediction.

In many ways, his whole life would be built around that prediction: around a climb toward that single, far-off goal. As a young congressman in Washington, he was careful not to mention that ambition to the rising young New Dealers with whom he was allying himself, but they were aware of it anyway. James H. Rowe Jr., Franklin Roosevelt's aide, who spent more time with Johnson than the others, says, "From the day he got here, he wanted to be President." When old friends from Texas visited him, sometimes his determination burst out of him despite himself, as if he could not contain it. "By *God,* I'll be President someday!" he exclaimed one evening when he was alone with Welly Hopkins. And an incident in 1940 showed the Texans how much he wanted the prize he sought, how much he was willing to sacrifice to attain it.

Lack of money had been the cause of so many of the insecurities of his youth, and his election to Congress, far from soothing those fears, had seemed only to intensify them: he talked incessantly about how his father, who had been an elected official himself—a six-term member of the Texas House of Representatives—had ended up as a state bus inspector, and had died penniless; he didn't want to end up like his father, he said. He talked about how he kept seeing around Washington former congressmen who had lost their seats—as, he said, he would inevitably one day lose his—and were working in low-paying, demeaning jobs; over and over again he related how once, while he was riding in an elevator in the Capitol, the elevator operator had told him that *he* had been a congressman. Hungry for money, he had already started accepting, indeed soliciting, financial favors from businessmen who wanted favors from him, and had been pleading with two important businessmen—George R. Brown of the Texas contracting firm of Brown & Root and the immensely wealthy Austin publisher, real estate magnate and oilman Charles Marsh—to "find" him a business in which he could make a little money of his own. So when, one autumn day in 1940, the three men—Johnson, Brown and Marsh—were vacationing together at the luxurious Greenbrier Hotel in West Virginia, lying on a blanket in front of their adjoining cottages, and Marsh offered Lyndon Johnson a business in which he could make a lot of money, the two businessmen were sure the congressman would accept it. Marsh, who, in Brown's words, "loved Lyndon like a son," told him he could have his share in a lucrative oilfield partnership, a share worth three-quarters of a million dollars, without even putting up any money; he could "pay for it out of his profits each year." To the surprise of both men, however, Johnson said that he would have to think about the offer—and after a week he turned it down. "I can't be an oilman," he said; if the public knew he had oil interests, "it would kill me politically."

Believing they understood Johnson's political ambitions—Lyndon was always telling them about how he wanted to stay in the House until a Senate seat opened up, and then run for the Senate, about how the Senate seat was his ulti-mate goal in politics; never had he mentioned any other office, nor did he men-tion one during his week at the Greenbrier—Marsh and Brown were shocked by his refusal. Being known as an oilman couldn't hurt him in his congressional dis-trict, or in a Senate race in oil-dominated Texas. But then they realized that there was in fact one office for which he would be "killed" by being an "oilman." And then they understood that while Lyndon Johnson might hunger for money, that hunger was as nothing beside his hunger for something else.

And unlike others—the many, many others—in Washington who wanted the same thing he did, who had set their sights on the same goal, Lyndon Baines Johnson, born August 27, 1908, had mapped out a path to that goal, and he refused to be diverted from it.

The path ran only through Washington—it was paved with national, not state power—and it had only three steps: House of Representatives, Senate, pres-idency. And after he had fought his way onto it—winning a seat in the House in 1937 in a desperate, seemingly hopeless campaign—he could not be persuaded by anyone, not even Franklin Roosevelt, to turn off it. In 1939, the President offered to appoint him director of the New Deal's Rural Electrification Adminis-tration. The directorship of a nationwide agency, particularly one as fast-growing, and politically important, as the REA, was not the kind of job offered to many men only thirty years old, but Johnson turned the offer down; he was afraid, he said, of being "sidetracked." In 1946, he was urged by his party to run for the governorship of Texas. If he did, he knew, his election was all but assured, and at the time his path seemed to have reached a dead end in Washington: stuck in the House now for almost a decade, with little chance of any imminent advancement to its hierarchy, he seemed to have no chance of stepping into a Senate seat. In the 435-member House, he was still only one of the crowd of ju-nior congressmen, and, as a woman who worked with him when he was young put it, he "couldn't stand not being somebody—just could not *stand* it." But he still wouldn't leave the road he had chosen as the best road to the prize he wanted so badly. The governorship, he explained to aides, could never be more than a "detour" on his "route," a detour that might turn into a "dead end." (Some years later, when his longtime assistant John Connally decided to run for the governor-ship, Johnson told him he was making a mistake in leaving Washington. *"Here's* where the power is," he said.) In 1948, still stuck in the House, he was about to turn forty, and a new assistant, Horace Busby, saw that "He believed, and he believed it really quite sincerely . . . that when a man reached forty, it was all over. And there was no bill ever passed by Congress that bore his name; he had done very little in his life." Hopeless though his ambition might seem, however, Lyndon Johnson still clung to it. Instructing Busby to refer to him in press releases as "LBJ," he explained: "FDR–LBJ, FDR–LBJ. Do you get it? What I want is for them to start thinking of me in terms of initials." It was only presi-dents whom headline writers and the American people referred to by their initials; "he was just so determined that someday he would be known as LBJ," Busby recalls.

That year, frantic to escape from the trap that the House had become for him, he entered a Senate race he seemed to have no chance of winning; during the campaign, and during post-campaign vote-counting, he went beyond even the notoriously elastic boundaries of Texas politics, and won.

But the Senate, into which he was sworn in January, 1949, was also only a step toward his goal, only the second rung on a three-rung ladder.

It was a rung on which he seemed very much at home. Lyndon Johnson was, as I have written, a reader of men. He had promulgated guidelines for such reading, which he tried to teach his young staff members. "Watch their hands, watch their eyes," he told them. "Read eyes. No matter what a man is saying to you, it's not as important as what you can read in his eyes." Teaching them to peruse men's weaknesses, he said that "the most important thing a man has to tell you is what he's not telling you; the most important thing he has to say is what he's trying not to say"—and therefore it was important not to let a conversation end until you learned what the man wasn't saying, until you "got it out of him." Johnson himself read with a genius that couldn't be taught, with a gift that was so instinctive that one aide, Robert G. (Bobby) Baker, calls it a "sense." "He seemed to *sense* each man's individual price and the commodity he preferred as coin." And Johnson also had a gift for using what he read. His longtime lawyer and viceroy in Texas, Edward A. Clark, was to say, "I never saw anything like it. He would listen *at them* . . . and in five minutes he could get a man to think, 'I like you, young fellow. I'm going to help you.' " Watching Lyndon Johnson "play" older men, Thomas G. Corcoran, the New Deal insider and quite a player of older men himself, was to explain that "He was smiling and deferential, but, hell, lots of guys can be smiling and deferential. Lyndon had one of the most incredible capacities for dealing with older men. He could follow someone's mind around, and get where it was going before the other fellow knew where it was going." These gifts served Lyndon Johnson better in small groups—men marveled at his ability to "make liberals think he was one of them, conservatives think he was one of *them*"—since that tactic worked best when there was no member of the other side around to hear. It worked best of all when he was alone with one man. "Lyndon was the greatest salesman one on one who ever lived," George Brown was to say. These gifts had gone largely wasted in the House, whose 435 members "could be dealt with only in bodies and droves," but the first time Lyndon Johnson walked into the Senate Chamber after his election to that body, he muttered, in a voice so low that his aide Walter Jenkins, standing beside him, felt he was "speaking to himself," that the Senate was "the right size."

This assessment proved accurate. With ninety-six men in that body, there were only a relatively small number of texts to be read, and because of senators' six-year terms, these texts were not constantly changing, as they were in the House, and therefore could be perused at length—some Senate subcommittees had only three members, so on these subcommittees it was literally necessary for the great salesman to sell only one man to obtain a majority for his views—and he rose to power in the Senate with unprecedented speed. In a body previously dominated by the strictures of seniority, he became Assistant Leader of his party in 1951, two years after he arrived there; in another two years, still in his first term, he became the party's Leader; two years later, in 1955, when the Democrats became the majority party in the Senate, Lyndon Johnson became the youngest Majority Leader in history, the most powerful man in the Senate after just a single term there.

The youngest—and the greatest. By 1955, in the opinion of its journalistic chroniclers and a growing number of historians and political scientists, the Senate was the joke it had been for decades, only more so—so much an object of contempt that, more and more frequently, a suggestion was being heard that perhaps the institution might be dispensed with entirely: its "obsolesence," said the era's most authoritative work on Capitol Hill, George B. Galloway's *The Legislative Process in Congress,* "may lead the American people in time to recognize that their second chamber is not indispensable." Revolutionizing the Senate, not only pushing long-stalled social welfare legislation through it but making it, for the first time in over a century, a center of governmental energy and creativity, Lyndon Johnson brought a nineteenth-century—in many ways an eighteenth-century—institution into the twentieth century. The role of Leader—legislative leader—was, furthermore, clearly a role he was born to play. As he stood at the Leader's commanding front-row center desk in the Senate Chamber directing the Senate's actions with the surest of hands, as he strode the aisles of the Chamber and Capitol with colleagues addressing him by title—"Good morning, Leader." "Could I have a minute of your time, Leader?" "Mr. Leader, I never thought you could pull that one off"—he was completely in charge, a man at home in his job. His twelve years in the Senate, his wife, Lady Bird, was to say, "were the happiest twelve years of our lives."

To him, however, the Senate remained only a rung on the ladder—as was demonstrated in 1956, at the Democratic National Convention in Chicago. He had stayed out of the primaries and other pre-convention maneuvering because he had concluded he had no chance to win the party's presidential nomination, but when at the very last moment, on the very eve of the convention, he suddenly came to feel that he *did* have a chance, he grabbed for the prize. Although his effort lasted only two days, the frenzied urgency with which, during these days, he grabbed ("Deep down, he understood the realities," Jim Rowe recalls, "but he wanted to be President *so much.*" Adds Tommy Corcoran: "On most things, you could talk sense to Lyndon. But there was no talking to him about this") showed how desperately he wanted it. And when the two days were over, and with another two days still remaining before the actual balloting, it became clear that the ballot would be only a formality and that Adlai E. Stevenson of Illinois was assured of an overwhelming victory, Johnson, in the past invariably the most pragmatic of politicians, nevertheless refused to withdraw his name—against all logic, in the face of every pragmatic consideration—his supporters felt they understood the reason. After explaining that Johnson's actions "made no sense to anyone, myself included," John Connally added that in politics "you can always have a dream," that "you always have hope"—and that Johnson had simply been unable to bring himself to give up his great dream. "He wanted it so much he wasn't thinking straight," Corcoran said. Resting up at Brown & Root's hunting lodge in Falfurrias, Texas, after the convention, Johnson spent hours talking to George Brown, who says, "He hadn't thought he would be so close . . . and then when all of a sudden, he felt he was close, he got carried away with the thought that he might get it, and he simply couldn't bear to just admit he didn't have a chance." That was the explanation, Tommy Corcoran agrees; Johnson hadn't withdrawn "Because he couldn't bear to." And these men knew he would try again—at the next convention, in 1960. Standing ankle-deep in discarded sandwich wrappers, coffee containers and Johnson placards on the Convention floor after Stevenson had won (he received 905 votes, Johnson 80), Connally shouted defiantly, "Don't you worry, this was just a practice run. We'll be back four years from now!"

ONE OBSTACLE MADE CLIMBING TO the next—the top, the ultimate—rung, reaching the prize of which he had so long dreamed, especially difficult for him. He was from the South, from one of the eleven states that had seceded from the Union and formed the rebel Confederacy, and that, despite America's Civil War almost a century before, still largely denied basic civil rights to their black citizens—to the indignation and anger of the heavily populated northern states, the states whose convention votes determined the Democratic nominee. With growing black protests focusing attention on southern injustice, northern anger against the South was mounting steadily during the late 1950s. No southerner had been elected President for more than a century,* and it was a bitter article of faith among southern politicians that no southerner would be elected President in any foreseeable future; when members of the House of Representatives gave their Speaker, Sam Rayburn, ruler of the House for more than two decades, a limousine as a present, attached to the back of the front seat was a plaque that read "To Our Beloved Sam Rayburn—Who Would Have Been President If He Had Come from Any Place but the South."

During his first twenty years in Congress, through 1956, Lyndon Johnson's 100 percent southern voting record on civil rights and his work as a southern strategist, a Richard Russell lieutenant, against rights bills—work that had won him the trust and respect of the "Georgia Giant" so completely that Russell

---

*Since Zachary Taylor in 1848. Andrew Johnson of Tennessee was not elected but completed Abraham Lincoln's term.

anointed him to one day succeed him, and the Southern Bloc raised him to the Senate leadership—had put what one journalist called "the taint of magnolias" on Lyndon Johnson; in 1956, there had been no realistic possibility that the North would support him for the nomination, or that it would, should he be nominated, vote for him for President. He could never scrub off that taint completely, but during the year following the 1956 disappointment, he managed to remove part of it. Throughout his life, there had been hints that he possessed a true, deep compassion for the downtrodden, and particularly for poor people of color, along with a true, deep desire to raise them up. During his previous career, that compassion, subordinated always to ambition, had revealed itself only in brief flashes, quickly suppressed, but in 1957, compassion and ambition had finally come into alignment, pointing at last in the same direction. His allies in Washington told him bluntly what he already knew: that the crux of the North's animosity to him was its belief that he was opposed to civil rights, and that the only way to dilute that animosity was to pass a civil rights bill. "Consequential action . . . is essential for LBJ," warned a confidential memo he received from his supporter Philip Graham, publisher of the *Washington Post.* Otherwise, Graham told him, he might wind up his career as only another southern legislative leader, "only to be (another) Dick Russell." Corcoran, that ultimate Washington insider, was, as always, blunter; he was to recall telling Johnson flatly in 1957 that "If he didn't pass a civil rights bill, he could just forget [the] 1960 [nomination]." And these warnings were being given to a man who didn't need them. "If I failed to produce on this one," Lyndon Johnson himself said, "everything I had built up over the years would be completely undone." In 1957, he set out to pass a civil rights bill. And when, after months of effort, that attempt seemed to have failed, and he retreated to his ranch, as if to avoid being identified with another civil rights defeat, Rowe pursued him with a memo warning him that he had no choice but to come back and fight: "This is Armageddon for Lyndon Johnson. . . . I would not like to see the 1960 nomination go down the drain because of . . . 1957." It had been upon receipt of that memo at the ranch that Lyndon Johnson had returned to Washington, and, in a monumental feat of legislative maneuvering, of bullying, cajoling, threatening, of lightning tactical decisions on the Senate floor, and of parliamentary genius on a grand scale, including a strategic masterstroke that brought into line behind his efforts, in a single transaction, a dozen western senators, had succeeded in persuading his twenty-one fellow southern senators—the mighty "Southern Caucus"—to allow the passage of the first civil rights bill since Reconstruction, eighty-two years earlier. It was not a strong bill. By the time Johnson had finished fashioning a compromise that the southerners would accept, provisions that would have enforced school desegregation and banned racial segregation in housing, hotels, restaurants and other public places—provisions liberals considered essential—had been removed; only a single civil right, voting, remained, and the provisions for enforcing that lone right proved largely useless. But the mere fact of the bill's passage—that after eighty-two years in which every civil rights bill that reached the Senate had died there, one had finally been passed—was of historic signifi-cance. "It opened a major branch of American government to a tenth of the pop-ulation for which all legislative doors had been slammed shut," Johnson's longtime press secretary, George Reedy, said. And Johnson argued—in a con-tention that would be vindicated by history—that although there was only one right remaining in the bill, that was the right that mattered: that it gave blacks the power to at least begin fighting for other rights. Furthermore, he pointed out, once a bill was passed, it could be amended to correct its deficiencies. "It's just a beginning," he said. "We'll do it again, in a couple of years. . . . Don't worry, it's only the first."

Although passage of the 1957 Civil Rights Act did not eliminate the distrust with which liberals viewed him—far from it; his previous record on civil rights was too long, and too southern, for that, the bill he had forced through too weak—his Washington allies felt that the sharpest edges of that distrust had been blunted. As for the southern senators, a key reason they had allowed the measure to pass was their hope that enactment of a bill with which Johnson was identified might, by lessening northern distrust of him, enable the South to get its first Pres-ident in a century; they were confident that as President, Johnson would keep civil rights reform to a minimum. He had, in years of private conversations, con-vinced the southerners that in his heart he was on their side. "We can never make him President unless the Senate first disposes of civil rights," Russell had explained to Reedy. So if he ran for the 1960 nomination, expectations were that the eleven southern states would be solidly behind him—a bloc of 352 votes out of the 761 needed for nomination in the Democratic convention. And he had a real chance, political observers said, to go into the convention with a large bloc of votes from the West as well. Now, at last, was the moment Lyndon Johnson had been waiting for all his life. While Adlai Stevenson was still the idol of many Democratic liberals, his two losses in presidential campaigns disqualified him in the eyes of party professionals, and anyway he had said quite definitively that he would not be a candidate. The party's perennial hopeful, Estes Kefauver of Ten-nessee (Adlai's running mate in 1956), was distrusted by these same profession-als because of his stubborn independence. And Kefauver, like the other potential candidates, John F. Kennedy of Massachusetts, Hubert Humphrey of Minnesota and Stuart Symington of Missouri, was a senator, and he, Lyndon Johnson, was the Senate's *Leader, their* leader, the man they had to come to—and *had* been coming to, for years—for every large and small favor in the Senate pantry. As Lyndon Johnson surveyed the field in early 1958, none of these men seemed a particularly formidable opponent.

If he won the nomination, furthermore, he would not have to face Eisen-hower, since the beloved President would have served the two terms the Consti-tution allowed. Neither of the two potential Republican nominees—William Knowland of California and Eisenhower's Vice President, Richard M. Nixon—

would be nearly as formidable. Lyndon Johnson had positioned himself as well as was possible for a southern candidate. Now was the moment to strike.

BUT HE DIDN'T.

Sometime in 1958—no one involved knows the exact date—he summoned to his LBJ Ranch six or seven men who were veterans of previous campaigns, greeted them on the front lawn that sloped down from the house to the little Pedernales River, asked them to pull the lawn chairs into a semicircle around him, and told them he had called them together to discuss his upcoming campaign for the presidency. "He was convinced that he was the best man to be President," recalls one of the group, Texas State Senator Charles Herring, and "he was convinced that he could be nominated and win if we'd work hard enough." "I'm going to be President," he told them. That was his destiny. "I was *meant* to be President."

Having worked for Johnson in earlier campaigns—Herring, for example, had been a part of the first Lyndon Johnson campaign, two decades before, when he ran for Congress in 1937, and of every campaign since (the other five congressional races, and three races for the Senate: the losing campaign in 1941, the legendary eighty-seven-vote victory of 1948 and the walkaway of 1954); Joe Kilgore, now a congressman, had worked the Rio Grande Valley for Johnson in '41 and carried it with him in '48 and '54—the men in that group had heard similar speeches at the start of campaigns, of so many campaigns, in fact, that among themselves they had given the speech a name: "The sales pitch." No matter what office he had been running for, he "would make that pitch: that he was going to be President one day," Kilgore recalls.

This occasion seemed no different. As Lyndon Johnson sat in front of his big white house under a majestic oak tree, facing the men and the long, sloping lawn behind them, wearing a rancher's khaki pants, open-necked shirt and high boots, the men there remember him, as Kilgore says, "leaning out of his chair like he always was." He was a big man—just under six feet four inches in height—and everything about him was outsize, dramatic: his arms long even for a tall man, his hands huge, mottled; the powerful shape of his massive head emphasized because his thinning, still mostly black, hair was slicked down flat on it. His face, unblurred by excess flesh because, ever since his 1955 heart attack, he was keeping his weight thirty or forty pounds below its previous level, was a portrait in aggressiveness: between the long ears the sharp, jutting nose; the sharp, jutting jaw; under long, heavy black eyebrows penetrating, intimidating eyes so dark a brown that they seemed black. And as he talked, leaning forward out of his chair, his belief in his destiny poured out of Lyndon Johnson with such passion and intensity that, as had been said about him, "He was big all right, but he got bigger as he talked to you." And now, on the ranch lawn in 1958, "he was very aggressive," Herring says. "Anyone who didn't agree with him was wrong. He knew he was going to win. He knew in his own mind that he was destined to be President of the United States." He didn't use the word "destined," Herring says. "That wasn't a word in his vocabulary." But he used other words that conveyed the same meaning. "He told us, 'I'm going to be President. I was *meant* to be President. I was *intended* to be President. And I'm *going* to be.'"

These men had also heard before some variation of the words Lyndon Johnson spoke next. If we do *everything,* we'll win, he told them. It was simply a matter of hard work. In every campaign, as in every aspect of his life, Herring, Kilgore and the other men in the little circle knew, Lyndon Johnson had driven himself, and had driven his men, reciting that mantra, "If we do *everything,*" and now he told them what "everything" was going to mean in the campaign for the nomination: They would each shortly be assigned a group of states for which they would be responsible, and they would make contact with—and try to win to Johnson's side—every member of those states' convention delegations. Between them, and others who would be brought aboard and assigned responsibility for other states, "we were," Herring recalls, "going to see every Democratic delegate in the United States." So, having heard similar sales pitches before, they felt they knew what would quickly come next: the list of states to which each of them was assigned and then the barrage of orders telling them what they were to do to win those states' delegates for Lyndon, orders that would include details of each delegate's political, personal and financial situation, and then the follow-up calls from Johnson—the calls, often in the middle of the night, in which he did not bother to identify himself but simply began, as soon as the telephone receiver was picked up, to ask questions, demand answers (Had this been done? Had that been done? Why hadn't more been done?) and to give new assignments.

But this time, as month after month passed in 1958, nothing came, not even the list of assigned states. "We didn't hear anything at all," Kilgore says. And when, puzzled, they called the two men they normally called when they had questions—John Connally, who had left Johnson's staff to become attorney for the wealthy oilman Sid Richardson but who would, Johnson had told them, be running the campaign, and Walter Jenkins, the member of Johnson's staff most able to convey Johnson's thinking—the answers they received were evasive. Oh, he would be running, Connally and Jenkins told them. Of course he would be running. He just wasn't running yet.

But, as month followed month, and 1958 drew to a close, and the convention and election year of 1960 drew closer, the assignments were still not forthcoming.

MEN WERE PUZZLED in Washington, too. When a group of attorneys—a dozen leading legal and political minds of the New and Fair Deals—had, in 1957, been brought together in the conference room at Corcoran & Rowe to devise wording that would facilitate passage of the civil rights bill, the senior partner of that influential Washington law firm had told them, "You know, we're all pros here, and we can talk to each other. We know we're here to elect Lyndon Johnson President." And now, in 1958, with the bill passed, "it was," Reedy says, "time to move." Hardly had the year begun when the firm's other name partner was sitting in Johnson's office in the Capitol explaining what Johnson had to do.

He had to broaden his support beyond the South, Jim Rowe said, but the big northern states were controlled by a few bosses—Dick Daley of Illinois, Dave Lawrence of Pennsylvania, Mike DiSalle of Ohio, Carmine De Sapio and Mike Prendergast in New York, John Bailey of Connecticut. To win the support of these hard-eyed men, and of party chieftains in smaller northern states, he would have to demonstrate that, although he was a southerner, he could attract support in non-southern states, not in liberal strongholds like Illinois or Pennsylvania or New York, perhaps, but certainly in the border states, and in the western and Rocky Mountain states. That could only be done, Rowe said, if he entered some of the Democratic primaries that would be held in 1960. There would be sixteen of them, and some of them seemed naturals for Johnson: Indiana, for example, a conservative state with strong ties to the South; and West Virginia, whose junior senator, Robert C. Byrd, a Johnson acolyte, was already urging him to run, promising to deliver the state for him—a state so overwhelmingly Protestant that even if a Kennedy candidacy had somehow managed to pick up steam, it would be derailed there. He had to decide which primaries he was going to enter, Rowe said, and he had to decide quickly. While the primaries might be two years away, it was none too early to begin setting up organizations—statewide organizations, county-wide organizations, organizations in each state's individual congressional districts. He had to start immediately making trips to states that would not hold primaries as well as to those that did, meeting the men who would select and, in some cases, control the delegates who would cast votes at the convention; he had to establish personal relationships with them—personal and other kinds: had to find out what they wanted, what promises (of positions in a new presidential Administration, for themselves or for their allies; of rewards even more pragmatic) would enlist their support; what issues they cared about, cared about deeply enough that a candidate's position on them would be a decisive factor in whether or not they supported him. And, Rowe said, it was important to start doing that, too, as soon as possible: to lock up delegates before they were locked up by someone else.

Lyndon Johnson had, George Reedy was to say, "an almost mystical belief in Jim's powers" because of a memorandum that Rowe had written to President Harry Truman in 1948, at a moment when Truman's re-election campaign looked hopeless. Johnson knew that Truman had kept the memorandum—thirty-two single-spaced typewritten pages, containing a campaign strategy of great specificity and pragmatism, with every one of its recommendations based not on ideology but on what the memo called "the politically advantageous thing to do"—in the bottom drawer of his desk in the Oval Office all during the campaign, using it as a blueprint for his come-from-behind victory over Thomas Dewey. Having read it himself, Johnson believed that its brilliance had been proven by Truman's victory. Feeling that Rowe might be able to do the same for him—could give him, too, a blueprint for reaching the goal that flickered always before him—he had often, as in the case of the "Armageddon" memo, given heavy weight to Rowe's opinions. But this time, when Rowe gave his advice, Lyndon Johnson rejected it—all of it.

He wasn't going to enter any primaries, he told Rowe. He wasn't going to run around the country giving speeches. He was going to make no overt move at all to get the nomination. Instead, he was going to stay in Washington and stick to running the Senate; he was going, he said, to "tend the store." He had a responsibility to do that, he said; being Majority Leader was a full-time job, and he was going to concentrate on that job, and simply stay in Washington and do it. The country would see that he was doing it, he said; the country knew what he had accomplished as Majority Leader, and would see that he was doing the responsible thing.

He would pick up plenty of non-southern support without running around the country, he said. He would get that support right out of Washington. For one thing, he had Mr. Sam. The Speaker, he said, had an awful lot of representatives who owed him favors and who wanted favors from him. And he himself, he said, had his senators. He could count on them, he said, senators like Carl Hayden, Mike Mansfield, Clint Anderson and Dennis Chavez. Ol' Carl had promised him Arizona; in Montana, he had Mike; Clint and Denny would take care of New Mexico. Let the other candidates run around the country, he said. Since none of them were particularly strong, they would kill each other off in the primaries. None of them had a chance of coming into the convention with anything near the necessary 761 votes. The convention would therefore be deadlocked, he said— and then the party would turn to him, for in the event of a deadlock, the nomination would be decided by the party's bosses. They wanted a winner; they weren't going to go for Adlai, a two-time loser whose indecisiveness had exhausted their patience; they weren't going to go for Hubert—he was so liberal he could never win. Symington was hardly known outside his own state. Kennedy was campaigning all over the country, but he not only was young—forty-one—but looked much younger, far too young to be a President. Furthermore, he was a Catholic. The veteran big-city bosses were Catholics, all of them: Daley, Lawrence, DiSalle, De Sapio, Prendergast, Bailey. They would never put a Catholic at the head of their party's ticket. As *Newsweek* analyzed their feelings, "Thirty years have passed since the defeat of Al Smith, but they still remember vividly the violent anti-Catholic feeling which the 1928 campaign engendered." Who would take Kennedy seriously anyway? Johnson said. He knew him from the Senate, and he was little more than a joke there: a rich man's son, a "playboy," and, he said, "sickly" to boot, always away from Washington because of some illness or other, and never accomplishing anything when he was present. "He never said a word of importance in the Senate, and he never did a thing," he was to say. And he himself would have, between his southern support and the additional states his senators delivered to him, a substantial bloc of votes of his own with which to bargain. And the old leaders wouldn't require much persuasion anyway; they knew the importance of experience and responsibility in a candidate. They would go for him. For example, he had already had discussions with De Sapio and Prendergast; he would have plenty of support in the New York delegation.

The men to whom Johnson explained this reasoning—and soon he was having to explain it not only to Rowe but to Corcoran and other New Deal lawyers like Ben Cohen and Abe Fortas ("I was so anxious for him to announce," Fortas would recall), and to many other men in Washington—felt that it might have a certain degree of validity. His position as Leader made him vulnerable if he declared his candidacy. "I'm trying to build a legislative record over there," he told one of Rayburn's assistants, D. B. Hardeman. "The Senate is already full of presidential candidates. If I really get into this thing, they'll gang up on me and chop me up as Leader so that I'll be disqualified for the nomination." "Speculation [over whether he is a candidate] merely adds to the burden of his leadership," John Steele of *Time* magazine explained to his editors on March 4, 1958, in a memo following a conversation with Johnson. But the validity, these men felt, was only to a point. For one thing, Johnson's belief that senators (and members of Rayburn's House) would control delegations had long been disproved. Senators spent much of their time in Washington, and that made a difference. W. H. Lawrence was to point out in the *New York Times* that for decades, "the Congresional [*sic*] bloc has not been dominant in either party's national conventions. . . . In convention delegations, governors—enjoying state-wide patronage and constantly on the job at home—usually exercise much more influence than do Senators and Representatives." In fact, Johnson had seen this for himself. In 1952, another Senate Majority Leader, Robert Taft, had relied on senators to get him the Republican nomination against Eisenhower, with notable lack of success. And while Johnson may have believed that his triumphs in the Senate had given him national recognition, men like Rowe and Corcoran knew that this belief was unfounded. Outside of Washington, people simply weren't that interested in the Senate, didn't even know what a Majority Leader *did*. As a Johnson ally explained to Walter Jenkins, "You can cross the Potomac River and get out in the country and those folks haven't the slightest idea how legislation is brought up—they don't even know that Lyndon Johnson has the power to schedule legislation." Moreover, Johnson's strategy rested on his belief that the bosses would turn to him if there was a deadlock. But they wouldn't turn to him unless he had proven that he could win outside the South. That meant entering the primaries, and Johnson was saying he wouldn't enter any primaries. If he wouldn't do that, there was a slim chance—very slim, but nonetheless a chance—that he might be able to demonstrate that he could connect with northern delegates by going to their states, meeting them, speaking at their meetings. And, of course, he had to meet, and make allies of, the bosses themselves, some of whom he had met only once or twice—if at all. But Johnson was saying he wouldn't do even that. "I'm not going to get the nomination by running around with my shirttail hanging out hollering for it," he said. He refused to do any form of campaigning in northern states. "He said he wasn't going to do *anything*," Jim Rowe recalls.

It wasn't that Lyndon Johnson didn't want the nomination, these men saw. All during 1958, he swung back and forth between his desire for the presidency, and his refusal to reach for it. A few days after he was so adamant with one of them (or sometimes on the same day, in another conversation with the same man), he would begin talking—"endlessly," Corcoran says—about delegate counts, analyzing how he was going to put together the necessary 761, and about the best arguments to use to win over some specific big-state leader, analyses that showed them that he wanted the nomination as desperately as ever, that he was thinking constantly about it, and that he understood the need to start taking steps to get it. Nonetheless, all through the year, he drew back from taking any steps. Having "seen in '56 how much he wanted it," Rowe says, he didn't take seriously Johnson's disavowal of interest, and early in 1958, "I wrote him a memo whose theme was the need to 'position yourself for '60' " without delay. "He said that's a good memo," and asked Rowe to expand it into a detailed campaign strategy, similar to the one he had written for Truman, for winning the Democratic presidential nomination. When, in August, Rowe told Johnson that the document was nearing completion, Johnson asked him to come to the ranch to discuss it. Just a day or two later, however, with the memo not yet finished, he told Rowe not to bother going on with it. Rowe told Johnson that they both knew he would eventually get in the race, and that if Johnson waited too long, "It won't do you any good. You will be doing it too late." Johnson's response was to tell him again that "he wasn't going to do anything." And he didn't. Kilgore, who had seen, close up, how hard Lyndon Johnson worked during campaigns, realized that this time "he wasn't really trying."

"One so often thinks of Mr. Johnson as being a decisive man," George Reedy was to say. "On most issues he is. On this one he was not. . . . That was a confused period, extremely confused, in which I believe he was a man badly torn."

IN ATTEMPTING TO EXPLAIN why he was torn, why he wasn't really trying—in attempting to explain why Lyndon Johnson, who had schemed and maneuvered so endlessly, worked so hard, to become President, now, when the prize was closer than ever before, when it was perhaps almost within his reach, was refusing to reach for it—the men, in both Texas and Washington, who had worked longest with Lyndon Johnson come to the same conclusion. Connally, who had once confided to a friend that "He's never had another thought, another waking thought, except to lust after the office," had been told by Johnson that he would be managing the campaign for that office, but he had still been given no campaign to manage. Asked, years later, for an explanation, Connally said that as much as "He [Johnson] wanted the nomination, he did not want to be tarred" with—did not want the stigma of—"having lost it." And, Connally says, "If he didn't try, he couldn't fail." Says Jim Rowe: "He wanted one thing. He wanted it so much his tongue was hanging out; then he had another part inside him that said, 'Why get my hopes up? I'm not going to try. If I don't try, I won't fail.' "

And indeed, as the men who had worked with him longest knew, failure—the dread of it, the fear of losing, that is a factor in the equation that makes up the personality of many men, perhaps most men—was a factor possessed of a particularly heavy weight in the very complex equation that was the personality of Lyndon Johnson. When Bobby Baker had first been assigned the job of counting votes for Johnson in the Senate, Walter Jenkins, who, like Connally, had been working for Johnson since 1939, warned him never to overestimate the number of votes that Johnson would have if he brought a controversial bill to the floor, because then the measure might be defeated, and defeat was something the Chief wanted to avoid at all costs. *"Never"*—that was the operative word, and Baker learned quickly that the warning had not been overstated. Other senators might want Johnson to make a fight even on an issue on which he might lose because it would enable them to make "a fighting record in behalf of their causes," Baker says. But "Pyrrhic victories were not Lyndon Johnson's cup of tea. . . . He saw no value in glorious defeats." "Johnson feared losing," Baker was to say. He had a deep "fear of being defeated. He always was petrified by that notion." He was, Baker says, "haunted by fears of failure."

"Petrified. Haunted." Strong words—and other men who had known Lyndon Johnson a long time use words equally strong. Luther ("L. E.") Jones, a member of the debate team he coached at Sam Houston High, recalls that when, in the final round of the Texas State Debate Championship tournament, the judges voted against his team, two to one, Johnson rushed to a bathroom and vomited. "He had a horror of defeat," says Jones, who was later to work for Johnson, "an absolute horror of it." And the people—his relatives and the residents of Johnson City—who had known Lyndon Johnson longest, who had known him in his boyhood, felt they understood at least something about the roots of that fear. They felt those roots lay in the little house—a shanty, really, a typical Texas Hill Country "dog run": two box-like rooms, each about twelve feet square, on either side of a breezeway, two smaller "shed rooms" and a kitchen, all connected by a sagging roof—where Lyndon Johnson had lived from the age of eleven until just after his fourteenth birthday, for it was there that his father had failed.

Sam Ealy Johnson Jr. had brought to that dog run not only his family—his gently reared wife, Rebekah; his elder son, Lyndon; Lyndon's brother, Sam Houston Johnson; and their three sisters—but also his dreams: big dreams. The land on which it sat had once bordered the legendary "Johnson Ranch," whose corrals, in the days of the Texas Cattle Kingdom, had stretched for miles along the banks of the Pedernales River; during the 1860s and '70s, its owners, Lyndon's grandfather Sam Ealy Johnson Sr. and Sam's brother Tom, had driven huge herds north to Abilene through Indian Country, returning with saddlebags stuffed with golden eagles; Sam's wife, Eliza Bunton, a heroine of the Hill Country, had ridden out alone in front of the herd to scout, a rifle across the pommel of her saddle. The Johnson brothers had gone broke and lost the ranch, but Sam and Eliza had later saved enough money to buy an adjacent 433-acre parcel on the Pedernales, and Sam Ealy Jr. had grown up there. In 1919, after his parents' deaths, his eight siblings wanted to sell the place, but Sam, a romantic and a dreamer, wouldn't hear of it; the Pedernales Valley had been "Johnson Country," he said, and it was going to be Johnson Country again. A touch of grandiosity in his nature, and the lure of high cotton prices, which had been soaring for years and seemed likely to continue to do so (he was planning to raise cotton until he made enough money to re-establish a Johnson cattle herd), led him to end a tiresome bidding war by paying far too much for the land—much more than he could afford.

At the time he bought the ranch, Sam Ealy Jr. had been quite a figure in the Hill Country: tall, with a jutting nose and jaw, long ears and piercing eyes, outgoing, friendly, and eloquent. Despite a streak of idealism that made him a fervent Populist and put him at odds with the "interests" who dominated the Legislature, during his six terms in the Texas House he was surprisingly successful in getting bills passed. He and his growing family lived in Johnson City. The town, whose population during Lyndon's high school years was 323, was one of the tiny towns, miles apart from each other, that dotted the vast emptiness of the Hill Country, a little huddle of houses so cut off from the rest of the world by a sea of land that one of its residents called it an "island town"; with no paved roads, it took hours to reach Fredericksburg or Austin, even when roads were passable. But the Johnsons' house was comfortable. "The Hon. S. E. Johnson," as the local newspaper called him, the only man in Johnson City who always wore a necktie, was for a while so successful in "real-estatin' " that he bought his wife the first automobile anyone in the town had ever owned, and provided her with a chauffeur to drive it. "You can tell a man by his boots and his hat and the horse he rides," he said, and his hand-tooled boots and pearl-gray Stetson were the most expensive money could buy. And his demeanor reminded people of an old Hill Country saying: "Johnsons always strut; they even strut sitting down." Johnson City was a religious town—fundamentalist, revivalist, hard-shell religious—but everyone knew that Sam believed in the Darwinian theory, that he attended church (on the irregular Sundays on which he attended church) only to please Rebekah, and that he would take a drink now and then, although, as Johnson City knew, "sneaking a beer by Jesus is like trying to sneak daylight by a rooster." His financial success brought him respect, and he was so smiling and friendly, always so willing to spend days helping an old rancher get a pension, that he was a popular figure in the little town.

All that changed when, in January, 1920, Sam moved his family to the ranch. The next years were years of drought, and as Sam's cotton was dying under the blazing Hill Country sun, so was the cotton market, as prices fell from forty cents a pound to eight cents. In September, 1922, when Lyndon was fourteen, Sam had to sell the ranch for whatever he could get—which wasn't nearly enough to cover his debts.

The Johnsons moved back to their house in Johnson City, but they were able to keep it only because Sam's brothers periodically made payments on the back interest on the mortgage. Often, there would have been little to eat in that house if it hadn't been for the covered dishes neighbors brought. There was no money in the house; the ranch had broken Sam's health, and it was always frail after that.

In any small town, a world to itself, such a transformation would have been dramatic; in Johnson City, an unusually isolated town—in which, as late as 1922, there was not a movie house or, except for a few outmoded crystal sets, a single radio—its residents' interest in each other, and particularly in the fall of its most famous resident into ruin, was unusually intense. Sam Johnson became, in a remarkably short time, a figure of ridicule, as if Johnson City had been eager to turn against a man whose views—on Darwin, on Prohibition—violated deeply held beliefs. He didn't run for re-election, and he probably wouldn't have won anyway. A potential opponent coined a saying: "Sam Johnson is a mighty smart man. But he's got no sense." The remark was first delivered at a political barbecue. Everyone roared. The interests in Austin made sure Sam didn't get a state sinecure: the only job he could find at first was a two-dollar-a-day post as a state game warden. He was to die—in 1937—as a penniless bus inspector; the only thing he had to leave his children was a gold watch and a legacy of the townsfolk's sneers. He couldn't pay what he owed to the local merchants, and he and his wife and children had to walk every day past stores whose owners were writing "Please!" on the bills they sent every month; they had cut him off from further credit, so that he had to shop—and to run up bills which he also couldn't pay—in other towns. A remark made by the Johnson City druggist soon gained wide circulation: "Sam Johnson," the druggist said, "is too smart to work, and not smart enough to make a living without working." His wife's education (she was the only woman in the area with a college degree) and "pretensions" (her inability, for example, to work in the fields like other Hill Country wives) now made her almost a joke, too. And the children of Sam and Rebekah shared in their shame. One of Lyndon's classmates at Johnson City High School, Truman Fawcett, was sitting on his uncle's porch one day when Lyndon walked by. "He'll never amount to anything," the uncle said, loud enough for Lyndon to hear. "Too much like Sam." The Johnsons were, for the rest of Lyndon's boyhood, the laughingstocks of Johnson City.

The scar that his father's failure left on Lyndon Johnson was shown by the way he talked about it. "We had great ups and downs in our family," he would recall. "One year . . . we'd all be riding high in Johnson City terms. . . . But then two years later we'd lose it all. . . . We had dropped to the bottom of the heap." Once in later years a reporter asked him about life on the ranch. "We lived there just long enough to go broke," he replied. And the depth of the scar was, perhaps, shown even more clearly by the rarity of such remarks. Lyndon Johnson very seldom talked about his youth—or, to be more precise, very seldom talked about it frankly: he tried to conceal its circumstances by weaving, for journalists and biographers, a mythical boyhood, a tapestry of anecdotes, told with the vividness and plentiful detail of a great storyteller, that, as his brother sums up, "never happened."

NO TRANSFORMATION CAUSED by Sam Ealy's failure was more complete than the one it effected in his relationship with his elder son.

Before the Johnsons moved to the ranch, the relationship had been strikingly close: when Lyndon was a little boy, his favorite outfit was one that made him look like his father, right down to a scaled-down version of Sam's big Stetson hat. Lyndon imitated his father, tagged along with him everywhere—"right by the side of his daddy wherever he went," an aunt says.

When Lyndon was ten, Sam began taking him to Austin. "I loved going with my father to the Legislature," Lyndon would say. "The only thing I loved more was going with him" during his campaigns for re-election. "We drove in the Model T Ford from farm to farm, up and down the valley, stopping at every door. My father would do most of the talking . . . local gossip, talk about the crops and about the bills he'd introduced . . . and always he'd bring along an enormous crust of homemade bread and a large jar of homemade jam. . . . We'd stop by the side of the road. He sliced the bread, smeared it with jam, and split the slices with me. I'd never seen him happier. Families all along the way opened up their homes to us. . . . Christ, sometimes I wished it could go on forever." Other children in Johnson City remember how, while they were playing outside, Lyndon and his father would be sitting together in the swing on the Johnsons' screened back porch, holding "long conversations . . . friendly conversations. Those were the only times that I ever saw Lyndon quiet and relaxed." By the time Lyndon was thirteen or fourteen, and about six feet tall, there was a particularly conspicuous aspect of the resemblance between them. The tall man with the big ears and nose was very physical in conversation. His arm would go around the shoulders of the legislative colleague to whom he was talking, his other hand would grasp the man's arm or lapel, his face would bend very close to him. Legislators saw Sam's son adopting the same technique. "He was a gangling boy, very skinny," Wright Patman would recall. He had the same huge ears, the same big nose, the same pale skin, and the same dark eyes, and "Lyndon clutched you like his daddy did when he talked to you. . . . He was so much like his father that it was humorous to watch." Legislators saw what playmates saw: a quite unusual bond between father and son.

After Sam's fall (and the change was so dramatic that, as the first volume of this work relates, it is possible to date it), his relationship with Lyndon was very different: cold—hostile, in fact—with Lyndon refusing his father's requests and orders, defying him so blatantly that, legislators say, "He wouldn't pay attention to anything his father wanted."

It was at this time, too—the time during which his father was failing on the ranch—that Lyndon began making the prediction; it was at the school he attended when he was thirteen, the tiny school in the little village of Albert, four miles away, that he first began making it: a classmate, Anna Itz, remembers that during a recess, when a group of children were sitting under a hackberry tree near the school, "All of a sudden, Lyndon looked up at the blue sky and said, 'Someday, I'm going to be President of the United States.' We hadn't been talking about politics or the presidency or anything like that. He just came out with it." (Mrs. Itz says that the other children laughed at him and said they wouldn't vote for him, and Lyndon replied, "I won't need your votes.")

In the opinion of men and women who were children with Lyndon Johnson, his father's fall affected him all his life. His brother, Sam Houston, says that "the most important thing for Lyndon was not to be like Daddy." That feeling had several dimensions: for example, Sam Ealy was an idealist, a romantic, a dreamer, a man who had "no sense"; it was important—terribly important—to Lyndon that he be regarded as a man who scorned ideals and causes as impractical dreams, that he be regarded as pragmatic, cynical, tough, shrewd. But another dimension had to do with Lyndon's feelings about failure and defeat. His father's fall had shown him that failure could mean not merely failure but terror, the terror of living in a house that, month by month, you were afraid would be taken away from you by the bank; that failure could mean not merely terror but ruin, permanent ruin; that failure—defeat—might be something from which you would never recover. And failure in public—failing in a way that was visible: having to move off your ranch; having your credit cut off at stores you had to walk past every day; no longer holding your public office—could mean a different, but also terrible, kind of pain: embarrassment, disgrace, humiliation.

When, in 1948, the place he had wanted so long—a seat in the United States Senate—finally opened up, Johnson had not leapt at the opportunity as his allies had expected him to do, but instead had vacillated endlessly, until it was almost too late to enter the race, agonizing over the decision as to whether or not to run; his allies had finally threatened to run John Connally instead of him to nerve him up to announce his candidacy. And those men understood what was holding him back. Lyndon Johnson had long had the habit, in times of crisis, of telephoning Ed Clark, "the Secret Boss of Texas," at six o'clock in the morning to discuss the situation and ask for advice, and in 1948, in these calls, Ed Clark heard, over and over, one word. " 'Humiliation,' " Clark would recall. "That was what he kept repeating. 'I'll be humiliated. I'll be ruined. If I run, I'm going to lose—I'll be humiliated.' " Now, in 1958, a race for a much greater prize stretched before him—a race for a prize so vast that the attention not just of a state but of an entire country would be focused on it. So the possibility of defeat—of humiliation—loomed before him larger than ever, and *"If he didn't try, he couldn't fail."*

So he didn't try.

On the Senate floor, in 1958, he was the same as he had always been: a man in command—from the moment, just before noon each day, when he pushed open the tall double doors at the rear of the Chamber so hard that they swung wide as he strode through them, and came down the four broad steps to the front-row center Majority Leader's desk.

No assistant accompanied him as he walked down to the little clutch of journalists waiting for him in the well below his desk. He knew all the details himself: the intricacies of bills, not only major bills but minor ones, too; the number that each bill had been assigned on the Senate Calendar; where in the subcommittee or full committee approval process it stood at the moment; what new amendments had been added to the bill, or defeated, that day, and why they had been added or defeated; what the arguments on each side had been; when the bill would be brought to the floor for a vote.

And there was never any question of him making a slip and giving the journalists information he didn't want them to have. "You didn't get any more than Lyndon Johnson wanted to tell you," one of them says. "Never. . . . He knew exactly what he wanted to say—and that was what he said. Period. I never felt in all those years that he ever lost control [of one of those briefings]. He was always *in charge.*"

In charge—"in command"—journalists said about him. In part, they say, it was because of the aura around him, what one of the journalists says was "the knowledge we had of what this guy *had* done, of what this guy could do. Of what he wanted to be." But there was something more. As another reporter says: "Power just emanated from him. There was that look he gave. There was the way he held his head. Even if you didn't know who he was, you would know this was a guy to be reckoned with. You would feel: don't cross this guy. . . . He would look around the Chamber—it was like he was saying, 'This is *my* turf.' "

Prowling the Chamber during debates, he would put a long arm around a senator, grasp his lapel firmly with the other hand, put his face very close to his colleague's as he tried to persuade him. His hands never stopped moving, patting a senator's shoulder, straightening a senator's necktie, jabbing a senator's chest, gesturing expressively, his face breaking into a grin if the senator agreed to the proposition being made, turning cold and hard if he didn't. He would be snatching a tally sheet out of Bobby Baker's hands—or, dispatching Bobby on an errand, grabbing his shoulders and shoving him violently up the aisle if he wasn't moving fast enough; rasping at the assistant of some other senator, who was still back in the Senate Office Building, "Get your fucking senator *over* here!"

During votes he controlled the very rhythm of the roll call. For some reason—perhaps all his senators were present, and there were absentees on the other side—he might want the roll call to be fast, before anything could change.

Or, if he didn't have all his men there, he wanted the vote to be slow. Standing at that front-row desk, towering over the well, dominating the Chamber of the Senate of the United States, Lyndon Johnson would raise his right hand high in the air and make "revving-up circles" to hurry the clerk through the names, or make a downward shoving motion with his hands meaning "slow down," "for all the world," as *Time* said, like "an orchestra conductor" leading the Senate as if it were an obedient orchestra. "It was a splendid sight," the journalist Hugh Sidey would recall years later. "This tall man with . . . his mind attuned to every sight and sound and parliamentary nuance. . . . He signaled the roll calls faster or slower. He'd give a signal, and the door would open, and two more guys would run in. My God—running the world! Power enveloped him!"

And one of the key elements in Lyndon Johnson's command of his world—the Senate world—was his decisiveness.

During the previous four years of his majority leadership (the situation would not be ended until a Democratic landslide in November, 1958) he was usually operating with a mere one-vote margin, and in a Senate in which both parties contained differing, hostile blocs, the vote on proposed measures was constantly shifting, changing; amendments that could alter the balance were constantly being introduced, so a Leader had to know the moment at which to allow (or not allow) an amendment, or the moment at which, if he called a bill to the floor, it would pass—to know the moment, and to seize the moment. Month after month, year after year, when those moments came, Lyndon Johnson knew them—and seized them, with a decisiveness so quick and firm that it obviously came naturally to him, that it was obvious that deciding—acting—was something he enjoyed doing, something that he had the will, the desire, the need to do.

And in his office after the day's session, in that incredible office with its desk up on a low pedestal so that he sat higher than his guests and its spotlight in the chandelier focused on his chair, that office so opulently furnished that it was nicknamed "the Emperor's Room" and "the Taj Mahal," he was in 1958 the same as always, too. Holding court for senators and favored journalists, with his feet, clad in either highly polished black shoes or elaborately hand-tooled "LBJ" boots, up on his desk and a glass of Scotch in his hand (he would hold it out, rattling the ice in it, to summon a pretty secretary for a refill), he would dominate the conversation as he recounted the day's triumphs and the next day's strategy: at ease, confident, purposeful, assured.

EXCEPT WHEN THE SUBJECT turned to the presidential nomination.

George Reedy or Walter Jenkins might bring in a sheaf of speaking invitations—they were pouring into Johnson's office every day from all over the country. The boots would come off the desk, and Lyndon Johnson would begin to pace back and forth around the office. Or he would walk over to the window, plunge his hands into his trouser pockets, and stand looking out for long minutes, his tall figure, silhouetted against the fading late-afternoon light, very still—except that his assistants would hear a continual low jingle as his hands restlessly shuffled the coins and keys in his pockets. Returning to the desk, he would agonize over each invitation, unable to decide whether or not to accept it, at one moment saying he would, the next moment changing his mind, wavering back and forth.

Almost always, he wound up declining—declining even invitations that a candidate (even an unannounced candidate) for the presidency would obviously be well advised to accept; among the seventeen invitations to deliver major speeches he received during March, 1958, were personal requests from the *grande dame* of his party, Eleanor Roosevelt, for a speech before the American Association for the United Nations, and from the governor of Iowa, Herschel C. Loveless, who had recently announced that he had not decided whom his state's delegation would support in 1960. Sometimes, Johnson would accept one or another invitation—but then invariably would change his mind and refuse (as he did eventually with every one of the seventeen March requests), and then would regret that he had refused. Finally, in October, he agreed to visit six states in which Democratic candidates for the Senate were involved in tight races, and he told Reedy to set up small private meetings in his hotel suite after each appearance so that he could meet local political leaders. But at these meetings, he told the leaders he had come to their state strictly in his capacity as Senate Majority Leader, to help the Democratic senatorial candidate get elected; when they asked him if he would be a candidate for President, he said he would not, and said it so emphatically that they believed him. And then, as soon as he returned to Washington, he, in secret, took a step in the opposite direction. While in Tennessee, he had spoken at a Democratic fund-raising dinner that brought in $10,000 for the Democratic Senatorial Campaign Committee. Instead of having the money used in Tennessee, he directed the committee's chairman, Senator George Smathers, to have it sent to West Virginia, to be used by Democratic officials who would have influence in that state's 1960 Democratic primary, and to make sure the officials knew the money was coming at his, Johnson's, direction. He told Smathers he wanted the committee's resources husbanded for the moment—so they could be used in 1960. All through 1958, Johnson wavered between his yearning for the prize and his fear of being seen to yearn for it.

His explanations for not becoming an active candidate—for not traveling to other states to rally delegates and leaders to his cause—varied widely. One day he would give someone the "tending the store" explanation, saying he wouldn't campaign, at least not for a while, because that was the best strategy to win the nomination; he was going to remain the responsible leader above the fray, minding the nation's business, while the other candidates killed themselves off in the primaries; then, when the party was deadlocked, it would turn to him. *Time* magazine's Hugh Sidey, who spoke to Johnson frequently during this time, says that he "had decided . . . that being above the battle was the big thing." The next day—or to someone else the same day—he would say he didn't want the nomination: that the South's power was on Capitol Hill ("This is my home," Corcoran recalls him saying. "This is where *we* have our strength") and that he had decided to stay there, in the Senate. On other occasions he said he wasn't running because it was impossible for him, for anyone from the South, to win the nomination, that he was tarred not only with being a southerner but, despite his refusal of Charles Marsh's offer, with being an oilman as well, since he had supported legislation benefiting his state's oil interests; even if he received the nomination, the North would never accept him, and he could not possibly win the election; therefore he would not allow himself even to be drafted; if he was drafted, he said, he would refuse. His decision, he would say on these occasions, was final.

The year was summed up in his relationship with Rowe, who kept urging him to run. But "he didn't do anything, said he wasn't going to do anything. This went on for a long time. Any reasons? Just that he couldn't make it. My argument was that you certainly can't make it if you do nothing." The harder Rowe pushed, however, the more adamant Johnson became. A few days after the end of the year, Rowe finally gave up, in a way that dramatized the validity of at least one aspect of his warning. He had been telling Johnson that one reason he couldn't wait— that while he could say publicly that he wasn't a candidate, he had to let party insiders, men with influence or power over other delegates, know that he would announce his candidacy when he judged the time right—was that these insiders were choosing up sides; many of them favored him, Rowe said, but for these political pros, not having a candidate in the race was an unsupportable idea: if he convinced them he wouldn't be a candidate, they would select someone else. He himself was in that situation, Rowe had been warning him. "I finally said, 'I want to get into the campaign, and if you're going to go, let's go. If you aren't, I'm going over and join Humphrey.' I talked this way to him for two or three months, and he said, 'I am not going. You can count on it. I am not going to run.' "

"I think you are making a mistake," Rowe wrote him. "But I will *not* press you again." He signed up with Humphrey—and the day after Rowe's decision was announced in the press, Johnson had a few words on the subject with Tommy Corcoran. "Jim betrayed me," he said. "He *betrayed* me!" He was going to need Jim when, at the proper time, he stepped in to get the nomination, he said, and now Jim wasn't going to be available. Corcoran tried to point out that he had told Rowe something else, but, Corcoran says, "You couldn't reason with him."

HAD IT NOT BEEN for one factor, Lyndon Johnson's strategy—whatever its roots: calculation or fear—might have worked. Johnson did, after all, possess a number of assets the other candidates did not: a solid, substantial bloc of delegates—the South's—that would be behind him when the convention started; the support of his senators, and of Sam Rayburn. And the fact that each of the other contenders had at least one major liability (Humphrey's extreme liberalism; Symington's lack of national recognition; Stevenson's and Kefauver's previous losses) while Kennedy had two (his youth and his Catholicism) made Johnson's belief that none of them would be able to command a majority on early ballots seem, at the beginning of 1958, well founded, as did his belief that therefore the convention would be deadlocked and thrown into the hands of the big-state leaders, who would turn to him.

But there was the one factor: this great reader of men, this man who thought he could read any man, had read one man wrong.

2

The Rich Man's Son

LYNDON JOHNSON MIGHT have been excused for misreading John Kennedy. A lot of people in Washington had misread him. When he arrived on Capitol Hill as a newly elected representative from Boston in January, 1947, he was twenty-nine years old, but so thin, and with such a mop of tousled hair falling over his forehead, that he appeared even younger. He was the son of a rich man, a very rich man—a legendary figure in American finance: Joseph P. Kennedy, who had made millions in the stock market on its way up during the Roaring Twenties, and then, selling short on the eve of the 1929 Crash, had made millions more on its way down; who had then turned from amassing wealth to regulating it, as Franklin D. Roosevelt's dynamic chairman of the new Securities and Exchange Commission; who had been FDR's ambassador to the Court of St. James's; who had then, through investments in real estate, and movies (and, some incorrectly said, through bootlegging), turned millions into tens and then hundreds of millions—into one of America's great fortunes, into wealth that seemed almost limitless, and into influence, in Hollywood, in the media, that seemed to match. Everyone in Washington seemed to know that the ambassador had given Jack—along with each of his other eight children—his own million-dollar trust fund, as everyone in Washington seemed to know that the ambassador had bought Jack his seat in Congress with huge campaign expenditures. And for some years after Jack Kennedy's arrival on Capitol Hill, that was all he seemed to be: a rich man's son.

His appearance reinforced the stereotype. He was not only thin—barely 140 pounds on a six-foot frame—but, in the words of one House colleague, "frail, hollow-looking," and below his tousled hair was a broad, gleaming, boyish smile; when a crusty Irish lobbyist, testifying before one of Jack's committees, repeatedly addressed him as "laddie," he did so not out of disrespect, but, as James MacGregor Burns wrote, because "it was just the natural way to talk to someone who seemed more like a college freshman than a member of Congress"; one of Kennedy's fellow members, in fact, once asked him to bring him a copy of a bill, under the impression that he was a page. The college-boy image was reinforced by the fact that he dressed like one, not infrequently appearing on the House floor in crumpled khaki pants and an old seersucker jacket, with his shirttail hanging out below it; sometimes he wore sneakers and a sweater to work. And when he wore a suit, so loosely did it hang from his "wide, but frail-looking shoulders" that he looked, in one description, like "a little boy dressed up in his father's clothes." And reinforcing the image was his attitude: his secretary, Mary Davis, a woman who had worked for other congressmen, liked Kennedy "very much" when she met him: "He had just come back from the war and wasn't in topnotch physical shape. He was such a skinny kid! He had malaria, or yellow jaundice, or whatever, and his back problem"; his suits, she says, were just "hanging from his frame." But she grew annoyed by his cavalier attitude toward his job: by the way he would toss a football around his office with friends; once when she complained about his absences when there was work to be done, he said, "Mary, you'll just have to work a little harder." "He was rather lackadaisical," she says. "He didn't know the first thing about what he was doing. . . . He never did involve himself in the workings of the office." For constituents' problems, he had little patience: once, having set aside two days to see them in his Boston office, he gave up after the first day, telling another secretary, "Oh, Grace, I can't do it. You'll have to call them off." His service in World War II had included a highly publicized exploit in the Pacific—a long article had been written in *The New Yorker* about it—but in 1947 there were scores of men in Congress with celebrated war records, and some of those records wouldn't stand close scrutiny: the new senator from Wisconsin, for example, liked to be known as (and sometimes referred to himself as) "Tail-Gunner Joe" McCarthy and had received the Distinguished Service Medal, although he had never been a tail (or any other variety of) gunner but rather an intelligence officer whose primary duty during the war had been to sit at a desk and debrief pilots who had indeed flown in combat missions; Lyndon Johnson himself, who constantly wore his Silver Star pin in his lapel, was given to regaling Washington dinner parties with stories of his encounters with Japanese Zeroes, although his only brush with combat had been to fly as an observer on a single mission, during which he was in action for a total of thirteen minutes, after which he left the combat zone on the next plane home. Exaggeration was a staple of the politician's stock-in-trade; understanding that, congressmen discounted stories about wartime heroism. And stories about a war faded before Jack Kennedy's conduct in Washington, for sometimes he seemed to be doing his best to reinforce the stereotype. Everyone on Capitol Hill seemed to know that he lived in a Georgetown house that was so filled with his friends, and with movie industry friends of his father's, dropping in from out of town, that it seemed like a fraternity house, or, as one friend said, "a Hollywood hotel"; that he had his own cook and a black valet, who delivered his meals to the House Office Building every day. And everyone seemed to know about the glamorous women he dated—one, whom he dated until he told her he couldn't marry her, was the movie star Gene Tierney; sometimes his charming, apparently carefree smile would be in magazines after he was photographed with these women in New York nightspots, and he would drive them around Washington in a long convertible with the top down: the very picture of a dashing young millionaire bachelor playboy. Watching Jack stroll onto the House floor one day with his hands in his pockets, a colleague said his attitude suggested: "Well, I guess if you don't want to work for a living, this is as good a job as any."

And he was on Capitol Hill much less than he was supposed to be. During his first year in Congress, he took an active role on the Housing Committee, giving a series of speeches on the postwar housing crisis, and when the Taft-Hartley Act was introduced, he opposed it on the House floor. But that fall, while he was vacationing in England after Congress had adjourned, he fell ill, and although when Congress convened in 1948, he was back on Capitol Hill, announcing that his attack of "malaria" was over, he was no longer active at all, and thereafter his rate of absenteeism was one of the highest in the House. "He had few close political friends," one of his biographers puts it, and even those few could not pretend he was an effective congressman. His closest friend—"about his only real friend on Capitol Hill"—Florida congressman (later a senator) George Smathers, recalls that "he told me he didn't like being a politician. He wanted to be a writer. . . . Politics wasn't his bag at all." And, Smathers recalls, "He was so shy . . . one of the shyest fellows I'd ever seen. If you had to pick a member of that [1947] freshman class who would probably wind up as President, Kennedy was probably the *least* likely." The House bored him, said his father's friend Supreme Court Justice William O. Douglas. "He never seemed to get into . . . political action, or any idea of promoting this or reforming that— nothing. He was sort of drifting. . . . He became more of a playboy." The men who ran the House agreed. Sam Rayburn called him "a good boy" but "one of the laziest men I ever talked to."

In 1952, he ran for the Senate, against the widely respected incumbent from Massachusetts, Henry Cabot Lodge Jr.

Favored when the campaign began, Lodge was overwhelmed by the Kennedy organization, directed for the first time by the candidate's younger brother Robert, and by Kennedy innovation. Tens of thousands of women voters were invited—by hand-addressed, handsomely engraved invitations—to meet the candidate and what one writer called "his large and fabulous family," including "his comely mother and three attractive, long-legged sisters." He was overwhelmed as well by Joe's money—some people "could live the rest of [their] lives on [the campaign's] billboard budget alone," one observer remarked; among the ambassador's outlays was a $500,000 loan that rescued from bankruptcy the publisher of the *Boston Post,* which shortly thereafter endorsed his son—and by Jack's charm: the attraction of his "boyish, well-bred emaciation" for women of all ages ("every woman who met Kennedy wanted either to mother him or marry him," the *Saturday Evening Post* reported) was so intense it might have been humorous were it not later to become a central fact of American political life, and indeed to play a role in altering America's political landscape. During the campaign Jack Kennedy showed a new side of himself: from Monday to Thursday, he still seemed, in Washington, merely the Georgetown playboy; from Thursday night through Sunday, he raced over Massachusetts from one end to the other; "no town was too small or too Republican for him," an aide was to recall. By the end of the campaign, the *Saturday Evening Post* reported, "Jack was being spoken of as the hardest campaigner Massachusetts has ever produced." But once he was in the Senate the House pattern was repeated (even down to elevator operators misled by his boyish looks; one of the Senate operators told him to "stand back and let the senators go first").

During his first year in the Senate, 1953, he not only made major social news, with his spectacular marriage to Jacqueline Bouvier, but also, during the 1953 and 1954 sessions, developed proposals for New England economic expansion and took at least one stand that lifted him above the role of a senator from just a single state or region, supporting the St. Lawrence Seaway, a project long opposed by Massachusetts and New England due to apprehension over its impact on Boston's seaport. But even during this period, he seemed to be sick quite a bit, first with one illness, then with another, although he always made light of his ailments; in July, he was hospitalized with another attack of "malaria." And his bad back was getting worse; the marble floors of the Senate Office Building and the Capitol were hard on him; by the spring of 1954, he was on crutches; he tried to hide them before visitors entered his office, but sometimes when he went to committee meetings, there was no place to put them, and he would have to lean them against the wall behind him, in full view. He tried to play down the seriousness of his back condition, and it didn't seem all that serious, because he was so insouciant about it. Trying to spare himself the walk through the long corridors, he requested a suite nearer the Senate floor, but he didn't want to draw attention to the situation by emphasizing it too strongly to his party's Senate Leader, Lyndon Johnson, and his low seniority meant that he kept the office he had. He finally stopped going back to his office between quorum calls, staying in the cloakroom or in his seat on the floor instead. Senate rules require a senator to be standing when he addresses the Chamber; his Massachusetts colleague, Leverett Saltonstall, obtained permission from the presiding officer for him to speak while sitting on the arm of his chair.

And then, in October, 1954, there was an operation on his back. Like so many of his medical procedures, this was performed while Congress was in recess for the year: most senators weren't around, and the press wasn't focusing on Capitol Hill. His staff made it seem as if the operation were just a run-of-the-mill back operation. When the Senate reconvened in January, 1955, he was still in the hospital, and when it was learned that he had had a second operation, on February 15, 1955, it was obvious that there were complications. Ambassador Kennedy reportedly broke into tears in a friend's Washington office, and said Jack was going to die. But the ambassador's friend, the publisher William Randolph Hearst Jr., quieted the rumors by saying that he had visited the ambassador's Palm Beach residence, where Jack was convalescing, and found him "looking tanned and fit again"; for the next few weeks there were continuing reports of his imminent return to Washington, and he gave interviews in Palm Beach, after which the reporters commented on his tan. Although, in an interview at Palm Beach on May 20 with a journalist from the *Standard-Times,* he did make one remark out of character—"I'll certainly be glad to get out of my 37th year"—he quickly caught himself and assured her that everything was going well, and that his situation had never been serious. "If the Senate hadn't kept such long hours, I could have taken it easy—perhaps I mightn't have gone to the hospital last fall. But . . . there's so much walking to do at the Capitol." And when a few days later, he finally returned to the Senate, he did so with a quip, saying that during his time away, he had read the *Congressional Record* every day; "that was an inspiring experience." Acknowledging that there had been rumors that he wouldn't return, the *New York Herald Tribune* said that nonetheless, "young Jack Kennedy comes from a bold and sturdy breed, and he's back on the job again." His concept of the job continued to differ from that of harder-working senators, however. Although upon his return, he had been "applauded by colleagues, they nevertheless found it hard to take him seriously," says one of his biographers. "He was still young, inexperienced, ill, and, despite his marriage, a playboy with pretensions."

Then, in Chicago in 1956, after Stevenson had startled the convention by throwing open the vice presidential nomination, suddenly Kennedy was running for it. " 'Old pal, you've got to do me a favor,' " George Smathers said Kennedy told him, telephoning at 1 a.m. " 'You've got to nominate me for vice president.' I said, 'For vice president? You're running for vice president? . . . You've got to be kidding.' " Kennedy explained that he wanted the nominating speech to be made by House Majority Leader John McCormack of Massachusetts, but that McCormack wasn't answering his phone: thirty minutes had been allotted for the speeches of each nominee, Kennedy said, "and you may have to take all the thirty minutes." Delivering the speech the next morning, Smathers was having difficulty filling the time—"I couldn't really think of anything he had done except he was very strongly for education"—but as it turned out he didn't have to fill it all. "All of a sudden I had this very sharp pain in my back," he was to recall—and then another one, and another. "I thought, 'I'm having a heart attack.' " But looking over his shoulder, he saw that the pain was being caused by the handle of the convention chairman's large gavel, which was being jabbed vigorously into his spine. "McCormack is here! McCormack is here!" the chairman rasped. "Sam Rayburn [was] sticking me in the back . . . to get me to shut up . . . so that McCormack" could speak.

DESPITE HIS DEARTH of accomplishment, Kennedy had two things going for him at the 1956 convention: his effective star turn as the on-screen narrator of a filmed tribute to the Democratic Party that had been shown at the convention's opening night; and the determination of party professionals to deny the vice presidential nomination to the other man trying for it: Tennessee senator Estes Kefauver, anathema to the South because of his support for civil rights and to the party's northern big-city bosses because of his sensational, nationally televised, investigations that had too often hinted at links between big-city machines and organized crime. (Johnson disliked him for a personal reason—Kefauver's refusal to accord him the deference he demanded: after maneuvering secretly for years to deny Kefauver committee assignments to which he was entitled by seniority, in 1955 the Leader had told him openly that he wouldn't put him on the Foreign Relations Committee because he had a "team," of which he was captain, and Kefauver wasn't on it; the price of Senate advancement, Johnson told him, was "to *want* to be" on that team.) Although at one point on the second ballot Kennedy was just thirty-eight votes short of the nomination—Johnson had taken Texas into his camp—Kefauver had enough devoted rank-and-file supporters to win. (The nomination of course was meaningless, given the Eisenhower landslide.) And in 1956 and 1957, Kennedy's record in the Senate was little better than before. "In the terms that mattered to Johnson—which senators got things done in the Senate—Kennedy didn't measure up," Kennedy's aide Ted Sorensen was to say. "So Johnson underestimated him; he, who had done everything, felt that he didn't have to take him seriously."

When, in January, 1957, another vacancy opened on Foreign Relations, Joe Kennedy importuned Lyndon Johnson to fill it with his son instead of Kefauver, "telling me that if I did, he'd never forget the favor for the rest of his life," and Johnson agreed. Later, he would say that he had done so because "I kept picturing old Joe Kennedy sitting there with all that power and wealth feeling indebted to me for the rest of his life, and I sure liked that picture." But the real reason was 1960: although as it would turn out, Kefauver would not be able to make a serious bid for the 1960 Democratic nomination, in 1957 it seemed that he would be able to—he had, after all, won all those primaries in 1952 and had won some in 1956 before bowing out of the race in Stevenson's favor—and at that time Johnson regarded him as a serious threat for the nomination. Lyndon Johnson did not regard John Kennedy as a threat; in fact, he felt he might be a useful asset: a southern presidential candidate—a candidate from Texas, for example—would need a running mate from the Northeast; it wouldn't be a bad idea to build one up, particularly one who had a father as powerful as Jack Kennedy's.

Before the 1957 session ended, Kennedy rose on the Senate floor to deliver a speech on foreign relations: on the Algerian struggle for independence, criticizing not only the French refusal to allow it, but the American government's support of the French policy. Although the historian Arthur M. Schlesinger Jr. wrote that in Europe the speech identified Kennedy "for the first time as a fresh and independent voice of American foreign policy," and the editorial page of the *New York Times* applauded it, it aroused anger in the foreign policy establishment; "even Democrats drew back." And aside from that speech, his career in the Senate continued on a course that, in Capitol Hill terms, was charted toward mediocrity. Anecdotes—possibly exaggerated but certainly striking—abounded about his absenteeism and his irresponsibility. When he was asked to chair a new Foreign Relations subcommittee on Africa, it was recounted, Kennedy replied, "Well, if I take it, will it ever have to meet?" and accepted only when he was assured it wouldn't. (Actually, it seems to have met at least once.) The fact that, due to his father's fame, his speeches attracted more attention than those of other senators did not lead to more respect for him among his colleagues, but to the opposite: senators liked to categorize their colleagues as either "work horses," men who studied hearing transcripts and department reports, did the donkey work on committees behind closed doors, and really made the Senate work, and "show horses," men in the Senate only for the publicity it could bring them. Kennedy was, in the opinion of the "Old Bulls" who ran the Senate, a prime example of the latter breed. Looking back on Jack Kennedy's Senate career decades after it had ended, Smathers had the same opinion of it that he had had in 1956: "not in the top echelon at all. . . . While he did from time to time make some brilliant speech about something or other . . . he was not what you would call a really effective senator. . . . He had a couple of pretty good ideas that he talked about, but I don't know that anything he ever really passed . . . was of great significance."

As for Lyndon Johnson, his opinion was that the young senator from Massachusetts was a "playboy" and basically lazy. "He's smart enough," he told Bobby Baker at the time, "but he doesn't like the grunt work."

"Kennedy was pathetic as a congressman and as a senator," Johnson was to say. "He didn't know how to address the Chair." He was, he said on another occasion, "a young whippersnapper, malaria-ridden and yellow, sickly, sickly. He never said a word of importance in the Senate, and he never did a thing." During his retirement, describing Kennedy as a senator, in phrases that he knew were being recorded for posterity, Johnson used similar adjectives—and added to them four final words that were, in the lexicon of Lyndon Johnson, the most damning words of all: as a senator, Lyndon Johnson said, Jack Kennedy was "weak and pallid—a scrawny man with a bad back, a weak and indecisive politician, a nice man, a gentle man, but not a man's man."

THERE WERE, HOWEVER, ASPECTS of the life of Jack Kennedy of which Lyndon Johnson was unaware—and which, had he known about them, might have led him to a more nuanced reading. He might have read him differently had he known what Kennedy had gone through to get to Capitol Hill—and why he hadn't accomplished more once he was there.

Behind that easy, charming, carefree smile on the face of the ambassador's second son was a life filled with pain—and with refusal to give in to that pain, or even, except on very rare occasions (and never in public), to acknowledge its existence.

Born on May 29, 1917, Jack Kennedy, even as a boy, seemed always to be falling ill—and doctors were never able to determine what was wrong with him. At the age of fourteen, already strikingly thin, he began to lose weight and said he was "pretty tired" all the time, and one day he collapsed with abdominal pain. The undiagnosed illness forced him to withdraw from boarding school. At Choate, where he enrolled the next year, he was frequently in the infirmary with severe stomach cramps, high fever and vomiting, and then, in January, 1934, when he was sixteen, he had to be rushed by ambulance to a hospital in New Haven, where he was kept for almost two months of humiliating and painful tests. "We are still puzzled as to the cause of Jack's trouble," the wife of headmaster George St. John wrote Jack's mother, Rose. "I hope with all my heart that the doctors will find out . . . what is making the trouble." But they didn't. For a while, the diagnosis—an incorrect one—was leukemia; prayers were said for him in chapel; later the diagnosis was changed to hepatitis, also incorrect. In March, doctors released him without having been able to determine what he had suffered from; some of the symptoms had cleared up, but he still vomited frequently, and had periodic high fevers and severe cramping pain in his stomach, and almost constant fatigue, and no matter what he tried, he couldn't gain weight.

In June, ill again, he was sent to the Mayo Clinic in Rochester, Minnesota, and then to a hospital there. "The Goddamnest hole I've ever seen," he wrote his friend Lem Billings. "I wish I was back at school." The tests lasted for a month. "I now have a gut ache all the time." "Shit!!" he wrote eight days later. "I've got something wrong with my intestines. In other words I shit blood." There were constant tests. "I've had 18 enemas in three days!!! . . . Yesterday, I went through the most harassing experience of my life. . . . They put me in a thing like a barber's chair. Instead of sitting in the chair I kneeled . . . with my head where the seat is. . . . The doctor first stuck his finger up my ass. . . . Then he withdrew his finger and then, the schmuck, stuck an iron tube 12 inches long and 1 inch in diameter up my ass. . . . Then they blew a lot of air in me to pump up my bowels. I was certainly feeling great. . . . I was a bit glad when they had their fill of that. . . . The reason I'm here is that they may have to cut out my stomach—the latest news." For a while the tentative diagnosis was that he had chronic inflammation of the colon and small intestine, so severe that it could become life-threatening, but at the end of the tests, as Joseph Kennedy wrote Dr. St. John, "they were unable to find out what had caused Jack's illness." And because of the fears about the leukemia and hepatitis, he had to live with frequent blood counts: "7,000—Very Good," he reported to a friend once. But when Mrs. St. John visited him in the hospital, he never stopped kidding with her—"Jack's sense of humor hasn't left him for a minute, even when he felt most miserable," she wrote Rose. In the Mayo Clinic and the Rochester hospital, he charmed his nurses and doctors. And at Choate, when he wasn't in the infirmary, he was the center of a circle of friends, some of whom, like the loyal Billings, he kept for life. "I've never known anyone in my life with such a wonderful humor—the ability to make one laugh and have a good time," Billings was to recall. "Jack was always up to pranks and mischief," says another friend. "Witty, unpredictable—you never knew what he was going to do." And except for the occasional letter to Billings, "He wouldn't ever talk about his sickness," another friend says. "We used to joke about the fact that if I ever wrote a biography, I would call it 'John F. Kennedy: A Medical History.' [Yet] I seldom ever heard him complain." And thin as he was, he never stopped trying to make the Choate football team.

During most of Jack's senior year at Choate, he stayed out of hospitals; in 1935, at Princeton, however, "He was sick the entire year. . . . He just wasn't well," had to withdraw—and spent nearly two months at Peter Bent Brigham Hospital in Boston. "The most harrowing experience of all my storm-tossed career," the eighteen-year-old youth wrote Billings. "They came in this morning with a gigantic rubber tube. Old stuff, I said, and rolled over thinking naturally that it would [be] stuffed up my arse. Instead they grabbed me and shoved it up my nose and down into my stomach. Then they poured alcohol down the tube. . . . They had the thing up my nose for two hours." The blood counts were very bad. "My . . . count this morning was 3500," he wrote Billings. "When I came it was 6000. At 1500 you die. They call me '2000 to go Kennedy.' " A few days later, he wrote again. "They have not found anything as yet. . . . Took a peak [*sic*] at my chart yesterday and could see that they were mentally measuring me for a coffin." But when the next year, during what a biographer calls a "brief Indian summer of good health," he enrolled at Harvard, he tried out for end on the freshman football team. "He was pathetic because he was so skinny. You could certainly count his ribs," one member of the team recalls. The captain, Torbert Macdonald, who was to become another lifelong friend, counted something else, however. "As far as blocking and that sort of thing, where size mattered, he was under quite a handicap," he was to write. But, he added, "Guts is the word. He had plenty of guts." He made the freshman second team, until coaches found out about a party he organized at which a number of players, in his words, "got fucked," after which he was demoted to the third team. Nonetheless, although he had barely made the team, he had made it.

By 1938, he was back in a hospital, "trying to get rid of an intestinal infection I've had for the last two weeks." And for the next three years, he would be in and out of hospitals, with a pain in his stomach that he told Billings felt "like a hard knot," and that never seemed to leave him, and with chronic vomiting and diarrhea and fever, and unending concern about his weight and his blood count. But when he wasn't in the hospital, he was always organizing pranks and parties, and never talking, except, it seems, to Billings, about what was going on in the intervals. Many years later, Billings told an interviewer: "Jack Kennedy all during his life had few days when he wasn't in pain or sick in some way. Jack never wanted us to talk about him, but now that Bobby has gone and Jack is gone, I think it really should be told."

• • •

LATE IN 1940, having turned his Harvard honors thesis into a best-selling book, *Why England Slept,* he felt a sudden pain in his lower back, as if "something had slipped," and not long afterwards his back started to hurt him so badly that he was hospitalized; some years later, when he was operated on, the surgeons would find puzzling deterioration in his lumbar spine, with "abnormally soft" material around the spinal disks, almost as if the spine had rotted away; there would be speculation then that adrenal extracts which had been prescribed for his stomach and colon problems had caused his spine to deteriorate. He was forced to wear a canvas-covered steel brace. But when, in the summer of 1941, it became obvious that war was coming, he tried to enlist. And when, despite his attempts to conceal his condition, he was unable to pass physical examinations for either the Army or Navy, he kept trying—first spending five months trying to build up his back through calisthenics so that he could pass another examination and, then, when that didn't work, insisting that his father arrange for a special, in effect fixed-in-advance, examination by a Navy Board of Examiners that, in October, cleared him to enlist.

His back spasms grew rapidly "more severe," and the pain "very bad"; during training, he had to sleep on a table instead of a bed. Despite his efforts to hide his condition, he had to go to a Navy doctor, who declared him unfit for duty; he was given permission to visit the Mayo Clinic, where he was told an operation to fuse his spine was necessary. But he chose sea duty instead, and used all his father's influence to get it—once, when his father, worried about his condition, didn't move fast enough for him, he went to his grandfather, former Boston mayor "Honey Fitz" Fitzgerald, who interceded with Massachusetts senator David Walsh, whose word as chairman of the Senate Naval Affairs Committee was law with the Navy—and the duty Jack Kennedy chose was, of all possible assignments, one for which a man with a bad back was particularly unsuited: service on speedy patrol torpedo boats. With a back as sensitive as Kennedy's, any jolt hurts, and on the small, thin-hulled PT boats, it sometimes seemed that every wave was a jolt; "the bucking bronchos of the sea," a magazine writer named them after spending a day aboard—"ten hours of pounding and buffeting. . . .Even when they are going at half speed it is about as hard to stay upright on them as on a broncho's back." And at top speed, "planing over the water at forty knots and more, with bows lifted, slicing great waves from either side of their hulls, they gave their crew 'an enormous pounding.' " Kennedy "was in pain, he was in a lot of pain," a fellow trainee was to recall. "He slept on that damn plywood board all the time and I don't remember when he wasn't in pain." In desperation, he went to his father, hoping that an operation could be arranged, and that he could recuperate quickly enough to go back on duty. "Jack came home," his father wrote Jack's older brother, Joseph P. Kennedy Jr., "and between you and me is having terrific trouble with his back." But the lengthy recuperation period that would be required for an operation made that plan unfeasible, and Lieutenant Kennedy went back to duty, persuading Senator Walsh to arrange his immediate transfer to the South Pacific—where, on the night of August 1, 1943, the boat he was commanding, *PT-109,* was part of a patrol torpedo squadron sent to intercept a Japanese convoy of troop carriers, escorted by destroyers, as it came through a strait in the Solomon Islands.

The action was not successful—it was, according to one account, "the most confused and least effective action the PTs had been in"; only half the boats fired their torpedoes, and none caused any damage—but if, in a starless, "pitch dark" night with only four boats equipped with radar and all the boats enjoined to radio silence, there was confusion, there was none about what happened after a Japanese destroyer, looming suddenly out of the dark, smashed into *PT-109,* slicing it in half.

One half of the boat sunk immediately, the other half remained afloat. Two of the crew were dead; Kennedy and ten others were alive, he and four men on the hull, the others widely scattered, including two, Charles Harris and the boat's thirty-seven-year-old engineer, Pat "Pappy" McMahon, who were near each other about a hundred yards away. All were wearing their kapok life jackets. Harris shouted, "Mr. Kennedy! Mr. Kennedy! McMahon is badly hurt." Shedding his shoes, shirt and revolver, Kennedy swam to the engineer, whose hands, arms and neck were so badly burned that they were only raw flesh, and began towing him back to the half of a hull. A wind kept blowing the boat away from them. Harris, swimming beside him, said, "I can't go any farther."

"For a guy from Boston, you're certainly putting up a great exhibition out here, Harris," Jack Kennedy said. Harris stopped talking and kept swimming, and eventually the three men reached the hull. Like the others, they fell asleep on the tilted deck.

As John Hersey related in *The New Yorker,* after interviewing Kennedy and members of his crew some months later, there wasn't room on the hull for all the men, and it was beginning to sink, so when daylight broke, Kennedy ordered the uninjured men into the water, and went in himself. All morning they clung to the hull, and finally Kennedy decided they would swim to a small island, one of a group of little islands about three miles away. Nine of the men made the swim hanging on to a large timber from the boat. Pappy McMahon was unable to do even that. Slicing loose one end of a long strap on McMahon's life vest, Kennedy took the end in his teeth, and told McMahon to turn on his back. Then he towed him, swimming the breaststroke, his teeth clenched around the strap.

The swim took five hours. After he pulled McMahon up on the beach, Kennedy lay on the sand, exhausted. "He had been in the sea, except for short intervals on the hull, for fifteen and a half hours," Hersey relates. But he lay there only for a few minutes, and then he got up, and tied his life vest back on to go back into the water. He had realized that beyond the next small island was Ferguson Passage, where PT boats sometimes patrolled. His men tried to dissuade him from going, saying he was tired, and that the currents in the passage were treacherous. Tying his shoes around his neck, he swam out into the passage, carrying a heavy lantern wrapped in a life vest to signal passing boats. It took him about an hour to swim out far enough into the passage so that he felt a boat could see him, and he stayed there, treading water, holding the heavy lantern, for hours, until, finally, he realized that no boats would be coming.

Trying to get back to the island, he was too tired to fight the current, which carried him right by it. He stopped trying to swim, and, as he later told Hersey, "seemed to stop caring. . . . He thought he had never known such deep trouble. . . . His body drifted through the wet hours, and he was very cold." He got rid of his shoes. But the lantern was his only means of signaling, and he never let go of it. "He drifted all night" with his fist "tightly clenched on the kapok." When the current, which had carried him during those hours in a huge circle, finally deposited him back on the second small island, he was still holding it. Crawling up on the beach, he vomited, and passed out.

The next day, he decided they would have a better chance of finding food, and of making contact with the Navy, on another of the islands. Swimming to it took three hours, the other men hanging on to the timber again, Kennedy again towing McMahon by clenching the strap in his teeth.

Hungry and thirsty, his men started to despair, but Kennedy never stopped trying to get them rescued. The cuts on his bare feet from the sharp-edged coral reefs were so festered and swollen that his feet "looked like small balloons," but he and one of his men crossed other reefs and swam to another island, where they found a Japanese cache of food to take back to the rest. Then he found a native canoe. With the wind rising, he had to order a member of his crew to help him take the canoe with the food out into Ferguson Passage: "the other man argued against it; Kennedy insisted." Waves five and six feet high swamped their canoe, and as the two men clung to it, the tide carried them toward the open sea while they pushed and tugged the craft to try to turn it toward the island. "They struggled that way for two hours," Hersey wrote, "not knowing whether they would hit the small island or drift into the endless open." Eventually the tide carried them toward the island, but first they struck a reef around it; the waves crashing on the reef tore them away from the canoe, and spun Kennedy head over heels so that "he thought he was dying" until he suddenly found himself in a quiet eddy. While he was away on one of his trips, two friendly natives came upon the crew and told them their squadron had given them up for lost. When he returned, Kennedy scratched a message to his squadron on a coconut shell for the natives to take away with them, and two days later, on the sixth day of their ordeal, his note having been delivered, they were rescued.

DURING THIS EPISODE, the pain in his back had grown worse, and so had his stomach, but he insisted he was all right. New PT boats were being fitted out with heavier guns, and he wanted command of one. "He wanted to get back at the Japanese," his squadron commander was to recall. "He got the first gunboat," *PT-59*. And the commander would recall that "I don't think I ever saw a guy work longer, harder hours," as it was being made ready for sea. His crew were all volunteers, five of them from *PT-109*—one remembered how they went down to the dock where the skinny lieutenant was fitting out the new ship. "Kennedy said, 'What are you doing here?' We said, 'What kind of a guy are you? You got a boat and didn't come get us.' Kennedy got choked up. The nearest I ever seen him come to crying." His new executive officer later said that "what impressed me most . . . was that so many of the men that had been on *PT-109* had followed him to the *59*. It spoke well of him as a leader."

Kennedy had six weeks of action on *PT-59,* on one occasion sinking three Japanese barges. Finally, he was no longer able to walk without the aid not only of a back brace but of a cane as well, he was terribly thin, and his stomach pain had become so intense that he had to see Navy doctors, who found "a definite ulcer crater." X-rays of his back found a chronic disk disease that had obviously been aggravated by the pounding inflicted on the boats. Shipped home, he had his back operated on in June, 1944, but the operation, for a ruptured disk, didn't work; obviously something else was wrong: the "abnormally soft cartilage" was found; the degeneration of his lower spine was wider than had been feared—the surgeons had no real explanation; when he tried to walk again, the pain was so bad that it could be controlled only by what one of the surgeons calls "fairly large doses of narcotics."

"PT-109" WOULD BECOME a highly publicized saga of courage and duty— members of Jack Kennedy's crew would talk in later years of his obvious feeling of obligation to get as many of them back to safety as possible, no matter what the cost to himself. The courage required for that episode, however, had had to last for only six days. What came next in Jack Kennedy's life—his campaign for the House of Representatives in 1946—would require courage for much longer than that, and on more levels.

His older brother, Joe Jr., had been the one who had been supposed to make that race; he was the Kennedy boy, handsome, poised, outgoing, who was destined for politics and who embraced the destiny, but Joe had been killed in the war. No one could have seemed less suited to take over his role than Jack. "Joe used to talk about being President some day, and a lot of smart people thought he would make it," his father was to say. "He was altogether different from Jack— more dynamic, sociable and easygoing. Jack in those days . . . was rather shy, withdrawn and quiet." He did not, the ambassador was to say, have "a temperament outgoing enough for politics." "His mother and I couldn't picture him as a politician. We were sure he'd be a teacher or a writer."

And his health had not improved. "He looked jaundiced—yellow as saffron and thin as a rake," says a friend who saw him when he came back from the war. To try to build himself up, in 1945 he went to the Camelback Inn in Arizona. A couple who sat at an adjoining table for a month saw an "ill, sad and lonely young man," so pale and gaunt that they thought he was "trying to recover from shock." So bad was his back that he went to the Mayo Clinic again, but no one there had anything new to suggest. In August, he had a violent incident of stomach pain, vomiting and high fever. But, also in August, his father wrote to a friend that while Jack was "very thin . . . he is becoming quite active in the political life of Massachusetts." Ill suited though he might have seemed for his brother's role, he was accepting it. (He would say later that it was because of his father. "It was like being drafted," he would explain. "My father wanted his eldest son in politics. 'Wanted' isn't the right word. He demanded it.") "I'm just filling Joe's shoes," he told friends. "If he were alive, I'd never be in this." There had, however, also been hints that there might be reasons that had little to do with his brother. In the Pacific, Jack's squadron commander was to recall, "We played a lot of cards. Jack never played cards. He spent most of his time looking for officers who weren't in any game, as he did with me. We'd sit in a corner and I'd recall all the political problems in New Jersey and Long Island, where I come from. He did that with everybody—discussed politics." The politics Kennedy discussed, morever, was politics with a purpose. Says the commander of another PT boat in the squadron: "He made us all very conscious of the fact that we'd better do some reading, we'd better be concerned about why the hell we're out here, or else what's the purpose of having the conflict, if you're going to come out here and fight and let the people that got us here get us back into it again. . . . He made us all very aware of our obligations as citizens of the United States to do something, to be involved in the process." Whatever the reasons, in 1946, John Fitzgerald Kennedy announced that he was running for Congress, in Boston, in Massachusetts' Eleventh Congressional District.

HIS FATHER'S MONEY played a huge role in the campaign, buying unprecedented amounts of radio, newspaper and billboard advertising, but his father's money couldn't get him onto the street corners, and into the bars—couldn't help with his shyness. Although the Eleventh District included Harvard, most of it was a tough working-class area. An old Irish pol who was "handling East Boston" for him recalls that at first, "He was very retiring. You had to lead him by the hand. You had to push him into the poolrooms, taverns, clubs. . . . He didn't like it at first. He wanted no part of it." Says another campaign aide: "He was not the ordinary type of campaigner in the sense that he was not affable or easygoing. . . . His shyness came through." It was, another aide recalls, "Very hard for him to go up to someone he'd never met, and say, 'I'm Jack Kennedy.' "

Hard though it may have been, however, he did it, walking down the aisles of trolley cars between the seated passengers, then going to a subway and repeating the process. And he got better at it. Watching Jack shaking hands with a group of longshoremen, asking each one for his vote, his father, standing across the street, said to a friend, as he recalled, "that I would have given odds of 5,000 to 1 that this thing we were seeing could never have happened. I never thought Jack had it in him."

His father's money couldn't help with the speeches.

At a talk he gave at a Rotary Club, not only was he so thin that, in the words of one Rotarian, "the collar of his white shirt gape[d] at the neck" and his suit "hung slackly" from his shoulders but the speech itself contained "No trace of humor. . . . Hardly diverging from his prepared text, he stood as if before a blackboard, addressing a classroom full of pupils." His early speeches all seemed to be, a biographer has written, "both mediocre and humorless . . . read from a prepared text with all the insecurity of a novice," in a voice "tensely high-pitched," and with "a quality of grave seriousness that masked his discomfiture. . . . He seemed to be just a trifle embarrassed on stage." Once, afraid he was going to forget his speech, his sister Eunice mouthed the words at him from the audience as he spoke.

There were, however, moments even in these early speeches when something different happened. When he stumbled over a word, "a quick, self-deprecating grin" would break over his face—and, a member of one audience remembers, it "could light up the room." And there was, however much he stumbled over his words, "a winning sincerity" in his speeches.

And sometimes what happened during a speech was something special. At one forum in which all the candidates spoke, the master of ceremonies, no friend to Kennedy and eager to emphasize that he was a rich man's son, made a point of introducing each of the others as "a young fellow who came up the hard way." Then it was Kennedy's turn. "I seem to be the only person here tonight who didn't come up the hard way," he said—and suddenly there was the grin, and the audience roared with laughter, and that issue was dead. On another occasion, he walked into a hall late, while his leading opponent, Mike Neville, a former mayor and a popular state legislator, was speaking. "Here comes the opposition," Neville sneered. "Maybe he's going to talk to you about money and how to manage a bank." Without a pause, Kennedy said, "I'm not going to talk about banking, Mike. I'm going to talk about you." And Neville was thereafter in about the same position as the issue. The tough Boston pols who had been hired with the ambassador's money started to realize that the ambassador's son not only had quite a quick wit but could think on his feet—could think fast.

And sometimes there was something more than wit. A pol from the district's tough Charlestown area, Dave Powers, who had turned down Kennedy's offer of a campaign job, saying he was a friend of one of his opponents, saw it happen one night when Jack Kennedy was addressing a meeting of Gold Star Mothers, mothers who had lost a son in the war. Kennedy's prepared speech was just something he read from a text, but at the end, as he was about to step down,

Jack Kennedy paused, and said in a slow, sad voice, "I think I know how all you mothers feel because my mother is a Gold Star Mother, too."

Suddenly women were hurrying up to the platform to crowd around Jack Kennedy and wish him luck, coming up to try to touch him. "I had been to a lot of political talks in Charlestown but I never saw a reaction like this one," Powers was to recall. "I heard those women saying to each other, 'Isn't he a wonderful boy, he reminds me so much of my own John, or my own Bob.' They all had stars in their eyes. They didn't want him to leave. It wasn't so much what he said but the way he reached into the emotions of everyone."

Everyone. Not just the mothers. As Jack Kennedy was walking out of the hall, Powers told him what a "terrific" speech he had given. "Then do you think you'll be with me?" Kennedy asked.

"I'm already with you," Powers said.

AND HIS FATHER'S MONEY couldn't help with the pain.

Jack was better when he rested a lot; a long, strenuous day intensified the symptoms—the nausea and the gripping stomach cramps—that the doctors couldn't explain, and of course a long day put more strain on his back. But his days were very long. He was up early—early enough to be standing at the gates of the district's factories so he could shake hands when the morning shift arrived at seven o'clock, and then he would go house to house through the district's working-class neighborhoods, then ride trolley cars and subways and return to the factories at four, when the next shift arrived, then to his hotel for a long soak in a hot tub to ease the pain in his back, and then, in the evening, out to speeches at local clubs and organizations and to house parties arranged by his sisters, where, as a biographer wrote, "he was at his best, . . . coming in a bit timidly but with his flashing picture magazine smile, charming the mothers and titillating the daughters."

In the Eleventh District, campaigning in the neighborhoods meant climbing stairs, for these were neighborhoods with block after block of "three-deckers," three-story tenement buildings, in which often every floor had to be visited because there were different tenants on every floor, and stairs were very hard on Jack Kennedy's back—he could climb them only one step at a time: by putting a foot on each step, and then pulling the other foot up next to it. The old Boston pols recruited by Joe Kennedy's allies and Joe Kennedy's cash to take him around looked askance at "the millionaire's kid" at first—"It was tough to sell the guy," one recalls. "We had a hell of a job with him. Young Kennedy, young Kennedy, we kept saying. But they didn't want him in the district. . . . They called him the Miami candidate. 'Take the guy and run him down in . . . Palm Beach.' " The pols came to think more of him, however. They would watch him tear off his clothes when he got back to his room at the end of a long day campaigning and sink into a tub of water as hot as he could bear, and they would watch as he climbed out, and strapped on a heavy corset and, on top of it, wrapped tightly around himself for extra support, a wide elastic bandage. And they would watch as he headed out on the evening's campaign trail. "The guy was in agony," one of them came to realize. But "off we'd go again, until eleven or twelve at night, never wasting a minute," as another of them put it. And he never complained. Another, Tom Broderick, watched the millionaire's kid limping into a meeting. "I knew his back was bothering him, and we had to walk up three flights of stairs. When we came downstairs, I said, 'You don't feel good?' And he said, 'I feel great.' . . . He never would admit that he felt the least bit tired or anything." Nor was he going only where he had been scheduled. At the end of his last scheduled event of the evening, he'd turn to the campaign aide who was almost always with him, Billy Sutton, and ask if there was anywhere else he could go. "I'd say, 'Well, do you want to go to ——?' And he'd say, 'Yes!' "

On the last day of the campaign, there was a parade, the annual Bunker Hill Day parade, a five-mile walk on a hot June day, during which spectators kept running up to him and grabbing his hand, which of course pulled at his back. "Jack was exhausted," recalls a supporter, a Massachusetts state senator. At the end of the parade he collapsed. Carried to the senator's home, "he turned very yellow and blue," the senator says. "He appeared to me as a man who probably had a heart attack." His friends took off his clothes, "and we sponged him over." When they got in touch with the ambassador, he said it was a malaria attack and asked if Jack had his pills with him. When he took them, he started feeling better, and the next day, he won the election.

AND SO, if after his promising first, 1947, session in the House of Representatives, his work there fell off, part of the reason could be attributed to something other than laziness.

While visiting his sister Kathleen in England after the session, he fell so ill that he was rushed to a London hospital, where there was finally a definitive diagnosis: he had Addison's disease, an illness in which the adrenal glands fail— and that includes among its symptoms the nausea and vomiting, loss of appetite, inability to gain weight, fevers, chronic fatigue and yellow-brown coloring from which he had been suffering for years—and whose sufferers have a high mortality rate. So ill was he that the examining physician told Pamela Churchill, "That young American friend of yours, he hasn't got a year to live." Brought back to America in the ship's hospital of the *Queen Elizabeth*, he was given last rites by a priest who came aboard in New York. He was taken on a wheeled stretcher, ghostly pale, horribly thin, so weak he couldn't raise his head, to a chartered plane, and then by ambulance to New England Baptist Hospital, where "it was touch and go" for a while. But he recovered, with the help of new drugs that had been causing the mortality rate from Addison's to drop dramatically. In 1949, moreover, a new drug, cortisone, would prove to be a "miracle drug" for Addison's: thereafter, every three months 150-milligram pellets, first of cortisone and later of corticosteroid, a cortisone derivative, were implanted in his thighs, and he took 25 milligrams orally every day; his weight became normal at last, and from that time on, the abdominal symptoms didn't bother him as much. Cortisone gave him, as a friend wrote, "a whole new lease on life."

As soon as he started to recover, there became more and more evident another aspect of the text that was Jack Kennedy, an aspect previously not as visible as the pain and the struggle against it—an aspect that Lyndon Johnson might have read with a particularly deep understanding.

Even before cortisone—in 1948 and 1949—while he was still so ill and had barely arrived in the House of Representatives, "Jack was aiming for higher office," a friend says, and in 1950, he was spending three or four days a week traveling by car all over Massachusetts. Henry Cabot Lodge Jr. would be running for re-election to the Senate in 1952, and Kennedy was going to be running against him.

His back was getting worse, and he was frequently on crutches. There was, again, in 1952, the sheer, brutal impact of his father's money—the gigantic outlays for billboard and other advertising, the $500,000 loan to the newspaper. But the cost to the ambassador was one he could easily pay; the cost to the son was not so easy to pay—although it was paid without a murmur.

Arriving for a speech, he would conceal his crutches in the back seat of his car, and his aides would see him gritting his teeth in pain as he climbed out and walked to the front door. "But," as Dave Powers was to recall, "then when he came into the room where the crowd was gathered, he was erect and smiling, looking as fit and healthy as the light heavyweight champion of the world." After the speech, and after standing in the receiving line, he would walk, still smiling, back to the car, and the smile would still be on his face, until the door was closed behind him. Sometimes, as they drove to the next stop, Powers would turn around and see the candidate leaning back against the seat, his teeth gritted again against the pain, his eyes closed. There was a big state to be covered; he didn't talk about the pain, but about the need to make himself known in every section of it. Powers had tacked a map of Massachusetts on the wall of Jack's Boston apartment and would stick colored pins in each town or city where Jack had spoken. Studying the map, Jack would point to some area with insufficient pins. "Dave, you've got to get me some dates around there," he would say, and, Dave says, by Election Day, when Kennedy was elected to the Senate, by 70,737 votes out of a total of 2,353,231, it was "completely covered with pins."

The first issue he chose in the Senate—the St. Lawrence Seaway project—was one that transcended the interests of his state or region, and that was a major part of the reason it was chosen; as the veteran journalist Jack Bell puts it, Kennedy "just made up his mind that if he was ever going to be bigger than Massachusetts, then he'd better go against public opinion in his state." He started giving speeches on foreign policy; by April, 1954, the *Brooklyn Eagle* was saying, "Keep your eye on young Democratic senator Jack Kennedy. He's been getting a build-up for a nationwide campaign." Though he had reached the Senate so young, the Senate was not the goal he was aiming at.

It seemed that his back was going to stop him. By the spring of 1954, the pain was so bad that, Billings wrote, "he could no longer disguise it from his close friends, and the toll it was taking on his mind and body was tremendous." The crutches were often leaning against the wall behind him in committee hearings; he even had to hold himself up on them while delivering a speech in Massachusetts. Even with their help, he could hardly walk; it simply hurt too much.

Only an operation—a complicated fusing of two areas of the spine, with a metal plate inserted to stabilize it—could enable him to walk, doctors agreed, but an operation would be extremely dangerous because of the havoc that Addison's played with the body's ability to resist infection; "even getting a tooth extracted was serious," said a doctor at Boston's Lahey Clinic, and surgeons at the clinic flatly refused to operate; that same year, as Doris Goodwin reports, "a 47-year-old man with Addison's underwent an appendectomy and died three weeks later from a massive infection that antibiotics were unable to treat."

His father tried to dissuade him from having the operation by telling him that he could live a full life even if he was confined to a wheelchair; look at Roosevelt, he said. Nonetheless Kennedy told his father he had decided to have it; his mother was to write that "He told his father that . . . he would rather be dead than spend the rest of his life hobbling on crutches and paralyzed by pain." The operation took place at a New York City hospital on October 21, 1954. "Thirty-seven years old, a United States senator with a limitless future before him, he succumbed to the anesthesia knowing he had only a 50-50 chance of ever waking up again," Goodwin wrote.

Three days after the operation, the infection materialized; his longtime secretary, Evelyn Lincoln, was told that doctors did not expect him to live through the night; his family gathered at his bedside while a priest administered last rites; his father, coming from the hospital and needing someone to talk to, wandered, almost in a daze, into the office of his friend the columnist Arthur Krock; "he told me he thought Jack was dying and he wept sitting opposite me." Recalls Rose: "It seemed inconceivable that he could once again be losing his eldest son." Gradually recovering from the infection, Jack remained in the hospital for eight weeks, but his back wouldn't heal—the huge incision, more than eight inches long, around the plate refused to close. In Palm Beach, where he was taken to recuperate, the scar still refused to heal, and he couldn't walk; he could only lie on his back, in pain, "and the doctors," as Goodwin writes, "would not say whether he would ever walk again, let alone walk without crutches."

On February 15, 1955, a second operation was performed, and the metal plate was removed, and he began to heal—somewhat. Three months later, on

May 23, he returned to the Senate, coming down the steps from his plane, and, on Capitol Hill, walking to his office, without crutches, a smile on his face. He was "tanned and fit," the *Herald Tribune* said. "Aside from experiencing some difficulty in walking, the Senator looked to be in excellent shape," the *Boston Post* said. But the reality was very different—as a new physician, Dr. Janet Travell, saw three days later when, in desperation, he came to consult her for the first time in her office on the ground floor of a New York brownstone.

She had read the news stories about his return to Washington, Dr. Travell was to recall. "It must have taken tremendous grit for him to create that effect." The young senator could barely get down the few steps to her office; the taxi driver had to help him. As he sat in her office, she saw that he was too thin, and that under his tan he looked pale and anemic; "he moved guardedly" and "couldn't turn to face her . . . without turning his entire body." He answered all her questions, but did so reluctantly, "as if he were retelling a boring story. . . . He seemed tired and discouraged. . . . When I examined him, the reality of his ordeal was brought home to me by the callus under each armpit . . . where the skin had borne his weight on crutches for so long."

Dr. Travell's treatment—injection of the muscles in spasm in Kennedy's back and legs with a solution of procaine and Novocain—worked to a considerable extent, and in remarkably short order. The pain was still there, although far less than before, and so was the brace; but the hated crutches were gone. After he began using a rocking chair she prescribed, sitting became much easier. And the cortisone kept the Addison's, except for isolated incidents, under control: his face was no longer gaunt; he was no longer tired so often; he was, in fact, filled with energy. And after so many years of thinking he would die young, he had a different view. "Jack had grown up thinking he was doomed," Lem Billings was to say. "Now . . . instead of thinking he was doomed, he thought he was lucky." And by the 1956 convention, when he grabbed at the vice presidency, it was apparent that that was not the "higher office" he had in mind. "I'm against vice in all forms," he joked not long thereafter, and by 1957, a large map of the United States was always spread out on a table in Palm Beach. Jack Kennedy, and his father, and visiting politicians—and they were visiting from all over the United States—would pore over it, noting "potentially valuable contacts."

And Jack Kennedy made the contacts—and turned contacts into allies—in person, crisscrossing the country again and again. In September, an infection around the spinal fusion required hospitalization and a "wide incision," and thereafter, as he recuperated in Hyannis Port, was so painful that his father made what must have been a difficult telephone call for him. "Maybe Jack should stop torturing himself and he should call the whole thing off," Joseph Kennedy said to Dr. Travell. "Do you think he can make it? There are plenty of other things for him to do." Calling it off, however, was not something Jack Kennedy was considering. Visiting Hyannis Port, Dr. Travell sat with the senator studying his schedule for the next five weeks, and trying to find time in it for rest periods.

"There was," she wrote, "scarcely a free hour." The senator told her the schedule couldn't be changed.

Lyndon Johnson might well have read John F. Kennedy differently than he did—more accurately. He was, in fact, particularly well qualified—almost uniquely well qualified—to do so. For all the differences between the two men, there was at least one notable similarity, and it had to do with their campaigns for office, starting with each man's first campaign. Jack Kennedy was not the only one of the two men, after all, who had, during his first campaign for Congress, driven himself to the limit of his physical endurance, and then beyond, until at the end of the campaign—but not until the end—he had collapsed in public. Kennedy's collapse had been in that Bunker Hill Day parade on the last day before the election; Johnson's, during *his* first campaign for Congress, in 1937, was two days before the election, in the Travis County Courthouse. All during that campaign—a campaign it seemed all but impossible for him to win—he had been losing weight; during it he lost about forty pounds from an already thin frame, until his cheeks were so hollow and his eyes sunk so deep in their sockets that, as I have written, "he might have been a candidate by El Greco." Then he began vomiting frequently, constantly complaining of stomach cramps, sometimes doubling over during a speech. The complaints were not taken seriously because he never slackened the pace that led to Ed Clark's comment that "I never thought it was *possible* for anyone to work that hard," but on a Thursday night in the courthouse—the election was on Saturday—he was delivering a speech, holding on to the railing in front of him for support, when, doubling over, white-faced, he sat down on the floor. He got up, finished the speech and then was rushed to an Austin hospital, where doctors, finding his appendix was about to rupture, operated almost immediately. Jack Kennedy was, moreover, not the only one of the two men who had fought through pain—great pain—in a later campaign. During his 1948 race for the Senate, Johnson was suffering from a kidney stone and kidney colic, an illness whose "agonizing" pain medical textbooks describe as "unbearable." His doctor said he didn't know "how in the world a man could keep functioning in the pain that he was in." But he kept functioning, smiling through speeches and receiving lines even though, in the car being driven to them, his driver, looking in the rearview mirror, often saw him doubled over in pain, clutching his groin, shivering and gasping for breath. A temperature of over 104 degrees left him racked alternately by fever and violent chills. Refusing for long days to be hospitalized despite warnings that he was risking irreparable loss of kidney function, he suspended his campaign only (and even then against his will) when he could no longer control his shivering, and could barely sit upright. When, in the hospital, doctors told him that an operation to remove the stone was imperative—that with his fever, caused by infection, not abating, and the possibility of abscess and gangrene in the prognosis, his situation was becoming life-threatening—Johnson nevertheless refused to agree to one because the lengthy recovery time would end his hopes of winning the campaign, finally persuading surgeons to try to remove the stone by an alternative procedure that they were doubtful would work, but which in fact succeeded. Throughout his life, Lyndon Johnson had aimed at only one goal, and in his efforts to advance along the path to that goal had displayed a determination—a desperation, really—that raised the question of what limits he would drive himself to in that quest, and indeed whether there *were* any limits. Had Johnson read Jack Kennedy more accurately, he might have seen that the same question might have been asked about *him*. The man Lyndon Johnson was running against—this man he didn't take seriously—not only wanted the same thing he did, but was a man just as determined to get it as he was.

As determined as he was, and much better at running for the presidency than Johnson had thought possible.

One of Jack Kennedy's most impressive characteristics was an ability to observe—and to generalize from his observations, to understand the implications of what he was seeing—no matter how hectic his pace might be: to "learn on the run," as one of his aides would put it. And as he raced back and forth across the United States in 1957, and continued to do so at the beginning of 1958, he had drawn one definite conclusion: that, as he told a friendly reporter at the end of 1957, "The Senate is not the place to run from"—that not only was being a United States senator not much of an advantage when it came to running for the presidency, it might even on balance be a disadvantage, and quite a considerable one at that.

While newspaper and magazine coverage of the Senate, of necessity consisting of hard-to-follow explanations of arcane legislative technicalities, didn't translate into public interest in that body, and the benefit to a presidential candidate in being an active senator was therefore very limited, the liability inherent in such a role wasn't limited at all. A senator was constantly being forced to take stands on controversial issues, and such stands antagonized one side or the other—which meant antagonizing individuals or groups whose support a senator needed if he wanted to be President. One reason that Kennedy had lost the vice presidential nomination to Kefauver was the refusal of Midwest states to support him because of a vote he had cast against an Eisenhower Administration bill to prop up farm prices. And then there had been the Joe McCarthy issue: McCarthy was a friend of Joseph Kennedy Sr., a friend of the whole Kennedy family; in fact, Kennedy had been the only Democratic senator not to vote for McCarthy's censure. Kennedy had hoped that the fact that he had been in the hospital for much of the censure debate might insulate him from criticism for not voting; it hadn't. In the history of the United States, only one senator—Warren Gamaliel Harding in 1921—had ascended to the White House directly from the Senate, and Kennedy understood why: "No matter how you vote, somebody is made happy and somebody unhappy," he explained. "If you vote against enough people, you are dead politically."

Jack Kennedy had the ability not only to "learn on the run" but also to act on what he learned, to act rationally, dispassionately, coldly. Spending time in the Senate was a drawback, so he would spend as little time as possible there: that meant not doing the job to which he had been elected. He would be criticized—for absenteeism, for shirking his duties. But he had calculated that, in terms of his presidential run, such criticism would be far outweighed by the benefits from campaigning across the country; it was a criticism that would have to be accepted—and he accepted it.

Not only was Kennedy learning who had what Theodore H. White calls the "pieces of power," he was learning who didn't have them—which meant that he was learning, firsthand, the hollowness behind Lyndon Johnson's belief that the Old Bulls of the Senate ruled their home-state pastures. Politics was changing, the old-style organizations were no longer so dominant, and as part of the change, in every state younger men—in 1957, about Kennedy's age: forty—were rising up on the political ladder, some still on the lower rungs, some just entering politics, many of them war veterans like himself; they identified with him, were willing to work for him. Kennedy organizations were being set up in many states; thousands of names were being indexed at Kennedy headquarters. "Johnson thinks the campaign is in Washington," Kennedy said one day to Ted Sorensen. "It's not. It's out here."

And, of course, there was the new factor in politics, the factor that was to transform politics, the medium—television—that could transmute a little-known senator into a national figure in a moment.

Jack Kennedy had had that moment, at the 1956 Democratic convention in Chicago—had had, at that convention, two moments, in fact. The first had been on its opening night. The lights in the hall dimmed, a huge movie screen unrolled above the podium, and a dramatic and moving documentary, *The Pursuit of Happiness,* on the history of the Democratic Party, made by the Hollywood director Dore Schary, was shown to the eleven thousand delegates—and to forty million viewers watching the convention on television. The shots of Roosevelt and Truman brought the delegates to their feet with a roar—and so did the film's on-screen narrator, Jack Kennedy. Schary, sitting on the convention floor, saw that the personality of the young, handsome senator "just . . . jumped at you on the screen." Jack Kennedy, the *New York Times* reported, "came before the convention tonight as a movie star."

Then, two nights later, came his daylong battle with Kefauver, which for a few minutes he appeared to have won, but which he lost at the wire. Television loves a drama, and that neck-and-neck race was a riveting drama—and so was Kennedy's appearance on the rostrum to concede.

Biographies of Kennedy almost unanimously say he was smiling as he conceded. He wasn't. This was Jack Kennedy in defeat: below him, waving in his

face as he came out on the platform, was a sea of signs—"Win with Estes!"—
celebrating the man who had beaten him. There was no trace of a smile on his
face. For once, his attire wasn't impeccable; one wing of his shirt collar stuck out
of his jacket. Sam Rayburn had handed him the big gavel as he stepped up to the
podium, and as he said the few necessary words ("I want to take this opportunity
first to express my appreciation to Democrats from all parts of the country—
North and South, East and West—who have been so generous and kind to me. I
hope that this convention will make Estes Kefauver's nomination unanimous"),
his hands never stopped turning it restlessly around and around. As his beautiful
young wife watched him from a box in the hall, her face, above her black dress
and pearls, was sad. Thinking his words had completed his chore, he turned to
step down from the podium, but Rayburn took his arm firmly and turned him
back, saying he had to make a formal motion that the nomination be made unanimous, and as he stepped back to the microphone, he did so with an air of resignation before walking off again, while the band played Kefauver's theme song,
"The Tennessee Waltz." This was the first time in his political career that Jack
Kennedy had tasted defeat, and it was apparent that he didn't like the feeling at
all. Yet not only his words but his demeanor, if resigned and disappointed, had
been gracious—the demeanor of a handsome young man dignified, even gallant,
in defeat. "And then he was gone, the underdog candidate who had intrigued and
captivated the hearts and minds of millions of Americans," as one historian put it.
"The dramatic race," which "had glued millions to their television sets," was "his
great moment—the moment when he passed through a kind of political sound
barrier to register on the nation's memory," wrote another.

Kennedy realized that. About a year later he ran into Jim Rowe at some airport and the two men sat down for a chat, and Kennedy said, "Jim, do you know
who's the most well-known senator in the United States?"

"Kefauver," Rowe replied, thinking of the Tennessean's nationally televised
organized crime hearings, and, he recalls, Kennedy said, "That's right. And do
you know who the second most well-known senator is?"

"Who?" Rowe asked.

"I am," Jack Kennedy said. "And do you know why? It was the half hour on
national television when I ran against Kefauver for the vice presidency."

While in hindsight, the transformation that television was to make in American politics seems obvious, at the time few politicians recognized this new reality as Kennedy did. Seizing every opportunity to be on-screen, he appeared not
only as a guest on the Sunday interview shows from Washington, but also, for
example, as narrator on two programs that the popular show *Omnibus* presented
on the Mideast crisis. Moreover, his good looks and relaxed charm made him naturally suited to the new medium that was becoming a fixture in America. Television critic Jack Gould called him "the most telegenic person in public life." And
his popularity on television brought him a flood of invitations to appear before
Democratic groups all over the country. To dispel doubts about his health, he
played golf and touch football with photographers present, but in reality the con-

stant traveling was hard on him; his back began giving him trouble again, but as long as he wore both the brace and the elastic bandage, his back held up; by the end of 1957, he had made hundreds of speeches, in forty-seven states.

AND THOSE SPEECHES were increasingly effective.

During his six unproductive years in the House of Representatives, when Mary Davis, his secretary, had been so annoyed by his "rather lackadaisical" attitude toward work, there had, nonetheless, been "one thing" about Jack Kennedy "that really surprised me"—the speeches he dictated to her.

"He wrote his own," Ms. Davis was to recall. "He appeared to be such a disinterested guy, not involved, couldn't care less, but then he'd say, 'Mary, come on in.' Then he would start dictating off the top of his head. The flow of language, his command of English, was extraordinary. It would come out beautifully— exactly what he wanted to say. And I'd think, 'This—coming from *you*.' I surprised myself, but I came to the conclusion that he was brilliant—the brightest person I've ever known."

Brilliant though the content of the speeches that Jack Kennedy dictated during those six years may have been, however, audiences were less than impressed, because of the way he delivered them. Despite magical moments like the one with the Gold Star Mothers, most of his talks were still delivered much too fast, with his smiles so fleeting and mechanical that their brightness hardly registered, and his physical appearance—the gaunt cheeks, the stiffness with which he moved, the suits hanging too loosely—did not add to their effectiveness. Occasionally, if he got caught up in what he was saying, his right arm would come up, and his hand would be extended to emphasize a point, but the gesture was a tentative one, the arm usually not coming up very far, and quickly coming down again. And during his first three years in the Senate, of course, before Dr. Travell, he was all too often delivering his speeches while he was in pain; several times he was forced to give them while standing on those crutches, with their big, padded crosspieces.

After the cortisone and Dr. Travell, however, his face became fuller (sometimes, in fact, too full for his liking; the drug sometimes caused a slight puffiness around his jaw). His body filled out, too; he seemed healthy, full of energy. The grin was, really, the same grin, but it beamed out now from a face that was very handsome but in a different way from before: confident, strong. The way he delivered his speeches changed, too. His suits now looked casual and debonair, made elegant by his bearing as much as by the fabric; only late in the day, when the press of the suit jacket had wilted and the jacket clung to his frame a little bit, would the outline of the brace be even faintly visible. And the right arm was coming up more and more, higher—to shoulder level, often—and the hand was jabbing forward more and more emphatically as he made his points. And there was something different about the way he was starting to hold his head: sometimes it would tilt a little to the right, and his chin would come up, and out:

strong, self-assured. His voice, with its distinctive New England accent, had always sounded earnest; now it was becoming more emphatic; sometimes, in fact—not often but sometimes—it was starting to have quite a ring to it. Lyndon Johnson might still be clinging to the image of a frail, ineffectual Jack Kennedy, but, month by month, as Kennedy crisscrossed the country in 1957 and 1958, speech following speech, that picture was changing: the chin coming up more and more, not just confident but a bit cocky, combative, ready for any challenge; the hand, when he got carried away, often up above his shoulder now, the forefinger jabbing at the sky, the fist punching at the audience, then the hand reaching to the crowd, palm up in entreaty and exhortation. And if, after the speech or during a press conference, he got hostile questions, which were mostly about his Catholicism, the chin would cock up a little more, the gesture would be more emphatic, and he would answer with a mixture of sincerity and self-deprecatory humor that brought audiences over to his side. "I have never seen anybody in my life develop like Jack Kennedy did as a personality, and as a speaker, and as an attractive person, over the last seven, eight years of his life," George Smathers was to say. "It was just a miracle transformation." In addition, during the same time that this was happening, there were, month after month, the feature stories in national magazines—on him, and on his glamorous wife, and, after November, 1957, on his little daughter Caroline, and on his whole glamorous, talented, wealthy family: "The Rise of the Brothers Kennedy" in *Look,* "The Amazing Kennedys" in the *Saturday Evening Post* (which called its readers' attention to "the flowering of another great political family, such as the Adamses, the Lodges, and the La Follettes")—the cover stories in *Time, McCall's, Redbook,* one after the other, so that Jack Kennedy's broad, open, assured grin, under that trademark unruly forelock, seemed to be beaming constantly from newsstands.

Being out on the campaign trail meant he wasn't in the Senate—during his eight years in the Senate, according to one estimate, Kennedy was away from Washington at least half of the time it was in session—and conventional political observers complained bitterly about the dereliction. "This man seeks the highest elective office in the world not primarily as a politician, but as a celebrity," one wrote. Said *New York Post* columnist William V. Shannon: "There is a growing tendency on the part of Americans to 'consume' political figures in much the same sense we consume entertainment personalities on television and in the movies. Month after month, from the glossy pages of *Life* to the multicolored cover of *Redbook,* Jack and Jackie Kennedy smile out at millions of readers; he with his tousled hair and winning smile, she with her dark eyes and beautiful face. We hear of her pregnancy, of his wartime heroism, of their fondness for sailing. But what has all this to do with statesmanship?" The answer was: Nothing. While Lyndon Johnson's assessment of Jack Kennedy as a senator—"He never did a thing"—is an exaggeration, its import is, on the whole, not far wrong. "His Senate career," concludes one of his biographers, Robert Dallek, "produced no major legislation that contributed substantially to the national well-being." Misgivings about his lack of accomplishments were drowned out by the ubiquity and attractiveness of his media appearances, however. By May of 1957, the nationally syndicated columnist Marquis Childs would write, "Seldom in the annals of this political capital has anyone risen as rapidly and as steadily in a presidential sweepstakes as Jack Kennedy." The effect of his celebrity was evident even in the enclave that was home to many of the capital's political elite. During the spring of 1958, Kennedy had a drink with the columnist Joseph Alsop at Alsop's home on Dumbarton Avenue in Georgetown. As he was making his farewells on the high stoop of the house, some of Alsop's neighbors, looking out their windows, happened to see him. Opening the windows, they began to applaud. Lyndon Johnson had been visiting homes in Georgetown for almost a quarter of a century. No one had ever applauded him. By that spring, Kennedy had reversed his standing against Kefauver in the Gallup Polls; now, instead of trailing him by eleven points, as had been the case the year before, he was ahead by eleven. Kefauver, in fact, was all but out of the race; in 1952 and 1956 he had made himself a threat by his relentless and effective campaigning; there was an equally relentless, and more effective, campaigner in the race now. In March, 1958, *Time*'s Washington bureau chief felt "by general agreement," Kennedy is "the early-season favorite" to win the Democratic nomination; unless he was stopped, he would "win on the first ballot."

BUT THERE WAS also general agreement that he *could* still be stopped.

"Enormously successful" though Kennedy's campaigning had been, "it was not enough," an historian was to write. "And he knew it was not enough." Popular though he may have been with the public at large, he wasn't the leader in the polls of Democratic delegates and party officials who would cast the actual votes that would determine the nominee. With them Adlai Stevenson was still ahead. Symington, who had also won a landslide re-election campaign in November, and Humphrey appeared to have substantial blocs of delegates plus the possibility of winning more in primaries, and Johnson had his four hundred or so from the South and border states; favorite sons like Governors Robert Meyner of New Jersey and G. Mennen "Soapy" Williams of Michigan were still in the running. There appeared to be every chance that Kennedy would not be able to win 761 delegates, and that, after a number of indecisive ballots, the convention would still be deadlocked, and the battle would move into the back rooms—where Johnson wanted it, where the decision would be made by the old bosses who were still put off by Kennedy's youth, inexperience and religion. Johnson was sure he would win in these rooms, and he was not alone in that feeling. "If the convention ever went into the back rooms, we'd never get out of the back rooms," Sorensen was to say.

Favorite though he might be, *Time* said, "Jack Kennedy could turn out to be one of the flowers that bloom in the spring," and might well do so; "the battle for the 1960 nomination" still "shaped up as one of the grandest, free-swinging, rough and tumble in years."

3

Forging Chains

In his January, 1959, letter telling Johnson that he had decided to cast his lot with Humphrey, Jim Rowe agreed with *Time*'s assessment. "I still think you have a chance for the nomination, despite [the] obvious political handicaps both of us know you carry with you, *if* you would go after it in the way I have urged you should," Rowe wrote. "You would have had a better chance a year ago than now, but it is still possible, however remote. But, as I said, and as you agreed, you have *no* chance whatsoever if you 'wait.' By 'waiting' I mean staying always in Washington and doing only a superb job as Leader. . . . I did not make the rules that must inevitably be followed to win the Presidential nomination. . . . But I know, as do you, that they must be followed."

Rationally, Johnson knew that Rowe's argument was correct ("You agreed," Rowe reminded him), but it wasn't the rational that was governing Lyndon Johnson now—as 1959 was to demonstrate.

He was running all right. Since running would create two problems for him in Texas, early in the year he took steps to solve both of them.

The first was a prohibition in Texas law against anyone being a candidate for two offices in the same election. Johnson wanted to be a candidate for two in 1960. His Senate term expired that year, and if he received the Democratic presidential nomination but lost to Richard Nixon or whomever the Republican candidate might turn out to be, he wanted to retain his Senate seat. While his re-election to the Senate would not be in doubt—he had won in a landslide in 1954, and his position in Texas had only strengthened since then—under that law, he couldn't be on the ballot for senator if he was on it for another office.

Solving that problem required no more than a phone call—which he made to Ed Clark. The state's "Secret Boss" took care of the matter in the Legislature: on April 20, 1959, over the violent objections of a little band of liberals, it passed a special act which preserved the two-office prohibition—except in the case of a candidate who had been nominated for both a statewide office (such as United States senator) and "for the office of president or vice president of the United

States." And when, later, a lawsuit was filed challenging the constitutionality of this "Johnson for President" bill, Johnson simply made another call to Clark, this time asking him to bring to the Johnson Ranch a list of lawyers who could defend the suit. Clark watched Johnson's big thumb move down the list, as slowly as it moved down Senate tally sheets, pausing as he considered the pros and cons of each name, until he got to "Jaworski"—Leon Jaworski, a respected Houston attorney who had two additional qualifications: first, as Johnson put it to Clark, that "He's never been mixed up with Brown & Root"; second, that he was a friend of the state's senior senator, Tom Connally, whose son, United States District Court judge Ben Connally, would probably be presiding over the case. "Will Leon Jaworski take this suit?" Johnson asked Clark. "I said Yes. You don't even have to call him. I'll take care of that." (The suit never reached Ben Connally's court; it was dismissed at a lower level.)

The other problem required a lot of phone calls, and delicate ones, since they involved a figure from Johnson's past whom he had been hoping to keep in the past: George Parr—George Berham Parr of Duval County in the Rio Grande Valley, the legendary "Duke of Duval," the most powerful of the despotic *patrones* or *jefes,* who controlled the Valley and its votes.

Confident though Johnson might be about a Senate re-election race, the situation in Texas would be very different should he be the presidential candidate. The state had gone Republican in the last two presidential elections—Dwight Eisenhower had carried it by more than 200,000 votes in 1956—and while part of the explanation was Eisenhower's personal popularity, part was the fact that traditionally Democratic Texas was becoming steadily more conservative. Johnson might need every vote he could get.

Parr could produce a lot of votes for him; he had, in fact, done so in 1948, when, late on election night, with Johnson still far behind Coke Stevenson, the two counties the Duke controlled personally—Duval and Starr—and other Valley counties controlled by the Duke's satraps suddenly produced 20,000 new votes for Johnson; the vote in Duval was 4,195 for Johnson, 38 for Stevenson: a margin of more than a hundred to one. And, six days later, with all the late returns supposedly counted and Johnson still behind by a few votes, a Parr-controlled precinct in adjoining Jim Wells County suddenly announced that its returns had somehow not been counted, and the two hundred new votes for Johnson from this precinct—votes cast by people who had all written their names in the same ink, in the same handwriting, and who had voted in alphabetical order—gave Johnson the lead in an election he won by eighty-seven votes. With Parr still in power, still able to produce what was needed if he wanted to, Johnson had to make sure he wanted to.

That required taking a hand in another legal case: Parr's 1957 conviction for mail fraud. Johnson had assisted the Duval *patrón* on the legal front before: helping Parr obtain, in 1946, a presidential pardon for a conviction for income tax evasion for which he had served time in a federal prison. Now, in 1959, Parr wanted help again. Having lost his appeals of the mail fraud conviction, he had only one remaining hope—a very slim hope: that the United States Supreme Court would take the case. He needed a lawyer with very good Washington credentials, and, with federal prosecutors having seized his assets, he had run out of funds with which to hire one. Johnson had another incentive to help: his fear, as Ed Clark's law partner Donald Thomas explains, that Parr might decide to talk publicly about 1948. He asked Abe Fortas, whose legal brilliance had rescued his '48 victory from a federal investigation, not only to take the mail-fraud case but to take it without a fee; as Fortas' biographer Bruce Murphy writes, "In return for Parr's silence, Johnson asked Fortas if he would take the case *pro bono*." Fortas agreed, later assuring Johnson that he "had not asked for any money" from Parr, and the case was soon on the Supreme Court's docket, which "is the best break we have had in the case thus far," Fortas' partner Paul Porter told Jenkins. "If they had refused to review it . . . Parr was just on his way to the clink." (In 1960, Parr's conviction would be reversed: "We got him off on a technicality," another of Fortas' partners, Charles Reich, explains.) Anxious that his role in helping Parr not become public, Johnson wanted nothing in writing. He told Fortas and Porter to keep Jenkins informed of the appeal's progress through telephone calls, and told Jenkins to "burn your memo up on [those] phone calls." All through 1959, he monitored the case closely, however, and those involved knew why. "He was looking ahead to 1960," Ed Clark says.

BUT IF IN TEXAS—and in Washington, too, where at the opening of the 1959 Senate session he easily quashed a revolt by liberal senators against his iron rule—he was moving with a sure hand, in the rest of the country it was a very different story.

Part of his strategy for obtaining the nomination was based on invalid assumptions—assumptions explained by the fact that he had lived so much of his life in Washington, where the Senate was a focus of intense interest, senators figures of power, and he, as the Senate's Majority Leader, a cynosure of attention, his remarkably successful maneuvers through the arcane thickets of Senate rules and precedents chronicled in detail in the *Washington Post* and the *Washington Star*, marveled at during Georgetown dinner parties. He assumed that senators could deliver their state delegations to him, and that his announcement that Senate business required him to forgo campaigning would be understood, indeed hailed, by the country as proof of his indispensable devotion to the national welfare.

Another part of his strategy—his plan to keep anyone else (and anyone else was starting to mean John F. Kennedy) from winning the nomination—might have been valid, as sound a strategy, perhaps, as could be devised for a southerner who could not hope to win the votes of 761 of the 1,521 delegates. If he could indeed get enough delegates—add enough, mostly from the western states, to his southern votes—he would have enough, in combination with those of other candidates, not to win the nomination, but to deny it to Kennedy, to throw the choice, after a number of inconclusive ballots were taken, into the back rooms (the "smoke-filled rooms" of political legend) that were the domain of the big-state bosses.

It was in these rooms, from these men, that Lyndon Johnson indeed had his best chance of obtaining the nomination. He would be negotiating with them—and he was of course a great negotiator—meeting alone with one or another of them: the greatest salesman, selling himself. Lyndon Johnson's confidence that he would get what he wanted from any man if he was only able to spend time alone with him had not, in the major episodes of his life, often proved to be over-confidence. He would be negotiating, furthermore, with men who talked the idiom of hard, tough, pragmatic politics, the language not of the Senate floor but of the Senate cloakroom—Lyndon Johnson language. "It is the politician's task to pass legislation, not to sit around saying principled things," he often declared. In the conversation of these men, "principled things" were not a prominent motif; what they talked about was winning.

For this strategy of the back rooms to succeed, however, there was a *sine qua non.* To these men who wanted to win, he had to prove that he could do so, had to demonstrate to the northern bosses that he could carry states outside the South in November. He had to enter some non-southern primaries—Indiana and West Virginia, for example—and do well in them. If he didn't show these men that he was a winner, no sales talk would help.

What he could have done, were he to campaign in the North, was demonstrated when finally, on May 7, 1959, he accepted an invitation to speak there—before six thousand Pennsylvania state employees who, at the behest of Governor David L. (Don't Call Me "Boss") Lawrence, had anted up a hundred dollars per ticket to attend a "Democratic Victory Dinner" that overflowed the main auditorium in Harrisburg's Zembo Mosque as well as two smaller dining rooms and two huge tents that had been set up outside, so that scores of Democrats had to eat their dinner in the mosque's kitchens.

The star attraction proved worth the price of admission. "Never had Lyndon looked more vigorous as he raced from tent to tent, dining room to dining room, greeting Pennsylvanians," John Steele of *Time* reported in a memorandum to his editors. Tall, slender, smiling broadly, "daisy-fresh in a neat, dark blue single-breasted suit, white shirt, and dark tie . . . his laugh at the quips of others infectious," he entered the mosque by bounding up its several flights of steep stairs "like a high hurdler" as if to put to rest once and for all any doubts about his health (meanwhile the aides who had accompanied him were quietly letting reporters know that his health was so good that he'd just qualified for an additional $100,000 of life insurance).

Calling his 1957 civil rights bill "weasel-worded," the NAACP's Pennsylvania Chapter had protested the invitation to Johnson, calling him "one of the foremost enemies of civil rights in the Senate." Lawrence, however, had somewhat more experience than they with the difficulties in passing legislation, and he dealt with that subject when he introduced Johnson. "For eighty-two years men talked and talked—and did nothing—about civil rights legislation," the governor said. "But it was a Democratic Congress which in 1957 passed the first civil rights bill since Reconstruction." It was a Democratic Congress that had in 1956 and 1957 passed disability insurance, minimum wage, public housing, and public works measures. "Lyndon Johnson is . . . the man who guided through the Congress the programs upon which the Democratic Party rests its case with the people." And when a beaming Johnson rose to speak, with the crowd, stirred by Lawrence's introduction, giving him a warm welcome and the band playing "Deep in the Heart of Texas," he threw up both arms in an "Ike-like" gesture, and, after a few quips—"You discovered oil in Pennsylvania but we get all the blame"—delivered a powerful message: that indeed the Democratic programs would keep America true to its ideals, and, what's more, would bring the world to America's side: "Flung down before us now is a Communist challenge to wrestle for the soul of uncommitted lands. The struggle is not to be won by arms—it is to be won by the force of the examples of our two systems—and the century itself is the prize." Johnson's "approach varied from . . . the shouted, flourished" challenge to "the confidential conversational of the great FDR speeches," Steele told his editors. And the audience interrupted him twenty-three times with applause, and gave him a standing ovation when he finished.

"For years," Steele wrote, "Lyndon . . . had turned down by the bushel basket full [sic] invitations to invade the unfriendly North . . . which he needs but which for so long he has timidly distrusted." The warmth of the Pennsylvania reception would change his attitude, Steele believed. Decades later, remembering the scene, Steele said, "You felt that surely, now, he would campaign in the North—and that he was going to make everyone who heard him rethink what he was all about." Reedy felt the same way. After such a triumph, he felt, Johnson would see the possibilities: he had thought he couldn't win over a northern audience, but now he had finally appeared before one—and had won it over. Surely he would now agree to more speaking engagements in the North, perhaps even agree to enter primaries there. When, however, a month or so later, Reedy handed his boss an invitation to address another Democratic event in Pennsylvania, the response, after long minutes of poring over the invitation, was, "I don't want to get into a hostile audience." His excuse for declining invitations was the press of Senate business, but the Senate adjourned for the year in August; five months were open before the next session. Although he had accepted invitations for events during these months, again and again he pulled back as the day approached, often at the last minute telling his staff that he wouldn't go, to make some excuse; often he blamed the staff, saying he had never agreed to go, even though of course he had—in a pattern that became so familiar that his aides grew to dread accepting an invitation, since they knew that later, after the invitations had been printed and mailed and all arrangements made, they would probably have to call the event's organizers and tell them the featured speaker wouldn't be there. Jim Rowe saw a man being "torn"—"tortured, almost"—between his desire for something, and his desire not to be seen to be desiring it.

Johnson's strategy also required winning western votes. Winning the West—in political parlance, "the West" in 1960 didn't include California (deemed too urban to fit that category) but ten other states: Oregon and Washington in the far Northwest; the seven so-called "Mountain States" (Idaho, Montana, Wyoming, Colorado, Utah, New Mexico and Nevada) that ran southwest down the long line of the Rockies; as well as Arizona—should have been easy for Lyndon Johnson. Not only had he, as Senate Leader, consistently been the West's ally on mineral rights, irrigation and reclamation projects, and other issues important to the region, he had made himself its champion in 1957 by maneuvering through the Senate the long-stalled authorization for a great federal dam on Hells Canyon on the Snake River that would provide the inexpensive "public power" so vital in the West not only to Oregon and Idaho, the two states separated by the Snake, but to other western states linked to the dam by long transmission lines. What's more, since the ten states had only small black populations, civil rights was not a major issue; Johnson's southernness wouldn't hurt him there. And although, compared with the heavily populated northeastern states, the western states individually had few delegates, together they had 172.

In addition to the virtually solid support from the 352-delegate Southern Bloc, Johnson was anticipating all the votes of at least two border states, Oklahoma (29 votes) and Kentucky (31), and a scattering of votes from other states—a total of perhaps 430 or 440 delegates out of the 1,521 who would be voting at the convention. If he could add to that number the bulk of the 172 western delegates, he would arrive at the convention with 550 or more. Hubert Humphrey would have 31 from Minnesota, and expected to win the same number in the primary in neighboring Wisconsin—so identified was Humphrey with that state's battle for milk price supports that he had been called "Wisconsin's third senator"—and to add more from other Upper Midwest farm states; he had been the region's leading spokesman for years; it was expected that Humphrey would arrive at the convention with at least 150 delegates. Symington would have perhaps 100, including 39 from his native Missouri. Several favorite sons, including two governors—Robert Meyner of New Jersey (41 votes) and George Docking of Kansas (21)—were adamantly refusing to bow out of the race. Other delegates would hold out to the end for Adlai Stevenson. If Johnson did indeed get the bulk of the western delegates, Kennedy would have little chance of getting the 761 he needed on the first ballot.

And Johnson *could* have won the West. The Kennedy assigned—in September, 1959—to canvass for western delegates was the youngest brother, twenty-seven-year-old Ted. Amiable, gregarious, open, Ted was nonetheless a natural and keenly observant politician, and on this, his first political foray, he quickly realized, he recalls, that the West "was very sympathetic to" Johnson.

"They sweet-talked me about my brother. But they said, 'The reality is: This is Johnson Country. We know how he stands on minerals, on grazing issues, on . . . We know he's been a friend of the West. . . .' They felt enormously committed to him on the issues. He [Johnson] could have locked that place up without any difficulty at all."

Locking it up, however, meant courting the western delegates as individuals. To find out what issues were important to a man or what pragmatic considerations—a federal job, a contract, cash—a man really wanted, it was necessary to talk to him in person. And while in the western states there were no statewide bosses, in many cases four or five delegates might be controlled by, or subject to the persuasion of, some local political leader or businessman. Johnson had to learn the identity of the local leaders who held these "pieces of power," and bring them, too, to his side.

Lyndon Johnson could have learned all that, could have found out whom he needed in various states. There was nothing in politics that Lyndon Johnson couldn't learn—couldn't learn "very fast when he had to," in Jim Rowe's words. And nothing did he learn faster than who had the power in any group. But learning would require him to travel to the different states, meet the delegates—he would have to, in short, *campaign.* Unless he did that, his strategy had no hope of success. But campaigning would have meant admitting that he was trying—and in 1959 he still wouldn't, still seemingly *couldn't,* admit that.

Denying in public that one was a candidate was, naturally, par for the political course; in Johnson's case, however, the denials were made, with seeming conviction, even to men who had worked with him a long time.

Though to these men, his maneuvers in Texas were definitive proof (not that they needed proof) that he was a candidate, he kept refusing to admit that to them, refusing even to say that he would eventually, at the proper time, become a candidate. "You can count on it. I am not going to run"—that was still his mantra. On the subject of primaries, he was equally unequivocal. Primaries produce an unambiguous, undeniable result: there is a winner—and there are losers. Johnson was adamant: he wouldn't enter any primaries.

On every other subject related to a presidential candidacy, equivocation was, in 1959, the order of the year. At one moment, he would be telling an ally or aide, with apparent great sincerity, that his health made running an impossibility; sitting with Bobby Baker in the Senate Chamber after adjournment one evening, he said in a quiet, earnest voice: "Bobby, you've never had a heart attack. Every night I go to bed, and I never know if I'm going to wake up alive the next morning. I'm just not physically capable of running for the presidency." At another moment he would be explaining that his recovery from his attack had been complete (as indeed it had, and the sixteen- and eighteen-hour days he was putting in proved it), pulling out of his breast pocket a laminated copy of his latest cardiogram as documentation. Or he would make the "our home is here" argument, saying that the South's strength—"our strength"—was on Capitol Hill, and that therefore not only was he not running for the presidency, he didn't want the job, wouldn't accept it even if it was offered; if the convention were to draft him, he would say, he would refuse to accept the draft; he would probably not even attend the convention: that would make a draft less likely. The next moment he would be explaining that his "tending the store" stance was the best strategy to get the nomination: at these times, Baker says, "his attitude was, 'I'm not running, but I'm gonna win.' " Out would come another laminated card: this one with a precise state-by-state delegate count, and he would analyze exactly *how* he was going to win: state-by-state rundowns that would lead to a deadlock on the first ballot, state-by-state switches that would give him additional votes on later ballots. Fresh from a conversation in which Johnson assured him he wasn't running, Baker would watch Walter Jenkins (who never, as Baker knew, "took the smallest step without his [Johnson's] consent") "hand wads of hundred-dollar bills to Johnson loyalists as they fanned out to many states." Not that Jenkins was any less confused than he. Johnson had indeed told Jenkins—in May—to start setting up state-by-state "Johnson for President" organizations. He had also ordered Jenkins, however, to keep their existence secret. Complying with that order was difficult. One of the putative organizers was to ask Walter a little plaintively if it would be possible for him to speak directly to Johnson, because "I want to ask the Senator just how he wants me to do this [set up a statewide organization] behind the scenes."

And while Johnson was equivocating in 1959, Jack Kennedy was sending into the field against him a brother a lot less amiable than Ted—one who, in addition, had had Lyndon Johnson fixed in his sights for a long time.

THE FIRST TIME that Lyndon Johnson met Robert Kennedy was an encounter that the two Johnson staffers who were present would never forget.

It occurred early one morning in January, 1953, in the Senate cafeteria on the second floor of the Senate Office Building—there was only one Senate Office Building then—next door to Johnson's office. Johnson would often have breakfast there, usually with Horace Busby, on this morning also with George Reedy.

Just to the left of the cafeteria entrance was a cash register, and beyond it was a large round table, at which, every morning, Joe McCarthy sat, with three or four staff members from his Senate Investigations Subcommittee, and this morning there was a new staff member at the table: the subcommittee's newly appointed assistant counsel, twenty-seven-year-old Bobby Kennedy.

As Johnson, Busby and Reedy walked by, McCarthy, as was his custom, jumped up to shake Johnson's hand, calling him, as senators were already starting to do, "Leader," and McCarthy's staffers also rose—except, quite conspicuously, for Bobby, who sat unmoving, with a look on his face that Busby described as "sort of a glower."

Lyndon Johnson knew how to handle that situation. Moving around the table, he extended his hand to take McCarthy's and those of the standing staffers, and, when he got to Bobby Kennedy, stood there, with his hand not exactly extended but, in Busby's words, "sort of half-raised," looking down at Kennedy. For a long moment Kennedy didn't move. The glower had deepened into something more. "Bobby could really look hating," Busby says, "and that was how he looked then. He didn't want to get up, but Johnson was kind of forcing him to," and finally, without looking Johnson in the eye, he stood up and shook his hand.

Later, after the Johnson group had finished their breakfast and were leaving the cafeteria, Busby asked, "What was that all about in there?" and Johnson replied, "It's about Roosevelt and his father." Busby and Reedy knew what that meant. The long relationship between Joseph P. Kennedy and Franklin Roosevelt had ended in acrimony and bitterness, and Johnson, the young congressman, was a Roosevelt protégé. Moreover, the relationship's denouement had included one particularly vivid scene—at which Johnson had been present. The President, suspecting that the real purpose of a trip the ambassador made back to the United States from England during the 1940 election campaign was to denounce him for bringing the United States closer to war and to announce his support for Republican nominee Wendell Willkie, lured him down to Washington and tricked him. When a secretary announced that Ambassador Kennedy, who had returned that day, was calling, Johnson reported, the President had turned to him and said, "Oh boy, this is a real problem and I've got to handle it." Johnson related how Roosevelt, in his booming voice, had said, "Joe, how are ya? Been sittin' here with Lyndon just thinkin' about you, and I want to talk to you, my son. Can't wait. . . . Make it tonight," and then, hanging up the phone and turning to him, had said, with a smile, "I'm gonna fire the sonofabitch." The trick had worked; Kennedy made a very effective radio broadcast supporting Roosevelt, and then, the day after the election, his resignation was announced. The story was a dramatic one—and for years Johnson, the great storyteller, had been telling it with drama, using his gift for mimicry to repeat "Joe, how are ya?" in the President's booming voice, and his "I'm gonna fire the sonofabitch" in FDR's confidential whisper. And, exaggerated or not—and it may not have been *too* exaggerated, for Johnson had indeed been in Roosevelt's office the day Joe Kennedy's plane arrived from England—Johnson had told the story many times; "For decades," Hugh Sidey would write, "evenings in the capital were enriched with stories like the one about Franklin Roosevelt coaxing Ambassador Kennedy [down to Washington] and then with great relish firing him," a story which of course made Joe Kennedy look foolish. Bobby Kennedy's tribal loyalty to his family—"Bobby's a tough one. He'll keep the Kennedys together, you can bet," Joe Kennedy said— and in particular his adoration for his father were very deep; it took only a hint of a slighting reference to the ambassador to arouse him to fury, and Lyndon Johnson's story was far more than a hint. But as other breakfast encounters in the cafeteria and repetitions of the first scene took place during 1953, it became apparent to Busby and Reedy that Johnson's explanation must be only partially correct. "Bobby was there more than once in the morning when we came in, and Johnson always forced him to shake hands," Busby says. "He enjoyed it." Aware of "the discomfort he was causing" Bobby, "he'd get out in the hall and he'd laugh about it." And sometimes the Leader and the young staffer would pass in a Senate Office Building corridor. "Did you ever see two dogs come into a room and all of a sudden there's a low growl, and the hair rises up on the back of their necks?" George Reedy asks. "It was like that. . . . Somehow he and Bobby took one look at each other"—the one look, Reedy explains, was in the cafeteria that day in 1953—"and that was it."

Robert Francis Kennedy was shorter, slighter and much shyer than his two tall older brothers (and, in time, than his younger brother) and with none of their jaunty, glowing air and easy charm. He was all but written off by his family ("Forget Bobby; let's talk about Joe and Jack," one of his sisters said), most notably by his father, who once called him the family's "runt" and who didn't include him in his discussions of politics with Joe and Jack. Whatever the reasons may have been, many of his biographers have speculated, as one puts it, that he had "no ambition save one": to please that demanding figure whose insistence on toughness and victory was so uncompromising; "he was willing to do anything to get his father's respect." And, in addition, there had, since his boyhood, been visible in Robert Kennedy, born November 20, 1925, a streak often characterized as ruthless, but that could also be called just simply "mean"—or cruel. There was a tenderness in him, too—it would become apparent after he began having children of his own—but the other quality was always there. At Harvard (when he wrote his father, "I wish, Dad, that you would write me a letter as you used to Joe & Jack about what you think about the different political events and the war as I'd like to understand what's going on better than I do now"), there was raw courage (small and slight, he "didn't have any great God-given ability," the freshman football coach recalls, "but he had great determination. You'd have had to kill him to make him quit. He had a temper. . . . He had a determined and belligerent look. His attitude was always, 'We'll settle this thing right now and I'm willing to go all the way to do it' "): on the varsity, the 230-pound fullback told the coach, after the 155-pound Kennedy kept hitting him head-on, "For Christ's sake, stop him before he gets killed"; he once broke his leg but went on playing, tears of pain streaming down his face, but, as one biographer wrote, "Kennedy did not just play furiously. He was furious," spoiling, off the field as well as on, for a fight—often for senseless fights. One took place in a Cambridge bar where Bobby, celebrating his birthday with a group of friends, including the football captain, Ken O'Donnell, was picking up everyone's bar tab. Another Harvard student, John Magnuson, happened to be already celebrating *his* birthday there, and his friends began singing "Happy Birthday" to him. Infuriated over what he apparently regarded as an intrusion into his celebration, Bob walked up behind Magnuson and hit him over the head with a beer bottle, sending him to the hospital for stitches. (A few days later, Ken O'Donnell apologized to Magnuson; Bobby hadn't come himself, he said, because "it just wasn't his nature to apologize.") The journalist Anthony Lewis says that at Harvard, "I didn't like him and thought he was callow and tough." In another fight, with a man who, unaware that Joe Jr. was dead, made light of Bobby's attempts to quote him as an authority on some subject, "Bobby would have killed him if we didn't pull him off. We had to pry Kennedy's fingers off his neck. It really scared us." At law school, at the University of Virginia, "he became more insensitive and selfish . . . known for his rudeness . . . a bit of a lout," with an anger so close to the surface that it showed as clench-fisted rage. He also became known, and regarded warily, for his huge dogs. He would "always have these colossal dogs around him," at one time a large German police dog "who liked to bite"—and whom he kept unleashed; at another time two fierce Doberman pinschers that, another friend says, "we had a terrible time with." And he was still spoiling for fights—some, of course, over his father; when the school newspaper criticized Joe Kennedy after he gave a speech at the university urging isolationism, Bobby showed up in the paper's office "ready to punch someone in the nose." And there were, during this time, incidents which went beyond rudeness. Once, at Hyannis Port, Bobby took a friend,

> who could not sail, out in one of the family sailboats. The wind was fading, and as lunchtime approached, Kennedy realized that they might not make it ashore in time for lunch. Obsessed with his father's insistence on punctuality, he simply dove overboard and swam for shore, leaving his helpless crewmate to fend for himself. After flailing about, the friend was rescued by a passing boat. Kennedy made no attempt to apologize. Bobby was not a boy at the time. The incident occurred in 1948, when he was twenty-two years old.

In 1953, his father got him the job with McCarthy's committee. Later his work with this committee would be glossed over, excused by saying he didn't really believe in McCarthy's anti-Communist campaign. He did. "I felt it was work that needed to be done then," he was to say. And on another occasion: "At the time, I thought there was a serious internal security threat to the United States . . . and Joe McCarthy seemed to be the only one who was doing anything about it." When he resigned in July of that year, it wasn't because he disapproved of McCarthy's tactics, but because of a feud with chief counsel Roy Cohn—whose job he wanted, and didn't get, and with whom he almost came to blows—and because he didn't get a promotion on the committee staff. And he remained loyal to McCarthy, in 1955 walking out of a banquet because the speaker, television commentator Edward R. Murrow, was going to attack the senator; in 1957 not only attending McCarthy's memorial service in Washington but flying to Wisconsin for the demagogue's funeral. And when he returned to the committee after the Democrats took over the Senate and made him counsel in January, 1955, the belligerence, unabated, was given the armor of governmental authority, and what friends already saw as an extremely moralistic view of the world became even more apparent.

"For him the world is divided into black and white hats," his wife, Ethel, once said. "Bobby can only distinguish good men and bad." In a nationally televised series of hearings he brought the black hats—organized crime figures tied in with labor unions such as Momo "Sam" Giancana, "Crazy Joey" Gallo, Anthony "Tony Ducks" Corallo, Joey Glimco—before the Senate Rackets Committee, where they found themselves confronted by a young man with icy blue eyes staring, glaring, at them with an unnerving intensity. As he questioned them, hunching forward over the committee dais as if he wanted to get at them physically, his right arm would jab out with each question in a movement reminiscent of his brother's when his brother was giving a speech, except that Jack Kennedy's hand was open for emphasis and entreaty; Robert Kennedy's hand was balled up; sometimes the thumb stuck up from it, sometimes the forefinger pointed out, but essentially it was a fist. And the questions the chief counsel asked made it clear that to him a witness's invocation of the constitutional right against self-incrimination was proof of guilt (Giancana: "I decline to answer because I honestly believe my answer may tend to incriminate me." Kennedy: "Would you tell us anything about any of your operations or will you just giggle every time I ask you a question?" Giancana: "I decline to answer." Kennedy: "I thought only little girls giggled, Mr. Giancana." To Glimco: "And you defraud the union?" "I respectfully decline to answer." "You haven't got the guts to answer, have you, Mr. Glimco?"). The chief counsel was no less confrontational when the microphone was off—"You're full of shit," he kept repeating to one witness during a brief recess—or in private, as in a meeting in his office with Joey Gallo. "I walk into Kennedy's office and he gets mad at me. He says, 'So you're Joey Gallo, the Juke Box King. You don't look so tough. I'd like to fight you myself.' I hadda tell him I don't fight."

It was conservatives who would, later, first call him a "Torquemada," but many liberals wouldn't dispute the comparison. The liberal journalist William Haddad was told by a friend to go down to the hearings if "I wanted to see a fascist at work," and came back feeling, "He was in the McCarthy mode."

The only time Kennedy himself seemed on the defensive—"a little keyed up, a little tense"—was when Joe Kennedy showed up to watch a hearing. He had more respect for his son now. "Bobby hates like me," he is reported to have said.

The union leader Bobby focused on was Jimmy Hoffa of the International Brotherhood of Teamsters, a man in whom, he said, he saw "absolute evilness." In his dealings with Hoffa, Robert Kennedy demonstrated another trait. He tried to trap Hoffa on a bribery charge, boasting that the case was so airtight that if the Teamster boss wasn't convicted, he would jump off the Capitol dome. But Hoffa wasn't convicted. Then he indicted him on an illegal wiretapping charge; when, at a first trial, the jury deadlocked, he brought the union leader to trial again on the same charge, and he was acquitted. "Frustrated to the point of fury," as one account put it, Kennedy never stopped trying to influence the public against Hoffa, through reports of his committee, a steady stream of inflammatory press releases and the use of "friendly reporters to propagate" the image of Hoffa that he himself saw; one reporter was given a key to the committee offices so that he could obtain information about Hoffa while Kennedy could deny he had leaked it. And when, in 1961, Kennedy would become attorney general, and had at his command, as the journalist Nick Thimmesch writes, "the full arsenal" of the government's legal powers, he used them. Forming an elite "Get Hoffa" squad in the Justice Department, he launched an all-out campaign against the union leader, in which he also deployed the FBI and the Internal Revenue Service. At one time, fourteen separate grand juries were probing the Teamsters. Protests over Kennedy's tactics came not just from congressmen and senators of both parties who felt that Hoffa's corruption and brutality did not justify the tactics that Kennedy was using against him, but from the American Civil Liberties Union. Kennedy never changed them, and, finally, in 1964, he got a conviction. It had taken seven years—but he had gotten it. "When Bobby hates you, you stay hated," Joe Kennedy told a friend. And he hated Lyndon Johnson. Years before, the two men would pass in the halls of the Senate Office Building. "This was the Leader, the *Leader*," says a reporter who covered the Senate. "Everybody gave him deference. Bobby could barely look at him."

As for Johnson, his feelings were in many respects the same. He took every opportunity to rub in his dislike of Robert Kennedy. Passing Bobby in the Senate corridor, he would greet him as "Sonny Boy." The difference, at this stage in their careers, was their status. Johnson, whose eye missed nothing in the Senate world, was watching Bobby's work with the McClellan Committee. "He's a snot-nose, but he's bright," he told Bobby Baker. And once he gave him a compliment. When, after the Soviet Union beat the United States into space by launching *Sputnik* in October, 1957, proposals were being made for a Senate investigation, Johnson said that an investigation would be successful "if it had someone like young Kennedy handling it." But these were the compliments of a senator about a staffer. In the Senate world, staffers were employees, and that was all they were—on a decidedly lower level than senators, and so they were regarded. If Johnson had some matter regarding the McClellan Committee to discuss, he discussed it with McClellan, Kennedy's boss. He disliked Kennedy but didn't take him seriously.

Yet Bobby Kennedy understood things about running for the presidency that Lyndon Johnson didn't. He had learned some of them on the floor of the 1956 convention during the brief, hectic battle with Estes Kefauver. When he had asked his senatorial boss and patron, John McClellan, to give his brother Arkansas' vote, McClellan had told him, "Just get one thing through your head. . . . Senators have no votes; I'm lucky to be a delegate; Orval Faubus is the Governor of Arkansas, and that's it, and where he goes the Arkansas delegation goes." Bobby

Kennedy had learned what Lyndon Johnson hadn't: the insignificance of senators in the convention equation; Lyndon Johnson didn't realize that but the young staffer did. And he had learned that he didn't know who *did* have significance. At the 1956 convention, "Bobby and I ran around like a couple of nuts" trying to get votes, Ken O'Donnell was to recall. "A joke; we didn't know two people in the place." That was not a situation that Bobby let continue. Jack Kennedy had learned that it was the young people who mattered; Bobby Kennedy knew *which* young people mattered, and how to win to his brother's cause the ones who mattered, how little courtesies could mean a lot. "It really struck me that it wasn't the issues which matter. It was the friendships. So many people said to me . . . they were going to vote for Estes Kefauver because he had sent them a card or gone to their home. I said right there we should . . . send Christmas cards and go to their homes."

And he had learned other lessons after the convention, traveling on the campaign trail with Adlai Stevenson. Adlai's people didn't like him—Arthur Schlesinger, a Stevenson man then, remembered that Bobby, "making notes, always making notes . . . huddled by the window in the rear of the bus or plane, seemed an alien presence, sullen and rather ominous, saying little, looking grim and exuding an atmosphere of bleak disapproval"—but they had little choice other than to accept his presence; they needed the Catholic vote, and they felt the Kennedys could deliver it. If Schlesinger, by accident, got to know him better, and to like him (finding themselves seatmates, "we fell into reluctant conversation. . . . To my astonishment he was altogether pleasant, reasonable and amusing. We became friends at once"), for most of the rest of Stevenson's entourage, getting to know him didn't work the same way; by the end of the campaign he had thoroughly alienated them. Nonetheless, the notes he had taken became a case study of how to run (actually, since it was Stevenson he was observing, how not to run) a campaign. As one journalist put it, "after the Stevenson campaign . . . Bobby knew every single thing there was to know about a campaign. He just squeezed all that absolutely dry." During 1957 and 1958 and part of 1959, he spent most of his time on his McClellan Committee job (and in 1959 he wrote a book, *The Enemy Within,* about his work with the committee), but, in September, 1959, the book completed, the committee post resigned, Bobby Kennedy headed out—full-time—on the campaign trail. Christmas cards were not the only message he was sending now. "Bobby Kennedy holds his head down and looks up through his eyebrows," one newspaperman wrote. "Throw an arm around those shoulders and the big white teeth might snap at you. . . . The Kennedys are chill dishes indeed. But you feel they know what to do in a hot fight." This impression was not exaggerated. Old-time politicians—men familiar with the harsher aspects of politics—would talk for years about Bobby Kennedy on the trail of the votes his brother needed.

Governor Mike DiSalle controlled Ohio's delegates, and he wasn't for Jack Kennedy; he had opposed him in 1956. But DiSalle wanted the honor of running as Ohio's favorite son candidate in the state's primary. The Kennedys told him he could run unopposed if he publicly endorsed Jack Kennedy, and committed the delegation to him before the convention. If he didn't, DiSalle was told, he would find himself in a fight in the primary against an old rival, Ray Miller, Cleveland's Democratic leader, who had been trying, thus far unsuccessfully, to win control of the state for himself—and Miller would be backed by the Kennedys. Aware that Kennedy backing meant not only Kennedy endorsements but Kennedy money, DiSalle, nonetheless, in a tense meeting with Jack Kennedy, remained evasive, thinking he was in a negotiation. His next meeting was with Jack's brother. Connecticut's boss John Bailey, who accompanied Bobby, "does not shock easily," O'Donnell was to recall, but "he told me later that he was startled by the going-over that Bobby had given DiSalle." Precisely what he told him has not been recorded—did he warn DiSalle that the Kennedys would, by backing Miller, take the state away from him? DiSalle was to describe the session as "stormy" and Bobby Kennedy as "fierce"—but at the end the Kennedys had what they wanted. "What could I have done?" DiSalle was to tell friends. "Those Kennedys play real rough." Out beyond Ohio, in those crucial western states, Bobby worked on the men who held the "pieces of power," turning into votes the friendships his brother Ted had made with them.

Newspaper articles were beginning to appear about Bobby Kennedy now. In describing him, many of them used the same adjective: "ruthless." Bobby hated that adjective. Men who dealt with him, however, did not feel it was inaccurate.

LYNDON JOHNSON'S SUPPORTERS SAW how much his wavering was hurting his chances. Rayburn told Johnson's aide Booth Mooney that he had tried "to get Johnson to let it be known quietly, without any public announcement, that he would" eventually become a candidate; "That was the only way, the Speaker said, to prevent . . . men of power . . . from lining up behind some other candidate," but Johnson still wouldn't allow that. His insistence on secrecy hamstrung Jenkins' organizing efforts. The Kennedy organization was "extremely effective," George Reedy was to recall, "and most of us really wanted to get out and counter, and we thought it could be countered . . . despite the fact that he [Johnson] was a southerner. After all, Kennedy was . . . testing the old saw that a Catholic could not be President; and we saw no reason why we couldn't test the old saw that a southerner couldn't be President . . . , especially since this was a southerner who actually managed to pass the first civil rights bills through the Congress in eighty-two years. . . . We wanted to get out, and really fight at it. But he would not permit us to do it." "We've had more trouble between us about this damn campaign than anything within my memory," Rayburn told Bobby Baker. "Lyndon's using his friends to raise money and court delegates and he's making them as well as himself look silly."

· · ·

"*SILLY.*" ALL THROUGH 1959, he wavered back and forth, until his wavering, his circling about the prize, this vacillation by a man usually so single-minded, tough and decisive, contained elements not of failure alone, but of farce.

A celebration he staged that year at the LBJ Ranch in honor of the President of Mexico, Adolfo López Mateos, was quite a spectacle: a fleet of eight helicopters, bearing, among others, Rayburn, Truman, Secretary of the Treasury Robert B. Anderson and Texas Governor Price Daniel, circled the ranch. When Mateos' helicopter touched down on the runway, a red carpet was rolled out to it, and the visitors were greeted by a large mariachi band; at lunch, as the 450 guests ate barbecue on the front lawn, the band played and there was a lasso-twirling exhibition by the gaily costumed Mexican Charro Association of San Antonio, while all during lunch, on the far side of the little river, mounted cowboys herded longhorn cattle back and forth; the *Dallas Morning News* called the luncheon "one of the most dramatic outdoor shows since they produced *Aida* with live elephants." And the most prominent decoration, looming over the guests while they ate, was a large, brightly colored banner that had been hung from a branch of the big live oak tree in the ranch's front yard. Newsmen who had been assured by the ranch's owner—assured by him over and over, in the most earnest of tones—that he was not a candidate for President, that he was not running for the job and didn't want it, arrived at the ranch to find the banner the owner had had hung at his front door: "Lyndon Johnson Será Presidente."

Despite his insistence that he wasn't a candidate, when someone took him at his word his reaction was pique. Convinced by his assurances, six Washington journalists, writing a book of profiles on major candidates, hadn't included one on him. Although Johnson had accepted an invitation to the book party, when, on the day of the party, he learned of his omission, he let it be known that he took it as a personal insult, and refused to attend. Or the reaction was sulking. Asked by someone at his table at a White House dinner to list the leading Democratic candidates, President Eisenhower treated the matter as a joke, naming Rayburn and a number of Democratic senators who were obviously not candidates. Johnson, reading about this exchange in Drew Pearson's column, didn't take it as a joke at all. The next time he was in the White House (at another social gathering), he sat pouting, as the President's diary was to relate, "in almost complete silence." When Eisenhower, attempting to draw him out, asked him direct questions, he "answered only in monosyllables." And when the next day Eisenhower telephoned with an apology ("Just kidding. This was all in the most laughing kind of thing"), it took a while for Johnson to accept it. "I have no ambitions," he assured the President. "I'm not even going to the Convention. At an appropriate time, I will tell them that. [But] I was distressed that the one whom I had admired and had attempted to cooperate with as much as I have . . ."

Farce—unless Lyndon Johnson in 1959 was viewed as a man throwing away his chance at the thing he had wanted all his life, in which case there were elements in the performance that might more aptly be fitted into a different theatrical genre: tragedy.

On the evening of December 7, 1959, in New York City, the Democratic Party was turning out in force for a lavish dinner in honor of the idolized and influential Eleanor Roosevelt. Johnson, who had refused invitations to every other major Democratic event in this state he was counting on as a keystone in his presidential bid, was invited to give a short speech at this one, as were all the other leading candidates. Kennedy, Humphrey, Symington—even Adlai Stevenson—of course accepted. Johnson declined. And then he accepted two other speaking invitations for the same date: one before a fifteen-dollar-per-plate fund-raising dinner sponsored by a Democratic club in a small town in Kansas, the other to a sewing bee in a small town in Iowa.

"As usual," James Reston wrote in the *New York Times,* "these moves by the Democratic majority leader are a mystery to friend and foe alike. . . . Even his enthusiastic supporters cannot make sense out of these decisions." (What made them even more senseless, to those rooting for Lyndon Johnson, was another demonstration of what might have been: following his speech in Kansas, a *Times* reporter asked one of the guests, Would you vote for a southerner? "I didn't think of him that way when he was speaking," the man replied.)

The targets of his fearsome rages had always been men and women at whom they could be directed with impunity: subordinates who had no choice, if they wanted to keep their jobs, but to accept his tongue-lashings; junior senators who, needing his favor, also had no choice. With men *he* needed, there was not rage but only humility, deference; with Herman Brown of Brown & Root, or the Old Senate Bulls whose support was still essential to him, he had always been as obsequious as he was overbearing with others. Now, so intense was the conflict within him that it exploded as well against men he needed, at least once in a way very damaging to his hopes.

Trying to decide whom to support, California governor Pat Brown, whose state was very much up for grabs, flew across the country to Washington in 1959 to evaluate the candidates and, accompanied by his aide, Fred Dutton, met with Johnson in the Taj Mahal.

The meeting went on far longer than Brown had expected, ninety minutes, and, as Brown later related, "Senator Johnson did all the talking," explaining, among other things—many other things—why he was not electable. "For the first half hour," Brown was to say, he was "rather impressed"; during the second half hour, "he was not so impressed." And then, as the meeting entered its third half hour, Brown, perhaps trying merely to get in a word or two, used the wrong one, saying that he agreed that northern hostility made Johnson not "electable."

Johnson's reaction "astonished" Dutton. "Brown was a Governor, and here Johnson was just *tongue-lashing* him," he says. "He towered . . . his desk was higher; it was on a platform. 'Don't you ever say I'm not electable! What do *you* know about national politics?' "

The reaction cost Johnson any chance of Brown's support. The governor, who was to tell a friend that during the third half hour he became "downright angry," didn't respond at the time. "It just wasn't in Pat Brown's nature to answer back," Dutton says. He responded on national television—in a particularly effective way, using an appearance on *Face the Nation* to spotlight the issues most damaging to Johnson, saying that California "probably would not vote for him because of his associations with the South and the oil interests."

Late in the year, trying to solve what *Look* magazine called "The Number One enigma of United States politics," Jack Kennedy dispatched Robert to the Johnson Ranch to decipher his intentions face-to-face.

The trip did little to ease the tension between the two men. There was a deer-hunting trip—Bobby didn't want to go but Johnson insisted—and when Bobby fired the powerful shotgun he had been given, instead of the rifle customary on deer hunts, the unexpected force of its recoil knocked him to the ground. Helping him to his feet, Johnson said, "Son, you've got to learn to handle a gun like a man." Nor did it do much to solve the enigma. Assuring Bobby that he had decided not to run and to stay neutral as the other candidates fought it out, Johnson made these statements so convincingly that Bobby returned north to tell his brother that Johnson probably *wasn't* running. While Bobby had been in Texas, however, an interview with Johnson had appeared in the *Christian Science Monitor.* To the interviewer's inquiry about the burgeoning number of "Johnson for President" clubs, he had replied, "I hear what some of my friends are doing, and I see what they are doing. The people usually have a way of selecting the person they think best qualified"—the strongest public indication he had yet given that he was running. Then there was an interview in *Time* magazine. "I am not a candidate and I do not intend to be," Lyndon Johnson said. Soon thereafter, Jack Kennedy found himself on a train from New York to Washington with Texas reporter Leslie Carpenter, and, Carpenter was to say, Kennedy "spent the whole time trying to find out what I knew about whether Lyndon Johnson was actually going to be more than a favorite son candidate." Kennedy remained puzzled. He was sure that Lyndon Johnson was running—but how could he be running if he was acting like this?

THEN IT WAS 1960 — if he wanted to reach for the prize, he couldn't wait any longer. Within Lyndon Johnson's inner circle there was no longer any pretense that he wasn't running. He had persuaded Sid Richardson to lend John Connally to him for the campaign—he considered that very important; he felt, Busby says, "that Connally was the only man tough enough to handle Bobby Kennedy"—and John was directing the work of a full-scale national campaign headquarters: a twelve-room operation in an Austin hotel with fourteen paid staff members and scores of volunteer workers. Walter Jenkins was organizing new "Johnson for President" clubs every day; by the end of January, they would be operating in twenty-seven states. Speechwriters were being hired; Theodore H. White was one of those recommended, but White said he was going to be working on a book in 1960. A score of surrogates were fanning out across the country talking up his candidacy before local Democratic groups, and thanks to Rayburn, they were very well-connected surrogates: Oscar Chapman, former secretary of the Interior, for example, and India Edwards, a onetime vice chairman of the Democratic National Committee. In 1959, Jack Kennedy had sent an emissary to ask Mrs. Edwards, in her words, "what it would take to get me on his bandwagon," and she had refused, feeling he was "too young and inexperienced." But when Sam Rayburn asked her to work for Johnson, of course she accepted. And all these operations were funded with a lavishness awesome to anyone not familiar with the scale, and casualness, of campaign financing Texas-style. "I have some money that I want to know what to do with," George Brown said in a call to Johnson's office on January 5. "I . . . will be collecting more from time to time." He collected a lot more. Envelopes stuffed with cash cascaded up to Washington, for the other Texas oilmen were aboard. Booth Mooney had left Johnson's staff to work for oilman H. L. Hunt, and, he was to relate, "Twice I personally carried packets of a hundred hundred-dollar bills, the common currency of politics, to Jenkins."

ON THE EVE of the New Year, at the end of December, 1959, Lyndon Johnson convened a meeting at the ranch to begin a drive to capture those ten western states that were the key to his plan.

There was a lot of power at that meeting: Mike Kirwan, a senior member of the House Appropriations Subcommittee that approved (or disapproved) western public works projects; Governor Buford Ellington of Tennessee; a couple of western senators; Bobby Baker, "the man who knew where all the bodies were buried"; as well as the right guy to scout the western political landscape—Irvin Hoff, Washington senator Warren Magnuson's administrative assistant, who had been loaned to Johnson because of the expertise he had demonstrated while running senatorial campaigns in several western states. When, however, just after the first of the year, Hoff headed into the West, he found that "Wherever I went, Bobby Kennedy had been there."

"He was easy to track—and the tracks were everywhere," Hoff says. And whatever Bobby had done to tie delegates to the Kennedys, he had been very effective. "People who would normally have been with Johnson had been approached six months earlier, and had already had the halter and bridle. By the time I got there, it was already too late." In every state that Hoff visited, a smoothly functioning Kennedy organization had been in place for some time. When Hoff asked Larry Jones in Johnson's Austin headquarters about their own western organizations, the report was clear: "We have no organization in the state of Montana, either contacting potential delegates or delegates; nor do we have an organization building popular support. . . . We have no organization in the state of Idaho." Even as Hoff was traveling, Johnson organizations were being set up, but it was too late. Rowe's warning two years earlier that ignoring western delegates could be "disastrous" had been borne out. Johnson's headquarters was sending the new organizations crates of buttons bearing the legend "All the Way with LBJ." Hoff telephoned Austin to say it would be necessary to design a different button: "Many people do not know what LBJ means."

The accuracy of Rowe's prediction struck George Reedy at about the same time. While Johnson was still refusing to leave Washington on days when the Senate was actually meeting, "quick weekend trips"—in a specially equipped twin-engine Convair that Johnson had leased for campaigning—were possible, and the first of those trips was to Wyoming, a state Reedy (and Johnson) had believed bore the "LBJ" brand.

That belief didn't last even as long as it took Reedy to get out of the Cheyenne airport. Piling into a car along with several Washington newsmen to follow Johnson to the hotel at which he was to speak, Reedy found himself sitting next to a man he didn't know. One of the reporters asked the man whom Wyoming would be supporting at the convention. "Oh, Kennedy," the man replied matter-of-factly. Startled, Reedy asked the reason. "He's the only one who's been out here and asked us for our vote," the man said. The man turned out to be Teno Roncalio, chairman of Wyoming's Democratic Party. Reedy had never heard his name, but learned that his preference was quite firm. "Wyoming was a state that Lyndon Johnson should have had; and we would have had if we had merely done some organization work in it a few months earlier," Reedy was to say. Johnson's fear of trying had held him back until now—and now it was too late.

In addition, while he was at last actively planning his campaign within his inner circle, outside that circle he was still refusing even to acknowledge that he would one day become a candidate. His public refusals might be laid to the fact that by saying—so often and so convincingly—that his Senate responsibilities were his first priority, he had trapped himself: with the Senate still in session, how could he openly run for President? But that explanation doesn't make clear why he didn't say—*wouldn't* say; adamantly refused to let his representatives like Irv Hoff say, even in private—that he would announce his candidacy after the Senate adjourned. And he *wouldn't* say that, or let men like Hoff say it, not even in private, not even in the West, where he had to have delegates if he was to stop Kennedy, not even to men in the West, who, if he didn't say it, would—with the time before the convention growing short—align themselves irrevocably to another candidate.

Despite the Kennedys' activities, there was still solid Johnson sentiment in the West, but politicians there had to be assured that the sentiment would be requited. "They're a pretty cagey bunch of guys out there, and they're not going to support someone who maybe won't run, and then they've alienated the guy who was going to win," Hoff said. "It was pretty hard to sell a guy if all you could say was: 'Maybe he's going to run.'" Flying back to Washington, Hoff told Johnson that he had to give western delegates at least an assurance that while he was not announcing at the moment, he would eventually do so. "I said, 'Senator, I've got nothing to sell. The media out there all want to know if you're running. What can I tell them?' He said, 'Irv, I'm not at this point saying. I have ten bills I have to pass here.'"

At one point, Hoff thought he had made Johnson understand. In Idaho, where the Hells Canyon Dam was rising day by day, and where political leaders knew who had gotten them the dam at last, the Democratic state chairman, Tom Boise, had told Hoff that, despite all the Kennedy efforts, many party leaders were still considering supporting Johnson. "These guys were *for* Johnson," Hoff says. "If we had been able to tell them that he was going to run, we'd have had that delegation." He explained this to Johnson, and Johnson accepted an invitation to speak in Lewiston, Idaho, and afterwards to have a drink with Boise and his leaders in a hotel suite. But in the suite, Johnson said all the right things— except the one thing it was necessary for him to say. "Lady Bird had gone to bed in another room, and he was in his living room, walking around in his pajamas holding a drink, stirring it with his big finger. They said, 'We're for you, but we need to know if you're going to run.' He said, 'What the hell do you think I'm out here for—catching butterflies? Do you see me carrying a net?' " But there were future government positions at stake, careers at stake, issues at stake—with the convention so close, rhetorical humor wasn't enough. They pressed him further. But all Johnson would say was, "I'll let you know. . . . You'll be the first to know." Recalling the scene years later, Hoff would say, "It was like he couldn't bring himself to say it. He had flown out there to say it, but he couldn't bring himself to get the words out." Witnessing similar scenes, Bobby Baker felt he understood them, that "The problem was LBJ's fear of being defeated": that saying it would be admitting that he was trying, and trying might mean failing, "so he couldn't bring himself to say it." After Johnson had gone to bed, Boise told Hoff quietly that Johnson's assurances had not been adequate. "He said, 'We've got to know, and we've got to know pretty soon. I'm for him one hundred percent, but we've got to know.' " Hoff understood, but when he raised the subject the next day, Johnson again refused to authorize him to give Boise any firm assurance.

And at least Johnson was willing to go to Idaho, where people were friendly. To any suggestion that he visit a state where his reception would be problematical, he was still shying away, quite violently.

There was a hint of desperation now in the telephone calls that Walter Jenkins was receiving from California. An opening—an 81-vote opening—was ready to be exploited there, he was being told. Pat Brown's attempt to keep his delegation uncommitted until he could decide on a candidate was falling apart, and despite the governor's hostility to Johnson, "If I could bring Lyndon in contact with" the delegates themselves, "he would own them like he does everybody he meets," Judge Walter Ely told Jenkins on January 25.

The old problem remained, however. Among the key California Democrats favorably disposed toward Johnson was the delegation's vice chairman, Clinton D.

McKinnon. "I asked him if he would help," Leonard Marks reported to Jenkins. "He says he can't make a commitment until he knows for sure that Johnson is a candidate. He says when I ask him to help Johnson I am talking about some very practical things in his life, and something that might affect his future so he wants to make sure that he is a candidate."

Yet Johnson wouldn't even visit California. After first accepting, and then declining, a number of speaking engagements there in January, he repeated that performance in February. At the end of March, Hoff, who had been touring California sounding out individual delegates, sent Jenkins two memos telling him that although "Johnson hadn't even set foot in California for too many years," he still had a chance to win a substantial number of delegates there. "The California delegation is far from being committed to anyone," Hoff said. "Kennedy may have a few more commitments than anyone else but all the delegates are very friendly to Johnson." But, Hoff said, if he "is going to get any place in this delegation, he has just got to come out here." There was simply no alternative. "They all know who he is but don't know him. You can't turn the Johnson sentiment into solid support without Johnson coming out."

Johnson then agreed to go during the Senate's Easter recess, and Bobby Baker told Ely to arrange a statewide tour, saying, "I can practically guarantee you he will be there." The guarantee proved worthless, however; at the last minute, Bobby had to tell Ely that "The senator is disinclined to come." In desperation, Ely tried to telephone Johnson directly; Johnson refused to take the call. Phoning Jenkins, Ely said that many of the delegates were saying of Johnson, "Oh, he is the best man, but . . . he is not a real candidate."

"Hell, Walter, he either wants it or he doesn't," Ely said, "and he has never even been out here to make a speech. . . . Walter, he simply must let people see him. It is when they meet him and shake his hand that they are won over. I just don't believe he can do it unless he comes. . . . There comes a time when you can't just continue to keep fighting for a phantom."

To make matters worse, civil rights came up again. The assurance Johnson had given liberals to persuade them to support the weak 1957 Act—that it would be quickly amended to strengthen it ("Don't worry, we'll do it again in a couple of years")—had not been redeemed in 1958 or 1959; in '59, in fact, Johnson's power had been the principal obstacle. Emboldened by the 1958 elections, which had given liberals an overwhelming two-to-one (64 to 34) majority in the Senate, liberal senators moved to amend Rule 22, the "filibuster rule" that ensured the tactic's effectiveness. Johnson placed himself in their path. "Jesus, it was rough," recalled one of them. "Lyndon was going around with two lists in his inside pocket. One was for committee assignments and anything else you wanted, and the other was for Rule 22. He didn't talk about the first until you'd cleared on the second, and that was all there was to it." With no new legislation to strengthen the civil rights bill in 1958 or 1959, he had to produce some in 1960 if he was to reduce the hostility of northern convention delegates.

Liberals were insisting now on the part of the 1957 bill that had been cut out: Part III, the section that would ban segregation in public venues such as theaters, restaurants, hotels, buses and trains—and in schools, where, six years after the *Brown vs. Board of Education* decision, only a tiny percentage of black children were going to school with white children in the South. Without enactment of Part III, the federal government would still in effect have done nothing about the most painful injustices to which millions of American citizens were subjected because of their race.

Johnson had hoped that Richard Russell, understanding Johnson's need to placate liberals, would compromise as he had done in '57, but, as I have written, "However much affection Russell might feel for Lyndon Johnson, the overriding reason that Russell wanted him to become President was to protect the interests of the South; when Johnson's interests collided with those interests, it was the South's, not Johnson's, that would be protected," and to Russell, Part III, in any form, struck at the heart of the southern way of life. By banning segregation in social settings, it would, Russell felt, inevitably lead to what was for the Georgian the horror of horrors: what he called the "mongrelization" of the noble white race. When, in January, 1960, Johnson tried to explain that he had no choice but to bring a civil rights bill to the floor, Russell, "cool" and "aloof," said, "Yes, I understand that you let them jockey you into that position. I understand." A Johnson proposal to bypass the southern-controlled Judiciary Committee and bring the bill to the floor by adding its provisions to a House measure on an unrelated topic caused the first rupture in the eleven-year alliance of the two legislative titans; Russell called the move "a lynching of orderly procedure in the Senate."

Johnson's angry response—that "this was the only kind of lynching he had ever heard Russell object to"—was blurted out only in private, to two staffers in his limousine; Johnson had had no choice but to repair the breach. Though he made a show of attempting to break a Russell-led southern filibuster, with around-the-clock sessions, veteran Senate observers saw that it was all a charade, "a cozy and often rather jolly affair"; "bonhomie has been rampant," one was to write. "The Senate has never seemed more like a gentleman's club." Never had the South's power been more clearly demonstrated than in the 55–42 vote against cloture: not only had liberals been unable to muster the necessary two-thirds vote, they hadn't even been able to get a majority. Working with Eisenhower's attorney general, William P. Rogers, Johnson then watered down Part III until by the time it passed little remained but an amendment that supposedly strengthened the voting rights provisions of the 1957 bill but from the start proved next to worthless. Although Russell made a show of dismay at the bill's passage, it was, Jacob Javits of New York said, "a victory for the Old South." Accusing Johnson of collaborating with Russell to reduce the measure to "only a pale ghost of our hopes of last fall," Pennsylvania's Joseph Clark turned to the southern leaders on the Senate floor, and said, "The roles of Grant and Lee at Appomattox have been reversed. Dick, here is my sword. I hope you will give it back to me so that I can beat it into a plowshare for the spring planting."

Having given it what it wanted—a civil rights bill so weak as to be virtually no bill at all—Johnson got the South back, from Russell and the southern senators down to the man in the street: a Gallup Poll showed Johnson with "a wide edge" (35 percent to 20 percent for Kennedy, the runner-up) in the former Confederate states. Liberal magazines and newspapers, on the other hand, with the notable exception of Philip Graham's *Washington Post,* found in the weak bill confirmation of their long-held suspicions about him.

Even in the earlier stages of the 1960 fight, before his alliance with the South had become obvious, the issue had hurt him with liberals. On March 6, before his statement against the original Part III—at a point where he was still ostensibly fighting for a strong bill—James Reston reported that he had nonetheless "lost support in the North."

"The explanation of this odd paradox," Reston said, "is that the debate, accompanied by demonstrations against segregated restaurants in the South, has dramatized the race issue and evidently convinced the Democratic politicians in the large Northern cities that a Texan, even one responsible for putting over a good civil rights bill, would not be a popular candidate in the urban North." And when, a few days later, it became apparent that the bill Lyndon Johnson was putting over was not at all a "good" bill, liberal distrust of him was back, stronger than ever. Joseph L. Rauh Jr., probably the single most influential figure in the civil rights camp—former chairman of both Americans for Democratic Action and the Leadership Conference on Civil Rights, and chief counsel of the United Automobile Workers—had, in 1957, "hated his guts for what he was doing for school desegregation; that was a crime against the Negroes when Lyndon Johnson knocked out Part III." He had nonetheless persuaded other civil rights leaders to support the bill partly because it was important to show that a civil rights bill could be passed, and largely because of Johnson's promises to revisit and amend it. Now he "hated his guts more than ever—if possible." The 1960 bill, Rauh says, was "a pile of rubbish and garbage" disguised as a statute. It "was a joke," he says. "Everybody knew it was a joke. Nobody who was really for civil rights then could have supported it," much less have pushed it through the Senate. And Johnson was *not* really for civil rights, Rauh felt. Not that he was against civil rights; he was simply for anything—on either side—that would help him become President. "It wasn't that he was a conservative or a radical or anything else; it was simply that he was trying to be all things to all people." The revered liberal senator Paul Douglas of Illinois went further. Johnson had remained at least ostensibly neutral in the cloture fight only because he had known the South would win, Douglas said; had the result been in doubt, Johnson would have thrown his full weight behind the filibuster. Liberal opinion was hardening. JOHNSON REJECTED, said the *ADA World,* making clear that what Johnson was being rejected for was the Democratic nomination. The article quoted a liberal congressman who said, "ADA, union officials and colored leaders may not have the votes to put a presidential candidate across at the convention, but they sure have the votes to block a man." On May 29, speaking before the American Jewish Congress, Roy Wilkins, executive secretary of the NAACP, praised the civil rights record of Nixon and "all the Senator-candidates" for the presidential nomination "except Senator Lyndon B. Johnson."

LYNDON JOHNSON MIGHT HAVE BEEN able to blunt at least the sharpest edges of the suspicions of blacks and liberals: to emphasize that, however weak the 1957 Civil Rights Act might be, its very passage was an historic achievement, and it was he who had gotten it passed; to explain that voting was indeed the most important right; to sell them on the idea that he had done all that he could, and would eventually, as soon as possible, do more. Men and women who had watched him sell that idea in Washington felt he could have sold it anywhere. But it was a very difficult sale—and no one could make it for him.

The proof of that came in his attempts to let others make it for him—in his decision to stay in Washington instead of traveling to northern states and explaining his civil rights stance in person.

Trying to persuade black political leaders in Detroit to withdraw their opposition to his candidacy, Johnson asked Hobart Taylor, a young black assistant district attorney in that city whose father was a longtime Johnson ally in Texas, to invite the leaders to meet not with Johnson but with four of his Texas surrogates. The room full of black faces and southern accents must have made an interesting scene. And although young Taylor was a popular figure, and the Texans did their best, they weren't Lyndon Johnson. After the meeting, one of the leaders told a reporter that they "tried to convince us that Senator Johnson was a friend of the Negro and was trying to help them to the best of his ability. We were told that if we withdrew our opposition as a race, it would help Johnson's campaign, and would help us. . . . We were not convinced." Another said simply, "They are wasting their time."

And it wasn't just northern blacks whom Lyndon Johnson was failing to placate on the civil rights issue. He wasn't doing any better in the North with whites, as India Edwards was finding out. "I talked to the northern delegations, and *that* was some experience," she was to recall; at a meeting of the Minnesota delegation, "They laughed at me. . . . When I began telling them that Lyndon Johnson would be a liberal President, well, the delegates just put their heads back and screeched; it was the funniest thing they ever heard."

After another discussion in Detroit—this one on March 28 in a hotel room—David S. Broder, a young reporter from the *Washington Evening Star*

who had been allowed to attend, on condition that he not identify the participants, felt that he understood the problem: that Johnson hadn't come to Detroit
himself.

The discussion took place after the annual dinner of the Democratic Midwest Conference, which had been attended by three of the four invited
speakers—Kennedy, Humphrey and Symington—but of course not by Johnson.
For hours, a Johnson aide tried to persuade two key Michigan politicians—one a
high-level aide to Governor Williams—to support Johnson, with a lack of success so total that, in Broder's words, the participants "were on the verge of
exhaustion and tears."

"The coolness toward Senator Johnson rests not on what he has done, but on
what he has not done," Broder wrote. "He has not taken the Michigan Democrats
into his confidence and made them feel they have a part in his efforts. For all their
carping about his compromises, Michigan Democrats—whose own Governor
has faced a Republican legislature for 12 years—have an underlying sympathy
for the frustrations that beset" a leader facing a Senate with such a powerful conservative wing. "If Senator Johnson had visited the state, they would [have been]
reminded of these facts." Had he done so, and explained the facts to Michigan
Democrats (as Broder had watched him do with such success in Washington, to
so many groups of varying political sympathies), they would have seen "what
larger purpose animates Senator Johnson's technical maneuvers." But nothing
but such a visit, and such discussions, would help, Broder explained. "So long as
he leaves them in ignorance, they find it easy to accept the popular liberal char-
acterization of him as a representative of a Texas dominated by segregationists
and oil barons."

The Johnson aide had given the standard explanation for his absence: that
the Majority Leader would have "neglected his duties" had he come to Detroit.
That argument might be valid, Broder wrote, "but unless Senator Johnson can
find some means of communicating directly with his fellow Democrats in states
such as Michigan, it is difficult to see how he can satisfy the ambition no one
doubts he harbors."

BRODER'S BELIEF IN Johnson's ability to win over even blacks suspicious of
him if only he communicated with them "directly" was validated during a long
plane flight in 1960, for on that flight he communicated with one man quite
directly.

The man was Howard B. Woods, the editor of a black newspaper, the
St. Louis Argus, and his presence aboard Johnson's Convair was the outgrowth of
a conversation between Johnson and one of his largest campaign contributors,
August Busch, owner of the Anheuser-Busch Company, during a visit to Busch's
country home outside St. Louis. When Johnson began complaining about how
blacks didn't appreciate—or, apparently, even know about—his accomplish-

ments in civil rights, Busch telephoned Alfred Fleishman, a St. Louis public relations man, and put Johnson on the line. When Johnson told Fleishman that if he could only dispel the image that he was an anti–civil rights southerner, "lightning might strike" at the convention, Fleishman suggested that he allow himself to be interviewed by Woods, and a week or two later, the short, bespectacled editor found himself on Johnson's Convair.

Lady Bird and Lucy Baines* were aboard, and his secretary Mary Margaret Wiley, and several Texans, and Woods was made uneasy at first by what he was to describe as "a cabin filled with yards and yards of honey-coated southern drawl." But all his misgivings vanished after Johnson came over, and sat down facing him across a narrow table. The Senator, tie-less and in shirtsleeves, was eating cookies and drinking a tall, and stiff, Scotch, but when Woods asked him about the civil rights bill "which seems to please no one," saying, "Senator, the bill, as it was finally passed, was admittedly watered down," Johnson forgot about the cookies and the Scotch, and leaned forward across the table, looking Woods "straight in the eye" in a way the editor found quite memorable.

"When we say every man has a right to vote, that is not watered down," Lyndon Johnson said. "The important thing in this country is whether or not a man can participate in the management of his government. When this is possible, he can decide that *I'm* no good." George Reedy slipped into the seat next to Woods', but Johnson didn't need Reedy now. "Civil rights are a matter of human dignity," he said. "It is outrageous that all people do not have the dignity to which they are entitled. But we can't legislate human dignity—we can legislate to give a man a vote and a voice in his own government. Then with his vote and his voice he is equipped with a very potent weapon to guarantee his *own* dignity."

Johnson continued talking for quite some time, Woods was to write, and he "does not exude" at all "the craftiness and cunning attributed to him. Rather, he is homespun, warm"—and utterly convincing. "You ask me if I'm a Southerner or a Westerner," he said to Woods at one point. "I don't think it makes any difference." And, he said, it didn't matter if he was a Protestant or "a Catholic, or a Jew, white or colored. I am an American."

A man's religion didn't matter, shouldn't matter, Lyndon Johnson said, and neither did the region of the country he came from. "What is the difference if it's LBP or LBW?"—Lyndon B. Protestant or Lyndon B. Westerner? And a man's color shouldn't matter, either, he said, and, extending his huge hand across the table, he took Woods' hand in his, and stroked it—"vigorously," in Woods' terms—as if to rub its color off.

The more trips Lyndon Johnson took into the North, the more black people who actually got to meet him—"the better it will be for him," Woods wrote.

•   •   •

*Lucy changed the spelling of her name to Luci in February, 1964.

HIS REFUSAL TO ADMIT that he was a candidate was still leading to scenes that would have been funny, except to those who, like Sam Rayburn, saw him throwing away his great chance at the prize he had worked for so long and so hard. "Horace, what's wrong with him?" the Speaker asked Busby once.

One of these scenes took place at a busy Washington intersection. National campaign headquarters were being set up on the entire mezzanine floor of the Ambassador Hotel at the corner of Fourteenth and K Streets. Furniture had been rented, telephone lines were being installed. But the existence of a campaign headquarters was proof that there was a campaign, so even while Johnson was staffing it himself—personally giving out assignments—he wanted its existence kept secret. And then suddenly, there was a story about it in Sarah McClendon's column.

"Who told her this!?" Johnson screamed. At first, recalls Ashton Gonella, one of his secretaries, he blamed Bobby Baker. " 'Boy, that office better be closed by *tonight*! You're trying to *ruin* me!' He pinned him up against a wall. *'I didn't give you permission!'* " When Johnson was very upset, he would pace back and forth with lunging, somewhat awkward strides, making gestures with his long arms so frenetic that Marie Fehmer calls them "flailing," and he was pacing and flailing now. He ordered Connally to find out where McClendon had gotten her information, and finally ascertained that one of his own lawyers, Leonard Marks, had let something slip while chatting with her at a cocktail party. And then, five days later, embarrassment escalated. Baker had indeed closed the office, the furniture and telephones had been removed, but someone had forgotten that large signs—one for the K Street side of the Ambassador, one for the Fourteenth Street side, each proclaiming in huge letters, NATIONAL HEADQUARTERS—LYNDON B. JOHNSON FOR PRESIDENT CITIZENS COMMITTEE, had been ordered. No one had canceled the order. All at once reporters were calling, and Johnson's horrified staff learned that the signs were being hoisted into place at that very moment, and that television crews had arrived, along with newspaper photographers. Telephoning the sign company, Jenkins demanded that the signs be taken down immediately, but when workmen started to do so, it turned out that while the company had a permit to erect the signs, a different permit was required to remove them. A patrolman ordered the workmen to stop, and when they tried to go ahead anyway, the patrolman called for backup, and a patrol car arrived. It took two hours for *that* matter to be resolved, and for the signs to come down, and there were photographs in Washington newspapers the next day, and headlines like the one in the *Post:* PREMATURE BOOM A DUD—JOHNSON-FOR-PRESIDENT SIGNS GO UP, THEN DOWN IN TEXAS-SIZED FAUX PAS.

Then, in March, Israeli Prime Minister David Ben-Gurion visited the United States. New York attorney Edwin Weisl, a major financial supporter of both Israel and Johnson, had arranged for the two men to meet in New York. Saying that the meeting would make him look like a candidate, Johnson backed out at the last moment, however, and wouldn't meet with the prime minister in public even when Ben-Gurion came to Washington. Johnson was finally taken secretly, without reporters being informed, to talk with Ben-Gurion at Abe Fortas' Georgetown home.

Telephoning Jenkins, the economist Eliot Janeway—a Weisl friend and another longtime Johnson ally in New York—told him that Johnson's actions made no sense. "Why didn't he publicize it?" he asked. "He is his own principal source of defeat."

"He makes the stories to flog him with," Janeway told Jenkins. The nomination wasn't going to be won "as an inside job. . . . He better come out and be a candidate. . . . You ought to call off this cloak and dagger business. . . . They are all laughing at Johnson."

And, in fact, they were: journalists, politicians, his own supporters—their puzzlement over his tactics was turning to ridicule. Even Charlie Herring, loyalest of the loyal followers of his standard through so many campaigns, was losing faith. "We *DO* have a candidate, don't we?" he asked Jenkins in a call on March 23. "He isn't going to run out on us, is he?"

"I wear the chain I forged in life," Marley's ghost admits to Ebenezer Scrooge. "I made it link by link." During the early months of 1960, Lyndon Johnson was forging, link by link, his own chain, and it was a heavy one. "Humiliation" had always been what he most feared; during these months, again and again, through his own actions, he was bringing upon himself what he most feared.

HIS LAST-DITCH ATTEMPT to reach for the prize was being hamstrung as well by another aspect of his personality. When Lyndon Johnson was fighting hard for something—and he was fighting hard now, even if only behind the scenes ("It was like the old days," Ed Clark says; "I could set my watch by getting a call from him at six o'clock in the morning")—an aspect of the determination he always displayed during such efforts was conviction, a seemingly total belief in what he was fighting for. He felt that victory *required* belief. As a boy, friends recall, "he was always repeating" the salesman's credo that "You've got to believe in what you're selling"; decades later, in his retirement, he would say: "What convinces is conviction. You simply *have* to believe in the argument you are advancing; if you don't, you're as good as dead. The other person will sense that something isn't there." And Lyndon Johnson could make himself believe in an argument even if that argument did not accord with the facts, even if it was clearly in conflict with reality. He "would quickly come to believe what he was saying even if it was clearly not true," his aide Joseph Califano would write. "It was not an act," George Reedy would say. "He had a fantastic capacity to persuade himself that the 'truth' which was convenient for the present was *the truth* and anything that conflicted with it was the prevarication of enemies. He literally willed what was in his mind to become reality." He would refuse to hear any facts which conflicted with that "reality," to listen to anyone who disagreed with him. His oldest Texas associates, men like Clark, called the process the "revving up" or the "working up," explaining, "he could start talking about something and convince himself it was right" and true—even if it wasn't. The argument Johnson was advancing now was that Kennedy, needing to win on the first ballot if he was to win at all, would not be able to win enough primaries or enough delegates to win on that ballot—and he had convinced himself of that so completely that he discounted any suggestion to the contrary.

James C. Wright, a third-term congressman from Fort Worth, had long been a true believer in Lyndon Johnson's political acumen; "I was one of his eager disciples during the 1960 campaign," he was to say. But now Johnson sent him to speak on his behalf at the state convention of the Kansas Democratic Party. It had been agreed that each speaker would talk for about twenty minutes, and Wright had spoken for that length of time, as had Hubert Humphrey.

And then, Wright was to recall, he saw Jack Kennedy speak for the first time. "He spoke for about eight minutes," and "that was all he needed. When he sat down he had that crowd in the palm of his hand. He had the gift of leaving them wanting more. I saw the Kennedy magic then that I had not really appreciated." Feeling that Johnson had not sufficiently appreciated the impact that Kennedy was making, "when I got back to Washington, I asked to see Lyndon and I told him I thought he should get out on the hustings more." But, Wright says, "he rejected my suggestion." The reason Johnson gave, Wright says, was that "I've committed myself" to remain in Washington doing his Senate work, but the real reason was that "he just didn't believe" Wright's assessment of Kennedy's effectiveness as a speaker. "He thought I had been overly impressed by Kennedy." For the first time, the "eager disciple" began to doubt. "I wondered when I left [Johnson's office] if Lyndon was taking that seriously enough."

He refused to hear anything he didn't want to hear. When his longtime ally Richard Berlin, publisher of the Hearst newspapers, tried to tell him that he was losing his chance in California, he "just pooh-poohed the idea," as Berlin said in a telephone call to Jenkins. "You know Lyndon—he believes what he wants to believe." At a meeting where he was receiving reports from his emissaries to the western states, the man responsible for Wyoming began saying that "Jack Kennedy had Wyoming locked up." Johnson cut him off. "Next!" he said curtly. Later, Johnson "told Walter Jenkins the man was 'a defeatist,' and soon he was no longer" on the payroll. "Consequently, fewer and fewer people who had Johnson's ear told him the truth as they saw it."

Men who did not know Johnson as well as Wright or Berlin—and who were aware of the steadily rising total of Kennedy delegates—were startled by the strength of his conviction. Johnson asked a young congressman, Thomas P. O'Neill Jr. of Massachusetts, if he could come by O'Neill's office; there was no more making men come to him now, not if they could help him at the convention, and although "Tip" O'Neill was only in his eighth year in the House, he was, as a protégé of Majority Leader John W. McCormack of Massachusetts, a rising figure there—he would one day be Speaker, and was already known as a congressman with connections beyond Massachusetts' borders. O'Neill, a congressman from Kennedy's own state, could not imagine what Johnson wanted—and when he found out what it was, he was astonished.

"After some small talk," O'Neill was to recall, Johnson said, "Now I realize you're pledged to the boy, but you and I both know he can't win. He's just a flash in the pan, and he's got no record of substance to run on. Will you be with me on the second ballot?"

O'Neill knew nothing of the sort, and since he had already tangled with the Kennedys in Massachusetts, he tried to explain the situation. "I said, 'Mr. Leader, let me tell you something. Jack Kennedy is going to be the nominee for President. He's going to win on the first ballot for several reasons—because of the innovative methods the Kennedys use, the untold wealth they have, and the long arm of Joseph Kennedy.' " But Johnson, O'Neill realized, "couldn't believe what he was hearing. 'You're a professional,' he said, 'you *know* the boy can't win.' "

"He can and he will," O'Neill said. "When we get to the convention, there won't even *be* a second ballot." As it happened, at the moment of the conversation, O'Neill's estimate of Kennedy's strength was slightly exaggerated. But Johnson, he saw, was unwilling to concede even that Kennedy had a chance. "I could see that Johnson thought I was nuts," O'Neill recalls. Shaking his head at O'Neill's words, the Leader said, "Come on, Tip, you know better than that. That boy is going to die on the vine. I'm asking you for some aid and support in New England after he fails." O'Neill saw that "he just couldn't imagine that Jack Kennedy was going to win."

AND THEN CAME the primaries. Johnson had been confident that the other candidates would kill each other off in those primaries: that Kennedy would win some, Symington perhaps one or two, Humphrey a few—including, certainly, the first one in which he took on Kennedy head to head, since it would be held, on April 5, in his neighboring state of Wisconsin. Kennedy won Wisconsin, though his margin over Humphrey was not decisive, and, more important, had come from Wisconsin's four predominantly Catholic congressional districts. Since Humphrey had won the state's four Protestant districts, the vote, as Theodore White reported, was read "as a Catholic-Protestant split"; it "would convince none of the bosses who controlled the delegates of the East that [Kennedy] was a winner." The religious issue was more alive than ever. When, on primary night, one of Kennedy's sisters asked him, "What does it mean?" he replied, "quietly yet bitterly," that "We have to do it all over again." A Humphrey victory in the next significant primary—West Virginia on May 10—would be taken as proof that Kennedy couldn't carry a heavily Protestant state; it would, White said, "all but end John F. Kennedy's chance of nomination" because it would "throw the nominating decision into the back rooms," exactly what Johnson had been hoping for; as Roland Evans and Robert Novak wrote in their widely syndicated "Inside Report" column, it would "open up the party to a whole series of new arrangements and deals, a fluid situation tailored to Johnson's skills." Johnson began helping Humphrey in West Virginia, working through Senator Byrd, who put his organization behind the Minnesotan. (Kennedy, realizing what was happening, paid a call on Johnson in the Taj Mahal on April 8 and asked him, according to Johnson's account, "to get Bob Byrd 'out of West Virginia.' " Johnson said he had nothing to do with Byrd's activities. "I reminded him that this is Byrd's own state and I couldn't get him out if I was foolish enough to try.") A lot was riding on that state, and Johnson played the card that, thanks to Brown & Root, had been the ace in his hand for all his political life. His first campaign for Congress had been the most heavily financed congressional campaign in the history of Texas; his two campaigns for the Senate had been the most lavishly financed senatorial campaigns in the state's history; and now, in West Virginia, a state where politics was very much for sale, he played the money card again, pouring cash into the state on Humphrey's behalf. But it was to no avail. It was after West Virginia that Johnson said to Jim Rowe, "How the hell does Joe Kennedy move money around like that?" And, like the rest of Johnson's efforts, the money card was played too late. Television documentaries and telethons have to be produced in advance to be effective, local organizations require time to be set up and financed. A last-minute half-hour statewide telephone call-in telethon for Humphrey, staged with almost no preparation at all, was embarrassing: authentic, unscreened questions put the candidate on the defensive.

The Kennedys held other cards, too, and in West Virginia they were played in a manner that cast a revealing light on Jack Kennedy's "cool rationality." The ambassador had arranged for Franklin D. Roosevelt Jr. to campaign for his son—a masterstroke in itself since President Roosevelt was idolized in the state—but, as Doris Goodwin wrote, FDR Jr. "did not confine his role to nostalgia." The Kennedy campaign had provided him with documents allegedly showing that Humphrey had sought draft deferments during World War II—although, in fact, he had attempted to enlist in both the Army and the Navy but had been rejected because of physical disabilities. Although FDR Jr. was reluctant to use the documents, Bobby insisted, and Roosevelt displayed them to audiences, implying that Humphrey had been a draft dodger by saying, "I don't know where he was in World War II." Humphrey made what he was to call "repeated contacts with the Kennedys" proving the charge was untrue, but Roosevelt continued making it. Asked about this, Jack Kennedy said, "Any discussion of the war record of Senator Humphrey was done without my knowledge and consent, as I strongly disagree with the injection of this issue into the campaign"—a statement which, notes one of his biographers, "did not challenge the accuracy of what Roosevelt said"; Goodwin was to write that "As Kennedy perfectly understood, the deed was already done." And in fact FDR Jr. went on with the injections.*

And they had the trump card: Jack Kennedy—his willingness to confront an issue, and his ability, his unique gifts as an orator, in doing so.

With the focus now, more than ever, on Kennedy's religion, polls in West Virginia, where only 5 percent of the population was Catholic, showed that the tide had turned to Humphrey.

Kennedy's advisers were split on how to handle the issue, with most of his Washington staff telling him to avoid it because it was too explosive. Kennedy decided to meet it head-on. Two days before the primary, on a paid telecast, he discussed in detail the importance of the separation of church and state. And then, looking directly into the camera as he spoke, he said, "so when any man stands on the steps of the Capitol and takes the oath of office of President, he is swearing to support the separation of church and state; he puts one hand on the Bible and raises the other hand to God as he takes the oath. And if he breaks his oath, he is not only committing a crime against the Constitution, for which the Congress can impeach him—and should impeach him—but he is committing a sin against God." And at this point, as Theodore White describes it, John F. Kennedy "raised his hand from an imaginary Bible, as if lifting it to God, and, repeating softly, said, 'A sin against God, for he has sworn on the Bible.' " It was, White wrote, "the finest TV broadcast I have ever heard any political candidate make." During the remaining two days before the primary, every other card in the Kennedy deck was played as well: the money, the bands of brothers and sisters roving the state, the "handsome, open-faced candidate" on masterfully produced documentaries opening with a shot of a PT boat cutting through the waves. After the telecast in which Kennedy raised his hand to God, "With a rush, one could feel sentiment change," White recounts, and he took more than 60 percent of the West Virginia vote. Flying off to Maryland, where he had campaigning to do, for its primary was a week away, Kennedy said, "I think we have now buried the religious issue."

HE HAD BURIED Lyndon Johnson's hopes as well.

When Johnson picked up the next morning's *New York Times,* he read that "Washington heard the unmistakable sound of a bandwagon calliope today." There was a quote from New York City's mayor Robert F. Wagner, who said he "would do nothing which might interfere with Jack's candidacy." Johnson had been counting on support from New York, but, the *Times* reported, "West Virginia's primary election victory appeared . . . to have all but guaranteed" Kennedy the bulk of that state's 114 votes. "Mr. Kennedy is beginning to take on

---

*FDR Jr. was later to call this maneuver "The biggest political mistake" he had ever made. After the campaign, he went to Humphrey's office and apologized, but Humphrey never forgave him.

an air of inevitability," James Reston wrote. "The road to victory in Los Angeles suddenly seemed free and clear to him," W. H. Lawrence chimed in.

At a press conference, Johnson could not hide his dismay. In his hand was a statement George Reedy had prepared—"The West Virginia primary demonstrated that voters are not going to pick a candidate on the basis of an irrelevant issue such as how he worships his God"—but he couldn't even look at it. To questions about the effect of Kennedy's victory, he replied only "I don't know" or "I have nothing to say." Sarah McClendon, who had covered him for many years, was shocked at what she saw in his face. He "slumped further in his seat," she reported. "He had circles under his eyes and looked sad. He was much quieter" than usual. And when, a few minutes later, he went into the Senate's Democratic cloakroom, the little knots of senators abruptly stopped talking; the senators had been saying that Kennedy had it locked up, that Lyndon Johnson had made a huge mistake by not campaigning. What he feared most was happening to him even in this room in which he had for years reigned supreme, in this room in which, of all the rooms in the world, he had been most assured of respect.

AND THEN, when it was in effect too late, when his dream was all but dead, when his chances for the great prize were all but gone, Lyndon Johnson showed how much he had wanted it all along. By the morning after that sad press conference, he had pulled himself together, and during the two months remaining before the Democratic convention, he made a desperate lunge for the prize.

With Humphrey effectively out of contention, Jim Rowe no longer had a candidate. Johnson had refused Rowe's offers of assistance for years. Now he telephoned Rowe, and Rowe said, "If you want some help, I will be delighted to help you."

"Fine," Lyndon Johnson said. "I need all the help I can get."

And now that he was no longer trying to conceal his ambition, the effort that he was willing to make in its service became visible—and, although he was older now, the way he campaigned was a reminder of Ed Clark's remark that "I never thought it was *possible* for anyone to work that hard."

His days, as one reporter wrote, "were all 18-hour days." As soon as the Senate adjourned on the Friday after the West Virginia primary, he flew to Indianapolis, because the Indiana primary bound the state's delegates only on the first ballot, and Senator Vance Hartke had just assured him again that if only he could hold on through that ballot, many of the delegates would switch from Kennedy to him on the second round. As the plane was passing over the Alleghenies, on the way to Indiana, ten thousand feet up, Johnson tapped a reporter on the shoulder, and pointed to a cluster of toy-size houses in a bend of a river: Morgantown, West Virginia. "See those houses yonder?" he said. "In those houses— like all over the country—there are people who want what is good for America.

They are looking for leadership. They must have it." And for half an hour, until the plane touched down, Johnson kept reminding the reporter that it was leadership that was needed, and that he was the Senate's *Leader,* that he had proven he could *lead.* Leaving the plane, he held a press conference at the airport ("The American people are looking for leadership . . ."), then a second, because some local reporters had missed the first, then gave a speech at the Indianapolis Gridiron Club dinner, and met the delegates in a hotel suite afterwards. It was almost midnight before he stopped working on them, singly or in little groups, and climbed into a car to take him back to the plane.

The Convair was not equipped with a bed. Lady Bird urged him to close his eyes and nap in his seat, but there were other reporters to be told about the need for leadership, and, as one of them wrote, as the plane "thundered through the cloudy night," Johnson's voice never stopped. Lady Bird said, "Please." "I'll get my sleep on the ranch," Johnson replied. But after the plane finally landed at his airstrip, at four o'clock in the morning, there wasn't much sleep. He was up very early Saturday making telephone calls, and the next day, Sunday, he headed back to Washington.

And then, on the next Friday, on the eve of a long Memorial Day weekend, after another week of long days as Majority Leader—he was convening the Senate promptly at ten o'clock every morning now—and long strategy sessions every evening with his campaign team, he headed into the West, for a five-day speaking tour of six western states, beginning with Iowa, where Governor Loveless, whose invitations he had been rejecting for two years, had agreed to come out to the Des Moines airport and meet with him aboard the Convair. Then he went on to Idaho Falls (where the mayor had declared "Lyndon Johnson Day," saying, "This is the biggest day ever to happen to Idaho Falls"). For more than two years, he had been refusing every suggestion that he let western officeholders know he was a candidate. Now, when it was all but too late, he let them know. In the same Idaho Falls hotel suite in which, three months before, he had refused to give Tom Boise the assurance he required, Johnson was approached now by another key Idaho Democratic leader, Lieutenant Governor William E. Drevlow. "I can't say whether I'm with you or not, because I don't know whether you're a candidate," Drevlow said. "Are you a candidate?"

"You're damn right I am," Lyndon Johnson said.

He asked Drevlow to join him on the rest of the tour, and Drevlow agreed.

Then came Saturday, "a day that," as one report described it, "started in Idaho Falls, swept through Spokane, side tripped to Coeur d'Alene," and ended in Pierre, South Dakota—at 3:30 a.m.

When the Convair landed at the little airport in Pierre, a cold, cutting wind was blowing, and it was dark, although there was the first faint pink smudge of dawn in the sky. And as the reporters filed down out of the plane, they saw, silhouetted black against that smudge, a big Texas Stetson. South Dakota's governor, Ralph Herseth, had come to the airport, and Johnson had "bounded out of the plane" to meet him, and as the journalists walked past on the tarmac, he was pumping the governor's hand, talking away, with the only expression on his face a broad, confident smile; if Lyndon Johnson was tired, he wasn't letting anyone know it.

Not long before he left, Kennedy had given him an opening, and he charged through it. An American U-2 spy plane had been shot down over Russia, and Soviet premier Nikita Khrushchev, demanding that President Eisenhower apologize, had broken up a scheduled summit conference. Criticizing Eisenhower for authorizing a flight when it would jeopardize the conference, Kennedy said that had he been President he would have sent "regrets" to Khrushchev.

Even as Kennedy was making his statement, the country was already rallying behind its President, as Americans had traditionally done in foreign affairs crises, and Johnson told his western audiences that that was what they should do now. "I want our President to be successful in his dealings with foreign nations," he said. "If we get into trouble, it won't be our President who is in a jam—it will be our nation that is in a jam." Khrushchev was trying to divide the American people, he said, and "We ought not to be doing the job for him." Kennedy's statement gave him the opportunity to remind his audiences that supporting Eisenhower was what he had been having his Democratic senators do for eight years.

As for apologizing, "It was Mr. Khrushchev who . . . broke up the summit meeting by refusing to talk to the President other than in insulting language. It is not the American President who ought to apologize to Mr. Khrushchev. It is Mr. Khrushchev who ought to apologize to the American President."

Audiences responded. "At every stop, with increasing fire and to increasing applause, he is holding up the hand of the President in the new cold war," the columnist Mary McGrory wrote.

Sharpening his rhetoric, he trained it on the candidate who had suggested "regrets." By the time he reached Spokane, where he spoke to the Washington State Democratic Convention, he was shouting, "I am not prepared to apologize to Mr. Khrushchev. Are you? I am not prepared to send regrets to Mr. Khrushchev. Are you?" And to each question, the audience shouted back: "No. No."

And it wasn't only an issue that was working for Lyndon Johnson in the West—it was also his personality.

Stiff, stilted and unconvincing though he had been when delivering prepared speeches during his congressional and Senate campaigns, shouting sentences without inflection, his gestures as awkward as his phrasing, when in the latter stages of some of those campaigns he had realized he was losing and in desperation threw away his text and spoke directly to his audience, he was suddenly something quite different. Lyndon Johnson without a speech in his hand, as I wrote about his first, seemingly hopeless campaign, "Lyndon Johnson alone and unprotected on a flatbed truck: no paper to hide behind, nothing to look at but the faces of strangers; Lyndon Johnson with nothing to rely on but himself," was suddenly, gangling and big-eared and awkward though he remained, a candidate with a remarkable gift for establishing rapport with an audience. In 1960, of course, his platforms were not flatbed trucks but elaborately bunting-draped stages, and the candidate was no longer skinny and gangling, but on this trip into the West there were nonetheless moments that recalled those desperate early days.

On the Saturday of that hectic trip, he was so far behind schedule that Governor Herseth had provided a helicopter; it wasn't the tiny Sikorsky "Flying Windmill," that then revolutionary machine, in which he had swooped across Texas in '48, but it was a helicopter, and the plains he was flying over were plains as flat as those of Texas. And the audiences he spoke to during these days in the West had issues they shared with Texans, and those were the issues he spoke about.

Back in his plane, he was flying over the great West's rivers—the Columbia, the Colorado, the Snake, the Pecos, the Platte—and over the tiny gray-white lines across them that were the great dams the government had built to tame their floods, to make their waters work for electricity and irrigation; he flew, on the second of those western days, over Hells Canyon itself. Dams were the symbol of what government could do for the West, and he told his audiences about the dams he had built in Texas, and what they had done for the people of the Hill Country. Flying over Oregon, he had noticed strange lines on the earth far below, and someone had explained to him that they were ruts left by the wagon trains in which settlers had come into the Northwest. Those tracks had reminded him of the wagon trains that had come into the Texas Hill Country, he said, and had reminded him also that "those who remain behind in older sections don't grasp the West, don't understand it—and that is the West's Number One roadblock and problem." He spoke sometimes in terms out of another era—of the era of the Populists, of the People's Party, which had been founded in the Hill Country not far from Johnson City. He told western ranchers that the "world of high finance" was cheating them; that its bias against the West was reflected in high interest rates on the financing for the development projects the West needed, and in discriminatory freight rates when they sent cattle and goods to market. That's why the West needed "leadership which understands not how to keep the West in its place but how to give the West its place in the sun."

"The West," Lyndon Johnson said, "needs a champion in Washington."

In Theodore White's book on the 1960 presidential campaign, he linked the name of Lyndon Baines Johnson with the name of a Democratic presidential candidate from another century. If Lyndon Johnson could become "the candidate of the West" as well as the South, White wrote, if he could add its delegate votes to those of the South, "he could stand as the candidate of the wide-open spaces, the candidate of the William Jennings Bryan crescent, against the preponderant Northeastern bloc." And if he could do that, White wrote, if he could in effect become another Bryan, he had a realistic chance of winning the Democratic

nomination. "Let Kennedy be stopped . . . on the first ballot or two, and this crescent would close on the Northern delegates and roll east to victory." Whether or
not the people Lyndon Johnson was talking to now ever thought of Bryan's
name—and no newspaper mentioned it, and this author has been able to find no
book other than White's that does, either—the people to whom Lyndon Johnson
was speaking recognized the similarity between his background and theirs. The
fact that he was wearing boots didn't hurt, of course, and neither did the accent:
the southernness had faded from his voice; it was a West Texas twang now. A
Wyoming rancher, trying to explain to Mary McGrory why he was for Johnson,
said, "He has an honest-sounding voice."

Whatever the reason, the lieutenant governor of one western state was
aboard his plane, and the governor of another, South Dakota's Herseth, told
reporters, "There's no question but that he's picking up support." Returning from
the western trip, the columnist Doris Fleeson wrote that on it Lyndon Johnson had
been "a lion on the platform, a charmer in cozy conferences with delegates." Journalists reported that, as one of them wrote, "party leaders as well as correspondents traveling on the plane with Johnson agreed that he had improved his
position in the presidential sweepstakes in every state." *The West?* Had he only
started campaigning earlier, "he could have locked that place up without any difficulty at all," Ted Kennedy said. Looking at that trip that Lyndon Johnson finally
made at the end of May, 1960, it is easy to speculate about what he might have
cost himself by his years of procrastination. If he had held the West, the convention might well have been deadlocked, been thrown into the back rooms from
which, he was certain, he would emerge as the nominee.

And, it is easy to speculate, had he only started sooner, he *could* have held
the West.

BUT NOW IT WAS too late. The Kennedys had been sowing in the West for two
years. And now, almost as soon as Johnson returned from his Memorial Day trip,
the Kennedys began to reap.

Although none of the reporters understood the significance, there had been
indications that during the trip itself it was too late. Seven states, not six, had
been on the original itinerary; one of the seven—Montana—had been quietly
dropped even while the Convair was heading west. Confident that he could count
on that state—one of its senators, Mike Mansfield, was his Assistant Leader,
after all—Johnson had told Rowe to schedule a full day of appearances there.
Montana was Rowe's home state, however, and when he began telephoning his
old political allies, the reports he received were so disturbing that he contacted
Johnson, who was already on his way, and told him to postpone his visit.

(The reports were correct, as Rowe was to find when, two weeks later, he
arrived on the scene himself, to prepare for the Democratic State Convention in
Helena on June 27. Reporting to Jenkins over the phone on June 23, he told him

that Kennedy was ahead in Montana, "and Symington next. Symington has seven people in here plus two airplanes and they are really covering the territory." The Kennedys were playing hardball with the delegates, he said. "We had to do everything very quietly because every single time somebody comes out in the open [for Johnson], the Kennedy crowd move in [on him]." Just before the convention, Mansfield finally arrived in Helena—only to inform Rowe that, in Rowe's words, "he's for Johnson, but he won't tell anyone who to vote for." Though Johnson had been planning to address the convention on the morning it opened, Rowe telephoned him and said: "Don't come. We are going to get badly licked.")

Another indication had come in Idaho—at the Idaho Falls airport, where the delegation welcoming Johnson had been led by thirty-five-year-old Frank Church, who was, in the Senate, a favorite of the Majority Leader: Johnson had given him a key role in the '57 civil rights battle, and then a seat on Foreign Relations, simply bypassing half a dozen senators with greater seniority to do so.

Having assessed Church's ambition, he had once scribbled a note to him at a committee meeting to assure him he would help him realize it: he had, the note said, asked Drew Pearson "to help me give you a buildup over the years" so that one day "you can . . . be our President." A faster buildup had been promised by the Kennedys, however: in return for his support they had offered Church, a stirring orator, the role of keynoter in Los Angeles, a role that Church believed would catapult him to national prominence. Church had agreed. Johnson had heard rumors that this was the case, and, reading the young senator's eyes over the toothy smile he gave him at the airport, he saw it was true. Walking toward the terminal, he told Horace Busby: "The little sonofabitch has already sold out. They bought him."

"The halter and bridle" had been slipped on western delegates by Robert Kennedy, and Robert Kennedy was not a man to allow someone who had accepted the halter to take it off. One of Idaho's delegates, a state legislator, had been moved by a Johnson speech, but had earlier given his pledge to Bobby Kennedy. When a reporter asked him if he would change, he replied that he "simply couldn't." Bobby, he said, was not a man who ever forgave a broken promise.

In the weeks after his return to Washington, Johnson frantically worked the telephone for hours every day, and, since the time was earlier in the West, for hours every evening. His father had been a farmer, he told the head of a Minnesota farmers' grange. The Hill Country was a land of farmers. "You and I have got a lot in common, and I don't think you and your people have any with Boston." And he was flying—to New York, to Oklahoma, back to Iowa: in May and June, 1960, Johnson logged 31,250 miles back and forth across the United States, making thirty-six speeches and holding twenty-seven press conferences. But, state by state in rapid-fire order now, his mistake in relying on senators was exposed. With Anderson and Chavez behind him, he had taken New Mexico for granted. Every delegate count on those laminated cards in his breast pocket had

had all seventeen states from "Texas's backyard" in the Johnson column. But when, a week after his western trip, New Mexico's Democrats held their state convention, at which the delegates were actually selected, [Kennedy] received seven of the seventeen. The "successful [Kennedy] raid . . . deep in [Johnson's] southwestern backyard" shook the Johnson camp, the *New York Times* reported.*

Then there was Carl Hayden's Arizona. That state had a unit rule, and suddenly Kennedy had all seventeen of its votes. In Colorado, Edwin (Big Ed) Johnson was denied even a seat on the delegation. Montana, New Mexico, Arizona, Colorado, Wyoming—by the end of June, the West was gone. For so many months, Irv Hoff had urged Lyndon Johnson to campaign in the West. "He had put it off, and put it off, and put it off as long as he could," Hoff would say. "And he put it off too long."

THE DESPERATION WITH WHICH Lyndon Johnson was trying for the nomination now was visible not only in public but behind closed doors—Rowe and Corcoran and Connally and Clark saw that they had been right all along: that because "he wanted it *so much*," "eventually he was going to do it," was eventually "going to get in—get in all the way."

Having finally accepted Rowe's offer of help, he asked him for advice, and when Rowe told him bluntly, "Kennedy has got this. There's only one way to stop him that I can see. That's for Adlai to give a signal [that he was willing to be drafted]," he acted on it.

If the two-time nominee could attract enough votes, Rowe was saying, they might, combined with Johnson's and a few from Symington and the favorite sons, be enough to deny Kennedy a first-ballot victory. Long though that shot may have been, Johnson tried it, suggesting, in a number of conversations with Stevenson, that Adlai "let his people be more active." Johnson's argument, according to a Stevenson aide, was, "Now listen, Adlai, just hang loose here. Don't make any commitments. You may still get it. Don't help that kid, Kennedy. Just stay neutral." And the argument may have been persuasive: "I believe that Governor Stevenson . . . made a commitment to him that he would do that," the aide says. At the end of the month, when Arthur Krock told Kennedy that Adlai had started making a real effort for the nomination, Kennedy said, "And how!"

ON CAPITOL HILL, Johnson held a lot of cards, and now he was playing them. In several states crucial to his presidential hopes, Senate seats were becoming vacant in 1960, and some of the Democrats running for them—Thorn Lord of New Jersey and Representative Lee Metcalf of Montana, for example—had been

---

*In later maneuvering before the convention, Johnson would get three of them back.

promised financial support by the Senate Democratic Campaign Committee. Now these candidates were told that that support would be rationed out in inverse proportion to their support of Kennedy. And not only cash but committee assignments were in Johnson's hand. What had he said to Governor Loveless in that brief meeting aboard his plane? Loveless was to tell an Iowa politician that his Senate assignments were going to depend on his convention activities. To all these men, it was becoming apparent, Johnson was saying, in effect, Vote for me if you can, but if you can't, just don't vote for Kennedy. And to all these men the message had been delivered in firm terms. After talking to Loveless, the Iowa politician said, "Rough stuff. These boys aren't playing for peanuts." "I'm not what you call a Kennedy fan," one unidentified governor told the *Wall Street Journal,* "but these Johnson tactics almost have me mad enough to become one."

One card in Johnson's hand could be played only if Sam Rayburn, who held the same card, agreed to play his. The Speaker had been reluctant to play it, telling Johnson its use would be "too raw," but Representative Richard Bolling, a witness to some of their discussions, says that at seventy-eight "Sam was just old now; Lyndon finally wore him down." On June 29, without warning, the two Texans suddenly announced that rather than Congress adjourning for the year before the convention, as had been expected, it would instead immediately recess, and return to complete the session on August 8—after the convention.

Longtime congressional observers could recall only one maneuver even faintly comparable: Harry Truman's 1948 masterstroke, following the Republican convention, of calling the Republican-controlled Congress back into session, and challenging it to deliver on the convention's campaign platform. Truman, however, had been challenging a Republican Congress, in which he had limited influence. Johnson and Rayburn were talking about a Congress *they* controlled. Rayburn's "word is virtually law among Democrats in the House," James Reston noted. Power over legislation senators and congressmen wanted—or needed, to satisfy demands of their constituents—was in the hands of the two Texans, and in the hands of the committee chairmen who wanted Johnson to get the nomination. With the new congressional schedule, Johnson and Rayburn would be holding this legislation over the heads of senators and representatives in Los Angeles; as James Reston wrote, "The theory . . . was that the two Texans would be able, by their influence over legislation in the recessed session, to induce forty or fifty delegates to support Mr. Johnson."

Evans and Novak were to call the "audacious" maneuver "blatant political blackmail." As the Senate, in previous years so efficient under Johnson, had dawdled through the year, there had indeed been speculation that the Majority Leader had, as the *New York Times* was to put it, "engineered a Senate slowdown to keep control of the fate of major bills during the Democratic convention." (The speculation had been discounted because the maneuver would be "too extreme [an] exercise of power.") There was, in reality, not much chance it would succeed—for the same reason that Johnson's reliance on senators wasn't succeeding. While he had power over them, they didn't have power over their delegations. His use of it made clear, however, the lengths to which he was going in his last-ditch effort to get the nomination.

"WORKED UP," "revved up" now, Lyndon Johnson had convinced himself he was going to defeat Kennedy. He believed that thoroughly now. It was, after all, his destiny. "I was *meant* to be President." Governor Lawrence had seen it. "The man has sold himself." Now Johnson, meeting with a group of senators in the Taj Mahal, waved a copy of a newspaper article predicting a Kennedy win, and laughed at it. The winner was going to be *him,* he said. "The bandwagon is rolling, boys. You might as well get on board."

AND HE WAS WORKED UP about his opponent. While he had begun deriding Kennedy as soon as the Massachusetts senator began running for the presidency, calling him "the boy," or, in a contemptuous tone, "Sonny Boy," or "Johnny" or "Little Johnny," saying that he was just a rich kid whose daddy was trying to buy him the nomination, in public, for a time, he confined himself to the age issue ("He's a nice, attractive young man," he would say, heavily underlining the final adjective) and the absenteeism issue ("Jack was out kissing babies while I was passing bills, including his bills"), and the contrast between their roles in the Senate. Johnson "likes to portray himself as the man who made Senator Kennedy what he is today by securing him choice committee assignments," David Broder reported. "He looks with paternal pride on the accomplishments of Kennedy, Symington and all the others . . . who flourished so well under his care."

As it became apparent that Kennedy's bid was serious, however, in public the paternalistic note faded, and the jabs became sharper. To a press conference question about Kennedy, he responded that with the Cold War in such a serious phase, the United States shouldn't be represented in world councils by someone "second-class." After Kennedy said he would have expressed regret to Khrushchev, the word "guts" became a standard word in Johnson's platform rhetoric, and the jabs started to be thrown in combination. "It is up to the American people in their wisdom to judge whether a man of that age can lead the country. . . . The next President should have a little gray in his hair, wisdom in his heart, and guts under his belt." A full-page newspaper ad which his campaign took out in May in eighteen cities across the country said, "We cannot afford to gamble with inexperience, immaturity." Jack Kennedy's father had been an appeaser, Lyndon was to say. "I wasn't any Chamberlain umbrella man. I never thought Hitler was right."

In private he was funnier. Riding in an elevator in the Capitol with a Republican congressman, Walter Judd of Minnesota, Johnson asked him, "Have you heard the news?" "What news?" Judd responded. "Jack's pediatricians have just given him a clean bill of health!" Johnson said. And not so funny. Although Humphrey and Symington would make "small cracks" about Kennedy, Hugh Sidey would observe, "they were never bitter. They knew the game, and the closest they'd get to being bitter was that he was a rich, spoiled kid who had never had to make it. . . . The most vicious evaluation of Senator Kennedy was from Johnson, and that got quite violent at times." After a campaign trip to Oklahoma in June, he offered Peter Lisagor of the *Chicago Daily News* a ride back to Washington on the Convair, and, Lisagor was to recount, "all of the enmity and hostility that he held for the Kennedys came out. He called Kennedy a 'little scrawny fellow with rickets' and God knows what other kind of diseases. He said, 'Have you ever seen his ankles? They're about so round.' " And Johnson made a tiny circle with his fingers.

There were other flights with Lyndon Johnson, jacket and tie off, sitting beside other reporters pouring out his feelings about "the boy," the Texas twang clear and sharp through the hum of the engines. Even reporters who had covered Johnson for years were startled by the depth of his feelings. "It is amazing to note the changes that have come over the man," Robert G. Spivack wrote on June 27. "One day he is the ingratiating, let's-all-be-friends . . . political gladhander; the next day he is a rough-tough, kick-and-gouge fighter who will destroy anyone who gets in the way. Johnson seems determined that no matter what happens to his presidential ambitions, the one who must not become President of the United States is the man he contemptuously calls 'Johnny' Kennedy."

One issue he had stayed away from was health: for a candidate who had suffered a major heart attack, health wasn't a sure winner. But now any card he held had to be played. A decade before, as the chief counsel of Johnson's Preparedness Investigating Subcommittee, Donald Cook had impressed Johnson as a very sharp lawyer and investigator. Now he was president of the American Power Company, but at the end of June Johnson drafted him to investigate Jack Kennedy's health.

Going directly to Frank Brough, who, as president of a pharmaceutical manufacturing company, "has," as Cook was to tell Walter Jenkins, "a great many doctor contacts around the country," Cook quickly struck pay dirt. "Brough told me about this Addison's Disease," he told Jenkins. "Kennedy . . . was treated for it in the Lahey Clinic in Boston. . . . I am told he not only *had* it but *has* it now and is receiving treatment for it."

By the next day, Cook had the name of a doctor, Lewis Hurxthal, who he said had treated Kennedy for Addison's disease at Lahey, and the fact that "the records of [the] case are not kept in the general clinic files, but in Hurxthal's personal records." He told a Johnson aide, Arthur Perry, to tell Johnson that Kennedy was under Hurxthal's "care . . . right down to the present time" and that the medication given for Addison's "creates what the doctors call a psychic problem," including "a split personality and . . . very neurotic behavior patterns." Cook suggested that the story be leaked to "some newshound . . . without involving the Senator," but Johnson took a role himself, telephoning a California internist who had once worked at Lahey in an attempt to confirm that Kennedy had the disease. Despite the doctor's refusal to provide this confirmation, however, Johnson decided to make the issue public—not himself, of course; publicly he stayed above the fray, refusing to get into the health issue at all, but having John Connally and India Edwards hold a press conference in which Mrs. Edwards said that Kennedy did indeed have Addison's disease, which she defined as "something to do with lymph glands." She added that "Doctors have told me he would not be alive if not for cortisone."

But the Kennedys deflected the attack with their usual skill. Seizing on the fact that the classic cause of Addison's was tuberculosis, which Jack Kennedy did not have (his Addison's was caused by other factors), Robert Kennedy said that his brother "does not now nor has he ever had an ailment described classically as Addison's Disease, which is a turberculose destruction of the adrenal gland"; that his brother had only "some adrenal insufficiency" which "is not in any way a dangerous condition"; and that "any statement to the contrary is malicious and false . . . despicable tactics . . . a sure sign of the desperation of the opposition. Evidently there are those within the Democratic Party who would prefer that if they cannot win the nomination themselves they want the Democrat who does win to lose in November." Sorensen went further. Evidently feeling himself justified by the fact that Kennedy was taking not cortisone but a cortisone derivative, he told a reporter flatly, "He is not on cortisone." And when the reporter asked him what other drugs Kennedy might be using, he said, "I don't know that he is on anything—any more than you and I are on." So successful were the Kennedys that the next day New York's Carmine De Sapio, friendly to Johnson, had an intermediary relay a message to the candidate: that Mrs. Edwards' statement had backfired "and was going to hurt badly" not Kennedy but Johnson, and that "Johnson should disavow" it—which Johnson did.

None of his cards took a trick. It was just too late. On July 5, with the convention just six days away—standing, as Mary McGrory sarcastically put it, "before the barn door" and "declaring that the horse has not been stolen"— Lyndon Johnson said the words he had never said before: "I am, as of this moment, a candidate for the office of President of the United States." His voice suddenly broke as he was reading that sentence; "I had never heard him do that before," Horace Busby says. (The announcement, delivered in the auditorium of the new Senate Office Building, packed with reporters and cheering Senate staffers, and with Rayburn's bald head shining in the front row, was filled with jabs at his leading opponent's failure to condemn McCarthy—he himself, he said, had been "a working liberal when Joe McCarthy had been at the height"; at his absences from the Senate—he himself had stayed on the job while "those who have engaged in active campaigns have missed hundreds of votes. . . . The next President is not going to be a talking President or a traveling President. He is going to be a working President"; and at his inexperience: the "forces of evil in this world . . . will have no mercy for innocence." If the next President "is inex-perienced in making government work, he becomes a weak link in the whole chain of the free world.") Then, after a last visit to the White House with Ray-burn to try and persuade Eisenhower to publicly criticize Kennedy—the Presi-dent was to recount that the two Texans felt he was "a mediocrity in the Senate . . . a nobody who had a rich father. . . . And they'd tell some of the God-damndest stories"—on Friday, July 8, he flew to Los Angeles. Excoriating his top campaign workers ("He got mad," Herring says. "He felt we hadn't done our job. He didn't feel we had done enough with the delegates. 'If you'd done the job you were supposed to have done, I wouldn't be in this situation' "), he told them he was going to win despite their incompetence. Listing the states that were going to switch to him after the first ballot, he said, "It was going to be nip and tuck but he still felt he would win." But an article on the front page of Saturday's *New York Times* showed how unrealistic it was for him to hope for the support of any substantial number of northern liberals. "Top-level labor leaders passed the word to union delegates to the Democratic National Convention today to give no aid to Senator Lyndon B. Johnson for nomination to any office," it said. At a meeting of union leaders, one after the other had denounced what they called the "Johnson operation" to "hold liberal and labor legislation hostage to his candi-dacy," it said. While the article contained no direct quotes from the meeting— that was evidently the condition on which a description of it had been given to reporter Joseph Loftus—Loftus got the wording across nonetheless: the most powerful leader, gruff old George Meany, president of the fifteen-million-member-strong AFL-CIO, had, the article said, "left no doubt . . . that Senator Johnson should be regarded by all union delegates as an arch foe of labor."

And, liberal leaders said Sunday, of civil rights as well. All the candidates had been invited to a rally organized by the NAACP that evening to support a civil rights fight in the convention's platform committee, and Johnson had accepted. Now he said he wasn't coming, sending former Interior Secretary Chapman in his place. The audience, about six thousand persons, mostly African-American, was tough on all the candidates except for Humphrey, who was cheered when he rose to speak. When Kennedy was introduced, some boos mingled with the applause; he spoke in generalities, making no specific pledges on Negro rights, but apparently convinced the audience of his sincerity; at the end of his talk, the applause was no more than polite, but there were no boos. Then Chapman spoke. As soon as he mentioned Johnson's name, the jeering and angry shouts were so loud, and went on so long, that for a time it seemed he would not be allowed to continue. When, finally, he was, he said, "If I did not think Senator Johnson would support the Supreme Court decision [on school desegregation] wholeheartedly, I would not support him." The skeptical reaction drowned him out again.

One by one, all that weekend, delegations came down for Kennedy. Calling on Johnson in his suite—7333—in the Biltmore Hotel on Saturday morning,

De Sapio and Prendergast delivered in private the news that Mayor Wagner, who hadn't come, would announce publicly that afternoon: that Kennedy would receive 104 or 105 of New York's 114 votes. On Saturday also, Governors Docking and Loveless announced that they would release the Kansas and Iowa delegations from their favorite-son candidacies; although Kennedy had only a bare majority of Kansas' 21 votes, under the unit rule if the delegation was released, Kennedy would get all 21. The big headlines in the Sunday newspapers said: MOVE TO KENNEDY NEARS STAMPEDE; JOHNSON SEEMS HEADED FOR POLITICAL ALAMO. And later on Sunday, Dick Daley let it be known that Kennedy would get all but a handful of Illinois' 69 votes.

THERE REMAINED just one hope: what Joseph Alsop called "the single major herd of delegates that is . . . genuinely uncommitted. This is the Pennsylvania delegation, 81 strong, sternly commanded by the Sphinx of Harrisburg, Gov. David Lawrence."

Slim though the chance might be, it was definitely a chance. Despite the headlines, if Kennedy didn't take almost all of Pennsylvania's votes, he might still be well short of the 761 he needed. Pennsylvania would not caucus until Monday morning, and, as Alsop wrote on Friday, the result of that caucus would be "decisive" for Kennedy's chances. "Everything depends on Pennsylvania," Lyndon Johnson said that weekend. "If we could have held Pennsylvania," John Connally was to recall years later, "we would have stopped him." And that weekend Lawrence was doing—as he had been doing for more than a year—everything he could to keep his state out of Kennedy's column.

The son of an Irish teamster, David ("Don't Call Me 'Boss'") Lawrence had dropped out of high school at fourteen to run errands for a Pittsburgh alderman, and thereafter his education had been as a politician, and a formative moment had come in 1928. Idolizing another poor and uneducated Irishman up from the slums, Alfred E. Smith, for the social reforms Smith had enacted as governor of New York, Lawrence had thrown himself and his Pittsburgh machine into Smith's presidential campaign. The storm of anti-Catholic prejudice that sent the "Happy Warrior" to overwhelming defeat—fiery crosses had blazed on midwestern hills as Smith's campaign train passed—had burned into Lawrence the belief that Roman Catholicism was an insurmountable handicap in American politics; in 1932, despite his admiration for Smith, he took his machine into Franklin D. Roosevelt's camp, "solely," Lawrence's biographer wrote, "on the religious issue." Then, in 1958, after four terms as Pittsburgh's mayor, he ran for the governorship. Until the end of his life, he never stopped talking about what had happened to him in that race: about the hate-filled letters that poured into his home, some of them worded so violently that he feared for his family's safety; about the ministers in Pennsylvania's rural Dutch districts who warned their congregants not to vote for a Roman Catholic; about how, although he had come out of Pittsburgh and Philadelphia, and the hard coal counties, with a huge plurality, he had almost lost anyway, when the vote from the non-Catholic areas came in. On the morning after a Jefferson-Jackson Day Dinner in 1959, Lawrence had attended a Sunday Mass together with Richard Daley, Robert Wagner, Carmine De Sapio, Mike DiSalle and Pat Brown—a communion of the bosses—and during break-fast after church Lawrence delivered his sermon: that Kennedy "just can't win. Districts that have always gone Democratic I lost because I was a Catholic." Now, on the eve of the 1960 convention, the stocky, grizzled ruler of the Penn-sylvania Democrats was convinced that, despite West Virginia, nothing had changed; Kennedy's victory there might have eased the fears of some of those other leaders about anti-Catholic prejudice; it had done little to ease Lawrence's. "I figured . . . he'll lose Pennsylvania sure," he was to recall. And he was afraid that Kennedy's name at the top of the ticket would, by arousing anti-Catholic sentiment in those "Dutch Democratic districts," drag other Pennsylvania Democrats down with him. Says an old friend who talked to Lawrence shortly after West Virginia: "What he wanted was to win. He was convinced that the whole ticket was going to go down the drain because you couldn't elect a Roman Catholic." An ambitious program he wanted to pass as governor depended on his narrow margin in the legislature. If Kennedy was the nominee, Lawrence recalls, "I could see losing . . . the Legislature."

And there were, besides, his feelings about Adlai Stevenson, feelings which one reporter called "an almost youthful adoration," the admiration, almost awe, of the tough old boss, with little formal education, for Stevenson's learning, wit and brilliance. He had played a crucial role in getting Adlai the nomination in 1952 and 1956, and, Lawrence's son was to say, in 1960 "though I don't think his political sense was with Stevenson . . . his heart was with Stevenson." Lawrence himself would say, "I was very enamored of Stevenson, because I think of him as one of the ablest men in the world and the ablest man I ever met."

The Kennedys had been working on Dave Lawrence not for months but for years; Joseph Kennedy had made a substantial contribution to his 1958 guberna-torial campaign. ("Why would you want to contribute in Pennsylvania?" Lawrence's protégé, Joe Barr, had asked the patriarch at the time.) In Pennsylva-nia's own, non-binding 1960 primary, more than 175,000 Democrats, an aston-ishingly high number, had written in Kennedy's name, and more than half the state's eighty-one delegates were for him. But Lawrence wouldn't budge. "We were all furious" at him, Rose Kennedy would recall. "Joe has worked with Lawrence all winter, but he still can't believe a Catholic can be elected. He has been one of the most exasperating and tantalizing forces."

That didn't mean that Lawrence was for Johnson. If he felt a Catholic couldn't win, he had the same feeling about a southerner, even after Johnson's speech at the Zembo Mosque. On a visit to the Taj Mahal near the end of May, he was "given the 'full treatment.' " Emerging "in a daze," he "sought refuge" in the office of Pennsylvania Senator Joseph Clark, and told him, "in wondering tones," that "the man has sold himself on the idea that he is going to be our nominee and the next President. Now how can I ask Pennsylvania Democrats to vote for Lyndon Johnson?"

Over that weekend in Los Angeles, Johnson was working furiously to hold the Pennsylvania delegates. His partner in the effort was a key player in the Pennsylvania game, John L. Lewis, president of the United Mine Workers, who had been his ally—a secret ally, since labor union support was not a political *desideratum* in Texas—for years; the UMW's chief counsel, Welly Hopkins, a onetime Hill Country legislator for whom Johnson, as a young man, had campaigned in Texas, had carried cash back to that state for both of Johnson's Senate campaigns.

In any state with as much coal as Pennsylvania, of course, the mine workers would be a potent political force; Lewis had already dispatched UMW Secretary-Treasurer Tom Kennedy to Los Angeles, and, on Lewis' instructions, Hopkins had been discussing with Johnson ways in which Johnson might hold at least a substantial bloc of the Pennsylvania delegation.

The last chance melted away due to Stevenson's indecisiveness. Arriving in Los Angeles, Lawrence found that more of his Pennsylvania delegates than ever were for Kennedy, and Chicago's Daley let him see with his own eyes that Stevenson had little support even from his own state, inviting Lawrence to attend the Illinois caucus on Sunday, in which Stevenson received only a handful of votes. Nevertheless, meeting Sunday night "with the man he had championed for almost a decade," Lawrence pleaded with him to announce that he was a candidate. "You'll have eighty-five percent of the Pennsylvania delegation," he said. "I can hold it. They're going to kill me, but I can hold it. They're all on the [state] payroll." And if he held Pennsylvania, Lawrence said, Kennedy couldn't win on the first ballot, "and this guy is dead if it goes to a second ballot. He's dead!" But Pennsylvania was going to caucus the next morning. "You've got to tell me right now."

Adlai was Adlai. "If the party wants me . . ."

"No, no, Governor," Lawrence said. "Right now. I have to know *right now!*"

Finally, Stevenson said cavalierly, "Do what you have to, Dave." Adlai's aide Willard Wirtz said in despair, "Governor, are you sure that's the message you want to give Governor Lawrence?" but Stevenson said it was. "Adlai could have said anything but that and he [Lawrence] would've stopped Pennsylvania from going to Kennedy," said another Stevenson aide. Lawrence had given Stevenson a last chance—and Stevenson had refused it. Lawrence told Stevenson that Pennsylvania would go for Kennedy at the caucus. All during that weekend, Welly Hopkins says, the UMW's Tom Kennedy had been working the Pennsylvania delegates, and "there was some reason to believe that there might be a last-minute gambit . . . through Lawrence that they be put in Lyndon's column," but "he wasn't able to put it over although he tried."

Late Sunday night Johnson learned what Pennsylvania was going to do when it caucused Monday morning. Nonetheless, that morning, before the actual vote he had to attend a breakfast meeting of the Pennsylvania delegation, where he, Kennedy, Symington and, speaking for Stevenson, Mike Monroney would give brief talks to the delegates before they voted; he had to sit beside Kennedy all through that breakfast, keeping a smile on his face. At one point, Lawrence opened the doors and let photographers in. Leaping to his feet, Johnson stood between Kennedy and Symington, who had remained seated, and put a hand on each of their shoulders so that in the photographs he would be the dominant figure. But after the photographers were ushered out, the doors were closed again, and Lawrence introduced the speakers. Johnson received polite applause. Then Lawrence introduced Kennedy. With a spontaneous roar, the delegates stood and cheered him. After the talks, the speakers left, and the doors were closed again. Back in his suite at the Biltmore an hour later, Johnson got the exact count: he had received 4 of Pennsylvania's 81 votes, Stevenson 7½, Kennedy 64 (1½ had gone for "others"). Later that day he had to keep a commitment to speak to New York. "I am not a naïve person," Lyndon Johnson said. "I know that a preponderance of the cards are stacked against me here." Of the 114 delegates in the audience facing him, 4½ would vote for him. That night, he sat watching the opening of the convention in his suite at the Biltmore, alone except for Jim Rowe. Rowe was staring at the screen when he heard a voice beside him say softly, "I don't see how we can stop this fellow."

TUESDAY BROUGHT TWO EPISODES of note. One was the wild demonstration touched off by Senator Eugene McCarthy's emotional speech placing Stevenson's name in nomination, a riotous parade around the convention floor that moved television commentators to speculate that the convention might be stampeded for Adlai. The political pros in the hall, however, noticed that very few of the paraders were delegates; in terms of changing votes, the demonstration had little significance.

In those terms, the other episode didn't have much significance, either—but it may have given Lyndon Johnson a new appreciation of John F. Kennedy.

Trying to give as many delegates as possible a chance to meet Kennedy, his campaign headquarters had sent a telegram, signed by him, to the chairman of each delegation, asking for permission to address it "to explain my views and to answer their questions." The chairman of the Texas delegation was Lyndon Johnson, and no one had thought to omit him from the list.

It was only a form telegram, but when Johnson received it, he seized upon it as the opening he had been waiting for: the opening that could, even at this late moment, change everything—a chance to trap Kennedy into a debate.

"I want to get on the same podium with Jack," he told Irv Hoff. "I'll destroy him."

Connally, Reedy and Busby, when they were called in, were unanimously enthusiastic; "One major error" by Kennedy, Connally felt, and the Kennedy bandwagon, which he believed was not yet on completely firm ground anyway, would be overturned. A reply from Johnson was drafted, ostensibly "in response to your request" but in terms that would elevate the event to a more significant level: a debate between the two leading contenders for the nomination. It challenged Kennedy to "appear together" with him at three o'clock that afternoon before a joint caucus of the Texas and Massachusetts delegations "and debate the major issues," and on Tuesday morning, even before it was sent to Kennedy, Johnson called a press conference and read it to reporters. "It would be in the interest of our party that this session be open to" television coverage, it said. "If it went well, enough delegates would be watching to tip the balance," Reedy said.

Kennedy had every reason not to accept, and his advisers told him not to: as the front-runner, he had a lot to lose and not much to gain. But Kennedy did not look at it that way. His father heard about Johnson's telegram that morning as he was sitting next to the swimming pool at the Marion Davies estate, which he had rented for the duration of the convention, giving an interview to the friendly journalist John Seigenthaler. His son would be "a damned fool" to accept, the ambassador said. But Jack's sister Jean Kennedy Smith said, "I know, Daddy, but he's challenged him to a debate." To Seigenthaler, she said, "You'll see. That's the way they are. He'll debate him." He announced he would.

In describing Johnson's reaction, Philip Graham was to call it "tremendous exhilaration. Once again he was a candidate for the presidency with a chance, even an unlikely one." He told Graham what he wanted to say, "which seemed a bit harsh and personal. . . . He began talking in *ad hominem* terms about Kennedy," and Graham tried to dissuade him, saying, "No, we're not going to say that sort of thing. We're going to talk about . . . the world situation." And he wrote a ten-minute "high road" statement for Johnson to use.

In accepting Johnson's invitation, Kennedy had said that he had appeared before many delegations, and "I have never found it necessary to bring the Massachusetts delegation with me. I will appear alone before the Texas caucus." Trying to elevate the newsworthiness of the event, Johnson had announced that Kennedy was violating the terms of his invitation, and Kennedy finally said he would try to round up some Massachusetts delegates, but there weren't more than a handful or two in the Crystal Ballroom of the Biltmore Hotel when Kennedy arrived, with his brother Robert and a few aides, a little after three o'clock. The entire sixty-one-man Texas delegation seemed to be there, as well as scores of other Texans, the men in big Stetsons, the women wearing "All the Way with LBJ" pins; under glittering chandeliers, the huge ballroom was jammed wall to wall with reporters; "TV cameras bristled like machine guns from every point in the ornate gallery," one wrote.

As he took his seat on the stage, Kennedy wasn't at ease—a reporter noticed his leg shaking under his trousers—but no one seeing only his face would have known it. And when he rose to speak, looking out at the ballroom that, one Texas reporter wrote, "Johnson had packed full of his folks," Kennedy said with a smile that he was glad the vote for the nomination wasn't being taken there. "I doubt whether there is any great groundswell for Kennedy in the Texas delegation," he said. The audience chuckled at that, and laughed when, after promising to campaign for Johnson if Johnson won the nomination, he said, "And if I am nominated, I am confident that Senator Johnson will take me by the hand and lead me through the length and breadth of Texas." He said he wasn't going to argue with Johnson on the issues—"because I don't think Senator Johnson and I disagree on the great issues that are facing us"—and said he admired him for his work as Majority Leader. "If [I am] successful in this convention," he said, "it will be the result of watching Senator Johnson . . . for the last eight years. I have learned the lesson well, Lyndon, and I hope it may benefit me in the next twenty-four hours. . . . So I come here today full of admiration for Senator Johnson, full of affection for him, and strongly in support of him—for Majority Leader." The audience laughed again. When Kennedy sat down at the end of his opening statement, there was quite a bit of rather warm applause.

Johnson started off on Phil Graham's "high road," although it was an arm-waving, blustering journey—"And when I take the oath of office next January . . ."—but before long he veered off.

He had gotten a civil rights bill through the Senate, he said, but not every senator had been present to help him. "Six days and nights we had 24-hour sessions," he said, shouting every word. "Lyndon Johnson answered every one of the fifty quorum calls. Some men who would be President answered none." He had voted in all forty-five roll calls, he said. "Some senators missed 34." A Texas legislator, George Nokes, leaned over and whispered loudly to the other people in his aisle, "Lyndon sure bear-trapped him, didn't he?"

After a brief, whispered conference with his brother, Kennedy rose to reply. Johnson's face had been grim as he spoke. On Kennedy's face was a grin. Senator Johnson had criticized some senators, he said, but he had not identified those he was talking about, so "I assume he was talking about some other candidate, not me."

The grin broadened. "I want to commend him for . . . a wonderful record answering those quorum calls," he said.

People in the audience started to chuckle, and then others started to laugh, and a wave of laughter swept over the hall. Turning to Johnson, Kennedy shook his hand for the photographers, and walked out of the hall, his little band following him.

Watching Johnson as Kennedy spoke, Arthur Schlesinger saw his face change. "Johnson felt that Kennedy had the drop on him," he was to say. That was what the Texas delegates thought, too—even those who, like Jim Wright, had been Johnson's "eager disciples." Wright, a very tough politician—he would later rise to Sam Rayburn's place as Speaker of the House—heard Johnson's attack, and then, he was to recall decades later, saw Kennedy give that "big Irish grin of his, and say, 'Since Lyndon mentioned no names, I'm sure he wasn't talking about me.' Then he began bragging about Lyndon. By the time he ended, he had won our admiration—begrudging but admiration." In fact, in describing the debate, Wright bestowed on Kennedy what was, for a Texan, the highest accolade possible. Jack Kennedy, he was to recall, had reminded him that afternoon of the legendary Texas Ranger who was sent in 1906 to a city down on the Rio Grande border in which a riot was raging. The city's sheriff had telegraphed Ranger headquarters for assistance, and had been told it would arrive on the next train. When the train pulled in, and only one man disembarked, the dismayed sheriff asked, "Only one Ranger?" "Only one riot," the Ranger explained. When Jack Kennedy had walked into that hostile ballroom, packed with his enemies, Wright said, "Came in all alone, walked in bareheaded, I made that comparison in my mind. By the time he finished, we were all identifying with that old Texas Ranger." Even Johnson's most loyal staff members felt the same way. "Really, it didn't come off as we had expected it to," Jake Jacobsen says. Months earlier, Jim Wright had tried to warn Lyndon Johnson about "the Kennedy magic." Now Johnson had experienced it for himself. "He got cured once and for all of getting into a debate with Jack Kennedy," Irv Hoff says.

AFTER THE DEBATE, less than twenty-four hours remained before—on Wednesday, July 13, in midafternoon—the convention would be called to order to nominate the candidates, and those hours were filled with a desperate last round of infighting. Delaware and North Dakota were both states with eleven votes—which would, in both cases, be cast as a unit—and in both states a delegate with half a vote held the balance; Kennedy held North Dakota, but Johnson brought Delaware into his camp. And Robert Kennedy and John Connally were both pleading with Robert Meyner, Kennedy for New Jersey to throw its forty-one votes to his brother on the first ballot, Connally for the state to stick with Meyner as a favorite son on the first ballot at least, and Connally won. Johnson raced from delegation to delegation in a last-minute attempt to pick up some votes. Bumping into Jack Kennedy once, he accused him of using unfair tactics. "Johnson's eyes were like flamethrowers," said a man who was present. His bile against Kennedy was spilling over. Before the Washington State delegation, he attacked the Kennedys, father and son, saying again that the father had been a "Chamberlain umbrella man" while he himself had "never thought Hitler was right," and bringing up Joe McCarthy. The Kennedys, he said, had advised the Wisconsin senator on strategy and contributed money to his campaigns, and, of course, Jack had not voted with the rest of the Democrats to condemn his methods. "I was not contributing comfort to his thinking or contributions to his campaign," Johnson said. "When he was on the march in this country and someone had to stand up and be counted," every Democratic senator "stood up and voted with their Leader," he said. "That is, all those who were present." And more personal feelings spilled out as well. "No one handed any wealth down to me," he told the Kentucky delegation. "I haven't had anything given to me. Whatever I have and whatever I hope to get I got through my own energy and talents." He had helped Kennedy in the Senate, he said, and "Now this young man I appointed to the Foreign Relations Committee claims he knows more about foreign affairs than I do. You know, there are some people who will throw crutches at their doctor and get smarter than their daddy."

Johnson's emotions were no hotter than those of the Kennedy who hated him. Bobby Baker, to whom politics was all a game, if a dirty one, was slow to realize this; "as one accustomed to the rough-and-tumble of politics, after which foes might sit down together over a drink," he had "thought nothing" of Johnson's attacks, and noticing Bobby Kennedy outside the Biltmore coffee shop where he and his wife, Dorothy, were eating, he invited him to join them. Then, however, in the course of what he regarded as "normal banter between political adversaries," he ventured to remark that some of the Kennedy criticisms of Johnson had been "a little rough."

In an instant, Robert Kennedy's face had flushed so deep a red that Baker "thought he might have a stroke."

"You've got your nerve," he said. "Lyndon Johnson has compared my father to the Nazis, and John Connally . . . lied in saying my brother is dying. . . . You Johnson people are running a stinking damned campaign, and you're gonna get yours when the time comes!" Baker tried to calm him, but there was no calming Robert Kennedy when his family was concerned. "Leaning forward, clenching his fists, thrusting his face into mine," he went on shouting, until he finally jumped up, threw some money on the table and stalked off, on his face that glare that men feared.

AFTER THE CONVENTION was gaveled to order at three o'clock that afternoon, Sam Rayburn got out of his seat in the Texas delegation's section to make the first nominating speech, and the two thousand delegates on the floor of the Los Angeles Memorial Sports Arena rose in a great ovation as they saw the familiar bald head moving through a crowd to the high platform. Johnson had sent Lady Bird and his two daughters to his box in the arena; Mary Margaret Wiley and Johnson assistant Bob Waldron were in his suite with him, and George Reedy was in and out; Johnson sat on the edge of a sofa, hunched forward, watching the Speaker on the television screen.

Rayburn's speech was a very personal one. "I am going to present to you today . . . a man that I have known since his babyhood," he said. "I knew his pioneer father and mother, who faced the ravages of the great West when there was little or no civilization there." Lyndon Johnson, he said, was "a poor boy who dreamed great dreams. A young man who worked his way through school, a young man in his youth who did menial work, who climbed with an ambition, superb and superior." During his forty-seven years in Congress, Rayburn said, he had served with three thousand men and women. He knew leadership when he saw it, and Lyndon Johnson was a leader.

In the left-hand pocket of Lyndon Johnson's suit jacket as he sat in his suite watching Rayburn was a folded sheet with the delegate count, and it showed that Kennedy was going to have enough votes to win on the first ballot—just barely enough, but enough. Despite those hard figures, Johnson was evidently unable to give up his hopes. Perhaps feeling that Rayburn's speech might sway a few delegates' votes, and at the very last minute start a drift away from Kennedy, he tried a last maneuver. As the nominating speeches for other candidates dragged on into the early evening, he phoned John Connally, reaching him on the telephone that had been set up next to the Texas delegation's standard on the convention floor, and told him to suggest to the convention's chairman, Governor LeRoy Collins of Florida, that, since it was growing late, the convention should recess after the speeches and postpone the voting to the next day. Connally made the request, but Collins quickly rejected it. At about 9:15, the voting began. By the State of Washington, Kennedy's count was 710; at West Virginia, it was 725; after Wisconsin, 748. Johnson had 405. The next state was Wyoming, Wyoming that Johnson could once have had so easily, but that he hadn't bothered to visit until it was too late. Teno Roncalio still only had ten of its fifteen votes for Kennedy; the other five were under the control of the delegation's chairman, Tracy McCracken, a "very, very conservative" publisher who was "a strong Johnson person."

Ted Kennedy was standing with the Wyoming delegation. That morning Bobby, counting delegates, had told him that the first ballot might come down to those five votes. Ted hadn't believed him, but he had gone to McCracken and asked him, "If it comes down to Wyoming, will you cast all fifteen votes for my brother?" McCracken said, "I can't believe that after all those states, it will come down to those five votes." But he said that if it did, he would cast the whole fifteen votes for Kennedy. And now it did. "Wyoming casts all fifteen votes for the next President of the United States," McCracken announced. Kennedy had 763. Sam Rayburn shut his eyes, and began to cry. He put his head down on a friend's chest, and tears ran down his cheeks. After a while, he sat up in his seat, squared his shoulders, lit a cigarette and took a long puff.

After several states, seeing that Kennedy had won, switched to him to be with the winner, Kennedy finished the first ballot with 806 votes. Johnson had 409. All the other possibilities—Symington, Stevenson, Humphrey and the various favorite sons—had a total of 306.

FOR A WESTERN STATE to have cast the decisive votes was a fitting denouement to the fight for the nomination, for it was western votes that had given

Kennedy victory, and denied the possibility of victory to Lyndon Johnson. His boasting during the Kennedy debate that he had passed a civil rights bill had cost him some southern support—at the last minute Mississippi had switched its 23 to Governor Ross Barnett and Florida its 29 to Senator Smathers as a protest—but he had still received 281 votes from the South. He had added to those the 54½ he had expected from border states Oklahoma and Kentucky, and 40 scattered tallies from other states. But out of the 172 possible votes from the western states, he had received only 22½. (Kennedy had received 119, other candidates a total of 30½.) Had he received more—had he held the West—would Kennedy have won on the first ballot, or would the convention have ended with a different outcome?

McCracken's announcement came at ten minutes before eleven. Johnson had changed into pajamas and bedroom slippers as he saw how the vote was going, and was sitting on a couch sipping a Scotch and soda, and that's how Lyndon Johnson was watching when he lost his chance at the prize he had yearned for all his life.

Summoning Reedy and Busby, he told them, "I want to send a telegram to the nominee and pledge my full support." They should draft one, bring it back for his approval, and then, to make absolutely sure Kennedy received it, make two copies, one to be sent by Western Union to the nominee himself, and one for Connally to deliver personally to the Kennedy people. They should do it as quickly as possible, he said. "I'm going to sleep. I don't want to talk to anybody."

4

The Back Stairs

AND THEN, the next morning, Thursday, July 14, at about eight o'clock, the telephone rang in the darkened bedroom of Lyndon Johnson's suite.

Its jangling woke Lady Bird, and when she picked it up, it was Senator Kennedy, asking to speak to Lyndon, who was still asleep in the other bed. Saying "Just a minute," she shook him awake, and when he picked up the phone, Kennedy said he would like to come down to talk to him, and it was agreed he would do so at about ten o'clock.

Jumping out of bed, Johnson went into the suite's living room and told a secretary to have it neatened up. And then, going back into the bedroom and sitting on the bed, he began making telephone calls. One was to John Connally, who was shaving. "Jack Kennedy just called me," Johnson said. "He wants to come down and see me. What do you think he wants?"

"I think he wants to offer you the vice presidency," Connally said—and Johnson knew Connally was right.

He called Jim Rowe. "We had lost and it was over," Rowe was to recall. "I was still asleep." "Kennedy is coming down here in a few minutes," Lyndon Johnson told him, "and I think he's going to offer me the vice presidency. What should I do?"

Still "half asleep," Rowe mumbled, "What do you want that for? You've got the power now."

The next words in his ear woke him up. "Power is where power goes," Lyndon Johnson said. "I'll still control the Senate." And "the way he said it, all of a sudden a bell rang in my head, as sleepy as I was: 'This guy is really thinking about it!' "

IN ALL THE REAMS of speculation that had been printed during the previous weeks and months about the eventual makeup of the Democratic ticket, there had been very little about the possibility that Lyndon Johnson would be in its second slot. Almost no one in the political world even suspected that the Majority Leader of the Senate would seriously consider trading that position for the vice presidency. During Johnson's six years in the job, the leadership had been a position of immense power, "the second most powerful man in Washington," and the vice presidency was a position of almost no power at all—virtually its only constitutional responsibility that of presiding over the Senate ("but shall have no vote" except in case of a tie; of so little power, in fact, that its first occupant, John Adams, called it "the most insignificant office that ever the invention of man contrived or his imagination conceived." Its powerlessness was a staple of Washington humor: everyone in the capital, it seemed, knew the joke about the unfortunate mother who had two sons who were never heard from again: one was lost at sea, and the other became Vice President; everyone quoted—actually misquoted—the remark that one Vice President, the Texan John Nance Garner, had made about the job: "It's not worth a bucket of warm spit." (Actually, as Johnson knew because Rayburn had told him, Cactus Jack had said that what the job was not worth was "a bucket of warm piss.") Any holder of the job became automatically a figure of ridicule in power-obsessed Washington, and, indeed, in the world beyond: the obscurity of the office had been the comic theme of a popular American musical of the 1930s, the Gershwins' *Of Thee I Sing,* which won a Pulitzer Prize for its depiction of a presidential campaign: in an early scene, none of a political party's leaders can recall the name of the party's vice presidential candidate—and neither can the presidential candidate, John P. Wintergreen. The name is Alexander Throttlebottom, and when he arrives on stage, it is to tell the leaders that he wants to resign from the ticket; the shame that would be brought on his mother should he win—and actually *be* the Vice President— might be too much for her to bear, he says. Although he is talked out of quitting and his ticket wins, he is still unrecognized; after the election the only way he can get into the White House is by joining a guided tour. And Johnson himself had repeatedly said, whenever the subject was raised by a reporter in 1958 and 1959, and, indeed, in the early months of 1960, that he would never consider leaving the Senate, and the leadership, for the vice presidency, in which his role in the Senate would be only to preside over it; "I wouldn't trade a vote for a gavel" was his invariable remark. The remark was delivered, what's more, with seeming conviction. When Hugh Sidey had persisted in probing Johnson about the possibility during a visit to the ranch in the spring of 1960, Johnson "got irritated and stormed . . . He declared that the vice presidency was a worthless job compared with being Senate leader, related the sad tenure of 'Cactus Jack' Garner . . . and said Speaker Sam Rayburn had told him to stay far away from it. If he could not be President, he would stay in the Senate, Johnson had told me with such rage and finality—his nose an inch from mine—that I chalked him off." But in fact Johnson had for some time been seriously thinking about making the trade—as Jim Rowe himself realized as soon as he became fully awake after talking to Johnson that morning.

Rowe should have been more aware of that possibility than almost anyone, he would recall years later with a wry smile, since he himself had been not only an eyewitness to, but the key go-between in, a previous Johnson effort to make that precise trade. Following the failure of Johnson's bid for the Democratic presidential nomination at the party's 1956 national convention, the Majority Leader had made a try for the vice presidential nomination, sending a message ("Tell him I want it") to presidential nominee Adlai Stevenson—and it had been Rowe whom Johnson had selected to carry the message. Stevenson, who was about to startle the convention by announcing that he would not suggest a vice presidential nominee but would let the delegates freely choose one, responded to the message noncommittally, and when Rayburn heard about Johnson's attempt, he reacted with such furious disapproval ("I saw that red [flush] coming up over his neck and head, and I just said to myself 'Uh-oh,' " Tommy Corcoran recalls) that Johnson hastily sent the embarrassed Rowe back to withdraw the demand.

Several considerations made him think about it seriously.

Some of them were merely tactical. No matter who won the presidency that November—Kennedy or the as-yet-unnamed GOP nominee—if Lyndon Johnson continued as Majority Leader he would still, within the world of the Senate, maintain much of the unprecedented power he had created for himself. Emboldened by the liberal success in 1958, Senate liberals had challenged him not only on the filibuster but by demanding that the Democratic conference or "caucus" take up a number of measures to end what Wisconsin's William Proxmire called his "one-man rule," including a resolution that the caucus, not the Leader, name the members of the Policy Committee. Liberal senators had delivered fiery speeches, and the Washington press corps had taken this threat to Johnson's rule seriously, but the definitive verdict on its seriousness had been the number of votes this key liberal proposal had actually received in the caucus: twelve. Johnson had received fifty-one. Richard Russell said that the liberals' "position reminded him of a bull who had charged a locomotive train. . . . That was the bravest bull I ever saw, but I can't say a lot for his judgment." No Majority Leader in history had ever accumulated anything remotely comparable to the powers Johnson had accumulated; that was why he was able to run the Senate as no other Leader had run it. So long as the Democrats controlled the Senate, and the southern Democrats who controlled the Democratic Caucus (and the chairmanships of virtually all of the most powerful Senate committees) supported him, his power within the institution itself would remain solid; the Senate leadership would still be immensely more powerful than the position he was trading it in for. Should Kennedy win, on the other hand, Johnson's position in relation to the world outside the Senate would be diminished both symbolically (he would no longer be the highest elected Democratic official in the country) and in a very concrete way as well: to the extent that there had been a Democratic legislative agenda during the past six years, he had had a major role, perhaps *the* major role, in setting it; now that agenda would be set by the White House: legislation—Democratic legislation—would be sent to the Senate for him to pass. "Although Johnson's power emanated from the Senate, he had made the Senate felt across the land," Evans and Novak wrote. "For the past half dozen years . . . he, more than any other single Democrat, spoke for his party." Now, if Kennedy won, that would no longer be the case. And if he proved insufficiently compliant with a Democratic President, that President could always move against him. An antagonistic President of his own party could make life difficult for any Majority Leader.

Other considerations, however, were much more than tactical—because they related not so much to a comparison between the Senate leadership and the vice presidency but to the great aim of his life: the job he had spent so many years scheming and sacrificing to obtain.

His chance to win his party's nomination in 1960 was gone now, and if in the general election Kennedy defeated the Republican nominee, and served his full two terms, he might not get another chance until 1968. There was of course a possibility—Kennedy might lose to the Republican—that he would get another chance at the nomination in 1964, but Kennedy, despite his loss, would be coming into that convention as the party's last standard-bearer, and would be even harder to beat than he had just been; it wasn't much of a possibility. Eight years would probably be how long Lyndon Johnson would have to wait. And in eight years Lyndon Johnson would be sixty—and that was an age that throughout his life had loomed before him with a grim, talismanic significance. All during his boyhood, he had heard relatives repeating a piece of family lore: that all Johnson men had weak hearts and died young. Then, while he was still in college and his father was barely fifty years old, Sam Ealy's heart had begun to fail, and he had died in 1937, twelve days after his sixtieth birthday. Two years later, one of his father's two younger brothers—Lyndon's uncle—had died suddenly of a massive heart attack, at the age of fifty-seven.* Lyndon, always conscious of his remarkable physical resemblance to his tall, big-eared, big-nosed father, was convinced—convinced, one of his secretaries says, "to the point of obsession"—that he had inherited the Johnson legacy. "I'm not gonna live to be but sixty," he would say. "My daddy died at sixty. My uncle . . ." With attempts to argue him out of this belief he had no patience; once, when Lady Bird was trying to reassure him that he would not die young, he looked at her scornfully and said flatly: "It's a lead-pipe cinch." And then, in 1955, at the age of forty-six, he had had his own massive heart attack. Now, in 1960, with the nomination lost, he felt he couldn't wait eight years for another chance to win it. When, following Kennedy's victory on Wednesday night, Reedy and Busby had been called into his suite, they had seen how depressed he was, and Reedy had tried to console him by pointing out that he would have another chance in eight years. There was a long pause before Lyndon Johnson's reply, and when it came it came in a very low voice. "Too long," he said. "Too long."

In addition, waiting—whether it was for eight years or only four—might

---

*The other uncle lived to seventy-one, but after suffering a heart attack in 1946, at the age of sixty-five, and a second in 1947, spent his last years as a near invalid.

not help, so long as while he waited he continued as Senate Leader. As long as he stayed in that job, in fact, waiting might make his chances worse instead of better. If Lyndon Johnson's age was one compelling consideration in his thinking, another was that "scent of magnolias." Hard as he had tried—supreme as had been the effort he had made in passing those two civil rights bills—to scrub off the southern taint, it still clung to him, almost as strong as ever. And the reaction to the 1960 bill had shown him how hard it would be to ever scrub it off completely as long as civil rights were an issue—and, of course, civil rights would always be an issue: *the* issue. With civil rights militancy mounting by the month, it was clear, as Johnson had often explained to aides and colleagues, that the issue was going to become steadily bigger. Whenever he tried again for the nomination, he would be caught again in the trap in which he had found himself during the last congressional session: the South, the southern supporters he could not afford to alienate in the Senate, would demand the weakening, or death, of any civil rights bill—a demand which, if he complied with it, would antagonize the North even more. Scrubbing off the scent was going to be difficult, if not impossible, so long as he remained in the Senate.

And of course if the scent of magnolias remained, it would taint him not only in the convention, but, should he by some long chance win the nomination, in the country as a whole. Should he win the nomination but not the presidential election which followed, he would be only a footnote in history, just another defeated presidential candidate. He wasn't interested in being a footnote. He was interested in being "LBJ." And was it possible for him to win a national presidential election with the scent still on him? Was it possible for *any* southerner to win? The last southerner to be elected to the presidency, Zachary Taylor, had been elected in 1848—more than a century before. Would it be possible for a southerner to be elected now? A southern candidate would have the eleven southern states behind him, of course, but with the states of the Northeast, and California, and the Republican Midwest so solidly against him, it was difficult to see how. Lyndon Johnson did not see how. "I don't think anybody from the South will be nominated in my lifetime; if so, I don't think he'll be elected," he had said flatly to one journalist. As long as he was Senate Leader—held responsible by civil rights militants, and segregationist militants, by northerners and southerners, and by the media, for the fate of civil rights in that institution— he would not be able to escape being viewed as a sectional candidate, from the wrong section. Lyndon Johnson's path to the presidency—that route he had mapped out for himself so long before—had always been narrow, twisting. He had navigated so many treacherous turns—had come much farther along the path than might have been thought possible. But he could go no farther. That route was closed.

But there was another route—and he had reconnoitered it.

Sometime early in 1960, he had had his staff look up the answer to a question: How many Vice Presidents of the United States had succeeded to the presidency? The answer was ten: John Adams, Thomas Jefferson, Martin Van Buren,

John Tyler, Millard Fillmore, Andrew Johnson, Chester A. Arthur, Theodore Roosevelt, Calvin Coolidge and Harry Truman. That route was well traveled.

Furthermore, for a Texan who had only one goal, that route had some obvious advantages over the Senate leadership. The vice presidency might be a meaningless position, a joke position, when looked at as it was generally looked at: in terms of itself. When looked at as a means of becoming President, it took on a different aspect. For one thing, a Vice President was a national figure. As a Leader raised to Senate power by the South, Johnson had little choice but to represent southern interests, to be a sectional leader. He would continue to be, as he had been, bound to the South (just as—as a senator from Texas—he was bound to Texas oil interests, which were also unpopular in the rest of the country). To realize his great dream, those southern and Texas ties needed to be cut.

As Vice President, those ties *would* be cut, to a considerable extent. He would no longer have to represent Texas: the national Administration of which he would be a part represented not a state but a country. He would no longer have to represent the South—the South would be only one section of the country. His positions on issues could be those of an official representing the whole country— positions that would help, rather than hurt, in a future bid for the presidency. In addition, a Vice President was the logical candidate to succeed the President when his four or eight years in office ended, the natural heir to the presidency.

And of course a Vice President might not have to wait that long. The alternative route had an abbreviated version—and Lyndon Johnson had reconnoitered that, too.

He had his staff look up a second figure: How many Presidents of the United States had died in office? The answer was seven. Since thirty-three men had been President,* that was seven out of thirty-three: The chances of a Vice President succeeding to the presidency due to a President's death were about one out of five. And when that question was asked about Presidents in modern times, the odds against such an occurrence got shorter—better. During the last hundred years before 1960, five Presidents had died in office—Abraham Lincoln in 1865, James Garfield in 1881, William McKinley in 1901, Warren Harding in 1923 and of course Franklin Roosevelt in 1945. During that time span, in other words, a President had died in office approximately every twenty years. There had been eighteen Presidents during that time, and five out of eighteen were odds of less than one out of four.

Furthermore, those odds seemed even shorter—much shorter—when compared with the odds of a Senate Majority Leader, or, indeed, any senator, being elected President. If John F. Kennedy made it to the White House straight from the Senate, he would be accomplishing something that only a single senator— Harding—had accomplished before him. And the odds were perhaps even more favorable when compared with the chances of Lyndon Johnson, the southerner,

---

*There had been thirty-four presidencies, but Grover Cleveland had served two separate terms.

being elected in 1964 or 1968 with the civil rights issue still burning in America. Johnson was to reiterate even during his retirement his belief that no southerner would be elected President in the foreseeable future, as when, in 1969, he told Texas' young lieutenant governor, Ben Barnes, the state's new rising political star, that the only way for a Texan to reach the presidency was through the vice presidency. He never referred to his analysis of the odds in public, of course, and so far as the author of this book can determine, he never referred to it in private during his vice presidency, except on the evening of its first day, the day on which he was inaugurated. Sitting beside him that evening on a bus carrying high-level guests to the Inaugural Ball, Clare Boothe Luce, the former congress-woman and the wife of *Time,* Inc. publisher Henry R. Luce, asked him why he had agreed to accept the vice presidential nomination, and he replied: "Clare, I looked it up: one out of every four Presidents has died in office. I'm a gamblin' man, darlin',' and this is the only chance I got." But during the period immediately following the convention, he explained his thinking several times. Robert M. Jackson, editor of the *Corpus Christi Caller-Times* and a longtime ally, was to tell his reporter James M. Rowe (not the James H. Rowe Jr. of Washington) that, encountering Johnson at the Corpus Christi Airport during this period, he had asked him, "Lyndon, why in the world did you accept the nomination?," and that Johnson had replied, "Well, six of them didn't have to get elected." When he was asked the same question by intimates in Texas, the precise figure, as often with Johnson, varied from telling to telling, but the theory remained the same: that because it was so hard for a Texan to be elected President, becoming Vice President was a Texan's best chance to reach the Oval Office. "Well," he replied when Joe Kilgore asked the question, "six of them [Vice Presidents] didn't have to be elected [in order to become President]." "You know, seven of them got to be President without ever *being* elected," he told Ed Clark.

AND, OF COURSE, if the odds paid off, it might not require waiting eight years for them to do so.

The possibility that fate might intervene was vivid in the mind of anyone who had been in Washington on April 12, 1945, and especially vivid to members of Sam Rayburn's basement "Board of Education" in the Capitol, where Harry Truman had often sat having a late-afternoon drink—and where he had been having a drink when, that day, the summons had come from the White House that had been Franklin Roosevelt's. Lyndon Johnson hadn't been in that room when the summons came, but he arrived there a few minutes later. He had known Truman for years as a senator, and then Harry had been plucked from the Senate to be Vice President—and then, less than four months after he had been sworn in, he was President.

The possibility had been kept vivid in Washington by what had happened during the presidency of Truman's successor. Three times in twenty-six months, Dwight Eisenhower had been hospitalized with serious illnesses (in 1955, a heart attack; in 1956, an attack of ileitis, an abdominal obstruction that required sur-gery; in 1957, a stroke), and each time the capital seethed with rumors that the President might die—or that he *had* died and that Richard Nixon would become President, or, particularly in the case of the stroke, that Eisenhower might be dis-abled, and that Nixon would, while remaining Vice President, assume presiden-tial duties and powers. If John Adams had once called the vice presidency "the most insignificant office," he had also, on another occasion, made a statement that cast the position in a different light. "I am Vice President," Adams had said. "In this I am nothing, but I may be everything." All his life, Lyndon Johnson had aimed for a single goal. The path he had originally chosen, he now realized, might be closed to him by the magnolia taint. But there might be another path. As long as he had felt he had a good chance to win the presidential nomination—as he *had* felt, until the West Virginia primary—this alternative route had remained only a dim possibility, and consideration of it had stayed on a back burner; it was winning that nomination that he was focused on. But West Virginia had wakened him to reality. That primary had been held on May 10. Thereafter, even while he was continuing to try to obtain the presidential nomination by deadlocking the convention, he was careful not to close the door to that alternative route. While before the primary, he had been so definitive about never accepting the vice pres-idential nomination—angrily dismissing reporters' questions on the subject—when, shortly after West Virginia, the question came up at a press conference, he was suddenly not so definitive. That's a "very 'iffy' question," he said, and then added: "When and if my country wants me to serve her, I will give it every con-sideration."

Private as well as public signals were soon being sent out. Ending a conver-sation with Ted Sorensen in June, Bobby Baker suddenly said, "Maybe the ticket will turn out to be Kennedy and Johnson."

"I think that would be wonderful, but I doubt very much that the second man on that ticket would agree to it," Sorensen said.

"Don't be too sure," Bobby Baker said, and walked away.

And with men whose voices would carry weight in discussions about the vice presidency, Johnson made very sure indeed that the door was not closed, even if keeping it open required him, on one occasion, to do what he almost never did—disagree, to his face, with Sam Rayburn.

The disagreement occurred in late June while he and Rayburn were meeting with Governor Lawrence and the powerful Democratic fund-raiser and Kennedy supporter, contractor Matt McCloskey. To McCloskey's suggestion that "It would make a great team if you would take the second spot," Rayburn exploded, "We didn't come down here to talk about the second spot, we came here to talk about the first spot," but Johnson said, "Now, wait a minute, Sam, I don't want these boys to go out of here and not know where I stand. First of all, I am a Democrat, and I am going to do anything my party wants me to do." (So firm was that statement that Lawrence would mention it to Kennedy at the convention, saying that because of it, he, Lawrence, "guaranteed" that Johnson would take the job if it was offered.)

Reiterating a week before he left for Los Angeles the phrase that had caught his fancy, Johnson responded to a reporter's query about the vice presidency by saying, "Well, that is a very iffy question, and I wouldn't want to have it even thought that I would refuse to serve my country in any capacity, from running the elevator to the top job, if I felt that my services were needed." Even at the press conference at which he at last formally announced his presidential candidacy, he was sending the signal. When a reporter offered him, as the *New York Times* put it, "an opportunity to rule himself out as a possible nominee for Vice President," he "passed [it] up," saying, "I have been prepared throughout my adult life to serve my country in any capacity where my country thought my services were essential."

These signals were overlooked, largely because, before West Virginia, he had been saying for months—often, and in seemingly unequivocal terms—that he would never, under any conditions, accept the vice presidency, and because prominent figures in the Kennedy campaign—including the most prominent figure—had been saying for months that Johnson would never be offered the vice presidency. Ken O'Donnell, the campaign's liaison with the country's top union officials, was to write that "The labor people had warned me repeatedly that they did not want Johnson on the Kennedy ticket. I had promised them that there was no chance of such a choice." These reassurances had continued right into the convention; when some liberal delegates, wavering up to the last minute between Kennedy and Adlai Stevenson, had said they were leaning to Stevenson because they feared there was a chance—no matter how slim—that Kennedy might select Johnson, O'Donnell gave them "the same assurance." And this assurance came right from the top; O'Donnell says that he had made his promise "with [Jack] Kennedy's knowledge." O'Donnell had not the slightest reason to doubt that the promise would be honored. During the months prior to the convention, he had flown thousands of miles with Jack Kennedy, he was to recall, "and once in a while we'd discuss the vice presidency and he never mentioned Lyndon Johnson's name." Some black delegates and civil rights leaders had the same concern as the "labor people," and to Joseph Rauh, Jack Kennedy made the same promise—not through intermediaries but in person. A month before the convention, when Rauh told Kennedy that it was important to him that "It not be Johnson," Kennedy replied, "It will not be Johnson." "Kennedy promised me it would be—and this is a direct quote—'Humphrey or another midwestern liberal,' " Rauh says. And in the last days before the balloting that assurance was repeated to other liberals. The assurances were repeated also by the candidate's brother. Robert Kennedy "pledged to a number of those working with him—including Rauh, who was trying to deliver the District of Columbia [delegation]—that Johnson would not be on the ticket," the *Washington Post* was to report. After Humphrey removed himself from contention by refusing to endorse Kennedy, the candidates most often mentioned for the ticket's vice presidential slot were

Stuart Symington, Governor Orville L. Freeman of Minnesota and Senator Henry M. (Scoop) Jackson of Washington. "The one name never mentioned was Lyndon Johnson," Arthur Schlesinger states. "Quite the contrary: the Kennedy people told everybody as categorically as possible that he was not in the picture." This was the stance not only in public but behind closed doors. "There was *never* any talk in the office that Mr. Johnson was to be the running mate," Evelyn Lincoln was to recount.

But now, after Kennedy called, Johnson said to Rowe, "Power is where power goes," and Rowe knew "He was really thinking about it."

HE HAD TWO HOURS before Kennedy came down to his suite at ten o'clock, two hours not to decide what he was going to do, because he knew what he was going to do—but to check to see if there was anything he had overlooked. This was no time for the second string, or for anyone who, like Reedy, was intelligent but sometimes flinched from looking harsh realities in the face, for the realities now were very harsh, the choice very tough. Three men were called to the Johnson suite: "the man who knew where all the bodies were buried"; the man who had written the Truman memo; and the man who was the most pragmatic of all his aides—not his confidant, for Lyndon Johnson had no confidant, but the man who would "do *anything* for him," and who was also "the only man who was tough enough to handle Bobby Kennedy." And when Bobby Baker, Jim Rowe and John Connally had arrived, Johnson told them to lay out the reasons why he should or shouldn't accept the vice presidency, should Kennedy offer it. He told Connally to start off, but the three men found themselves in agreement on all the key points, pro and con.

"We were not trying to persuade him of the virtues and glories of the vice presidency," Connally was to recall. "We were looking at it more from a negative point of view: where does your risk lie?" And he and Rowe both concluded that, in Connally's words, "Your risk lies in declining to accept it."

Johnson had a lot to lose by not accepting, they agreed. If he didn't accept, Kennedy would probably lose the election. "He'll never beat Nixon in Texas unless you're on the ticket," Connally said. "Texas was discussed at considerable length." Without Johnson on the ticket, in fact, Kennedy might not, against Nixon, a conservative and heir to Eisenhower, be able to win back the Solid South Eisenhower had broken so decisively. And if Kennedy lost the election, Johnson would be blamed for the loss by northern liberals who already, in Baker's phrase, "hate your guts"—they already felt he was "not a fully committed Democrat," Baker said; Johnson's refusal to join the ticket would confirm them in that belief. And, the three men agreed, he would be blamed by Kennedy; "it could make Kennedy angry and bitter," Baker recalls saying. Connally recalls telling Johnson that if Kennedy lost, "you're going to be blamed—because they'll try to ensure that you'll be blamed. And [therefore] you'll have a large segment of the party against you." If Johnson ever wanted to try for the nomination again, that would make it even harder than it otherwise would be. And if he didn't accept and Kennedy won, the situation might be even worse. As Baker recalls saying, "A strong Democratic President will send his own programs up from the White House," would create a legislative agenda that the Majority Leader would have no choice but to follow. "He would have to carry that program unless he wanted to have an open break with the President," Connally explains. Even if he carried it, moreover, an "angry and bitter" President could make life difficult for a Senate Leader; if he didn't accept, and Kennedy won, Lyndon Johnson would still be Leader, but the leadership might not be nearly as desirable a job to have. And, Connally recalls, "I even expressed the thought that he might not *be* Majority Leader. The Kennedys play for keeps. I said, 'You assume that you're still going to be Majority Leader, but why do you assume that? The Kennedys play for keeps. Bobby plays for keeps. They might say: We won without him. What the hell do we need him for? We don't need him.' I told him, 'I'd hate to see you try to hold on to it [the leadership] in the face of opposition from the President.' "

By accepting, they felt, Johnson ran far less risk. In fact, Baker said, "I don't think you have a thing in the world to lose by running with Kennedy." Connally told Johnson that the arguments on that side—that Johnson had no choice but to accept—were overwhelming. For one thing, Kennedy might lose. There were few downsides to *that*. "Suppose you take it, and he's defeated—you'll still be Senator. And you'll still be Majority Leader." If Kennedy lost, "you can't really be hurt."

And what if he took it, and Kennedy won? There were definitely downsides to that, as Connally pointed out: "You're totally at his command. You almost can't leave town without his permission. You're going to have to listen more than you've ever done." But, the three advisers said, there might be upsides, too, even if these could only be touched upon delicately, in oblique phrases. One had to do with Sam Rayburn. Even if Kennedy won, and Johnson was only his Vice President, "You'll still have the Speaker," is how Connally remembers putting it. He meant that as long as Johnson had Rayburn on his side, he would have power behind him. "No one thought he could be forced out as Speaker, or that the President could do much trying to go around him in the House," he would remember years later. As long as a Vice President had Sam Rayburn behind him, the Vice President couldn't be ignored. (Connally, tough though he was, was careful to look around before he said even "You'll still have the Speaker"—to make sure that the Speaker hadn't somehow entered the room. "We didn't [want to] make that argument when the Speaker was there, because we would be presuming," he explains.)

And then there was another possible upside—one that was in the minds of all three advisers even though, pragmatic and tough though they were, they mentioned it only in another oblique phrase, in part because, perhaps, they were not able to think about it other than obliquely, for thinking about another man's mortality often leads to thoughts of one's own mortality, and these are thoughts difficult to confront directly.

The phrase was *"a heartbeat away."* "I felt—you're a heartbeat away from the presidency," John Connally says. Asked if he had actually used even that direct a phrase during the conference that morning, he says he can't remember, but Bobby Baker, brasher—and younger—says that *he* used it; he recalls reminding "Mr. Leader" that as Vice President, he would be "one heartbeat away from the presidency." Rowe couldn't bring himself to say those words. He stayed mostly silent during the conference, and after Johnson had dismissed them, saying Kennedy would be arriving in a few minutes, and Rowe had returned to his own room, he telephoned Johnson, and said only, "On balance, I would take it. I want to see you President one day." Asked by the author almost a quarter of a century later for his reasons, he listed many, in his careful, lawyerly manner. Then there was a pause, quite a long one.

"And that one heartbeat . . . ," Jim Rowe said.

DURING THE CONFERENCE with the three men, Johnson was "quiet, sober, reflective—obviously analyzing all of it," Connally was to recall. He didn't say much. But what he did say gave them a clue as to what his thinking was. Near the end of the discussion, after he had been, in Baker's word, "passive" for a long time, he said, perhaps thinking of the intense dislike of many Texans for the Kennedys, "Well, I'll probably have some trouble with my Texas friends if I decide to run." And when Connally had finished his argument that Johnson had no choice but to accept the vice presidency, Johnson said quietly, "Well, I don't disagree with that." And during the conference there was a call from Texas congressman Homer Thornberry, who was phoning to offer condolences for losing the presidential nomination. When Johnson told him that there might be a vice presidential offer, and Thornberry blurted out, "Oh, you can't do that," Johnson said, "Well, here's my problem," and listed all the reasons why he had no choice but to accept, listed them so persuasively that Thornberry changed his thinking, and, a few minutes later, telephoned back to tell him, "I was wrong": that if the nomination was offered, he should accept. Lyndon Johnson wasn't merely thinking about it. He wanted it.

ONE GREAT OBSTACLE stood in his way. John Nance Garner had been Sam Rayburn's friend, his mentor in many ways, and Rayburn had seen what happened after Cactus Jack—a mighty figure on Capitol Hill, with the power he wielded as Speaker of the House spilling over to the other side of the Capitol ("No man was more influential in the Senate than Garner," one observer noted)—accepted the vice presidential nomination from Franklin Roosevelt in 1932; had seen how the President increasingly ignored his advice to end what that Texas conservative came to call, privately at first but only at first, "This New Deal spending orgy." Garner came to regard Roosevelt as a power-hungry "dictator," Roosevelt saw him as an ignorant reactionary, and after Garner split with him for good over Roosevelt's attempt to pack the Supreme Court (it was he whom the Senate chose to deliver the news—"Cap'n, you are beat"—to the President), Garner's expectations of succeeding the President were over, as was his career. When Roosevelt sought a third term, he enlisted in a "Stop Roosevelt" movement, and on Roosevelt's third inaugural day, in 1941, Garner was back in the little Texas town of Uvalde, where he was to live out the rest of a long life as a pecan farmer. "I saw Jack Garner agree to run twice with Roosevelt . . . and go back to Texas a bitter man for life," Rayburn told a friend. Loving Lyndon Johnson as the son he never had, Mr. Sam was firmly opposed to him even considering the vice presidential nomination. The night before he left for Los Angeles, the Speaker told his friends Gene and Ann Worley, "The first thing I'm going to do when I get off that airplane tomorrow is to announce to the world that Lyndon Johnson ain't interested in second spot on a ticket with Kennedy." And after Wyoming's votes had ended Lyndon's dream, and Rayburn had cried, he had squared his shoulders and sat up—and then had picked up the telephone in the Texas delegation's section and called Johnson, because, as one observer put it, "He had had a premonition." "They are going to try to get you to go on the ticket," he said. "You mustn't do it. It would be a terrible thing to do. Turn it down." *Power is where power goes.* Whatever the equation of power that Lyndon Johnson was using as the basis for his calculations, Sam Rayburn was a major factor in it. Lyndon Johnson couldn't defy him. Whether he wanted the vice presidential nomination or not, he couldn't take it if Rayburn didn't want him to. So after his conference with Connally, Rowe and Baker had ended, he telephoned Earle Clements, with whom Rayburn was comfortable, and asked him to come to the suite, and when he arrived, told him about the vice presidential offer he expected—told him in such a way that, Clements was to say, it was "obvious he wants it." And when Clements advised him to accept, Johnson said, "Then I wish you'd go down and convince Rayburn. He's right down the hall."

THE DRAMA THAT WAS to consume the rest of the day—Thursday, July 14, 1960—would play out on two sets in Los Angeles' Biltmore Hotel.

One was on the hotel's ninth floor. It consisted of a large three-room suite in one corner of the floor, together with a series of individual standard hotel bedrooms that stretched along a rather dimly lit corridor. All the inner-connecting doors had been unlocked so that the suite and bedrooms comprised a single unit. During the hectic days earlier that week, this "Kennedy suite" had become known by the number on the door of the big corner suite: 9333. The candidate himself slept every night in a hideaway apartment his father had rented for him, but during the day 9333 was his headquarters.

The other set, two floors below and in the corresponding corner and corridor, also with a large suite and adjoining bedrooms stretching down the corridor, was 7333, the Johnson suite. (Johnson and Lady Bird slept there during the convention, as did their daughters.) John Connally was in the first of the bedrooms, 7331, Walter Jenkins in 7330, and the rest of the staff had bedrooms further down the hall. Separating the two sets was the eighth floor, on which Robert Kennedy had a suite, 8315. Governer Lawrence had the big suite on the tenth floor, Stuart Symington on the sixth. Rayburn's suite was on the seventh floor with Johnson's, but at the opposite end of the corridor.

The elevator in this section of the hotel was located near the far end of the line of bedrooms at the end of the corridor furthest from the corner suite. That morning what one reporter referred to as the "pushy, sweaty mass" of the press— newspaper and magazine reporters and photographers, television cameras, cam- eramen and correspondents—was clustered around the elevator's doors. Kennedy had arrived at his suite very early, before any reporters had arrived, and it was assumed he was still at his apartment and would come up in the elevator, and might emerge and provide them with a clue as to the identity of the vice presi- dential nominee.

There was another connection between the two sets, however: a back stair- case almost directly across from the 9333 door in the floor's corner, not a narrow back stairway but a broad one, with a broad open landing on each floor, as dimly lit as the corridors. If someone stepped out of the 9333 door of the Kennedy suite and walked almost straight across the hall and down the stairs, he had a good chance of avoiding the press, and that was what Jack Kennedy did, successfully, at about 10:15 that morning. Descending down the two flights of stairs, he knocked on the door of 7333.

Johnson opened it. The corridor outside was empty. Reporters and photog- raphers had been stationed outside the rooms of the men considered likely vice presidential nominees, but Johnson was not one of them. Johnson led Kennedy into the living room, and they sat down on a couch, each at an end, half turned to face each other, two very tough, very smart men. Someone closed the door to the living room.

Johnson congratulated Kennedy on winning the nomination, and then the talk turned to Kennedy's running mate. When Kennedy asked Johnson, as Kennedy was to recall it, "if he were available for the vice presidency," Johnson "told me that he was. He then suggested that I discuss the matter with various party leaders." Johnson's recollection of his response was that he would consider the offer, but that before he could give an answer, "there are a couple of problems that have got to be worked out." The main one was that he couldn't even think of taking the job unless Sam Rayburn agreed, and that Rayburn was "dead set" against it. "You'll have to get him to withdraw his objection." Also, he said, "a lot of your own people are going to be madder than hell. . . . You'll have to straighten them out." Kennedy said he had already checked with some of the northern bosses—Lawrence and De Sapio were mentioned—and that they approved. Johnson said Kennedy should talk to labor and liberal leaders— "people like" Walter Reuther and Soapy Williams. He said Kennedy had said he would do that, and then had turned to the Rayburn situation. He asked Johnson, as Johnson was to recall, if Rayburn had anything against him personally, and whether Johnson would mind if he himself—Kennedy—tried to persuade the Speaker to change his mind. Johnson said he wouldn't. Kennedy said he would call back in a couple of hours, and left, "with quick nods and a smile" to Connally and Baker and Walter Jenkins, who had come into the suite.

Whatever had been said between Kennedy and Johnson, it had been said in terms vague enough so that their purport could be denied. The talk had taken about half an hour, and by the time Kennedy left there was a reporter, Marvin Miles of the *Los Angeles Times,* outside the door. "We talked mostly about what happened last night," Kennedy told him. When Miles asked him if the vice presidency had been discussed, Kennedy said, "Nothing specific," before heading back up the two flights of stairs to his suite, and Johnson was similarly noncommittal. Whatever had been said, however, it was said clearly enough so that both men understood it the same way. Calling Baker, Connally and Jenkins into the living room—he couldn't locate Rowe—Johnson told them, "You were right. He offered me the vice presidency." ("He said he had declined, but Kennedy had insisted," Jenkins recalls.) Walking back up the stairs to his suite on the ninth floor, Kennedy was joined a few minutes later by a group of northern bosses, and informed them, as Ken O'Donnell was to put it, "that he had just talked to Lyndon, who wanted a little time to think it over, but it looked as though Johnson would take it."

AS WORD OF KENNEDY'S VISIT SPREAD, emotions boiled over among Johnson supporters who hated the Kennedys. Oklahoma's burly senator Robert Kerr came "barreling into" the Johnson suite, livid with rage, shouting at Johnson, Lady Bird and Baker, "Get me my .38, I'm gonna kill every damn one of you. I can't believe that my three best friends would betray me." Johnson motioned Baker to take Kerr into the bathroom and calm him down, but as soon as the bathroom door closed behind them, Kerr slapped Baker across the face so hard that "It sounded like a dynamite cap exploding in my head! I literally saw stars. My ears rang. 'Bobby, you betrayed me! You betrayed me!' " Baker explained the reasoning ("Even if Kennedy-Johnson loses, LBJ gets better known nationally. . . . If he's elected vice president, he'll be an excellent conduit between the White House and the Hill . . ."), and Kerr calmed down, apologized to Baker and, leaving the bathroom, hugged the Johnsons.

Emotions were boiling over upstairs, too. Bobby Kennedy was later to state that his brother's offer to Lyndon Johnson had been strictly *pro forma,* a courtesy to a powerful member of the party, and that he had neither expected him to accept the offer nor wanted him to. "The idea that he'd go down to offer him the nomination in hopes that he'd take the nomination is not true. . . . *He never dreamt that there was a chance in the world that he would accept it.*" Bobby said that when Jack returned from Johnson's suite, he said, " 'You just won't believe it.' I said, 'What?' And he said, 'He wants it,' and I said, 'Oh, my God!' He said, 'Now what do we do?' " And, Bobby said, "The only reaction that the President [Jack Kennedy] had after talking to Lyndon Johnson was just surprise and then concern that he would take it. He never dreamt—he never considered that he would take it. After that, there was a good deal of time spent in trying to get him off the ticket."

Bobby's statement is buttressed by a remark that Jack Kennedy made a few days later to a friend, the syndicated columnist Charles Bartlett, a statement made off the record and not put in print by Bartlett until 1964. According to Bartlett, Kennedy told him that his offer to Johnson had been merely a "gesture"—and not much of a gesture, hardly an offer at all. "I just held it out like this," he said, holding his hand two or three inches from his pocket, "and he grabbed at it." The Kennedys, Bartlett wrote, were "shocked" when Johnson "seized the offer and held fast to it."

Those accounts are given weight by many historians because of Robert Kennedy's repeated, and emphatic, reiterations of them, and because of the acceptance of those reiterations as accurate, and the restatement of them in books and articles by Arthur Schlesinger, whose writings on John and Robert Kennedy have for decades set the template for the image of the two brothers in history. In 1984, Schlesinger would still be writing, "As Robert Kennedy's oral history makes clear, the offer of the vice-presidential nomination was *pro forma;* the Kennedys never dreamed Johnson would accept." Those accounts are not, however, supported by a number of actions that John F. Kennedy actually took that day.

The first had occurred before his visit to Johnson's suite—had occurred first thing that morning, at about 6:30 a.m. Telephoning Bobby in Suite 8315, he asked him to find out the number of electoral votes that could be won, in the November election, in the northern industrial states "plus Texas." A few minutes later, Ken O'Donnell and Kennedy press secretary Pierre Salinger were summoned to 8315. Bobby was in the bathtub, but called out to them through the door, "How many electoral votes are we going to get if we capture the East, Northeast, and the solid South?"

The solid South, Salinger realized, included Texas. "Are you talking about nominating Lyndon Johnson?" Salinger asked in astonishment. "You're not going to do that!"

"Yes, we are," Bobby Kennedy said. Jack would be going down to Lyndon's suite at ten o'clock to make the offer. "Thereupon," Salinger says, "there ensued a violent argument between Kenny and I, and Bobby." Bobby's response was to point out that Johnson had great strength in the South.

The second action that Jack Kennedy took occurred after his trip down to Johnson on the seventh floor—immediately upon his return to his own ninth-floor suite. Before going down to see Johnson, Kennedy had telephoned Governor Lawrence—his quarters were on the tenth floor—to remind him of his "guarantee" that if the vice presidential nomination was offered to Johnson, he would accept it, and Lawrence, anxious to have Johnson on the ticket because he felt southern electoral votes were necessary for victory, had not only come down the flight of back stairs to reaffirm his guarantee in person, but had also brought the witness to Johnson's words—Matt McCloskey—with him. Kennedy had taken them into 9333's bathroom for privacy, and then had said, as McCloskey recalls it, "I don't want to go down and ask that guy [if he won't accept the offer]. Are you sure now?" Lawrence and McCloskey had reassured him—had, in fact, in McCloskey's words, "authorized him to say to Johnson that . . . the two of us had assured him that this was what Johnson had said." Now, having met with Johnson, Kennedy returned to 9333, moments before Lawrence and McCloskey came back in, to be followed shortly by Governors DiSalle and Ribicoff and Mayors Daley and Wagner, along with Connecticut's Bailey and Tammany's De Sapio and Chicago's Jake Arvey—the "old pros from the North," as one reporter put it. When Jack told the group that "it looked as though Johnson would take it," Lawrence, with a happy grin on his weathered old Irish face, reached out and grasped Kennedy's hand in congratulation, to be met with a matching smile from the young candidate. Suddenly, in O'Donnell's words, "all of them"—all the northern bosses who could count, and who had not previously been able to count enough electoral votes for Kennedy to win—"all of them milling around Jack Kennedy [were] congratulating him for offering the vice presidency to Johnson." Lawrence was telling him that "Johnson has the strength where you need it most."

"I could have belted him [Lawrence]," O'Donnell was to recall. He had become very emotional. When Bobby had shouted out the news from his bathtub, "I was so furious I could hardly talk. I thought of the promises we had made to the labor leaders and the civil rights groups, the assurances we had given that Johnson would not be on the ticket. . . . I felt that we had been double-crossed." Telling Bobby, "Now Nixon can say Kennedy is just another phony politician who will do anything to get elected," he had demanded a chance to talk to Jack Kennedy himself, and Bobby had brought him upstairs so that he could do so. Seeing the expression on O'Donnell's face, Jack took him into the bathroom and closed the door behind them—and attempts to maintain that Kennedy's offer was *pro forma,* that he really didn't want Johnson, have to take into account O'Donnell's story of what happened when O'Donnell began to argue against the choice of Johnson.

"Wait a minute," Kennedy said. "I've offered it to him, but he hasn't accepted it yet and maybe he won't." But, Kennedy said, "if he does accept it, let's get one thing clear." He then pulled out all the arguments that might work with O'Donnell's labor and liberal clientele, none of the arguments terribly convincing (one was: "I won't be able to live with Lyndon Johnson as the Leader. . . . Did it occur to you that if Lyndon becomes the Vice President, I'll

have Mike Mansfield as the Leader . . . somebody I can trust and depend on";
another that the offer had been made to keep Johnson—and Rayburn—friendly,
so that liberal-labor legislation could be passed in that upcoming rump session of
Congress; "Lyndon Johnson we don't worry about, but Sam Rayburn is a tough
cookie, and well liked and respected"). One other argument would be, in retrospect, terribly poignant: it didn't matter who was Vice President, Jack Kennedy
said. "I'm forty-three years old, and I'm the healthiest candidate for President in
the United States. You've traveled with me enough to know that I'm not going to
die in office. So the vice presidency doesn't mean anything." But whether
O'Donnell's clients were persuaded by those arguments or not, Jack Kennedy
said, and whether O'Donnell himself was persuaded by them or not, that was the
way it was going to be. "You get your tail over and get your labor friends," he
said. "You get them and tell them this is the way it has got to be."

"He wanted no back talk," O'Donnell recalls. Kennedy said Johnson had
surprised him by being receptive, but the important thing was to get him on the
ticket. "He said getting Johnson on the ticket was worth it and I was to go to my
clientele and make them see it."

There followed summonses to the top Kennedy staff people such as
Lawrence F. O'Brien, his National Campaign Director, to come to the ninth floor,
and when they arrived, they learned that, as O'Brien puts it, "Jack Kennedy had
made a decision that he'd like to have Lyndon Johnson as his running mate." For
a moment, O'Brien recalls, "I was stunned . . . it was out of the blue"; he had
never, he said, given "any serious thought" to the possibility that Kennedy would
offer, or that Johnson would accept, the vice presidential nomination ("If I ever
really gave more than a fleeting thought to Lyndon Johnson, it would be 'He's the
Majority Leader. He isn't going to sacrifice what he has to be on this ticket' ").
But the moment he began giving it serious thought, O'Brien, a keen political
strategist—and one who knew the importance of counting—understood Jack
Kennedy's logic. The night before—and for so many months before that, ever
since 1958, in fact—the Kennedy camp had been counting convention delegate
votes, the votes necessary to win the nomination. As soon as the nomination was
won, Kennedy had begun counting the Electoral College votes necessary to win
the real prize, the presidency—and even a quick, preliminary look at those votes
showed that without Texas' twenty-four votes, and at least a few of the other
southern votes, in his column, Jack Kennedy stood almost no chance at all of
defeating Richard Nixon or any other Republican candidate. Extended analysis
was not required, O'Brien was to explain. Jack Kennedy hadn't needed input
from others; he had selected Lyndon Johnson because "he was perhaps the first
to focus on 'Are you going to be a footnote in history as a nominee for the presidency or are you indeed going to achieve election?' " The presence of Lyndon
Johnson on the ticket was the single best way—by far—of assuring that the name
"Kennedy" would not appear in history books only in small type at the bottom of
a page. "With him [Johnson], you had the South and the Southwest. . . . It was a

stroke of genius." And O'Brien understood also, from Jack Kennedy's mouth, that the decision was firm. His trip to Kennedy's suite "was just an unbelievable experience," O'Brien recalls. "When I got the call that morning," he had felt that "obviously . . . the subject [was going to be] now let's go over the list [of possible vice presidential candidates] and let's get a consensus." But "there would be no list. It would be Lyndon Johnson." Orders were given on the assumption that Johnson would accept. "People fanned out and there were tasks to do. You had to decide who was going to place him in nomination, who was going to second the nomination."

The offer, O'Brien was to say, had been couched in terms of "a feeler" because if Kennedy had made a formal offer, "and it was turned down, that could be adverse to his campaign." But the offer had been understood. "Did Kennedy come back from that meeting with the notion that Johnson would accept it?" O'Brien was asked. "That he would be thinking about it," O'Brien replied.

In contrast to Bobby Kennedy's account that Jack's offer had been *pro forma,* that he had not wanted Johnson to accept and had hoped he wouldn't, and that Jack Kennedy had vacillated for some hours over whether or not to withdraw the offer, O'Brien says the opposite was true. Asked whether "the offer was intended as one that Johnson would decline," O'Brien replied, "Oh, no." On the contrary, he said, the ninth floor was worried because "we were not at all sure that he would accept. . . . The word would come back, 'Well, no, he's not going to take it,' and then, 'Well, he'll think about it some more.' This sort of thing just went on and on." But through it all, O'Brien says, one thing did not change: Jack Kennedy's decision. "Jack Kennedy had made up his mind this was absolutely the right thing to do, and there were no alternatives."

And perhaps most definitively, the story that Kennedy's offer to Johnson was only *pro forma* and that Kennedy had not wanted it to be accepted is made less credible by what Kennedy did that morning to solve the problem of Sam Rayburn. Johnson had said he couldn't even think of accepting the offer unless Rayburn agreed—so Kennedy went down the back stairs again, this time to Rayburn's suite to try to persuade him to agree.

Johnson himself had begun the persuasion process even before Kennedy came down and made the offer, sending emissaries to soften Mr. Sam's opposition: not just Clements but Homer Thornberry and Wright Patman. "Sam was in the bathroom in his shorts, and he was shaving," Patman was to recall. "He was blistering mad about Lyndon's even considering the vice presidency."

As soon as Kennedy left him, Johnson sent another emissary, Tommy Corcoran, and asked Clements to go back again. Corcoran knew how important his mission was: "Johnson was going to do whatever Mr. Rayburn told him to do," he was to say. But neither he nor Clements had any luck with the Speaker. "Rayburn was adamant about it," Clements was to confess. "I wouldn't say I made any headway with him." As Corcoran was walking away from Rayburn's suite, however, he encountered in the corridor a member of Rayburn's House team, Majority Whip Hale Boggs of Louisiana, a state which had voted for Eisenhower in 1956. Boggs told Corcoran that Johnson's presence on the ticket would guarantee that Louisiana wouldn't vote Republican again. Corcoran had him go in and tell that to Rayburn—and Boggs pulled out another argument, one that evidently had some impact on the Speaker. Rayburn's distrust of Richard Nixon was legendary in Washington; Boggs told him that without Johnson and the South in the Democratic column, Nixon would win the presidency. "I knew that this was the one thing he didn't want to happen," Boggs was to recall. And Johnson himself telephoned Rayburn. Mr. Sam "reiterated strongly that he felt it would be a mistake for me to take it," he was to recount. The Speaker added to his other objections (among them: "He said I could do a better job for the Democratic Party and the country as Majority Leader") one that was very personal—and poignant— coming from a childless man who for years had been able to work closely every day with a young man who said he looked on him as a father: "He said he would not be happy without me on the Hill." Johnson emphasized how much the nomination meant to him, however, and when he asked Rayburn to hear Kennedy out if he telephoned, Rayburn said he would. "I think Jack will be calling you soon," Johnson said.

"John, I've got to think a little bit," Rayburn said to his aide John Holton, and Holton gave him the key to his room, and "twenty, thirty minutes later" Rayburn emerged, and told Holton that if Kennedy met certain conditions, he would advise Johnson to accept. And when Kennedy did call, and came down to see Mr. Rayburn, Rayburn gave his conditions, and Kennedy agreed to them. Within a few weeks—the interview transcript is dated "Summer, 1960"—Rayburn gave another assistant, D. B. Hardeman, his account of what had happened when Jack Kennedy came down to see him.

> I told him, "I'm dead set against this, but I've thought it over, and I'm going to tell you several things: if you tell me that you have to have Lyndon on the ticket in order to win the election, and if you tell me that you'll go before the world and tell the world that Lyndon is your choice and that you insist on his being the nominee, and if you'll make every possible use of him in the National Security Council and every other way to keep him busy and keep him happy, then the objections that I have had I'm willing to withdraw."
> Kennedy said to me, "I tell you all those things."

Kennedy walked out of Rayburn's suite. "He was positively exuberant," says Boggs, who saw him emerge. Returning to his suite upstairs, he told O'Brien and other aides to set the wheels in motion for Johnson's nomination; O'Brien, for example, was to inform the campaign's various state coordinators that Kennedy had decided on Johnson. If these were the actions of a man who had made a *pro forma* offer, and was hoping it would not be accepted, they were strange ones. Rather, they were the actions of a man who very much wanted Lyndon Johnson on the ticket—and who was determined, despite opposition, to persuade him to accept his offer.

When Kennedy left his suite, Sam Rayburn walked—"briskly," according to a *Dallas Morning News* reporter who saw him—down the hall to Johnson's suite. Taking Johnson and Connally into a bedroom, he had Connally run through all the reasons why he felt Johnson had no choice but to accept the nomination. When Connally finished, the great bald head nodded. "I don't like it," he said to Lyndon Johnson. "But I don't think you *do* have any choice." Jokingly, Johnson said Rayburn had evidently changed his mind since the previous night. "I am a wiser man than I was last night," Rayburn said. The three men assumed, Connally was to say, that everything had been settled.

"AND THEN," Connally was to say, "Bobby Kennedy showed up, and said he wanted to see Mr. Johnson"—and from that moment, and for approximately the next three hours, nothing was settled, and during those hours what had previously remained, despite all the tension, within the boundaries of normal political behavior, was transformed, with the admixture of personal hatred, into confusion and chaos, a chaos whose aftermath would, during the next eight years, affect profoundly the shape of American politics and, to a lesser but still surprisingly significant degree, the shape of American history.

No two people of the many who were involved can agree on anything that happened during those hours. Each account, and some are quite detailed and convincing, contains statements that are impossible to reconcile with, or that directly contradict, statements in other accounts—which are also quite detailed and convincing. To try to reconcile the recollections of those hours is to be reminded, again and again, of what Theodore White wrote (after trying to reconcile them): "It is a trap of history to believe that eyewitnesses remember accurately what they have lived through." Chronologies of that afternoon's events were later compiled by more than one of the participants—but no two chronologies are the same. There is no agreement, to take just a single example, about the number of meetings that Robert Kennedy held with Johnson, Rayburn and Connally—either with one of them alone or with various combinations of the three Texans. Arthur Schlesinger says there were two, Connally says there were three, in fact there were probably four—all that is certain is that for three; hours Robert Kennedy ran up and down those back stairs. There is no agreement on the number of telephone conversations Jack Kennedy held with Johnson and his allies. Philip Graham, who was in Johnson's suite during part of the three hours and later wrote a memorandum trying to recount what had occurred during that time, says there were four such conversations, Rowe says there were three. In the various versions of the afternoon's activities, two meetings (or three) are conflated into one, or what happened in one meeting is divided as if it occurred in two (or three). The only summary statement about the meetings that can be made without dispute is that each of them was a drama in itself, a vivid, tension-fraught drama of powerful men in confrontation.

In what may have been the first of them (it occurred at about 1:30)—the one at which, unexpectedly, "Bobby Kennedy showed up, and said he wanted to see Mr. Johnson"—Bobby did not in fact see Mr. Johnson. "I don't want to see him," Johnson said. Lady Bird said she didn't think Lyndon should see him, so, John Connally says, "Rayburn and I saw him."

Rayburn and Connally were waiting, in Graham's phrase, "for the obvious"—the formal offer of the vice presidential nomination; they were expecting Bobby to formalize the offer his brother had made to Johnson that morning by inviting him, in so many words, to be on the ticket—but the obvious was not what they got. The young man sitting before them in the suite's living room was upset, "his hair all hanging down in his face," in Rayburn's description. He "told me that there'd be a fight over Lyndon." In Connally's recollection, "Bobby said, 'We've got to persuade Lyndon not to take this vice presidential thing. I don't know why my brother made the offer, but it's a terrible mistake. There's a revolt brewing on the floor. Labor is off the reservation. The liberals are in revolt. You've just got to persuade him not to accept this.' " And he asked if Johnson would, instead, accept the chairmanship of the Democratic National Committee. Rayburn refused that invitation with a single word: "Shit," and went into a bedroom, where Johnson, Lady Bird and Graham were sitting on the twin beds, to tell Johnson that perhaps he should talk to Bobby in person. "Lady Bird intervened, apologizing by saying she had never yet argued with Mr. Sam, but repeating that she "felt L.B.J. should not see Bobby." Agreeing with her, Graham told Johnson that his position should be that "You don't want it, you won't negotiate for it, you'll only take it if Jack drafts you, and you won't discuss it with anyone else."

"All of us were pacing around the bedroom, in and out of the bathroom," Graham says. And "finally, in that sudden way decisions leap out of a melee, it was decided": Rayburn would return to the living room and tell Bobby that Johnson would indeed accept the nomination, but only if Kennedy "drafted" him (by which, it soon turned out, Johnson meant merely that Kennedy would have to publicly make him a formal offer), and "I [Graham] was to go phone Jack" and tell him Johnson's position directly. Rayburn went back and delivered that message to Bobby, whose response, according to Rayburn, was: "Then it's got to be Lyndon. I'm going up to tell Jack." Racing out of the room ("Suddenly, the door burst open, and Bob Kennedy ran out and up the steps two at a time," the *Dallas Morning News* reported), brushing past reporters, Bobby shouted, "I can't say anything now!"

This was the formal offer—or as formal an offer as Bobby was ever to make, and one not made directly to Johnson.

Meanwhile, Graham, pulling Rowe along "as witness," went into a vacant bedroom down the hall to telephone Jack Kennedy and tell him Johnson's position.

Jack's response did little to immediately firm up the situation. "He said something to the general effect that he was in a general mess because some liberals were against L.B.J.," Graham was to recall. "He said he was in a meeting with others right then and that people were urging that 'no one had anything against Symington': . . . He then asked me to call back for a decision 'in three minutes.' "

When Graham *did* call back, not in three minutes but in about ten (he and Rowe "both agreed that 'three minutes' in these circumstances mean ten minutes"), the confusion vanished, as far as Jack Kennedy was concerned. "Jack was utterly calm," Graham says. "It's all set, he said. Tell Lyndon I want him and will have (Gov.) Lawrence nominate him, etc." The confusion was not ended in Lyndon Johnson's suite, however, for Bobby Kennedy was to return there, several times.

On what appears to have been the second of his trips, apparently made while Jack was in the meeting with the liberals upstairs, Bobby was, for a moment, alone with John Connally in the living room, but only for a moment. Connally may have been tough enough to handle Bobby Kennedy, but Connally knew someone who was tougher—and he knew he needed that man now. Going out into the corridor, he started looking for Sam Rayburn. Encountering Horace Busby, he shouted, "Come with me!," grabbed his arm and dragged him back to the suite. "Bobby Kennedy's in there," he said. "You go in there and make sure he doesn't leave until the Speaker gets here."

Busby went in, "and there was Bobby Kennedy pacing furiously, just furiously, you know, just, almost at a trot." The glare he gave Busby was the glare he had given Busby before—in the Senate cafeteria, seven years before, when Lyndon Johnson had come over to the table at which Bobby was sitting with Joe McCarthy. "It was the same expression that I told you about," Busby told the author. It had nothing to do with him personally, he knew. "It was just that I was a Johnson man." It had lost none of its ability to intimidate the timid little speech-writer, and anyway he was no Rayburn or Connally, and he knew it. "So I came back out. . . . There wasn't a point in me saying anything to him, I could tell. And I came back out into the anteroom (the suite's vestibule) and told John—who was on the phone—I said, 'I'll try to tackle him from out here, but I'm not staying in there with him.' And at this moment the Speaker arrived—you know the Speaker was a short fellow and bald-headed, completely bald—and he . . . looked at me and he said, 'Where is the little son of a bitch?' And I said, 'He's in there.' And he said, 'What the goddamn hell is he trying to do now?' " The short bald-headed man opened the door, and went in to see Bobby Kennedy. He wasn't in there long, and then "the door burst open, Bobby sprinted past us out in the hall, disappeared." Rayburn came out right behind him. Connally was standing in the vestible, and Walter Jenkins had come in, and everyone asked Sam Rayburn what had happened inside. And none of them would ever forget Sam Rayburn in that moment. He was old, and he was blind, and, as would soon become apparent, he was very, very ill. But, as he told them what had happened, he didn't seem old, or blind, or ill. He said that Bobby Kennedy had told him that liberal and labor leaders were going to stage a floor fight against Johnson's nomination, and that perhaps Johnson would prefer to withdraw. He said he asked Bobby one question: "Are you authorized to speak for your brother?" Bobby said no.

"Come back and see the Speaker of the House when you are," Sam Rayburn said.

AND THAT WAS NOT THE END of the confusion, because that was not the last of Bobby Kennedy's trips downstairs.

During the next hour, there was one—the consensus among the accounts makes this the third meeting—at which he met John Connally. Rayburn refused to see him again, so Connally saw him alone. "It's getting worse. You've just got to convince Lyndon not to take it." Connally reiterated Rayburn's stance, saying that Jack had made the offer, and if the offer was to be withdrawn, it had to be Jack who withdrew it. "I said, 'This is a very simple matter. All your brother has to do is call Mr. Johnson and say, "I've re-evaluated the situation and I want to withdraw the offer." ' He said, 'He can't do that.' I said, 'Why in the hell can't he? I'll tell you this: Mr. Johnson's not going to be persuaded by the conversations that are taking place here.' "

Bobby then said—Graham puts the time at "roughly, 3:00"—that Jack would phone at once to make the formal offer. No call came, however, and, Graham says, Johnson "was considerably on edge." Graham telephoned Jack, saying, "Johnson hasn't heard from you, and you'd better call him." Jack said he had assumed the message—"It's all set"—he had sent through Graham would suffice, and "He said he'd call at once." (But he also mentioned again the "opposition to LBJ." Graham responded that he should "stop vacillating," and, Graham says, Kennedy "agreed about the finality of things.") Rowe went down the hall to Johnson's suite. "Just don't go wandering," he told him; Kennedy was about to call. He did, at perhaps 3:30. "Johnson took the call sitting on one bed; I was on the other." Kennedy read Johnson a press release saying he had selected him as the vice presidential nominee. "Do you really want me?" Lyndon Johnson said. Rowe says he could hear Kennedy say, "Yes, I do." "Well, if you really want me, I'll do it," Johnson said.

"EVERYBODY SORT OF RELAXED, thought it was all settled," Jim Rowe recalls. A statement accepting the nomination had been typed up, and Johnson was preparing to go out into the corridor, now jammed from wall to wall with reporters, photographers and television lights and cameras, and read it. But, in fact, the worst of the confusion, fueled by hatred, was yet to come. For there was one more trip downstairs by Robert Kennedy, and on this trip he met, alone, with Lyndon Johnson.

Not long, perhaps half an hour, after the phone call from Jack Kennedy to Johnson, Graham and Rowe were sitting in a bedroom down the hall that they had commandeered, when suddenly, as Rowe recalls it, a young man "whom I had never seen before"—it was a young Johnson aide named Bill Moyers—came running in, yelling, "Graham, my God, Bobby is in the room." Grabbing Graham's arm, he dragged him out into the crowded corridor, and, pushing through the crowd with Rowe behind them, down the hall to Johnson's suite, where they learned Bobby Kennedy had just left after being closeted alone with Johnson in the suite's living room.

The only people who could say what occurred in that room were Lyndon Johnson and Robert Kennedy. In his account of what had happened there, Kennedy let all his hatred and contempt for Johnson spill out.

> There were just the two of us. He was seated on the couch, and I was seated on his right. I remember the whole conversation. . . . I said, "There's going to be a lot of opposition." . . . It was going to be unpleasant, that we were going to have trouble with the liberals. They were going to get up and fight it, and the President [Jack Kennedy] didn't think that he [Johnson] wanted to go through that kind of an unpleasant fight.

Therefore, Robert Kennedy said, repeating the offer that Connally and Rayburn say he had made to them earlier, perhaps Johnson would like to become chairman of the Democratic National Committee.

> The President [Jack Kennedy] wanted to have him play an important role, and he could run the party—the idea being that to run the party he could get a lot of his own people in; and then if he wanted to be President after eight years or something, he could have the machinery where he could run for President or do whatever he wanted. That was the idea at the time. We didn't really know whether he'd want to go through it [a floor fight], and, in any case, the President wanted to get rid of him.
>
> He [Johnson] is one of the greatest looking sad people in the world—you know, he can turn that on. I thought he'd burst into tears. He just shook, and tears came into his eyes, and he said, "I want to be Vice President, and, if the President will have me, I'll join with him in making a fight for it." It was that kind of a conversation. I said, "Well, then, that's fine. He wants you to be Vice President if you want to be Vice President."

Going back into the other bedroom, Lyndon Johnson yanked off his jacket and tie. He couldn't sit still. With the connecting doors between the suite and the adjoining bedrooms open, he paced back and forth in his shirtsleeves through the long line of rooms with awkward, lunging strides, his arms flailing, a towering distraught figure. Trying to find a place in which he could talk with his advisers, he walked into a room in which his staff had been entertaining some fifteen delegates from Hawaii. Saying, "Thank you, boys, thank you. Thank you for all you did," he shooed them out.

Then he was alone with Lady Bird, Rayburn, Connally, Graham, Rowe and Bobby Baker. "LBJ seemed about to jump out of his skin," Graham said. He told them that Robert Kennedy had said, "Kennedy doesn't want me." He asked them, "What am I going to do?" Jim Rowe, who had been with him in a score of crises over the course of more than twenty years, says, "I'd never seen him in such a state of—not panic—confusion."

Through the "hubbub" that followed, Rayburn's voice cut through: "Phil, call Jack." Returning to the bedroom, and sitting on a bed, Graham did—and as soon as that call went through, the confusion was over, at least for the day. " 'Oh,' Jack Kennedy said—as calmly as though we were discussing the weather—'that's all right; Bobby's been out of touch and doesn't know what's been happening.' " When Graham asked, "Well, what do you want Lyndon to do?" Kennedy replied, "I want him to make a statement right away." He had, he said, "just finished making mine." Graham said, "You'd better speak to Lyndon," and a moment later Johnson, sprawling across the other bed, was agreeing to make his statement. Graham then told Jack Kennedy, "You'd better speak to Bobby." Baker went out to get Robert Kennedy, who came into the room looking exhausted; his face was white and, in Graham's description, "sullen" and "dead tired." He took the phone, and as Graham walked out of the room, he heard Robert Kennedy say to his brother, "Well, it's too late now."

Johnson didn't look any better. He and Lady Bird, standing amid a cluster of men in the suite's vestibule, resembled two people who "had just survived an airplane crash," Graham says. Through the double doors to the corridor, they could hear a babble of voices: the press corps. Johnson was still holding the typed statement accepting the nomination. Before Bobby had come down, "I was just going to read this on TV . . . and now I don't know what I ought to do," he told Graham, who relates that "With more ham than I ever suspected myself of, I suddenly blurted: 'Of course you know what you're going to do. Throw your shoulders back and your chin out and go out and make that announcement.' " Someone shouted approval, and swung open the door, and someone pushed Johnson and Lady Bird "out into the TV lights and the explosion of flashbulbs." A couple of chairs were brought out and they were helped up to stand on them, "and," Graham says, "as they rose their faces metamorphosed into enthusiasm and confidence."

Behind them, in the bedroom of the Johnson suite, only two men were left: Jim Rowe and Robert Kennedy. "Jim, don't you think it is a terrible mistake?" Kennedy asked. He leaned his head against a wall. "My God, this wouldn't have happened except that we were all too tired last night," he said.

• • •

WHILE JACK KENNEDY HAD BEEN READING his statement and answering questions at a crowded press conference a few minutes earlier (the announcement was greeted by "gasps of surprise," the *New York Times* said), he made one or two minor gaffes, very unusual for him, referring to Symington, at one point, as the "Senator from Illinois," but there was no other sign of fatigue or tension. He seemed, in fact, quite at ease; he looked, as the *Washington Post* put it, "as though he had spent the day at the beach."

In his efforts to "get him off the ticket," to try to persuade Lyndon Johnson to withdraw, was Robert Kennedy acting without his brother's knowledge?

Even Philip Graham, the man who raised that possibility in the memorandum he wrote shortly after the convention, found it impossible to resolve that question. ("I urged [Jack] Kennedy to offer the Vice Presidency to Johnson. He immediately agreed. . . . Kennedy was decisive in saying that was his intention. . . . 'Bobby's been out of touch and doesn't know what's been happening.' . . . I later learned he [Bobby] had . . . assured several liberal delegates it would *not* be Johnson. My guess is that he made that assurance on his own and tried to bring it about on his own during his dealings with Johnson and Rayburn.")

"Did Jack offer the VP hoping LBJ would turn it down?" Graham wrote. "Did LBJ really want it? Did Bobby try to sabotage the offer? And if so, did he do so on his own or with Jack's approval? I have no confident answer to any of those questions."

When the possibility that Bobby had made the effort on his own became a public issue—and it became a very public issue when Graham's memorandum was published in 1965, and again, as will be seen, in 1967—Bobby indignantly denied it. No one but he and his brother knew what had happened, he told two interviewers, Arthur Schlesinger and the journalist John Bartlow Martin, who, in a series of oral history interviews, recorded his reminiscences for posterity. "The only people who were involved in the discussions were Jack and myself. Nobody else was involved in it." Graham's memorandum—the claim that "I went down by myself and on my own"—"flabbergasted me," he said. "Obviously, with the close relationship between my brother and me, I wasn't going down to see if he would withdraw just as a lark on my own. 'My brother's asleep, so I'll see if I can get rid of his Vice President.' " He had, Robert Kennedy said, "worked out" with Jack that he would tell Johnson that "the liberals . . . were going to get up [on the convention floor] and fight it," and that Johnson could have the Democratic National Committee (DNC) chairmanship instead. "That was the idea," he said. "In any case [JFK] wanted to get rid of him. . . . During that whole three or four hours, we just vacillated back and forth as to whether we wanted him or didn't want him. And finally we decided not to have him, and we came upon this idea [offering him the DNC chairmanship] of trying to get rid of him. And it didn't work."

Descriptions of some telephone conversations tend to support the view that Bobby Kennedy was acting on his own, without Jack's knowledge: the four conversations reported by Philip Graham, in an account corroborated by Rowe (who says about one conversation, "I could hear [Jack] Kennedy talking," and about another that Graham had, immediately upon hanging up, told him what Kennedy had said)—the conversations in one of which, Graham wrote, Jack Kennedy told him, "It's all set"; in next of which Kennedy had said he had thought that first message would suffice to let Johnson know he was his choice; and in the last of which he said, "Bobby's been out of touch" and that he, Jack, had already made his public statement announcing that Johnson was his choice.

Robert Kennedy explained these conversations by saying that at the time Jack first dispatched him to make the DNC offer, Jack had *not* yet made the public statement and still wanted Johnson off the ticket. Bobby says that Jack's decision to publicly announce Johnson's choice was made between the time he, Bobby, left to see Johnson and the time he returned to Jack's suite, and that Jack had made that decision because, Bobby says, during that interval Jack had received a telephone call from "somebody" saying he had to stop vacillating, and had therefore decided to make the announcement.

Whatever the explanation for what happened during that long afternoon, however, it is difficult to credit Robert Kennedy's explanation. His initial acceptance of his brother's decision, conveyed to Ken O'Donnell and Pierre Salinger from the bathtub early that morning, appears to have faded quickly, perhaps partly because he accompanied O'Donnell when Ken, following Jack Kennedy's instructions to "Get your tail over and tell your labor friends," went to UAW President Walter Reuther's suite at the nearby Statler Hilton Hotel, where labor and liberal leaders had gathered. The reaction from this group of men whom O'Donnell and Bobby (and perhaps Jack) had unequivocally assured that Johnson would never be Jack Kennedy's choice was "violently angry," O'Donnell was to relate. Joe Rauh had somehow already heard the news, and as one of the labor leaders, UAW vice president Leonard Woodcock, was heading up to Reuther's suite, suddenly in front of him was "Joe Rauh, who had tears literally rolling down his cheeks. Have I heard the news?" Woodcock hadn't heard it, and as Rauh told him that Kennedy had chosen Johnson, "It seemed" to Woodcock "that Kennedy had betrayed us all. Well, I, very frankly, was shocked, because our whole theme had been to unite behind Kennedy to stop Johnson." Up in the suite, there were shouts of "Double-cross" and "sell-out" from a group that included George Meany of the AFL-CIO; Jack Conway, Reuther's top political aide; and Alex Rose of New York, president of the Cloth Hat, Cap and Millinery Workers International Union. In O'Donnell's recollection, Bobby was attacked "savagely." Jabbing a finger at him, Rose shouted that if Johnson's name was on the ticket, Kennedy would not receive the Liberal Party designation in New York State. Conway started for O'Donnell as if he were going to hit him. "I don't think that Bobby Kennedy fully realized the predicament that Jack had put us into until we walked into the room at the Statler Hilton," O'Donnell was to relate. The labor delegates said that they, in combination with civil rights and other liberal groups, would nominate their own candidate for the vice presidency to oppose Johnson that evening. "Bobby was shaken."

But while Bobby Kennedy may have changed his mind, Jack appears never to have changed his. And emotional though the scene at the Statler Hilton may have been, it doesn't explain Bobby's repeated attempts, attested to not only by Johnson but by Rayburn and Connally, to persuade Johnson to withdraw from the ticket. O'Donnell, who says he was present when Bobby reported back to his brother on his meeting with the angry union and liberal leaders, says that Bobby asked Jack, "Do you want me to tell Lyndon that there's a possibility of a floor fight?" and that Jack replied, "Maybe you better go downstairs and tell him that. I doubt that it will bother him, but we ought to let him know that there might be a floor fight against him, in case he doesn't feel up to facing it." According to O'Donnell, that was all Jack said. He didn't, according to O'Donnell, tell Bobby to try to persuade Johnson to withdraw. And throughout that afternoon, Jack's determination to keep Johnson on the ticket appears never to have wavered. As liberal outrage mounted, he treated it with cool indifference. At one point, as Kennedy was meeting in his suite with a group of southern governors exuberant over Johnson's selection, Soapy Williams unexpectedly walked in. Shocked by what he was hearing—the governor had just been assuring his Michigan delegation that rumors they had been hearing about Johnson's selection were false—he shouted that he would lead a floor fight against it. Several of the southerners threatened to punch him, and were actually advancing on him when cooler heads pushed them back. All during the scene, Jack Kennedy, "sitting in an armchair with one leg hanging over its arm, watched without saying a word," O'Donnell says. Asked whether, during the course of the long afternoon, "Jack Kennedy ever seem[ed] to waver on [the choice of Johnson]," Larry O'Brien says, "Not to my recollection." (Kennedy had asked David Lawrence to nominate Johnson, and all during the time Bobby was making his trips down the stairs to the seventh floor, Lawrence's speechwriters were drafting the nominating speech.) And of course when Philip Graham telephoned Kennedy while he was in the middle of a meeting with a group of angry liberals, Kennedy asked him to call back in three minutes, and when Graham did, Kennedy's answer, "utterly calm," was "It's all set. Tell Lyndon I want him." Some minutes later, after Bobby had finished his one-on-one session with Johnson, during which, Johnson said, Bobby had told him, "[Jack] Kennedy doesn't want me" (Bobby explains that meeting by saying, "The President wanted to get rid of him"), Graham spoke to Jack Kennedy again. Saying, "Oh . . . Bobby's been out of touch," Jack told Lyndon to make his statement accepting the nomination immediately, because he himself had already made his, announcing that Lyndon was his choice. And Jack's statement to Johnson was accurate. He *had* made his announcement, some minutes earlier.

Robert Kennedy could of course have been doing what he thought his brother wanted him to do but didn't want to put into words, even to him, or he could have been hearing—hearing through the haze of his hatred for Johnson—

what he wanted to hear. But there is another possible explanation. Close though the two brothers may have been, in their relationship it was only the elder brother who made the decisions. "As the years went on," O'Brien says, "Jack Kennedy never at any fleeting moment was other than the President of the United States. His brother was the attorney general and his brother was his confidant and adviser, but the decision maker sat in the Oval Office and the decision maker sat in the suite that day." And it may be that the elder brother had not, before he got the nomination, allowed the younger brother to know what he was planning to do after he got it because if anyone, including his brother, knew, it would make it harder for him to get it. In his biography of Robert Kennedy, Evan Thomas, after summarizing Robert's account of the long afternoon, says, "That was [Robert] Kennedy's story, but it wasn't the whole story or, the evidence suggests, an entirely accurate account. . . . Robert Kennedy later said the complete story would never be known, but that may be because he hoped it wouldn't. Jack Kennedy relied on his brother, trusted him, needed him, but he didn't always tell him everything he was thinking or doing."* More than one Kennedy adviser arrives at the same conclusion. Fred Dutton, for one, says, "I always suspected that Jack didn't tell Bobby everything about LBJ because Jack figured Bobby would try to stop him."

It may be that Jack Kennedy didn't always tell *anyone* everything he was thinking or doing. In attempting to understand why he declared to his journalist friend Charles Bartlett that his offer to Johnson had been merely a gesture ("I just held it out like this, and he grabbed at it")—a statement at direct variance not only with Johnson's account of the conversation but with what Kennedy himself told O'Donnell, O'Brien, Governor Lawrence and others immediately after it took place—one possible explanation is that since he had allowed unequivocal "promises . . . assurances" to be given in his name to liberals and labor leaders that Johnson would not be offered the vice presidency, the easiest way to explain why the offer had been made was to say he *hadn't* really offered it, had only "held it out like this," and that Johnson had, "to his shock," "grabbed at it," and he, Kennedy, then had had no choice but to let the offer stand.†

---

*Jeff Shesol, in his book about the Johnson–Robert Kennedy feud, also concludes that "Bobby's case is not persuasive." He feels that his account "cannot responsibly be dismissed as duplicity. It is more believable that Robert Kennedy, who despised LBJ even in 1960, remembered events as he saw them."

†Philip Graham interprets his telephone conversations with Kennedy—in one of which Kennedy said he was in a meeting with liberals and "was in a general mess because some liberals were against LBJ" and to call back "in three minutes" and another of which he mentioned "opposition to LBJ"—to mean that Kennedy was wavering, but that interpretation conflicts with what in fact Kennedy actually *did* at each of those moments: when Graham *did* call back, Kennedy, with the liberals now gone, said simply, "It's all set," and added that he had already arranged for Lawrence to nominate Johnson; in the call in which he mentioned "opposition to LBJ," he then also "agreed about the finality of things." And in the last call, he had already delivered his formal statement announcing that he had picked Johnson.

That explanation raises the possibility that Jack Kennedy may have known all along—for months, perhaps for years—that if he won the presidential nomination he would try to persuade Lyndon Johnson to join him on the ticket, and that he simply hadn't dropped a hint of that to anyone, even his brother. Such an explanation suggests, of course, cold calculation—very cold; it suggests the existence of a deep reservoir of calculation and reserve beneath Jack Kennedy's easy charm. But that explanation—that for months he had concealed his true intentions from his brother, his closest adviser—is not definitive, nor is any other. All it is possible to say is that however shrouded the events of that afternoon in Los Angeles may remain for history—however undefinitive, resistant to proof, every explanation subject to contradiction—that is nonetheless one possible explanation for them.

Since rumors and the reports of rumors, confusion and conflicting stories, are a staple of all contested political conventions, the questions surrounding Lyndon Johnson's acceptance of John F. Kennedy's offer to be his Vice President, and Kennedy's decision to make (or not to make) the offer to him, might not warrant as much consideration—so much effort to resolve them—as they have, for decades, been given, except that, because of November 22, 1963, the events of that long afternoon in 1960 were to affect so profoundly the course of American history. As Evans and Novak were to write, the alliance between John Kennedy and Johnson "that opened to Johnson the door of national power set in motion the mutual suspicion between" Johnson and Robert Kennedy "that would grow in importance and depth as the years went by." After that afternoon, Robert Kennedy wasn't the only one of the two men who hated the other. Whatever Lyndon Johnson's feelings toward Robert Kennedy had been before, the events of that afternoon had intensified them. He never blamed Jack Kennedy for the uncertainties and indignities—and the attempt to destroy his hopes, to snatch away from him the opportunity he so much wanted—that were visited upon him that afternoon. He knew who was behind them, he felt. "Bobby was against my being on the ticket in 1960," he was to say years later. "He came to my room three times to try to get me to say we wouldn't run on the ticket." At the end of that long afternoon, after he had stepped down from the chair in the Biltmore corridor on which he had stood to make his acceptance statement, he came back into his suite, and closed the door behind him, and cursed Robert Kennedy. He called him, Bobby Baker was to write, " 'that little shitass' and worse." Perhaps much worse. John Connally, who during long days of conversation with this author was willing to answer almost any question put to him, no matter how delicate the topic, wouldn't answer when asked what Johnson said about Robert Kennedy. When the author pressed him, he finally said flatly: "I'm not going to tell you what he said about him." During the months after the convention, when Johnson was closeted alone back in Texas with an old ally, he would sometimes be asked about Robert Kennedy. He would reply with a gesture. Raising his big right hand, he would draw the side of it across his neck in a slow, slitting movement.

Sometimes that gesture would be his only reply; sometimes, as during a meeting with Ed Clark in Austin, he would say, as his hand moved across his neck, "I'll cut his throat if it's the last thing I do."

The nominations for Vice President were to begin, in the Los Angeles Coliseum, where the convention's final session was being held, at eight o'clock, and for a couple of hours there was, as Ken O'Donnell recalls, "the possibility of a messy floor fight over Johnson's nomination."

The gasps from reporters that had greeted Kennedy's announcement of his choice were echoed even by seasoned politicians. When a reporter said "It's Johnson" to FDR's tough old Democratic Party national chairman, "Farley's jaw dropped." "Why that's impossible!" he exclaimed. And, *Newsweek* reported, "Jim Farley's reaction was typical of the stunned disbelief that swept over the delegates to the Democratic National Convention at the news that Jack Kennedy wanted Lyndon Johnson." The Michigan delegation, which included a large bloc of UAW delegates from the Detroit auto factories, declared that other candidates would be nominated for Vice President, and that there would be a floor fight, complete with a roll call, and members of several other delegations, including California, New York and Wisconsin, followed suit. Checking with Reuther's aide Conway a little later, O'Donnell was told that the Michigan delegation would "definitely" nominate a candidate to oppose Johnson and was planning "a fight to the finish" against the Kennedy-Johnson ticket. "It looked like a bad night for all of us," O'Donnell was to recall. The threat was less that Johnson might actually be defeated than that an open battle over Kennedy's choice, the first decision he had made as the nominee, would embarrass him—and of course the man he had chosen. That threat of embarrassment "was," in O'Donnell's words, "very strong and real that afternoon." Though Kennedy would win the fight, it would handicap his campaign at its very start, O'Donnell felt. "When you were on national television . . . the speeches were going to get a little rough after a while and would advertise . . . the split in the Democratic Party. It was going to be real, real tough. You were going to get into the Negro thing. You were going to get into the southern versus the northern."

To Lyndon Johnson, already strained to the breaking point, the threat certainly seemed real. On the television set in his suite Robert Nathan, chairman of the District of Columbia delegation, was telling CBS News that the delegation had decided on its candidate: Minnesota Governor Orville Freeman. That "revolt" against Kennedy's choice was spreading, commentators said. "I don't believe his managers or lieutenants can put this down," Edward R. Murrow said. "He is going to have to deal with this himself." The "humiliation" of defeat had loomed ominously before Johnson when he had been fighting for the top spot on the ticket. Now, was there to be a fight over even the second spot—with "humiliation" a possibility at the end of that fight, too? A new figure—a tall one—

appeared on the back stairs. Rushing up the two flights to the Kennedy suite, Johnson conferred with Larry O'Brien about a floor fight: "He was concerned that . . . it could turn out to be a debacle, and that would be devastating not only to us but to him, too." He talked with Jack Kennedy, and then they stepped out into the hall, and photographers caught their smiles: Jack's wide, Lyndon's wary—so wary that in some of the photographs it is more a grimace. Going back down the stairs, he picked up Lady Bird and left for their quarters, a model home that had been built by a real estate developer next to the coliseum, where he was to wait for the nominations, and as he was stepping out of his hotel suite—Lady Bird beside him with the set-in-stone smile for once chipping away at the edges into something on the verge of hysteria—a reporter asked him, "Are you going to the Arena later?"

"That depends on developments," Johnson replied.

Just as he was about to enter the door of the model home, reporter Bill Downs of CBS shouted at him, and Johnson turned to face him as Lady Bird continued through the door, standing with television lights glaring on his face. Fleshy though it was, his face was gaunt and haggard, the circles under his eyes so dark they looked like bruises. Downs' next words were a brutal reminder that Johnson had once hoped to be the presidential, not vice presidential, nominee. "Senator, this is the first time you've been out to the Arena," the reporter said. "We expected you to come out in a different role." Johnson smiled wanly, without a word. "How's it feeling, huh?" Downs asked. Seeing that something was wrong, Lady Bird came back and took her husband's arm. Lyndon Johnson stood there a moment in the glare of the television lights. Then, still without a word, he went inside.

But the liberal bravado faded in the face of reality. The reality was the numbers: the figures in the Electoral College were all that mattered now. Thirteen-year-old Lucy Baines, tired out from crying over her father's loss the night before, had been napping during the day's developments, but she understood that reality as soon as she awoke, and was told that her father had accepted the nomination. "Kennedy couldn't win without Daddy," she said. An older person—and one with more experience with numbers—understood it, too. The economist John Kenneth Galbraith got the news from Robert Kennedy, who telephoned him and said, "Jack's decided, and you've got a revolt on your hands. . . . Go out there and see what you can do." Galbraith started circulating among liberal delegates, reminding them that the move was not unprecedented—after all, Roosevelt had picked the Texas conservative Garner—and had been made for the same reason: FDR needed Garner if he was to win. "For God's sake, give Kennedy the same right that you would have automatically given FDR," Galbraith said.

The man who was probably best of all at realities was immediately confident of the wisdom of his son's decision. That evening, in the courtyard of Joe Kennedy's rented mansion, as Robert was on the telephone to the convention floor monitoring the vice presidential proceedings while Jack read a newspaper, both Kennedy brothers seemed in low spirits. Robert, Charles Bartlett felt, was "in near despair." "Yesterday was the best day of my life," he told the columnist, "and today is the worst day of my life." Then, "their father appeared in the doorway" in a smoking jacket, and, standing there "in a very grand manner with his hands behind his back," said, "Don't worry, Jack, in two weeks they'll be saying it's the smartest thing you ever did."

It didn't take even two weeks. Alex Rose was calmed down within minutes by his longtime ally, and fellow power in New York liberal politics, David Dubinsky, president of the International Ladies' Garment Workers' Union. Telephoning Dubinsky to tell him of Johnson's selection, Rose expected him to be as angry as he was, but Dubinsky's immediate reaction was "Kennedy is making a smart move!" A moment later, he went further. "I think it's a good ticket," he said. "I think it's a ticket that can win." "A political masterstroke," he said. On the coliseum floor, Soapy Williams angrily demanded of Abe Ribicoff, "Why retreat . . . from principle?" "We want to win," Ribicoff replied. And, as the AFL-CIO's general counsel, Arthur Goldberg, told Kennedy that day, labor and the liberals would have no option but to go along with his choice. They would hate the idea, he said—"Meany has developed a vendetta [against Johnson]"— but labor would certainly endorse him because under no circumstances could it support Nixon; "they had no choice." (Besides, Goldberg was to recall, "I rather discounted the [importance of] the Vice Presidency. Who thought this young fellow might be assassinated? He [Johnson] will be just another Vice President, which you don't take seriously.") Forty-eight hours later, the *Herald Tribune* would be reporting that "the consensus of America's traditional politicians, Republican and Democratic, is that the Democratic Kennedy-Johnson ticket is a 'brilliant stroke.' No question about it, the professionals see in" Kennedy's choice "a swift, bold strike . . . a bridge to the South . . . by way of Texas." Johnson's selection, Doris Fleeson said, was simply "a decision to win the election." And the reality went beyond the math. The southern delegations were enthusiastically for Kennedy's choice (more than one southern governor told Kennedy it was "the only way" to hold the South); the most powerful of the northern big-city bosses were enthusiastically for it—and as for the liberals, as *Newsweek* put it, "they had no place else to go." Bitter though Joe Rauh might be, he saw that. "What can I do—work for Nixon?" he said. And, finally, there was the overwhelming fact, what the *Washington Star* called "the tradition that a Convention does not deny a presidential candidate the right to pick his running mate." Labor leaders bowed to these realities. "If Jack wants Lyndon, I'm for Lyndon," David McDonald of the United Steelworkers of America said. Meany and Reuther were finally persuaded to pass the word to the union members in the New York, Michigan, and California delegations not to fight—word of that order was passed to O'Donnell, who had been working frantically with delegates on the floor, at 7:30, just a half hour before the nominations began. Orville Freeman told the District of Columbia delegates "very firmly" not to nominate him. "Although I am not completely enthusiastic about his [Kennedy's] choice of a vice presidential candidate, I am certainly not prepared to nominate him yesterday and to oppose his choice for the vice presidential seat today," he said.

As eight o'clock neared, and the hopelessness of opposing Kennedy's choice became apparent, the District's delegation—and some liberal delegates in other delegations—remained determined, even if they did not nominate other candidates, to withhold their votes from Johnson, but in fact they were unable to register even this form of protest because Sam Rayburn knew how to make sure they wouldn't be able to. After Johnson had been nominated by Governor Lawrence and seconded, and bands had played "The Eyes of Texas" and "The Yellow Rose of Texas" while delegates paraded through the hall in his honor (it was noticeable that few northern delegates got out of their seats, but the southern delegations, including those who had not joined the parade for Kennedy the night before, marched in strength), Rayburn's Majority Leader in the House, John W. McCormack, made a motion: to suspend the convention rules (which allowed other nominations), and nominate Johnson by acclamation. Explaining that such a motion required approval of two-thirds of the delegates, Chairman Collins called for a voice vote. Estimates of whether there were more "ayes" or "nays" were to vary from newspaper to newspaper—in the opinion of most they were about evenly divided—and Collins hesitated, as a rising murmur began in the coliseum, during which the harsh, commanding voice of a bald old man in the Texas delegation could be heard, shouting, "Say 'aye'! Say 'aye'!," and Rayburn's man on the platform, the convention's parliamentarian, Representative Clarence Cannon of Missouri, whispered something in Collins' ear, and Collins announced that the rules had been suspended, and that Lyndon Johnson "has been nominated for Vice President by acclaim."

While the parade in his honor had been going on, Johnson and Lady Bird had come out of the model home at the head of his entourage to walk the few yards to the coliseum. As he emerged, Ed Murrow said to Walter Cronkite, "Johnson looks considerably older than when he arrived here, doesn't he, Walter? Shows the strain."

"He certainly does," Cronkite replied. "He looks exceedingly tired—and I would say somewhat downcast." But while he waited behind the podium, the bands playing his songs, Chairman Collins announced that he was, by acclamation, the Democratic nominee for Vice President, and then he came out on the high platform above the crowd, and his smile broadened into a big smile, and he threw up his long arms in the "V for Victory" sign.

5

The "LBJ Special"

DURING THE CAMPAIGN that followed the convention, the campaign between the Kennedy-Johnson ticket and the Republican slate of Richard Nixon and Henry Cabot Lodge, it was important to Jack Kennedy's chances that there be harmony, so when, the very morning after the vice presidential nomination, Robert Kennedy bumped into George Reedy, he said, in the friendliest manner, "Everything's all right now, George." Following a joint planning session at the Kennedy compound in Hyannis Port, and the rump session of Congress—which, with its true purpose now gone, accomplished nothing: not one of the four major legislative proposals brought up was passed—Kennedy and Johnson opened the campaign by appearing together on Labor Day in Boston and later that week in cities across Texas, and the two candidates thereafter waged largely separate campaigns, on the same platform only a few times during the two months before Election Day. There was a minimum of interaction, or friction, between the Kennedy and Johnson camps.

Johnson's job was to hold the South—or, to be more precise, since Eisenhower had won five of the eleven states of the Old Confederacy in 1956, to win it back: a tough assignment, due to southern misgivings about the strong civil rights platform the Democrats had adopted in Los Angeles, and due also to Kennedy's liberalism, civil rights views and religion. Kennedy's hope that he had "settled the religious question for good" in the West Virginia primary proved, in Theodore White's word, "naïve"; by September, "the old fears were boiling to the surface. . . . The reports from the South were bad; Baptist ministers had begun to preach against the Church of Rome and 'its' candidate." Though Kennedy lanced the boil again in a speech before the Greater Houston Ministerial Association, under the surface the issue still festered. A Gallup Poll at the end of September found the Kennedy-Johnson and Nixon-Lodge tickets in a dead heat in the South: 46 percent to 46 percent, with 8 percent undecided.

Johnson's campaign in the South included some very tough behind-the-scenes arguments to the most influential southern Democrats, such as the handful of key Florida leaders he flew to Miami to meet—in a very private meeting. So far behind did Kennedy's private polls show him in that state that he had all but written it off, but Johnson, his face grim and his eyes blazing, told the Florida leaders that "This boy Kennedy is going to win, and he's going to win big, and if he wins without the South, I'm warning you—I'm warning you—you bastards are going to be dead. You'll get nothing out of the next Congress, and you won't get anything out of the Kennedy Administration." And "after that," columnist Drew Pearson was to write, Florida's top Democrats "really began to work."

And his campaign included a "whistle-stop" train tour down through the South on a thirteen-car "LBJ Special," pulled by two locomotives, that chugged out of Washington's Union Station in mid-October to spend five days wending its slow way through the little towns and cities of eight southern states.

He designed the format for the stops himself, and, as George Reedy put it, "they were potent." As the LBJ Special entered the outskirts of a town, its public-address system would be switched on, and over it would come the stirring strains of "The Yellow Rose of Texas." At first the tune would be played at low volume, but as the train approached the town's center, where advance men would have gathered a small crowd, "the volume would be turned up to a point where the tune could be heard from blocks away." Record player and engine would stop simultaneously, a dark blue curtain that had been hung over the doorway onto the rear platform would be pulled aside, and the tall figure of Lyndon Johnson, waving a ten-gallon hat, would step through. Following him would be the town's mayor and sheriff and perhaps the district's congressman, and other local dignitaries, and Johnson would introduce them, perhaps say a word or two about one or another, and then shake their hands as they stepped down from the platform into the midst of their constituents. Then he himself would be introduced, in introductions that emphasized that he was from the South and the significance of that fact. Tennessee's governor, Buford Ellington, who made a lot of the introductions, riding the train for the entire five days, would tell the audience that the platform adopted in Los Angeles didn't really matter; "The main thing is to have a Southerner on the ticket." Or an introduction might remind the crowd that Kennedy had been attacked for putting a southerner on the ticket. "Are we going to sit idly by while this great southerner is abused in this manner?," Virginia's governor, John S. Battle, demanded at one stop. And Johnson would step forward, sometimes throwing his Stetson into the crowd (where an advance man was supposed to retrieve it and bring it back; Stetsons were expensive), sometimes simply placing it conspicuously on the railing in front of him, to say he was happy to be back "in the land we love, with the people we love" (although he would then add that "In our campaign, there's no North, South, East or West—it's for all America").

His talks were brief—ten or fifteen minutes, generally—but very southern in their message. "Why, oh why, should the great state of Virginia ever vote Republican?" he asked at one stop. "This high-talking, high-spending crowd has never done anything for the South. It has no interest in Virginia or any other southern state. What excuse have you got for not voting with the party of your fathers?"

Often he told his audience that he had come because he had been reading about southern defections to the Republicans. "We just decided we'd come down and see who deserted us and where they've gone." Or he would talk about his daddy, his father who had been dying in a hospital, but when he, Lyndon, had come to see him, had said, "Son, get me my britches. I'm going home." He had reminded his daddy that he would get better medical care in the hospital, Lyndon would say, but his daddy had said, "I want to go back among our people, where they know when a man's sick, and they care when he dies." That is the difference between Democrats and Republicans, Johnson would say. "Democrats *do* care when a man is sick, and they care when he dies, and Democrats care year in and year out." Republicans care, too, he said—"just before every election time."

And his talks were very southern in their delivery: old-fashioned stump speeches, "real stemwinders": shouted out, with the points he wanted to make delivered in a bellow, so that his voice was continually hoarse, and as he shouted, his arms flailed, and he would raise an arm—or two—high above his head, and jab a finger toward the sky. Among his gestures was one in which, a reporter wrote, "the Johnson hands went up beside his ears and wavered there like a television commercial on headache misery."

And some of the points he made were unforgettable, for if Lyndon Johnson reading from a prepared speech was stilted and unconvincing, Lyndon Johnson without a speech—Lyndon Johnson alone with an audience he had to persuade— was still the Lyndon Johnson who had, in his early Texas campaigns, shown that in a state with a history of great stump speakers, he was one of the greatest of them all.

Was the religious issue—Kennedy's Catholicism—a menace to the Democrats? Jack Kennedy had met the issue in his way, with the carefully reasoned speech to the ministers in Houston. Lyndon Johnson met it in *his* way.

The "hate campaign" being waged against Jack Kennedy because of religion was a shame, he said, particularly the attacks by Baptist preachers from the pulpit. Jack Kennedy had had an older brother, Joe Jr., he told the huddles of people at the whistle-stop towns of the South. Jack Kennedy had loved Joe Jr., he said. But Joe Jr. was dead now. He had been killed in the war. He had been killed when he volunteered to pilot a plane on a suicide mission. And when Jack's brother took off that morning, on that mission from which he knew he would never return, "nobody asked him what church he went to." And after he died— after he "went down in a burning plane over the English Channel so that we could have free speech and a free press and live as free men, not a soul got up in a pulpit and asked what church he went to." And as Lyndon Johnson told the story of Jack's brother, his voice wavered and almost broke, and, in town after town, a deep hush fell over the crowd gathered around the train platform.

As he was talking, Lyndon Johnson had of course gotten "worked up," and often, as the train pulled out, with "The Yellow Rose" blaring again, he would think of additional points he wanted to make, and, with the train already in motion and pulling away from the crowd, would turn back to the microphone, waving and shouting to make them, so that as the train disappeared down the tracks, the sound of his voice remained behind with its final message, as when he shouted while the train was chugging away from the station in a little town in Virginia named Culpepper: "Good-bye, Culpepper. Vote Democratic. What has Dick Nixon ever done for Culpepper?" Since often the public-address system was still turned on as the train left, his audiences could also hear his asides to his staff. "Good-bye, Greer," he shouted to a little South Carolina town rapidly vanishing down the tracks. "Good-bye, Greer. God bless you, Greer. Bobby, turn off that 'Yeller Rose.' God bless you, Greer. Vote Democratic. Bobby, turn off that fuckin' 'Yeller Rose.' "

So wound up would he become that, sometimes, at the end of the day, he couldn't stop talking. One day his last stop was in Atlanta, Georgia, and the Special didn't pull into the yards behind Atlanta's Terminal Station, where a small crowd was waiting on the crossties, until after eleven o'clock. He was still speaking at midnight—when he was drowned out by a loud hiss as the train's engineer shut down its air brake for the night. His speech was very effective, reported Eugene Patterson of the *Atlanta Constitution.* "What he was doing was speaking the language. . . . He was likeable. He was folksy . . . earthy. . . . It was clear what his job is—to speak to the people in their own tongue while Kennedy addresses his broad A to the ages. Kennedy looks good on the white horse. Johnson dominates the caboose." And while the engineer had cut off Lyndon Johnson's speaking for the day, there were other means of campaigning. Grabbing a packet of Kennedy-Johnson campaign cards from an aide, Johnson climbed down from the rear platform, and, leaning "comfortably" against the steps, started handing them to the people filing by, like a blackjack dealer dealing cards. "His fawn Stetson sat on the back of his head," a reporter wrote. "A quizzical smile, hinting of spoofery, played around his mouth and eyes under the bright light. A card here, a card there, when he would lick his thumb and deal. . . . Imagine a blend of Harry Truman and Marshal Dillon dealing a hand of poker in the railroad yard near midnight and you've got a picture of Lyndon Johnson's visit to Atlanta."

"He seemed to like what he was doing," Patterson wrote—and the crowd "liked him."

And as that very perceptive reporter, Mary McGrory of the *Washington Evening Star,* put it, effective as Johnson was as a southern stump speaker, "the Senator was doing his best work not on the observation platform" of the train's last car but in the car in front of that one, which she called the train's "equivalent of the Senate cloakroom" (a southern reporter called it "a portable smoke-filled room").

That car—a parlor car with roomy, comfortable seats—was filled with southern politicians: a constantly changing cast of politicians. The local dignitaries who stepped out onto the rear platform with Johnson and got off in their town had boarded the train at the previous town, climbing into the parlor car to be offered drinks by Johnson's pretty secretaries and have impressively large "Official Party" badges pinned to their lapels. As soon as Johnson had finished his speech in that town, he and Lady Bird had come back into the parlor car to have their picture taken with the officials, and he would chat with them, charm them, and warn them what would happen to the South if Nixon won—or if Kennedy won without its support. Then there would be an announcement: "Five minutes till the next stop." The secretaries would line up the officials behind Johnson, and they would walk into the rear car and then to the rear door of the train, and, as "The Yellow Rose" blared and the train pulled into their town's station, would come out on the rear platform behind him, in front of their constituents, waving to them as if—"as befitted their importance"—they had been aboard the train for a long time, and would climb down into the midst of the hometown crowd. For a moment the parlor car would be empty, except for the secretaries. And then, as Johnson began his speech, a new group of dignitaries, from the next town down the line, would come aboard, climbing into the parlor car, to be handed their drinks and badges.

The efficiency of this technique maximized its impact: during the five days that the LBJ Special chugged through the Southland, the incredible number of 1,247 dignitaries—governors, senators, congressmen, state legislators, mayors, councilmen, sheriffs, bankers, businessmen and other pillars of local communities—were entertained in that parlor car. And maximizing its impact also was the unique ability of its host; after interviewing a group of local officials who had just descended from the train, McGrory summarized their comments: "In explaining the political realities, he remains peerless."

Coverage of the LBJ Special in northern papers was relatively cursory, and tinged with condescension (among themselves, reporters had dubbed the train the "Cornpone Special"), but in the South the headlines grew steadily larger—JOHNSON HAILED BY S.C. CROWDS; "LADY BIRD" MAKES BIG HIT AT PRESS SESSION; SOUTHERN DEMO POLITICOS FLOCKING TO JOHNSON'S SPECIAL; CANDIDATE FOR VICE PRESIDENT OF U.S. TO BE IN GREENVILLE 5:25 TODAY; JOHNSON MAKES FIERY TALK HERE; JOHNSON BRINGS CAMPAIGN TO MERIDIAN; JOHNSON SPEAKS HERE TODAY; LBJ'S SPECIAL CARAVAN SHARP, EFFICIENT SHOW; LBJ ON WAY, PARADE SLATED—and so did the crowds: two thousand in Clemson, three thousand in Meridian, five thousand in Gaffney, until, in an end-of-the-trip climax, Johnson led and then reviewed a Mardi Gras preview parade in New Orleans before one hundred thousand spectators. And the tour accomplished its purpose. Republican strategists saw its effect: the astute White House counsel Bryce Harlow told Nixon that he was "being religioned right out of this campaign. Lyndon is talking religion at every stop. . . . You're just flat losing the campaign on religion. . . . It's a calculated stance. Kennedy can't talk it. Lyndon can and Lyndon's talking it." Southern Democratic politicians aboard the LBJ Special were saying that, as Mary McGrory reported, "two weeks earlier, the Republicans would have won the election [in the South] if it had been held then, but that now the South had rejoined the flock." Skeptical though she had been when the tour started, at its conclusion McGrory wrote that Lyndon Johnson "has justified his existence on the Democratic ticket." Said another observer: "master of the political coup has done it again."

HOLDING HIS OWN STATE — or, to be more precise, bringing it back into the Democratic column after Eisenhower's lopsided victories there—was perhaps the toughest job of all. The anger of the state's conservatives over his decision to join Kennedy's ticket and thereby in effect run on the liberal Democratic platform had only intensified since the convention; signs with the word "Judas" on them had been waved at his every appearance in Texas. As always with Lyndon Johnson, the spectre of "humiliation" loomed before him. Writing John Connally on October 18 that he was "deeply disturbed about Texas," he added: "We just must not win the nation and lose Texas. Imagine when we win how the next Administration will look upon us." "The ever haunting fear of losing Texas never left him for a second," Jim Rowe was to recall; "he was wound up tight like a top." When he and Lady Bird arrived in Dallas on November 4, four days before the election, to attend a Democratic rally in the Adolphus Hotel, it appeared the fear might well prove justified; his private polls were showing the Democratic ticket to be slightly, but clearly, behind.

On that day, however, he got a break. An hour before the Democratic rally, there had been a Republican event at the Adolphus, attended mainly by wealthy right-wingers—many of the women were Dallas Junior Leaguers, wearing red-white-and-blue Nixon costumes. Hearing that the Johnsons would be arriving shortly, they crowded into the hotel's lobby, their hatred simmering, joining a group of placard-carrying men who had been organized by the state's only Republican congressman, Bruce Alger of Dallas, and as Lyndon and Lady Bird entered the lobby, they swarmed around them, shouting and cursing. Alger was raising and lowering his big sign, LBJ SOLD OUT TO YANKEE SOCIALISTS, like a piston, and it came dangerously close to Lady Bird's head. One woman snatched the gloves out of Lady Bird's hand, and threw them on the floor, and there was spitting in her direction. At one point, she fell several steps behind her husband, and there was a frightened expression on her face. Several Dallas policemen were escorting the Johnsons, but Lyndon told them to stand aside, and when General Carl L. Phinney, commander of the Texas National Guard, tried to step between Johnson and the demonstrators, Johnson said, "I want you to get away from me." It took the Johnsons thirty minutes to negotiate the seventy-five feet between the front door of the Adolphus and the elevators that took them up to the ballroom, where two thousand Democrats were waiting to greet them.

Not everyone who witnessed the scene was sure it had had to take that long. "LBJ and Lady Bird could have gone through that lobby and got on the elevator in five minutes, but LBJ took thirty minutes to go through that crowd, and it was all being recorded and played for television and radio and the newspapers, and he knew it and played it for all it was worth," says D. B. Hardeman, Rayburn's aide and a Johnson admirer. Bill Moyers says: "He knew it got votes for him. He could never have calculated that scene or fixed that situation or arranged for it. He didn't know how he was going to carry Texas, and he greatly feared losing Texas because he thought it would discredit him totally in the nation and with Kennedy. If he could have thought this up, he would have thought it up. Tried to invent it. But the moment it happened, he knew." Some Johnson admirers feel that was the reason he sent the policemen away. But whatever the reason, television that evening showed Lady Bird's frightened face and Lyndon saying, at the Democratic rally, that he had told the police to leave because "I wanted to find out if the time had come when I couldn't walk with my lady through the corridors of the hotels of Dallas." The incident turned the tide in Texas. Editorials in newspapers across the state echoed the *Abilene Reporter-News* comment that "a mob in Dallas yesterday wrote a new chapter that stands to the shame of our state and people, of whatever political shade." The next day, the Johnsons flew to Houston. Ashton Gonella recalls that "we had been told ahead of time that it [Houston] was really going to be ugly to us because they were very conservative; up to then, Texas had really not been that much for Kennedy-Johnson." When the Johnson plane arrived at the Houston airport, however, "it couldn't have been more overwhelming. Everybody had signs: 'WE APOLOGIZE. WE LOVE YOU.' " And during the remaining time before the election, the Johnsons were greeted everywhere in Texas with standing ovations.

LYNDON JOHNSON HAD something else on his side in Texas. His investment in George Parr was paying off.

In the election, on November 8, the Kennedy-Johnson ticket carried Texas, 1,167,932 votes to 1,121,699; Kennedy won by 46,233 votes out of 2,311,670 cast, winning 50.5 percent of the votes to 48.5 for Nixon (1 percent were cast for candidates of two minor parties). Hardly had the votes been tallied when Texas Republicans charged that tens of thousands of them were fraudulent—and that tens of thousands of other votes, legitimate votes, had fraudulently been invalidated, and not counted. The GOP complaints dealt not primarily with the state's big cities—Nixon carried Dallas, Fort Worth and Houston by almost 100,000 votes—where voting machines were used, but rather with the scores of counties in which voting was still by paper ballot, and in which voters had to sign numbered "poll lists" which made it possible for officials to know for whom they had cast their ballots, making a mockery of the concept of the secret ballot; well over half the ballots cast in Texas in 1960 were paper.

GOP complaints about most of the state centered on a technicality. Under a new state law—the 1960 election was the first time it was in effect—voters who used paper ballots were required not only to mark the candidate of their choice, but also to cross off the candidates they opposed, not only the candidate of the other major party, but the candidates of the two minor parties as well. Although one of the law's other provisions allowed judges to count votes (even if this requirement was not complied with) if the voter's intent was clear, the GOP, noting that the longtime Democratic dominance in the state meant that the election machinery—from precinct judges to the State Board of Elections canvassers—was overwhelmingly Democratic, charged that in pro-Nixon precincts many ballots were invalidated, in pro-Kennedy precincts far fewer. Republicans said that a spot check of just ninety-four precincts showed that fifty-nine thousand ballots had been invalidated; in some precincts, heavily pro-Nixon, the disqualification rate was 50 percent, they said. About certain areas of Texas, however—the sprawling Mexican-American slum in San Antonio that was known as the "West Side" and the impoverished Mexican-American counties south of San Antonio in the Lower Rio Grande Valley that formed the border between Texas and Mexico—the Republican complaints were not about technicalities.

In these areas—then known in a Texas political euphemism as the "ethnic bloc"—Mexican-American Catholics made up a substantial portion of the population, and the Kennedy edge in these areas has been generally attributed to his Catholicism, as well as to the activism of the younger Mexican-American World War II veterans who had established "Viva Kennedy" committees. Kennedy's Catholicism, the *Texas Observer* noted, had contributed to his victory in the thirty-nine counties throughout Texas in which Catholics comprised a majority of the population: while Eisenhower had carried twenty-eight of them in 1956, Kennedy carried thirty-five in 1960. This analysis, however, omits the factor considered decisive by some Texas political figures, including the two key ones, John Connally, who would in 1962 be elected the state's governor, and Edward A. Clark, the onetime Secretary of State and longtime "Secret Boss" of the state, a factor whose significance is demonstrated by the fact that while in the "Catholic" counties outside the San Antonio–Rio Grande areas, the shift from the Republican ticket in 1956 to the Democratic ticket in 1960 fell generally within limits that might be expected in elections held in a democracy, in San Antonio and the Rio Grande counties, the shift was outside those limits, and the majorities recorded for the Kennedy-Johnson ticket were startling in comparison with those recorded in the previous presidential election.

In that 1956 election, San Antonio (which used voting machines) supported the Republican ticket by a margin of 12,000 votes. In 1960, it supported the Democratic ticket by a margin of 19,000 votes. "This is a reversal of 31,000," former San Antonio Congressman Paul Kilday wrote Johnson. "We are quite proud of the results." The reversal was due largely to results from the West Side, which was run, with an iron hand, by Kilday's brother, Sheriff Owen Kilday. The West Side went for Kennedy-Johnson by a margin of 17,017 to 2,982, just over 14,000 votes. In one precinct (or "box") in that area, which had given Eisenhower a substantial majority in 1956, sentiment had evidently changed. Kennedy won, 1,324 to 125. Other West Side boxes recorded margins for Kennedy of 880 to 55 and 799 to 48.*

In the Valley border counties, the results were even more dramatic. For decades, as I wrote in *Means of Ascent,* the results reported from the "ethnic" towns

> had little to do with the preferences of the Mexican-Americans. The overwhelming majority of their votes had been cast at the orders of the Anglo-Saxon border dictators called *patrones* or *jefes,* orders often enforced by armed *pistoleros* who herded Mexican-Americans to the polls, told them how to vote, and then accompanied them into the voting cubbyholes to make sure the instructions were followed—if indeed the votes had been actually "cast" at all; in some of the Mexican-American areas, the local border dictators, in Texas political parlance, didn't "vote 'em," but rather just "counted 'em." In those areas, most of the voters didn't even go to the polls: the *jefes'* men would, as one observer put it, simply "go around to the Mexicans' homes. Get the numbers of their [poll tax] receipts. Tell them not to go to the polls. Just write in a hundred numbers, and cast the hundred votes yourself," or, after the polls closed, would simply take the tally sheets and add to the recorded total whatever number was needed to give their favored candidate the margin he desired. "You get down on the border, and it didn't matter how people [the Mexican-Americans] felt," Ed Clark would explain. "The leaders did it all. They could vote 'em or count 'em, either one."

Between 1948 and 1960, little had changed. In the latter election as in the former, George Parr counted them for Lyndon Johnson. The first sign was the pace of the counting. By the evening of election day, several hours after polls had closed, veteran reporters had noticed what one called the "slow-motion count of votes" in Duval—they knew what that meant; that the Duke was holding back a final tally until he saw whether the race was close, so that if it was, he could give his allies the votes they needed. At midnight, only one of Duval's ten precincts had reported a final tally. Then, finally, came the count itself. The Duke controlled not only Duval County but Starr County as well as a personal fiefdom. Duval voted for Kennedy-Johnson by a margin of 3,803 to 808, Starr by 4,051 to 284. In a petition for a recount filed with the state canvassing board three days after the election, Republicans charged that pistols were carried by "[election] judges and others in Duval County so that voters were intimidated and coerced."

*The vote for Bexar County as a whole was 75,298 for the Democratic ticket, 63,931 for the Republican.

Then there was Jim Wells County, or to be precise, the county's Precinct Thirteen: "Box 13," the precinct, already legendary in Texas political history, that in 1948 had provided the decisive margin for Lyndon Johnson by giving him two hundred new votes—the votes that were cast in alphabetical order and all in the same handwriting six days after the polls had closed. The Mexican-American reform movement had taken control of most of Jim Wells from Parr, but not the thirteenth precinct, the poorest Mexican district in the county seat of Alice. In 1960, that box gave Lyndon Johnson's ticket a margin of 1,144 to 45, or twenty-five to one, so the ticket came out of the heart of the Duke's Rio Grande domain with more than 88 percent of the vote—and a plurality of more than 7,800 votes.

The results were almost as lopsided in the counties controlled by Parr's allies, who followed his lead. In Webb County, it was 10,059 to 1,802, more than five to one; in Jim Hogg County, 1,255 to 244, more than five to one; in Brooks, 1,934 to 540, almost four to one. The nine counties controlled by Parr and his allies reported a total of 37,063 votes to the Texas Election Bureau. Almost 30,000 of them—29,377, or 79 percent—were for Kennedy-Johnson.* The Democratic ticket therefore came out of those counties with a plurality of 21,691.

"One charge of vote-buying and voter-herding," Earl Mazo reported in the *New York Herald Tribune,* "involves some Democratic leaders who are said to have purchased poll tax certificates in blocks of 300 to 3,000 at $1.75 for each certificate for use in precincts near the Mexican border," precincts which, he noted, "produced sizable Democratic majorities." There was, the GOP alleged, no secrecy in voting in these areas: in Precinct 8 of Benavides, in Duval County, a "local machine" supervisor kept a list of persons "voting against the machine." The Valley *patrones* who had given Johnson huge majorities in his 1941 and 1948 Senate races (and who would have done so in his 1954 race had they been needed) were still for Johnson, Clark and Connally explain. The Valley was still "strictly L.B.J. country," Duval County political operative O. P. Carrillo was to say. Catholicism was not the key, Connally says: "the basic core of the Johnson adherents in the Hispanic community"—he meant Parr and his allies—"were all still there [in 1960] and still loyal to him." When Clark was asked about the role of Catholicism and the "Viva Kennedy" organizations in the vote in Parr's Valley domain, he gave a slight smile, shook his head no and said that rather, "Our old friends stood by us."

Most important, George Parr had stood by Lyndon Johnson, and the reason, says Clark, was the Supreme Court decision. "He were grateful for the reversal," Clark was to say in his East Texas patois.

In the aftermath of Lyndon Johnson's 1948 election victory, an investiga-

---

*For the nine counties—Starr, Duval, Webb, Jim Hogg, Jim Wells, Brooks, Maverick, La Salle and Zapata—the major-party totals were 37,063 votes, of which Kennedy-Johnson received 29,377, or 79.3 percent, and Nixon-Lodge received 7,686, or 20.7 percent. In contrast to the 21,691 plurality, in 1956 these counties had given a plurality of only 7,432 votes to the Democratic ticket.

tion had been conducted by federal Masters in Chancery, appointed by a federal judge. The Chancery hearings were cut short by an order from United States Supreme Court Justice Hugo Black after arguments were made before him by Abe Fortas; enough witnesses had testified so that one of the Masters, the only one to comment, was to conclude, "I think Lyndon was put in the United States Senate with a stolen election." No investigation was ever made of the 1960 results. The Republican petition, alleging "numerous and widespread frauds," was brought before the three-man state canvassing board, whose members were Governor Price Daniel, Attorney General Will Wilson and the board's chairman, Secretary of State Zollie Steakly—three of Johnson's most active supporters in the campaign (Daniel and Wilson had been on the same ballot with him). Steakly said Texas law gave the Board no authority to investigate the returns, and hearings were simply delayed until after December 19, when the national Electoral College, using the totals furnished to them by the various states, the Texas total by the canvassing board, certified the overall vote. The truth of the Republican allegations was never examined in the depth necessary to ascertain their validity (as was also the case in Dick Daley's Illinois, where the results were even closer and where widespread fraud was also alleged).

The attention focused on fraud in the 1960 presidential campaign has during the intervening half century centered on Illinois, not Texas. The Republican allegations, not only about voting in the Valley but about the invalidating of ballots under the new state law, have never been examined in the depth necessary to ascertain their validity, much less to determine how many votes were affected if indeed the allegations were true. Nor have the many other factors—from demographic shifts in the state's population to the scene in the Adolphus Hotel—ever been examined in the necessary depth. Today, the passage of time has made it difficult—impossible, really—to ascertain, in trying to assess the election results in Texas, the weight that should be assigned, in an equation that contains so many factors, to the vote from the "ethnic bloc." Paul Kilday wrote of the 31,000-vote "reversal" in San Antonio, which of course included the 14,000-vote plurality the Kilday machine produced in that city's West Side. It would be misleading to speak of a "reversal" in the Valley, since George Parr and his allies could simply produce whatever result they wanted there. But Parr had demonstrated before that when he became angry at what he construed to be an inadequate lack of allegiance by some public official, he would retaliate in the next election by throwing the Valley's bloc vote to the official's opponent. How he might have reacted had Lyndon Johnson not assisted with his court case can be today, long after his death, a matter only for speculation, since, so far as the author can determine, no historian or journalist raised the matter with him before his death. But the point is moot in any event: Johnson produced the legal help, and Parr produced the votes—the 21,000 plurality. Thirty-one thousand and 21,000—in an election that was decided by 46,000 votes, the weight of those votes could hardly have been a minor factor. Whatever the explanation for the results from the "ethnic bloc" in Texas, John Kennedy had selected Lyndon Johnson in part to take back Texas for the Democratic presidential ticket, and Johnson had done it.

HE HAD TAKEN back the South, too.

"Republicans were stunned by their poor showing in Dixie," Evans and Novak were to write. Before Johnson was nominated, Republican strategists had been confident—in a confidence bolstered by poll results—that Nixon would hold all five of the former Confederate states that Eisenhower had carried in 1956—Texas, Louisiana, Florida, Tennessee and Virginia—and would pick up the two Carolinas as well, for a total of seven. In the event, it was Kennedy who carried seven; Nixon won only three southern states: Florida, Tennessee and Virginia. (Mississippi voted for a slate of independent electors.) Texas and Louisiana were brought back into the Democratic column, and both Carolinas stayed there—by very narrow margins. There were southwestern and border states in which Johnson's presence on the ticket may have been crucial—New Mexico's Clinton Anderson was to say flatly that without Johnson that state would have gone Republican; and in Missouri, as *U.S. News & World Report* reported, Johnson "is given much of the credit" for the narrow Democratic victory, but it is not necessary to go beyond the South in showing his impact on the result. Together, the Carolinas had 22 electoral votes, Louisiana 10, and of course there were Texas' 24—a total of 56 votes. The electoral vote by which Kennedy defeated Nixon was 303 to 219. Had those four states gone Republican, Kennedy would have had 247 electoral votes—and Nixon would have had 275.

On a national scale, of course, other factors were more significant in the 1960 campaign: Kennedy's triumph over Nixon in the televised debates; his courageous speech before the ministers in Houston; the telephone call he made to Martin Luther King's wife when the minister was arrested in Atlanta; the style, the elegance, the wit, the charisma of the handsome, debonair candidate that brought larger and larger, and more and more frenzied, crowds out to greet him in the cities of the Northeast. Despite all these factors, however, Kennedy might not have been elected President without Johnson. "John F. Kennedy could not have been elected President without the South," Evans and Novak were to conclude. "Could he have carried enough southern states to win" without Johnson on the ticket? "Probably not." "The key to the election had been in the South," said *U.S. News & World Report.* "And this was the land of Lyndon Johnson. It had backed him for the presidency and he had been put on the Kennedy ticket to hold it for the Democrats. Mr. Johnson did the job. He campaigned and cajoled and persuaded and wound up by getting almost all of the top-level Democrats in the South out fighting for the ticket." In Kennedy's suite at the Biltmore Hotel the morning after his nomination, the southern governors had told him, one after the other, that the only way to hold their states was to put Johnson on the ticket. Kennedy had put him on—and the states had been held. Eighty-one of the South's 128 electoral votes had gone to Kennedy-Johnson; Nixon had received only 33 (14 went to Mississippi's independent slate).

As the decades have rolled by since that election, the picture of the Kennedy campaign etched at the time by the journalists traveling with it and by the campaign's first—and most famous—chronicler, Theodore H. White, became a staple of American political legend. Lyndon Johnson was only peripherally a part of that legend. In the 173 pages in *The Making of the President 1960* that White devoted to the post-convention campaign, the Adolphus incident is mentioned only in a phrase, as was Johnson's role in the South as a whole; his name appears in those pages exactly seven times, always as a brief mention. In a vivid portrait of efficiency and sophistication, of Ivy League charm and a group of brilliant young men transforming American politics, what room remained for a tall, thick, bellowing figure with his arms flailing above his head, shouting, "What has Dick Nixon ever done for Culpepper?," for the endless blaring repetition of "The Yellow Rose of Texas," for the "Cornpone Special"? In the years since White's book established the terms of reference by which the 1960 campaign is considered, there has been scant reference to the scene at the Adolphus. Even in discussions of possible fraud in the election, and of how it might have changed the overall result, it had been Illinois on which most of the focus has remained, not those border counties down on the Rio Grande. But Johnson should have been a part of the chronicles, as one of Kennedy's intimates, Ted Sorensen—the only one, really, to give Johnson more than passing mention—acknowledges. Noting that Kennedy's margin of victory in Texas had been 46,000, and that a switch in votes by 23,000 voters would therefore have turned the tide, Sorensen wrote that "The maltreatment to which he [Johnson] and his wife were subjected by a shoving and booing crowd of disorderly Republican fanatics in Dallas undoubtedly helped switch more than the 23,000. . . . And had it not been for the return of Texas and Louisiana to the Democratic column . . . and for the Carolinas staying Democratic against a predicted Republican victory, Nixon would have won the election." Kennedy had "gambled" on Lyndon Johnson, Sorensen wrote. "That gamble paid off." Jack Kennedy himself was to say to Ken O'Donnell in 1962: "You have to admit I was right. We couldn't have won without him."

On election night, from Austin, Johnson made a call to Jack Kennedy. "I am carrying Texas," he said. "I hear *you* are losing Ohio, and *we* are doing fine in Pennsylvania." Kennedy turned away from the phone with a smile. "We?" It was *he* who was going to be President. Lyndon Johnson was going to be Vice President.

Part II

"RUFUS CORNPONE"

6

"Power Is Where Power Goes"

"POWER IS WHERE POWER GOES": the most significant factor in any equation that adds up to political power, Lyndon Johnson had assured his allies, is the individual, not the office; for a man with a gift for acquiring power, whatever office he held would become powerful—because of what he would make out of it.

Johnson felt he had that gift—"I do understand power, whatever else may be said about me," he had once told an aide. "I know where to look for it, and how to use it"—and nothing in his career, at least nothing in his career before he began running for the presidency, made that assessment seem immodest. At every stage in his life, from college onward, he had demonstrated not only that he possessed the gift, but that he possessed it in a particularly rare and creative form: the ability to look at an organization that had little or no political power, to perceive in it political potentialities that no one else had ever seen, to acquire a position in the organization, and then to transform the organization into a political force, so that the office he held, and he, as its holder, became powerful. At every stage, the gift had been maximized by the ruthlessness with which he grabbed for the power he perceived and with which he wielded the power once he had it, but nothing could diminish the brilliance of the perception.

At college—a sleepy teachers college deep in the Texas Hill Country—the organization was a small social club, the "White Stars." Becoming its leader, he turned it into a political organization, disciplined and secret, brought it into campus politics—"he *created* campus politics, really"; previously, "no one even cared" about campus elections—and through means that included a stolen election and the use against a young woman student of what his lieutenants called "blackmail," made himself, an extremely unpopular young man on College Hill, the student with the most influence there. Then he persuaded the college president to give him a say over which students would get campus jobs. At this "poor boys' school" the choice was often stark: get a teaching diploma or live out a life of drudgery on your family's lonely farm or ranch. The wages from a campus job were often a student's only hope of paying his tuition. "Twenty cents an hour and you either went to school or you didn't," one says. "And Lyndon would say [who would] get that job."

The gift worked on Capitol Hill as well as on College Hill. There, the organization was the "Little Congress," an almost moribund debating society of congressional aides that had degenerated into little more than a poorly attended social club, and the office he acquired was its Speaker. After Johnson won that office, in an election, in 1933, that also would not bear close scrutiny, the organization was transformed, an invitation to address it now prized in Washington, and the Speaker became one congressional aide who had access to powerful congressmen and senators, and prestige as well: seeing Johnson striding self-importantly down a Capitol corridor, a newly arrived congressional aide asked who he was, and was told, "That's the Boss of the Little Congress."

The Democratic Congressional Campaign Committee, with two employees and little cash, was, in 1940, another almost moribund organization that no one took seriously—except Lyndon Johnson. The junior congressman saw two things that no one else saw. The first was a possible connection between two groups that had previously had no link: conservative Texas oilmen and contractors—most notably his financial backer, Herman Brown, of Brown & Root—who needed federal contracts and tax breaks and were willing to spend money, a lot of money, to get them; and the scores of northern, liberal congressmen, running for re-election, who needed money for their campaigns. The second was that he could become that link. Although the only position he could obtain with the committee was a vague, informal one, without any title at all, with it he forged the link: made himself the conduit through which the Texas contributions passed, the congressman to whom, junior or not, other congressmen had to appeal for campaign financing. By the end of the 1940 campaign, the committee had become a key funding source, and at the age of thirty-two he had his first toehold on national power.

Hardly had he arrived in the Senate in 1949, after the most notorious of his elections, when he began seeking the post of his party's Assistant Leader, or "whip." Two years later, he got it—got it easily: no one else wanted it; it was, everyone agreed, a "nothing job." But Johnson made it a significant job, and then became Leader, a position historically so powerless—"I have nothing to threaten them with, nothing to promise them," one of his immediate predecessors as Leader had said—that no one really wanted that job, either; the most influential and respected senators routinely refused to take it; previous Leaders' inability to actually lead the Senate, or even to control it, had for years made Leaders figures of ridicule. Johnson took it—sought it, maneuvered for it—and so transformed it that a journalist, watching him run the Senate, said he seemed to be "running the world!" and journalists in general bestowed on him the title "The second most powerful man in the country." All his life Lyndon Johnson had been taking "nothing jobs" and making them into something—something big.

And now, no sooner had he been elected to the vice presidency than he tried to do the same thing with that office.

THE CONSTITUTION OF THE UNITED STATES says that the Vice President shall preside over the Senate, "but shall have no vote, unless they be equally divided." It says that in case of the President's "death, resignation or inability to discharge the powers and duties of said office, the same shall devolve on the vice-president." And, in regard to the powers of a Vice President, that is all it says.* With the exception of his ability to cast a vote to break a tie in the Senate, the document that created the office attached to it, not a single specific power. Provisions in the Constitution, moreover, stand in the way of a Vice President's acquiring power. Its very first lines—Article I, Section 1—state that "All legislative powers herein granted shall be vested in a Congress of the United States," that the Congress "shall consist of a Senate and a House of Representatives" and that the Senate "shall be composed of two senators from each state." Of senators only—no mention of a Vice President. The Founding Fathers were concerned that the mere fact of the Vice President presiding over the Senate might blur the overarching principle of separation of powers, that the office, as Hugh Williamson of North Carolina put it during the Constitutional Convention of 1787, would then "mix too much of the Legislative and Executive, which . . . ought to be kept as separate as possible." "In particular," as one study of the office put it, the Founders "seem to fear that the President would somehow gain ascendance over the Senate through the Vice President." They needn't have worried. No body could have been a more staunch guardian of the separation principle, more fiercely jealous of its independence from the executive branch. The Senate, the Constitution says, makes its own rules, and its rules (together with its precedents) grant only to senators (and, upon appropriate notice, former Presidents) the right to address the body or to participate in debate. It doesn't give that right to a Vice President. He could sit in the presiding officer's chair in the Senate; he couldn't be a part of it, couldn't even speak on the floor except with its consent. As for the authority given him by his right of presiding over it, the Senate had, after some decades in the early nineteenth century in which Vice Presidents had indeed intruded, taken care that its rules and precedents would in future keep such intrusion by the executive branch to a minimum, had done so

---

*The Twelfth Amendment to the Constitution, adopted in 1794, says that he "shall open" the envelopes containing the certifications from the various states of their electoral votes in presidential elections, but opening them (and perhaps announcing the results: the amendment is unclear about that) is his only function in this ceremony. The Twenty-fifth Amendment, dealing with the death or disability of a President and the Vice President's assumption of his powers, would not be adopted until 1967.

with such thoroughness that in fact by 1960 a Vice President possessed no significant power that couldn't be exercised just as well by the newest freshman senator, if *he* was presiding in the Vice President's place (and in fact, with Vice
Presidents having little taste for the almost purely ceremonial role, it was often
freshmen senators who were assigned to sit in the presiding officer's chair).

Article I of the Constitution deals with legislative powers. Article II deals
with executive powers. "The executive power shall be vested in a president of the
United States of America," states the Article's first lines. In the President—not in
any manner in the Vice President. Succeeding sections of that Article enumerate
the presidential powers—to act as commander in chief of the armed forces, for
example, or to veto legislation passed by Congress, or to grant pardons. No provision in the Constitution authorizes a President to delegate any of these
powers—any of "the executive power"—to a Vice President. Even should
Congress wish to, it can't get around that barrier. "Any formal allocation of
power to the Vice President would conflict with the clause in the Constitution
vesting the undivided 'executive power' in the President," stated one study of the
situation. There was, moreover, a further barrier. The various great departments
of government—not only the Department of Agriculture, the Department of the
Interior, all the departments whose heads sat as the President's Cabinet—but
other major if non-Cabinet-level federal agencies as well had been established by
law: by statutes enacted by Congress. In establishing these departments, Congress had laid out boundaries, statutory boundaries, of their authority. Powers
delegated to a Vice President by a President might infringe on those statutory
powers. This conflict—and the weakness of the Vice President's role in it—had
become clear during a President's attempt to give his Vice President what was
accurately called "the only big job ever handed a Vice President" during the
almost two centuries the United States had been in existence: the executive order
that Franklin Roosevelt issued in July, 1941, after, with war looming, he had
declared a state of national emergency. "By virtue of the existence of the emergency," he created an Economic Defense Board to coordinate planning for the
looming war with broad powers over areas such as imports, exports and the
stockpiling of strategic materials, and made Vice President Henry A. Wallace its
chairman, in a position that gave Wallace broad authority in such areas. No
sooner had the board been created, however, than the inherent conflict between
the Vice President's role and the powers of other Cabinet members had erupted
in open hostility. In their conflict with Wallace, the Cabinet members had Congress behind them. No President since then had made any similar attempt.

As for the possibility of a President making a more informal delegation of
powers to a Vice President, that possibility was hazy. Nothing specific stood in the
way of his being given major responsibilities within the executive branch—should
the President wish to do so. But there was a practical consideration that might
make him reluctant to do so. Under the Constitution, the Vice President is not a
subordinate of the President; the document mentions only one method of remov-

ing a vice president from office—through impeachment by Congress; it confers on a President no power to remove him (as he could remove a Cabinet officer, for example) should he use the delegated powers to initiate policies that conflicted with a President's wishes, or to defy a President. For a President to confer power on someone whom he can fire is one thing; conferring power on someone he can't fire is a risk, and a big one. At the beginning of 1961, the Vice President had only one position to which he was entitled by law—membership in the National Security Council, a body that had been created not to make decisions but to advise a President. Kennedy had proposed that another law be passed that would make Lyndon Johnson not merely a member but chairman of the National Aeronautics and Space Council, but this, too, was an advisory, not a decision-making, body. Kennedy also told Johnson that he wanted him to succeed his predecessor Vice President, Nixon, in another virtually powerless role: the chairmanship of a committee monitoring racial discrimination in government contracts. When Johnson analyzed the three positions he would be holding, "he discovered something very quickly," George Reedy says—that they carried with them only "a derivative power of the President. . . . He discovered that none of the power was his . . . that any power that a vice president has is just power which has been given him by a president and can be taken back." When, shortly after his inauguration, Johnson asked Deputy Attorney General Nicholas de Belleville Katzenbach for a study of other possible duties in the executive branch, he would be told that "the nature and number of" those duties "are, as a practical matter, within the discretion of the President." In later decades, the role of the Vice President would be gradually and substantially enlarged—at the discretion of the President—but at the time of the 1960 election, that was where the office stood. No legislative powers, no executive powers, and obstacles, hitherto insurmountable obstacles, to obtaining any— except what the President might choose to give him.

But "power is where power goes." Hardly had he been elected to the vice presidency than Lyndon Johnson launched a campaign, unprecedented in American history on several levels, that, had it succeeded, would not only have dramatically transformed the nature of the office—but would also, in the process, have undermined the concept of the separation of executive and legislative powers embedded in the Constitution.

THE LYNDON JOHNSON WHO was maneuvering for power now, however, wasn't the Lyndon Johnson who throughout most of his career had calculated so thoughtfully, made his moves so subtly, demonstrated always so deft a hand, when he was seeking power. He was the Lyndon Johnson of the last year or two, when, with the great prize so close at last, the fear of failure so great, he had made, over and over again, the stops and starts, the frantic flurries of desperation— when he would listen to nothing he didn't want to hear, when "you couldn't reason with him."

The campaign had two fronts, a mile and a half apart on Pennsylvania Avenue.

One was on Capitol Hill. The formal conference, or "caucus," of the Senate's Democratic members had traditionally been presided over by the senator who had been elected their Leader: Johnson, of course, had been the conference chairman for the past eight years. Now Johnson asked the senator who was to succeed him as Majority Leader—his Assistant Leader, Mike Mansfield—to allow him to continue as conference chairman. He assured Mansfield that the chairmanship would be merely a symbolic honor in recognition of his past services, a *pro forma* position, as Mansfield was to put it; Johnson may have said— he was to use this argument later—that since the Constitution already gave the Vice President the duty of presiding over the Senate as a whole, presiding over a party caucus was only another, similar function.

Persuading Mansfield was not difficult. The Montanan was a quiet, accommodating, philosophical man who, as one account noted, "owed his prominence in the Senate solely to Johnson's selection of him as his Assistant Leader," and who in that job had had, as he himself said, "no work to do: he [Johnson] kept control even when he went to Texas" through "his conduit, Bobby Baker." Taking Johnson at his word—"In my view," Mansfield was to say, "this would constitute (only) an honorary position, and I had no objection"—he agreed.

This, in itself, would have been a revolutionary step. As Evans and Novak were to say, Mansfield was agreeing to do "what no other Senate had ever done: breach the constitutional separation of powers by making the Vice President the presiding officer of all the Senate Democrats whenever they met in formal conference." But Johnson was not in fact intending the chairmanship to be *pro forma* at all—as became clearer when he also persuaded Mansfield to let him retain what was to Washington the symbol of his senatorial power: his awesome "Taj Mahal" office. Although this office, convenient to the Senate Chamber, had been the Majority Leader's office, Mansfield agreed to let Johnson keep using it, saying he himself would be more comfortable operating from a less pretentious suite. Then it was announced that the conduit through which the power flowed would remain in place as well; Bobby Baker would stay on as secretary for the majority. "I think that Mansfield inherited Baker passively," Larry O'Brien says. "Baker had the job, and he wouldn't throw him out any more than he would demand the Majority Leader's office and that the Vice President remove himself from it."

But Johnson also had to persuade senators far less malleable than Mansfield—and that proved a very different story.

Sometime in December, with Mansfield's agreement secured, Johnson invited four longtime senatorial allies—Robert Kerr, Hubert Humphrey, George Smathers and Richard Russell—to a meeting not in the Capitol but in a private dining room at the Sheraton-Carlton Hotel, "probably hoping," as Humphrey puts it, "to keep it a secret," and told them of his plan to retain the caucus chairmanship.

It was obvious to the four senators that Johnson's plans for the post included more than merely presiding over the caucus. "He had often controlled, constantly influenced the course of legislation" from that "powerful position" for eight years, Humphrey was to say, and now he was planning to continue doing so, to use the chairmanship, in Humphrey's words, "to hang on to [the power] he had wielded as Majority Leader" as a *"de facto* Majority Leader"; Johnson "had the illusions that he could be in a sense, as Vice President, the Majority Leader."

His proposal violated what was to these senators one of the Senate's most sacred precepts—its independence of the executive branch; he was proposing that a member of that branch preside over their meetings. Misgivings were voiced, but, as Humphrey puts it, "Johnson was not an easy man to tell you can't do something," and he evidently felt he had persuaded his old allies. Summoned to the Taj Mahal, Baker found "a buoyancy about him that lately had been missing." "Bobby," he said, "I've been thinking about where I can do Jack Kennedy the most good. And it's right here on this Hill. All those Bostons and Harvards don't know any more about Capitol Hill than an old maid does about fucking. I'm gonna keep this office, and help Mike Mansfield and Bob Kerr and Hubert Humphrey pass the Kennedy program. It's gonna be just the way it was! You can keep on helping me like you've always done. . . . Bobby, I'm working it out."

And, in fact, had Johnson's plan succeeded, in many ways it would indeed have been "just the way it was." In several conversations during this period, he also mentioned, seemingly casually, that he planned to "sit in" on meetings of the Democratic Policy and Steering Committees. These committees—the first, known for years as "Johnson's rubber stamp," exercised considerable control over the fate of legislation Democratic senators wanted passed; the second had absolute control over the committee assignments crucial to senators' careers— had been keys to his domination of his party's senators; most of their members had been his allies, long accustomed to accede to his wishes; that was why they were on the committees. He had always been able to count on them to do his bidding and evidently felt they would continue to do so. Had his plan succeeded, although he would no longer be Majority Leader in name, both of these key instruments through which he had controlled the Senate would still be in his hands, not in those of the "amenable" Mansfield. "He was going to be vice president *and* Majority Leader," Ken O'Donnell says. And if he was—if the Vice President was also the leader of the Senate majority—the Vice President would possess a source of power totally outside the executive branch, power separate from, and independent of, the President. Kennedy would not be able to deal with him as if he was merely a subordinate. Johnson had told Baker that he was keeping the caucus leadership to "help Jack Kennedy's program." But what if he opposed some aspect of that program, this leader with a firm control of the Senate? His opposition might have behind it an institution that, as he had already demonstrated, could be quite successful in opposing a President.

However, Johnson's belief that his plan would be accepted was only another example of how his loss of confidence had eroded his gift. Certain though he was that it would succeed, it never really had much of a chance. When Baker heard it, he was to recall, "I was both astonished and horrified. If anyone knew the United States Senate, its proud members and its proud traditions, it was Lyndon B. Johnson. Surely he knew that the prerogatives of membership were jealously guarded, that no member of the Executive Branch—even a Lyndon Johnson—would be welcomed in."

Though "I saw a disaster in the making," Baker says, when he attempted to "interpose reservations . . . , I had a hard time doing so." Having worked himself up into believing that the plan would succeed, willed himself into the state in which he believed that whatever was in his mind was reality, Johnson just talked over him. "Blinded by his plans, his ego and his past Senate successes," Baker says, he refused to listen to anything he didn't want to hear. As had been the case ever since he had accepted the vice presidential nomination, in fact, this "revving up" was at a level of intensity rare even for him. Baker had often seen him in what he calls a "manic mood"; this time, he says, Johnson "seemed excessively manic."

An aspect of the relationship between Lyndon Johnson and power that had been evident through his life was that the more of it he got, the more intoxicated he became with it. Now he had had a lot of it ("My God—running the world!"), and had had it for a long time: the eight years he had been the Democratic Leader of the Senate, minority and majority. And there was on Capitol Hill an understanding that he had restored the Senate to respect it had not enjoyed for more than a century, that he had transformed the institution from something very near a joke into a force to be reckoned with, and had therefore transformed its members as well, so that being a senator now meant so much more than before. Surely, he felt, these men wouldn't want to go back to the situation that existed before he became Leader. He had boasted to his aides that he had the Old Bulls who ran the Senate in the palm of his hand, and indeed he did; the feelings of many of them toward him were almost paternal. As long as he had them behind him, the more junior senators didn't much signify. But, he felt, the juniors, too, must of course be grateful for all he had done for them: changing the seniority system to place them in their freshman year in prestigious committee seats it would previously have taken them years to attain, giving them in other ways, too, opportunities to play a significant role in achieving governmental objectives of which they could be proud. *They were his children; it was his Senate.* "I feel sort of like a father to these boys," he had explained to reporters. "A good father uses a gentle but firm rein." He had been "enveloped" by power ("Good morning, Leader," "Could I have a minute of your time, Leader?" "Mr. Leader, I never thought you could pull that one off"). Of course, they would be happy to let him keep running it. "He thought he *was* the Senate," Neil MacNeil says.

Johnson's reasoning was overlooking two factors. One was personal, and had to do with those young senators he treated like "boys." As had been the case throughout his life, the more power Johnson acquired, the more cavalier he became in its use; respectful, even obsequious to men whose backing he needed to get power, as soon as he didn't need them anymore, he became overbearing, domineering, in his dealings with them. In the Senate, too, that had been the pattern—not with the most powerful of the Old Bulls: "He didn't rant and rave at the Harry Byrds of the world," George Smathers would say. "Oh no, he was passive, and so submissive, and so condescending, you couldn't believe it! I've seen him kiss Harry Byrd's ass until it was disgusting"; with these powerful committee chairmen, he was as fawning as he had ever been—but with the younger senators. Another continuing motif of Lyndon Johnson's career—one that had been repeated in every institution in which he had climbed to power—was that the more power he acquired, the more he reveled in its use, flaunting it, using it often just for the sake of using it, bending men to his will just to show them he could, as, at college, no student was given one of those desperately needed jobs just because the student needed one, or because the student was a friend, no matter how close a friend, of Lyndon Johnson's. *"You had to ask."* And when the power had been solidified—when he was in charge, and confident of staying there—the flaunting was as dramatic as the fawning had been. "During his early years as Leader, he put on a humble-pie act that would have done credit to Ella Cinders," George Reedy was to say. "This faded overnight." With senators other than the Old Bulls, he made it clear that no disobedience to his wishes would be tolerated, that his leadership had to be accepted completely, that as he had told Estes Kefauver, a senator who wanted to get ahead in the Senate not only had to be on his team but had to *"want* to be on that team." Senators who accepted the rein received rewards from his hand—prize committee assignments; prize office space; prize junkets; a place for their bills at the head of the Senate calendar. Those who didn't, he not only ignored but humiliated—in the hundred ways a Leader could humiliate a junior senator. And not all senators, no matter how junior, liked being reined in, liked having to ask for things to which, under Senate rules and traditions, they were entitled, liked having to beg. And those of them who were liberal—and this included not only junior senators but longtime liberal stalwarts like Herbert Lehman, Paul Douglas and Albert Gore of Tennessee—felt, as well, that by allying himself on crucial matters with the southern Bulls, Johnson was the most formidable obstacle to the achievement of liberal objectives. They were already, in Evans and Novak's description, "brooding that Johnson would try to run the Senate from the Vice President's chair, with Mansfield, the self-effacing, introspective former professor who was uncomfortable with power, deferring to him," and they felt their misgivings deepen as news leaked out about his plan. "Having watched him operate for eight years, Democratic senators were fearful of what he might do now if he got a toe in the door. An unspoken sentiment among many senators was the fear that if Johnson became *de facto* chairman of the conference, he would use that position to become *de facto* Majority Leader, with tentacles of power into both the Steering and Policy Committees," which he, not Mansfield, would still control.

The feelings of these senators didn't matter so long as Johnson still had the Old Bulls behind him, as the 51–12 vote on Proxmire's resolution had proved. But Johnson was not taking into account that the particular issue at hand—allowing a Vice President to preside over the Democratic Senatorial Conference—was one issue on which the Old Bulls wouldn't be behind him. Strong as was their affection for Johnson, they loved the Senate more, and the heart of the Senate to them was its independence of the executive branch.

Johnson must have been aware of their feelings, and of their reverence for this Senate tradition, and if he needed to be reminded, both Humphrey and Baker tried to remind him. But, having worked himself up, he wasn't listening to anything he didn't want to hear.

And then he had no choice but to listen. At 9:45 a.m. on January 3, still a senator—he would not resign until the new Senate convened at noon—and still Majority Leader and Caucus chairman, he strode into the Democratic Caucus with a broad, confident smile on his face, sat down at the small table that had been placed in the front of the room, gaveled the caucus to order, and said that the first order of business was to elect a new Leader. After Mansfield was elected (by acclamation), however, Johnson did not hand him the gavel and surrender his chair. And Mansfield, sitting down instead in a chair next to Johnson's, made a motion, the minutes state, that "the Vice President–elect preside over future conferences."

"Can you imagine that?" Robert Byrd of West Virginia, a Johnson team member but also a very firm believer in senatorial precedents, was to ask. "This action . . . reflected the quiet and unassuming nature of Mike Mansfield, but it was a mistake." Another historian writes that until that moment, "Despite Johnson's signals, few senators [had anticipated] the extent of his power grab." Now, with understanding suddenly dawning, one by one, liberals—Douglas, Gore, Joseph Clark—rose to stand at their seats, right in front of Johnson, to denounce the proposal to his face. "I don't know of any right for a Vice President to preside or even be here with senators," Gore said. "This Caucus is not open to former Senators." Johnson's face flushed with anger.

While objections from liberals could, of course, be disregarded, other hands were being raised—the hands of Old Bulls. One after another, Johnson recognized them, expecting them to support Mansfield's motion; one after another, they attacked it. Even Clinton Anderson, one of Johnson's closest allies in the Senate, attacked it, saying that "to allow a member of the Executive Branch to preside over the Conference would not only shatter the principle of separation of powers but would make the Senate look ridiculous." Johnson's face, so red a few minutes before, had turned ashen. All of the Old Bulls included praise of Johnson in their remarks, Baker says, "but there was no getting around that they were inviting him out of their inner circle." Insisting that he had no intention of "sharing either [his] responsibility or authority," and that he had intended the motion only as recognition of Johnson's achievements, Mansfield said the motion was entirely his own idea. He repeated this several times. "With each repetition, fewer members believed that to be true," says a Mansfield aide who was present. "Instead, the murmurs of disbelief indicated that they were beginning to suspect that Mansfield had been had by Johnson." When Mansfield made a personal appeal for his proposal, a vote was taken supporting it, "but," as Baker says, "everyone in the room knew that Johnson had been rebuffed." Hardly had the Democrats left the caucus room when word began circulating through the Senate Office Building that if necessary there would be another vote—one that would have a different result. When several friendly senators tried to make this clear to Johnson, they found only a reluctance to face reality—"It was too much for him to leave that center of power," Humphrey says. "He was just very reluctant to give up those reins." The senator to whom he had to listen was delegated to make him face it, and after Richard Russell spoke to him, he did: at the next day's Democratic Caucus, there was only one chair at the presiding officer's table, and Mansfield was sitting in it; Lyndon Johnson was not present. As always, he had a vivid phrase to describe what had occurred. "I now know the difference between a caucus and a cactus," he told Baker. "In a cactus, all the pricks are on the outside." But no words could hide the pain. "Those bastards sandbagged me," he told Baker. "They had to humiliate me in public."

THE OTHER FRONT OPENED BY JOHNSON in his campaign for power as the Vice President was a mile and a half west on Pennsylvania Avenue. Previous Vice Presidents had had their office in the Capitol; no Vice President in the country's history had had one in the White House. Johnson asked Kennedy for an office there, and not just any office but a room right next to the Oval Office. Johnson's predecessors had had staffs of their own, but rather small ones, housed either in the Capitol or some government office building. Johnson wanted a large staff—a very large one; he had had some fifty persons working for him as Senate Majority Leader, and he seems to have envisioned keeping most of them as Vice President. And he didn't want them set off from Kennedy's staff. He was to ask Kennedy for permission "to appoint a staff within the Executive Office of the President." And this would have been quite a staff. "He told me, 'I want to establish a little Joint Chiefs of Staff in my office,' " says Colonel Kenneth E. BeLieu, a longtime Johnson aide and at that time executive officer to Secretary of the Army Frank Pace. So confident was Johnson that he would be allowed to establish one that he told BeLieu to begin interviewing senior military officers for the posts; BeLieu, taking into account what Johnson wanted in his advisers, had to tell one candidate, an Army colonel otherwise well qualified, that "You have a habit of telling people when you think they're wrong, and I don't think you'd get along with Lyndon." (Actually, BeLieu explains, with a smile, the first time the colonel disagreed with Lyndon, "Lyndon would have crucified him.")

And then there was the proposed executive order that Johnson, shortly after the disastrous Senate caucus, sent to the White House for President Kennedy's signature.

The date and exact wording of the order originally sent to Kennedy's office, and of a letter, also drafted by Johnson for Kennedy's signature, that accompanied it, are unknown. No copies can be found in either the Lyndon B. Johnson Library or the John F. Kennedy Library. Several persons who saw the order at the time say it would have given the Vice President "general supervision" over a wide range of national security issues. After discussing the matter with the Harvard historian Richard Neustadt, who was advising Kennedy on the transition, Doris Goodwin was to write that the "unusual" document, "outlining a wide range of issues over which the new Vice President would have 'general supervision,' " also "put all the departments and agencies" concerned with national security "on notice that Lyndon Johnson was to receive all reports, information and policy plans that were generally sent to the President himself." The draft of the order and the letter would be revised, perhaps on suggestions from the White House before Kennedy himself saw them. The revised drafts finally submitted to the President—they have been preserved for history—do not contain the words "general supervision." Instead the draft of the executive order states that "in order to provide a more effective coordination of the departments and agencies of the government concerned with national security, the Vice President is hereby designated and empowered to exercise continuing surveillance and review, and to advise the President, with respect to the integration of domestic, foreign and military policies relating to national security."

Vague though the "surveillance and review" phrase may have been, succeeding clauses in this final draft of the executive order made it more specific. One authorized the Vice President "to obtain all pertinent information concerning the policies and operations of" the State Department, the Defense Department, the Central Intelligence Agency, the Budget Bureau and the Office of Civil and Defense Mobilization as well as "other Government departments involved in national security matters." Another clause said that "in the performance of [these] functions," the Vice President, "whenever necessary and with the approval of the head of the department or agency concerned," was authorized to use their "established facilities and personnel." And another clause would make it difficult for a department or agency head to refuse that approval whenever the Vice President asked for it. "All elements and agencies of the United States shall cooperate fully with the Vice President in the carrying out of these assignments," it said.

The order was not written by, or, during its preparation, even seen by, the man who had for the past decade been so successfully playing the key role in drafting Johnson documents: George Reedy. Lyndon "did not like opposition, and was in a mood where he was bypassing me on projects to which he suspected I might be negative." And "He was right about this one," Reedy says. When he finally got a glimpse of it (BeLieu showed it to him), he knew at once that it was "a blunder on his part—far greater than his misreading of the Senate Democrats." No opportunity was given him to offer any input, however. "Before I could protest, it was on its way to the White House." A friend—apparently Jim Rowe—to whom Johnson showed it after it had already been sent was, Evans and Novak wrote, "flabbergasted." It was, Rowe said, "frankly, the most presumptuous document any Vice President had ever sent to his President."

Of even more significance was Kennedy's handling of the executive order and letter that Johnson was suggesting he sign. When Johnson met with Kennedy in the Oval Office on January 28, no executive order but only a letter ("Dear Mr. Vice President . . .") was handed back to him, and it contained no authorization for him to conduct "continuing surveillance" or "general supervision" of anything; no such phrases remained in the letter, and neither did the phrase "I am directing you"; all the letter said on the subject of national security was "I am hereby requesting you to review policies relating to the national security"—a meaningless phrase that conferred no power at all. There was no provision in Kennedy's letter for any additional staff—there was no mention in the letter of any staff at all. There was no mention of any use by the Vice President of the agencies' "facilities and personnel"; all Kennedy was now saying was that he would expect the agencies "to cooperate fully with you in providing information." As for the proposed executive order, that had disappeared from the scene entirely. Kennedy did not hand Johnson any version of an order at all, edited or otherwise; no executive order bearing on the Vice President and national security was ever issued.

REEDY HOPED AGAINST HOPE that no word of the incident would leak out, but these hopes were dashed on February 9 when the nationally syndicated columnist Marquis Childs walked into his office and said, as Reedy later reported to Johnson, that "he understood the relations between you and the President were 'like this' (making jabbing motions with his hands like two men fighting)" and mentioned that "a very responsible White House official" had told him that there had been an incident between the two men that was "so major that a parallel could not be found in history without going back all the way to Seward's letter to Lincoln." The White House official, Childs said, "declined to describe the incident other than in terms of the" Seward parallel, but since Seward's letter to Lincoln—actually a memo sent by Secretary of State William H. Seward shortly after Lincoln's inauguration—had sought extraordinary power for himself at the President's expense (it would have made him, an historian wrote, the equivalent of "a prime minster, with Lincoln the figurehead"), Reedy knew that the Kennedy official had been referring to Johnson's proposed executive order.

Aside from one rather oblique reference in Childs' column ("There were predictions that Johnson would insist that . . . he should be at least equal [to the President] in executive authority. Knowing persons suggested a parallel between

Abraham Lincoln and . . . Seward") and in a few others, the incident received little publicity—a fact that is perhaps the most significant aspect of the incident.
Kennedy simply didn't publicize it and, except to a very few close aides, didn't
even disclose it. Lincoln had handled Seward's power grab by all but ignoring it;
he wrote a response to Seward—if a policy was to be carried out, he said, "*I* must
do it"—but never sent it; it remained buried in his papers until it was discovered
decades later. As one of his biographers later wrote: "Had Mr. Lincoln been an
envious or resentful man, he could not have wished for a better occasion to put a
rival under his feet," even, perhaps, by dismissing him, but instead he demonstrated an "unselfish magnanimity" which was "the central marvel of the whole
affair." John Fitzgerald Kennedy had handled Johnson's power grab the same
way, as Reedy saw: thanks to Kennedy, he was to say, "the whole thing was
lost in charitable silence." The President had handled it magnanimously and
casually—as if there had been no reason to take it seriously.

He handled the same way all Johnson's attempts of those first very early
days to expand the vice presidency's formal, institutional powers. When Johnson's suggestion that he be given an office next door to the Oval Office was mentioned to him, Kennedy was "flabbergasted," his secretary Evelyn Lincoln
recalls. "I have never heard of such a thing," he told her, but his response was to
simply instruct her to instead give him one "over in the Executive Office Building," across from the White House. Johnson's suggestion of his own staff within
the President's Executive Office would be brought up again; Kennedy simply
ignored it. (When Johnson said there was virtually no provision for staff aside
from positions allowed a Vice President on the Senate payroll because of his
"presiding" role there, Kennedy allowed him sixteen posts that he could fill—
attached not to the executive office but to the Department of Defense.)

At the end of all his scheming and maneuvering, what he got—the only
new responsibilities Kennedy gave him—were the chairmanships of two committees: the National Space Council and the President's Committee on Equal
Employment Opportunity. The impressive ring to the assignments—the nine-
member Space Council had been created as a central coordinating body for
America's growing involvement in space, and the CEEO to prevent racial discrimination by companies that received government contracts—was hollow to
someone who understood them, and Johnson's understanding was thorough, particularly about the Space Council, since it had been he who, leading the Senate's
investigation in 1957 of America's space program following Russia's launching
of *Sputnik,* the first man-made satellite to orbit the earth, had introduced the legislation setting it up, and had thereafter watched President Eisenhower rapidly
reduce it from a coordinating to a purely advisory body, "not one that makes
decisions."

The limits on the amount of advice Kennedy was willing to receive from the council became apparent with that body's first task: to recommend an administrator for the National Aeronautics and Space Administration. Kennedy asked for the recommendation from his science adviser, Jerome B. Wiesner, not from the Space Council or from Johnson himself. Only after Wiesner's recommendations—nine in all—proved, one after another, unacceptable was Johnson's opinion finally solicited. And the man selected on his recommendation, James E. Webb, a former Budget Bureau director who had become an executive in Senator Kerr's oil and gas empire, quickly learned, as he was to put it, that Kennedy "wanted to control the agenda of the Council, that he wanted to determine those items on which he would accept advice," and, most crucially, that he wanted the all-important budget for space projects to be drawn up not by the council but by the Budget Director. Kennedy "was not about to abdicate those decisions to anyone," Webb says.

The council's other members included the secretaries of state and defense, Dean Rusk and Robert McNamara, and the atomic energy commissioner, Glenn T. Seaborg, all of whom had staffs of technical experts to prepare their positions on issues that came before the council; Johnson didn't. Attempting to obtain funds to hire some, he requested a doubling of the previous year's half-million-dollar appropriation for the council—and the Senate rejected his request, a further rebuff from that body which left him "bitter and hurt." The *Times* would soon be reporting that it was known at NASA that "Mr. Johnson's hand, if it has been laid upon that organization at all, has been light, indeed." Aside from Webb's appointment, "Mr. Johnson's activities and influence there are scarcely visible."

If the first chairmanship was frustrating, the second—of the Committee on Equal Employment Opportunity—carried with it a threat of damage to his ambitions. If you accept the post, Rowe wrote him in alarm, "You will become the target of . . . the 'advanced' liberals because you are not doing everything and also the target of the southerners every time you try to do something even minor. . . . It will be impossible to satisfy either group no matter what you do." The warning was unnecessary; Johnson was well aware that no proposal had enraged southerners more than attempts to force employers to hire black men and women for jobs in which they would be working in proximity to white men and women; Richard Russell, outflanked by Franklin Roosevelt in 1941, when, after the Georgia Giant had blocked the creation of a Fair Employment Practices Commission in the Senate, the President had created it by executive order, had been hamstringing its activities ever since by slashing its appropriations, and by amendments limiting its jurisdiction and activities. Complaining to aides that as committee chairman "I don't have any budget, and I don't have any power, I don't have anything," Johnson tried to refuse the job by arguing that it exceeded a Vice President's constitutional responsibilities, but found that refusal was not an option. Kennedy, he was to say, replied that "You've got to do it because Nixon had it before"; since the committee had been chaired by the Vice President in the previous administration, his own administration, to show its commitment to civil rights, could do no less than have *its* Vice President take over the job. Johnson asked for an executive order that would assure him that the Vice President had authority to chair such a committee—thinking that the order would, incidentally, give him specific powers. Kennedy agreed to the request, and an order was drafted, by Robert Kennedy's aide Nicholas Katzenbach; when Johnson read it, however, he found that it provided only the assurance, not the authority, reorganizing the committee in ways that made Johnson's dilemma worse than before. While the order indeed enlarged the committee's powers, they were to be exercised not by the chairman but by the vice chairman, Secretary of Labor Arthur Goldberg, who shall have "general supervision and direction of [its] work . . . and of the execution and implementation of the policies and purposes of this order." The vice chairman was empowered to appoint an executive vice chairman to run the committee's day-to-day operations, and Goldberg appointed a man from Texas, not one of Johnson's allies in the state but Jerry R. Holleman, longtime president of the Texas AFL-CIO and a key figure in the liberal—anti-Johnson—wing of the state's Democratic Party. "Under the way in which the executive order was written, Jerry Holleman has control over the staff and the best we can do is review his proposals," Reedy told Johnson. Was that not bad enough? Holleman appointed as his second-in-command—committee executive director—John G. Feild, an aggressive, militant official of the Michigan Fair Employment Practices Commission (FEPC) and the very epitome of an "advanced" liberal. Johnson tried to keep a measure of control over the committee by having its staff communicate with Holleman through Reedy. Johnson should insist on this, Reedy told him. "Administration is in the hands of Goldberg and Holleman. Nevertheless, in the public mind, the responsibility for this Committee inevitably falls upon the Vice President and therefore there should be the closest liaison in terms of . . . approving actions." Holleman refused even this suggestion. The next memo from Reedy reported that "Jerry Holleman is going to insist [that] I contact the committee staff only through him."

Frantic, Johnson asked Reedy and Abe Fortas to find a way to get out of the chairmanship, only to be told there wasn't one. "It is going to be somewhat difficult to drop the . . . committee without some form of achievement first," Reedy wrote him on February 8. Johnson had insisted on an executive order—and he had gotten one.

By the time all these initial maneuvers were over—by the end, certainly, of the first month of the Kennedy presidency—the misreading of John F. Kennedy by Lyndon Johnson was over, too. He had read him now, all the way through: The younger man was a lot smarter than Johnson had thought he was—and a lot tougher, too. He was always, without exception, whatever the provocation, the gentleman—but a very tough gentleman. Nothing could have been more gracious than the way he had handled Johnson's requests—and nothing could have been more unyielding. Some months afterward, Johnson would be talking off the record to Russell Baker of the *New York Times,* and, Baker was to write years later, "there was a tribute [from Johnson] to the steely strength with which President Kennedy dispatched his enemies"—a tribute couched in rather remarkable words: Johnson described Kennedy "when he looks you straight in the eye and puts that knife into you without flinching."

THE INAUGURATION OF JOHN FITZGERALD KENNEDY was one of the memorable days of American history, for a presidential inauguration is a day for inspiration. "Let the word go forth from this time and place, to friend and foe alike, that the torch has been passed to a new generation of Americans"; "Let every nation know, whether it wishes us well or ill, that we shall pay any price, bear any burden, meet any hardship, support any friend, oppose any foe, to assure the survival and the success of liberty"—the phrases of Kennedy's inaugural address were so gloriously inspiring even before the ringing voice said, "And so, my fellow Americans, ask not what your country can do for you—ask what you can do for your country" that they summoned up, and, in some ways, summed up, the best of the American spirit, igniting hopes so that, almost on the instant it seemed, they summoned up a new era for Americans, an era of ideals, of brightness, of hope. "Oh, Jack," his wife said afterwards, her hand stroking his face, "Oh, Jack, what a day!"

It was a very different kind of a day for Lyndon Johnson. The stands erected for the inauguration were in front of the Capitol's long eastern façade. During Johnson's time as a young congressional aide, he had passed along the length of that façade every morning on his way to the House Office Building from his basement room, with its uncovered steam pipes running across the ceiling, in a shabby little hotel near Union Station. The young woman who worked in the same office with him, and who would sometimes see him coming to work, noticed that as he was passing the façade, he almost always broke excitedly into a run, as if the façade's sheer majesty, with its towering white marble columns and its parapets and friezes jammed with heroic figures, all gleamingly, dazzlingly white as they were struck full by the early-morning sun, had, perhaps, in its symbolic evocation of what he was aiming for, and in its contrast with the shabby little houses of the Hill Country from which he had come, touched something deep within him. Perhaps Lyndon Johnson had dreamed on some of those mornings of a presidential Inauguration Day. But he certainly hadn't dreamed of a day like this one; whatever he had dreamed, it had not been of sitting on the inaugural platform, squinting into the sun, listening to another, younger man speak. And as he sat there on this day, he knew that his plans to obtain some measure of independent power of his own, separate from the new President's, had been thwarted. He was going to be completely dependent on whatever that younger man chose to give him—for years to come.

7

Genuine Warmth

HOW MUCH OF WHAT FOLLOWED can be laid at that young man's door is obscured by his manners, his graciousness and his opacity.

Arthur M. Schlesinger, Jr., whose books set the lens through which history has viewed the relationship between Kennedy and Johnson, wrote that Kennedy "liked Johnson personally, valued his counsel on questions of legislation and public opinion and was determined that, as Vice President, Johnson should experience the full respect and dignity of the office. He took every care to keep Johnson fully informed. He made sure he was at major meetings and ceremonies. Nor would he tolerate from his staff the slightest disparagement of the Vice President." He "always had a certain fondness for Lyndon Johnson," Schlesinger wrote. "He saw his Vice President, with perhaps the merest touch of condescension, as an American original, a figure out of Mark Twain, not as a threat but as a character." Occasionally he called him, in that context, "Riverboat." Theodore Sorensen, who did similar lens-setting himself in his first two books before a drastic, and very honorable, readjustment in his final book (and in interview after interview with the author of this book) was, in those first two books, equally effusive. "The President and Vice President, to the astonishment of many and somewhat to the surprise of them both, got along famously," he wrote. "Their initial wariness gave way to genuine warmth. Johnson's vast energies were enlisted in a wide range of undertakings. . . . The President . . . took pains to have him present at all the major meetings. . . ."

Certainly, many of Kennedy's instructions to his aides—at least during his Administration's early days—support this view. "I can't afford to have my Vice President, who knows every reporter in Washington, going around saying we're all screwed up," he told his appointments secretary, Ken O'Donnell, "so we're going to keep him happy." Telling O'Donnell that that was *his* assignment— that he was, as O'Donnell puts it, "in charge of the care and feeding of Lyndon Johnson"—he told him to handle the job with sensitivity. "Lyndon Johnson was . . . the number one Democrat in the United States elected by us [Democratic senators] to be our leader. I'm President of the United States. He doesn't even like that. He thinks he's ten times more important than I am, he happens to be that kind of a fellow. But he thinks you're nothing but a clerk. Just keep that right in your mind. You have never been elected to anything by anybody, and you are dealing with a very insecure, sensitive man with a huge ego. I want you literally to kiss his fanny from one end of Washington to the other." He told O'Donnell that he had given Johnson permission to enter the Oval Office unannounced, through the doors that led out into the Rose Garden, although it appears to be understood that this was a *pro forma* courtesy; if Johnson ever took advantage of it, no one in the White House can remember the occasion. Summoning his chief of protocol, Angier Biddle Duke, the President said, "I want you to take care of the Vice President and Mrs. Johnson. I want you to watch over them and see that they're not ignored. . . . Because I'm going to forget. My staff is going to forget. We're all going to forget. We've got too much to do around here . . . and I want you to remember."

Kennedy instructed his legislative assistant Lee White that the Vice President was to be included in all major meetings—not only of the National Security Council, of which he was of course a statutory member, but of the Cabinet and the regular Tuesday breakfasts with legislative leaders—and when, at a meeting during the first weeks of his presidency, Kennedy noticed that Johnson was not present because White had forgotten to notify him, he said, in an angry tone, "Don't let this ever happen again. You know what my rules are, and we will not conduct meetings without the vice president being present." And there is even a statement supporting that view from Reedy, who, during a conversation with Schlesinger, said, "President Kennedy was rather generous to Vice President Johnson." ("But that didn't mean that Vice President Johnson appreciated it in the slightest," Reedy added. "Johnson was insatiable," Schlesinger said in reporting this conversation. For him, "no amount of consideration would have been enough.") And that view has been accepted by historians, both by historians who wrote about it first—"The President made of Johnson, as much as any President can make of his Vice President, a working participant in national affairs," Theodore H. White wrote in 1964—and by those who wrote about it decades later. Kennedy "had genuine regard for Johnson as a 'political operator' and even liked his 'roguish qualities,' " Robert Dallek wrote in 1998. "More important, he viewed him as someone who, despite the limitations of the vice presidency, could contribute to the national well-being in foreign and domestic affairs and, by so doing, make Kennedy a more effective President."

A number of incidents that occurred during the next three years, however, raise the question of whether that setting of the lens was quite as precise as it might have been.

Some, at least in the early days of the Kennedy Administration, were the result of Johnson's attempts to create an image of himself as one of its key players, a valued adviser (more than an adviser: in a way a partner of this younger, less experienced man); of his attempts to push himself forward into that position; and of the fact that he was dealing with a man who didn't like to be pushed—and who wasn't going to be pushed, certainly not by someone he didn't need anymore.

There was, for example, the scene that occurred just before the first weekly 9 a.m. breakfast meeting of the legislative leaders—Rayburn, McCormack and Majority Whip Carl Albert of the House; Mansfield, Majority Whip Humphrey and Smathers from the Senate—in the Cabinet Room in the West Wing of the White House, just down the hall from the Oval Office, on Tuesday, January 24. On Monday, Johnson had telephoned Kennedy to suggest that he come to the Mansion (the central portion of the White House, in which the President's living quarters are located) about a half hour before the meeting, so that he could discuss matters with the President, and that they then walk over to the meeting together, and Kennedy had agreed. Now, emerging from the rear of the Mansion just before nine, they walked along the colonnade behind the White House to the West Wing, Johnson, in Evelyn Lincoln's recollection, "talking and gesturing," very much the man giving advice. Kennedy let him talk, but he didn't let him walk into the Cabinet Room with him. Just as they reached its door, Mrs. Lincoln saw, Kennedy motioned to Johnson to go in. He himself walked past the door and into the Oval Office.

"Mr. Kennedy stopped by his desk, glanced at his schedule for the day, had a few words with . . . Kenny O'Donnell, looked at the clock, pushed back the hair from his forehead, seemed to wait a moment," obviously killing time, Mrs. Lincoln was to recall. "And then he slowly walked through the door," out through her office, and only then entered the Cabinet Room, where the legislative leaders—and Johnson—were standing waiting for him. He hadn't wanted to walk into the meeting with Johnson beside him. And when he walked into the meeting, Johnson hadn't *been* beside him.

Then, when the meeting ended, Mrs. Lincoln says, "Mr. Johnson followed Mr. Kennedy right into the President's office." During the next fifteen minutes or so, she came into the office several times with telephone messages for Kennedy. Each time she came in, Johnson, standing in front of Kennedy's desk, was talking, his right arm raised and his forefinger jabbing at Kennedy. "In a loud voice he would preface his remarks with, 'Now let me tell you, Jack.' " And each time she came in, Kennedy, saying "very little," was shuffling through papers on his desk. Finally, he stood up, looked pointedly at his schedule and said, "That's fine, Lyndon," and Lyndon left.

That scene—Johnson lecturing and jabbing, Kennedy "fiddling with papers"—"was one that I was going to see many, many, many times whenever Johnson was in that office alone with Mr. Kennedy," Mrs. Lincoln says. But, in fact, there weren't all that many times. During the entire year of 1961, Mrs. Lincoln was to calculate from her diary entries, Johnson spent a total of ten hours and nineteen minutes alone with Kennedy—less than an hour per month. During that year, he had breakfast alone with the President twice. He had had more breakfasts, many more breakfasts, alone with a President—President Roosevelt—when he had been a junior congressman twenty years before.

And if that incident was a response to Johnson's pushing, there were others that couldn't be laid at the Vice President's door.

Kennedy's instructions that Johnson be invited to the large formal meetings of the Cabinet, the National Security Council and the legislative leaders were followed, at least for a while. In the Kennedy White House, however, as Theodore Sorensen was to admit, it was not in such formal meetings but in "the smaller and more informal meetings" of presidential intimates that "the final decisions were often made"—and to such meetings, from the early days of the Kennedy presidency, Kennedy quite often "did not invite him."

Johnson's exclusion was particularly striking in the area in which he had expected to play his most significant role: guiding the Kennedy Administration's program through Congress. Lawrence O'Brien was put in charge of that task, and Kennedy made it clear that O'Brien was, in fact, the man to see. When a senator or a congressman called the President, Kennedy would ask: "Have you talked to Larry O'Brien about this. . . . You should talk to Larry." As O'Brien puts it: "It didn't take long for them to recognize [that] Larry O'Brien spoke for the President." Not long at all. Within a few days Johnson realized that he wasn't the man whom senators and representatives were calling when they were negotiating about something with the Administration, or asking it for some favor.

There were, of course, some strategic explanations for Johnson's exclusion. One was his reputation, the aura of legislative genius that surrounded him in the eyes of newsmen who had watched his mastery of the Senate. One of the new President's characteristics was an affection for the spotlight—and a disinclination to share it. To the suggestion that the renowned poet Robert Frost be given a role in the inauguration, he had responded with approval—and caution. The role should not be a speech, he said. "Frost is a master of words. His remarks will detract from my inaugural address if we're not careful. Why not have him read a poem—something that won't put him in competition with me?" Johnson was a master of something, too—legislative tactics—and, as one historian writes, Kennedy "did not want [Johnson] managing [the Administration's] legislative program and creating the impression that the President was following the lead of his Vice President, a more experienced legislator." Another explanation was Johnson's ego, which, as O'Brien aide Myer Feldman puts it, Kennedy felt "was so great it might handicap the Administration." Once Lyndon Johnson was again roaming free on Capitol Hill, his native habitat, there would be no controlling him. "If he had been unleashed he would have found it hard to refrain from running the whole show," his aide Harry McPherson says.

Considerations of policy may also have played a role. "If Kennedy had allowed Johnson to conduct his congressional relations, he would in effect have made the Vice President the judge of what was legislatively feasible and therefore lost control over his own program," Arthur Schlesinger wrote. "This was something no sensible President would do. Kennedy therefore relied on his own congressional liaison staff under Lawrence O'Brien, calling on the Vice President only on particular occasions."

Johnson's exclusion from this area of political activity extended to advice as well as participation, however. "Never in about two years" had O'Brien so much as stopped by his office to ask for any, he would tell McPherson near the end of 1962. O'Brien, a tough Irish pol, had great admiration for Johnson, as it happened, and was always "tactful and courteous" with him, but there was a line he never permitted Johnson to cross. On Sundays, O'Brien and his wife, Elva, invited senators, representatives and journalists to mingle with Administration insiders at brunch at their house in Georgetown. At one time—during his twelve years in the Senate, in fact, and, indeed, even before that, during his later years in the House—Lyndon Johnson's house had been the place to be on Sundays if you wanted to know what was really going on on Capitol Hill.

Not anymore.

AND ON THOSE OCCASIONS WHEN, as at one of the Tuesday breakfasts, he offered his opinion on legislative matters, it was not treated with particular respect. "He was so resentful of being at the breakfasts with . . . Mansfield and Hubert Humphrey, who was quite voluble, speaking on every issue," says O'Donnell. "And they sort of all treated Lyndon like he was one of them and he didn't want to be treated like he was one of them. If he did say something, they'd say, 'I don't think you're right. You haven't been up there lately.' " These were men who had once shown him deference, and more than deference. Once, after Johnson had given Hubert Humphrey an order on the Senate floor and he hadn't moved fast enough to suit the Leader, Johnson, snarling "Get goin' now!," had kicked him—hard—in the shin to speed him on his way, and Humphrey had accepted the kick without complaint, had even pulled up his pant leg the next day to proudly show a reporter the scar. Now Humphrey talked back to him, told him he was wrong.

Estelle Harbin, the woman who had worked in the same office with Johnson when he first came to Washington, had observed that even as a new congressional aide, he "couldn't stand being just one of a crowd—just could not *stand* it." Congresswoman Helen Gahagan Douglas, who had come to know him later (and who became his mistress), had noticed the same characteristic: watching him on the floor of the House when he had been just another representative, she had seen "the picture of boredom, slumped in his seat with his eyes half closed. Then suddenly he'd jump to his feet, nervous . . . as if he couldn't bear it another minute." That was the picture of Lyndon Johnson at social as well as political gatherings; at dinner parties, he wanted to monopolize the conversation; if other guests persisted in talking, he would close his eyes and go to sleep, or at least appear to, until a gap in the conversation let him start talking again.

And if the senators didn't listen to him, certainly the bright young men of the Administration who attended the leaders' breakfasts—O'Donnell, O'Brien and O'Brien's aides Feldman and White—didn't. Says an occasional attendee, Wilbur Mills, chairman of the House Ways and Means Committee, "The President had more or less shelved the Vice President, . . . turned him out to pasture." The congressional leaders saw that the Administration's men didn't put much stock in his opinions. So why should they? No one listened to him. "The greatest legislative prestidigitator of his time" had been stripped of any opportunity to use his sleight of hand.

In status-conscious Washington, it did not take long for such a dramatic change to be noted. By March 19, Tom Wicker of the *New York Times* was writing that "Those who have watched his giant strides about Washington this past decade" are "puzzled." The Administration has kept this "proud and forceful figure . . . out of sight and out of print."

Johnson's response to the new position in which he found himself was to hardly talk at all at Cabinet, National Security Council and legislative leaders' meetings—even when directly invited by the President. Kennedy would ask him for his recommendation on the particular issue at hand, or, if a decision was being taken, whether he approved of it. Johnson would answer in monosyllables—and in a voice so soft that sometimes it could not be heard, so that he would have to be asked to repeat himself. One of his tactics throughout his life—one of the techniques he employed to bend people to his will—had been to make them feel sorry for him, to pity him, until, moved at last by his distress and his sad state, they gave way, at which point he would promptly revert to his normal self, with a speed and thoroughness so dramatic that they made it obvious that this sad demeanor was indeed only a tactic. This technique had had success even with people as familiar with it as Jim Rowe. Having observed Johnson close up for more than twenty years, Rowe was aware, he says, that Johnson would always use "whatever he could" to "make people feel sorry for him" because "that helped him get what he wanted from them." But that awareness didn't help Rowe when, in 1956, the person from whom Johnson wanted something was *him*. Having observed also how Johnson treated people on his payroll, he had for years been rejecting Johnson's offers to join his staff, and had been determined never to do so. But Johnson's heart attack in 1955 gave him a new weapon—and in January, 1956, he deployed it, saying, in a low, earnest voice, "I wish you would come down to the Senate and help me." And when Rowe refused, using his law practice as an excuse ("I said, 'I can't afford it, I'll lose clients' "), Johnson began telling other members of their circle how cruel it was of Jim to refuse to take a little of the load off a man at death's door. "People I knew were coming up to me on the street—on the *street*—and saying, 'Why aren't you helping Lyndon? Don't you know how sick he is? How can you let him down when he needs you?' "

Johnson had spoken to Rowe's law partner, Rowe found. "To my amazement, Corcoran was saying, 'You just can't do this to Lyndon Johnson!' I said,

'What do you mean I can't do it?' He said, 'Never mind the clients. We'll hold down the law firm.' " Johnson had spoken to Rowe's wife. "One night, Elizabeth turned on me: 'Why are you doing this to poor Lyndon?' "

Then Lyndon Johnson came to Jim Rowe's office again, pleading with him, crying real tears as he sat doubled over, his face in his hands. "He wept. 'I'm going to die. You're an old friend. I thought you were my friend and you don't care that I'm going to die. It's just selfish of you, typically selfish.' "

Finally Rowe said, "Oh, goddamn it, all right"—and then "as soon as Lyndon got what he wanted," Rowe was forcibly reminded why he had been determined not to join his staff. The moment the words were out of Rowe's mouth, Johnson straightened up, and his tone changed instantly from one of pleading to one of cold command.

"Just remember," he said. "I make the decisions. You don't."

Now this technique was used with Jack Kennedy. At meetings, the soft voice was coupled with a face that varied between sullen and sorrowful—the look of a very sad man. And if pressed particularly pointedly by the President for an explanation or a recommendation, he would say, "I'm not competent to advise you on this," sometimes adding that he didn't have enough information on the subject, statements that Kennedy viewed, in Sorensen's phrase, as being Johnson's "own subtle way of complaining to the President" about his treatment.

With Kennedy, however, the tactic had no success at all. "I cannot stand Johnson's damn long face," the President told his buddy Smathers. "He just comes in, sits at the Cabinet meetings with his face all screwed up, never says anything. He looks so sad. . . . You've seen him, George, you know him, he doesn't even open his mouth." Smathers suggested foreign travel. "You ought to send him on a trip so that he can get all of the fanfare and all of the attention . . . build up his ego again, let him have a great time"—and also, although Smathers didn't say it, get him out of Kennedy's hair. "You know, that's a damn good idea," Kennedy replied—and at the beginning of April sent him to Senegal, which was celebrating the first anniversary of its independence.

ONE EARLY INCIDENT is difficult indeed to reconcile with statements that Lyndon Johnson was being included "at all the major meetings," that he was being made "a working participant in national affairs."

On Saturday morning, April 15, he flew to Norfolk on a Military Air Transport Service plane, to crown his daughter Lynda Bird as Virginia's Azalea Queen. As it happened, other military planes were in the air that morning: eight old B-26 bombers were bombing and strafing airfields in Cuba as a prelude to the Bay of Pigs invasion, which would take place in two days. Johnson did not know the bombing was taking place—or that the invasion was imminent. He may not have known that there was going to *be* an invasion. Shortly after the inauguration, he had attended a few meetings on the general Cuban situation, but from the moment serious planning began, he was, in Dallek's words, "systematically excluded" from any part in it. During the month before April 15, meeting after meeting had been held at the White House and State Department to plan for the attempt to overthrow Cuban dictator Fidel Castro. Johnson had participated in none of them. Kennedy had, in fact, made sure that he wouldn't even be in Washington on the weekend of the invasion. He had asked the Vice President to entertain German Chancellor Konrad Adenauer that weekend—on his ranch in Texas.

Flying there directly from Norfolk, Johnson was waiting at the ranch when the chancellor arrived. On Sunday, with the fourteen-hundred-man Cuban Exile Brigade at sea and heading for Cuba, Johnson was introducing Adenauer at the Gillespie County Fair in Fredricksburg, the German town near his ranch. And on Monday, the day the Brigade landed, to be pinned down on the beach and eventually forced to surrender—those of them who survived—to Castro's forces, Johnson was introducing the chancellor before his speech to the Texas Legislature in Austin. Only that evening did he return to Washington.

The next day Johnson was invited to attend a meeting on Cuba—a *postmortem* on what had gone wrong. Whatever mistakes the President had made in authorizing the invasion (which had left more than one hundred members of the Brigade dead, with an additional twelve hundred taken prisoner, and the strengthening of Fidel Castro's position; it was, the historian Theodore Draper said, "one of those rare events in history—a perfect failure")—an invasion in which, in an attempt to conceal American involvement, Kennedy refused to send air cover even when the men on the beach, encircled by thousands of Fidel Castro's troops and being strafed by Soviet-made MIG-15 fighters, were asking for the American air support they thought they had been promised—the President accepted the blame for them. Misled though he had been by the CIA and the Joint Chiefs of Staff ("Those sons-of-bitches with all the fruit salad" who "just sat there nodding, saying it would work") about the invasion's chances of success, he took every bit of the blame. "There's an old saying that victory has a hundred fathers and defeat is an orphan," he said; not this defeat. "President Kennedy has stated from the beginning that as President he bears sole responsibility," a White House release declared. "He has stated it on all occasions and he restates it now. . . . The President is strongly opposed to anyone within or without the administration attempting to shift the responsibility." No matter how upset he was by having had to leave men on the beach (Salinger found the President crying in his bedroom the morning after the invasion; when he came downstairs later, he looked a little disheveled, his hair not combed right, the knot of his necktie slightly askew; more than once in the days that followed the Bay of Pigs, friends saw John Kennedy talking to himself; sometimes he would blurt out, in the midst of conversations on other topics: "How could I have been so stupid?"), no matter how the realization of the cost of his miscalculations tormented him (walking into Ken O'Donnell's office one morning, he told him he had had a sleepless night: "I was thinking of those poor guys in prison down there"; when

he was arranging the ransom of the prisoners the next year, "It was," Richard
Cardinal Cushing of Boston said, "the first time I ever saw tears in his eyes"), no
one was taking the blame but him. During the *postmortem* meeting on the catastrophe, however, Johnson launched into what has been described as "a general
criticism of" the CIA. Kennedy said, "Lyndon, you've got to remember we're all
in this, and that, when I accepted responsibility for this operation, I took the
entire responsibility on myself, and I think we should have no sort of passing of
the buck or backbiting, however justified." At the first meeting on the Bay of Pigs
to which Johnson was invited, he had been rebuked by the President in front of
the other men at the table.

PART OF THE EXPLANATION for the attitude of President Kennedy and many
members of the Kennedy Administration toward Lyndon Johnson was suspicion
and fear—of this figure who for so long had loomed so large over their lives, as
the Leader, as their most feared opponent in the fight for the presidential nomination: of what he might do, this master of politics, if they gave him the slightest
opening. All but unmentioned though the "Seward" episode may have been in
the press, it wasn't forgotten by the men who knew about it—White House aides
were still repeating around Washington that Lyndon Johnson had tried "to pull a
William Seward"—and it proved to them that the Vice President would grab
power at the slightest opportunity; "newspapermen" were still telling Reedy and
Busby, as Busby reported to Johnson, "that the White House is unhappy over the
Vice President seizing power." One journalist, *Time*'s Sidey, was later to write
that "At least part of the problem in Johnson's vice presidency was LBJ's personality and lust for power. The more restless he got, the more suspicious of him
Kennedy's people became." Part of the explanation was the fact that Johnson, as
Kennedy put it, "knows every newspaperman in Washington," and could, and
probably would, leak to journalists any information they let him have. So they
made sure he had as little as possible.

Another part of the explanation was Johnson's natural aggressiveness—
which manifested itself to them in ways that confirmed their feelings that he was
still trying to grab a bigger role in the Administration than they wanted him to
have; that, as Evelyn Lincoln was to say, his "immediate thought was of his
image," not of the President's. A constant reminder of this was Johnson's unending appeals, when the two men were traveling to the same city, to be allowed to
fly with Kennedy on Air Force One, appeals that Mrs. Lincoln felt were being
made so that he would be photographed getting out of the plane with the President, share in his spotlight. This "constant argument," as Lincoln calls it,
"cropped up every time the two men were going to make a joint appearance."
"You don't mean to say that Mr. Johnson is again insisting on riding with me,"
Kennedy would say. "How many times must I tell him that the President and
Vice President, as a matter of security, should never ride on the same plane."
(The requests were always refused, and the refusal to be allowed to ride on Air

Force One "bothered the Vice President more than anything else," Lincoln says.)

After he moved into his office in the Executive Office Building, Johnson unveiled a new strategy to demonstrate how close to the President he was, how much an insider in the Administration. His car, a long black Cadillac, with its impressive license plate, "111," familiar to Washington journalists, would pull onto West Executive Avenue, the narrow street between the White House and the Executive Office Building, and Johnson would get out and walk, not into the EOB, but along the rear of the White House on a concrete sidewalk, past the doors to the Oval Office, until he came to the next door, that opened into Evelyn Lincoln's office, and walk inside. After glancing into the Oval Office—which was almost invariably empty; Johnson arrived rather early, before the President—he would stand in Mrs. Lincoln's office, chatting with the Administration staffers and officials who were coming in and out. After a while, he would leave by the other door in her office, on a route which took him by the press room, where a group of journalists would be sitting, before walking across to the EOB. Mrs. Lincoln felt she understood why Johnson was doing this. "By coming into my office, Mr. Johnson was creating the image of working closely with Mr. Kennedy," she was to write, especially if he was in her office "when any of the Cabinet men or other officials came in." And by emerging from the President's part of the White House when he walked by the journalists, he would give them the same impression. And she felt she understood why Johnson's car would remain standing outside the West Wing all the time he was inside—as an advertisement that he was inside.

Part of the explanation for the Kennedy attitude, however, was more personal. If there exists copious documentation of the President's remarks demonstrating "genuine warmth" toward the Vice President, there were nonetheless other remarks. "Kennedy is funny about LBJ," Ben Bradlee was to write. "He really likes his roguish qualities, respects him enormously as a political operator, a politician who can get things done, and he thinks Lady Bird is 'neat.' But there are times . . . when LBJ's simple presence seems to bug him. It's not noble to watch, but there it is." Sometimes in the President's descriptions of his Vice President an adjective would slip in that wasn't all that funny. "The President used to say he wasn't like anyone he'd ever known . . . somewhat monstrous . . . larger than life . . . with a comic side," Joseph Alsop recalls.

And if Kennedy had given instructions to his aides to avoid "the slightest disparagement of the Vice President," to let him "experience the full respect and dignity of the office," they were not always being followed to the letter. Not long after the denouement of the "Seward" episode, Johnson dispatched Horace Busby on what amounted to a peacemaking expedition to Ted Sorensen. Busby began by asking Sorensen to spell out what role he thought Johnson should play in the Administration. Sorensen, always determined to find *les mots justes,* paused, and then found *mots* that could not have been more disparaging. Johnson's role, he said, should be "Salesman for the President's program." During the conversation that followed, it became clear to Busby, as he reported in a memo to Johnson, that the Administration was determined that that role would not include a leading part on Capitol Hill. "In and out, during the conversation, various assistant secretaries from HEW and Budget" would be coming into Sorensen's office, conferring about legislation about to be introduced. When Sorensen introduced Busby to them ("perfunctorily," in Busby's account, saying only "Mr. Busby, with the Vice President"), their reaction was "invariably the same—with transparent impact on Sorensen. They would say—two of them, separately, used virtually identical words—'Oh, gee, I wish we could get the Vice President to work on our bill— that is what would make the difference.' " (And in each case "Sorensen hastened to prevent my direct response.") Summing up the conversation in the memo to Johnson, Busby said, "I felt, as I left, that I had been to a summit conference, held on an iceberg, between two [men] who, while members of the same political faith at the moment, each brought—and left with—his own God."

As for Ken O'Donnell, if indeed he had, as he maintains, been put in charge of keeping Johnson happy, he was not fulfilling his responsibility. Feeling that "Johnson was a liability who would say or do things that would reflect badly on the Administration, he wanted to keep close reins on him"—and he did. He informed Johnson's staff that all vice presidential speeches and statements had to be approved in advance by the White House. "He couldn't issue a press release without it being cleared," says Ashton Gonella. "Imagine if you had been king and then you had to clear everything you said."

Clearance was required in other areas as well. During the new Administration's first months, Johnson's Air Force aide, Colonel Howard L. Burris, simply submitted a request to the Air Force each time Johnson was scheduled to travel somewhere. Johnson was often chagrined by the response to the requests, since he was not routinely assigned one of the three Boeing 707s—the same model as Air Force One—in the pool of planes the Air Force maintained for travel by high-level government officials, but was sometimes given, despite his protests, a Lockheed JetStar, a ten-passenger plane originally designed as an executive jet. The contrast between his plane and Air Force One was further heightened by the fact that instead of having "United States of America" painted on its fuselage, the lettering on the sides of the JetStar was "United States Air Force," and two prominent insignias on each side of the plane identified it as part of the Air Force's Military Air Transport Service. Descending from so small a plane before a welcoming delegation of local dignitaries Johnson considered an embarrassment. There was a more substantive problem as well: none of the MATS JetStars were outfitted with the powerful communications equipment that kept Air Force One in continual touch with the White House, and when Johnson asked that one JetStar be assigned permanently for his use, and that the equipment be installed, he was rebuffed. For a while, however, at least no barriers were placed to his requests for a plane to travel in. Then, however, that changed, and he was informed that before his requests could be submitted to the Air Force, they had to be approved by the White House, specifically by Special Assistant to the President Ralph

Dungan. "You had to ask for, and get approval," every time Johnson wanted to travel by plane, says Marie Fehmer, who went to work for Johnson as a secretary in June, 1962. "How do you think that made him feel?" And the plane he was assigned was, all too often, the detested JetStar. After many requests, the Air Force agreed to remove the MATS insignia; when he asked that "United States of America" be painted on its side, Burris had to report to Johnson that "Mr. McNamara's office was informed" of the request and "the determination was to retain" the wording. His LBJ Company then leased a larger Grumman Gulfstream, which could carry up to twenty-four passengers, for his use on trips he made for political purposes—to speak at a Democratic Party Jefferson-Jackson Day Dinner, for example—but this attempt was curtly rebuffed. A message from the White House was dictated over the phone to Walter Jenkins: "The President has reached the following conclusion on travel policy: Both the President and Vice President will use Government planes whenever the occasion requires for both official and unofficial trips, including trips for political purposes."

Some of the insults were inadvertent. When Kennedy staffers, accustomed to calling him "Lyndon," continued to call him that instead of "Mr. Vice President," "he just couldn't stand that; he felt they were doing that deliberately to humiliate him," Sam Houston Johnson says.

One insult, which O'Donnell was to excuse in his memoirs as merely a "terrible mistake," involved a sixty-four-year-old lawyer and longtime Johnson ally from Dallas, Sarah T. Hughes. Early in 1961, Johnson asked Robert Kennedy to nominate Mrs. Hughes for a Federal District Court judgeship, but the reply from the Justice Department, which was trying to get younger judges on the federal bench, was that she was too old. Telling her that she couldn't have the appointment, Johnson had then offered it to another Texas lawyer.

In turning her down, however, the Kennedys had been unaware of a salient fact: Ms. Hughes was an ally not only of Lyndon Johnson but of Sam Rayburn. Rayburn did not contact them on the subject, but after several months Robert Kennedy realized that a bill important to him, one that he had expected to make its way smoothly through the House Judiciary Committee, was in fact making no progress at all. He asked Rayburn for an explanation—and got it. "That bill of yours will pass when Sarah Hughes gets appointed," the Speaker said.

Bobby explained that she had been ruled too old for the job. "Sonny, everybody seems old to you," Rayburn replied. Ms. Hughes' appointment was announced the next day.

Rayburn's remark—and Hughes' appointment—had occurred while Johnson was on an overseas trip for the President. When he returned, O'Donnell says, "You never saw such an outrage. . . . He went through an act which is beyond belief with the President and me. 'Mr. President, you realize where this leaves me? Sarah Hughes now thinks I'm nothing. The lawyer I offered the job to—he thinks I'm the biggest liar and fool in the history of the State of Texas.' " The outrage was understandable. In the Evans and Novak summary, "The Speaker had demonstrated that he possessed" enough power "to make the Attorney General waive [the] age requirement"—and that Johnson didn't. And, of course, "the story of how Sarah Hughes got to be a judge quickly made the rounds" in both Washington and Texas. "Johnson felt . . . his reputation" had been unfairly damaged, O'Donnell says, "and he was right, he was totally right. . . . It was a mistake."

And some of the insults weren't inadvertent. As Johnson's "laments" had multiplied, O'Donnell says, he and Kennedy had "worked out a set routine for handling" them. "The President would first hear him out alone, and then call me into his office and denounce me in front of Johnson—'Damn it, Kenny, you've gone and done it again'—for whatever the Vice President was beefing about. I would humbly take the blame and promise to correct the situation, and the Vice President would go away somewhat happier." On one occasion, however, a different routine was prepared—one that didn't leave Johnson happy at all.

Once again, it involved Rayburn. Having to deal with the Speaker on his legislative program had made John Kennedy more aware than ever of his power; appointing his friend, the painter William Walton, to the chairmanship of the federal Fine Arts Commission, he had only one instruction for him: "Don't get me crossways with Rayburn." And he was aware also of how much Johnson needed the old man—and of how wary Johnson was of doing anything to irritate him. And when, suddenly, there was a possibility of a dispute between the two Texans, the President knew just what to do about it, and worked out with O'Donnell a scenario designed for Johnson's maximum discomfiture.

The potential dispute was over an appointment to an Agricultural Department commission. With little interest in Texas patronage—except for old friends who needed jobs—Rayburn had been allowing Johnson to clear all appointments for Texas (Kennedy had agreed that Johnson could do so), but he had an old friend who had been on the commission for years until he was removed by the Eisenhower Administration, and he wanted him back on it. Rayburn's friend had once annoyed Johnson, but Rayburn wasn't aware of this—and in the case of an old friend it would not have mattered to him if he *had* known. When O'Donnell asked if the appointment had been cleared with Johnson, Rayburn said, "I don't care. I want this fellow." Appearing some hours later in O'Donnell's office, Johnson told him that Rayburn's friend was an alcoholic who was "going to embarrass the President," added flatly, "I don't want that fellow appointed" and reminded O'Donnell of his appointment-clearing agreement with Kennedy.

Saying he would have to let the President decide, O'Donnell ushered Johnson into the Oval Office, where the President, after listening to the dispute as if he'd never heard about it before, told Johnson, "Well, I'll stick by my agreement." Swiveling his chair, he stared out the window as if he had no further interest in the matter—and the scenario began to unfold. O'Donnell put his hand on the telephone on Kennedy's desk.

"Who are you calling?" Johnson asked.

"The Speaker," O'Donnell replied.

Hurriedly stretching out his hand, Johnson put it on top of O'Donnell's to prevent him from lifting the receiver. "What are you going to tell him?" he asked. O'Donnell said he was going to tell him that Johnson wouldn't clear the appointment.

"You can't do that!" Johnson said. "You tell him that *you* don't want him appointed." O'Donnell said that was impossible, that he had no power over appointments. "Mr. Vice President, it's either you or the President that's not going to appoint him, and it's not going to be the President."

The President, O'Donnell recalls, was still staring out the window, "enjoying the whole scene." There was a long silence—during which Johnson's hand never left O'Donnell's. Finally Johnson said, "Well, don't call him." Telling O'Donnell to let the matter rest until he made a decision, he walked out. A few minutes later, Walter Jenkins telephoned to say that Johnson was withdrawing his objection.

WHAT WAS THE EXPLANATION for treatment of Johnson that had such a personal edge?

Was part of it—an understandable part of it—the simple fact that Jack Kennedy had been too close to death too many times to want to be reminded of his mortality, and that his Vice President was, by his very existence, the most vivid of reminders?

Sometimes Kennedy would bring up the subject of presidential succession in kidding terms, in what Sorensen calls "casual banter." Dressing in his bedroom for a flight to Ohio that was going to be made through a storm, he said, "with a laugh," to Sorensen, with the presidential valet, George Thomas, listening, "If that plane goes down, Lyndon will have this place cleared out from stem to stern in twenty-four hours—and you and George will be the first to go." And sometimes when he spoke of the subject, there was, in Jack Kennedy's tone of voice, no banter at all. Walton, wanting the Fine Arts Commission to preserve two red-brick-and-white-trim townhouses diagonally across Lafayette Park from the White House that were about to be demolished for a modern office building, was considering combining the townhouses and making them the official residence of the Vice President. When he raised the suggestion in the Oval Office, however, the reaction was emphatic: "You think I want Lyndon listening across the park for my heartbeat? *No!*" (The townhouses were instead used for the commission's own offices.)

And was part of the explanation something beyond reminders of mortality?

Unlike Robert, Jack Kennedy appeared not to care that Johnson had, for years, been telling insulting stories about his father—and about *him:* that Johnson had called him nicknames, like "Sonny Boy"—stories that had surely gotten back to his ears. Did he really not care?

Had he "forgiven"—but not forgotten—India Edwards? Says Ted Sorensen, the aide who was as close to Jack Kennedy as anyone ever got, about India's statements that Kennedy "wouldn't be alive" without cortisone: "That was about as low as anyone could go."

There had been years—eight years—when the young senator "could not get consideration for a bill until I went around and begged Lyndon Johnson." How much had Jack Kennedy resented having to beg? Whatever the reasons for a personal edge in his dealings with Johnson, the edge, no matter how many historians and Kennedy aides deny its existence, was definitely there.

THEN, DURING THE FOURTH OF JULY WEEKEND OF 1961, while Sam Rayburn was back in Bonham, he felt a terrible pain in his back. Despite his failing eyesight and the way age had shrunken his body, he had been, at the age of seventy-nine, in relatively good health up until then, occasionally even giving one of his rare smiles as a milestone neared for him: on June 12, 1962, he would be Speaker of the House twice as long as anyone else in American history; in January, 1963, he would celebrate his fiftieth year—a half century—in the House, a milestone that also meant a lot to him.

His decline after the Fourth of July was rapid. Back in Washington, he had no appetite and began losing weight; he had cancer, probably pancreatic (no one knows for sure). He didn't want the House to see him like this; he was going to "get away from here so the boys won't see me until I lick this thing," he told a friend. On August 16, he told a shocked and silent House that he was returning to Texas for medical treatment.

He didn't leave for a few more days, and during those days there was a moment Lady Bird Johnson never forgot. On the weekend of August 18, Lyndon Johnson was in Berlin, as President Kennedy's representative to assure that city of American support in a Russian-instigated crisis, and when he returned to Washington, Lady Bird was waiting for him at Andrews Air Force Base.

Almost twenty years before, in January, 1942, Lyndon Johnson and John Connally had been boarding a train at Union Station, for war service which would presumably take them to the South Pacific. Lady Bird and Nellie Connally went to the station with them, and, at the last moment, Rayburn said he was going, too. He didn't presume to intrude on the two young couples as they said their good-byes; he stood well behind them on a platform in the giant terminal. Lady Bird would always remember that short, blocky figure—so massive and strong, then—standing, unmoving and unsmiling, grim as always, amid the tumult of young men rushing for the trains that would take them off to war, and the young couples kissing good-bye; she had never forgotten how hard this man who could never be cheerful tried to be cheerful to her and Nellie as, after Lyndon and John's train pulled out, he said, very gruffly, the only words he could think of to cheer them up: "Now girls, we're going to get us the best dinner in Washington."

Now, in 1961, waiting for her husband's plane to touch down at Andrews,

Lady Bird happened to glance behind her, and there, to her surprise, standing on the tarmac, shrunken and almost blind, still as grimly expressionless as ever, was Sam Rayburn.

"Dear Mr. Speaker," she wrote him a few days later. "As I stood by that airplane in the gray, grizzly morning waiting for Lyndon, I looked up and saw you and my mind went back to so many times and so many trouble-fraught situations when you have stood by our side. . . . Next April is my twenty-fifth anniversary as a wife of a member of Congress. This quarter century of our lives has been marked most by knowing you." On August 30, Rayburn wrote back, even in this last letter stilted and formal: "Dear Bird, Your note was very refreshing and highly appreciated by me."

Here are the words I wrote in the first volume of this work:

"Although the pain was very bad that day, the hand that wrote that letter did not shake. There was not a tremor in the name 'Sam Rayburn.' The next morning, Rayburn went home to Bonham to die."*

"YOU'LL STILL HAVE THE SPEAKER," John Connally had told Johnson in Los Angeles, advising him to accept the vice presidential nomination: as long as he had Rayburn behind him, he would have power in dealing with the Kennedys.

Now he no longer had the Speaker behind him. He no longer had the Senate behind him. He had no one behind him in Washington. "Was it worse for Johnson after Rayburn died?" the author once asked John Connally.

"Yes," Connally replied.

LYNDON JOHNSON, WHO HAD DEVOTED all his life to the accumulation of power, possessed now no power at all, and as Vice President the only power he would ever possess was what the President might choose to give him. He understood that now: understood that it was imperative for him to remain in the President's good graces. All his life Lyndon Johnson had been as obsequious to those he needed as he had been overbearing to those he didn't—and now he needed Jack Kennedy desperately.

He gave him gifts: four Hereford heifers, two with calves, all granddaughters of Real Silver Domino 203rd, "Bridwell's top bull," which, he informed Jack Kennedy after a legislative leaders' breakfast in 1961, he was having sent to the estate, Glen Ora, that the Kennedys had rented in the Virginia hunt country; a pony for four-year-old Caroline (he suggested the name "John Jr." but Jackie preferred "Tex")—and he got as much mileage out of the gifts as possible, telling the President he would like to be at Glen Ora when the cattle and pony arrived so that, Mrs. Lincoln writes, "he could see that they were in good order." And he

---

*The 1942 episode, with much of the same wording, is from *The Path to Power.* The story of Sam Rayburn is in that volume, in the chapter entitled "Rayburn."

said he would like to have a picture of Tex with all of them together—Jack, Jackie, Caroline and him—on the White House lawn.

The photo session went off smoothly—after Mrs. Lincoln had recovered from her surprise when, one morning, she glanced out her window and saw a strange pony grazing outside the Oval Office. She arranged for a photographer to snap a picture of Tex with Caroline in the saddle, Jack and Jackie standing behind her, and Lyndon holding the reins, and "You could tell Mr. Johnson was really enjoying this, because he strolled around patting Caroline on the head and patting the horse." Nonetheless, these gifts were not a total success. When the Vice President saw Caroline in Mrs. Lincoln's office a few days later, he told her, according to Mrs. Lincoln's recollection, "I'm your Uncle Lyndon, remember? I'm the one who gave you that fine riding horse, Tex. . . . Now remember what I told you, Caroline. I want you to call me 'Uncle Lyndon' whenever you see me." Caroline, as it happened, already had a pony—Macaroni—whom she had been learning to ride, and a couple of uncles. Although she and the Vice President often bumped into each other in Mrs. Lincoln's office, "She never . . . called him 'Uncle Lyndon,' nor did he ever mention it to her again."

As for the cows, raising cattle had not been what Jackie had in mind when she acquired a country home. She didn't know what to do with them. The first year, the heifers and their calves were pastured on a neighboring farm, but the farmer said he wouldn't have room for them the next year. And, in the course of nature, the gift kept multiplying. By 1962, there would be eleven cows, and Jackie, in the process of renting another hunt-country estate, had to write Lyndon a letter: "I can see myself plodding down a dusty lane—beating the rumps of a lowing herd in front of me—which is what your cows have now grown into." There wasn't going to be room for the cows on the new estate, she said, so she had two suggestions: either "We give them back to you—with all the new ones they have produced" or "We sell them . . . and with the money give a present in your name to the White House." The letter was as gracious as possible under the circumstances ("It was so incredible of you to give them to us. I love animals so much I feel badly to have any that I can't care for properly. . . . The only sad thing about having cows is the little calves you love the most always end up at the butcher. So the one thing I won't do is eat any of them—as I have loved them so much"), but the message was clear: the present was being disposed of. (In the event, Johnson sold the herd, and with the proceeds bought a Lincoln manuscript for Jackie's White House restoration project.)

With livestock failing to produce the desired effect, there was an escalation—to pearls. On Christmas, 1961, while the Kennedys were vacationing in Palm Springs, they received presents from the Johnsons which Jackie found "unbelievable." "Jack is enchanted with his pearl cufflinks—and has dressed for dinner with them two nights in a row," she wrote Lady Bird. "As for me—a black pearl was always the most romantic exotic piece of jewelry—which I never imagined I would be fortunate enough to have—I wear it on my little finger."

• • •

MATCHING THE GIFTS in extravagance was the deference. Over the same Christmas, at the Johnson Ranch, a great deal of care was going into a letter to Kennedy which was edited and re-edited, and then copied out by Johnson by hand so that it would seem more personal. It was a paean of praise for the President. "Sitting in front of the ranch fireplace at Xmas Lady Bird and I had many long, long thoughts. This year has been one of peaks and depths for us. The loss of the Speaker as well as many people dear to us put many sad milestones in our lives. But there have been many joys. Never was I prouder than the day last January 20 when I sat on the platform and heard my President rally his country to 'begin now.' I am even prouder at the year's end to look back and see where you have been and see ahead and know where you are going." The paean swelled. "Winning the peace is a lonely battle, as you have said so well. . . . But you have inspired so many. You will win it for us all." And the letter ended with a coda of loyalty.

"Where you lead, I will follow," Lyndon Johnson wrote.

Similar pledges of loyalty were delivered orally, for conveyance to the President's ears, to Johnson's few friends in the Administration. "I want you to get that point over to him that I'm not playing any games here," he told Angier Duke. "I'm sincere. I would like to be part of his team and play on the team. If he thinks I'm out playing for myself . . . it's not so. How can I get that through to him?"

And, during the almost three years of Lyndon Johnson's vice presidency that followed the failure of his "Seward" campaign, the pledges were honored. All his life, since his youth in the Hill Country had taught him the horror of defeat and public humiliation, Lyndon Johnson had done whatever he had to do to avoid them, willing himself, whenever he was in trouble, to do whatever was necessary to win; willing himself into those efforts that astounded men who were close enough to grasp their dimensions, that made Ed Clark say he had never thought it *possible* for anyone to work so hard. What Lyndon Johnson had to do now was very hard. In a way, for this man to whom it had always been so terribly important that other men know he had power and that they know also how shrewd he had been in acquiring it, and in using it, and how he reveled in its use, few things could have been harder. But he did it.

During the summer of 1961, the Washington bureau chiefs of several magazines were invited to the Taj Mahal. The scene was one they had witnessed before, during Johnson's days as Majority Leader: the big desk on its platform, the big man behind it, spotlit from above, doing all the talking, in what one of the newsmen, *Time*'s John L. Steele, described, in a memo to his editors, as a "three-hour monologue." The monologue's theme, on the other hand, could not have been more different from those of the earlier era, which had invariably been Lyndon Johnson's power and shrewdness. The theme of this one was that Lyndon Johnson had no power—that on his foreign trips, for example, he was no more than a messenger boy for the President—and that he didn't want any. Before he left on those trips, he told the journalists, "I had President Kennedy write down for me what he wanted in the communiqués for every country I visited," and he said he had stuck to the letter of what the President had written. He had, he said, carried messages not only from but *to* the President: "Ayub told me to tell the President . . . ," "I was taking a message for the President from de Gaulle." The startled Steele told his editors: "He is, by his own words, a mouthpiece, a message bearer . . . surrendering any notion that he had an important substantive impact himself."

That was his attitude not just about foreign policy, but about every aspect of his job, Johnson told the journalists. All he wanted to be, he said, was "the kind of Vice President I would want if I was President." And, Steele wrote, that was what Johnson was, in fact, succeeding in being. "There is about Lyndon Johnson these days a quiescent air, an attitude of submission to the young President. . . . The surprise of the first six months of the Kennedy Administration is the 'new' LBJ—far quieter, far less aggressive and considerably less exciting. He isn't running the Senate, he isn't running anything except his office. . . . By every word and deed [he] is the President's man."

If this was a mask, it was one in which not a single crack was allowed to appear. Precautions were taken against the utterance of a single wrong word—or against a single word that could be interpreted wrongly. He announced that he would hold no press conferences, so that, as Jack Bell of the Associated Press explained, reporters would have no opportunity to "get him into a position at cross purposes with the President," and for some time except for occasions—such as a return from a foreign trip—when a press conference was unavoidable, he adhered to that ban. Reporters weren't able to get him into that position in private, either. "In private, serious talks about John F. Kennedy, there was never a hint of criticism from the Vice President," wrote Evans and Novak, with whom Johnson would have such talks. The two columnists, who had seen a lot of Johnson over the years, noted that "For Johnson, whose pleasure in mocking competitors and politicians behind their backs was legendary in Washington, that self-control must have stretched his endurance." Stretched or not, however, it held.

It had always been so important to him that the world know he was on the inside of things, and all his life, what's more, he had used inside information, the "inside story," as a tool to woo journalists and dominate conversations, vividly leaking details and anecdotes—some true, some partly true, some false (but during the Senate years he had been leaking to a captive Senate press corps that generally never questioned what he said)—about policies and maneuvers and individuals. Now that changed—completely. One reporter, looking for news, and feeling, from past experiences, that Johnson was always good for some, recalls that he "made an appointment with him and rode from the Capitol to the White House, and tried to talk with him about [some] situation, and he said absolutely nothing." This experience jibed with that of other reporters: "He was maintaining a very rigorous self-imposed silence."

With his staff—or old allies from Texas—he would sometimes burst out in anger against Bobby Kennedy's latest affront or comment acidly on mistakes he felt the Administration was making, but these outbursts were very rare. And they were never about the President. "Even in his most private harangues, LBJ never denounced John Kennedy," as one account says. And not only would he permit no word of criticism of the President to cross his lips, he would permit no word to be uttered in his presence. In the fall of 1961, the Johnsons, together with their daughters, seventeen-year-old Lynda Bird and fourteen-year-old Lucy Baines, moved to 4040 52nd Street Northwest, in Washington's Spring Valley, into a house, in the style of a small French château, that had been owned by the Washington hostess Perle Mesta, who had named it "Les Ormes" for the big trees outside. (Johnson changed the name to its English translation, "The Elms," and added a heated swimming pool and piped-in music.) When, at a dinner there, a former staff member, Mary Fish, who had been working for the State Department in Europe, repeated a joke about the Kennedys that was circulating there, Johnson told her to "Either quit talking that way or quit your job!" It wasn't only with his staff that he acted like this. "Even old Johnson friends in the Senate did not receive any signal by word or inflection of significant disagreement with Kennedy," Evans and Novak write. Looking back later on his entire vice presidency, Charles Bartlett, the columnist who was John Kennedy's friend, would write, "There was never *any word* that ever drifted back to Jack Kennedy of any criticism from Lyndon Johnson. . . . There was certainly not one word—and I'm very sure of this—of disloyalty that the Vice President ever uttered in terms of the President, no comment, no criticism."

At the outset of his vice presidency, his silence at meetings had been a kind of sullenness, an attempt to evoke Kennedy's pity. There was more behind it now. When asked a question directly, he would say, "I agree with what the President said." He told journalists that when he was at a meeting, "I always hope that the President won't turn to me and ask, 'Lyndon, what would you do?' " The President had a terribly difficult job, he said. "There were difficult, terrible decisions to make and there was only one person to make them: the President."

Of all the types of loyalty that Lyndon Johnson could have demonstrated, verbal restraint must have been one of the hardest for him to impose on himself. "For a man given to majestic displays of rage, to shouting and swearing and pounding on desktops," to nonstop monologues, Johnson's restraint was uncanny, the historian Jeff Shesol writes. "His ability to suppress explosive emotions . . . revealed a personal power few had ever seen." A journalist calls his vice presidency "a triumph of self-discipline." Difficult though the restraint may have been, however, it never faltered. Hard as it must have been for him to honor his pledge of loyalty, honored it was.

His loyalty didn't do him any good, however. Walking across West Executive Avenue and into the White House, he would enter Ken O'Donnell's office and say he would like a minute or two of the President's time when he was free, and sit by O'Donnell's desk waiting for an opportunity.

But others would also be waiting. They would be put in the Cabinet Room or the Fish Room to wait, and sometimes the appointments were so closely stacked that, O'Donnell recalls, both rooms "would be filled with callers," and others would be put in other aides' offices, "or any place in the West Wing where a few feet of empty space happened to be available." And these callers had specific business, often urgent, with the President—matters on which he had asked to see them. He would buzz out to O'Donnell or Evelyn Lincoln to bring one of them in; the visitor would be ushered into the Oval Office as Lyndon Johnson still sat outside. Or there would be emergencies, and "Dean Rusk or another State Department officer would want thirty minutes of the President's time for an urgent discussion involving top-priority national security matters"—audiences "that could not be denied." Sometimes Lyndon Johnson had to wait quite a long time to see the President.

And sometimes, after he finally *did* get in to see him, the meetings weren't that satisfactory. More than once, when Johnson was in the Oval Office with the President, Robert Kennedy simply walked in and interrupted to discuss some new matter, "without," as one account puts it, "so much as a nod of apology toward LBJ." Nor was it only the President's brother who was permitted to interrupt. Once, for example, Arthur Schlesinger, sticking his head through the open door behind Mrs. Lincoln, saw Johnson sitting next to Kennedy's desk, and "began to retreat," but the President beckoned him to come in. Johnson was being treated as if he were simply another member of Kennedy's staff.

He was reduced to begging—although he did it, at least mostly, through aides. "Charlie," Liz Carpenter asked Charles Bartlett, "could you get the President to check with Lyndon once in a while on matters of foreign policy that he's considering?" She said, in Bartlett's recollection, that "the Vice President was very frustrated by the fact that he was out of these deliberations; he felt a little bit sort of out of it, and perhaps if the President would just call up once in a while and ask his opinion, it would be a great help." Bartlett did bring the matter up with Kennedy, asking him, "Why don't you call Lyndon more often and ask his opinion?" Replying that he really should have done so more often, Kennedy said, "You know, it's awfully hard because once you get into one of these crunches you don't really think of calling Lyndon because he hasn't read the cables. When you get into one of these things you want to talk to the people who are most involved, and your mind doesn't turn to Lyndon because he isn't following the flow of cables." That explanation might have been valid except that Kennedy, had he wanted to, could simply have included Lyndon as one of the people who got the cables.

In any case, the begging didn't help. It wasn't simply foreign policy from which Johnson was being excluded. Consideration was being given to changing the jurisdiction and procedures of the Committee on Equal Employment Opportunity, of which he was the chairman, by an executive order. "For nine months," Shesol was to report, "memos [about the changes] circulated between the White House and the Justice Department. . . . At no point did a copy reach the vice president."

DURING THE ADMINISTRATION of John F. Kennedy, Washington was Camelot, and in Camelot, the political world included parties. Johnson was always invited to formal state dinners; he and Lady Bird would be escorted upstairs to the family quarters in the White House with the evening's other honored guests, so that they could come down the staircase with the President, a careful several steps behind him, taking their pace from him, and they would be part of the receiving line. And they were invited to some smaller dinners in the White House, too, including some of the black-tie, candlelit dinners—the "dazzling mixture of 'beautiful people' from New York, jet-setters from Europe, politicians, reporters who are friends and Kennedy relatives," at which "the crowd is always young, the women are always gorgeous," described by Ben Bradlee—to which invitations were highly prized; they were invited, that is, if Kennedy was directly asked about including them. Recalls Angier Biddle Duke: "I would get the list pretty late and see that the Vice President wasn't on it, and call the White House—it was often in the afternoon of the day of the party—and remind—usually it was Kenny O'Donnell, that [since it was so late] the President himself would have to invite the Johnsons," and "he would, and they would come."

But Johnson felt just as out of place at the parties as in the West Wing. Everyone—Schlesinger, the Galbraiths, the Bundys—seemed to know everyone else so well. He didn't. And in Washington, parties are a place for conducting business; after dinner, two or three men would be holding a quiet conversation. None of the business was with him. "Nobody was terribly interested in him," Duke says. Things got worse. At the third White House dinner-dance, on November 11, a particularly dazzling affair which lasted until 4 a.m. and at which the champagne flowed quite freely, Lester Lanin's society orchestra played, and many of the eighty guests began doing a new, hip-swiveling dance called the twist. Johnson asked the scintillating Helen Chavchavadze (who, as it happened, was one of the President's mistresses) to dance—and slipped and fell on her, knocking her to the floor. It took a minute or two for him to be helped to his feet. By noon the next day, word of Johnson's fall, couched in vivid phrases ("He lay on her like a lox," one of the other guests reported), had reached Camelot's most distant frontiers—as Johnson was well aware.

And sometimes he *wasn't* invited—and he seemed simply unable to accept that. Evelyn Lincoln picked up her phone one day to find the Vice President on the line; "Mrs. Lincoln," he said, "I've just looked over some of the lists of dinners to be given by Mr. Kennedy and on one of them I don't find my name. I wonder if you would check and see if there has been a mistake." The dinner in question was one for the President's personal friends, she was to recall. When she told Kennedy about Johnson's call, Kennedy asked, "You mean he called and wanted to be invited?" Mrs. Lincoln said that was correct. "Call and tell him that you have checked and you found that there was no mistake," Kennedy said.

WASHINGTON HAD IN MANY WAYS always been a small town, and in small towns gossip can be cruel, and the New Frontiersmen—casual, elegant, understated, in love with their own sophistication ("Such an in-group, and they let you know they were in, and you were not," recalls Ashton Gonella)—were a witty bunch, and wit does better when it has a target to aim at, and the huge, lumbering figure of Lyndon Johnson, with his carefully buttoned-up suits and slicked-down hair, his bellowing speeches and extravagant, awkward gestures, made an inviting target. "One can feel the hot breath of the crowd at the bullfight exulting as the sword flashes into the bull," one historian wrote. In the Georgetown townhouses that were the New Frontier's social stronghold "there were a lot of small parties, informal kinds, dinners that were given by Kennedy people for other Kennedy people. You know, twelve people in for dinner, all part of the Administration," says United States Treasurer Elizabeth Gatov. "Really, it was brutal, the stories that they were passing, and the jokes, and the inside nasty stuff about Lyndon." When he mispronounced "hors d'oeuvres" as "whore doves," the mistake was all over Georgetown in what seemed an instant.

His accent—his pronunciation of the personal pronoun ("Ah reckon," "Ah believe," "Well, ahm just an ol' country boy"); the way he slipped into saying "nigrah" instead of "Negro" no matter how hard he tried—his clothes (for one white-tie dinner-dance, he wore, to the Kennedy people's endless amusement, not the customary black tailcoat but a slate-gray model specially sent up by Dallas' Neiman-Marcus department store): all were grist for the Georgetown mill, as were his loquacity and his endless, corny stories. Any lull in the conversation could be filled with a question based on his rapid descent from power to obscurity: "Say, whatever happened to Lyndon Johnson?" Nicknames—shorthand for that fall—were coined for him: "Judge Crater," for example, after a New York City judge who, during the 1920s, had disappeared one day, never to be seen or heard from again. Some of the New Frontiersmen had a gift for words, and the terms that finally became the accepted nicknames for Lyndon Johnson in their social gatherings—"Uncle Cornpone" or "Rufus Cornpone"—were, in their opinion, so funny. They had a nickname for Lady Bird, too, so when the New Frontiersmen referred to the Johnsons as a couple, it might be as "Uncle Cornpone and his Little Pork Chop." The journalists who, as members of the in-group, were at the parties would hear a West Winger laughingly refer to "Lyndon? Lyndon Who?" and references to the situation would creep into print.

8

"Cut"

THE LARGE, FORMAL MEETINGS that were the only ones to which the Vice President was invited were becoming more and more infrequent. Regarding them as "a waste of time," Kennedy cut back on sessions of the Cabinet and the National Security Council; soon the Cabinet was meeting less than once a month. And with the Space Council running itself and the Committee on Equal Employment Opportunity being run by Labor Department officials, Lyndon Johnson had very little to do. He spent a lot of time at the Capitol, in the Taj Mahal and, sometimes, presiding over the Senate, sitting on that dais on which, even as a freshman senator years before, he "couldn't bear" to sit, so removed was it from the action; presiding often over a Chamber in which a senator would be giving a speech to rows of desks empty except for two or three colleagues. During the early weeks of his vice presidency, he would sometimes, during a speech, step down from the dais to the Chamber floor and begin to make conversation with a senator. The senator would be polite, but often he would have to break away after a bit—he had other things to do. After a while, Lyndon Johnson stopped coming down to the floor. And once he came into the Democratic cloakroom, where, for eight years, he had been the cynosure of senators' attention, where he had stood dispatching senators to the floor for a speech or a parliamentary maneuver, leaning over to hear as Bobby Baker or some senator whispered in his ear, senators clustered around him, trying to catch his eye. This time, when he came in, a few senators were in the cloakroom, sitting in armchairs or on the sofas, reading newspapers or chatting. He greeted them. They greeted him back. Then Lyndon Johnson stood in the center of the cloakroom for a few minutes. No one stood up to talk to him. No one invited him to sit down. One of the men who was there that day says, "I don't think he ever came into the cloakroom again."

His big car would take him the mile and a half back up Pennsylvania Avenue. He had a suite, EOB 274, of three rooms on the second floor of the Executive Office Building, and his private office was high-ceilinged with ornate moldings, a marble fireplace and tall windows—which looked almost directly down, across the narrow pavement of West Executive Avenue, at the entrance to the West Wing of the White House, with the cars pulling up at it and the men getting out of them to hurry inside to important business.

It was so close. He couldn't seem to take his eyes off it. His chair faced away from the window, but it was a swivel chair. In the midst of talking to someone—usually an aide: Buzz or Reedy or his Air Force aide, Colonel Howard Burris; he had few other visitors—talking across a desk that was all too empty of anything that mattered, he would swing the chair around so that he was facing the window, and then jump up and stare out so that he could get a better look, a tall figure silhouetted against a tall window, looking out at the place he had always wanted to be. He couldn't stay away from it. Suddenly he would stride out of the office, without a word of explanation, and "you knew where he was gone to," Horace Busby says. He had no reason to be in the White House, of course—no assignment from the President required his presence. He might give O'Donnell some reason he wanted to see the President, and sit there beside O'Donnell's desk, waiting for a few minutes of another man's time. The door would open; a group of men would come out, chatting, perhaps laughing, with one another. He wouldn't know what they had been talking about. He might be told to go in then—or he might not. Or he would walk around the halls. "This was a period in which he proceeded to 'hang around' the outer offices of the White House—something like a precinct captain sitting in the anteroom of a ward leader hoping to be recognized," George Reedy was to write. "It was not a very prepossessing sight and certainly not worthy of a man of his stature." And in so many rooms in the White House, it seemed, there would be meetings going on: the smaller, informal conferences through which much of the business of the Kennedy Administration was conducted. The halls were filled with men walking and talking together, or standing in little groups, having come out of one of the offices, and continuing their discussion in the corridors. "The White House is small," Lyndon Johnson was to recall years later, "but if you're not at the center, it seems enormous. You get the feeling that there are all sorts of meetings going on without you, all sorts of people clustered in small groups, whispering, always whispering. I felt that way as Vice President."

Among Johnson's assistants were men who loved him, and they could hardly bear to watch the way their Chief was being treated. The adoring Horace Busby, to whom Johnson would have been a father figure had Busby loved and revered his father, was, in fact, physically unable to bear it. Going across to the West Wing one day on some errand, he saw Johnson "wandering around, kind of your obedient servant just waiting for somebody to say, 'Lyndon, would you run down and get the President an apple or something,' . . . just kind of exposing himself so they would notice that he was on call." And he saw what the Kennedy staffers were doing to Johnson: ignoring him. Returning to the Executive Office Building, he went into a bathroom and vomited. Lyndon's brother couldn't bear it. His visits to Washington became increasingly infrequent, Sam Houston was to say, "because I didn't want to be a firsthand witness to my brother's day-to-day humiliation."

In the little world of Washington, what's more, everyone knew the situation: knew that Lyndon Johnson was no longer on the inside of anything. The discipline with which, during the early months of his vice presidency, he had imposed on himself a policy of silence with journalists who had previously known him as a master leaker of inside information was no longer necessary, since, as Booth Mooney puts it, "he could no longer be regarded as an important news source."

Where at one time influential members of the Washington press corps had pleaded for a few moments of his time, the situation was reversed now. "He used to call me—he was very lonely," *Time*'s Sidey recalls. " 'Hugh, you haven't been to see me, you haven't called me.' Lonely. Pathetic." But Sidey had no reason to call him now. "He wouldn't know what the President was going to do. He couldn't talk about things in detail like he used to do."

Spotting Russell Baker of the *New York Times* outside the Senate Chamber one day, he "clapped my back, mauled my hand, massaged my ribs . . . all the time hailing me as though I were a long lost friend and simultaneously hauling me into" the Taj Mahal, where he launched into a seemingly endless monologue. "Torrents of words poured out of him"—on a dozen subjects. Although Baker had covered him in the Senate for years, Johnson didn't know his name. Sometime deep into the monologue, he scrawled a few words on a slip of paper, and called in a secretary to take it, and, Baker recalls, "a few minutes later his secretary brought him back a message" on another piece of paper, which Johnson looked at, and then crumpled up and threw into a wastepaper basket. When Baker was finally able to leave, he bumped into a friend who had been in Johnson's outer office when the secretary came out with Johnson's note. The friend told Baker that Johnson's note asked the secretary: "Who is this I'm talking to?" Aware of Baker's name or not, however, he had found a journalist willing to listen to him for a while, and the "torrent of words" went on. The monologue had a purpose. "Its central theme was his devotion to John F. Kennedy." He put on a front. "To hear him tell it, there had never been a happier second banana. Never mind that the Kennedys' glittering young courtiers—the 'Harvards,' as Johnson called them—joked constantly and cruelly about him. . . . Never mind realities. On this day, playing to a nameless Capitol reporter, he spoke of the vice-presidential life as a friendship with a man he admired extravagantly. . . . He was making it plain what the headline should say: 'Lyndon Johnson Utterly Devoted to John F. Kennedy!' " But Baker, of course, recognized the truth: that Johnson "knew he was the butt of cruel humor among many of President Kennedy's people, and was trying to pretend it wasn't so, that he still counted as he had counted back in the Fifties when he was Johnson the Genius Who Ran the Senate. . . . I felt sorry for him. If you had once been the great Lyndon Johnson . . . it was painful to be laughed at and called 'Cornpone' by people you thought of as arrogant, smart-ass Ivy League pipsqueaks. Here was greatness comically humbled."

It wasn't only newspapermen who had stopped calling. Washington was a Kennedy town now; it wasn't a good idea for Lyndon Johnson to be able to say he had been talking with you. A friend who visited him in EOB 274 says, "I couldn't believe it. I sat there for an hour and the phone didn't ring." When old allies from Texas—who, not being familiar with vice presidential traditions, assumed that a Vice President would have an office in the White House—visited Washington, he was ashamed that he didn't, so he would bring that fact up himself, as if doing so made it less bad. Charlie Herring came by, and Johnson said, "You know, I feel like I've got nothing to do. I don't even have an office in the White House. Let's go out for a while." Supreme Court Justice Tom Clark of Texas, an old ally, was at home, and they dropped in on him "just to have something to do." Dropping by for another visit some months later, Herring found that nothing had changed. "He was completely at loose ends. He had nothing to do. He said, 'We might as well get out and see the country,' " and in the middle of the day they drove down to Fairfax, Virginia, to see a facsimile of George Washington's will.

THE FORMAL MEETINGS in the Cabinet Room—of the Cabinet or the National Security Council—at which Johnson sat, in the center of one side of a long table, directly across from President Kennedy, were particularly terrible hours for Lyndon Johnson. Not just his desire, his *need,* to dominate, but also his need to decide—his will for decision, his will to *act,* what Theodore H. White was to call his "yearning" to act—were fundamental to his inner being. But if at first his reluctance during the Kennedy Administration to speak at such meetings had been a manifestation of sullenness or self-pity, or a bid for sympathy, or a desire to show his loyalty ("I agree with what the President said"), another consideration had now, with the increasingly open hostility of the New Frontiersmen, been added to the list of those that militated silence: any comment that he made in a meeting seemed to be quoted—or misquoted—to the press, in ways that made him seem southern, or militaristic, or uncouth. "I don't want to debate these things around fifteen men and then have them all go out and talk about the Vice President and what he thinks," he explained once. So while other men discussed, while another man decided, Lyndon Johnson sat silent, in a role that was, like so many aspects of the vice presidency, foreign to his very nature, sat so silent that people who had watched him at meetings in earlier years marveled at what they were seeing now, at what Dean Rusk was to call the "great self-discipline and strength," the "self-control," that enabled Johnson "with all that volcanic force that was part of his very being . . . [to] fit into that new role." Not even when the discussion turned to problems with Congress would he comment unless asked directly by the President, and then the answer would be brief. "He had to sit there . . . and observe controversies and frustrations which for years he had managed, and be totally passive," his old friend Elizabeth Wickenden points out.

His hands revealed how hard it was. Sometimes, as he sat at the long table in the Cabinet Room, listening to other men talk, those big hands would be

Majority Leader Lyndon B. Johnson

1957: Senators celebrate the Leader's
forty-ninth birthday. Left to right:
Richard Russell, unidentified,
Harry Byrd, William Knowland,
George Smathers, LBJ, Sam Ervin
(behind LBJ), J. William Fulbright,
Hubert Humphrey, John F. Kennedy,
Robert Kerr

Joseph P. Kennedy with sons
Joe Jr., John and Robert

June, 1946: Congressional candidate
John Kennedy leads Boston's Bunker
Hill Day parade minutes before
collapsing. The next day he won the
primary.

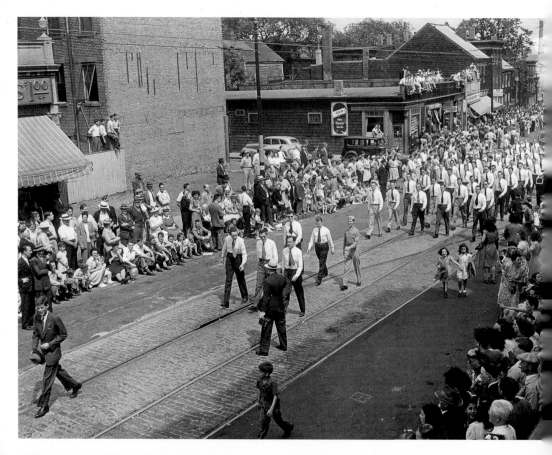

The brothers. (*Above*) Conferring in JFK's office, May, 1959, and (*below*) questioning a witness at the McClellan Rackets Committee (RFK was chief counsel)

The 1960 Democratic National Convention. (*Above*) Lucy, Lady Bird, LBJ, Lynda. (*Below*) LBJ and JFK at the Pennsylvania caucus. (*Opposite above*) LBJ and RFK listening as John Kennedy speaks at the Massachusetts/Texas delegation debate. (*Opposite below*) RFK whispers to LBJ after his arrival at the Los Angeles Coliseum.

JFK chooses LBJ as his running mate:
July 14, 1960. (*Opposite above*)
8 a.m.—JFK calls Lyndon to request
a meeting. (*Opposite below*) 10:45—
Returning from the meeting, JFK
announces its result, and Pennsylvania's
Governor David Lawrence congratulates
him. Looking on: Matt McCloskey.
(*Above*) Late afternoon—LBJ, RFK
and JFK discuss threats of a floor fight.
(*Right*) The Kennedy brothers at the end
of the day.

(*Above*) The candidates and their wives together at Hyannis Port after the convention
(*Below*) The candidates, with Congressman Albert Thomas, campaigning in September
in Houston

The "LBJ Special" whistle-stop tour of the South

LBJ campaigning (*above*) in Oklahoma, and (*left*) in Pennsylvania

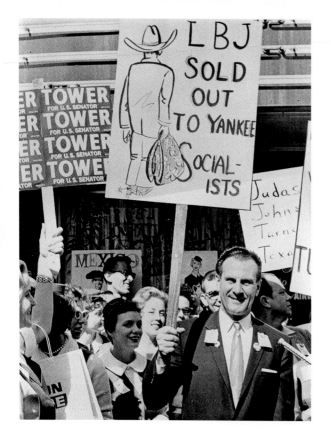

The incident at the Adolphus
Hotel in Dallas that turned
the tide for the Democratic
ticket in Texas

January 20, 1961: Inauguration Day. Speaker Sam Rayburn swears in Lyndon Johnson as Vice President. Dwight D. Eisenhower and John F. Kennedy are on the left; Richard M. Nixon is on the right.

(*Above*) The new President and Vice President review the inaugural parade.
(*Below*) A Texas Society reception for Johnson: Lynda, Lady Bird, LBJ and Lucy, who is kissing Sam Rayburn.

The Vice President overshadowed. (*Opposite above*) The President pledging support for Equal Employment Opportunity as LBJ looks on. (*Opposite below*) The President signing a bill at his desk in the Oval Office as LBJ looks on. (*Above*) The President confers with a congressional delegation.

The Cuban Missile Crisis. October 29, 1962: ExComm meets in the cabinet room. Around the table, clockwise, from Attorney General Robert Kennedy (standing at left): Deputy USIA Director Donald Wilson; Special Counsel Ted Sorensen (behind him Executive Secretary NSC Bromley Smith); Special Assistant McGeorge Bundy; Secretary of the Treasury Douglas Dillon, Vice President LBJ; former Ambassador to Russia Llewellyn Thompson; William C. Forster; JFK; Secretary of State Dean Rusk; CIA Director John McCone (partially obscured); Secretary of Defense Robert McNamara; Deputy Secretary of Defense Roswell Gilpatric; Chairman of the Joint Chiefs of Staff Maxwell Taylor; Assistant Secretary of Defense Paul Nitze clasped together, the intertwined fingers working nervously, so hard that his knuckles were white with the effort he was making not to speak. Sometimes, as Kennedy, directly opposite him across seven feet of polished mahogany, ran the meetings with his easy air of command, he would look away from the President for long minutes, staring down the length of the table, a faraway expression on his face. Sometimes he would put his elbows on the table and his head in his hands and stare down at the mahogany. Then he might raise his head, and lean forward across the table, a hand shielding his eyes, as if from the sunlight streaming in the windows behind the President. At the weekly legislative leaders' breakfasts now, he "rarely said a word," wrote Doris Kearns, whose future husband, Richard Goodwin, attended some of them. "His face appeared vacant and gray; he looked discontented and tired." Even when, in response to a direct question from Kennedy, he offered an opinion, "he tended to mumble, his words barely audible to the person sitting beside him. On rare occasions, when he was particularly excited or perturbed, he would suddenly raise his voice for a few moments to its customary shout, only to let it sink again into an unintelligible murmur."

And by the summer of 1962, his predicament was in the press; for this man who so dreaded public humiliation, the spectre had arrived at his front door—in the newspapers that were delivered to The Elms each morning. And waiting for him each morning at his desk in the Taj Mahal were articles that had been scissored out of other newspapers by his staff and placed in a folder for his perusal. By the end of the day, each would have scribbled across it the big *L* that signified that he had seen it.

WHERE'S LYNDON? asked a headline over a syndicated article that asked, "Why has Lyndon Johnson gone into eclipse?" LYNDON JOHNSON GUESSING GAME was another headline; the article under it asked the question, "why Johnson does not make the headlines now that he did once," and answered it: "It is John F. Kennedy who makes the decisions—and gets the headlines." In a syndicated column that appeared in scores of Hearst newspapers Marianne Means wrote, "He is usually so thoroughly ignored that it is hard to tell if he is here at all," and, noting that, in conferences, "basically, Johnson remains an observer, not a participant," mocked his "extraordinary efforts to keep himself in check. . . . None of these were Johnson traits before the vice presidency. His egotistical temper rarely has permitted him to share the credit for anything. Thus, Johnson appears to be working very hard at his tiny job." One aspect to the mockery must have cut particularly deeply, to a man to whom it was so important to be thought of as shrewd, tough, always outsmarting other men, using them, and never being used himself. "Now that Johnson has served his purpose"—to get southern votes for Kennedy—"perhaps Kennedy was simply tossing him aside," the *Chicago Tribune* speculated. And as the number of such articles increased, the headlines seemed to boil down to a single mocking question, repeated in a dozen newspapers: WHATEVER HAPPENED TO LYNDON JOHNSON?

On one such article, Johnson, in his agony, scribbled a note to his aide Charles Boatner: "Chas—Why? Not True." But it *was* true, and he knew it.

IT WASN'T ALL THAT HARD to break Lyndon Johnson. What lay beneath that blustering, bullying exterior was too fragile—had been broken too many times in his youth. Ever since those terrible years growing up in the Hill Country, ever since those years whose shadow never left him, any disparagement, any criticism, had hurt so deeply because it was cutting into a wound too deep ever to have closed. "*It was most important to Lyndon not to be like Daddy*"—not to become what his father, once so respected, had become: the object of public ridicule, of public scorn. But the parallel was inescapable now. His father had become a laughingstock. Now, so had he.

His whole demeanor showed what had befallen him, showed that the effort he was making came at a very high price, that the self-discipline it took for him to act against his nature, the "self-effacement" that Arthur Schlesinger says "was for him the most unnatural of roles," came at "a growing psychic cost." The price was registered in his weight, which was dropping off him because he wasn't eating much; although he ordered new suits, they were soon hanging loosely on his shoulders, his trousers, which he always liked cut full anyway, bagging around his shoes. It was registered in his face, which had become gaunt, haggard, so thin that the long lobes of his ears, the jut of his big nose, his heavy black eyebrows and the dark circles under his eyes—eyes sunk deep in his head now—were more prominent than ever, and the gauntness was accentuated by his expression, so gloomy, with the corners of his mouth pulled down and the jowls hanging down, that more than one journalist called it a "hangdog look." It was registered in his stride: the old, long, imperious Texas lope was gone; he walked more deliberately, with shorter steps; his shoulders were slumped; when he was in the President's presence, he seemed sometimes to be actually bending his knees a bit, as if he wanted to conceal the fact that he was the taller man. Bill Moyers—who had, within a few weeks of the inauguration, become publicity director for Kennedy in-law Sargent Shriver of the Peace Corps—felt that Johnson's self-confidence was gone, that he was "a man without a purpose . . . a great horse in a very small corral."

Others described the cost in terms of an image—not a pleasant image when applied to a man to whom being "a man" was all-important. Daniel Patrick Moynihan was to recall looking into Lyndon Johnson's eyes during his vice presidency and thinking, "This is a bull castrated very late in life." Nor was it only other men who applied that image to Johnson. He applied it to himself. In later years, when the vice presidency was behind him, he would apply it jokingly. "A vice president is a steer," he would say. "You know what a steer is? A steer is a bull who has lost his social standing." But there was no joke in the way he used it now. Late one afternoon, while Sam Rayburn was still alive, Johnson walked into

Rayburn's Board of Education. Instead of walking over and kissing Rayburn, as he usually did, he sat down without a word in one of the dark leather easy chairs, and put his head in his hands. Then he sat there for long minutes, oblivious to the other men in the room. His head kept dropping lower, until it was barely above his knees. And then, in a very low voice, Lyndon Johnson said, "Being vice president is like being a cut dog."

TALKING TO THE PRESS was too hard. The big names had stopped interviewing him, but there were still requests, relayed to him through Reedy, from other Washington reporters, or from reporters from Texas and foreign papers. "I am too worn out," he said to one request; on another, he scribbled a single word: "No." He couldn't bear to appear on television, turning down even the popular *Today* show; he told Reedy to simply reply to television requests by saying that he didn't go on television. Reedy, reluctant to make this bare, almost unbelievable statement—that the Vice President of the United States doesn't go on television—resorted to different excuses, but they wore thin. In March of 1962, Adlai Stevenson's press secretary, Clayton Fritchey, telephoned Reedy, an old friend, to say that the U.N. ambassador had agreed to host a program on outer space and international cooperation, and wanted Johnson to appear on the show, and Reedy pointed out to Johnson that, as chairman of the Space Council, it was only logical that he do so, and that if he didn't, Fritchey would get someone else, perhaps one of Johnson's space aides, like James Webb. Johnson told him to refuse, but instead Reedy sent Johnson a memo which he wrote and rewrote, trying to make Johnson see the folly of what he was doing. "After considering it from every angle I would like to suggest that you reconsider your refusal," he wrote. "This program would definitely give you an opportunity to be associated with the space program, above and beyond almost anything else you could do. . . . The spotlight would be on you." When Johnson told Reedy to say what he had been told to say, Fritchey's response was curt. "I called Clayton Fritchey and told him that you do not go on TV shows," Reedy reported. "His exact response was: 'All right! I might invite Jim Webb then. We want someone from Washington. I appreciate your efforts, George. So long.' "

He couldn't bear to stay in Washington. After Kennedy's triumphant confrontation with Big Steel in April, during which, to battle inflation, the President forced the United States Steel Corporation to rescind the price increases it had announced—a four-day-long episode in which Johnson played no part—he began spending more and more time on his ranch, leaving Washington on Thursday and not returning until Monday. But he couldn't relax there. To while away the time, he played endless games of dominoes with his ranch foreman, Dale Malechek. And he couldn't sleep there, either. Malechek, milking cows at 4 a.m., suddenly felt a presence behind him, and, turning on his stool, saw Johnson standing behind him in his bathrobe.

With the weather turning warmer in Washington that summer, he would invite Texas allies over to The Elms to swim or sit around the pool and then have dinner, but, one of the frequent guests, Congressman Jim Wright, recalls, he kept "grabbing the phone impatiently and calling somebody. He couldn't relax, you couldn't keep his mind on one subject."

And when he did sleep, his dreams—his nightmares—were of what Doris Kearns Goodwin, to whom he was later to recall them, called the "utter power-lessness" of being trapped, and the trap in which he was caught in his dreams was, in fact, the one in which, in daylight hours, he lived. In the dream that particularly tormented him, he was seated at his desk in the Executive Office Building, so near, and yet so far, from the White House just beyond his window. "In the dream," he told Goodwin, "I had finished signing one stack of letters and had turned my chair toward the window. The activity on the street below suggested to me that it was just past five o'clock. All of Washington, it seemed, was on the street, leaving work for the day, heading for home. Suddenly, I decided I'd pack up and go home, too. For once, I decided, it would be nice to join all those people on the street and have an early dinner with my family. I started to get up from my chair, but I couldn't move. I looked down at my legs and saw they were manacled to the chair with a heavy chain. I tried to break the chain, but I couldn't. I tried again, and failed again. Once more and I gave up: I reached for the second stack of mail. I placed it directly in front of me, and got back to work."

In desperation he turned back to the staff member on whom he had relied for so many years, instructing George Reedy to draft one of his long memos laying out a strategy to deal with the predicament. But as always, he got from Reedy the truth: that there was, really, no way of dealing with it. "The question raised by so many newspapermen—'What is the Vice President doing?'—is not going to be answered satisfactorily by more activity or by public relations moves," Reedy told him in a memo. "They are accustomed to thinking of you as the man who for eight years was one of the dominant movers and shapers on the American scene and this does not accord in their thoughts with the picture of a man . . . meeting officials at the airport and going down to the White House to give advice but not to make decisions. . . . The question 'What is the Vice President Doing?' is going to persist with unfavorable undertones until they find some area in which you are actually making decisions." And, Reedy went on, "Because of the inherent nature of the Vice Presidency, it is very difficult to put you in a decision-making role. . . . For the time being there is no conclusive answer to the 'What is the Vice President Doing' question. We have no choice other than to struggle along doing the best we can while laying our plans for the future."

Reedy was telling him that there was no way out of the trap in which he had caught himself. If, during the vice presidency's early days, a gloomy demeanor had been a pose Johnson adopted to elicit sympathy, it was no longer a pose. He began telling even his most trusted staff members that they should start looking for other jobs. John Connally, running for governor of Texas, asked Ken BeLieu to leave Washington and join his staff in Texas. When BeLieu reported this to Johnson, Johnson replied: "Go. I'm finished. You follow him."

HIS MANNER WAS PARTICULARLY NOTICEABLE when John Kennedy was present, as Evelyn Lincoln noticed. As the President's "sureness and independence increased, the Vice President became more apprehensive and anxious to please," she was to recall. Sometimes, on the increasingly rare occasions when he was in the Oval Office, with Kennedy leaning back, relaxed and at ease in his chair, Johnson, sitting facing him in a chair beside his desk, would be on the edge of his seat, leaning forward as he talked, his pose that of a schoolboy trying to win a teacher's favor.

And, in the fall of 1962, in response to further humiliation from the Kennedys, he groveled even more deeply than before.

In September, James Meredith's attempt to become the first of Mississippi's one million black residents to attend the state university was met by the defiance of Mississippi Governor Ross Barnett, touching off two weeks of tense negotiations with the White House before, over the last weekend in the month, the tension erupted in violence that left two dead and scores injured, and in the dispatch of hundreds of United States marshals and the federalizing by Kennedy of the Mississippi National Guard. Johnson was not involved in the negotiations; during the crucial weekend he was not even in Washington but down at the ranch. Unfortunately, that fact became known, and on Monday morning the *Houston Chronicle* asked its congressional correspondent, Vernon Louviere, to ask the Vice President for comment. Strolling with an affectation of casualness up to the Senate Press Gallery, Boatner managed to get a look at the story in Louviere's typewriter. "He has written only one paragraph," he reported to Johnson, "but it was to the effect that the man who carried the South for President Kennedy apparently had not been called in for discussion of the Mississippi situation." Telephoning Louviere, Johnson tried frantically for thirty minutes to convince the reporter that his information was incorrect, that in fact the White House had been constantly consulting him that weekend, that even when he had been out boating on a lake near the ranch, he had had a ship-to-shore telephone with him. But the information was accurate, and the article, which ran on Tuesday, reported that "over the weekend—one of the tensest in the nation's history—Johnson was not in . . . close personal contact with the White House. He was relaxing at his ranch in Texas."

Johnson's response to the story was panic—that it might offend the President. Telephoning Dean Rusk, the Cabinet member friendliest to him, he asked him to get a message to Kennedy—which Rusk did by passing it on to White House aide Dungan. The message was that the information in Louviere's article had not come from him or anyone on his staff—that he had never discussed the

Meredith situation with any journalist or leaked any information that would suggest discord within the Administration. And the message didn't stop there. He wanted the President to know, it said, that "the situation in Mississippi had been handled better than he could ever have thought of handling it"—and that "He felt that he had been treated better than any other Vice President in history and knew it."

THEN, A FEW MINUTES BEFORE NINE O'CLOCK on Tuesday, October 16, 1962, as President Kennedy, still in his pajamas, was sitting in bed reading the morning newspapers, there was a knock on the door, and McGeorge Bundy came in, and under his arm was a sheaf of photographs—and the thirteen days of the Cuban Missile Crisis had begun.

When, at 11:50 a.m. that Tuesday, the photographs—barely discernible lines and dots that were, a CIA analyst explained, missile sites that Russian technicians were assembling in Cuba for missiles, capable of carrying nuclear warheads, that would be able to reach targets in most of the United States and that would soon be operative—were shown to the group, mostly members of the National Security Council, that Kennedy had assembled in the Cabinet Room, Johnson, as a member of the NSC, was among them. The first reaction was shocked disbelief; for months the Russians had been assuring Kennedy that they would not put offensive weapons in Cuba. And when opinion in the group (which, during the Thirteen Days, would come to be known as "ExComm," for the executive committee of the National Security Council) came down in favor of quick action—an immediate air strike, delivered without warning against the missile sites, or a broader, more massive bombing campaign, or some other form of quick military action—Johnson was part of that hawkish majority. Prodded by Kennedy—"You have any thoughts, Mr. Vice President?"—after he had remained silent all afternoon, Johnson said he wanted to hear the recommendation of the Joint Chiefs of Staff, who were meeting at the Pentagon. But, he said, "the question we face is whether we take it [the missile sites] out or whether we talk about it. And, of course, either alternative is a very distressing one. But of the two, I would take it out—assuming that the commanders felt that way." He would not, Lyndon Johnson said, consult with America's allies, or with its senators or congressmen. "I'm not much for circularizing it over the Hill or with our allies, even though I realize it's a breach of faith, not to confer with them. We're not going to get much help out of them. . . . Tell the alliance we've got to try to stop the planes, stop the ships, stop the submarines and everything else they're [the Soviets] sending. Just not going to permit it."

THE JOINT CHIEFS ADVOCATED a surprise air strike, not just against the missile sites but against airfields and possibly other targets in Cuba, with a simultaneous buildup for a possible invasion. Kennedy ordered ExComm's members to drop whatever else they were doing and analyze his options. Action was imperative, Kennedy said—"I don't think we've got much time on these missiles. We can't wait. . . . We're certainly going to do [option] number one. We're going to take out those missiles"—but, he said, he wouldn't act immediately. He ordered more photographic reconnaissance flights; "We had to be sure," in Sorensen's words, "of what we were facing, had to have the most convincing possible evidence" to present to the world, had to know "what else was taking place throughout the island." The President made a plea to the group for secrecy, until the evidence—and our response—was determined. "Any premature disclosure," in Sorensen's words, "could precipitate a Soviet move or panic the American public." And if negotiations were decided on, leaks would make them more difficult. He and the Vice President, Kennedy told ExComm, were both scheduled to campaign for congressional candidates that week, and, so that the press wouldn't get wind of the crisis, they would both keep those commitments until the group united behind a recommendation. Johnson was scheduled to leave the next day for appearances in the Midwest and West, and then Hawaii, but Kennedy's appearances were in the East until Friday, so he could sit in on at least some of the group's meetings.

NEAR THE END of that evening meeting, at which Johnson had again sat silent, Kennedy had pressed him—"Mr. Vice President, do you have any thoughts?"—but Johnson this time declined to give any. His only response was, "I don't think I can add anything that is essential."

His silence at the meeting did not, however, mean he was silent everywhere. Despite his statement that "I'm not much for circularizing it over the Hill," he evidently decided to circularize it to at least one man on the Hill. Telephoning Richard Russell, he told him about the photographs—"The first word about the existence of those missiles came [in a telephone call] from Johnson," says William H. Darden, chief clerk of Russell's Senate Armed Services Committee. Kennedy had asked that that information be kept secret, and among those from whom he was undoubtedly most anxious it be kept secret were the members of the congressional hawks whom he called the "war party." Johnson had given the information to the war party's chief. (That during the next six days—before Kennedy made the information public in a television address—it remained secret was proof of the fact that coexisting with Russell's monumental racism was what a friend called "a monumental sense of honor." During the quarter of a century of Russell's dominance in the Senate Armed Services Committee, he regarded his responsibility to America's fighting men as a sacred trust: he never leaked confidential information to journalists, and members of his committee, even the most publicity hungry of them, were aware of what his attitude would be if *they* did. Once, after a closed committee hearing, Wayne Morse of Oregon, looking for headlines, leaked a piece of secret military information. Cornered for a comment by journalists the next day, Russell said he would give one not on the information but on the leak; the comment was a single word: "dishonorable." He shared the information Johnson gave him about the Cuban Missile Crisis with no one, waiting for the time when he could discuss it with the President.)

DURING A BREAK in one of the meetings in the Cabinet Room that day, Kennedy inadvertently left the tape running, and it captured a private remark Johnson made to McNamara, not about the missile crisis but rather about the plane he had leased. "I have a Grumman Gulfstream that I've leased. I want you to lease it for MATS [the Military Air Transport Service] after the election," he said, apparently asking for the Defense Department to pick up the cost of the plane. And he wanted better communications equipment installed on it. "I wonder if there's any good reason why you shouldn't go to somebody and put" better equipment on the plane, he said. McNamara appears to have had other things on his mind: "Oh, sure, sure," he said to Johnson, brushing him off.

CAMPAIGNING IN THE WEST, Johnson was away from Washington during what Sorensen calls the first week's "blur" of "the crucial meetings" at which "the basic decision was hammered out."

Early in that week, the tone of ExComm's discussions changed—and the catalyst for the change was Robert Kennedy. At some point, when the general opinion was still for a surprise bombing attack to be delivered the following Sunday, and much of ExComm was pressing the President to authorize it, Bobby passed a note to his brother: "I now know how Tojo felt when he was planning Pearl Harbor."

Reminding the group, in what Sorensen was later to describe as "rather impassioned tones," that the Japanese sneak attack on Pearl Harbor, the day "that will live in infamy," had occurred on a Sunday, Bobby said that the contemplated Sunday air strike on Cuba would be "a Pearl Harbor in reverse, and it would blacken the United States in the pages of history." And it wasn't just the Pearl Harbor comparison that bothered him, Bobby was to recall. "I could not accept the idea that the United States would rain bombs on Cuba, killing thousands and thousands of civilians in a surprise attack. Maybe the alternatives were not very palatable, but I simply did not see how we could accept that course of action for our country." Every time opinion around the table seemed to be hardening behind the air strike, he spoke against it. "For 175 years we have not been that kind of a country," he said. "A sneak attack is not in our traditions." While he wanted steps that would make clear America's determination to get the missiles out of Cuba, he felt the Russians must be allowed room for maneuver, an avenue along which to pull back without losing face. The onetime rabid anti-Communist was viewing the Cuban problem not just in military but in moral terms.

Listening to Robert Kennedy analyzing all sides of the situation, with his emphasis on the moral rather than the military—"We spent more time on this moral question during the first five days than on any single matter," he was to say—Undersecretary of State George Ball was "very much surprised." He had always felt that Bobby's ideas were "much too simplistic and categorical—either you condemn something utterly or you accept it enthusiastically . . . and there seemed no intermediate positions," but now "he behaved quite differently." And, Treasury Secretary Douglas Dillon was to say, Bobby spoke "with an intense and quiet passion" that swayed ExComm. "As he spoke, I felt that I was at a real turning point in history"; after listening to him, "I knew then that we should not undertake a strike without warning." It was "Bobby Kennedy's good sense"—his "good sense" and "his moral character"—which were, perhaps, "decisive" in ExComm's debates, said the State Department's U. Alexis Johnson. (Dean Acheson felt differently: he was to say with contempt that Robert Kennedy had been "moved by emotional or intuitive responses more than by the trained lawyer's analysis.")

The President had not sat in on all ExComm's meetings: he wanted to stay away from some of them, his brother would explain, because he didn't want the discussions to be "inhibited"; "personalities change when the President is present." But he was kept apprised. Returning from a campaign trip to Connecticut on Wednesday evening, the President found his brother and Sorensen waiting for him at the airport, sitting in his car to avoid reporters' attention. "I have the most vivid memory of the smiling campaigner alighting from his plane, waving casually to onlookers at the airport, and then instantly casting off that pose and taking up the burdens of crisis as he entered his car," Sorensen was to recall. But Johnson was not present as the tone in the group, prodded constantly by the President for new ideas, probed by him to make sure that no one was merely trying to guess his own views and agree with them, swung slowly away from the Joint Chiefs' insistence on immediate bombings and possibly invasion and toward an intermediate step: a naval blockade, or "quarantine," of Soviet ships heading for Cuba with new equipment.

A blockade would not necessarily lead to bloodshed, and it would be coupled with a demand that Khrushchev remove the missiles already in Cuba, and with attempts, despite the Soviet premier's deceit in previous dealings, to find some basis for negotiations with him. And the possibility of gradual military escalation would be kept open; preparations for air strikes of varying size, and for an invasion later if necessary, would go forward. On Saturday, October 20, ExComm decided on that recommendation, and Robert Kennedy called his brother, who was campaigning in Chicago, and the President, pleading a cold, came home; Bobby, sitting on the edge of the White House pool while the President was swimming to ease the pain in his back, gave him the recommendation and the President accepted it.

• • •

LYNDON JOHNSON WAS also summoned back on Saturday, but since he was on his way to Hawaii, he did not arrive in Washington until Sunday, October 21; that evening, he was briefed at The Elms by CIA director John McCone.

Although McCone laid out for Johnson "in considerable detail" the thinking that had gone into Kennedy's decision, the Vice President did not agree with it, according to a "Memorandum for the File" that McCone wrote the next day. A blockade, Johnson said, would be "locking the barn after the horse was gone" since missiles were already in Cuba. He was also not in favor of gradual escalation, which he called "telegraphing our punch." Instead, he wanted "an unannounced [air] strike"—bombing Cuba without warning. (The scale of the strike he was advocating is not made clear in McCone's memo.) He "finally agreed reluctantly [with the blockade plan] but only after learning among other things the support indicated by General Eisenhower," McCone wrote.

Johnson's attitude can be partly explained by the fact that he had not been sitting in on the deliberations of the intervening days, when the pros and cons of the various options had been explored, and, of course, he was not the only member of ExComm—General Maxwell Taylor, McCone and Dillon were among the others—who were urging, in one form or another, a harder line. But during the next five days—on the first of which Kennedy went on television to tell America that Communist nuclear missile sites were being built in Cuba; that Russian bombers, capable of carrying nuclear weapons, were being assembled just ninety miles from America's shores; that he was immediately instituting a "quarantine" under which "all ships of any kind bound for Cuba" would be halted, boarded, searched, and "if found to contain . . . offensive weapons, be turned back"; and that if the offensive buildup continued, "further action will be justified" ("I have directed the Armed Forces to prepare for any eventuality")—Johnson was part of ExComm's deliberations. There were moments when he was on the side of caution—once, when ExComm was mulling the utility of nighttime photography of the sites, which would require the use of flares, he said, "I've been afraid of those damned flares ever since they mentioned them. . . . Imagine some crazy Russian captain doing it. The damned thing [the flare] goes 'blooey' and lights up the skies. He might just pull a trigger. Looks like we're playing Fourth of July over there or something. I'm scared of that." But in general, Johnson's attitude didn't change.

These were days of terrible moments. Every day the photos, enlarged, placed on easels in the Cabinet Room and interpreted by CIA experts, showed that construction of the missile sites was not being halted but speeded up. "That is one launch pad there. . . . The conduiting goes back through this blast wall here. Here are the cables that come out of the control bunker. . . . This is the other launch pad over here. And here is where we think is probably one of the nuclear storage bunkers." Work on the launch pads, by thousands of Russian technicians and soldiers, was going on day and night now; some of them would become operational in a matter of days. And when they were—if America had not attacked before then, if America had waited too long to attack—then, if America did attack, the missiles, with nuclear warheads, could be launched against American cities in retaliation. Once "nuclear warheads were in place and pointed at the United States," the balance of power in the Cold War would have changed.

The Russian ships kept coming. A quarantine line—the line at which armed American sailors would board Cuban-bound vessels, just the type of action that could lead to escalation, and then to war—had been established five hundred miles off Cuba, and on Wednesday, October 24, two Russian ships were within a few miles of the line. And just after ExComm convened at 10 that morning came the news that a Russian submarine had moved into position to protect them. An American aircraft carrier, the *Essex,* with helicopters carrying anti-submarine depth charges, had been ordered into the vicinity. "It's a very dangerous situation," McNamara said in that hushed Cabinet Room. "We'll declare radio silence. And therefore neither we nor the Soviets will know where our Navy ships are for much of today."

"This was the moment . . . which we hoped would never come," Robert Kennedy was to recall. In that moment Bobby saw only his brother. "His hand went up to his face & covered his mouth and he closed his fist. His eyes were tense, almost gray, and we just stared at each other across the table. Was the world on the brink of a holocaust and had we done something wrong?" For a few fleeting seconds, it was almost as though no one else was there, and Jack was just his brother again, not the President. "Inexplicably, I thought of when he was ill and almost died . . . when we learned that our oldest brother had been killed, of personal times of strain and hurt. The voices droned on, but I didn't seem to hear anything. . . . I felt we were on the edge of a precipice with no way off. . . . One thousand miles away in the vast expanse of the Atlantic Ocean the final decisions were going to be made in the next few minutes." Then a messenger came into the room, and handed a note to John McCone, and McCone announced that the Russian ships had stopped, and might be starting to turn around. "The meeting droned on," Robert Kennedy said. "For a moment the world had stood still, and now it was going around again."

The danger was far from over: some Russian ships, further from the quarantine line, were still continuing toward it at full speed; and even if no more missiles arrived, the ones already in Cuba were still there, and the work on them was continuing. But the constant in all these moments was the determination of the two brothers to give Khrushchev every chance to reconsider, to pull back; the determination to avoid war—and above all, to avoid it through miscalculation. The President had read Barbara Tuchman's *The Guns of August,* and, sitting in the Oval Office after the ExComm meetings with his brother, Sorensen and O'Donnell, "he talked," Robert Kennedy recalls, "about the miscalculations" that had exploded into the First World War. "They somehow seemed to tumble into war, he said, through stupidity, individual idiosyncrasies, misunderstandings and personal complexes of inferiority and grandeur. . . . 'The great danger and

risk in all of this,' he said, 'is a miscalculation—a mistake in judgment.' " He
was determined to do anything possible to avoid one. That Wednesday, not long
after the tension had been eased, it was ratcheted up again—in minutes of confusion over whether all of the Russian ships had stopped, or all but one, the
Kimovsk, which might be turning back, or was simply moving in a circle, as if it
still might challenge the blockade. There were American planes overhead; the
Soviet sub was there—and the *Essex;* it was just the type of situation in which
someone out in the Atlantic might make a mistake. And the time for the mistake
was—"right now," McNamara said; it was 10:40 a.m., almost the moment at
which an American destroyer was scheduled to hail the *Kimovsk,* and demand
that it halt and submit to a search. "Check first," John Kennedy ordered. "We
ought to maybe wait an hour on the *Kimovsk.* To see whether. . . . It seems to me
you want to give that specific ship a chance to turn around. You don't want to
have word going out from Moscow: 'Turn around,' and suddenly we sink a ship."
Tell the *Essex* "to wait an hour and see whether that ship continues on its course,"
he ordered. And in fact the *Kimovsk was* turning around; by Thursday, sixteen of
the twenty-five Russian ships heading for Cuba had stopped dead in the water or
reversed course.

The next day, Thursday, one of the nine other Russian ships, the *Bucharest,*
was still steaming toward the quarantine line. Because it was a tanker, it almost
certainly didn't carry any missiles or other armament, but, as Robert Kennedy
recalls, "there were those on the Executive Committee who felt strongly that the
Bucharest should be stopped and boarded, so that Khrushchev would make no
mistake of our will or interest." John Kennedy assured them that the Navy would
stop and board one of the ships. Just not this one at the moment, he said. He
would make a decision by nightfall, he said. But that evening, "after further
heated discussion," Kennedy made a final decision to let the *Bucharest* proceed
to Havana. "Against the advice of many of his advisers and of the military he had
decided to give Khrushchev more time. 'We don't want to push him into a pre-
cipitous action—give him time to consider. I don't want to push him into a corner from which he cannot escape.' " Over and over again, Kennedy delayed a
decision to take a step that would require force and might be met by force—and
therefore might escalate into the war that would destroy mankind. Over and over
again, he tried to give Khrushchev more time to think—until on Friday night, a
cable clattered over the State Department teletype, a long, rambling message
from Nikita Khrushchev. It contained an offer to trade: in return for America's
pledge not to invade Cuba, the missiles and the Russian technicians and soldiers
would be withdrawn. And it contained also "very personal" sentences about the
Russian premier's own fears that mankind was on the edge of the abyss of
nuclear war, as well as a statement—"Mr. President, we and you ought not now
to pull on the ends of the rope in which you have tied the knots of war; because
the more the two of us pull, the tighter this knot will be tied." That message "for
the first time," Robert Kennedy said, gave his brother hope that he was not the
only one of the two leaders who was trying to pull mankind back from the abyss.

• • •

DURING THESE FIVE DAYS—from Monday, October 22, through Friday, October 26—Lyndon Johnson was in the Cabinet Room hour after hour as ExComm met, but he hardly spoke, at least while the group was sitting around the Cabinet table with the President presiding. According to Robert Kennedy and Ted Sorensen, he would, however, speak after the meeting was over and the President had left the Cabinet Room, having switched off the tape recorder. "Frequently, after the meetings were finished, he would circulate and whine and complain about our being weak, but he never made . . . any suggestions or recommendations," Robert Kennedy would say. "He was displeased with what we were doing, although he never made clear what *he* would do. He said he had the feeling that we were being too weak, and that we should be stronger."

He didn't speak even at one meeting at which he might particularly have been expected to.

On the Monday of that week, just before his telecast, President Kennedy met in the Cabinet Room with twenty congressional leaders, hastily ferried back to Washington by Air Force planes from all over the country, to inform them of the decision he had made, and of the reasons behind it, and he had Johnson attend the meeting.

Nineteen of the leaders were learning the scope of the Russian buildup for the first time; Richard Russell, of course, was not, thanks to Johnson; he had had a week to think about what should be done,* and he did not accept Kennedy's reasoning. "Mr. President," he said, "I could not stay silent under these circumstances and live with myself. I think that our responsibilities to our people demanded stronger steps than that. . . . We're at the crossroads. We're either a first-class power or we're not." The United States should invade, and invade immediately, he said. It would not be an invasion without warning. "You have warned these people time and again. . . . They can't say they're not on notice. You have told them not to do this thing. They've done it. And I think you should assemble as speedily as possible an adequate force and clean out that situation." Why had the President been waiting so long to act if he knew work on the missiles was going forward? Russell demanded. "Why didn't you start when you first got these notifications of all these [missiles] down there? It's been over seven days. . . . I think we can die by attrition here. . . . Our authority and the world's authority will hinge on this decision."

Foreign Relations chairman agreed with Armed Services chairman. "I think a blockade is the worst of the alternatives because if you're confronted with a Russian ship, you are actually confronting Russia," J. William Fulbright told the President.

---

*Although, in the week since Johnson had leaked his information, electronic launching systems had been installed at the missile sites. When, now, Kennedy revealed this, Russell said, "they'd be ready to fire now? . . . My God."

"What are you in favor of, Bill?" Kennedy asked him.

"I'm in favor . . . of an invasion, and an all-out one, and as quickly as possible," Fulbright replied.

Every congressional leader who spoke at the meeting agreed with Russell. This was indeed the "war party," and it included the leaders, perhaps *all* the leaders, of Capitol Hill.

Kennedy was jolted. Later, Robert Kennedy would write that his brother's meeting with the congressmen had been "the most difficult meeting. . . . it was a tremendous strain." And during it, he had received no help from Lyndon Johnson. Kennedy may have expected that his Vice President would help. The men in that room were his longtime allies; moreover, the Vice President had been a part of the ExComm deliberations: he knew, and could explain in terms they understood, the arguments that would temper their opposition. The meeting had lasted for an hour, and during it Lyndon Johnson had not said a word. Given a chance to help the President, he hadn't used it.

DURING THOSE FIVE DAYS, furthermore, Jack Kennedy's insistence that ExComm explore each option, think through the consequences of each course of action, had won most of the committee's members over to his side, and while some, the most hawkish, still felt his response was too weak, the attitude of most of them had been softened. But Johnson was one member of ExComm the President hadn't won over at all, whose attitude had not softened at all, as became apparent on the sixth day after the Vice President's return from Hawaii, the twelfth—and climactic—day of the Cuban Missile Crisis: Saturday, October 27.

Hardly had ExComm convened in the Cabinet Room just after 10 a.m. that Saturday when, as Theodore Sorensen puts it, "our hopes," raised by Khrushchev's letter, "quickly faded." The Soviet premier had sent a new letter, this time a public message, "raising the ante": a no-invasion pledge was no longer all he was asking for in exchange for removing his missiles; the new letter also demanded the removal of American Jupiter missiles based in Turkey.

Since the Jupiters were, in fact, all but obsolete, the United States had been considering their removal for some time before the crisis, assuring Turkey that Polaris nuclear submarines in the Mediterranean offered far more protection, not pursuing the matter because of Turkey's strenuous objections, and Khrushchev's proposals immediately appealed to Kennedy. But because Khrushchev had made the demand publicly, America's agreement to it would appear to our allies, as one of them, British Prime Minister Harold Macmillan, was to put it, as "a sign of weakness," of appeasement—a sign that Khrushchev had, by putting missiles in Cuba, forced the United States to withdraw weapons from an ally. Accepting Khrushchev's deal would appear to demonstrate that to remove a threat to itself, America had sacrificed an ally; "anything like this deal would do great injury to NATO," Macmillan said. "All credibility in the American protection of Europe would have gone."

That second letter began what Robert Kennedy was to call "the most diffi-cult twenty-four hours of the Missile Crisis."

All that day, the news got steadily worse. "To add to the feeling of forebod-ing and doom, Secretary McNamara reported increased evidence that the Rus-sians in Cuba were now working day and night, intensifying their efforts on the missile sites." There were indications that some missiles were being moved into ready position for firing. The Russian Ilyushin-28 bombers—the bombers capa-ble of carrying nuclear warheads—were being uncrated and assembled. Time had all but run out for America. And nine ships were still steaming across the Atlantic; one of them, the *Grozny,* was less than a hundred miles from the quar-antine line and heading straight for it; McNamara said the Navy was readying destroyers to board it. Joining the meeting, the Joint Chiefs delivered their rec-ommendation: an air strike on Monday, followed by an invasion.

The President kept postponing his decision. Leaving the Cabinet Room, he and his brother would walk down the hall to the Oval Office to talk privately there, occasionally calling in Sorensen: still hopeful that Khrushchev, despite his second letter, might be searching for a way out of the crisis, they were trying to find a way to help him do so, and finally they felt they had: that the President sim-ply ignore the second letter, including the demand about the Jupiters in Turkey, and reply to the first, accepting the deal *it* had offered—to withdraw the missiles in exchange for a no-invasion pledge. Returning to the Cabinet Room, he left Sorensen drafting the reply.

And then, in the evening, as Sorensen was still working, came news of an American U-2 spy plane that had been photographing the missile installations. Momentarily rattled when he heard it, the President said, "A U-2 was shot down? Well now, this is much [*sic*] of an escalation by them, isn't it? How do we explain? . . . How do we? . . . I mean that must be—"

Days earlier, ExComm had decided on the actions to be taken if a U-2 was shot down—"immediate retaliation upon the most likely SAM [surface-to-air missile] site involved," coupled with an announcement that if another U-2 was hit, "we'll take out every SAM site"—and now a U-2 *had* been shot down, its pilot was lying dead in the wreckage, and from all along the long table came angry demands that that decision be carried out. "They've fired the first shot." "We should retaliate against the SAM sites and announce that if any other planes . . . It's what we agreed to two [*sic*] days ago." "It looked good then and it still looks good to me." Carried out immediately. "You can go against one SAM site, can't you?" McGeorge Bundy said. "Now? Tonight?" "The hawks, dream-ing of a Monday morning war, rallied behind the hard line," Arthur Schlesinger writes, and it wasn't only hawks who were following that line now. "I think tomorrow morning we ought to go in and take out that SAM site and send our surveillance in with proper protection immediately following it. . . . Shoot up that SAM site and send in—" Robert McNamara said. "There was," in Robert Kennedy's words, "almost unanimous agreement that we had to attack early the next morning."

"The noose was tightening on all of us," he says.

But again his brother pulled everyone back. The letter to Khrushchev was almost completed; it might work. "It isn't the first step that concerns me, but both sides escalating to the fourth and fifth step—and we don't go to the sixth because there is no one around to do so," the President said. He left the Cabinet Room with his brother to see how Sorensen was coming with the letter, and when he returned about ten minutes later, leaving his brother and Sorensen working on the draft, he changed the subject: "Gentlemen, come up and sit here now. Gentlemen. Let's talk a little more about the Turks, how we're going to handle that. NATO and the Turks, that's the one matter we haven't settled today." Discussions went on, about the Jupiter trade, about how to get Turkey and NATO to agree to it.

DURING MOST OF THAT SATURDAY, Lyndon Johnson had had, as usual, little to say, but that evening, President Kennedy and his brother having left the Cabinet Room, suddenly the Vice President was talking—harshly criticizing what the President was trying to do.

If America agreed to trade the Turkish missiles for the Cuban missiles, he said, "Radio and TV reports will give the impression that we're having to retreat." And, he said, those reports would not be wrong. "We're backing down." In fact, he said, "I think we've been [backing down] gradually from the President's speech."

Re-entering the room at that moment, Robert Kennedy heard Johnson's remarks. "[Who] feels we're backing down?" he demanded.

"We've got a blockade, and we're doing . . . this and that and the [Russian] ships are coming through," Johnson replied.

"No, the ships aren't coming through," Kennedy said. "They all turned back. Ninety percent of them, they haven't been running for twenty-four hours."

"I don't think we can justify, at this moment, [the argument] that it looks like we are as strong as we were the day of the President's announcement," Johnson replied.

Bobby left, to rejoin his brother in the Oval Office, and Bundy started trying to explain that the Navy was still "waiting for up-to-date information on" the *Grozny*'s position—how close it was to the quarantine line—but Johnson returned to the subject of the President's speech of October 22, in which Kennedy had promised further action if the missiles were not removed. The public was going to start asking why the President had not carried out that pledge, Johnson said—"Since then why we . . . I don't say [unclear], I don't say it's a lie. I just say that's what happens [with public opinion] when it's 101 degrees [hot]. And I think they would see this whole thing, they see the U-2 shot down, and they say, 'What's your response?' "

For the first time during the crisis, Johnson was doing a lot of talking, and he was talking—the Texas twang authoritative, insistent, overriding other voices—with a fervor that held the table, and shifted the mood of at least some of the men around it.

With both Kennedys out of the room, he was running the meeting. "Did we get off this letter of points [to Khrushchev] . . . ? Is that finally put in, Mr. Secretary?" "Well, then, to summarize it [the situation] . . . What has been done today? Let's just see how he [Khrushchev] is looking at our performance today before he shot down this plane." When Rusk tried to answer his questions, Johnson interrupted him.

The concept of the trade—removing the Jupiters from Turkey if Russia removed its missiles from Cuba—had a great drawback, Johnson said. The trade would leave Russian bombers and troops still in Cuba. To get them out, he said, the United States would be forced to trade again: to agree to remove our bombers from Turkey—the Jupiters might be obsolete, but the planes weren't; and having them based close to Russia's borders was a vital strategic advantage for the United States—and our troops as well. "I guess what he's [Khrushchev] really saying: I'm going to dismantle the foreign policy of the United States for the last fifteen years in order [for the United States] to get those missiles out of Cuba. Then we say we're glad and we appreciate it, and we want to discuss it with you."

And even more important, Johnson said, accepting a trade showed weakness. "Look, the weakness of the whole thing is, you say, 'Well, they [the Russians] shot down one plane, and they [the Americans] gave up Turkey. Then they shoot down another, and they [the Americans] give up Berlin.' You know, like a mad dog—he tastes a little blood, he . . ."

Showing weakness to a mad dog was always a mistake, Lyndon Johnson said. "He's [Khrushchev] got to get a little blood." And now, by shooting down the U-2, "he's *got* it." And America was still not responding. "Now, when they realize that they shot down one of our pilots, we're letting this ship go through and that ship go through . . ." What was needed was strength, action. The American people were going to demand action, he said. "I think you're going to have a big problem right here, internally, in a few more hours in this country." An American plane had been shot down, and the President was taking no action. "This ought to start the wires [coming] in now from all over the country, the states of the Union: 'Where have you been? What are you doing? The President made a fine speech. What else have you done?' . . . They see that there's some ships coming through. There's a great feeling of insecurity."*

He was pounding home the idea that the time for negotiation—at least for negotiation alone—was over, that immediate military action was needed, rallying the hawks. In the midst of an exchange with two of them, Treasury Secretary Dillon and former ambassador to Russia Llewellyn Thompson, he demanded: "You just ask yourself what made the greatest impression on you today, whether

*Earlier that evening, Johnson had appeared to be endorsing the trade, but that had been before he understood the terms Khrushchev was proposing.

it was his [Khrushchev's] letter last night, or whether it was his letter this morning, or whether it was that U-2 boy going down?"

"The U-2 boy," Dillon replied. "That's exactly right; that's what did it," Johnson said. "And that [attacking a SAM site] is what's going to make an impression on him [Khrushchev]—not all these signals [letters] that each one of us write. He is an expert on that palaver."

Johnson was making an argument with the force—so long held in check—that carried all before it, and by the time President Kennedy returned to the Cabinet Room, about 7:20, the effect he had had on the hawks was obvious. Bundy told the President that "There is a very substantial difference between us," and Dillon and Thompson made that clear. Dillon said, "It would probably be more effective and make more of an impression on him if we did do what we said we were going to do before, and just go in and knock out this one SAM site. . . . Don't say anything. Just do that." "They've upped the price and they've upped the action," Thompson said. "And I think we have to bring them back by upping our action." And Johnson for once engaged Kennedy in an exchange, which showed how substantial a difference there was between *him* and the President. When Kennedy tried to explain that escalation such as knocking out a SAM site might well end in invasion, and "We can't very well invade Cuba, with all this toil and blood it's going to be, when we could have gotten them [the Soviet missiles] out by making a deal on the same missiles in Turkey," Johnson interrupted him.

"It doesn't mean just missiles," he said. To get the Russian bombers and troops out of Cuba as well, another trade would be necessary. And if America took its planes and troops out of Turkey, "Why then your whole foreign policy is gone. You take everything out of Turkey. Twenty thousand men, all your technicians, and all your planes and all your missiles. And crumble."

"How else are we going to get those missiles out of there [Cuba] then?" Kennedy said. "That's the problem."

He was still playing for time—time that could bring peace, not war. He wanted to see if his letter to Khrushchev, which he had had his brother hand-deliver to Ambassador Anatoly Dobrynin, had any effect, and in the meantime he wasn't taking any action. Everyone should "get a bite to eat," he said, and reconvene at nine o'clock. Then "we'll see what we do about the plane," he said, and discuss "this Turkish thing."

AS THE FIFTEEN MEMBERS of ExComm were filing out of the Cabinet Room to go to dinner, a quiet word was said to eight of them—Robert Kennedy, of course; Sorensen, Bundy, Rusk, McNamara, Ball, Thompson, and Deputy Secretary of Defense Roswell L. Gilpatric—to join the President in the Oval Office for another, more private, discussion. This smaller group included hawks as well as doves—Thompson, Gilpatric and Bundy were, to varying degrees, in the first category—but it did not include the Vice President. "Lyndon Johnson was not invited to that meeting," Sorensen says. Whether it was the harsh words he had spoken to the Kennedys that evening—If you do the Turkish trade, you *"crumble,"* he had told the President; "We're backing down," he had said to Robert—or his complaints during the entire week ("about our being weak"); or his silence when the President had needed his help with the congressional leaders; or the fear that he could not be trusted not to leak confidential information; or the unalloyed hawkishness he had displayed from the first day of the crisis through that very evening toward the "mad dog" in the Kremlin, whatever the reasons, he had his dinner downstairs in the White House mess.

The subject of the discussion in the Oval Office upstairs was what Robert Kennedy should say to Dobrynin, who was probably waiting for him already at the Justice Department. "One part of the oral message we discussed was simple, stern, and simply decided," Bundy was to recall. It was the same message sent in the President's letter to Khrushchev: remove the missiles, and there would be no invasion. "Otherwise further American action was unavoidable." But now Dean Rusk proposed a second, very secret, part: that Bobby should tell Dobrynin "that while there could be no [public] deal over the Turkish missiles, the President was determined to get them out and would do so once the Cuban crisis was resolved."

"The moment Rusk made his suggestion it became apparent to all of us that we should agree," and they did, Bundy says.

And they agreed on something else: the nine men in that room swore themselves to secrecy. All were aware, as Bundy later put it, that if word of the missile trade—a "bargain struck under pressure at the apparent expense of the Turks"—leaked out, it might undermine the Atlantic alliance, and that "the potential political cost of appearing to 'appease' the Kremlin" would also be high. "Aware as we" also "were from the day's discussion that for some, even in our closest councils, a unilateral private assurance might appear to betray an ally, we agreed without hesitation that no one not in the room was to be informed of this additional message," Bundy was to write. The deal remained secret for years. The most important decision of the Kennedy Administration was made without Lyndon Johnson's knowledge.

AT HIS MEETING with Dobrynin, Robert Kennedy told the Soviet ambassador that a letter had just been sent to Khrushchev repeating the offer of a no-invasion pledge if all offensive weapons were removed from Cuba: "I said that those missile bases had to go and they had to go right away. We had to have a commitment by at least tomorrow. . . . He should understand that if he did not remove those bases that we would remove them. His country might take retaliatory action but he should understand that before this was over, while there might be dead Americans, there would also be dead Russians." Then Kennedy said, not in writing but only orally, so there would be nothing on the record, that while there could be no direct *quid pro quo* for the Jupiters, "if some time elapsed . . . I mentioned 4 or 5 months—I was sure that these matters could be resolved satisfactorily." Dobrynin did nothing to commit his country, and Robert returned to the White House, about 8:40 p.m., to give his brother, who was having dinner with Dave Powers, a report so pessimistic that Powers, listening to it, says, "I thought it was my last meal."

WHEN EXCOMM RECONVENED about nine o'clock that Saturday evening, the two brothers were a little late—and during the few minutes before they arrived, there were more strong words from Lyndon Johnson about how to handle the Russians, and, listening to him, Sorensen suddenly felt "chilled." It wasn't just the bellicosity of the words but the force behind them: Lyndon Johnson could persuade men, and, without the countervailing presence of the brothers, he might, Sorensen saw, be persuading these.

"The hawks were rising," he recalls. "Bobby wasn't there, and I was rather concerned about that. The President wasn't there, so I didn't have my strongest allies there. Johnson slapped the table. 'All I know is that when I was a boy in Texas, and you were walking along the road when a rattlesnake reared up ready to strike, the only thing to do was to take a stick and chop its head off.' There was a little chill in the room after that statement."

There were strong words, also, from other hawks, these after the President and Bobby had entered the room, for there had still been no American retaliation for the death of an American pilot; Russian ships had been allowed through the quarantine line, and others, notably the *Grozny,* would reach the line Sunday morning; and the missile sites were about to become operational.

"Do anything about the SAM site that shot down our plane?" Dillon demanded. Temporizing, the President said the guilty site had not yet been definitively identified. "We don't know [which one] yet, Doug," he said. McNamara said, "If our planes are fired on tomorrow, we ought to fire back." Kennedy wanted to delay even that, to give negotiations more time, in hope that the messages delivered to Dobrynin might work. "Let me say, I think we ought to wait until tomorrow afternoon, to see whether we get any answers. . . . We're rapidly approaching a real—" Wait until tomorrow, he said. "If tomorrow they fire at us and we don't have any answer from the Russians, then Monday it seems to me" would be time enough. "And then go in and take *all* the SAM sites out." The fate of mankind might hang in the balance; surely the chance for peace could be given one more day; "I think we ought to keep tomorrow clean," Jack Kennedy said.

There was still the *Grozny.* It was going to reach the quarantine line at about 8:15 or 8:30 Sunday morning. This time, it was the younger brother who spoke, in a low, very soft voice. "It's just a question of whether we want to intercept that at all tomorrow, or let it go through. . . . Whether this ship gets in or not, it's not really going to count in the big picture. . . . Isn't it possible to decide tomorrow?" "Yes, we can wait until about noon tomorrow," McNamara said. And finally, Jack

Kennedy decided. "Give them that last chance," he said—and peace had one more day.

THERE WAS LITTLE OPTIMISM that that extra day would bring peace. "Saturday night was almost the blackest of all," Schlesinger was to recall. "Unless Khrushchev came through in a few hours, the meeting of the Executive Committee on Sunday might well face the most terrible decisions." Strategic Air Command bombers were circling endlessly over the Arctic that night; the crews of other bombers were being handed their target packets for bombing runs they might have to make the next day; American destroyers were circling in the Atlantic—with, a few fathoms below them, enemy submarines; the Fifth Marine Expeditionary Brigade began boarding ships to invasion staging areas; watching the sun set that Saturday night, McNamara wondered if he would live out the week. "But the next morning, a golden autumn Sunday morning," the *Grozny* suddenly came to a dead stop, and the nine o'clock newscasts were interrupted by a bulletin: Khrushchev had accepted Kennedy's terms, the no-missiles, no-invasion terms to which the President had brought him back by ignoring the second letter. The letter ended with this salutation to John Fitzgerald Kennedy: "With respect for you, Khrushchev."

ExComm met that Sunday at eleven. When the President walked into the room, everyone stood up, standing silently until he sat down. As he began the meeting, there wasn't, Ted Sorensen recalls, "a trace of excitement or even exultation" in his bearing.

IT HAD BEEN NO OVERSIGHT that Lyndon Johnson wasn't invited to that crucial conference in the Oval Office on Saturday evening.

On Sunday, after the final ExComm meeting, Jack Kennedy said to his brother that this was the night he should go to the theater, like Lincoln after the Union victory in the Civil War, and Robert—the subject of assassination having been raised, and with it, of course, the reminder that the Vice President would thereupon become President—said that "if he was going to the theater, I would go too, having witnessed the inability of Johnson to make any contribution of any kind during all the conversations." In later years, he would recall Johnson's displeasure "with what we were doing," the way, in Bobby's words, that "he would circulate and whine and complain about our being weak," while never making "any suggestions or recommendations" himself. The people who "had participated in all these discussions," Robert Kennedy was to say, "were bright and energetic people. We had perhaps amongst the most able in the country, and if any one of half a dozen of them were President the world would have been very likely plunged in a catastrophic war." Lyndon Johnson, he would make clear, was one of that half dozen. Jack Kennedy, as always, was more oblique, but, through the means of another, shorter, list, he also made his feelings clear. Recalls his friend, the journalist Bartlett: "He said after the Cuban Missile Crisis that there were three men on that Executive Committee that he would be glad to see become President of the United States: McNamara, Dillon, and his brother Bobby. He said that a couple of times." Three men whom John F. Kennedy would be happy to have succeed him as President. The Vice President wasn't one of them.

"You must know as well or better than I President Kennedy's steadily diminishing opinion of him," Jacqueline Kennedy would, years after the assassination, write in a private letter to Ted Sorensen. "As his term progressed, he grew more and more concerned about what would happen if LBJ ever became President. He was truly frightened at the prospect."

EARLY IN DECEMBER, Lyndon Johnson received a note from Robert Kennedy saying that he, "together with some of the other Executive Committee members," was buying a Christmas present for the President "in remembrance of our days together" during the Cuban Missile Crisis. "We are not yet certain of the cost but when that small matter is worked out I will write you a letter asking for a 'voluntary' contribution," Kennedy said.

While Johnson had not been one of the ExComm members who had planned the gift—a sterling silver plaque showing the month of October with the thirteen days of the crisis in bold numerals—the note at least implied that he would be invited to the presentation. "Mac Bundy will be in touch with you about" the arrangements, it said. When, however, on December 17, Bundy's secretary called one of Johnson's secretaries, Winnie Coates, to inform her that the presentation would be the next morning at 8:15, the call was not exactly an invitation. "She said Mr. Bundy felt it would not be necessary for everybody to be there at such an ungodly hour," Winnie reported.

Johnson got the idea. He didn't attend. But when he was asked for the contribution—"The happy, joyful ceremony . . . must now be paid for," Robert Kennedy wrote him. "I would greatly appreciate it, therefore, if you would send me a check for $200.00 which will cover your assessment"—he sent the check right off.

"AFTER THE CUBAN MISSILE CRISIS," Evelyn Lincoln was to write, "Mr. Kennedy seemed to be less concerned with making sure the Vice President was occupied, and from then on, he let Mr. Johnson seek his own place in the Administration." Johnson's response was the technique he had always used with people who had more power than he, as Mrs. Lincoln observed with barely concealed contempt. "The Vice President became more apprehensive and anxious to please. He tried even harder to enter into activities and become part of them. Whenever anyone mentioned Mr. Kennedy's name he would immediately tell them what a good job he was doing. He praised the efficiency of the Kennedy staff and the soundness of the Kennedy ideas. Time and again, as they filed out of the Cabinet Room, I would hear Mr. Johnson making these glowing compliments." Elbowing his way through a group standing in her office after one meeting, "he came up to the President. He stuck out his hand and said, 'That was a fine speech, Jack.' " But he wasn't dealing with elderly senators now. Fawn over Jack Kennedy though he might, Mrs. Lincoln says, "The President was . . . sending him fewer memos and giving him fewer assignments, and as a result, Johnson was fading into the background." In 1963, "One saw much less of him around the White House than in 1961 or 1962," Arthur Schlesinger was to write, and this wasn't a mistaken impression; in 1961, according to Mrs. Lincoln's detailed diaries of the President's activities, Johnson had spent only ten hours and nineteen minutes alone with the President, a meagre enough figure; in 1962, the figure had been smaller; in 1963, the Vice President was alone with the President for a total of one hour and fifty-three minutes. And Kennedy's attitude was reflected in the attitude of his staff. "I hate to admit it but in planning the surprise birthday party for Mr. Kennedy on May 29th, I forgot all about inviting Mr. Johnson," Mrs. Lincoln says. "And no one reminded me."

The President was still, of course, dispatching him on foreign trips, and assigning him routine ceremonial duties. "The vice presidency is filled with trips around the world, chauffeurs, men saluting, people clapping, chairmanships of counsils [*sic*], but in the end it is nothing," Lyndon Johnson was to say years later. "I detested every minute of it." And when he tried to make something more of the foreign trips, steps were taken to make sure he couldn't. During his September, 1963, visit to Finland, recalls America's ambassador to that country, Carl Rowan, "there was an earthquake in Iran, and he [Johnson] wanted to go there to demonstrate American caring. The White House said no." It said no as well to the very possibility of another trip. In a casual conversation in the embassy in Helsinki one evening, Johnson, boasting about his ability to read men, said, in Rowan's recollection, "that he could look into the eyes of the Soviet leaders and see what was in their hearts." This statement was relayed to Washington, which evidently became concerned that the Vice President might try to visit Finland's neighbor Russia. "I got a secret back-channel message saying, 'Do what you must, under any circumstances, to prevent Johnson from going to the Soviet Union,' " Rowan recalls.

And, as Schlesinger was to write, "the psychological cost was evidently mounting." Historian and secretary use the same phrase: "He seemed to have faded astonishingly into the background," he says. People who remembered him, tall and lean and bursting with energy, emanating power and authority as he strode through Capitol corridors and commanded the Senate Chamber from his front-row center desk, were shocked when they saw him now. His complexion was gray, and on that canvas face, now so gaunt, was painted sadness. Sitting at meetings in the Cabinet Room, gray, withdrawn and silent, he "appeared," in Schlesinger's phrase, "almost a spectral presence." When some official did telephone him, he seemed unable to stop talking, until the official, the brief purpose of the call accomplished, became desperate to get off the phone. Social occasions could be poignant. Invited to a fund-raiser at the Fifth Avenue apartment of a wealthy New York couple, "like a fool I went," he told Harry McPherson. "The President was there, sitting in a big easy chair, and everyone was in a circle around him, leaning in to hear every word. I was leaning over, too, and suddenly I didn't want to do that, to be leaning over listening to Jack Kennedy." Walking over to the French doors, he stood there alone, staring out over Central Park, until the hostess noticed, and asked a group of young guests, "Will somebody go and talk to the Vice President?" A beautiful young heiress, Jeanne Murray Vanderbilt, said, "I'll talk to him, but what can I talk to him about?"

The hostess, who knew Johnson, told Vanderbilt, "Don't give it a thought," and, Vanderbilt was to say, "She was right. He never stopped talking and he was so charming." After they had talked for some time, Johnson offered her a ride home—and as he let her out of the car, he said, "I'll never forget how nice you were to me tonight."

And, of course, with the blood in the water so plainly visible now, the journalistic swarm was more avid than ever. "It would be a rich treasure for historians if there were a tape recording of the talk Jack Kennedy gave to Johnson in the Biltmore Hotel in Los Angeles to persuade him to accept the nomination. . . . Few men in American history have given up so much for so little," the *Miami Herald* said. By the end of the year, the boast he had once made was being used to taunt him. In an article in *The Reporter* magazine under the now-familiar headline WHAT EVER HAPPENED TO LYNDON JOHNSON?, journalist Ward Just wrote that once "Johnson had said, 'Power is where power goes.' . . . It has not worked out quite that way, as LBJ would probably admit. . . . The man of power who suddenly finds himself short of it is a fascinating study. Lyndon Johnson seems determined to shun controversy. With newsmen he is strictly for 'background only.' The result . . . is that LBJ has all but disappeared from official sight. . . . The relationship between Kennedy and Johnson is one of the most curious in Washington. . . . Is there, in fact, any business relationship at all?" Said a *Time* article in January, 1963: " 'Power is where power goes,' Johnson confidently told a friend before taking office as Vice President. He was wrong—power has slipped from his grasp." All of the jobs he had been given—the chairmanships of the Space Council and the CEEO, the membership on the National Security Council—"all of this together adds up to only a fraction of his old power and influence. He is free to speak up, but nobody, really, has to heed him anymore." The popular television show *Candid Camera* asked random passersby: "Who is Lyndon B. Johnson?" Not one knew. One of those questioned said he couldn't be expected to know: "I'm from New Jersey." "Well," said another, "he's not President. Am I getting close?"

• • •

AND IN 1963, also, his predicament was growing worse due to another factor. Over Jack Kennedy's dealings with his Vice President there was painted—even if only lightly and only in public—a tint of respect, and of the wry amusement that made the President call him "Riverboat." Now Lyndon Johnson found himself increasingly dealing with—increasingly in confrontation with—the President's brother.

The hatred that Lyndon Johnson felt for Robert Kennedy on that terrible afternoon in Los Angeles had never faded. It would never fade; he would talk about that afternoon for the rest of his life. Years later, back on his ranch after his presidency, not long before he died, he would seize visitors' lapels and bend his face into theirs in the intensity of his effort to make sure the visitor understood that it hadn't been Jack Kennedy but Bobby who had wanted him to withdraw from the vice presidential nomination. Recording his thoughts to guide the ghostwriters of his autobiography, he made sure they understood. "He came to my room three times to try to get me to say I wouldn't run."

Time was curing nothing between the two men. The traditional seating arrangement for Cabinet meetings, established in the chronological order of the creation of the different departments, placed the attorney general next to the Vice President. Saying he didn't like that arrangement, Bobby had his place moved. With no formal seating arrangement at National Security Council meetings, sometimes the two men found themselves sitting side by side, and, as Richard Goodwin, seated against the wall behind the President, noticed, "They literally couldn't look at each other."

And as Johnson knew—or thought he knew, or said he knew—who had been responsible for his humiliation in Los Angeles, he knew, or thought he knew, or said he knew, who was responsible for all the humiliations of the following three years. "Jack Kennedy's just as thoughtful and considerate of me . . . as he can be," he told Bobby Baker. "But I know his snot-nosed brother's after my ass."

Such statements were made with a conviction that persuaded assistants and allies that Johnson believed what he was saying to be true, but the more perceptive of them wondered if the remarks were yet another example of him believing what he wanted to believe—in this case, what he felt he *had* to believe. Feeling as he did that the fulfillment of his dream—of his life—depended on his staying on as friendly terms as possible with the President, anger at Jack Kennedy wasn't an option. And therefore, Doris Kearns Goodwin was to write, "Johnson projected his feelings onto . . . Bobby." During her conversations with Johnson at the ranch, she says, "It was Bobby he reserved his anger for.

"It was Bobby who was cutting him off the list of invitees at the White House. . . . If he had submerged feelings towards Jack—and they had to be there—then Bobby becomes the target of those feelings. He blamed him for the ill treatment—he couldn't afford to blame Jack Kennedy—although clearly Bobby wasn't acting in any way his brother would disapprove of." Everything was Bobby's fault. "He couldn't be rational where Bobby was concerned," Bobby Baker says. Says Ashton Gonella: "He thought he was sneaky, he thought he lied—I can't say the rest. He just *hated* him."

There was an additional, ironic, note. In explaining to his angry allies why he had accepted the vice presidential nomination, Johnson had said, in a phrase he used repeatedly, that if he couldn't be "The Number One Man" in Washington, he would at least be "The Number Two Man." Now, however, *Life* magazine's issue profiling Bobby bore the headline "THE NO. 2 MAN IN WASHINGTON," and *U.S. News & World Report*'s said, "ROBERT KENNEDY: NO. 2 MAN IN WASHING-TON," and *Time*'s said simply, "NO. 2"—each headline another dash of salt in Lyndon Johnson's wounds.

And Johnson had read at least one aspect of Bobby Kennedy well enough to know the feelings were mutual. "When this fellow looks at me, he looks at me like he's going to look a hole right through me, like I'm a spy or something," he told John Connally.

But to a man whose life is based on calculations of power, the crucial factor in any equation is who possesses it, and Lyndon Johnson's eyes, so keen at these calculations, knew the answer; knew the headlines had ranked Bobby correctly. By the beginning of 1963, all Washington understood that Robert Kennedy had transformed the Justice Department, turning it into a newly aggressive foe of organized crime and juvenile delinquency, and that his role in government had been expanded far beyond his department—that, following the Bay of Pigs deba-cle, his brother had assigned him foreign policy responsibilities as well, had in fact brought him into the inner circles in which foreign policy is decided. But Johnson saw more than that. He saw the signs that, to the skilled calculator of power, meant more than the assignments: who entered a meeting beside the Pres-ident, which meant that the President had been consulting with him before the formal deliberations began; who the President quietly asked to stay behind after the meeting; whose views at the meeting were embodied in the presidential deci-sion that followed. "Every time they have a conference, don't kid anybody about who is the top adviser," Johnson blurted out one day. "It isn't McNamara, the chiefs of staff, or anybody else like that. Bobby is first in, last out. And Bobby is the boy he listens to." Nor was it merely a matter of advice: Bobby was more than an adviser; he was a brother, in a family in which the blood tie meant all. The attorney general was unfailingly formal during meetings, never forgetting that he was addressing "Mr. President," but sometimes on the way out, in a brief huddle together, the names the attorney general and the President called each other in private slipped out: "Johnny"; "Bobby." It was the way that they some-times communicated without words, the reaction of one brother to the other's statement being conveyed in a shrug of the shoulder or a shake of the head. It was the way that, as Arthur Schlesinger wrote, "They . . . always talked in the cryptic half sentences that bespoke perfect understanding," the way they finished each other's sentences. Watching them at a formal state dinner, where they were sitting far apart, a guest was struck by how each heard, through the chatter, what the other was saying, and chimed in on it. "They hardly had to speak with each other," the guest said. "They understood each other from a half word. There was a kind of constant, almost telepathic, contact between them." Asked once to explain, Jack Kennedy said, "It's by osmosis." Lyndon Johnson heard and saw it all. He sued for peace.

The suit was pursued first through a subordinate. John Seigenthaler, the aide perhaps closest to Robert Kennedy, received a telephone call from Walter Jenkins. "We have to work together," Jenkins said. "We have to keep these two fellows from embarrassing themselves" by publicly feuding. The call, Seigenthaler says, "was basically to say, 'No hard feelings' " about anything in the past—and Jenkins made clear that his principal was willing to go more than halfway to effect a rapprochement. Mentioning some matter that the Vice President wanted to discuss with the attorney general—that was merely an excuse to make the call, it was clear—Jenkins said Johnson would come to the attorney general's office at any time that was convenient for him. "Well, what time would you prefer?" Seigenthaler asked. "No," Jenkins said, "what's convenient for *you?*" Seigenthaler said he was sure a mutually convenient time could be worked out, but such an arrangement would be contrary to the instructions Jenkins had been given, and he said, this time with agitation in his voice, "No, no, it's got to be convenient for the Attorney General. Would you check with the Attorney General?" And when, although the appointment was granted, and Johnson made his visit to the Justice Department, the situation did not improve, he pressed the suit in a more informal setting—an upstairs kitchen at the White House, where, after a dinner-dance in January 1963, guests were scrambling eggs for an after-midnight snack. Approaching the attorney general, Johnson said, "I don't understand you, Bobby. Your father likes me. Your brother likes me. But *you don't like me.* Now, why? Why don't you like me?"

Bobby, in the recollection of Charles Spalding, one of the other guests in the kitchen, "agreed to the accuracy of all this"—but Johnson wouldn't let it drop. "Why?" he kept asking. "Why don't you like me?" He was begging, crowding against Bobby, and Bobby kept retreating—and letting him beg. "It was a role . . . Bobby was enjoying. . . . The discussion was completely in his favor and in his hand," Spalding says. And although Johnson asked the questions "again and again" (it seemed to Spalding that "this went on and on for hours")—"Why don't you like me? I don't understand it. Now, why?"—Bobby wouldn't answer them.

Finally, Johnson said, "I know why you don't like me." The reason was a misconception, he said: the press had misquoted statements he made at the 1960 convention. "You think I attacked your father," he said. "But I never said that. Those reports were all false. . . . I never did attack your father and I wouldn't, and I always liked you and admired you. But you're angry with me and you've always been upset with me." That explanation, though, didn't have the desired effect at all. A day or so later Kennedy repeated Johnson's explanation to Seigenthaler, who, as a reporter for the *Nashville Tennessean,* had in fact been present in 1960 at Johnson's speech to the Washington State delegation in which he had called Joseph Kennedy a "Chamberlain umbrella man," and said, "I never thought Hitler was right." Kennedy asked Seigenthaler, "Do you remember what he said?"

"Yes, I do," Seigenthaler said, and repeated Johnson's words. When Kennedy told Seigenthaler of Johnson's claim that his remarks had been misquoted, Seigenthaler said, "Well, he's not telling the truth." Looking up microfilms of the articles on Johnson's attack that had run in the *New York Times* and other newspapers, he sent reproductions to Kennedy with a note: "There can't be much doubt . . . that he was vicious." Kennedy told him dryly the next time they met, "If the press misquoted him, it's a general misquoting."

Among the aspects of Robert Kennedy's character most conspicuous to his intimates was what *Life* magazine called his "genuine contempt for liars." "He could forgive anything in a staffer except lying," one aide says. "If you tried to fool him . . ." The only result of the encounter in the White House kitchen was a reinforcing of his convictions about Lyndon Johnson. "My experience with him since [the convention]," he was to say, "he lies all the time, I'm telling you, he just lies continually about everything. . . . He lies even when he doesn't have to lie."

NOT THAT HIS CONVICTIONS needed reinforcing.

Bobby Kennedy's behavior during the Cuban Missile Crisis had not been the first indication that behind the Torquemada glower, the prosecutor's jabbing fist, the bullying, the insistence that all surrenders be unconditional that made the adjective "ruthless" an apt description no matter how deeply he resented it, beneath the idolization of his father, the need to attain his approbation, which seemed to be the constant motivation in his life—that beneath all this, there was something more, something quite different, within Robert Francis Kennedy.

Hints of it had appeared long before the Cuban crisis—before he had become attorney general; in fact, even before he had been Joe McCarthy's assistant; before he had even entered government. His father was an anti-Semite—no matter how biographers may try to gloss over that trait, it was there: Jews were the problem with the movie industry, Joe Kennedy had found when he first went out to Hollywood; "a bunch of ignorant Jewish furriers" had taken it over "simply because they had unethically pushed their way into a wide-open virgin field"; Jews were a problem in government, too: "There is a great undercurrent of dissatisfaction with the appointment of so many Jews in high places in Washington," Joe wrote his friend, the British press czar Lord Beaverbrook, in 1942; behind Joe's tolerance of Hitler, a biographer notes, was a willingness "to write off . . . the Jews as well as almost anyone else to achieve peace." But when Bobby himself, still the religious teenager, the most devoutly Catholic of Rose's children, encountered anti-Semitism, he could not contain himself, even though the sentiment "came clad in priestly robes."

Listening to the fascist diatribes of the anti-Semite Father Feeney on Boston Common, something made Bobby burst out, interrupting the priest to tell him that what he was saying contradicted the Catholic principles he was being taught in school. ("I was horrified," Rose said. "My own son arguing with a priest. But when the Vatican excommunicated Father Feeney, I knew Bobby had been right.") After Bobby's graduation, with C's and D's, from Harvard in March, 1948, his father arranged for him to tour the Middle East (and arranged also for him to be accredited as a correspondent for the *Boston Post*). Crossing the Atlantic on the *Queen Mary,* he dined, at his father's insistence, with Beaverbrook, who explained to him that the United States was "a subjugated nation to a Jewish minority." But when he arrived in the Middle East and saw, with his own eyes, Jews fighting for their existence against overwhelming odds, and was told by a twenty-three-year-old Israeli woman ("I never saw anyone so tired," he wrote his mother) about her four brothers fighting in the Haganah, the views he expressed in his articles for the *Post* were not the views of his father. "The Jews in Palestine have become an immensely proud and determined people . . . a truly great modern example of the birth of a nation," he wrote. They have "an undying spirit" the Arabs could never have; as for the United States, its failure to come more strongly to Israel's assistance should be a matter of shame. "We are certainly not the good little saints we imagine ourselves." And there was another noteworthy aspect to the articles, written as they were by such a mediocre student: they showed, as Arthur Schlesinger writes, "a maturity, cogency and, from time to time, literary finish" quite "creditable for a football player of twenty-two."

It wasn't only his reaction to Jews that gave the hint, it was his reaction to the embattled, to the oppressed—to anyone, it began to become apparent, who was the underdog (as, in that family in which he had had "to struggle to survive," *he* had been the underdog).

At law school at the University of Virginia, where, as usual, "nothing came easy" to him (he graduated fifty-sixth in a class of 124), he became president of the organization that invited outside speakers, and invited his father, his father's friends like Supreme Court Justice Douglas and Joe McCarthy—and Ralph Bunche, the black United Nations peace negotiator who had won a Nobel Peace Prize. When Bunche replied that he never spoke before a segregated audience, Bobby asked the student council to pass a resolution requesting the university to make an exception to its segregationist policy. The southern students on the council were willing to vote for the resolution but not to sign it individually, since after graduation they would have to practice law in Virginia. Bobby refused to understand their problem. "It [was] his black and white view of things," an unsympathetic classmate says. His temper was still uncontrollable, and he had none of his brother's eloquence; after shouting, "You're all gutless," he became almost incoherent with rage. Refusing to let the issue drop, he brought it before the law school's governing body, the Board of Visitors, where, again, he lost his temper, and "the madder he got, the worse he got at talking. Very little came out." But the audience at Bunche's speech was integrated.

The portrait that was Robert Kennedy had always been heavily layered, with the harsh, dark colors—the rudeness, the ruthlessness, the rage; the desire to please and emulate his father—so dominant that it had been hard to see the glimpses of brighter hues. But they were there. They seemed to become more apparent, to be brought out—in this young man who had never been a reader of books—when he saw things with his own eyes. Robert Kennedy "possessed to an exceptional degree an experiencing nature," Schlesinger has written; what he actually saw, came into personal contact with, he learned from, and moreover, felt—and felt deeply. And when what he saw were the embattled, the oppressed, when he saw injustice close up so that, reader or not, he understood it, he felt it so deeply that he would argue against it, fight against it, as if even the teachings of his father faded before something deeper within him.

Then there was the way he acted with children. By 1963, he and his wife, Ethel Skakel (daughter of a wealthy midwestern industrialist), had seven; they would eventually have eleven. When he had been younger, no matter how much work he had, he would leave Capitol Hill at 5:30 each afternoon to be with them; the work would be finished at night, after they went to bed. Now, as attorney general and the President's principal adviser in every crisis, "Bob was," Seigenthaler says, "overloaded with work"—there was no more leaving at 5:30—"but he *always* took time for those children."

As he was shaving in the morning—he arose early so he could spend time with them before he went to work—they would come into the bathroom and squirt shaving cream, shouting happily; taking the blade out of a razor, he'd hand the razor to his daughter Kathleen, and she would shave along with him. For half an hour—7 to 7:30—he tossed a football around with them. Over breakfast, he fired questions at them on current events, as his father had tossed questions (not at him so much, but at Joe, Jack, and his sister Kathleen). "Unlike his father," Bobby "was careful to include all the children, the youngest and smallest, too," one of his biographers notes. In the evenings, on the rare weekday evenings when he was home, he knelt with them beside their beds as they prayed (ending with, "And please make Uncle Jack the best President ever and please make Daddy the best Attorney General ever").

On weekends, there was, from this man who disliked being touched by adults, "a lot of physical affection," Kathleen says. "All the children would pile into my parents' bed and tickle each other; it was called 'tickle-tumble.' " On the sweeping lawns of the rambling Civil War mansion in McLean, Virginia, called "Hickory Hill," a place Bobby and Ethel had filled not only with the seven children but with a donkey, two horses, three ponies, five goats, ten ducks, rabbits (thirty-two one day, forty a few days later), snakes, a burro, a tortoise, hamsters, a cockatoo and a parakeet (and, for a while, a sea lion in the swimming pool)—and seventeen servants—he and the boys would roll on the ground in playful wrestling matches, grunting ferociously, "exchanging," as a frequent visitor recalls, "terrible threats and mock punches" in a "Donnybrook that left everybody all laughed out and tearfully exhausted." If one of the children started crying, Bobby would hug him, saying soothingly, "Hush, now, Kennedys don't cry."

When he couldn't get home enough, he'd bring the children to his office, as if, as one writer puts it, he "cannot bear being away from them for long." That started when he was working for the McClellan Committee. "My father very much believed that we should know what was going on in the world, and wanted to engage us in what he was doing, so it was interesting and fascinating," Kathleen says. "Oftentimes when other children were swinging on swings, we went to the Senate Rackets Committee hearings and listened to him cross-examine Jimmy Hoffa. There was always a sense of right and wrong. I didn't realize until much later that 'Teamsters' wasn't a term for bad guys." He put up their crayon drawings in the vast, somber, walnut-paneled attorney general's office. And no matter how busy he was, if they showed up in the office, he would always stop to hug them and talk with them for a few minutes. "There wasn't a problem that the kids had that he wouldn't interrupt whatever he was doing to solve," says a friend.

As striking as the amount of time spent with them was the tenderness with which he treated them. While he was splashing violently in the pool with the older boys in wild games of water polo, one of the very young girls would come to the pool's edge to be taught to swim. As her father's arms came up to get her, they came up slowly, carefully, as gently as he then cradled her in the water.

His gentleness with children wasn't only with his own. If he was sometimes still inarticulate with adults, he always knew exactly what to say to *them*. Particularly with children who were underdogs. "Children in neglect, privation, distress wounded him, like an arrow into the heart," Schlesinger was to write. Coming across a group of about a hundred black boys and girls from an orphanage being herded through the corridors of the Justice Department by a rather indifferent tour guide, he watched for a moment, and then invited them to come into his office. He showed them pictures of his own children, telling anecdotes about them until the orphans relaxed, and started asking him questions. "Can you all see me?," he said, and climbed up on his desk before explaining to them what his job entailed. "Children dissolved his reticences, released his humor and his affection, brought him, one felt, more fully out of himself and therefore perhaps more fully into himself," Schlesinger wrote.

The gentleness wasn't only with children after, in December, 1961, a stroke left his father permanently crippled and virtually unable to speak. Bobby maintained that Jack, "because he really made him laugh," was "the best" with Joe Kennedy after the stroke, but others had a different opinion, although with

Bobby it wasn't always about laughing. "Bobby would fly down to Palm Beach at 6 AM, and be back at noon, just to say hello for fifteen minutes," says White House Social Secretary Tish Baldridge. During summers at Hyannis Port, he would exercise with his father every day in the swimming pool. Says one of Joe Kennedy's nurses: "During the years that followed [the stroke], I watched Bobby strengthen his father, laughing with him, praising him, then he would swim away. His eyes would fill with tears, and a look of deep sorrow would cloud his face, but he would quickly compose himself, and begin once more doing what he could to assist him in his therapy." Once, in Palm Beach, when Jack and Bobby were visiting him, the old man rose from his wheelchair to try to walk, but began to fall. Bobby grabbed him, but his father, in frustration, began to struggle, wildly swinging his cane at him. When, with the help of a doctor, he was finally back in his wheelchair, he kept screaming and shaking his fist at his son. Bobby leaned over and kissed him. "Dad," he said, "if you want to get up, give me your arm and I'll hold you till you get your balance. . . . That's what I'm here for, Dad. Just to give you a hand when you need it. You've done that for me all my life, so why can't I do the same for you now?"

There were hints in the way he acted with everyone who was a member of his family when there was trouble.

When, after the 1956 convention, his pregnant sister-in-law, Jacqueline, was rushed to a hospital in Newport, Rhode Island, at 2 a.m., it was not her husband but her brother-in-law, with whom she had never been particularly close, who was sitting by her bed when she awakened from the anesthetic. "Jack," as another of Bobby's biographers, Evan Thomas, puts it, "was off cruising in the Mediterranean with two of his fellow pleasure-seekers, his brother Ted and Senator George Smathers." When Rose had called Bobby to tell him what had happened, he had driven through the night from Hyannis Port to be there with her. It was Bobby who told her that she had lost her child. When Jack, as Thomas puts it, "did not rush back," it was Bobby who arranged for the infant's burial. He never told Jackie that; when, years later, after they had endured other troubles together, she learned that it had been he who had done so, she said she wasn't surprised to hear it. "You knew that, if you were in trouble, he'd always be there."

And it was the way he acted sometimes with people who were not members of the family, like an elderly Supreme Court Justice, too old to remain on the bench: at one of Felix Frankfurter's last public appearances before he retired, the justice, confined to a wheelchair, made a rambling speech that went on for a very long time. Notes were passed, someone even whispered to him that he had spoken long enough; but he went right on. People were restless. One who wasn't was Bobby Kennedy. Driving away, he said to a friend, "If that experience gave the old man half an hour of pleasure, no one in the room had such pressing business that he couldn't stay for a few extra minutes."

"It's pretty easy to see somebody compete fiercely and see a grimace on his face or see what looks like a snarl as he really is . . . just trying as hard as he can . . . and trying harder than he thinks he can," says Charles Spalding, who had known Robert Kennedy since he was a boy. "You can see that and then you translate that into terms of ruthlessness. But what you don't see is the softness because it's been disciplined not to show." It didn't show much now, when the runt of Old Joe's family was attorney general of the United States. "It was his most tenaciously maintained secret: a tenderness so rawly exposed, so vulnerable to painful abrasion, that it could only be shielded by angry compassion at human misery, manifest itself in love and loyalty toward those closest to him," Richard Goodwin says. Joe's son may have taken great pains to conceal that tenderness, but it was there.

DURING THE TWO YEARS since he had come to power, moreover, new colors had been added to the portrait: elements of personality of which there had previously been no indication at all in Robert Kennedy.

Some had been added to what had always been one of the portrait's least appealing features: the Manichean "black and white view of things," Robert Kennedy's previous tendency to see the world and individuals as either evil or good.

In no area had this view been more stark than in his attitude toward Communism and the Soviet Union. His enlistment with Joe McCarthy and his belief in McCarthy's cause had been just one token of it. In 1955, he had taken a trip—arranged, of course, by his father—to the Soviet republics in Central Asia with Supreme Court Justice William O. Douglas. (Douglas, who had previously spent time with Bobby, was reluctant to take him along, but Joe Kennedy insisted.) A foreign service officer reported hearing the same story from local officials at each stop. "We liked Justice Douglas. . . . But [great sigh, looking at the ground] with him there is Mr. Kennedy. He seems always to be saying bad things about our country." The young man, Schlesinger was to write, "carried mistrust to inordinate extremes." Claiming that Russian food was dirty, he ate as little of it as possible, "subsisting," during the month-long trip, "mainly on watermelon." When their guide brought them a container of caviar, he was so suspicious that he wouldn't even taste it. When, in Omsk, he became ill, running a high fever, he said, "No communist is going to doctor me"; only Douglas' insistence—"I promised your daddy I would take care of you"—persuaded him to allow a physician to examine him. Administering not poison but penicillin, the doctor told Douglas, "This is a very disturbed young man." He arrived home so pale and thin from illness and lack of food that when Ethel saw him, she shouted at Douglas: "What have you done to my husband?"

Two years later, neither his attitude nor his manners had changed, as State Department aide Harris Wofford found when his boss, Chester Bowles, planning a Central Asian trip of his own, sent him to Kennedy for advice. "Already Bobby's reputation was that of an arrogant, narrow, rude young man," Wofford was to recall. Shown to a chair on the far side of Kennedy's Rackets Committee office, he was kept waiting for almost an hour while Kennedy "ate his lunch, talked on the telephone, worked on his papers." Finally waving to Wofford to approach, he "gave a short, glum account of [his] Russian trip, warned that they spied on you day and night . . . and said he had nothing special to suggest. Then he went into a diatribe against the Soviet regime, which he explained was a great evil and an ever present threat, and bade me good-bye." Inclined though Wofford had been to support Jack Kennedy for President, the encounter gave him pause: "If the senator was not guilty by association with his father, there was this insufferable brother." Within the first few months after Bobby became attorney general, however, he was not only meeting frequently and secretly with Soviet diplomat Georgy Bolshakov but had made a friend of him, using him as a back-channel conduit for personal messages between Jack Kennedy and Nikita Khrushchev. By 1962, the role he had played in devising compromises over crises in Berlin and Laos had made the Russians trust him enough so that they let Washington know they would be pleased if he was appointed ambassador to Moscow. Although Bobby tossed off the proposal with a quip—"In the first place, I couldn't possibly learn Russian; I spent ten years learning French"—it was evidence of how much, in his biographer Thomas' words, "the bullyboy of the 1940's and 1950's, so quick to pick a fight," had "quite quickly developed a more balanced, neutral way of dealing with the Kremlin." Part of this moderation came, of course, "on the direct orders of his brother," but part was due to something in Bobby himself. "While his first instinct was" still "to strike a blow, his second was to listen carefully" and try to find a way in which both sides could preserve face—and peace.

And people who remembered "the old Bobby" were startled also by what he did with his new job—the post of attorney general of the United States which his brother had handed to him although he seemed utterly unqualified for it: a lawyer who had never tried a case in court.

In hiring a staff, he selected men who possessed not only the qualifications he lacked, but stature far above his. His top deputies—the famous Byron "Whizzer" White, the all-American football player and Rhodes Scholar; Nicholas deBelleville Katzenbach, former editor-in-chief of *The Yale Law Journal* and Rhodes Scholar; the renowned legal authority Archibald Cox, holder of an endowed chair at Harvard Law School; Burke Marshall, former editor of *The Yale Law Journal* and an attorney deeply respected in the Washington legal community—were, as one historian described them, among "the sharpest lawyers of his generation." Another historian called them one of "the most impressive groups ever assembled in the top jobs of one government agency," and the selection showed something about Bobby, too: that, as Evan Thomas puts it, "he did not feel upstaged by men who had more experience, credentials, than he." The legal scholar Alexander Bickel, who had once criticized his McCarthy-like tactics, now said, "One immediately had the sense of a fellow who wasn't afraid of having able people around him and indeed of a fellow who had an ideal of public service that would have done anyone proud."

Younger and more inexperienced than they were, he nonetheless inspired them. One of White's newly appointed assistants, Joseph Dolan, remembering Kennedy as the bully from the Rackets Committee, "thought he was an absolute disgrace [there]. I thought I was going back to save the country from Robert Kennedy." But Dolan saw something different now. Bobby was still given to quick, impulsive, harsh judgments, he saw—until he realized that the subject he was dealing with was important. Then he would stop, catch himself—as if, by an effort of will and self-discipline, he was making himself change. "Once he realized something was significant, he became the most deliberate, most thoughtful, most intense man." Listing, years later, the qualities that had made him admire, and want to follow, Robert Kennedy, Archibald Cox would include "his willingness to listen and reconsider his initial reactions."

Standing behind his desk, jacketless, shirtsleeves rolled up, necktie pulled down, talking to them about what he thought the Justice Department should be doing, "he had," one of them says, "a way of creating an impression that if he thought something was wrong, he'd do something to right it. He had a way of saying it, a lilt to his voice. I can still hear it, a little higher pitch. . . . He had a passion." Says another: "He had that quality of leadership that made us all play above our heads," the quality of "bringing out the very best in everyone who worked for him." He inspired them, and bound them to him, by his commitment to social justice, by an instinct for what was right, and by his insistence on doing it—at once. "Bob never pauses to regroup and say, 'Now what shall we do?' " Dolan recalls. "When he is saying, 'What shall we do now,' he is doing something." "Don't tell me what I can't do," he told them. "Tell me what I can do." They learned he was willing to take on the most unpleasant tasks himself, that if one of them made a mistake, he would stand behind him. They started to roll up their own sleeves, to pull their own neckties down. Bobby was always quoting Shakespeare to make a point, and after he recited some lines from *Henry V* one day to tell them what he thought of them, they were very proud, and they started to call themselves "the band of brothers."

Aides outside this inner circle were treated with the same lordliness with which he treated everyone else. He was, one biographer notes, "in the manner of the very rich, rather spoiled." Some staffers were "less [than] amused about getting his laundry" or carrying his shirts, which he changed several times a day. "If you want to be secretary of state, you have to know how to get those shirts out of their plastic bags," one said. But, roaming the halls of the Justice Department, bursting into the offices of lawyers who had never seen the attorney general up close before, asking them about their work, he filled the vast building with new life. Ramsey Clark, the son of a former attorney general, Tom Clark, was working for Kennedy now, and he said, "It was a quiet and sleepy place until January of '61. . . . Then it came *alive.*" Flying around the country to visit departmental outposts, Bobby took a special interest in the work of young lawyers. "That was one of his great gifts," says Robert Morgenthau, the new United States attorney in New York, "to make people feel they were part of the team."

And he made people have a broader, deeper idea of what the team should be doing. By the end of 1962, Justice had taken a newly active role in fighting not only organized crime but juvenile delinquency; once, testifying before Congress, the man who had been an arrogant prosecutor blurted out a sentence that wasn't in his prepared testimony: "I think some of us who were more fortunate might also have been juvenile delinquents if we had been brought up in different circumstances," he said. A broader role was being taken against many forms of social injustice. Looking back on his prosecutorial days, it was possible now to see that there had been hints of such concerns visible even then. In *The Enemy Within,* he described attending a Mass at a workingman's church and seeing "the strong, stern faces of people who have worked hard and who have suffered."

And there were other new shadings in the portrait. The moody and indifferent student now started to read, quite extensively, in history and biography. Since there weren't enough free moments for the reading he wanted to do, he took the speed-reading course that Jack had taken. He began the practice, which he was to follow to the end of his life, of listening to recordings of Shakespeare's plays while he was shaving and playing with his children in the morning. In 1961, he instituted a series of evening seminars at Hickory Hill at which leading thinkers discussed their areas of expertise. "They sound rather precious," Alice Roosevelt Longworth said, "but there was nothing precious about those lectures." The questioning of the speakers was quite intense—and the most intense of the questioners was often the attorney general (even though, sometimes, his old pugnacity reappeared: "That's the biggest bunch of bullshit I've ever heard," he told one lecturer—who was, after all, a guest in his home).

An observer as acute as Budd Schulberg, the novelist and screenwriter who in 1961 was asked to write a screenplay of *The Enemy Within* because his masterpiece, *On the Waterfront,* dealt with corruption in a labor union, saw the depth of these concerns. During their first meeting, over dinner at Hickory Hill, to discuss Schulberg's ideas for the screenplay, there was for some time a noticeable lack of rapport between the two men. And then Schulberg blurted out that he wasn't interested in writing a script merely about the labor rackets investigation, that he felt the movie's broader theme should be that there was something at the core of America as a whole that had begun to rot.

Suddenly the man across from him was a different man. Yes, Robert Kennedy said, that was what he was interested in, too. In fact, he said, that "seems to me the only real reason for making the picture. If it comes out as well as *Waterfront,* it could help shake people out of their apathy." He spoke in terms of his brother—"The creeping corruption, it is something the President hopes to check, to give the people a new sense of idealism, a sense of destiny that isn't just money-making or pleasure-seeking"—but, Schulberg realized, it wasn't just the

President whose feelings Bobby was expressing. Robert Kennedy spoke "with quiet fervor," the writer was to recount. "He cared about it. He felt it. . . . He said he thought the next ten years would produce the turning point in our history— either an America infected with corruption or the rebirth of a spirit and idealism with which we had begun."

The movie was never made—the producer who hired Schulberg died, and there were threats from corrupt labor bosses against studios that were considering making it—but during the year and a half that Schulberg was working on it, he spent days with Robert Kennedy at Justice, including the day the attorney general was directing efforts to get James Meredith enrolled, and he heard him say to one of his men in Mississippi, "I know it's only *one*—but it's the first one, and then two and then four, eight. . . . We have got to enforce the Constitution. . . . We've got to—it's the *law,* it's our moral obligation." He hung up the phone, and then said, in a tone that Schulberg felt was a "human outcry," "Oh, God, I hope nothing happens to Meredith. I feel responsible for him. I promised we'd back him up. I'm worried for the marshals. It seems so simple to us, and down there it's bloody hell." Having seen him up close, in that and other moments of crisis, Schulberg was to write that "No one can ever tell me that Bob Kennedy was merely going through the motions. When something struck him as wrong or evil, it was his nature to root it out, or to try like hell—not tomorrow, but now."

And, of course, the Cuban Missile Crisis had brought out all these new elements in Robert Kennedy, made them clear and vivid; during those thirteen days in October, there was unveiled in the Cabinet Room a portrait of a master of compromise, of diplomacy, of diplomacy with a moral element, of diplomacy that was, in fact, in some ways grounded in "the moral question": there was the insistence that "a sneak attack is not in our traditions," that America was not "that kind of a country." And there had been, as well, the passion with which Kennedy presented his arguments, the "intense but quiet passion" that moved one of the hardened, pragmatic men around the long Cabinet table to say that "as he spoke, I felt that I was at a real turning point in history." So many elements in the portrait came together during those thirteen days—as if, as his biographer Thomas was to write, "the worst of times brought out the best in Bobby Kennedy." An aide who came into his office during the crisis said, "Something's different in here." "I'm older," Kennedy replied. But the difference was due to more than age. So dramatically had Bobby Kennedy changed that the men around the Cabinet table were startled—"very much surprised," in George Ball's words. "He made believers of men who expected less of him," Thomas says.

IN SOME WAYS, however, Bobby Kennedy had changed not at all. The old, dark hues—the rudeness, the anger, the belligerence, the "mean streak"—were sometimes still visible under the new, brighter colors.

Sometimes belligerence was employed as an instrument for his brother, a tool with a very rough edge, even when it was being wielded against grand (or formerly grand) old men of the Democratic Party establishment. The seventy-year-old railroad magnate W. Averell Harriman, former ambassador to Great Britain, ambassador to Moscow, expediter of Lend-Lease, adviser at Yalta, not to mention governor of New York, found himself being ordered about at his own dinner table. Asked by Bobby about a report the President had requested, he said he was still doing research on it. "Well, get on it, Averell," Bobby snapped at him, in a tone as cold as his eyes. "See that you do it tomorrow." Said one of Harriman's other guests, Rowland Evans, Bobby "couldn't have cared less [who Harriman was]. . . . Bobby was giving an order, and it happened to be Averell Harriman; it could have been anybody." Undersecretary of State Chester Bowles, another former governor (of Connecticut) and a revered figure to American liberals, whose backing of Jack Kennedy in 1960 had been a key factor in softening liberal opposition to his candidacy, had not supported the Bay of Pigs invasion, and after its failure, had let that fact be known. Suddenly confronting Bowles after a White House meeting, Bobby had snarled, "You should keep your mouth shut. As of now, you were *for* the Bay of Pigs"—and, to emphasize the point, had jabbed a finger into Bowles' chest. Bowles was, in addition, too wordy and slow-moving for the Kennedys, who, following the Bay of Pigs, were looking for a way to remove Castro from power. At a National Security Council meeting with the President in the chair, Bowles delivered a summary of State Department reports that concluded Castro was now firmly in control of the island and could be removed only by the full-scale American invasion that the Kennedys were determined to avoid. Jumping to his feet, Bobby slammed the reports down on the table. "This is worthless," he shouted. "What can we do about Cuba? This doesn't tell us anything. You people are so anxious to protect your own asses that you're afraid to do anything. All you want to do is dump the whole thing on the President." He went on shouting for ten minutes. And then he glared directly at Bowles. "We'd be better off if you just quit and left foreign policy to someone else," he said.

As Bobby's tirade continued, the President didn't interrupt, but simply sat silently, tapping the metal rim of the eraser on his pencil against his front teeth. Watching from his seat against a wall, Richard Goodwin "became suddenly aware," as he was to write, that "there was an inner hardness, often volatile anger beneath the outwardly amiable, thoughtful, carefully controlled demeanor of John Kennedy." He had no doubt that Robert Kennedy was "communicating exactly what his brother wanted said"—that the President wanted Bowles out of the Administration, but, because of his popularity in liberal circles, didn't want to fire him, and that Bobby's tirade was a way to force Bowles to resign (and, in addition, to deter him from leaking information that would undermine the Kennedy image; and to let the other officials watching the scene see what might happen to them if *they* leaked). Goodwin's suspicion was confirmed when, not long thereafter, Bowles not having taken the hint, the President began easing him out of his job.

Sometimes, however, Bobby's manners had nothing to do with the President, and were a reminder that there had always been that "mean"—cruel—streak in him. As the adulation from the press for the Kennedys, for their graciousness and charm, mounted and mounted, and Bobby's face, boyish and open and grinning, became a fixture on newsstands, dissenting voices were drowned out, but they were there. If within his "band of brothers" there was a sometimes forced but nonetheless humorous badinage, he had lost none of his brusqueness with other subordinates; "Kennedy's most obvious fault is rudeness," wrote a young Justice Department staffer who was not a member of the in-group. "His face, when it lacks that boyish, photogenic grin, is not a pleasant sight. It has a certain bony harshness and those ice-blue eyes are not the smiling ones that Irishmen write songs about. It is with this stern visage that Kennedy confronts most of the world. . . . His friends call this shyness, but the historians of the 1960 campaign do not record that he was ever shy in pursuit of a stray delegate." A CIA official giving him a report he didn't like saw "his eyes get steely and his jaw set, and his voice get low and precise." An Army general who tried to tell him that a request would be very difficult to meet was asked, "Why would it be difficult, General?" and, wrote a witness to the encounter, "learned that there are few experiences in this world quite like having Robert Kennedy push his unsmiling face towards yours and ask, 'Why?' "

He had lost none of his insistence on the importance of winning. An autographed picture of heavyweight champion Floyd Patterson hung on the wall of his office—until Patterson lost the title to Sonny Liston. The next day, the photograph was gone. Even while Hickory Hill touch-football games were becoming fixed in American myth as boyishly friendly, visitors who played in one for the first time got a somewhat different view. "Even approaching forty," wrote a Washington newsman, "Bobby was playing touch football with the callow ferocity of a fraternity boy." Said another: "I'd like to hit him right in the mouth. Every time I went up for a pass, he gave me elbows, knees, the works. Then our team got within one touchdown of his team, by God he picked up the ball and said the game was over."

"Just when you get Bobby typed as the white hope, compassionate, he'll do something so bad it'll jar you completely, destroy your faith in him," a journalist wrote. "And just as you're ready to accept the excessive condemnations, to accept him as ruthless and diabolical, he'll do something so classy it stuns you. The inescapable truth about Robert Kennedy is that the paradoxes are real, the conflicts do exist." Said another, "From one day to the next, you never know which Bobby Kennedy you're going to meet."

And he had lost none of the quality—the capacity for hatred—that had made Joe Kennedy begin to respect him. After his brother's defeat at the Bay of Pigs, Robert Kennedy's determination to, in Bowles' phrase, "get Castro" was so intense that one of his key advisers on Cuba said he seemed to regard the failed invasion as "an insult which needed to be redressed rather quickly." "It was almost as simple as goddammit, we lost the first round, let's win the second,"

McGeorge Bundy was to say. "We were hysterical about Castro," Robert McNamara says. Setting up a special CIA operation, later code-named "Mongoose," Bobby kept pushing the CIA. Over Thanksgiving weekend in 1961, he repeatedly telephoned CIA Director of Operations Richard Bissell at home to tell him to "get off his ass" on Cuba. Following Bissell's replacement by Richard Helms, Kennedy made it clear to Helms, as he records, that Castro was "the top priority of the United States Government—all else is secondary—no time, effort, money or manpower is to be spared." That directive was followed, with the CIA ceaselessly trying to set up raids by Cuban exiles, blow up bridges and factories. There were efforts of another type as well. The CIA would carry out eight separate assassination attempts on Castro's life, continuing into 1965. Did Robert Kennedy authorize them, or know about them? "The Kennedys made clear their desire to 'get rid' of Castro," Evan Thomas wrote. But did they authorize his assassination? "The truth is unknowable," Thomas concludes.

Despite his coolheadedness and caution during the Cuban Missile Crisis—and his delicate and successful negotiations beginning a month later to free the Bay of Pigs prisoners—Robert Kennedy's attitude toward Castro didn't change; in April, 1963, for example, he was proposing sending a five-hundred-man raiding party into Cuba, a proposal which somehow, luckily, faded away. Over and over during that year he would telephone Helms. "My God, these Kennedys keep the pressure on about Castro," he recalls.

He kept the pressure on also in his vendetta against Jimmy Hoffa. When Bobby had left the Senate Rackets Committee in 1959 to run his brother's presidential campaign, he had failed, "despite 1,500 witnesses and 20,000 pages of testimony," to win a conviction against the Teamsters' boss. But, he told his aides, "the game isn't over." No sooner had he assumed command of the Justice Department than he set up an elite "Get Hoffa" squad that reported directly to him. Were Justice's resources not adequate? The Internal Revenue Service and the FBI—with "walkie-talkies, electronic recording devices, cameras, informers, pressure, harassment, every conceivable tactic"—were deployed "to pin a criminal charge on Hoffa," as one of Kennedy's biographers puts it. At one time, fourteen grand juries had been impaneled in different cities. Not scrupling to employ the press as a weapon as well, while Hoffa was under indictment, he orchestrated a *Life* article that painted the Teamsters' boss in unflattering terms. "It would be hard to find a man of the law who would consider it ethical for the Attorney General of the United States to work behind the scenes to discredit a citizen under federal indictment," wrote Nick Thimmesch, another of Bobby's biographers. So relentlessly did he pursue the labor leader "that he accomplished the truly stupendous feat of making people feel sorry for Hoffa"; the American Civil Liberties Union filed a brief on his behalf. It would eventually take seven years, but in 1964, Jimmy Hoffa would indeed be convicted. "Bobby hates like me," Joe Kennedy said. "When I hate some sonofabitch, I hate him until I die."

And Bobby Kennedy hated Lyndon Johnson. During oral history interviews he gave to the journalist John Bartlow Martin, on May 14, 1964, he began discussing his brother's feelings about Johnson—"I'm affected considerably by, I suppose, what . . . the President thought of him, by, for example, the President's resentment that he wouldn't speak at meetings"—and then moved beyond his brother's feelings to his own, to his feelings about Johnson's constant lying, for example, and about his treatment of subordinates. "They're all scared, of course, of Lyndon," he said. "He yells at his staff. He treats them just terribly. Very mean. He's a very mean, mean figure." And then, comparing him with his brother, Robert Kennedy made a more general statement. "Our President was a gentleman and a human being," he said. "This man is not. . . . He's mean, bitter, vicious—an animal in many ways." Robert Kennedy told Bobby Baker, "You're gonna get yours when the time comes!"—and now he seemed to feel the time had come.

The reins on the Vice President were tightened by his hand. Johnson's requests for planes—not for the foreign trips he took on presidential orders but for domestic trips—would be ignored until the last minute, and then the planes he was assigned were generally the small Military Air Transport Service planes with the wording he hated on their sides; it became more and more difficult for him to travel on a plane he considered appropriate for a Vice President. It was made clear now that not only his speeches but his brief introductory remarks—his every public utterance—had to be approved, and not only by the White House but by the attorney general. Working with the Justice Department on Committee on Equal Employment Opportunity matters was necessary almost every day, and Johnson's secretaries and assistants, telephoning Bobby's office, felt the contempt. "They went out of their way there to make you know that they were in and you were not," Gonella says. "We just dreaded having to call over there." So integral a part of the Hickory Hill gang's culture was the contempt that at least once it was expressed, without thinking, in Johnson's presence. Two middle-level Administration officials, Ron Linton and John J. Riley, were chatting at a cocktail party when Linton realized that someone was standing next to them, wanting to be part of the conversation. The listener was Lyndon Johnson. They didn't stop talking. After a while, Johnson walked away. And when Linton said, "John, I think we just insulted the Vice President of the United States," Riley blurted out, "Fuck him"—loud enough for Johnson to hear. Whirling around, he stared at the two men for a moment. But what was there to say? Turning again, he walked away.

In attempting to understand Robert Kennedy's treatment of Lyndon Johnson, is there a clue in his treatment of Chester Bowles while his brother was watching, not interrupting because Bobby "was communicating exactly what his brother had wanted"? Was Bobby, with Lyndon Johnson, also serving as a weapon for his brother? Did the President want Johnson kept under tighter rein than ever—and was Bobby his instrument for doing this?

Whether or not that was one of the reasons, other—political—considerations may have militated such treatment. Robert Kennedy, after all, had been part of the Senate world on days—and there had been many days—when that world marveled at the genius and power of Lyndon Johnson, when word spread through the Senate corridors (and down to the basement office of the Senate Rackets Committee) of how, up on the Chamber floor, the mighty Leader had just done it again: of how, with a vote seemingly sure to go against him, he had somehow once again turned defeat into triumph. Bobby had left the Senate Office Building very late on so many nights, to turn and see the lights still burning in the Leader's office; he had said on one such night, "No one can outlast Lyndon."

Because of the contempt with which Robert Kennedy always treated, and generally spoke of, Lyndon Johnson, many historians have felt that contempt was his basic attitude toward him; the title of the most detailed book on their relationship is, in fact, *Mutual Contempt.* But when Robert Kennedy was talking to men close to him, very different feelings emerged. "I can't stand the bastard," he once said to Richard Goodwin, "but he's the most formidable human being I've ever met." "He just eats up strong men," he said on another occasion. "The fact is that he's able to eat people up, even people who are considered rather strong figures." "Contempt" was not at all an accurate summation of his feelings about Lyndon Johnson, and powerless though Johnson might be at the moment, as Vice President he was still a threat. The more perceptive members of the staffs of both men understood this. Says Harry McPherson, who had worked for Johnson before the vice presidency, "If your brother is President, and you've got this powerhouse accustomed to being in command as Vice President, it would make you as suspicious as anything." Kennedy's aide William vanden Heuvel says that Robert Kennedy saw Johnson as "a manipulative force" who could, if he ever got off his leash, be very difficult to rein in again. So the leash had to be kept tight.

But there was also the aspect that lay beyond the political, and beyond analysis, too, the aspect that led George Reedy to ask, "Did you ever see two dogs come into a room . . . ?" There was Bobby's hatred for liars, and his feeling that Lyndon Johnson "lies all the time . . . lies even when he doesn't have to lie." There was his hatred for yes-men—and for those who wanted to be surrounded by yes-men—and Johnson's insistence on being surrounded by such men, an insistence which, Bobby was to say, "makes it very difficult, unless you want to kiss his behind all the time." He detested the politician's false bonhomie, and Johnson embodied that bonhomie. "He [Bobby] recoiled at being touched," and of course Lyndon Johnson was always touching and hugging. And talking. "It was southwestern exaggeration against Yankee understatement," Arthur Schlesinger has written. "Robert Kennedy, in the New England manner, liked people to keep their physical distance. Johnson . . . was all over everybody." So many of Bobby Kennedy's pet hates were embodied in Lyndon Johnson.

"No affection contaminated the relationship between the Vice President and the Attorney General," Schlesinger writes. "It was a pure case of mutual dislike." Lyndon Johnson, he writes, "repelled Robert Kennedy." The two men were, as he portrays them—in the portrayal that has become the model for other historians—opposites, and certainly in many ways, in all the obvious ways, perhaps, they were.

YET, IN SOME WAYS, "opposite" is not at all an apt adjective to apply to Lyndon Johnson and Robert Kennedy, as is shown by their approach to two of the most fundamental elements of politics.

One was counting votes.

"Vote-counting"—predicting the count for or against an issue or a candidate in advance of the actual ballot—is, as I have written, "one of the most vital of the political arts, but it is an art that few can master," subject as it is to the distortions of sentiment or romantic preconceptions. A person convinced of the arguments on one side of a controversial issue feels that arguments so convincing to him must be equally convincing to others, a belief which leads to wishful thinking and to overoptimism in vote predictions. Even as a congressional aide—not even a congressman, yet—Johnson had been known among young Washington insiders as "the greatest vote-counter."* In the Senate, leading a party that often had only a one-vote majority, a party with fiercely opposed liberal and conservative blocs so that the Democratic coalition was shifting constantly beneath his feet and he almost always had to cobble Republican votes together with it, he had almost never, during his six years as Majority Leader, lost a vote on a major bill. During the days leading up to the vote, he kept his count on the long, narrow Senate tally sheets, and his thumb, moving down the sheet from name to name, moved very slowly as he reflected, not moving on to the next name until he was certain about this one. To a staff member who, after talking to a senator, said he "thought" he knew which way the senator was going to vote, he would snarl, "What the fuck good is *thinking* to me? Thinking isn't good enough. I need to *know*!"

In 1960, the man counting votes against Lyndon Johnson was Robert Kennedy, and Kennedy's men had learned he didn't want optimism or wishful thinking. "I don't want generalities or guesses," he told them when he gathered them together before the convention. "There's no point in our fooling ourselves. I want the cold facts. I want to hear only the votes we are guaranteed to get on the first ballot." He wanted to *know*, to know beyond doubt; he insisted on knowing: "He insisted practically on the name, address, and telephone number of every half vote," someone who watched him recalls. And he *knew*. He couldn't be wrong: "If we don't win tonight, we're dead." Ben Bradlee was to remember "Bobby, literally sick with fatigue, going over the . . . first ballot with me at two o'clock in the morning, one last time, delegate by delegate." Getting the necessary majority was going to be so close. He couldn't be wrong—and he wasn't.

*See *Master of the Senate*, p. 389.

He had told Ted that the outcome was going to come down to those last five votes from Wyoming, and that was just how it turned out.

Johnson, who, after his long indecision, was battling in the last days before the 1960 convention for every delegate vote as the count swayed back and forth—Delaware hinging on a single vote, North Dakota on half a vote—was keeping his own tally. A master of an art recognizes another master when he encounters one, and Johnson knew there was a master battling—and counting votes—against him.

The other element, as important as counting votes, was holding them. When he was Majority Leader, nobody had been better at holding votes than Lyndon Johnson: keeping the vote of a senator who, after he had pledged him his vote, received a better offer—or a more effective threat—from the other side. "Destroy" was a verb he used to men who, having pledged him their support, were thinking about changing their minds: "I'll destroy you." "Ruin" was a verb he used. "I'm going to give you a three-minute lesson in integrity," he told one politician. "And then I'm going to ruin you." And, as he tried to take votes away from the Kennedys in 1960, there had been someone on the other side holding them fast, someone who, having slipped on "the halter and the bridle," would not allow them to be slipped off. There were, moreover, other qualities to which the word "opposite" did not apply. Was Lyndon Johnson a smearer of opponents, a destroyer of reputations, without scruple? Watching Franklin Roosevelt Jr. destroy Hubert Humphrey in West Virginia with the "draft dodger" fabrication, Johnson knew who had orchestrated the tactic. "That's Bobby," he had told Tommy Corcoran—and he had been right. In some ways, Robert Kennedy and Lyndon Johnson were very different—and in some ways they weren't.

Lyndon Johnson recognized the caliber of the man he was dealing with. He had recognized it even before the campaign. It had been in 1957, when he was the Majority Leader and Robert Kennedy had been a thirty-two-year-old Senate staffer, that he had said that an investigation of America's *Sputnik* disaster might succeed "if it had had someone like young Kennedy handling it." All during his life, words would, as if despite himself, burst out of him that revealed that he recognized Bobby's abilities. Back on his ranch in retirement, watching on television the bumbling attempts of Edward Kennedy and a retinue of Kennedy advisers to explain away the Chappaquiddick drowning, he would say, "Never would have happened if Bobby was there." And, recognizing that caliber, he was, as Richard Goodwin says, "always afraid of Bobby. It was more than hatred. It was fear."

And hatred and fear, no matter how deep they went, were not Lyndon Johnson's only feelings about Bobby Kennedy, for the President's brother had come to embody to him something deeper than the political.

Hickory Hill, that most "in" of all Camelot's social "in" places, was the catalyst for these emotions. He and Lady Bird were almost never invited, of course, and in a town where everyone was talking about the gossip columns' description of the previous evening's dinner party, he would invariably be asked if he had been there, and would have to say no. On those occasions when an invitation to the Vice President and his wife was unavoidable, they were seated at Ethel's "losers' table." While at the White House, protocol and the President's expressed desire that the Vice President be treated with respect maintained a patina of courtesy—he and Lady Bird may have come down the staircase behind the President and the visiting head of state, but at least they came down the staircase, and then stood in the receiving line with them—at Hickory Hill, there was no patina at all. Hugh Sidey was to call the mockery of the Vice President at Ethel's parties "just awful . . . inexcusable, really." At one party, to "overwhelming merriment," Bobby was presented with a voodoo effigy of Lyndon Johnson for him to stick pins into.

Hickory Hill hurt especially deeply because of the way it fit into the pattern of his life. It wasn't the first place from which Lyndon Johnson had been excluded—the Hickory Hill regulars not the first in-group that had rejected him. His youth had, after his father's failure, been years of rejection. The Johnson City families that didn't have to work with their hands—the owners of the stores in the little town who were, more or less, its little social hierarchy, the merchants who wrote "Please!" on the Johnsons' bills, and made clear their feelings that the crucial fact about Lyndon was that he was "a Johnson," that he was "too much like Sam"—had cut him off from more than credit. His high school girlfriend was his classmate Kitty Clyde Ross, daughter of E. P. Ross, "the richest man in town," until her parents ordered her to stop dating him, and encouraged a rival suitor by lending him their car so the young couple could drive around Johnson City in the evenings. "I saw how it made Lyndon feel when that big car drove by with Kitty Clyde in it with another man," says his cousin Ava. "And I cried for him." At college, there had been an in-group, a social club called the "Black Stars," which included the athletes and the other big men on campus, and the prettiest girls, the group that "everyone wanted to be part of." Lyndon tried very hard to become part of it, pressing one Black Star or another to put his name up for membership in meeting after meeting, and every time he was voted down. "He wanted so badly to belong to the 'in' crowd," says a classmate, Ella So Relle. "To be accepted by them. But they wouldn't let him in. He was just not accepted."

As a youth, Lyndon Johnson had been very aware—as how could he not be?—of exactly where his family stood. "We had dropped to the bottom of the heap." There had been moments during that youth that revealed an insecurity so deep that they raised the question of whether anything could ever convince him that he had respect; of whether anything could make him, deep inside himself, feel secure. Hickory Hill, and its master, seemed to bring back those insecurities, to arouse in him emotions that went deeper than politics—to the very depths of his being.

Washington social pages and gossip columns were filled with details of life at Hickory Hill, the dinner parties at tables set up around the swimming pool, the brunches filled with pranks and charades, the mixture of gaiety and serious discussion. He would pore over the names of the people who had been in attendance, parsing them for a common denominator that might be an excuse why they had been included and he hadn't, each story—each name of a couple that had been invited while he and Lady Bird hadn't—a little dart of pain. At one, Ethel Kennedy and Arthur Schlesinger and other guests fell or jumped or were pushed into the pool, and the stories about that party leapt into prominence across the country, and of course he was asked over and over if he had been there, and he had to invent some excuse to explain why he hadn't been.

And then there was "Hickory Hill U.," the seminars that one participant said summed up "the humane and questing spirit of the New Frontier," while another thought they were "all sorts of fun." Led by renowned intellectuals like Isaiah Berlin and Schlesinger, they included, in addition to diplomats and Cabinet members, Harvard professors and deans like Mac Bundy and graduates of the university's colleges and graduate schools such as Dillon and McNamara—and of course sometimes the President. The "Harvards," Johnson called this group when he was talking with his own aides. He understood the quality of his education. It wasn't just that he hadn't gone to Harvard, he hadn't even gone to the University of Texas, the school, in Austin on the edge of the Hill Country, where the few young men and women from the Hill Country's farms and ranches who had the marks—and the tuition—went to college. He had gone to Southwest Texas State Teachers College, and he knew what that was: "the poor boys' school," he called it. "Most of the kids were there because they couldn't afford to go anywhere else," one of Johnson's classmates was to say. So low were its standards—its fifty-six faculty members included exactly one holder of a doctorate—that the year Johnson arrived there was the year the college graduated its first fully accredited class. Another classmate, who became a professor at Bryn Mawr, says that when he first came to Bryn Mawr, "I felt so inadequate—that I had so much to catch up. . . . I could not go to a dinner party, and participate intelligently in the conversation. And this is a terrible feeling. I don't think anyone who hasn't experienced this feeling can understand how horrible it is. At San Marcos I got cheated out of an education."

Johnson knew they were laughing at him at Hickory Hill. Did something in his life, deep within him, something created by the years of being laughed at in his youth, feel the laughter was justified? "They're trying to make a hick out of me," Johnson said. Did he himself feel like a hick—feel that there was a chasm dividing him from the Kennedys, and that the ground on their side of the chasm was higher ground, ground to which, because of the circumstances of his youth, he could never climb? When his assistants are asked to describe his feelings toward the Harvards, they respond with words that have little to do with politics, words like "hurt" and "rage" and "jealousy," and the last of the three words is one that is heard often. He was caught in a "storm of jealousy about the 'Kennedy

class,' " a storm so violent that at times it "threatened to drown him," Joseph Califano says. And his feelings centered, with a growing concentration that seemed
to leave none for other targets, on the slight figure of Bobby Kennedy. "As LBJ
saw it, there was a poor kid working around the clock at . . . San Marcos and
there was a rich kid partying through the ivy halls of Harvard with plenty of time
to acquire the social graces" he himself lacked, Califano says. He was, Califano
says, "possessed by an internal class struggle . . . , and tortured by an envy he
could not exorcise." Princeton professor Eric Goldman, who would come to
work for Lyndon Johnson later in his presidency, learned that "the response that
Robert Kennedy evoked in Lyndon Johnson was hugely disproportionate to the
political realities. Something beyond politics was at stake." The disproportion
was already visible as 1962 turned into 1963, and Richard Goodwin felt he
understood. "Bobby symbolized everything Johnson hated," he was to say. "He
became *the* symbol of all the things Johnson wasn't . . . with these characteristics
of wealth and power and ease and Eastern elegance; with Johnson always looking at himself as the guy they thought was illiterate, rude, crude. They laughed at
him behind his back. I think he felt all that." And the intensity of his feelings
about Bobby made them something that cause Johnson's associates, in describing them, to use words that have nothing to do with politics. "Whatever realistic
basis there was for dislike or fear, it cannot explain the almost obsessive intensity
of Johnson's feelings towards Robert Kennedy," Goldman says. His feelings
weren't "totally rational," Goodwin says. "He just couldn't be rational where
Bobby Kennedy was concerned," says Bobby Baker.

AND IN 1963, Bobby Kennedy was becoming not only a symbol or an obsession to Lyndon Johnson, but, in a very concrete way, a threat—to his gaining the
prize he had always pursued. He had accepted the vice presidency, and was
enduring all the humiliations that went with it, was bearing an all but unbearable
burden, because he had felt that doing so was his best chance, quite possibly his
only chance, of obtaining the Democratic presidential nomination in 1968. But
by 1963 Washington was becoming aware that the President's brother had set his
sights on the same prize.

In the March issue of *Esquire,* Gore Vidal predicted that Johnson wouldn't
be the nominee in '68. "Time is no friend to Johnson's candidacy," he wrote.
"The public . . . has already forgotten the dynamic Lyndon Johnson who was
once master of the Senate. Eight years of vice presidential grayness will have
completed his obscurity; nor is there any way for Johnson to gain political attention. . . . How does the ceremonial presiding officer of the Senate make a new
record for himself?"

Bobby's situation was the opposite, Vidal wrote. "During the next few
years, he will be continually in the headlines and" by 1968 "even his numerous
enemies will have a hard time trying to pretend he is not 'experienced.' " He will

"have the support of the Kennedy political machine, easily the most effective in the history of the country. . . . One cannot imagine any Democrat seriously opposing Bobby at the '68 convention."

Vidal was no friend of Bobby's; his views, however, were echoed by the Washington press corps. LBJ MAY FACE BOBBY IN 1968, said the headline over a Roscoe Drummond prediction in the *Herald Tribune*. It was true, the columnist said, that Bobby would thus be trying to succeed his brother, but he wouldn't wait for 1972. "No Kennedy likes to wait too long." Another columnist, Gould Lincoln, wrote that "a great many have speculated that the [1968] Democratic presidential candidate would be Robert F. Kennedy." On March 1, Bobby denied such predictions, saying he was "emphatically not" planning to run for the nomination in 1968. "This certainly ought to be a relief to Lyndon Johnson, if it's true," Republican Senator Barry Goldwater said. But any relief was short-lived. Addressing the same subject three days later, Bobby added an additional phrase: "I have no plans to run at this time," he said.

When these stories first began appearing, Johnson, seeing Bobby's hand behind everything, thought they had been planted by the attorney general with friendly journalists; he seemed unable to believe that a man so young (Bobby had just turned thirty-seven), whose qualifications even for attorney general had been suspect only two years before, was now a leading candidate for the presidency. After checking in with the columnists, however, Reedy had to report that they were writing what they believed. "The Washington press corps is convinced that there is a well organized move afoot to groom Bobby Kennedy for the Presidency in 1968 and shove you aside," he told Johnson. And Johnson felt he was helpless to fight the move. "My future is behind me," he told Busby.

9

Gestures and Tactics

ON FEBRUARY 24, 1963, Johnson received a letter from Mrs. Fannie Fuller-wood, of St. Augustine, Florida, an African-American cleaning woman who was president of the local branch of the National Association for the Advancement of Colored People. Because it was George Smathers who had asked him to do so, he had agreed to give two speeches in St. Augustine on March 11, one at a banquet that would kick off a year-long celebration of the four hundredth anniversary of St. Augustine's founding, the other at one of the area's most important industries, the Aircraft Division of the Fairchild Stratos Corporation. Pointing out that there had been recent instances of police brutality toward blacks in a city that was a bastion of racial segregation, Mrs. Fullerwood told him that no blacks would be allowed to attend the banquet, nor was there one on the planning committee for the anniversary. "It is impossible for us to see how you can" come "under such conditions," she wrote. Johnson's response was immediate—and firm. "I cannot go unless we get this worked out," he told Smathers, and Smathers assigned his administrative assistant, Scott Peek, to work it out. Peek tried to assure Johnson that the letter was "nothing to get excited about," that it represented the views of only one branch of the Florida NAACP, a "very small" branch at that, and said that "if the State NAACP knew anything about this they would raise hell with the local chapter." Peek added that any interference by Johnson would embarrass Florida Senators Smathers and Holland, who would also be attending the banquet, because they would be caught in the middle of a racial dispute; moreover, the chairman of the four-hundredth-anniversary celebration—and of the banquet—was St. Augustine banker Herbert E. Wolfe, one of Florida's leading political fund-raisers, and, in fact, treasurer of Smathers' next senatorial campaign. When Johnson told George Reedy to look into the situation, however, Reedy learned that the local chapter was planning to picket the banquet if blacks were not allowed to attend, and to picket Fairchild as well. A telephone call to Fairchild elicited the information that of the one thousand employees at the plant, exactly sixty-two were black, none of them executives. A Fairchild official explained the situation by telling him that "St. Augustine does not have many colored people and it is difficult to get the few that are there out of grade school." (The "best solution" to the lack of black executives, the official said, would be "some colored office workers . . . and he is going to redouble his efforts to find some.") But, Reedy added in his report to Johnson, Peek had also said that "if necessary, the local people can probably get a Negro table set up at the banquet," and "if a Negro table could be set up . . . you could well emerge as a hero."

A hero, Johnson knew, was not a role the Kennedys had in mind for him; their attitude toward his involvement in civil rights matters had been demonstrated just five months before when they had completely cut him out of any deliberations on the James Meredith crisis. Not only would any racial dispute be a thicket of complications, he would be stepping into it without any assurance of support from the Administration. Yet almost immediately Johnson began to get excited as he had not been for months. Busby and Reedy understood the reason: they had witnessed themselves, or had heard about from other Johnson aides, the immediacy and passion with which Johnson had reacted in the past when confronted by examples of racial injustice; how, with barely a moment's pause, in almost the very instant he was told that a Mexican-American war hero had been denied burial in a whites-only cemetery in South Texas, he had blurted out, "By God, we'll bury him in Arlington!," how this reaction was "*immediate . . . instinctive. . . . It had to do with outrage*"; how, when Johnson described his longtime African-American cook driving back and forth to Texas across the South without being able to find a gas station or motel that would allow her to go to the bathroom so that she had to "squat in the road to pee," his words would be underlined by an indignation "that was straight from real feelings," straight from anger, "sometimes just about to tears." Johnson told Reedy to get in touch with the St. Augustine NAACP and to see what could be worked out. That proved logistically difficult—Mrs. Fullerwood was constantly having to break off phone calls to get to her housecleaning jobs—but otherwise easier than Reedy expected, because the St. Augustine civic leaders planning the celebration were anxious not to have it marred by a picket line. Peek, through whom Reedy dealt with these leaders, found them amenable to the "Negro table," and Reedy then persuaded the NAACP leaders to agree not to picket if two conditions were met: first, that there actually be such a table and, second, that the St. Augustine City Commission agree to meet with the NAACP after the banquet to discuss not only the police brutality issue but the desegregation of city-owned facilities. The civic leaders agreed to that: a time for the commission meeting—9:30 a.m. the very day following the banquet—was set, and Wolfe persuaded the hotel to allow the Negro table. But that wasn't enough for Johnson; he knew about "Negro tables" at southern dinners, he told Reedy; he didn't want it placed in the rear of the hall or off to one side. And he didn't want just one table, but at least two. It wasn't just the banquet that he wanted desegregated, moreover; he didn't want the races to be separated at his speech at Fairchild Stratos, or at any other event at which he spoke. Reedy insisted on all this, and by March 1, Peek was able to assure Johnson that invitations to all events were being extended to NAACP leaders and that "They will not be stuck off in a faraway corner" at the banquet. "No event in which I will participate in St. Augustine will be segregated," Johnson wrote Mrs. Fullerwood, dispatching Reedy to Florida to make sure that would be true.

JOHNSON'S VISIT TO ST. AUGUSTINE started at an old mission that housed the casket of the Spanish explorer who had said the first Mass at the site of what was to become the city, and he was very silent as a priest guided him through the buildings, until, coming to the coffin, he saw the dates of the explorer's birth and death—1519 and 1574—and then the only words he spoke were a number: "Fifty-five." *He* was going to be fifty-five on his next birthday; he seemed unable to escape reminders that time was running out on him. But when he was met at the gates to the Stratos plant, there was a black man on the welcoming committee, which sat behind him on the platform as he spoke. Sitting in the audience, Reedy heard people saying that, as he was to report to Johnson, "This was probably the first time in the history of the County that a Negro had appeared on the same platform with a white speaker." At his next speech, at the dedication ceremonies for a memorial to St. Augustine, there was also a black face on the platform. And at the banquet, there were two "Negro tables," and they were, Reedy says, "good tables close to the speakers' platform." Reedy and Peek were sitting at these tables when Peek suddenly got word that Johnson wasn't coming down from his suite until it was time for his speech. He understood that Johnson was nervous—"he didn't want to have anything that was a situation"—but he went upstairs to Johnson's suite to protest, telling him that not showing up for dinner would give the appearance that he was boycotting the blacks. "I'm *eatin'* with 'em," Peek said. "At least you can come." Johnson came downstairs with a grim expression on his face that Reedy knew only too well. But as the Vice President looked out over the hall he seemed to relax, and his speech went well. While members of the audience were coming up to his table to shake his hand afterwards, he caught Reedy's eye, with a look that Reedy understood; he and Peek brought the little group of African-Americans up to the dais, and Johnson was, Peek says, "very cordial with them, very cordial—they had a good time talking to him." As he turned away after a while, one said, "Don't forget us, Mr. Vice President." His flight back to Washington that night was in the small MATS Jet-Star he detested, but, flying back with him, Peek, who during his eleven years as Smathers' assistant had spent enough time with Johnson to know his moods, saw that he was "very happy." "Happier than he had been for months," Reedy says.

IN A MEMO summarizing the St. Augustine trip, Reedy wrote that "a major breakthrough on the color line was achieved" because, in allowing the events to be integrated, and in agreeing to negotiate about segregation in the city in general, "local people [had] made . . . concessions, which in light of the history of St. Augustine, are startling."

This evaluation was to prove overoptimistic. When the next day at 9:30 a.m., a nine-member NAACP delegation went to City Hall for the promised meeting, there to greet them in the commission chamber were no commissioners but only a tape recorder sitting on a bare table; a city functionary told them they could record their complaints on that; the commissioners had been unable to attend, he said.

Leaning forward one by one to talk into the recorder, the black men and women asked for the removal of "Colored Only" signs at least in city-owned facilities, for the inclusion of at least one black person among poll watchers at elections, and for the end of various other humiliations routinely inflicted upon black residents of the city. One of the nine, a carpenter, said that when his sister had died recently, and he and his family had gone to City Hall to obtain a death certificate, "we had to stand on the outside to give the information they wanted. . . . It was cold and raining." No response would ever be vouchsafed to the delegation's requests—no attempt by the commissioners to live up to their promise to Reedy. With Johnson gone, the leader of the delegation came to realize, he had lost any leverage with the commission. A report later sent to Washington concluded that St. Augustine officials regretted the extent to which they had cooperated with Johnson: "They feel that they went even further than they should have gone to accommodate the Vice President when he was here."

Yet despite this denouement, and despite the fact that he had no power to do anything to change the situation, Lyndon Johnson had not accomplished nothing, in George Reedy's opinion. The mere fact that blacks had been in the banquet hall had not been meaningless, he said. "One of the Negroes said that never before in the history of the hotel had a Negro eaten in it except in the kitchen. . . . The whites . . . have had the experience of sitting down in the city's finest banquet hall with Negroes to eat a meal. The roof did not fall in and the walls did not collapse. Furthermore, they have had the example of one of the highest officials of the United States insisting upon equality."

And the incident in St. Augustine had an effect also on that official. Fighting on a civil rights issue—taking a step, however small, against racial injustice; trying to do something for people of color—had always roused something in Lyndon Johnson. That had happened again, from the moment he insisted that the hall in St. Augustine not be segregated. After his return to Washington, his staff saw, he was "revved up" as he hadn't been since the start of his vice presidency.

His depression was gone. After months of refusing to give interviews, now, when Reedy left him a note saying that Jack Bell of the Associated Press wanted one, back came a note saying, "Set up a date." He even agreed to do one on television—his first since the earliest days of his vice presidency. "LBJ last night broke his self-imposed silence to deny allegations that his post of Vice President is a comedown," Evans and Novak reported on March 28. Facing three reporters from ABC, he seemed calm, poised and content as he said, "I am very happy. I have everything a man could want. I have a lovely family. I enjoy my work. . . . I have never felt that the vice presidency was a comedown from anything except the presidency." The only tense moment came when a questioner noted that Johnson had once "reached for the presidency" himself. "I don't consider that I ever reached for the presidency," he said. "My friends put me in the race. . . . I didn't feel I was a candidate. I didn't go into any of the primaries."

Now that he was involved in civil rights again, the uncertainty was gone. He understood the importance of gestures, gestures that indicated respect, to people starved for respect, and he knew just what gestures to make. The great African-American singer Marian Anderson was giving a concert in Austin. The city's university-centered liberal community welcomed the news, but there was a studied disdain from its conservative establishment; Johnson invited her to visit—and stay the weekend—at his ranch. He knew just what words to use. Every year the press club for African-American journalists in Washington tried to get a high-level speaker from the federal government, sending invitations first to the President, then to the Vice President, "and so on down the Cabinet," as a club officer put it. None had ever been accepted. But in 1963, the club was able to stop with the Vice President. The other speaker was a southern governor, Terry Sanford of North Carolina, who called for "moderacy and restraint" on the civil rights issue, "sounding," in the opinion of the *Washington Afro-American,* "like the siren call of the last 100 years . . . like the last grunt to the chorus of the 'Volga Boatman.' " And then the Vice President spoke. "The sands of time are running out," Lyndon Johnson said. "The hours are short and we have no moral justification in asking for an extension." Six years earlier, he recalled, when the first civil rights law had been passed, he had said that half a loaf was better than none. Now, he said, "It seems to me that we are well past the stage where half a loaf will do." He understood, the *Afro-American* said, "the reasons that drive colored men and women to fight for their rights these days." Before he spoke, a young black woman, shortly to graduate from a Washington high school, had been called to the stage and awarded a scholarship to enable her to go to college. At the end of his speech, Johnson turned to her and said she would probably need more financial aid than the scholarship would provide; she should come to his office, he said—he would see she got it. While he was shaking hands after the speech, an African-American woman came back to her table holding one hand in the air. "I shall never wash this glove," she said.

HE DECIDED TO ACCEPT an invitation to deliver the Memorial Day speech at the Gettysburg Battlefield in Pennsylvania, where, one hundred years before, Abraham Lincoln had given a speech. He had received the invitation months before, but had told his assistant, Juanita Roberts, a former WAC colonel, to decline;

among other reasons, he was afraid his speech would be compared to Lincoln's Gettysburg Address. But Horace Busby had begged Colonel Roberts not to send the letter, and she, aware of how often Johnson changed his mind—and hoping he would change it this time—simply filed the invitation away. Now, after his success in St. Augustine, he asked her if she had replied to the invitation. When she said she hadn't, he told her to accept.

A few days before the Memorial Day weekend, he had Busby come out to The Elms, and they sat by the swimming pool and talked, with Johnson doing most of the talking, about what should be in the speech. He expected Busby to follow their usual practice and turn his rough views into a polished speech, but this time the speechwriter didn't think much polishing was required. "I knew what I had heard," he says. He had been writing speeches for Lyndon Johnson for fifteen years, and he felt that this time Johnson had said exactly what he wanted to say. In Busby's car was a large, clumsy recording device, and, he recalls, as he was driving away from The Elms, "I stopped the car a half a block away and recorded what we'd been saying pretty much as" he remembered it, and the next morning took the recording to his office and had his secretary transcribe it, "and when I saw the transcription, I got very—uh, huh!" He added two introductory paragraphs, and one at the end, and took back to Johnson essentially what Johnson had said to him by the pool.

It was a very short speech—much shorter than the usual Johnson speech—and he had expected Johnson to discuss it with him, to change and edit it, and to tell him to add to it. And he had expected Johnson to tell him to clear it with the Kennedys. "But," he was to recall, "I didn't hear any more from him." The next thing Busby saw or heard about the speech was when he read it—in the *Washington Post*; as the lead story in the *Washington Post*.

So short was the speech—barely two typed pages—that it had taken Johnson only eight minutes to read it, but Lincoln's speech had been short, too, and, the *Post* said in an editorial, this one, too, had "eloquence . . . political courage . . . vision."

"One hundred years ago, the slave was freed," Lyndon Johnson had said. "One hundred years later, the Negro remains in bondage to the color of his skin. The Negro today asks justice. We do not answer him—we do not answer those who lie beneath this soil—when we reply to the Negro by asking, 'Patience.' . . . To ask for patience from the Negro is to ask him to give more of what he has already given enough. . . . The Negro says, 'Now.' Others say, 'Never.' The voice of responsible Americans—the voices of those who died here and the great man who spoke here—their voices say, 'Together.' There is no other way."

And, for a while, it seemed that the speech would be just the start. His long-time Texas allies had phrases to describe how Lyndon Johnson threw himself into a cause, even if it was sometimes a cause in which he had not previously believed, even if it was in fact a cause he had previously opposed—phrases to describe the "revving up," the "working up," when he made himself believe in the cause absolutely, with total conviction, when, as Ed Clark puts it, "He could . . . convince himself" something "was right, and get all worked up, all worked up and emotional, and work all day and all night, and sacrifice, and say, 'Follow me for the cause!'—'Let's do this because it's *right*!' " And, Clark says, Johnson would believe it *was* right—no matter what he had believed before, so that, as Reedy says, "he acted out of pure motives regardless of their origins."

And in the case of helping people of color, there had always been something very pure about Lyndon Johnson's motives. Definitive though his twenty-year record of voting against and carrying out southern strategy against every civil rights bill might seem, it was not in fact the whole story. Even during the early years of his life, the story had had a very different side. At the age of twenty, he had been a teacher in the "Mexican school" in the desolate South Texas town of Cotulla; no teacher had ever really cared if the Mexican children learned or not—until Lyndon Johnson came along. And it was not only the children whom Lyndon Johnson taught; to help the school's janitor, Thomas Coronado, learn English, he bought him a textbook, and before and after classes each day, sat tutoring him on the school steps. The anger, "sometimes just about to tears," of which aides spoke was something they saw often when Lyndon Johnson was talking about the indignities that his black household staff had to suffer in their daily lives. Whether it was because he had had to do "nigger work" as a youth—picking cotton, chopping cedar in the Hill Country—or because as "a Johnson" he had felt the sting of unjust discrimination, there had always existed within Lyndon Johnson genuine empathy and compassion for Americans of color. Hidden though it had been for years—twenty and more—because during those years compassion conflicted with the ambition that was the force that drove Johnson more than any other, when, in 1957, compassion had, for the first time, coincided with ambition, the compassion had been released. And it was released now. May of 1963 had been the month of Birmingham—of Martin Luther King's desperate decision to throw his last resource, children, into the fight to desegregate that tough southern city—the month of the fire hoses ("They've turned the fire hoses on a little black girl. . . . They're rolling that little girl right down the middle of the street") and of the dogs, the big German shepherds that Bull Connor's police kept on leashes, but not tightly. And all that month, the President and the attorney general and their aides were discussing what to do in Birmingham, and whether or not to propose new civil rights legislation, and what that legislation should be, but they hadn't been discussing it with him. On Sunday, May 12, after bombs had exploded in front of the home of King's brother, and at the motel where King himself was supposed to be staying, Kennedy headed back from Camp David for a long day of crisis meetings with his aides and Cabinet members, who arrived at the White House in a procession of limousines; the Second Infantry Division and the 82nd Airborne were put on alert, and the paperwork was drawn up to federalize the Alabama National Guard at a moment's notice. None of the limousines contained the Vice President; that afternoon, he was at a garden party at the home of Congressman Hale Boggs, where the gathering buzzed with rumors of what was happening at the White House, so all the guests were aware that whatever was happening, the Vice President was most definitely not a part of it. The Administration was drawing up civil rights legislation, but he was not part of that either. For the past two and a half years, Johnson's response to such exclusion had been to retreat into silence and sulking, but he didn't retreat now. He asked to meet with the President, and when he was put off, he kept repeating the request, finally, on Saturday, June 1, telling O'Donnell—this is what Lyndon Johnson had been reduced to—that, in the words of one Administration official, "he thought he should have fifteen minutes alone with the President."

At 10 a.m. on Monday, June 3, Johnson was allowed into the Oval Office, with Robert Kennedy and O'Donnell and Sorensen already there, discussing the civil rights bill, but in the course of a very brief meeting the President asked him if he had anything to add—and he told the President what he thought should be done about the legislation, and after listening to him, Kennedy asked him to repeat his thoughts, in detail, to Ted Sorensen, and said Sorensen would be calling him, which Sorensen did, that afternoon.

AND SINCE, AT LAST, the President had asked Lyndon Johnson for advice about civil rights, he gave some.

It was advice on two levels.

One, the lower level, was about tactics, and it was advice from a master of tactics, from the most effective Senate Leader in history, a leader who had, in fact, done what the President was saying he wanted to do now: pass a civil rights bill.

He didn't know exactly what was in the Kennedy civil rights bill, he told Sorensen. "I've never seen it. . . . I got it from the *New York Times*. . . . I haven't sat in on any of the conferences they've had up here with the senators. I think it would have been good if I had." But sending any civil rights bill to Congress at the present moment was a tactical error, he said.

It wasn't that he didn't want a bill, Lyndon Johnson said. But other major legislation that Kennedy needed hadn't yet been passed. Sending up a civil rights bill before all other major legislation was disposed of was a very bad idea. A traditional southern tactic—one that had been perfected by Richard Russell in a score of civil rights fights—was to delay consideration of other major bills in the Senate while waiting to take up civil rights. If the other major bills had been disposed of by the time a civil rights bill arrived on the Senate floor and precipitated a filibuster, it would be the only major piece of unfinished Senate business. But if other major bills remained to be disposed of at the time a filibuster brought Senate activity to a halt, other senators would be faced with an unpleasant reality. There were only two ways to end a filibuster: by a cloture vote or by abandoning the bill that was being filibustered, withdrawing it from the floor. Since, as the

1960 cloture vote had demonstrated yet again, winning such a vote was highly unlikely, senators would realize that if the civil rights bill was not withdrawn—if the southerners were not allowed to win; if instead the Senate decided to fight it out on the filibuster front as long as it took and not move on to other business—the other necessary legislation might not be taken up. Those other bills would therefore become hostages to civil rights—hostages held in southern hands. They couldn't be released until the filibuster was ended—and the southerners wouldn't allow the filibuster to be ended until the civil rights bill was abandoned. Eventually the pressure to pass those bills would become so great that civil rights *would* be abandoned. "So," Lyndon Johnson said, "I'd move my children [the other bills] on through the line and get them down in the storm cellar and get it locked and key, and then"—and only then, when the other bills were safely passed—"I'd make my attack." But Kennedy wasn't doing that; a number of necessary bills—most notably his proposal for a tax reduction that would give a boost to a stalled economy—were still in the legislative process, still before committees in either the House or Senate that hadn't yet released them to the floor so that they could be debated and voted on. By sending up a bill at the present moment, without getting the other important bills out of the way, Kennedy would simply be playing into the southerners' hands. The year was half over—"we've got six months, we haven't passed anything!" Johnson told Sorensen. "I think he ought to make them pass some of this stuff before he throws this thing out [introduces the civil rights bill]." The southerners and the Republicans were just laughing at them for introducing it now, Johnson said. "They're sitting back giggling. If I were Kennedy I'd pass my program" before proposing a civil rights bill. "He's got plenty of time to propose. . . . You ain't going to get even started discussing it until September anyway. You got to pass your tax bill. You got to pass some of your other bills. September is just about the time."

He tried to warn Sorensen—tried, really, to warn the President through Sorensen, since the President wouldn't give him the time to explain it to him directly—about other traps ahead, and how to avoid them.

He tried to explain to Sorensen how the Senate works: that when the time came for the vote on cloture, you weren't going to have some of the votes you had been promised, because senators who wanted civil rights also wanted—*needed,* had to have—dams, contracts, public works projects for their states, and those projects required authorization by the different Senate committees involved, and nine of the sixteen committees (and almost all of the important ones) were chaired by southerners or by allies they could count on. And then, should the authorizations be passed, the projects would require appropriations, the approval of the actual funding for them, and the Appropriations Committee was stacked deep with southerners and their allies—who took their orders from Richard Russell. Or senators needed to have other, non–public works legislation vital to their states, and such legislation often faced other, but also southern-controlled, congressional barriers.

Senators weren't going to be told that a project they desperately needed depended on their voting against cloture; no direct *quid pro quo* was going to be mentioned; the southerners weren't that crude, and crudeness wasn't necessary: after a senator's pet project simply didn't move forward, week after week, month after month, in the Appropriations process, and week after week, month after month, he couldn't seem to get an answer as to why, he would eventually figure out the answer for himself. And the same was true, if to a somewhat lesser extent, in the House. "When he [Kennedy] sends this [civil rights] message . . . Howard Smith [chairman of the House Rules Committee] is going to be in the lead in one place and Dick Russell in the other place, and they're going to sit quietly in these appropriation committees and they're going to cut his outfit [his sexual apparatus] off and put it in their pocket and never mention civil rights." So before the message was sent to the Hill, Kennedy should make sure he had the committee chairmen behind him. "He ought to get his own team in line about chairmen of committees." The Administration seemed to think it meant something that Hubert Humphrey, the Assistant Leader, was for the bill; what power did Humphrey have? "What the hell is Humphrey? . . . We've got to get some other folks . . . to get that cloture." That meant sitting down with the chairmen, discussing the proposed legislation with them, hearing their views and their objections, incorporating them in the legislation, getting their support in advance, before the bill was introduced. Waiting until a controversial bill was introduced to do that was to help doom the bill before it ever arrived.

The other level on which Lyndon Johnson talked to Ted Sorensen was a very different level, a level on which Johnson seldom talked, for he despised politicians who talked about "principled things," and it was principles—a moral commitment—that he was talking about now.

"I think that I know one thing," he said, "that the Negroes are tired of this patient stuff and tired of this piecemeal stuff and what they want more than anything else is not an executive order or legislation, they want a moral commitment that he's behind them." Kennedy hadn't given them that commitment, he said. Legislation—no matter how well written it was—was only part of the answer to the civil rights problem, he said. "The Negroes feel and they're suspicious that we're just doing what we got to do [to keep their vote]. Until that's laid to rest I don't think you're going to have much of a solution. I don't think the Negroes' goals are going to be achieved through legislation. . . . What Negroes are really seeking is moral force and to be sure that we're on their side . . . and until they receive that assurance, unless it's stated dramatically and convincingly, they're not going to pay much attention to executive orders and legislation recommendations. They're going to approach them with skepticism."

And only the President himself can give them that assurance, Johnson said. "What they want to know is the President's own heart is really on their side." If he said so, "I believe they'd believe us." But he has to say so—himself. No legislation, no spokesman will do it. "We got a little popgun, and I want to pull out the cannon," Johnson said. "The President is the cannon."

"This aura, this thing, this halo around the President, everybody wants to believe in the President and the Commander in Chief," Johnson said. That was the weapon that could beat the South on Capitol Hill, Johnson said. "As it is now," he said—without such a commitment—"the President's message doesn't get over."

THE TELEPHONE CALL WAS almost over. "The President asked me this morning, 'Do you have any suggestions?' " Lyndon Johnson said. Yes he had, he said. "I've had some experiences. . . . Whenever he wants them, I'm available."

"Well, I'll pass all this on to him, you can be sure," Ted Sorensen said.

Throughout the conversation, Sorensen had been carefully noncommittal, but he apparently passed enough on to the President so that the next morning Johnson met with Kennedy again. And that afternoon was the first of a series of meetings that had been scheduled with leaders of various groups—this one was with a hundred executives of America's largest retail chains—to mobilize opinion behind the civil rights effort. Kennedy had invited him at the last minute. And when he spoke, some members of the Kennedy Administration who had never seen Lyndon Johnson "revved up" saw it now. Sitting in the rear row of straight-backed gilt chairs in the East Room behind the executives, Arthur Schlesinger felt almost as if he were watching "a Southern preacher." Kennedy was "wholly reasonable, appealing to the intellect. Johnson was evangelical. He was eloquent, all-out emotionally." Whatever doubts Schlesinger had entertained about his sincerity on the issue evaporated that afternoon. He realized now, he was to say, that Johnson was "a true believer." Six more of these meetings would be held during the next month, and Johnson would be at all of them. And anyone who observed the courtesy with which the President treated him at these meetings might have imagined for a moment that Lyndon Johnson was being given, at last, a significant role in the Administration. Sometimes the President referred to him almost as if he was a partner. "This is a very serious fight," he said at one meeting, of leaders of civil rights organizations. "The Vice President and I know what it will mean if we fail." He began to invoke him as an authority. When at another meeting, labor union heads asked that a Fair Employment Practices law be included in the civil rights package, Kennedy said it had been decided not to do so because there was not the slightest chance of its passage. He and the Vice President had discussed this with congressional leaders, he said, and they were both certain of that. Sometimes, during this period, Johnson's demeanor seemed to be changing back to what it had once been. "For a couple of weeks there, he started to look almost like the old Lyndon," George Reedy says. His monologues were starting to be punctuated with dramatic gestures again. Once, in the Taj Mahal, while he was explaining to his own aides what points the President should make in a speech on civil rights, he said that Kennedy should make the point that while he could order Negroes into a foxhole in a foreign country to fight for the American flag, he couldn't get them into southern restaurants while they were on their way to join their units to go to the war. They couldn't get a cup of coffee while they were on the way to die for the flag, he said, and with his huge hand he grabbed the flagpole of the American flag that stood beside his desk, and shook it in his rage at the injustice.

But only for a couple of weeks—thanks to Robert Kennedy.

At a meeting on June 22 in a crowded Cabinet Room with twenty-nine civil rights leaders, the President had to leave early, for a trip to West Germany, and he asked Johnson to preside in his place. As Johnson was speaking, Bobby, sitting on the opposite side of the long table, beckoned to one of the men standing against the wall, the black newspaper publisher Louis Martin, deputy chairman of the Democratic National Committee, and when Martin bent over him, he whispered, "I've got a date, and I've got to get on this boat in a few minutes. Can you tell the Vice President to cut it short?"

Having worked with both men—and being, therefore, more than a little afraid of both—Martin was, he says, "absolutely thunderstruck" by this assignment. Trying to dodge it, he went back to his position against the wall, "and did nothing." But Bobby motioned him over again. "Didn't I tell you to tell the Vice President to shut up?" he said, with the glare that Martin had learned to fear; "I can't explain and describe adequately how he could talk to you," he says. "But anyway I was in such a dilemma I had to do something. The Vice President was going full steam." Edging his way around the table and coming up behind him, Martin bent over and whispered, "Bobby has got to go and he wants to close it up." This time the glare was from piercing dark eyes instead of pale blue, and he "didn't stop for a moment. He just kept going. . . . I didn't really know what to do. . . . I knew the Vice President, once he was aroused, was a pretty tough gentleman. I was really sick." Luckily, after "another ten or fifteen minutes," the meeting came to what seemed to be a natural end.

During this same period the Kennedy Administration, casting about for areas in which it could quickly demonstrate its concern for civil rights, was eyeing the CEEO. Enlarging the committee's powers—or, to be more precise, giving it some in fact rather than in theory—would have enlarged Johnson's, so that wasn't in the cards. What it was decided to enlarge instead was its jurisdiction: an executive order was drafted giving it authority not only over the federal government's own construction projects but over all construction projects—state, local and private—that were financed even in part by federal funds. The executive order would thus allow the committee to identify more instances of discrimination while leaving unchanged its inability to act effectively against them. Essentially meaningless though the order was, it would nonetheless be a fundamental change in the committee's mandate, and it was discussed during several weeks of meetings in the White House, with Robert Kennedy a central figure. Not only was the committee's chairman not included in the discussions, he was not told about them. Lee White, who was coordinating them, was to explain that he simply forgot. "I checked with every damned guy in government, I think, except Johnson! There was nothing deliberate about it. . . . There's no god-damned rational explanation for it except [that] in my mind . . . he wasn't part of the machinery." He wasn't even told about the executive order on the day, June 22, it was issued. "I've never seen a more surprised, disappointed and annoyed guy than Lyndon Johnson when the President of the United States issued [the] executive order changing the jurisdiction of his committee," White says. He accepted the slight with as much dignity—"about as good as a guy can get when he gets a mackerel in the face!"—as possible.

And then there were two meetings of the committee itself.

With the battle of Birmingham still raging and civil rights on everyone's tongue, Conference Room B at the State Department was filled for both meetings, with Johnson and Hobart Taylor, his young black supporter from Detroit whom he had made the CEEO's executive director, sitting at the head of the long conference table: around it high-ranking officials—Cabinet members, agency heads, liberal luminaries like UAW President Reuther and Dean Francis B. Sayre of the Washington National Cathedral—and sitting against the wall a full complement of their staffers. And, unfortunately for Johnson, also present at the first of the meetings was Lady Bird's brother Antonio Taylor, whom he had invited so that Taylor could get a view of him in action.

When Johnson called this meeting to order, the attorney general's chair was vacant, but he came in a few minutes later, Burke Marshall behind him, and, recalls Reuther's assistant Jack Conway, "within a matter of three or four minutes, the Vice President found himself on the defensive because Bobby just tore in," demanding precise statistics on Negro employment in federal agencies in Birmingham from Hobart Taylor. When Taylor tried to explain that the statistics were not yet available, because a new form that would show them had just been developed, Kennedy demanded, "Well, where is the form?" Taylor said it was in the final stages of preparation by the Budget Bureau and that he expected it to be ready shortly—and to have the statistics by the next meeting. Kennedy was not satisfied. "Where in the Budget Bureau is it?" he demanded. "He wanted to know where it was right then because he would expedite its completion," Judge Marjorie Lawson says. The young man sitting beside Johnson—the man he had brought in to run the committee—"was now getting quite upset." When an "embarrassed" Johnson tried to intervene, on his face a dark flush and his voice almost inaudible, Kennedy "snapped a few more questions" not at his aide but at him. "At this point Bob turned to someone and wanted to know about the [Negro] apprenticeship program." But while the official he addressed was still talking, "Bob got up and without a word to excuse himself" walked out of the room.

The second meeting, on July 18, was a repeat performance by Kennedy, except that this time—after again arriving late—he lashed into not only Taylor but also into Johnson's other man on the committee, NASA director James Webb, firing a barrage of questions at him, as Webb, not knowing the answers, kept turning to an aide named Hartson, behind him—who, it became clear, didn't know them either. When Webb tried to defend Hartson, Kennedy interrupted. "Excuse me. This committee and the President of the United States are interested in this program. I don't see that the job will be done. . . . This gentleman over here [Hartson] that spent a year and a half on this program . . . I don't think he is going to get the job done. . . . I am trying to ask some questions. I don't think I am able to get the answers, to tell you the truth."

"It was," Conway says, "a pretty brutal business, very sharp. It brought tensions between Johnson and Kennedy right out on the table and very hard. Everybody was sweating under the armpits. . . . And then, finally, after completely humiliating Webb and making the Vice President look like a fraud and shutting up Hobart Taylor completely," Kennedy abruptly stood up. Johnson had started trying to explain the situation to him. "For your information, Mr. Attorney General, we of the committee have met with the leading agencies who have the most contracts, namely the Department of Defense. . . . The Defense Department told us they had some 30 or 40 people working on this. . . . Mr. Webb doesn't do that. This man here [Hartson] doesn't do it anymore than you try to call a case in the Department of Justice. You have got a District Attorney down there that does that." To Judge Lawson, "It was very obvious that he was angry . . . but he was clearly more in control, or more dignified in the encounter, than Bob was." But as he was speaking, Kennedy started walking out of the room. Then, changing his mind, he walked around the table to where Conway was sitting, shook his hand, and stood there chatting with him, in Conway's words, "about how things were going here, there, and every place," as casual and relaxed as if nothing else was going on—and then, while Johnson was still talking to him, walked out the door.

As the door closed behind him, "There was a great silence for a while" before the meeting resumed, Judge Lawson says. If Bobby Kennedy was still trying to get revenge for Los Angeles, he got a full measure of it that day.

AFTER THAT MEETING, Lyndon Johnson wasn't wound up anymore. "In the late summer of 1963," Harry McPherson says, Johnson "looked miserable," more depressed, Horace Busby says, "than I had ever seen him. Nothing to do—frustrated." Friends invited to swim and have dinner at The Elms were shocked when they saw him in a bathing suit. His weight had always fluctuated wildly; now he had gone from thin to fat—very fat. "His belly . . . enormous," McPherson says. "He looked absolutely gross." His face was flushed and mottled—"maybe he had been drinking a good deal." Sitting by the pool, he seemed unable to relax for a moment. Grabbing the phone impatiently, he would make a call, his conversation jerking without transition from one topic to another. Then, hanging up abruptly, he would make another call, and another.

The fact that Robert Kennedy had not only harassed him ("humiliated" was the word he used; "he humiliated me") but had done so in public (and, in fact, in a setting—a meeting packed with government officials—that ensured that the scene would become known throughout the capital) had, in Johnson's mind, the most ominous implications: that it was no longer just 1968 that the Kennedys were thinking about but 1964; that they must be planning to drop him from the ticket in the next election because Bobby would never have made him look ineffectual and incompetent if he was still going to be his brother's running mate. He felt his suspicions were confirmed when Kennedy loyalists began spreading the story of the meeting around Washington.

Washington had had its suspicions even before the confrontation. By the summer of 1963, speculation was rife that he was going to be dumped from the ticket.

Dampening the speculation was the fact that every time the President was asked about the rumors, he denied them. "There have been rumors in print and out that Vice President Johnson might be dropped," a reporter asked him on one occasion. "I am sure that the Vice President will be on the ticket if he chooses to run," Kennedy replied. "We were fortunate to have him before—and would again. I don't know where such a rumor would start." "Assuming that you run next year, would you want Lyndon Johnson on the ticket, and do you expect he'll be on the ticket," he was asked at another press conference. "Yes, to both of these questions," Kennedy replied. "That is correct." Denying the rumors in private, he was equally emphatic. When Ben Bradlee asked him, after a quiet dinner for the two men and their wives upstairs in the White House in October, if he was considering dumping Johnson, he said, "That's preposterous on the face of it. We've got to carry Texas in '64, and maybe Georgia." When George Smathers, riding with him on Air Force One in November, said, "Everybody on the Hill says Bobby is trying to knock Johnson off the ticket," he said, "George, you have *some* intelligence, I presume. . . . Why would we want to knock Lyndon Johnson off the ticket? Can you see me now in a terrible fight with Lyndon Johnson, which means I'll blow the South? I don't want to be elected, do you mean? You know, I love this job, I love every second of it. . . . I don't want to get licked . . . and he's going to be my vice president because he helps me."

"What do you mean, am I going to dump Johnson?" he had demanded when his friend Paul B. (Red) Fay visited him in the Oval Office in the spring. "What do you ask a question like that for? Of course I'm not. He's doing an excellent job in the most thankless position in Washington. He's my man for the job. He's going to be my man in '64, and I don't know why you're asking." No denials could have been more unequivocal. John Kennedy's assurances, in public and private, that Johnson would be on the ticket were, in fact, as unequivocal as his assurances in 1960 that Johnson would not be on the ticket. No one could have echoed the denials more firmly than Robert Kennedy—"There was no plan to dump Lyndon Johnson," he would say in his oral histories. "There was never any discussion about dropping him"—unless it was Lyndon Johnson in his later years. "Reports . . . that I was going to be dumped from the ticket . . . were rumors and nothing more," he wrote in his autobiography. "I had every reason to

believe that he intended for us to go forward together. . . . What some people did
not understand was that our relationship . . . had always been one of mutual
respect, admiration, and cooperation." The denials made their way into the historical record. "The ticket was definitely to be the same," Arthur Schlesinger
would write in 1978; he knew because Kennedy's brother-in-law and campaign
strategist Stephen Smith had told him so—"emphatically." Indeed it has become
an historical axiom, totally accepted, that there was never any serious discussion
of dropping Johnson from the ticket; that, as Schlesinger put it in 1980, "There
was no discussion. This idea is total fantasy." "I have never encountered anything
that corroborates that story" (the story that he would be dropped), journalist Max
Frankel says, adding that in addition to the political considerations there was
John Kennedy's personality: "Whether he would have . . . been capable of the
ultimate, really, destruction of Lyndon Johnson—I would doubt it." Johnson's
conviction at the time that he would be dumped—and in complete contrast to
later statements, his conviction at the time was firm ("In the back room they were
quoting Bobby, saying I was going to be taken off the ticket")—is explained
away by amateur psychoanalysis; "obsessed" is the word Reedy uses to describe
this conviction. "His complaints against Bobby Kennedy may have bordered on
the paranoiac," is Bobby Baker's analysis; "among the other things Bobby was
doing to him was to drive him from the national ticket." The axiom has endured
to this day. Yet, in fact, as summer turned to fall in 1963, the question of whether
Lyndon Johnson would be on John Kennedy's ticket again was beginning to be
shrouded in ambiguities.

His value to a Kennedy ticket had rested on very solid ground in 1960:
Kennedy had needed at least a few southern states, and in particular Texas, to win
the presidency—and the best way to win these states was to have Lyndon Johnson as his running mate. By 1963, however, that ground was shifting beneath
Kennedy's feet—and it was shifting fast. In 1960, Kennedy's civil rights record
had been inoffensive enough to minimize the antagonism of southern white voters, and therefore it was possible for him to win some southern states and Texas
if he had a southern running mate. But in 1963, there had been his outmaneuver-
ing of Governor Wallace, and on June 13 he had delivered an inspiring televised
address in which he said that civil rights was "a moral issue"—"as old as the
scriptures and . . . as clear as the American Constitution." And not paranoia but
only polls were required to explain Lyndon Johnson's fears.

One, taken in September, 1963, by the Democratic National Committee,
showed that if the election were held then, Kennedy would lose not only Texas
but Georgia, Louisiana, Arkansas and both Carolinas, the states whose electoral
votes were largely responsible for his victory in '60. Another, by the Gallup
Organization, showed that winning the South would not only be much more difficult for him in 1964, but that it might, in fact, be all but impossible if the Republican candidate was one whose stance on civil rights was attractive to that region,
and by the fall of 1963, it was becoming increasingly likely that the Republican

candidate would be one with a very attractive stance: Senator Barry Goldwater of Arizona. Gallup pitted Kennedy against Goldwater head to head in a thirteen-state bloc, the eleven of the Old Confederacy and Kentucky and Oklahoma on its borders—the result was Kennedy 41 percent, Goldwater 59 percent.

And Johnson's own stance on civil rights had changed, of course, and while it had given him a new popularity in liberal precincts of the North, it hadn't had the same effect in the cotton mills of the South—as conversations in the Senate cloakroom showed. "I don't know what's got into Lyndon, but he's outtalking Bobby Kennedy in civil rights," one southern senator said. "Lyndon never had a more devoted admirer than myself," said another. "Now I wouldn't give two cents for his winning an election in my state." And those mills were significant to Kennedy's re-election plans. Johnson had held the South for Kennedy in 1960; he might not be able to hold it in 1964. Democratic political strategists, interviewed by the *Philadelphia Inquirer* in the summer of 1963, "said they doubted whether . . . Johnson would be able to overcome anti-Kennedy sentiment in the Deep South stirred by civil rights unrest." "The President and his political advisers probably have written off the South for 1964 on the civil rights issue," the *Cleveland Plain Dealer* said. "If they haven't, they should."

Polls were showing, as well, that holding the South might no longer be imperative for Kennedy's re-election, so long as he did better in the North than he had in 1960, and they were showing also that his popularity was holding fairly steady there, at about 60 percent. Strength in the North (holding the big northern states he had won in 1960 and picking up states such as Ohio that he had lost) and picking up also some electoral votes in the West, most importantly California's thirty-two, that he had lost in '60 might be the key to victory in '64; it might be more important he have a running mate who added strength to the ticket in those areas rather than in the South. Which led of course to the subject of Lyndon Johnson. "If the solid South is to be written off in 1964, the question is whether Mr. Johnson will be retained on the ticket and if so what his function will be," the *New York Times* asked. The question was being asked more and more by Democratic strategists, however much the Kennedys denied it—asked so frequently that in October the syndicated columnists Robert S. Allen and Paul Scott could write that a "new political strategy [is] being hammered out at the party's secret deliberations," a strategy which "calls for major Democratic efforts to increase the party's vote in all the northern industrial areas to offset expected Republican gains in the South." Specific names were starting to be mentioned: Pat Brown of California, for example. If the Democrats have "written off the South for 1964 . . . the question becomes whether they should recognize this fact publicly and go west for a vice presidential candidate. . . . Kennedy strategists are saying that they may have to carry California to win next year. But California is where Barry seems to be running best. Will the President decide that his best chance lies with a Californian or some other westerner as his running mate?"

• • •

AND THEN THERE WAS the situation in Lyndon Johnson's own state. Carrying Texas against the conservative tide rising there had, of course, been hard even in '60 (even with those votes from the Rio Grande Valley), and since '60 that tide, strengthened by a backlash against civil rights, had been rising even faster. In 1961 John Tower became the first Republican United States senator elected from Texas since Reconstruction—and, as the United Press reported on October 2, "The mere mention of Goldwater as the GOP presidential nominee in 1964 has caused thousands of conservatives" to change party affiliation, sending them into a booming Republican Party in Texas. Were the Arizona conservative to be the nominee, state GOP leaders were predicting, he would carry the state by about the same 200,000-vote margin Eisenhower had rolled up. Kennedy's approval ratings in Texas, which had been slipping steadily, falling to 59 percent in May, had been plummeting since then, and in September, according to the state's definitive Belden Poll, were down to 50 percent. Johnson's popularity, tied to his, had dropped to the same level.

His identification with Jack Kennedy was only one of his problems in Texas. What George Reedy had warned against two years before—that he would be "forgotten" in his home state—had in fact occurred: after three years of trying to stay out of the news, to the mass of the state's voters he was no longer nearly as towering a figure as he had been. And with the Texans who mattered most in the state's politics—the reactionary, in fact ultra-reactionary, business establishment: the oilmen and big government contractors, who had always been the source of his most important support, financial and otherwise—with these men his position was even more precarious. Haters of Roosevelt, of the New Deal, of liberals in general, they had never really forgiven him for going on Kennedy's ticket; they had taken his decision to do so, after they had contributed so generously to his campaign against Kennedy, as an act of betrayal. And that decision had, in their eyes, been only the beginning of his apostasy. They had believed all those years—because he had made them believe—that he felt the same way as they did about people of color. ("Basically, Lyndon was more conservative, more practical than people understand," George Brown says. "You get right down to the nut-cutting, he was practical. He was for the Niggers, he was for labor, he was for the little boys, but by God . . . he was as practical as anyone.") Reading what Lyndon was saying about civil rights now, they wondered if he had been deceiving them all along.

During the three years since 1960, moreover, there had been what was, in their minds, a more mortal sin, one that involved not philosophy but money. To cool their rage over his acceptance of the vice presidential nomination, he had told them that by becoming a part (an important part: the "Number Two Man") of the Kennedy Administration, he would be in a position to moderate its policies from the inside, to act as a rein on liberal tendencies, and in particular he had let them understand that he would be able to be a force within the Administration against the tendencies that mattered most to them: tendencies to regulate, and reduce, their wealth. Business regulation, tax reform, all forms of government intervention in their enterprises—these matters, as Brown & Root lobbyist Frank C. ("Posh") Oltorf was to put it, "transcended ideology. . . . That's how they viewed politics. 'Any son of a bitch who makes me a million dollars can't be all bad.' As long as you put dollars in their pockets, they'd forgive your ideology." When it became apparent to them that Johnson did not in fact have the power to protect them from the liberal impulse—*that,* to them, was the unforgivable sin. Early in 1963, a quote from a Texas businessman appeared in the "Washington Whispers" column of *U.S. News & World Report:* "Lyndon as vice president just can't do as much for Texas any more as he could as Senate Leader." That quote was mild; what was being said about Lyndon Johnson in the Petroleum Club of Houston and the Riata Club of Dallas and the other big business watering holes of Texas wasn't. "He had promised to protect them," says Ed Clark, attorney for some of the biggest of them, "and he couldn't deliver. He couldn't *deliver!*" Kennedy was still proposing tax reform legislation, bills to close tax loopholes. "*Loopholes!* Those were *their* loopholes he [Kennedy] was talking about!," Posh Oltorf says. In particular, there was the oil depletion allowance. Although the Kennedy plan ostensibly kept the rate of the allowance at $27\frac{1}{2}$ percent, the oilmen's attorneys, analyzing the measure, had concluded that changes proposed by the administration in the tax code would cut the effective rate to $17\frac{1}{2}$ percent. To the rest of the world, such a reduction would be only justice—or at least the beginning of justice. To the oilmen, it was robbery. The change—together with the elimination of some of the hundred hidden tax breaks for oil in the Internal Revenue Code—would cost them millions, perhaps billions, of dollars a year. These big businessmen who controlled so much of the state's political machinery were no longer enthusiastic about controlling it on behalf of Lyndon Johnson, not at all. He was "losing some of his grip on the . . . party machinery of that state," *U.S. News* reported.

As Johnson's star had been waning in Texas, furthermore, another star— that of John Connally, elected Governor in 1962—had been rising. The same Belden Poll that showed Kennedy-Johnson's approval at 50 percent put Connally's at 61 percent, and likely to go higher; formerly undecided voters had begun swinging over to him. Lyndon Johnson's onetime assistant was heading rapidly toward the pinnacle he would one day occupy as a three-term governor, one of the most popular and powerful in the history of the state. No sooner had Connally moved into the Governor's Mansion in Austin, moreover, than he began to demonstrate that the organizational and political skills he had deployed for Lyndon Johnson were just as effective on his own behalf. Sitting on the fence of his ranch in Floresville just after sunrise one morning decades later, watching Mexican vaqueros exercising his stable of quarter horses, he would say, "One thing I'm proudest of: We built the strongest organization in the history of the state while I was Governor." His pride was justified, and the base of his power was the people who controlled Texas: the powerful conservative establishment. Lyndon might have turned liberal; they didn't have to worry about John. He was already, in the first year of his governorship, showing that he was willing to lower taxes on banks and business, and to fight proposals by liberals in the legislature for increases in the minimum wage. They saw, also, that he was, as governor, talking the same way he had talked as Lyndon Johnson's aide and Sid Richardson's lawyer, as he had been talking all his life; he shared their views—with the fervency of the true believer. Johnson and Connally "still had the same political base," Joe Kilgore says, but, as the congressman adds, it had become "just a little bit more John's political base than Lyndon's."

Adding to the significance for the Kennedys of the Texas businessmen's affection for the governor they were starting to call "Big John," was the pivotal role that Texas traditionally played in the financing of Democratic presidential campaigns. The Kennedys were counting on major help from Texas now. And the businessmen would contribute at Connally's direction. "John controlled the money in the state now," Kilgore says. All through 1962, the President had been asking Johnson to arrange a fund-raising trip to Texas, and there had been no result. The President may once have thought that Johnson could again deliver the Texas money, but by 1963 the White House had begun to recognize that that was no longer the case. For two decades, Lyndon Johnson had been the key to the electoral votes and the money of the great province in the Southwest. He wasn't anymore, and he knew it. He was telephoning Kilgore "almost every night" now, and the congressman felt he knew why: "because I was close to John. He was scared to death that John would control the state in 1964, and might not be controlling it entirely for him."

Kilgore, who had traveled the Valley with Johnson and Connally during two long election campaigns, knew Johnson's worries were baseless; that however much the quarter-century-long ties between the two men—the "loyalty," the psychological ties—that bound Connally to Johnson might fray, in the end they would hold. "Of course, John would have been for him when the chips were down," he says. But Lyndon wasn't confident of that: the "falling out" had to come to an end. "After the talk [started] of Kennedy replacing him in 1964, we were in constant contact," Connally says dryly. "He and I talked about" the possibility that he would be dropped from the ticket. "He told me, 'Bobby's around talking about dumping me. We've got to show him that we've got the power down here.'" Connally knew that Johnson was calling him now because he needed him. "He knew I controlled the Texas delegation"—and Texas, he was to tell the author. And he knew why Johnson and Kennedy needed him. "I had frankly been elected by the people that President Kennedy needed most, by the moderates and conservatives of the state. . . . [They] were not supporting him" and "he was looking at a tough election, at least in our part of the country, in 1964." He understood that when Johnson talked about the necessity of showing the Kennedys that "we've got the power down here," he really meant showing the President that he, Lyndon Johnson, had power—that he still had power. Connally was very careful to try to leave that impression in the White House, and to make it clear that Johnson would be the same asset to the ticket in Texas that he had always been, and that he, the governor of Texas, considered it imperative that Johnson be Kennedy's running mate. After one conversation with Connally, Jack Kennedy told Evelyn Lincoln, "The one thing I noticed above everything else was his concern about Lyndon being on the ticket."

Jack Kennedy was not an easy man to fool, however. Johnson "did not want the President to see for himself how little prestige and influence the Vice President then had in his own home state," Ken O'Donnell was to write—in a comment that shows that the President *had* seen. "The more liberal Texas Democrats . . . had always been against him," O'Donnell wrote, and "since he had joined the New Frontier, his fellow conservatives had turned against him."

By early 1963, the President was becoming quite insistent on arranging that fund-raising trip to Texas, but Johnson, aware that funds would be raised only on Connally's say-so, had had to admit that the matter should be arranged through the governor. And Connally, "who had," as O'Donnell understood, "no desire to be marked as a Kennedy supporter in Texas, had been stalling off the President," using as an excuse the fact that he was in the midst of his first legislative session as governor. Finally, during a presidential swing through the West in June, Kennedy, Connally, and Johnson were alone in a hotel room in El Paso. "Well, Lyndon, are we ever going to get this trip to Texas worked out?" Kennedy asked—but as Connally knew, while "he was addressing Vice President Johnson, he was speaking to me." And Johnson's reply—"Well, the Governor is here, Mr. President, let's find out"—was a tacit admission that decisions about the trip were Connally's to make.

"I knew at that point my string had run out," Connally was to recall, but he asked Kennedy what kind of a trip he had in mind, and Kennedy proposed that the trip revolve around Johnson's birthday, August 27, and that there be five separate fund-raising dinners in the state's five principal cities—Dallas, Houston, Fort Worth, San Antonio and Austin. Connally, shocked at the scope of the proposal, said he would "like to think about that." Holding the dinners on Johnson's birthday would be "a serious mistake" because it was too hot in Texas in August; people weren't interested in politics in August: it was, he told Kennedy, "the worst month of the year to have a fundraising affair in Texas."

During the summer, Johnson kept trying to persuade Connally to accept the multi-dinner proposal, and Connally kept replying, "Well, that is a mistake." Kennedy was later to tell his wife that "John Connally wanted to show that he was independent and could run on his own and . . . he wanted to show that he didn't need Lyndon Johnson." Indeed, he didn't, and the polls that summer were proving that, and the Kennedys read polls. And if Connally didn't need Lyndon Johnson, was Johnson really what Jack Kennedy needed in Texas? If Connally was more popular and also controlled the money he needed, perhaps it was Connally he should be working through instead. Furthermore, Connally would be running for re-election in November, 1964. Whether or not Lyndon Johnson was Jack Kennedy's running mate, the name of a powerful, popular Texan would be on the ballot with him.

The whole situation in Texas was an irritant to Kennedy. His Vice President was from Texas, yet he was being told it would be difficult to carry the state. "That thought irked him," Connally was to say. "We shouldn't have a hard race in Texas," the President told the governor.

A FEUD, PERSONAL AS WELL as political, between Connally and United States Senator Ralph W. Yarborough had split the state's Democrats into two bitterly hostile factions. A presidential candidate wants a united party behind him in key states when he is running; "The last thing we want is a big political fight in Texas in 1964," O'Donnell had told Yarborough back in January. But since then the feud had grown only more bitter, and the Vice President wasn't helping to mend it, and Kennedy had become aware that he *couldn't* help much, that, as the President was to tell Ben Bradlee that fall, Johnson had become "a less viable mediator than he had been." If Johnson wasn't the best person to raise money for him in Texas, if he wasn't particularly popular in Texas, if he wasn't a particularly viable mediator in Texas—what was the reason to keep him on the ticket?

ON SEPTEMBER 2, 1963, Johnson was to leave for Stockholm and a fifteen-day tour of five Scandinavian nations, and about a week before the trip he told Ken O'Donnell that, as Charles Bartlett relates, "He'd like to see the President before he went and have a little bit of a send-off from the President to boost his own role."

"One of the weaknesses of the Kennedy White House staff was that individuals became rather arrogant," Bartlett was to recall. "O'Donnell said it was impossible." Reedy went hat in hand to Kennedy's military aide, Major General Ted Clifton, who went directly to the President, and Kennedy said that Johnson's plane could touch down at Hyannis Port on its way to Stockholm and the Vice President could have a brief talk. Kennedy had asked a houseguest, his old friend Red Fay, if he'd like to sit in on the talk, and Fay was "strongly conscious," as he was to write, "of the contrasts in the room," the President in a sport shirt and blazer, the Vice President too formal in both appearance—overdressed, as someone overdresses out of insecurity, "in a double-breasted blue suit that seemed unusually somber in contrast to Kennedy's casual attire"—and manner, sitting "forward uncomfortably on the edge of his chair," very "deferential, . . . very grateful" to have been granted the audience. "The apparent uneasiness and unsureness of the Vice President surprised me," Fay was to write.

The conversation couldn't have done much to boost his confidence. After discussing his Scandinavian itinerary, he said he would like permission to add a visit to Poland, saying, as Fay recalls, that "it would be a dramatic sign of our desire to be friendly with the countries behind the Iron Curtain . . . that have shown a desire for freedom."

Permission was refused. "Has this been cleared by the State Department?" Kennedy asked, and when Johnson said it hadn't because he wanted to get Kennedy's reaction first, Kennedy said he didn't think it was a good idea "at this time." "Maybe some time later," he said.

Then Kennedy asked to see the prepared speeches for the trip, and when Reedy provided him copies, not only read them, but edited them, turning the pages rapidly, crossing out paragraphs and lines. When he finished he simply handed Johnson the pages. They were "very good," he said. "I have crossed out a few short sections which won't hurt the speech[es] but which are better left unsaid." A few minutes later, the visit was over; Johnson and Reedy were out the door. Johnson hadn't been asked for comment on Kennedy's changes; he had been treated like a speechwriter, and not a particularly respected one at that.

ON OCTOBER 4, John Connally flew up to Washington to participate in a number of meetings on Texas problems, including one with President Kennedy to make definite plans for the President's trip to the state. He had told Johnson he was coming to Washington, and Johnson had invited him for dinner that evening at The Elms. But he hadn't told Johnson he was meeting with the President—and neither had the President.

Connally was to say that when he entered the Oval Office he "frankly was a bit surprised that the Vice President wasn't there. But he wasn't." The meeting was very cordial. Connally proposed that Kennedy's visit, for which the dates of November 21 and November 22 had been tentatively set, include visits to five cities, as Kennedy wanted, but only one fund-raising affair: a hundred-dollar-per-plate dinner in Austin, on the 22nd. Otherwise, Connally said, " 'people down there are going to think that all you are interested in is the financial rape of the state,' and I used those words," and Kennedy said he would accept Connally's judgment.

When Connally arrived at The Elms that evening, Johnson "already knew that I had been with the President." His first words were: "Well, did *you all* get the trip worked out?" The Vice President, he was to say, "was considerably irritated with me." "Irritated," Connally said, wasn't quite the right word. "Hurt" was the right word. But what could Connally say? "I suppose you think I don't have any interest in what is happening in Texas," Johnson said. "No," Connally said, "I know you are extremely interested in what is happening in Texas."

"Why didn't you tell me?" Johnson asked. Connally said he had assumed he knew about the appointment, "trying to alibi any way I could because I recognized that he was really irritated about it." But Johnson kept pressing him. Connally didn't want to hurt him any more than he had already been hurt, but he finally had to give him the only answer he could: "I assumed if the President wanted you there, you would be there." But he and Lyndon Johnson had had so many years together. "I'm sorry," he said. "I should have talked to you before I went in to see the President." While he had apologized, however, the fact remained that the President hadn't wanted Johnson there. The arrangements for a major political event that the Administration was holding in his state had been made—and he hadn't been told about them.

10

The Protégé

IN OCTOBER, 1963, also, there was gathering, over the darkened landscape of Lyndon Johnson's life, a thundercloud even more threatening than those already overhead.

The first faint rumble of the approaching storm had come on that Scandinavian trip—on Friday, September 13, in Copenhagen, just after he had returned to the Royal Hotel from luncheon at the palace with the Danish king and queen.

It came in a telephone call from Walter Jenkins. Reporters didn't know about the call. All they saw was that, as Bart McDowell of the Associated Press was to put it, on that day in Copenhagen "there was a change in" Lyndon Johnson's "personality . . . a great change." There were changes in his schedule, too. "Whatever plans that were on the docket for him, he scratched and spent the entire day locked up in his room." Several times that afternoon, Reedy emerged to deliver announcements: the trip was being shortened; "The press of business in the United States made it impossible" for Johnson to visit Greenland on Monday, as had been planned; the Greenland trip was canceled; the Vice President would be returning to the United States a day earlier than had been scheduled.

Those would not be Reedy's last announcements of schedule changes. A full-dress inspection of the Danish Navy scheduled for Saturday was canceled, as were other events for Sunday, so that, as a Danish newspaper put it, "An official guest could hardly see less of Denmark." On Sunday, in fact, the Vice President didn't emerge from his suite the entire day. Reedy told newsmen that, as one of them recalls, Johnson had remained in his bedroom, "closed the door, and spent the day on the telephone."

"We assumed that it was—heaven knows what," McDowell says. Reedy tried to scotch rumors that the Vice President was ill, or exhausted from the trip, but "the press of business" was the only explanation he had been authorized to give. "We were just in the dark . . . totally," McDowell says.

Sunday evening, at 8:25, Johnson finally emerged from his suite with Lady Bird, his entourage behind him, for the lone event that day that had not been canceled: a visit to Copenhagen's famous Tivoli Gardens amusement park, where he was to appear with the Tivoli Marching Band. His lips were pressed into a thin line, and his eyes were narrow and hard. "He had spent the whole day on the phone, and when he finally emerged to march in this lighthearted parade, he was obviously very grim and preoccupied," McDowell says. The mood of the people walking behind him reflected his. "You could sense a change in the whole party." No one in the group said a word as they walked downstairs to the waiting limousines.

His expression hardly changed during the parade. It would have been a festive scene as the band, colorful in white trousers, red jackets and tall black bearskin shakos, its tubas and trombones glinting in the light of bright lanterns, marched through the park's gaily colored thrill rides and turreted mock castles, playing lively tunes—except that the tall man in an overcoat striding with it was "as grim as a pallbearer."

Though the Greenland visit had been canceled, there was still a visit to Iceland scheduled for Monday, and a formal state dinner given by Iceland's prime minister, and Johnson had been scheduled to fly back to Washington on Tuesday, arriving in the evening. But he told the State Department aides who had been rescheduling and rescheduling the trip that it was very important that he get back to Washington earlier than that, and he left the dinner early and took off Monday night, setting down at Andrews at one o'clock in the morning.

THE CALL HAD BEEN about Bobby Baker.

On September 9, Ralph Hill, the president of a firm that installed vending machines for coffee, candy and cigarettes in factories and collected the profits from them, had filed a lawsuit in United States District Court in Washington against another vending machine company, the Serv-U Corporation—and against Baker. The suit alleged that Baker had taken $5,600 from Hill to use his influence with the defense contractor North American Aviation Corporation so that one of its subcontractors would allow Hill to place his vending machines in its plant—and that Baker had then turned around and persuaded the subcontractor to oust Hill, and replace his company's machines with Serv-U's machines; that Baker had thus, as one writer later put it, "taken money to use his influence with a defense contractor and had then double-crossed the man who bought him." Jack Landau, a reporter for the *Washington Post* who covered the District Court, was given a tip that there might be something interesting in the suit. The matter seemed minor—a dispute over a contract between businessmen—and Baker, an official of Serv-U assured Landau, had no connection with the company, and, it was later to be recalled, there was "considerable initial soul-searching by the *Post*'s editors" over whether to run a story about it, but it had finally been decided to do so, and on Thursday, September 12, while Johnson was in Scandinavia, the story was published, buried inside the newspaper's city section, but with the headline SENATE OFFICIAL IS NAMED IN INFLUENCE SUIT. A couple of *Post* reporters were assigned to look further into the matter, as were a reporter or two from other papers—and by Friday morning, reporters had started calling Jenkins, which is when he telephoned Johnson in Copenhagen. And by Sunday—the day Johnson spent the entire day in his room, the day he became so "grim" and "preoccupied"—Jenkins had other news to report. The reporters had come across the fact that the vending industry's trade journal, *Vend* magazine, had been looking into Serv-U for some time and, in fact, was about to run an article on the company in its next issue. And the article's author, G. R. Schreiber, had allowed the *Post* to see the article, on condition that the newspaper not print any of its material before the magazine appeared—and the reporters, having seen it, had begun calling Jenkins with more serious questions because, *Vend*'s article said, with detailed documentation, that Baker, whom the article identified as the "protégé of Vice President Lyndon B. Johnson," was, despite all the assurances, not only connected with Serv-U but was in fact one of its stockholders, and in addition had substantial business dealings with the company; that the company, which had been founded in December, 1961, had enjoyed "remarkable" growth in the less than two years it had been in business; that in fact its annual gross income (the income of this firm intimately connected with a Senate employee whose salary was $19,611 per year) was "at or in excess of" $3.5 million—and that every cent of that amount came from companies that were in the aerospace industry and that were all "sizable contractors with Uncle Sam." And *Vend* reported that Ralph Hill's suit alleged that Baker had obtained the vending machine contracts for Serv-U because, "as Secretary of the [Senate] Majority, [he] was able to, and did, represent . . . that he was in a position to assist in securing defense contracts." "In view of the phenomenal growth of Serv-U over a 20-month period in a handful of plants owned by corporations who do billions of dollars in business for Uncle Sam," *Vend* said, "the question of any relationship between Serv-U and [Baker] needs an answer."

WHAT JOHNSON WAS DOING behind the closed door of his suite in Copenhagen was telephoning—and panicking. "He panicked on Bobby," George Reedy was to say. He "absolutely panicked." He was scared—"timorous," in Reedy's word. "The way that man could panic. And when he panicked, he had this animal instinct: cover up." With reporters badgering him for an explanation for the Vice President's day-long seclusion in his suite, Reedy tried to tell Johnson he had to give them some explanation, but the response was a shout: "Don't say a thing!" When Reedy, as always, tried to reason with him, Johnson said, "Don't tell them a *thing*!" and went into his bedroom, slamming the door in Reedy's face.

Johnson telephoned Abe Fortas, who had gotten him out of some of the tightest spots in his career—the federal judge's decision to hold hearings on the vote-counting in the 1948 election, for example. But those had been legal difficulties. Fortas was indeed what Johnson considered him, one of the sharpest of lawyers, but this new problem was at the moment a public relations problem, and public relations was not the area of Fortas' expertise. When, however, he gave Johnson advice that fit in with the "cover-up" instinct, Johnson followed it. Fortas suggested that reporters should be told that he, Johnson, really wasn't all that close to Bobby Baker, and never had been—that Baker had been selected as Senate secretary not by Johnson but by vote of all the Democratic senators; that, in fact, he had hardly seen Baker since he had left the Senate.

"Oh my God, that was incredible," Reedy was to say. "That was just stupid. Abe was the one who came up with this. . . . 'All the Senate Democrats elected Bobby secretary of the majority.' Well, for the love of God, they all elected him because LBJ told them to"—and, of course, everyone knew that. While Reedy didn't have to deliver that line himself, at least not for a while—the reporters who were accompanying Johnson in Denmark knew nothing about the matter— Johnson telephoned Jenkins and told him to take that line with the reporters asking him questions in Washington; meanwhile, he told Jenkins, he was rushing home.

JENKINS HAD RECEIVED one call that was particularly disturbing. Harry Provence, editor of the *Waco News-Tribune* and an editor who had been working closely, and subserviently, with Johnson for years, had telephoned from Texas to say that one of the reporters who was looking into the lawsuit had already written a draft of a story about it, and had sent it to him.

The reporter, fifty-three-year-old Sarah McClendon, wrote a column that ran weekly in the *News-Tribune* and six other Texas newspapers and was also a one-woman news bureau who submitted articles to newspapers around the country and to a small New York–based wire service, the North American Newspaper Alliance, in hopes that they would publish them. She was regarded by the rest of the Washington press corps, in the words of one article, with "a mixture of derision and respect," the former for her practice of shouting down other reporters at presidential news conferences—in a loud, shrill, gravelly Texas voice—and asking accusatory questions that were all too often based on conspiracy theories, the latter for the courage she displayed in her struggles to make a career (and support her daughter; her husband had abandoned her when he learned she was pregnant) as a woman journalist in Washington at a time when the National Press Club didn't even admit women. "She didn't know how to be discreet," her colleague Andrea Mitchell was to say. "She was as aggressive as hell. Objectivity was not her concern. That was bred from years of having to be outrageous to be heard." And while her stories were sometimes filled with overstatements and unsupported generalizations, this time her story was understated—and filled with facts.

McClendon's article did not merely give the details of the lawsuit against Serv-U, it identified one of Baker's co-defendants, Fred Black, as a lobbyist employed by North American Aviation "for the purpose of securing contracts from the United States government," and said Black had worked with Baker to do that. And her article was not limited to the suit, or to Serv-U. It reported that the Senate employee was operating other businesses as well—"businesses of a varied nature in Washington and South Carolina." It reported that he had built and operated the Carousel, a motel in Ocean City, Maryland, that was a "recreation spot for . . . top officials of government." Nor was it limited to Baker's private business interests. He was, the article said, "one of the chief dispensers of lush Democratic campaign funds." And, it said, Baker was Johnson's "protégé and close personal friend."

Provence read McClendon's article to Jenkins over the telephone, and then Jenkins had the editor dictate it to a secretary, and then Jenkins either read it to, or discussed it with, Johnson in Copenhagen. And at about 5:30 on Monday, about the time that Johnson was boarding his plane in Iceland for the flight back to Washington, Jenkins telephoned Ms. McClendon and asked her to come to his office in the Senate Office Building, and, she says, when she arrived, took the line that Abe Fortas had laid out. "We have your story," he told her. "We know that you've been trying to peddle it all over the country for days." The story was "just not true," he said. "Baker is no protégé of Mr. Johnson. Baker was here before Mr. Johnson ever arrived in the Senate. Mr. Johnson hasn't seen him in ages. Mr. Johnson has barely seen him since he became Vice President. He never sees him, on social occasions or otherwise." Ms. McClendon says that Jenkins ordered her to stop trying to "peddle" the story. "We know you're trying to get it out. We want you to stop it. You are not to print this story." It was no use trying to get it out, he said. Telephone calls had been made. "The impression" he "passed on to me [was] that no one would print the story, that all lines of getting the story out . . . had been closed off." She had better stop trying to get it out, he said. "I was given the impression that if I persisted my bosses in Texas were ready to act."

Jenkins' statement that Ms. McClendon had been trying to sell her story was correct; she had sent it to all her other Texas newspapers. His statement that no one would print it was correct—as far as Texas was concerned. Every one of her Texas clients had rejected it.

But, she says, while "Walter knew what papers I worked for, he didn't know about" (or had forgotten about) the North American Newspaper Alliance—"the little wire service in New York." Feeling that "in justice" she owed it to the wire service to tell it that there might be consequences if it sent the story out to its subscribers, she went straight from Jenkins' office to her telephone in the Senate Press Gallery, glanced around to make sure that no one could overhear her, and called the service's editor, warning him that "He'll [Johnson] make trouble. He's going to make an awful lot of trouble."

The editor said it was too late to stop the story from going out. "It's already on the wire." Only one newspaper, the *Des Moines Register,* printed it, but on

Wednesday, September 18, there it was, on the *Register*'s front page, and the next day the *Charleston (South Carolina) Courier* picked it up, and the *Chicago Tribune* assigned its top Washington correspondent, Willard Edwards, to it, and on the 23rd, his article ran; not only did it contain the story of Baker's ties to Serv-U, whose rapid growth made it "the talk of its industry," it also contained the same phrase McClendon had used: "Lyndon's protégé." And that same day, *Vend* was published; "it was," as one account put it, "one of those rare instances when a highly specialized trade journal became a newsstand sellout in Washington"— and suddenly not a few but a pack of reporters were investigating the case of Bobby Baker, and the next Monday he was in a national magazine, *Newsweek,* its headline calling him "THE SERV-U MAN." The text had an amplified identification: Bobby Baker, it said, was "so much the protégé of Lyndon Johnson . . . that he is known as 'Lyndon's Boy.' "

THE CASE THAT HAD BROUGHT Baker to national attention had no direct connection with Lyndon Johnson, and possible connections would never be definitively explored; the only senator who would ever be directly linked with Serv-U was Robert Kerr, one of whose banks had, before his death, made a major loan to the company. The only journalistic references to a possible connection would be hints—all of Serv-U's contracts were "with plants in the aerospace industries," and "among several hats worn by the Vice President is that of chairman of the Space Council"—or gentle sarcasm ("It is, of course, only accident that Lyndon Johnson is chairman of the National Aeronautics and Space Council and that Bobby Baker is his protégé," Murray Kempton wrote in *The New Republic*). And it was also, of course, possible that Baker had been invoking Johnson's name without his consent or knowledge. Johnson did his best to keep such hints to a minimum by, on the record, silence ("Don't tell 'em a thing," he kept saying to Reedy; the single sentence Reedy was authorized to give to reporters was "No comment on a matter pending before court") and, off the record, denials ("Just trying to sell that line that 'he hardly knew Bobby Baker,' " in Reedy's words. "You just couldn't sell that ridiculous story," Reedy says. Johnson kept trying to sell it, however; Reedy was to recall one "horrible" session at which he had to watch as Johnson denied to reporters a relationship which they, often in company with Reedy, had witnessed, year after year, with their own eyes). The Vice President also stopped communicating with Baker, never speaking to him during this period and ordering his aides not to speak to him. The single telephone call from The Elms that Baker received, late one evening, wasn't from the man with whom he had, for years, right up to the time Johnson left on the Scandinavian trip, spoken almost daily.

"Bobby," Lady Bird Johnson said, as Baker recalls the conversation. "Lyndon and I just want you to know we love you. You are like a member of the family and we are so grateful for all you've done for us. Our prayers are with you." Then she changed the subject.

No sound came over the telephone line to indicate that anyone was in the room with Lady Bird, but Baker was sure someone was. "I knew while she was talking on the phone, he was lying right beside her listening," he was to say. He understood the reason for the call, he was to say. It was to keep him friendly. "He probably was . . . concerned that I might become miffed at his inattention and say something harmful to the detriment of his career. . . . He's using Lady Bird to soft-soap me." And, he was to say, he knew the reason for the silence. "I was thinking: *LBJ's right there by her side, but he won't talk to me because he wants to be able to say that he hasn't.*" It was very important to Johnson that he be able to say that, Baker says. "I knew Johnson was petrified that he'd be dragged down" by being connected with him. And, Baker says, there was valid reason for Johnson's concern. If he had revealed their many connections, Bobby Baker would say, "Lyndon B. Johnson might have incurred a mortal wound by these revelations. . . . They could have . . . driven him from office." "He lied. He knew *exactly* what I was doing."

Johnson would be able to go on saying that for quite a long time. From the moment in Copenhagen that he learned of the lawsuit until—almost exactly nine years later—Baker visited him for a day at his ranch in October, 1972, "We spoke not a word and communicated only through intermediaries" (and, even through intermediaries, very rarely). Lyndon Johnson didn't speak to Bobby Baker during the years before 1967, when Baker was convicted of larceny, fraud and tax evasion in an unrelated campaign funds case, and sentenced to three years in prison, or during the years in which Baker was appealing the conviction, or when Baker finally went to jail. And even on that ranch visit, there were moments hurtful to someone who had so worshiped the man he called simply "Leader." When, in 1973, Walter Jenkins telephoned to invite him and his wife, Dorothy, to the ranch, he included the caveat that "This is to be very private. No publicity before, during or after." Meeting the Bakers at the Austin airport, Jenkins "quickly ushered us into his car as if eager to hide us." At the ranch, Johnson tried to create an atmosphere of old times, but Baker noted that Johnson wanted to know about the memoir he had contracted to write. "Is it going to be one of those kiss-and-tell books?" And when Baker asked him to "put in a kind word for me" with the Justice Department, which was investigating him again ("I don't want to go back to jail"), he turned cold. As the Bakers were leaving, Bobby noticed the ranch guest book on a table by the front door. He knew how insistent Johnson was that every visitor sign the book. He stood there until "it became too obvious that my old leader" wasn't going to ask him to sign.

No matter how completely Johnson cut himself off from Baker, however, he couldn't do so in the press. Baker *was,* of course, his protégé—"Lyndon's Boy," "Little Lyndon." Any new revelations about Baker (and the new revelations would come fast upon each other's heels, including the fact that according to a financial statement he filed in 1954—the last financial statement he filed before Johnson had him elected majority secretary—his net worth was $11,025, and in 1963, according to another financial statement he filed, it was $1,791,186) would reflect upon Johnson himself. "The man most harmed by Baker's fall from grace is his long-time sponsor, Vice President Johnson," Doris Fleeson wrote. And while no direct connection may have existed between Johnson and Baker's activities with Serv-U, there were connections between him and Baker in other areas, and when Johnson was leafing through the *Washington Post* on the morning of October 6, and reached page B-6—ever since the first story by Jack Landau had appeared in the city section, he had taken to looking through that section as well as the national section every morning—he realized that at least one of those connections was about to come to light, for the article contained the name of Don B. Reynolds.

REYNOLDS' NAME WAS there because a senator had begun looking into Baker's business dealings—from Johnson's point of view, the worst possible senator.

Although John J. Williams, a Republican from Delaware, was not a junior senator—in 1963, he was a year away from completing his third term and was the ranking Republican member of the Senate Finance Committee—no senator could have been more isolated from the Senate's ruling inner circle, because he wanted it that way.

Williams hadn't been a politician but the owner of a livestock and poultry feed company when, in 1946, at the age of forty-two, he decided to run for the Senate. Arriving in Washington, he shunned the social circuit that politicians frequent; reinforcing his appearance of shyness was his demeanor on the Senate floor, where his voice was so soft that it was often inaudible to reporters in the Press Gallery, who gave him the nickname of "Whispering Willie." A tall, spare man with, as one journalist put it, "friendly lines grooved at the corners of his mouth," he soon had a reputation for fierce independence. Although, as one account was to say, "Washington folklore holds that any Delaware politician jumps when DuPont snaps its fingers in Wilmington," he opposed, and defeated, a proposal that would largely have freed DuPont stockholders from taxes on a particularly profitable company transaction, and, although a rigid conservative about social mores, he voted to censure Joe McCarthy because he disapproved of his methods. The niche he carved out for himself in Washington was an unusual, perhaps unique one. Becoming curious about complaints that "something was wrong" in the Wilmington office of the Internal Revenue Service, in 1949 he launched an investigation, not through a Senate committee with its attendant glare of publicity but largely on his own, that went on for three years and by 1952 had resulted in no fewer than 125 convictions for bribery, extortion and falsification of records. During the years since then, he had conducted more investigations, again not through Senate committees but on his own, relying on information supplied by the Government Accounting Office and on tips from men and women in the government. Of all the scandals involving Harry Truman's "cronies" that had marred his presidency, none resonated more with the public than the one involving Truman's old friend and military aide General Harry Vaughan, described by the press as perhaps the ultimate White House "crony," who helped obtain government contracts and favored treatments for businessmen, and accepted from one of them—and arranged for another to be given to First Lady Bess Truman—an expensive food storage "deep freeze." Although Vaughan said the freezers were merely "an expression of friendship," and although there was nothing illegal in what he had done, the "deep freeze" had, in headlines and cartoons, come to symbolize "the mess in Washington." Williams, who spent three years looking into the Vaughan situation, was to add a dimension to the story: it wasn't only businessmen who had benefited from Vaughan's influence, he revealed, but businessmen associated with the underworld. During the Korean War, one of them had been given a government post "solely upon" Vaughan's recommendation. And during the Eisenhower Administration, Williams, although he was a Republican, had been one of the first senators to demand the investigation of, and then the dismissal of, Eisenhower's "assistant president," White House Chief of Staff Sherman Adams, who had intervened with federal agencies on behalf of Boston textile magnate Bernard Goldfine, and who, the investigation revealed, had accepted expensive gifts from Goldfine, including an Oriental rug and a vicuña overcoat.

Williams seemed not to care where his investigations led. One was into the overseas junkets taken by members of Congress—which didn't increase his popularity with his colleagues. But while the Senate inner circle and the reporters who crowded close to it and seemed to regard themselves almost as a part of it sneered at Williams, journalists of a more independent bent had made his qualities known to the public. "His performance has not included TV spectaculars," the *New York Times* was to observe. "He has no power of subpoena. He has no sleuthing staff, no special counsel serving as prosecutor." Yet, as the *Times* wrote, by his investigations "Senator Williams has perhaps brought down more wrongdoers operating in the United States Government, or chiseling from it, than any other man." "A growing army of men and women . . . confide in Senator John J. Williams," Doris Fleeson wrote. Thanks to these journalists, "Whispering Willie" was not John Williams' only nickname; he had another one: "The conscience of the Senate." The fiery investigative reporter Clark Mollenhoff of the *Des Moines Register,* who admired him—as much as Mollenhoff could admire anyone—said that despite the softness of Williams' voice, what he said "usually echoed with a roar throughout the entire federal government." And, late in September, Williams had begun an investigation into Bobby Baker.

He did so in his usual low-key manner, inviting Serv-U's Ralph Hill to his office and asking him for the names of other persons he could speak to if he wanted to learn more about Baker's business interests, and then he started inviting these people in, and one of them was Don Reynolds.

The October 6 article contained Reynolds' name only on a list of persons Williams had interviewed, identifying him as an insurance broker from Silver

Spring, Maryland; it gave no hint of what subjects he had discussed with
Williams. But Johnson knew what subjects Reynolds might be discussing with
Williams—and, it would turn out, was indeed discussing with the senator.

Reynolds told Williams that in 1957, having been advised that a "political
connection" would be helpful in building up his insurance business, he contacted
Bobby Baker, a fellow South Carolinian, and they entered into an agreement
under which he would make payments to Baker "because," as Reynolds was to
put it, "of his social contacts and his wide knowledge of people [whom he] could
present to me." Baker had shortly thereafter introduced him to Walter Jenkins.
Johnson, that same year, had mentioned to Baker that he was having difficulty
obtaining life insurance because of his heart attack, and Baker, as he would
recall, "told Senator Johnson about my partnership with Don Reynolds, and we
agreed to seek the policy through him." Reynolds secured Johnson $100,000 of
insurance (in 1961, the amount would be increased to $200,000), whose pre-
mium, he learned, would be paid not by Johnson but by the LBJ Company, with
the checks signed by Lady Bird—and when Reynolds obtained the policy, Baker
brought him to the lobby outside the Senate Chamber so that he could hand it to
Johnson personally.

Johnson told him jovially that, as Reynolds was to recall, "he was going to
rib his bigshot friends from Texas" that with all their insurance company connections, "they were unable to insure him and a country hick came up here from
South Carolina and got it for him"; Reynolds, Baker was to say, "was delighted"
to be "doing business with the big man."

The delight was soon to fade. Reynolds never spoke to Johnson again, but
he did speak to Jenkins, because Jenkins called him in to tell him that in return
for being allowed to write the policy and obtain the commission, about $2,500
per year, he would be required to purchase advertising time on the television station in Austin, KTBC-TV. When, Reynolds said, he protested that it made no
sense for a Maryland insurance broker, unknown in Austin, to advertise on television there, Jenkins said that didn't matter. Baker, Reynolds said, "prodded"
him to buy the time. And after Reynolds made the purchase, buying $1,208 of
airtime, another type of purchase was required. The Johnsons wanted a new
stereo set, Baker told Reynolds, and Reynolds would have to supply it. Reynolds
did, obtaining catalogs from various companies and giving them to Baker to give
to the Johnsons; Lady Bird selected a Magnavox S-44 model in a cherrywood
cabinet, an expensive set selling for about $900 in stores. Reynolds managed to
buy it wholesale through a friend for $542.25; when Lady Bird wanted it deliv-
ered quickly for a party she was giving, he had it delivered airfreight, which cost
an additional $42.50. Although Jenkins would later deny, again and again, the
advertising time and stereo set demands, Baker would confirm them—"He
[Johnson] took the stereo, and he required Don Reynolds to buy the . . . advertising. . . . It was a kickback pure and simple," he was to say—as would Reynolds,
who called the demands a "shakedown." And when Williams asked Reynolds if
he had proof of what he was saying, Reynolds produced it, and brought it to the

senator's office: the invoice from the Magnavox Company for the stereo, to be shipped to "Sen. Lyndon B. Johnson" and billed to "Mr. Don Reynolds"; the canceled check, signed by Reynolds, with which he had paid Magnavox; the canceled checks—one for $1,000, one for $208—signed by him that he had written to the Johnson television station for "advertising," on the back of which were stamps showing they had been deposited to the account of "THE LBJ COMPANY."*

While these transactions were illegal—insurance laws in both the District of Columbia and Maryland prohibit an insurance salesman from sharing with a policyholder any commission or premium he collects, laws designed to prevent kickbacks or rebates being used by brokers as an inducement to buy insurance"—they were small in amount (although, Baker was to write, that was "precisely my point. . . . You may be thinking that Senator Johnson spent a great deal of time and effort to clear a very modest profit." He did, indeed. "He was always on the lookout for the odd nickel or dime"). They nonetheless made clear the crucial connection, documenting the link between Baker and Johnson that Johnson had been trying so desperately to deny. The kickback on the insurance policy that Baker had arranged had been demanded by Baker not for himself but for Lyndon Johnson. Dealing with Little Lyndon had meant, in at least one instance, dealing with Big Lyndon—the invoices and checks proved that. According to Reynolds' statements to Williams, and according to the written evidence that supported them, the Bobby Baker story was also the Lyndon Johnson story.

And while a stereo set was a small item in the great scheme of public life, was it any smaller than a freezer, or a vicuña overcoat? Johnson had held a front-row seat at both the Truman "crony" and Sherman Adams scandals—had seen a cold-storage container and an overcoat wreck the reputations of two prominent officials, drive one of them, a man second in power in the executive branch only to the President, out of government. In a way, the fact that freezers and vicuña coats—and top-of-the-line stereo sets—were minor but expensive items, the type of material possessions a newspaper reader could visualize and relate to (and wish he could afford to buy), made them political bombshells that could do as much, or more, damage as revelations of much more significant transgressions. Lyndon Johnson was very well aware of what an expensive gift could do to a political career. The whole Bobby Baker case, in fact, had unfortunate echoes of the Truman scandal, including the fact that each had had a memorable noun for the headlines: "protégé" was a word with an unfortunate ring to it—like "crony." "He hated that word 'protégé'—just hated it," George Reedy said. "Every time he saw it, it just seemed to drive him up the wall." No one outside Williams' office was yet aware of what Reynolds had told the senator—even,

---

*The television checks are made out to the "KTBC Cable and Television Station and the Mid-Atlantic Stainless Co., Inc." because Reynolds, in an attempt to recoup some of the $1,208 he was being forced to spend for advertising that could have no possible benefit to him, had resold part of the advertising time to the Mid-Atlantic Company, a manufacturer of pots and pans.

really, that Reynolds had any significant connection to Johnson at all—but from the moment Johnson saw Don Reynolds' name, says Horace Busby, he knew the statements the insurance broker might be making, and how damaging they might be to him if they ever became public. "He knew it in a moment," says Busby, "it was trouble."

More important, small an item though the stereo gift might be in itself, its disclosure might open up questions about Lyndon Johnson that were not small at all. The premiums on Johnson's life insurance had been paid by the LBJ Company. There had been speculation for years about Johnson's relationship to that company. Lady Bird had purchased one small radio station in 1943 for $17,500. Since then, thanks in part to a twenty-year-long string of strikingly favorable rulings by the Federal Communications Commission (which, among other aspects, had left Austin as one of the few metropolitan areas with only a single commercial television station), the company had burgeoned into a chain of immensely profitable radio and television stations the length of Texas, and by 1963 it owned as well 11,000 acres of ranchland and major shareholdings in nine Texas banks. Johnson had quieted the speculations by his unequivocal denials that there was any relationship. He had said, over and over, for twenty years, that the LBJ Company was entirely his wife's business and he had nothing to do with it; that, as he claimed in one of many such statements, "All that is owned by Mrs. Johnson. . . . I don't have any interest in government-regulated industries and never have had." But if Lyndon Johnson had no interest in the LBJ Company, why was it taking out insurance on his life? And, of course, his denials had omitted the salient fact. Texas was a community-property state, and therefore since Lyndon Johnson had an interest—a half-interest—in all the company's income, he had become rich. If Reynolds' statements became public, it would cast doubt on Johnson's claim that there was no connection between LBJ and the LBJ Company—and once that connection was established, the company's financial dealings would become a subject of journalistic inquiry. Johnson had arrived in Congress poor, and during his career had ostensibly had no source of income other than his government salary. He had been boasting to friends for years that he was a millionaire. By 1963, he, a man who had never held any job but his government positions—whose salary had never been more than $35,000 per year—was not merely a millionaire but a millionaire many times over. That fact had never become known to the press or the public. How would it look if it did?

Furthermore, once reporters started looking into the LBJ Company, they might look not only into its wealth, but into how that wealth had been accumulated, and one area of that accumulation—the key area—was particularly vulnerable to journalistic inquiry: precisely the area with which Don Reynolds had been involved. The insurance broker had been forced to buy advertising time that he didn't need on KTBC-TV in return for receiving something from Lyndon Johnson. This had long been Johnson's practice—and, as readers of the second volume in this series, *Means of Ascent,* may recall (and if they don't, they can look on pages 101 through 106), what they were often receiving, often getting in return for their payments, was Lyndon Johnson's political influence on their behalf; they had been buying, he had been selling, political influence. Sometimes the payments were made not in cash but in kind—in material things that Johnson wanted for his home in Washington or for his ranch, in what KTBC's general manager, Earl Deathe, called "trading out." A stereo was only one of many such items "traded out." Deathe was to recall television sets—large sets, the newest model, enough of them for both the main house and the guest houses Johnson was building on his ranch—as well as tractors and cars. "It was a means of getting material things without paying for them," he explains.

And, Deathe says, there was "so much of it." Johnson, he says, "lived in fear" that such dealings would be exposed; "he just lived in fear of that—and I think rightfully so. He had been involved in so much." The "Bobby Baker thing" made this fear very real, says Deathe. Johnson had "traded out" with so many people, he says. What if one of them came forward with a statement to the press? And if Reynolds' statements became public, would others be encouraged to come forward?

Reynolds was, in his talks with John Williams, opening up other areas as well. He was telling the senator about campaign contributions Baker had made— and, as it happened, on the very day, October 6, on which the first article containing Reynolds' name appeared, there was another development: one of the senators to whom Baker had offered a contribution that year came forward voluntarily to talk about it, and about what Baker had wanted in return.

No sooner had he arrived in the Senate in January, 1963, as a newly elected senator from New Hampshire, than Thomas J. McIntyre was approached in the Democratic cloakroom by Baker, who, McIntyre said, told him, "I understand you have some campaign debts. Well, I have a few friends who would be willing to pick up the tab." McIntyre did have debts, $17,000 worth, but decided to check with an older senator before accepting the offer, and was told, "Don't touch it or you'll be in the bag to the oil interests."

McIntyre's statement—he was to issue a formal typed version—was self-serving. "The important point here was that I did not accept the offer because of the possibility that such a sum of money was coming from a single source," it said, and its timing was interesting; as *Newsweek* was to comment: "The exchange [between Baker and McIntyre] might have been lost.... But it cropped up because Bobby Baker is in trouble, trouble especially titillating because he is so widely regarded as Lyndon Johnson's protégé that he is known as 'Lyndon's Boy.' " To Johnson the disturbing point was that Baker's role in the dispensing of campaign funds had made an appearance in the public gaze. These funds, startlingly large amounts of money, and much of it in cash, had been raised and dispensed at Johnson's direction. How long could it be before *his* role was in the public gaze as well?

• • •

THE SENATE'S REACTION to the Baker revelations had been indignation—at
the fact that someone had had the effrontery to make them. Baker had not been
asked to resign, Majority Leader Mansfield told reporters on October 4; he had
not offered to resign—and there was no reason he *should* resign. "Bobby's work
in the Senate has been excellent," he said. "The other matter [Serv-U] affects his
activities outside the Senate." Even in that other matter, he said, Baker might vin-
dicate himself. "We will not attempt to prejudge it." Some senators tried to duck
reporters—Majority Whip Humphrey, cornered by the Associated Press shortly
after a visit to Mansfield's office and asked if they had talked about Bobby Baker,
replied, "Not entirely"—and others, even Wayne Morse of Oregon, usually as
far outside the Senate establishment as Williams, tried to defend the eager little
man who had done them all so many favors. Speaking "for once with the united
voice of the Senate," as Murray Kempton put it, Morse said on the Chamber floor
that "Bobby Baker performed many effective services for each and every one
of us. . . . I am not going to walk out merely because a friend may have made
mistakes."

However, Williams kept bringing Mansfield and Republican Leader Everett
Dirksen reports on what his interviews were turning up, and Mansfield asked
Baker to meet with him, Dirksen and Williams on Monday, October 7, to give his
side of the story, and that morning, Lyndon Johnson didn't have to leaf through
the *Washington Post* to find the story he was worried about: there it was, big and
black in a headline that stretched across the top of the front page: BAKER CALLED
IN INFLUENCE PROBE.

Bobby Baker knew what his side was. Had he talked, he was to write in his
memoirs, "many senators would have found themselves in highly embarrassing
circumstances, to say the least." And so would the man he revered. The "wound"
Johnson "might have incurred" by his revelations could indeed have been "mortal," he said. "They could have denied him the presidency, or driven him from
office." Shortly before the meeting was scheduled to begin, he resigned, and the
next day, the storm broke on the front page of every major newspaper in the
United States, and almost every article, it seemed, not only contained the word
that Lyndon Johnson hated, but gave short shrift to his contention that it had not
been him who had raised Baker to power. "Baker is a protégé of Vice President
Lyndon B. Johnson," the *Washington Post* explained. "Johnson named Baker to
the position of Secretary to the Senate Majority. . . . At the time, Baker was
twenty-six and still at law school." "Theirs was a close relationship," Mary
McGrory explained to the readers of the scores of newspapers that ran her column; during the 1960 campaign, "it was he [Baker] who put 'The Yellow Rose'
on the record player. And Mr. Johnson, to please Bobby, made a long detour to a
South Carolina mountain hamlet called Rocky Bottom, where Bobby was
greeted triumphantly as a native son who had made good."

Baker had hoped, he was to say, that his resignation would make the affair "magically disappear from the front pages and come to a grinding halt," but nothing could have been further from the truth. Declaring on the Senate floor that "the integrity, not just of Baker, but of the Senate," is involved, Williams said the case "cannot be closed by resignation," and introduced a resolution calling for a Senate investigation. The Senate had little choice but to pass it. Although it had been expected that the investigation would be carried out by the Senate Permanent Investigations Subcommittee chaired by the hard-bitten Senator McClellan, it was referred instead to the Rules Committee, a decision which, as *Newsweek* said, "had old Senate hands chuckling. . . . The Rules Committee has as its most weighty duty, approving Senate press passes." The committee's chairman, sixty-seven-year-old B. Everett Jordan, a first-term southern conservative from North Carolina, was slow-talking and slow-thinking—even Baker had to say he was "something of a bumbler"; in contrast to McClellan, one columnist was to say, "He is as hard a negotiator as Neville Chamberlain." Not only had he been an admiring, indeed subservient, "Johnson Man" during Johnson's time as Majority Leader, moreover, Jordan had been a "Bobby Baker Man" as well. He was fond of telling how much he had relied on Bobby; asked how he had spent his first day in the Senate, he said, "Oh, I went over to the Senate Chamber, and I stayed there until Bobby Baker told me I could come home." Although he now hastily removed it, an autographed picture of Bobby had hung in a prominent position on the wall of his office. And he was almost immediately to confirm fears that, as one columnist delicately put it, he "is too soft-hearted to head the investigation," by postponing indefinitely what the *Chicago Daily News* called "the logical first step in a hard-hitting investigation—a request to examine Baker's income tax returns and the sworn statements of his assets that he had given to various federal agencies."

But Williams was still conducting his own, independent investigation, and so now was a whole pack of reporters, and all through October there was a drumfire of disclosures in the press: that Baker was a partner not only in Reynolds' insurance business and in the vending machine company that was the talk of its industry, but also in a travel agency and a law firm; that the Carousel wasn't the only motel in which he had an interest: he was a partner in one in North Carolina as well; that he had, not a month before the investigation opened, moved from a modest home to a $125,000 "mansion" in "swank" Spring Valley—"near the home of Lyndon Johnson"—where, the *Chicago Daily News* reported, "a Chinese houseboy fends off callers." And then, as the month was coming to an end, and October, 1963, was drawing close to November, 1963, the stories began growing bigger and bigger, for the Bobby Baker case, it was revealed at the end of October, had every ingredient necessary for it to become a scandal of truly major proportions—not only money, it was turning out, but sex as well.

During the last week of October, newsmen, searching through District of Columbia real estate transactions, had discovered that Baker was the owner not only of the Spring Valley house but of a Capitol Hill townhouse—one that was occupied by shapely twenty-four-year-old blond Carole Tyler of Tennessee, a former Miss Loudon County, who had been Baker's administrative assistant before he resigned, and who had continued as his mistress. And they discovered, and began to print, at first in hints and then more openly, that at the townhouse "chain-smoking, martini-drinking, party-loving" Carole and a group of other "attractive young women" were assigned "to dwell and entertain," in all-night parties at which "Baker's high-flying circle of acquaintances" entered and left through a back door; headline writers named it the "party house."

And a "party house" was, innuendo-wise, thin gruel beside another venue that, over the weekend of October 26 and 27, began to appear in newspaper stories as part of the Bobby Baker case. It was a small hotel, the Carroll Arms, situated not a hundred yards from the Senate Office Building, "just an ice cube's throw from the Capitol," as one article put it. On its second floor, the stories said, was an "intimate" club, a "discreet little private club," "smoky and dimly lit," a spot where "the ceiling is red and the lights are low"—an "intimate and elegant gathering place" named the "Quorum Club" that Baker had, the stories said, organized for "romantic caucuses" of senators, lobbyists and congressmen. And there were stories also about the caucusees, the young women, the "hostesses," or "party girls," the articles called them, in a euphemism for call girls—and in particular about one of the hostesses. For those who didn't prefer blondes like Carole Tyler, this one was a brunette—and on any scale of scandal material, she was off the charts.

"Clad," as one account put it, "in a brief, revealing, skin-tight costume and black net stockings," sultry, dark-haired, dark-eyed Ellen Rometsch, the spectacularly exotic and sensual-looking wife of an East German army sergeant, had worked at the Quorum Club, and at the Carousel Motel, for more than two years before, in August, 1963, she had been expelled from the United States and hustled back to East Germany because, as Clark Mollenhoff reported that weekend in the *Des Moines Register,* she had been "associating with congressional leaders and some prominent New Frontiersmen from the 'executive branch'"—and because of fears that she was an East German spy.

As it happened, Lyndon Johnson had no more association with Elly Rometsch than he had with the Quorum Club, which had not even been established until after he left the Senate; he was not even a subject of her boasts. The official with whom she was rumored to have had sex was John F. Kennedy. Apparently she had bragged that she had had sex with the President, and in July, 1963, an informant had reported the boast to the FBI, which was already investigating rumors that she was a spy, the agency's suspicions "fueled," as one account puts it, by her "expensive lifestyle," which, the FBI investigators concluded, "hardly could have been maintained on the pay of a German army enlisted man."

The FBI had found no evidence to corroborate either rumor; a summary, written in July, of its preliminary inquiries concluded that "Investigation has not substantiated the security allegations against subject nor does she apparently have the high-level sex contacts she originally boasted of." Not a week earlier, however, Harold Macmillan had resigned as prime minister of Great Britain, brought down by the "Profumo Affair," in which the British defense minister, John Profumo, was caught in "impropriety" with a call girl who was also the mistress of a Russian naval attaché—a concatenation of circumstances that raised the spectre of security breaches. The parallels between the Profumo affair and the rumors about Elly Rometsch's White House connections and about her spying would turn her boasting into a big story if the press got wind of it. Robert Kennedy, who, as Evan Thomas puts it, "From the outset . . . understood that the merest whiff of a sex-and-spies scandal could be threatening to the president," had, in August, arranged to have her quietly deported, and the matter had appeared closed.

If she had no connection to Johnson or Kennedy, however, Ms. Rometsch certainly had one to Bobby Baker's club, and now, with Baker big news, she was news, too, and she certainly had the figure (35–25–35) and face (an "Elizabeth Taylor look-alike," one reporter called her) and, apparently, sexual proclivities ("Lesbian prostitute," was how Mollenhoff described her in his notes; the German Defense Ministry was to mention her "somewhat nymphomaniacal inclinations"; another source said simply, "She would do anything") to elevate a scandal to new heights. OUST BEAUTY TO HEAD OFF DC SCANDAL was the *New York Daily News* story that Sunday: "A beautiful German beauty with a lusty yen for men was rushed out of the country in August after bragging about affairs with important Washington figures, informed sources disclosed tonight." And with reporters tracking down every fact and rumor about her, how long could it be before the identity of the most "important Washington figure" of all was in print? HILL PROBE MAY TAKE PROFUMO-TYPE TWIST was the *Washington Post* headline over a story that promised "a spicy tale of political intrigue and high-level bedroom antics" when the Senate Rules Committee took up the Baker case that week.

Robert Kennedy headed off the threat to his brother. On Monday morning, October 28, he asked J. Edgar Hoover to persuade Senate leaders that the Rules Committee investigation should not include sexual matters, and Hoover, meeting with Mansfield and Dirksen, did so, assuring them that none of Rometsch's—or Bobby Baker's—activities had anything to do with national security. The attorney general may have had to guarantee the FBI director that his job was secure to persuade him to do it. But nothing could head off the threat to Johnson. Rometsch was undoubtedly linked to Bobby Baker—and Bobby Baker was Lyndon Johnson's protégé. And the issue of *Life* magazine that landed on newsstands during the first week of November had Baker on the cover, and inside, illustrating a story headlined THE BOBBY BAKER BOMBSHELL, was not only a full-page photograph of Bobby and Lyndon grinning together in their Senate heyday (the caption was "Legman and Leader") but, on the page facing them, two other photographs, one of Elly Rometsch, one of Carole Tyler—the brunette hugging some sort of fluted upright object, the blonde bounding out of ocean surf in a white bathing suit, every inch the beauty contest winner—that guaranteed the attention of at least the male portion (and, in the case of Ms. Rometsch, perhaps of part of the female portion, too) of *Life*'s thirty million readers.

ON OCTOBER 30, Lyndon Johnson had attended Tom Connally's funeral in Marlin, Texas, flying to Waco, the nearest city with a sizable airport, and then continuing on by a small plane to the little town.

All during Johnson's years as a congressman's secretary and a congressman—and into his first term as senator, until Connally retired in 1953, at the age of seventy-six, at the end of his fourth term in the Senate—Connally had been a great power in Washington, chairman for almost a decade of the Foreign Relations Committee, as well as an icon in Texas, his frock coat, string tie, black hat and great mane of silver-gray hair familiar in every corner of the state: a man to be courted and feared. As a newly elected senator in 1948, Johnson had made a pilgrimage to Marlin to solicit Connally's help with committee assignments, and had been careful not to take offense when Connally patronizingly refused it. Johnson had told his staff never, under any circumstances, to antagonize him. But in 1963, Connally had been retired for ten years, and the turnout of officials at his funeral was slim. Although Presidents Kennedy and Truman had sent elaborate floral arrangements, the Presidents weren't there themselves, and neither were any senators or congressmen, not even the representative from the local district.

After the funeral ceremony in Marlin's First Methodist Church, mourners filed past the open coffin, and when it was Johnson's turn, the line stopped as he stood looking down at Connally's face. He put on his glasses, and continued looking, for a long moment, and then walked out of the church, and the harsh Texas sun spotlit his face, on which was written a depression so deep that Posh Oltorf, who had known Johnson for many years, was shocked.

After following the coffin to the cemetery and watching it being lowered into the ground, Johnson came to Oltorf's house. "I think it's a disgrace that there was no delegation there from Congress," he said, as Oltorf recalls it. "As powerful as he was, and with all he had done, if he had died when he was in office, you wouldn't have been able to get into Waco for all the airplanes."

"I had seen him low before," Oltorf was to say, "but I had never seen him that low." And having heard Johnson tell him more than once how meaningless a job the vice presidency was—how only the presidency meant anything—Oltorf felt he understood Johnson's feelings. Tom Connally had been a powerful senator, but no one remembered him. Lyndon Johnson had been a powerful senator. He was thinking he would never be President—and no one would remember him, either.

IN EARLY NOVEMBER, 1963—the exact date is not clear—Senator Williams asked Reynolds to come to his office again, and Reynolds told him about another insurance deal.

In the spring of 1960, Reynolds said, Baker had invited him to a meeting in the Capitol at which the upcoming bidding for the contract to construct a District of Columbia stadium was discussed. Present were the chairman and the chief clerk of the House District of Columbia Committee, and Matt McCloskey, the contractor and Democratic fund-raiser who had been active in the 1960 convention and then had been named Kennedy's ambassador to Ireland, and who now announced, as the others in the room already seemed to know, that he was going to be one of the bidders. Baker told McCloskey that Reynolds was his business associate and that if McCloskey won the contract, he would like to have McCloskey consider retaining Reynolds as the broker for the performance bond which would be required. McCloskey won—and selected Reynolds as the broker for the bond, on which McCloskey had paid a $73,631 premium, out of which Reynolds had, he said, kept $10,000 as a commission, and paid $4,000 to Baker as what Reynolds was to describe as a "payoff." And again, Reynolds produced for Williams documents that he said supported his story: an invoice for a $73,631 premium from the insurance firm through which Reynolds had secured the bond, his check to that firm for $63,631 (the amount of the premium minus his $10,000 commission)—and a personal check, signed by "Don B. Reynolds," for $4,000, made out to, and endorsed for deposit by, "Robert G. Baker."

That was all Reynolds told Williams during that interview, but during another session, not long thereafter, he told the senator that there had also been another, more hidden, side to the transaction: that the entire deal had been structured in such a way that it would provide not only the $4,000 payoff to Baker, but a $25,000 contribution to Lyndon Johnson's campaign for the Democratic presidential nomination.

The amount of the premium had been $73,631, Reynolds said, but that hadn't been the amount that McCloskey & Company had actually paid. McCloskey had paid $109,205, with the understanding that of the approximately $35,000 overpayment, Reynolds would receive a second $10,000 for being the "bag man" and the remaining $25,000 would be given to what Reynolds described as "Mr. Johnson's campaign." Reynolds said he was instructed to deliver the money to Baker in cash—in installments that were never to be more than $5,000 each. He said he made three such deliveries—each of fifty hundred-dollar bills—although, since the performance bond was not written until after the Democratic convention, McCloskey did not pay the $109,000 until October 17, 1960, and the cash was delivered not for Lyndon Johnson's campaign but for the "Johnson-Kennedy campaign."*

If Reynolds' story was true, the District Stadium deal violated at least three federal laws: one prohibiting political contributions of more than $3,000, one prohibiting corporations from making any political contributions at all, and one prohibiting the charging of a contribution to a government contract. Reynolds

---

*No explanation was given for the discrepancy between the $25,000 Reynolds was supposed to deliver and the $15,000 he actually delivered.

told Williams that he didn't have the check that would document his story—the $109,000 check from McCloskey & Company, to be held up against the $73,000 bill to McCloskey & Company—but Williams would try to find a copy and would eventually succeed, obtaining a photostat of the check from someone, never identified, who wanted to cooperate with his investigation; Reynolds' story was therefore documented. And Baker would, years later, confirm it. Reynolds, who would later discuss other alleged transactions involving Lyndon Johnson and himself, exaggerated about some of them, Baker was to say, and made up others out of whole cloth (and it appears that Reynolds may indeed have done so), but he was apparently telling the truth about the McCloskey deal: "I was the man who put Reynolds and McCloskey together, so I know what the understandings were," Baker was to say. Reynolds "told the truth with respect to . . . the DC Stadium deal." (McCloskey was later to admit the $35,000 overpayment, but said it had been merely a clerical error that had gone undetected until the Baker investigation started; that someone in his company had assumed the extra $35,000 was the premium on another insurance policy. "Somebody in our organization goofed. We make goofs like that every once in a while.") And while Senator Williams did not, during that early November interview, learn the whole story of the stadium contract, Bobby Baker knew it—knew it included the cash for the Lyndon Johnson campaign—and Johnson knew that Williams had been talking again to the insurance broker who had been central to it. Suddenly another link between him and Bobby Baker was on the verge of coming to light.

ON WEDNESDAY, NOVEMBER 13, the President convened the first major strategy session for the 1964 campaign in the Cabinet Room at the White House. It included the men who would be directing the campaign: from the family, the attorney general and Stephen Smith; from the White House staff, O'Donnell, O'Brien and Sorensen; from the Democratic National Committee, Chairman John Bailey and Richard Maguire; from the Census Bureau, Richard Scammon, "an expert," in O'Donnell's words, "on population trends with many interesting ideas on where to find the most Democratic votes." It was a long meeting, lasting from four o'clock until the President broke it up well after seven, saying he had a busy week ahead of him, and then, the next week, his trip to Texas.

Lyndon Johnson was not at the meeting, and neither was any member of his staff, a fact that might have had no significance (a Vice President is not invariably included in campaign strategy sessions) except for two factors: first, the main topic of the meeting was the South—the difficulty of holding the gains made there in 1960, and the region's long-term future in the Democratic Party—and in 1960 the South had been his responsibility; second, that there was such intense speculation over whether, in fact, he would be on the ticket.

In these circumstances, his absence, as Arthur Schlesinger was to put it, "led to a burst of talk"—another burst—"that the Kennedys were planning to dump Johnson." Such talk, Schlesinger says, was wrong. "The non-existence of any dump-Johnson plan is fully and emphatically confirmed by Stephen Smith," he was to write. "Johnson's place on the ticket was not discussed on November 13 because (barring illness or scandal) it was a given," is a summary in a book published in 1977 that is in line with that given in virtually all books on Kennedy or Johnson. But of course there had never been any discussion about putting Lyndon Johnson *on* the ticket in 1960—not even with Bobby—until Jack Kennedy suddenly announced, to the astonishment of everyone, that he was doing so. And, in fact, Evelyn Lincoln says that when, the morning after the strategy session, she was reading material from the meeting and Kennedy came over to her desk, he made a remark that contradicted his other quotes. She was to write that when she told the President that the 1964 convention wouldn't be as exciting as the 1960 version, "because everyone knows what is coming," he replied: "Oh, I don't know, there might be a change in the ticket," before walking away. And, she wrote, when a week later Kennedy, sitting in a chair in her office, started talking about the reforms he wanted to make in government if he was re-elected, he said, "To do this I will need as a running mate in sixty-four a man who believes as I do. . . . It is too early to make an announcement about another running mate—that will perhaps wait until the Convention." When she asked whom the announcement might name, she wrote, Kennedy didn't hesitate. Looking straight ahead, he said, "At this time I am thinking about" another, more moderate, southerner, the young governor of North Carolina, Terry Sanford. "But it will not be Lyndon," he said.

Mrs. Lincoln says that she wrote down the conversation "verbatim in my diary," but before her book, *Kennedy and Johnson,* was published in 1968, at a point at which, it should perhaps be mentioned, Robert Kennedy was hoping for Johnson's support in his campaign for the presidency, Schlesinger saw an advance copy, and, he says, "alerted Robert Kennedy," who reiterated that there had been no intention of dumping Johnson, and added, "Can you imagine the President ever having a talk with Evelyn about a subject like that?" The reaction of the Kennedy partisans to her book is a case study in reversal. Prior to its publication, references to Mrs. Lincoln in their books and oral history reminiscences had all emphasized the respect Jack Kennedy had for her ("in eleven years he never called her Evelyn," Sorensen wrote) and her faithfulness to the President; "soft-hearted" is an adjective used about her by Sorensen, who calls her "unruffled and devoted," and praises her "unfailing devotion and good nature"; Schlesinger talks of her "welcoming patience and warmth" with people insistent on seeing the President. When, decades later, the author asked these same partisans about this woman, whom President Kennedy had regarded highly enough so that he kept her as his private secretary for eleven years, she was described to the author by these same men as a flighty, rather rattlebrained woman. Following the publication of her book, the terms they use to describe the conversation she claims to have had with Kennedy about the 1964 ticket are skeptical; she "claimed to remember" the conversation, Schlesinger said. When the author of this book went to see her himself, she repeated the conversation as she had written it, saying that the President wanted Johnson off the ticket, and "the ammunition to get him off was Bobby Baker."

AND FOR LYNDON JOHNSON, the stories were beginning to come closer and closer. Hitherto, during the two months in which the scandal had been unfolding, it had, despite the frequent mentions of Johnson's name, been primarily a scandal about Bobby Baker, but that was about to change.

On November 15, two liberal Democratic senators, Stephen M. Young of Ohio and Quentin N. Burdick of North Dakota, called in reporters and told them that, in early January, 1961, while Johnson was still contemplating keeping control of the Senate, Baker had kept them from seats on the Judiciary Committee by telling the Democratic Steering Committee, falsely, that neither had any interest in serving on the committee; two Johnson allies, his junior senator from Texas, William A. Blakley, and Edward V. Long of Missouri, were named instead. And on November 18, a *New York Daily News* columnist drew the lesson that the two senators' disclosures were not about Baker's personal financial maneuvers but about his impact on the governmental process, that he had been an "instrument" of the Senate's inner circle, and, specifically, of Lyndon Johnson—"As Baker was Johnson's errand boy, would he have given the Steering Committee the wrong information all by himself?" And, in the *Daily News,* perhaps for the first time in print, appeared the suggestion that the witnesses summoned to testify should include not only the instrument but the man who, the *Daily News* said, had wielded it: the man who was now Vice President of the United States. "If Baker is to be quizzed by the investigating Senate Rules Committee about this specific incident, it would appear only fair to have the Vice President called to give his version." On that same day, November 18, the Monday of the week the President was to leave for Texas, a new *Life* article hit the newsstands. Its headline was still THE BOBBY BAKER CASE (SCANDAL GROWS AND GROWS IN WASHINGTON), and the text, written by Keith Wheeler and based on the work of a nine-member *Life* investigative team, was in part merely a recounting of Baker's personal financial saga that had been public since the filing of the Serv-U suit and of the role of sex in his rise to wealth ("in the peculiar Washington world here under review, wives were not the only women included in social activity. . . . One way or another, young women become more or less legal tender in the ancient and crafty commerce of getting things done"), although it added, in chops-licking prose, some new details—one of the Quorum Club hostesses "kept a tambourine and harem pants" handy "as costume for the oriental dances she sometimes performed. . . . Sometimes she did other dances which required no costume whatever"; during one exercise in which a number of naked young women poured champagne over each other in a bathtub, Elly Rometsch was bitten in the behind by another bather but "apparently bore her wound with fortitude and no ill will"—and was illustrated by a new photograph of Carole Tyler, no longer a blonde but a brunette, who had "posed graciously for *Life*'s cameras," not in the surf but on a sofa, in a demure suit. But the article was also about the Senate—and about Lyndon Johnson.

The Senate had been Baker's "base of operations," Wheeler explained, and the Senate was controlled "rigidly" by a small group that was its "Establishment," and "In a very real sense the . . . Establishment is the personal creation of Lyndon Baines Johnson who, from the day he took over as majority leader until he went to the Vice Presidency, ruled it like an absolute monarch. . . . It was Johnson who sponsored Bobby Baker's election as majority secretary and fashioned him into his legman, mouthpiece and satrap of power."

And the article demonstrated that Johnson had used Baker in that way at the beginning of his vice presidency as well. Quentin Burdick had been independent, *Life* said, quoting "a man in a position to know," and "Lyndon Johnson wasn't likely to forgive" that. "So Bobby Baker shivved Burdick. It was typical."

The article gave examples of Baker's use of campaign funds—how he gave Paul Douglas only $3,000 of the $12,000 that had been donated for him—and an example of how, as Wheeler put it, such "campaign money might carry its own corrupting price tag": "In 1958, when Frank Edward Moss was running for the Senate in Utah, an emissary was dispatched from Washington to offer him 'a big chunk' of money to boost his campaign along. . . . But then the messenger let him know there was a catch. He could have the swag only in return for his signature on a letter avowing that he had studied the 27½% oil depletion allowance and concluded that its continuance was in the national interest." And the article disclosed, in addition, that much of the campaign funding was in cash. "When there was a lot of it, somebody—not necessarily Baker, but somebody in the entourage—carried it in a money belt strapped around his belly." But the article also made clear that it wasn't Baker who had directed the collection and distribution of the money. He had done so, the article explained, in his post as secretary of the Democratic Senatorial Campaign Committee. "It was a committee in name only, for Johnson controlled it absolutely," *Life* said, and money was given only to senators and senatorial candidates whom Johnson felt he could control; in the words of a Senate insider quoted by the magazine, "what Lyndon wanted was a nice, cozy little majority . . . with no back talk. No mavericks." Bobby Baker, this source said, had simply been "Lyndon's bluntest instrument in running the show." Famous though Bobby might have become, he was no more than Lyndon's acolyte. "He always spoke of LBJ as 'The Leader.' . . . He even tried to *be* Johnson. He copied Johnson's clothes and mannerisms. When he came into the Senate chamber, he'd take the Johnson stance." After the publication of that article, in that immensely influential magazine, it was clear that the Bobby Baker case was inevitably going to become the Lyndon Johnson case as well.

• • •

FOR SOMEONE WHO was poring over every word in the *Life* article—as Lyndon Johnson was poring over every word—one of those words in it was, according to George Reedy, particularly distressing. Baker's new home, it said, was near "millionaire Lyndon Johnson's" home. "Millionaire"—this was perhaps the first time that Johnson had ever been identified as such in print, at least in a national publication; he had perhaps never been identified in a national publication even as a wealthy man, let alone a very wealthy man; for *Life* to do so, it must know something about his personal fortune that he had previously been able to keep hidden.

And, in fact, it did.

The magazine's investigative team had been working since the end of October, and, during that time, says its leader, Associate Editor William Lambert, "I began to pick up all these hints" about Lyndon Johnson, not merely about Johnson and his relationship with the newly rich Bobby Baker, but about Lyndon Johnson "and the acquisition of *his* fortune." Following up on the hints, the team had found, in the words of Russell Sackett, one of its members and also an associate editor, that "The deeper you got, the more serious they were; he was far richer than anyone had expected," that he was, in fact, very rich indeed.

"I was very indignant," Lambert said, and during the week of November 11, he had gone to the office of George P. Hunt, *Life*'s managing editor, and said of Lyndon Johnson, "This guy looks like a bandit to me." Although "bandit" is, of course, a synonym for "robber" or "thief," Lambert didn't feel he was misusing the word. "I felt that he had used public office to enhance his private wealth." He told Hunt, "We're going to have to spend some money [to investigate]. I need some people, and a lot of time." Johnson's entire financial picture should be looked into, he said. "It was almost a net worth job, and you know that takes an enormous amount of time. I told Hunt, 'He's got a fortune, and he's been on the [public] payroll ever since he got out of college. And I don't know how he got it, but it's there.' " By the time he went in to see Hunt, Lambert was to recall, "We knew he was a millionaire many times over."

After listening to Lambert's description of what the investigation had uncovered thus far, Hunt agreed to allocate the manpower Lambert wanted (the managing editor warned him to be "very careful" in checking the facts "because he [Johnson] is only a heartbeat away from the presidency"), and, Lambert recalls, "we put together a kind of task force," and by the end of that week, no fewer than nine reporters were digging, not only in Washington but in Austin and Johnson City, into a story which, if it was told in any detail, would be a story that was being told for the first time: what Sackett calls "The story of Lyndon Johnson's money." By the middle of the week of November 18, even while Wheeler's Bobby Baker story was still on the newsstands, the investigative team had uncovered enough new material so that, in Sackett's words, "We knew there was a much bigger story. We were finding more and more on Lyndon." Wheeler and Lambert felt Hunt should be informed about their findings, and a meeting in the managing editor's office, at which all the members of the team who were in New

York would be present, was scheduled for the late morning of that Friday, November 22.

And also on that Friday, for the first time a Lyndon Johnson financial transaction was going to be described by a witness, seated beside his lawyer, to representatives of the United States Senate—for on November 22, 1963, the witness in a closed hearing with the staff of the Senate Rules Committee was going to be Don B. Reynolds.

He began testifying that morning at ten o'clock.

LYNDON JOHNSON HAD FLOWN to his ranch on Friday, November 15. The President and Jackie were to spend the following Friday night—the 22nd—and Saturday at the ranch after the fund-raising dinner in Austin. Kennedy wasn't looking forward to the visit—when O'Donnell and Dave Powers tried to get out of accompanying him, he told them they didn't have a chance: "You two guys aren't running out on me and leaving me stranded with poor Jackie at Lyndon's ranch. If I've got to hang around there all day Saturday wearing one of those big cowboy hats, you've got to be there, too"—but since he was going to be in his Vice President's hometown, not visiting the ranch would have added to the speculation Kennedy was trying to avoid. The Johnsons had flown down a week ahead of time to prepare for the visit.

Tight as were the political tensions—the Senate investigation, the Yarborough feud—that were wound around Lyndon Johnson that week, the visit, being social, gave the screw another twist. "This was important to him to have this go off well," his secretary Marie Fehmer says. "He was quite tense." Liz Carpenter recalls "much cleaning and directing of servants to have everything spick-and-span." Everything had to be perfect. When the President had been asked if there was anything he'd like to do at the ranch, he had said that perhaps he'd like to ride. This casual remark brought an influx of new horseflesh. Wesley West's thoroughbreds were the finest in the Hill Country; eight of the best were brought to the Johnson Ranch. A Tennessee walking horse, with its easy gait, might be a good horse for Jackie; Lady Bird's Tennessee walker was at that moment back in Tennessee, undergoing further training; a horse trailer was dispatched to get it back before the Kennedys arrived. Supplies of the President's preferred beverages—Poland water, Ballantine's Scotch—were laid in; inquiries were made to determine the temperature ("tepid") at which he liked to drink the water. Jackie sometimes preferred Newport cigarettes, sometimes Salems; adequate supplies of both were laid in. The champagnes she preferred had of course been purchased, but then it was learned that she sometimes liked to drink them over ice; Bess Abell was assigned to show one of the housemen, James Davis, "This is how you pour champagne on the rocks for Mrs. Kennedy." A trip to Austin produced new terry-cloth hand towels for Jackie. Then it was learned that she preferred smooth hand towels; another 120-mile round-trip was made. Liz Car-

penter recalls "many telephone calls and drives into town . . . to bring back the
very nicest perfumes, scented soaps for Mrs. Kennedy's bathroom." And one
thing wasn't perfect. The bedboard and horsehair mattress for the President's bad
back hadn't arrived on schedule, and the empty bed seemed to loom over all the
preparations; Mrs. Abell kept thinking, "Will he wander in to bare springs?" And
there was one piece of information that it had proven impossible to determine:
the duration of the Kennedys' visit. Would they be staying until Sunday?
Repeated inquiries to the Kennedy staff had produced no response. As Friday
neared, "that was still very much a question mark," Mrs. Abell says.

Then there was the question of entertainment. The ranch's specialty was a
sheepherding show in which two sheepdogs rounded up a small herd of sheep
and moved them from one pen to another; it had been decided to stage that show
for the Kennedys because it would, Ms. Carpenter says, give them "a real flavor
of the hillside of Texas, which Mrs. Johnson wanted very much to show them,"
but the decision was continually revisited. "On one hand," writes one of Mrs.
Johnson's biographers, Jan Jarboe Russell, "she wanted to entertain Mrs.
Kennedy in her own unpretentious way, out of doors. . . . Yet she was also eager
to avoid playing the part of the rube." And Lady Bird had an additional
concern—indeed, horror. Because the paved path from the ranch's airstrip led
not to the front door of the ranch house but to the kitchen door in back, she had
fallen into the habit of bringing visitors into the house by that entrance, so that
they entered through a little room containing a washing machine and dryer, and
then came into the kitchen, with its corkboard filled with scribbled messages, and
she seemed unable to break herself of that habit. "The image of Jackie Kennedy,
immaculately dressed . . . , being herded through the busy ranch kitchen seemed
like a waking nightmare to Lady Bird," Russell writes. "If you don't do anything
else for me, please be sure that I get the President and Mrs. Kennedy into the living room door and not the kitchen door," she told Mrs. Abell. "I'm sure to forget
about it." The President was to land at San Antonio's Bergstrom Air Force Base
at 1:30 on Thursday afternoon, November 21, lead a motorcade through the city
to the new Aerospace Medical Center, then fly on to Houston for another motorcade and an Albert Thomas Appreciation Dinner in the Houston Coliseum that
evening. After the dinner, he would fly to Fort Worth, where on Friday he would
give a breakfast speech before flying to Dallas for another motorcade, which was
scheduled to end at the Dallas Trade Mart, where he was to give a luncheon
speech before flying down to Austin for the hundred-dollar-a-plate dinner, and,
later that night, to the LBJ Ranch. When, on Thursday, at 11:20 a.m., the Johnsons left the ranch in their Beechcraft Bonanza for the short flight to Bergstrom,
where they would greet the President, they left behind them a staff still agonizing
over details of the Kennedy visit.

The President's arrival at Bergstrom brought with it more trouble for Lyndon Johnson—political trouble, but with a personal twist.

Close behind the President and Jackie as they came down the steps of Air
Force One was Ralph Yarborough, who, along with most of the twenty-member

Texas congressional delegation, had flown to Texas with the President. The senator, Ken O'Donnell was to say, had boarded the plane "in a rage," having just learned that there was going to be no seat for him at the head table at the Austin dinner and no invitation at all for him to Connally's reception for the President at the Governor's Mansion. On the flight down, Ken O'Donnell says, his anger had boiled over when reporters asked his reaction. "I'm not surprised," he said. "Governor Connally is so uneducated governmentally, how could you expect anything else?" If his anger required additional fuel, it was provided by a group of supporters who, as he came down onto the Bergstrom tarmac, crowded around him to tell him, as one of them says, that "what Connally and Johnson are trying to do to you" was public knowledge. And, as it happened, he did not have to wait more than a few minutes for an opportunity to retaliate for these slights—delivering one of his own that was particularly painful to a man who lived in dread of public humiliation.

A motorcade was forming on the tarmac for the drive from the airport to the Aerospace Medical Center. Behind the lead police car was the long, midnight-blue presidential convertible, carrying the Kennedys and Connallys, followed by the Secret Service security car, which reporters had dubbed the "Queen Mary," an open, armored, four-ton rolling arsenal with four agents inside and four more standing on the running boards; and then, after the requisite seventy-five-foot security gap, the rented convertible for the Vice President and a rented car containing his Secret Service detail; and then a car for the four-man press pool, a press bus for the forty reporters not in the pool, a caravan of open cars crammed with still photographers and newsreel cameramen, and other convertibles for congressmen and local officials. Yarborough had been assigned by O'Donnell to ride with the Johnsons—but now he refused to do so. When the chief of Johnson's Secret Service detail, Special Agent Rufus W. Youngblood, a lanky, balding Georgian with an easy drawl, tried to direct the senator to Johnson's car, he simply ignored him. Turning to San Antonio congressman Henry Gonzalez, he asked, "Henry, can I hitch a ride with you?" and got into his car instead.

The motorcade pulled away on its sixteen-mile trip to the medical center, and hardly had it entered the streets of San Antonio when huge crowds were waiting for it, packed four-deep on sidewalks, jumping and screaming and shouting, "Jack! Jackie!" as it approached, with thousands of children, released from school for the day, waving little hand-colored American flags. In the presidential limousine, the Kennedys and Connallys, two handsome, poised men and their wives, Jackie radiant in a stylish suit, Nellie Connally, once "Sweetheart of the University" at the University of Texas, still beautiful at forty-four, basked in the adulation, smiling and waving at the crowds and chatting together. Behind them came a long line of open cars, jammed to the gunnels with congressmen and camaraderie; in one convertible two congressmen sat in front with the driver, and five more were crammed in behind them, three sitting in the back seat and two on the top of the seat, with their legs hanging down into the car. And in the midst of this procession of smiling, waving men crowded happily together was one car in

which, in the wide back seat (too wide in the circumstances; the Johnsons' situation was "awkward," said one account, "no matter how wide they spread themselves, they were obviously missing a passenger"), the Vice President of the
United States sat alone with his wife, unaccompanied except for the driver and
Youngblood in the front seat, because the man who had been assigned to ride
with him had refused to do so.

Alone, and naked to the gaze of the reporters behind him, who knew he
wasn't supposed to be alone—Ken O'Donnell had given them a list of the car
assignments for the principals in the motorcade—and who knew why he was.
When, later, a reporter asked Gonzalez what the day's main story should be, the
congressman said it should be the tumultuous reception San Antonio had given
the President. No, the reporter said, the headline was going to be, "Yarborough
Refuses to Ride with Lyndon Johnson." Johnson knew the reporters had been
given the list. He knew that they knew why he was alone. The trip from
Bergstrom to the medical center took a little more than an hour. It must have been
a long hour for Lyndon Johnson.

AFTER KENNEDY'S SPEECH at the medical center, there was another motorcade, to the planes that would carry the party to Houston. Yarborough got into
Gonzalez's car again, and Rufus Youngblood got out of Johnson's and went back
to the senator, to ask him to ride with Johnson. With a curt wave of his hand,
Yarborough had him go away. Returning to Johnson's convertible, Youngblood
slid into the front seat, turned to Johnson and spread his hands in a helpless gesture, saying simply, "Well, I told him." The reporters were watching.

Then there was Houston: another airport, with Johnson (whose plane had of
course landed first) waiting at the foot of the ramp to welcome the Kennedys and
Connallys (and Yarborough) as if he was the state's official greeter, another
motorcade through cheering crowds that weren't cheering for him, with him and
his wife again conspicuously alone in their car (new attempts to persuade
Yarborough to join him had been made by Congressman Thomas, the honoree of
the evening's dinner, and by Youngblood—"I've bugged him enough," the agent
said when he came back to Johnson's car this time). And then, during a three-
hour rest stop at Houston's Rice Hotel before the dinner, Jack Kennedy asked
Lyndon Johnson to come to his suite, and the door was shut behind them—and
there were, perhaps for the first time since Kennedy had been elected, loud,
angry words directly between the President and Vice President.

No one knew quite what those words were; Johnson was later to deny there
had been any: "There definitely was not a disagreement. . . . There was an active
discussion"; he and the President had been "in substantial agreement," he said.
The hotel waiters who came in and out of the suite, interviewed later by the
author William Manchester, told him, in his summation, that they "heard Yarborough's name mentioned several times," and that they had received the impression
that Kennedy "felt the Senator [Yarborough] was not being treated fairly, and

that he [the President] was expressing himself with exceptional force." Jackie Kennedy, rehearsing her speech for that evening's dinner in the next room, heard raised voices, but said only, "There was all of this [talk] about people not wanting to ride in the car with him." After Johnson had left, she asked her husband, "What was that all about? He sounded mad." "That's just Lyndon," her husband replied, seeming amused. "He's in trouble." On a later occasion, she said, "I remember asking Jack . . . what the trouble was. He said that John Connally wanted to show that he was independent and could run on his own . . . and he wanted to show that he didn't need Lyndon Johnson, or something. And that part of the trouble of the trip was him [Connally] trying to show that he had his own constituency."

That day, Kennedy had asked Albert Thomas to intercede not just with Yarborough but with Connally, to bring the party-splitting feud to an end, and on the brief flight from San Antonio to Houston, Thomas had in fact asked Connally to allow Yarborough a more prominent role at the Austin dinner. Thomas had had to report to Kennedy that Connally had not been receptive. One of the purposes of the trip—to create the party unity Kennedy needed for his re-election campaign in a key state—was not being accomplished. The President may, behind that closed door at the Rice, have let his anger loose at the Texan he had put on his ticket but who was proving not to be a "viable mediator" at all. And Johnson may have responded that it was not his fault that Yarborough was still hostile— that Yarborough wouldn't even ride in his car. Whatever was said, when Johnson opened the closed door, nothing had been settled. Johnson came rushing out into the corridor with an angry expression on his face; "he left that suite like a pistol," one of the Secret Service agents on duty outside said.

AFTER THE DINNER, the President rode to the Houston airport with the *Houston Chronicle*'s publisher, John T. Jones Jr., and his wife, Winnie. Jones shared with the President the results of a Texas poll that would be published in his newspaper on Friday. It showed Yarborough's approval rating—57 percent—above that for a Kennedy-Johnson ticket. *"He's in trouble,"* Kennedy had said about Johnson, and whatever the President had meant when he said it, that poll—which, of course, reinforced the other Texas polls he had seen—indeed meant trouble for Johnson. He had been supposed to be holding together the conservative and liberal wings of the Texas Democratic Party. The conservative leader, Connally, had been trying to demonstrate to Kennedy that he didn't need Johnson—and the demonstration had been convincing. The liberal leader, Yarborough, didn't need Johnson, didn't want him—wouldn't even ride in a car with him. And both Connally and Yarborough were running well ahead of the Kennedy-Johnson ticket. They didn't need Kennedy nearly as much as he needed them. Not only might his Vice President no longer be a "viable mediator" in the feud, he was beginning to seem, in a way, almost irrelevant.

Part III

DALLAS

11

The Cubicle

FRIDAY, NOVEMBER 22, 1963, began for Lyndon Johnson with the headline he saw on the front page of the *Dallas News* that morning: YARBOROUGH SNUBS LBJ—hard to think of a verb that would have hurt him more than that one.

At about eight o'clock Texas (Central Standard) time—the time in Washington (Eastern Standard) was an hour later—Johnson, in his suite in Fort Worth's Hotel Texas, telephoned George Reedy in Washington to find out how other newspapers had covered the trip. Reading Johnson the passages that mentioned him, Reedy cringed inside, for every detail of the previous day's humiliation had been chronicled. "Twice at San Antonio . . . Johnson sent a Secret Service man to invite Yarborough to ride with him in his car. Both times the senator ignored the invitation and rode with someone else," the *Los Angeles Times* reported. The *Chicago Tribune* noted the "curt wave of his hand" with which Yarborough had sent the Vice President's emissary packing. The feud—and not Kennedy's triumph—was the main story of Kennedy's trip not just in Texas but across the country. Lyndon Johnson sat there with the Texas papers in front of him—there were four separate stories in the Dallas paper alone: in addition to the SNUBS story, others were headlined STORM OF POLITICAL CONTROVERSY SWIRLS AROUND KENNEDY ON VISIT; PRESIDENT'S VISIT SEEN WIDENING STATE DEMOCRATIC SPLIT; NIXON PREDICTS JFK MAY DROP JOHNSON—and then he had to go downstairs for an early-morning rally of five thousand labor union members, and join Kennedy, Yarborough, Connally and some local congressmen, all of whom had of course read those headlines. As they walked across the street to the rally, a light drizzle was falling. Johnson was wearing a raincoat and a hat; Kennedy, as always, was bareheaded and lithe in an elegant blue-gray suit. Johnson hastily snatched off his hat. His assignment, as usual, was to introduce Kennedy, and as he finished, the crowd roared for the young man beside him. Explaining why Jackie wasn't there ("Mrs. Kennedy is organizing herself. It takes her a little longer, but of course she looks better than we do when she does it"), Kennedy was easy and charming. Johnson had had to ask Kennedy for a favor: to be allowed to bring his youngest sister, Lucia, and her husband, Birge Alexander, who lived in Fort Worth, to meet him; shaking hands with Kennedy in his suite after the rally, she was thrilled; she had always wanted to shake hands with a President, she said.

Getting dressed that morning, Kennedy, after strapping the brace around him tightly, had wrapped over it and around his thighs in a figure-eight pattern an elastic Ace bandage for extra support because it was going to be a long day. Now it was nine o'clock, time for a breakfast speech to the Fort Worth Chamber of Commerce in the hotel's ballroom. "All right, let's go," he said.

NINE O'CLOCK IN TEXAS was ten o'clock in Washington: at about the same time that Kennedy was heading downstairs in Fort Worth, Don Reynolds, with his attorney beside him, walked into Room 312 of the Old Senate Office Building on Capitol Hill to begin answering questions from the Senate Rules Committee.

Reynolds was not under oath—it was expected that he would shortly testify to the committee itself under oath; the purpose of this interview, conducted by Burkett Van Kirk, counsel to the committee's Republican minority, and Lorin Drennan, an accountant from the General Accounting Office who had been assigned to assist the committee with its investigation of the Bobby Baker case, was to determine which areas the committee should pursue when Reynolds appeared before it. But on the advice of his counsel, James F. Fitzgerald, who was seated beside him, Reynolds had brought documents with him that he said would prove his contentions about a number of Baker's activities, two of which—the purchase of television advertising time and an expensive stereo set in return for the writing of an insurance policy; and Matthew McCloskey's payment of $109,000 for a performance bond that had only cost $73,000—related to Lyndon Johnson.

In New York, the meeting of the *Life* investigative team in George Hunt's office began at about 11:30, with a dozen reporters and editors present, and it soon became apparent that the meeting was going to be a long one, for there was much to report to the managing editor.

Even in the day or two since Wheeler and Lambert had last spoken to Hunt, the reporters who had been sent to Texas had found new areas ripe for inquiry. For one thing, they had begun searching through deeds and other records of recent land sales in county courthouses not only in Blanco County, but in Gillespie and Llano as well, and in Austin, and had found that the real estate transactions of the LBJ Company were on a scale far greater than had previously been suspected. And other reporters were digging into the advertising sales and other activities of KTBC, and these too were turning up one item after another that the reporters felt merited looking into. "With every day that week," the story "had kept getting bigger and bigger," Lambert says, and it was no longer a Bobby Baker story but "a Lyndon Johnson story." But, he says, so many reporters were working in Johnson City, Austin and the Hill Country that "they were tripping all over each other." The areas for further investigation had to be weeded down to the most promising, and reporters divided up among them. Moreover, Wheeler, who had written the story that was already on the newsstands that week, said that enough material had already come in so that he could write another one—immediately. A decision had to be made on whether he should do that, or whether the material already in hand should be held until more was available, and combined into a multi-part series on "Lyndon Johnson's Money"—the "net worth job"—that would run in several issues.

As DON REYNOLDS was providing the Rules Committee staff with information that might—and very shortly—produce headlines, and as *Life* was mapping out assignments for an investigation that might produce even bigger headlines, the presidential motorcade was pulling away from the hotel in Fort Worth for the airport, and the brief flight to Dallas.

In Lyndon Johnson's lapel was a white carnation that had been pinned on him at the Chamber of Commerce breakfast, and in his car was Ralph Yarborough. "I don't care if you have to throw Yarborough into the car with Lyndon," Kennedy had told O'Brien that morning. "Get him in there." He told O'Donnell to give Yarborough a message: "If he doesn't ride with Lyndon today, he'll have to walk." And while these statements may have been a bit of presidential bravado, the President himself had had a few words with the senator that morning. When, after he asked Yarborough to ride in the car to which he had been assigned, the senator had remained evasive, Kennedy spoke another sentence in a quiet voice. If he valued his friendship, the President told him, he would ride with Lyndon. Yarborough took a good look at the President, and shortly thereafter spoke a few words to O'Brien, and when Johnson came out of the hotel for the motorcade, O'Brien was able to tell him, "Yarborough's going to ride with you." ("He is?" Johnson said. "Fine.") On the thirteen-minute flight to Dallas, the President took care of the other public aspect of the feud. Taking Connally by the arm, O'Donnell pushed him into Kennedy's cabin and closed the door. "Within three minutes," he was to recall, the governor had agreed to invite Yarborough to the reception at the Governor's Mansion and to seat him at the head table at the Austin dinner. Emerging, Connally asked, "How can anybody say no to that man?"

As AIR FORCE ONE was heading for Dallas, the last of the clouds cleared. "Kennedy weather," O'Brien said.

It seemed as if it was going to be a Kennedy day. As Air Force One touched down at Dallas' Love Field at 11:38—12:38 Washington time—everything seemed very bright under the brilliant Texas sun and the cloudless Texas sky: the huge plane gleaming as it taxied over closer to the crowd pressing against a fence; the waiting open presidential limousine, so highly polished that the sunlight glittered on its long midnight-blue hood that stretched forward to the two small flags fluttering on the front bumpers. There was a moment's expectant pause while steps were wheeled up to the plane, and then the door opened, and into the sunlight came the two figures the crowd had been waiting for: Jackie first ("There is Mrs. Kennedy, and the crowd yells!" the television commentator yelled), youthful, graceful, tanned, her wide smile, bright pink suit and pillbox hat radiant in the dazzling sun; behind her, the President, youthful, elegant ("I can see his suntan all the way from here!" the commentator shouted), with the mop of brown hair glowing, one hand checking the button on his jacket in the familiar gesture, coming down the steps just so slightly turned sideways to ease his back that it wasn't noticeable unless you looked for it. A bouquet of bright red roses was handed to Jackie by the welcoming committee, and it set off the pink and the smile.

No time had been built into the schedule for the President and Jackie to work the crowd, but who could resist doing it, so adoring and excited were the faces turned toward them, so imploring the hands stretched out toward them, and they walked along the fence basking in the smiles and the sun, grinning—laughing, even—at things people shouted as they stretched out their hands, in the hope of a touch from theirs. "There never was a point in the public life of the Kennedys, in a way, that was as high as that moment in Dallas," a reporter who had covered the entire presidency was to write.

Taking Lady Bird by the arm to bring her along, Lyndon Johnson walked over to the fence and started to follow the Kennedys, but the faces remained turned, and the arms remained stretched, toward the Kennedys even after they had passed, and Johnson quickly moved back to the gray convertible that had been rented for him. O'Brien made sure Yarborough got in. The senator sat on the left side of the back seat, behind the driver, a Texas state highway patrolman named Herschel Jacks, the Vice President on the right side, behind Secret Service Agent Youngblood. Lady Bird, sitting between Yarborough and her husband, tried to make conversation but soon gave up. The two men weren't speaking to or looking at each other—the only noises in the car came from the walkie-talkie radio that Youngblood was carrying on a shoulder strap—as the motorcade pulled out.

SENATE HEARINGS NORMALLY break for lunch, but at 12:30, after two and a half hours of explaining his overall business relationship with Bobby Baker, Reynolds had begun telling his two Rules Committee questioners—Van Kirk and Drennan—specifically about the pressures that had been brought on him to purchase advertising time on Lyndon Johnson's television station, and they didn't want him to stop. They sent a secretary out to bring back sandwiches and milk, and Reynolds continued talking.

• • •

THE FIRST FEW MILES of the presidential procession were along an avenue
flanked by low light-industrial factories, and relatively few people were watching as the motorcade swept past: an unmarked white police lead car, and hel-
meted motorcycle police outriders; then the Kennedys and Connallys in the
presidential limousine with the flags fluttering from its bumpers and two motorcycle escorts flanking it at the rear; then the Queen Mary armored car with four
agents erect on the running boards and Ken O'Donnell and Dave Powers in the
jump seats; then, after the careful seventy-five-foot gap, the gray vice presidential convertible and vice presidential follow-up car, the press cars and buses and
the rest of the long caravan. But then the motorcade reached Dallas' downtown,
and turned onto Main Street. For a while, Main was lined on both sides by a
row of tall buildings, so that as the cars drove between them, they might have
been driving between the walls of a canyon, not a New York–height canyon, of
course, but deep enough, and the windows of the buildings were filled, floor after
floor, building after building, with people leaning out and cheering, and on the
sidewalks the crowds were eight people, ten people deep. Overhead, every hundred yards or so, a row of flags hung vertically from wires stretched across the
street, and at the end of the canyon, after the buildings ended, was a rectangle of
open sky.

As the procession drove further into the canyon, the noise swelled and deepened, becoming louder and louder so that the motorcade was driving through a
canyon of cheers. Every time the President waved, the crowd on the sidewalk
surged toward him, pressing back the lines of policemen, so that the passage for
the cars grew narrower, and the lead car was forced to reduce speed, from twenty
miles an hour, to fifteen, to ten, to five. Every time Jackie waved a hand in its
white glove, shrieks of "Jackie!" filled the air. As the tall governor with the leo-
nine head of gray hair waved his big Stetson, the cheers swelled for him, too. The
four passengers in the presidential limousine kept smiling at each other in
delight. "Mr. President, you certainly can't say that Dallas doesn't love you!"
Nellie Connally said; the President's "eyes met mine and his smile got even
wider," Mrs. Connally was to recall.

TRAILING THEM in his rented car, driving between crowds of people cheering
but not for him, sharing a seat with a man who had humiliated him, Lyndon Johnson was far enough behind the presidential limousine that the cheering for the
Kennedys and Connallys—for John Connally, some of it, for his onetime assistant who had become his rival in Texas—had died down by the time his car
passed, and most of the faces in the crowd were still turned to follow the presidential car as it drove away from them. So that, as Lyndon Johnson's car made its
slow way down the canyon, what lay ahead of him on that motorcade could, in a

way, have been seen by someone observing his life as a foretaste of what might lie ahead of him if he remained as Vice President for the next five years: five years of trailing behind another man, humiliated, almost ignored—most important, powerless. The vice presidency, *"filled with trips . . . chauffeurs, men saluting, people clapping . . . in the end it is nothing."* He had had three years of that nothing; to stay as Vice President might mean five years more of it.

And if there was nothing at the end of the Dallas canyon but empty sky, what, the observer might have asked, would there be for him at the end of that five-year-long canyon; what would there be at the end if he stayed on as Vice President? He had accepted the vice presidency because he had felt that at the end might be the presidency. Now there was another man who wanted the presidency. And in five years, Bobby Kennedy would have had five more years to build up a record. He would have had five years to hold other positions besides attorney general: secretary of Defense, perhaps—whatever positions he wanted, in the last analysis. And could Lyndon Johnson realistically believe, after watching the rapport between John Kennedy and his brother, that if President Kennedy had to choose between him and his brother to be his successor, he would choose Lyndon Johnson? Observing Lyndon Johnson's life, one might have wondered if what was waiting for him at the end of the vice presidency, in that empty space at the end of it, was only that slight, hunched figure he had long hated and now had learned to fear?

And what if his vice presidency wasn't five years longer, but only one? What if he was dropped from the ticket in 1964?

He had been saying for some time—had apparently convinced himself—that that was the probability. That belief—that fear—may, or may not, have been justified before the call to Copenhagen, before Bobby Baker had been on magazine cover after magazine cover, before the name of Don Reynolds had entered the picture; and before this trip to Texas. Given what the President was seeing for himself in Texas, given what was happening at that very moment in the Senate Office Building, the President's assurances that he would be on the ticket might start to have a hollow ring indeed. Whether he had another term as Vice President or not, Lyndon Johnson's prospects may indeed have justified the adjective he had been applying to them: *"finished."*

LEAVING BEHIND the deep crowds of Main Street, the motorcycle police, the lead car and the presidential limousine swung right onto Houston Street and then left onto Elm, which sloped slightly downhill toward a broad railroad overpass; on the right was a grassy open space, with scattered spectators standing in it, called "Dealey Plaza." In Washington, at just about the same time, Don Reynolds was showing the Rules Committee investigators the papers—the invoices from the Magnavox Company, the checks made out to KTBC—which he said proved his charges against Lyndon Johnson, pushing the documents, one by one, across the witness table. In New York, the *Life* editors were assigning reporters from its task force to investigate specific areas of Lyndon Johnson's finances while still debating whether the magazine should run a story on Johnson's wealth in the magazine's very next issue. Ahead of the vice presidential car, the spectators in Dealey Plaza began to applaud the Kennedys and the Connallys as Johnson followed in their wake.

There was a sharp, cracking sound.

It "startled" him, Lyndon Johnson was to say; it sounded like a "report or explosion," and he didn't know what it was. Others in the motorcade thought it was a backfire from one of the police motorcycles, or a firecracker someone in the crowd had set off, but John Connally, who had hunted all his life, knew in the instant he heard it that it was a shot from a high-powered rifle.

Rufus Youngblood didn't know what it was, but he saw "not normal movements" in the presidential car ahead down the incline—President Kennedy seemed to be tilting toward his left—and in the Queen Mary immediately ahead of him, one of the agents was suddenly rising to his feet, with an automatic rifle in his hands. Whirling in his seat, Youngblood shouted—in a "voice I had never heard him ever use," Lady Bird says—"Get down! Get *down*!" and, grabbing Johnson's right shoulder, yanked him roughly down toward the floor in the center of the car, as he almost leapt over the back of the front seat, and threw his body over the Vice President's body, shouting again, *"Get down! Get down!"* By the time, a matter of only eight seconds later, that the next two sharp reports had cracked out—everyone knew what they were now—Lyndon Johnson was down on the floor in the back seat of the car, curled over on his right side. The sudden, loud, sharp sound, the hand suddenly grabbing his shoulder and pulling him down—now he was on the floor, his face on the floor, with the weight of a big man lying on top of him, pressing him down; Lyndon Johnson would never forget "his knees in my back and his elbows in my back."

He couldn't see anything other than Lady Bird's shoes and legs in front of his face—she and Yarborough were ducking forward as far as they could. Above him, as he lay there, he heard Youngblood yelling to Herschel Jacks to "Close it up! Close it up!"—the Secret Service agent still wasn't sure what had happened, but he knew he would have the most protection if he stayed close to the car ahead of him that was packed with men and guns; and, lying on the floor with Youngblood on top of him, Lyndon Johnson felt the car beneath him leap forward as Jacks floored the gas pedal, and he felt the car speeding—"terrifically fast," Lady Bird was to say, "faster and faster"; "I remember the way that car . . . zoomed," Johnson was to say—and then the brakes were slammed on, and the tires screamed almost in his ear as the car took a right turn much too fast, squealing up the ramp to an expressway, and hurtled forward again. "Stay with them—keep close!" Youngblood was shouting above him. The shortwave radio was still strapped to Youngblood's shoulder, so that it was almost in Johnson's ear. The radio had been set to the Secret Service's Baker frequency, which kept Youngblood in touch with the vice presidential follow-up car, but now Johnson heard the agent's voice above him say, "I am switching to Charlie"—the frequency that would connect him with the Queen Mary ahead of him. For a moment there was, from the radio, only crackling, and then Johnson heard someone saying, "He's hit! Hurry, he's hit!" and then "Let's get out of here!"—and then in his ear a lot of almost unintelligible shouting, out of which one word emerged clearly: "hospital."

He still couldn't see anything, so he didn't see what Youngblood was seeing, as, sitting more erect now, the agent stayed on top of him, shielding his body with his own. He didn't see what Youngblood was seeing ahead: as the third shot had rung out, a little bit of something gray had seemed to fly up out of Jack Kennedy's head; then his wife in her pink pillbox hat and pink suit, that seemed suddenly to have patches of something dark on it, was trying to climb onto the long trunk of the limousine, and then was clambering back into the car, where her head was bent over something Youngblood couldn't see; one of the agents on the Queen Mary's running board, Clint Hill, had, a moment after the first shot, sprinted after the limousine as it was accelerating, leapt onto its trunk, grabbed one of its handholds, and was now lying spread-eagled across the trunk of the speeding vehicle, but he managed to raise his head, look down into its rear seat, and then, turning to the follow-up car, make a thumbs-down gesture.

The agents in the Queen Mary were waving at Jacks to stay close. The patrolman, a laconic Texan—"tight-lipped and cool," Youngblood was to call him—pulled up within a few feet of the armored car's rear bumper, and kept his car there as the two vehicles, with the presidential limousine not many feet ahead of them, roared along the expressway and then swung right at an exit ramp.

The man underneath Rufus Youngblood was lying very quietly, seemingly calmly, except when his body was jolted forward or back as the car braked or accelerated or swerved. His composure would have surprised most people who knew Lyndon Johnson, but not the few who had seen him in other moments of physical danger, including moments when he was under gunfire. Johnson's customary reaction to physical danger, real or imagined, was so dramatic, almost panicky, that at college he had had the reputation of being "an absolute physical coward." All during World War II he had done everything he could to avoid combat. Realizing, however, that, "for the sake of political future," as one of President Roosevelt's aides wrote, he had to be able to say he had at least been in a combat zone, he went to the South Pacific and flew as an observer on a bomber that was attacked by Japanese Zeroes. And as the Zeroes were heading straight for the bomber, firing as they came, its crew saw Lyndon Johnson climb into the navigator's bubble so that he could get a better view, and stand there staring right at the oncoming planes, "just as calm," in the words of one crew member, "as if he were on a sight-seeing tour." Although his customary reaction to minor pain or illness was "frantic," "hysterical"—he would, says Posh Oltorf, "complain so often, and so loudly" about indigestion that "you thought he might be dying"— when in 1955, in Middleburg, Virginia, a doctor told Johnson that this time the "indigestion" was the heart attack he had always feared, Johnson's demeanor changed. Lying on the floor of Middleburg's "ambulance"—it was actually a hearse—as it was speeding to Washington, he was composed and cool as he made decisions: telling the doctor and Oltorf, who were riding in the ambulance, what hospital he was to be taken to, which members of his staff should be there when he arrived; telling Oltorf where his will was, and how he wanted its provisions carried out. It was a major heart attack—when he arrived at the hospital, doctors gave him only a fifty-fifty chance of survival—and at one point during the trip Johnson told the doctor that he couldn't stand the pain. But when the doctor told him that giving him an injection to dull it would require stopping for a few minutes, and that "time means a lot to you," Johnson said, "If time means a lot, don't stop." There were even wry remarks; when the doctor told him that if he recovered, he would never be able to smoke again, he said, "I'd rather have my pecker cut off." Lady Bird was always saying that her husband was "a good man in a tight spot." Oltorf had never believed her—until that ambulance ride. He had thought he knew Johnson so well, he was to say; he had realized on that ride that he didn't know him at all. This, in Dallas, was a tight spot. Lying on the floor of the back seat with Youngblood still on top of him, Johnson asked the Secret Service man what had happened. Youngblood said that "the President must have been shot or wounded," that they were heading for a hospital, that he didn't know anything, and that he wanted everyone to stay down—Johnson down on the floor—until he found out.

"All right, Rufus," Lyndon Johnson said. A reporter who later asked Youngblood to describe the tone of Johnson's voice as he said this summarized the agent's answer in a single word: "calm."

A moment later, the voice on the shortwave radio told Youngblood that they were heading to Parkland Hospital, and the agent, shouting, he was to recall, against the noise of the wind and the wail of police sirens, told Johnson what to do when they arrived: to get out of the car and into some area the Secret Service could make secure without stopping for anything, even to find out what had happened to the President. "I want you and Mrs. Johnson to stick with me and the other agents as close as you can. We are going into the hospital and we aren't gonna stop for anything or anybody. Do you understand?"

"Okay, pardner, I understand," Lyndon Johnson said.

THERE WAS another squealing turn—left onto the entrance ramp to the Parkland Emergency Room; the car skidded so hard that "I wondered if they were going to make it," Lady Bird said—and then the brakes were jammed on so hard that Johnson, and Youngblood, were slammed back against the seat. Then Youngblood's weight was off him; hands were grabbing his arms and pulling him roughly up out of the car and onto his feet. The white carnation was still in his lapel, somehow untouched, but his left arm and shoulder, that had taken the brunt of Youngblood's weight, hurt. There were Secret Service men all around; police all around; guns all around. Then Youngblood and four other agents were surrounding him, the hands were on his arms again, and he was being hustled—almost run—through the entrance to the hospital and through corridors; close behind him was another agent, George Hickey, holding an AR-15 automatic rifle at the ready. He was later to say that he had been rushed into the hospital so fast, his view blocked by the men around him, that he hadn't even seen the President's car, or what was in it. Lady Bird, rushed along right behind him by her own cordon of agents, had seen, in "one last look over my shoulder," "a bundle of pink, just like a drift of blossoms, lying on the back seat. I think it was Mrs. Kennedy lying over the President's body."

Lyndon Johnson was being hustled, agents' hands on his arms, down one hospital corridor after another, turning left, turning right; his protectors were looking for a room that could be made secure; then he was in what seemed like a small white room—it was actually one of three cubicles in the Parkland Minor Medicine section that had been carved out of a larger room by hanging white muslin curtains from ceiling to floor. Two of the cubicles had been unoccupied; in the third, a nurse was treating a patient; the agents were pushing nurse and patient out the door; they were pulling down the shades and blinds over the windows. Then he and Lady Bird were standing against a blank, uncurtained wall at the back of the furthest cubicle. Youngblood was standing in front of them, telling another agent to station himself outside the door to the corridor, and not to let anyone in—not anyone—unless he knew his face. Three of the other agents were stationed in the cubicle between this one and the corridor. Someone was saying Youngblood should get to a telephone and report to his superiors in Washington; Youngblood was saying, "Look here, I'm not leaving this man to phone *anyone*." Remembering that a Vice President's daughters did not normally receive Secret Service protection, he asked Lady Bird where the girls were at the moment (Lynda Bird was at the University of Texas, Lucy at her high school in Washington), told one of the agents to call headquarters and have guards assigned to them immediately, and then to get back to the cubicle as fast as possible.

Someone brought two folding chairs into the cubicle, and Lady Bird sat down in one. Lyndon Johnson remained standing, his back against the far wall. As had been the case in every crisis in his life, a first consideration was to have people loyal to him around him, aides and allies who could be counted on to take his orders without question. He knew the Texas congressmen who had been in the motorcade must be nearby, and he asked Youngblood to have them found, and Homer Thornberry was brought in, and after a while Jack Brooks. His aide Cliff Carter came in and handed him a container of coffee, which he drank.

And then, for long minutes, no one came in. Lyndon Johnson stood with his back against the far wall. It was very quiet in the little curtained space. "We didn't know what was happening," Thornberry was to recall. "We did not know about the condition of the President. . . . I walked out once to try to see if I could find out what was going on, but either nobody knew or they didn't tell me." Johnson asked Youngblood to send an agent to get some news, and he returned with Roy Kellerman, chief of the White House Secret Service detail, but Kellerman didn't provide much information. "Mr. Johnson asked me the condition of the people and the Governor," he was to relate. "I advised him that the Governor was taken up to surgery, that the doctors were still working on the President. He asked me to keep him informed of their condition."

There was more waiting. "Lyndon and I didn't speak," Lady Bird Johnson says. "We just *looked* at each other, exchanging messages with our eyes. We knew what it might mean." Johnson said very little to anyone, moved around very little, just stood there. Asked to describe him in the hospital, Thornberry uses the same word Youngblood used to describe him in the car. "All through the time he was . . . very calm," Thornberry was to say. Kellerman's deputy Emory Roberts came in and said that he had seen the President as doctors were working over him in the emergency room, and said, as he was to recall, that "I did not think the President could make it"—and that Johnson should leave the hospital, get to Air Force One "immediately," and take off for Washington. Youngblood agreed. The word "conspiracy" was in the air. Not merely the President but the governor had been shot; who knew if Johnson might himself have been the next target had not Youngblood so quickly covered his body with his own? The Secret Service wanted to get Johnson out of Dallas, or at least onto the plane, which would, in their view, be the most secure place in the city.

But Johnson did not agree. No one had yet given him any definite word on the President's condition; no one had yet made, in that little curtained room, any explicit statement. In Brooks' recollection, he said, "Well, we want to get the official report on that rather than [from] some individual." He wouldn't leave without permission from the President's staff, he said, preferably from the staff member who was, among the White House staffers in Dallas, the closest to the President: Ken O'Donnell. Youngblood and Roberts continued, in Youngblood's phrase, to "press Johnson" to leave the hospital "immediately"—they "suggested that he [the Vice President] think it over, as he would have to be sworn in"—but Johnson didn't change his mind "about staying put until there was some definite word on the President."

And there was still, for minutes that seemed very long, no definite word. "Every face that came in, you searched for the answers you must know," Lady Bird Johnson was to say. Lyndon Johnson still stood against the wall in that small, curtained space, his wife sitting beside him, two or three men off to one side, standing silent or occasionally whispering among themselves; standing in front of him, "always there was Rufe," Mrs. Johnson says. Johnson stood there for about thirty-five minutes. Then, at 1:20, O'Donnell appeared at the door and crossed the room to Lyndon Johnson, and seeing the stricken "face of Kenny O'Donnell who loved him so much," Lady Bird knew.

"He's gone," O'Donnell said, to the thirty-sixth President of the United States.

When the first calls came into George Hunt's office at *Life* reporting "that Kennedy had been shot—at first, that's all: just that he had been shot," Russ Sackett recalls—the meeting broke up immediately, with editors and reporters running back to their offices.

While, during the next few minutes, the news was trickling in from Dallas, one decision was made quickly: Keith Wheeler's proposed second article on Lyndon Johnson would not run in the next issue of the magazine: there was obviously going to be so much other news that there would be no room for it. About a week later, William Lambert went in to see executive editor Ralph Graves and told Graves that any further investigation into Johnson's finances should be postponed. "I told him I thought we ought to give the guy a chance," he said about the President, and Graves agreed, saying, in Lambert's recollection: "If you hadn't said that, I was going to tell you that."

No one thought to notify the four men meeting behind closed doors in Room 312 of the Old Senate Office Building about what was happening in Dallas, and Don Reynolds continued giving his account, and pushing his checks and invoices across the table to Van Kirk and Drennan. According to the most definitive account of the Bobby Baker case, it was shortly after 2:30 Washington time (1:30 Texas time), about ten minutes after O'Donnell had told Lyndon Johnson, "He's gone," that Reynolds finished, and just as he did, a secretary "burst into the room . . . sobbing almost hysterically," and shouting that President Kennedy had been killed. Reynolds, saying that since Johnson was now President, "you won't need those," reached for his documents to take them back, but Van Kirk refused to let him take them, saying that they now belonged to the Rules Committee.

At the moment the news from Dallas reached Abe Fortas' office, he was conferring with Bobby Baker, who had retained him as his attorney in the Rules Committee investigation, and in any criminal prosecutions that might follow.

"As soon as" the news came, Baker recalls, he realized that if Fortas continued to represent him, the attorney might find himself in "a conflict-of-interest situation." Telling Fortas, "I know Lyndon Johnson will be calling on you for advice," he released him as his attorney.

12

Taking Charge

"HE'S GONE," Ken O'Donnell said—"and right then," Homer Thornberry says, "he took charge."

Even before O'Donnell came in, as Lyndon Johnson had been standing against the back wall of that curtained cubicle in Parkland Hospital, there had been something striking in his bearing, something that had first shown itself that day in the tone of his voice as he lay on the floor of a speeding car, with a heavy body on top of him and the frantic voices on the shortwave radio crackling in his ears. Johnson's aides and allies knew that for all his rages and bellowing, his gloating and groaning, his endless monologues, his demeanor was very different in moments of crisis, in moments when there were decisions—tough decisions, crucial decisions—to be made; that in those moments he became, as his secretary Mary Rather says, "quiet and still." He had been very quiet during the long minutes he stood there in the little room—"very little passed between us," Homer Thornberry says; no words even to Lady Bird; as he stood in front of that blank wall, carnation still in his buttonhole, there was a stillness about him, an immobility, a composure that hadn't been seen very much during the past three years. Though he had been for those years restless, unable to sit still, unable to keep his mind on one subject, unable to stop talking, he wasn't restless in that little room.

And the hangdog look was gone, replaced with an expression—the lines on the face no longer drooping but hard—that Jack Brooks describes as "set." Lyndon Johnson's oldest aides and allies, the men who had known him longest, knew that expression: the big jaw jutting, the lips above it pulled into a tight, grim line, the corners turned down in a hint of a snarl, the eyes, under those long black eyebrows, narrowed, hard, piercing. It was an expression of determination and fierce concentration; when Lyndon Johnson wore that expression, a problem was being thought through with an intensity that was almost palpable, a problem was being thought through—and a decision made. That expression, set and hard, was, Busby says, Lyndon Johnson's "deciding expression," and that was his expression now. To Lady Bird Johnson, looking up at her husband, his face had become "almost a graven image of a face carved in bronze."

What was going through Lyndon Johnson's mind as he stood there history will never know. The only thing that is clear is that if, during those long minutes of waiting, he was making decisions—this man with the instinct to decide, the *will* to decide—by the time O'Donnell spoke and the waiting was over, the decisions had been made.

O'Donnell and the Secret Service agents were still urging him to leave the hospital and fly back to Washington at once. "We've got to get in the air," Emory Roberts said again. The possibility of "conspiracy" was looming larger, because Johnson now learned, or was reminded, that six members of the Cabinet—including Secretary of State Rusk and Treasury Secretary Dillon—together with Press Secretary Pierre Salinger were not in Washington but in a plane en route to a conference in Japan; in fact, they were at that moment somewhere west of Hawaii. Johnson, as one account puts it, was "disturbed to learn that half the Cabinet [was] five time zones away, somewhere over the vast Pacific Ocean," and all together on the same plane. The Dallas motorcade had been one of the rare occasions when President and Vice President were not only both out of Washington but both in the same motorcade; with so many other officials away from Washington at the same time, and bunched together on the same plane, the shots at the President had been fired at a moment when the government of the United States was unusually vulnerable. Was that fact only a coincidence, or was it the reason the moment had been chosen? The possibility that the shooting was "part of a far-ranging conspiracy" that "had not yet run its course" was "in the thoughts of everyone," Youngblood recalls. Among the reporters being herded into a nurses' classroom at the other end of Parkland Hospital that was going to be the press briefing room, there was, as Charles Roberts, *Newsweek*'s longtime White House correspondent, recalls, "a fear that—perhaps a lot of people thought, as I did, of Lincoln's assassination, where not only Lincoln, but four or five of his Cabinet were marked for assassination, that it might be, just might be, an attempt to literally wipe out the entire top echelon of government. We certainly had no way of knowing that it was a lone . . . gunman." The urging from the three men standing in front of Johnson intensified. "Sir," Youngblood said, "we *must* leave here immediately." O'Donnell told him "that in my opinion he ought to get out of there as fast as he could." "We've got to get in the air," Emory Roberts said.

But Johnson reached a different decision—and he announced it as quickly as if he had already thought through all the options and decided what he would do. When O'Donnell kept pressing him to leave Dallas, he asked him, "Well, what about Mrs. Kennedy?" and when O'Donnell said that she was determined not to leave her husband's body (at that moment, she was standing, shocked and silent, in a corridor outside the room in which the body was lying) and that Johnson should fly back without her, while she and her husband's body and aides followed in another plane, Johnson said he wasn't going to do that—that he would take her back on the same plane with him. O'Donnell said she would never leave the hospital without the body. Johnson said in that case he would leave the hospital but not Dallas; he would go to the plane, but he would wait aboard it for the coffin, and the widow, to arrive. A contrary course continued to be urged. A new adjective entered the descriptions of Lyndon Johnson. He was, Youngblood says, "adamant."

He wasn't ignoring the conspiracy possibility; in fact, he "mentioned . . . the attempt on the life of Secretary of State Seward at the time of Lincoln's assassination," O'Donnell says. Therefore, Johnson said, since they were going to leave the hospital, they should leave immediately. Exchanging quick sentences, he and Youngblood agreed that because of the possibility of another assassination attempt, the trip back to Love Field should be made in as much secrecy as possible: by different hospital corridors from the ones they had run through on the way in; in different cars from the ones they had arrived in; by a different route from the one the motorcade had taken into the city. Youngblood said that when they started moving, they should move fast, and should use black, unmarked cars, with Johnson and Lady Bird in separate cars, and Johnson told him to have the cars gotten ready, and Youngblood sent an agent to do so, telling him to have the cars waiting, with their motors running, in the ambulance bays at the emergency room entrance, and to make sure the drivers knew backstreet routes to the airport so they could use them if necessary. "Quick plans were made about how to get to the car . . . who to ride in what," Lady Bird was to say. Her husband, she was to say, "was the most decisive person around us. Not that he wasn't willing to listen . . . but he was quick to decide."

A MOMENT LATER, another decision had to be made. The press secretary on the Texas trip, Salinger's assistant Malcolm Kilduff, came into the curtained room to ask Johnson's permission to announce Kennedy's death to the press corps that was waiting in the nurses' classroom.

"Mr. President," he began. It was the first time that anyone had ever called Lyndon Johnson that, but when he answered Kilduff, it was a President answering, firm and in command. "He reacted immediately," Kilduff was to recall. Immediately, and unequivocally. "No," he said, don't make that announcement yet. "Wait until I get out of here and back to the plane before you announce it. We don't know whether this is a worldwide conspiracy, whether they are after me as well. . . . We just don't know." And get in touch with that plane carrying the Cabinet, he said. Get that plane turned around.*

He made his dispositions. There hadn't been many allies in that motorcade; three whose loyalty he could count on were the Texas congressmen, and he told the two who were in the room, Homer Thornberry and Jack Brooks, to ride back

---

*The Cabinet plane, notified of the assassination by the White House, had already turned around, but neither Johnson nor anyone in the room with him was aware of that.

to the plane with him. He wanted every one of the few aides who had accompanied him to Dallas rounded up: he told Cliff Carter not to leave the hospital with
him, but to find Liz Carpenter and Marie Fehmer and bring them to the plane.
That still wasn't much staff. Among the handful of people in his party was a
Houston public relations man, Jack Valenti, who had caught Johnson's attention
a few years before by writing favorable newspaper columns about him, and who
had worked with him on arrangements for the Albert Thomas Appreciation Dinner. He told Carter to find Valenti, and bring him. Carter and his crew would need
a driver, he told Youngblood, and Youngblood assigned an agent to wait at the
ambulance bays until they arrived. Then he was ready. "Homer, you go with me,"
he said. "Jack, you go with Bird."

In a rush—not running, because that would call attention to them, but walking as fast as they could—they left the cubicle, through hospital corridors, following a red stripe on the floor to the emergency-room exit where the cars were
waiting, Youngblood first, his head turning ceaselessly from side to side as he
searched for danger, Johnson second, his eyes down as if he didn't want to catch
the eye of anyone who might be watching, then the two congressmen, and then
two more Secret Service agents, and Lady Bird, who kept breaking into a trot as
she tried to keep up. "Getting out of the hospital was one of the *swiftest* walks I
have ever made," she was to recall. The White House press corps was gathered in
the nurses' classroom at the other end of Parkland Hospital, waiting for word on
Kennedy's condition. As the new President of the United States headed out of
the hospital, Robert Pierpoint of CBS News caught a glimpse of him, but didn't
follow him. No other reporter followed him, or, apparently, even knew he was
leaving. "We weren't thinking about succession," *Newsweek*'s Roberts would
explain. "I don't remember anybody saying, 'My God, Johnson is President.' . . .
There was almost no focus of attention on him, and this was true as they left the
hospital. . . . Nobody made any attempt to follow him, although he was then
President of the United States." One photographer, official White House photographer Captain Cecil Stoughton of the Army Signal Corps, happened to be standing by the emergency-room reception desk at the moment the little procession
hurried by. Suspecting that Kennedy was dead, he decided to follow and caught a
ride a few minutes later with Carter and Valenti.

Getting into the back seat of the first car, Johnson sat behind the driver,
Youngblood by the window on the other side of the back seat, in the place where
the Vice President normally sat, so that if someone fired at the person in that seat,
thinking it was the Vice President, the bullet would hit him instead of Johnson.
Thornberry sat in front. Youngblood told Johnson to keep below window level,
and he slouched down on his shoulder blades.

As they were pulling away from the hospital, another piece of protection
was added. Congressman Thomas, standing near the ambulance bays, saw the
cars, and motioned for them to stop for him. Youngblood told the driver to keep
going, but Johnson said, "Stop and let him get in." Thomas got in the front seat,

beside Thornberry. As the car started moving again, Johnson told Thornberry to climb across the back of the front seat, and get in the rear. Thornberry did, but did not wind up sitting in the vacant space between Johnson and Youngblood. Instead, Youngblood was to report, he "took a position on the window side" behind the driver, where Johnson had been sitting. Whether Johnson had changed seats by accident or design, he now had a human shield between him and any bullets on the left side as well as the right.

One of the motorcycle policemen in front of them began to sound his siren. "Let's don't have the sirens," Johnson said. As they sped through the Dallas streets, Lady Bird, following in the second car, saw, atop a building, a flag at half-mast: "I think that was when the *enormity* of what happened first struck me." And then they were on the Love Field tarmac, and, Youngblood was to recall, "suddenly there before us was one of the most welcome sights I had ever seen"— Air Force One. The staircase to the rear door and the presidential quarters was in place, and he and Lyndon Johnson "practically ran up" the steps.

ENTERING THE REAR of the plane, Johnson walked forward down a narrow aisle, past a sitting area with six first-class-type plane seats, and then past the small bedroom with beds for the President and his wife—"I want this kept strictly for the use of Mrs. Kennedy, Rufus," Johnson said; "see to that"—and into the President's stateroom, a compartment sixteen feet square with a small sofa attached to a wall; a small desk, with a high-backed armchair, for the President; and a small conference table with four chairs. A handful of crew members and White House staff, including two secretaries, were watching the television set. Back at Parkland Hospital, Kilduff had announced Kennedy's death, and Walter Cronkite of CBS News was reporting it to the country. Youngblood was shouting to everyone to pull down the window shades; the possibility of a conspiracy, and of snipers at the airport, still seemed "very real indeed," the agent was to say. From the secretaries came the sound of weeping.

The stateroom was already warm. Having been alerted to prepare for an immediate takeoff, Air Force One's pilot, Colonel Jim Swindal, had disconnected the air-conditioning unit, mounted on a mobile cart, that kept the plane cool on the ground. The plane's own air-conditioning functioned only when the plane's engines were running. Swindal had only one running, at a low speed that provided electricity for lights in the cabins but not air-conditioning.

For a few minutes, there was a hurried conference between Johnson and the three Texas congressmen, because there were decisions to be made: when and where to take the oath of office, whether here, in Dallas, or in Washington, where there could be a formal ceremony, in an appropriate setting, with the oath administered by Chief Justice Earl Warren, as Warren had administered it to John F. Kennedy at his inauguration. Harry Truman, another Vice President brought to the presidency by the sudden death of his predecessor, had not been sworn in for two hours and twenty-four minutes after Franklin D. Roosevelt's death (and almost two hours after he had been notified of it), waiting until the Cabinet, congressional leaders and several other key government officials could be assembled in the Cabinet Room at the White House to watch Chief Justice Harlan Stone swear him in. Thornberry argued for Washington, Thomas and Brooks for Dallas, so that the country would immediately see that the succession had taken place: "Suppose the plane is delayed?" Thomas asked. But a few minutes was all that the discussion lasted. There were reasons for the swearing-in to take place quickly: the fact that the President had been assassinated, and that a wider conspiracy might be involved, made the need to establish a sense of continuity, of stability, more urgent; should the Russians try to take advantage of the situation, there should not be the slightest doubt about who was in command. A panic on Wall Street that was to wipe out more than ten billion dollars in stock values within slightly more than an hour was already under way. Although the taking of the oath was a merely symbolic gesture—no one but a Vice President had ever ascended to the presidency when a President died, so precedent had established that a Vice President became President automatically, immediately upon a President's death—it was a powerful symbol. To Johnson it seemed particularly meaningful, as if, despite the fact that he had actually been President since the moment Kennedy died, it would be the taking of the oath that would truly make him President; later, discussing November 22, he would say: "I took the oath. I became President." During the discussion, a crew member saw that Johnson was "very much in command," and as soon as Thomas finished arguing for taking the oath in Dallas, he said, "I agree."

IF COOLNESS and decisiveness under pressure were components of Lyndon Johnson's character, there were, however, as always with Johnson, other, contrasting components.

Aware though he was of considerations that militated against anyone entering the presidential bedroom, that it should be kept "strictly for the use of Mrs. Kennedy," as he had instructed Youngblood, there now arose another consideration. He had telephone calls to make, including one of a particularly delicate nature, and he wanted privacy while he made them.

Privacy was available in the stateroom where he was standing (as it happens he was standing right beside a telephone); doors on either side of the room could close it off completely from the rest of the plane; he could have asked the people in the room to leave and closed the doors. But he had more privacy in mind than that. Leading Marie Fehmer—and Youngblood, who said he would not leave his side until the plane was in the air—into the Kennedys' bedroom, he closed the door, pulled off the jacket of his suit and sat down, sprawling down, on one of the beds.

And these other components were demonstrated also by the identity of the person to whom the delicate phone call was made, and by the questions Lyndon Johnson asked during the call.

Objective, rational reasons can explain why Lyndon Johnson called Robert Kennedy. One of the purposes of the call was to obtain a legal opinion on a matter of governmental policy, and Kennedy was the country's chief legal officer. And, the decision to take the oath having been made, the wording of the oath was needed, and there was also the question of who was legally empowered to administer it, and these pieces of information could be obtained most authoritatively from the same source.

And there were strategic reasons for him to have called Bobby. Lyndon Johnson seems to have had even in this first hour after John F. Kennedy's death feelings that would torment him for the rest of his life—feelings understandable in any man placed in the presidency not through an election but through an assassin's bullet, and feelings exacerbated in his case by the contrast, and what he felt was the world's view of the contrast, between him and the President he was replacing; by the contempt in which he had been held by the people around the President; and by the stark geographical fact of the location of the act that had elevated him to office. Recalling his feelings years later, in his retirement, he would say that even after he had taken the oath, "for millions of Americans I was still illegitimate, a naked man with no presidential covering, a pretender to the throne, an illegal usurper. And then there was Texas, my home, the home of . . . the murder. . . . And then there were the bigots and the dividers and the Eastern intellectuals, who were waiting to knock me down before I could even begin to stand up." He seems to have felt even in this first hour that the best way to legitimize his ascent to the throne, to make himself seem less like a usurper, would be to demonstrate that his ascent had the support of his predecessor's family. The decision to be sworn in immediately, in Dallas, instead of waiting until he returned to Washington, had been made, but he wanted that decision to be approved by the man whose approval would carry the most weight.

There were, of course, reasons for him not to have called Robert Kennedy, reasons for him to have obtained the information he wanted from someone else—from anyone else. The questions he asked on the call—whether the swearing-in could take place in Dallas? what was the wording of the oath? who could administer it?—were not complicated questions, and could have been answered by any one of a hundred government officials. One of them, in fact, was an official he had already dealt with extensively on questions of vice presidential procedure—on the drafting of the executive order establishing the Committee on Equal Opportunity, for example—and whom he trusted and even felt a rapport with: the number two man in the Justice Department, Deputy Attorney General Nicholas Katzenbach.

And there were other—non-governmental—considerations that might have led him to telephone Katzenbach or some other official rather than the one he called, considerations of humanity rather than of politics. But none of these more personal considerations appear to have had much weight with him (unless, perhaps, they did). Whatever the reasons, a half hour after Robert Kennedy had been told that the brother he loved so deeply was dead, the telephone rang again at Hickory Hill, and when Kennedy picked it up, he found himself talking to the man he hated so deeply—who was asking him to provide details of the precise procedure by which he could, without delay, assume his brother's office.

ROBERT KENNEDY HAD BEEN having lunch with Ethel, United States Attorney Robert Morgenthau of New York and Morgenthau's deputy Silvio Mollo by the side of the swimming pool at Hickory Hill. It was a bright, sunny day, warm for November. At the top of the lawn sloping up from the pool, workmen were painting a new wing that had been added to the rambling white house. Suddenly, Morgenthau saw one of the workmen start running toward them. He was holding a transistor radio in his hand, and he was shouting something that no one understood. Just then a telephone rang on the other side of the pool, and Ethel walked around the pool to answer it, and said it was J. Edgar Hoover, and Bobby walked over to take the call, and Morgenthau saw him clap his hand to his mouth and turn away with a look of "shock and horror" on his face. "Jack's been shot," he said. "It may be fatal." He walked back to the house, and tried to get more news, and a few minutes later—at 2:25, according to White House phone logs—he got it, from a White House aide, and a few minutes after that it was confirmed by Hoover, and then, at 2:56, Lyndon Johnson was on the phone.

This call—and a second one between Johnson and Robert Kennedy six minutes later—was not recorded, and, as had been the case with the meetings of the two men in Los Angeles three years before, their recollections differ. The only witnesses to the calls—Rufus Youngblood and Marie Fehmer—heard only one side of them, and their impressions of what occurred differ markedly from those of Katzenbach, to whom Robert Kennedy spoke both between the two calls, and immediately afterwards. But whatever the differences, there emerges from the recollections and impressions a picture of two conversations between a man who knew exactly what he wanted and what to say in order to get it, and a man so stunned by grief and shock that he hardly knew what he was saying, or even, to some extent, what he was hearing.

Johnson would give accounts of the telephone calls several times, both in the months immediately following the assassination, and in 1967, when the dispute over the conversations grew so public and bitter that it, along with the dispute over his Los Angeles meetings with Robert Kennedy, not only became a crucial element in this great blood feud, perhaps the greatest blood feud of American politics in the twentieth century, but also one that played a role, small but not insignificant, in decisions that shaped the course of American history. By his account, he telephoned Kennedy because "I wanted to say something to comfort him in his grief." And, by Johnson's account, he succeeded in this purpose, bringing Kennedy's mind around to practical matters. "In spite of his shock and sorrow," Johnson said, Kennedy "discussed the practical problems at hand with dispatch"; he was "very businesslike." They discussed "the matter of my taking the oath of office," and "the possibility of a conspiracy," Johnson was to say. Kennedy, he says, "said that he would like to look into the matter of" when and where the oath should be administered, and "call back," and when Kennedy called back, "he said that the oath should be administered to me immediately." Kennedy's accounts of the conversations, including one he gave that evening to Ken O'Donnell after O'Donnell had arrived back in Washington, were different. Johnson had, Bobby said, told him that "a lot of people down here had advised him to be sworn in right away" and asked if he had any objections. When there was no immediate reply, Johnson pressed him, asking, "Do you have any objections to that?" Bobby said he hadn't replied to the question. "I was too surprised to say anything about it. I said to myself what's the rush? Couldn't he wait until he got the President's body out of there and back to Washington?" Johnson, in this account, took—or used—silence as assent. "He began to ask me a lot of questions about who should swear him in. I was too confused and upset to talk to him about it." In a later conversation Bobby taped for posterity, he said he had never told Johnson that the oath should be administered immediately. "I was sort of taken aback at the moment because I didn't think—see what the rush was." In fact, he says, his wishes were the opposite of what Johnson portrayed them to be. "I thought, I suppose, at the time, at least, I thought it would be nice if the President came back to Washington [as] President Kennedy." The only aspect of the conversation that is agreed on was that Kennedy said he would look into the matter and call Johnson back.

Kennedy called Katzenbach, who recalls him saying: "They want to swear him in right away in Texas. That's not necessary, is it?"

"No, not necessary," Katzenbach replied. And when Kennedy asked who could swear him in, Katzenbach said "anyone who can administer an oath," a category that included any federal judge or hundreds of other federal officials; the place or exact time of the swearing-in didn't matter; "You become President when the President dies—that's accepted. It's not a question."

Katzenbach was to say he agreed that an immediate swearing-in, while not necessary, was desirable, "given its symbolic significance." But, he told the author, he was "absolutely stunned" that Johnson had made the call to Bobby Kennedy so soon after his brother's death. So many federal officials could have given Johnson the information he was seeking, he says. "He could have called *me*. I was in my office." He felt Johnson might have made the call because "he may have wanted to be absolutely sure that there wouldn't be an explosion from Bobby's end"—wanted to ensure that Bobby would not later say that the immediate swearing-in showed a lack of respect for the dead President. But, he says, given Bobby's "feelings about Johnson, and about his brother," the fact that Johnson had called Bobby so soon after his brother's death "frankly appalled" him. "Calling Bobby was really wrong."

Then there was a second call—the return call from Robert Kennedy to Lyndon Johnson—about which, as William Manchester writes, "the facts are unclear and a dispassionate observer cannot choose." Johnson was to say that on this call Kennedy advised him "that the oath should be administered to me, immediately, before taking off for Washington, and that it could be administered by any judicial officer." During the call, however, it became clear that the questions of when and where the oath should be administered were in fact now moot, and that all Johnson wanted from Kennedy was the oath's precise wording. Kennedy said he would have Katzenbach dictate it; telephoning his deputy again, he said, "They're going to swear him in down there, and he needs the oath." Katzenbach pulled a copy of the Constitution off his bookshelf, and read the thirty-seven-word declaration that is in Article II, Section 1: " I do solemnly swear (or affirm) that I will faithfully execute the office of president of the United States, and will to the best of my ability, preserve, protect and defend the Constitution of the United States."

Johnson had told Marie Fehmer to go out to the staff section of the plane and take down the wording. "Bobby started it and turned the phone to Katzenbach," she recalls. (Katzenbach apparently patched in to this second call.) What was Katzenbach's voice like at that time? she is asked. "It was controlled; he was like steel," she replies. "Bobby's was not when he started. I kept thinking, 'You shouldn't be doing this.' " When Katzenbach finished, she says, she asked him, " 'May I read it back to you?' Which I afterward thought may have been a little cruel, but yet I wanted to check it." As for her own emotional state at the time, she says, "I was all right. I broke up later that night, but I was all right. You get that feeling from him [Johnson]. He taught you that, by George, you can do anything. . . . There was a job to be done."

Whatever the disputes over the telephone calls, the oath was dictated, and typed out, and if the desired assent by Bobby Kennedy to its immediate administration was not obtained, at least he had been asked whether he objected to that, and had not replied, so it would be difficult for him to criticize it later; the possibility of public criticism from the President's brother had been muted (as it would turn out, only for a time). The call to Hickory Hill had achieved its purpose. Whatever the details of the conversation between Lyndon Johnson and Robert Kennedy, when Johnson hung up the phone he had gotten enough of what he wanted so that he could go ahead.

HANGING UP THE PHONE, he began giving orders. Any federal judge could swear him in, he had been told. He knew what judge he wanted—and she was right in Dallas.

"As much as any single person possibly could," an historian has written, this judge had "personified Johnson's utter powerlessness" during his vice presidency. He had been unable to secure her appointment; she had been named to the Federal District Court in Dallas only after Sam Rayburn had intervened, a fact which had made Johnson feel like "the biggest liar and fool in the State."

"Get Sarah Hughes," he told Marie Fehmer.

Judge Hughes' law clerk told Ms. Fehmer he didn't know the judge's whereabouts—the last he knew, he said, she had been at the Trade Mart luncheon waiting for the President to arrive—and Fehmer told Johnson that.

He told her to call the clerk back, and picked up the receiver himself. "This is Lyndon Johnson," he said. "Find her."

She was found, and she hurried to Love Field.

HE WANTED SOMETHING MORE from the Kennedys, and he got that, too.

No single gesture would do more to demonstrate continuity and stability— to show that the government of the United States would continue to function without interruption despite the assassination of the man who sat at its head— and to legitimize the transition: to prove that the transfer of power had been orderly, proper, in accordance with the Constitution; to remove, in the eyes of the world, any taint of usurpation; to dampen, so far as possible, suspicion of complicity by him in the deed; to show that the family of the man he was succeeding bore him no ill will and supported him, than the attendance at his swearing-in ceremony of the late President's widow.

Was this consideration part of the reason—in addition to the humanitarian consideration that he didn't want her left behind in Dallas—that when the Secret Service and Ken O'Donnell had told him that Jacqueline Kennedy would follow in another plane, he had refused to leave Dallas without her? Certainly some of the Kennedy loyalists harbored that suspicion. "Some of us did feel that he was using Mrs. Kennedy and the Kennedy aura when he stage[d] his oath-taking ceremony . . . with her present, and so he could arrive in Washington with her and President Kennedy's casket," O'Donnell was to write. History will never know the answer to that question. All history can know for certain is that now, on Air Force One, he moved with determination to obtain her presence.

HIS EFFORTS WERE almost derailed at their very start by a moment of awkwardness.

While he was making phone calls—not only to Bobby Kennedy but to Walter Jenkins and McGeorge Bundy—in the plane's bedroom, hammering began on the other side of the bulkhead that separated the bedroom from the rear seating compartment, and when Fehmer went out into the corridor and asked what it was, crew members told her that four of the six seats in the compartment were being removed to make room for Kennedy's heavy bronze coffin, which was about to be brought on board through the plane's rear door, followed by Jackie and Kennedy's aides.

Kennedy's aides were to say later that they weren't aware at that moment that Johnson and his party were aboard the plane, that they had assumed that he had returned to Air Force Two, and in fact had already taken off for Washington.

In the confusion, they hadn't noticed that Air Force Two was still parked nearby. As soon as the Kennedy party was on board, while the coffin was being lashed to the floor, Jackie, seeking a few moments alone, walked past it and opened the door to the bedroom, thinking it would be empty—and instead encountered Lyndon Johnson. Whether, when she opened the door, Johnson was, as Manchester wrote after talking to her, "reclining on the bed" in his shirtsleeves, or whether, as Fehmer later stated ("in an effort to clear up the bedroom thing"), he had already risen from the bed and was about to leave the bedroom when, "as he opened the door, there was Mrs. Kennedy," she was evidently shocked; hastily retreating to the rear compartment, she told O'Donnell, he relates, "something that left me stunned: When she opened the door of her cabin, she found Lyndon Johnson." She wasn't the only one who retreated. "She was entering her private bedroom," Fehmer says. "She . . . saw a stranger, in his shirtsleeves yet . . . in the hallowed ground. . . . We, of course, scurried out of that bedroom. It was really embarrassing."

Returning to the rear compartment, Jackie sat down in one of the two remaining seats, across the aisle from the coffin. In a moment, Lyndon, having collected Lady Bird from the stateroom, came back to see her. "It was a very, very hard thing to do," Lady Bird Johnson was to recall. "Mrs. Kennedy's dress was stained with blood. One leg was almost entirely covered with it and her right glove was *caked*—that *immaculate* woman—it was caked with blood, her husband's blood. She always wore gloves like she was used to them; I never could. Somehow that was one of the most poignant sights . . . [Mrs. Kennedy] exquisitely dressed, and caked in blood." Shocked though she was at Jackie's appearance, Lady Bird found the right things to say: "Dear God, it's come to this . . . ," and Jackie responded, making "it as easy as possible. She said things like 'Oh, Lady Bird . . . we've always liked the two of you so much.' She said . . . 'Oh, *what* if I had not been there. Oh, I'm so glad I was there.' " Only once did Jackie's voice change: when Lady Bird asked her if she wanted to change clothes. Not right then, Jackie said. "And then . . . if with a person that gentle, that dignified, you can say had an element of fierceness, she said, 'I want them to see what they have *done* to Jack.' " And Lyndon finally raised the subject. "Well—about the swearing-in," he said—according to Manchester, he had to use the phrase twice before Jackie responded, "Oh, yes, I know, I know." "She understood the symbols of authority, the need for some semblance of national majesty after the disaster," Manchester was to write; whether she agreed explicitly or not, there was an understanding that when Johnson took the oath, she would be present.

AND WITH HIS WORK with the Kennedys done, Lyndon Johnson headed back to the stateroom.

It was crammed now with people—Secret Service agents; the three Texas congressmen; Kennedy's aides and secretaries who had come aboard with the coffin; two uniformed generals, Kennedy's military aides Clifton and Brigadier General Godfrey McHugh; Johnson aides Carter, Valenti, Fehmer, Liz Carpenter; Bill Moyers, who, hearing of the assassination while in Austin on a trip for the Peace Corps, had chartered a plane, flown to Dallas and come aboard Air Force One; two presidential valets, Kennedy's Thomas and Johnson's Glynn— all crowded together in a sixteen-by-sixteen-foot square that was so dimly lit (with the shades still drawn across the windows, the only lighting came from dim fluorescent bulbs overhead) that the generals' gold braid glinted only faintly in the gloom, and that, with no air-conditioning, had grown so hot and stuffy that, one man says, "It was suffocating in there; it was hard to think." The low, penetrating whine of the single jet engine that was operating never stopped. There was weeping in the room, and whispering—and confusion. Kennedy's aides had been able to remove the dead President's coffin from the hospital only after an angry confrontation with the Dallas County medical examiner, who, insisting that an autopsy had to be performed first, had stood in a hospital doorway to block them, backed by a policeman. They had literally shoved the examiner and the policeman aside to get out of the building, and now, on the plane, O'Donnell says, he "kept looking out the window, expecting to see the flashing red lights" of police cars, "coming with a court order to stop our takeoff." Not knowing when they came aboard that Johnson had decided to wait for Judge Hughes and take the oath on the ground (not knowing for some minutes, in fact, that Johnson was even on board; he was at that time behind the closed door of Kennedy's bedroom), General McHugh had gone forward to the cockpit and ordered Colonel Swindal to take off immediately. Swindal couldn't—the plane's forward door was still open, with the ramp still pushed up against it—and by the time the door was closed, Malcolm Kilduff had come to the cockpit to tell him that the plane wouldn't be taking off until after the swearing-in ceremony. When McHugh, who had apparently passed Kilduff in the aisle without knowing what message the press secretary was bearing, realized the plane wasn't taking off, he rushed back to the cockpit to repeat his order, and Kilduff countermanded it. Not until O'Donnell, "in a highly desperate strait," he says, headed for the cockpit himself did he learn of Johnson's plans. The conflicting orders were less the bitter series of confrontations between Kennedy and Johnson aides that would be later pictured than a misunderstanding, but they added to the confusion. McHugh and other Kennedy aides were still pushing back and forth down the crowded aisle in the passenger portion of the plane, and in the stateroom men and women were asking each other what was happening, what was going to happen, without anyone really knowing.

And then, in the narrow doorway that led back toward the presidential bedroom, there suddenly appeared, in Jack Valenti's words, "the huge figure of Lyndon Johnson."

The carnation was gone; the dark gray of his suit, which appeared black in the dim light, was relieved only by the tiny Silver Star bar in his lapel and a corner of a white handkerchief peeking out from the breast pocket. His thinning hair was slicked down smooth, so that as his head turned from side to side as he surveyed the cabin, checking on who was there, there was nothing to soften that massive skull, or the sharp jut of the big jaw and the big nose, and his mouth was set in that grim, tough line.

Seeing him standing there, Valenti, whose acquaintance with Lyndon Johnson had taken place mainly during his vice presidency, was startled. "Even in that instant, there was a new demeanor in him," he was to say. "He looked graver." The restless movements were gone. "Whatever emotions or passions he had in him, he had put them under a strict discipline" so that "he was very quiet and seemingly very much in command of himself." There had, Valenti says, been "a transformation. . . . [He] was in a strange way another man, not the man I had known."

Other Johnson aides, who had known him longer, saw, after he had returned to Washington that night, the same transformation, but found nothing strange in it. The Lyndon Johnson that Horace Busby saw in Washington that night was a Lyndon Johnson he hadn't seen for three years, but it was a Lyndon Johnson he remembered very well. The Johnson he saw—and that George Reedy and Walter Jenkins and other longtime aides saw—was simply the old Lyndon Johnson, the pre–vice presidential Lyndon Johnson. And Busby understood why he had changed back, and why he had been able to change back so quickly. "You see, it was just that he was coming back *to himself,*" he says. "He was back where he belonged. He was back in command."

As the people in the stateroom noticed Johnson standing in the doorway, the ones who had been sitting rose to their feet. The whispering stopped—even, for a moment, the weeping.

"When I walked in, everyone stood up," Johnson would write in his memoirs. "Here were close friends like Homer Thornberry and Jack Brooks; here were aides. . . . All of them were on their feet. . . . I realized nothing would ever be the same again. . . . To old friends who had never called me anything but Lyndon, I would now be 'Mr. President.' " In the memoir, he says that this "was a frightening, disturbing prospect." But if it was, he gave no sign of that at the time. In the silence, Congressman Thomas said, "We are ready to carry out any orders you have, Mr. President." Walking into the stateroom, as the people made way before him, he sat down in the high-backed President's chair. Beckoning Kilduff over, he told him to make sure a photographer and reporters were aboard to record the swearing-in ceremony. "Put the pool on board," he told him. He beckoned over Valenti. "I want you on my staff," he said. "You'll fly back with me to Washington." And when an order was challenged, no challenge was entertained. When O'Donnell and O'Brien came up to him and asked if the plane could take off immediately, he said: "We can't leave here until we take the oath of office. I just talked on the phone with Bobby. He told me to wait here until

Sarah Hughes gives me the oath." (Then he added a line with connotations. "You must remember Sarah Hughes," he said.) O'Donnell didn't believe him—"I could not imagine Bobby telling him to stay"; Johnson had become President the moment Kennedy died; "the oath is just a symbolic formality"; "there is no need to hurry about it." (And later that night, at Hickory Hill, his skepticism would be confirmed. "Bobby gave me an entirely different version of his conversation with Johnson.") Whether O'Donnell believed him or not no longer signified, however. Johnson's expression hardly changed as he spoke; his voice was so low that, one observer says, "he was almost whispering." But if the voice was soft, that was not the case with the message. "Johnson was adamant that the oath be administered by Judge Hughes," Larry O'Brien was to say. "There was adamancy. It became clear that the oath was going to be administered on the ground." General McHugh was still pushing up and down the aisle, trying to get the plane to take off, not having talked to Johnson directly, but O'Brien and O'Donnell stopped arguing.

Standing up, Johnson moved to the center of the crowded little room (he was, as was the case in most rooms he was in, the tallest person in it), and through the recollections of people present in that room, there runs a common theme: a sense that, out of aimless confusion, order was quickly emerging.

If one reason for his insistence that the swearing-in take place at the earliest possible moment was to demonstrate, quickly, continuity and stability to the nation and the world, then it was important that the nation and the world *see* that a new President had taken office.

Luckily, White House photographer Cecil Stoughton had come aboard, and almost as soon as Johnson had told Malcolm Kilduff to make sure a photographer was present at the ceremony, Kilduff bumped into him in the aisle. "Thank God you're here," Kilduff said. "The President's going to take the oath." And when Stoughton, carrying two cameras, entered the stateroom, seeing "Johnson in there, standing tall," Johnson asked him, "Where do you want us, Cecil?" Stoughton told him that the room was so small that he would have to place his own back against a wall, and, to gain height for a better view, stand on the sofa, and that Johnson and the judge should be directly in front of him, but back a few feet; Johnson began moving people around, directing them to their places with jerks of his thumb—"taking command," in Stoughton's words. Witnesses were important; Kilduff asked Johnson whom he wanted present; "as many people as you can get in here," he replied. Witnesses whose presence—whose photographed presence—would be testimony of continuity and legitimacy, of the Kennedy faction's sanction of his assumption of Kennedy's office, were particularly desirable; two of Jackie's secretaries, Mary Gallagher and Pamela Turnure, were in the forward cabin, crying, and he dispatched Kilduff to get them, and they came in, and so did General Clifton.

And he wanted from the Kennedy people another, more durable, demonstration of continuity; Judge Hughes had not yet arrived; there were a few minutes to spare; he used them.

Sitting down again, he changed both his chair (to one at the conference table; the fact that he was not in the President's chair "in itself did not go unnoticed" by the two men he beckoned over to sit with him) and his tone—in a change so abrupt and dramatic that it would have been startling to anyone who had not witnessed, over the years, Lyndon Johnson's remarkable ability to alter tone completely and instantaneously to accomplish a purpose. Where, just a few minutes before, in his conversations with O'Donnell and O'Brien, there had been "adamancy," in full measure, now—in a new conversation with the same two men—there was humility, and in the same measure.

He wanted them to remain in their White House posts, he told the two Irishmen, still in the first throes of grief for their dead leader, because the best tribute that could be paid to President Kennedy would be passage of the programs he had believed in; they and he should fight for them together, he said, "shoulder to shoulder." And, he said, leaning across the table toward them and looking into their eyes, they should stay on because he needed them. He had so much to learn about his new responsibilities, he said, and he just didn't absorb things as quickly as Jack had. Jack had had not only the experience but the education and understanding; he didn't. "I need your help," he said. "I need it badly. There is no one for me to turn to with as much experience as you have. I need you now more than President Kennedy needed you."

He only had a few minutes to make the plea—hardly had he finished when Judge Hughes arrived. But although O'Donnell and O'Brien made no response at the time—"We can talk about all that later," O'Brien said; O'Donnell was to describe himself as "noncommittal"—events were to prove that his plea had softened their feelings toward him.

JUDGE HUGHES ARRIVED, a tiny woman in a brown dress decorated with white polka dots, and Johnson showed her to the place Stoughton had selected, in front of the sofa on which the photographer was standing, and someone put a small Catholic missal in her hands. Then, a moment later, three reporters— Newsweek's Roberts, Merriman Smith of UPI and Sid Davis of Westinghouse Broadcasting—came on board after a wild trip to Love Field in a police car, with the uniformed officer who was driving them speeding through red lights, avoiding tie-ups by bumping over median strips and driving against oncoming traffic; despite their pleas, the driver had refused to notify their editors of their whereabouts, telling them, Davis recalls, that radio silence had to be maintained because "They don't know whether there is a conspiracy or not." "We were speculating on 'Are they going to try for Johnson, and where have they taken him?' 'Are the Russians trying to take over Berlin?' " Roberts says. Seeing them enter the stateroom, Johnson said, "We've got the press here, so we can go ahead."

•   •   •

HE MADE HIS FINAL ARRANGEMENTS. Crowded though the stateroom was, a few more witnesses could still be crammed in. Raising his voice so that he could be heard in the forward cabin, he said, "Now we're going to have a swearing-in here, and I would like anyone who wants to see it to come on in to this compartment," and, Judge Hughes says, "in they came, until there wasn't another inch of space"—until twenty-seven people were wedged into the stateroom, among the desk and the table and the chairs.

The Kennedy presence was still not all he wanted it to be. "Johnson particularly wanted Evelyn Lincoln," Judge Hughes was to recall, "but when she came, she stood in the midst of the crowd behind him, so that she was not sufficiently prominent; he made a gesture and she squeezed forward until she was standing directly behind him. He made sure his position in front of the judge was precisely where Stoughton wanted him, and placed Lady Bird on his right. He had Kilduff, who had obtained a Dictaphone machine, kneel on the floor next to the judge to record the ceremony.

ONE WITNESS WAS STILL MISSING, the most important one. He told Judge Hughes that, as the judge recalls his words, "Mrs. Kennedy wanted to be present and we would wait for her." "Do you want to ask Mrs. Kennedy if she would like to stand with us?" he asked O'Donnell and O'Brien. When they didn't respond at once, the glance he threw at them was the old Johnson glance, the eyes burning with impatience and anger. "She said she wants to be here when I take the oath," he told O'Donnell. "Why don't you see what's keeping her?"

The scene was still eerie: the gloom, the heat, the whispering, the low insistent whine of the jet engine, the mass of dim faces crowded so close together. But one element had vanished: the confusion. Watching Lyndon Johnson arrange the crowd, give his orders, deal with O'Donnell and O'Brien, Liz Carpenter, dazed by the rush of events, realized that there was at least one person in the room who wasn't dazed, who was, however hectic the situation might be, in complete command of it. "Your mind was so dull, but one of the thoughts that went through my mind . . . was 'Someone is in charge.' . . . You had the feeling that things were well in hand." Carpenter, like Valenti, was an idolater, but the journalists had the same feeling. On the ride out to the airport, Sid Davis, who, as he recalls, "had not known this man except as Majority Leader, and as someone who was . . . thought of by some . . . as 'Colonel Cornpone,' " had said to his colleagues in the car: "It's going to be hard to learn how to say *President Lyndon B. Johnson.*" As Davis watched Johnson in the stateroom now, it was, suddenly, no longer hard at all: "Soon—immediately—we started to see the measure of the guy and his leadership qualities." Part of the feeling stemmed from his size. As he stood in front of Judge Hughes, towering over everyone in the room, Stoughton realized for the first time how big he was: "Big. *Big.* He loomed over everyone." But part of it was something harder to define. As Lyndon Johnson arranged the crowd, jerking his thumb to show people where he wanted them, glancing around with those piercing dark eyes, Valenti's initial feeling that this was a different man was intensified; Johnson was suddenly "something larger, harder to fathom" than the man he had thought he knew. He looked, in fact, for the first time in three years, like the Lyndon Johnson of the Senate floor. Now he had suddenly come to the very pinnacle of power. However he had gotten there, whatever concatenation of circumstance and tragedy—whatever fate—had put him there, he was there, and he knew what to do there. When O'Donnell, obeying his order, went to her bedroom and asked Jacqueline Kennedy if she wanted to be present at the swearing-in, she said, "I think I ought to. In the light of history it would be better if I was there," and followed O'Donnell out, to the door of the stateroom.

"A hush, a hush—every whisper stopped," Roberts recalls. She was still wearing the same suit, with the same bloodstains. Her eyes were "cast down," in Judge Hughes' phrase. She had apparently tried to comb her hair, but it fell down across the left side of her face. On her face was a glazed look, and she appeared to be crying, although no tears were coming out. Johnson placed her on his left side, and nodded to the judge, who held out the missal. He put his left hand on it—the hand, mottled and veined, was so large that it all but covered the little book—and raised his right hand, as the judge said, "I do solemnly swear . . ." Valenti, watching those hands, saw that they were "absolutely steady," and Lyndon Johnson's voice was steady, too—low and firm—as he spoke the words he had been waiting to speak all his life. In the back of the room, crowded against a wall, Marie Fehmer wasn't watching the ceremony because she was reading the oath to make sure it was given correctly. ("He taught you that, by George, you can do anything.")

The oath was over. His hand came down. "Now let's get airborne," Lyndon Johnson said.

Part IV

TAKING COMMAND

13

Aboard Air Force One

THE DEATH OF A PRESIDENT — with the necessity for the sudden transfer of his enormous powers—is in many ways a supreme test for a democratic government.

For what if the transfer did not go smoothly? What if policies were changed—foreign policies: what if a détente was ended, new orders given; what if, along a border, the border between East and West Berlin, perhaps, tensions rose; what if tanks began to rumble forward, troops began to march; what if, in the harbors of naval bases, anchor chains began to rattle aboard so that fleets could sail? Or domestic policies: what if interest rates set by a government agency of which people had previously been only vaguely aware suddenly began to be raised, and raised too high—what if, as a result of that change, businesses that had planned to borrow money to expand suddenly found the cost of money too high, and had to contract instead, laying off employees? What if the rates were lowered—and lowered too far—and, as a result, inflation rose, and rose too far; what if currencies crumbled, life savings were eaten away, elderly couples suddenly facing impoverished old age? What if tax policies, or depreciation allowances, were changed, so that corporations abruptly found that expansions planned under the old policies would now be unfeasible, so they could no longer afford to add employees? What if previously announced government appropriations were suddenly rescinded or the schedule of their payments stretched out so that schools, hospitals, clinics, day-care centers, suddenly had bad news for students and patients; what if decisions were made not to build dams or roads on which people had been counting for employment? What if naval yards, aircraft factories were closed, their thousands of employees thrown out of work? What if adjustments were made in government health-care policies, so that families that had been struck by illness but had believed that at least their medical expenses were covered found all at once that in fact they weren't?

And beyond institutions and policies, what of the man—the new President? The old President had been elected to that office, installed in it by the will of the people, by the hard, concrete totals of the ballots they cast, his place, his author-

ity, "legitimated," in the word used by Richard Neustadt, perhaps the era's leading analyst of the presidency, "by a national election after national campaigning." The people he was governing had given him the authority, legal and moral,
to govern them. Although his successor was of course entitled under the Constitution to the office to which he was succeeding, and the electorate was of course
aware when it voted for the ticket of which he was a part that he would occupy
that office should the President die, the possibility of the President doing so had
not been prominent in its mind—it never is: voters focus on the candidate at the
head of the ticket, not on his running mate, and they focus on the candidate, not
on what would happen should the candidate, having been elected, suddenly die.
The draping over a Vice President of the mantle of authority that had been conferred on the President is not guaranteed to be straightforward. For what if,
because of the new President's early actions in his new office, the people found
that they did not have confidence in him? What if they felt that the government
had abruptly altered course to a wrong course, or that the firm hand at the helm of
state was not a firm hand, and that therefore the circumstances of their own lives,
dependent in so many ways (they suddenly realized now that the President's
death had made them think of it) on presidential performance, were suddenly
more uncertain than before? If there was no confidence in the continuity and stability of the new government, no feeling that, despite a President's death, someone competent was in charge, what then might be the consequences for a
democracy?

In America, the test is made easier to pass because under the Constitution
the transfer of power is swift and unquestioned. Seven of the nation's thirty-five
Presidents had died in office before John F. Kennedy died; in each case, presidential power had passed to the Vice President in a smooth and systematic manner, even in the case of the two deaths that had come at particularly crucial
moments of history—Lincoln's and Franklin Roosevelt's, both of which presidencies had ended as the great wars they had directed were ending, with postwar
decisions immediately ahead; Roosevelt's death, just eighteen years before
Kennedy's, had elevated to the place FDR had filled so long that many Americans could hardly envision anyone else holding it a man largely unknown to
America, and seemingly very ill fitted for the office, yet the transfer had been
instantaneous and smooth. Aspects of the transfer of power which made such
transfers fraught with uncertainty and danger in other nations had barely even
been thought of, if indeed they were thought of at all; as one political scientist
was to put it, the questions that were not raised at the time of Roosevelt's sudden
death—and that were not raised at the time of other presidential deaths, either—
"illustrate how fundamental and implicit is the commitment to" America's governmental institutions; "it is, for example, not so much that the American
military did not attempt to take control of the government; it is that no one even
thought to ask where the military's support lay." Harry Truman, raising his hand
in 1945 to take the oath as Roosevelt's successor before a group of officials in the

Cabinet Room of the White House, realized that "although we were in the midst of a great war, only two uniforms were present," and, noting that "this passed unnoticed" by anyone but him, understood the significance of that fact: "the very fact that no thought" was "given to it demonstrates how firmly the concept of the civil authority was accepted in our land," he wrote.

Yet in certain crucial aspects Lyndon Johnson's ascension to the presidency—the presidential transition of 1963—took place in uncharted waters, in circumstances that made it different from, and in some respects significantly more difficult than, any of the seven previous transitions, even the one that had followed the death of Franklin Roosevelt.

Two of these circumstances were products of the age in which this transition occurred, for 1963, unlike 1945, was the age of television, and of nuclear weapons.

Roosevelt's death, the death of this President who had become a father figure to much of America, was a shock, and resulted in immense grief and anxiety: would, for example, the war drag on longer, now that the great leader was dead? Nevertheless his death, of a stroke after years of failing health that had become increasingly apparent, was a natural death; as one writer put it, "violence was missing from the story of Roosevelt's demise; as it must to all men, death came to him." And there was in effect no television; only a few thousand American families had a set; FDR's funeral ceremonies in Washington and at Hyde Park were moving, but while the radio let America listen to them, America couldn't watch them while they were taking place; could see them only in still newspaper photographs and newsreels, after the fact. John F. Kennedy's death was unnatural, terrible: violence, murder, blood—and mystery; as Air Force One was flying back to Washington, commentators were speculating, and America was wondering: murder by whom, and at whose orders? Forty minutes into the flight, it was announced that a Dallas policeman had been shot, and, a few minutes later, that a twenty-four-year-old man, Lee Harvey Oswald, had been arrested in connection with that slaying, and that "he also is being questioned to see if he had any connection" with Kennedy's assassination, and then, an hour later, that he was "a definite suspect in the assassination," and then there were rumors that he had not been the only gunman. And Kennedy's death was made more terrible because of television. Television had, during the almost three years of his presidency, brought JFK and his wife and children into America's homes: the first detailed study of America's reaction to the assassination found that four out of five of those surveyed (79 percent) felt with the "very deepest feeling" or "quite deeply" that not just a President but "someone very close and dear to them," almost like a member of their own family, had died when JFK died. And television intensified the shock and horror—the unnaturalness—of the death of a President who had been the epitome of youth and promise by the rapidity with which it broke the news, the report of the assassination crossing the country, *Newsweek* said, "like a shock wave." By the time Air Force One touched down in Washington, 92 per-

cent of the American people had heard the news; television, almost instantaneously, it seemed, bound an entire nation together in "a communion of disbelief, sorrow and anger." And two days later the shock would be multiplied by
television, for on that day the murderer was murdered, on live television, the shot
fired and Oswald's face contorting in pain as the nation watched—and more
questions were raised, about what had really happened at Dealey Plaza, and why
it had happened.

During the day of the assassination and the next three days, furthermore,
the nation would be bound together by television not only in shock but in mourning. From shortly after the shots in Dallas on Friday to the conclusion of the
funeral services in Arlington National Cemetery on Monday, America's three
television networks canceled all regular programs and all advertising, and carried only news related to the assassination and the events that followed, in coverage uninterrupted by commercials. As the day of the assassination and the three
days of memorial pageantry for John Fitzgerald Kennedy unfolded in Washington, America sat before its television sets watching it as if the country was gathered in one vast living room: a nation that was, for those four days, a single
audience—in a way that had never happened before in history. A survey by
the A. C. Nielsen Company, the leading commercial firm conducting television
surveys, showed that during these four days approximately 166 million Americans in fifty-one million homes were tuned in at some time to the Kennedy
coverage—and surveys by Nielsen and social science organizations showed that
in most homes the time was substantial: during the three days, according to these
surveys, the average American family watched the ceremonies for an almost
incredible total of 31.6 hours, almost eight hours per day. The pervasiveness as
well as the immediacy of television coverage made the assassination and the
events following it an event "probably without parallel in the past," the Social
Science Research Council said. Not only was "President Kennedy's loss the first
loss of a national leader reported in any such detail on the picture tubes of a
nation," but "For all practical purposes there was no other news story in America
during those four days," a study by the National Opinion Research Center concluded. "There were times during those days when *a majority of all Americans*
were apparently looking at the same events and hearing the same words from
their television sets—participating together . . . in a great national event. Nothing like this on such a scale had ever occurred before." After President Roosevelt's death—the event social scientists consider most similar to Kennedy's in
American history—only 88 percent of Americans said they listened to the radio
"at *some* time during the three days" that followed. A characteristic of television
is its ability to magnify and reinforce emotions. "It seems more personal when
you see something happening on TV than just listening about it," as one viewer
said. "It brought you there as if you were one of the close spectators. . . . You felt
as if you were one of the people watching on the scene," another said. "When
President Franklin D. Roosevelt died, there were memorable radio reports,"

wrote Jack Gould, the television critic for the *New York Times,* "but the person at home mourned through the eyes and ears of the unseen commentator." But the Kennedy ceremonies were carried on television. "To read or hear about a nation in the agony of unexpected transition is one thing; to see it in terms of close-ups of persons who are familiar faces in one's own home is searing." All sudden, unexpected transfers of presidential power produce shock and anxiety and uncertainty; by reinforcing and magnifying these emotions, while blanketing them in a mantle of grief that made them stronger still, the new medium of mass communication intensified, sharpened, deepened, the impact of the assassination, and therefore the concern about whether the government would continue to function, whether it would be stable, whether its reins would be in firm hands. The National Opinion Research Center survey would not be begun until five days after the assassination, and would not be completed for another three days, an eight-day interval following the assassination during which such anxieties had been eased, and even so, almost half those surveyed were still "worried" with the "very deepest feeling" or "quite deeply" about how it "would affect our relations with other countries" or how it "would affect the political situation in this country" or "how the United States would carry on without its leader."

And television was only half of the new equation. The year 1963 was the age of the Bomb, and America was only a year away—the Cuban Missile Crisis had taken place in October, 1962—from being dramatically reminded of the implications of that fact. The questions that were raised now—was the assassination of the President an isolated act or was it part of a conspiracy to leave the government leaderless, or in disarray, so that, as Tom Wicker put it, "the Soviets might try something, in Cuba, again, or in Berlin, that might rapidly lead to escalation, and the possibility, in a nuclear age, of annihilation"—possessed more urgency because of this new factor. Presidents had always had a large measure of what Neustadt calls the "terrible responsibility for the use of force," but now, because the force a President could employ—and that could be employed against us—was nuclear, a decision a President made might be a decision which could not be called back, might be a decision which was irreversible and irreparable. In the past, during every previous transition, a snap decision by the new President— a wrong snap decision, perhaps: a miscalculation—might mean war. Now it might mean the end of much of mankind. The number of Americans who might die in the first hours of a full-scale nuclear exchange with the Soviet Union, the Atomic Energy Commission had calculated, was thirty-nine million. This was a situation that was new, unprecedented, in presidential transitions. No situation even remotely similar had confronted any of the seven other men who had been suddenly placed in the presidency by death. This new President, a man made President in an instant, without being elected to the presidency, held in his hands the fate of mankind. "The advent of nuclear weapons, together with the fact that another nation—a foe—also possessed nuclear weapons," Jonathan Schell was to write, "has done nothing less than place the President in a radically new relation to the whole of human reality. He along with whoever is responsible in the Soviet Union has become the hinge of human existence." Lyndon Johnson was the first President ever to have been given, without being elected, such power, such responsibility; the American people hadn't given him that power, and didn't know him very well, as the *Candid Camera* show had demonstrated. The death of a President, and the resultant sudden transfer of power, had always produced a measure of anxiety. But on November 22, 1963, there was a new, overriding, reason for anxiety. "Lyndon Johnson's ascent to the presidency," says presidential historian Henry Graff, "came at the most traumatic moment in American political history."

AND OTHER CIRCUMSTANCES surrounding the presidential transition of November, 1963, made it unprecedented in American history, circumstances that had nothing to do with the age in which it occurred.

Vital as are continuity and stability—and the impression of continuity and stability—in any sudden transfer of power, now, given the unprecedented shock and anxiety of November 22, that impression was needed more than ever, and a crucial element in creating it would be the continuation in office of the men John F. Kennedy had appointed to the Cabinet and to key, visible White House staff positions, men who were linked in the public mind with his Administration. If "some or most of them moved out of their old jobs," Evans and Novak were to write, "the country would draw an obvious conclusion: these Kennedy men did not choose to work for Johnson. That could destroy confidence." He had to prevent "even the appearance of an exodus." And merely keeping them in their jobs wouldn't do the trick: the press would be watching to see whether these men were working at them as diligently as they had worked under Kennedy, whether they were taking the new President's orders, giving him loyalty. But these were—many of them—the same men who had been sneering at Lyndon Johnson for years, who had called him "Rufus Cornpone" behind his back, and "Lyndon" instead of "Mr. Vice President" to his face, who had snickered as people asked whatever had become of him, and roared as pins were jabbed into his voodoo effigy. Besides, many of them had come to Washington not to work for a President but to work for John Fitzgerald Kennedy; they—men like O'Donnell and O'Brien and Dave Powers—had followed his banner for years, since the long days campaigning across Massachusetts. Others, like Secretary of the Interior Stewart Udall and Freeman and Salinger—and, most of all, Sorensen—had been inspired and thrilled by Kennedy, and their devotion to him was deep and personal. If he was gone, would they want to stay? "We came down to be with Kennedy, and he [is] no longer President, so perhaps we ought to leave," legislative aide Mike Manatos said on one of the first days after the assassination. And some of these men were aware that their leader had lost confidence in Lyndon Johnson; they had, for example, noticed who wasn't invited to the decisive meeting on the missile crisis. The "noncommittal" response of O'Brien and O'Don-nell to his plea on Air Force One that they stay had demonstrated how difficult preventing an exodus would be.

As vital as an impression of continuity was an impression of competence, of decisiveness—an impression that the new President was immediately filling the office as it should be filled—and that impression, that image, would be hard to create for the same reason: that the men *this* new President was taking charge of, or trying to take charge of, had little respect and in not a few cases actual con-tempt for him. If that attitude wasn't changed, they would communicate their feelings to the journalists who would be creating the impression in their articles about the transition. Making it even harder to create was the existence of the same attitude among some of the journalists themselves, the men and women he lumped together as "the Eastern intellectuals," journalists who had asked the "whatever happened" question in print, and had joined in the mockery of Lyndon Johnson at Georgetown dinner parties. And not only had the new President not been elected to the office, his predecessor had not merely died but had been assassinated ("I always felt sorry for Harry Truman and the way he got the pres-idency, but at least his man wasn't murdered," Lyndon Johnson was to say)—and, in addition, assassinated in his own state; "A Texas murder had put a Texan in power," as one Kennedy partisan was to say. Johnson himself felt this deeply. *"I was still illegitimate, a naked man . . . , a pretender . . . , an illegal usurper. And then there was Texas, my home, the home of . . . the murder."*

And of course taking charge would mean dealing—successfully—with Capitol Hill.

The upper house of Congress had rejected him emphatically three years before, the respect and fear with which the Senate had once regarded him evapo-rating since without a trace, and the senatorial snubbing was merely one aspect of a situation on Capitol Hill that made Johnson's ascension to the presidency especially difficult.

Just ten days before President Kennedy had left for Texas, Democrat Thomas J. Dodd of Connecticut had risen in the Senate to publicly assail Major-ity Leader Mansfield—"I wish our leader would be more of a leader . . . [or] we shall go on dribbling our way through the legislative session"—and had, as *Newsweek* put it, "thereby opened the cloakroom doors and let the nation in on the gossip" that had been rampant in Washington all year: that Congress was in stalemate, and that there was no sign that the stalemate was being broken.

A number of factors had contributed to the deadlock, but the key factor was the one about which Lyndon Johnson had, through Ted Sorensen, tried to warn Kennedy in June: not to send Congress a civil rights bill until all his other major bills had been disposed of, lest the other bills be held up, as hostages against civil rights. Kennedy had sent Congress the civil rights bill anyway—and now the other bills were being held up. These included bills to provide health insurance for the elderly, to assist education, including a bill to finance desperately needed

construction of new school buildings, foreign aid bills, even routine appropriations measures. Kennedy's other major legislative priority had been a bill to
reduce income and corporate taxes by a total of $11 billion per year, a reduction
that many economists felt would provide a stimulus to the economy perhaps
three times the amount of the reduction (about $33 billion per year, in other
words) and would therefore not only ease a persistent unemployment problem
but would also, despite the reduction in rates, increase tax revenue, thereby providing funds for the expansion of government spending on social programs liberals advocated. That bill had arrived on the Hill in January, along with a plea from
the President. Noting that without the bill, "you increase the chances of a recession," and that unemployment was already uncomfortably close to an unacceptable 6 percent, the President said the bill was "the first priority. . . . Nothing
should stand in its way. . . . We have to get a tax cut this year." Priorities, however, are in the eye of the beholder—in this case in the eye of Harry Byrd of Virginia, chairman of the Senate Finance Committee. Byrd hadn't even begun
public hearings on the measure until October 15, and had announced that scores
of witnesses who had already testified before the House Finance Committee
would be welcome to repeat their testimony before the Senate committee. And
the pace of the hearings had been kept very slow. Byrd didn't press his committee's seventeen members to attend; sometimes there weren't enough of them to
make up a quorum; that didn't perturb the chairman; the hearings would just be
postponed to another day. When a hearing *was* held, moreover, the pace was
leisurely, starting late, finishing early—and with absolutely no feeling that the
members should limit their participation. The tax reduction bill affected many
industries; many of the senators had good reasons to speak, to make a record for
their constituents; Byrd made clear that he wouldn't even consider trying to stop
a United States senator from expressing his views in full. It was November now.
The list of witnesses still to be heard seemed endless; there was absolutely no
sign that the committee was anywhere near ready to start voting on the bill; it
hadn't even begun taking up the list of proposed amendments to the measure,
each of which might be discussed in detail, and there were, at the moment, thirty
amendments, with more being submitted all the time.

As for the civil rights bill, the demonstrations throughout the South were
continuing and rising in intensity, but the bill hadn't even arrived in the Senate.
Having finally been reported favorably out of the House Judiciary Committee, it
had passed into the hands of the House Rules Committee, without whose
approval no bill could be sent to the floor. And the Rules Committee's chairman,
Judge Howard J. Smith—of Virginia—was refusing even to set a date on which
its hearings on the measure would begin, much less give an estimate of how long
the hearings might last.

The inefficiency of Congress was nothing new, of course—the only period
since the Civil War that the pattern had been broken in the Senate, the principal
logjam, was the six years of Lyndon Johnson's leadership—but now, in both

houses of Congress, it was escalating to a new level, a level at which some analysts were questioning the efficiency of the governmental framework of which Congress was so pivotal a part. In a book, *The Deadlock of Democracy,* published earlier in the year, the distinguished historian—and unabashed Kennedy admirer—James MacGregor Burns said that "we are at the critical stage of a somber and inexorable cycle that seems to have gripped the public affairs of the nation, . . . mired in governmental deadlock, as Congress blocks or kills not only" Kennedy's programs but Republican programs as well. Concluding that "We . . . underestimate the extent to which our system was designed for deadlock and inaction," he said that perhaps the system would have to be changed. Writing shortly before Kennedy's assassination, the respected columnist Walter Lippmann said: "This Congress has gone further than any other within memory to replace debate and decision by delay and stultification. This is one of those moments when there is reason to wonder whether the congressional system as it now operates is not a grave danger to the Republic." Commenting that the Eighty-eighth Congress had "sat longer than any peacetime Congress in memory while accomplishing practically nothing" and that "feebly led, wedded to its own lethargy and impervious to criticism," it is "a scandal of drift and inefficiency," *Life* magazine said that "This scandal has put our whole system of parliamentary democracy in question."

The extent of the impasse on Capitol Hill was just beginning to be discussed in all its ramifications during the last few days before Kennedy had left for Texas—in discussions of which the word "impossible" had been not infrequently employed to describe the prospects for breaking it. "It has seemed impossible to bring about any resolution of the deep and embittering divisions in Congress," the columnist Marquis Childs wrote. In his final press conference—on November 14—Kennedy, instead of repeating his demands for speedy passage of the two key bills, had spoken of an "eighteen-month delivery," which would mean that the tax cut bill, at least, would pass by mid-1964, and the civil rights bill by the end of that year. But, Childs noted, in an opinion that was, in the days before Kennedy's death, starting to be heard more and more frequently as more and more observers began to focus on the realities on Capitol Hill, "there was no assurance in view of the sit-down strike of the southern committee chairmen and the certainty of a filibuster conducted with all the resourcefulness of such an implacable enemy as Senator Richard Russell of Georgia that action will come on the rights" in 1964—or at any other specific date. In its first post-assassination issue, *Life* magazine said that "Congress is reluctant to bypass Judge Smith because of its respect for its own hoary rules and seniority rights. Senator Byrd enjoys a similar veto over the tax bill. . . . Ours is still a system of divided and mutually checking powers." No matter who is President, *Life* said, Congress would still be the same Congress.

And yet, it was felt, a civil rights bill *must* pass. There must be a release for the emotions boiling up in the streets of the South, release—or explosion. The stalemate in Congress "is, here and now, the great test of the American system," Evans and Novak wrote. The system's "constitutional fragility" has been exposed by the inability of the Administration to move its crucial legislation through Congress. And, they wrote, the stalemate is due primarily to civil rights. "For the last six months, the country has been torn apart on the civil rights issue. . . . This is the underlying reason for the legislative stalemate." The stalemate could wreck America's image in the eyes of the world. "We are now the center of the world stage. Every nuance, every subtle shift of policy, every shift of an Assistant Secretary of State have their implacable effect on international politics. But compared to these, the sudden, involuntary change of an entire Administration is an incalculable disaster. That is why the transition of power today, with its brutal finality, places on the American people a terrible responsibility." And, they wrote, it is on Lyndon Johnson that the responsibility rests; "To break" the congressional stalemate "now becomes the new President's high responsibility."

THE FACT THAT THE HEART of the stalemate was civil rights made the problem of Congress even more difficult for Lyndon Johnson to solve than it would otherwise have been, a problem that was not only personal but political. His passage of civil rights legislation in 1957 and 1960 hadn't eliminated the suspicion with which he was regarded by many liberals, and neither had the two "Negro tables" at the St. Augustine banquet or the speech at Gettysburg. Some liberals, indeed, saw a change in him; the New York Post said, in a profile of the new President, "A man who wore a ten-gallon Stetson and spoke with a magnolia accent had little hope of winning the Democratic nomination in 1960. . . . But the mantle of national office wrought change." To most liberals, however, the operative facts were still the accent and the Stetson—the fact that Lyndon Johnson was from the South, that hated South which, in recent months, had, with its fire hoses and its police dogs, reminded the rest of America that the South was still the South. No southerner had been elected to the White House in a century; that was still the case, although a southerner would be sitting in it now. The very raising of the civil rights issue had hurt Johnson in 1960 because for Washington observers it was a reminder of his twenty-year record as a southern vote and a southern strategist, and of the fact that he was Richard Russell's protégé; most liberals viewed Johnson's more recent civil rights record—the two bills, the Gettysburg speech—with distrust, as maneuvers by a man who was, as Joseph Rauh had said, "trying," because of his presidential ambitions, "to be all things to all people." The taint of magnolias still remained to be scrubbed off.

So deep were the suspicions of Lyndon Johnson that the only way of reducing them would be by concrete achievement: the passage of laws that the liberals wanted—the tax bill, for one, but especially the civil rights bill. Kennedy had spoken eloquently for a civil rights bill, had promised one; eloquence and promises wouldn't be enough for Johnson. He would have to deliver, would have to have a record of his own in civil rights to run on. For him to be assured of the nomination of his party if he decided to run for President in his own right in 1964—for him to obtain his party's endorsement for the post to which he had been raised only by accident—he would have to have the support of northern liberals because it would be the big northern liberal states that would hold the balance of power at the 1964 Democratic convention, and political observers agreed that, without the passage of a civil rights bill, that support was far from assured. Telephoning political observers the day after the assassination to get their opinion on Johnson's problems, reporter Vincent J. Burke of the *Los Angeles Times* found them agreed on one point: "Mr. Johnson needs a meaningful civil rights bill much more than did Mr. Kennedy, whose favorable 'image' among Negroes was so solidly fixed that apparently nothing could undercut it." "Mr. Johnson," Burke said, "is now more appealing to the conservative elements of the party than to liberals who comprise the dominant factor in the party. . . . To strengthen his position for the 1964 election campaign, party liberals and professionals generally agree that he needs from the balky Congress a meaningful civil rights bill." "As the first southerner in the White House in over a century, this will be an absolute necessity for him," the liberal columnist William V. Shannon wrote in the *New York Post.* It would, in other words, be an absolute necessity for him to break the stalemate in Congress over civil rights—a stalemate it seemed impossible to break.

AND THEN THERE WAS the element of time—in a number of permutations.

The most obvious was in itself daunting. Taking over the machinery of government—selecting a Cabinet, a White House staff, filling as many as possible of the seven hundred high-level governmental posts within a President's discretion, drafting a legislative program, preparing for decisions on urgent foreign policy and defense questions left unresolved by the previous Administration, writing an inaugural address that would be measured against the great inaugural speeches of the past—is, even under normal circumstances, difficult enough. Prior to passage of the Twentieth Amendment in 1933, a President-elect had had four months—from Election Day in November to March 4 of the following year—to prepare to be President; after the amendment, he had between ten and eleven weeks. "The eleven weeks," wrote Neustadt, who advised Kennedy on his transition, "are hazardous because they are so few. They leave but little time to turn a campaign into an Administration." John F. Kennedy, assigning men to begin analyzing the "problems in the executive branch" because "If I am elected, I don't want to wake up [the next morning] and have to ask myself, 'What in the world do I do now?,'" had found those weeks to be barely enough time. Lyndon Johnson had less time than that. One moment he was not President—and the next moment he was. The interval between the moment he arrived in the cubicle at

Parkland Hospital and the moment he took the oath on Air Force One—the time he had in which to prepare himself—was slightly less than two hours.

Then there were, looming dead ahead, startlingly close, various dates.

One was the date of the next presidential election: November 3, 1964—less than a year away. Of the seven Vice Presidents who had previously succeeded to the presidency due to the death of the President, five—John Tyler, Andrew Johnson, Chester Arthur, Theodore Roosevelt and Harry Truman—had done so with more than three years remaining before the next presidential election; one, Millard Fillmore, had done so with more than two years remaining; only one, Calvin Coolidge, had come to the office with less time remaining than that, and even Coolidge had had well over a year—more than fifteen months.

And Lyndon Johnson was facing deadlines that were even closer.

While the election would be in November, 1964, the Democratic National Convention, at which it would be decided whether he would receive the nomination to run in the election, would begin on August 24, 1964, a date only nine months away.

Like so many other aspects of Lyndon Johnson's assumption of the presidency—the presidential transition of 1963—the imminence of those dates made it a transition unlike any other in American history. No Vice President had ever come to office with so little time in which to establish a record on which he could run in his own right. Johnson, Neustadt was to write, "faced the unprecedented challenge of assuming office and then running for election in the same first year." Needing a record on which to run, he had very little time to create one.

Those were political deadlines. Other deadlines were governmental. The President had to deliver the State of the Union address when Congress reconvened, and in 1964 Congress was scheduled to reconvene on Monday, January 6—in six weeks. By law—an unbreakable deadline, the Budget and Accounting Act of 1921—the President was required to submit his budget for the next fiscal year to Congress fourteen days after that Monday, on January 20: in eight weeks.

During the very next week in this November—the week in which President Kennedy was to be buried—an arbitrator's decision on railroad featherbedding was scheduled to be filed with a United States District Court. The decision, fraught with implications both for railroad labor unions and for presidential relations with them, was being warily awaited both by the unions and by the railroad companies, and it had been warily awaited by the White House, too, because of the presidential actions that might be required as a result of it. A few days after the arbitrator's decision, a presidential decision was supposed to be made on the wage-price guidelines vital to the economy. Now, suddenly, the decision on these issues would not be Kennedy's but Johnson's. And, excluded as he had been from Administration discussions, he was only vaguely familiar with the issues involved.

And tangled with and complicating the time factor—and every other factor associated with the transition; looming over every aspect of Johnson's ascension to the presidency—was one that made that ascension uniquely difficult, a complication that wasn't out of the new age but seemed rather as if it were out of an age long past, a complication that required to plumb its depths not a Reston but a Shakespeare. The President, the King, was dead, murdered, but the King had a brother, a brother who hated the new King. The dead King's men—the Kennedy men, the Camelot men—made up, in Shakespearean terms, a faction. And it was a faction that had a leader. An election was coming in less than a year, and a convention in nine months, but due to the faction and the brother, these were not the crucial dates. Because if the King's faction, and the King's brother, decided to contest Lyndon Johnson's right to the nomination, the crucial date would be the first of the party primaries which preceded the convention—the New Hampshire primary, on March 10, less than four months off. Unprecedented shock and grief and anxiety; unprecedented danger to America and the human race. Unprecedented time pressure, and problems with staff and Cabinet made uniquely difficult by the brother factor. Even Truman's transition problems, Neustadt was to conclude, had been "easier" than Johnson's. "Johnson's situation was extreme." Although seven Vice Presidents before him had suddenly been thrust into the White House by the President's death, Johnson's situation—the problems that confronted him, and that would confront America should he fail to solve them—were indeed in many ways without parallel in the transitions that had come before his.

AND AS WAS ALWAYS the case with Lyndon Johnson, in addition to the obstacles before him there were the obstacles within, the emotions inside him that had been rubbed raw by that terrible youth in the Hill Country, the scars so deep that they raised the question of whether they would ever be healed—of whether anything could make him feel secure.

When he looked back on his ascension to the presidency in later years, these feelings were still vivid in his memory. The fact that he hadn't been elected to the office was an objective consideration. But the words in which he described that aspect of his ascension went beyond the objective. "Illegitimate," "naked," "pretender," "illegal." And "the bigots and the dividers and the Eastern intellectuals, who were waiting to knock me down before I could even begin to stand up. . . . The whole thing was almost unbearable." Fears, doubts, almost unbearable fears and doubts.

The need for continuity in personnel—the need to keep the Kennedy men from resigning, to keep Cabinet and staff in place—was a genuine need, an objective, rational, political consideration. But in describing that need, Johnson went beyond the political. "I simply couldn't let the country think that I was all alone," he was to say.

His education—his lack of a good one, of even an adequate one—added fuel to those emotions, because of the way he felt about that education. During his presidency he would often say that when he convened a meeting of his top advisers, at the table would be men with Harvard degrees, Rhodes Scholars, Phi Beta Kappas—"and one from Southwest Texas State Teachers College." The story was supposed to be funny, but when at the end, he laughed, he "always laughed loudly—too loudly," says the reporter Hugh Sidey, who heard it many times. "He obviously was only half joking." And once, during the very early days of his presidency, Sidey, walking out of the Oval Office after an interview, heard behind him words from Lyndon Johnson that were not spoken loudly but very quietly, as if he was speaking to himself: "I'm not sure I can lead this country and keep it together, with my background." His staff heard many similar remarks. "He felt a lack of sort of erudition," Walter Jenkins says. It wasn't just that he was not well educated. It was that he knew he wasn't—and that that knowledge hurt.

The Kennedy men, the "Harvards," in his term, were so brilliant—"a lot of damn smart men," he would call them—and his men weren't. That was how he saw it. At a meeting on economic policy a few weeks after he became President, Horace Busby found himself disagreeing with two key economic advisers who had been appointed by Kennedy, Kermit Gordon and Walter Heller. Sneaking a glance at Johnson, Busby saw that he was very disturbed, and after the meeting the President, taking him aside, told him angrily, "You just came here to embarrass me. Here you've got Rhodes Scholars and you've got Ph.D.s and all like that and . . . you're telling them that they don't know what they're talking about. Don't you understand? These are the people that Kennedy had in there. They're *ipso facto* a hell of a lot smarter than *you* are." And the key word that let him understand Johnson's feelings, Busby says, was "embarrass"—"He was embarrassed."

Not only were the men on his staff not smart enough, he believed, he also felt that his personal acquaintance didn't include as many "smart" men as he was going to need to bring into the Administration. Among the "things he envied about the Kennedys most of all was that their old school ties go back so many years and so when Kennedy became President, he had people he could really trust because he'd gone to prep school with them, college with them and all that. Johnson didn't have these old school ties and friendships," says his aide James Jones. However unjustified Johnson's statement about his lack of "smart" men— and it was quite untrue; it would have been hard to find a political strategist more astute than George Reedy, who had, after all, been at Johnson's right hand during all the years of his ascent to power in the Senate; Busby, forgotten though he may be by history today, was to Lyndon Johnson what Ted Sorensen was to Jack Kennedy, a wordsmith with a rare gift for turning his principal's thoughts into memorable prose—that was nonetheless how Johnson felt. In an indication of his feelings, Lady Bird would say, "Our pool of high-calibre brains . . . is not too deep and wide." Nothing the Kennedys felt about Lyndon Johnson could be any worse than what Lyndon Johnson felt about himself.

The strength of these feelings, these insecurities—these terrors from his youth that combined to create a fear of failure so strong that, in words he frequently used to describe himself, they "immobilized" and "paralyzed" him—had been dramatically apparent in the effectiveness with which they had kept him from entering the race for President until it was too late.

And now, stepping into the presidency, if he failed, the failure would be on a gigantic scale, on the largest scale of all, under the brightest lights of all, before an audience that would be the entire nation.

WHILE SOME COMPONENTS of Lyndon Johnson's character added to the difficulties of his ascension to the presidency, there were, however, within that complex persona, other components.

One was the fact that in addition to his knowledge of governing, his understanding of the craft of governance—and no one understood that craft better than Lyndon Johnson—he possessed something that was beyond knowledge and understanding, that was instinct. It is possible—probable, in fact—that he had thought through long before November 22 what he would do if he suddenly became President. But unless one believes that he planned or in some way was aware in advance of the assassination (and nowhere in the letters, memoranda and other written documents in the Lyndon B. Johnson Library, the John F. Kennedy Library and the other public and private collections the author has reviewed—and nowhere in the interviews that the author has conducted—has he found facts to support such a theory), he couldn't have foreseen the unprecedented circumstances under which it actually happened. Nonetheless, he seems to have known instantly—or at least by the end of those minutes in the Parkland cubicle—what had to be done.

"Everything was in chaos," he was to recall years later. "We were all spinning around and around, trying to come to grips with what had happened, but the more we tried to understand it, the more confused we got. We were like a bunch of cattle caught in the swamp, unable to move in either direction, simply circling 'round and 'round. I understood that; I knew what had to be done. There is but one way to get the cattle out of the swamp. And that is for the man on the horse to take the lead, to assume command, to provide direction. In the period of confusion after the assassination, I was that man."

And there was his willingness to do it—his will to decide, his will to *act,* to use power. During the last three years, the ability to use power had been taken from him, but with the crack of that gunshot in Dallas, he had power again, had again the ability to act. Fears had to be overcome for him to do so, for him not only to act but to act firmly and decisively; there was more reason than ever before—far greater possibilities for failure—for him to be "immobilized," "paralyzed" now. His memories of that time reveal how clearly he understood the possibility of failure before him. Recalling for his memoirs how he felt after O'Donnell told him "He's gone," he said, "I was a man in trouble, in a world that is never more than minutes away from catastrophe"; "I realized that ready or not, new and immeasurable duties had been thrust upon me. There were tasks to perform that only I had the authority to perform. . . . I knew that not only the nation but the whole world would be anxiously following every move I made—watching, judging, weighing, balancing.

"I was catapulted without preparation into the most difficult job any mortal man could hold. My duties would not wait a week, or a day, or even an hour."

But this time he couldn't give in to his feelings. "I knew I could not allow the tide of grief to overwhelm me," he was to say. "The consequences of all my actions were too great for me to become immobilized now with emotion. . . . I knew it was imperative that I grasp the reins of power and do so without delay. Any hesitation or wavering, any false step, any sign of self-doubt, could have been disastrous. The nation was in a state of shock and grief. The times cried out for leadership. . . . The entire world was watching us through a magnifying glass. . . . I had to prove myself."

And, knowing what had to be done, and that only he could do it, he did it.

LIFTING AIR FORCE ONE off the Love Field runway in the takeoff so steep that to Sid Davis, watching from the tarmac, it seemed "almost vertical," Colonel Swindal turned northeast. He had leveled off at twenty-nine thousand feet when his Air Force command post advised him of tornadoes over Arkansas, dead ahead. Taking the big blue-and-white jet up to forty-one thousand feet, high enough to fly over the storm, he roared toward Washington, with a strong tailwind behind him, at more than six hundred miles per hour. At every Air Force base along his flight path, jet fighter planes sat on runways with their pilots already strapped into the cockpits, ready to take off at the first hint of danger; in the bases' radar shacks, men sat watching for any unidentified blip on their screens, for who could know yet whether the assassination had been the first step in some Soviet or Cuban plot, and Air Force One the next target; "who knew then," as Tom Wicker was to write, "who had pulled the trigger or ordered the shots," who knew whether Lyndon Johnson, "even while aloft on the way to Washington . . . might have to confront a fearful challenge?" Along the Rio Grande, the Mexican border was being sealed to keep conspirators from escaping.

AS THE PLANE carrying two Presidents, "one alive and one dead," as a journalist was to put it, flew across the country, beneath it, all along its route, and in a thousand towns and cities from coast to coast, flags were being lowered to half-staff, and the bells of churches were starting to toll.

In Los Angeles, the rush of automobiles on the freeways began to slow, and then to halt, as drivers stopped their cars as they heard the bulletins coming over their radios. Motorists behind them, jumping out of their cars to expostulate, got the news from the drivers ahead, and stood in stunned silence, listening to the bulletins through the windows. In New York, traffic came to a standstill on a thousand streets and avenues across the five boroughs—and angry horns would start to blare, and then, the *New York Times* reported, "went soundless as word of the President's death filtered from driver to driver." On Manhattan's crowded streets and avenues, at every red light "the cry," as the *Times* reported, "cascaded from car to car, from pedestrian to motorist: 'Is it true?' " A driver whose car didn't have a radio stopped in the middle of traffic, walked over to a sidewalk lunch stand, and asked the question of the vendor, who was sitting on a stool, staring down at the sidewalk. "Yes," was the reply, "he's dead." In cars that had pulled over to the curb, radios were playing, and the car windows were open, and around them, knots of people were standing, and as they heard the bulletins, people clapped their hands to their mouths in horror.

Dusk had begun to fall, and marquee lights had been lit at Broadway's theaters in preparation for the evening's performances. First at one theater, and then at another and another, the lights went off, and after a while signs were posted that the performances were canceled. At dusk, automatic timers switched on Times Square's huge, garishly illuminated signs. One by one, the signs went dark. Along Fifth Avenue, stores had already put up their Christmas lighting and installed their spectacular Christmas displays in their windows. They turned off the lighting, and the windows went dark—except for a few: in one of them, at Saks Fifth Avenue, salespeople came into the window and carried away the mannequins, and then carried in a large photograph of President Kennedy, which they placed on a chair, and flanked it with urns filled with red roses. A crowd gathered in front of the window, crying. In the windows of other stores, television sets had been placed, and crowds stood in front of them, watching the news. And over the noises of the avenue came the sound of bells; the chimes of St. Patrick's Cathedral had begun to toll.

The news came so fast. The first bulletins (SHOTS FIRED—PRESIDENT HIT—UNKNOWN HOW BADLY) had begun at about 1:34, Eastern Standard Time—but they were confused, unclear. As Air Force One was turning northeast toward Washington, it was still barely an hour since Walter Cronkite had said it was apparently official: the President was dead. Pearl Harbor had been, as one historian was to put it, "the last thunderbolt of comparable magnitude," but it had "belonged to another communications era. Radio was in its heyday then. . . . Now it had been replaced by TV and the transistor." Speed—together with the fact that the news came as a running account, almost as it was happening—intensified the shock. America was convulsed with grief and horror.

ONE ELEMENT IN THE UNCERTAINTY was the fact that for some time the United States did not know the whereabouts of its new President. The exact time John F. Kennedy died—whether he was killed by the bullet that shattered his brain at 12:30 p.m. or whether his time of death was the time, "approximately one o'clock," at which the doctors at Parkland pronounced him dead—would become the subject of endless dispute, but the time at which it was announced to the world, by Malcolm Kilduff to the press corps in the nurses' classroom at Parkland, was 1:36, more than half an hour later than the doctors' pronouncement. So for a period of time that was at least thirty-six minutes and possibly more than an hour, the world did not know that Kennedy was dead. Lyndon Johnson had been President for at least thirty-six minutes before the world knew it. And when the world found out that he was President, it was still not told where he was. Kilduff told the press corps that, as the *New York Times* reported, "Mr. Johnson, who had not yet been sworn in, was safe . . . at an unannounced place." Walter Cronkite had to say, on CBS, that "Vice President Johnson has left the hospital . . . but we do not know to where he has proceeded." ("We began to be concerned about where Lyndon Johnson was, and when—and where—he might be taking the oath of office," Cronkite was to recall.) The place was not announced for about an hour. At 2:04, when Johnson was back on Air Force One, ABC still had to report that "there has been no immediate word on when (or where) Mr. Johnson will take the oath of office." Two thirty-five p.m. was when ABC reported that "we have learned from our man in Dallas that Lyndon Johnson will be sworn in shortly at Love Field." (He was sworn in at 2:38.) So for about an hour, an hour of tension and fear, America was not sure of the whereabouts of its President. During this period, little more than rumors ("It appeared Vice President Johnson might have been struck. He walked into the hospital holding one arm as if he had been hit by one of the bullets"; "We now have a report that is unconfirmed, I repeat this is unconfirmed, that Vice President Johnson has suffered a heart attack")—rumors quickly denied—were all the world was told about him. It was not until 2:49, eleven minutes after Johnson had taken the oath from Judge Hughes, and Sid Davis had left the plane and given a pool report to the press—after Air Force One had taken off—and reporters had raced to find telephones to call their city desks, that the world was given definite information. Then, for more than two hours, while Johnson was on Air Force One, America, except for the handful of people contacted over the plane's radio, was again out of touch with its President.

Anxiety and uncertainty about more than the new President. As Air Force One flew—eight miles up—across America, the country beneath it was being swept with rumors.

Twenty minutes into the flight, television networks announced the death of the Dallas police officer, J. D. Tippit, and twenty minutes later that a former Marine named Oswald had been arrested, and then facts, or rather alleged facts, started to emerge about Oswald's stay in Russia, about his application for Soviet citizenship, and his links with pro-Castro groups. Little was known definitively about him as yet, however, and there was no conclusion about whether one man or several men had fired at the presidential car: according to some reports, two heads had been seen at the window from which the shots were reported to have come; other reports said that shots had been fired not only from that window but from the triple overpass or the grassy knoll.

And these rumors fed deep fears: was the assassination a coup? Was it part of a plot—a wider plot—to take over the government? Might the implications even go beyond a coup?; while Air Force One was aloft, there were vague reports of a troop alert in Germany; the alert was, in fact, only part of a general step-up in the level of defense status ordered for all United States forces by Secretary McNamara, but, as one observer was to write, "the German alert seemed especially ominous, hinting at massive troop concentrations throughout Europe." "People were desperately unsure of what would happen next," Wicker was to write. "The world, it seemed, was a dark and malignant place; the chill of the unknown shivered across the nation."

Newspapers that sent reporters out into the street to obtain reactions received many comments like the one made by Ulrick O'Sullivan of Chicago. "It could mean an awful change in the world. It all depends on how Johnson handle[s] it."

ABOARD AIR FORCE ONE, there were, behind the cockpit, three sections, and two of them were so filled with grief that there seemed room for no other emotion. In the front section, the main passenger compartment, the two reporters aboard, *Newsweek*'s Charles Roberts and the AP's Merriman Smith, were sitting in two seats with fixed tables in front of them so that they could type, in the midst of Kennedy staffers and Secret Service men, and Roberts would remember the strangeness of the flight—with the air-conditioning working now, the oppressive heat was gone, but the window shades remained closed, so "the ride back was," he says, "like going back in a tunnel, flying 650 [*sic*] miles per hour in a plane we couldn't see out of"—and the sobs. Evelyn Lincoln and Pamela Turnure sat together, not speaking but "sobbing every now and then," their faces streaked from the tears that had run down through their mascara; other Kennedy staffers sat silently, with their heads cupped in their hands—Roberts felt they were doing that to hide their tears, but it was obvious that they were crying, too. As he began typing his story, Roberts tried for a while to get more details from Roy Kellerman, who was sitting across the table from him, but he didn't have the heart for it. There were no tears on Kellerman's face, the reporter was to recall, but "his eyes were brimming"—he was one of the "strong men crying on the plane that day."

In the rear section, the part of the plane that contained the President's bedroom and, behind it, the rear sitting area, Jacqueline Kennedy, sitting in one of the two remaining seats, was with O'Donnell, O'Brien, Powers and General McHugh—and what she was to describe as "that long, long coffin." Her thoughts were on her husband ("This is my first real political trip," she said. "I'm so glad I made it. Suppose I hadn't been there with him.") and on her duty to him: she had appeared beside Lyndon Johnson at the swearing-in; sending for Kilduff now, she told him, "You make sure, Mac—you go and tell [Roberts and Smith] that I came back here and sat with Jack." When the White House physician, Dr. George G. Burkley, suggested she change her bloodstained clothes, she repeated what she had said to Lady Bird: "No. Let them see what they've done." O'Brien seemed a man resigned, drained of all vitality; Powers couldn't stop talking about the Celtic songs Kennedy had loved. McHugh kept repeating, "He's my President— my President." After a while, they decided to drink, and asked Jackie if she wanted one, and she had a Scotch, the first Scotch she had ever had; she felt it tasted like medicine, and she never learned to like it, but in the weeks to come, Scotch was the only whiskey she would drink; it was a sort of reminder of things she felt she shouldn't forget.

But in the middle section—the President's stateroom, where the swearing-in had occurred—there was not only grief but an air of decision, of purposeful-ness, the same feeling that had come over Liz Carpenter when Lyndon Johnson had come into that room to arrange the swearing-in: the feeling that "someone was in charge."

He didn't have much time. The flight was going to take only two hours and six minutes. In 126 minutes, he was going to have to step off the plane as President—and be ready to *be* President. The stateroom was equipped with small notepads, each page embossed with the presidential seal and the words "Aboard Air Force One." Sitting down in the President's high-backed chair, Lyndon John-son pulled a pad toward him, and wrote on it:

1) Staff
2) Cabinet
3) Leadership

The meaning of those words—that there should be meetings, at which he would speak, of the White House staff, the Cabinet, and the congressional lead-ership as soon as possible after he landed—was apparent when, a few minutes later, General Clifton ("Watchman" in the Secret Service code names assigned to all members of a presidential or vice presidential traveling party) spoke from the cockpit of Air Force One to Gerald Behn, chief of the President's Secret Service detail, at the White House (named "Duplex") to relay instructions Johnson had just given him.

"Duplex, Duplex, this is Watchman. Over," Clifton said, his voice crackling over static on the radio.

"Go ahead, Watchman. This is Duplex. Over," Behn replied.

"President Johnson wants to meet the White House staff, the leadership of Congress, and as many of the Cabinet members as possible at the White House as soon as we get there," Clifton said. "The *key* members of the White House staff. That is, Sorensen, Bundy, et cetera."

Those instructions proved difficult to carry out. "I needed that White House staff," Johnson was to recall. "Without them I would have lost my link to John Kennedy, and without that I would have had no chance of gaining the support of the media or the Eastern intellectuals. And without that support I would have had absolutely no chance of governing the country." The overtures he had made to the two key members of that staff who were aboard Air Force One, Ken O'Donnell and Larry O'Brien, had already been rebuffed, however, and when he tried O'Donnell again, sending Moyers to ask him to come forward to the stateroom, and, when he came, asking him to stay on as appointments secretary, O'Donnell remained, he was to say, "non-committal." Some time later, Johnson sent Moyers back again, this time to ask O'Donnell to come forward and discuss the mechanics of calling a meeting of the National Security Council; O'Donnell refused to come, telling Moyers, "Bill, I don't have the stomach for it." For the rest of the flight, Johnson didn't press him—or O'Brien—again, and before the flight was over, the staff meeting had been canceled. And much of the Cabinet, of course, was still over the Pacific on its return flight. The Cabinet meeting, too, was postponed until the next day. Only the congressional leadership would assemble that night.

But if "leadership" as he wrote it on the pad referred only to a meeting of congressional kingpins, the word also had broader connotations, and he showed not only that he knew what to do—but that he had the will to do it. Other arrangements (for Air Force One's arrival at Andrews Air Force Base, presidential logistics for the rest of the evening) had to be made, and these arrangements—the impression they added up to: the country's first impression of Lyndon Johnson as President—could not be postponed, for that impression was symbolically important, crucial in fact, to what Johnson wanted to accomplish. The arrival itself, a plane carrying a President and his just-murdered predecessor, would be unprecedented in its drama. And during the plane's flight back to Washington, shock and uncertainties had been heightened by the news of the policeman's murder and Oswald's arrest and by the rumors about his Communist connections. "None of us had any idea whether this was a conspiracy, whether Johnson was the next victim," O'Brien was to say. Reassurance was more necessary than ever. It was important that Lyndon Johnson show himself to an anxious, worried nation as a man in whom it could have confidence, as a man firmly in charge, in full command of presidential duties—that he demonstrate that under his command the nation's government was continuing to function normally despite the terrible event that had occurred and the suspicions about the motives behind it. Martin Van Buren had said in 1867, "The Presidency under our system like the king in a monarchy never dies." The first moments at Andrews Air Force Base would be the moments to demonstrate that that statement was true in the twentieth century as well.

And it was not just America that had to be shown, Johnson felt. Sitting at the President's desk in the stateroom, he said, "It's the Kremlin that worries me. It can't be allowed to detect a waver. . . . Khrushchev is asking himself right now what kind of a man I am. He's got to know he's dealing with a man of determination."

The line between showing that he had assumed and was exercising the President's duties and making the family and followers of the late President feel he was in too much of a hurry to assume those duties was a delicate one. Many decisions to be made about the arrival in Washington and his logistics were complicated by that fact. They were nonetheless decisions that had to be made—and they were made.

In the stateroom, General Clifton and Kilduff were called over to receive instructions to be relayed over the plane's radio to the White House, and they hurried forward to the cockpit. Orders began to crackle out over the plane's radio, orders in which a key word was "normal." Before Johnson had boarded the plane in Dallas, Secret Service headquarters in Washington had instructed Swindal that, on landing at Andrews, he was to taxi to an isolated area of the base and park there, away from public and press, so that the plane could be more easily guarded. Now, from Air Force One, those orders were countermanded. The plane would park in its customary parking space directly in front of the terminal, where President Kennedy had always descended on his return from trips. "Next item, Duplex. Next item," Clifton told Behn. "The press, according to Lyndon Johnson, the press is to have its normal little corral at Andrews . . . a normal press arrangement." Kilduff ("Warrior") had been dispatched to the cockpit to call deputy press secretary Andrew Hatcher at the White House. "Winner, Winner, this is Warrior. Will you please advise press that normal press coverage, including live TV, will be allowed at the base." Continuity was important. As he had wanted his predecessor's widow next to him at his swearing-in, so he wanted her next to him when he first appeared before the television cameras. "According to plan, once we landed the President would go immediately to the rear of the plane and depart the aircraft alongside Mrs. Kennedy and the coffin of President Kennedy," Jack Valenti was to write. The Secret Service agents in Kennedy's detail and O'Donnell, O'Brien and the other Kennedy men were to carry the coffin down the stairs from the rear door; most of the agents, Mrs. Lincoln, Mrs. Gallagher and other Kennedy aides were sitting in the front compartment, and Jackie sent General McHugh to tell them, "I want his friends to carry him down." Johnson didn't want to appear "all alone." When he came down the stairs, he said, "I want my staff behind me and then the Texas members of Congress."

"*Staff,*" he had written on the notepad. Continuity wasn't the only reason he needed the Kennedy men to stay on. Almost no one on his staff had ever exercised any substantial governmental responsibility or authority, and no one on the plane at all: Cliff Carter's job had been setting up a political organization in Texas; Liz Carpenter, also on board, was there to assist Lady Bird, and Marie Fehmer, of course, was only a secretary. Almost no members of the staff from his senatorial days back in Washington, except for Jenkins and Reedy, were still with him.

Moyers was on the plane, however, and Johnson knew his abilities. And so was Valenti, the Houston advertising man, who had, he was to say, no idea why he was aboard except that the President had wanted him to come to Washington with him; Johnson had only intermittent dealings with Valenti, but he had evidently seen something. There would have to be a statement from him when they landed at Andrews. Motioning over Moyers, Valenti and Liz Carpenter, he said, "I want you to put something down for me to say when we land. Nothing long. Make it brief. We'll have plenty of time later to say more."

Together the three Texans composed a draft, and Fehmer typed it and gave it to him. It was short, but Johnson could always improve a statement—and this one didn't have to be cleared with anybody. He made it more personal, changing their line "The nation suffers a loss that cannot be weighed" to "We have suffered a loss that cannot be weighed," and more dramatic, reversing two phrases in the last sentence. The draft said, "I ask God's help and yours"; he changed it to "I ask for your help—and God's."

The question of where the congressional leadership meeting would be held was important. McGeorge Bundy seemed to feel that Johnson could hold it in— and indeed could immediately begin to work out of—a number of places in the West Wing. Over the radio he told Clifton, "Tell the Vice President the Cabinet Room is under rearrangement. But the Oval Room will be ready . . . both the Fish Room and the President's study, and we will try to have the Cabinet Room. But that's a detail. We can work that out." Clifton had had very specific instructions from Johnson, however. No, he said, that was not merely a detail. "He [Johnson] does *not want* to go in the Mansion, or in the Oval Room, or the President's study or the President's office." There was the question of where he was to live. Youngblood was sent to the cockpit. "Dagger to Duplex. Messages from Volunteer and Victoria. . . . Volunteer will reside at Valley for an indefinite time." Of arrangements that had to be made there: The telephone lines there should be disconnected immediately, and secure lines installed.

There were telephone calls he had to make, to Jenkins telling him to arrange to have helicopters at Andrews for transportation to the White House, and who would ride in each of them; a brief call to McGeorge Bundy, who told him, he was to recall, "that he must get back to Washington where we were all shaky." And calls that he had to make together with Lady Bird, to Nellie Connally. "Nellie, do you hear me?" "Yes, Bird . . . the surgeon just got done operating on him. And John is going to be all right."

And one that was harder to make. "Crown, [this is] Air Force One," Swindal said. "Volunteer requesting a patch with Mrs. Rose Kennedy."

Mrs. Kennedy was patched in to the plane. Kennedy's steward, Sergeant Joseph Ayres, holding the line in the stateroom, handed the phone to Johnson. Putting his hand over the phone, Johnson said, "What can I say to her?" He said, "I wish to God there was something that I could do, and I wanted to tell you that we were grieving with you. Here's Lady Bird."

There was a lot to do in two hours. But by the time Air Force One started its descent it had been done, and in a manner that, Liz Carpenter says, made her keep recalling what Lady Bird had said about her husband in an emergency. In this emergency, Charles Roberts was to say, Lyndon Johnson had been "masterful." "After all," the reporter was to say, since "he was the first President ever to" be on the scene at "the murder of his predecessor, he could have been forgiven if he hadn't been too cool. But the fact is, he was cool." Thornberry, who had known him for so many years, says he was "as calm and collected" as he had "ever seen him." As Air Force One touched down, taxied toward the terminal, and came to a stop in its usual place, he stood up with Lady Bird, told his aides, "Let's get everybody together," and headed down the narrow aisle toward the rear until he was stopped, between the door to the President's bedroom and the rear sitting area where the coffin was lying, by the jam of Secret Service men and Kennedy aides filling the aisle behind Jackie, waiting to carry the coffin off, and he stood there, just behind the Kennedy people, with his own entourage behind him.

AND THEN BOBBY KENNEDY came on board.

After his conversations with Johnson on the telephone, Bobby had walked, head down, hands in pockets, back and forth on Hickory Hill's lawn, his huge Newfoundland, Brumus, trailing at his heels. Several aides had hurried out from the Justice Department, and he talked with them, telling Ed Guthman, "There's so much bitterness. . . . I thought they would get one of us, but Jack, after all he'd been through, never worried about it. . . . I thought it would be me." He tried to comfort them—"He had the most wonderful life," he said—as he did his children, who, brought back from school, came running across the lawn to him, and hugged him. But he wasn't fooling his friends—or his wife; she handed him a pair of dark glasses to hide his red-rimmed eyes.

Arriving at Andrews about a half hour before Air Force One landed, and seeing the television cameras and floodlights being set up, he climbed into the back of an Army truck parked on the tarmac so he wouldn't be seen, and sat there unnoticed even after the lights were turned on to illuminate the runway in a garish, almost eerie light. When the plane landed, and the floodlights were turned off so the pilot could see his way to his parking spot, he got out of the truck. The huge jet rolled like a shadow out of the darkness and came to a stop, and as a movable flight of stairs was rolled up beside its front door and the door was opened, he ran up the stairs and ducked inside the plane, just as the floodlights were turned on again, unseen by anyone on the ground, and rushed toward the rear of the plane, pushing past people in aisles. "Where's Jackie?" he said. "I want to be with Jackie." When he reached the Texas group behind Johnson, he pushed his way through them, too. He "didn't look to the left or the right," Liz Carpenter says—"his face looked streaked with tears and absolutely stricken," she says—but simply pushed through the group, saying, "Excuse me. Excuse me." He pushed past Lyndon Johnson, too, almost touching him, but saying nothing. Valenti felt he was so distraught that he didn't even see Johnson; he "couldn't see anything or anybody." Johnson was "impassive," Valenti says. "No change in expression." At the same time, the Secret Service agents and Kennedy aides who had been in the front of the plane were, in response to Jackie's request, coming back to help carry off the coffin, and as Bobby pushed past Johnson they followed him. "Everyone," as William Manchester was to write, "seemed to have priority over the chief executive." Johnson found himself, in Valenti's word, "trapped" behind the agents and Kennedy aides, unable to move forward, jammed against the wall of the narrow plane corridor.

"Hi, Jackie," Bobby said when he reached her. "I'm here." "Oh, Bobby," she said. Was she thinking of how Bobby had driven through the night so that he could be with her when she had lost her child? She told Manchester that when she saw Bobby now, "She thought how like Bobby this was; he was always there when you needed him."

A truck lift, a large yellow-painted metal container, almost the size of a small room, that was used to transport the meals served to passengers on a plane, drove up, and was raised so that its floor was level with the rear door; standing atop it was a young Navy lieutenant, in dress blues, hand to cap in a rigid salute; he was to say that the sight of the long red-bronze coffin had disturbed him, because, in Manchester's words, he felt that "a fallen chieftain should be shielded by a flag; he wished he had brought one with him." The agents and the aides got the coffin into the lift. Watching on television, Americans saw them carrying what looked at first only like a long box, glinting in the glare of the floodlights. Then they realized what it was. Jackie and Bobby stepped in beside it; he was holding her hand. That was the first time America saw the stains on Jackie's suit. The agents and aides stepped in, too. The crowd was so silent that Theodore White "yearned for a cry, a sob, a wail, any human sound."

The lift was lowered. Since only the lift, not a stair ramp, had been placed at the plane's rear door, there was now nothing between the door and the ground. A gray Navy hearse was backed up to the lift, and the coffin was put in it. As it was being put in, Lyndon and Lady Bird came to the rear door, expecting to descend to the ground. But there were no steps there. Jackie and Bobby got into the hearse and drove off, leaving the President and First Lady in the doorway.

THE NEXT DAY, according to a diary kept by a Cabinet member—apparently Orville Freeman—who spoke to Johnson, "He [Johnson] said that when the plane came in . . . [they] paid no attention to him whatsoever, but they took the body off the plane, put it in the car, . . . and departed, and only then did he leave the plane without any attention directed or any courtesy toward him, then the President of the United States. But he said he just turned the other cheek . . . he said, what can I do? I do not want to get in a fight with the family and the aura of Kennedy is important to us."

Turning the other cheek must have been hard, as was evidenced by remarks he made in a television interview during his retirement. Asked about the incident, he said at first that he couldn't recall it. Even if such a thing had occurred, he said, "I would not have felt any offense in a critical period like that and carrying the burden and troubles that he [Bobby] was carrying." But then, when asked whether the manner of "the removal of President Kennedy's body" had been "a surprise to you," he replied, "Yes . . . it didn't occur to me that the ramp would be removed and we would not be privileged to go down the same ramp with the body." He had never asked why that had been done, he said. "I just observed it, as I did a good many things." He was to call Bobby's actions, in the words of one writer, "a deliberate snub." "He ran so that he would not have to pause and recognize the new President," he said to another.

THE TELEVISION CAMERAS at Andrews had shown America—an America that had been out of touch with its President for more than two hours—the darkened runways at the air base, and then the plane's long shape gliding out of the shadows, taxiing toward the spectators and a group of Cabinet officials, and then turning so that its whole length was in front of them, still in the dark. And then the floodlights were switched on, and for a moment, as one observer wrote, "the scene, the waiting for Air Force One beneath the glare of television klieg lights," seemed to be one that "had been enacted many times in the past when the President was returning from a triumphant tour of Europe or a 'non-political' jaunt" across America. But this time a truck, with atop it an hydraulic lift holding the room-size metal container, brightly lit inside and open at both ends so the watchers could see into it—in a way, it was a giant picture frame—was wheeled up to the plane's door, and when the door was opened, "there was," as Mary McGrory wrote, "no familiar, graceful figure, fingering a button of his jacket, waiting to smile, waiting to wave." Instead, what appeared in the frame were the backs of a little group of men, bent over, holding something heavy and tugging it into the container—and then the viewers could see what they were tugging: the reddish-bronze box, glistening in the light as it lay on the floor of that brightly lit yellow frame. Then the men straightened up, and "there in the frame" was what McGrory called "the old guard of the dead President"—and his wife and brother.

The container—the tableau inside: of the box, and the men standing beside it, and the widow and the brother—was lowered to the truck bed. The gray ambulance-hearse backed into position near it, and a ten-man Marine honor guard marched up beside it, and the coffin was lifted into the hearse, and then Jackie and Bobby got in, and the ambulance pulled away, followed by a line of limousines. The television cameras swung to follow the ambulance as it left the airport, driving past another honor guard, rifles at the salute. As it was leaving, a television reporter said, "President Lyndon B. Johnson and Mrs. Johnson are standing in the door of the plane," but the cameras did not swing to show the new President and his wife until the ambulance had disappeared out of the airport. Then there was the pause while the white presidential stairs were wheeled up to replace the truck lift. It wasn't long—less than two minutes—but it was a pause, a gap during which, after the hearse pulled away, the Johnsons were kept waiting in the door.

And after they came down, Youngblood behind them, the agent's eyes flickering constantly around the figures in the darkness beyond the floodlights, there was another delay. About a dozen microphones for radio and television stations, poles with speakers on them at which Johnson was supposed to give his statement, had been set up on a broad expanse of the tarmac. There was no podium, no presidential seal, only the cluster of poles. When he walked over to them, after getting a report from Bundy ("that there was no indication of a [foreign] plot" since no country—including the Soviet Union—was doing anything to exploit the situation), the roar of the engines of the two Army helicopters waiting to take him and his party to the White House, and the *thump-thump* of their whirling rotors, was so loud that he realized no one would be able to hear him. He sent Youngblood to speak to the pilots, but the noise didn't abate noticeably, and he motioned the agent over to him again, and said, "Are we ready? Ask them if they're ready," and Youngblood went over again. The noise remained deafening, and the lights were glaring blindingly into the Johnsons' eyes. He and Lady Bird had to stand alone before the little group of microphones on the bare, garishly lit concrete, in a setting with no dignity about it at all, for a long, awkward, few minutes—until the engines were throttled back a bit; despite Youngblood's requests, the pilots didn't turn them off, saying they needed to keep them warm for a quick takeoff.

Although it was a situation in which it was difficult for a person to keep his poise, Johnson kept his. He showed not a trace of irritation. The command he had imposed on himself did not slip for an instant; his face remained expressionless as he and his wife stood alone in the harsh lights. He read his few words, with their poignant ending—"I will do my best. That is all I can do. I ask for your help—and God's"—slowly and solemnly. "He was very reassuring, and I think for the country to hear the new President was a reassuring thing," said one TV newsman, even though, as another said, "Because of the noise in the place it was hard to hear his words." He assigned people to the helicopters (making himself heard was so difficult that he cupped his hand around Valenti's ear as he shouted, "Get in the second chopper and come to my office as soon as you can"), climbed into the first one, and they lifted off and wheeled toward Washington, their blinking red lights disappearing into the darkness. The flight was only eleven minutes long, but before it was over, sitting in the front compartment with Lady Bird, McNamara, Bundy and Ball, he asked the right questions—"Any important matters pending?" to McNamara: what was the impact of the assassination on foreign governments—to determine that the foreign situation was, indeed, stable, and found the right words, eloquent words. He had to keep these men in his Administration. Leaning toward the three Kennedy men, hunched forward in his intensity, he said, "President Kennedy did something I could never have done. He gathered around him the ablest people I've ever seen—not his friends, not even the best in public service, but the best *anywhere*. I want you to stay. I need you. I want you to stand with me."

The job had been done. "No other words could have better appealed to

Bundy's sense of himself and his duty to the Presidency," his biographer said; the shakiness he had felt when he spoke to Johnson in Dallas was, suddenly, gone now; Ball, who found Johnson "surprisingly stable—more so than I would have been," felt that his words were "especially moving"; McNamara was, as always, McNamara: cold, efficient, focusing on the task to be done. All three remained in their posts. Then, all at once, the windows of the helicopter were filled with a huge, shining white shape—the floodlit Washington Monument—and, swerving close around it, the helicopter began to descend. The reporters gathered on the South Lawn of the White House had seen red lights blinking far out beyond the monument, and heard a faint *pop-pop* sound from the whirling rotors; then, seemingly in an instant, the *pop-pop* had become a deafening roar, the helicopter was hovering over the lawn, a second copter in view now right behind it, the wind from the big blades shook the trees around the lawn as if there was a storm, and cut through the tall spraying waters of the fountain beyond the lawn, one reporter wrote, "like an invisible knife."

Following Youngblood down its steps, holding Lady Bird's arm, Johnson told Liz Carpenter, "Stay with Lady Bird and help her all you can," and the two women headed for a limousine that would take them to The Elms. (In the car, after rolling up the glass that separated them from the driver "so we could talk," Ms. Carpenter said, "It's a terrible thing to say but the salvation of Texas is that the Governor was hit." "Don't think I haven't thought of that," Lady Bird Johnson replied. "I only wish it could have been me"—her words revealing the depth of both Texas defensiveness, and of her love for her husband; Secret Service agents speak of being willing "to take the shot for the President," of an agent being willing to sacrifice his own life for his leader's; Lady Bird Johnson was saying that if by being shot, she could have removed the tarnish that she feared would attach to her husband because the assassination that had elevated him to the presidency had occurred in his state, she would have willingly accepted the bullet.) Johnson, with Moyers and several other men behind him, and Youngblood walking stride for stride next to him, so close that their shoulders kept touching, headed for the White House. The doors of the Oval Office were open, so that the President's desk, on a new red carpet Jackie had had installed while he was away in Texas, was visible, but before he reached those doors, he veered to the right, so abruptly that his right shoulder banged into Moyers. "Don't you want to go in?" someone asked. "I'll use my office," he said, and, entering the White House through the doors to Mrs. Lincoln's office, walked through her office, into the corridor outside, down the stairs, and across West Executive Avenue to the Executive Office Building.

THE WHITE VICE PRESIDENTIAL FLAG behind his desk in 274's ceremonial office had been replaced with the blue presidential flag, and the vice presidential seals above the outer doors with presidential seals. As soon as his junior military assistant, twenty-four-year-old Army Lieutenant Richard H. Nelson, had heard the news from Dallas, there had flashed into his mind something he had been taught as a political science major at Princeton, and how it related to his boss's return to Washington: "He had to come back not as the Vice President and not as the acting president, [but] as the President of the United States. Because this was always drummed into us in everything, the continuity of government, that the American people will carry on, will survive." Dragooning a White House guard to help, Nelson ran down to the basement, found an old presidential flag and some seals, and installed them in 274—"just the symbols, that when he walked into the Executive Office Building office, he was walking into the office of the President, not the Vice President."

But that was the only aspect of 274 that was presidential. It was still the same undistinguished, fluorescent-lit three-room office. He would still need the large room, the ceremonial room, for meetings, and while previously there had been two desks in the secretaries' office, there would have to be a lot more people working in the suite now: not only the staff he had left in the Capitol offices, Jenkins, Reedy and their secretaries, but the three additions, Moyers, Valenti and Carter, he had made on Air Force One. No one knew where they would sit, or what their assignments would be.

Already in the EOB elevator when he, Jenkins, Bundy and Moyers stepped in was Colonel Juanita Roberts. They shook hands "with a sort of reassuring pat," and when they got out on the second floor, and he was going into 274's conference room, he said, "Walter, let's have Marie take the phone calls; Juanita can take care of the people who are coming, and make my appointments. You and Bill come in here." He went into the large room.

"Nothing worked," Nelson was to recall. "Government officials [were] competing with telephone men" laying new wires. Among the people crowding in were Senate Foreign Relations Committee chairman J. William Fulbright and veteran Democratic foreign policy adviser Averell Harriman. The Secret Service blocked off the corridor outside, so no one else could enter, but every phone in the three rooms seemed to be ringing. Marie Fehmer wouldn't get there for a while—having landed in the second helicopter, she had been separated from the rest of the group, and not knowing where Johnson was, went home, where she found messages telling her to come to 274—and Carter and Jenkins were answering the phones, Carter "just inundated by calls," Jenkins, an oasis of calm, sitting with his yellow pad in front of him, taking notes in Gregg shorthand. The staff was crowding in: Mildred Stegall, Dorothy Territo, Valenti, Nelson, Ivan Sinclair. There was no place for them all to sit, so Nelson and Sinclair pushed in more desks and chairs. More telephone men arrived, trying to set up a hotline to Moscow and enough regular lines for all the people who were going to need them. Every few minutes a man Colonel Roberts had never seen before rushed in and handed her wire-service copy from the White House pressroom tickers for her to give Johnson—"I didn't know him; he didn't know me," she recalls; it was

Mac Kilduff. "Much chaos, and a lot of people running helter-skelter," Fehmer says. But, she says, at the center of the storm, there was a calm: her boss. Young Nelson, when Johnson had come in, saw the same thing in this man he had known only as Vice President: "Total command—I mean, just his bearing. He somehow appeared to me to have grown about seven, eight inches in the course of the day. He seemed bigger than when I saw him off on the plane to Texas." Fehmer saw the change—"almost a different person," she says. "Many, many phone calls," she says, "both coming in and going out," but "there was no more of that hurrying. We may have all been hurried and flurried inside, but he set the pace," and the pace was "deliberate." "There was no lost motion; it wasn't neces- sary for us to talk," Colonel Roberts says. "He would say, 'I want such and such,' and we would . . . do it. We knew his ways. And we had always known that when there was a difficult problem, this would be the time when you would work fastest and with very little conversation." Bundy "was in and out, and the Presi- dent was" giving him "instructions" about one matter after another; "a person who wouldn't know either one" of the two men would "have assumed that they had . . . worked with each other forever."

Foreign worries were the first priority—Johnson saw Fulbright and Harri- man first, and fast—and then he started making his calls: to his three living pred- ecessors (to Eisenhower Johnson said, "I have needed you for a long time, but I need you more than ever now"; according to Reedy, he used similar words to Truman; Herbert Hoover's son, Allen, said his father was too deaf to use the phone); to J. Edgar Hoover to direct him to throw the FBI's full resources into investigating the assassination (hanging up the phone, Hoover ordered thirty additional agents to Dallas); to Sargent Shriver to express condolences. He called the treasurer of the Democratic National Committee, Richard Maguire, a Kennedy man. A lot of money had been raised on the fatal Texas trip; it had gone to the committee. He told Maguire how much he needed him ("I've got to rely on you more than he did"), and, in what might be an indication that he was thinking ahead to the 1964 election, said, "You be giving some thought to what needs to be done, and when we get these things behind us the next day or two, then we'll get together"). And there were calls to two of the "damn smart men" who had given Jack Kennedy the brilliant concepts and the brilliant words that Johnson admired. "You're going to have to do some heavy thinking for me," he said to Supreme Court Justice Arthur Goldberg. "I want you to be thinking about what I ought to do. . . . I want you to think . . . just *think* in capital letters, and *think, think, think.* And then—then talk to me tomorrow or the next day. . . . There's nobody in town that I believe in more than you and I've just *got* to have your help." Then he called the Kennedy aide he felt he needed more than any other; in explaining on the plane the importance of keeping the Kennedy team, he had said, over and over, "especially Sorensen." Of all Kennedy's men, none had been hit harder. McGrory had seen him, at Andrews, "white-faced and stricken, unsee- ing and unhearing"; as Johnson walked through the West Wing on the way to his office, Ted Sorensen had been sitting alone at the Cabinet table, weeping. "Kindly, strongly, generously he told me how sorry he was, how deeply he felt for me, how well he knew what I had been to President Kennedy for eleven years, and that he, LBJ, now needed me even more." Sorensen said, he was to recall, "Good-bye and thank you, Mr. President." Hanging up the phone, he broke into tears again, "unable to face the fact that I had just addressed that title to someone other than John F. Kennedy." Arriving at the White House, the congressional leaders had headed for the Oval Office, only to be directed across the street. Jenkins seated them at the conference table in 274's outer office while Johnson, who had hurriedly gone into the inner office, made more calls until they were all present. His three years of sitting silent at leaders' meetings was over. He knew what he wanted to say—that they couldn't let other countries get "wrong ideas" that America's foreign policies might be changed as a result of a "very abrupt and sudden transition," that it was important to show that the country was unified, that he needed the support of both parties in Congress—and what he wanted them to say to waiting reporters at the conclusion of the meeting. He had, in fact, already had Reedy draw up a statement expressing the desired sentiments and had edited it, rewriting it heavily. Reading it to them now, he got their agreement to have Reedy issue it on their behalf; as they were filing out of 274, Reedy was typing it for distribution to the press.

Writing in later years about that Friday night, Hugh Sidey said that it was in Johnson's meeting with the congressional leaders "that perhaps more than in anything else lay the real clue to his flawless assumption of power." "The meeting had no real purpose," Sidey wrote—yet it was very important. "It was a kind of tribal ritual of those men who wielded the power in the legislative halls [where] meetings are a way of life and a sign of authority." Once Johnson had called such meetings, summoning such men. He hadn't called one for three years. But now he had called one again. And, Sidey wrote, "these men understood."

THAT STATEMENT for the press wasn't the only thing Lyndon Johnson wrote that evening. Sitting at his desk in his inner office, door closed against the voices outside, he wrote two letters in longhand. "Dear John," said the first, "It will be many years before you understand fully what a great man your father was. His loss is a deep personal tragedy for all of us, but I wanted you particularly to know that I share your grief—You can always be proud of him." The second said, "Dearest Caroline, Your father's death has been a great tragedy for the Nation, as well as for you, and I wanted you to know how much my thoughts are of you at this time. He was a wise and devoted man. You can always be proud of what he did for his country." He signed them both, "Affectionately, Lyndon B. Johnson." Even Manchester had to write, of those letters, "He would never be a simple man. He was capable of tactlessness and tenderness, cunning and passion." Then he was almost done with his office work for the evening. He telephoned the young man who had always been closer to him than any of his other aides, and to whom he talked in a kidding tone that he didn't use often with the others. "I'm going to be leaving here soon," he said without preamble when Buzz picked up the phone. "I'll come by and pick you up—you wait at the curb." And when Buzz, knowing that with the world watching on the evening of an assassination, the new President should not stop on Connecticut Avenue and pick someone up, said that he would drive to The Elms in his own car, Johnson asked, in the old kidding tone, "What's the matter? Are you running from the press?"

IT WAS 9:24 P.M. Valenti, who had received an order to get on the plane, and then one to get on the helicopter, now received one to get in the car ("Drive home with me, Jack. You can stay at my house tonight and then we will have a chance to do some talking. Are you ready to leave now?"), still, he was to say, "not quite sure precisely why I was even here in the first place." Gathering up Carter and Moyers as well, Johnson led them out to his car, two Secret Service agents in front of them, two behind, Youngblood at his shoulder. Two agents were already sitting in the front seat, a convertible full of agents behind; as Johnson got into the car, two of the agents stood up, automatic rifles in their hands; then as the White House gates swung open ahead of them and the two cars pulled out onto Pennsylvania Avenue, a half dozen waiting police motorcycle outriders swung out in front of them, their sirens wailing. At the other gates—at The Elms—men were holding shotguns as well as pistols; the street around them was filled with reporters, television mobile units, telephone trucks and telephone linemen hooking up the new, secure lines, and a cluster (surprisingly small, in reporters' memories) of neighbors and onlookers.

Busby, arriving at The Elms a few minutes earlier, had seen at once that "the aura of the office preceded" the man he had worked for for so long. No one wanted to be in the foyer when the new President came in; it was "conspicuously empty; when people crossed through it, they hurried their steps." Yet they wanted to see him coming in; "whenever the front door opened to admit a Secret Service agent or a telephone installer, faces appeared" at the five other doorways that opened off the foyer, "peeking around doorframes to see if the sound meant that he had come." When he did indeed come, Busby counted sixteen faces (including "my own") at the doorways.

Walking through the hallway to the sunroom at the back of the house, Johnson sprawled down in the big green chair. Framed in each of the French doors, there was, suddenly, a Secret Service man, his back to the windows. Asking for a glass of orange juice, Johnson raised it in a toast toward the grim photograph on the wall. "Hello, Mr. Sam. Sure wish you were here tonight," he said.

Dr. J. Willis Hurst, Johnson's cardiologist, was waiting in the sunroom; hearing the reports that Johnson had gone into Parkland Hospital rubbing his left arm, Dr. Travell had called him. Johnson told Hurst he had no pain in his arm, and observing him, Hurst was reassured about his health. Busby, observing him from a different perspective, was reassured in other ways; he saw in an instant that his calmness was only a façade: "he was more controlled than calm." But he saw also that the control—the "composure and coolheadedness"—was complete.

After watching television for a few minutes, Johnson said, "I guess I know less than anybody about what's happening in the United States." Then the films on the screen were of Kennedy's appearance in Fort Worth that morning. Raising his hand as if to shield his eyes from the screen, he said, "I don't believe I can take that. It's too fresh," and the channel was changed to one showing, first, films of Kennedy's early career and then films of his own. An announcer mentioned the plane bringing the Cabinet members back to Washington. "That's the last damned time that the President, the Vice President, and six Cabinet members are going to be out of Washington at the same time, I can tell you that," he said. Calling in the head of the Secret Service, James J. Rowley, he told him about Youngblood protecting his body with his own. "I want you to do whatever you can, the best thing that can be done for that boy," he said. He told Busby to get Nellie Connally on the phone, and asked her about the governor's condition. "Take care of Johnny," he said at last. "I need him now." He told Valenti, Moyers and Carter that they could sleep at The Elms, told Valenti he could stay there—or at the White House when he, Johnson, moved in—until he found a place to live in Washington. And in a low voice, "almost to himself," he repeated, over and over, as if he was working himself up, preparing himself, the same sentence: "We really have a big job to do now."

At about midnight, Busby left for his home, after a conversation in which Johnson said, "You know, almost all the issues now are just about the same as they were when I came here thirty years ago." Those issues were still on the table, he said, and he intended to get action on some of them. He went upstairs, and directed Moyers, Valenti and Carter to the bedrooms they were to use, but they had only begun undressing when he called them on the intercom and told them to come to his room because "I want to think out my agenda."

Johnson was in bed, in striped pajamas, propped up against a pillow, with memoranda and reports spread out around him; Mrs. Johnson was in bed in another room. The three men pulled chairs up next to the bed.

The men didn't talk much; very little input from them was required. Lyndon Johnson just wanted, Carter was to say, "a sounding board."

The "agenda" he was planning was his schedule for the next day—what he had to do, what people he should see, what he should say to them. There was the Cabinet meeting: What time should it be? What White House staffers should be invited to attend? What should he say there? He had to meet with Eisenhower: What did he want to accomplish at that meeting? What did he want to say to him? Buzz should be told to draft talking points. Pulling out a notebook, Valenti started scribbling frantically. What legislation was most urgent? What could he do to get it passed? Who in the House and Senate should he talk to about it—the budget, and the tax bill that was tied in with it, in particular? How to deal with Harry Byrd? Harry Truman had given an address to a joint session of Congress the day after Roosevelt's funeral; he wanted to give one, too—when should it be scheduled?; what should he say in it?; who should draft it? "We sat and talked so long, we were talking about the many, many details of things that needed to be done, the bases that needed to be touched with foreign governments, with governors, with senators, congressmen, mayors, certain things with the Cabinet members," Cliff Carter was to say. Some of the things were sensitive, because if he appeared to be assuming power quickly he might offend the Kennedys, but if he didn't, the public might not see that the government was in firm hands: "Everything was weighed out . . . to make sure that he was walking this chalk line not to overdo but yet where the people had confidence that he could do the job." All this time the television set was on, and the newscasters' words would remind him of other things: Harry Truman was mentioned; "By God, I'm going to pass Harry Truman's medical insurance bill," he said. The three men around the bed sat silently; the man in the bed talked, and talked—he didn't want advice; he knew what should be done the next day; he just wanted to lay it out. "That whole night he seemed to have several chambers of his mind operating simultaneously," Moyers was to say. "It was formidable, very formidable." Valenti kept scribbling things to be done on his pad—ten pages were to be covered with notes; he gave them the next morning to a secretary to have them typed up, but they were lost; "do you realize how valuable they would be?" he was to moan to the author years later. There was the question of who was going to carry out the tasks listed on the pad. Johnson made clear that they were all on his staff now: "He told Moyers that he wanted him back from the Peace Corps," Carter says. He told Valenti to take a two-year leave of absence from his public relations firm because he would be working at the White House, and he told Carter "to move over to the Democratic National Committee to represent his interests there." Johnson started to firm things up, mapping out an hour-by-hour schedule of what he would be doing Saturday. He stopped talking at about three a.m. It was about twenty hours since he had woken up in Fort Worth that morning. "Well, good night, boys," he said. "Get a lot of sleep fast. It's going to be a long day tomorrow."

14

Three Encounters

AT ABOUT 4:30 A.M., while Johnson was sleeping, the autopsy was finally completed at Bethesda Naval Hospital, and the coffin was brought by that gray Navy ambulance to the White House, Bobby and Jackie sitting in the back beside it—Jackie was still wearing the pink suit—and was carried into the East Room by a Marine honor guard. Jackie had sent word that she wanted the room to look "as it did when Lincoln's body lay there," Dick Goodwin recalls, and sketches from 1865 had been located, and black crepe had been draped in folds over the long gold curtains and the three crystal chandeliers. A catafalque, similar to Lincoln's, a black stand on a black base, had been found, and set up in the center of the room. A group of Kennedy aides was standing in a far corner of the room when the coffin was carried in. Jackie followed it, Bobby beside her, Kenny and Larry behind. "Her face was fixed straight ahead, lovely, painful to see," Dick Goodwin says. Walking over to the coffin, she knelt on the floor, turned her face away so that the watching group could not see, and rested her cheek on the flag that draped the long box. Then she put her arms around it. Anyone who hadn't been crying before was crying now. After a while, she got up; the aides followed the Kennedys out of the room. There was still a decision to be made—Jackie wanted the coffin closed, so that the world would remember her husband as he had been; McNamara said it must be open, because the world would demand to see the body of a head of state—a hard decision, so it was made by the man who made those decisions. Going back into the East Room alone, he had the casket opened so he could see his brother's face. After a while, he came out, and asked Arthur Schlesinger to go in and look. "For a moment, I was shattered," Schlesinger recalls; "It was not a good job." "Close it," Robert Kennedy said. Tall candles stood flickering at each corner of the catafalque, and at each corner, also, was a man in uniform with his rifle at parade rest, guarding it; at the head of the coffin stood the honor guard's commander, a Navy lieutenant, of course, rigidly at attention. At two wooden prie-dieux knelt two priests in cassocks, praying.

• • •

ROBERT KENNEDY'S FACE had remained pale and sad, but set, resolute, and, apparently, calm. He went up to the Lincoln Bedroom, still seemingly so "controlled," says Charles Spalding, who went upstairs with him. "There's a sleeping pill around here somewhere," Spalding said, found one, gave it to him, and then closed the door. "Then I just heard him break down. . . . I heard him sob and say, 'Why, God?' "

FOR LYNDON JOHNSON, Saturday could hardly have gotten off to a worse start.

Arising after only a few hours' sleep, he breakfasted and left for the White House at 8:40, planning to begin working on the agenda he had outlined during the night. Instead, he began with a confrontation with Robert Kennedy.

McGeorge Bundy had told Johnson Friday evening that he would be able to move into the Oval Office Saturday morning, but subsequently the national security advisor had learned that that would not be a good idea, and, going to the Executive Office Building early Saturday morning—8:05 a.m.—he left a note for Johnson there, telling Mildred Stegall to give it to him as soon as he came in. "When you and I talked last night about when the President's office in the West Wing would be ready, I thought possibly it would be immediately," the note said. "However, I find they are working on President Kennedy's papers and his personal belongings and my suggestion would be that—if you could work here in the EOB today and tomorrow, everything will be ready and clear by Monday morning." Johnson, unfortunately, didn't get the message. Emerging from his limousine at about 8:55, he didn't go to the EOB, but walked into the West Wing instead—to the Oval Office—and walked in on Evelyn Lincoln as she was beginning to pack up Jack Kennedy's belongings. "I have an appointment at 9:30," he said. "Can I have my girls in your office by 9:30?"

That would give her a half hour to pack. "I don't know, Mr. President," she said. "Grief-stricken and appalled," in a friend's words, she walked out of the office and began to cry—just as Bobby walked in. Sobbing, she said, "Do you know he asked me to be out by 9:30?"

At Bethesda Hospital the previous evening Bobby had been, Evan Thomas says, "a commanding figure," making funeral arrangements, giving orders "in Jackie's name, just as he had in Jack's." He had kept telling little jokes, trying to keep everyone's spirits up. "Composed, withdrawn, resolute," was how Arthur Schlesinger saw him; he was "clearly emerging as the strongest of the stricken," Ben Bradlee said. But, Schlesinger says, "within, he was demolished. . . . He didn't know where he was. . . . Everything was just pulled out from under him." Only the two words Spalding heard because Bobby Kennedy didn't know anyone would hear had revealed the depth of his anguish. But when Mrs. Lincoln told him what Johnson had asked her, he blurted out, "Oh, no!" Not wanting to talk to Johnson in the office that had been his brother's, he went with him into the small adjoining private office and told him that crating his brother's possessions would take time, and asked him if he could wait until noon. Johnson said he could, that the only reason he had wanted to move in was that his advisers had insisted that he should. He quickly walked downstairs to the Situation Room for a briefing from Bundy and CIA Director McCone, and then went across the street to Room 274. He didn't return to the Oval Office at noon; he didn't return to it for three days.

The confrontation had been due to a misunderstanding—"a mix-up," Bundy called it—and he explained that to both Kennedy and Johnson later that day, but between these two men the blackest interpretation was placed on every action; a misunderstanding was only a new cause for rage. Johnson felt that in pushing past him on the plane at Andrews Bobby "ran so that he would not have to pause and recognize the new President." "Perhaps some such thought contributed to Robert Kennedy's haste," Schlesinger commented. "But a man more secure than Johnson would have sympathized with the terrible urgency carrying him to his murdered brother's wife." And he saw not only personal but political motives in the Oval Office scene. To Johnson, it was part of a plot. "During all of that period," he was to say years later, "I think [Bobby] seriously considered whether he would let me be president, whether he should really take the position [that] the vice president didn't automatically move in. I thought that was on his mind every time I saw him in the first few days. . . . I think he was seriously considering what steps to take. For several days he really kept me out of the President's office. I operated from the Executive Office Building because [the Oval Office] was not made available to me. It was quite a problem." And that afternoon, at 2:30, was the Cabinet meeting, and the attorney general was a member of the Cabinet.

It couldn't have been an easy meeting for the Kennedy men, who had sat at the Cabinet table or, like Ted Sorensen, against the wall behind the man who had presided over past meetings, his personality dominating the room. Now Jack Kennedy was lying in a coffin not far away; several of the Cabinet members and White House staffers had come to the meeting directly from the East Room with its catafalque; as they entered the Cabinet Room, they could see, in the hallway beyond it, by the Oval Office door, Jack Kennedy's rocking chair sitting, upside down, on a mover's dolly. Bundy had written a note to Johnson, advising him to keep the meeting "very short. . . . A number of them and perhaps still more of the others who regularly attend the Cabinet are still numb with personal grief." It couldn't have been an easy meeting for Lyndon Johnson. It had been in the Cabinet Room that he had had to sit, powerless and silent, through so many meetings; in the Cabinet Room that, during the Cuban Missile Crisis, Robert Kennedy's hostility to him had been so vividly displayed. The men sitting around the long table knew who had thereafter been invited to the final decision-making meeting on Cuba—and who hadn't.

As Johnson, sitting now in the President's place, opened the meeting with a prepared statement, one chair at the table was empty—the attorney general's. Robert Kennedy had agreed that the meeting should be held, his only request was that there be "*no* pictures." At the last minute, however, he may have been unable to bring himself to attend it—"I was upset" by the conversations he had had with Johnson in Dallas and by the morning's confrontation, he was to explain, "so by this time I was rather fed up by him. . . . But I went by and Mac Bundy said it was very important that I come in. So I went." Bundy himself said that "Bobby was late and perhaps would not have attended if I had not told him he must"; he had "virtually to drag" him into the room, he was to say—if those statements are correct, the national security advisor may have made another mistake.

When Bobby entered the room, his face so racked with grief that men who hadn't seen him since the assassination were shocked, Johnson was speaking, but several of the Cabinet members stood up and remained standing as the attorney general walked to his chair. Johnson didn't stand up, and as soon as Kennedy sat down, continued his statement. To Agriculture Secretary Orville Freeman, watching Robert Kennedy, it was "quite clear that he could hardly countenance Lyndon Johnson sitting in his brother's seat." When Johnson finished—"The President is dead. The President must keep the business of this government moving. None of us in this room can really express the sadness we all feel. Yet we have work to do. And must do it. . . . I want you all to stay on. I need you"— Dean Rusk and Adlai Stevenson spoke, pledging their support to the new President, and the meeting quickly ended.

"Awful" was how Willard Wirtz described it—"almost mechanical"; "a drab little meeting," Bundy said. Back in EOB 274, Johnson raged about Kennedy. When Orville Freeman, who was taking every opportunity to be in Johnson's presence, walked over to the EOB to discuss the meeting with him, Johnson said that Kennedy had arrived late on purpose to ruin the effect of his statement; he had already learned, he said, that Kennedy had told "an aide" that "We won't go in until he has already sat down." "There was real bitterness in Lyndon's voice on this one," Freeman wrote in his diary. (When Manchester later passed on this story, Arthur Schlesinger wrote, "Kennedy expressed amazement at first, then amusement.")

Bitter or not, however, Lyndon Johnson had to deal with Robert Kennedy again that afternoon, for there was still the question of when he should address Congress. Harry Truman had delivered his speech to the joint session on the day following Franklin D. Roosevelt's funeral, believing that to reinforce the aura of continuity it was important that the nation hear the new President in a formal setting "as soon as possible." Another argument to support Johnson's feelings that his speech should be given the day after Kennedy's funeral—on Tuesday, in other words—was that Thursday was Thanksgiving, and, wanting to be home for the holiday, many congressmen might be leaving Washington on Wednesday. "I'll make it Tuesday if I can," Johnson told House Speaker McCormack. "I can't sit still. I've got to keep the government going." But there was the matter of keeping "the Kennedy aura." "I don't want the family to feel I have any lack of respect . . . so I have a very delicate wire to walk here." (If Johnson had any doubts about which of the two considerations—continuity or aura—was more important, McCormack, a very shrewd politician, helped dispel them, if tactfully. "On the question of Tuesday or Wednesday," he said, "don't you let that disturb you at all. . . . It's a delicate field for all. You should *respect* the delicacy. . . . That's all I say, and this is of paramount importance and gravity.") A Tuesday speech, Johnson told a visitor that day, "might be resented by the family."

When Johnson suggested Tuesday, he found out how deep that resentment might be. "I didn't like that," Robert Kennedy was to recall. "I thought we should just wait one day—at least one day after the funeral." He communicated his feelings to Bundy, but Johnson sent Bundy back to him to say that "they [the 'they' was unidentified] want it on Tuesday." Kennedy's response was an angry "Well, the hell with it. Why do you ask me about it? Don't ask me what you want done. You'll tell me what it's going to be anyway. Just go ahead and do it." Johnson didn't give up, sending a Kennedy relative—Sargent Shriver—as an emissary, but Kennedy's response was even angrier: "Why does he tell you to ask me? Now he's hacking at you. He knows I want him to wait until Wednesday." Shriver reported this response to Johnson. Without a word, the President picked up his telephone, and, angrily, punching one button after another, said a single terse sentence to each person he was calling: "It will be on Wednesday."

Lyndon had had to deal with Robert Kennedy three times Saturday. After the first of those encounters, he had had to retreat from the Oval Office, the second had resulted in his Cabinet meeting being "ruined," in the third he had had to give in on the scheduling of his speech. In some ways, that Saturday was a reprise of his three years as Vice President: constant conflict with Robert Kennedy—and constant defeat. Given the importance of keeping the support of the Kennedy faction, there was nothing he could do about it. He told Reedy to announce that he would not move into the Oval Office until Tuesday, the day after the funeral. For three days—Saturday, Sunday and Monday—he would work out of Room 274.

15

The Drums

A HARD RAIN had begun to fall just before daybreak on Saturday; through it, on the television cameras shooting with long-range lenses from Lafayette Park across Pennsylvania Avenue, the White House looked gray, the November-bare limbs of the trees in front of it black from the rain, the remaining leaves sodden and dark. Through the rain, all that day, black limousines pulled up to the North Portico, with its familiar lantern and its black-draped doorway, one after the other, in an endless line, and as the car doors opened, Marines snapping to attention with their heels hitting the pavement so loudly that the click was picked up by television microphones, out stepped senators and ambassadors (Dobrynin clasping his hands together and trying to keep his composure), generals and admirals, in uniforms stiff with medals and braid; men who had to be identified by the newscasters (seventy-one-year-old John McCormack, with his shock of snow-white hair, eighty-six-year-old Carl Hayden, laboriously climbing the stairs with a cane supporting him on one side and a policeman on the other), and men with faces everyone knew: Truman, Eisenhower. One by one, or couple by couple, they walked up the steps between rigid men in dress uniforms with rifles held high. The chief justice and his wife; when they emerged after viewing the casket, Mrs. Warren could no longer maintain her composure, and, during the long minutes while the Warrens waited on the portico for their car to pull up, she stood weeping.

Dusk fell, the rain continued, through it the great lantern shone; as each car was pulling up to the stairs, its headlights swept across the white columns; on the second floor of the White House, to the left of the portico, in the living quarters, there was a single lit window.

And television, cutting away from the portico to West Executive Avenue, showed America other pictures that day: of "the removal of the late President's personal effects from the White House office—cartons of files, a large globe, a model of the aircraft carrier *Enterprise,*" TV newscaster David Brinkley said in his dry voice. They were taken out the West Wing door and trundled on movers' dollies across to the EOB, where they would be stored temporarily. Then another artifact came out. When Brinkley had finished explaining to his viewers about the rocking chair, he bit his lip. Television showed the President's mother, veiled and holding her Bible, supported by two men as she made her way to morning Mass in Hyannis; they couldn't show the father, for he didn't come out of his house, but TV told the world that President Kennedy's youngest brother, Teddy, and his sister Eunice had flown to Hyannis to break the news to the patriarch: "It is said that he took [it] remarkably well," television reported. Television didn't get a glimpse of Jack Kennedy's children that day, and there wasn't too much information about how they had been told, or about how they had reacted, but television showed a lot of film of John Jr. and Caroline playing in the Oval Office, romping with their father; viewers could imagine how they had reacted.

Over and over on Saturday television showed the scenes that had occurred at the White House during the previous night—at 4:30 a.m. It showed the White House and the marble gates to the horseshoe driveway brilliantly white in TV floodlights, and the Marine honor guard drawn up in the driveway. As the cameras swung toward the gates, a dark shape appeared beyond them in the darkness, and, as it came into the lights, it was seen to be the ambulance bringing the President's body from Bethesda. Television showed the honor guard marching, rifles high at port arms, in front of the ambulance to the portico—to the tall columns and the hanging lantern behind them, and the doorway draped in black—and it showed the coffin, covered now in a flag, being lifted out by uniformed men and carried up the steps, past other guards, hands at the salute, staring straight ahead when the widow, still in the pink suit, and the brother walked past them. Most of the country had been sleeping when those scenes occurred, but television showed them, over and over, that Saturday, so the country saw them as if they were happening then, that day. And before dawn television crews had been briefly allowed into the East Room, and the film they had taken there was shown over and over again that day, so that over and over again America saw the black catafalque, like Lincoln's catafalque, the black crepe on the draperies and chandeliers—and America saw, too, two workmen, after finishing some task in the East Room in those pre-dawn hours, start to leave and then stop at the two prie-dieux, and kneel, and cross themselves, and pray.

Interspersed with all this were documentaries of Kennedy's life—images of his smile, remembrances of his wit; pictures of him with his wife and children. And then there were replays of significant television programs in which he had participated. One of them was an hour-long interview he had held in the Oval Office with the three network correspondents, sitting relaxed and easy in the rocking chair. The country therefore saw him in his rocker, and then saw the rocker being trundled out on a dolly.

There were pictures of Lyndon Johnson, too, that Saturday, of the new President inside his car, face grim, as he left The Elms and as he turned into West Executive Avenue that morning, of him walking quickly into and out of church from his car, of him walking across West Executive to the Cabinet meeting, a Secret Service agent holding an umbrella over his head.

There were no television cameras in 274, as there were none in the White House; still photographs of him sitting at the conference table with Rusk and then McNamara were shown—"the first pictures . . . of him at work, as President," Brinkley said—but they didn't have much impact beside pictures of Jackie Kennedy following the coffin, or beside pictures of the honor guard, or beside pictures of what one broadcaster called "the mighty of the land filing into the White House . . . for a mournful adieu to President John F. Kennedy." The Cabinet meeting had drama to it, but there were no pictures of that, live or still; indeed television mentioned it only briefly. There was no hint at all of what had happened between Johnson and Bobby Kennedy that morning. The new President did appear on television to read his proclamation establishing Monday as a day of national mourning, but he simply walked up to a makeshift microphone, quickly read the statement in a minute and a half, and left the room without another word. "He apparently decided just to read the proclamation and let it go at that," a newscaster said. After summing up the day's dramatic events in the White House, Brinkley added that "President Johnson in the meantime was across in the Executive Office Building . . . carrying on his business, meeting with the Cabinet. . . ." "President Johnson," said another newscaster, "has been shall we say a little bit in the background today."

Newspapers covered his activities more thoroughly, running long articles about them on the front page. "President Lyndon B. Johnson took firm control of the reins of government," the *Washington Post* said. "Mr. Johnson's day was one of brisk activity," the *New York Times* said. And the headlines about him were banner headlines—all across the top of the front page—just as were the headlines about Kennedy and Oswald. But the headlines about him had none of the drama of the headlines about Kennedy and Oswald. Across the top of the *Washington Post*'s front page, for example, the headlines were: NATION'S GREAT FILE PAST KENNEDY BIER: BODY LIES IN STATE AT CAPITOL TODAY; JOHNSON MOVES TO CARRY ON POLICIES. In the *New York Times* the banners were: KENNEDY'S BODY LIES IN WHITE HOUSE; JOHNSON AT HELM WITH WIDE BACKING; POLICE SAY PRISONER IS THE ASSASSIN. The stories about him weren't the lead stories, but only the second lead. And in any event it wasn't from newspapers, but from television that America was getting its news that day.

AND THEN, the next morning, Sunday morning, began the roll of the drums.

As the sun rose that morning, the rain gone, the pale blue sky seemingly without a cloud, the broad avenues between the White House and the Capitol were waiting, their roadways empty, the crowds lining them on the pavements packed solid, standing in silence.

In front of the White House, the sounds were of horses' hooves and the creaking of harnesses, and of rolling wooden wheels. A bare black wooden platform—a caisson, or artillery gun carriage—on four black wheels was pulled into the driveway and up to the North Portico by six matched gray horses in pairs, a rider on the left-hand horse in each pair, the saddle on the right horse empty, as was military custom for a fallen leader. Two heavy black straps had been attached to the caisson. It stood there, in front of the portico, for a while, black and bare, the straps dangling. Then, without ceremony except for the coming to attention, rifles held high, of the dress-uniformed men flanking the doorway and the steps down to the driveway, eight military pallbearers brought the flag-draped coffin out of the doorway and down the stairs, and lifted it onto the gun carriage. The straps were laid across the coffin, black against the bright red and white stripes, and buckled fast so that it couldn't fall off.

There was a pause, and suddenly, in the doorway, there she was.

Jacqueline Kennedy was dressed all in black; she wasn't crying—at least there were no tears on a face that might have been the model for a portrait of Grief. On either side of her was a small figure, dressed in a sky-blue coat, and she took their hands. Standing behind her, a little to the side, was Robert Kennedy, expressionless, still as a statue.

They stood there while the caisson began to move away down the driveway toward Pennsylvania Avenue, between soldiers and sailors holding the flags of the fifty states, who dipped them in salute as the caisson passed. The first of a line of black limousines pulled into the portico, and the Kennedys walked down the steps as Clint Hill opened the back door of the car. Behind them the figures of Lyndon and Lady Bird Johnson came into view, and came down the steps; they and the Kennedys were to ride in the same car together. They got in, Jackie and Lyndon in the rear seat, with Caroline and John Jr. sitting next to their mother, Lady Bird and Robert in the jump seats, which faced forward, with Lady Bird in front of her husband. The car pulled slowly down the driveway behind the caisson. It waited at the end of the driveway, so that as the caisson came out between the gates, it came out alone. And as it came out, the drums began.

Few people in Washington—few people in America, perhaps—had ever heard the sound of muffled drums, the tension on each drumhead loosened so that the resonance was deadened. With a whole corps playing muffled drums, as they were playing now, the roll of those drums filled the air—melancholy, ominous, final. And it was to that sound that the caisson came out onto Pennsylvania Avenue to take its place in a column—ahead of it, after the drum corps, priests marching abreast, three of them with their black robes billowing behind; warriors marching abreast, their medals glinting in the sun: the dead President's military aides, the Joint Chiefs of Staff, other generals, other admirals, a company of sailors with fixed, shining bayonets; an honor guard carrying the flag of his country, and, just behind the caisson bearing the dead President, carried by a single tall sailor, his own flag, the presidential standard. Shielded by the portico, the standard had hung limp, but as it came out between the gates, it was caught by a gust of wind so that it blew straight out, and the golden presidential seal, with its eagle holding an olive branch in one talon and arrows in the other, stood out for a moment bold against the navy blue background. Behind that flag came a riderless horse, a magnificent tall black gelding, sword in its scabbard hanging from the saddle, but in the stirrups, boots turned backward to symbolize the fact that his fallen rider would never ride again; since the days of Genghis Khan and Tamerlane, a riderless horse with boots reversed in the stirrups had followed fallen chieftains to their graves. Black Jack was a restless animal, always hard to control; he was prancing nervously now, tossing his head, trying to rear against the bit. Following him came the limousine carrying the Johnsons and the Kennedys and then a line of other limousines with Kennedy relatives and the dead President's closest aides. None of the cars had its top down this time.

After three blocks, the procession wheeled around the corner by the Treasury Building, and suddenly, facing the marchers a mile away, rearing up—huge, gleaming, almost dazzlingly white against the clear blue sky, thrusting up out of a base so long that it seemed to fill the horizon—was the dome of the Capitol. Stretching along the base, the building that held the two chambers of Congress, were tall white marble columns and the pilasters that are the echo of columns, and the dome was circled with columns, too, circled by columns not only in its first mighty upward thrust, where it was rimmed by thirty-six great pillars (for the thirty-six states that the Union had comprised when it was built), but circled by columns also high above, hundreds of feet above Pennsylvania Avenue, where, just below the Statue of Freedom, a circle of thirteen more slender shafts (for the thirteen original states) made the *tholos,* a structure modeled after the place where the Greeks left sacrifices to the gods, look like a little temple in the sky. As the long procession moved down that broad avenue before the packed, silent throng, to the thunderous roll of the muffled drums, it was moving toward columns atop columns, columns in the sky—a procession carrying the body of a republic's slain ruler, in all the stateliness and pomp a republic could muster, toward a structure that represented, and embodied, all a republic's majesty.

For long minutes the drums would roll and the air reverberate with their sad, fateful sound, then the drums would stop, and so quiet was the watching crowd that in those intervals the clatter of hooves, Black Jack's and those of the matched grays, and the rhythmic tread of the marching sailors echoed down the avenue. "Block by block, the hush deepened," an observer wrote. General Clifton, marching with the other military aides, was to recall that "All you could hear was the drums and the clump of the horses"—"the drums, the terrible drums," another marching general was to say.

The procession from the White House to the Capitol took about forty-five minutes. As the lead limousine came out of the White House gates, there was, Lady Bird Johnson was to recall, a "sea of faces stretching away on every side— silent, watching faces." She would remember the flags at half-mast all along the avenue, and the sailors marching in front of her, "and always there was the sound of muffled drums in the background." But "most vivid of all was the feeling of a sea of faces . . . and that curious sense of silence, broken only by an occasional sob."

Lady Bird sat next to the man her husband hated—and who hated him. Robert Kennedy's "face was grave, white, sorrowful," she was to recall. John-John, "in a peripatetic mood," kept jumping back and forth from the back seat to his uncle's lap and back again, until finally Robert said, "John-John, be good, you be good and we'll give you a flag afterwards." The "only time the Attorney General said anything else," she says, was as the car passed the Old Senate Office Building. "The Attorney General looked over and said . . . as though to himself, or perhaps to the children, 'That was where it all began. That was where he ran for the presidency.' "

"There was a flinching of the jaw at that moment that almost made—well, it made your soul flinch for him," she says.

Otherwise, Lady Bird says, "we were a pretty silent group as we rode along, each wrapped in his own thoughts." She was to sum up that ride in a single word: "interminable."

IN THE PLAZA before the Capitol's East Front, Lyndon and Lady Bird got out of the car, and he helped the children and Mrs. Kennedy out. Robert got out last without looking at Johnson.

The staircase on the East Front, broad and tall, was lined now on each side with a double row of men in dress blues and white gloves, rigid in salute, and the coffin of the dead President was carried up between their bayonets, flag of his country fluttering ahead of him, his own flag fluttering behind, to lie in state in the soaring, stone-floored Rotunda under the dome, with its friezes and paintings commemorating historic moments in the nation's past. As the coffin went up the steps, a Navy band played a sailor's hymn asking for help "for those in peril on the sea," for the President had once been in peril on the sea—and played also "Hail to the Chief," but in an unusually slow tempo, so that as it was played for the last time for John Fitzgerald Kennedy, it was played as a dirge. "Nothing could be harder to endure than 'Hail to the Chief,' " Kennedy's sister Jean felt.

In the Rotunda, the coffin lay on the very catafalque on which Lincoln's body had lain after *he* had been shot. In front of the circle of statues of great men of the nation's past was a circle seven or eight deep of the major figures of the present, and there were eulogies from McCormack, representing the House; Mansfield, representing the Senate; and the Supreme Court's Warren. During the speeches, Mrs. Kennedy stood holding Caroline's hand; John-John had been taken away to Speaker McCormack's office, where one of McCormack's aides was amusing him by letting him play with flags, one of which attracted his interest. "Can I have that one?" he said. "I want to take it home to my Daddy." Jackie turned her face attentively toward each speaker, a reporter saw. Sometimes, he wrote, "there was the shine of tears in her eyes, but her lips never trembled," her face was still the immobile mask. They didn't tremble even when Mansfield told how in Dallas she had taken the ring from her finger and put it in the coffin. "For an instant, her eyes closed, her shoulders sagged," but she caught herself and stood erect again. During the last speech she swayed for a moment, but then "the soldierly figure . . . firmed again." Another of Jack Kennedy's sisters, Pat, was thinking, *If Jackie can do it, I can.* Says Lady Bird Johnson, "Her behavior from the moment of the shot . . . was, to me, one of the most memorable things of all. Maybe it was a combination of great breeding, great discipline, great character. I only know it was great." Sometimes, Lady Bird says, she herself wanted to cry, but felt that she couldn't permit herself "the catharsis of tears." One reason for that, she says, "was that the dignity of Mrs. Kennedy and the members of the family demanded it." After the speeches, during which Lyndon Johnson stood in the third row of spectators, behind the Kennedy family, came his moment in the ceremonies, a somewhat awkward moment. He had to place a wreath by the coffin, and the wreath, a large one on an easel, was to be carried in front of him by an Army sergeant. For some reason, the sergeant walked backward as he carried the wreath and easel, facing Johnson, matching his steps to Johnson's, so that their approach to the casket resembled, to one observer, an odd dance. And then, immediately after Johnson had returned to his former place, came another moment. Jacqueline Kennedy and Caroline walked forward to the coffin and knelt beside it. "You just kiss," Jackie had told her daughter, and Jackie knelt, touched the flag covering the coffin, and kissed it. The little girl beside her touched the flag, too, but, as if she couldn't get close enough to her father that way, then put her hand under the flag to touch the coffin. The Joint Chiefs of Staff were standing at attention, tears running down their cheeks.

AFTER THE CEREMONIES, the Johnsons followed the Kennedys down the broad steps, and they drove away, this time in separate cars. And as soon as the dignitaries had left the Rotunda, the people who had been waiting were admitted.

While the ceremonies had been going on, crowds that had been waiting outside to view the coffin had been joined by crowds from Pennsylvania Avenue who had followed the procession to the Capitol, and now the building was surrounded by a throng which filled the plaza all the way to the Supreme Court Building and the Library of Congress, filled the streets around the Senate and House Buildings and spilled down the hill toward Union Station. And the crowd was growing. Every highway leading into Washington "seemed to be jammed for miles with cars bringing more people."

There would not be much to see when these people got inside—just the coffin and its guard of honor—and they would have time only to file past it, and kneel quickly if they wished, yet more and more came. Dusk fell, the temperature dropped into the low thirties, yet the line of people grew longer as people joined it faster than people could be admitted to the Rotunda. The lights were turned on, the great dome was illuminated by floodlights so that it loomed, beautiful and majestic, in the dark. By midnight, when perhaps a hundred thousand people had passed by the coffin, the line, five abreast, of people waiting to get in was three miles long, and still getting longer. The people who entered the Rotunda at 2:30 a.m. had been waiting in line in the cold for eight hours. At 5:45 Monday morning, a policeman near the end of the line told people who were just arriving that they might as well go home because the doors had to be closed at 8:30, and "only 85,000 more can get in," and there was no chance that they would be among them.

MONDAY WAS THE DAY of the funeral itself.

As a procession was bringing the coffin back from the Capitol to the White House, to be taken from there to St. Matthew's Cathedral for the funeral Mass and then to Arlington National Cemetery for burial, the pageantry was suddenly at a new level. The honor guards were in it, and the flags, and Black Jack, and there were also bands, their brass instruments agleam in the sun: the Marine Band, in scarlet tunics, its muffled drums draped in black, playing "Onward, Christian Soldiers"; the Navy Band marching behind the caisson; tall tartan-clad figures, bagpipers of Scotland's "Black Watch," the Royal Highland Regiment, which had played for President Kennedy at the White House; and troops of marching men, West Point cadets in gray uniforms, striding with their famed precision, the gold insignia of their headgear shining; Annapolis midshipmen in Navy blue and white; Air Force cadets in lighter Air Force blue—close to half a mile of bands and troops. And when, at the White House, other marchers fell into line to walk behind the coffin the eight blocks to the cathedral, it became a procession that was, in the *Times'* description, "extraordinary."

First came Jackie Kennedy, walking between Robert and Edward, her face veiled in black, but her shoulders back, behind them a group of other Kennedys; then the Johnsons—he had been advised not to walk but to go to the cathedral inside a car but had refused, and around him the heads of Secret Service agents swiveled back and forth as they scanned the roofs along the route, and the windows. And after them came what the *Times* called an assembly of the world's leaders "such as this city has never seen." In the first row behind the Johnsons were a king, Baudouin of Belgium; a queen, Frederika of Greece; a prince, Philip of England; three Presidents, Lübke of West Germany, Macapagal of the Philippines and General Park Chung Hee of South Korea—and two figures who, each in his own way, stood out in even this assemblage, one, quite tall, de Gaulle of France, erect and dignified in a soldier's plain khaki uniform, not a decoration on it, the other, quite short, the Lion of Judah, Emperor Haile Selassie of Ethiopia, in a uniform all but aglow with medals and braid. And behind this group came a throng of other heads of state and world leaders, more than a hundred of them.

And after the service there was another moment. Three-year-old John F. Kennedy Jr. was standing next to his mother on the sidewalk outside the cathedral as John F. Kennedy's coffin was lifted onto the caisson for the last time, and the horses began to pull it away to lead the procession to Arlington. As his father's body passed, the little boy in his blue coat drew himself up to attention, and standing stiff as a soldier, raised his hand to his forehead in a salute.

At Arlington, with the troops drawn up below the grave site—massed soldiers among the graves of soldiers fallen—fighter jets screamed overhead, with, as was military custom, one plane missing from the formation, and then Air Force One flew over, very low, and Colonel Swindal dipped its wings in farewell, and then there was the rifle salute and taps, and the lighting of the eternal flame, and, as the last of the dignitaries left, the crowds began to trudge up the hill.

NEVER IN AMERICAN HISTORY — never in the history of any republic since, perhaps, the great pageants of Rome—had the passage of power been marked by such pageantry, pageantry which made the three days of funeral ceremonies for John F. Kennedy three of the most memorable days in American history.

The images of those days—of the coffin on the gun carriage; of the widow in her veil, erect and tearless in grief (tearless in public: inside the cathedral, she broke down once, crying and shaking uncontrollably); of her children, Caroline and John-John, the little girl's hand creeping under the flag, and the little boy's hand up in salute; of the long processions; of a hundred heads of state walking behind the caisson; of Black Jack and the matched grays; of Air Force One dipping its wings over Arlington—were poignant, dramatic, indelible.

And they were engraved, indelibly, on the consciousness of the nation, and, to a remarkable extent, of the world, in a way that had never before happened with a major historical event, because these images were *seen,* seen live, as they were happening, which added to the drama, to the viewers' sense of involvement, and to the viewers' emotions. "The juxtaposition of tapes of the happy Mrs. Jacqueline Kennedy, touring at her husband's side in the Texas morning, with the live pickup of her arrival behind her husband's coffin in the Washington evening were almost too much to bear," Jack Gould wrote. Television had given "a new dimension to grief," he said. People didn't have to be satisfied with a description of the great parades; they saw the parades for themselves. And it wasn't only funeral ceremonies that were seen live. "He's been shot! He's been shot! Lee Harvey Oswald has been shot! Pandemonium has broken out!" an NBC announcer shouted, and then viewers saw police officers swarming over a balding man with a gun. Oswald's mortal wounding, and Jack Ruby's arrest, "marked," as the *Times* said, "the first time . . . that a real-life homicide had occurred in front of live cameras." It wasn't grief alone that, during those three days, had been given a new dimension. "For total horror," Gould wrote, "nothing could quite compare with . . . Oswald's death" on . . . live TV. "Through television the shock of history reverberated in every home," Gould wrote. "Clustered around millions of television screens, most Americans were involved in the death and burial of Kennedy to a degree unimaginable before the age of electronic communications," wrote Louis Heren, then chief Washington correspondent of the London *Times*. "The grief and pride of those . . . days became a collective national experience surely unprecedented anywhere in the world and anytime in history."

"And," Heren says, because of television, Americans were involved to a similar extent not only in Kennedy's death but "in his life." During those three days, he says, "Thousands of feet of film were shown, of Kennedy on the campaign trail, at home, as President, and even speaking in Texas a few hours before he was killed." "No man, living or dead, had ever been given such concentrated exposure." Television, the medium Jack Kennedy had understood before other politicians understood it ("Do you know who's the most well-known senator in the United States?"), the medium that had done so much to make him his party's nominee, and then had done so much to make him President, had now during those three days transmuted him into a figure of legend and myth.

DURING THOSE THREE DAYS, the focus of America and the world was on Washington, but on the White House and the Capitol and the cathedral and the cemetery. Very little was on the Executive Office Building.

On Sunday and Monday, Lyndon Johnson's relegation to the "background," to the "sidelines" of the events unfolding in Washington that had begun on Saturday, continued. The television cameras across Pennsylvania Avenue could have panned slightly and shown the side entrance of the EOB as well as the North Portico, but there was no Marine honor guard at the EOB, no long line of limousines pulling up to it, no long line of the "mighty of the land" going in, just the very occasional car with a Cabinet member—Rusk or McNamara—getting out quickly and hurrying through the door. There were no television cameras inside EOB 274, and what would they have shown had they been there?—just Johnson talking on the telephone or sitting at the conference table talking to Rusk or McNamara. Indeed, each time a conference was finished, the photographers—still photographers—were called in, and the pictures were taken, and newspapers ran them: obviously posed pictures, static, dull.

And indeed the setting in which Lyndon Johnson was working hardly seemed one in which memorable events would occur, particularly in contrast with the majestic settings—the East Room, the Rotunda—in which the vivid pageantry of those days was being played out. It hardly seemed presidential: just a governmental office suite, a little more elegantly decorated than most, that, with all the new staff members working in it, was overcrowded, cluttered. Johnson himself was to remember these days in terms of a contrast—of what he called "a strange counterpoint"—between "the harsh glare" of the fluorescent "office lights burning deep into the night, then the somber hush and the dim, soft light in the East Room from the four large candles flanking John F. Kennedy's coffin," between "the frenzied pace of meetings and briefings held behind closed doors, then the measured cadence of the funeral march."

At least on Sunday some of the banner headlines had been about Johnson. Not so on Monday. Most of Monday's banners didn't even mention Lyndon Johnson. PRESIDENT'S ASSASSIN SHOT TO DEATH IN JAIL CORRIDOR BY DALLAS CITIZEN; GRIEVING THRONGS VIEW KENNEDY were the headlines across the top of the front page of the *New York Times,* for example. None of the stories at the top of that front page were about him. The two huge pictures on the page were of Caroline putting her hand under the flag and of Oswald grimacing as Ruby shot him, the detective next to Oswald aghast, his mouth open in shock. The *Washington Post*'s photos were of the grimace and the grays, as the horses pulled the caisson away from the White House. Johnson barely made the front page of that paper at all; the only story on the activities of the new President was squeezed onto the bottom of the page. Television reported on his activities but television was the realm of the picture, and what pictures could compare with the tape of Oswald's shooting, which was shown over and over that day, or with the live coverage of the incredible procession and the funeral and the foreign leaders following the coffin and the Kennedys? "The drama" of the three days following Jack Kennedy's assassination "centered on the flag-draped catafalque in the East Room," Hugh Sidey was to write. "Beyond the legend of the dead Kennedy which was then being magnified in every hamlet was the presence of the Kennedy family. Johnson could not compete with them. . . . The great and the near-great came in waves for three days. Charles de Gaulle was a more imposing and fascinating figure than the new President." Then there were Selassie, Macapagal, "Germany's Ludwig Erhard, Queen Frederika, Ireland's marvelous old De Valera, . . . Mikoyan. Lyndon Johnson had less glamour than any of them." During those three days, he "stayed in his old office . . . only on the edge of the drama."

He would stay in his own home, too. Asked by reporters when the Johnsons would be moving into the executive mansion at the White House, Lady Bird replied, "I would to God I could serve Mrs. Kennedy's comfort. I can at least serve her convenience." Jacqueline and her children would move out on December 6th, the Johnsons would move in the following day. And although the address of The Elms was being printed in newspapers and television was showing pictures of the house during those three days, the number of persons standing outside remained surprisingly small. The President of the United States was living there—and, during those three days, the world didn't seem particularly interested.

But for anyone who cared about the art of governing, about political power—about the art of assuming, and employing, power in sudden, unexpected, without warning, crisis; about governing a nation, soothing its fears, restoring its confidence, keeping it on course and moving in such a crisis; about governing with hardly a moment for preparation—for anyone who cared about that, what was happening in EOB 274 during those three days was memorable, too.

Part V

TO BECOME
A PRESIDENT

16

EOB 274

SOME OF THE ITEMS on the list Valenti had scribbled in Lyndon Johnson's bedroom were ceremonial, symbolic: to demonstrate appropriate respect on the part of the new President—respect for God: infrequent though his visits to church had been, one should be made on Saturday; respect for his living predecessors: not merely to telephone but to meet face-to-face with the two (Truman and Eisenhower) physically able to come to Washington (and to elicit from Eisenhower, still the most popular Republican in the country, an expression of support to foster the picture of unity he wanted to paint). Some were to demonstrate sympathy—"Call widow of Officer Tippett [*sic*]," Valenti's list said, and of course there would have to be ceremonial calls on another widow as well—some to demonstrate continuity (and to get briefings on the international situation) by conferring with, and being photographed conferring with, prominent members of the late President's Cabinet, in particular Rusk and McNamara. Some items were both symbolic and substantive: a foreign affairs briefing in the White House Situation Room. These items were quickly arranged and easily scripted. There wasn't much time on Saturday for church, but the most convenient house of worship—St. John's Episcopal Church, right across Lafayette Square—was also the most appropriate: it was called "the Church of Presidents" because many of them had worshiped there. After a visit to St. John's pastor to request a special memorial service for John F. Kennedy that the new President would attend, the Secret Service assured Juanita Roberts, as she put it in a memo to Johnson, that "Services will be simple and will last approximately ten minutes." Since Johnson's attendance mustn't appear to be a bid for publicity but rather a simple expression of sorrow and faith, presidential panoply would be kept to a minimum, her memo assured him. While there would be a full complement of Secret Service agents inside the church, only one "will be on the street in front at time of arrival." He "will meet the President and Mrs. Johnson, take them into the church. Rev. Harper will lead the President and Mrs. Johnson down the aisle to second row. Turn left for sitting in the center."

Bill Lloyd, one of Johnson's aides, had drafted talking points for the call to Marie Tippit, widow of the Dallas police officer Oswald had killed, and Valenti had redrafted them: "Mrs. Tippit, I know that words are not very useful when your grief runs so deep. But Mrs. Johnson and I wanted you to know that you and your children, Allen, Brenda Kay and Curtis Ray, are in our thoughts and prayers." Colonel Roberts put a slip in front of him. "Mrs. Tippit is at the . . . funeral home now arranging for the funeral. She will be home after 1 pm, EST." In his call, Johnson made the words more personal; "I just want to say 'God bless you,' and I know you're a brave and a great lady," he concluded. "I certainly appreciate your praise of him. It's quite a consolation," Marie Tippit replied. "Could I get your address there?" Johnson said. "I want to drop you a little note too," and he scrawled an outline for Valenti to flesh out.

Johnson began to move down the list with the briefings on the international situation, and here, in a tour d'horizon from Bundy and CIA director John A. McCone in the Situation Room, the news was good, with no sign that any foreign country was attempting to exploit the assassination—no troubling movement anywhere, not in Cuba, not in Vietnam ("It was," Johnson was to say later, "almost as if the world had provided a breathing space within which I could concentrate on domestic affairs"). McCone explained the "President's Checklist" ("with which," he noted in a confidential memo for CIA files, Johnson "was not familiar"), the summary of international developments prepared by the CIA each morning for the President's information. To Johnson's request that he stay on as director, he simply replied he would do so, as did the next person Johnson conferred with: Secretary of State Rusk.

While he was talking to Rusk in 274's conference room, however, Colonel Roberts came in and handed him a note—"J. Edgar Hoover is calling on the White House line"—and throughout that day he would be interrupted by a torrent of calls from Hoover and McCone about new "developments" in the FBI and CIA investigations of Oswald: that in the past few weeks the assassin had visited the Soviet Embassy in Mexico City, for example.

And all that day, Saturday, November 23—and during the next two days—there would be other new developments for which no script had been prepared, but about which decisions had to be made.

It had been expected, of course, that some world leaders would attend the funeral, but Bundy, repeatedly ducking in and out of EOB 274 those three days, kept adding names to the list—until it was obvious that leaders would be arriving in Washington in unprecedented numbers; one after another was notifying the State Department that he was coming. "There will be de Gaulle, Erhard, Douglas-Home—separate category, Mikoyan,"* Bundy said in one call; scores were coming; Johnson would not be able to meet with all of them individually after the funeral; but did he want to meet with some of them, and if so, which

---

*British Prime Minister Alec Douglas-Home and Soviet Deputy Premier Anastas Mikoyan.

ones?; it was important not to offend any—"I need your personal guidance on it. . . . It's going to be awfully difficult to pick and choose here" but "I think in fact to have them come and go and *not* meet with you will be equally foolish." And if he met with them, what, exactly, should he say to each one—in meetings in which every word counted? This was dangerous ground. These meetings would be foreign leaders' first impression of Lyndon Johnson, and first impressions could influence the policy of nations; look at what had happened after Khrushchev, in Vienna, had met Kennedy for the first time! "Need to do," Johnson scribbled on a notepad in front of him. "De Gaulle—Hume [*sic*]—Mikoyan."

Then there was Congress: the stalemate of the Administration's legislative program on many fronts, including civil rights and the intertwined budget and tax cut proposals that had been held up, month after month, in Harry Byrd's Senate Finance Committee.

Because of his exclusion from Kennedy's legislative efforts, he didn't know what he needed to know about the status of those proposals; much of what he knew—not only about the tax cut and civil rights stalemates but about the reasons behind the seeming paralysis on other fronts as well—he knew only because, as he had told Sorensen in June, he had "got it from the *New York Times.*" But it was his Administration now, his legislative program; he was going to be held responsible for its success or failure; he had to find out what the situation was on Capitol Hill.

To find out, he turned not to the Senate Leader, Mike Mansfield, because he felt that would be no help, but to a senator who knew how to count. Johnson had, in fact, turned to the suave Floridian George Smathers for help in counting before, during his time as Majority Leader, appointing him his "whip," or Assistant Leader. The independent Smathers later refused Johnson's request that he stay in the job, telling him flatly, "I don't want to be your assistant." (Johnson had flown into a rage. "What are you saying?" he demanded. To Smathers, "It was just as though you had unleashed an awful smell. His nostrils flared, his eyes sort of looked funny.") Since Smathers' counting ability (and unapologetic pragmatism) made him too keen-edged a tool to be discarded, however, Johnson had found another use for him—raiser and dispenser of campaign funds as chairman of the Senate Democratic Campaign Committee—until the end of his time as Leader, and now, three years later, needing him again, he telephoned him at 2:10 on Saturday afternoon.

The purpose of the call was to obtain information, and "you don't learn anything when you're talking." So, from Johnson, there wasn't any talking. For ten minutes after Smathers began explaining the tax cut bill's status, the only sounds Johnson made were noncommittal little grunts. And by the time Smathers finished, Johnson had learned that the situation was worse—far worse—than Marquis Childs or James Reston realized.

For one thing, he had learned that Byrd's opposition to the tax bill was linked to his feelings about the budget Kennedy was to submit to Congress in January. Smathers, a member of Byrd's Finance Committee, said that on Kennedy's behalf he had gone to Byrd, and learned that what he "was really trying to accomplish [was] to hold up the tax bill until he could see and prove that" Kennedy's budget would be "over a hundred billion dollars"—in other words, that if it was above that figure, he wouldn't approve the tax cuts. Then Smathers had tried to broker a deal with Byrd under which "the President would . . . tell him now . . . what he thought his budget would be" (Treasury Secretary Dillon thought that getting it down to a figure not too far above $100 billion would satisfy Byrd—"Current expectations were for $101.5 billion to 102 billion," Dillon was to tell Johnson—and apparently Kennedy did, too), and in return Byrd would speed up the committee's hearings.* But that proposal had foundered, because, Smathers said, "he [Byrd] really doesn't *want* it, you know. He's really *against* the tax bill." Then, Smathers said, he had, also on Kennedy's behalf, tried to "go around Harry Byrd in the committee," but going around a committee chairman was something very seldom done in the Senate—and never to Harry Byrd; although two Democratic members of the committee had pledged their votes to Smathers on the "going around" maneuver, after each had been summoned to a face-to-face meeting with Old Harry, each had withdrawn the pledge. Smathers had done some counting—of some of the seventeen committee members to ascertain how many votes the Administration proposals would have in a showdown with Byrd: not enough. "At the last legislative breakfast," which Johnson, in Europe at the time, had not attended, the possibility of getting the tax bill to the floor had been raised, but Mansfield hadn't been much help—he didn't know "how many votes we got, I don't know if the leadership isn't in the dark"— and, in the crunch, neither was the President: "Kennedy was there; he wasn't pushing it too hard," Smathers said.

Johnson asked whether there was any possibility that Byrd would agree to deal with the proposed amendments to the bill in a "reasonable time" and "pass it this year"—before Congress adjourned for the Christmas vacation and the end of its 1963 session.

"I don't think Byrd will . . . make that kind of an agreement," Smathers replied. He told Johnson that in his opinion there was nothing that could be done about getting the tax reduction bill passed before Christmas. He himself, he said, evidently forgetting Dallas for a moment, but then catching himself in mid-phrase, would "do anything short of, you know, *anything* to try to get it passed." But, he said, passing the bill before Congress adjourned would be simply impossible. There was so much "strong feeling" against the Kennedy measures not only in the committee but in Congress as a whole that Johnson should just aban-

*According to Evans and Novak, who had evidently been allowed to read a report Heller had prepared on the subject, "Kennedy had set an arbitrary [budget] ceiling of 101.5 billion dollars," although even after he did so in internal memos the figure of $102 billion kept cropping up.

don the fight: perhaps "the smart thing to do . . . would be for you to get the appropriation[s] bill[s] through real quick, and then just" adjourn for the year.

Johnson told Smathers why he couldn't do that (or at least one of the reasons why he couldn't do that).

"No, no," he said, "I can't do that. That would destroy the Democratic Party and destroy the election—destroy everything. We've got to carry on. We can't abandon this fella's [Kennedy's] program because he's a national hero and . . . these people [the Kennedy Cabinet and aides] want his program passed, and we've got to keep the Kennedy aura around us through this election."

But when he himself, during the same call, got down to another count—of the days remaining before adjournment—he learned how hard passing the tax bill, much less the rest of Kennedy's program, was going to be. "Where are your holidays? . . . What are you planning for Thanksgiving?" he asked, and Smathers replied that because of the imminent holiday, the Senate wouldn't be doing much work that week; "Byrd doesn't plan any hearings—he couldn't get a quorum, he told me." And, Smathers said, "that puts us into December"—and the Christmas recess.

"I tell you, Mr. President, I'd hate to see you make that [the tax bill] a big issue because I'm afraid we're not going to be able to do it."

DISCOURAGING AS WAS the news on the tax bill, that same day—his first full day as President—he also got the news on the budget that was tied in with it. It came in an urgent memo on that budget—the so-called "1965 budget" that covered the fiscal year between July 1, 1964, and June 30, 1965—from Budget Bureau Director Kermit Gordon. "We stand at a critical stage in the 1965 budget process," Gordon wrote. "Every agency has submitted its budget requests, and we are now about half-way through our intensive review of these submissions," after which Kennedy's economic team had been scheduled to meet with the President "to present our recommendations," and explain the conflicts between these recommendations and the higher amounts requested by individual departments and agencies so that he could resolve them.

The budget determined many government actions and policies. "Despite the fact that the time is late, I know that you will want to make this budget *your* budget," Gordon wrote. "Accordingly, I hope we can sit down with you very soon." And the memo closed with a list of dates—"the time schedule against which we must work"—that showed what "very soon" meant.

As it happens, Gordon had the date at the top of the list incorrect. His memo said that January 19 was the date by which, under law, the "Budget [must be] submitted to Congress." The correct date was January 20. January 20 was almost two months off. But that was the end date on the list. The line underneath it said "January 9—Budget message locked up." By that date, all decisions on the message—on the final budget that would be submitted to Congress on January 20—had to be finalized, because it would take eight days for the final figures for expenditures to be calculated, and totaled, and measured against tax revenues, and for the message, the huge 439-page document, to be prepared and printed. And underneath January 9 were other dates: "December 26—Final day for decisions on proposed legislation": on the bills, complicated bills that had to be drafted with care, that would authorize the creation of new federal programs that the President wanted funded in the budget. But before this legislation could be drafted—before *any* legislation for programs, either new or existing, could be drafted—decisions would have to be made on the individual requests from the departments and agencies: whether to approve or reduce them; which programs to continue or reduce or eliminate. Those decisions had to be made by the President—had to be made by *him*—after meetings in which, as Gordon's memo said, we "present the major policy issues involved in the budget and obtain your guidance on how we should proceed." Three weeks had been allowed for such meetings, so the final dates in the memo were "December 2–20—Final decisions on agency programs under existing legislation. (Defense and space decisions must be virtually complete by December 10.)" December 2 was a week from Monday, the day of Kennedy's funeral. But, Gordon's memo said, "very soon" meant even sooner than that. The economic team's crucial meetings with President Kennedy "to present our recommendations [and] obtain his decisions" had actually been scheduled "to begin next Wednesday," a day four days off.

At 7:40 Saturday evening, another member of the economic team, Walter W. Heller, chairman of the President's Council of Economic Advisers, was shown into 274's inner office, and while underlining to Johnson Gordon's urgency—"I told him [Johnson] we were pretty deeply in the process already, and that sometime in December or early January he would have to make final decisions," Heller was to recall—he added an additional point: that Kennedy had received budget briefings and "a coordinated budget, revenue and economic picture" from the economic team on a regular basis, so that he had been familiar with many of the considerations that would be involved in making the impending budgetary decisions. Johnson had never received any such briefing.

And tight as the time schedule was, it wasn't the hardest problem confronting Johnson on the budget. The document, with its setting of governmental priorities, was a key battlefield in the war between liberals and conservatives. Liberals wanted a larger role for government, wanted bigger, and new, government social welfare programs and therefore a larger budget. They believed the $11 billion tax cut would, by putting more money into people's pockets, stimulate the economy and thereby increase tax revenues, and the money the government would have available for these programs. Conservatives, uneasy about an expansion in government's role and about the proposed new programs, were opposed to the deficits that would be produced by the higher spending, and believed the deficits would be increased by the tax cuts. So Johnson, in starting to deal with the budget, would immediately find himself plunged into the middle of the intense ideological warfare between conservatives and liberals.

That very Saturday began a battle to influence the new President's thinking on the budget–tax cut issue—a battle, Willard Wirtz said, "for his mind." The militant conservative and former Treasury Secretary Robert Anderson, whom Eisenhower had urged him to see, was Ike's crack general on financial issues, and, in a long telephone conversation somehow crammed into Johnson's schedule that Saturday, Anderson told him that the surest way to restore confidence was to cut the budget and reduce the deficit. The Cabinet's most aggressive liberals, Udall, Wirtz and Freeman, had all urged Johnson in the opposite direction, Freeman in a note which, mindful of what he knew about Johnson, he was careful to keep to one page.

Anyone who thought Johnson's mind could be captured didn't know it. He knew what his most important priority was. Leaving 274 that evening, Heller had opened the door—only to find it shut again, by Johnson's big hand. Drawing him back into the room, Johnson said, "Now I want to say something about all this talk that I'm a conservative who is likely to go back to the Eisenhower ways or give in to the economy bloc in Congress. It's not so, and I want you to tell your friends—Arthur Schlesinger, Galbraith, and other liberals—that it is not so. I'm no budget slasher. . . . If you looked at my record, you would know that I am a Roosevelt New Dealer. As a matter of fact, to tell the truth, John F. Kennedy was a little too conservative to suit my taste." But the liberals didn't have the votes in Congress, didn't have the nine votes necessary to get the tax cut bill out of the seventeen-member Senate Finance Committee. The economy bloc had the votes, and they had Harry Byrd. Smathers had summed up the prospects for passing the tax cut bill: "We're not going to be able to do it."

THE PROBLEMS WITH Congress that he was aware of—not only the intertwined tax cut and budget bills and the eleven unpassed appropriations bills that were also tied in with them, but civil rights, foreign aid and school construction—were difficult enough, particularly because the deadlines for solving them were so close, but on Saturday, talking with Mansfield and Humphrey, he was suddenly made aware of another problem on Capitol Hill, one on which, to his surprise, the deadline was much closer.

As part of his attempts to ease tensions with the Soviet Union, President Kennedy had, in October, offered to help alleviate its serious food shortage by selling it wheat from America's surplus, and by allowing Russia, short of foreign exchange reserves, to finance the purchase on credit from the United States Export-Import Bank.

Helping Russia out of a jam was anathema to Capitol Hill hard-liners. Calling Kennedy's plan "indefensible," one of the hardest, Republican Senator Karl E. Mundt of South Dakota, had attached an amendment to the foreign aid bill prohibiting the Export-Import Bank from extending the credit.

The amendment would probably kill the wheat deal. It would certainly infringe on the President's authority in foreign affairs. On November 14, a week before the President left for Texas, the Kennedy Administration had tried to defeat Mundt's prohibition in the Senate—and had failed, mustering only forty votes. Mundt was then persuaded to withdraw it, so that the foreign aid bill could proceed—not that it *did* proceed—but only by Mansfield's promise that he would be allowed to submit it as a separate bill and to have a vote on it on an early date, which had been set for Tuesday, November 26. At the legislative leaders' breakfast on November 21, the day Kennedy left for Texas, Kennedy had insisted that the Mundt bill must be defeated. From the report Mansfield and Humphrey now gave Johnson, however, the former President's words had little relation to reality: the bill, they reported, was probably going to be passed.

In reporting this to Johnson, Mansfield and Humphrey seemed to feel that they were talking only about a vote on a wheat sale, and Smathers hadn't considered the Mundt bill important enough to mention it, but none of these senators were Lyndon Johnson, who as master of the Senate had demonstrated a gift, an intuition, for seeing, in a vote on some individual bill, larger implications seen by no one else. In the instant the wheat sale vote was mentioned to him—"just the moment he heard about it," George Reedy says—he knew that because of Kennedy's death and the resultant change in Presidents, the vote was now about more than the wheat sale, that it now possessed a far broader significance.

In confrontations with the former President during the past three years, Congress, and in particular the Senate, had won so often, had blocked so many Kennedy legislative proposals, that Congress now felt that in such confrontations, power rested on Capitol Hill, not in the White House. And the confidence among congressmen that they could win battles with the President had made them more willing to fight them, had emboldened them to contest the Kennedy program. "They've got the bit in their teeth," Johnson was to explain to his aides.

That was under the former President. A vote on the Mundt bill on November 26, the day after Kennedy's funeral, would make that measure the first bill to be considered by Congress under the new President. The wheat sale vote was going to be Congress's first confrontation with the Johnson Administration—and therefore its result would be an indication of whether, under the new Administration, the situation would remain the same, or if power would shift. The result, Johnson saw in an instant, would be crucial. The feeling on Capitol Hill had to be changed. If Congress won, its confidence that it could still defeat the President would make subsequent battles—over civil rights, for example, or the tax cut—much more difficult for him. "We could not afford to lose a vote like that, after only four days in office," he was to explain in his memoirs. "If those legislators had tasted blood then, they would have run over us like a steamroller [on future votes], when much more than foreign aid would depend on their actions." The Mundt bill had to be defeated; the issue, as a journalist was later to report after Johnson's aides had explained it to him, "was simply" whether "presidential dominion over Congress" would be "reasserted"—or not.

Since Johnson, at his ranch in Texas preparing for Kennedy's visit, had missed the last leadership breakfast, he hadn't been aware of the bill's status. Learning it from Mansfield and Humphrey sometime on Saturday, he tried to rescue the situation, but when he gave the two leaders the instructions that to him were so elementary—not to schedule the vote on the bill until they were certain they had the votes to defeat it—he was informed that the vote had already been scheduled, for Tuesday. And when he told them to delay it—there was a perfectly good excuse for a brief delay, he said: the President's assassination, and the resultant need for a new Administration to get its bearings—the answer from Mansfield was that he wasn't willing to do that: he had promised Mundt the vote would be on Tuesday, he said, and he wouldn't go back on his word. The leaders weren't sure if they had the votes to defeat the bill. Johnson couldn't even find out what the vote count *was.* "They don't know how many votes they have," he told Reedy in a tone of disbelief.

Humphrey of course said he was sure they would have the votes, but Johnson, having had experience with Humphrey's counts in the past, had no confidence in them, and the lack of confidence proved justified. "They told me that the Mundt bill's pretty close," he was to say, "but when [we] checked it down, why they [the bill's supporters] had a good many votes to spare." He had three days— the vote would be held Tuesday afternoon—to turn the vote around, and not only did the leaders not know what the count was or which senators had to be turned around, the man who might know, Larry O'Brien, had made it clear that, at least for the moment, he didn't even want to discuss working for Lyndon Johnson. When Johnson tried to reach O'Brien that Saturday, he was told that he was tied up—and would remain tied up for the next couple of days, helping with preparations for the funeral.

HE HAD FOUR DAYS—until Wednesday at noon—before he would have to stand before a joint session of Congress and deliver his first speech as President. He would want to emphasize continuity in the speech, of course—to make clear that he was carrying on Kennedy's program—and he knew who he wanted to write it: Kennedy's speechwriter. He gave Ted Sorensen credit for the ringing phrases in Kennedy's speeches; perhaps Sorensen could give his own some of that magic. At the conclusion of Saturday's Cabinet meeting, he had walked over to Sorensen, sitting against the wall, and asked him to begin working on it. But Sorensen was still dazed by the "grief and disbelief" that had gripped him since he first heard the news. He was to say forty-five years later that he had never been able to remember "the details of that awful weekend . . . unreal . . . unbelievable . . . a blur of pain and tears." That evening Johnson tried again in the inner office in 274. "I do not recall much" of that meeting, Sorensen was to say, "but I was blunt and unsmiling." Most of the meeting, Sorensen was to say, "was devoted to his request that I stay: 'I need you more than he needed you,' " but, as best as he could recall, his response was, "I've given eleven years of my life to John Kennedy, and for those eleven years he was the only human being who mattered to me." Johnson may have intended to ask him again that evening to draft the joint session speech, but the request was not made.

And all the time, the calls kept pouring in. "Gov. [George] Romney [of Michigan] is at the airport. An aide is asking if he [the governor] could talk to you if he came over," said a note Roberts handed him that Saturday. "Aide holding on 304," said another note a few minutes later. Picking up 304, Johnson said a few words to Romney, who might be his opponent in a few months. "Governor Lawrence . . . would like to stop by at your convenience," said a note from Jenkins. "Harry Provence is at the Washington [Hotel], Room 432, and is waiting." Suddenly Jenkins was coming in to tell him that McCone was in the outer office; he motioned to Jenkins to show him right in; entering, McCone closed the door behind him before he spoke: Oswald, the CIA had learned, had visited not only the Soviet Embassy in Mexico City but the Cuban Embassy as well. There was even a call from Ralph Yarborough; when, after a while, Johnson hadn't returned it, the senator left a message with Jenkins: "The President will have my complete support in Texas and in the Nation. . . . If the President had lived another day, he would have seen some harmony in Texas." (Returning the call after he received that message, Johnson said, "You're wonderful, and I'll be in touch with you—I appreciate it more than you know." "I have no ideological problem; I'm willing to give at least 90 percent—" Yarborough said. "That's right. Always have," Lyndon Johnson interrupted. "Always have. I know that. Thank you, my friend.") There was, Reedy was to say, "one call after another, all day" from Hoover and Bundy. There were the things to do that no one had thought of but that were essential. A presidential proclamation had to be issued to designate Monday, November 25, the day of the funeral, as an official "day of national mourning." After it had been written and approved, a memo that Reedy stuck in front of him told him that something had been left out. The proclamation authorized the closing of all government offices, but no one had thought of the banks. "Apparently because of a legal quirk, we have not given the nation's banks authority to close Monday. A bank can be sued if it is not opened during regular hours, and the only way in which they are safe from such suits on Monday is if the day is proclaimed a legal holiday."

By the time Saturday was over, Johnson had, since his confrontation with Robert Kennedy that morning, met with his Cabinet as a group, and with three of its key members—Rusk, McNamara and Labor Secretary Wirtz—individually; with Eisenhower and Truman; with leaders of Congress; with the CIA director; with Supreme Court Justice Goldberg; and, over and over, with his national security advisor; had gone to church; paid his respects to the dead President and to the dead President's widow in the White House; and had talked on the telephone with, and won firmly to his side, perhaps another forty people.

Arriving in the office on Sunday with a list of problems that must be faced immediately, he was handed the instructions for his participation in the day's memorial ceremonies, which, he saw, would consume a substantial portion of the day. ("The President and Mrs. Johnson . . . will follow the casket through a cordon of honor troops from the East Room to the North Portico entrance where the casket will be placed on the caisson. . . . The President should place his right hand over his left breast while the casket is being placed on the caisson. . . . The President and Mrs. Johnson will board vehicle No. 1 for procession to the Capitol. . . . At the conclusion of the last eulogy the President will move from his position to the base of the catafalque where the wreath bearer will assist him in placing a wreath.") And then he was told that also riding in vehicle No. 1 would be the attorney general. Just a few minutes later, as he was waiting in the East Room to step on the portico, an usher told him that Dean Rusk wanted to speak to him on the phone, and Rusk told him that Lee Harvey Oswald had just been shot "on television." Shortly after the procession arrived at the Capitol, the assassin was pronounced dead, murdered by another assassin—and immediately the second murder, fostering as it did the impression that the assassination was part of a conspiracy, created a huge problem. Obviously some sort of major investigation was necessary—but what type of an investigation, and by whom?

ONE PROBLEM he dealt with that Sunday seemed somewhat less pressing than the others. After his return from the Capitol (faster coming back, with motorcycle outriders clearing the way, no Kennedys in the car with him) there was a meeting in his office—on Vietnam.

Ambassador Henry Cabot Lodge had returned from Saigon to report on the effects of the coup that had, three weeks previously, resulted in the assassinations of South Vietnamese President Ngo Dinh Diem and his brother, secret police chief Ngo Dinh Nhu, and the installation of a new government led by General Duong Van (Big) Minh. Most of America's major newspapers had welcomed the end of the repressive Diem regime, and there had been relatively few public statements about the coup from Capitol Hill; Senate Foreign Relations Committee chairman Fulbright would soon be telling Johnson that he saw no need for any immediate action on his part: "I think we ought to give this new man a chance to see what he can do for a little while." And the meeting didn't make Johnson, who, Valenti recalls, had "talked little of Vietnam that first night," feel the need for immediate action. Lodge, who had not been at all opposed to the coup, said that it had improved prospects for victory. None of the others sitting around the conference table in 274—Rusk, McNamara, Bundy, McCone and Ball—agreed with this prediction; McCone, in fact, said that the new military leaders were having difficulty organizing a government, that Viet Cong activity seemed to have increased since the coup, and that he saw no reason for optimism. But there was no strong feeling from anyone but McCone that there had been substantial deterioration, either, and Johnson was to recall that he found the "net result modestly encouraging." A preliminary plan for covert operations against North Vietnam had been approved at a conference in Honolulu two days before Kennedy's assassination, and it was decided at the meeting in 274 that when the plan had been refined, it would be sent to the President for approval.

The "breathing space" in foreign affairs appeared to include Vietnam; of all the potential trouble spots in the world, Johnson would recall in his memoirs, "Only South Vietnam gave me real cause for concern. . . . But, compared with later periods, even the situation in Vietnam appeared to be relatively free from the pressure of immediate decisions." The solution seemed the same as in domestic matters: continuity—the continuation of Kennedy policies. Reinforcing that conclusion, furthermore, was a simple political calculation; as Bundy was to say, a presidential election was less than a year away, and major decisions on Vietnam in an election year were something no President would want to make. "It was so under Johnson, and it would [have been] under Kennedy as well. Neither man wanted to go into the election as the one who either made war or lost Vietnam. If you could put it off, you did."

With political calculations Johnson was at ease. While the range—from Lodge to McCone—of the assessments of the Vietnam situation may have been mixed, Johnson's response wasn't. When, at the end of the discussion, Lodge told the President that unfortunately hard decisions would be necessary on Vietnam, Johnson barely hesitated, and his instructions to Lodge, Wicker was to write, were "firm." There had been, the President said, too much bickering among the various American agencies in South Vietnam—the Army, the CIA, the USIA, the Joint Chiefs of Staff, the State Department—over our aims there. "We had spent too much of our time and energy trying to shape other countries in our own image." There would be time enough for broader objectives later, he said. At the moment, "The main objective" was to just "win the war—he didn't want as much effort placed on so-called social concerns." He told Lodge to return to Vietnam and assure its new government that his Administration would continue Kennedy's policy of helping Saigon to fight the Communists.

"I am not going to lose Vietnam," he said. "I am not going to be the President who saw Southeast Asia go the way China went." Lodge raised a question about political support. "I don't think Congress wants us to let the Communists take over South Vietnam," Johnson said, noting that "strong voices" in Congress were urging the United States to take more forceful action in Vietnam.

A tentative step in a different direction had recently been announced by the Kennedy Administration. On October 2, McNamara and Taylor, returning from an inspection trip to Vietnam, had recommended stepping up the training of the Vietnamese army so that American military personnel could be withdrawn from Vietnam, and had said that if this was done, "It should be possible to withdraw the bulk of US personnel" by the end of 1965. Their report concluded that a thousand Americans could be withdrawn by the end of 1963. "We need a way to get out of Vietnam, and this is a way of doing it," McNamara said. At the close of Kennedy's meeting with his two envoys, on October 2, Pierre Salinger had publicly announced that the President had endorsed their recommendations, saying that the President accepted "their judgment that the major part of the US military task can be completed by the end of 1965. . . . They reported that by the end of this year . . . 1,000 military personnel can be withdrawn." The number of American personnel in Vietnam at the time was 16,732, and it was forecast that by the end of the year, the number would be reduced to about 15,700. That had been before the coup. Whether Kennedy, despite the coup, would have kept the pledge to withdraw the thousand troops is unknown, but the pledge was on the public record. Johnson, calling in reporters after his meeting with Lodge and the others, "reaffirmed," the *New York Times* said, "the policy objectives of his predecessor regarding South Vietnam." The *Washington Post* reported that after the meeting "White House sources said the late President Kennedy's statement" about the troop withdrawals "before the end of the year remains in force."

Johnson's statement said: "First, the central point of United States policy on South Vietnam remains: namely to assist the new government there in winning the war against the Communist Vietcong insurgents. The adoption of all measures should be determined by their potential contribution to this overriding objective. Second, the White House statement of Oct. 2 on the withdrawal of United States troops from South Vietnam remains in force. This statement . . . said the program for training of Vietnamese troops should have progressed by the end of this year to the point 'where 1,000 United States military personnel' can be withdrawn."

Two days later, on November 26, the reaffirmation—all the conflicting parts of it—was given official status. On November 21, the day before Kennedy's death, Bundy had drafted a National Security Action Memorandum, a formal notification to the heads of government agencies of a presidential decision, and directives to take steps required to implement it. On November 26, Johnson approved the memorandum, NSAM 273. It emphasized that the Vietnam conflict was a war against Communism, and a war that had to be won, and that "It remains the central objective of the United States in South Vietnam to assist the people and Government of that country to win" it.

The specific withdrawal goals enunciated under Kennedy—a thousand by the end of 1963, "the bulk" of the rest by the end of 1965—"remain as stated," the NSAM declared. Among the directives included in the document, however, was one for the planning of "possible increased [military] activity," a reference to the plan for covert military operations against North Vietnam (CINCPAC Operations Plan 34-A-64, or OPLAN 34-A) that had been discussed and approved at the November 20 Honolulu conference.

IF VIETNAM SEEMED — no matter how misleading the impression—"relatively free from the pressure of immediate decisions," without deadlines by which specific actions had to be taken, little else was. All during those three days—"days filled with people, days filled with telephone calls," in Juanita Roberts' recollection—the crises never stopped. She, Marie Fehmer, Cliff Carter and Mildred Stegall would funnel the more important calls to the desk at which Walter Jenkins sat, taking notes on his legal pads, quiet, outwardly calm, the only sign of tension the steady reddening of his face as the day went on. A light on one of the buttons on the telephone console on Jenkins' desk showed when Johnson, in his private office, was talking on that line. Except when Johnson was talking to someone in person in his office, one of the buttons was almost always lit. When, for a moment, Johnson was alone in his office and the buttons were suddenly all dark, Jenkins would seize the opportunity, snatching up his pads and going in, to read Johnson the messages that required immediate attention. The buzzer from the inner office would sound on their desks. Johnson would tell them to set up an appointment with someone, or to get someone else on the phone. "Sometimes he would buzz out and say, 'What have you got?' and we'd tell him," Colonel Roberts says. Sometimes he would come out, into the two rooms with the desks crammed together and the phones ringing and people hurrying in and out, "and," Roberts says, "if he'd pass our desks and we had something we thought he should see, we'd give it to him."

There was so much to do. "He was working as rapidly as he possibly could," she recounts. And, of course, she says, "he was constantly having to leave for [the] ceremonies" for his predecessor. But, as had been the case Friday night, there was, during those next days in EOB 274, very little conversation, "no lost motion; it wasn't necessary for us to talk." To Marie Fehmer, her boss was "a changed man, transformed." At first she couldn't understand why he looked so different from the Lyndon Johnson for whom she had been working, but she came to realize, she says, that the very movements of his body were different; that instead of the awkward, almost lunging, strides and "flailing" movements of his arms that had previously often characterized Johnson under tension, now his stride was shorter, measured, and his arms were staying by his sides, hardly moving at all; that "there was no flailing," that "only his head moved. It wasn't just that there was no flailing emotionally. There was no flailing physically either. It was as if he was actively controlling his body." Not only his movements but his voice was transformed, she says. It had none of the impatience in it that was often—usually—present, none of the anger and rage into which impatience so often morphed, none of any of the emotions with which it was generally filled. "His voice was not low so much as it was level—it didn't fluctuate in tone. He was keeping it under control, calm."

It was an iron control, a discipline that, during those three days, never slipped. "I've never seen him as controlled, as self-disciplined, as careful and as moderate as he's been this week," Bill Moyers told *Time*'s Loye Miller. "He's remained calmer . . . he's been more careful to sort out and reason his feelings and his thoughts, and he's been good to work with. You know very well how he used to thrash around and blow his top so often. It seemed like he had a clock inside him with an alarm that told him at least once an hour that it was time to go chew somebody out. But he hasn't lost his temper once since two PM last Friday."

"It is remarkable, really," Miller reported to *Time*'s editors in New York. "Some of us who have seen Lyndon at his most cantankerous in times of lesser stress were wondering what sort of tantrums he must be having behind the office doors as the immense pressures of his new job and necessity for seizing it quickly bore down on him. But . . . my every inquiry brings the reply" that there were no tantrums—none of the cursing, none of the glass-throwing, none of the vicious rages. And the replies Miller received were accurate. There was never a crack in the calmness, the aura of command, the sense of purpose. The few reporters who were allowed to spend time in 274 during those days saw it for themselves, and those of them who had known Johnson for years were startled by what they saw now. Hurrying from 274 to *Time*'s offices to describe Johnson in a wire to New York, John Steele used adjectives like "direct, calm, deliberate," and nouns like "composure and sense of being collected." Hugh Sidey felt he was showing more of such qualities than he had *ever* demonstrated before. "There were questions, decisions to be made, just flooding in on him one after the other," he says. "He just handled them, one after the other," without a pause. Business in 274 "seems to be progressing matter-of-factly," another reporter wrote, "and actually quite well compared to the tumultuous office atmosphere which has often surrounded Johnson in the past."

Conferring with Johnson on Saturday, Abe Fortas was struck by his "studied calm." *"Studied."* Other aides also felt the calm was a mask, and they had reason to feel that way. On Saturday night, after a twelve-hour working day, Johnson was having dinner at The Elms with Busby and Thornberry. At dinner, he was rather quiet, in a mood Busby recognized. "He was thinking things through," he says. "Very intense. You could smell wood burning." Going upstairs after dinner, he asked Busby to sit in his bedroom until he had fallen asleep, and after the lights had been turned out, Busby did that, until, after about a half hour of silence, he thought it was safe to leave, and started tiptoeing toward the door.

"Buzz," said Lyndon Johnson's voice out of the darkness. "Buzz, is that you?" And when Buzz said that it was, the voice said, "Buzz, I'm not asleep yet."

Returning to his chair, Buzz waited for a while longer, but again, when he tried to leave, Johnson asked, "Buzz, are you still there?" Busby assured him he was, and that he had just been walking over to the window to adjust a curtain. It took several more attempts, and several more "Buzz, are you still theres?" before he finally made it out of the room. Busby, who loved him, didn't mind waiting, he was to say. He had done it before, when Lyndon Johnson found it hard to get to sleep. "Anything I could do to gentle him down," he says. "His mind just wouldn't stop working, working, working."

ALTHOUGH DURING THOSE three days he didn't have the use of the White House or adequate space for his staff while the Oval Office and its adjoining rooms stood empty across the narrow street, he had the telephone, and he used it—as only Lyndon Johnson could use it.

"I knew I had to secure the cooperation of the . . . natural leaders of the nation," he was to say, and it was over the telephone that he did it. For the sake of the country, he wanted unity behind his presidency, and for the sake of his political future—the 1964 election, and the convention, and the string of primaries and deadlines that loomed so imminently—he wanted it within his party, wanted to forestall any liberal attempt to contest his nomination, and wanted it fast. The leaders who would (in addition to the Kennedy faction, of course) be most reluctant to support him were the leaders who had opposed him so violently when he ran for the presidency in 1960: the liberal leaders of the great labor unions and the major civil rights organizations, the leaders who had opposed him even for the vice presidency, and who had called the nomination a "double-cross," and threatened to stage a floor fight, even to name a rival candidate, against him. Although the hostility of some of these men had softened during his vice presidency—some of them regarded themselves as his friends now—he couldn't feel confident of their support, particularly if in 1964 a rival candidate for the nomination was supported by the Kennedy faction, or was, in fact, *named* Kennedy. The hostility of many of them—perhaps most of them—had not softened at all; despite the St. Augustine tables and the Gettysburg speech, they still felt that at heart he was a Texas conservative, still felt that whatever he might have been saying for the last three years, Lyndon Johnson was still in reality what he had, in their opinion, always been: anti-union and not enthusiastic about civil rights, not a liberal at all. And among the union leaders whose hostility remained unabated was the most powerful of them, the man Lyndon Johnson called labor's "stud duck" because other union chiefs followed his lead, the man who in 1960, calling him "the arch foe of labor," had staged a "vendetta" against him, a vendetta in which, during the intervening three years, he had called no truce.

In dealing with these men now, however, Johnson possessed advantages he had never had before—not only the power of the presidency but what the presidency symbolized, and the desire, evoked by that symbol, of Americans to support their President, a President who had taken office at such a difficult moment. The first call Lyndon Johnson made when he arrived in EOB 274 on Saturday morning demonstrated how much that might mean. "George," Lyndon Johnson began. "Mr. President," George Meany replied.

"George," Lyndon Johnson said, "you know how tragic this whole thing is. And I just called to tell you that you have been of inestimable help to this administration and to your country, and I need you as we've never needed you before."

"I'm still in a state of shock," Meany said. But if the President needed him, he would be there. "I can tell you, we'll go down the line with you and you have got an awful job. But I'm sure you can do it!"

Johnson went on telling him how much he needed him. "I know I'm totally inadequate to it. But maybe with friends like you . . . and the phone's always there . . . and you just let me know and come over." He said it was time for enemies to unite. "Let's try to pull our country . . . close ranks, and pull it out of this terrible situation in which we find ourselves."

Meany tried to encourage him. "It's a tough job but I'm sure you can do it," he said. "I think you, with your training and everything else, Mr. President, you can do it. And you'll have me and all of our gang back of you one thousand percent."

"I want your counsel and I want your friendship," Lyndon Johnson said.

"Well, you have it," Meany replied.

By "our gang" Meany meant labor leaders like Reuther of the Autoworkers, McDonald of the Steelworkers, Rose and Dubinsky of the Garment Workers. Despite Meany's assurance that Johnson would have them behind him, Johnson telephoned each of them himself, telling them that, as he said to Reuther, he would be loyal to the Kennedy program, the liberal program—that he wouldn't "abandon the ship," that "we're going to turn our sails into the wind and we're going places and we're going to carry on," telling McDonald, "I want to meet the needs of our people and there are many unfulfilled ones" so he would ask Congress to "do more good and less economizing. . . . We'll just have to go after them, and we'll need you then. You better stand ready and be armed." He had the key line pretty well down now. When Reuther said, "Mr. President, [you have] my prayers, and my friendship, and *every* possible help that I can offer," Johnson said, "Well, I need it all. I never needed it as much in my life." And the line worked. "Anytime that you need me, you call and I'll be there," Reuther said.

Arthur Goldberg, now a Supreme Court Justice but once, as general counsel to the Steelworkers, at the heart of labor's hierarchy, had telephoned Reedy that morning and advised him that, as Johnson was to put it, Meany "liked the visible signs of consultation," public acknowledgment of his importance—and wanted also acknowledgment that he was labor's leader. Reedy had typed up this advice and handed it to Johnson. The call to Meany, Reedy's memo said, "should be told to the press." The calls to Reuther, Rose and the others "should remain off the record"—so that Meany would believe he had been the only leader called. Johnson told Reedy to make sure reporters knew he had telephoned Meany—and to make sure reporters didn't find out he had telephoned the others.

Then he turned to leaders of the civil rights movement. He told them his problems. "It's just an *impossible* period," he said to Martin Luther King Jr. "We got a budget coming up that's—we got nothing to do with it, it's practically already made. And we got a civil rights bill that hadn't even passed the House, and it's November, and Hubert Humphrey told me yesterday everybody wanted to go home. We got a tax bill that they haven't touched." He went to considerable trouble for them, graciously, warmly. When, at the end of his conversation with Johnson Sunday evening, Whitney Young of the National Urban League mentioned that he had "sort of expected" tickets for himself and his family to the Kennedy funeral services, but hadn't received them, Johnson said "Bobby," not he, was handling the funeral arrangements, but "Let me inquire on it," and added, "I'm taking my family and I'd almost take you as my guest if I can get an extra ticket." He said he would get back to Young Monday morning, but then apparently realized that might be too late, arranged for the tickets with Sargent Shriver, and called Young back to tell him he had done so, and to tell him that if there was any problem with the tickets, he should call Moyers at once. ("God bless you," Young said.) He made them laugh, using a Texas axiom to assure Young he wouldn't stop fighting for civil rights. "We'll keep coming," he said. "Kind of like the fella who said, 'What's the difference between a Texas Ranger and a Texas sheriff? Well, when you hit a Ranger, he just keeps coming.' " Solemn though the day may have been, Young burst into laughter. He told them they could depend on him. When Dr. King mentioned Kennedy's "great, progressive policies that he sought to initiate," Johnson said, "Well, I'm gonna support them all, and you can count on that." He told them he needed their support. "I'll have to have you-all's help—and I never needed it more than I do now," he said. And they told him he would have it. "Just feel free to call on us for anything," Dr. King said.

One of the most difficult problems that had faced Johnson when he was thrust into the presidency was the dislike and suspicion with which he was regarded by not a few leaders of the labor and the civil rights movements whose support was indispensable to him if he wanted to unite the Democratic Party, and if he wanted to secure its presidential nomination. He didn't solve that problem—didn't eradicate those hard feelings—during his first three days in the presidency but, by the end of those three days, he was on his way to a solution.

WANTING, NEEDING to unify more than the party, from one telephone call to another he shifted from one tone to another, and back again. Had he told a liberal that he was going to ask Congress for "less economizing"?—to the conservative Robert Anderson he said he was going to ask Congress for more: "to try to watch expenditures." With Democrats, he invoked Truman's name, telling Carl Albert he wanted to speak to a joint session "similar to what President Truman had after President Roosevelt died"; with Republicans, it was Eisenhower's name: he had just been in an "elevator with President Eisenhower," he mentioned to Everett Dirksen. "He had lunch with me and we were talking. . . . It might be a good thing . . . to have a Joint Session. . . . Ike thought I ought to." Liberals he told that they should support him because he was going to reform the system, Republicans that he was going to preserve it, hinting to them that because of things that had not yet come to light about the assassination, the system (under which of course their wealth had been accumulated) might be under attack, telling his key link to Wall Street, Ed Weisl, that "your folks" should be given a hint that "this thing . . . this assassin may . . . have a lot more complications than you know about. . . . It may lay deeper than you think" ("Oh, no," Weisl interjected), but that his folks shouldn't be afraid because "we're going to preserve this system"; therefore it was vital that the financial world show confidence in him. He himself called Frederick Kappel, president of the country's largest corporation, American Telephone and Telegraph, and chairman of the influential Business Council, to tell him,

"We've got to preserve this system, my friend. And there's a good deal more." The key to the financial world was Wall Street—it had panicked on Friday on news of the assassination; based on the experience with previous sudden presidential deaths, it would rebound when it reopened on Tuesday, as long as it had confidence in the President. Picking up the phone to call Bundy, Johnson told him that Treasury Secretary Dillon and Federal Reserve Chairman William McChesney Martin should make "a statement about continuity, stability or something, and express their confidence" before the market opened. After letting Weisl know that "I've been visiting with President Eisenhower" and that "I was thinking of you and I never needed you as much as I do now," he told him to "tell Bobbie [Robert Lehman of Lehman Brothers] and some of his group—you just say that it's very tragic, but you have great confidence in me and my experience, so on and so forth. . . . We don't want anybody to panic."

And all the time other calls were pouring in, from congressional leaders, from governors like Pat Brown, whose previous experience with Lyndon Johnson had been so unpleasant but who now wanted to "offer you all the help a governor can give to you" ("Pat, you're wonderful and I appreciate it, and I sure reciprocate it, my friend. And I've never needed help as bad as I need it now"), from governors two at a time, John Reynolds of Wisconsin and Karl Rolvaag of Minnesota, both in Washington for the funeral, on the line at the same time. Mentioning that they had visited him on one of his trips to the Mayo Clinic, Johnson said, "You came to see me when I was sick. I don't forget. Now you let me know if there's anything I need to know out there. I'm going to depend on you."

OF ALL THE PROBLEMS facing Lyndon Johnson, one of the most delicate—and, to his mind, most urgent—was to persuade key Kennedy Administration figures to remain in their jobs. While his plea on Friday that they stay on had worked with McNamara, Rusk and Bundy, it hadn't with O'Brien, O'Donnell or Sorensen, and on Saturday it quickly became apparent how difficult it was going to be to keep with him some of the other most visible symbols of the Administration. When, early Saturday morning, Johnson woke its public face, Press Secretary Pierre Salinger, to ask him to stay in his job, Salinger agreed to do so—through Monday. Telling his friend the journalist William V. Shannon that he would handle press arrangements through Monday's funeral because he wanted everything to go as smoothly as "the President"—he didn't mean the new President—would have wished, he said he would resign first thing Tuesday morning. As for Arthur Schlesinger, not a significant figure within the Kennedy Administration but, to liberals, the very embodiment of liberalism, on Saturday, while President Kennedy's body was still lying in the East Room, he convened a lunch in a private dining room in Washington's Occidental Restaurant. Present, along with their wives, were Walter Heller; Heller's fellow economists Ken Galbraith, Sam Beer and Paul Samuelson; William Walton and Richard Goodwin.

The topic was the possibility of denying Johnson the nomination at the 1964 Democratic convention by running a ticket of Robert Kennedy and Hubert Humphrey.

In trying to persuade the Kennedy men to stay in their jobs, Johnson had working for him, to a varying degree in each case, of course, fundamentals of human nature—the desire to hold on to position and power and the perquisites that came with them—but he was confronted, again to varying degrees depending on the man he was talking to, with a quality not universal at all: the feelings of the Kennedy men about a dead leader who, as far back as *PT-59,* had elicited an unusual depth of loyalty in men who served under him. "Almost all Presidents evoke intense loyalty from their aides; a few, something quite beyond," Eric Goldman says. "These men had not only admired John Kennedy as President but had been entranced by him as a human being and had found a good deal of the excitement and of the meaning in their own lives through their feeling of closeness to him." On the evening of Kennedy's funeral, Schlesinger wrote in his journal, "I keep supposing that tomorrow morning, I will come down to the White House, Evelyn will be in her office and Kenny in his, and in a few minutes the President will be along, with some jokes about the morning papers. The thought that we will never see him again is intolerable and unacceptable and unendurable." To an unusual degree, the loyalty was to the man—and now the man was gone. "We came with him, we should leave with him," William Walton said.

Complicating Johnson's task were the feelings of the Kennedy men about him, Lyndon Johnson—the contempt many of them felt for him exacerbated now by contempt for his state that had turned into hatred because it was there in that outpost of braggadocio and prejudice that their leader had been murdered. Walking into Ted Sorensen's office, Kennedy aide Ted Reardon shouted, "I'd like to take a fucking bomb and blow the fucking state of Texas off the fucking map." Sorensen wasn't a shouter; his quiet words to Reedy—"George, I wish to hell that goddamned state of Texas of yours had never been invented"—let Reedy understand how deep his feelings ran. In addition, they had seen the way he treated his staff, and the cost exacted by such treatment. "Johnson really took from Walter Jenkins his substance," Ralph Dungan was to say. "He is that way with people. . . . He really took the substance, the psychological and spiritual substance of people and sucked it right out like a vampire. . . . He could not leave a man whole with his own dignity and his own self-esteem." And what programs would the new President ask them to support? They had believed not only in a President but in a program, a liberal program, and they believed—many of them and perhaps almost all of them—that Lyndon Johnson was, despite his recent statements about civil rights, fundamentally a Texas conservative. Joining anyone else's team after working for John F. Kennedy wouldn't have been easy; joining the team of Lyndon Johnson would be particularly hard.

With each of them, Johnson employed the same basic line: "I need you more than President Kennedy needed you." Comparing notes, they realized they had all heard the line, and mimicked it, exaggerating the Texas drawl—"Ahhh need you, really ah do"—laughing about it among themselves. And journalists would repeat their mockery, enshrining it in print, as if Johnson was simply repeating the same line over and over. But, although no one realized it, in each case that line had been subtly altered, tailored to the man he was talking to, by this great reader of men—tailored, for example, not only to Kenneth Galbraith's idealism but also to his ambition to be what Kennedy hadn't allowed him to be: an insider like his friend Schlesinger. He, Lyndon Johnson, and Galbraith had both been young men in Washington in the early days of the New Deal, Lyndon Johnson reminded him; they had both believed in the ideals of the New Deal, he said; they both still did—wouldn't Ken help him turn those ideals into reality? And he had that joint address to give to Congress, he said; he would appreciate it if Ken could get up a draft for him as quickly as possible. Tailored to Schlesinger's intellectual arrogance: "I just want to say that I need you far more than John Kennedy ever needed you. He had the knowledge, the skills, the understanding himself. I need you to provide those things for me. . . . You have a knowledge of the programs, the measures, the purposes, of the history of the country and of progressive policies, you know writers and all sorts of people. I need all that, and you must stay." With Adlai Stevenson, he played on ambitions, thwarted ambitions, and, it may have been, on regrets, on thoughts of what might have been. "I know, and you know, that you should be sitting behind this desk rather than me," Lyndon Johnson told him. Played on resentments. "There has been no consultation around here," he told Stevenson. "You know, they put in the tax bill without ever talking to me . . . I know they haven't consulted you either. So far as I'm concerned, that is all changed. . . . I want you to play a big role in the formation of policy."

And it wasn't just the line, or the variations on the line, but the way it was delivered. He humbled himself before these men, abased himself. He wasn't as smart as Jack Kennedy, he told them. He needed them to think for him—to "*think, think, think.*" He didn't absorb things as fast as President Kennedy, he said. "Don't expect me to absorb things as fast as you're used to." They would have to be patient with him, he said. When one of them suggested that because of the strain he was under he should consider going to the ranch for a vacation over the upcoming Thanksgiving weekend, he said, "I'm afraid to. I don't have enough time to keep abreast. . . . I just haven't read one-third of the stuff I need to read, and I read until two o'clock in the morning." He pleaded with them. He was helpless because of his background, he said—in his notes on his conversation with Johnson, Heller wrote that the President had said that "he did not have the education, culture and understanding that President Kennedy had . . . but he would do his best"—and because he didn't even know people as smart as them to staff the government. "I don't know the kinds of people that we're going to need—I don't have anyone to replace you with," he told one man. "Please stay—I don't know *anybody,*" he said to another. "In these early days," as Doris Kearns

Goodwin puts it, he "spoke to the Kennedy men with a subdued tone. He requested rather than ordered; he spoke of his shortcomings and shared his doubts." Evans and Novak, who interviewed many of these Kennedy men during this period, were to write in their study of Johnson and *The Exercise of Power* that "In [these] first few days . . . Johnson subdued his energy, lowered his voice and assumed a posture of humility. . . . Old friends and aides remarked they had never seen him so self-possessed, so humble."

If the humility, the deference, he showed was a mask, as it had invariably proven to be in the past—after he had cried in front of Jim Rowe years before, for example—it was a mask that, in those crucial days, never slipped. Men who had watched Johnson for years could hardly believe the depths of the humility they were seeing now. His onetime aide Harry McPherson was in the inner office in 274 when "McGeorge Bundy entered with several cables and memoranda. They were not urgent but the President should see them before evening. Johnson was extremely deferential. He said, 'Whenever you need me, let me know.' Bundy replied, 'Oh, Mr. President, you let *me* know when you need *me*.' That made sense; Presidents pushed the button to summon aides, not the reverse. But I wondered if there was, in his correct, fluid response, the tone of a professor gently chiding a student who'd got it wrong." Johnson gave no indication that he had noticed the tone. Kennedy aides gave him advice—lectures, in some cases, so all-knowing was their attitude—on how best to get the tax cut and civil rights bill passed, lectures on legislative strategy to the master of the Senate. Johnson sat and listened, attentively, earnestly; it seemed all he could do to keep himself from taking notes.

Moreover, as Doris Kearns Goodwin says, "Never once did he permit himself even to imply that, however things were done before, this was now *his* White House. Where one might have expected bitterness—for all the slights received from some of these same men when he was Vice President—Johnson showed only benevolence." In fact, quite deliberately, he was telling them that it was still going to be *their* White House. "I knew how they felt," he was to tell Goodwin. The impact of Kennedy's death was evident everywhere—in the looks on their faces and the sound of their voices. "He was gone and with his going they must have felt that everything had changed. . . . So I determined to keep them informed. I determined to keep them busy. I constantly requested their advice and asked for their help." *"Never once."* His "restraint," as Goodwin wrote, was "continuous." Summing up descriptions of Johnson conversations they received from a dozen Kennedy aides, Evans and Novak said that his "restraint" was "magnificent."

And the restraint and humility got him what he wanted—"induced in these men the very cooperation and submission that Johnson was after," as Goodwin was to comment. By Sunday night, as one reporter wrote, "he obviously had good news he wanted to share," and although he restrained himself from making the announcement himself, "associates of President Johnson" told reporters that

"President Kennedy's Cabinet will be kept virtually intact until after the 1964 election." As for the Kennedy staff, Salinger had intended to brief the press for the last time on Monday; on Tuesday, he was still briefing, "with swollen eyes," one reporter wrote. Adlai Stevenson had been so thoroughly convinced that he would be playing "a big role in the formulation of policy" that he couldn't resist gloating over the alteration in his status. Johnson and he "talk the same language," he told Schlesinger; in fact he felt that had he "said the word," Johnson would have fired Rusk and Bundy, "but I told Johnson . . . that they should both be kept." "You know," he told Schlesinger, "things are ten times better for me now than they were before." Adlai would remain as ambassador to the United Nations until his death in 1965. When, during his conversation with Schlesinger, Johnson saw that the historian's resistance might have withstood the "need" plea, he lightened the mood with a little joke, saying about Schlesinger's letter of resignation, "If you act on it, I will have you arrested." Still trying to demur, Schlesinger said that every President should have his own men around him. Johnson said, "I consider you one of my men."

"I hope you will consider yourself that way too," Johnson went on. "I just want you to know that I have complete and unlimited faith and confidence in you. I want you to stay. I know it will be a sacrifice for you, and I know that you have many other things you can do. But I am asking you, for my sake and for the sake of the country, to stay with me for at least a year. By that time I hope I will have earned from you the same confidence and faith which I know you had in John F. Kennedy."

"He said all this with simplicity, dignity and apparent conviction," Schlesinger was to write in his journal that evening. "I am a little perplexed as to what to do. I am sure that I must leave, but I can see the problem of disengagement is going to be considerable."

Disengagement was, in fact, to prove to be impossible, at least for a time. Schlesinger, still speaking frequently with Robert Kennedy about strategies for 1964, would remain in his White House office until the end of January.

To the idealistic Sorensen, who despised him—"To me, he personified the kind of hyperbole and hypocrisy that defined the worst aspects of politics in my eyes," he was to say—his appeal was based on Sorensen's loyalty to the Kennedy program, and to his love for the man himself. When Sorensen mentioned that he had already submitted a letter of resignation, Johnson said, "I know. I got it." He didn't mention it again. Instead, he said, "I want you to draw the threads together on the domestic program." In another meeting, he asked him to draft the address to the joint session. These were the right notes to hit. "I agreed [to draft the speech]," he was to say. "I wanted to help commit LBJ to carrying on Kennedy's program for 1964, and Kennedy's legacy for the ages; and I wanted him to invoke these policies and words specifically as well as the late President's name." And, in addition, "I knew that JFK would not have approved my leaving during the brutal, grim post-assassination transition."

Johnson was aware of the significance of his accomplishment. "By remaining on the job, they helped give the government and the nation a sense of continuity during critical times—a sense of continuity which in turn strengthened my hand as Chief Executive," he was to write in his memoirs. Washington insiders were aware of it, too—and were aware also of how difficult that accomplishment had been. Familiar with the feelings of the Kennedy men toward the new President, many insiders had considered it simply impossible that Johnson would be able to persuade more than a few of them to stay. He had persuaded all of them to stay. And he had done it so fast! Johnson's "intensity and persistence . . . in carrying out this job was . . . extraordinary," Evans and Novak wrote. "There was no hesitation, no ceremony, no delay." Almost the entire job had been carried out in three days—Saturday, Sunday and Monday—those three days during which the nation had paid little attention to what Lyndon Johnson was doing. By the time on Monday afternoon that their beloved leader's body had been laid to rest, his men had agreed to stay and serve under his successor's flag.

"THE END OF THE SERVICE at Arlington," to McGeorge Bundy, "was like the fall of a curtain, or the snapping of taut strings"—and when the curtain came up again, it came up on Lyndon Johnson.

After Kennedy's body was lowered into the ground at 3:34 p.m. that Monday, Johnson was driven back to the Executive Office Building. The vote on the Mundt bill was less than twenty-four hours away. Larry O'Brien had had enough time to mourn. When Johnson telephoned him, at 4:40 p.m., he was sitting in his office with Ken O'Donnell, who was drinking, and, intermittently, crying, and when the President called, O'Brien was reluctant even to talk to him. When Johnson used the same line he had used with him on Air Force One—"I'm most anxious for you to continue just like you have been, because I need you a lot more than he did"—O'Brien sighed audibly into the receiver and said, "Mr. President, did you—Ken is here with me. Did you—do you have any immediate problem?" Johnson said "no," that he "just wanted you to know . . . how strongly I felt about you. . . . I think you know . . . the admiration I have for you, and—" O'Brien interrupted him. "I know that, Mr. President," he said in a very flat voice. Johnson said, "I don't expect you to love me as much as you did him, but I expect you will, after we've been around awhile." "Right," O'Brien replied.

But the time for that line—the time for begging—was over. If O'Brien truly cared about Kennedy's memory, he had a duty to it—and Johnson summoned him to his post. "I think it would be a terrible thing to Kennedy's memory to have this wheat sale thing repudiated," he said. O'Brien had to agree. "Yeah," he said. And Johnson's next words to Kennedy's congressional vote-counter were less emotional than professional: one pro speaking to another. "I hope they got the votes in the Senate," he said. "Do you know anything about it?"

How could O'Brien respond to a summons like that but obey? "I'll check that," he said, and with those words became, whatever his feelings about Johnson at that moment, effectively a member of his team. "Now, what's important is that we check those votes pretty carefully," Johnson said. "Right," O'Brien replied.

"I want somebody to give it a little attention . . . and then you let me know any suggestions you have because we're in this thing, right up to our ears," Johnson said. "I did tell Mansfield that I thought it would be a terrible thing to Kennedy's memory and a helluva way to launch a new administration," Johnson said. "I agree," O'Brien said; "I agree." Changing out of the formal striped trousers and black tailcoat he had worn for the funeral and into a business suit, he had himself driven to Capitol Hill and went to work.

Then Johnson had to meet with Adlai Stevenson on a problem that was, Theodore White wrote (after talking to Stevenson), "abrupt, urgent, unpostponable." Stevenson had been scheduled to address the United Nations on Tuesday—in less than twenty-four hours—on America's policy on orbiting armed spacecraft; he felt the speech could not be canceled, lest that arouse suspicions of disarray in the American government. Instead of spacecraft, he felt, the subject should be the strongest possible reassurance to U.N. delegates, who were worried about Johnson's views, that the new President supported the international organization. Johnson approved the change in topic, and the text. "President Johnson has directed me to affirm to this Assembly that there will be no 'Johnson policy' toward the United Nations—any more than there was a 'Kennedy policy,' " Stevenson told the U.N. the next day. "There was—and is— only a United States policy." Then it was time for the State Department reception for the foreign leaders who had come to Washington—except that the Democratic chairman of California, Jesse Unruh, whose support he might need in a few months, accompanied by two other key California Democrats, had been waiting at Cliff Carter's desk "hoping," as Carter's note to Johnson said, for "a quick visit with you." The visit was held ("as quick as possible," noted one of Johnson's secretaries)—and then he was at the State Department.

This appearance, his first public appearance since the funeral, was before a small but very select audience, about as select an audience as could be found on the face of the earth, and there was, as one account put it, "electricity"—the glamour and glitter of this "unprecedented gathering of world power under one roof"—in State's three brilliantly lit top-floor reception rooms with their view of the Potomac and, beyond it, Arlington Cemetery. The rooms were filled with sashes and turbans and medals; Queen Frederika of Greece led Emperor Haile Selassie to a couch, while, nearby, Mikoyan of Russia fenced with de Gaulle of France; everywhere one turned there was a world-famous face. And as Johnson stood before a fireplace receiving heads of state, with Secretary of State Dean Rusk standing at his shoulder, two of Rusk's aides—his executive secretary, Benjamin H. Read, and State's chief of protocol, Angier Biddle Duke—watching nearby, were apprehensive. These leaders were there, Duke was to say, to "take the measure" of Lyndon Johnson, and the State Department officials were anx-

ious about how the measuring would go. If there was a focal point—in addition
to the Kennedy circle, of course—for uncertainty about the new President, it was
at State, not in Dean Rusk's office but among the officials below Rusk, the officials who, rightly or wrongly, had quailed at Johnson's openness and exuberance
on his foreign travels, embarrassed at the impression of America that they felt he
was conveying to the world, and who, aware of Kennedy's orders that he not be
allowed to visit Russia, felt that their embarrassment had been shared by the late
President. Read was to recall that State's attempts to keep Johnson informed on
foreign policy "had never worked out terribly successfully. . . . I think it would
be foolish to pretend that it was otherwise because it wasn't." Whatever their
feelings about Johnson, furthermore, State's diplomats knew that one wrong
word could bring international complications, and knew also that there had been
no time for them to give Johnson any but the most cursory briefing on the right
words. Looking at the big Texan (he towered over everyone in the room but
de Gaulle), who he felt had done such a poor job representing the United States
in the past, Read didn't know, he was to say, what to expect at this reception.

But, he was to say, he certainly didn't expect what he got.

"The President had had a terribly busy day," he was to say, "doing the
thousand-and-one things that he needed to do in those desperate early days. And
the briefing time was just non-existent." Read had typed notes on five-by-eight
white cards, and "we would put these little cards into his hand just moments
before he would be greeting these people." Carrying out the instructions on some
of the cards required delicacy: for Prince Kantol, prime minister of Cambodia, a
country with whom American relations were in an advanced state of deterioration, the card read: "Tone—firm, no nonsense, though kindly. . . . President
Kennedy had a high regard for Prince Sihanouk; you share that regard. President
Kennedy personally investigated the charges of U.S. complicity in the Khmer
Serei plots and gave Prince Sihanouk his categorical assurances that they were
false. . . . The U.S. respects Cambodia's desire for neutrality and supports it, but
if international guarantees are wanted, the right way to get them is not to begin
by continuing to accuse the U.S. of complicity in plots." Watching Johnson now,
however, Read started to relax. Glancing at each card for a moment, the moment
that was all he had, "grasping the essence of it" in an instant, "he would work
into the conversation points which we had suggested."

Nor was it just with talking points that Johnson was making an impression.
As each minister or prime minister or prince came up to him, Johnson would
shake his hand. But then that hand wasn't released. Still holding it, Johnson
would grin—and in almost every case, the prince or prime minister would grin
back. From his earliest days campaigning in the Texas Hill Country as a gawky,
awkward young politician, Johnson had displayed a remarkable gift for making
an immediate connection with people he had never met before. Part of his technique was a handshake, which he turned into more than a handshake. Max
Frankel of the *New York Times,* watching nearby, wrote, "The average dignitary

received a firm handclasp that was held for minutes, if necessary, until condolences and wishes had been expressed. Older acquaintances received not only the prolonged handshake but also the covering clasp of the left hand; they were held there through longer remarks and, usually, broad smiles." Held firmly—but also in a friendly way. It was a technique that had worked with farmers and their wives, and it worked now with prime ministers. The State Department men saw, as Duke put it, that Johnson "understood . . . how he was being measured by them." And they saw that the foreign leaders were impressed. "He was marvelous," Duke says. "He came away with a good . . . deal of respect."

Mikoyan approached, flanked by Ambassador Dobrynin and an interpreter. A private meeting had been scheduled for the following morning with "the shrewdest man of the Russian leadership," but this tonight was a first impression. State wanted Johnson to project willingness to continue his predecessor's efforts to ease tensions between the two superpowers—together with firmness in protecting America's interests. Taking Mikoyan's hand, Johnson chatted with him for about ninety seconds and posed for a photograph, "without smiles." Although the expression on Johnson's face was not unpleasant, the photographs showed a very shrewd man squinting up at a very tough one.

And then came the one-on-one meetings, in Rusk's office on the seventh floor, with Ikeda of Japan and Pearson of Canada—after, of course, de Gaulle.

Johnson had met with the French President once before, and it had been an unpleasant occasion as de Gaulle, with his customary haughtiness, had lectured Johnson on America's role in the world. The unpleasantness had been rekindled in Johnson's mind by a report Bundy had handed to him that morning: at a recent meeting between de Gaulle and "an allied Ambassador," the report said, de Gaulle had indicated that despite America's NATO commitments, Western Europe would not be able to rely on the United States in the event of a Soviet invasion; in both world wars, he had said, America had arrived late—only Pearl Harbor had brought us into the second one. When, shortly before the reception, Bundy had told him that his first private meeting would be with Le Grand Charles, Johnson had for a moment reacted with a lack of enthusiasm so noticeable that Bundy asked, "Does that bother you?"

"Naw—a little," Johnson had said. He had been hoping his talk with de Gaulle could be brief. "I thought I'd sandwich him in . . . disagreeable. See, he had urged that we—" But then he caught himself. He was President now. "All right," he told Bundy. "I'll follow your judgment." When de Gaulle now asserted, in Johnson's recollection, that differences between the two countries had been exaggerated and that Frenchmen knew they could always count on the support of the United States, "I suppressed a smile," Johnson was to recall—and he evidently suppress[ed] it successfully. No one watching the two men talk would have suspected there had ever been anything "disagreeable" in their relationship. Watching from across the room as Johnson met one on one with "the real heavyweights" was, Read says, "quite a sight. . . . It was done with real skill by him under the maximum of difficulties." What were his feelings about Johnson by the end of the reception? "The greatest feeling of admiration. . . . It was quite a show."

Then he had to rush back to the Executive Office Building.

As he had been walking down the hill at Arlington that afternoon, he had noticed a number of state governors in the crowd, and "their presence," as one account gives it, "had suddenly registered on him," and he had realized that, trying as he was to meet with the nation's leaders to build rapport with them and to build their confidence in him, here, in the governors, were whole handfuls of key leaders, chief executives of the states of the Union, all in Washington at the same time, ready to hand. And he had thought, moreover, thought in an instant— biographies of a writer or an artist would call such a moment an "epiphany"—of a way to make use of governors. To break the logjam on Capitol Hill, he needed to influence senators and representatives—needed levers outside Congress to put pressure on it—and he had learned during the 1960 campaign that governors could put quite a bit of pressure on senators and representatives. Immediately after his return to 274 after the funeral, he had told his staff to invite the governors to a meeting in his office at eight o'clock that evening; with the funeral over, some of them would probably be leaving already, he said: stop them. William Scranton of Pennsylvania was, in fact, waiting in line to board an airplane back to Philadelphia when he was asked to return. It wasn't possible to get them all, but the staff got thirty-five, and they were waiting in 274's conference room when he hurried in at 8:30, apologizing for being late, saying he had just been talking with General de Gaulle and the talk had lasted longer than expected.

The conference table had been pushed back against the rear wall to make more room—three photographers were standing on it—and folding chairs had been brought in and placed in rows facing his desk, but there weren't enough of those chairs for all the governors, and some were sitting in the green conference table chairs that were now flanking his desk and others were crammed onto a couch flanking the desk on the other side, and aides and a few reporters lined the walls; so overcrowded was the room that it wasn't just the fluorescent lights that kept the setting from being dignified or impressive.

But the setting wasn't going to matter.

Talking points for the meeting—mostly platitudes—had been hastily prepared by Valenti, and they were lying on the desk in front of him, but after a minute or two, the platitudes were forgotten, and Lyndon Johnson got to the point.

"We do have this problem tonight, and that is the business of the government going forward," he said. "We live under a system of checks and balances," he said, and "I will tell you the Congress has exercised its power to check the Executive all right."

He told them how bad the problem was—in terms they could all understand, for they were chief executives, too, which meant they also had budgets to pass, and resistance against passing them from legislators.

"I have a budget that has to go to Congress December 15th," he said. There were demands on him to increase the budget. "The Secretary of Defense told me last night that he would have to have close to a billion dollars extra to keep up our defense guard. The Space Administrator said that unless we want to cut back and abandon our trip to the moon he has to have three-quarters of a billion more than he had last year." Congress had blocked passage of the budget. It had blocked passage of the civil rights bill. "We have a good education bill which has passed the House, and it is over in the Senate. We have one that has passed the Senate and is over in the House"—so an education bill was blocked, too. Other important bills were blocked. "Congress has gone a record ten months without finalizing action on many of these bills. . . . This is November, and this is the first time in thirty-two years that we have not passed an appropriations bill.

"So," he said, "I need your help."

He explained what type of help he was thinking of. "I want to appeal to you . . . to get your delegations"—their congressional delegations: their states' senators and representatives—"to help us break through this impasse." He needed them to help influence public opinion back in their states. "I not only need your hands; I need your voice," he said. He couldn't "make Congress legislate" by himself, he said. "If there is anything you can do to help us get action in this period of time when we are faced with this tragic experience of ours, we will be grateful."

The budget had to have enough money for defense, he said. "We have had hopes" of easing tensions with Russia, he said, "but that does not mean we have to lessen our strength. That means we have to maintain it. We have to lead from a position of strength, so we have to maintain that defense posture, because if we let down our guard, that is a written invitation for more trouble instead of less tension."

He appealed to their pride in their country. "I am seeing fifteen leaders in the morning from foreign countries, and all of them have their doubts as to what is going to happen in America. . . . To hesitate the slightest, I think, would be a great risk in compromising our whole system as a leader of the world."

And he explained to them why they should help regardless of their party affiliation. "You are great patriots and no single party has a single mortgage on patriotism. I have been a Democrat all my life. I cannot point to any members of my party who are more patriotic than members of the other party." Ike understood this, he told them. "I sat here yesterday with the great President of this country who led our forces to victory. . . . He came in yesterday to offer his help. He spent two and a half hours here. . . . We did not discuss his party or politics. We just discussed what needed to be done in this country to save it."

He was getting worked up now—"revved up." His desk was up on blocks, so that he would appear bigger than he was, but he didn't need the blocks to look bigger now; as he went on, emotions, passion, began to pour out of him so that he was again, for the first time in three years, the Lyndon Johnson who "got bigger as he talked to you." And suddenly his talk was on a different level—about larger issues than budgets or bipartisanship.

"We have hate abroad in the world, hate internationally, hate domestically where a President was assassinated and then they take the law into their own hands and kill the assassin," he said. "That is not our system. We have to do something about that. We have to do something about this hate, and you have to get to the root of hate. The roots are poverty and disease and illiteracy."

He had been sitting erect behind his desk, smiling, friendly, dignified, at the beginning of his talk; he wasn't erect now but hunched forward over the desk, arms leaning on the pages that he had long since stopped reading from, and as he talked he leaned further and further forward toward the men sitting in front of him, his hands sometimes open in entreaty and sometimes clenched into fists.

He had noticed something in the State Department briefing cards, he said. "The people I talked to tonight, out of a hundred nations, there are only six of them that have an income of as much as eighty dollars a month. We don't really recognize how lucky and fortunate we are until something tragic like this happens to us. Here is our President shot in the head and his wife holds his skull in her lap as they drive down the street. Here is our Governor who looked around and said, 'Oh, no, no, no,' and because he turned a bullet just missed his heart. It went down through his lung into his leg and tore his left hand off. And, then, yesterday, they take the law into their own hands. We have to do something to stop that hate, and the way we have to do it is to meet the problem of injustice that exists in this land, meet the problem of inequality that exists in this land, meet the problem of poverty that exists in this land, and the unemployment that exists in this land."

"The best way" to meet those problems, Lyndon Johnson said, "is to pass the tax bill and get some more jobs and get some more investments and, incidentally, get more revenue and taxes, and pass the civil rights bill so that we can say to the Mexican in California or the Negro in Mississippi or the Oriental on the West Coast or the Johnsons in Johnson City that we are going to treat you all equally and fairly, and you are going to be judged on merit and not ancestry, not on how you spell your name."

Forget your party for a moment, Lyndon Johnson told the men before him. "We are going to have plenty of time after the conventions to get out . . . and campaign and talk about ourselves and our merits. Let's talk about the country until then."

And "let's not just talk about it," Lyndon Johnson said. "Let's get some action on it and do something."

"*Do something.*" Lyndon Johnson wasn't smiling and friendly anymore. When he said the *Let's do something,* "he just snarled it," Valenti was to say. There had been exaggeration in his description of the scene in Dallas. John Connally's hand had not been torn off. But there was a vividness in the description, too—not John Kennedy's head in Jackie's lap but "his skull in her lap"—the vividness of a great storyteller whose words caught men up in their grip. And there was a vividness in the part of his talk that wasn't exaggerated that caught them up, too. "The only thing you could see moving in that room was the reporters' pencils," Valenti was to recall. "No one moved. No one budged. The room was absolutely still. No one took their eyes from his face." Reedy was very proud; others were finally seeing what the Senate cloakroom had seen.

Johnson finished by talking for a moment about himself. "I am not the best man in the world at this job, and I was thrown into it through circumstances, but I am in it and I am not going to run from it," he said. "I am going to be at it from daylight to midnight, and with your help and God's help we are going to make not ourselves proud that we are Americans but we are going to make the rest of the world proud that there is an American in it."

Some of the governors facing him had risen to their office through their capacity for leadership, and others had learned leadership since they were in the office, but one way or another many of them had learned to know leadership when they saw it. When Johnson finished, they stood and applauded him. A reporter asked Pat Brown his reaction to the speech. This was the Pat Brown who, three years before, had been thoroughly repelled by Johnson's manner.

"Astounded," Brown said.

OTHERS SAW IT, too—including men more accustomed to dealing with hard, cold numbers than with intangibles: the economists who had been preparing President Kennedy's budget.

Six of them had been waiting outside during Johnson's meeting with the governors: the Administration's three top advisers on economic policy—Dillon of Treasury, Heller of the Council of Economic Advisers and Gordon of the Bureau of the Budget—who called themselves Kennedy's "troika," after a Russian sleigh that is pulled by three horses; and their top assistants, Treasury Undersecretary Henry H. Fowler, Gardner Ackley of the Council and Budget Deputy Director Elmer Staats.

As soon as Johnson began talking to them, they realized that the sleigh had a very different driver now.

They were conscious, they were to say, of some of what Johnson had done that day: marching in the procession past a thousand windows after his predecessor had been shot from a window, attending the funeral, dealing with de Gaulle and Mikoyan and scores of foreign leaders, and then, as they sat waiting outside, with the governors, dealing with the investigation of the murders in Dallas—as well as, they were sure, carrying out a dozen other tasks of which they were not aware. They knew his day must have begun early that morning—actually it had begun at about 6:30 in the morning, and their meeting began at 9:15 that night, almost fifteen hours later—but, Ackley was to record in his notes on the meeting, "The President showed no signs of his tiring day, looked fit and vigorous, was affable and relaxed, but always in command."

"*In command.*" "The most impressive thing," Ackley wrote, "was the confident way in which he approached the whole problem—not necessarily implying that he knew the answers, but that he knew the score, and that the problem could be solved. All we had to do was to decide how to tackle it." And a moment later, they realized that he *had* decided: that he already knew how he was going to deal with the problem—of getting a tax reduction bill through Congress—that had stymied them for almost a year.

"What about your tax bill?" he asked Dillon—and before Dillon could reply, Ackley wrote, "he answered his own question." Dillon and the other members of Kennedy's economic team had believed that getting the budget down to $101.5 or $102 billion—reasonably close to the $100 billion figure Harry Byrd kept mentioning—would satisfy Byrd and his fellow Finance Committee conservatives. The previous year's budget had been $98.8 billion. Mandatory "built-in" increases would add $1.8 billion more, new expenses required under legislation already passed and signed an additional $1.6 billion. Even if no department or agency was given a raise, the total therefore currently stood at $102.2 billion. Dillon felt that figure might possibly be reduced to the $101.5 billion figure but no further. But Johnson told Dillon that he had been checking with senators on Finance ("The President indicating pretty clear knowledge of every vote," Ackley noticed) and the team's belief was wrong: the $100 billion wasn't an estimate, a rough figure, but a hard one, not an approximation of what Byrd wanted but a limit, "a psychological barrier that should not be breached," in the words of one senatorial observer, a "magic number" with a deep symbolic significance to the chairman; no peacetime budget had ever reached that figure, and he was determined that this budget wouldn't reach it either; unless the budget was reduced below that figure, the tax bill, with its savings to taxpayers of $11 billion and the resultant three-to-one stimulus for the economy that would produce badly needed new jobs and programs, wasn't going to be released by the committee and sent to the full Senate for a vote. There was no choice, Johnson told Dillon: "We won't have the votes to get it to the floor unless we tell them the budget will be about one hundred billion."

"It was as simple as that," Johnson said, according to Ackley's notes. "If you want to get an $11 billion tax bill, you're going to have to give up $1, 1½ billion of expenditures. Which would you rather have?"

The troika began to tug against the reins. To get the budget down to $101.5 or $102 billion, Kermit Gordon said, they had already had to cut from it so many items that shouldn't have been cut, including every single new dam and irrigation project, and to drastically reduce expenditures for reclamation and rural electrification. Johnson interrupted Gordon. "He knew about what $101.5 meant," he said. "He'd been hearing about it from Freeman, Wirtz and company—all of Heller's liberal friends." In a manner that Ackley described as "half-jokingly, but pointedly," he told Heller, "Tell them to lay off, Walter. Tell them to quit lobbying. I'm for them." He was a liberal, he said. "I want an expanding economy." The budget should actually be far higher than the figures they were talking about, and he knew it. "They don't need to waste my time and theirs with their memorandums and their phone calls." But if they didn't get the budget down below $100 billion, Byrd was not going to allow the tax bill to get to the floor. Heller tried to argue that the $101.5 billion budget already represented such substantial economies that the President could defend it persuasively. "*I* can defend one hundred and one point five," Lyndon Johnson said. "*You* take on Senator Byrd." He had talked with the conservatives and knew what they wanted. "Unless you get that budget down around one hundred billion, you won't pee one drop."

They seemed to feel there were alternatives to giving Byrd what he wanted, he told the six economic advisers; there weren't, and he gave them a lesson in political realities.

You couldn't get around the Senate, he said, telling them about a President, a President at the very height of his popularity, who had tried it, attempting in 1938 to unseat southern conservative senators by going into their states to campaign against them. "Of course, you could try to take it to the country. FDR tried that, with his tremendous majority, and got licked," he said. "It wouldn't work" if they tried it now, either. He gave them a lesson in parliamentary tactics—a master class in Senate tactics. As Ackley recorded, "The civil rights bill came up. The President said he [had] told President Kennedy not to send it up at least until after the appropriations [bills] were passed. Once it was sent up, Russell gave the orders to stall, to do nothing, and that's what happened." And that's what was going to continue to happen on the tax bill, and the budget, and the appropriations bills unless the conservatives got what they wanted. Economists could talk all they wanted, he told the economists; the reality was the Senate, the Senate Finance Committee—and Harry Byrd. "You had to give up something to buy off Byrd," he told them, and what they had to give up was that billion and one hundred and fifty million.

His message hadn't gotten through to the Administration before. But it was his Administration now, and they heard what he was saying. "Dillon agreed that you had to pay the price to get the tax bill, but it was worth it," Ackley's notes say. ("Then when you have it, you can do what you want," Dillon added, and Johnson agreed: "Like Ike did . . . talked economy and then spent.") And "at the end Heller agreed that if it were a real choice between a tax bill right away and one and a half billion of expenditure . . . it was worth the price." The deal would be made, Johnson indicated. "It might take a week to work [it] out."

The troika and their deputies filed out. They had been meeting with Johnson for about an hour. When the meeting had started, they had felt the tax bill was stalled. Now they saw a way it could be passed. They felt it *would* be passed. Had the governors been impressed with Lyndon Johnson? So were they. The budget–tax bill situation contained so many complexities. They had been grasped so quickly. Decisions had had to be made. They had been made—so quickly. When the economic advisers had entered his office, their tax bill and budget had been trapped, the government still operating, as it had been operating for months, under a makeshift budget, with the budget for the year to come still in limbo. If, to use Lyndon Johnson's terms, they had been mired in a congressional swamp, "caught . . . unable to move . . . simply circling 'round and 'round," needing someone "to assume command, to provide direction," needing, in other words, a leader, by the time they left, an hour later, they felt they had one, "affable and relaxed, but always in command . . . confident . . . that the problem could be solved," a leader who might, in fact, have found at last a way out of the swamp.

As for America as a whole, during the past three days the country, its eyes riveted on the memorial ceremonies for John F. Kennedy, had paid little attention to Lyndon Johnson, and there was widespread uneasiness about what lay ahead—a nation's need to feel that, its leader dead, it had a new leader. But by the end of those three days, while America as a whole had not yet paid much attention to Lyndon Johnson, people who had, during those days, dealt with him in person, face-to-face or over the telephone—the troika, the governors, the princes and prime ministers, the worried young State Department aides, his own ministers: Bundy, Rusk, McNamara—those who had watched him up close as he wrestled with problems that had to be resolved, that could not wait, knew, by the end of those three days, that America did in fact have one.

The drama into which Lyndon Johnson had been plunged was a drama that had begun with the transfer of power—great power—in an instant, without warning. It had continued with the assumption and use of that power in its very early stages—in its first three days, in what is called the "transition" between the Kennedy and Johnson Administrations, the passage of power from one Administration to the other. And in these early stages, already perilous because of circumstances that made it difficult for him to create an impression of continuity and confidence, it was a passage through uncharted waters, a passage that in significant ways was without parallel in American history. No precedents existed to guide Lyndon Johnson through some of the problems that confronted him. He had had to create his own precedents, and had done so with such success that *Time*'s Sidey, writing years later, said, "Even now . . . one must marvel at Johnson's total grasp of the machinery of government." There was "no script" for what he had done, Sidey said, and yet "his assumption of power" was "flawless."

AND BY THE END of the third day—or, to be more precise, by early the next morning, Tuesday morning—America had a leader who had assured himself of victory in his first battle.

"I want somebody to give it a little attention," Lyndon Johnson had told Larry O'Brien about the Mundt bill, and O'Brien had gone to work—and no sooner had Johnson finished with the troika at about 10:15 Monday night than he gave it a little attention himself, working to defeat the bill by telephoning not only senators who were undecided about it, but senators who had announced unequivocally that they would support it. There was no time to lose. The vote was only a few hours away. "All of us worked far into the night on that," Johnson was to write. He had a strong argument to use: that a vote for Mundt would be a repudiation of Jack Kennedy—and of him. "He came hard to the point," reported Evans and Novak, who spoke to several of the recipients of his calls, transforming the issue "from a question of foreign policy toward Moscow . . . into a vote of confidence in the new President. In essence, he said: Do you want the first action of the United States Senate to be a posthumous repudiation of John F. Kennedy and a slap in the face of Lyndon Johnson."

Framing the issue that way changed votes, and by about eleven o'clock that night, he had enough so that he knew he had won.* But for his purpose—to show he was in charge—he wanted not just a victory, but a rout. "That wheat thing—I hope that gets *murdered,*" he said. He kept making calls. And the vote against the bill the next day would be 57 to 36. "WHEAT BILL—FIRST JOHNSON VICTORY," the headlines said.

During his years in the Senate as, year by year, during his time as Assistant Leader and then Leader and Majority Leader, the legend of Lyndon Johnson had grown, one element that had contributed to his mastery of the Senate had been his intuition, his rare gift for seeing the larger implications in an individual bill. Another element had been his decisiveness: his gift, equally rare, not only for sensing in an instant, in the midst of the cut and thrust and parry of debate on the Senate floor, which way the Senate's mood was running on a bill, and not only, if the mood was running in the wrong direction, for sensing the moment at which the tide might be turned, but a gift as well not only for sensing the moment, but for seizing it—for launching, on the instant, maneuvers that turned the tide.

Three years though it had been since he had had an opportunity to use those gifts, he hadn't forgotten how.

THOUGH THE SCENES Lyndon Johnson had played that day—with the hundred heads of state, the thirty-five governors, the troika—had been crucial, they had been played before small audiences, and before such audiences, the smaller the better, he had usually performed well throughout his career. But on Wednesday, in his address to the joint session of Congress, he was going to have to appear before the entire country.

He was well aware that, as *Newsweek* warned its readers that week, while he could be "charming, informed and persuasive in man-to-man talk, he often seems corny and tedious in public address"—in prepared, full-length speeches to large audiences. With very rare exceptions, such as the talks at the Zembo Mosque, in formal addresses before large audiences he had, all his life, been unable to conquer his tendency to talk too fast, to rush over—and blur—the points he wanted to make. And the audience for this address would be not merely the thousand or so people seated before him and in the galleries above

---

*Among the senators whose vote he changed were two Democrats, Russell Long of Louisiana and Thomas McIntyre of New Hampshire.

but the tens of millions who would be watching him on television—the medium that had always been particularly unkind to him, the medium in which the impression he made with his bellowing, hectoring, vigorously gesticulating style had almost invariably merited the "corny" and "tedious" adjectives, and other adjectives as well: ponderous, dogmatic, loud, overbearing, irritating, off-putting. On Wednesday, in addition, he would be following onto the television screen a very hard act for anyone to follow: the greatest political performer who had ever appeared on television, one whose grace and wit, handsome face and boyish smile had been made newly vivid to America by the replays of his speeches and press conferences that had been on that screen, hour after hour, for three days.

A lot was riding on this speech for Lyndon Johnson. The country wasn't familiar with him, didn't feel it knew him. This address would, to a great extent, be its first impression of him—and first impressions can be lasting. As *Time*'s Loye Miller put it, "Overshadowing everything else" Johnson had done since taking office, "it would be beyond doubt the most important speech of his political life, because from it a very shaken citizenry would form judgments" of him, "take away impressions and opinions which it would" be hard to change. The American people, Miller wrote, "are anxious to size up their new President, anxious to believe that he has what it takes." But if, at the end of the speech, they didn't believe that, everything he had accomplished in the past three days wouldn't matter very much. "If it failed, all the doubts, oh, more than doubts, all the suspicion of him would only be fortified, and nothing he said in the future would erase that original mistake," another Miller, the author Merle Miller, was to write. Johnson himself was aware of the stakes. As Bill Moyers told Loye Miller, "He knew that the people watching it were burning with the question, 'Who is this man?' He felt that it would be setting off a chain reaction of opinion about the President. And he felt that since he was in office by accident, it was very important to show people right now that his Administration would not be government by accident." But what if he didn't show them that? He had understood from the first moments after the assassination the importance of instilling confidence in him in the American people. After the speech, they would either have confidence in him—or not. And if they didn't, all the assumptions about the inevitability of renomination for a sitting President would be meaningless. Speculation about rival candidates would begin immediately.

A lot riding for him—and a lot riding for America. Should the speech fail to instill confidence in him, the anxiety and unease would still be there, and John Kennedy's programs—civil rights, the tax cut, education, foreign aid, all the legislation that had been stalled for so long in Congress—would still be stalled.

MEN WHO REGARDED themselves as his friends, who had known him or worked with him for a long time and had heard him make many speeches, were very worried. Congressman Kilgore, who had, over the years, sat in on many

(*Above*) Arriving in Texas, November 21, 1963: (from the top) Representative Jack Brooks, unidentified, Senator Ralph Yarborough, Representative Albert Thomas, Governor John Connally, Nellie Connally, President and Mrs. Kennedy greeted by Vice President and Mrs. Johnson. (*Below*) November 22: President Kennedy speaking in Fort Worth. Behind him, from the foreground, LBJ, Governor John Connally and Senator Ralph Yarborough

LIFE

CAPITAL BUZZES OVER STORIES OF MISCONDUCT IN HIGH PLACES

THE BOBBY BAKER BOMBSHELL

NOVEMBER 8 · 1963 · 25¢

The Bobby Baker scandal had already erupted and on November 22 was heating up in Washington and New York.

From the Senate up—and down—a dark trail of misconduct

THAT HIGH-LIVING BAKER BOY SCANDALIZES THE CAPITAL

The dread cry of scandal, bane of all establishments, burst like a bombshell across the Washington autumn. It associated the name of Bobby Baker, the plausible young man on the opposite page, with an incredible mingling of high office, high influence and high living. This Baker, a onetime Senate page, had served long and diligently as secretary to the Senate majority under the former majority leader, Lyndon Johnson, marshaling votes, handling campaign funds. He was known as "Lyndon's boy."

Last week a Senate committee was investigating Bobby Baker. He had quietly resigned after a former vending-machine business associate sued him, charging use of Baker's influence in placing machines in defense plants. Then the German call girl, Elly Rometsch, shipped back to Germany in August, implied she knew Bobby socially, as well as Baker's blond secretary, Carole Tyler. Then there was the Quorum Club, where lobbyists and legislators go to mingle; Bobby was an organizer and Elly had hung around it. Some among the Washington mighty might well be shuddering as the Senate committee set out to learn how this young Baker fellow came so far so fast.

GERMAN CALL GIRL. At U.S. government request Elly Rometsch and husband, a German army sergeant, were returned to Germany after her partying with unnamed U.S. officials.

SECRETARY. Carole Tyler, former beauty contest winner from Lenoir City, Tenn., worked on Bobby's secretary, lived in his town house. He listed her on mortgage records as a cousin.

LIFE
Vol. 55, No. 19   Nov. 8, 1963

LEGMAN AND LEADER. For Lyndon Johnson when he was Senate majority leader—and for Mike Mansfield, his successor—Bobby was an indispensable confidant. He was a messenger, a pleader of causes, a fund-raiser and a source of intelligence. Another Senate aide remembers that "Bobby was the man you called. He had the head count. He knew who was drunk, who was out of town, who was unreachable. He knew who was against a bill and why, and he maybe knew how to approach a senator and get him to swing around. Bobby was it."

Dallas: the motorcade

(*Above*) LBJ leaves Parkland Hospital after the death of JFK. Secret Service Agent Rufus Youngblood is at left, and Representative Homer Thornberry at right. (*Below*) Back in Washington, at Andrews Air Force Base, the new President speaks to the nation.

On Air Force One in Dallas, LBJ—with Lady Bird and Jacqueline Kennedy by his side—is sworn in as President by Judge Sarah T. Hughes.

(*Above*) November 23: President and Mrs. Johnson leave the East Room after paying their respects. (*Below*) November 24: The procession from the White House to the Capitol.

The casket is carried into the Capitol, followed by Jacqueline Kennedy and the family.

Leaving the Capitol after the eulogies, Jacqueline Kennedy with Caroline and John, (behind them) RFK, Sydney Lawford, Patricia Kennedy Lawford, Peter Lawford; Jean Kennedy Smith, Stephen E. Smith, LBJ and Mrs. Johnson. Rufus Youngblood is left of Johnson.

(*Above*) LBJ in the Oval Office. (*Below*) Moving in to the White House: Lucy is escorting the beagles; Lady Bird is carrying her favorite picture of Sam Rayburn.

Taking command. LBJ meets (*above*) with the state governors in the Executive Office Building; (*below*) in the first meeting on Vietnam, with (from left) Ambassador to South Vietnam Henry Cabot Lodge Jr., Secretary of State Dean Rusk, Secretary of Defense Robert McNamara and Undersecretary of State George Ball;

. . . (*above*) with the press; and (*below*) with members of Congress at a White House breakfast. To LBJ's right is House Speaker John McCormack, to his left is Senate Majority Leader Mike Mansfield.

In Texas, over Christmas. The first state visit: German Chancellor Ludwig Erhard, happy with his new ten-gallon hat, with the Johnsons at the barbecue state dinner in the Stonewall High School gymnasium, near Fredericksburg

(*Above*) LBJ strides across a field on his ranch with reporter James Reston and his white-faced Herefords, and (*below*) chats with the press in his living room.

The Harry Byrd lunch: wooing him in the White House

The State of the Union address, January 8, 1964

President Lyndon Baines Johnson in charge

Robert Kennedy in mourning

coaching sessions in which Johnson was told not to wave his arms and bellow and talk too fast and who had, many times, watched Johnson try to follow that advice, and fail, telephoned Liz Carpenter to tell her he must follow it this time, that this was "the most important speech he would ever give," and that "he must not wave his arms from the rostrum of the House, he must not shout or speak too fast . . . and he must say the right things." Having worked with Johnson for a long time, Kilgore expected the response to such advice to be rage; instead, on Tuesday, Johnson invited him to the White House to review drafts of the speech, and also to ride in his limousine when he went to Capitol Hill to deliver it. (When he went to the White House that Tuesday, Kilgore didn't wear his customary pearl-gray Texas Stetson. The Texas image was more infuriating than ever to some people at that moment, he was to explain. "The worst service his friends could perform for Johnson would be to strut in and out of the White House wearing Stetson hats." And he told Johnson he wouldn't ride to the Capitol with him. "The best help he could give his old friend, he told the President, was to stay away from him in public. . . . The President must" not "convey the impression that his closest friends were conservative Texas politicians." He went to the speech in a taxi.)

JOHNSON KNEW SOME of what he wanted to say. Telling Busby on Sunday morning to begin drafting the speech, he mentioned a phrase Kennedy had used in his inaugural address; he wanted to play on that phrase. Also, on a notepad on his desk in 274, he had begun scrawling words among the doodles, and one of the words was "hate." "[Assassination] product of hate," he scribbled. "Get rid of Hate." And he knew who he wanted as the speech's principal drafter: the man he felt was the finest speechwriter of them all. When, on Saturday, he had asked Ted Sorensen to begin putting some thoughts together, the young Nebraskan had been too dazed with grief to respond, but when Johnson telephoned him again on Sunday, he agreed, because of his love for and loyalty to his dead leader—and to what he had stood for to "commit LBJ to carrying on Kennedy's program." Although drafts had been solicited from State and Treasury and from individuals like John Kenneth Galbraith, following Sorensen's agreement, all drafts were submitted to him, even Busby's; Sorensen gave them short shrift, except for one three-paragraph segment from Busby—the segment that made use of Kennedy's inaugural phrase—that was so good (and that dovetailed so perfectly with Sorensen's purposes) that it stayed in through every draft.

Sorensen's final draft was very much a tribute to Kennedy from Johnson; it included the line "I who cannot fill his shoes must occupy his desk." That sentence, not surprisingly, didn't survive, as was the case with the most extravagant of Sorensen's other tributes to Kennedy: "No man has ever done so much for so many in so little time," for example. Johnson liked the rest of the draft, although, feeling it needed what Abe Fortas called "a little corning up," he had Fortas and the master of corn, Hubert Humphrey, come to The Elms that evening.

After dinner Fortas, Humphrey and several other Johnson allies worked on the speech at the dining room table. While the corning was completed rather quickly, a fierce debate then erupted—over the emphasis to be given in the speech to civil rights. "A great issue was whether he would recommend congressional action" on rights, Fortas was to recall, "and, if so, whether he should put that as a number one item." Several of the men at the table said that pressing for passage of a civil rights bill would jeopardize the tax cut, and the appropriations bills, and would shatter Johnson's relationship with the southerners who had always been the base of his strength in Congress, and whose support he would need there now. The discussion had gone on, Fortas was to say, "for hours"— until about 2:30 in the morning—with Johnson sitting silently listening when, Fortas says, an "incident" occurred "which renewed my pride in him."

"One of the wise, practical people around the table" urged Johnson not to press for civil rights in his first speech, because there was no chance of passage, and a President shouldn't waste his power on lost causes—no matter how worthy the cause might be. "The presidency has only a certain amount of coinage to expend, and you oughtn't to expend it on this," he said.

"Well, what the hell's the presidency for?" Lyndon Johnson replied.

THEN THE SPEECH WAS FINISHED. It was sent off to the White House to be typed, in large type, and placed in the black loose-leaf notebook Johnson would take to Capitol Hill with him. The next morning, at about eleven o'clock, he closed the door to the Oval Office, and worked alone editing the speech. Moyers had "never seen him do [that] before."

His edits were small, but they added drama. The text in front of Lyndon Johnson included the phrase "the dream of education for our youth." Johnson changed it to "the dream of education for our *children.*" The text spoke of "the dream of jobs for all who seek them." "For all who seek them—*and need them,*" Johnson wrote in. The text urged the passage of Kennedy's tax bill "for which he fought." "For which he fought—*all this long year,*" Johnson added. It urged the passage of Kennedy's civil rights bill "for which he fought." "For which he fought *so long,*" Johnson added.

And the text wasn't being edited just for drama.

It was being edited—by this man who knew he had never been able to speak effectively before large audiences—to help him speak effectively this time, the most important time. To try to keep himself from rushing through it, blurring its meaning and its force—as, for thirty years, despite every effort, he had almost invariably done—he had it retyped in one-sentence paragraphs in an attempt to make himself pause between the sentences. Then, because he had used that device before and it hadn't worked, he reinforced it by writing in, in hand, between many paragraphs a reminder to himself: *"Pause."* And then, as if he was afraid that he would nevertheless still speak too fast, he wrote in *"Pause—*

Pause." Before a one-line paragraph he wrote in *"Pause Pause."* Then, after the paragraph, he wrote again, *"Pause Pause."* For thirty years, talking too fast, he had almost invariably rushed through key words he should have emphasized. When he finished editing this text, it was filled with underlining of words he wanted to emphasize.

Then he was in the car with Sorensen, O'Brien and Salinger, motorcycle outriders in front, Secret Service and staff cars behind, driving—fast—past a hundred flags flying at half-mast from the government fortresses along Pennsylvania Avenue, with above them, on the buildings' roofs, policemen with rifles outlined black against the sky; spectators, however, were "sparse," Tom Wicker noticed. "Even in the East Plaza of the Capitol, as he got out of his car, only a few people watched and applauded." Then he was standing in a corridor outside the House Chamber, behind Doorkeeper Fishbait Miller, and then the tall double doors swung open and Fishbait stepped through and announced, "Mr. Speaker— the President of the United States," and started to walk up the center aisle to the dais, and Johnson walked in behind him.

The Chamber, bright in the glare of television lights, was jammed—every seat taken, in the galleries above people jammed even on the steps in the aisles: in the presidential box, Lady Bird and his daughters; the family retainers, Zephyr and Sammy Wright; and the others he had placed there: Mayors Wagner and Daley and Governors Lawrence and Sanders and liberal symbol Schlesinger; in the press gallery, photographers elbowing each other for a better angle for their bulky cameras. Sitting in the front rows below the dais were the black-robed Supreme Court Justices, the bemedaled Joint Chiefs, ambassadors of foreign nations, and the Cabinet (Robert Kennedy, gaunt and wan, was sitting at the end of the Cabinet row, staring at the floor) as Johnson walked down the center aisle, his face set and unsmiling, and went up to the dais and opened the notebook for the speech on which so much depended.

"ALL I HAVE I would have given gladly not to be standing here today," he began.

The sentence was eloquent, sorrowful. A hush fell over the Chamber, the hush of hundreds of men and women so intent on a speaker's words that they barely moved.

"The greatest leader of our time has been struck down by the foulest deed of our time," he said. "Today John Fitzgerald Kennedy lives on in the immortal words and works that he left behind. He lives on in the mind and memories of mankind. He lives on in the hearts of his countrymen."

The next lines on the page in front of Lyndon Johnson were "No words are sad enough to express our sense of loss. No words are strong enough to express our determination to continue the forward thrust of America that he began." But the words as Johnson spoke them *did* express that sense and that determination—because of the way he spoke them: so slowly, with a deep, grave dignity behind them, that they seemed to reverberate across the rows of listeners before him and above him. He stood erect behind the rostrum, in dark blue suit and tie, a tall, strong figure, and there was an air of command in the way his big head turned from side to side as he spoke, taking in the Chamber, his dark eyes intense behind the rimless glasses. And when he spoke of "determination" and the need to thrust forward, so caught up was he in what he was saying that his head and shoulders thrust forward as if his entire body was pounding home the words, his eyes narrowing, his jaw jutting, and his lips tightening into a straight, grim line in an expression the senators below him remembered from another time: the expression of a Lyndon Johnson determined to win. The audience broke into applause.

He defined the dreams that Kennedy had "vitalized by his drive and by his dedication"—"The dream of conquering . . . space—the dream of partnership across the Atlantic—and across the Pacific as well—the dream of a Peace Corps . . . the dream of education for all of our children." He would carry on the fight for those dreams, he said: "now the ideas and the ideals which he so nobly represented must and will be translated into effective action." America "will keep its commitments from South Viet-Nam to West Berlin," he said.

And then he arrived at the paragraphs that picked up on Kennedy's inaugural phrase.

"On the 20th day of January, in 1961, John F. Kennedy told his countrymen that our national work would not be finished 'in the first one thousand days, nor in the life of this administration, nor even perhaps in our lifetime on this planet. But,' he said, 'let us begin.' "

Johnson paused, and there was the thrust of his head again and the narrowed eyes, narrowed almost into slits, and the stern hard mouth and the jaw jabbing out as he said, "Today, in this moment of new resolve, I would say to all my fellow Americans, let us continue.

"This is our challenge," Johnson said, "not to hesitate, not to pause, not to turn about and linger over this evil moment, but to continue on our course so that we may fulfill the destiny that history has set for us."

"Pause Pause," Johnson had written at that point. He would have had to do that anyway—because of the applause.

WHEN HE RESUMED, he said that "Our most immediate tasks are here on this Hill"—and then he told the senators and representatives before him what the first task was.

He had not, it now turned out, accepted the "wise, practical" advice tendered at The Elms. "First," he said, "no memorial oration or eulogy could more eloquently honor President Kennedy's memory than the earliest possible passage of the civil rights bill for which he fought so long. We have talked long enough in this country about equal rights. We have talked for one hundred years or more. It is time now to write the next chapter, and to write it in the books of law."

"Write it in the books of law." He had written civil rights into the books of law, written it twice, and his next words were a reminder of that. "I urge you again, as I did in 1957 and again in 1960, to enact a civil rights law." The legislation he had been forced to settle for then, in those years, had been inadequate, and he admitted that, urging the legislators before him to enact this time a law that would "eliminate from this Nation every trace of discrimination and oppression that is based upon race or color."

Later, in another speech, he would explain that if he hadn't been able to do more for civil rights before, the situation was different now. Referring to the brown-skinned children he had taught in Cotulla, he would say, "I never thought that I might have the chance to help the sons and daughters of those students . . . and people like them all over the country. But now I do have that chance. And I'll let you in on a secret. I mean to use it." Although he didn't make that personal explanation now, in this first speech, he nonetheless got the point across. Before he had finished with his sentences on civil rights, the House Chamber erupted in applause, the longest and loudest of his entire speech.

Not everyone was applauding, of course. Sitting in the second and third rows of seats, directly behind the Cabinet, since, as senior members of the Senate, they had led the procession of senators into the Chamber and had been seated first in the Senate section, were two rows of southern senators: Russell, Byrd, Eastland, Talmadge, Thurmond, and the rest, the men who had raised Lyndon Johnson to power in the Senate and had supported him for President, who had swallowed the 1957 and 1960 civil rights bills because (in addition, of course, to the fact that they were weak bills) of their belief that "he'd be with them forever," that the civil rights bills he had passed and the civil rights speeches he had made were merely gestures he had had to make because of his presidential aspirations, that "he was with us in his heart," and that the interests of the South—of segregation—could best be served by making him President. St. Augustine and Gettysburg had been, they believed, merely similar gestures, and they clung to that belief now. Herman Talmadge of Georgia, whom Johnson had spent "hours and hours" cultivating, who felt that Johnson viewed the relationship between whites and Negroes as "master and slave," Talmadge, whom Johnson had assured so earnestly "I'm one of you," felt that Johnson still was one of them; asked by the author of this book years later if his opinion had changed during that joint address on November 27, he replied, "Not then, no." As for Russell, monumental as was his racism, it was no more monumental than his patriotism; an aura surrounded the presidency, and the occupant of that office; Johnson had asked him the previous day to continue calling him "Lyndon"; Russell never again called him anything but "Mr. President." With Russell, what's more, there was something harder to define, more poignant, something that had to do with the small apartment Richard Russell lived in alone, and the long evenings where his only companions were his books, something that had to do with the companionship of the younger man, and the dinners after work ("You're gonna have to eat somewhere, you know") at the Johnsons', and the brunches with the gentle wife and the two girls who called him "Uncle Dick." And it had to do also with what it would mean to face the fact that he had raised to power a man who was committing himself to the destruction of the way of life he treasured. Nonetheless, they did not of course applaud, but while from those two rows, and from the clusters of southern representatives around the Chamber, there was no applause, these were islands of silence in a sea of cheers.

He went on to the other tasks. "Second, no act of ours could more fittingly continue the work of President Kennedy than the early passage of the tax bill for which he fought all this long year," he said. And, he said, there were "the pending education bills . . . the pending foreign aid bill . . . the remaining appropriation[s] bills."

These were the tasks of Congress, he told them. He was a child of Congress, he told them. "For 32 years Capitol Hill has been my home," he said. He knew the right words to use with Congress. He couldn't do what he had to do without their help, he told them. "An assassin's bullet has thrust upon me the awesome burden of the Presidency. I am here today to say I need your help; I cannot bear this burden alone." What was needed from them was action. "This Nation has experienced a profound shock, and in this critical moment, it is our duty, yours and mine, as the Government of the United States, to do away with uncertainty and doubt and delay, and to show that we are capable of decisive action; that from the brutal loss of our leader we will derive not weakness, but strength; that we can and will act and act now. . . . I firmly believe in the independence and the integrity of the legislative branch. And I promise you that I shall always respect this. It is deep in the marrow of my bones." But it was necessary for Congress to act, and to act quickly. "The need is here. The need is now. I ask your help."

There were words on hate. "The time has come for Americans of all races and creeds and political beliefs to understand and to respect one another. So let us put an end to the teaching and the preaching of hate and evil and violence." And then there were the final lines of the speech—from a song. He spoke them in a very soft voice, very slowly, with so much emotion that his voice seemed on the verge of breaking. No one listening to those last lines would recall that Lyndon Johnson was not an eloquent speaker.

"America, America, God shed His grace on thee," Lyndon Johnson said. "And crown thy good with brotherhood, from sea to shining sea."

Although the speech had been interrupted thirty-one times for applause, the applause had not come from everyone in the Chamber. Republicans had not applauded many of his points, and the southerners had applauded none that dealt with civil rights. But as Lyndon Johnson spoke those last words, and closed his notebook, and took off his glasses, the Chamber—to the last man and woman in it, it seemed—rose to its feet, and began clapping. And as Johnson walked off the dais, and back up the center aisle, the applause didn't stop. It didn't stop until he had left the Chamber. Yet it wasn't the applause that most forcefully struck some of the reporters watching the scene from the Press Gallery, but the tears. "Every-where you looked," Hugh Sidey said, "people were crying."

THE APPLAUSE WAS echoed in the press. Newspapers across the United States and, indeed, the world used "triumph" and synonyms for that word to describe the speech. "In the most important address of his life," Evans and Novak were to write, "Johnson achieved a *tour de force.*" And filled as it was with eloquent, memorable phrases—"All I have I would have given gladly"; "The greatest leader . . . the foulest deed"; "let us continue"; "I cannot bear this burden alone"—the power of Lyndon Johnson's first speech as President, his "Address Before a Joint Session of the Congress" on November 27, 1963, lay as much in the manner in which the words were delivered as in the words themselves: "It was," Wicker wrote in the *New York Times,* "the way the President spoke, the dramatic force of his delivery . . . that impressed a city long accustomed to think-ing of Mr. Johnson as flamboyant."

The awkward, bullying gesticulations—the upraised hand with the jabbing forefinger, the upraised arms with the clenched fists pounding the air—the off-putting delivery, alternating between ponderous and rushed, with shouting as the principal vocal means of emphasis, that had characterized Lyndon Johnson's for-mal speeches during his decades in public office were totally absent during the twenty-seven minutes he had spoken to Congress. During the entire speech, his hands had lain flat on the lectern, moving only to turn the pages of the notebook; "his only gesture," as the *Times* reported, "an occasional forward snap of his head to emphasize his points." There was no shouting. "Several times, his voice dropped almost to a whisper; at other times, it rang out challengingly," the *Times* said, but never in a "flamboyant" way. And no rushing: Rather, the *Washington Post* said, the speech's "most striking" aspect was its "delivery, slow, solemn, measured. . . . Missing totally were the excesses of speech so widely associated with his earlier career." The words used to describe him were unlike any words that had been used about him before; he had, the *Boston Herald* said, "demon-strated a sense of the grandeur of language that we did not think was one of his talents." A headline in the *New York Times* said, JOHNSON EMERGES GRAVE AND STRONG. Analyzing the speech's impact, the *Times*' Washington bureau chief, James Reston, wrote that "It would have been so easy in the emotion of the moment for him to have gone too far today, or, being deeply moved, to have choked on the lovely cry 'America, America' at the end. But he was both bold and restrained." Trying to find words to praise him adequately, Reston gave him what was for the columnist his highest compliment: "He sounded for all the world like Mr. Sam Rayburn today, ever so slow and serious, but with repressed emotion always behind the deep strong Texas voice." Sitting in the rows of con-gressmen looking up at the House dais, Joe Kilgore, who had been so worried, could, he says, "hardly believe" what he was seeing. "I had never seen him speak in public like this," he says. "Never." The discipline that Lyndon Johnson had imposed on himself within EOB 274—that he had imposed on himself for five days—had held firm in what was, for him, the most difficult setting of all.

Beyond merely avoiding the mistakes of the past, moreover, he had—for this one speech, at least—transformed himself into what the *New York Times* called "an orator," and a remarkable one.

The manner in which he spoke of his grief—the moving first line of the speech and the apparent sincerity and deep, solemn emotion with which he delivered it, together with the many lines thereafter in which he spoke of John Kennedy—accomplished what may have been the most difficult feat of all: to convince even men and women who, long familiar with Johnson and his ambitions as well as with his ostracism by the Kennedys, had not been disposed to accept his sincerity. Perhaps no columnist fell more completely into that category than Mary McGrory, but, she wrote, "No one doubted for a moment that he spoke nothing but the truth when he said, 'All I have I would have given gladly not to be standing here today.' No man, regardless of his ambition or his drive, would have wanted to stand in Lyndon Johnson's shoes on Wednesday." Said Doris Fleeson: "His grief was obvious for all to see." And his determination to continue, and to push toward enactment, Kennedy's policies had been convincing, too—because of the determination written on his face as well as in the pages of his notebook.

He had wanted the speech to reassure the country about its government, to give it confidence in the continuity and stability of the government's policies, to make it feel that policies would not be suddenly changed but would in fact continue unchanged. The speech had done that. "President Johnson has seized the New Frontier in an all-encompassing embrace under the slogan: Let us continue," Doris Fleeson wrote. And he had wanted it to reassure the country about himself, to give the nation confidence in him, to show a people that had not elected him to the presidency that he was competent to handle the job, to demonstrate to a country that was worried, uncertain, anxious for someone to "take the lead, to assume command, to provide direction," that it had someone to do that: a new leader to replace the old one. He had wanted to show the country that he was in charge—that he knew what to do, and that he would do it. And the speech had done that, too. It had not been merely the words—"The need is here. The need is now"; "We must act, and act now"—that had done it. It had been the determination with which the words were spoken—the determination and the air of command. The big head had swung slowly, deliberately, back and forth as he spoke, traversing the ranks of faces below him, with the same air with which he had once looked around the Senate, an air that had once moved a reporter who covered the Senate to say, "It was like he was saying, 'This is *my* turf,' " an air that made a watching nation feel not only that he knew what should be done, but that if Congress resisted he knew how to get Congress to do it—and *would* get Congress to do it. As Lyndon Johnson's narrowed eyes, tightened lips, and jutting jaw filled the television screen with fierce resolve, no one could doubt his willingness to act, and to triumph. "Across the nation and around the world," *Newsweek* said, "there was evident relief in the strength . . . he showed."

The speech reminded journalists and congressmen as well that in fact he *had,* for six years, gotten Congress to do it—had made the Senate act, and not only act but take the initiative in governmental action, as no other senator in American history had done. Johnson, Reston wrote the next day, is "something different in the Congressional mind" from Kennedy or Eisenhower or Truman. When he was Majority Leader, Reston wrote, "He ran the place, and without his special magic and cunning, his urgent energy, and his bag of tricks and treats, nothing has quite seemed to run as well on Capitol Hill since he left . . . [Johnson] is, to use his own inelegant phrase, 'a gut fighter' . . . and a parliamentary tactician with few equals. Congress did not always like him—often it hated him—but it never trifled with him."

In trying to illustrate his meaning, Reston found an apt quotation. It came from Woodrow Wilson, who wrote, "When you come into the presence of a leader of men, you know you have come into the presence of fire—that it is best not incautiously to touch that man—that there is something that makes it dangerous to cross him."

Congress was going to be a lot less willing to cross Lyndon Johnson than it had been to cross John Kennedy, Reston wrote. "President Kennedy had a way of seeing all sides of a question. . . . President Johnson has a way of concentrating on his own side of a question." When a congressman disagreed with him, Reston wrote, Johnson will say, " 'I know how you feel, but can I count on you?' . . . and when the thing is put that way, upstairs in the White House, with Lyndon's long arm on a man's shoulder, voting suddenly becomes slightly complicated."

The tragedy of Kennedy's death had changed Washington, Reston wrote. "He is very much on the memory and the conscience of the Congress. . . . [He] apparently had to die to create a sympathetic atmosphere for his program." And in Johnson there was a man who could take advantage of that atmosphere. Between the tragedy and Johnson's abilities, Reston wrote, "the mind and spirit of [Washington] have been transformed."

Making the triumph even more dramatic was the fact that it was so unexpected. After an entire career, three decades, spent anxiously but unsuccessfully attempting to overcome his faults as a speechmaker, Lyndon Johnson had, in the most important speech of his career, overcome them completely. A headline over David Lawrence's column summed it up: JOHNSON'S SPEECH: HE MET THE TEST.

Before the speech, during the five days since Ken O'Donnell had told him "He's gone," he had met other tests; thrust without warning into a crisis with potentiality for disaster, he had risen to the occasion—to every occasion. And now, on what may have been for him the toughest occasion of all, he had risen again.

The feeling of confidence, in his Administration and in him, was, furthermore, described by journalists who had known him for years in words—or rather, in *a* word—that demonstrated that it was not just a city but a man who had, during crucial days, a crucial moment in American history, been transformed.

To Chalmers Roberts of the *Washington Post,* watching from the Press Gallery, the man below him, whom he had known for so long, all at once had "established himself as the dominant personality in American life." Suddenly, Roberts wrote, below him "there stood Lyndon B. Johnson, President of the United States."

"President." The applause at the end of the speech was "for the tradition he had summoned and so well embodied, and for the dead President whose programs he had taken as his own," *Time* magazine said. But there was another reason for the applause as well, *Time* added: "The formidable and elusive Majority Leader of the United States Senate sounded like a President."

"Not a fluke of history," the *Herald Tribune* said, "but a President."

17

The Warren Commission

AND, AT LAST, he was in the President's office.

There hadn't even been an oval-shaped office in the White House until 1909, when one was built as part of William Howard Taft's expansion of the West Wing, and that one had been in a different part of the building. The room into which Johnson walked on Tuesday morning had been created only twenty-nine years earlier by Franklin Roosevelt, who in 1934 had the President's office moved to the West Wing's southeast corner, from which it was easier to roll in his wheelchair to his living quarters in the Mansion, and who, working with the architect Eric Gugler, designed the room himself. As soon as John Kennedy had left for Texas, it had been redecorated with a red carpet and red-trimmed white drapes, ordered, as a surprise for her husband, by Jackie Kennedy.

When Lyndon Johnson walked into the room at 8:50 a.m. Tuesday, two white couches were still standing in front of the fireplace at one end of the room, along with lamp tables and a coffee table with a telephone console on it at the room's other end, in front of three tall windows; the American and presidential flags still were standing behind a desk, a large, standard-issue government desk, bare except for another telephone console, that had been brought in the night before, along with Johnson's big leather desk chair, his own rocking chair, a side table and a couple of chairs to put in front of the desk. Colonel Roberts had had these items moved in on Monday night, along with a bust of Franklin Roosevelt that Johnson had told her to bring, and framed photographs of Lady Bird, Lynda, Lucy and John Kennedy. But Kennedy's rocking chair, the *Resolute* desk, the coconut shells and the ship models were gone, as were the naval paintings and the books. Noticing that there were not even any shades on the windows, Roberts had located a White House seamstress, and had had her run some up, and Roberts had carried over two vases, and put flowers in them, but without paint-ings on the walls or books on the shelves, there was nothing to soften the bare-ness of the long curving white walls, newly painted and gleaming, except for a lone pair of sconces.

• • •

THE ORNAMENTATION OF THE ROOM—an oval thirty-five feet, ten inches long and twenty-nine wide at its widest point, with a ceiling rising in a gentle arch from a cornice sixteen feet high—was restrained. The symbols of power in it— on the ceiling, in plaster, the presidential seal; above French doors classical pediments and representations of "fasces," bundles of bound rods with an ax protruding, that in ancient Rome symbolized a magistrate's authority—were muted, subtle, in low relief and painted to blend in with the ceiling and walls. The room was gracious and serene, the four doors leading out of it to other parts of the White House set flush into the walls, so that, closed, they didn't interrupt the walls' long, graceful curves, which were broken otherwise only by bookshelves set into them and topped by graceful seashell designs. Through the French doors one could glimpse a garden with a row of rosebushes along one side. Yet despite the restraint in its decoration, there was something about the room that made it seem special, somehow larger and more imposing than its dimensions, something dramatic, memorable—unforgettable, in fact.

Its shape had something to do with that. So rare in America were oval rooms that on entering this one you felt immediately that you were in a place that was out of the ordinary. And with the four doors set flush into its walls, those walls curve in an unbroken sweep, imposing, powerful; the shape of the room somehow imprints itself on the consciousness. From the time it was first built, newspapers and magazines started referring to it not simply as "the President's office" but, more often, as "the oval White House office" or "the President's oval office in the White House." The silence inside it had something to do with it, too. With the glass in the windows and French doors layered three inches thick, thick enough in 1963 to stop an assassin's bullet, few noises penetrated from outside; there is a particular intensity to the quietness in that oval room. And it is special because of the light that suffuses it. The artificial lighting set invisibly behind the cornice that rims the room is very bright, but artificial light is the least of it. At one end of the room, filling its southern curve, behind the President's desk, are three great windows, each eleven and a half feet tall. In its eastern wall are the three tall French doors. On clear days, the room was bathed in light, sunshine pouring in through all this glass in a flood of light so brilliant that, together with the expanse of white walls—during the twenty-nine years since the office had been built, the walls had always been white—it seemed as luminous and dramatic as a stage set. Because the room is an oval, furthermore, there are no corners in it, no shadows, no darker areas. Day or night, there was nothing to dim the brightness of the Oval Office of the White House.

But the room seemed special mostly because of what had happened in it.

History had happened in it. Franklin Roosevelt had sat at that desk in front of the flags and windows bantering with reporters as he guided a nation through a great depression and a great war; hidden below the desk, his paralyzed legs. Harry Truman had stood behind the desk to announce Japan's surrender, had later placed on it the plaque that said "The Buck Stops Here." Television had made the nation familiar with the setting—the President at the desk, flags flanking him—as a grim-faced Eisenhower announced in 1957 that he was sending troops into Little Rock or, smiling his wonderful smile, stood behind the desk, bantering with the press corps, or as Kennedy, sitting at the desk, told the nation about the missiles in Cuba, or leafed through papers while his little son peeked out of the desk's cubbyhole. The room had an aura of great events. And since the desks of all of the four Presidents who had occupied it—Roosevelt, Truman, Eisenhower, Kennedy—had been placed at one end of the oval in front of the tall windows and the tall flags, over three decades the setting had become emblematic of the presidency. So familiar was it becoming by November, 1963, thanks to Kennedy and television, that journalistic references to the office were changing, and, as with all things involving Kennedy and television, they were changing fast. The room was, in fact, well along the road to becoming simply the capitalized, iconic "Oval Office," perhaps the most famous room on earth.

THE AURA WASN'T misleading. In that room, history was just a button away. The telephone consoles on the desk and coffee table resembled ordinary telephone consoles, albeit with an unusually large number of buttons: twenty-seven. While twenty-five of the buttons were the customary transparent, whitish buttons of the ordinary console, two, however, were not. One was amber in color, the other red. Both were linked directly to the "war room" in the Pentagon and to the office of the Joint Chiefs of Staff. Both were linked also to an army switchboard, and through it to the Secretaries of Defense and State, to the directors of certain crucial government agencies, and to key members of the White House staff. And when a President pushed the red button, he would also be connected through the war room to Strategic Air Command bomber bases, to other military commanders, and to the heads of government of America's allies. When the red button was pushed, moreover, the President's telephone line would be scrambled electronically so that he could be understood only by men with a similar line on their desks. And on a late November day, like the day Lyndon Johnson took possession of the Oval Office, when the leaves were off the trees beyond the three tall windows, visible through the windows and the bare branches beyond was a reminder of history's ultimate prize, for beyond the windows and the branches was the great, shining white marble pillar, the Washington Monument, towering over the capital as a symbol of a President who achieved immortality, as a reminder of what the man behind the desk can become, of what the stakes are for him now, of the prize he can win in history's great game for which he has at last a seat at the table.

LYNDON JOHNSON HAD BEEN in that room many times before, of course, many times with Roosevelt as a young congressman, two or three times with Truman, often with Eisenhower, and then with Kennedy, but always on the other side of the desk. He wasn't on the other side now. Sitting down behind it, he telephoned the Senate offices to order the desk he had used in his Majority Leader's office delivered, and then directed his secretaries to start placing calls.

THAT FIRST DAY, and the next, were devoted mostly to preparing his Wednesday speech to the joint session, but there was a major problem he hadn't addressed, and on Thursday he turned his attention to the investigation into his predecessor's murder.

THE PROBLEM OF who was going to investigate the assassination, and the assassin's murder, had to be addressed, he knew—"The atmosphere was poisonous and had to be cleared"—for he was aware of the directions in which the poison might spread. "Russia was not immune," he was to write in his memoirs. "Neither was Cuba. Neither was the State of Texas. Neither was the new President of the United States." The rumors about Russian or Cuban involvement in a conspiracy, rumors being kept fresh every day with new reports, mostly false, of Oswald's connections to the two Communist countries, had "very dangerous implications," he felt, since "if they got a headstart"—if suspicions mounted that Khrushchev or Castro was responsible for Kennedy's death, or if, in Russia, fears about America's suspicions, and about the possibility that they might cause America to retaliate, created a feeling that perhaps Russia should move first—they contained the seeds of escalation, in an age in which escalation could mean annihilation. Jack Ruby had added fuel to the fire, he was to write. "With that single shot the outrage of a nation turned to skepticism and doubt"—to heightened fears of conspiracy, international or not, that further unsettled a country to which he was trying to bring a feeling of calm and stability.

Intensifying the sense of urgency was the fact that Congress was already busily circling around the bright lights in which any assassination investigation would be bathed. The House Un-American Activities Committee, which saw a Communist under every bush, had already announced it would hold an investigation, as had the Senate Judiciary Committee, chairman James Eastland, whose obsession with Communists might, in other circumstances, have been a joke: If the Mississippi River flooded, Johnson himself had said, Eastland would say "the niggers" had caused it, "helped out by Communists." "Vying for the limelight," as one account was to put it, other committees, in both the Senate and the House, were proposing their own investigations—investigations with their inevitable attendant television cameras, leaks, baseless speculation, half-truths and innuendo. More anxiety, more danger.

In his attempts before Thursday to deal with this problem, however, Johnson had shown none of the sure-footedness with which he had dealt with the other problems that had confronted him since November 22. To cut off the congressional publicity hunt ("a lot of television show," as he put it) in its infancy, he wanted the investigation carried out by some other entity, but his first suggestion, made, after consultation with Abe Fortas, on the evening of November 25, the day of Kennedy's funeral, was that the entity be either the Federal Bureau of Investigation, which of course was already investigating, or a special "Texas State Court of Inquiry," staffed only by Texans, that would be convened by the state's attorney general, Waggoner Carr.

There were legal, jurisdictional, rationales for his suggestion. The murder of a President, or of the President's murderer, was, under criminal justice law, no different from other murders; they were not federal but state crimes, and prosecutable only under state, not federal, law. And there were political rationales as well. Fortas was later to explain that he had advised Johnson against the formation of any special new national investigating body such as a presidential commission on the grounds that its formation would be counterproductive to the aim of tamping down suspicions of a broader conspiracy since "people would gather there was more to" the two murders "than appeared on the surface"; therefore, he said, "ordinary procedures"—like the Texas court of inquiry and the FBI investigation—should be followed. Fortas was also "leery" of having Johnson appoint the investigating body, since that might raise suspicions among those who believed the President himself might have had a role in the conspiracy. Personal, subjective considerations figured in the decision as well: the state with the legal authority to investigate the murders was Texas, *his* state, its name already blackened by November 22 and November 24. To turn over that authority to an outside body would, Johnson felt, be an admission of the state's lack of competence to conduct the investigation. The reaction to Fortas' suggestion was predictably unenthusiastic. Deputy Attorney General Katzenbach told Fortas it would be a "ghastly mistake"; explains one account, "Texas justice was so tainted that any purely state verdict on what happened would not be credible"; as for the FBI, liberals' distrust of that agency "would undermine the credibility of any report it issued"; only a special national commission composed of men of national prominence and respect, and endowed with broad investigating latitude, would command the necessary credibility.

Johnson's first responses to that reaction were ones that would have been expected from the pre–November 22 Lyndon Johnson: anger, a refusal to change his mind, and a secretive move designed to ensure that his solution would be the one adopted. He quietly gave Carr his approval of the state Court of Inquiry proposal—"Good idea, but purely a state matter. Can't say President asked for it," was the word Cliff Carter passed to the Texas attorney general—and after Kennedy's funeral on Monday, Carr announced its formation. So were his next responses. Learning that the *Washington Post* was planning to run an editorial on Tuesday calling for the creation of a national commission, he had Fortas telephone its two top editors to try to kill it, and he himself made three calls for the same purpose: to J. Edgar Hoover, asking him to use his contacts on the *Post* to explain that an investigation by a commission might expose FBI sources and methods; to the paper's publisher, Katharine Graham; and to *Post* columnist Joseph Alsop. During his conversation with Alsop, the calm cracked—for the first time in any call during this period that has been recorded, Johnson's voice rose as he railed against Bobby Kennedy's lawyers: "they thought of the blue-ribbon commission first at Justice. And we just can't have them lobbying against the President, when he makes these decisions." He was yelling into the phone as he said, "They lobbied *me* last night! . . . I spent the day on it. . . . I spent most of my day on this thing yesterday," and in describing the proposed commission he used the term that, to any Texan, was particularly pejorative. "We don't send in a bunch of carpetbaggers," he told Alsop. "It's the worst thing you could do right now. . . . We don't want to be in a position of saying we have come into a state . . . with some outsiders, and have told them that their integrity is no good, and that we're going to have some carpetbagger trials. . . . We can't haul off people from Dallas and try them in New York. It's their constitutional right." But while, after those calls, the *Post* did tone down its editorial—it no longer mentioned a presidential commission—it nonetheless still said that "No state or local inquiry will meet the situation, in view of the dreadful record of justice miscarried that already has been made," and that the inquiry must be prosecuted by "the Federal Government." And outside Texas, almost no one was buying the Texas Court of Inquiry proposal; the reaction of newspapers across the country to its formation was "generally scathing."

Two days later, Johnson reversed his course. On Friday, November 29, he created, by Executive Order No. 11130, a "Special President's Commission on the Assassination of President John F. Kennedy," a seven-member bipartisan body (five of its members, in fact, were Republicans), "to satisfy itself that the truth is known as far as it can be discovered," and to report its findings and conclusions to him, the American people and the world. His order gave the commission powers so broad that they superseded all other inquiries, including those by the FBI or any state agency.

IN FORMING HIS COMMISSION, Lyndon Johnson displayed another of the qualities that had made him, to men and women who had worked for him over the years, a figure who inspired not only fear and respect, but awe: his ability that had led to his reputation as "the greatest salesman one on one," to persuade someone to do something he didn't want to do—to do something, in fact, that the person had been determined not to do.

The purpose of the commission was to reassure the country, so he felt its members must be public figures whose very presence on it would be reassuring, "men," in his phrase, "known to be beyond pressure and above suspicion." When, in response to his request, Robert Kennedy suggested two names—former CIA director Allen Dulles and a longtime adviser to Presidents, John J. McCloy, both of them Republicans—Johnson made them two of the seven, along with three respected Capitol Hill figures, Senator John Sherman Cooper of Kentucky, a Republican, and, from the House, Democratic whip Hale Boggs of Louisiana and Republican Gerald R. Ford Jr. of Michigan, a young representative who had risen fast in the House hierarchy. But it was the two other men he wanted to appoint whose presence on the commission he considered indispensable.

Its chairman had to be not only a Republican, he was to say, but a Republican "whose judicial ability and fairness were unquestioned." Although he had only a passing acquaintance with Earl Warren, chief justice of the United States Supreme Court ("We had never spent ten minutes alone together"), "to me he was the personification of justice and fairness." As for the other man whose presence Johnson considered essential, he was less well known nationally than the chief justice, but to Capitol Hill Richard Russell personified, in every area but race, similar attributes, and if the commission's investigation and subsequent report should prove to be controversial, his unrivaled power there would be an effective means of keeping the controversy under control. Johnson may have been remembering, too, another investigation, one that had taken place at a time when America had been "as close to a state of national hysteria as it had ever been before in its history," a crisis that in its challenge to civilian authority over the military had threatened constitutional upheaval: the controversy that had erupted in 1951 over President Truman's firing of Douglas MacArthur. Johnson, then a junior senator, had observed how his seniors, even those most avid for publicity, had shrunk from the responsibility of chairing Senate hearings on MacArthur; had seen how, in a time of crisis, even though the Senate's militant liberals generally regarded Russell as the Enemy, "that did not prevent them from running to him for shelter." And Johnson had witnessed the results: how the calmness and patience with which Russell conducted months of hearings—a "firmness, fairness and dignity" that *Life* magazine said was "almost unmatched in recent Congressional history"—had taught the country that "things were more complicated than they had seemed," calming its passions in what one historian called "a demonstration of what the Senate at its best was capable of doing." The intervening twelve years had done nothing to diminish the reputation of the Georgia Giant; when, during their discussions of the executive order, Johnson told Fortas he wanted Russell on the commission, the lawyer, normally reserved, burst out, "Oh, I would too. *Yes sir.* I'd rather have him than most anybody for anything." He hadn't mentioned Russell's name himself, Fortas said, only "because I thought it would be foreordained."

A further consideration was that a President appointing a commission or committee to investigate a controversial issue wants to have an ally on it—someone he can trust, a member who will quietly keep him informed about the investigation's course and its findings, and about the conclusions of the report the panel is likely to issue, so that, if necessary, there can be intervention to effect an alteration in course or a change in emphasis in the report, a member who would be, in the political parlance of the day, the President's "man" on the panel.

Richard Russell, of course, would never be anyone's "man" on anything, yet he and Johnson had, over the years, quietly worked hand in glove on so many sensitive issues (and for similar aims: on most questions—almost all, really, that did not involve race—their views were very much alike) that the quiet rapport between them was an established element of their relationship; private discussions of the commission's work would be only normal for them.

Nor were these the only reasons he wanted Russell on the commission. There was only one head of the table at which the Southern Caucus met: wherever Richard Russell sat; the southern senators, so many of them powerful in their own right, looked to him for guidance on many issues, and followed his lead all but automatically. On racial issues—on the great civil rights fight to come— he and Russell would be unalterably opposed, but there would be other issues. The more of them on which he could make Russell an ally—strategizing and persuading together as they had in the past—the easier things would go for him in the Senate.

There was, however, a problem. Warren and Russell were both very strongminded men, and neither wanted to serve on a commission investigating the assassination. Indeed, each of them had made up his mind not to do so.

Warren had strongly held views about Supreme Court justices serving on what he called "extrajudicial bodies." No justice, he felt, should ever do so. Every time that precept had been violated, he felt, the results had been unfortunate. "The service of five justices" on the commission investigating the Hayes-Tilden election of 1876 had, he was to write, "demeaned" the Court; the appointment of Justice Owen Roberts as chairman of the presidential commission investigating Pearl Harbor—and the resulting criticism of that commission's report—had tarnished the Court's august image; and he had several other examples to prove his point. During his tenure as chief justice, in fact, the justices had discussed the question, and "I was sure that every member of the Court was of the opinion that such appointments were not in its best interest." The formation of a presidential commission now was undoubtedly necessary, he felt: to have several congressional investigations going on at once "would have been chaos." But he was not going to serve on it. When, at Johnson's request, Deputy Attorney General Katzenbach and Solicitor General Archibald Cox called on him in the Court at 2:30 in the afternoon of November 29, to sound him out about accepting the chairmanship, he "told them," he was to recall, that "I thought the President was wise in having such a commission, but that I was not available for service on it." He told the two men to tell the President that if he was asked to serve, he would refuse, and, he says, "I considered the matter closed."

As for Russell, one of his reasons—the emphysema that was draining his energy so that he worried, with reason, that he was not fulfilling his Senate responsibilities as he once had—was poignant. When Johnson telephoned him at his home in Winder that afternoon, and asked him to serve on the commission, Russell's reply was "Oh, no, no. Get somebody else now. I haven't got *time*." His health simply wouldn't permit him to assume any new duties, he said. Not being appointed would "save my *life, I declare.* I don't want to serve on that committee."

Johnson didn't press the point, because the call had other purposes: to conceal from Russell, at least for the moment, any connection between the commission on which he was being asked to serve and the two men whom Russell distrusted above all others in public life—one of whom, Robert Kennedy, Johnson had allowed to name two members of the commission, the other of whom, the man who had led the Warren Court to foist the *Brown* decision on the South, he wanted to be its chairman. The concealment required an outright falsehood. During the call, Russell asked Johnson, "Now you [are] going to let the Attorney General nominate someone, aren't you?" Johnson's reply was "No, uh-uh," although, of course, he not only had asked Robert Kennedy to nominate someone, but had already accepted both his nominees, Dulles and McCloy. On another point, there was, if not falsehood, indirection. During his conversation with Russell, Johnson had said to Moyers, "Bill, give me that list of people" he was considering so that he could read it to Russell "to get your reaction to it." But he read only six of the seven names on the list: he didn't read the seventh name, the one that in fact headed the list. Throughout the long, rambling call, Johnson never revealed that Warren was being actively considered for membership on the commission, let alone for its chairmanship: the closest he came was to say that for the seventh member he was considering "maybe somebody from the Supreme Court." At one point he dropped a hint, asking Russell, "Who would be the best one if I didn't get the Chief?" But his next words obscured it. He understood that "none of the Court" would want to serve because of the past history of justices in non-judicial roles, he said. And, he said, "that's why he's [Warren] against it now." And there were other words to obscure it. Since he didn't think any member of the Supreme Court would accept an appointment to the commission, he brought up the possibility of naming a judge from a lower court, even asking Russell's opinion of several. The call ended with Russell saying that he was sure Johnson could get "the name of some outstanding circuit court judge," and Johnson saying, "Okay. You be thinking." Russell, too, assumed his refusal had closed the matter.

But Lyndon Johnson never took no for an answer, and he wasn't going to take no now. As soon as he was informed of Warren's refusal to serve, he telephoned the chief justice and invited him to the Oval Office. Warren, a man of great determination, may have been determined not to serve, but when he arrived, as he was to recall, there were "only the two of us in the room." Lyndon Johnson had him one on one. The chief justice may have believed that there were no words that could move him, but Johnson found some. Reminding Warren that he had served in the Army during World War I, the President said he was sure that if he asked him to put on his uniform again, he would do it, "and you'd go fight if you thought you could save one American life."

It wasn't just one American life that might be involved now, Lyndon Johnson said. It was thirty-nine million. "If Khrushchev moved on us, he could kill 39 million in an hour," and "these wild people are charging Khrushchev killed Kennedy, and Castro killed Kennedy, and everybody else killed Kennedy," and if Khrushchev felt threatened because of what these rumors might cause America to do, he just might move on us. "And all I want you to do is look at the facts, and bring any other facts that you want in here and determine who killed the President," and end the rumors, Lyndon Johnson said. "But here I'm asking you to do something and you're saying *no,* when you could be speaking for 39 million people. Now I'm surprised that you, the Chief Justice of the United States, would turn me down."

Tears came to Warren's eyes, Johnson was to write in his memoirs. Warren does not confirm that in *his,* merely writing that he said, "Mr. President, if the situation is that serious, my personal views do not count. I will do it." Then, says Warren, "he thanked me, and I left the White House." It hadn't even taken that long—according to the White House log, twenty-two minutes at most. It's possible to make a sale quickly, even a very big sale, if the salesman is good enough.

THAT LEFT RUSSELL. Johnson had had to do a quick reading of Warren; he had had years to read Richard Brevard Russell, and he had read him all the way through. Russell may have thought his refusal to serve on the commission had ended the matter, but a few minutes after Johnson had put down the receiver at the end of his call to Winder, he picked it up again to call Everett Dirksen and tell him the names of the panel's members, and Russell was one of the names. "He didn't want to take it, but he will," Johnson said. "I'm going to *make* him do it." And he knew how to make him do it: he had Pierre Salinger type up, and hand to the White House press corps, a press release announcing the formation of the commission, and the names of the seven people he had appointed to it, and Russell's name was one of the seven.

He waited awhile, because he didn't want Russell to know about the announcement until newspapers had set it in type, and until presses were rolling with the next day's editions. Then, at 8:55 that evening, he had the White House operators put in another call to Winder.

When Richard Russell picked up the phone, he was in a good mood. When Johnson said, "Dick, I hate to bother you again, but—" he interrupted his caller to say in a friendly tone, "That's all right, Mr. President." But that mood didn't last long. "I wanted you to know that I'd made the announcement," Johnson said. "Announcement of what?" Russell asked in a puzzled tone. Johnson read him the text of the press release: "The members are Chief Justice Earl Warren, chairman; Senator Richard Russell, Georgia. . . ." Russell protested. "Well now, Mr. President, I . . . just can't serve on that commission. . . . I couldn't serve there with Chief Justice Warren. I don't like that man. . . . I don't have any confidence in him."

"Ah, Dick," Johnson said. "It's already been announced. . . . It's already done. It's been announced."

In an astonished tone of voice, Russell said, "You mean you've given that—"

"Yes, sir, I mean I gave it—I gave the announcement and it's already in the papers, and you're on it."

Russell didn't go quietly. "Mr. President, you ought to have told me you were going to name Warren," he said, and when Johnson said, "I told you! I told you *today* I was going to name the Chief Justice, when I called you," Russell refused to let that misrepresentation stand. "No, you did not!" he said. "You were talking about getting somebody on the Supreme Court. . . . You didn't tell me you were going to name him." But the arguments Johnson used on Russell—and their effect on Russell—showed how deeply he had read into the text.

He used the arguments he had used with Warren—in very much the same words, because Russell, too, had served in the armed forces: "We've got to take this out of the arena when they're testifying that Khrushchev and Castro did this and did that, and that—kicking us into a war that can kill 40 million Americans in an hour. And . . . you'd put on your uniform in a minute"—and when at first they proved less effective than they had with the chief justice, he appealed to the motivation that always worked most effectively with Russell: his patriotism and sense of duty, telling him that he might not want to serve with Warren, but "you can do anything for your country. And don't go to giving me that kind of stuff about you can't serve with anybody. You can do anything.

"You never turned your country down," Lyndon Johnson told Richard Russell. "This is not for *me,* this is your country."

There was, furthermore, a new tone, a tone of command, as if to remind Russell that it was not just Lyndon Johnson talking now but the President. When Russell continued to protest, the Texas twang rode over the Georgia drawl. "You're *my man* on that commission. And you are going to do it! And don't tell me what you can do and what you can't, because . . . I can't arrest you. And I'm not going to put the FBI on you. But you're goddamned sure going to serve, I'll tell you that!" And when Russell continued to balk—"I think you're sort of taking advantage of me, Mr. President"—the attack switched from the patriotic to the personal. "I'm gonna take a helluva lot of advantage of you, my friend, because you—you *made* me and I know it, and I don't ever forget. . . . I'll be taking advantage of you a good deal," Johnson said. "I'm a Russell protégé, and I don't forget my friends." The childless Russell was paternally fond of his nephew Robert E. Lee Russell Jr., and Johnson had, over the years, invested time in making a friend of Bobby Russell, and he brought his name in. "You are going to do what's right, and if you can't do it, you get that damned little Bobby up there, and let him twist your tail and put a cocklebur under it." There was a hint of the possibility of a federal appointment. "Where is he?" Johnson asked. "You just tell him to get ready, because I'm going to need him."

The conversation continued, for the senator received a much harder sell than the chief justice, and although there were signs that Russell was weakening, Johnson still didn't have him. "I don't know when I've been as unhappy about a thing as I am *this*"—"This is awful," Russell said. "I *can't* do it," he said. "I haven't got the *time.*" When Johnson said, "I don't want to beg you, by God, to serve," Russell replied, "I know, but this is a sort of rough one now."

It had been essential to stop the other investigations, Johnson said to Russell, and his use of Russell's name had done that. "Jim Eastland, he said this is the best thing that ever happened." Before Russell's name was invoked, "they had a full-scale investigation going, Dick, with the TV up there." He had had no choice but to appoint him, Lyndon Johnson said, and his voice dropped to the earnest deferential tone of a protégé talking to "the Old Master." How else could he have stopped the congressional circus that would have been so harmful to America, Lyndon Johnson asked Richard Russell. "How do I *stop* it? How do I *stop* it, Dick? Now don't tell me that I've worked all day and done wrong!"

And that last twist did the trick. "I didn't say you'd done wrong!" Richard Russell said. "If it is for the good of the country you know damned well I'll do it. And I'll do it for you, for that matter." And when, despite this remark, an instant later Russell was still expressing reservations so that Johnson still could not be certain that his acceptance was final, Johnson resumed the tone, reminding Russell of a very intimate—and significant—moment in their relationship.

"Dick," he said, "do you remember when you met me at the Carlton Hotel for breakfast in 1952? When we had breakfast there one morning, and I became Leader?"

"Yes, I think I do," Russell said. No one can be certain of what was said at the breakfast, but it had occurred on November 9, 1952, a week after the elections in which the Senate Democratic Leader, Ernest McFarland of Arizona, had lost his Senate seat.

Russell could have had the leadership for the asking, but as had always been the case, he didn't want it, and during that week he had several conversations with Johnson, who did, and in one of them, reported Evans and Novak, who interviewed both men that month, Russell suggested that Johnson should take the job, and Johnson's reply was that he would do so—on condition that Russell would change his desk in the Senate Chamber so that he would be sitting directly behind the Leader's desk; he needed Russell close to him, Johnson said, because he would be constantly asking for his guidance. Now, in this November, 1963, call, he was saying that he still needed Russell, that that was why he had appointed him to the commission. "Do you think I'm kidding you?" Lyndon Johnson asked.

Over the telephone line from Winder—heard clearly in the recording of this conversation—came a chuckle from the old senator, amused, fond. "No, I don't think you're kidding me," Richard Russell said.

And the bottom line was the ineluctable fact: the announcement of Russell's appointment to the commission had already been made, was already public knowledge—and therefore Russell's refusal to accept it would be not merely a quiet refusal but a public rejection of an assignment that the President considered important to the country, a slap in the President's face from a man who revered the institution of the presidency, and a public slap as well in the face of a man with whom he had worked for many years, and who was, indeed, his protégé, a slap in the face of a man with whose wife and family he had spent so much time. "If you hadn't announced it, I would absolutely" have refused it, Russell said, quite firmly. "Yes, I would." But Johnson's announcement had left him no choice, and he knew it. "I'm not going to say any more, Mr. President, because I'm at your command, and I'll do anything you want," he said. "I hope to God you'll be just a *little* bit more . . . deliberate and considerate next time. But this time, of course, if you've done this, I'm going to do it and go through with it, and say I think it's a wonderful idea."

"Well, you are damned sure going to be at my command—you are going to be at my command as long as I'm here," Johnson said, and, "worked up," "revved up" by this time, he didn't stop escalating his appeals even after Russell's surrender. "I don't give a damn if you have to serve with a *Republican,* if you have to serve with a *Communist,* if you have to serve with a *Negro,* if you have to serve with a *thug,* you're going to serve," he said, and then switched abruptly to the personal again. "No one has ever been more to me than you have, Dick—except my mother," he said. "I bothered you more and made you spend more hours with me telling me what was right and wrong than anybody except my mother." Was "mother" insufficient? A man had, after all, two parents. "I haven't got any daddy, and you're going to be it," he said. Richard Russell laughed—although the man who hated the "Warren Court" was now a member of the Warren Commission.

THE FORMATION of the commission was greeted with an overwhelming chorus of praise—for both its mandate and its membership. The huge headlines in the Republican *Herald Tribune* might have been written by Johnson himself: WARREN HEADS PRESIDENT'S PANEL, they said. ITS PURPOSE—TO REVEAL EVERY FACT.

The commission's membership "represents a broad power structure, cutting across party and executive lines," the *Herald Tribune* said. "It includes leading figures ranging from Mr. McCloy" to Ford, "a leading congressional Republican. . . . In Mr. Dulles, the President has selected one of the most famous intelligence experts in U.S. espionage history." And the inclusion of the two men Johnson considered key had the effect he wanted; almost immediately the body became known as the Warren Commission, and with the announcement that Russell was on the investigating panel, talk of other congressional investigations quickly died away. Although it had taken a few days for Johnson to understand that the Texas course on which he had originally been insisting was misdirected, when he did, he demonstrated on the new course the same sureness of touch he had been exhibiting in other areas. He had come to the presidency with an understanding of the need to build confidence, and of the need, as a crucial element in accomplishing that end, to end "skepticism and doubt" about the assassination, particularly because of the possibility—in that Cold War era—of doubts escalating into disaster. Far-fetched? No more so than a Balkan bullet leading to a world conflagration. And, with the appointment of the Warren Commission, he may have felt—and, for a time, the country felt—he had accomplished that end. The widespread praise for its creation was echoed, ten months later, by the reaction when it issued its report, which found that a single gunman, Oswald, was responsible for the assassination of John F. Kennedy, that no conspiracy was involved, either by the Soviet Union or Cuba or anyone else. Before the Warren Commission's report, only 29 percent of the American public had believed Oswald had acted alone; a poll taken shortly after the report's release showed that that percentage had risen to 87. That confidence would not last for long, in part because of the discovery of gaps in the commission's work, in part because of a flood of books—a flood that has continued to this day—that claimed to have discovered evidence of conspiracies, involving, among others, the CIA, the Mafia, and Lyndon Johnson himself. A House of Representatives Select Committee that was established in 1976 to restudy the assassination did little to resolve the controversies; its report, released in 1979, concluded that John Kennedy was probably assassinated as a result of a conspiracy, but while it ruled out the Soviet Union or Cuba as the origin of this conspiracy, it said it was unable to identify who had been involved in it. By 1983, 75 percent of Americans disbelieved the lone gunman theory, and felt a conspiracy was involved, and the percentage has held relatively steady in polls taken since. In no poll was there consensus about the conspiracy's origin or members; in a 2003 Gallup Poll 18 percent of Americans felt Lyndon Johnson was indeed involved. Since that time, more books, as well as television programs, have put that theory forward. However, as I've said earlier, nothing that I have found in my research leads me to believe that whatever the full story of the assassination may be, Lyndon Johnson had anything to do with it. At the time, the crucial weeks and months following the assassination, the formation of the commission accomplished its purpose. The fact that the crime was being investigated by a commission of men with reputations for integrity, that its chairman was a public figure with a uniquely high reputation for integrity, and that its report initially was greeted with respect, helped calm America's unease over the assassination of its President. The Warren Commission "brought us through a very critical time in our history," Lyndon Johnson would write in his memoirs. "I believe it is fair to say that the Commission was dispassionate and just." The second sentence in that statement would not, if evaluated at the time this book is published, enjoy universal acceptance. But the first sentence should. And the country had been brought through that "critical time"— that crisis in the national history, those initial days and weeks after the assassination in which anxiety about conspiracies could have escalated— because of Lyndon Johnson's decision to create the Warren Commission. It was a difficult decision for him to make. It went against his nature—against his desire, his need, for control, and for the secrecy which is a form of control—control and secrecy that he would have had had he insisted that the investigation into the assassination be made by a Texas court of inquiry that was under his thumb and by an FBI headed by a longtime ally. But he made that decision, sacrificed control and secrecy, and, moreover, turned over the investigation to a man he hardly knew and whose independence was already a legend, when, that Friday afternoon, he asked Earl Warren to come to the Oval Office. It was not his speech to Congress alone that had demonstrated, in these early days, that Lyndon Johnson was "not a fluke of history, but a President."

18

The Southern Strategy

THEN HE HAD to turn back to Capitol Hill—to Congress.

Much of Lyndon Johnson's accomplishment thus far in his presidency—creating an impression of continuity by holding the Kennedy men and of competence by his first speech—had been, while important, symbolic in nature. Dealing with Congress wouldn't be symbol but substance, indispensable substance, the very essence of governing in a democracy, for in dealing with Congress a President was dealing with a democracy's very heart: the creation of the laws by which it was governed.

The creation of the laws most needed if America were to fulfill the ideals on which it had been founded had proven to be very difficult for Presidents—for a very long time.

The stalemate between the White House and Capitol Hill had begun not a few years but a quarter of a century before, under not JFK but FDR, because it was Franklin Roosevelt who, in 1937, exuberant over his landslide re-election and with unprecedented Democratic majorities in Congress (seventy-six of the ninety-six senators, a fifty-six-seat plurality in the House), had attempted to pack the Supreme Court, and, in a titanic struggle with the Senate, had been defeated.

The defeat had repercussions beyond the Court. For almost a century before Roosevelt, the Senate, with its unbreakable filibuster and its six-year terms—staggered, moreover, so that public opinion could never touch more than one-third of the body at any one election—had stood like a mighty dam, towering and impregnable, against social-reform legislation, no matter how strong the tide of public opinion the legislation might have behind it. During the first term of his presidency, not just during its first hundred days but during the almost four years thereafter, Roosevelt had broken through the dam, stripping Congress of its power. The Court-packing proposal had brought together in opposition Republicans and conservative Democratic senators, particularly from southern and border states—and Roosevelt had thereby inadvertently handed the Senate back its power. For four years, uneasy though those senators had been over the New

Deal's agenda of social reform, they had been awed by Roosevelt's seemingly unchallengeable popularity into going along with it. Their victory over the President on Court-packing reminded Republicans and conservative Democrats of their strength if they stayed together, and made them realize also the similarity in their philosophies, uniting them against the New Deal, as an historian has written, "in a way they would have been completely incapable of achieving on their own."

Powerful in both houses of Congress, the new coalition was virtually invulnerable in the Senate, as Johnson had reminded his troika; Roosevelt's 1938 "purge" campaign against southern Democratic senators had resulted in nothing but defeats for the President. Year by year thereafter, for a quarter of a century, the power of the southern Democrats grew. Congress gave Roosevelt a free hand in running the Second World War; in domestic affairs, on the other hand, he never got a single major social reform bill through Congress during the eight years of his presidency remaining after the Court fight.*

The Fair Deal fared little better. Harry Truman's program was a far-reaching attempt to alleviate social and economic injustices in a nation which, rich though it was, had left most of its citizens unprotected against the ravages of old age and unemployment; a nation in which an inexcusably high percentage of the population—not Roosevelt's one-third of a nation, perhaps, but not much less—was still ill fed, ill clothed, and ill housed; a nation which denied to millions of its citizens, those whose skin was black, the most fundamental rights of citizens. After Capitol Hill gave Truman almost nothing of what he asked during the three and a half years in which he was filling out Roosevelt's term, and he made the "Do-Nothing Congress" the issue in the 1948 election campaign, and won a stunning victory in his own right, the new Democratic majority in Congress and a rising public outcry against Jim Crow gave liberals confidence that the long-awaited day of social justice was at last at hand. It wasn't. The election had changed nothing in the South; every southern senator who was up for re-election had won; in both House and Senate, key committee chairmanships, with their immense, all-but-unchallengeable authority, would still be held by southerners. The southern Democrat-Republican coalition was actually stronger than ever; the frustrated liberal senator Paul Douglas was to write of how it flaunted its power, "as when Harry F. Byrd and [Republican Leader] Robert A. Taft sat together on the floor checking the list of senators and sending out for the absent" or laying down the law to "the few recalcitrants." When Truman left office four years later, his only victories in civil rights had been the limited ones—most notably desegregation of the armed forces—that he had obtained by executive orders which did not require Capitol Hill's assent. As for the rest of his program, Congress had given him only a patch on the nation's needs. His proposals for

*This discussion of presidential-congressional relations is adapted, sometimes with direct quotes, from *Master of the Senate*.

national health insurance, for expanded unemployment insurance, for reduced taxes for the poor, for the expansion of federal aid to education—every one of those proposals died on Capitol Hill. And even those few victories which Congress allowed him—a meagre increase in the minimum wage, a small expansion of Social Security—would, thanks to Congress, prove even less meaningful than they had first appeared. Housing was an example. In 1949, more than ten million American families were still living in houses and apartments that didn't meet even the lowest standards for decent housing. Congress grudgingly enacted legislation authorizing construction of eight hundred thousand housing units, far fewer than Truman had asked for. But it didn't appropriate funds for the eight hundred thousand units in 1949—or during the rest of his term. The appropriation bills Congress passed were, in fact, so small that by 1955, six years later, only three hundred thousand units had been built, not even enough to keep up with the increase in population. The number of Americans living in substandard housing was still over ten million. As for the minimum wage, one increase, Congress had apparently decided, was plenty. In 1955, it still stood at a pathetically inadequate seventy-five cents an hour. During two years of Truman's term, the Senate was controlled by Republicans, but the identity of the party in power didn't matter. It was the southern-conservative coalition that mattered—and the southern-conservative coalition held firm. Bills that passed the House dashed themselves against the Senate dam—and died.

When during the 1950s the dam's gates swung briefly open at last, it wasn't the President, Dwight Eisenhower, who forced them open; the bolts were pulled back from within, by Lyndon Johnson, who as Senate Majority Leader from 1955 through 1960 not only won an increase in the minimum wage* but extended its coverage to millions of workers who hadn't been earning even that minimum, broke the housing impasse by raising appropriations to a level that would realize the goal set in the 1949 bill, and even accomplished what seemed impossible to accomplish: passage by the Senate of the first civil rights bill since Reconstruction.

No sooner had Johnson left the Majority Leader's desk than the gates swung shut again—more firmly than ever. While the stalemate hadn't begun under Kennedy, it had grown worse under Kennedy. The sure touch the young President demonstrated on foreign affairs (a sure touch amounting to diplomatic genius in the Cuban Missile Crisis), the programs—the Peace Corps, the Alliance for Progress, the nuclear test ban treaty—which embodied an idealism that was the best of America, the mastery he showed on the podium and in press conferences, the ability he displayed there to inspire a nation and rally it to its better, most humane impulses, did not, during the three years of his presidency that was all he was allowed, carry over to the implementation of those ideals in

---

*The brilliant legislative maneuvers by which Johnson won the minimum-wage increase are described in *Master of the Senate,* pages 609–12.

domestic reforms, did not integrate into American life the ideals he so movingly enunciated.

In 1961 and again in 1962, he had sent Congress health-care-reform legislation, including, most importantly, a proposal—"Medicare"—for health-care insurance for the elderly. The House Ways and Means Committee had not agreed until November, 1963, even to hold hearings on that proposal. In 1961 and again in 1962, he had sent Congress education legislation, to provide federal aid for college loans for students who otherwise couldn't afford college, for vocational training, and for urgently needed classroom construction for elementary and secondary schools and colleges. The construction bills had finally passed the House and Senate in November, but in versions so different that it appeared likely that any version which reported out—if in fact *any* version was reported out—by the conference committee would fail of passage. The other education proposals were stalled completely.

The few successes he had enjoyed in Congress—manpower-training legislation, a farm bill, increases in Social Security benefits and the minimum wage— were exceptions, and relatively minor ones. In 1961, Congress had passed his Area Redevelopment Program to provide aid for depressed areas. The program had been hailed as a major achievement. In 1963, Congress was asked to authorize funds that would enable the program to continue. It declined to do so. And his record on other legislation was even bleaker. Bills to create a Youth Conservation Corps and other programs to combat juvenile delinquency, to create a Cabinet-level Department of Urban Affairs, to provide funds for urban mass transit, to preserve natural resources—not one of these had been passed. Civil rights was only one of the logs caught in the jam. The bill that, along with civil rights, he considered most important—the tax cut bill that, saying, "Nothing should stand in its way," he had sent to Capitol Hill in January—was still lodged in Harry Byrd's Senate Finance Committee, with endless amendments still to be disposed of, and even a committee quorum apparently difficult to obtain. Of his major domestic legislative proposals—Medicare, federal aid to education, the tax cuts, civil rights—nearly three years into the administration of John F. Kennedy, not one had become law. Nor, in November, 1963, had his request for $4.5 billion in foreign aid been passed: it had already been whittled down to $3.6 billion by the Senate, and the House was just waiting to get its hands on the measure and reduce it further. When Lyndon Johnson became President, the deadlock in Congress that the press called a "logjam" had, except for its breakup during his majority leadership, lasted for twenty-six years.

DURING 1963, it wasn't merely major legislation that had become caught in the jam. Appropriations bills, too, weren't moving normally through the congressional machinery—hadn't been moving normally for months.

Each year, twelve appropriations measures had to be passed to pay the operating expenses of the government's departments and agencies, for under the Constitution no government agency can spend any federal money unless it has been appropriated by Congress. Although these bills were nothing more than routine "housekeeping" measures that simply provided the funds necessary to carry out decisions already made by Congress to appropriate, for example, money for public works projects like dams, reclamation projects that Congress had already authorized, traditional congressional inefficiency had often kept a few appropriations bills for each fiscal year—the government's fiscal year begins in the middle of the calendar year, on July 1, so the current bills were to pay expenses for the period July 1, 1963, through June 30, 1964—from being passed until late in each congressional session, sometimes at the very last minute before adjournment. Never, however, had so many of them not been passed this late. The twelve bills sent to Capitol Hill by the White House early in the year had been referred to each Chamber's appropriations committees. Four had been passed by both houses, but in different forms, and, although there seemed to be no major points at issue, were tied up in conference committees. Four had been passed by the House but not by the Senate. As a result, with eight bills not passed, eight departments had been limping along for months under "continuing resolutions," renewed and then re-renewed every month or so, which allowed them only to proceed with projects and programs already under way, but not to undertake any new ones, and which required them to hold their overall spending to the level of the previous fiscal year, and not spend at the higher levels that would have been authorized under Kennedy's proposed more liberal 1964 fiscal year appropriations. For almost half of 1963, July 1 through November, therefore, spending had been held to the previous year's level, and no new projects, not even ones that had been authorized by Congress, had been begun. The delay had already given conservatives a solid, measurable victory, by the measure that counted with them: a reduction in government spending, a lessening of the impact of the government they mistrusted. So long had the appropriations bills been delayed that even were they to be approved now, the eight departments would not have time to spend the money authorized in them: some $2 billion that would have been spent was, in effect, lost forever. "The longer these bills are delayed, the . . . less of a drain on the Treasury," explained the chairman of the House Appropriations Committee, Clarence Cannon of Missouri.

What was happening in 1963 had gone beyond the traditional. Never in history had so much of the federal government remained unfunded so late in the year. The general slowdown on Capitol Hill had also reached new levels, observers said. "This Congress has gone further than any other within memory to replace debate and decision by delay and stultification," Walter Lippmann wrote. Calling Congress "a scandal of drift and inefficiency," *Life* pointed out that it has "sat longer than any peacetime Congress in memory" without producing needed legislation; "the least productive Congress in memory," William Shannon called it. And there was no sign of the deadlock being broken. Education, health insurance, foreign aid, tax cut, civil rights bills—"everything" seemed "stalled, stalled completely" on Capitol Hill.

ALTHOUGH A FEW LONGTIME congressional observers had, during the very last days of the Kennedy Administration, begun to glimpse a pattern—a strategy— behind the delays in congressional, particularly senatorial, action on a wide variety of legislation, the explanations offered by most Washington commentators, and by senators like Dodd and Clark, still focused on the familiar villains: congressional inefficiency caused by absenteeism, "archaic rules," a seniority system which left the committee chairmanships in the hands of elderly men, or lack of leadership. If there was a unifying strategy behind the various delays, very few people were aware of it. But Lyndon Johnson, surveying the Capitol Hill battlefield for the first time as President, appears to have seen the pattern, and recognized it at a glance—as was understandable, since it was a strategy that during his very first months in the Senate, fourteen years before, he had helped carry out.

Public outcry for civil rights—for an end to Jim Crow—had been rising in 1949, too, in the wake of Truman's dramatic 1948 campaign, in which he had committed himself to that cause, and the Democratic recapture of Congress, which brought outspoken civil rights advocates like Paul Douglas and Hubert Humphrey to the Senate. Believers in social justice were confident that the Southern Caucus would no longer be able to stand in its way. Expressing a viewpoint found in many liberal journals after the election, the columnist Thomas L. Stokes wrote that "The President can get most of his program, and without so much compromise, if he constantly calls upon the great public support manifest for him in this election."

Richard Russell's public stance was an admission that the odds against the South were long. "It is clear that the only thing we can do now is gird our loins and shout the cry of centuries: 'The enemy comes: to our tents, O Israel!' " he said. Behind the Senate scenes, however, he wasn't bewailing the odds but shortening them.* He drew up a list of all federal laws that would expire during 1949 if they were not renewed by Congress to see, he quietly explained to his troops, "if there are any of them . . . that will build up a logjam . . . behind . . . the civil rights bills," and found one in particular that the Administration could not afford to have delayed. Unless Congress extended federal rent-control laws—the only protection against exorbitant rents for millions of families in northern cities— they would expire on March 31. And then he simply delayed the progress of the bills that would have extended rent-control (and the other expiring laws), by having them held in Senate committees controlled by southerners or delayed at some

---

*For a more detailed discussion of Russell's 1949 victory over civil rights, see *Master of the Senate,* pp. 215–18, from which this summary is adapted.

other point in the Senate process, while on the floor his southern senators conducted a filibuster—not on the civil rights bill itself but on the motion to bring the
civil rights bill to the floor. Should the South lose that battle, should cloture be
imposed to end the filibuster on the motion, he would still have another line of
defense, a filibuster against the bill itself, to fall back on.

Falling back, however, would not be necessary. As February became March
in 1949, editorialists thundered against the filibuster, and public demand for cloture rose, but somehow the votes for cloture were never there, and the focus was
shifting to the bills that were soon to expire, and the Senate Majority Leader,
Scott Lucas, calling the "logjam" in Senate business intolerable, warned that
"rent control would go out the window" if civil rights was not withdrawn from
the floor.

Withdrawal would be surrender: the only senators who could withdraw the
bill were the liberals who had introduced it. But many of the constituents of these
senators lived in northern cities. If they didn't withdraw civil rights—and rent
control therefore expired—their constituents would be the ones who were hurt.
The bill was withdrawn. The South had won—again. (The southern senators
knew who deserved the credit. "With less than 25 percent of the membership of
the Senate, the Southerners have won one of the most notable victories in our history," Harry Byrd said. "The credit goes mainly, of course, to our great leader,
Dick Russell. . . . I do not think that even Robert E. Lee . . .")

The newly elected Lyndon Johnson had been one of the senators who in
1949 sat around the oval table in Richard Russell's office as that strategy was laid
out, one of the soldiers who carried it out—one of the southern sentries stationed
in relays on the Senate floor "to see," in Russell's instructions, "that no legislative trickery is employed to secure the passage of any of these bills" ("Relative to
my 'guard duty,' I will do my best," Johnson assured him), one of the speakers in
the filibuster, the deliverer, on behalf of "We of the South," of a major, thirty-
five-page speech defending the right of unlimited debate that Russell called "one
of the ablest I have ever heard on the subject," and that moved southern senators
to line up at Johnson's desk to congratulate this fresh recruit to their cause.

RECOGNIZING THE STRATEGY—to defeat a civil rights bill by holding other
bills hostage until, to secure their release, the White House or liberal senators
agreed to withdraw it—Johnson recognized something else: that if something
were not done to counteract it, the strategy would succeed now, as it had succeeded not only in 1949 but at several other times in the past, because it enlisted
on the side of Russell's embattled southern minority in the Senate a reliable ally:
time.

Time had not been on the side of the great general to whom Russell was
continually being compared. When Lee, on the defensive in 1865 as Russell was
on the defensive now, was desperately improvising one maneuver after another

as Grant pressed him back and back, he had known in his heart that each strata-
gem was merely a delaying action that might postpone, but could not avert,
defeat. Time was on Russell's side, however. His battlefield was both sides of
Capitol Hill. Southern strategy in Senate and House was coordinated; explains
Strom Thurmond's administrative assistant, Harry Dent, "No one had had to say
anything, they [southern representatives and southern senators] had been doing it
so long. Things were understood without any words having to be spoken." But
the Senate, with its filibusters, was the last redoubt. And in the Senate, time—the
use of time, the use of delay while the days of the calendar drifted away—could,
if enlisted on the side of a cause, mean victory even if majority opinion among
the American people and majority opinion in the Senate itself, factors which in
theory meant victory in a democracy, were united on the other side.

For Lee, there had been no time limit to the war, no point at which, if he
could delay Grant until then, hold out until then, a final armistice would be
declared, so that the South would not lose. But in Congress—in the Senate that
was Russell's final redoubt—there was always a time limit, always a deadline,
always a point at which time would run out for supporters of civil rights if he
could just hold out until then: the end of each two-year Congress. A bill that has
not been passed at the end of a Congress dies, and must start over, from scratch,
in the next Congress: must be reintroduced, must negotiate again all the preliminary procedures in both houses, must be passed again by both houses. The effectiveness of the legendary Senate rules and precedents as traps in which, year
after year, decade after decade, hopes for social justice were ensnared and died
was in many crucial aspects a function not only of the gavel but of the clock and
the calendar. So long as a civil rights bill remained on the Senate floor, so long as
the southerners were filibustering it to prevent it from coming to a vote, they
could prevent any other bill from being brought to the floor—not a White House
bill essential to an Administration's program, not a bill essential to an individual
senator's political survival (for example, a bill he needed to get passed to satisfy
his constituents, bills to authorize a public works project, perhaps, or, if the project had already been authorized, to have funds appropriated for its construction,
in one of the twelve appropriations bills). So long as civil rights remained on the
floor, these bills would be held where they were, held hostage, imprisoned in
committee or on the Calendar, until the civil rights bill was removed from the
floor. Senators who might have supported civil rights, seeing time running short
at the end of a session, would become more amenable to dropping the civil rights
bill (only for this session, of course, they could rationalize; it could be brought
back in the next session).

A filibuster could be ended in only one of two ways. One was by a cloture
vote to end debate and force a vote on the bill. That method would be difficult—
very difficult. In 1963, sixty-seven votes, two-thirds of the Senate, were necessary to cut off debate so that a bill could be voted on; without such a vote a bill
could not be voted on, could not be passed, could not become law. In the history

of the Senate, there had never been enough votes to end a civil rights filibuster by cloture; since 1938 alone, there had been eleven such attempts, and every one had failed. And Johnson, in his brief time in the presidency, had already found there were still "not enough votes" for cloture. Or a filibuster could be ended if its sponsors voluntarily withdrew it from the floor, thereby surrendering by abandoning the bill and admitting defeat. And therefore as the end of a session grew closer, as time grew short, it would be not merely individual senators but the White House, with its vital major measures, like the tax cut and education bills (not to mention the appropriation bills), still being held hostage, that would begin to feel pressure to obtain their release by withdrawing the civil rights bill.

And Johnson recognized something else. Not only had the strategy already been implemented, it was already working. Even while Kennedy had been in Texas, the southerners had been reinforcing their lines. One of the eight unpassed appropriations bills, for example, was the measure that would fund the operating expenses of three departments—State, Justice and Commerce. Sent to Capitol Hill by the White House, like the other appropriations measures, early in the year, it had been passed by the House on June 18. Then it had been referred to the Senate Appropriations Committee, which referred it in turn to a subcommittee chaired by John McClellan of Arkansas, which referred it in turn to a subcommittee of McClellan's subcommittee—the "Department of Commerce and Certain Related Agencies Subcommittee of the Subcommittee on Departments of State, Justice and Commerce," as this final subcommittee was familiarly known—which was chaired by Spessard L. Holland of Florida, but with McClellan as its dominant member. McClellan was a tough, very shrewd, subtle legislator. During Johnson's days as Leader, a young staff member had once reported back to him on negotiations with McClellan that the staffer felt had gone well; "Unzip your fly and take a look," Johnson had told him. "There's nothing there." McClellan, he said, "just cut it off," with a razor so sharp "you didn't even notice it." During the five months since June 18, McClellan had never even hinted at any connection between the State-Justice-Commerce appropriations bill and the civil rights bill. He had simply found a number of projects unrelated to either measure with which to occupy himself: high-profile projects—an investigation of a possible scandal in a Defense Department award of a contract for the TFX fighter plane; televised hearings about the Mafia. "Everybody could see how busy McClellan had been," a Washington columnist, one of the few who glimpsed the strategy, was to note. "Nobody could prove that he was holding up an appropriations bill deliberately to slow down the legislative process and thus jam up the civil rights bill and other legislation"—like the tax cut bill—that "he didn't fancy." But the subcommittee of the subcommittee had been too busy to hold even a single hearing on the bill, and when, on November 21, an angry liberal, Joseph Clark of Pennsylvania, introduced a resolution on the Senate floor that would have taken the bill away from Appropriations and brought it to the floor for debate, vote and, hopefully, passage, the presiding officer had asked if there were any objections, and Richard Russell, sitting at his desk, had raised his arm, and said calmly, "I object." The two words meant that a vote would have to be taken first, not on Clark's resolution, but on Clark's motion to bring the resolution to the floor. There could be a debate on that motion—and the debate could continue as long as Russell's southern senators wanted it to continue; there could, in other words, be a filibuster against the motion to bring the resolution to the floor. And if the filibuster was, by some chance, ended and the resolution made it to the floor, there could be a debate on the resolution itself, and then a filibuster against any attempt to bring the debate to an end and actually vote on the bill.

The State-Justice-Commerce bill was just one of the eight appropriations bills that had not yet been released and reported to the floor by the Senate Appropriations Committee, which of course would act only after the bills had been reported back to it by its subcommittees. The Appropriations Committee was dominated by southerners and their allies, so each of the remaining bills was in the hands of a subcommittee dominated by the South, stacked deeply enough with southerners and their allies to ensure that in the unlikely event that a revolt should be mounted against a subcommittee chairman, it would have little chance of succeeding. And even if a bill was reported out by a subcommittee, it would still have to be voted on by the full twenty-seven-member committee, and the date of the vote would be whatever the committee's chairman, Carl Hayden of Arizona, staunch ally of the Southern Caucus, decided.

The stalemate on Capitol Hill was "unprecedented," the *Congressional Quarterly* said. A new continuing resolution had been proposed to provide funds until January 31 for the agencies affected. If it was approved, "it will be the first time in memory that Congress" has "been forced to provide for such a blanket carryover," the *Washington Post* noted. The appropriations backlog had, in fact, resulted in another situation which not even the oldest congressional observers could recall: an Administration was in the latter stages of drawing up the budget for the next fiscal year—in this case the budget that would cover the year beginning July 1, 1964, the budget about which the troika had conferred with Johnson—while Congress had not yet passed bills to make funds available for the current fiscal year. Nevertheless, a continuing resolution seemed the only choice; Russell's troops weren't budging, and neither were Republican conservatives, as they were pleased with the results of the delay. The GOP's Mundt (who sat on no fewer than six of the twelve Senate appropriations subcommittees) said that since "already too much money is being spent, and spent too rapidly, I am perfectly content to let the appropriations bills wait until next March."

And appropriations were just some of the bills that Congress had not sent on to the White House, and the list ran on beyond major measures like Kennedy's education bill. Bills before Russell's own Armed Services Committee had not moved at the anticipated pace; some were not moving at all. Bills were not the only problem. Nominations had been made a part of the strategy; the hearings on Kennedy nominees, for example, were droning on endlessly.

• • •

THE MOST IMPORTANT HOSTAGE being held to stop the civil rights bill was of course the tax cut bill.

Kennedy's pleas for passage of the tax legislation, now in its eleventh month before Congress, had been reiterated shortly before his departure for Texas. "This nation urgently needs [its] earliest possible passage," he had said on November 16. "Clearly no single step can be more important . . . as insurance against recession. . . . This is a good bill, and we need it now." In addition to Harry Byrd's other reasons for holding the tax bill in his Finance Committee, however, another reason was the civil rights bill.

No one understood better than he the horrific consequences that would follow the enactment of such a bill. The *Brown* decision had been bad enough. When a federal judge had issued a ruling to enforce it in Byrd's native Virginia, the senator had pointed out the dangers. Six-year-old children of both races were going to be "assembled in little huts before the bus comes, and the bus will then be packed like sardines," he said—and everyone knew what would come of that: "What our people most fear is that by this close intimate contact future generations will intermarry." Intermarriage! Miscegenation!—the "mongrel race" of which Dick Russell warned. Byrd had called for "massive resistance by the white people of this country" to all court rulings which might foster integration.

And now there had come upon the South this new civil rights bill. He was ready to do his part to stop it. He didn't let the fact that Kennedy's decision in June to send civil rights to Capitol Hill had played into the South's hands make its way into Washington or New York newspapers, but talking that June to a *Richmond Times-Dispatch* reporter who was an old friend, he let that fact slip, saying, as the reporter summarized his views, that "the new civil rights legislation from President Kennedy would bring on a Senate filibuster that . . . would probably delay hearings on the tax bill before the Senate Finance Committee." The tax bill hearings, in other words, would not be brought to an end; they would still be going on—the bill was not going to be freed from the Finance Committee—until the civil rights bill had been disposed of, either by being withdrawn or by being sufficiently weakened. That had been back in June. It was five months later now. The civil rights bill hadn't been disposed of—and Byrd was still holding his endless hearings on the tax bill, implementing Russell's strategy of delaying Administration bills in the Senate so that they would still be available as hostages against civil rights when the rights bill came over from the House. Kennedy had handed him a hostage, an extremely valuable hostage, and he was holding it fast. If the President wanted his tax cut bill, he was going to have to abandon or gut his civil rights bill. Other southern committee and subcommittee chairmen were doing their part, holding their own hostages. If you don't get your other bills "locked and key," Lyndon Johnson had warned, these other bills would be stalled. His advice had not been heeded. And the other bills were stalled.

• • •

AND NOT ONLY had the civil rights bill not yet reached the Senate, there was no indication of when it would.

The first step in the southern strategy of denying supporters of civil rights sufficient time to pass the bill in the Senate was to delay the moment at which the Senate could begin considering the bill—to delay, in other words, the time at which the bill came over from the House, to have Chairman Smith keep it bottled up in his House Rules Committee as long as possible, and Smith had already begun doing that.

On November 21, after a five-month-long battle in the House Judiciary Committee, the bill had finally been reported out—not to the House floor, but only to Smith's Rules Committee, since no bill can go to the House floor without an accompanying "rule" setting the length of debate and whether amendments to the bill can be offered. On the morning of November 22, at about the time Kennedy was speaking at the Chamber of Commerce breakfast in Fort Worth, House Speaker John McCormack was asking Smith when Rules might take up, and report out, the bill, so that the House could vote on it; Smith had said blandly that he didn't know. Not enough time remained to hold hearings before the Christmas recess, he said. The hearings would have to begin after Congress reconvened in January.

Trying to bargain with him, McCormack said that if Smith would agree to hold hearings before the recess, he in return would agree not to call the bill up for floor action until after Congress reconvened. Smith wasn't interested in bargaining. He told the Speaker he wouldn't agree to anything. He refused even to say when in January the hearings would begin, or how long they might last after they had begun. He would discuss that matter with members of his committee, he said, but he wouldn't begin those discussions until after Congress reconvened. When, on November 29, Johnson asked McCormack, "He won't give you a hearing of any kind [before the recess]?," McCormack's reply was a flat "No." "He was frank about it," McCormack said. "He won't do anything to help [the bill] along." Asked about his plans for the bill by the *Washington Post,* Smith was equally frank. "No plans," he replied. He would make plans in January, he said.

Smith's statement to McCormack—that he would not begin discussing the starting date and the duration of the Rules Committee hearings on the civil rights bill until after Congress reconvened—had ominous implications. If he had not agreed before the Christmas recess on a date for the beginning of the hearings, what would begin when Congress reconvened was not the hearings but only the discussions with committee members: the negotiations between Smith and liberal committee members over the date. And if Smith had not agreed before the recess on a date by which the hearings would end, that date as well would have to be negotiated in January. Negotiations with Judge Smith could be lengthy negotiations. The hearings themselves might not begin until quite some time after Congress had reconvened.

Understanding the strategy, Johnson explained it to people whose support he needed. "He [Smith] won't do one damned thing," he told Robert Anderson in a telephone call on November 30. "His idea, of course, is that he'll run it [the civil rights hearings] over until January. And then in January they'll be late coming back [getting back to work after the recess], and he'll piddle along and get it into February, and then maybe they won't get it out [of the full House] until March. And then in March, the Senate will be able to filibuster it until it goes home, and there'll be nothing done." Understanding it, he explained what had to be done to defeat it—to, for example, break the Rules Committee impasse immediately, before Christmas, 1963, since otherwise there would be little hope of passing civil rights by July, 1964.

"We're going to have to do it now," he told Katharine Graham in another call. "If we don't, they're going to start quitting here about the eighteenth of December, and they'll come back about the eighteenth of January. Then they'll have hearings in the Rules Committee until about the middle of March. And then they'll pass the bill and it will get over [to the Senate], and Dick Russell will say it's Easter and Lincoln's Birthday, and by the time he gets them [the civil rights bill], he will screw them to death, because he is so much smarter than they are." Understanding the strategy, Lyndon Johnson understood that it was working— both parts of it. The southern tactics were designed to prevent any progress on the civil rights bill until Congress reconvened in 1964—to keep the bill stalled during the three weeks remaining before the Christmas recess—and that's what the South was doing, at both ends of the Capitol. And it was far from clear that progress would be made in January; on the main battlefield, the Senate, Byrd's refusal to accelerate his pace meant that his hearings might not resume until Congress got down to business in mid-January; the amendments to the tax bill would still be before his committee then, still to be debated and voted upon, when the civil rights bill arrived in the Senate. The tax bill would still be imprisoned in committee, still available as a hostage.

And of course the civil rights bill wasn't even in the Senate yet—and there was no schedule to get it there. Chairman Smith was refusing to even discuss the Rules Committee's hearings on the bill. His tactic (in Johnson's words, to "run it over into January," to "piddle along and get it into February") was already under way. If civil rights wasn't moving through the congressional roadblocks before Christmas, the chances of its passing in July were slim.

And it wasn't moving.

MAKING OTHER CALLS that weekend, Johnson checked up on the most recent attempts to accelerate the tax bill's progress through the Finance Committee.

They hadn't succeeded. "If we don't have [Harry] Byrd" there was little hope of their succeeding, as Smathers told him on Saturday, November 30— "We'd need Harry Byrd." They didn't have Harry Byrd. The South was using the strategy that had worked for years. And it was working again. "To get the tax bill marked up it would be a miracle," Smathers said. Smathers was talking about a markup before Christmas, but an equally unequivocal statement about the Finance Committee situation made some years later by the committee's ranking majority member, second in power to Byrd, Russell Long of Louisiana, dealt with a longer time frame. "I couldn't move the bill out of committee," Long said. "He [Byrd] wasn't going to permit the bill to pass."

"Go around Harry Byrd?" Nobody was going to go around Harry Byrd. Even some of Kennedy's people had finally gotten the idea. "It was stalled. . . . The tax cut was stalled when Lyndon Johnson became President," Kennedy Budget director Kermit Gordon was to say. "Stalled completely," says Russell Long, the committee member with whom Kennedy's aides were working closely. The "two Virginians"—Byrd and Judge Smith—backed by the power of the Southern Caucus and directed by a master legislative strategist "had been thwarting Presidents almost, it seems, since time began," Richard Rovere wrote that November. It seemed clear that they would be able to do it again.

ONE SENATOR DID NOT share those feelings. "Smarter than they are" though Richard Russell may have been—smarter than his opponents in the Senate—it was not other senators who were Russell's real opponent now, but the new President, and Russell felt that fact would change everything. The Kennedy bills would be passed now, Russell told a friend. "He'll pass them, whereas Kennedy could never have passed them."

Lyndon Johnson, Russell felt, would even pass the bill against which Russell had been fighting, and winning, for thirty years. Discussing agricultural appropriations with Orville Freeman a few days after the assassination, Russell changed the subject and began talking about Lyndon Johnson. "He said that Lyndon Johnson was the most amazingly resourceful fellow, that he was a man who really understood power and how to use it," Freeman recalls. And then, Freeman recalls, Russell said, "That man will twist your arm off at the shoulder and beat your head in with it."

"You know," Russell said, "we could have beaten John Kennedy on civil rights, but not Lyndon Johnson." There was a pause. A man was perhaps contemplating the end of a way of life he cherished. He was perhaps contemplating the fact that he had played a large role—perhaps the largest role—in raising to power the man who was going to end that way of life. But when, a moment later, Richard Russell spoke again, it was only to repeat the remark. "We could have beaten Kennedy on civil rights, but we can't Lyndon."

19

"Old Harry"

SHORT AND SLIGHT, seventy-six-year-old Harry Flood Byrd walked softly (in recent years, as he grew older, in scuffed crepe-soled shoes and often with a cane), with a pigeon-toed, mincing gait, and talked softly, in a voice so whispery that his speeches could barely be heard in the high-ceilinged Senate Chamber in which he had sat for three decades. His manner, unvaryingly formal, with a graciousness that a friend described as "almost archaically elaborate," was mild and diffident, almost meek. His face, round, remarkably boyish, and very ruddy—since he owned the world's largest privately held apple orchards, generations of journalists had been unable to resist describing him as an "apple-cheeked apple-grower"—almost always bore a small but pleasant and friendly smile, and above the red cheeks shone a pair of blue eyes so bright they were continually being described as "twinkling." It might have been the face of a benevolent if aging cherub—if behind those twinkling eyes there had not been hatreds, hatreds so intense that sometimes they broke through the courtly façade; once, unable to restrain his rage when he saw NAACP President Roy Wilkins and lobbyist Clarence Mitchell, both black men, sitting in the gallery, he shook his fist at them, and in a voice quite loud enough to be heard throughout the Chamber, insulted them by likening them to Goldy and Dusty, the fictitious black twins whose ignorance and laziness enlivened a weekly radio comedy, shouting, "There they are—the Gold Dust twins!" His other hatred, an abhorrence of deficits, of big government and big government spending, was scarcely less intense; a biographer wrote of "his extreme obsessive hatred of debt, his dogged fixation on economy." Looking over the dollar numbers attached to some proposed new government program, he would jab his fingers into the offending figures; his voice would generally remain soft and courtly at such moments, but the red face would grow redder still. It might have been the face of an aging cherub had it not been for the way Harry Byrd—the man his Senate colleagues fondly called "Old Harry" or "Old Man Harry"—wielded power in the two domains over which he ruled: his state and the Senate Finance Committee.

"The name Byrd has been written across all the pages of Virginia's history" since William Byrd I sailed up the James River in 1674 to found what became, with the help of generations of slaves, a vast tobacco plantation, one chronicler wrote; among the other Byrds in the fourteen generations that followed were a captain in George Washington's army, a colonel in Robert E. Lee's, and a speaker of the Virginia General Assembly; as Richard Russell was a Russell of the Russells of Georgia, Harry Byrd was a Byrd of the Byrds of Virginia. And since becoming governor in 1926, he had written his own pages in that history, with a statewide political machine known simply as "the Organization." "The Byrd Machine is genteel," the liberal *Reporter* magazine had to admit. "There are no gallus-snapping or banjo-playing characters in Virginia politics." Its hallmark was courtliness, not the demagoguery prevalent in other southern states. "Virginia breeds no Huey Longs or Talmadges," John Gunther wrote in *Inside U.S.A.* "The Byrd Machine is the most urbane and genteel dictatorship in America." But a dictatorship it was. Candidates for office—almost any office, from state legislator down to local school board trustee—would, if the senator approved of them, receive an endorsement known as the "nod." Without the Byrd nod, it was all but impossible to win an election in Virginia. The state's last nine governors had all received the nod. As had, of course, Howard Smith of the House Rules Committee. And candidates who tried to win without it encountered tactics that had earned the Organization a different nickname: "the Steamroller." The Organization (or Steamroller) "runs the commonwealth as effectively as Prendergast ever ran Kansas City . . . though with much less noise," Gunther observed. "Because of its control over practically every office, no matter how minor, it is quite possibly the single most powerful machine surviving in the whole United States." Gunther had written that in 1947. Times might change—*had* changed, in some respects, since 1947. Virginia's demographic makeup had become dramatically more urban and African-American as the District of Columbia's suburbs spread into the state. But in 1963, the Organization, unchanged, was as powerful as ever. Voting by the newcomers hadn't altered the pattern of politics in the state, because, in general, the newcomers couldn't vote. Virginia's efficiency—Byrd's efficiency—in the use of the poll tax to restrict voting by the black people he hated was a model for the tactic. In the state's last gubernatorial election, in 1961, only 17 percent of Virginia's voting-age population had cast ballots. A very wealthy man, Harry Byrd lived in a colonnaded mansion, Rosemont, that, as one writer admiringly put it, "surmounts the nearby town of Berryville like a manor house over an English village," like "the seat of an all-powerful country squire." And that was still, well into his fourth decade of power, the way Harry Byrd—courtly, gracious, mild mannered—towered over Virginia politics. "The apparent invincibility of the organization makes it seem useless for the dissatisfied to oppose it," the *Reporter* said.

In his committee—"Senate Finance," as it was known on Capitol Hill—the same was true. No chairman could have been more considerate, more polite, to the committee members. Members were given all the time they required to be heard in committee sessions; these were senators, Old Harry would say; they shouldn't be cut off. The sincerity of his beliefs combined with the courtesy with which he fought for them won him the respect, and indeed affection, of opponents, even of Paul Douglas, not only a fervent liberal—the most liberal member of Byrd's committee—but an economist by training, the author of influential books espousing liberal economic policy. "He hated public debt with a holy passion," Douglas was to write of Byrd. "With little or no sympathy for poor people, and instinctively on the side of the rich and powerful, of whom he was one, he nevertheless had a certain rugged personal honesty and a genial air of courtesy toward his opponents, except when severely pressed. . . . I developed a real respect for him."

While he ran the committee graciously, however, he ran it unyieldingly. "He had a habit of slapping" a fellow senator on the back and laughing, "as if they were both enjoying a good joke," while he was denying a request, recalls the Republican committee member Norris Cotton of New Hampshire, and he did it when Cotton asked him for a hearing on a bill he had introduced. "He continued to pat me on the shoulder, and to laugh, but he said, 'Sorry, boy, you can't have a hearing on it.' " Cotton repeated the request several times, saying it would be embarrassing for him to have to tell constituents he couldn't get "even a hearing," but Byrd simply repeated the refusal each time. "Then, with a final hearty laugh and slap on the back, he ushered me out."

His economic philosophy was a businessman's philosophy. No one ever called him a reader or a particularly deep thinker, or even a man with more than a surface understanding of the field—the fiscal and tax policy of the United States—in which Senate Finance played so significant a role. He was, he often said, "blind to charts," on which economists rely so heavily. He couldn't understand them, he said; as a member of his committee was to recall, "he said . . . if you wanted to convince him you had to present it so he could understand it, and he could understand a column of figures." The figure that was important to him was the bottom line: one that showed a profit, or, in the case of government, a surplus, not a deficit. The "deceptively apple-cheeked apple-grower" had a "frank pleasure in the arts of business," the *Saturday Evening Post* noted; government, he believed, must be run like one, with debt kept to a minimum and the federal budget as firmly balanced as the ledgers of a successful corporation.

And if Harry Byrd's story was a businessman's story, it was the story of a very tough, and very shrewd, businessman. In 1902, his father, having lost what remained of the Byrd money, all but bankrupt and about to lose the local newspaper that was the last thing he owned, agreed to turn it over to fifteen-year-old Harry, who dropped out of school—he was to have no further formal education. He struggled for ten years to make the newspaper succeed under the load of debt that had been placed on it; since its credit had been cut off, he had to raise six dollars a day in nickels, dimes and quarters to pay, cash on delivery, for the newsprint on which the next day's paper would be printed. "When you have to hunt for them that way, you get to know how many cents there really are in a dollar," he was to say.

With the newspaper at last in the black, he turned to apples, first spraying orchards, then leasing them, saving every penny so he could begin buying them, working endless hours year after year, until his orchards, which produced a million bushels a year, stretched for miles across the Shenandoah Valley. Only then did he go into politics, running for governor.

Feeling, as a friend wrote, that "debt had robbed him of his youth and education," the "characteristic that distinguished him above anything else [was]" that "extreme obsessive hatred of debt," his "fixation" on frugality. The words he used on the subject had an almost religious intensity. "Improvident political promises and programs are sinful," he said once. "They are perpetrated on innocent citizens by demagogues." He said that "The American dollar is the only thing today that is holding the world together," and "Once the American dollar goes down, we will go into an age of international darkness." The role he could play in defending economy in government, in balancing the budget, was, to him, another friend said, "almost a sacred duty."

He "would have no truck with Keynesian theories," recalls Douglas Dillon, who as secretary of the Treasury dealt with the senator more frequently than any other member of the Kennedy Administration. Franklin Roosevelt had been all right for a while, Byrd was to say; the two governors had become personal friends; he had been an early supporter, the finance chairman, in fact, for FDR's first presidential campaign; "then this fellow Keynes got ahold of him." He liked to boast that "I am the only man left in the Senate who voted against the Wagner Act and the TVA." When President Kennedy, arguing that tax cuts would stimulate the economy and that the concept of a balanced budget was an outdated and "misleading . . . mythology," called, in one of his typically eloquent speeches, for "new words, new phrases" in economic theory, Byrd had been moved to make a speech of his own—in the old words and phrases. The "illusions," he said, were the ideas that budgets did not have to be balanced, that debt was not evil. No one who witnessed his frustration and genuine indignation at government's indifference to the old verities could doubt their depth. Jabbing his finger at a sheet of statistics on his desk, one day in 1962, he said, "The civilian employment in government went up 35,000 in just the last month." The red face turned redder with anger. Again and again the finger jabbed the paper. "Just think of that—35,000 in the last month."

BELIEVING THAT THE SIZE and cost of government should be reduced, that new government programs might be a menace to the American dollar, Byrd, Russell Long says, "measured his success as a senator not by what he passed, but what he stopped from passing." And at the moment, when the issue before the Finance Committee was the Kennedy tax bill, he was being quite successful.

His use of his powers as chairman—the virtually limitless powers of a chairman of one of the Senate's fifteen great Standing Committees, powers that, as was explained in the last volume, were almost never overruled—was of course not confrontational. "Senator Byrd was a gentleman of the old school, essentially a country gentleman," Dillon says. "Always most courteous in his relations with me and others." When, back in February and March, Kennedy had asked the senator to begin Finance Committee hearings on the tax bill without waiting for the House to pass the measure, all he had done was to explain that doing that would violate Senate procedure. "The old man won't begin [hearings on] the bill until it's sent over [from the House]," one senator said. "He's a stickler on this. Of course, one of the reasons for this is that he's opposed to doing anything anyway." When, in October, the hearings finally began, they moved very slowly, of course. Testimony thus far—in the hearings' sixth week—had all been on general topics; the committee had not yet taken up any of the individual amendments submitted by committee members. There were going to be quite a few individual amendments. The chairman had let it be known that members could submit as many of these "special provisions important to them" as they wished. Thirty had been submitted already—and more were coming all the time. And the chairman had let it be known that he understood how important these special provisions were to their sponsors, and that members would be allowed ample time to discuss them. On some days, there were no hearings. ("He couldn't get a quorum, he said.") To objections that Finance was hearing the same witnesses, and the same testimony, that the House had heard for months on end, Byrd said that senators had to have the opportunity to hear these views for themselves, had to be able to question witnesses themselves, had to have all the time they needed to express their own views on the testimony. He wouldn't even consider cutting off a United States senator. In dealing with the President's men, and with the President himself, he was unfailingly courteous, responding to each suggestion for speeding up the committee's work with some new, technical reason why it couldn't be speeded up, and unfailingly impossible to pin down. Doodling on a pad during one discussion, Kennedy had written: "Pillow fight in the dark with Harry Byrd."

Some of the Kennedy team did not seem to grasp the reality of what was happening. While describing Byrd's control of his committee as "absolute" ("nothing could be done that he [Byrd] opposed"), Dillon also says that although Byrd did not work actively to pass the Kennedy tax reduction bills, "he did not oppose them"—a statement that indicates the same lack of understanding of Byrd's tactics as the Treasury secretary had displayed about Byrd's mild suggestion that he would like to see the budget come in under $100 billion. He "*did not oppose them*"—that was true; all he was doing was delaying them. A "sweet dear guy—loved him," says the more realistic Russell Long, but "if he didn't want something to happen it usually didn't and vice versa. . . . Bills didn't move until he decided they would move."

No challenge from within the seventeen-member committee could threaten him. The Democratic Steering Committee, which appointed Democratic senators to committees, was dominated by southerners, and made sure that there was always a comfortable majority among his party's members of Finance of whose support Byrd could be certain; on the Republican side, the ranking member was Delaware's Williams, a close personal friend of Byrd and a fellow rock-hard fiscal conservative, and in general all seven Republican committee members were conservatives and behind the chairman; in 1963, in the event of a challenge to his authority, Byrd could count on the seven Republican votes and, on the Democratic side, in addition to his own vote, of five of the nine other Democrats—in all, a comfortable majority indeed. And, of course, behind him also was the interlocking power of the southern chairmen, and of the chairmen who stood with the South; seldom was that power (and its consequence for a senator who opposed a chairman) expressed as bluntly as it was on one occasion to Illinois' Douglas, who was opposing pork-barrel spending bills in several committees. He was informed that unless he stopped he would find "all public works projects for Illinois removed from" bills before Hayden's Appropriations Committee. Bluntness was not usually required, however. A senator who opposed Harry Byrd would simply find that a bill he had introduced—perhaps a bill he urgently needed to satisfy constituents without whose support he could not be re-elected—that was before Richard Russell's Armed Services Committee, or A. Willis Robertson's Banking Committee, or John McClellan's Government Operations Committee, or James Eastland's Judiciary Committee, or Allen Ellender's Agriculture Committee, or Lister Hill's Labor Committee, was simply not moving ahead within the committee process. He would eventually get the idea. Four Finance Democrats—Douglas, Gore, Hartke and Ribicoff—generally opposed Byrd. But they were four among seventeen.

And no challenge from outside the committee could threaten him, either.

Three Presidents had tried a challenge, each apparently believing that since Byrd's philosophy was so out of touch with that of the country at large, he was vulnerable, and that a President could exploit that vulnerability.

After Byrd had broken with him before the 1934 election, Roosevelt began funneling federal patronage through Byrd's political foes in Virginia. Byrd won re-election by forty thousand votes. And when Roosevelt tried another tactic, nominating a federal judge unacceptable to Byrd and to Virginia's other senator, Carter Glass, the vote against the nomination in the Senate was 72 to 9, the most one-sided vote in Senate history against a presidential nominee. Truman's attacks on him in 1952, Byrd said, had "actually helped me get re-elected." Kennedy had tried a different route, trying to go around Byrd by creating an alliance with Robert Kerr, then the Finance Committee's ranking Democratic member, and a Senate power himself, as part of which Kerr would have taken *de facto* control of the committee. While some members of the Washington press corps thought that the threat to Byrd's power was real, it never came even close to a showdown—Kerr, as Dillon noted, "always recognized the position of the chairman and worked with his approval and never against him"—before Kerr's death in January, 1963. Out of step with majority opinion in America though Byrd's philosophy may have been, it was what the residents of his state—or at least those residents who managed to vote—wanted. Every presidential attempt to challenge his power in Virginia had only strengthened that power. Harry Byrd's Finance Committee was a feudal barony within the governmental system of the United States. He was one of the mighty chairmen who ran their committees as independent fiefdoms—and who were, in effect, although it was never written about in those terms, in alliance against the President, an alliance, now a quarter of a century old, that no President had been able to break.

Two days before Kennedy had left for Texas, the *Washington Post*'s longtime Capitol Hill correspondent, Chalmers Roberts, had written that "probably" Byrd "has never been more powerful than he is today. . . . Right now he is all-powerful." *"Go around Harry Byrd,"* as the Kennedy legislative aides kept so blithely suggesting? Smathers wasn't the only senator who understood the impracticality of that suggestion. Johnson men, of course, had learned the lesson from Johnson. "You *couldn't* go around Harry Byrd," Horace Busby says.

DURING HIS YEARS in the Senate, Lyndon Johnson had spent a lot of time reading Harry Byrd.

At first, the book had been closed to him. During the first three of his Senate years, Byrd's attitude toward him had been so reserved that it sometimes seemed to border on dislike. Johnson had, nonetheless, never stopped trying to open the book, hadn't stopped "doing *everything*" to open it. Early in 1952, as was related in the last volume, Byrd's beloved thirty-five-year-old daughter, Westwood, died after a fall from her horse during a fox hunt. Rosemont was a two-hour drive from Washington, and heavy rain was falling on the day of the funeral. No other senators were planning to attend the services, but Johnson did, managing at the last minute to persuade another young senator, Warren Magnuson, to accompany him so he wouldn't be alone. And, Johnson told Busby later that day, as he and Magnuson stood in the rain across the grave from the Byrd family, holding their hats in their hands, the only senators present, Byrd suddenly looked up and saw them. "He looked at us, and then he looked back at me," Johnson told Busby. "I don't know what that look meant, but I'll bet . . . that was a very important look."

It was. Byrd's administrative aide John (Jake) Carlton told Johnson that he was welcome to drop around to Byrd's office when he had a problem he wanted to discuss. And Johnson used the privilege he had been given to make the impression he wanted to make on the courtly Virginian. He would always telephone ahead to Carlton for an appointment, but when he arrived at the office, even if Carlton said the senator was free and was expecting him and he could go right in, he wouldn't do so, "wouldn't walk right in even if I motioned to him that he could." Instead, to emphasize that he wouldn't even think of barging in, "he would wait until I got up and opened the door—so the Senator [Byrd] would know that he was going in only after I had opened the door." And once Johnson had the text open in his hands, he grasped and made use of the meanings he found within it. While Byrd's patrician aloofness made him unwilling to stoop to asking other senators how they were planning to vote, for example, he was nonetheless anxious to know what the vote would be on one of the tax or budget proposals about which he cared so deeply. After Johnson realized this, Byrd began getting this information without having to ask; Johnson, it was observed, "counted for him," having Bobby Baker do the asking and then relaying Baker's findings to Byrd—always offhandedly, casually, as if he didn't know how anxious Byrd was.

Then, as the years passed, the text grew easier to read—and it became easier for Johnson to make use of what he read, because Byrd, after all, was already sixty-seven years old when Johnson became Majority Leader.

After her conversations with Johnson, Doris Kearns Goodwin was to write that he recognized "that the older men in the Senate were often troubled by a half-conscious sense that their performance was deteriorating with age." "Now they feared humiliation," Johnson told her. "They craved attention. And when they found it, it was like a spring in the desert," and among its benefits was "dependence on me." Byrd's reluctance to spend money on hiring professional staff members made him particularly vulnerable as he grew older and was less able to do the work himself. More and more research that should have been done, reports that should have been written, were not being done or written—and he knew it. And sometimes, in the most delicate way, Johnson began asking whether perhaps George Reedy or another of his Senate aides, Gerry Siegel, might prepare a draft—just some suggestions, really—for the senator's approval. In addition, as I have written, "old men want to feel that the experience which has come with their years is valuable, that their advice is valuable, that they possess a sagacity that could be obtained only through experience—a sagacity that could be of use to young men if only young men would ask." Finding a word that evoked such feelings, Johnson used it with Byrd. He had a problem he didn't know how to solve, he would say. "Can I have a little bit of your wisdom?" He did a lot of thanking, using that same word. "Thanks for that wisdom," he would tell Byrd. "I *needed* that wisdom." And older men like deference, and with powerful older men Johnson took deference to extremes, and Harry Byrd was a very powerful man; were men astonished when they saw Johnson bend over and kiss Sam Rayburn's bald head?—with Byrd it was not the head but the hand over which he bent: expressing gratitude for some favor Byrd had done for him, or sometimes merely to show affection, he would take one of the old senator's hands in both of his, raise it to his lips, and kiss it. In the opinion of some of Lyndon Johnson's Senate colleagues, of course, Byrd's hand was not the only part of his body on which Johnson bestowed affection. With "the Harry Byrds of the world . . . he was . . . so submissive, and so condescending, you couldn't believe it! I've seen him kiss Harry Byrd's ass until it was disgusting: 'Senator, how about so-and-so?' . . . 'Can't we do this for you?' "

After Johnson became the Democratic Leader, he was not just Byrd's young friend but his reliable ally. No appointment was ever made to a vacancy on the Finance Committee without Byrd's approval; any bill, major or private, in which Byrd was interested was moved quickly to the head of the Senate Calendar; as Byrd passed the age of seventy, and moved well beyond it, and his stamina (although none of his mental acuity) began to fade, Johnson would, in the most tactful, considerate way, arrange with Byrd to have Louisiana's Long—an effective floor tactician and a senator Byrd trusted—manage some Finance bills on the Senate floor, constantly checking in with the chairman, of course.

Whatever the reasons for Harry Byrd's affection for Lyndon Johnson (one may have been his ill-concealed disappointment in his own son Harry Flood Byrd Jr.), the affection was deep. Ordinarily not a man to tolerate being kept waiting, sometimes, visiting Johnson in the hospital after Johnson's heart attack, he would find two visitors, the limit the doctors allowed at a time, already in his room, and others waiting on a bench in the corridor. Joining them on the bench, he would sit uncomplainingly, his dented Panama hat on his knee, waiting for his turn to be admitted. "Give Lyndon my best—Tell him the Senate is not the same without him," he wrote Lady Bird. When Johnson was trying to decide whether to run for President in 1956, Byrd pleaded with him to declare his candidacy; all he had to do was say yes, the Virginian had told him, and he would never have to think about Virginia again; its delegates would be solid for him until the end.

By the later years of Johnson's time as Leader, it had become known around the Senate that Johnson could occasionally—not often but sometimes—do what no one else could do: move the immovable Harry Byrd. Before one vote—on a measure about which Byrd did not have strong feelings but on which he would ordinarily have voted no—Johnson confided to a Senate aide that he might persuade him to abstain instead. "Harry Byrd is a man of principle," he said. "I can't ask Harry to do anything against his principles. But I *can* ask Harry Byrd—and he might oblige me—to stay away [during the vote]."

Reading the Byrd text, however, Johnson had found one point very clear: the unshakable, immovable solidity of Byrd's fiscal conservatism, of his belief in the importance, for America and the world, of the balanced budget and an end to deficit spending. For the Virginian there was a line, firm and hard, at which personal feelings, even paternal fondness, ended, and it was the line at which feelings collided with philosophy and issues based on that philosophy: nothing, not even Lyndon Johnson, could soften in the slightest Byrd's unyielding opposition to government spending and government debt.

Johnson knew that Byrd's references to a $100 billion budget were not off-hand, casual remarks; that to the Finance Committee chairman a budget over that figure would symbolize the launching of governmental spending into a new, unprecedented sphere. Under $100 billion, Johnson immediately understood, wasn't something Byrd was suggesting, it was something on which he was, in his bland, soft-spoken southern way, insisting. Johnson had also realized that Byrd was saying something else as well. When the chairman had told Smathers that he wanted to "see and prove" for himself that the budget was under $100 billion, those words had not been chosen casually, either. He had meant "*see and prove.*" He wanted to see the budget in writing. He wanted to be able to read it, and have congressional staff experts analyze it to ensure that the budget was truly under $100 billion, that that figure hadn't been lowered to that amount by some accounting or governmental gimmick. Johnson understood other aspects of the situation as well. For years, Harry Byrd had been trying to insist that government hold down spending, without much success. Now, however, for the first time, he had a bargaining chip, the tax bill, to force it to hold spending down, at least to a level he considered acceptable. And he was using that chip. What he was saying— even if no one in the Kennedy Administration seemed to have understood what he was saying—was that until he got a budget of under $100 billion from the President, got it in writing and had it analyzed, in detail, for himself, he was not going to release the President's tax bill from his committee. And, Johnson knew, if Byrd didn't release the tax bill, there wasn't going to *be* a tax bill.

TALKING WITH JOHNSON on the phone about the tax cut and budget, Robert Anderson, who during his years as Treasury secretary had often dealt with both men, told Johnson that the best hope of breaking the impasse might lie in Byrd's affection for him. "Harry Byrd *always* voted with the Republicans until you became the leader of the Democrats," he said. "And you could *bring* him to us once in a while and . . . finally, on every crucial vote, you *had* him. And you can get him again." Overstated though that analysis might be—only on rare occasions had Johnson won Byrd's support on a significant fiscal bill—it contained a germ of truth: he had indeed obtained Byrd's support on several occasions when doing so had seemed impossible. That, however, had always required a personal plea: no intermediary would do; he had always had to go to Byrd in person. He was reluctant to request a meeting with Byrd now, because making the request would weaken his negotiating position. He hoped the senator would make the first call, he told Anderson on November 29. "It would look a lot . . . a lot better if he was seeking the appointment." He asked Anderson to suggest to Byrd that he call, and when that didn't work, on December 3 he asked Mansfield, explaining, "I don't want to be asking him." But no call came.

Johnson had no choice. *You couldn't go around Harry Byrd.* Telephoning the senator on December 4, Johnson asked him to come to lunch, saying, "Harry, why don't you come down here and see me tomorrow. I want to get some of your wisdom." Hanging up the phone, Byrd turned to Neil MacNeil of *Time* magazine, who was sitting in his office, and said, "You know what that means. He wants to work on me a little bit." But, MacNeil recalls, as Byrd said that, his eyes were "twinkling," and there was a "fond note" in his voice.

• • •

PLANNING WENT INTO THAT VISIT. Every courtesy was observed, every gesture extended that would make Harry Byrd of the Byrds of Virginia feel that respect was being paid to his power—and to the power of the Senate that he represented. The White House limousine waiting for him at the steps of the Senate Office Building went without saying, but there was also a tour of the White House conducted by the President himself: of the Cabinet Room, the swimming pool, even what Byrd called "the little room where he gets his rub," and then the Oval Office—and, beyond it, the small office where they were to have lunch, with a menu selected by Johnson (potato soup, a Byrd favorite, and a salad). Byrd was the first person who had ever dined with him there, the new President said.

The only other person in the small office was Jack Valenti, and, thanks to his accounts, the lunch has previously been depicted as an unadulterated triumph for Johnson. By its conclusion, Johnson "had gotten a commitment out of Harry Byrd," Valenti has written in one of his many descriptions of the meeting, reporting that when Byrd said, "I want to get it down to one hundred billion," Johnson had asked, "Harry, if I do [that], will the tax cut come out of committee," and Byrd had replied, "In that case maybe we can do some business."

In reality, however, Byrd had not budged from his previous position on the budget during that lunch. Not only had he again insisted on the $100 billion limit, this very tough businessman had repeated his other conditions. Although Valenti doesn't mention this point, he had said that the tax bill might come out of committee, but only after he had been given the budget in writing, had seen it with his own eyes, and had had it analyzed.

In addition, it was not just he who would have to see it in writing, he told Johnson during that December 5 luncheon; it would also have to be shown to his committee's ranking Republican, John J. Williams, the same Williams who was investigating Bobby Baker, a senator as adamantly opposed to government deficits as Byrd himself. No negotiating had been possible about those conditions: Byrd had been immovable. Johnson understood the ultimatum; as he was to explain to a caller the next day: "They [the Finance Committee] are going to hold this thing [the tax cut bill] until they get a look at our budget and then decide what they do about our tax bill." And he understood that he had no choice but to accept the conditions. If he didn't, there might, at the end of all the months of effort, be no tax bill at all. In some ways, nothing had been changed by the lunch. "They'd like to get it [the tax bill] behind civil rights and not [pass] it . . . at all," he said. During that lunch, Byrd had received a commitment that he would get what he wanted, what he had been asking for for months: a budget that would be under his "magic figure" and proof—in writing—that it would indeed be under that figure. "If you don't mind," he said mildly to reporters after he got back to his office, "I wish you'd point out that this is what I've been asking for all along." And to Johnson's request that he speed up the Finance Committee's public hearings and vote on all of the committee members' individual amendments before Congress's Christmas adjournment so that when in January the budget was ready to be reviewed by him and Williams, the tax cut could come to the floor without further delay, Byrd told the reporters, "I told the President you simply can't rush through a complex bill that runs more than three hundred pages." Despite Valenti's depiction of the lunch as a victory for Johnson, the President emerged from it knowing as a certainty that there was no hope of having the tax cut bill pass before the end of the year and the current session of Congress, that, as George Smathers had told him in that first call about the congressional situation, he was simply "not going to be able to do it." And he emerged from the lunch knowing something else: the budget had been cut to $101.5 or $102 billion through the use of gimmicks, in particular the promise of future "supplemental" appropriations, and "the committee"—Byrd's committee—"knows how to spot the gimmicks," and knew all about supplementals. By the time Byrd saw the budget, it had to be not merely below $100 billion but far enough below $100 billion so that Byrd wouldn't feel that it had been reduced to that figure only by accounting tricks—wouldn't feel that the true figure was higher—and so that he would feel that federal spending for the year would still be below the magic figure even after the inevitable supplementals had been added later.

Nonetheless, hedged about by conditions though it was, a commitment had been made. If the conditions were met, "we can do some business." And of at least equal importance, there had been a renewal of old ties.

Cutting the budget to $101.5 or $102 billion hadn't really been all that difficult. But a lot more cutting was going to be necessary. The big hand grabbed the receiver. "Kermit, get in here, and bring your meat cleaver," Lyndon Johnson said.

AT DINNERS NOW, there would be senators and congressmen, Lady Bird Johnson was to write in her diary, and "the talk among the men was about the Tax Bill, the Tax Bill, the Tax Bill."

"He had to get that tax cut," Jack Valenti says. So many of the things Lyndon Johnson wanted to accomplish—so many of the subjects Valenti had listed on his notepad during Johnson's monologue in The Elms that first night—depended on the increased tax revenues that would be generated by an expanding economy. Without them, "it would be very difficult to do . . . the things he wanted to do. . . . It was his general feeling [that] everything [he] wanted to do would be hinged to the tax cut." After dinner, Lady Bird wrote, "he went back to his office and his telephone."

"I worked as hard on that budget as I have ever worked on anything," Lyndon Johnson was to say in his memoir, *The Vantage Point.* "The budget determines how many unemployed men and women are going to be trained; how many hungry schoolchildren are going to be fed; how many poor people are going to be housed . . . how our entire population is going to be protected against a possible enemy attack. Day after day I went over that budget. . . . I studied every line, nearly every page, until I was dreaming about the budget at night." Kermit Gordon seemed to be in his office every evening, Valenti says. "Then they would call in the department heads, one at a time, and work on them."

In memos to Cabinet members and agency heads, Johnson, in Gordon's words, made "abundantly clear his decision to tighten management and hold down employment in the federal government," and said he would personally review every request that would lead to an increase in a department's budget. In discussing with Gordon the Budget Director's meetings with Cabinet members, his tone was even tougher. "Is anyone going up on you?" he would demand. For those department heads who, like Fowler, Rusk and most of all McNamara, were cooperative, Johnson had a friendly voice. ("He's the only guy that's really try-ing to help me," Johnson said of McNamara in one call to Anderson. "And he *is* trying to help"; on December 7 the Defense secretary announced a series of steps that would lower his department's budget by an additional billion and a half dol-lars.) For those who weren't, there was a different voice, even for those Kennedy Cabinet members whom he had thus far been handling with kid gloves. The gloves had to come off now: the tax cut had to go through, and that meant the budget had to come down. To convince the country, and conservatives in Con-gress, that he was doing everything possible to economize, Johnson wanted a symbolic achievement: to be able to announce that the total number of federal employees under the new budget would be lower than under the old one. But although a number of departments were reducing their payrolls, some were resisting, including the Department of Agriculture.

The soft voice Johnson had been using with Walter Heller, and, through Heller, with Secretary of Agriculture Freeman, had evidently misled Freeman, who, despite the fact that Heller had given him Johnson's message to "quit lob-bying" for increased expenditures, had continued doing so, sending Johnson a stream of memos arguing for a substantial increase in the Agriculture Depart-ment budget. "Obviously, he knows I've been doing a bit of agitating," Freeman wrote in his diary, "but according to Walter this does not seem to irritate him."

The magnitude of that misconception should have become clear to him when, on December 11, he finally had an audience with Johnson in the Oval Office. He had expected, Freeman was to recall, "a philosophical discussion with the new President" about the overall goals of agricultural policy as laid out in his latest memo.

Johnson told him he hadn't even bothered to read the memo. Reminding Freeman that he had told him that he wanted him to deal personally with senators who were agitating for larger appropriations for various farm programs "and keep them off my back," he said that Freeman hadn't been doing that—and he wanted him to start. He had told Freeman that he had to get along better with Capitol Hill, to spend more time socializing with senators and representatives, and Freeman wasn't doing that. "You go up there as I told you to do originally and live with these people," he said. And when Freeman tried to tell him how hard he was working to cut the Agriculture budget, there was, the secretary says, a "minor explosion." Suddenly the President was standing very close to him, towering over him, and a long forefinger was jabbing his chest. "You've got about the biggest increase in personnel of anyone in the entire government," the President said. "We've got to get that budget down."

Evidently, however, the misconception still hadn't been cleared up. Freeman wrote another memo, apologizing for having made perhaps "a little more noise than anyone else" about the budget, but saying that there was no alternative "if Agriculture is going to get its day in court." His "vigorous management improvement program" had drastically reduced the number of additional new personnel he was asking for, he said, but the number was nonetheless still thirty-five hundred.

This time he didn't get even an audience. "Orville Freeman's got a memo here," Johnson told Gordon over the phone. "He's got plenty of time to write memos." He read Gordon a few lines from the memo: " 'Mr. President, your comments about the number of employees and increases in the Department of Agriculture concern me deeply. My concern does not represent personal sensitivity.'

"Ha, ha, ha!" Johnson said, in a voice that had no humor in it at all. He told Gordon to draft a reply for his signature—"To take this [memo] and not be unjust. But be just as close to being unjust as you can. . . . Say, 'Yes, you've given me seven reasons why you can't keep this thing down, but nevertheless we're *going* to keep it down.' " He didn't want any more discussions with Freeman, he said, and he didn't want any more memos. He told Gordon to draft a reply "that will get him away from writing memos, which take up my time . . . and cost us extra money, and see if he can't do some saving.

"Let's cut down on some of these employees," Johnson said. "I know the difference between adding 3,500 and subtracting 3,500." Tell him to "go back and work a little harder."

By December 17, despite a substantial reduction that Freeman, having evidently worked harder, had made in Agriculture, and reductions in other departments, the number of federal employees projected under the new budget was still seven thousand greater than under the old, and five thousand of the seven were in the Post Office Department. Citing a sharp increase in the volume of mail the Post Office was handling, and opposition from the powerful postal unions to any cuts in the department's budget that would reduce the number of projected jobs, Postmaster General John Gronouski had resisted any cuts at all in his proposed budget. When, on December 23, Johnson asked Kermit Gordon if Gronouski had agreed on a budget compromise, Gordon said, "We haven't agreed on anything—not yet."

"General," Lyndon Johnson said to Gronouski when he had him on the phone, he needed a compromise, "and they [the Budget Bureau] just said that if you'd give us a Christmas present and work day and night, you could squeeze that down. . . . Now don't you think you can?"

The inflection of the question was pleasant, but when Gronouski's answer was not an assent, the inflection hardened. "You've got five thousand of the seven thousand," Johnson told him. "We're trying to say we've got less employees next year than we had this year." Defense has cut its number, he said. State has cut its number. Interior has cut it. Agriculture has cut it. "I've just *got* to have some real pruning and some real cooperation. . . . You think about it."

There were ways in which the number could be increased later—after the budget had passed—Johnson said. "I wouldn't mind going up in December, after we get the election behind us, and giving you a little supplemental appropriation," he said. That possibility had to be kept secret for now, he said. "You've got to understand there's some bookkeeping here, and accounting, and we can't say that. But if you could just squeeze it out . . . and say you're going to get by on less than you had last year . . . even though the volume's way up . . . it would just help us, because you've got five thousand of those seven thousand jobs."

Gronouski continued to mention the strength of the postal unions, and the necessity, if cuts were made, of cutting back postal services. Johnson mentioned opposing arguments. "People are wondering about these extra employees," the President said. They might start wondering about the department's efficiency, he hinted. The postal service was a monopoly, he said, and "anybody that can't operate a monopoly at a profit, by God, we've got some serious problems. . . . If you give me a monopoly, I'll operate it at a profit: I'll guarantee you that." He had a list of the various departments before him—"every department," Lyndon Johnson repeated. "And of the 7,000 increase, 5,000 of them are in postal."

Gronouski tried to make a joke of it. "I've got them all, huh," he said with a little laugh.

"No," Lyndon Johnson said without a laugh. "You've got 5,000 of them, though."

The possibility that the press and Congress might get hold of those figures had sunk in. "Five thousand out of seven, right?" Gronouski said.

"And I don't think you want to be explaining that," Johnson said.

Ten days later, Gronouski announced that the Post Office Department had found it would be able to operate for another year at the current personnel level, so the five thousand extra jobs would no longer be needed. The budget was coming down.

ALTHOUGH HARRY BYRD had set tough conditions, he had said that if they were met, business could be done: the tax cut bill could come out of committee. And, it was turning out, Lyndon Johnson had again done with him what no one else could do. While Byrd still wasn't agreeing to end the committee's hearings on the original bill so that hearings could begin on the proposed amendments, now, when he gave a date by which those hearings on the bill might end—December 10—he appeared to mean it, and indeed they did end on that date. The atmosphere in the Finance Committee offices had changed. After a conversation with Finance Committee chief clerk Elizabeth B. Springer, Mike Manatos told Larry O'Brien, "If I am any judge of Mrs. Springer's feelings . . . she reflects a much more positive attitude about Senator Byrd's desire to cooperate. Obviously, the President's discussion with Senator Byrd has been most helpful."

Then came the committee members' thirty amendments. Byrd didn't want them all disposed of, because if, when he saw the budget, it wasn't below $100 billion, he wanted to be able to continue to hold the bill in the Finance Committee and not release it to the Senate floor, and an easy way of accomplishing that was simply to say that the committee was still dealing with amendments.

The chairman's handling, on December 11, of the first amendment (one that had been introduced by Russell Long on behalf of his state's oil oligarchy) was a case study in Senate procedure: that is, Senate delay. First, there was the question of whether, since the hearing was an executive session, a stenotypist should be present to record the proceedings: a simple question, but Byrd let discussion about it drag on for an hour and a half. Then one of the committee members asked a question about some unexplored aspect of the effect the amendment would have on the net amount collected through income tax, a technical question that had to be answered by the Treasury Department; Treasury officials had thought they had prepared for every question, but this one caught them by surprise; it could most easily be explained by graphs, they said, and it was decided that graphs should be prepared; the graphs couldn't be ready until the next day, so Byrd adjourned the hearings for this day. Some of Johnson's Cabinet members sometimes seemed to be working against him. The amendment wouldn't have received such serious consideration had it not been for a letter from Treasury supporting it. "I thought you had an agreement that you'd be against *every* amendment," Johnson reminded Treasury's Dillon on December 12. "Well, we're against practically every one," Dillon said; Long had insisted that Treasury support his—"that was the price" for his working with the Kennedy Administration to get the bill passed. If this amendment was passed, other senators would be encouraged to press for adoption of their own amendments, Johnson explained. "You'll have thirty more of them, if you start amending it." The following week would be the week before the Christmas recess; senators would begin leaving for home; "I'm afraid you won't have a quorum next week," Johnson said. When the Senate reconvened in January, 1964, there would still be many amendments left to dispose of. And even if Byrd was agreeable to disposing of them, that job wasn't going to be easy; it was going to be "a 9–8 thing every time" in the seventeen-member committee.

Johnson explained Byrd's tactics to Dillon. When Byrd had received Dillon's letter, he knew it would "delay things," but "the committee [Byrd] said, 'Hell, we don't care about delay. That's what we're in business for is to delay things.' "

And sometime in 1964, the civil rights bill was going to emerge from the House and go directly to the Senate floor. If that happened and "you don't have your tax bill," you will have to wait until after the civil rights fight—until after the civil rights filibuster—he reminded the Treasury secretary.

Dillon had to make more of an effort, Johnson told him. Every one of the committee's nine Democratic members had to show up for every meeting, so that there would be a quorum, and they had to vote against every amendment, to prevent any further delays. "You've got to get them all in there, and get them organized, and say, 'God almighty, fellows. We can't stand this. We can't have this follow civil rights. You're going to ruin us on our fiscal program.' " Exactly what he had feared would happen *was* happening. "I'm terribly distressed," he told Dillon. "I'm just distressed that it's going to get behind civil rights. If it does, it's Good night, Grace."*

The next day—December 13—there was another conversation between Johnson and Byrd. President though Johnson may have been now, he pleaded with Byrd, pleaded as if Byrd was not a foe but an ally. He was working to give Harry what he wanted on the budget, he told him. "I'm working in [*sic*] my budget every night. I was up till one o'clock last night. And I'm going to get you a budget I think you'll be proud of. . . . I'm going to help you with the budget." Pleaded as if Byrd was an old ally—and an old friend—who, like him, might see all their hard work go down the drain.

He found a line that worked. If the tax reduction bill was passed as part of the arrangement with the budget, he told the old senator, "You can tell your grandchildren you were the senator who finally got a President to cut his budget." And, having found the perfect line, he used it. Unless the bill had Harry Byrd's help, he told him, the bill might not pass.

"What we want to do, Senator, is to try to get those amendments voted on before we go home, or at least as many of them as we can," he said. "What I'm afraid of is" if the civil rights bill arrived on the Senate floor first, "if your [note the pronoun] tax bill got behind it, why all of our work would have been done in vain. So I'm just *so* anxious to run it [the hearings] morning, afternoon and night, and try to get these amendments voted on." They had both been working so hard, he said. "You help me . . . get that bill out. I know you're against it, but you're a good chairman, and you help them vote. You're tired of this talking yourself."

And he began to *make* him an ally—finally, during that December 13 call, began to "get him," as Bob Anderson had predicted he would get him, persuading Byrd to subordinate at least to a degree his desire to stall the tax cut bill, to subordinate it to this opportunity to realize the grand aim of his public life: to slow down government's headlong rush along the path of fiscal profligacy on which a budget over the magic figure would have been yet another step; to pass a

---

*Johnson was misquoting the words "good night, Gracie" that George Burns spoke to signal the end to each week's episode of the popular *George Burns and Gracie Allen Show.*

budget that might signal a beginning at last of a turn toward governmental prudence and economy.

Russell Long watched it happen. He had been unable "to move the [tax cut] bill," he was to recall. "I couldn't move the bill out of committee." Then, he says, "Johnson worked with Byrd—promised to cut spending, and Harry changed [his] attitude. Up until then he wasn't going to permit the bill to pass." But now, when Lyndon Johnson told Harry Byrd that he knew Byrd was "tired of this talking" and wanted his committee to send the tax bill to the floor, Byrd replied with a single word: "Right." From Harry Byrd a single word was enough. The amendments started to move faster.

20

"The Johnsons in Johnson City"

"I'D MOVE MY CHILDREN on through the line and get them down in the storm cellar" before "I'd make my attack" on civil rights, Johnson had told Sorensen in June. The tax cut bill wasn't down in the cellar yet, wasn't safely "locked and key," but it was—at last—moving through the line, and he had a commitment from Harry Byrd to keep it moving. And the time remaining during which Congress could pass a civil rights act was a lot shorter now than it had been in June. The moment for the attack had come.

Strong as was Lyndon Johnson's compassion for the poor, particularly poor people of color, his deep, genuine desire to help them had always been subordinated to his ambition; whenever they had been in conflict, it had been compassion that went to the wall. When they had both been pointing in the same direction, however—when the compassion had been unleashed from ambition's checkrein—then not only Lyndon Johnson but the cause of social justice in America had moved forward under the direction of this master at transmuting sympathy into governmental action. Now, in the days following the assassination, they were pointing in the same direction again—with every week that became more obvious; as one of Larry O'Brien's aides, Henry Wilson, was to put it to O'Brien, "I think civil rights is the total touch point for the press—if we passed it relatively intact plus the tax bill and nothing else . . . we'd be credited with having a good year," and if we don't, no matter what else was passed, "we'll be credited with having a bad year."

The highest hurdle in the path of President Kennedy's civil rights bill would be the Senate—decade after decade, civil rights bills that had passed the House had died there—and the reports Johnson was getting from the Senate indicated that nothing had changed. "They tell me they've [the South] got enough votes to never allow cloture. . . . They say they can never get the seventy [sic] votes we need," he told Andrew Hatcher. The bill hadn't even reached the Senate yet, hadn't even reached the floor of the House, where a vote would be required to send it to the Senate; it was still trapped in Judge Smith's House Rules Committee, and if Smith was allowed to "piddle along and get it into February, and then maybe they won't get it out [of the House] until March," the civil rights bill would be as dead in 1964 as it had been in 1963.

When, in the first days after the assassination, Johnson started exploring the civil rights situation, there was seemingly very little that could be done. A vote within the Rules Committee could be held, to have a majority of its fifteen members overrule its chairman and set a date for hearings. While ten of Rules' members were Democrats, however, three of them in addition to Smith were from the South, so there would be, at most, only six Democratic votes to overrule. At least two Republican votes would be needed to provide a majority. And every time the possibility of using Republicans to strip a committee chairman of his authority had been raised with House Republican leader Charles Halleck and his deputies, they had recoiled at the very hint of overturning the body's traditional procedures. There was only one other possibility ("the only thing we can do," Speaker McCormack told Johnson), a single remaining lever that might move the immovable judge: to obtain the signatures of a majority of the 435 House members— 218, in other words—on a "discharge petition," a resolution to discharge the Rules Committee from its control of the bill and send it to the floor. Although this was also, as the *New York Times* put it, "a procedure rarely invoked because it offends traditionalists to whom time-hallowed House rules are sacred," the procedure had in fact not only been employed against Smith before, in 1960, but employed successfully. As the number of signatures on that petition had slowly mounted, Smith, fearing what the *Times* called the "indignity of being relieved of responsibility for the bill," had given in; when the number reached 209, he had allowed his committee to release that year's civil rights bill to the floor. During the week following President Kennedy's assassination, a rebellious liberal congressman (a constant irritant to party leaders McCormack and Albert), Richard Bolling of Missouri, had introduced a discharge resolution, but when Johnson began looking into the civil rights logjam, a memo from O'Brien on November 29 told him that the discharge lever had been inserted into it too late to break the bill out of Rules before Congress adjourned. "Given signature of the . . . petition by a majority of the members of the House even immediately," the memo said, "it still would not be technically possible to put the bill on the floor" before December 23, by which date Congress would probably already have adjourned. House rules required a waiting period of seven business days after a petition acquired the 218 signatures, "and then can be called up [for a vote] only on a second or a fourth Monday [of a month]." The seven-day waiting requirement made a vote on December's second Monday, December 9, impossible. And getting a majority to sign was unlikely anyway. The 209 votes had been obtained in 1960 only because that petition had Sam Rayburn behind it; there was no Rayburn now, and without him, there was no one to persuade the House to bend its normal procedures. Of the 257 Democrats in the House, 90 were from the South, and others, from the adjoining border states, were allied with the South. The maximum number of Democratic signatures that could be hoped for was about 160. To reach 218, about sixty Republican signatures would be needed. The enthusiasm for civil rights expressed by many Republicans—particularly the GOP's large bloc of midwestern conservatives—was more on their lips than in their hearts. Committed though they were to vote for the bill itself, they would welcome any excuse—such as the inviolability of sacred House procedures—to avoid doing so. In addition, seeing the civil rights issue as one that split—and spotlit the split in—the Democratic Party, Republicans didn't want it settled. Reaffirming his opposition to the petition on the Thanksgiving weekend Sunday television talk shows, Halleck said that during his twenty-eight years in the House, "I've never signed one yet." In a Republican caucus the following day, he, other GOP leaders and even a key architect of the House civil rights bill—William M. McCulloch of Ohio—assailed the very concept of bringing a bill to the floor without the customary "rule" from the Rules Committee. As Henry Wilson reported, "Republicans have no intention whatever of pushing Smith into early action." And without Republican votes—without any realistic chance of passing the discharge petition—"our last threat to Smith will have been removed, and he could hold out forever," as Wilson gloomily put it in one of his memos to O'Brien.

But Lyndon Johnson was worked up now, "revved up," "all worked up and emotional, and work all day and all night, and sacrifice, and say, 'Let's do this because it's *right*!' " Those commentators who have questioned the sincerity of Lyndon Johnson's commitment to civil rights—questioning that persists to this day—simply haven't paid sufficient attention to the words that had burst out of him when he had been telling the governors why a civil rights bill should be passed: "So that we can say to the Mexican in California or the Negro in Mississippi or the Oriental on the West Coast or the Johnsons in Johnson City that we are going to treat you all equally and fairly." He had lumped them all together—Mexicans, Negroes, Orientals and Johnsons—which meant that, in his own heart at least, he was one of them: one of the poor, one of the scorned, one of the dispossessed of the earth, one of the Johnsons in Johnson City. What was the description he had given on other occasions of the work he had done in his boyhood and young manhood? "Nigger work." Had he earned a fair wage for it? "I always ordered the egg sandwich, and I always wanted the ham and egg." Nor was it financial factors alone that accounted for his empathy for the poor, for people of color—for the identification he felt with them. Respect was involved, too—respect denied because of prejudice. He had understood those kids in Cotulla, "the disappointment in their eyes . . . the quizzical expression on their faces: 'Why don't people like me? Why do they hate me because I am brown?' " They had been denied respect for a reason, the color of their skin, over which they had no control; so had he—for him the reason was his family, his father.

"Never amount to anything. Too much like Sam." He had "swore then and there that if I ever had the power to help those kids I was going to do it." And now, he was to say, "I'll let you in on a secret. I have the power." *"Well, what the hell's the presidency for?"* He could use only a modicum of presidential power as yet; he couldn't—daren't—rage and threaten and bully as yet. But whatever power he had, he was going to use—and no one knew how to use power better than he. If there was only one lever, Lyndon Johnson was going to push it.

Telephoning Bolling on Monday evening, December 2, after reading O'Brien's memo, he was cautious at the start, wary of saying something that, if quoted back to House leaders, would offend them as presidential interference in their affairs. He hoped Bolling would not discuss the call with them, he said. "I want to keep this secret. I don't want them to be thinking I'm going around them or anything. . . . You just keep this confidential, but give me your ideas about what are your prospects up there?" But when Bolling told him the prospects were "*bad*" ("our maximum Democratic signatures" on the petition—about 160— would be obtained "pretty quick," he said, but Republicans were balking, and Smith's flat refusal to "even set a date for" hearings "convinced me that we absolutely had to go this route or we wouldn't have any lever at all"), secrecy gave way to urgency, as Johnson spurred the congressman to the cause, rallying him as he had once rallied young senators to civil rights,* rallying him and guiding him, telling him what to say to colleagues uncertain about signing the petition. Was Smith refusing even to hold hearings?—"I think you can *really* make a point of that," he said. "Just say that the humblest man anywhere has the right to a hearing. . . . You [civil rights supporters] have been denied any opportunity to be heard at all, and the only way you *can* be heard is on the House floor itself," and therefore the petition should be signed so that the bill could be discharged to the floor for debate and a vote.

That was what should be said to Democrats, he told Bolling, who responded, "Right!" As for Republicans reluctant to sign, they should not be allowed to say they were in favor of a civil rights bill and were refusing to sign the petition only because they didn't want to overturn traditional House procedures. A vote against the petition was not just a procedural vote, he said. It was in reality a vote against civil rights because without the petition a civil rights bill had no chance of passage, and they should be told that. "Anyone who is for civil rights is going to be for signing this petition. If they are not for civil rights, all right. But don't hide behind a procedural thing. Anybody that wants to be anti–civil rights, that's their right. You've got no objection to that. They can do what they want to."

"Right," Bolling interjected.

"But they can't pretend to be for civil rights and then say they won't" sign the petition, Johnson said. "Let them sign the petition."

*For an example of him rallying, see *Master of the Senate*, pp. 970–75.

The number of signatures on the petition was important, the President told the congressman—"the more you get to sign it the better." Smith had released the bill in 1960 only after the Judge had realized that there was a real possibility that the bill might be taken away from him by force. Trying to ascertain exactly how many signatures Bolling was counting on, however, Johnson found the count disappointingly soft: "in the order of 160 Democrats," Bolling said; as for the Republican number, "Well, that's up in the air." The President got specific about one state. "Are you going to get any from Texas?" he asked. "Well, I don't know," Bolling said. Johnson said he would make calls to some Texas congressmen. The petition *had* to be filed, he said. "I think it's got to go." And when Bolling said, "This is the only lever we've really got in our arsenal," Johnson said, "I agree with you. I agree with you. I agree with you."

IF THERE WAS ONLY one lever, Lyndon Johnson was going to really lean into it.

The African-Americans who were the leaders of the five key civil rights organizations—Roy Wilkins of the NAACP, Whitney Young of the National Urban League, Martin Luther King Jr. of the Southern Christian Leadership Conference, James Farmer of the Congress of Racial Equality (CORE) and A. Philip Randolph of the Brotherhood of Sleeping Car Porters—had requested a group meeting with him, but a group meeting wasn't what he wanted. "What about one meeting a day for each?" were the instructions Juanita Roberts jotted down.*

His conversations with these men were conducted at the informal end of the Oval Office, the civil rights leader sitting on one of the couches in front of the fireplace, Johnson sitting in the rocking chair. Since the rocker was higher than the couches, the President towered over the men he was speaking to. Becoming worked up as he talked to them, he leaned forward in the rocker, over the coffee table, closer and closer to them, his eyes never leaving theirs. Coffee cups sat on the table between them, untouched, as he told them how to advance their cause, and tried to persuade them that he believed in it.

He persuaded them. Aware though these men were of the political considerations that motivated the President, from the descriptions of these conversations that they were later to furnish, there emerges a picture of a Lyndon Johnson who in their opinion had a genuine passion for social justice. Wilkins' feelings toward Johnson, for example, had always been ambivalent. "With Johnson, you never quite knew if he was out to lift your heart or your wallet," he was to write.

But now, seating Wilkins on one of the two sofas, Johnson pulled his rock-

*The one-on-one meetings had already begun, in a meeting with Wilkins, the dean of the group, on the Friday—November 29—of Thanksgiving weekend, and, on Monday, the day of his conversation with Bolling, with Whitney Young. Before the week was out, he would also meet with King, Randolph and Farmer.

ing chair, Wilkins says, "within a few inches of my knees" and began talking about the civil rights bill, and how hard the South was going to fight it. But Johnson also said, Wilkins recalls, "that such a law could be enacted if the people really wanted it. . . . He was asking us if we wanted it, if we would do the things required to be done to get it enacted." And Johnson said, as Wilkins recalls, that "the outcome, the very future of our country, depended on how we all handled ourselves over the next few months."

It wasn't merely the words but the passion behind them that moved Wilkins. "It was the first time I had really felt those mesmerizing eyes of Texas on me. When Lyndon Johnson wanted to sell an idea, he put all his being into the task. Leaning forward, almost touching me, he poked his finger at me and said quietly, 'I want that bill *passed.*' "

A passion rooted in empathy, a deep understanding of the indignities visited daily on black people in America. "Some of the southerners tell him that they'll buy the bill if he will take out the public accommodations section, but he can't do that because that's the heart of the bill as far as he is concerned," James Farmer recalls him saying, and, Farmer recalls, when he asked Johnson "how he got that way," the President told Farmer how when Lady Bird had told Zephyr Wright to take their dog to Texas when she drove down, Mrs. Wright had replied, "Please don't ask me" to do that, because "we're going to be driving through the South and our [trip] is going to be tough enough just being black without having a dog to worry about, too." And how Mrs. Wright had explained how hard it was in the South for a black person—even a college graduate like her—to find a place along the main highway to eat, or to go to the bathroom.

"Well, that hurt me, that almost brought me to tears, and I realized how important public accommodations were," Johnson told Farmer, and then the new President added that he had "determined that if ever I had a chance I was going to do something about it."

"He said he was running into great difficulty" with the civil rights bill, Farmer recalls, "but he's got to get that bill through, he's got to get it through, it's of vital importance."

And from these descriptions, also, there emerges a picture of a Lyndon Johnson who was hard, tough, canny—tough enough and canny enough to transmute passion and empathy into the legislative accomplishment that had been so lacking during the past three years.

When he had entered the Oval Office for his conversation with Johnson, Wilkins had not had much hope for the civil rights bill. If it passed, he felt, it might do so only in a drastically watered-down form. Kennedy, he was to recall, "believed that his package would have passed Congress by the following summer. I am not quite sure how much of it would have survived." But by the time the conversation ended, he had been "struck by the enormous difference between Kennedy and Johnson. . . . Where Kennedy had been polite and sympathetic on all matters of basic principle, more often than not he had been evasive on action.

Kennedy was not naïve, but as a legislator he was very green. He saw himself as being dry-eyed, realistic. In retrospect, I think that for all his talk about the art of the possible, he didn't really know what was possible and what wasn't in Congress. . . . When it came to dealing with Congress, Johnson knew exactly what was possible. . . . Johnson made it plain he wanted the whole bill. If we could find the votes, we would win. If we didn't find the votes, we would lose, he said. The problem was as simple as that." Wilkins had entered the Oval Office without much hope; that wasn't the way he left it.

The votes he was talking to them about now weren't for the civil rights bill, the President explained to them; they were for the discharge petition, because without the petition there might never be a vote on the bill. While he was talking to Young, who was sitting on the sofa to his right, Soapy Williams telephoned, and Johnson took the call, leaning in front of Young to lift the receiver off its cradle on the telephone console on the coffee table.

"We're going to go all out on this civil rights bill," Johnson told Williams. "But we've got to go the petition route, and that's a mighty hard route, as everybody knows." The public had to be made to understand that a vote against the petition was not a mere procedural matter but a vote against civil rights. "We've got to put the Republicans on the spot," he said. "Halleck was on television yesterday saying, 'Well, we've got to have hearings, and the bill was rushed through' [so it shouldn't be discharged by petition]. Rushed, my ass, it was there [in the Judiciary Committee] from May to November. But he was telling how it was rushed. . . . So we've got to find some way, somehow [to make the public understand that] these people [Republicans] either go with us [sign the petition] or they're [actually] anti-civil rights."

"I'll take care of the bill itself," Young heard the President say, but he needed help with the petition. "We'll all work on it. Everybody will have his assignment. . . . We're on the same team."

These black leaders had been fighting on the streets with, some of them, the tactics of the orator, and, some of them, with the tactics of the revolutionary. Sitting on the Oval Office couch, the long telephone wire stretching in front of their faces up from the telephone console on the coffee table to the receiver in Lyndon Johnson's hand, they heard, in a Texas twang, a President fighting with the tactics of the legislator. To a legislator, what counts is votes. Not merely explaining to Martin Luther King the importance of sufficient signatures on the discharge petition, he showed him a list of the congressmen who had not yet signed, pointed to the Republican names on it and told King to work on them.

The five civil rights leaders believed him, were convinced of his sincerity. Besieged by reporters, Young told them that "a magnolia accent doesn't always mean bigotry." The new President, he said, not only supported his predecessor's civil rights program but had "deep convictions" of his own.

The other leaders echoed Young's feelings. "I left the White House that day convinced that Johnson was willing to go much farther than he had ever gone before," Wilkins was to write. Despite his passage of the 1957 and 1960 civil rights bills, "there has been a lingering reservation in the minds of many Negro leaders whether Mr. Johnson, a Texan with close friendships among Southern legislators, whole-heartedly subscribed to the far-reaching Kennedy program," the *New York Times* said. His meetings with the five leaders, the *Times* said, had erased their reservations. (The statements some of them made to reporters as they left the White House showed a certain relief, summarized tactfully in Martin Luther King's statement that "As a Southerner, I am happy to know that a fellow Southerner is in the White House who is concerned about civil rights." Their feeling was not only for public consumption. Speaking privately to two of his aides later that day, King told them, "LBJ is a man of great ego and great power. He is a pragmatist and a man of pragmatic compassion. It just may be that he's going to go where John Kennedy couldn't.")

After these conversations, they believed *in* him. The speeches Lyndon Johnson had given as Vice President had made some of them start to look at him in a new light. To Wilkins, who had studied them closely, they could have been written "almost by a Negro ghostwriter." The descriptions the knowledgeable NAACP lobbyist Mitchell had been giving them for years about the difficulties in getting, in 1957, even the "half a loaf," even the "one crumb," that they despised, had finally made them understand the magnitude of what Johnson had accomplished. And now, sitting with him in the Oval Office, they had talked with him themselves, had looked into his eyes. They had felt what Howard Woods had felt three years before sitting across from Lyndon Johnson on the campaign Convair. One evening later that month, on December 23, the phone would ring in Roy Wilkins' apartment. It was 10:30, and Johnson was still in the Oval Office, "still signing mail," he told Wilkins, but he had something he wanted to tell him—that he was about to hire a black secretary, Gerri Whittington: "This Negro girl that's been working for Ralph Dungan. . . . She has good character and good ability. . . . You come on and you meet this woman the [next] time you're in this White House"— and "three or four things" he wanted to talk to him about: suggestions about whom to appoint to the Civil Rights Commission; what to include in his January State of the Union address; Wilkins' opinion of a California state official he was considering appointing to a White House job because he was not only competent but "a Mexican" and "They've had nobody" in the White House—it wasn't merely blacks he wanted to make a part of his Administration but other "minority groups" as well, he said. After those matters had been discussed, Johnson was about to hang up, but Wilkins had something he wanted to add. "Now, Mr. President," he said, "may I say just a word to you? I hope you're going to have, first, a Merry Christmas. . . . And I'd like to say this to you: *Please* take care of yourself."

"I'm going to. I'm going to," Johnson said.

"Please take care of yourself," Wilkins repeated. *"We need you."*

If Lyndon Johnson, dealing with Wilkins and Young and King and Randolph and Farmer about matters which concerned, at bottom, the color of their skin, was fooling these men, he was fooling men who were, where color was concerned, very hard to fool.

He wasn't fooling them, wasn't merely posturing. No television cameras had been present, no reporter taking down his words, when he had sat on the steps in Cotulla with the janitor Thomas Coronado.

IF THERE WAS ONLY one lever, Lyndon Johnson was going to put his shoulder into it, as became apparent on Tuesday, December 3.

Not only the civil rights organizations but civil rights' staunch ally, organized labor, had to be mobilized behind the civil rights bill, and labor's stud duck, who "liked the visible signs of consultation . . . the pictures of the two of you," was invited to The Elms Tuesday morning for breakfast, and a ride downtown afterwards. No sign of consultation was necessary to line up the staunch old leader of the unions behind civil rights; Meany had been behind that cause for thirty years. But he hadn't been behind Lyndon Johnson. As Johnson's limousine nosed slowly out The Elms' gates, the rear window was down, so that photographers could snap a picture of Meany in the back seat with the President. And at the White House, Johnson asked Meany if he'd like to come inside—and ushered him into the Cabinet Room to spend a few minutes at the legislative leaders' breakfast. When he emerged to be met by the waiting White House press corps, he said that the President would have labor's "full support" in the battle for the civil rights bill. Johnson would have had that even without the breakfast and the Cabinet Room, but, AFL-CIO lobbyist Andrew Biemiller would say, "This cemented Johnson with Meany."

After Meany had left, Speaker McCormack said Judge Smith's recalcitrance meant that getting the bill to the Senate early enough in 1964 for there to be any realistic hope of passage there was going to be difficult. "We cannot expect any action by Rules"—not even the setting of a date for hearings—"until the middle of January," he said. A discharge petition was "the only thing we can do," but "a lot of members don't like the discharge petition as a matter of policy."

Although he had given Bolling the go-ahead for the petition the previous evening, Johnson's first comment about the maneuver at the breakfast seemed to be merely an agreement with McCormack's reservation. Then he added, however, "psychologically it [the petition] would be good for the country. All you are asking is a hearing." Sentiment around the table moved toward a petition. Firming things up, he made sure they were all in agreement. "Does everybody agree that you get as many [Democratic] signatures [on the petition] as you can? Then tell the Republicans they must match us man for man." Bringing the discussion to an end, he said that when he himself had been in the House, "I was always reluctant to sign a discharge petition. But you have a great moral issue." McCormack had harbored some doubts, small but persistent, about whether Johnson's commitment to the bill was as strong in private as in public; had been hoping, he had told a friend the day before, for some "definite word." After that breakfast, he knew he had it. He told the waiting reporters that the discharge petition would be filed as soon as possible.

And Johnson was not only laying out a strategy on Tuesday, he was counting the votes that would be behind it.

The first counts he received were an illustration of why bills hadn't been getting passed. House Majority Leader Carl Albert of Oklahoma assured him of 165 Democratic signatures for the petition, but when Johnson asked the House Majority Leader—and the other leaders—specifically where those signatures would come from, since so many Democrats were from the South and border states, no one seemed to know. And even if the 165 number was correct, 53 Republican signatures would be needed to reach the required 218, and, as Albert was to confess, he had no idea how many Republicans would sign. When Johnson pressed the Majority Leader at the breakfast, his answers were the answers of a man who only thought he knew. "Where do you get your count of 165?" Johnson asked him. "We may have trouble getting it," Albert had admitted. "I think 150 would be more like it." "That includes twenty Republicans," Majority Whip Boggs chimed in.

"What good is thinking to me?" Telephoning Albert after the breakfast, Johnson asked, "Can we make a little poll of our own?" Congressmen should be asked one by one, each by the Democratic assistant whip responsible for knowing his views. "Just start going down them by whips," he said. And get answers that could be relied on. *"Thinking isn't good enough. I need to* know*!"* "Just say to each whip, 'Now we've got to know and this is it.' "

Counting the votes—and getting the votes. Larry O'Brien arrived on Capitol Hill with his assistants, and soon the Hill was buzzing with reports of the pressure the White House was putting on congressmen. And Meany was not the only labor leader Johnson was contacting. "We're going to either rise or fall . . . on the results of [the petition]," Johnson had told Dave McDonald of the Steelworkers, "and I think if there's ever a time when you really talk to every human you could . . . you ought to do it. If we could possibly get that bill out of the Rules Committee. . . . We've got to get 219 [*sic*]. . . . Until we get 219 we'll be a failure. And if we fail on this, then we fail in everything."

"I'll have all my legislative people report to Nordy immediately," McDonald had promised, and on this Tuesday, when his call to Johnson was put through while the President was talking to Martin Luther King, the Steelworkers lobbyists were working the Hill under the direction of Frank Nordhoff ("Nordy") Hoffman. "We've got thirty-three guys at work covering forty-five states," McDonald told Johnson. "Our boys are staying on top. We still haven't contacted North and South Carolina, Georgia or Tennessee, but that'll be done today."

"Well, you won't get that many [votes] there," Johnson said.

"No, but we can put the muscle on them," McDonald replied.

Getting the votes himself.

Albert's 165—or 150, or 130, or whatever—count of petition supporters did not include any from Texas. Since the state was still so overwhelmingly southern in its racial attitudes, getting any would be hard. A key to getting them, however, could be Albert Thomas, whose appropriations subcommittee chairmanships, and access to Brown & Root campaign funds, made him a congressman to whom other Texas congressmen paid attention.

Thomas was an advocate neither of civil rights nor of interference with House prerogatives, and when Johnson first asked him about the petition, he said he was against it. He was, however, an advocate of appropriations for Brown & Root projects such as the deep-ocean drilling project called "Mohole," and wanted assurances that Johnson's budget economizing wouldn't extend to the annual appropriation for that project that added so substantially to Brown & Root's annual profit. And he wanted to know also that he would continue to have the final say over matters before his subcommittees, that the new President wouldn't interfere with that. Giving him what he wanted, Johnson told Thomas that he would rely on "your judgment on the [National] Science Foundation before I send my budget up there," but coupled this assurance about Thomas' influence with a request that he use that influence for civil rights. When, that morning, Thomas had said he was against the petition, Johnson, as he was to relate to Homer Thornberry, "told him" that nonetheless "I sure hoped he'd sign it, and he said all right"; after all, Johnson said to Thornberry, Republicans, "the party of Lincoln wouldn't do anything" to help it pass—and in fact Thomas quickly called together the members of the Texas delegation whose districts did not include large numbers of African-Americans, and after that meeting Thornberry said the petition would have "six signatures from Texas," six more than it had had before.

Covering the House of Representatives for the *New York Times* that Tuesday, Anthony Lewis felt the mood shifting, and by evening, he understood the reason why. Sitting down at his typewriter, he wrote his lead: "President Johnson threw his full weight today behind the effort to pry the civil rights bill out of the House Rules Committee."

Pointing out that "It is extraordinary for any President to give direct support to a discharge petition," Lewis said that "The petition procedure is unusual, and it rarely works. . . . But the President's intervention could provide the psychological push to get past those obstacles." It hadn't taken long for the President's intervention to begin having an effect, he wrote. "By this evening," he said, "there was some evidence of a dramatic impact on the situation in the House." One veteran legislator, Lewis wrote, had told him, "It is too turbulent to predict anything certainly now, but I've never seen one before where we've had the President going, and the civil rights groups, and labor, and the church people."

AND IN FACT it didn't take long at all. The next day, Wednesday, December 4, the headlines were made by the Republican leaders of the House, who at a conference of the Chamber's Republican members that morning denounced the discharge petition ("This move for a petition is irritating some people" who other-wise would have supported the civil rights bill, warned Ohio's McCulloch, rank-ing Republican on the Judiciary Committee), announced that none of the leaders would sign it, and predicted that few other Republicans would, either. "The con-sensus appeared to be that the Rules Committee should be allowed a reasonable time to hold hearings and act on the bill before a . . . petition was used," Confer-ence chairman Gerald Ford told reporters. Not a single congressman had spoken in favor of a petition at the conference, Ford said. RIGHTS BILL STYMIED, the *Washington Star* was to proclaim the next day. HOUSE G.O.P. SCORNS PLAN TO FORCE ACTION ON RIGHTS, the *Times* said.

Those headlines, however, didn't take sufficient account of other meetings that day, among them two at which Johnson spoke: the first with the Business Advisory Council, eighty-nine of the nation's biggest businessmen; the second with the twenty-member AFL-CIO Executive Council. At both of the meetings the President showed again his gift for political phrasemaking. He had found his phrase now. Just as a key to his strategy was to make the public understand the issue—to make the public understand that Republican congressmen voting against the petition were actually opposing civil rights—another key was to make these congressmen wary of voting against it, to let them know that their vote could put them in an embarrassing position. And he had found a phrase that would dramatize the issue vividly, a phrase that would touch with Republican congressmen, because they were, after all, members of the party of the President who had freed the slaves. It was a phrase that had a ring to it, and Johnson knew it. Over dinner with old colleagues that evening, he told them what he had said at the two meetings: "I talked to both of them about the party of Lincoln."

He had indeed, and had hammered the phrase home. After telling the busi-nessmen that he knew that most of them were Republicans, and, due to funda-mental philosophical differences, might be his opponents, but that, nonetheless, "I am the only President you have; if you would have me fail, then you fail, for the country fails," he told them that at this moment they should be supporting him on civil rights. "I will say to those of you who belong to the party of Lin-coln," he said, "that the civil rights bill was sent to Congress in May," and Judge Smith was blocking it, and Republicans—members of "the party of Lincoln"—were supporting Smith. He had, he said, told the businessmen "that they either had to have two members [on the Rules Committee] from the party of Lincoln for civil rights, or they oughtn't to have one single Republican re-elected and they ought to have 60 or 70 or whatever you need on that petition—they're [the public is] going to know who's responsible and it's going to be right in the Republicans' lap."

To the labor leaders, he spoke as a general aware that he was speaking to men some of whom had been his enemies but who now should be his supporters—a general rallying troops. "I need you, want you, and believe you should be at my side," he said. "This nation will be grateful to you—and so will I." Labor

leaders showed their enthusiasm more visibly than business leaders. As he got
to the last sentences in his speech, all around him men were standing and
applauding.

He had rallied them to his side—and they came. The Steelworkers' thirty-
three lobbyists were already at work, and by the end of the day, the halls of the
House Office Buildings were filled with perhaps two hundred more "guys with
big stomachs and big watches," in the words of a congressional aide—lobbyists
from the Electrical Workers and the Auto Workers and the railroad brother-
hoods—with, behind them, the promise of labor's telephone banks, and labor's
field-workers, and labor's money for next year's election campaign.

And there was a third meeting that day—of the two hundred members of
the Leadership Conference on Civil Rights at a Washington hotel—and this time
the anger and bitterness of these men at social injustice had a focus. Congress
was no longer an amorphous problem that they couldn't solve; Johnson had
given them a clear target. Meany explained "that the discharge petition offered
the only method" that would work, the *Washington Post* reported, and Wilkins
"repeated the NAACP's intention of purging congressmen who voted against" it.
Johnson and O'Brien knew that the civil rights groups alone didn't have enough
broad strength to get the petition signed, but among the participants in the conference were leaders of religions organizations. Four thousand priests and ministers were at that moment in Philadelphia, attending a National Council of
Churches convention; the Leadership Conference decided to contact them and
ask them to return home by way of Washington so that they could visit their representatives and urge them to vote for discharge. By that evening, in fact, an
advance guard had already arrived on Capitol Hill. "Negro and labor leaders are
streaming in," Doris Fleeson reported, and there were clerics' collars in the halls,
too. Mail to congressmen about civil rights had been increasing. That afternoon,
it was, one report said, "heavy in favor of action now."

And all day the President hammered home, over and over again, the theme
he wanted emphasized, the phrase that would make it politically untenable for
Republicans to keep opposing the petition. "We've just got to [get] the party of
Lincoln on that goddamned spot and keep them there, and carry it right on
through the election," he told O'Brien. "If they're anti-civil rights, let's find out
about it right now. . . . We'll play it for keeps."

By the end of Wednesday, in fact, it was over. Despite the headlines, it
wasn't Wednesday morning's Republican conference with its defiant anti-
petition stance that was decisive but a quiet meeting Wednesday evening, mostly
unreported at the time, between Clarence Brown of Ohio, the pro–civil rights
Republican who was the GOP's ranking member on the Rules Committee, and
the committee's chairman.

Brown told Judge Smith, as a later account puts it, that "the heat was getting so great" that Republicans—by neither signing the petition nor voting
against Smith in committee, thereby in effect supporting him—were being put

in an embarrassing and politically untenable position. "Appealing to their friendship, Brown said he did not want to have to push him, but something had to be done." Whether or not Brown made a specific threat, he didn't have to, so clear was the situation. Two Republican votes could overrule Smith within his own committee and have the committee release the bill to the floor. Or enough Republican signatures could be added to the discharge petition so that it would have the necessary 218. Either course would be a public repudiation of Smith's authority. Smith agreed to issue a statement, which he did early Thursday morning.

This statement was somewhat different from earlier ones by the judge. Smith did not repeat that he had "no plans" for setting a date for hearings on the civil rights bill, and no estimate as to how long the hearings might last. Now the judge said he *did* have plans: to begin the hearings "reasonably soon" in January "after Congress reconvenes." The statement was allowed to be vague—to permit Smith to save as much face as possible—but the details of Smith's surrender were clarified by Brown, in a statement reinforced by Halleck. By "reasonably soon," Brown explained, the chairman had meant that he would begin the hearings in "early January"—it would soon become known that a firm date, January 9, had in fact been set—and that in fact they would run only from seven to ten days, in no event more than twelve. That meant the hearings would be over not in March, but in January. And Halleck said that at their conclusion, the five Republicans on Smith's committee would all promptly vote to send the bill to the floor—where it would be passed by the full House "by the end of January at the latest."

The press viewed the statements as merely a compromise. One of the few reporters who understood was the *Times'* Lewis, who noted that "it was a compromise that gave the President all he could reasonably have hoped for. . . . Johnson 'compromises' often have that character." While Johnson wouldn't have House passage of the bill in 1963, he would have it early enough in 1964 so that the scenario he had feared—the scenario that had in fact been unfolding until he stepped in ("they'll have hearings in the Rules Committee until about the middle of March," and by the time there was a House vote after that, and the bill finally reached the Senate, "Dick Russell . . . will screw them to death")—that scenario had been avoided. The "real problem" was still going to be in the Senate, but now there was going to be additional time, perhaps two months' additional time, to solve it. House observers who knew the judge knew why he had accepted the compromise—because by accepting it he had "spared himself the possible indignity of being relieved of responsibility for the bill," as the *Times* reported—and knew that he had been forced to accept it by the sudden new pressure behind the discharge petition from the White House. The civil rights bill was still going to face monumental difficulties when it reached the Senate in 1964, commented *Newsweek,* one of the few periodicals to grasp the situation, "but by then Mr. Johnson will have [given it] quite a head start."

• • •

JOHNSON'S STRATEGY WOULD WORK, of course, only if Smith didn't renege—start to delay again—when January arrived. The best way to ensure against that was to have the discharge petition still active—still on the floor, with a substantial number of signatures attached to it so that if delays began again, enough could quickly be added to pass it.

The petition was filed as scheduled on December 9. It was actually filed not by Bolling but by Judiciary Committee chairman Emanuel Celler, because of Bolling's unpopularity with the leaders, and because it was Celler's prerogative, as chairman of the committee that had passed the bill, to introduce it. But since Smith had agreed to a date for the hearings, many House members who had previously agreed to sign the petition were now unwilling to do so as long as Smith held to the schedule.

"Larry? Larry? How's that petition going?" Johnson asked O'Brien, who was on Capitol Hill monitoring its progress, that afternoon. There were only about one hundred signatures on it, O'Brien replied. "That's not as good as it should be." "No, it's not," Johnson said.

He put Jenkins to work applying pressure to wavering members of the Texas delegation, and four in addition to Albert Thomas' six signed before the day was over, but the total number at the end of the day was only 131. The number was small, however, because only a mere twenty-four Republicans had signed, and Clarence Brown had let Smith know that many more had agreed to sign in January, if the judge tried to delay then, so the number was high enough. "They'll sign it after the first of the year if he drags," Albert said. "We can get 218 members if he drags too long." And Smith knew it. The judge had confessed to Albert that many "members have been . . . threatening to sign" in January. It was too late for him to renege.

Thursday, December 5, the day Smith had surrendered, was also the day of Lyndon Johnson's lunch with Harry Byrd, the lunch at which the mood around the tax bill had started changing, so the lead headlines the next day, December 6, were not only ACTION IN JANUARY PLEDGED ON RIGHTS but also PRESIDENT WINS PLEDGE BY BYRD FOR TAX ACTION—headlines of triumph for Lyndon Johnson. Barely two weeks before, when he had become President, the two most important bills before Congress had been stalled, as they had been stalled for months, with no realistic sign of movement in any foreseeable future. Now, just two weeks into his presidency, both bills were moving.

They seemed to be moving, furthermore, in the order he wanted—the order this master of parliamentary strategy saw as crucial. If the tax bill wasn't cleared away—wasn't passed by the Senate—before the civil rights bill arrived on the floor, it would be used to delay and kill civil rights; the two bills would, in fact, be held hostage to each other, resulting, in all probability, in the death of both. Despite the tough conditions Byrd had set at their lunch, however, the senator had said that if they were met, he would bring his tax bill hearings to an expeditious end, and if he approved the galley proofs of the budget that would be ready for his perusal during the first week in January, he would release the tax bill to the Senate floor, where it could be passed not long thereafter. Since, under the schedule Brown and Halleck had announced, the civil rights bill would still be in hearings before Judge Smith's Rules Committee until mid- or late January, and then "by the end of January" it would be passed by the full House and sent to the Senate, if Byrd's schedule was adhered to, the tax bill would be passed—cleared from the Senate floor—before the civil rights bill arrived there from the House. "They'd like to get it behind civil rights," Johnson knew, and if it gets behind civil rights, "it's Good night, Grace." Good night for the tax bill, good night for the civil rights bill. Now, it seemed, he had made sure the tax bill wouldn't get behind civil rights, that it would be "down in the storm cellar" in time. Other Administration "children"—the appropriations bills, the education bill, the foreign aid bill—were also finally moving on through the line, and would be down in the storm cellar when civil rights arrived. And now, thanks to the discharge petition, civil rights *would* arrive.

ON ONE OF THE DAYS of that crucial, hectic, tension-filled week—the exact day is uncertain—*Life* magazine sent a photographer and a reporter to the Oval Office for a cover story that would run in the next week's edition.

The article was not the investigative article on Lyndon Johnson's money or on Bobby Baker and Don Reynolds that, had it not been for the assassination, might have been the magazine's cover story that week, but rather on the mastery Lyndon Johnson had demonstrated in taking over the presidency. The picture on the cover would be of him standing behind his desk in the Oval Office, leaning over it and resting his weight on his big hands, looking tall and strong in a dark blue suit with the two flags behind him, a picture that fit the headline over the article: TEXAN SITS TALL IN A NEW SADDLE.

The reporter was John Steele, who, having covered Johnson for many years, understood the significance of a small gesture Johnson made during the interview. On Johnson's desk was an in-box. Steele had seen that box in Johnson's vice presidential office, when there had been few documents in it—when, perhaps, it had been empty. Now it was filled, with documents that had to be dealt with, problems that had to be solved, decisions that had to be made. As Johnson was talking to him, Steele was to write, "Almost lovingly, he thumbed slowly through" its "jammed contents."

Steele had filed thousands of words on Lyndon Johnson over the years, but he felt the man he was seeing now was a man he had never seen before. "There is in Lyndon Johnson an inner calm, a certainty of purpose," he wrote. "The small vanities, the occasional petulance, the inordinate preoccupation with what men say or write about him are gone, at least for the present. There is about him now an aura of fulfillment which in all his prior years of public office never marked the man."

ON THE SATURDAY of that week—December 7—the Johnsons moved into the White House.

Lady Bird had insisted that Jackie and her children not be hurried out, but she had begun making plans for the move, on November 26, the day after President Kennedy's funeral, asking the man in charge of the internal administration of the White House—Chief Usher J. B. West—to come to The Elms. When West told her that Jackie would be taking only the furniture from her own bedroom and her children's, she said she would bring only the furniture from her own bedroom, and Lucy and Lynda's. She didn't want to alter the rooms Jackie had restored, she said. ("I especially love the Yellow Oval Room upstairs. . . . It's my husband's favorite color," she told West.) He quickly discovered, as he was to say, that "there was nothing tentative about Claudia Alta Taylor Johnson." Looking at him "intently," he was to say, she "emphasized, 'I want you to *run* the White House.'

"I've been running a house for thirty years, and I want to devote my time to other things," she said. She was highly organized, he realized, and had very clear ideas. "I like working in a room with one door so I can control my privacy," she said.

Jackie had moved out with her children, to a house in Georgetown made available to her by Averell Harriman, on the morning of the 7th, and Lyndon Johnson wanted to move in that afternoon. Feeling that December 7, a date with the aura of infamy about it, was not the best possible day for the move, Lady Bird had tried to persuade her husband of that, and thought for a time that she had done so. "I think we'll probably wait until after Pearl Harbor Day," she told West. In the event, however, her wishes had received the consideration they usually received. On the morning of the 7th, moving vans began pulling in to the driveway of The Elms, and at three o'clock, two cars pulled up to the White House, Lucy's white convertible, from which she emerged with the Johnsons' two beagles, Him and Her, on a leash, and a black White House limousine. (Lynda Bird had returned to the University of Texas in Austin.) When Mrs. Johnson stepped out of the second car, she was carrying only one possession: the large, framed photograph of the man with the grim face. "I had our favorite picture of the Speaker, Mr. Sam Rayburn, in my hand," she was to write in her diary. "His is the only photograph of a person that we keep in our living room wherever we are, and I wanted it with us at the White House."

West escorted Mrs. Johnson and Lucy up to the private, second-floor family quarters, where Lady Bird found a small vase of flowers from Jackie, and a note: "I wish you a happy arrival in your new house, Lady Bird—Remember—you will be happy here. Love, Jackie." He showed Lucy her bedroom. A telephone was on the nightstand next to the bed, and she asked him, "Does this telephone go just to my room or does it go anywhere else?" When he explained that it was connected only to the White House switchboard and not to any telephone on the second floor, she said, "Oh, good! In our house all our extensions were connected, and my daddy was always listening in on me."

Lucy's father was not as pleased with his new quarters. Two days after the Johnsons moved in, he told West, "Mr. West, if you can't get that shower of mine fixed, I'm going to have to move back to The Elms."

"He didn't sound as if he were joking," West was to say. And after the President explained that the water pressure was inadequate, and that he wanted the same elaborate, multi-nozzle arrangement that he had had at his former home, he repeated his threat to move out. Then, "without a smile, he turned on his heel and walked away."

A few minutes later, Mrs. Johnson asked West to come by the room she had chosen for her office, a small sitting room with one door. "I guess you've been told about the shower," she said, with a smile, and repeated to West what she said to all Johnson employees. "Anything that . . . needs to be done, remember this: my husband comes first, the girls second, and I will be satisfied with what's left."

As he became acquainted with the Johnsons, West was to write, "I soon could see that had been her life's pattern." Nothing, he came to see, could "faze her."

UNEXPECTEDLY, KARL MUNDT'S wheat amendment reared its head again. Despite Johnson's belief that he had "murdered" the bill, as it turned out, the death certificate bore only the Senate's signature. On December 16 the amendment was resurrected in the House, which passed it as an amendment to the foreign aid appropriations bill, and then refused to accept a conference committee report in which the Senate conferees tried to delete it. "Congress seemed ready to resume its rebellion against presidential authority," as Evans and Novak put it. Speaker McCormack again advised Johnson to let the whole foreign aid issue go over until January: for one thing, many House members had already left for the Christmas recess.

The advice wasn't accepted. Reminding his staff that the issue was not wheat but power—that the House as well as the Senate had to be shown who was in charge—Johnson worked on members of the conference committee, "demanding of Congress," Evans and Novak said, "what Congress had made clear it would not give," and on December 21 the conferees agreed on a foreign aid bill with no Mundt amendment in it. Then he ordered McCormack and the other Democratic leaders to call every Democratic congressman back to Washington for another vote in the House. When the leaders protested that the members wouldn't come, he wouldn't listen. Those who returned he invited to a December 23 Christmas party at the White House, at which he climbed up on a small gilt chair, and shouted, "You have labored through the vineyard and plowed through the snow." And on December 24, in a session held—"perhaps for the first time in history"—at 7 a.m. so that congressmen could get home for Christmas Eve, the House reversed itself, and on a party-line vote (189 to 158, with the 189 including only two Republicans), finally killed the Mundt amendment for good. The earlier victory had had to be revisited—it had been. He had won again—an even more impressive victory than before. He knew exactly what he had won. "At that moment," he was to write in his memoirs, "the power of the federal government began flowing back to the White House." His assessment was echoed by congressmen and by observers of Congress, one of whom said that if Johnson "had dodged this one," he might have been viewed on Capitol Hill as just another weak President, but by instead showing "steely nerve" in demanding the members' return, he had taught them once and for all that "a strong hand was at the wheel."

Two hours after the vote was counted, Air Force One was in the air, carrying him back to Texas, where he would spend thirteen days on his ranch over Christmas and New Year's.

2 1

Serenity

FROM BERGSTROM AIR FORCE BASE, outside Austin, three big olive-green Army helicopters lifted off and wheeled west. Down to the right, as Lyndon Johnson sat in the front seat of the first helicopter beside the pilot, was the pink granite dome of the State Capitol, in which as a boy he had stood, as content, perhaps, as he was ever to be, in the rear of the House of Representatives chamber while his father had had a seat there, and in which his father, after a while, no longer had had a seat, and near the capitol was Austin's other dominant building, the University of Texas Tower, centerpiece of the college he hadn't been able to attend because he had had to go to the "poor boys' school." And then, almost immediately, the helicopters were over hills; the passengers could see over the first ridges, over the ones behind them, could see the hills rolling away to the west as far as the eye could see, and Lyndon Johnson was, the moment the hills began, back in the landscape of his youth.

To the four pool reporters in the third helicopter, the land below, with its trees bare and meadows gray-brown in winter, was a shock; "sere and bleak" one was to call it, "so empty" another would say. "We had no idea of the emptiness." The fifty miles west of Bergstrom had only two tiny villages—Dripping Springs and Henly. The miles of Texas Hill Country between them were interrupted only by the occasional farm or ranch house, or by stone chimneys jutting up out of debris where houses had once stood before their owners gave up and moved away. The helicopters, their engines as loud as thunder in that silent landscape, roared over it, scattering herds of sheep and goats as they neared; even some of the placid white-faced Herefords were startled into lumbering a few steps. And then, down to the right, was a slightly larger huddle of houses and stores around a courthouse. When Lyndon Johnson had been growing up in Johnson City, the hills had added to the isolation of this "island town" surrounded by a vast sea of land, the only roads out of it unpaved, rutted, often impassable in winter. The helicopters made nothing of the hills; in no more than a minute or two after Johnson City, they were over the Pedernales Valley and the little river, as brown as the land, and were approaching the Johnson Ranch, a sprawling, comfortable but not huge house, only seeming huge in that land of little houses, a freshly painted white against the muted colors of the Hill Country, with the blue of the swimming pool beside it. And from the tall flagpole in front of the house, under the American flag, hung another flag, one that hadn't been there when he had last seen his ranch on November 21. The sky was literally cloudless on this day before Christmas—a bright and breezy day, as would be most of the thirteen days Johnson was to spend on the ranch over the Christmas break. It was that beautiful, glittering, pitiless blue sky, that "sapphire" Hill Country sky, at which his father and mother had stared day after day during those blazing Hill Country summers, looking in vain for a cloud that might mean rain, as their cotton and their dreams died in the drought. But fluttering against that sky now was a dark blue flag with a circle of white stars around an eagle holding an olive branch and arrows in his talons, the flag that meant that this house was the home of the President of the United States.

Lyndon Johnson's changes in mood had always been violent, veering from his sad, silent spells to the periods of almost frenzied euphoria that his aides called "highs." The depth of the depression he had been in when he left the Pedernales a month before was matched by the height of his elation now. He couldn't contain himself. It had been a long day, but Frank Cormier of the AP and the three other pool reporters were "whisked off by helicopter" to Judge Moursund's ranch, even deeper in the hills.

"A Johnson we had never seen emerged at the Moursund ranch," Cormier wrote. "Gone were the low shoes," the necktie and suit. The President was wearing hand-tooled cowboy boots, an open-necked khaki shirt and a tan Stetson, which he pushed back to "a rakish angle upon the familiar head." Moursund had two rifles in his hands, and Johnson took one. Telling the reporters "The Judge and I are goin' to do a little deer huntin' and you-all can tag along if you want to," he crammed them into the back seat of Moursund's convertible, and they headed off across the hills, bumping along rutted trails and lurching across gullies. Spotting a grazing doe, Johnson rested his rifle on the window to take aim, but lowered the gun, saying, "I haven't got the heart to kill her." The hunt ended without any shots being fired, but Johnson jumped out of the car happily. "I've only been here an hour and I feel better already," he said.

The next day, Christmas, a Wednesday, a brief photo session had been scheduled so that news photographers could take pictures of him on the lawn in front of the ranch—a full tour of the ranch house had been scheduled for Friday—and about fifty photographers, along with a dozen or so reporters hoping for a chance to ask a few questions during the photo session, had come out from Austin on a chartered bus. But when the picture-taking was over and they started to leave, he wouldn't let them go. His brother, his two surviving sisters, their children and other Johnson family members—twenty-seven in all—were at the ranch for Christmas dinner, and he had them come out of the house, and lined them up, ordering them about "as though they were junior senators," as one reporter put it, and introduced them to the press one by one.

"This is Aunt Jessie, Miz Jessie Hatcher, who did all my cooking, washing and sewing for me while I was in school in Houston.

"This is Uncle Huffman Baines. Uncle Huffman, how old are you?"

"I don't know," Uncle Huffman replied.

"A very sensible answer," the President said. "He's seventy-nine, but he looks fifty-nine, and he never had but one job in his life," a lifetime post as a telephone company engineer, he explained. "And this is Cousin Oreole, who keeps us fit" because her house was half a mile down the road from the ranch house, and he and Lady Bird walked down to see her almost every evening. "And when you sit down to visit with her, you have to be mentally fit." There were twenty-seven introductions to be made, with special attention to his daughters ("Her boyfriend is on his way here from Wisconsin," he said in introducing Lucy. "I mean one of her boyfriends"). Lynda was wearing her Christmas gift from her father, a loose-fitting red shift; he reached out and bundled up the fabric, to prove, he said with a smile, that she wasn't in a family way. Next he had the four secretaries he had brought from Washington—Marie Fehmer, Vicky McCammon, Yolanda Boozer and his new black secretary, Gerri Whittington—come out of the house, so that he could introduce them.

The photographers and reporters started to leave, but he still wouldn't let them. "Come in and see our house," he said, and asked Lady Bird if there wasn't time before dinner to take the group on a tour.

Actually, dinner was ready—and had been for some time. And parts of the house weren't in condition to be seen by journalists.

"Her mouth opened in wordless surprise and horror," one reporter was to write. "Why . . . yes," she managed to say. "But I'd just love to give them a wonderful tour when they come back Friday. The turkey is ready and the dressing is getting cold." There was a pause while she and her husband exchanged glances. "But whatever you say, darling."

He showed them the living room, with the enormous fireplace, and his desk ("Don't take any pictures of the desktop. I think there are some secret documents on it"), and the framed letter to Sam Houston from his great-grandfather ("He was a Baptist preacher, and he was writing to renew a note at eight percent interest"), and the paintings, including one that he told them was his favorite, of a farm girl standing happily looking up at clouds, that was named *First Rain*—he didn't tell them why it was his favorite—and they saw the only photograph in the room, the same photograph that was the only one Lady Bird had carried into the White House. He showed them the deer-head hat rack, with the deer's nose covered with red felt for Christmas. It was holding fourteen hats, and he told them anecdotes about several. The tour continued. The sixty journalists arrived at the master bedroom. The door was locked. He knocked, and then knocked again. "Mrs. Johnson has locked the bedroom on me," he said. She opened it a moment later; it was obvious, *Time* reported, that she "had just finished tidying up."

After he showed the group the other six bedrooms, Lady Bird was observed tugging on his sleeve, but all they had seen thus far was the inside. He showed them the swimming pool, and explained the heating system, and the family graveyard, and told them who was buried there, and the Friendship Walk, relating anecdotes about various famous guests on their ranch visits. "Go pipe that music in," he told Lynda, and the Muzak in the live oaks was turned on. "Overflowing with energy," Cormier wrote, "the President hopped up on a stone wall" overlooking the Pedernales and "assured us" the little stream "could become a raging torrent," told about various floods, including the one that had almost marooned Lady Bird on the ranch, and about the dam he had built across the river. Then, Cormier wrote, "with long strides, the President led us to the family hangar . . . to admire a new brown and white" plane the Johnsons owned, and then to the livestock loading pens and chutes. "That's where the cattle go out and the money comes in," he explained.

It might, it seemed, be time to leave. The press corps started to walk toward the buses. But as Johnson turned to go inside, he had a thought. "I've got something for you-all if you'll wait a minute," he said, and sent aides hurrying off to return with large cartons containing souvenir ashtrays bearing a map of Texas with the ranch's location indicated by a star. "Only take one," he said. In unwrapping them, some of the reporters dropped the cellophane wrappers on the lawn, and, one was to recall, "Our final view was of our Chief Executive stooping to retrieve them."

THEN, THREE DAYS LATER, on December 28, there was a state visit from the chancellor of the Federal Republic of Germany, Ludwig Erhard.

It began with the customary formalities that attended such visits, the nineteen-gun salute due a head of state as Erhard came down the ramp from his plane onto Bergstrom's red carpet, the long receiving line with Johnson at its head and the state's governor next to him, the military band playing the German and American national anthems, the honor guard parading the colors as the tall, bronzed President and the short, roly-poly, red-cheeked chancellor reviewed the ranks of rigid troops and then mounted, along with the governor, a small stand to make brief formal statements; the only disquieting notes were the cast on John Connally's arm, his face, gaunt and pale in the bright Texas sun, and the faces of the Secret Service men, "alert and obviously concerned"—were they remembering another big plane gleaming in the Texas sun, another red carpet, another receiving line with Johnson and Connally at its head? But then the helicopters lifted off and headed west into the hills, and from the moment, twenty-five minutes later, that they touched down at the LBJ Ranch, the visit became, in the words of one reporter, "nothing remotely like" any state visit that the journalists had ever seen.

In contrast to the formalities of Washington, here, festooning the balcony over the front door of the ranch house, was bunting in West Germany's red, yellow and black, a huge photograph of the chancellor and a sign saying "Willkommen!" After a photo and interview session for reporters with "diplomatic staffers who picked their way in shiny black street shoes across the ranch grounds," as *Newsweek* put it, Johnson met with Erhard, only interpreters present, in the living room while Secretary of State Rusk, German foreign minister Gerhard Schroeder and their staffs crammed into the smaller adjoining room—much too small for the group—for staff discussions. And then Johnson drove Erhard, Schroeder and Rusk out for a tour of the ranch, and stopped the car in the middle of a meadow, and the President and chancellor discussed affairs of state while white-faced Herefords moved closer to the car. Meanwhile, accommodations were being arranged: between the main house and the guest house, the ranch had eight bedrooms but the German party numbered twenty-five, and the State Department delegation eight. Lady Bird moved out of her bedroom, Lynda and Lucy moved out of theirs into a single smaller room, other staffers moved in with ranch foreman Dale Malechek, and his wife, Jewel—beds were found for everyone, and at dinner everyone crammed around three tables in the Johnsons' dining room.

The next day, Sunday, was spent in Fredericksburg, the community nineteen miles to the west down the Pedernales Valley that had been settled by an oxcart wagon train of Germans in 1846, after a harrowing, months-long journey through Comanche country. With its solid stone houses crowded close to the main street, the small, neat garden plots between them, and a church in early German Gothic style ("a rare bit of Nuremberg transplanted to Texas"), Fredericksburg was a tiny replica of Germany in the midst of the remote Texas Hill Country, and its residents clung to German folkways—there was an annual *Saengerfest,* or singing contest, and the *Schuetzenbund* held frequent shooting contests, and "Easter Fires" in the hills, and in its stores and streets German was heard at least as much as English. Along its main street, lined with German flags for the occasion, the names on the stores were Duecker's, Beckmann's, Kiehne's and Schroeder's, and the café was the Glockenspiel; the day's special, the sign in its window proclaimed, was "Eisbein [pig's knuckles] with sauerkraut." First the President and chancellor and their staffs and security men visited the Pioneer Memorial, an octagonal replica of the "Vereins Kirche," the church-fort built by the wagon-train pioneers. The welcoming speech by Fredericksburg's mayor was in German— and emotional. Bring our greetings back to Germany; "that is the homeland of our forefathers," he said. Erhard, replying, noted that Johnson had told him "that if I speak German, they will understand me better than they will understand him." Then they went to church, where the hymns and "Silent Night" were sung in German; when, after the ceremony, Erhard told the pastor he had been surprised by that, the pastor told him that the hymns were always sung in German.

THAT AFTERNOON WAS the state dinner, held in Stonewall, a wide spot in the road between the LBJ Ranch and Fredericksburg.

"No one who was there is likely to forget that dinner," Cormier was to recall. "The very idea of holding a state dinner in Stonewall, Texas, was daring . . . Barely a hamlet, Stonewall had just eight business establishments, three service stations, a café-motel, two grocery stores, a garage and a button factory—and even that listing makes it seem bigger than it really is." The venue for the dinner was the Stonewall High School gymnasium, a converted wooden Army barracks, rather rickety, which carpenters had been hastily patching and local housewives painting for several days in a vain attempt to conceal its imperfections.

Inside, the walls had been decorated with yellow, red and black bunting, and the basketball backboards with cutouts of German eagles. The rest of the décor was Texas. The narrow stage was a diorama of the state's symbols: Against its rear wall a corral fence had been erected with coiled lariats on its posts and a Western saddle and an Indian blanket on its top rail, from which dangled boots, spurs and a set of stirrups; propped against the fence were a wagon wheel and a banjo. Bales of hay completed the backdrop. In front of the fence, where the school's ancient, battered upright piano usually stood, was a huge, shining concert grand piano, so large that the stage seemed to sag a little under its weight. On the floor of the basketball court thirty tables had been set with red-and-white-checked tablecloths; kerosene lanterns were the centerpieces.

The dinner was Texas: a large chuck wagon had been parked near the front door by Johnson's favorite caterer, Walter Jetton of Fort Worth, "the Leonard Bernstein of Barbecue," and next to it were Jetton's barbecue spits on which, since 5 a.m., he and his sous-chefs, their Stetsons tilted back off their faces because of the heat, had been slathering his renowned special barbecue sauce onto vast expanses of meat—five hundred pounds of brisket and three hundred pounds of spareribs. The arriving guests, about three hundred natives and forty-five or fifty men in blue suits, were served the barbecue, together with hickory gravy, German potato salad, Texas coleslaw, ranch baked beans and sourdough biscuits. Then they went inside, Lady Bird escorting Erhard, Johnson behind them, "the leaders of two great nations carrying their own heaping plates" across the crowded gymnasium, filled with smoke and aroma from the barbecue spits. Dessert was a German chocolate cake baked from a recipe carried by the original pioneers, and the men in blue suits drank beer from paper cups, and, with dessert, coffee from tin cups. Strumming guitars, a country music band, the Wanderers Three, augmented to four members for the occasion, was "gathering rainbows and handing out schemes" with "a heart full of heather and a pocketful of dreams."

And the ambiance in the little country gymnasium was Texas, too, nothing at all like a formal state dinner in the White House—and in its informality and friendliness, very much like a typical Texas "speaking," the diplomats eating spareribs with their hands and making return trips to the chuck wagon. (Erhard's once-heaping plate was empty by the end of the meal.) A warm buzz of talk and laughter filled the hall—much of it in German as Fredericksburg's townspeople chatted happily with the representatives of the homeland. Up at the head table, Lady Bird and Erhard, despite their language differences, were talking together like old friends.

And, after dinner, the entertainment was also Texas.

The master of ceremonies was "Cactus" Pryor, "the George Jessel of Texas"; he apologized to the chancellor "because they had been unable to find a way to barbecue sauerkraut." There was a Mexican mariachi band, square dances by the Billyettes, a precision dance team (not all that precise) from Fredericksburg High School and then German carols sung by cowgirls—the St. Mary's High School choir in full cowgirl regalia: Stetsons, blue skirts, white blouses and red neckerchiefs—under the direction of a nun in head-to-toe black habit. They closed with "Deep in the Heart of Texas"—and that was in German, too. *"Die Sterne bei Nacht sind gross und klar / Tief in das Herz von Texas . . ."* After each couplet, the traditional four Texas claps. At the conclusion, a cowboy yell, echoed by the audience. Only after that did the explanation for the grand piano appear: tall, curly-haired Van Cliburn of Fort Worth, whom newspapers had been calling "the pride of Texas" ever since his victory in 1958 in the first International Tchaikovsky Competition in Moscow. The thunderous chords of the young virtuoso's selections from Beethoven, Brahms and other German composers filled the rickety little building.

FORMAL THE DINNER may not have been; it was, however, a triumph. Erhard's smile grew broader and broader with each German song; as the cowgirls were singing the carols, he leaned back, lit up a long cigar, and puffed on it for the rest of the meal, his bright blue eyes sparkling, his face a picture of red-cheeked contentment. When they got to *"Die Sterne bei Nacht,"* he "almost broke up with laughter," a reporter wrote. Leaning over to Lady Bird, he said, in English, "We know that in Germany, too." Johnson was carried away. He went from table to table shaking hands, on his face a broad smile that he rarely showed in public. And when he got back to the head table, the rapport between him and the chancellor was palpable. The dinner was to close with a Texas ritual, the presentation of big gray "ten-gallon" Stetsons to the guests, and Johnson, calling up the German diplomats one by one, trying hats on for size and then adjusting them to the right angle, kept up a running stream of remarks. When he got to Erhard, he remarked that the differences between the metric and imperial systems meant he was giving him a "forty-liter" hat. The audience started to applaud as Erhard turned to model it, and Erhard waved his hand in appreciation. Grabbing the chancellor's hand, the taller Johnson raised it above Erhard's head like a referee raising a boxer's hand in victory. The affection from the Fredericksburg natives, who had preserved for a hundred years the language and customs of the country from which their ancestors had come, toward that country's leader, who was right there in their town, filled the room, and they kept applauding as Johnson and Erhard stood there, Johnson still holding the chancellor's hand aloft, the two heads of state, one tall and tanned, the other short and rosy-faced, a study in physical contrast except for one similarity: the broadness of their smiles. And when Johnson and Erhard started to leave, they found they couldn't for a while. The people from Fredericksburg formed a long line so that they could, one by one, shake the hand of the chancellor from their homeland and of the President, their own "native son," as the *Fredericksburg Standard* called him the next day, who had brought him to their town.

THE ENTIRE STATE VISIT WAS a triumph.

The overcrowding at the ranch was part of it. "The fact that you couldn't be anything other than intimate helped the discussions" and "contributed to the good spirit," one of the German officials told a reporter. Lady Bird was part of it—her gift for making visitors welcome and at ease: the open arms and warm smile and "Hi! Now you all make yourselves at home!" with which she greeted guests. Turning to her and bowing during his toast at the barbecue, Erhard said, "The homelike atmosphere she created for our talks already was a guarantee of our success. I feel at home with you." When he left the ranch for Bergstrom that evening, she said, with that warm smile, "You all come back now, y'hear." When he was giving his farewell talk at the airfield, the chancellor said he was sure there would be other visits. The rapport between the two leaders played a part, too. Looking at Johnson as he spoke at the barbecue, Erhard said he had found that he and the President shared "the same moral views, the same spirit, the same political ideas." He had found, he said, that they "looked at the world with the same eyes."

In his talk at Bergstrom, Erhard said that he and Johnson had considered all the major issues facing their two countries. "All these questions were discussed in detail, and we have been able to state full agreement and full unity of views. This is not just a diplomatic statement; it is just the truth I feel." Landing in Bonn ten hours later, he told reporters there that he and Johnson had established a personal relationship "that I think you can call friendship."

Diplomatic correspondents who debriefed Erhard's aides and Rusk's after the visit felt that the chancellor had described his feelings accurately. He had, *Time* reported, been "enchanted by all the Texas trimmings. But he was even more taken with Johnson himself. . . . Erhard showed with genuine feeling that he had established a personal friendship with the President, and he was obviously moved when he made his farewell." *Newsweek* called the visit "Stetson Statesmanship" and the "Sparerib Summit"—and said "somehow it all worked."

IT HAD WORKED in another way, too. John F. Kennedy's state dinners had been fine wines and French cuisine. This state dinner was beer and barbecue. Beethoven and Brahms had been played this time not in the elegant formality of the East Room but in front of lariats and a saddle and bales of hay. It was a contrast that, of course, the press noted. Recalling a state visit on which "the Kennedys transported Washington society down the Potomac in boats to Mount Vernon and there served outdoor dinner by candlelight while violins played," Douglas Kiker of the *Herald Tribune* wrote that "Now Ludwig Erhard [gets] a barbecue at Stonewall High School, and [is] entertained by somebody named Cactus Pryor. . . . It is a long way from the banks of Mount Vernon."

And it was a contrast that Lyndon Johnson wanted noted. While he had still been back in Washington, at dinner at The Elms one Sunday evening with three or four couples he had known since his early days in the capital, he had said, "I've got to be thinking about my future. I have to carry out the Kennedy legacy. I feel very strongly that that's part of my obligation, and at the same time I've got to put my own stamp on this administration in order to run for office on my own." ("Johnson talked very freely at that Sunday dinner," one of the guests says.) During the month before he left for Texas—the first month after the assassination—the emphasis he had wanted in his Administration was continuity. But now, with a new year—1964, an election year—about to begin, the emphasis would have to change. While continuity would still have to remain a major element in it—there was still the "obligation" to "carry out the Kennedy legacy"—contrast would now be required as well; the Administration would have to bear "my own stamp." The image of his Administration, of his presidency, of himself, would have to change.

SINCE THE CREATION of an image is one of the political arts, Lyndon Johnson had always been a master of it: a dramatic showman on the Texas political trails during his early campaigns. Fully aware now that his personality was not firmly defined in the mind of a national public that had not known him well before he became President ("He was very, very conscious of that," George Reedy says) and that to the limited extent he possessed a national image, it was of a frenzied wheeler-dealer, an arm-twister, a restless, ambition-driven politician, he set out during his two weeks on the ranch to create a different one.

The Erhard state dinner, its pattern so dramatically different from the Kennedy pattern, was a vivid announcement of a new, contrasting pattern, the scene in the Stonewall High School gymnasium a scene that established that the new presidency was going to be, in its style at least, very different from the old, the new President very different from his predecessor. And that contrast, that theme, would be reiterated through the events—at least the public events—of the rest of Johnson's stay in Texas, in a performance, a creation of an image, that was quite a show.

The Johnson Ranch, of course, was a perfect setting in which to draw the contrast: it would be hard to imagine one less like Hyannis Port than the Pedernales Valley. And if the setting was perfect, the man at center stage made the most of it.

All during these two weeks, the big jets from Washington glided into Bergstrom out of the northeast, and the helicopters lifted off and beat their way across the hills to set down, in clouds of dust, at the LBJ Ranch, bringing men on business of state: generals—the morning after Erhard left, the beribboned Joint Chiefs of Staff arrived with Defense Secretary McNamara for discussions on the budget; ambassadors (Chip Bohlen from France and David Bruce from England for discussions about the strains Le Grand Charles was causing within the NATO Alliance); ministers (Cabinet Secretaries Rusk of State, Freeman of Agriculture, Wirtz of Labor) and undersecretaries; economists Heller and Gordon, each lugging a briefcase crammed with papers; the national security advisor, McGeorge Bundy; the director of the Central Intelligence Agency, John McCone, who, breakfasting alone with the President, told him that despite a civil war between Greeks and Turks on Cyprus, the seventeen hundred Americans on the island were safe and "the [military] situation appeared to be reasonably in hand," and then strolled with him along the dirt road by the Pedernales, Secret Service men in the pecan groves, and when the President asked him if Premier Khrushchev had done or said anything significant during the past few days, replied, as he recalls, "No, that I felt that Khrushchev was" still "pretty well consumed with his internal problems and the Sino-Soviet relationship and that he had been remarkably quiet with respect to the West." (The conversation turned to Cuba. The latest CIA "assessment" concluded that the Russians were turning the SAM sites over to Cuba, which could be "ominous," McCone said. "The President made no comment.") Ted Sorensen flew down, and was driven from the Johnson airstrip to the Lewis Ranch about twenty miles away; although Christmas vacation was Sorensen's visitation time with his three boys—he had recently been divorced, at least partly because, he was to admit, the life of a presidential speechwriter "had undermined our marriage"—the middle son, Stephen, then ten years old, recalls that in that ranch house, "We spent a lot of time by ourselves. . . . I remember him writing and writing and writing, holed up by himself in a study at one end of the house"; the State of the Union speech was scheduled for delivery on January 8. But the business was carried on in an atmosphere very unlike that of Washington—by a Lyndon Johnson who was, to the journalists' eyes, very unlike the one they had thought they knew.

Press conferences were held, of course—large press conferences: more than two hundred reporters, about a score of them from foreign countries, staying in Austin hotels, were periodically loaded into buses and driven out to the ranch—but they could hardly have been more informal. Many of the announcements made at them concerned the budget: Johnson's first priority was not only to get it down below Harry Byrd's $100 billion limit, but to demonstrate to Byrd and his conservative allies that he was going to run the government frugally. Standing on the lawn outside the house after giving a group of reporters and photographers a tour, he suddenly told an aide, "Run in there and ask them to bring me that order I was working on," and read aloud an executive order he was about to issue setting new maximum limits for employment in each of the various government agencies at the June 30 end of the current fiscal year, levels that, taken together, would reduce the overall number of federal employees below the figure in effect when he had assumed office. The order directed agency heads to immediately report the steps they were taking to effect those reductions, and to inform him immediately of target levels they would establish for the following fiscal year. And it told the agency heads that quarterly reports were to be made to him for his personal approval, beginning on April 1. "Finally, once I have given my approval to your new targets, they are not to be exceeded without my explicit approval," the order concluded. To make sure the reporters got the point, he added that "We are trying conscientiously to show the thrift we talked about in the message to Congress."

A more informal, spur-of-the-moment setting for an announcement of a major new government policy could hardly be imagined, reporters said. Except that, two days later, there was one even more informal—and more dramatic as well. This time, the full press corps was being given a tour of the ranch, three large buses squeezing through the cattle guards on the narrow roads, frightened sheep leaping into the air in panic as the buses passed—with Lady Bird as the tour guide on one bus, Lynda Bird on the second, and foreman Malechek on the third. When Lynda Bird's bus made a wide turn off one of the ranch roads, she quipped, "There go the winter oats"; Lady Bird's bus became mired in soft ground as it made a turn, and everyone had to climb out so the driver could maneuver out of the field. Late that afternoon, there was a Jetton barbecue, with hundreds of pounds of spareribs sizzling over hickory-fire grills that had been set up on the lawn between the ranch house and the Pedernales, guests sitting on bales of hay and acrid smoke curling through the live oaks. Dean Rusk and other men in blue suits were blinking away tears and rubbing their eyes; McGeorge Bundy couldn't rub his—with his briefcase in one hand and a greasy rib in the other, he didn't have a hand free. As one account put it, "Newspapermen from Europe and the Orient, as well as the White House press, discovered that pork ribs are delicious—finger-licking good—when consumed without benefit of silverware." A country music band was playing. And then suddenly the guitars stopped, and ranch hands were carrying out a portable lectern bearing the presidential seal and a microphone, and placing it, somewhat shakily, atop one of the bales, and the President, in khaki windbreaker, whipcord slacks and boots, was stepping behind it, and the newsmen had to, as one wrote, try "in vain to cope simultaneously with ribs, beer, pens and notebooks" because hard, substantial news was being delivered. Johnson introduced Secretary Freeman (in a suit), who, having evidently finally gotten the message, announced that he had reduced the number of requested jobs at Agriculture by four thousand. Then, after defending his decision to close thirty-eight defense bases, Johnson announced there would be more closings in the future. Secretary McNamara, he said, had, at his direction, appointed a board to intensify a study of various bases "with a view to eliminating those not needed." While he sympathized with congressmen and senators who didn't want local bases closed, he said, "every congressional district must understand that they are going to be reviewed from time to time. We are not going to be satisfied with the status quo." And then, following the business, came show business. The President walked over to the side of the house—where, the newsmen suddenly noticed, a tall black horse was tethered. Swinging up into the saddle, Johnson trotted a few steps while the photographers snapped away.

He added a bit of comic relief, calling over Pierre Salinger. The portly press secretary was already self-conscious because Johnson had insisted that he wear the short khaki windbreaker he had ordered for him, and Salinger was aware that the garment was particularly unflattering to a person of his girth. Johnson didn't put him any more at his ease now, telling the reporters jokingly, "I gave Pierre that jacket he has on today because it is too large for me to wear." And then he had another horse brought out, and told Salinger to get up on it. This was not good news for Pierre, but Johnson insisted. Salinger climbed aboard. Johnson reminded him to put his feet in the stirrups. Salinger's horse was a small, shaggy piebald. Astride it, next to the tall President on his tall mount, the rotund press secretary might have been Sancho Panza. Wheeling his horse and putting it into a canter, Johnson "rode off into the sunset," as the *New York Times* put it, with Salinger, trying to keep up, "clutching hard at any part of his horse he could grab," still astride—"when last seen."

"It is not to be believed," a French correspondent murmured.

American journalists agreed. "Members of the press had never seen anything like it," the *Times* reported. "The President of the United States held a news conference with a haystack as a rostrum. In the background, smoke drifted up from barbecue pits where Texas beef sizzled. After the conference, the President rode off on a horse."

Before cantering away into the distance, Johnson had let photographers snap their fill. What photo editor could resist? The pictures, some of Johnson alone, some with Salinger beside him, were on front pages all across the country, pictures of a President on horseback erect and commanding, every inch the western rancher, the self-made man who had pulled himself up by his bootstraps, and who, no matter how high he had risen, still had his roots firmly in his native soil—the very antithesis of the Washington wheeler-dealer (or, for that matter, of the touch football players at Hickory Hill).

IN THE CREATION of an image, reviewers—the press—are crucial, and they received a full helping of Texas hospitality.

Selected reporters, correspondents from the country's major newspapers, were driven over the bumpy roads of the ranch, with the President, a "jolly brown giant," in the words of one reporter, in his brown boots, khaki whipcord pants, khaki shirt, khaki windbreaker and tan Stetson, at the wheel of the big white Continental convertible.

The car was fitted out with a bullhorn which, at the touch of a button on the dashboard, emitted a loud moaning sound—*Oo-ooh-gah, Oo-ooh-gah*—like that of a bull in distress. Suddenly veering off the dirt track, the President would nose the Lincoln up to one of the Herefords, sounding the horn to try to get the bull to move. If it wouldn't, he would sometimes inch the car so close that its bumper touched the big, stolid animal, chewing solemnly on its cud. He would sound the horn again. The Hereford, alarmed at last, would amble away. Johnson would sound the horn in triumph. Or he might stop the car, step out and engage the bulls on foot. Noting that the Speaker of the House was next in line for succession to the presidency if Johnson died, Tom Wicker wrote that this "entertainment arouses in those who see it visions of John McCormack in the White House."

> Mr. Johnson strides vigorously at a monstrous Hereford, waving his arms and maybe his five-gallon hat, emitting a modulated roar that comes out something like: "Whooo-oo-oosh!" Herefords are both docile and well-fed and usually they back away or seek the protective company of their kind; Mr. Johnson will break into a trot, get in front of the animal, and whoosh it again . . . as it lumbers away.

Or he might point out its fine points ("See that flat back?") or go up to a bull, kick its hindquarters ("That's where the best steaks come from"). "But that's not why I bought him," he would explain with a grin, lifting up the bull's tail to display his huge testicles. "This one's a steer," he would say of another animal, giving his explanation that "A steer is a bull who has lost his social standing." He would tell hilarious anecdotes: getting out of the car and raising a Hereford's tail, he recalled a Swedish Minnesota congressman named Magnus Johnson who hadn't, he said, been very bright; once, during an impassioned debate on the House floor, Magnus had shouted, "What we have to do is take the bull by the tail and look the situation in the face."

Most days were warm enough for him to suddenly say, "Let's go for a boat ride." A helicopter would whisk the President and his guests forty-five miles across the hills to Lake Travis, to the house he had built there, and then the group would roar around the lake in an eighteen-foot speedboat, with two other speedboats filled with Secret Service agents trailing it to keep other boats away.

These outings would always end in time for the evening's six o'clock newscast, the group usually back in the lake house well before his wristwatch alarm went off. The President would sit in a rocker in front of the television set, sipping a Scotch and soda from a plastic glass, watching the news. Lady Bird, wearing a sweater, hand-tooled cowboy boots and riding jodhpurs, would pass around platters of crackers, sausage, smoked venison and cubes of cheddar cheese with toothpicks.

Half a dozen reporters were watching with him on the day—a Friday—that Barry Goldwater announced his candidacy for the 1964 Republican nomination. I wonder why he didn't announce on a Sunday, Johnson said. "He'd get more space in the Monday morning papers." When, on the set, a newscaster said, "At the LBJ Ranch, meanwhile, the nation's business was carried forward," he smiled broadly, and when one of the reporters asked him if Richard Nixon would get into the race, he said, "I don't know. I don't even know whether I will," with a grin. They all chatted for a while, and then the President ushered his guests into two waiting helicopters and they took off into a darkening sky for a dinner of fried catfish, coleslaw, cornbread and apple pie.

The two-week run of Lyndon Johnson on the Ranch (or, in the words of one headline, LBJ DOWN ON THE FARM) that he staged for the press had accomplishment—the budget announcements the centerpiece—as a theme, but accomplishment in an open, friendly, relaxed atmosphere. The script had homey lines—up at the lake house one evening, he was sitting in his rocker watching television with journalists when Lady Bird walked in; "Here comes the bride!" he shouted, jumping up and giving her an enthusiastic kiss—and colorful Texas idioms that he explained to the reporters. Judge Moursund, he said, was "a good man to go to the well with." Seeing puzzled looks, he said, "When the Indians were in these hills, raidin' and scalpin' during my granddaddy's time, you had to have somebody you could depend on to go with you when you had to draw water from the well." He told them, jokingly, the recipe for the spicy deer-meat sausage they were eating: "Half pork, half venison, and all pepper." He regaled them with stories—of his grandmother hiding in the cellar during an Indian raid and holding a diaper over her baby's face to muffle its crying.

He gave them gifts—gray Stetsons, among others; when Wicker dropped his in the mud, the President picked it up, pulled out a handkerchief, and wiped it off—including what were, for journalists, the most prized gifts of all: off-the-record anecdotes about his presidency, about his Cabinet members, about famous Washington figures. He did his imitations: "an incredible mimic," one reporter wrote. "When he mimicked Dean Acheson, you could see the mustaches quivering." He did them favors: one evening, he suddenly picked up the telephone, called Phil Potter's editor at the *Baltimore Sun,* and told him what a great job Phil was doing.

The show's set pieces were memorable. Every evening after dinner, for example, there was the excursion down the path beside the Pedernales to Cousin Oreole's one-room frame house, the President, wearing a peaked cap and Windbreaker against the night chill, leading the way.

"It is an experience," Wicker wrote. "Nights are dark in Texas and the stars tatter the velvet sky. The water pours over the dam, whispering in the vast stillness. Mr. Johnson goes ahead on the rocky road, a flashlight in his hand. . . . Beyond the road, in the soft darkness, there is movement, presence, a sense only. Nothing can be heard or seen, but the Secret Service agents are there, watchful in the night."

Rattling and banging on the locked screen door, the President would shout, "Cousin Oreole! Cousin Oreole! You in there?," explaining to the reporters,

"She's as deaf as a post," until the old lady finally came to the door in a gingham housedress. Generally, she would have been lying on the bed reading a Bible. The open Bible and a magnifying glass would be on the iron bedstead in the little bedroom–sitting room decorated with red plastic orioles and posters showing a younger Lyndon from his early campaigns ("For Roosevelt and Progress"), and the routine played out on this homey set was well established, with an accomplished actress in the supporting role. Lyndon would keep opening the door, saying the room was too warm; she would keep closing it, saying it was too cold. As he sat in a wicker rocking chair, she would pass around photographs of him as a boy, and tell an anecdote or two about his school days. She might admonish the newspapermen for unfair reportage (one had written that, on a previous visit, she had answered the door barefoot; "I don't go to bed with my shoes on," she said. "Don't you agree that was unfair?") and tell Lyndon his horoscope from an astrology magazine she had been reading ("It says you'll be a good President, but won't be re-elected," she said one evening. "The news," Wicker wrote, "was received in silence"). The President would josh her, saying, in a loud voice, that he had heard she was "courtin' a neighbor," and warn her that, now that he was President, she had to be careful: "Don't you pick up that telephone, Cousin Oreole. You might get Khrushchev." Walking back along the path one evening, he said, "The only car that comes by her house is the mailman once a day. So she backs her car out the other day just in time to hit him."

And there was variety—dramatic changes of pace—in the show's scenes. On a morning after Cousin Oreole, there were the Joint Chiefs of Staff. They, along with McNamara and Deputy Secretary of Defense Roswell L. Gilpatric, held a full-scale conference on the defense budget with the President in the ranch living room on the morning of December 30. When they emerged, Johnson told waiting reporters that "We had a fine meeting. It makes you very proud of your Defense Department. The Secretary and the Joint Chiefs are really on the ball this morning." It was a bitterly cold day—below freezing with a biting wind, the first cold day of the trip—and Johnson said, "I'm sorry these Joint Chiefs came down here, these warmongers, and brought a blue norther with them." It was Marine Corps Commandant David M. Shoup's birthday. A cake was suddenly produced. "Let's all sing 'Happy Birthday,' " Johnson said. "It was an Executive order," the *Times* reported. "The generals, Admiral McDonald, the Secretary of Defense, the photographers, six freezing reporters and the President of the United States raised their voices in the howling wind and sang."

And it all got great reviews.

As always with critics there were a few dissenters, reviewers unable to overcome earlier prejudices. Describing the Erhard visit and Van Cliburn in the gym through a scornful lens, one of the European correspondents, a "highly-sophisticated" one in the words of a colleague, said that they evoked "wistful recollections": "I couldn't help thinking of Pablo Casals playing the cello in the East Room." The *Los Angeles Times* reported that among the journalists the word "cornball" was still sometimes used to describe Johnson. But only a few. "There has been a notable lack of scoffing among the skeptical sophisticates as the new President works hard at proving . . . that he hasn't taken on a lot of high-falutin' airs since moving into the White House," wrote the previously hostile Peter Lisagor.

Most of the reviews were, in fact, unqualified raves whose wording showed how successful Johnson had been in creating the effect he wanted—and how successfully, also, he had impressed on them the contrast he had wanted to make clear. Driving back to Austin one evening, a reporter said, "Well, he's not Jack Kennedy." "No, he's not," another reporter said. "But then he never claimed to be." "They are two different men, and no doubt about it," wrote the *Herald Tribune*'s Kiker. "But the contrast between John F. Kennedy and Lyndon B. Johnson did not really present itself in dramatic form until the new President left the White House . . . and came home to Texas. . . . The nation has a new President now—a new, strong personality to get to know. Times have changed. You only had to see him get on that horse at his ranch and ride off into the sunset to realize that." By the end of that Texas trip, Lyndon Johnson had imprinted his own stamp—"his own brand," as *Time* magazine put it—on the presidency.

The dispatches from the Pedernales projected to the country the image he wanted. Journalists who, from their observation of Johnson in Washington— obsessed with politics and power, driven by ambition, ruthless and relentless— had believed they understood him revised their opinion during those thirteen days. This was, indeed, a different Lyndon Johnson, "a Johnson we had never seen." And this, they felt, was the real Lyndon Johnson. "Politics has been his life, and few play the game with more zest and skill," Wicker wrote. "But the four hundred acres of the Johnson Ranch . . . are where Mr. Johnson has his roots. He seems a casual king as he rides the acres, perhaps not so much because he is President as because he is LBJ." On this "hardscrabble land," he wrote, "the President is elemental in a different fashion" from the way he is in Washington, "this big, breezy, rough-cut man of the plains, the grass and the dust, of the arid Texas hills." Even as formerly hard-eyed a critic as Peter Lisagor now described him in adjectives like "unaffected" and "old-shoe." The President "has been full of surprises," the syndicated columnist told his readers. "President Johnson has delighted a host of citified strangers with his unaffected hospitality. [His] old-shoe approach shows Mr. Johnson as an earthy man of the people who loves the soil and the robust pleasures of the two-fisted outdoorsman." "Relaxed" was an adjective suddenly in print in newspapers from coast to coast—in the *New York Times* ("Around the ranch house, Mr. Johnson is . . . relaxed, talkative, entertaining") and the *Los Angeles Times* ("He is relaxed and confident here")—and in the national magazines: Did the *Times* call him "relaxed"? To *Time* magazine, he was "the very picture of relaxation." "Presidential home life at the ranch is a very relaxed affair," wrote the *Sun*'s Potter, a "zestful, breezy western 'open house' brand of togetherness. 'Ol' Lyndon,' as countless friends and neighbors in these parts know him, likes ranch-style beans and deer meat sausage. He likes to ride and does so with a rancher's practiced ease."

The reviewers predicted the show would have a long run. "Washington's canniest political thinkers have been astounded by the skill and swiftness with which President Johnson has moved to increase his family lovability rating," Russell Baker wrote. "By introducing the nation to Cousin Oriole [*sic*], who casts his political horoscope, and Uncle Huffman Baines, that dignified septuagenarian . . . , the President has quickly established himself as a man of wide, warm and charming family relationships. No Republican now in the field has a relative to rebut Cousin Oriole or Uncle Huffman." And, they said, it *deserved* to have a long run—because it was rooted in reality. No one could doubt the authenticity of the portrayal, the reviews said. In a magazine article he wrote some months later, after another visit to the ranch, Wicker said, "The one thing Lyndon Johnson's critics sooner or later question, the one thing his friends inevitably have to deal with, is his sincerity—whether he is the genuine article in his folksiness . . . his patriotism and fervor . . . in the whole of his evangelistic Presidency. But there is no such question about Lyndon Johnson, rancher, Texan, Westerner. . . . Down on the ranch, on the old home place . . . LBJ is all wool and a yard wide. In tan twill and leather boots he is at home, at ease—serene as a restless Westerner can be." This "perfect host," this "tall, genial man," had given the members of the Washington press corps lucky enough to have spent the vacation at the Johnson Ranch a vacation "none of them is likely to forget," *Time* said. His relations with reporters in Washington may have been testy, *Time* said, but that wasn't the real Lyndon Johnson. "If there was any lingering doubt that Lyndon Johnson likes his press relations on the easy going side, those doubts were removed last week."

WHILE LYNDON JOHNSON may have been putting on a great show, however, a show—a performance, an act—was what it was. True to life as was one point the Texas sojourn made with his journalistic audience—that he was placing his own stamp on the presidency—little connection existed between reality and the overall impression that reporters received and transmitted to their readers: that Lyndon Johnson in the Pedernales Valley, the "real" Lyndon Johnson, was a different, changed, man from Lyndon Johnson in Washington.

No change of scene could change Lyndon Johnson. The base of his personality was that potent inherited "Bunton strain" legendary throughout the Hill Country because of the grandeur of the ambitions, and the fierceness of the pragmatism with which those ambitions had been pursued, by generations of men, all of them well over six feet in height, all of them with big ears, the burning, piercing "Bunton eye," and the flaring Bunton temper, all of them with the "commanding presence" of the frontier hero who had made the name "Bunton" a "household word in all the scattered log cabins . . . of Texas"—and almost all of whose great dreams had come to nothing in the end. And that base had been hardened beyond possibility of alteration by the grimness of his youth. In fact, of all settings the Pedernales Valley, the place in which humiliation had been heaped on heredity, was the one particularly unsuited to Lyndon Johnson's peace of mind. Every time he stepped out the front door of his big house, down the river to the left was the pathetic little frame house, so similar to the one in which he had grown up, and had watched his father fail and his mother grow ill. Directly across the river from the front door was a stretch of highway on which he had pushed the fresno. Everywhere were reminders. Taking relays of reporters on tours of the ranch, Lady Bird would indicate a line from the river up past the house to the top of the ridge almost half a mile away, and say, in her chatty, pleasant way, "There used to be a ditch there deep enough to walk elephants in." That ditch was one feature of the ranch her husband never mentioned. The long, deep ravine had been, in a way, his father's last stand: the gully into which, day after day, under the broiling Hill Country sun, Sam Ealy, too old for such work, had shoveled wagonloads of soil, filling it with earth and planting cotton seeds in it, over and over, as his son Lyndon had watched, only to see the soil wash away every time in the next heavy rain.*

On Christmas Day, he and Lady Bird drove into Johnson City to deliver a poinsettia plant to his cousin Ava. There in her living room, over the threadbare sofa, was the double row of pictures. The last one—the one furthest to the right in the bottom row—was of him. The one next to it was of his father, and the next one was his grandfather, and the others were also of his forebears, and every one was a picture of a man with dark hair, pale skin, big ears, big nose, heavy eyebrows and dark, intense eyes, pictures of men who resembled his grandfather, resembled his father, resembled him—men who, almost all of them, had failed as his grandfather had failed, and his father had failed. His brother Sam Houston, telling the author that "the most important thing for Lyndon was not to be like Daddy," paused for a moment, and in a very quiet voice said that whenever the Johnson children were back at the ranch—as he and Lyndon and Rebekah and Lucia were back that Christmas—"Daddy and Mother were there, too." "Relaxed," "breezy," "serene"—the portrayal Lyndon Johnson was giving on stage during the show's two-week run, bantering and barbecuing with reporters, was letter-perfect. But during those two weeks he wasn't always on stage. Sometimes he was in his bedroom, with the door closed, alone or with only Lady Bird present. And sometimes, when he was in the paneled office or the small den, the doors to those rooms would be closed, and only Valenti or Jesse Kellam, general manager of KTBC and KTBC-TV, or one of his secretaries—or, sometimes, no one at all—would be with him. Behind those doors, he would be making telephone calls, in the den while sitting in the rocker, in the office in the recliner. The recliner tilted all the way back, so that most of his body might be horizontal, and

*Sam Ealy and the gully: *The Path to Power,* pp. 87–89.

the rocker tilted back, too, so he might have seemed relaxed if it hadn't been for the way in which, as he got to the point of the call, his shoulders would hunch forward and the eyes narrow above the receiver, which seemed surprisingly small in a huge, mottled hand, the left hand if the call was going the way he wanted, the right hand if the person to whom he was talking wasn't agreeing to do what he was asking him to do. On most of these calls, his voice stayed soft, although it didn't seem soft because of the twang in it—stayed calm, rational, reasonable. But if the journalists he was wooing had heard some of the things he was saying during these calls, "relaxed," "breezy," and "serene" might not have been the adjectives with which they described him.

All his life, Lyndon Johnson had made use of any political weapon on which he could lay his hand, or which he could invent, any power that he could find or devise, as a means to attain his ends, and he had employed these weapons to the hilt, with a ruthlessness startling even to men who had believed themselves inured to the ruthlessness of politics. A President had a lot of weapons—and during those two weeks on the ranch, behind those closed doors, he was beginning to use them.

SOME OF THE TARGETS on which he was using them were members of the journalists' own profession, for not all of Johnson's dealings with the press during those two weeks were on boat rides and at barbecues. *Life* magazine and Washington reporters may have given him a reprieve from the Bobby Baker scandal—although, as would become apparent within a very few months, not for long. But in Texas there was a reporter who hadn't—and he wanted her stopped.

Because for most of her professional life her articles appeared only in Texas newspapers, Margaret Mayer's work would never become as well known as that of colleagues on eastern and national publications. But, a very enterprising reporter, she would later, as chief of the *Dallas Times-Herald*'s Washington bureau, become one of the first women to head the Washington bureau of a major newspaper. In 1963, forty-one years old, she was a reporter in the *Times-Herald*'s Austin bureau, and had become curious about the many rumors she was hearing about Johnson's Texas Broadcasting Company and the way it attracted advertisers. "I had," she was to say, "questions about it even before the Bobby Baker thing started"—and, as Horace Busby, a longtime friend, has to admit, "Margaret always knew the right questions to ask." She had begun an investigation of KTBC and KTBC-TV, and when the stations' general manager, Jesse Kellam, refused to answer her questions, she put some of them—not particularly probing ones, just general questions about the scope of the stations' operations—in writing in a letter she sent him on December 17, a week before Johnson came to Texas. Kellam brought the letter out to the ranch on Saturday, January 4, and at 8:45 that evening the President telephoned the *Times-Herald*'s managing editor, Albert Jackson.

"I got a letter from Margaret Mayer worried me a little," Johnson said, as the taped recording of the conversation reveals, and he read Jackson some of her questions. Jackson was a longtime supporter of Johnson, continually trying to cultivate his acquaintance. The editor said he hadn't known about the letter, that "she certainly shouldn't be doing it," and "I can assure you that it'll be stopped."

That wasn't good enough for Johnson, however. When Jackson said he would "talk to our people" about the best way to stop it, Johnson told him what to say to those people. The names he mentioned during the conversation were those of the *Times-Herald*'s publisher and board chairman, John W. Runyon; the paper's president, James F. Chambers Jr.; and Clyde Rembert, president of the radio and television stations, KRLD and KRLD-TV, owned by the paper—and Johnson's instructions included references to the power of the federal government, and of the President in particular, and they included as well a hint that were Ms. Mayer not stopped, he might use those powers against the newspaper: that if the *Times-Herald* continued investigating him, he might investigate the *Times-Herald*.

"Tell them . . . that you all don't want to be picking a fight with somebody like this," Lyndon Johnson said. "We might want to ask [for] some of you all's records up there [in Dallas]. I imagine I could get that done."

If a newspaper was investigated by the federal government, a particularly vulnerable area would be its profitable radio and television stations, since all broadcasting stations are under the authority of the Federal Communications Commission, and in few businesses was the role of government as crucial as in broadcasting, for not only were the very licenses which allowed the use of the airwaves granted and periodically renewed solely at the FCC's sufferance, but the agency possessed virtually unchallengeable authority over every aspect of a station's operations. Johnson brought the Dallas stations' operations into the conversation. Under FCC regulations a significant criterion for its decision on the renewing of a station's license was a comparison of the percentage of the station's broadcast time that it had devoted to non-commercial—non-revenue-producing—public service broadcasting with the percentage of its "commercial," or revenue-producing, broadcasting. Too high a "commercial" percentage, too low a public service percentage, could imperil a station's license. Hinting that he had assisted KRLD in this area in the past, Johnson hinted also that he might, were Mayer's investigation not cut off, adopt a different attitude in the future.

"Get this goddamned Margaret Mayer satisfied . . . because I'll ask Clyde Rembert how much commercial he is," Johnson said. "I remember he was 98 percent when I was helping him." And there were other areas of the station's operations for which records might be requested, other questions that might be asked about KRLD if Mayer persisted in asking about KTBC, questions that related not to licenses and the FCC but to taxes, which would of course involve the Internal Revenue Service. "I hadn't been inquiring . . . what you make, and what your profit is, and what your estate tax was, and how much you paid . . . and all that kind of stuff," Johnson said.

At one point in the conversation with Jackson, Johnson may have dropped a hint that the areas of investigation could be broadened even further. "Just tell them," the President said to Jackson, "just tell Jim Chambers, whoever's running the show up there, just say, 'Listen, this guy [Johnson] might ask for some of yours, or some of our, records.' " His instruction to the newspaper's managing editor to warn Chambers, the newspaper's president, or "whoever's running the show up there," that the federal government might ask for "some of our records" evidently refers to the newspaper's corporate records. But Johnson was telling Jackson to warn his people also that federal agencies might ask not only for "some of our records" but in addition for "some of yours"—words that could be taken as a hint that not only corporate records but personal records, including tax records, might be investigated, audited, as well.

Don't let Mayer know he had intervened, Lyndon Johnson told Jackson. "A President oughtn't be calling about chickenshit stuff like this." But he wanted her investigation stopped, and he wanted it stopped fast. When Jackson said he would relay the message to the paper's owners, Johnson said, "Do that, and let me know in the morning." In the morning, at eleven o'clock on Sunday, the editor telephoned to reassure the President. "We'll take care of the thing tomorrow," he said. Margaret Mayer would not be told that Johnson had called him, he said. She would be told that Kellam had called "and asked what he should do about the letter" and that Kellam had been told to simply ignore it, "that we didn't want the information, if she'd written the story we wouldn't have published it."

Johnson, concerned that his involvement be kept secret, then said that he would prefer that Kellam send her a "cursory-like" letter, and send a copy to Jackson, and that "then, when you get it, you say [to Mayer] 'What in the hell is this? We don't want to spend all of our time inquiring into matters that's none of our business. They might be inquiring into some of our affairs that *are* their business.' " Jackson agreed to that approach.

STOPPING MARGARET MAYER had been easy. Another Texas journalistic enterprise on which Lyndon Johnson embarked during that Christmas trip was on a more difficult—and much more ambitious—scale. It involved not an individual reporter but an entire newspaper: the state's largest, and perhaps most influential, newspaper, the *Houston Chronicle* (circulation 259,000). The *Chronicle* had at times been critical of him, and had endorsed Richard Nixon in 1960. He set out that Christmas to stop the criticism, and to stop it immediately. And he set out to do more: to obtain the newspaper's unqualified support, and to obtain it not only for the near future, but for a considerably longer duration—for as long, in fact, as he held the presidency, no matter how long that might turn out to be. And he set out to get a guarantee of that support—in writing.

Ambitious though that objective was, Johnson had a weapon powerful enough to obtain it. The *Chronicle*'s president, John T. Jones Jr., was also the president of Houston's National Bank of Commerce, which had been attempting to merge with another Houston bank, the Texas National—and bank mergers require federal approval. Although the boards of directors of both banks had authorized the merger in July, the necessary approval had not been forthcoming due to opposition from the Federal Reserve Bank, which felt that the merger "would have a strongly adverse effect on competition," and from the Justice Department's Anti-Trust Division, which said, in a memo to Comptroller of the Currency James J. Saxon, that because both banks were strong, profitable institutions, a merger was not required, and that approval of this one "would set a precedent nationwide where all big banks in big cities would come flooding in asking for permission to merge." This, Anti-Trust's memo said, "is a very serious objection."

High stakes were riding on the approval. Stock market analysts felt that the merger would substantially boost the price of Commerce Bank shares—and the Houston Endowment, a charitable foundation with extensive business interests of which Jones was chairman, owned 2.75 million shares. With the Federal Reserve and Justice opposed, presidential intervention would be necessary to obtain the approval. And Johnson wanted Jones to pay for the intervention—with the written guarantee of his newspaper's support.

The President had spelled out the price of his intervention in a call from the ranch to Jack Valenti, who was acting as an intermediary because through his Houston advertising agency he was acquainted with Jones. In a telephone call to Valenti on Christmas Day, Johnson used the word "lung" to mean "voice"—the *Chronicle*'s "voice," or editorial support—but the quaintness of the synonym could disguise neither the harshness of the price he was demanding, nor his determination to exact it. "I ain't going to do it [approve the merger] . . . unless they give me their lung as long as I'm in public life," Johnson told Valenti. "And I mean when I call them and want them to run something, I want them to run it." The criticism in the *Chronicle* had to stop. "I've been hazed by it, and I'm tired of the hazing."

He told Valenti to arrange to have Jones come to the ranch for a meeting on December 27. The meeting should be kept "just as low [secret] as you can," he said. Because he hadn't dealt much with Jones, and the publisher might therefore not understand that when Lyndon Johnson set a price, he intended to get it, he told Valenti to have Jones bring along two Houston business tycoons with whom he had had dealings for many years, and who understood that point very well, George Brown and Gus Wortham, whose American General Insurance Company handled most of Brown & Root's insurance. Wortham had been pouring money into Lyndon Johnson's coffers for more than twenty years, through both the purchase of advertising time on KTBC and campaign contributions (because, George Brown was to say, "Herman [Brown] twisted his arm" to make him do so). And his insurance company owned 120,000 Houston Commerce Bank shares.

But Brown, who was in Houston's Methodist Hospital with a bleeding ulcer, couldn't make the trip—Albert Thomas, Brown & Root's representative in the

House of Representatives, came instead—and the meeting did not produce a satisfactory result, as the President informed Brown during a hospital room telephone call on January 2. Although during the visit to the ranch, Jones had expressed the *Chronicle*'s support, the expression had not been as unequivocal—and did not cover as long a time span—as Johnson wanted, he told Brown. "He [Jones] finally came around and said, 'Whenever you need anything call on us.' There's a hell of a lot of difference" between that and what he was asking for, he said.

He had made that clear to Wortham following the December 27 visit, he told Brown; had spelled out what he wanted in the written guarantee. "I told Gus [Wortham]—I told Jack [Valenti] to tell him [Gus] to get John Jones to write me a letter telling me he is our friend." Jones, he said, should write, "Dear Mr. President. . . . So far as I'm personally concerned and the paper is concerned, it's going to support your administration as long as you're there. Sincerely, your friend, John Jones." (Johnson's suggested text also contained a reference to another commitment he wanted. Jones, he said, should write "we're making arrangements for special coverage in Washington by the *Chronicle*"—by which, it would later become clear, he meant that the *Chronicle*'s managing editor, Everett Collier, would be dispatched to the capital to cover his presidency. Collier was prone to boasting that "I have been a close friend of the President for many years," and had in fact been a Johnson acolyte since he had been one of his students at Sam Houston High School, one who idolized him and was always following him around. "I was under his feet constantly there," Collier would say.)

"AS LONG AS YOU'RE THERE"—a commitment that the *Chronicle* would support him, not just for the moment, and not just through the next year's election campaign, but for as long as he was President, whether that be one year or five or nine. No mention in the letter of any specific Administration policies: the letter would be a commitment to support "your administration" whatever its policies might be. And the commitment was to be in writing, in a letter signed by the newspaper's president. Despite Wortham's assurances that the letter would be written, it still hadn't arrived, Johnson told Brown. And unless it did, he said, there would be no bank merger. "I'm not going to approve it. . . . I'm just not going to do it," he said.

Brown's response in this January 2 call was to mention a number of reasons that Johnson should approve the merger without insisting on a written guarantee.

One was a matter of discretion: of the inadvisability of putting in writing an arrangement that would, to anyone aware of Jones' interest in the bank merger, be a blatant *quid pro quo:* a trade of a government decision for a newspaper's support. "Albert [Thomas] thought it was too much of a cash-and-carry thing, [that] it was too much of a trade," Brown said. Anyone who found out about it would "say . . . they [the newspaper] had committed themselves to you, and you did something for them." Thomas says "they"—Jones and Wortham—"are com-

mitted [to you], but don't think they ought to do it in writing." Brown expressed
his own doubts on that point. "To have it in writing like that . . ."

Johnson dismissed that objection. The letter he had dictated took it into
account. "Well, I didn't tell him to mention the bank [in the letter]," the President
said. Brown chuckled as he got the point: that the letter would therefore contain
not the whole arrangement but only half of it—the *quo* but not the *quid,* no proof
in writing of the *quid pro quo.* "They don't have to be mentioning the goddamned
bank," Johnson said. The letter would contain only Jones' pledge of support, and,
Johnson said, "It ain't going to hurt me to have it in writing [from] any goddamned editor in the United States [to] say they're going to support me."

Brown mentioned other considerations that might, he suggested, be reasons
for Johnson to approve the merger without insisting on the letter.

One of them was a commitment that, Jones had been telling his friends,
President Kennedy had made to him: that Kennedy, as Brown put it to Johnson
now, had "said he was going to approve" the merger—without, although Brown
didn't put this point in so many words, demanding a written guarantee of the
Chronicle's support.

Johnson responded to that point by saying Kennedy had told him the opposite, that he was going to do exactly what he, Johnson, was doing: demand a letter. "He told me that he would get that *Chronicle* right in his hip pocket to
support him the rest of his life, or he wasn't going to give them the time of day."
In fact, Johnson said, it was because of the Kennedys—Bobby Kennedy's Justice
Department Anti-Trust Division—that he needed the letter. He wanted to let
Anti-Trust understand that reversal of its opposition to the bank merger would
ensure the *Chronicle*'s support for the Democratic ticket in 1964. He told Brown,
"What I was going to do was take the letter and . . . say, 'Now, here, goddamn it.
You-all've got jobs as well as we have. This fellow here [Jones] is important to us
and we've got to carry this state. And we've just got to do this. Period."

Johnson's statement about President Kennedy may or may not have been
accurate; there is certainly no confirmation for it that the author could find. But
whether or not Kennedy had made a commitment without demanding a specific
written *quid pro quo* in return, he, Lyndon Johnson, wasn't going to make one.
That wasn't his style. "If they [Kennedy] was committed, they ought not to be
committed unless it's a mutual affair," he said. He had the power to make Jones
and the *Chronicle* do what he wanted them to do—and he was going to make
them do it, in writing. "We want a very simple, easy little letter," he said. And
unless he got it there wasn't going to be a bank merger. "I ain't gonna do it otherwise. . . . You can just say you know me well enough to know that, by God,
that as long as that letter ain't there, the approval ain't there."

GEORGE BROWN *DID* KNOW Lyndon Johnson well enough. Perhaps, in matters
of business, no one knew him as well. "Let me talk to Gus," he finally said. "I can
explain things to him, without quoting you or anything, and he can go and get

John to do it." Johnson agreed to that, "but," he added, "you be damned sure that you and Gus . . . You get me that letter." There was a pause—a silence on the phone line. Lyndon Johnson wanted an answer. "Okay?" he asked. "Okay," Brown replied.

Brown got him the letter. John Jones wrote it the next day. While it didn't contain the precise words Johnson had used, the promise to "support your administration as long as you're there," the letter's wording—"While you have your capable hand on the reins of this administration, the *Chronicle* will do everything it properly can to help keep the Democratic Party in office"—was evidently close enough to satisfy Johnson, perhaps because the letter also contained a written promise of the "special coverage" in Washington that Johnson had demanded, and by the man he wanted for that coverage. "Everett Collier . . . leaves next week for Washington, where he has been assigned by me as a special editorial writer, background man or whatever is necessary," Jones wrote. "I think he can be helpful." On January 8, the President, back in Washington, telephoned George Brown from the Oval Office. "The letter came in just like it should have," he said. And, he said, he had kept his part of the bargain. "We signed that thing this morning and made them [the Justice Department] reverse themselves, and the consolidation's [merger] approved." He had to hang up now, Johnson told Brown, he had to work on his State of the Union speech, which he would be giving in a little more than an hour. He telephoned Jones. "John, much obliged for your letter," he said. "That thing [approval of the merger] signed this morning. . . . From here on out, we're partners." (Johnson got the date wrong. Although the approval of the merger had been finalized in principle by January 7, it wasn't until the 13th that Comptroller of the Currency Saxon announced that it had been formally approved.)

"We're partners"—Johnson's statement to the *Chronicle*'s publisher was borne out by the newspaper's eagerness to comply with their agreement. Even he could find no fault with the paper's efforts. Talking with Albert Thomas on January 20, he asked, "Is the *Chronicle* for us now?" and answered the question himself: "All out, all the time, aren't they?" ("They've been that for about two or three [weeks]," Thomas replied. "Every other page" had a favorable story now, the congressman said.) When, on February 9, Johnson told Valenti to plant "a paragraph" in the *Chronicle*, Valenti said he was confident William P. Steven, the *Chronicle*'s editor, would comply. "Bill Stevens [*sic*], every time I send him, ask him anything, boy, he has it in the paper the next day. . . . Stevens has been *real* good about it." The *Chronicle* was indeed to endorse Lyndon Johnson in 1964. It would not endorse another Democratic presidential candidate for forty-four years.*

THE POWER TO INVESTIGATE, the power to regulate, the power to license— those were not the only powers of government with which Lyndon Johnson,

---

*Until 2008, when it endorsed Barack Obama.

implacable, unyielding, refusing to accept anything less than exactly what he wanted, was, from behind closed doors at the LBJ Ranch, threatening the press during that Christmas vacation.

It wasn't only congressmen or senators to whom the closing of a military installation represented a threat. The closing of a base meant the departure of its personnel, and their salaries, some of which would have been spent in local stores and restaurants. The resultant reduction in those businesses' income would mean a reduction in their expenditures, including their expenditures on advertising—including newspaper advertising. And over Christmas, 1963, Johnson was contemplating the use of that threat against other newspapers, and against another reporter.

Shreveport, Louisiana, was the home of two daily newspapers, the *Shreveport Times* and the *Shreveport Journal,* and of Barksdale Air Force Base, home of the Strategic Air Command's Second Bomb Wing and its fifteen thousand military and civilian personnel. The *Times* and *Journal,* both supporters of racial segregation, had turned against Johnson as his support for civil rights had become clear, and during one of his telephone calls to Albert Jackson, who in addition to being Margaret Mayer's boss was president of the Southern Newspaper Publishers Association, Johnson asked, "What do we need to do about Shreveport? Do I need to really slug them, or just wait until they come around? . . . I can let them have it good with Barksdale Field and I'm tempted to, the editorials they're writing. . . . I'm almost inclined to let them have both barrels."

Jackson persuaded Johnson to wait "a little bit" on the Shreveport front.* He suggested that he come to Washington to advise Johnson on how to handle various publishers, both unfavorable and favorable. Taking him up on the suggestion, Johnson invited him to visit the Oval Office, "and let me and you sit there and have a drink, and call some of these folks, and just say hello to them, without [them] even knowing you're there."

On another journalistic front, however, Johnson wasn't willing to wait. Seventy-three-year-old Bascom Timmons, who had been reporting from Washington since 1912, had established his own news bureau, which represented more than a dozen newspapers in the capital. The *Fort Worth Star-Telegram* was the one to which he devoted most of his time, and the paper identified him as its chief Washington correspondent. A former president of the National Press Club, and a member of the Hall of Fame of Sigma Delta Chi, the national journalistic honor society, he was the dean of Texas newspapermen in Washington, and enjoyed, a colleague was to say, "the respect of all the newspaper people in town, and the love of many congressmen." Those feelings were not shared by Johnson. Timmons' articles and columns had been infuriating him for years, and during this Christmas vacation—on Christmas Day, in fact—he made a telephone call to the *Star-Telegram*'s owner, Amon Carter Jr. During the call, the recent decision to

*In the event, Barksdale would remain untouched.

close the Fort Worth Army Depot (with its twenty-six hundred soldiers) was mentioned by the President, as was Fort Worth's Carswell Air Force Base, home of six Strategic Air Command squadrons. And a non-military project, to link landlocked Fort Worth to the Gulf of Mexico, was mentioned also. The Trinity River Navigation Project, that would, through dredging and the construction of a series of dams, make the river navigable to barges all the way from the Fort Worth area to the Gulf 365 miles away, would cost an estimated billion dollars, but it had been a long-cherished dream of Amon Carter Sr., and after his death had been adopted by his son, and early in 1963, it had been approved by the Army Corps of Engineers, although the only funds thus far authorized had been for a minor first stage, a dam near Corsicana. And Bascom Timmons was mentioned, too, in a manner that made it seem that the President might be hinting at a connection between the journalist and the air force base, and between the journalist and the dream. After the exchange of Christmas good wishes, the President told Amon Jr., "Now, I want just to leave this one thought. . . . I'm going to get this budget down. And a lot of things are going by the wayside, and a lot of consolidation is going to take effect. And a lot of things are going to hurt people—like that Army depot the other day.

"We still got a lot of things there, like your Carswell, and your Trinity River, and things that you want. Now, you tell your crowd over at the *Star-Telegram* that you want to be damn sure that you've got as competent a man and as thorough a man and as attentive a man as the *New York Times* has got in those press conferences because you want the President's home state to be represented by *real* intelligence."

Carter understood what the President was getting at, because he knew how Johnson felt about Timmons; in fact, Johnson had complained to him already about the reporter. "We're going to try retiring Bascom, which is going to be pretty hard," the publisher said. "I know . . . you told me some things about him once before."

Understanding, however, was not what Johnson had in mind, and he was no longer merely a senator or Vice President. He became more explicit about what a President might do with his power. "You all ought to just get the best damn fellow you can for the *Star-Telegram*," he said. "And I'd have a man there, when he speaks up, he doesn't say, 'I'm Bascom Timmons' . . .

"And that," the President said, "will have its effect on other things. Because they're going to put a lot of Strategic Air Command bases together. They're going to phase out a lot of stuff. . . . It's going to be a complete overhaul. And if I were you, I'd just get the best damn person I could get and have him representing me. . . . I'd get me a good man covering the White House."

(Retiring Timmons was accomplished by the *Star-Telegram* sending, in 1964, one additional reporter, and, in 1965, another, to Washington to supplement Timmons' coverage for the paper and gradually phasing Timmons out of the paper. Timmons himself appears to have been unaware of Johnson's role in the phasing out. In an oral history interview he gave in 1969 he said only that "during his Administration, I didn't see him so much because I wasn't so active as I used to be." He continued reporting from Washington for other newspapers until his retirement in 1974.

Carswell Air Force Base continued in service, its Seventh Heavy Bomb Wing flying more than thirteen hundred bombing missions over Vietnam. As for the Trinity River Navigation Project, in 1965 the Johnson Administration proposed, and Congress approved, authorization for the Trinity River Barge Canal to connect Fort Worth to the Gulf at a cost of just under a billion dollars. At the end of Johnson's presidency, only a small portion of the project had been completed, and it was eventually abandoned.

THERE WERE OTHER TIMES also during that Christmas when he wasn't on stage, and during these other private interludes it was apparent that other traits—like ruthlessness, traits of Lyndon Johnson ever since his youth in the Hill Country— had not, for all his showmanship, been eliminated but were only being concealed.

There was, for example, his penchant for deception and secrecy.

He wasn't on stage in either his big white Lincoln Continental convertible or Judge Moursund's big white Lincoln Continental convertible. On seven of the vacation's thirteen days the two men were driving around together, two big good ol' boys with their hunting rifles and their Scotch and their tall stories and their Stetsons pushed back on their heads. Sometimes a secretary—either Vicky McCammon or Marie Fehmer—was with them, in the back seat, in case Johnson wanted to give instructions about what McCammon calls "White House business." Moursund, questioned by journalists the next year, would insist that his job as the principal trustee of Johnson's blind trust was "to see to it the Johnsons don't know what is going on," and, he would insist, that is what he did; "it's not at all tough for me to do what I'm supposed to do." Evidently, however, his job was tougher than he admitted. "With Moursund, he would talk about business, not White House business," McCammon says. "A. W. was a trustee, so there was a whole lot of discussion on different money matters." The two secretaries were not expected to deal with personal business matters. "Mr. Johnson and Judge Moursund would talk privately looking at things [those]," Fehmer says. She became so accustomed to such discussions that after a while "I didn't even take notice of it."

The President was also making arrangements so that the discussions could continue after his return to Washington. A new telephone was placed on a counter in the kitchen of Moursund's home. It was "linked by a private telephone circuit to the LBJ Ranch and the White House" so that the judge "can pick up his phone and talk almost instantaneously with the President," the *Wall Street Journal* was to report. (Although, Moursund insisted—in what the *Journal* described as a "heated" reply to its inquiries—that the Johnsons nonetheless "don't know what is going on" in their business.)

Moursund was not the only business associate with whom Johnson took drives around his ranch. Jesse Kellam sometimes accompanied him, and with KTBC's general manager, "the same thing," McCammon says. And Johnson was to talk regularly with Kellam, too, after he was back in the White House— although in Kellam's case the arrangements would be more complicated. Sometimes when Kellam was having dinner with friends in Austin the beeper he wore on his belt would buzz. He would excuse himself, saying he had to make a phone call, but he wouldn't make it from a pay telephone in the restaurant; he would return to his office, and make it from there.

Ed Clark understood why. The beeper was summoning Kellam to talk to the President, and the talk was to be conducted in privacy.

Another locale being linked that Christmas to the White House was the Johnson City office of the law firm of Moursund & Ferguson. The telephones on the desks of the two partners were replaced by new ones—with an added button; it "wasn't labeled anything, but when you pushed that, you got the White House's board in Washington," says Moursund's partner, Thomas C. Ferguson, an influential Hill Country politician, former district judge and chairman of the Texas State Board of Insurance. And while Moursund would maintain, over and over, during the entire Johnson presidency, that no business was discussed over those office lines, that is not what Ferguson says. When the author asked him whether Johnson conducted personal business over those lines, Ferguson replied, "Oh, yeah. He and Moursund were talking every day. . . . You see, Moursund was trustee of all his property: one of these blind trusts—it wasn't very blind." The author asked Ferguson if he himself had conducted business for Johnson during his presidency. "Myself? Oh, yes," Ferguson replied, and provided the details of several such transactions.

Other lines were installed—in the law firm of Clark, Thomas, Harris, Denius & Winters in Austin: one on Ed Clark's desk, one on Donald Thomas'; in Earl Deathe's office down the hall from Kellam's at KTBC. Another was placed in Deathe's home. By the conclusion of the Christmas trip, the phones were all in.

Calls were not restricted to office hours. Johnson wanted to be able to make calls to these men not only from the Oval Office but from his living quarters in the White House, and he didn't want those calls to go through the White House switchboard. "I want an outside phone [line] installed in my bedroom . . . like that other one, where I don't have to go through any operator," he told Walter Jenkins not long after his return from Texas. "Can I do that? . . . I'd like to make a private call. When I talk to A. W. Moursund, when I talk to any of them, I don't like the . . ." He *could* do that. Whatever it was he didn't like—perhaps the fact that a log is kept of all calls to and from a President that go through the White House switchboard, perhaps the chance that an operator might listen in on the call (the recording becomes too garbled at this point to understand his next words)—was promptly changed. The outside line was installed, and after it was, Marie Fehmer says, "We could not know the calls he had placed from the bedroom." White House phone logs and operators would have no record of them.

There would be a lot of such calls. "Every night he told Moursund what to do," Ferguson told the author. "A lot of [it] was Johnson saying to Moursund, 'Well, I want to do this,' 'I want to do that'—'I want to get this piece of land,' 'I want to stock [with cattle] certain places. . . .' And of course at that time anything Moursund said stood up throughout the Johnson properties . . . and he would carry out what the President would tell him he wanted done. . . . It was a very unblind trust as far as that trust was concerned." Moursund would arrive at the law firm office the next morning with instructions that Johnson had given him in calls to his home the previous evening. Often, he would tell Ferguson, Johnson had been lying in bed in the White House when he called. Earl Deathe also speaks of late-night—and some early-morning—calls from the White House. "Sometimes he'd call you three or four o'clock in the morning," he says. After these lines were installed, Clark says, Johnson wanted his dealings about his business interests conducted over these direct phone lines.

All during Lyndon Johnson's presidency, he, either himself or through a press secretary, would insist that he had divorced himself completely from his business interests. "As the American people know," George Reedy said in one of many such statements—all approved word for word by the President—"the President has devoted all his time and energy to the public business and he is not engaged in any private enterprise, directly or indirectly." And all during his presidency, the phones stayed in place, and the calls went on.

THERE WAS DECEPTION and secrecy during that Christmas trip in not only personal affairs but governmental.

If Vietnam initially seemed to him to be a part of the "breathing space" he had been provided on foreign affairs, the only immediate decisions necessary the ones he had made in his NSAM 273 of November 26, he had been quickly disabused of that impression. Within days, he was reading new reports: that the military situation, particularly in Vietnam's Mekong Delta, was "deteriorating," and that the new junta was disorganized. One report, from Lodge, said that in a key province, "The past thirty days have produced . . . a day-by-day increase in Viet Cong influence, military operations, physical control of the countryside."

The earlier reports, Johnson would say in his memoirs, using phrases that to him were particularly damning, were "wishful thinking": "We had been misled into over-optimism." He dispatched McNamara, along with McCone and Assistant Secretary of Defense William P. Bundy (McGeorge's brother), to Vietnam, giving McNamara "quite a lecture" expressing "concern that we as a government were not doing everything we should," and the Defense secretary's report, delivered on his return to Washington, on December 21, said that "the situation is very disturbing. Current trends, unless reversed in the next 2–3 months, will lead to neutralization at best and most likely to a Communist-controlled state. . . . We should watch the situation very carefully, running scared, hoping for the best, but preparing for more forceful moves if the situation does not show early signs of improvement."

McCone, in a brief report of his own, said he felt "a little less pessimistic [than McNamara]," but to Johnson the time for "less" pessimism, for "wishful thinking" in any form, was over. His views had been hardening—or perhaps only becoming more apparent. Strong as were the militant voices in Congress, there were voices on the other side, too—but the new President wasn't listening to them. Ill equipped though Mike Mansfield was to be Majority Leader, he was well qualified indeed to give advice on Vietnam, having been not only a professor of East Asian history but one with a thoughtful overview of that part of the world, and on December 7 he had given Johnson a memo saying continuation of the war there would be costly to America and urging less reliance on a military solution in Vietnam and more on a political. Johnson's response, in a conversation with Mansfield's aide Francis R. Valeo, secretary of the Senate, on the evening of December 23, the day before he left for Texas, was to ask for another memo from Mansfield, and he made the request in words that made clear the advice he wanted. "What are we going to do about Vietnam?" he said. "We're going to lose that war. Do you want that to be another China? . . . Get me a memo on it. . . . I don't want these people around the world worrying about us, and they are. . . . They're worried about whether you've got a weak President or a strong President." And when Mansfield didn't take the hint, saying in his second memo, "As you remarked to [Valeo] on the telephone, we do not want another China in Vietnam," but "neither do we want another Korea. . . . A key factor in both situations was a tendency to bite off more than we were prepared in the end to chew. . . . We are close to the point of no return in Vietnam," Johnson's response would be to solicit memoranda from McNamara, Rusk and Bundy to counter Mansfield's arguments. "The stakes in preserving an anti-Communist South Vietnam are so high that in our judgment, we must go on bending every effort to win," McNamara's said. Rusk arrived at the ranch with a memo that he handed to Johnson in which he wrote that there was need for a presidential statement emphasizing "the urgency of action to reverse the adverse trend in the war as well as reaffirming the United States policy of complete support for the Vietnamese government." And included in the President's response to McNamara's "disturbing" report was approval of two of its recommendations: that more United States advisers be sent from Saigon to the Mekong Delta and other embattled provinces; and that an interdepartmental committee, chaired by Marine Lieutenant General Victor H. "Brute" Krulak, be created to study OPLAN 34-A, the proposal for covert military operations against North Vietnam, and to designate those operations with the "least risk" and the most "plausibility of denial." The Krulak committee's report, which called for "progressively escalating pressure . . . to inflict increasing punishment upon North Vietnam," arrived at the Johnson Ranch on

January 2. Among the operations it recommended, all to be carried out during the next twelve months, were guerrilla raids against the Ho Chi Minh Trail, "hit-and-run" commando raids along the North Vietnamese coasts—and shelling by American warships of North Vietnamese military installations on the coast of the Gulf of Tonkin. "There's one of three things you can do" about Vietnam, the President would soon be saying in a telephone call from the ranch to John Knight of Knight Ridder newspapers, a supporter who nonetheless felt the United States might be "over-committed" in Vietnam. "One is run and let the dominoes start falling over. And God almighty, what they said about us leaving China would just be warming up compared to what they'd say now. . . . You can run, or you can fight, as we are doing, or you can sit down and agree to neutralize all of it. But nobody is going to neutralize North Vietnam, so that's totally impractical. And so it really boils down to one of two decisions—getting out or getting in. . . . But we can't abandon it to them, as I see it."

The great questions about the Vietnam War—including the questions of whether Lyndon Johnson had feasible choices other than the ones he spelled out in that telephone call; of whether it is true, as one of his biographers says, that "no President, especially an unproven, unelected one, could simply have withdrawn without some real hope that the South Vietnamese could have held off a Viet Cong–North Vietnamese takeover"; of whether, if other feasible options existed, Johnson pursued them with sincerity; and of whether, had John F. Kennedy lived, United States policy would have been different from the policy Johnson pursued—these questions are among those that must remain to be examined in the next volume of this work. However, two aspects of the early decisions on Vietnam, early steps on what was to be a very long road, that Johnson took during that Christmas vacation on the ranch, are clear: first, whatever steps he took during that vacation, he took as well steps to conceal them, to keep them secret from Congress and the American people; and, second, the steps he took had, as their unifying principle, an objective dictated largely by domestic—indeed, personal—political concerns.

By the time McNamara had completed his trip to Vietnam, "it was clear" that "the plan for withdrawing U.S. forces was no longer workable," says William C. Gibbons, author of a definitive study of Vietnam policy-making, but no announcement was made that the plan—the first stage of which was the withdrawal of a thousand troops "by the end of the year"—was not being carried out. Instead, there was, in Gibbons' phrase, "juggling the figures."

Every month, more than a thousand soldiers routinely left Vietnam as part of regular troop rotations, to be replaced by an equal number of new soldiers. During the first part of December, the rotation schedule had been on a pace to achieve the thousand-man reduction, but following McNamara's trip, while the rotation out of Vietnam was continued, "the replacement pipeline was slowed somewhat." The departure of the troops originally scheduled to be sent to Vietnam in the last weeks of December was delayed. They were simply sent in January and February instead. "In the last weeks of 1963 . . . plans for phased with-drawal of 1,000 advisers by end-year 1963 went through the motions by concen-trating rotations home in December and letting strength rebound in the subsequent two months," the *Pentagon Papers* explained. At the end of the year, the number of United States military personnel in Vietnam was 15,914, a number which, as the *Pentagon Papers* noted, "did not even represent a decline of 1,000 from the peak of 16,732," being, in fact, only 818 lower. Even the 818 figure was illusory. As soon as the year ended, the replacement pipeline was speeded up, and within a matter of weeks, troop strength was back at its peak level, so that there was in fact no reduction at all. December's "planned 1,000-man reduction [therefore] proved essentially an accounting exercise," the *Pentagon Papers* explained.

But Johnson was to announce that the plan had been carried out. "We have called back approximately 1,000 people," he said in a press conference on March 7, 1964.

In another development, the "more forceful moves" for which McNamara had said the Administration should be "preparing" were indeed being prepared. The Krulak committee's report, which had arrived at the ranch on January 2, would not be formally approved by the President until January 16, but the covert operations it authorized—including the ones around the Gulf of Tonkin—were to begin on February 1. The approval of the plan—in effect, an escalation of the war, although a minor one—was never announced to the public or revealed to Congress (although a few members may have been quietly advised of some of the details). A National Security Action Memorandum would have normally been signed by the President as a result of the approval. No such memorandum was ever signed.

The overriding aim of the withdrawal and covert operations decisions—and of other decisions about Vietnam during the early days of Lyndon Johnson's presidency—was to keep Vietnam from becoming a major political issue, "above all else," as Fredrik Logevall put it in *Choosing War,* a detailed study of American decision-making from 1963 through 1965, "to keep Vietnam from complicating his election-year strategy. . . . The president judged all options on the war in terms of what they meant for November." So close to his vest was Johnson holding his cards on Vietnam that even McGeorge Bundy, who was carrying out his strategy, wasn't sure what it was. When, on March 2, 1964, the national security advisor was driven to ask him, "What is your own internal thinking on this [the overall Vietnam situation], Mr. President?," Johnson gave him his clearest answer yet. "I just can't believe that we can't take 15,000 [*sic*] advisers and 200,000 people [South Vietnamese troops] and maintain the *status quo* for six months. I just believe we can do that, if we do it right." Six months might have been a minor miscalculation. Election Day, 1964—November 3—was not six months away, but eight. But it might not have been. The Democratic National Convention would begin on August 24, in slightly less than six months. Sitting President though he was, there was Bobby Kennedy to consider. Miscalculation or not, however, the President's aim was clear: the maintenance of the *status quo* until a date set by a political calendar.

RUTHLESSNESS, SECRETIVENESS, DECEIT — significant elements in every previous stage of Lyndon Johnson's life story. Not always, however, the only elements, not always the only character traits, contradictory though other traits might be. And sometimes these other elements—the anger at injustice, the sympathy, empathy, identification with the underdog that added up to compassion— had been expressed, by this master of the political gesture, in gestures so deeply meaningful, so perfect in their symbolism, that they reached a level for which "mastery" is an inadequate term. *"By God, we'll bury him in Arlington,"* he had blurted in the very instant he was told that a Mexican-American war hero had been denied burial in a whites-only cemetery in South Texas.* This stage of the story—Christmas vacation at the ranch—was no different. If most of the gestures Lyndon Johnson made during those two weeks in Texas were mainly for effect, stage business to reinforce the personal image he wanted to project, one gesture was something more.

Friends of Horace Busby were giving him a birthday party that New Year's Eve in Austin's Forty Acres Club, which was, like most of the city's clubs, rigidly segregated. Although many University of Texas faculty members had resigned from the club in protest the previous year after a black Peace Corps official had been told he couldn't have a drink there, the rule against any African-American being given a room, a meal or a drink was still firmly in place.

On New Year's Eve, however, Johnson went party-hopping in Austin. Lady Bird, exhausted, said she was staying home, so Johnson took his secretaries along on the helicopter ride to Austin, and then in his limousine, and one of the parties he went to was Busby's, and just before he entered the Forty Acres Club, he took Gerri Whittington's arm and put it through his.

The guests at Busby's party were standing around having cocktails and talking. "All of a sudden the Secret Service appeared," recalls a law professor, E. Ernest Goldstein, "and a few minutes later in walked President Johnson with Gerri Whittington on his arm, and she was beautiful and black."

No one told Johnson he and his companion couldn't come in; no one, in fact, made any fuss at all. To Moyers, trailing behind the couple, the striking fact about the guests' reaction was that there was none: "No gasp, nothing was made of it"; everyone studiously went on with their conversations.

"Does the President know what he's doing?" Goldstein asked Moyers.

"He always knows what he's doing," Moyers replied. The President stayed

*See *Master of the Senate*, pp. 740ff.

for about an hour, Gerri Whittington on his arm, chatting with the Busbys and their friends, and during that hour no one mentioned civil rights or desegregation. (Among the items of conversation was banter about how many supermarket trading stamps the White House must be accumulating because of all the groceries it had to order for dinner parties.) But the next day—the day following what Goldstein calls "that magnificent evening"—the professor telephoned the club to ask if he could bring black guests that afternoon. "The answer was laconic," he would recall. " 'Okay—no problem.' I insisted, 'Is the club really integrated?' The reply this time was loud and clear. 'Yes, sir. The President of the United States integrated us on New Year's Eve.' "

AND SOMETIMES, as in previous stages of Lyndon Johnson's life when compassion and ambition had coincided, during that Christmas in Texas the compassion was expressed in a manner that went beyond a gesture. During that Christmas, in fact, Lyndon Johnson was taking steps that would place his stamp on the presidency in a manner more significant than image, in not style but substance—substance, moreover, on the grand scale: in a program whose goal, the institutionalization of compassion in government policy, was, in fact, of a scope so vast that were it to be realized, it would transform a nation.

He had known back in Washington, of course, that new substance was a necessity: that while "I have to carry out the Kennedy legacy," "at the same time I've got to put my own stamp on this administration in order to run for office." The Christmas interlude on the ranch was the time to make the necessary preparations, for almost immediately after his return from Texas—at 12:30 p.m. on January 8, 1964—he would deliver the State of the Union address to Congress.

If he wanted to announce new policy, that speech was the place to do it. The origin of the annual address was the constitutional provision that the President "shall from time to time give to the Congress information of the state of the Union, and recommend to their consideration such measures as he shall judge necessary and expedient," and the speech had evolved over the life of the Republic into the vehicle in which a President, at the beginning of each congressional session, announced policy, revealed programs and set the agenda which his Administration would be pursuing; it was largely because of Woodrow Wilson's determination to take a more forceful role in proposing and pushing for the passage of legislation that he had, in 1913, revived the original practice—followed by George Washington and John Adams but abandoned by Thomas Jefferson*— of delivering the address in person instead of sending it to the Hill in writing; Franklin Roosevelt had announced many of his New Deal programs, Harry Truman all of his Fair Deal, in their State of the Union speeches. Because the speech

---

*Jefferson said he felt the practice was too similar to the address a British monarch makes to Parliament and was therefore too regal for a democracy.

was televised, furthermore, it was an opportunity for a President to talk beyond Congress to the people, to address the nation as a whole. Some of the agenda Lyndon Johnson would lay out on January 8 would still have to be Kennedy's: the tax cut and civil rights bills, still not passed by Congress, would have to be the first priorities; continuity would have to remain a theme in the speech—but, he knew, there would have to be something more, something new. It was time to make the presidency *his* presidency.

IRONICALLY, THE PROGRAM with which he did it had had its beginning under Kennedy. In 1962, Michael Harrington's book *The Other America,* together with a lengthy review of the book by literary critic Dwight Macdonald in *The New Yorker,* had aroused liberals and intellectuals to the dilemma of one-fifth of America's population, the thirty million people who, in the midst of a wealthy and prosperous nation, were living in poverty that seemed intractable; studies by sociologists were finding not only that the number of the poor was not falling but that it was rising, and was going to continue to do so. "There will be considerably more poor even with a more affluent America" because "They are not part of the economic structure," one study concluded. "Future economic growth alone will provide relatively few escapes from poverty," concurred a report by Walter Heller's Council of Economic Advisers. Existing government programs did not address that dilemma; "Social Security does not cover them. Minimum-wage laws specifically exempt them. . . . Government welfare unwittingly contributes to broken homes and illegitimacy. . . . School-lunch programs have not nourished the communities that could not afford to transport the surplus foods or the children who could not make even the token payments." Then, in early 1963, articles by Homer Bigart in the *New York Times* on the plight of coal miners in Appalachia stirred President Kennedy, reminding him of the conditions he had witnessed when he had campaigned in the region in 1960. "Anti-poverty," as an historian wrote, "was in the air" in Washington. When, in the spring of 1963, Heller asked the President for permission to conduct "a quiet investigation" into the problem of long-term, hard-core poverty in America with a view to developing a program to deal with it, Kennedy gave him the go-ahead, and early that fall a task force of Cabinet officers was organized, at first with Heller as chairman, for a rather vague purpose: as Heller's chief aide on the group, William M. Capron, was to put it, "to come up with suggestions for items that might be included" in proposals for legislation that would be introduced in Congress in 1964.

But it wasn't much of a beginning. Operating without clear direction from the President, the group produced results that were, in Capron's words, "perhaps predictably disastrous . . . a lot of . . . warmed-over revisions of proposals that had been around a long time, coming up out of the bureaucracy . . . programs that had already been rejected by Congress. . . . Little bits and pieces that didn't really hang together." Although in October, Sorensen took over the chairmanship of the group, "the agencies weren't paying a lot of attention because they weren't sure that the President really wanted it." At a White House meeting in mid-October, Sorensen told the task force to, in effect, "Go back and do some more homework." Heller was to recall him saying, "Keep at it, it's the kind of an issue we should sign on to, and it's a terribly important thing." Then, on November 13, during the first planning session for the 1964 presidential campaign—the meeting to which Johnson wasn't invited—Census Bureau director Richard Scammon, on whom Kennedy was relying to analyze the demographics of the 1964 election, told the President that "You can't get a single vote more by doing anything for poor people. . . . Those who vote are already for you," and advised him to concentrate instead on issues that would be popular in the rapidly expanding, vote-rich, middle-class suburbs. "I then heard from Ted Sorensen some rather disquieting comment about, 'We may have to put more emphasis on the suburbs,' " Heller says. Going directly to Kennedy, he asked the President to tell him his "current feelings." Heller left a number of versions of that meeting. According to one set of notes he made, Kennedy's response was "I am still very much in favor of doing something on the poverty theme to make sure we can get a good program, but I also think it's important to make clear that we're doing something for the middle-income man in the suburbs, etc. But the two are not at all inconsistent with each other. So go right ahead with your work on it." According to another version Heller left, the President told him to " 'Come back to me in a couple of weeks.' This is what Kennedy told me on November 19th."

With little sense of urgency emanating from the Oval Office, when Heller's aides tried to discuss specific legislative proposals with Cabinet officials, they sometimes had trouble even getting appointments—"Gordon's schedule was too jammed up or something," Capron recalls of one attempt. While it was still possible that some bills might be drawn up for 1964, "it was generally thought that they wouldn't be pressed very hard until after the 1964 presidential campaign."

In addition, that beginning had received scant notice from the press. Congress had never held a single full-scale debate on the subject. "Public awareness of poverty" as a governmental or political issue was, in Evans and Novak's term, "virtually nonexistent." An anti-poverty program would not—unlike the tax cut or civil rights—be identified with Kennedy, would not, in the public mind, be a Kennedy program that Johnson was continuing. It was an issue that he could make his own.

And he made it his own.

When Heller had first mentioned it to the new President, the response had a different tone from the one he had received from President Kennedy.

The mention, and the response, had occurred during Heller's first meeting with Johnson in the Executive Office Building on the evening of November 23, as the economist was briefing the new President about economic issues that had been under discussion in the Kennedy Administration. When he told Johnson about the poverty issue, "his reaction immediately was, 'That's my kind of program. I'll find money for it one way or another. If I have to, I'll take money away from things to get money for people.' "

That was the meeting at which, as Heller was leaving, Johnson stopped him, shut the door, and assured him that he was not a "conservative" but "a Roosevelt New Dealer," and "I should be sure to tell my friends that." The conversation at the door, Heller was to say, was a little "calculated . . . a play for support . . . there he was: Lyndon Johnson, the politician." There was, Heller felt, no calculation in Lyndon Johnson's response on poverty. That was "so spontaneous and so immediate . . . an instinctive and intuitive and uncalculated response." Heller then asked him "point-blank" how fast he wanted to move on anti-poverty. Johnson responded, in Heller's words, that "we should push ahead full tilt."

Arriving at the ranch on December 29, Heller and Kermit Gordon found that Johnson had been doing that on his own.

The emphasis on reducing the budget to satisfy Harry Byrd had led the two economists to concentrate on finding funds for the anti-poverty program within existing federal programs: on spending a portion of funds already earmarked for manpower training or youth employment, for example, on programs specifically directed at people below the federally defined poverty line. A total of $500 million had, in fact, been thus identified in a number of programs, and they had been lumped together and labeled an "anti-poverty program." The thinking in Washington was to use those funds on modest pilot projects—demonstration programs, some of them defined only vaguely, to test their workability. "We started out with the notion that we were not talking about big new budget resources, and that was a constraint," Capron says. "That's why . . . we talked about a targeted demonstration program. We used the argument that we were all terribly ignorant about poverty and programmatic ways to do something about it, that we had to learn a lot more. We were not talking about a massive" program at all. And even about these modest programs, there was mostly confusion and competition: Washington turf wars. A December 20 meeting of Cabinet officers and lower-level officials disintegrated into what participants call a "nasty jurisdictional dispute" with "angry arguments" among the Cabinet officers over who would control the various projects, with Sorensen, at the head of the table, too "morose" to take charge. "It was," Capron says, "clear that there wasn't going to be a big new program of any kind."

Immediately upon Heller and Gordon's arrival at the ranch, however, that clarity vanished. The two economists found that Johnson had found new money for the program—that he had meant what he said when he blurted out, "I'll take money away from things to get money for people." The overall budget was, of course, coming down; Johnson didn't want it to start going back up. McNamara's Defense Department economies had started to add up, however, and out of these savings, they found, Johnson had reserved money for the anti-poverty program—and the amount he had thus reserved was $500 million, which, added to the $500 million from existing programs, meant there would be twice as much, a billion dollars for anti-poverty, as they had been thinking about. And inadequate though the total might still be—1 percent of a nation's spending specifically directed at the 20 percent of its people who most needed help—a "billion-dollar" figure had a symbolic, significant, ring to it. "Gordon and Heller had been thinking of a pilot venture to be carried out in a limited number of 'demonstration project' cities," Johnson would write in his memoirs. "But I urged them to broaden their scope. [The program] had to be big and bold, and hit the whole nation with real impact." As he had earlier explained the congressional realities of the tax cut to Heller and Gordon, now he laid out for them a basic congressional reality that would confront an anti-poverty program: why a "limited number" of smaller projects would never pass; why the program would have to be "big and bold" if it was to have a chance of enactment. A small number of projects, he explained, meant that only a small number of congressional districts would receive the new federal funds, and the number of congressmen with a vested interest in supporting the program would therefore be small. "I was certain that we could not start small and propel a program through Congress," he was to say.

He wanted them to find new programs in which to spend it. There was a new urgency. He kept asking, "How are you going to spend all this money?," Heller recalls. "He was extremely demanding. Time and time again . . . he said, 'Look, I've earmarked half a billion dollars to get this program started, but I'll withdraw that unless you fellows come through with something that's workable.' "

There was a new demand for specifics. "He wanted something concrete," Heller was to recall. "He made it very clear that they [the programs] had to have some hard, bedrock content, and he kept referring time and again to his NYA [National Youth Administration] experience. He liked the idea of learning while doing, learning through doing." But he didn't want to go just back, but forward. "The challenge I presented to my advisors was the development of a new concept," he was to write. "I didn't want to paste together a lot of existing approaches. I wanted original, inspiring ideas."

Part of the explanation for Lyndon Johnson's enthusiasm for the anti-poverty program was, as was always the case with Lyndon Johnson, political.

All his efforts on behalf of the tax cut and civil rights bills had not come close to erasing liberal suspicions about him. On the day Johnson flew back to Washington from Texas, the liberal columnist William V. Shannon would tell his readers that the credit for anything the new President might have accomplished belonged not to him but to John F. Kennedy, that now the honeymoon was over and it was time for him to produce on his own—and that, judging from his record, it was doubtful that he could.

"All of us have been grateful to our new President," Shannon wrote, in a tone that suggested that he himself had not been overwhelmed by that emotion, "for the magisterial way in which he took hold of his responsibilities. His energy, self-confidence and natural energy have been therapeutic in a disheartening and troubled time. His conduct in the past several weeks which impressed everyone is already part of the history of the Kennedy period. It was a fitting epilogue to the Kennedy story."

Now, Shannon said, the time had come to view the Johnson Administration on its own. "It is time to examine President Johnson in the cold winter light of the problems and opportunities which confront him." The view was not reassuring. "History suggests that the martyrdom of a great man does not necessarily have positive political consequences." Lincoln's, for example, "led only to the failures of Reconstruction. . . . What was the political sequel to [Woodrow Wilson's] personal sacrifice" when he "broke his health in a stumping tour on behalf of the League of Nations? The isolation and corruption of the Harding Administration."

As for Johnson, Shannon wrote, he "is politically weak in the northeast and in the big cities generally . . . in the liberal, urban areas," and, he wrote, there was good reason for that weakness. "We have already witnessed the failures that occurred last month"—Shannon was classifying as failures the new President's inability to get the tax and civil rights bills through Congress before the end of the year—and, he said, those failures might be symptomatic of disturbing qualities in Johnson. "There are genuine ambiguities in his legislative record," and "moreover, as a legislator he overemphasized his talent for adjustment and compromise at the expense of . . . commitment. . . . We have to acknowledge that there are valid grounds for apprehension regarding Mr. Johnson or any other public man whose emphasis is almost wholly on means rather than ends. . . . The broker concept is inadequate for the far more demanding office of the presidency. What are a man's values, his moral ends, his vision of justice? These are the important questions." Shannon's was far from the only liberal voice still asking such questions. A campaign against poverty would strengthen Johnson in the "liberal, urban areas" in which he was weakest. And there was a political reason for launching the campaign quickly: an election that was now just ten months away.

But part of the explanation was, as always with Johnson, something more, something that had to do less with strategy than with memories. The ranch, with the pathetic frame house and the road across the river, was, after all, an appropriate setting for him to be thinking about poverty. And allusions in his conversation both in person and over the telephone—sentences, phrases, reminiscences—allusions that started to be heard as he chatted on the plane ride down to Texas, and that continued to sprinkle his speech during the two weeks on the ranch, show how fresh his youth was in his mind during that time. Talking to reporters on the plane about the federal budget, he had suddenly stopped and begun talking about himself. "I've always been an early riser," he said. "My daddy used to come to my bedroom at four-thirty in the morning when I was workin' on the highway gang, right out of high school, and he'd twist my big toe, real hard so it hurt, and he'd say, 'Git up, Lyndon, every other boy in town's got a half hour's head start on you.' " Making an early-morning call to an old Hill Country ally, E. Babe Smith of Marble Falls, he said he hoped he hadn't woken him up—and then said he was sure he hadn't because Smith had been "a poor boy," too, and therefore must have been getting up early all his life, as he himself did. "That's the only way we can keep up," he said. "Otherwise, they're too far ahead of us." Other old acquaintances recall similar early-morning calls from the Johnson Ranch that vacation. "We always get up early, don't we?" he told Fredericksburg attorney Arthur Stehling. "We can't make it unless we do." And at the age of nine and ten he had worked beside his cousin Ava, hauling the heavy bags of cotton, their backs stooped over in the burning sun, Ava to whom he had whispered as they worked, "Boy, there's got to be a better way to make a living than this. There's got to be a better way." Asked by the author twelve years after that Christmas trip what she and Lyndon had talked about that Christmas, Ava said she didn't remember, except that they had reminisced about their youth, and about the cotton picking. Whenever she and Lyndon reminisced, that subject came up, she said. "We always talked about the cotton. We just [had] hated that so much."

"Hate" is, in fact, a word that occurs frequently in descriptions of Lyndon Johnson's feelings about poverty. He "hated poverty and illiteracy," Dr. Hurst would say. "He *hated* it when a person who wanted to work could not get a job." Accompanying Johnson on a vice presidential trip to Iran, Hurst had seen his reaction when someone in the party said that a group of Iranian children they passed had "rags" for clothing.

"They did not," Johnson said. "Don't say that. I know rags when I see them. They had patched clothes. That is a lot different than rags." Hurst says that "I noted as the years passed that he reacted in the same way whenever he heard the word 'rags.' I realized that to him rags were the ultimate symbol of the poverty he detested." There had, after all, been patches on clothing worn by his brother and youngest sister, who had still been small when Sam Johnson went broke on the ranch, and that clothing certainly hadn't been *rags*!

From the moment Heller and Gordon arrived at the ranch that Christmas, Johnson "hounded" them to get him an anti-poverty package with hard, concrete, specific programs that would produce results. The two economists were quartered in the green frame guest house, and in the late evenings, when they, and perhaps Moyers and Valenti, were sitting around a little kitchen table littered with papers and coffee cups, its ashtray overflowing with cigarette butts, the President would suddenly appear in the doorway. He found the scene amusing, he was to recall: "Just a few feet from the window several of my white-faced Herefords were grazing placidly and a little noisily. It was an incongruous setting for Gordon and Heller, those two urbane scholars." Gordon was wearing one of his host's khaki western shirts, far too large for him, with "what we Texans called 'city-bought' trousers and low city shoes. Sitting down at the table, Johnson bantered with him about his half-hearted attempt . . . to blend in with his . . . surroundings." Johnson's mind was on the anti-poverty legislative program, however; when he was with the men working on it, all subjects, even their attire, were seen in their relation to that. When Gordon replied to the joking about his clothes by saying he was trying to blend urban and cattle country, "it struck me that the poverty program itself was a blend of the same: of the needs and desperate desires of the poor in the city ghettos and the poor in obscure rural hollows"—and that the new program must therefore include provisions not only for the urban slums on which attention was focused but also for rural areas, scattered, "obscure," in which needs were just as desperate.

Eager for new ideas, he even accepted one that had emerged from the President's Committee on Juvenile Delinquency and Youth Crime, chaired by a longtime Robert Kennedy friend, David Hackett.

While Johnson was talking about concrete, bulldozer projects, Hackett's committee had been urging him to make a concept called "community action"—a vague proposal to involve the residents of impoverished neighborhoods in programs that affected them—a key part of the program. Opposed to the idea at first as being too vague, not something that would give people jobs or children an education, Johnson changed his mind, according to Busby partly because it had emerged from a "Kennedy committee" and opposing it would therefore conflict with the continuity theme. "People would have said, 'Oh, he's not really sincere.'" Johnson's own explanation was that while "I realized that" the community action concept "might shake up many existing institutions, but I decided that some shaking up might be needed to get a bold new program moving."

While few specifics of the anti-poverty program had been decided upon when, on January 3, the two economists flew back to Washington from the ranch, by the time they left, the atmosphere surrounding the program bore little resemblance to the atmosphere that had existed before November 22. There was no more talk about "coming back in a couple of weeks." Instead, there were orders to have the Budget Bureau and the other government agencies involved draw up detailed recommendations, and to draw them up fast. By Monday, January 6, they were ready, and the two economists sent them to Cabinet members with a covering memo. "Your preliminary written reactions are required before the close of business, Thursday, January 9th," the memo said. Other deadlines were set—also tight deadlines. And by the end of the vacation, the program had a name. The "1964 State of the Union Message—First Draft" was completed in the little house on the Lewis Ranch on December 30, and a secretary was driven up to decipher and transcribe Ted Sorensen's tiny handwriting, and the draft's first page contained the words "Let this session of Congress be known as the session which . . . declared all-out war on human poverty and misery and unemployment in these United States," and the fifth page contained the words "This Administration hereby declares unconditional war on poverty in America."

While during the next week the message would go through many drafts, those sentences were to remain, essentially unchanged, in all of them. The provenance of the phrase "War on Poverty" is difficult to determine. When the author of this book asked Sorensen about it, Sorensen said that "it doesn't sound like something President Kennedy would have been comfortable saying, or that I would have been comfortable writing." In fact, however, President Kennedy *had* said it—in a little-noticed campaign speech in 1960, which, it appears, Sorensen wrote. Whether the phrase sprang from Sorensen's pen as he scribbled away in the guest house, or whether it was suggested to him by Lyndon Johnson in their early discussions about the speech, it caught Johnson's fancy—because it caught Johnson's feelings. Why wouldn't it? Lyndon Johnson knew what to do with enemies. And if, to destroy them, war was necessary, war it would be.

There would later—not at the time—be criticism of the phrases and sentences in which the war was declared for their overblown, hyperbolic quality, their gaudy rhetoric. But, says Elizabeth Wickenden, "The whole idea of declaring a big war on poverty and ending it for all time, all the rhetoric of it, appealed to him very much." By the time Johnson flew back to Washington, the speech had been finished in essentially its final form, and it laid out an anti-poverty program with only a few details filled in but designed to right, on a vast scale, vast wrongs. *"The moral arc of the universe bends slowly, but it bends towards justice."* Lyndon Johnson was trying to bend it faster.

THE STATE OF THE UNION came three days after he flew back from the ranch.

In the message, he gave Congress, as the mandate required, information—a startling announcement—about the budget for the next fiscal year. "Under the budget that I shall shortly submit," he said, there would be "an actual reduction in federal expenditures and federal employment."

A reduction in the number of federal employees, he said, would be "a feat accomplished only once before in the last ten years," and, he said, the reduction would be "substantial." As for the size of the overall budget, "It will call for total expenditures of $97,900 billion." Not only had he cut the budget below $100 billion, he had cut it so far below that magic figure that Harry Byrd wouldn't feel it had been brought in below only through accounting gimmicks. It was, in fact, lower, half a billion dollars lower, than the previous year's budget of $98.4 billion.

That announcement allowed him to segue into the need for a tax cut. A lower budget, he said, was an argument for lower taxes. Unemployment was still unacceptably high. "I would remind you that," despite America's prosperity, "four million workers . . . are still idle today." By creating an incentive for business investment, a reduction in the corporate tax rate would create jobs. "That tax bill has been thoroughly discussed for a year," he said. "Now we need action. The new budget clearly allows it. Our taxpayers surely deserve it. Our economy strongly demands it. . . . And the most damaging and devastating thing you can do to any businessman in America is to keep him in doubt and to keep him guessing on what our tax policy is."

THE TAX CUT, of course, was his predecessor's tax cut, and while President Kennedy's name was invoked only three times during the forty-three-minute speech, the invocations were couched in terms—Sorensen's terms—so stirring

("Let us carry forward the plans and programs of John Fitzgerald Kennedy—not because of our sorrow or sympathy, but because they are right") that the theme of continuity could still be heard in the address.

And then, about thirteen minutes into the speech, Lyndon Johnson introduced a new theme.

"Unfortunately," he said, "many Americans live on the outskirts of hope—some because of their poverty, and some because of their color, and all too many because of both. Our task is to help replace their despair with opportunity." His voice as he spoke those sentences was low, almost soft, reasonable in tone, but the next sentence rang out, with its Texas twang, across the big Chamber: "This administration today, here and now, declares unconditional war on poverty in America."

Retaining the words in Sorensen's draft, Johnson had added four words to them: Lyndon Johnson words. *"Today. Here and now."* So hard did he pound them in as they rang out across the rows of upturned faces before him that they might have been underlined in the air.

"It will not be a short or easy struggle," Lyndon Johnson said, "no single weapon or strategy will suffice, but we shall not rest until that war is won. The richest nation on earth can afford to win it. We cannot afford to lose it."

Although a few lines of attack were mentioned—"a special effort," an effort begun under President Kennedy, "in the chronically distressed areas of Appalachia"; enactment of new "youth employment legislation," reminiscent of the NYA, "to put jobless, aimless, hopeless youngsters to work on useful projects"—the speech was short on specific strategies for the war's prosecution. While the community action concept was endorsed, the endorsement came in terms too vague for its implications to be immediately apparent. "Poverty is a national problem, requiring improved national organization and support. But this attack, to be effective, must also be organized at the state and local level and must be supported and directed by state and local efforts," was what Johnson said on that subject. The war's causes—the reasons it was necessary—were made clear, however, as were, in general terms, the weapons that would be deployed, and the enemies at which he was aiming. "To help that one-fifth of all American families with incomes too small to even meet their basic needs," he said, "our chief weapons . . . will be better schools, and better health, and better homes, and better training, and better job opportunities to help more Americans, especially young Americans, escape from squalor and misery and unemployment rolls."

"Squalor." "Misery." "Unemployment." As Lyndon Johnson named those targets, his eyes, behind the thick glasses, narrowed, and his lips, set already in that grim, tough line, tightened and twisted into an expression close to a snarl. And he continued with words that, while none of them applied specifically to the circumstances of his own life, might nevertheless have had a special resonance for someone who had grown up in poverty, and who knew it was only because he hadn't been given a fair chance.

"Very often a lack of jobs and money is not the cause of poverty, but the symptom," he said. "The cause may lie deeper—in our failure to give our fellow citizens a fair chance to develop their own capacities, in a lack of education and training, in a lack of medical care and housing, in a lack of decent communities in which to live and bring up their children." He paused. "But whatever the cause, our joint federal-local effort must pursue poverty, pursue it wherever it exists—in city slums and small towns, in sharecropper shacks or in migrant worker camps, on Indian reservations, among whites as well as Negroes, among the young as well as the aged, in the boom towns and in the depressed areas."

And the aim of the war was made clear, too—and, as he enunciated it, it was titanic, nothing less than the unconditional transformation of a nation to eradicate a great injustice. "Our aim is not only to relieve the symptoms of poverty, but to cure it and, above all, to prevent it," he said.

Improved medical care was tied in with the war, he said. "We must provide hospital insurance for our older citizens financed by every worker and his employer under Social Security . . . to protect him in his old age in a dignified manner . . . against the devastating hardship of prolonged or repeated illness." Civil rights was tied in with it. While he had been in Texas, reporters in Washington, discussing with Mansfield, Dirksen and other Senate leaders the prospects for the civil rights bill, had concluded that its passage in its present form was all but impossible. The heroism on the streets of the South hadn't changed things. "The tumultous [*sic*] events of recent months have not altered the nose count in the Senate on civil rights," Marquis Childs wrote. "At most, 43 or 44 of the 67 Democrats will vote to shut off a filibuster. That is grim arithmetic. . . . It means that no fewer than 25 Republicans must vote for clo[t]ure. . . . Those 25 will be hard to come by." And because of that arithmetic, what the *New York Times* called "persistent reports" had begun circulating in Washington that in order to secure more votes, Johnson "might permit the [bill's] public accommodations section . . . to be eliminated or watered down." The State of the Union address laid that speculation to rest.

"Let me make one principle of this administration abundantly clear," Johnson said. "All of these increased opportunities—in employment, in education, in housing, and in every field—must be open to Americans of every color. As far as the writ of federal law will run, we must abolish not some, but all racial discrimination. For this is not merely an economic issue, or a social, political, or international issue. It is a moral issue, and it must be met by the passage this session of the bill now pending in the House.

"All members of the public should have equal access to facilities open to the public. All members of the public should be equally eligible for federal benefits that are financed by the public. All members of the public should have an equal chance to vote for public officials and to send their children to good public schools and to contribute their talents to the public good.

"Today," Lyndon Johnson said, "Americans of all races stand side by side in Berlin and in Vietnam. They died side by side in Korea. Surely they can work and eat and travel side by side in their own country."

• • •

IN SHARP CONTRAST to John Kennedy's State of the Union addresses, only about a quarter of Johnson's speech was devoted to foreign policy, and it was the last quarter. None of that portion was newsworthy, or even particularly significant, although its reference to Khrushchev's threat to "bury" the United States ("We intend to bury no one, and we do not intend to be buried," Johnson said) received, predictably, the loudest applause of any line he delivered. Vietnam was mentioned in this portion of the speech only once, when Johnson said America must be "better prepared than ever before to defend the cause of freedom, whether it is threatened by outright aggression or by the infiltration practiced by those in Hanoi and Havana, who ship arms and men across international borders to foment insurrection." In fact, the only other mention of Vietnam in the entire speech was the statement that Americans of all races stand side by side there.

POLITICALLY, THE SPEECH WAS a triumph. Clustering around Republicans as they left the Chamber, reporters found the expected hostile reactions muted, *pro forma,* a little lame. "He's proposing a cut-rate Utopia," was the best one GOP representative could come up with. The furthest Dirksen would go was to say that the message "seemed almost like a blueprint for the kind of paradise devoutly to be wished by everyone. But how do you all these things, and with less money?" And the press understood why. The House Republican whip, Leslie C. Arends of Illinois, said that Johnson "promises something for everyone." But if that was indeed what he had done, "everyone"—voters—might not be disposed to object. Saying that "Republicans found the speech hard to get at," the *Washington Post* quoted a Democrat in explanation: "It's the Sermon on the Mount. How can anyone attack it?" The *Post* said that "both his fellow Democrats and Republicans knew they had heard a consummate political artist at work," and that he had created a *tour de force* that was hard to criticize. JOHNSON MANAGES TO TOUCH ALL THE BASES IN A SHOW OF POLITICS AND STATESMANSHIP, a *Post* headline said, the analysis underneath it concluding that "There was something for everybody: economy for the conservatives; an anti-poverty program for the depressed one-fifth of our partially affluent society; a joyous tax cut [that will] give the economy a juicy shot by summer and fall. . . . In short, Mr. Johnson had his arm around the shoulder of so much of the Congress—and so many of the voters—yesterday that he didn't leave the Republicans much of a spot to take hold." No wonder senators and House members had sat like pupils being given "the lesson for tomorrow," the *Post* said. No wonder "they hung onto his every whisper" and applauded so often; "he took the high road of statesmanship and they knew he was making hay politically."

"Remarkable" was an adjective used in editorials and in columns like

Arthur Krock's ("remarkable for its bold sweep and the bold idealism of his programs, for its eloquence in composition and the masterly manner of its delivery"). "President Johnson's first State of the Union message today was a classic political document," the *Times* said.

And the triumph was also on a level above the political. "Masterful" as it was politically, *Time* said, "it was much more" as well. An editorial that may have proved particularly gratifying to Johnson, coming as it did in the *New York Post,* codifier of liberal opinion, said that the speech had "reinforced the image of a man who has risen resolutely to the tragic occasion under which he assumed office." It praised his budget. "The arithmetic of his argument may be subject to complicated dispute," its editorial said. "But even the most ritualistic 'budget balancers' cannot fail to be impressed by the boldness with which he and Defense Secretary McNamara have attacked the problems of waste in the military establishment. Military budgets have long been treated as politically untouchable. . . . President Johnson . . . has served notice that a day of real reckoning for the Pentagon has arrived." And then it added that "If excessive sums allocated for 'overkill,' obsolescence and other forms of military extravagance can be applied to positive social outcomes, the country can only be fundamentally stronger. And that seems to be Mr. Johnson's grand design."

"It was an address from which Americans could derive pride and inspiration," the *Post* said.

THE CHORUS OF PRAISE focused at first not on the anti-poverty program but on the budget reduction. This was "the stunner" in *Newsweek*'s account, a "near miraculous achievement" in the *Washington Post*'s. The key word in headlines across the country was not "poverty" but "economy." JOHNSON VOWS ECONOMY was the *Chicago Tribune*'s banner, PRESIDENT — ECONOMY VOW the *New York Herald Tribune*'s. The announcement that the budget was lower than Kennedy's was "the new President's most dramatic passage," the *New York Daily News* said. "No one had expected that," the *Times* chimed in. "The fact that it is lower is regarded as a considerable political coup for Mr. Johnson." The scope of the anti-poverty proposal took a few weeks to sink in, in part because there had been little preparation for it. "At least one public-spirited lobbyist in Washington who had been working long and hard to stir up a fight against poverty in the United States was caught by surprise to learn that President Johnson was declaring 'unconditional war' on the ancient enemy," the Washington reporter Douglass Cater wrote in *The Reporter* magazine in February. Despite his own longtime interest in the subject, Cater wrote, he himself had heard none of "the usual bureaucratic rumblings to indicate such a major governmental initiative in the making." By the end of those few weeks, however, the scope—the revolutionary ambition—of the proposal had begun to be understood. "The concerted effort at federal, state and local levels for which President Johnson is calling could inject government into social planning on a scale never before attempted," Cater wrote. Cater knew there was need for such an effort. "There is every reason why government cannot ignore the people who, in Johnson's phrase, are living on 'the outskirts of hope.' " Yet, he noted, "poverty has so far lacked a power base in Washington capable of sustaining its claims."

"Will Johnson show the perseverance to keep his program on target?" Cater asked. "Though his activities to date are largely on the propaganda side, there are some promising signs." And, despite the efforts of Kennedy adherents, who hurried to explain to columnists and reporters that the poverty program was really Kennedy's program, the program was accepted as Johnson's. "In launching a campaign against poverty President Johnson is carrying on what President Kennedy was intending to do," Walter Lippmann wrote. "I am told that the basic policy was Kennedy's, and that its translation into a program is Johnson's." But, Lippmann made clear, that quibble had little significance to him. The new President "knows about the hidden and forgotten American poor. . . . In style and in substance the President's message is an intimate and personal display of the political gifts for which Lyndon Johnson is celebrated. He shows himself to be a passionate seeker with an uncanny gift for finding, beneath public issues, common ground on which men could stand."

THE NEW PROGRAM he announced, combined with the demeanor with which he announced it, had achieved another of his purposes. "Once before, during the nightmare that was November, Lyndon B. Johnson stood at the Speaker's rostrum and addressed himself to Congress, but while the voice was the prairie drawl of President Johnson, the words echoed the program of the fallen President Kennedy. There was no mistaking either voice or words last week," *Newsweek* said. "This was President Johnson speaking, very much his own man in his first State of the Union Message, forcefully determined upon a program of his own making. . . . His own Administration had clearly begun."

The transition between the thirty-fifth and thirty-sixth presidencies of the United States, the period that had begun at the moment on November 22, 1963, when Ken O'Donnell had said of the thirty-fifth President, "He's gone," had been brought to an end with Lyndon Johnson's speech on January 8, 1964. It had lasted forty-seven days, just short of seven weeks. Now it was over. "I've got to put my own stamp on this administration," Johnson had known. In his State of the Union message he had done just that—had made the presidency his own, put a stamp, a brand, on it.

He had done it with an announcement of a program with goals so new and ambitious that it was necessary to go back to Franklin Roosevelt's New Deal to find, perhaps not an equal, but at least a comparison.

The ranch on which, during that Christmas vacation, he had created the program's outline was just down the road from the Junction School, where, as a small boy, he had scrawled his name across two blackboards in letters so large that schoolmates become old men still remembered the huge "LYNDON B." on one blackboard and "JOHNSON" on the other. The program he had announced in the State of the Union was of dimensions so sweeping that with it he was trying to write his name across the whole long slate of American history.

22

"Old Harry" II

AMONG THE HUNDREDS of representatives and senators crowded into the long curved rows of seats as Lyndon Johnson spoke of the state of the union was the one whose reaction was most crucial. From her front-row seat in the gallery above, Lady Bird Johnson was "searching for Harry Byrd every time the word 'budget' was mentioned."

The new President's efforts to bring Old Harry over, to "get" him as he had sometimes gotten him in the past, had been resumed before the speech, on the day following Johnson's return from Texas. The Finance Committee chairman had made his cooperation on the tax cut bill contingent on Johnson's promise not only to bring the budget in under $100 billion without gimmicks, but to show him and John Williams, Finance's ranking Republican, written documentation of that; despite the acceleration in his committee's processing of amendments, enough of them were being held in reserve to ensure that the Finance hearings could take whatever length of time the chairman desired. Knowing that the promise would have to be redeemed, Johnson's response when, on January 6, Kermit Gordon finally reported that the budget was "locked up," was to ask him, "When am I going to get the galley proofs" (of the final, printed version) and the "tally sheets" (the unofficial ledgers used by the Budget Bureau for its calculations)? "I'm going to have to show [them] to Harry Byrd sometime," he said. As soon as the proofs and sheets were ready the next morning, a car was sent to the Senate Office Building for Byrd and Williams.

"I've got a surprise for you, Harry," Johnson said when the two senators arrived at the White House. "I've got the damn thing down under one hundred billion . . . way under. It's only 97.9 billion. Now you can tell your friends that you forced the President of the United States to reduce the budget before you let him have his tax cut."

Not only was the budget indeed below Byrd's magic figure, there was magic also in Johnson's words, appealing as they did to an old man's pride in his principles and in the victory he had won for them—and appealing also to his pride in his power. Harry Byrd could indeed know that he had forced a President of the United States to bow to his demands: The President himself was acknowledging that, admitting it to his face. Given Johnson's hatred of losing, his feeling that any defeat was "humiliation," there was a sacrifice in Johnson's statement. He was admitting that he had lost, that he had been forced to bow to someone's demands, and he was admitting it face-to-face to the man who had beaten him. It was still the early days of his presidency—less than seven weeks after Dallas; if the price of achieving governmental progress was such a face-to-face admission, it was a price he was still willing to pay. And not only had he paid it, face-to-face, graciously, he had put it, from this man looking always for words that would "touch," in words designed to touch.

And they *did* touch. Byrd's reaction to the State of the Union speech—"I congratulate the President on his estimated reduction in federal expenditures and deficits. His references to cutting waste and extravagance have been impressive"—was all Johnson could have hoped.

The White House press office had been alerted to look for it. As soon as it clattered over the wire service ticker, a press office secretary tore it off, showed it to Pierre Salinger, ran with it into the Oval Office, and the President telephoned the senator and said, "I appreciate [it] very much."

In that call, the chord of pride he had newly struck in Byrd was struck along with the old one, Byrd's affection for him. "I've got to represent the whole country and do my best," the President said. "We're going to have some differences as we always do. . . . But I'll tell you this. . . . One thing I'm going to try to do— I'm going to try to stop and arrest the spending and try to be as frugal as I can make them be. . . . You're my inspiration for doing it. And I want to work with you. And I want you to advise me. . . . I want you to be proud that you supported me in 1960."

Byrd's response showed how strongly the chords resonated in him. Johnson said he wanted him to be proud of him—and the older man assured him that he already was. "That was an eloquent speech you made," he said. "You've made a good start," he said. And, as almost immediately became apparent, he was going to help him. The very day after their telephone conversation, the Finance Committee, in what the *New York Times* called a "speed-up," held an unusually long session, in which it defeated, often by a 9–8 vote, a number of amendments. By the next week, many journalists had noted that, as the *Washington Post* put it, "Byrd has been moving in high gear" in "what appeared to be a footrace with the Calendar."

"Harry started to regard the budget, well, almost as *his* budget—*he* had gotten it down," Neil MacNeil says. "And because the tax reduction [bill] was so tied in with it [the budget], and he had done so much work on that bill—well, it was almost as if the tax bill had suddenly become *his* bill, too."

All Byrd's help, and all his power, would be needed to get it passed. Developments that Johnson had not foreseen—a new line of attack orchestrated by

Richard Russell and a series of last-minute amendments introduced in the Finance Committee by Republican Leader Everett Dirksen and other GOP committee members, as well as by some Democratic members, to exempt the products of industries in their states from the excise taxes in the tax bill—threatened to upset Johnson's timetable: with Finance suddenly faced with more work than had been anticipated, and House Rules moving faster than had been anticipated, there was suddenly, thanks to Russell's maneuvers, the danger that Rules might complete its work before Finance, and send the civil rights bill to the Senate floor before the tax bill arrived there; there was suddenly, again, the possibility that the tax bill might get behind civil rights, that it would be "good night, Grace." But all that January the chords were played, in telephone calls in which Johnson used the tone he had used years before, as a young senator, when he had sat at Harry Byrd's knee, and pride and affection overcame even the fear of what might happen if black children and white children rode in school buses together. Harry Byrd no longer wanted the tax bill—*his* tax bill, now, in his mind—behind civil rights; he wanted his bill passed. He became, in Evans and Novak's phrase, "Johnson's secret ally"—and a very effective one. On Thursday morning, January 23, as the committee was about to complete its work, there was almost a derailment. Without warning, Dirksen suddenly introduced yet another new amendment, to repeal excise taxes on luxury goods such as jewelry and expensive handbags and luggage, and it was approved, 12 to 5. A "stunned" Treasury Department estimated that the amendment would cost the government $450 million—almost half a billion dollars—in tax revenue each year.

That vote broke the dam. Three Democratic committee members—Clinton Anderson of New Mexico, Vance Hartke of Indiana and Abraham Ribicoff of Connecticut—who had, in the interest of getting a bill passed, agreed to withdraw excise tax amendments that would benefit industries in *their* states immediately decided to resubmit them. Each amendment would have to be debated individually within the committee, and the debates, as senators fought for constituencies in their states important to them, might be long ones. And there remained the other amendments that had not been taken up by the committee: their sponsors might now want them debated individually as well.

JOHNSON LEARNED of these developments at thirty-four minutes past noon on the 23rd, in a panicky phone call from George Smathers, who told him that the previous agreement to get the tax bill out fast had fallen apart. "The goddamned thing came unglued," he said, and he didn't think there was anything that could be done about it in the committee. "I don't think there's anything we can do except . . . just take it [accept Dirksen's amendment] as it is."

Taking it as it was, however, would mean that all the careful balancing of the budget would be undone, and the careful scheduling to ensure the tax bill arrival on the Senate floor before civil rights might be undone, too. But Smathers was talking to the master of the Senate. Long before he was finished explaining that the problem was unsolvable, Johnson had thought of a way—possibly the only way—to solve it.

His solution would require two far-from-routine rulings from the committee chairman, rulings that would in fact fly in the face of the committee's vote that morning: first, that the Dirksen amendment could be brought back that afternoon and voted on again; and, second, that it be brought back by a motion that lumped in with it all remaining amendments before the committee, even those that had not yet been debated, so that a single vote by the committee—a vote to defeat the Dirksen amendment—would be a vote to defeat all the remaining amendments as well, thereby concluding the committee's work on the tax cut bill and removing the last obstacle to its release to the Senate floor. And since only five committee members had voted against the amendment before, Johnson's solution would require also that the three rebellious Democratic senators be persuaded not only to withdraw their amendments, but to reverse their vote on the Dirksen amendment, and this time vote to defeat it. Even their three votes would not provide the nine necessary to defeat it; not only Byrd's ruling to allow the motion but his vote against the amendment, a fourth vote that would be reversed, would be essential; it was going to be another "9–8 thing."

"I think we just got to go right on with the bill," Smathers said, but Johnson refused to accept that. "Can't you redo it in the committee?" he demanded. "Can't you repeal what you did in the committee? Can't you put those votes together?"

"I don't think so," Smathers said. "I just don't see how."

"That's what I'd try to do," Lyndon Johnson said.

There was little time to do it. He hung up the phone with Smathers at 12:42. The Finance Committee was scheduled to reconvene at two o'clock. He told Colonel Roberts to get the three Democratic senators on the phone.

Luckily, Anderson and Hartke had been in the Senate while Johnson was Leader. They knew that Lyndon Johnson was a bad man to cross but could be a good man to have on your side. And they—and Ribicoff—knew that a President had a lot of ways to help or hurt a senator. The persuasion went fast. Agreeing to withdraw his amendment, Anderson said Ribicoff would never withdraw his— "He won't do it! He won't go with anybody."

"If you go with us . . . I'll appreciate it and I'll remember it," Johnson told Ribicoff. He had *put* Ribicoff on Finance, he told him. "When you wanted to go on that committee, I just stood up and said, 'By God, it's going to be.' Now I just want one vote [one motion], and I want to get that bill out of there, and I've got to have it, Abe." Ribicoff said that his amendment "is for something in my home state that's already been announced" and that he had "a problem with saving [face]" with his constituency. "I'll save your face," Johnson said. "You save my face this afternoon, and I'll save your face tomorrow." "Okay, Mr. President," was the reply. When Hartke said he needed to have a separate vote on his amendment because it was vital to a company in Indiana, Johnson said he couldn't have it. "We want to just have a general vote. . . . See if you can't do that for me." Laughing, Hartke said, "All right."

"I'll do something for you," Johnson said.

"I know you will," Hartke replied.

Johnson's calls to the three senators had lasted a total of nine minutes.

But of course, despite his success with the senators, everything depended on Byrd, on his rulings—and on his vote, too. For all his telephoning Johnson was still one vote short. He telephoned Byrd to ask him to allow the motion for a single vote that very afternoon, and then, on that vote, to vote no. "I hope you can help," Johnson told the chairman in a call to Byrd's office at 1:17. "Because that [Dirksen amendment] throws *everything* out of caboodle if we lose 450 million"—all the careful budget calculations. "If you'll go with me on that, we can do it. . . . Just have one general motion that covers them all." Byrd said he would have a problem doing that because he had already committed himself to vote in favor of several individual excise tax amendments, but Johnson kept pleading. "I'll do the best I can," Byrd said finally. "Help me, Harry," Lyndon Johnson said.

Late that afternoon, Byrd called the Oval Office, getting the same White House switchboard operator on the line who had connected him to the President that morning. He was so excited that he delivered his news to her, not the President. "Well, I want to tell you—the President called me this morning in regard to votes," he said. "Yes, sir," the operator said. "We had a 9–8 vote," Byrd said. "My vote was the one that carried it his way."

"Ohhh, wonderful!" the operator said. The senator and the operator laughed happily together.

"Tell him, and I won't bother him, but I . . . Nine to eight was about cutting out these . . . reductions of the excise taxes, you know." The operator said she *did* know. Byrd told her that he had ruled that all the reductions "could be lumped together in a single bill," and "they were taken out of the bill by nine to eight."

The operator gave another long "ohhh" of admiration.

"My vote," the old senator said proudly.

THE CALL ENDED with the operator saying, "I'll tell him." She evidently did, because a few minutes later, her boss called Byrd. "That Harry Byrd," Lyndon Johnson said. "He can do anything."

It was a moment for remembering long-ago days. "You've learned to count since I left up there," Johnson said. "I used to do your counting, but when you can beat them nine to eight, you're doing all right."

THERE WAS STILL A NEED for haste. By that last 9–8 vote, the committee had finally finished its hearings on the tax bill, but it could not go to the Senate floor until the committee's majority report on the bill was written, printed and filed with the secretary of the Senate, and since a tax bill report was a complex document, the committee's staff usually took a week or more to write it. And over in the House, Republicans, eager to avoid further reminders about whose party they were the party of, had agreed that the civil rights bill would be reported out of Rules, and passed by the entire House, before members left town on February 8 to begin giving speeches for Lincoln's Birthday, February 12. "The clock is ticking," Johnson told reporters.

The staff couldn't take a week. "You make them write that Majority Report over the weekend, Harry," Johnson urged Byrd when he spoke to him that Thursday evening. "They're going to pass this other bill [the civil rights bill] before Lincoln's Birthday, and I want to get this tax bill out of the way before that civil rights bill gets there." Byrd made them—and Johnson made them. "Startled officials at the Government Printing Office" picked up their telephones to find that the caller was the President, ordering them not to close for the weekend in case the Finance Committee report was completed, one account said. Then a "flabbergasted" Elizabeth Springer picked up the phone to find the President of the United States on the line to tell her that the Printing Office was waiting for the manuscript. "No other President of the United States," this account said, "had ever been quite so familiar with the minutiae of the legislative process."

Springer's staff couldn't finish writing the report over the weekend, as it turned out, but they finished it on Tuesday, January 28—"record time," the *Washington Post* reported—and the Government Printing Office printed it the same day, and on that same day it was filed with the Senate, and Mansfield announced that no other matter would be allowed on the floor until the tax bill was passed, which it was on February 7, three days before the civil rights bill passed the House.

DIFFICULT THOUGH IT HAD BEEN to pass the tax cut bill, the effort would be justified by the results. The reductions instituted by the bill, and the increased spending they inspired, were a key element in what would become one of the longest economic expansions in American history. And the bill was passed because of what Lyndon Johnson had done during those first days after he was thrown, with no warning and no preparation, into the budget and tax cut fights, thrown into them and presented at the same time with deadlines that had to be met, and met very quickly. His grasp in an instant of the reality that underlay the haggling over the budget, that Byrd had to be given what he wanted; his promise to let Byrd see the figures for himself; and most important, his ability to take advantage of the affection and trust of an older man, to "get" the ungettable Harry Byrd—these were the crucial elements in breaking a deadlock that, before November 22, had seemed all but unbreakable.

23

In the Books of Law

THE CIVIL RIGHTS BILL ARRIVED in the Senate as early as it did—on February 10—because of the outcome of the early skirmish on that bill, the skirmish that had begun before Christmas to pry civil rights loose from Judge Smith's House Rules Committee. That encounter had ended almost on schedule—on the schedule which back in December Smith and House Republican Leader Halleck had agreed to accept.

Not that that had been an indication of good faith on the part of the judge.

Hardly had Smith gaveled the Rules Committee into order on January 9 to open its hearings on the bill when his agreement began to demonstrate a certain elasticity. During testimony by the very first witness, House Judiciary Committee chairman Emanuel Celler of New York, "the undercurrent of bitter feelings over the measure began showing," UPI reported, as Smith accused Celler of "railroading" the bill through his committee. "We don't railroad bills through," Celler said. "Do you prefer the word 'strong-armed'?" Smith asked, and it had immediately become apparent that "railroading" (or "strong-arming") was not a crime of which the judge himself was going to be guilty. He allowed each witness to testify at such length—asking them innumerable questions himself and allowing another southern stalwart, Representative William M. Colmer of Mississippi, to ask innumerable others, "going over and over the same points" hour after hour, the *Times* reported—that after seven days of hearings, only eight of the thirty witnesses scheduled to testify had been heard. At that pace, the schedule that had been agreed upon in December—that the hearings would not last longer than twelve days—was rapidly becoming meaningless.

That schedule was going to be accelerated, however.

Celler began mentioning to reporters the lever that Johnson had put in place in December with his telephone call to Richard Bolling, the lever behind which the President had thrown "his full weight," and that would, if pushed far enough, subject Smith to the "indignity" of having his committee discharged from consideration of the bill. Celler said he certainly expected Smith to live up to the agreement, and complete the hearings expeditiously. "But," UPI reported, "Celler also made clear that efforts to get enough votes for a discharge petition, which could bypass the committee if there were a prolonged stall, would not be abandoned." Johnson told Larry O'Brien to go back to work rounding up signatures to add to the 130 that had been placed on the petition before Christmas.*

And when that lever appeared to be stuck, Johnson inserted another one. Despite O'Brien's efforts, on January 18 the petition still bore only 178 signatures, forty short of the required number, and since 153 of them were Democratic signatures, not too many more could be expected from the Democratic side of the House. And while most of the necessary forty would have to come from the Republican side, Republican leaders, from Halleck on down, were still advising GOP congressmen not to circumvent traditional House procedure by signing. Republican members of the Rules Committee who wanted the bill released were getting the same advice, and, the *Times* reported, were still "reluctant to take it away from the chairman." But at noon on January 18, Charles Halleck was in the Oval Office. Using logic at first, as Johnson was later to recall, "I said, 'If I were you, Charlie, I wouldn't dare . . . go out and try to make a Lincoln Birthday speech that'll laugh you out of the goddamned park when Howard Smith's got his foot on Lincoln's neck. You'd better get that [the bill] out before then.' " And then he used a blunter weapon. Picking up the telephone, with Halleck sitting in front of him, the President called NASA Administrator James Webb about requests the Republican Leader had made of NASA, one of them concerning Purdue University in West Lafayette, Indiana, the largest educational institution in his congressional district.

"He wants to know what he can tell his people when he's running for reelection that he's done for them lately, and he wants to know what we *can* do for Purdue," Johnson told Webb. "I need to do anything I can for Charlie Halleck. Now isn't there something you can do?"

Webb replied that he would "talk with him" and "work out something that he'll come back to you and tell you he's pleased with." Johnson set up a time for the two men to meet. And then, after Halleck had left the Oval Office, Johnson got down to the nut-cutting. "Now, Jim," he said. "This is it. . . . Let's help him." Webb said that he would certainly "do everything I can, and I hope when he comes back to you he'll tell you that I've . . ." Hoping, however, was not what Lyndon Johnson had in mind. The civil rights bill was still stalled. "If he's not satisfied when he comes back to me, why, then, I'm going to be talking to you again," he said.

---

*He advised O'Brien what to say to Republicans. "What I'd say to them is this: 'I don't want . . . the party of Lincoln to go down in history as being unwilling to sign the statement [petition]. I don't want your name to be off of there. That's a golden honor roll. It's an honor roll. They are the men who care, [those men] whose name is signed to that. I want your name on it . . . in these towns.' "

Webb got the message. After meeting with Halleck on January 21, he telephoned the President. "I showed him that we could do some things at Purdue," Webb said, "a building that would run three-quarters of a million dollars, and we're talking about some research grants and contracts"—grants and contracts for which, he was careful to say, Purdue was well qualified. And Webb, having worked for Lyndon Johnson for fifteen years, knew that once Johnson had found a weapon that would help him control a man, he liked to keep it in place for further use. He had worked things out, the NASA administrator said, to facilitate Halleck's cooperation not only immediately but in the future as well. The key research grant "would be spread over three years and then renewed each year," he said. "The net effect, Mr. President, is that if you tell him that you're willing to follow this policy as long as he cooperates with you, I can implement it on an installment basis. In other words, the minute he kicks over the traces, we stop the installment."

"Sounds good," Lyndon Johnson said. Whether or not the contracts for Purdue had anything to do with it, the following day, January 22, some Republican members of the Rules Committee began doing what Halleck had previously advised them not to do: meeting with Democratic committee members to devise a move to force Judge Smith to speed up the civil rights hearings and release the bill to the floor. "All during" the next morning, Thursday, January 23, while the hearings were going on, "members were leaving the hearing to take calls from party leaders," the *Times* reported, and reports were circulating that Republican signatures, previously withheld from the petition, were about to be added to it. Just before lunch, Judge Smith surrendered. Saying "I have been here long enough to know the facts of life," he announced that he had agreed to a definite date on which the hearings would end—January 30—and said the bill "will be voted out" and sent to the floor on that date. "By the agreement," the *Times* said, "Mr. Smith was spared the humiliation of having the bill taken away from him by his committee." At a press conference on Saturday, January 25, Johnson said he was "very happy about the progress being made in civil rights. I have said to the [Republican] leadership that I . . . thought it would be rather unbecoming to go out and talk about Lincoln when we still had the civil rights bill that Lincoln would be so interested in locked up in a committee that couldn't act on it." Whatever the reasons, the Rules Committee sent the bill to the floor of the House on January 30, and the House passed it on February 10, sending it to the Senate. "Congress," Marquis Childs wrote, "is moving on the tax cut and civil rights at a pace that a short time ago seemed inconceivable."

THAT PACE WAS about to grind to a halt, for the bill was in the Senate now—the Senate that was the graveyard of civil rights bills. In the 1964 fight to pass John F. Kennedy's civil rights bill, Johnson would have a great advantage: the "transformation"—the "sympathetic atmosphere for his program"—that Kennedy's death had created in Washington. But sympathy for civil rights—majority opinion in the nation, majority opinion even in the Senate—had collided with the Senate's Southern Caucus before, and had lost every time. New lines of attack would be necessary.

One would be the line that Johnson had spelled out to Sorensen in June. Since the South used other Administration bills as hostages against civil rights, don't give them any hostages. By February 10, when the civil rights bill arrived in the Senate, the most valuable hostage, the tax cut bill, was out of the South's clutches, "locked and key" in the storm cellar of completed legislation, and so were the appropriations bills. And Johnson made sure that no other bills would wander onto the battlefield to be captured and held hostage. After the civil rights bill got to the floor (by a 54–37 vote that ended a determined Southern attempt to refer it instead to the Judiciary Committee chaired by Mississippi's Eastland), he told Larry O'Brien and his other legislative aides that no new bills would be sent to the Senate by the White House. "They can filibuster until hell freezes over," he said. "I'm not going to put anything [else] on that floor until this is done."

Then there was the question of compromises. The bill had finally been passed by the House Judiciary Committee largely because of the assistance of its ranking Republican member, William McCulloch of Ohio, a quietly determined champion of civil rights. Angered by the fact that desperately needed sections of both the 1957 and 1960 civil rights bills, in particular fair employment and public accommodations, had been bargained away in return for the South's agreement not to filibuster, McCulloch had, in dealing with Robert Kennedy and Justice Department aides Marshall and Katzenbach, made his support of the Kennedy bill conditional on a promise that, as Katzenbach was to put it, "we . . . not give away in the Senate" any provisions of the House bill. Not only was McCulloch's position on a civil rights bill influential with his GOP House colleagues, one tenet of GOP Leader Halleck's allegiance to House prerogatives was his policy of treating the ranking GOP member of each committee as, in effect, his party's chairman on that committee and supporting his recommendations—in this case McCulloch's no-compromise position—on legislation. Feeling therefore that only McCulloch's support could get the bill through Judiciary, Robert Kennedy had given him the unequivocal no-compromise promise he demanded. In the Senate, however, there was someone who was insisting on compromise, and he was the only senator who could deliver the Republican votes necessary for cloture. Everett Dirksen had promised Katzenbach in 1963—shortly before President Kennedy's assassination—that he would deliver them, that "this bill will come to a vote in the Senate." But Dirksen's promises always had considerable elasticity to them, and now, in 1964, discussing the bill with Katzenbach and Burke Marshall, the two Kennedy men discovered, as Katzenbach puts it, that "he obviously wanted the bill rewritten, to appear different, even if there were no substantive changes, so that he could explain to his colleagues all the changes he had negotiated." Changes—substantive or not—meant negotiations: compromise. And on two points—the public accommodations and fair employment sections—the changes Dirksen wanted *were* substantive. "Under [President] Kennedy," the conviction in Washington had been, as Evans and Novak expressed it, that "one or both of these sections would have been sacrificed . . . to eliminate or at least shorten a Southern filibuster," and that there would be other compromises as well, for, without them, the bill could not get through the Senate. And Dirksen was confident that the situation would be no different under the new President. The Republican Leader "expected President Johnson to be willing, as in the past, to negotiate some compromise," Katzenbach says.

Compromises had always been a key element in southern strategy because of the time element that was so decisive. Working out each one required lengthy negotiations behind closed doors and then lengthy discussions on the Senate floor—not filibusters exactly but a time-consuming, calendar-consuming part of normal legislative business. And each compromise meant, of course, that the Senate bill would be different from the bill the House had approved, and that therefore after the Senate passed its version of the bill, it would have to go to a Senate-House conference committee so that the changes could be reconciled, one of those conference committees behind whose closed doors bills could be emasculated, or delayed indefinitely, without public explanation. And, it would become apparent not long after the bill reached the Senate in 1964, compromise was going to be a southern tactic again. "We knew that there was no way in hell we could muster the necessary votes to defeat the civil rights bill, but we thought we could filibuster long enough to get the other side to agree to amendments that would make it less offensive," is the way Russell's Georgia colleague, Herman Talmadge, puts it.

Johnson refused to compromise. In public, in answer to a press conference question about the possibility of one, he said, "I am in favor of passing it [the bill] in the Senate exactly in its present form." In private, talking to legislative leaders, he had a more pungent phrase. "There will be no wheels and no deals." There was, as always, a political calculation behind his stance. "I knew," he was to tell Doris Goodwin, "that if I didn't get out in front on this issue, [the liberals] would get me. . . . I had to produce a civil rights bill that was even stronger than the one they'd have gotten if Kennedy had lived." And there was, as always, something more than calculation. Assuring Richard Goodwin there would be "no compromises on civil rights; I'm not going to bend an inch," he added, "In the Senate [as Leader] I did the best I could. But I had to be careful. . . . But I always vowed that if I ever had the power I'd make sure every Negro had the same chance as every white man. Now I have it. And I'm going to use it."

TELLING ROBERT KENNEDY "I'll do on the bill just what you think is best to do on the bill. . . . We won't do anything that you don't want to do," Johnson put the attorney general out front in the 1964 battle ("For political reasons, it made a lot of sense," Kennedy was to note; his partisans would have difficulty finding fault with the bill if he was in charge of it), and Kennedy and his Justice Department aides would play a key role in it. And since this was a battle in the Senate, a body fiercely jealous of its prerogatives, and a President's hand couldn't be too visible there, the floor leader of the bill, after Mansfield had declined the assignment, became the Democrats' Assistant Leader, Hubert Humphrey.

Summoning Humphrey to the Oval Office, Johnson told him, Humphrey was to recall, that "You have this great opportunity now, Hubert, but you liberals will never deliver. You don't know the rules of the Senate, and your liberal friends will be off making speeches when they ought to be present."

"I would have been outraged if he hadn't been basically right and historically accurate," Humphrey was to say. And, he was to say, Johnson was being accurate about him, too. "He had sized me up. He knew very well that I would say, 'Damn you, I'll show you.' " And then "having made his point he shifted the conversation and more quietly and equally firmly he promised he would back me to the hilt. As I left, he stood and moved towards me with his towering intensity: 'Call me whenever there's trouble or anything you want me to do.' "

"He knew just how to get to me," Humphrey says.

Humphrey had always had a gift for oratory, and for friendship, and all through the civil rights battle of 1964 he employed both gifts, in eloquent speeches, and in keeping the Senate debate as civil as possible. "I marveled at the way he handled the bill's opponents," a liberal senator recalls. "He always kept his ebullient manner, and would talk with the southerners. He was always genial and friendly, thus keeping the debate from becoming vicious." He had never had a gift for (or even much interest in) the more pragmatic requirements of Senate warfare: for learning, and using, the rules. (Russell "knew *all* the rules . . . and how to use them," Johnson had told him in that Oval Office lecture. "He [Johnson] said liberals had never really worked to understand the rules and how to use them, that we never organized effectively, . . . predicting that we would fall apart in dissension, be absent when quorum calls were made and when critical votes were taken.") Nor had he ever had a gift for organization; or for counting votes without false optimism. Now, however, he learned the rules; and he organized his forces so that the rules couldn't be so easily used against them. After the bill got to the floor, a series of Russell maneuvers delayed its being made the pending business until March 30, when the filibuster began. A key southern tactic had always been the quorum call: a demand, often in the middle of the night, that the chair call the roll to determine if the number of senators present was the number required—fifty-one—to conduct business. Each senator is allowed to speak only twice within a legislative "day." But if within the time limit, the required fifty-one couldn't be rounded up, the Senate was automatically adjourned. The next session would therefore be a new legislative day, and southern senators who had already spoken twice on the previous day could start all over again with two more speeches. Making sure that fifty-one senators could be rounded up was "perhaps the hardest part of managing the forces against" a filibuster, Nicholas Katzenbach was to say. Humphrey organized liberal Democrats, and the few liberal Republicans, into rotating platoons so that only once during the entire filibuster were the liberals unable to muster a quorum. To respond on the floor to southern attacks on the substance of the bill, he appointed floor captains, each with a team of four or five senators under him, to defend each major section. This gave the senators, as Humphrey noted, "a chance to debate the bill [and] get some press for themselves, to be known as part of the team fighting for civil rights. . . . They seemed to like it." Each morning, he, the liberal Republican Whip Thomas Kuchel of California, their floor captains, civil rights leaders, Robert Kennedy aides and lobbyists from organized labor met in Humphrey's office—one writer called it "a veritable war room with organization charts, duty rosters and progress calendars"—to anticipate southern maneuvers and map out ways to counter them.

And if Hubert Humphrey had never learned to count, now Lyndon Johnson taught him how. Suddenly his thinking was no longer so wishful. Of the sixty-seven Democrats, twenty-three or twenty-four were southerners or border state senators unalterably opposed to desegregation, so no more than forty-four Democratic votes could be counted on to vote for cloture. Liberal Republican votes, at most, brought the total to only about fifty-six or fifty-seven. "Somewhere we would have to pick up about ten or eleven additional votes," and, Humphrey saw, the only place to get them was from traditionally conservative midwestern Republicans, an unlikely source. And Johnson reminded him of what he knew: that there was only one way to get those votes. "He said, 'Now you know that this bill can't pass unless you get Ev Dirksen.' And he said, 'You and I are going to get Ev. . . . You've got to let him have a piece of the action. He's got to look good all the time.' "

Humphrey made the Republican leader look good. Seeing that "he had a sense of history," he gave Dirksen a place in it, a prominent place. Although Dirksen had announced his opposition to the fair employment and public accommodations sections, Humphrey, appearing on *Meet the Press* on March 8, ignored his statements. "He is a man who thinks of his country before he thinks of his party . . . and I sincerely believe that when Senator Dirksen has to face the moment of decision where his influence and where his leadership will be required to give us the votes that are necessary to pass this bill, he will not be found wanting."

"Boy, that was right," Lyndon Johnson said in a phone call afterwards, as Humphrey would recall. "You're doing just right now. You just keep at that. . . . You get in there to see Dirksen! You drink with Dirksen! You talk to Dirksen! You listen to Dirksen!"

"The gentle pressure left room for *him* to be the historically important figure in our struggle, the statesman above partisanship, the . . . master builder of a legislative edifice that would last forever," Humphrey was to say. But, he says, "as much as Dirksen liked the stroking . . . if he thought we had no chance, he would have kept his distance" or "insisted on major compromises as the price for his support." So therefore, Humphrey says, "of the greatest importance was President Johnson's public and private pronouncements that no compromises were possible this time," that "it was going to be a strong bill or nothing."

ALL THAT SPRING — all through April and May—the battle would go on.

In Mississippi, clergymen arriving from the North were given orientation sessions that included instructions on how to protect themselves after they had been knocked down (protection of the kidneys against assailants' kicks was emphasized), not that the instructions always helped: a Cleveland rabbi was seriously injured when he was hit in the head with an iron bar. These volunteers were, of course, joining local black civil rights workers who had been risking their lives for years, and, like them, were virtually without protection, with nowhere to turn for help; many of the beatings took place as policemen or state troopers watched. And looming over the volunteers always was the spectre of jail—and what might happen to them in jail. ("The officers forced me to unclothe and lie on my back. One of the officers beat me between my legs with a belt," wrote Bessie Turner.) The sacrifices made in Mississippi would include the lives of three young civil rights workers—James Chaney, Andrew Goodman and Michael Schwerner, a young black man and two young white Jewish men from New York City—who were arrested by a deputy sheriff, released into a Ku Klux Klan ambush and murdered. Eloquent though Martin Luther King's speeches might be, for his aides, each speech was an occasion for dread. "A mob might form," one explained. "They came right into the Negro neighborhood a few months ago to get them at the [civil rights] office." His public appearances had to be scheduled carefully. "I don't like to have Dr. King on the road at night."

In Washington, meanwhile, Students Speak for Civil Rights were holding daily rallies near the base of the Washington Monument. Making what they called a "pilgrimage" to Washington, students from seventy-five religious seminaries from around the country divided into three-member teams (a Catholic, a Protestant and a Jew) to begin a twenty-four-hour-a-day vigil at the Lincoln Memorial to pray for the bill's passage—a vigil they pledged wouldn't end until it passed. Clergymen were playing a larger and larger role. Meeting on April 1, the Leadership Conference on Civil Rights arranged for a daily prayer service, led by a rabbi or a minister or a priest, to be held in a Lutheran church on Capitol Hill one hour before the Senate convened each day. On April 28, a National Interreligious Convocation in support of civil rights began at Georgetown University. More than six thousand people attended. Ministers, priests and rabbis fanned out to Capitol Hill. They crammed the galleries, next to the observers, like Joseph Rauh and Clarence Mitchell, who had been there for years. "You couldn't turn around where there wasn't a clerical collar next to you," Rauh recalls. And they visited—delegation after delegation—the offices of the senators whose votes were needed for cloture.

The clergymen helped shift the tide of battle off the familiar—and hostile—terrain in which civil rights had, time after time, become mired in the Senate. "This was kind of like getting an army with new fresh guns, fresh rations. . . . It made all the difference in the world," Rauh says. These reinforcements concentrated their efforts in states, mostly midwestern, mostly Republican, mostly conservative, in which there had never been much interest in, let alone sentiment for, civil rights. In these states, labor unions and the NAACP and other African-American organizations had relatively few members. That wasn't true of churches. And the clergymen stayed in Washington to see the fight through. "This was the first time that I ever recalled seeing Catholic nuns away from the convents for more than a few days," says James Hamilton of the National Council of Churches. "There was agreement among religious groups that this was a priority issue and other things had to be laid aside." And the issue was, thanks to Johnson, finally understood. Senators from these states found themselves no longer able to maintain that they weren't against civil rights but only against changing inviolable Senate procedure by cutting off debate through cloture. "Just wait until [these senators] start hearing from the church people," Humphrey had predicted, and the prediction was borne out. Walking off the Senate floor after supporting the civil rights forces on a vote that defeated a Russell parliamentary maneuver, Mundt said, "I hope that satisfies those two goddamned bishops who called me last night."

As for the President, on April 29, Dirksen went to the White House. He went in blustering, telling reporters that he was going to let the President know that only compromise would produce the necessary Republican votes for cloture: "You say you want the House bill without any change. Well, in my humble opinion, you are not going to get it. Now it's your play. What do you have to say?"

His comments when he came out were in a very different tone. What Johnson had had to say was, apparently, very little—or, at any rate, nothing that Dirksen wanted to repeat. To reporters' questions about civil rights, the Republican Leader said that he and the President had barely touched on the subject.

Johnson maintained his public posture of knowing nothing about the tactics being used. "As President, I don't try to involve myself in the procedure of the Senate," he said during a press conference in May. "I think Senator Mansfield and Senator Humphrey are much closer to the situation than I am. I am not trying to dodge you. I just don't know." Asked during another press conference about a specific amendment that was being proposed, he said, "All I know is what I read in the papers." In reality, however, he knew all the tactics, devising many of them himself, thinking ahead to the tactics Russell would use to counter them and how those tactics could then be countered in turn. And the generals carrying out his tactics knew that he was looking over their shoulders—with little patience. After the weekly congressional leaders' breakfasts, which one leader likened to "battlefield briefings," Humphrey said that he often left the White House unable to remember whether or not he had actually eaten anything. And when, as spring was turning into summer, the votes for cloture were still not there, Johnson took, behind the scenes, a more direct hand.

Southerners were not the only Democrats opposed to the concept of cloture. Senators from sparsely populated states were reluctant to support it because the right to filibuster was their best defense against the power of the larger states. Many of the more sparsely populated states were western states, however— western states with requests (for dams, reclamation projects, irrigation projects, funding for their vast national parks) before the Department of the Interior. Johnson had Secretary of the Interior Udall tell western senators that while "I couldn't argue with them that they were wrong in principle, . . . I did suggest to them that they should make an exception in this case." Exceptions began to be made: by Anderson of New Mexico, Monroney of Oklahoma, Cannon of Nevada. No senator had been more adamantly opposed to cloture than Carl Hayden, but Hayden's lifelong ambition was to solve Arizona's water shortage with the Central Arizona Water Project, and, at age eighty-seven, time for satisfying ambitions was growing short. Johnson suggested that a Hayden vote for cloture would advance the project; Hayden said that if his vote was needed to obtain cloture, Johnson could have it. Acts of God—natural disasters—were enlisted in the cause. There was an earthquake in Alaska; Johnson wanted to send $50 million in emergency assistance, but Mansfield and Humphrey were afraid that if they allowed civil rights to be removed from the floor even temporarily to allow the necessary disaster relief bill to be brought there, Russell would block civil rights from being brought back. Johnson thought of a procedure that would prevent Russell from doing that, and telephoned Mansfield: "Mike. . . . These people [in Alaska] are suffering and they've got no money. . . . I don't want to be in a position of interfering with what you all are doing in the Senate, for obvious reasons. But . . . it is a *real* emergency, and there's a lot of suffering taking place." Alaska's two senators, Ernest Gruening and Edward L. Bartlett, wanted to get home as quickly as possible; they were told that Air Force Two was waiting for them at Andrews. On May 13 Gruening told Humphrey, "I am prepared, before long, to vote for cloture."

SACRIFICE, PRAYERS, PERSUASION — as May began, the votes were nevertheless still not there for cloture. And on July 7, the Senate was going to recess for the Republican convention, at which, it was now becoming more clear, the nominee was likely to be Goldwater, still unalterably opposed to cloture and the civil rights bill. His nomination would harden the resistance of conservative Republicans to both, since a vote for either one would be a vote against the position of their party's presidential nominee. And in November, there would be an election not only for President, but for thirty-three Senate seats. Humphrey knew, as one account of the bill says, that "the daily sessions would be drawn out until one-third of the Senate . . . would be anxious to get out campaigning." Time was growing very short.

The key—the only key—was still Dirksen. "Having learned" from his visit to the Oval Office, as another account puts it, "that the President was not going to make any deal," the Minority Leader had "decided it was time to talk with Humphrey and Company."

The courtship of Dirksen had never stopped. "We are carving out the states-man's niche and bathing it with blue lights and hoping that Dirksen will find it irresistible to step into it," a Democratic aide said. Other reasons for the Republican Leader to give in were becoming more compelling. It was an election year, and he didn't need the polls to know which way the political tide was running. And "after all," as one account puts it, "the Republicans were the party of Lincoln." Dirksen was from Illinois, Lincoln's state. His party were "inheritors of a grand legacy that Dirksen knew he could preserve or destroy." Watching the canny GOP Leader wrestle with civil rights, Herman Talmadge got the sinking feeling that "he wasn't about to let Republicans be on the wrong side of history." Anxious to show that he had contributed something to the bill, Dirksen proposed a series of amendments. "I'm going to be against them right up until I sign them," Johnson told Humphrey privately. Several (generally inconsequential in their effect) were cleared by Robert Kennedy with McCulloch to make sure he wouldn't object—and then were added to the bill on May 12. Dirksen agreed that the time for cloture had arrived. When Johnson telephoned him, the Republican Leader said he had told Russell that morning, "Dick . . . I think we've gone far enough." He promised Johnson, "We'll . . . see what we can do about procedure to get this thing on the road and buttoned up."

"You're worthy of the 'Land of Lincoln,' " Johnson said. "And the man from Illinois is going to pass the bill, and I'll see that you get proper attention and credit."

Persuading enough Republicans to go along would prove to be difficult. Although on May 20, following a bitterly divided Republican caucus, Dirksen called in reporters to tell them that the bill was going to pass because civil rights was "an idea whose time has come," he still didn't have enough votes, and neither did Humphrey. Russell suddenly began pressing for amendments to be brought to the floor. Amendments could be filibustered. Humphrey and Mansfield had to stall. "We need more time to nail down those cloture votes," Humphrey said on June 4.

The cloture motion was passed, by a 71–29 vote, on June 10, after a filibuster of fifty-seven days that was the longest in Senate history. Twenty-three Democrats voted against that motion; forty-four votes from the Democratic side was all it got. But, thanks to Dirksen, twenty-seven Republicans voted for it; only six, including Goldwater, remained opposed. There ensued another series of floor fights over proposed amendments to the bill, before its passage, 73 to 27, came on June 19. Thousands of people crowded around the Senate wing of the Capitol, cheering and applauding senators as they came out. When Humphrey emerged three hours later, they were still waiting to cheer him.

Because of the amendments that had been added, the bill then had to go back to the House, to Judge Smith's House Rules Committee, but, overriding the judge, McCulloch, Bolling, Clarence Brown and their allies got it released from Rules to the floor—with a rule allowing only a one-hour debate—on June 30, and the debate occurred on July 1. On July 2, it passed the House. Johnson signed the Civil Rights Act of 1964 into law that evening—eight days before the Republican National Convention, and the national presidential season, opened.

"We have talked long enough . . . about civil rights," Lyndon Johnson had said. "It is time . . . to write it in the books of law"—to embody justice and equality in legislation. It would require another piece of legislation, the Voting Rights Act of 1965, to give black Americans the weapon—the vote—that this master of power felt would be decisive because it would give them, he said, the power to "do the rest for themselves."

The 1965 Act would be passed after another titanic struggle, in which, with men and women (and children, many children) being beaten in Selma on their way to the Edmund Pettus Bridge, singing "We Shall Overcome" as they marched into tear gas and billy clubs and bullwhips, Lyndon Johnson went before Congress and said, "*We* Shall Overcome," thereby adopting the civil rights rallying cry as his own. (When Martin Luther King, watching the speech on television in Selma, heard Johnson say that, he began to cry—the first time his assistants had ever seen him cry.)* In 1965, Johnson was able to deploy from the Oval Office more weapons than he had available the year before. James Farmer, sitting beside the President as he used the telephone, heard him "cajoling, threatening, everything else, whatever was necessary," to get the bill passed. To bring black Americans more fully into the political system, he had to break the power of the South in the Senate—and he broke it. It was Abraham Lincoln who "struck off the chains of black Americans," I have written, "but it was Lyndon Johnson who led them into voting booths, closed democracy's sacred curtain behind them, placed their hands upon the lever that gave them a hold on their own destiny, made them, at last and forever, a true part of American political life." How true a part? Forty-three years later, a mere blink of history's eye, a black American, Barack Obama, was sitting behind the desk in the Oval Office.

The 1964 Civil Rights Act and the 1965 Voting Rights Act would not be Lyndon Johnson's only victories in the fight for social justice. Other bills passed during his Administration made strides toward ending discrimination in public accommodations, in education, employment, even in private housing. Almost a century after Abraham Lincoln had freed black men and women from slavery,

---

*For a fuller description of Johnson's speech, and its antecedents, and of Dr. King's reaction, see *Means of Ascent,* pp. xiii–xx.

"black men and women—and Mexican-American men and women, and indeed most Americans of color—still did not enjoy many of the rights which America supposedly guaranteed its citizens," I have written. "It was Lyndon Johnson who gave them those rights." Lincoln had been President during the nineteenth century. During the twentieth century, of all its seventeen American Presidents "Lyndon Baines Johnson was the greatest champion that black Americans and Mexican-Americans and indeed all Americans of color had in the White House, the greatest champion they had in all the halls of government. With the single exception of Lincoln, he was the greatest champion with a white skin that they had in the history of the Republic. He was to become the lawmaker for the poor and the downtrodden and the oppressed. He was to be the bearer of at least a measure of social justice to those to whom social justice had so long been denied, the restorer of at least a measure of dignity to those who so desperately needed to be given some dignity, the redeemer of the promises made to them by America." *"It is time . . . to write it in the books of law."* By the time Lyndon Johnson left office, he had done a lot of writing in those books, had become, above all Presidents save Lincoln, the codifier of compassion, the President who, as I have said, "wrote mercy and justice into the statute books by which America was governed." And as President he had begun to do that writing—had taken a small but crucial, ineluctable, first step toward breaking the century-old barriers that, at the time he took office, still stood against civil rights on Capitol Hill—with that telephone call he had made to Representative Bolling on December 2, 1963; with that decision he had made, so early in his presidency, to support the discharge petition; with that decision he made, when he realized that only one lever was available to him, to lean into it with all his might.

24

Defeating Despair

BACK IN JANUARY, when Lyndon Johnson had delivered his State of the Union address, the attorney general was sitting at the end of the row of Cabinet members. His presence at the speech, coupled with his return to his duties at the Justice Department, were celebrated the next morning on the front page of the *New York Times* under the headline ROBERT KENNEDY DEFEATS DESPAIR.

For those who had been watching him during the speech, however, it was difficult to credit that assessment. He applauded occasionally, but for the most part sat with his arms folded across his chest, his face expressionless, inscrutable, somber, withdrawn, as if he was remote from the scene in which he was participating. And friends and aides knew that if in fact despair was a foe, his battle with it was far from over.

During the three days of memorial ceremonies, he had never been far from Jackie's side, standing behind her, still as a statue, pale and grave but dry-eyed, resolute, seemingly calm; Chuck Spalding would have thought he was "controlled" had he not heard the question Robert Kennedy sobbed out when he thought no one could hear. In the weeks thereafter, however, his grief became so obvious that, his aide Ed Guthman says, "It was painful to see him." He lost so much weight that his collars gaped away from his neck, and his suits no longer fit. Some of the clothes that he insisted on wearing would have been too large for him anyway: an old tweed overcoat of his brother's; the President's bomber jacket with the presidential seal. As the weeks passed, he grew even thinner, the hollows in his cheeks and around his eyes deeper, "as if," a friend says, "he was being devoured by grief." For men who adored him, the fact that he so seldom spoke of what he was feeling was especially poignant. "It was, perhaps, that he held his grief inwardly so tightly that made it so hard for others to bear," Guthman says.

Douglas Dillon offered him his house at Hobe Sound in Florida for Thanksgiving, and he went there with Ethel and a few aides. "At Hobe Sound, the attorney general was the most shattered man I had ever seen in my life," Pierre

Salinger says. "Bobby had almost ceased to function. He walked alone for hours."

Try though he did to resume work at Justice, he couldn't concentrate on it. "In the middle of a meeting, his expression went blank and he would stare out a window, absorbed in his own thoughts . . . numbed by sorrow and depression." Sometimes, jumping out of his chair, he would hurry out of the room, and people would see him walking, often coatless in the freezing December weather, up Constitution Avenue, hunched, slight, frail-looking, unseeing. Long after midnight, the Secret Service agents on guard at Hickory Hill would see a light in the master bedroom go on, and a few minutes later Bobby would drive off, not to return until dawn. Sometimes he would have telephoned John Seigenthaler to tell him he would pick him up. "He was wearing that bomber jacket. 'Let's pay Johnny a visit.' " Arlington Cemetery would be locked, but Bobby had found a way in. "We scale the wall. . . ." Robert Kennedy would kneel—"sometimes for hours"—beside John Kennedy's grave. "He was just inconsolable," Seigenthaler says. "He was in perpetual pain. . . . It was awful to watch." Decades later, another aide, William vanden Heuvel, would say, "I don't think I ever saw human grief expressed as in the face of Robert Kennedy after the assassination." As another account puts it, "So complete was his withdrawal, so scant his interest in his own future in public life, that for a time members of the family felt that the political succession of the Kennedys, by Robert Kennedy's choice, might settle on his brother, Edward." Over Christmas, he and Ethel took their children on a skiing vacation in Aspen, and when, at the beginning of January, 1964, he returned, tanned, to Washington, he seemed, to reporters who didn't know him well, to have recovered himself. Returning to his office at Justice, "smiling," "relaxed," joking with the staff, he was, they wrote, "his old self," "as energetic as ever." Pledging loyalty to the new Administration, he said he would remain in office at least "through the election. . . . I'll do whatever anybody—the President or the Democratic National Committee—feels will be helpful." The pledge itself merited headlines: ROBERT KENNEDY STAYING ON.

Seeing the desolation in his wasted face when the smile faded, those closer to him remained uncertain about despair's defeat. To look into his eyes was to know "the suffering he had endured," a friend says. Though he was back in the office, his administrative assistant, Seigenthaler, says that "I didn't have the feeling that he really was part of the world in which he was working. I mean he was doing the job, answering the correspondence. . . . When I say he was not functional, I don't mean that he was not able to do what he had to do or that he didn't know what he was doing. . . . It was more that he did what he did through that sort of haze of pain that he felt." Calling on him in his office in February, the columnist Murray Kempton, an old friend, noticed that he hadn't regained any weight, that his collar was still "a little too large . . . and his cuffs a little too close to his knuckles, not as though he had wasted but as though he had withdrawn." The telephone rang, the caller happened to be a friend of Kempton's, Bobby handed him the phone, and Kempton began to banter and laugh with the friend.

Then he glanced over at Robert Kennedy. "The Attorney General was sitting and looking at his hands," and his face was "a face horribly lonely for a time when it had been part of a community with a place in it for careless laughter." New lines had been carved into his forehead and around his mouth. There was, suddenly, gray in the mop of ginger hair. "How his face had aged in the years I had known him!" a friend thought. "How do I look?" he asked Seigenthaler. "You look like hell," Seigenthaler replied. "I can't sleep. I can't sleep," Bobby said. He still, that February, drove at night to his brother's grave, still wore the talismanic bomber jacket or the tweed overcoat. On St. Patrick's Day, almost four months after November 22, he would be talking to Mary McGrory, whom, in the old days, he had once picked up and slung, the two of them laughing, over his shoulder. Trying to comfort him, she said, "You're young and you're going to be productive and successful." Suddenly burying his head in her shoulder, he gave a cry of anguish and, she would recall, "burst into tears." Time may have been blunting—slightly—the pain and desolation; it wasn't curing it. Time would never cure it. Almost half a century later, when she was the only one of the nine Kennedy siblings still living, the author would ask Jean Kennedy Smith about her brother Bobby and his depression over Jack's death. "When did he come out of that?" she repeated, and then said, "I don't think he ever came out of that."

SOME EXPLANATIONS FOR GRIEF of such vivid intensity were obvious. The brother who had died was not just a brother, but a brother with whom Robert Kennedy had been so close that they finished each other's sentences, or communicated without any words at all, in a "perfect," "almost telepathic" understanding. Strong-willed though Robert Kennedy was, he had at an early age subordinated his own aims and ambitions to his brother's, had subordinated them, submerged them, completely, investing himself totally in John Fitzgerald Kennedy's destiny. "Now he is alone," Kempton wrote. Bobby explained to a reporter "that he had to find a goal for the first time in his life because, for as long as he could remember, he had no goal that was not his brother's." Says a friend: "It was almost as if a part of *him* had died." Nor, on a less subjective level, was it merely a brother he had lost. In an instant, in the crack of a gunshot, he had lost power, too. "What is different now and what makes me sad is that I see a problem or someone tells me about a problem and I can't do anything about it," he told Kempton. "There was this time when if people had something and couldn't see my brother, they could always see me and I could pick up the phone and call him. . . . It's strange to think that you can't just pick up the phone."

Obvious as were these explanations, however, as weeks turned into months without the wound showing any signs of healing, friends began to wonder if there were less obvious ones as well. Seigenthaler was to say that he "sensed in the months after JFK's assassination that Robert Kennedy seemed haunted, as if he was holding something back."

To those searching for other explanations, there may—or may not—have been clues. Though Robert Kennedy's grief was "understandable," his biographer Evan Thomas would write, "yet it seemed too overwhelming, so all-consuming." McCone of the CIA, a close friend, remembered that, when he arrived at Hickory Hill not long after the terrible news, Bobby had asked him whether his agency was connected with the assassination; Bobby was later to say that he had asked McCone, a fellow Catholic, "in a way that he couldn't lie to me," and that McCone's answer had satisfied him that the CIA had not been involved. In 1975, when, during a congressional investigation, the CIA's assassination plots against Fidel Castro were revealed, McCone, suddenly recalling that question, had "a flash of recognition." "He had felt at the time that there was something troubling Kennedy that he was not disclosing," Thomas says. Operation Mongoose was still active on November 22; there had been eight separate CIA-sponsored assassination attempts on Castro's life since the beginning of 1961. Whether or not Robert Kennedy had been personally involved, did Castro feel he had been—that the Kennedys had been? Did the assassination in Dallas have anything to do with the attempts in Havana? During that 1975 investigation, as he learned more about anti-Castro intrigues, McCone, as Thomas writes, "began to suspect that Kennedy felt personally guilty" for what had happened in Dallas. Friends remembered remarks Kennedy had made not about Cuba but about the target of his other unrelenting campaign. On December 5, Arthur Schlesinger asked Robert "perhaps tactlessly, about Oswald. He said that there could be no serious doubt that he was guilty." But, he added, there was doubt—"argument" was the word he used—about something else: "whether he did it by himself or as part of a larger plot, whether organized by Castro or by gangsters." Ben Bradlee remembered President Kennedy, "obviously serious," telling him once that the Justice Department had discovered that an underworld enforcer had been given a gun fitted with a silencer and sent to Washington to assassinate the attorney general. When, later, the publicity-hunting New Orleans District Attorney Jim Garrison claimed to have discovered that the Dallas shootings—the two shootings—were part of an elaborate conspiracy, Kennedy asked his press secretary, Frank Mankiewicz, if he thought Garrison "had anything." "No, but I think there is something," Mankiewicz replied. "So do I," Bobby said.

Although he may, as Thomas says, have been "worried that his own aggressive pursuit of evil men had brought evil upon his own house," Robert Kennedy never went beyond such cryptic remarks, never told the Warren Commission of his suspicions about mobsters or Cuban exiles, never, in public, cast doubt on the single-gunman theory, never tried to have a more thorough investigation undertaken. "He never quieted his own doubts," Thomas writes. Though his "restless mind continued to torment him, he [was unwilling] to go where the facts might lead." He never pursued the question of who, or why. He "never really wanted any investigation," Katzenbach says. He just wanted to close the book. He "wondered," Schlesinger recorded in his journal after a talk with Robert Kennedy in 1966, "how long he could continue to avoid comment on the [Warren Commission] report. It is evident that he believes that it was a poor job and will not endorse it, but that he is unwilling to criticize it and thereby reopen the whole tragic business."

Such "clues" may, however, be clues to nothing at all. "I cannot say what his essential feeling was," Schlesinger finally had to confess—and neither, perhaps, can anyone else. No one knows whether there are explanations for Robert Kennedy's grief beyond the obvious ones. Half a century after John F. Kennedy's death there is still speculation among his brother's intimates about whether he was aware of any hard fact that might indicate that his crusades against the Cuban dictator or the underworld (or the Teamsters' boss) had backfired against his brother, about whether his grief was intensified by a sense of responsibility, even of guilt, about his brother's death. The fact that this speculation has never stopped is testimony not to any hard fact about his grief but rather to its unusual depth and duration, and to its effect on the man so many of them worshiped. For those who knew Robert Francis Kennedy well, the men and women who spent a lot of time with him, do not feel that he ever again became "his old self." Interview these men and women over and over, and one hears, over and over, the same phrase: "He changed."

EVEN TO DATE the change in Kennedy to the assassination may be misleading. It had been during the Cuban Missile Crisis a year earlier that the men sitting around the Cabinet table had seen the once "simplistic" Robert Kennedy behave "quite differently." But now, after the assassination, the evolution from Kennedy's old Manichean "black and white" view of life became, suddenly, much more noticeable. "It's an impressive thing now how well he grasps the gray areas," an old ally said. When, not long into the Johnson Administration, four Cuban fishing boats were seized just two miles off the Florida Keys, hawks in a National Security Council meeting wanted Johnson to view the incursion as a "test" of the new President, one that must be met by a show of force. Bobby advised viewing it instead as a mistake, "like a speeding, parking ticket . . . just tell them to get out of there and go home . . . if you wanted to fine them a couple of hundred bucks, fine them, but the idea of locking them up and creating a major crisis about it was foolish." (The fishermen were fined and sent home.)

In other respects, too, the "change" was more the continuation of an evolution.

The hints that there had always existed, beneath the rudeness, the anger, the belligerence, the "mean streak," the cruel streak; beneath the bottle over a student's head in the Cambridge bar, and the abandonment of a friend on a boat he couldn't sail—the hints that there had always been very different qualities in Robert Kennedy had always been just that: hints. Although vanden Heuvel, who went to work for him in 1955, says, "There was always something very vulnerable about Bobby," before November 22 there had been few signs of an awareness in Robert Kennedy that he himself might not be immune to the storms and terrors of life. Shielded by his father's wealth and calloused by his father's philosophy, and thrust at an early age into the roles of prosecutor and political campaign manager, he had lived a professional life more aptly described by the detested adjective "ruthless" than by the one vanden Heuvel chooses. If there was an awareness within him of, or any empathy for, the vulnerability of less protected human beings to the storms and terrors, the signs he displayed of it—tenderness, gentleness—had mostly seemed restricted to members of his family and to children. But now, following his brother's assassination, the hints began to become broader—in scenes that men and women who witnessed them never forgot.

About a month after the assassination, he attended the annual Christmas party at a Washington orphanage. Peter Maas, one of his journalist friends, had walked over from Justice with him.

"The moment he walked into the room [at the orphanage], all these little children—screaming and playing—there was just suddenly silence," Maas recalls. "Bob stepped into the middle of the room, and just then, a little black boy," six or seven years old, "suddenly darted forward and stopped in front of him, and said, 'Your brother's dead! Your brother's dead!' "

The words "knifed to the hearts" of the adults in the room. "You could hear a pin drop," Maas says. Some of the adults turned away. "There wasn't any place in the world any of us wouldn't have rather been than in that room," he says. "The little boy knew he had done something wrong, but he didn't know *what,* so he started to cry." Were there any words that could be said to him? "You wouldn't have thought so," Maas says. But then Robert Kennedy, picking him up "in kind of one motion," and holding him close, said, " 'That's all right. I have another brother.' "

There were other hints.

Appearing at the dedication of a Catholic home for the aged in Kansas City, Bobby moved through the wards followed by a throng of television cameras and reporters. Feeling they had enough pictures and quotes, all of them, with the exception of Ben Bradlee then of *Newsweek,* had left before he walked upstairs to a ward for the terminally ill. "He went from bed to bed, rubbing their hands, touching elbows, putting his head to their foreheads, comforting," Bradlee was to recount. Then he sat down "alone at the bedside of a woman whose eyes were tight shut, whose death rattle was the only sign [of] life," and for close to an hour "I watched with tears in my eyes as the 'ruthless' Bobby Kennedy stroked this unknown woman's hand, and spoke to her in a near whisper."

The gentleness and tenderness, the vulnerability, had always been present in Robert Kennedy, and yet had been subordinated to other, conflicting qualities, and had been hidden—"his most tenaciously maintained secret." But now he had had to look at that face that had once been so vibrant and charming but on which "not a good job" had been done—how could he not have learned more about vulnerability, realized that no one was invulnerable? How could he not identify more deeply than before with the injured, the wounded, of the world, after feeling himself such terrible pain? And, in a way, powerful though he still was, with the powerless of the world as well? His power now, though still considerable, was nothing beside his former power—much of that had vanished in an instant, in the moment he picked up the phone that day at Hickory Hill and heard J. Edgar Hoover's voice. He was still attorney general, he noted. "I have influence . . . but the influence is just infinitesimal compared to the influence I had before." After his return from Aspen in January, the deep wellsprings of compassion in Robert Kennedy, always present but heretofore only intermittently visible, began to rise to the surface in the objectives he pursued in government.

Some of his old objectives, ends to which he had devoted years of obsessive pursuit, seemed to interest him not at all. In March, a harpoon would sink into Jimmy Hoffa at last; found guilty of conspiring to fix a jury, the Teamster boss received an eight-year sentence. Bobby sat silent, melancholy, at the "Get Hoffa" team's celebration. Ken O'Donnell felt he understood. "There's nothing to celebrate," he said. "He had [had] enough tragedy of his own now." Several members of the team felt that he was, one says, "unhappy" that the Teamster boss had received such a long jail term. "He didn't like the idea of eight years," another says. From time to time thereafter, he would ask, "How's Jimmy doing?" Otherwise, "he had lost all interest in Hoffa," Murray Kempton was to say. "I never heard him say anything about Hoffa that really indicated much more than boredom with the subject in the last years of his life." The same was true of the Mafia. When the telephone rang at Hickory Hill that day, he had just been planning offensives against the underworld with District Attorney Morgenthau. "I saw him often after that, but he never mentioned organized crime to me again," Morgenthau says. Those intent on finding clues speculate that the subjects of Hoffa and the underworld were avoided because of an unwillingness "to go where the facts might lead," but Kennedy himself had a simpler explanation: "I'm tired of chasing people."

Even before the assassination, he had begun to take a more active role in the pursuit of social justice rather than of criminals, and it was to social problems, such as juvenile delinquency, that he turned now.

In part, he couched his interest in terms of his brother's legacy, of programs begun but not fulfilled because time had been cut short. Talking in his office with Arthur Schlesinger and Richard Goodwin that December, he explained why he wanted them to stay in their jobs. "What's important is what we were trying to do for this country. The thing is we worked hard to get where we are, and we can't let it all go to waste. My brother barely had a chance to get started—and there is so much now to be done—for the Negroes and the unemployed and school kids and everyone else who is not getting a decent break in our society. This is what counts. The new fellow doesn't get this. He knows all about politics and nothing about human beings. . . . A lot of people in this town . . . didn't come here just to work for John Kennedy, an individual, but for ideas, things we wanted to do. . . . I don't think people should run off." The power of the "Kennedy wing" of the party, he said, "will last for just eleven months"—until the election. Until that time, Johnson would need its support to win re-election. "After November 5th, we'll all be dead." But until November 5, he said, they would have enough power so that "when I talk to him, I am ready to be tough about what we must have" in return for that support.

His brother's programs would certainly have passed if he had lived: if they weren't passed during the remaining years of his first term, had he not been killed, they would certainly be passed during his second term. That was the mantra Bobby Kennedy repeated to his brother's men; that was the mantra they would repeat, in oral histories and interviews and speeches, as long as they lived. That was the mantra they would repeat in books—memoirs, biographies, scores of books. Those who wrote the books that originally influenced history, that set the template for the image of John F. Kennedy that has endured, would be reinforcing it in the books they wrote more than forty-five years later.

Regardless of the mantra's validity, however (and like so many other issues it must remain to be evaluated in the last volume of this work, for it is during the course of the years to be covered in that volume that the extent of its validity will become clear), the passion that lay beneath it—Robert Kennedy's passion for social justice—was genuine. With every month that passed after the assassination, his indignation at injustice seemed to rise. Even a newsman like Ben Bradlee, whose relations with him had been cool, saw the genuineness, realizing that the scene in the Kansas City home for the aged had been an accurate measure of something significant in Robert Kennedy's character, hidden and largely unrecognized though it had been. In an article he wrote after Robert's assassination in 1968, Bradlee said that during the years between the assassinations, "I had been slowly coming to sense this man's passion, his building rage at the persistent inequalities that plagued America, his readiness to embrace the homeless and enlist in their cause." During those years, Bradlee would write, "Bobby Kennedy's [almost] romantic determination to make a difference had deeply impressed me. There was no need to compare him with JFK, they were so different, except for that last name and that father. JFK was more intellectual, urbane, sophisticated, witty. RFK was more passionate, more daring, more radical."

ROBERT KENNEDY'S more pragmatic qualities, the ones that had earned him the adjective he so resented, would never disappear. "Anybody who writes that he looks like a choirboy should burn in hell," says a congressman who opposed one of his initiatives in 1967. His evolution would be a gradual one, and it was, at the time of his death at the age of forty-two, not so complete that the word "ruthless" would no longer apply. More than one of his intimates feel constrained to point out that the portrait was, thanks to another bullet, never finished, that, as one of them says, "Bobby Kennedy was always a work in progress." Unfinished though the portrait may have been left, however, its dominant tone had changed.

Having said he was "tired of chasing people," Bobby Kennedy had stopped chasing them. Was he tired of something else as well? In addition to "ruthless," "hate" was a word often applied to him in the past. *"Bobby hates like me." "When Bobby hates you, you stay hated."* But had the hatred for Jimmy Hoffa stayed? Perhaps not. Some people who knew Robert Kennedy well speculate that perhaps the death of his brother, combined with his father's helplessness, had altered that aspect of his character also. "Before that, perhaps the father and [the] brother had been the controlling forces in his life," vanden Heuvel says. "Before that, well, you know, the father had said, 'Bobby's like me'—and up to that point, he probably was." After his long talk with him in February, Murray Kempton wrote that "Robert Kennedy knew how to hate; he hated on his father's behalf; he grew up to hate on his brother's; but these last weeks that he has endured have now left behind a man we recognize as being unskilled at hating on his own." Examining Robert Kennedy's life following the gunshot in Dallas, it is possible to feel that, with one exception, that might be true.

With the exception of Lyndon Johnson.

There had been no change in Robert Kennedy's feelings toward him.

In conversation with other people, he never called him "the President." Whenever, for the rest of his life, all four and a half years of it, he used the phrase "the President," he was referring to John F. Kennedy. He called the new President "Johnson" or "Lyndon Johnson" or "the new fellow" or "this man." He couldn't bear to think of him sitting in his brother's place, a satyr to Hyperion. Some of the remarks he made about him showed a fundamental misunderstanding of his background. "What does he know about people who've got no jobs?" he asked Goodwin not long after the assassination. "Or are uneducated. He's got no feeling for people who are hungry. It's up to us." Johnson's success fed his bitterness. "All those things he's doing, poverty, civil rights, they're things we had just begun," he was to say to Goodwin some years later. "We just didn't have the time."

If, for reasons of politics, he covered up his feelings in public, he could not always contain them, even when he knew they were being recorded for history (or perhaps *because* they were being recorded for history). During the spring of 1964, he sat for a series of oral interviews being conducted for the John F. Kennedy Library by sympathetic friends like Arthur Schlesinger and John Bartlow Martin, and in these interviews his feelings poured out.

He tried to justify them. "There were three or four matters that arose during the period of November 22 to November 27 or so which made me bitter—unhappy at least—with Lyndon Johnson. Events involving the treatment of Jackie on the plane trip back and all that kind of business—when he lied again and where he treated Jackie, the whole business, very badly."

His brother had seen through Johnson, he said. His brother had "said to Jackie, talking about him, that Lyndon Johnson was incapable of telling the truth." His brother had "often said how lucky he was to have Lyndon Johnson

as Vice President, because otherwise, Lyndon Johnson would be Majority
Leader . . . and Lyndon Johnson would screw him all the time. . . . Lyndon Johnson never would have been loyal to him. So he was very pleased. He was more
pleased about having Lyndon Johnson Vice President because he was out of the
Senate than he was having him as Vice President."

And his brother's assessment of his Vice President had been correct. "He
was against our policy on Cuba in October of '62—although I never knew quite
what he was *for;* he was just against it. . . . He was shaking his head, mad."

The interviews reveal Robert Kennedy's resentment "that an awful lot of
things were going on that President Kennedy did that Johnson was getting the
credit for—and [that Johnson] wasn't saying enough that President Kennedy was
responsible for"; his resentment that columnists like Reston were comparing the
two men and not always favorably to President Kennedy; "I just don't think that
they understand it . . . in their buildup of Lyndon Johnson, comparing him to the
President."

He despised the way Johnson treated subordinates—"They're all scared, of
course, of Lyndon. . . . He yells at his staff. He treats them just terribly. Very
mean. He's a very mean, mean figure"—and resented the success of those methods, his ability "to eat people up, even people who are considered rather strong
figures. . . . Mac Bundy or Bob McNamara: There's nothing left of them." He
despised his methods: the way, for example, he made men beg. "Ralph Dungan
was trying to work out appointments. . . . And Johnson said he wanted to make
sure that everybody who was at all interested called him personally and ask him
for the person to be appointed so that they would know they'd be personally
indebted to him as President." But Robert Kennedy's feelings about Lyndon
Johnson went beyond such analysis. It was in one of these interviews that he
said, "Our President was a gentleman and a human being. . . . This man is
not. . . . He's mean, bitter, vicious—an animal in many ways."

As there had been no change in Lyndon Johnson's feelings toward Robert
Kennedy.

President though he was, fear—fear as well as hatred—was still a component in those feelings. The fear would always be there. Years later, in a conversation during his retirement, he would describe Robert Kennedy's 1968
announcement that he was running for President as "the thing I feared from the
first day of my presidency. Robert Kennedy had openly announced his intention
to reclaim the throne in memory of his brother. And the American people,
swayed by the magic of the name, were dancing in the streets."

Even the acclaim that had greeted his own performance after the assassination was soured for him by the "snot-nosed little runt," Johnson said in that conversation. "Every day as soon as I opened the papers or turned on the television,
there was something about Bobby Kennedy. . . . Somehow or other it just didn't
seem fair. I'd given three years of loyal service to Jack Kennedy. During all that
time I'd willingly stayed in the background; I knew that it was *his* presidency, not
mine. . . . And then Kennedy was killed and . . . I became the President. But

none of this seemed to register with Bobby Kennedy, who acted like *he* was the custodian of the Kennedy dream, some kind of rightful heir to the throne. It just didn't seem fair . . . " He railed about the "game of royal family" that was being played. "If Bobby Kennedy's name came up even by accident," Ken O'Donnell says, "he'd launch into a tirade about what a son of a bitch Bobby Kennedy was. Ninety-nine percent of the things were untrue. And it'd get back to Bobby Kennedy, and Bobby'd say something about Lyndon Johnson. . . . These two men . . . built up this picture of each other which was just incredible."

For a time, these feelings—on both sides—not only were kept out of public view, but were layered over when the two men were dealing with each other. Knowing how much he needed "continuity," Johnson did what he could to maintain a façade of cordiality with the living personification of the Kennedy legend, the man who had not only been the martyred President's most trusted counselor but who reminded people of him in the similarity of their accents and gestures. But Lyndon Johnson had the power now. Fortune's reversal could not have been more complete. Two men hated each other to the depths of their beings. For a time—three years—one had had power over the other, and had used it, used it ruthlessly, used it beyond the bounds of policy, used it to insult and humiliate the other. And then, in an instant, in a gunshot, the world of the two men was turned upside down. Suddenly the other man had the power. "You're gonna get yours when the time comes," Bobby Kennedy had vowed—and then the time had come: three years of it. Now that time was over. The other man's time—the time for vengeance—had not quite arrived. Lyndon Johnson couldn't afford to alienate the Kennedy faction yet; his strategy must still be one of restraint. Conscious though Johnson was of that consideration, however, his feelings about Bobby Kennedy were too strong always to be concealed. He was, furthermore, becoming more secure in the presidency, more euphoric from the adulation he was receiving, less guarded. Passion started to break through strategy's bounds. By mid-December, shortly before he left for the ranch, the rein he had kept on himself in his dealings with Bobby was starting to slip.

He fired a test shot, announcing that he had appointed Thomas C. Mann assistant secretary of state for inter-American affairs, a position from which President Kennedy had removed him because of a belief among Kennedy's Latin-American team that Mann was, in Goodwin's words, "a colonialist by mentality who believes that the 'natives'—the Latin Americans—need to be shown who is boss" and who had "a basic lack of belief in [Kennedy's] Alliance for Progress." Now, Mann would be in effective charge of the Alliance, and Goodwin, who wrote in his diary that the appointment had occasioned "real gloom among the" Kennedy crowd, went to see Bobby in his office at Justice along with Arthur Schlesinger.

It was at this meeting that Kennedy said that although "Our power will last for just eleven months," during these months—until Election Day, 1964—the power of the Kennedy faction would still be substantial. But that prediction did not survive its first test. The shot he fired back—a letter to Johnson protesting

Mann's appointment—went all but unheard. The public wasn't interested in Latin America. While the appointment drew some criticism in the editorial columns of liberal newspapers, it was buried in the wave of adulation for Johnson's successes.

"Johnson has won the first round," Schlesinger wrote Bobby. "He has shown his power to move in a field of special concern to the Kennedys without consulting the Kennedys. . . . We have underestimated the power of the Presidency. The President has nearly all the cards in this contest. . . . We are weaker— a good deal weaker—than we had supposed."

HAVING WON THE FIRST ROUND, Johnson, after his return from Texas in January, was ready for the second.

Trying to rouse Bobby from his apathy, Averell Harriman and McGeorge Bundy suggested that he be sent to Southeast Asia as a presidential envoy to informally mediate a territorial dispute between Indonesia's President Achmed Sukarno and the fledgling Federation of Malaysia. Unenamored of the idea, which, he complained to Bundy, had been proposed by "staff people who weren't thinking about the Johnson interest," Johnson was delaying a decision when the proposal was leaked to the *Washington Post*. Its editorial praising the idea as an indication of the President's laudable concern for the attorney general left Johnson, still trying to create the illusion of such concern, little choice but to approve. Speaking to Richard Russell, with whom maintenance of the illusion was unnecessary, the President said that at least the mission, seemingly foredoomed to failure, might make Bobby look bad. "I'm going to send Bobby Kennedy to Indonesia and just let him [Sukarno] put it right in his lap . . . let him go out there and have [a] row . . . with Sukarno."

The trip turned out to be the opposite of failure, although not for any reason Johnson or Kennedy had foreseen. Kennedy's meeting with Sukarno took place in Tokyo. On a previous visit to that city, in 1962, Bobby, speaking at Waseda University, had been heckled vociferously by both left-wing and right-wing students. Informed now by the American embassy that there was "insistent urging" from students that he speak again, he reluctantly agreed to do so. When he arrived, on a rainy day, the auditorium was jammed with students, and ten thousand more were huddled under umbrellas outside to hear him over loudspeakers. And when the professor introducing him said the name "Kennedy" for the first time, from inside and outside the auditorium there was a cheer that seemed to go on and on.

He spoke without a text, but since he was speaking about his brother, he didn't need one. "Tears were in his eyes, and in the eyes of many of the Japanese as he spoke about all the President had hoped to accomplish," Guthman was to recall, about how "he was not only President of one nation; he was President of young people around the world."

"If President Kennedy's life and death and his relationship to all in our age group mean anything, it means we young people must work harder for a better life for all the people in the world," Robert Kennedy said, as the cheering started again.

"It was a moment to remember," Guthman would recall. And, for "the first time," he says, Robert Kennedy "began to realize the magnitude of admiration for President Kennedy that existed overseas." A few days later, at the University of the Philippines, he spoke again. So large was the throng trying to get a glimpse of him that it broke through police lines. "I hadn't wanted to go on that trip, but afterwards I was glad I had," he was to tell Kempton. By the time he returned, he had decided—although he had not decided how he would do it—"to remain in public service and carry on his brother's work," Guthman says.

As a presidential envoy, he had expected to meet with the President alone to give his report, but on his arrival at the White House, he found, as Guthman relates, that the meeting would be "less than private," that Kennedy would be "required to brief him" in front of a roomful of congressmen and Cabinet officials. Afterwards, he and Johnson each spoke briefly before the television cameras—"We are of the unanimous opinion that he carried out his assignment constructively and with real achievement," the President said—so that Johnson got a picture of him and a Kennedy shaking hands, although Kennedy didn't look at him as he did so. Thereafter, the President never discussed the Sukarno-Malaysia controversy with him again, and the State Department showed little interest in his report. He told Theodore H. White that he felt he had been "used." As far as his relationship with Johnson was concerned, Guthman says, the episode left Bobby with "a bitter taste"—as if the taste hadn't been bitter enough already.

IN FEBRUARY, the rein slipped further, far enough so that words slipped out of Lyndon Johnson which he had for weeks restrained himself from speaking.

He said them to Robert Kennedy in the Oval Office. The two men were arguing over Paul Corbin. An eccentric, abrasive loose cannon of a political operative, Corbin had been useful to the Kennedys during the 1960 campaign as what Guthman euphemistically calls "a gutsy political infighter." Thereafter, however, he had proved troublesome because "He would do anything [President] Kennedy wanted (or that Corbin thought Kennedy wanted) whether or not Kennedy knew what he was doing," and he had been shunted into a low-level position at the Democratic National Committee. Early in February, he appeared in New Hampshire, where the first Democratic presidential primary would be held on March 10, organizing a write-in vote for Bobby Kennedy. Whether Corbin was operating on his own or under instructions is unknown—Bobby's closest aides, to a man, insist it was the former—but Johnson had no doubts. Summoning Kennedy to the Oval Office on February 11, he told him to have Corbin fired.

Bobby refused. He said he hadn't even known Corbin was in New Hampshire, and that he was a valuable political asset. Johnson said *he* knew Corbin was in New Hampshire, and that he wanted him out of that state, and off the DNC payroll. "If he's such a good fellow, you pay him," he said. "I know who he's loyal to. Get him out of there." Bobby continued to refuse. "I suggested that he find out himself whether" Corbin was actually in New Hampshire. "I'm not going to," he told Johnson. He said that Johnson should remember that Corbin had worked for President Kennedy, and that the President had thought highly of his work.

And Lyndon Johnson told Bobby Kennedy that his brother wasn't President now.

Bobby was to tell friends that Johnson, demanding Corbin's firing, had said, "Do it. President Kennedy isn't President anymore. I am." Johnson was not to deny expressing that sentiment, recalling it, during a recorded telephone conversation later that day with DNC Treasurer Maguire, in only slightly different words. Johnson told Maguire that "he [Bobby] said . . . that I must understand that he [Corbin] had worked for the President [Kennedy]" and that "the President liked the work he did. I said, 'I know it, Bobby, but *I'm* President, and I don't like what he's doing, and . . . I don't want him.' " "It was a bitter, mean conversation," Bobby Kennedy was to say. "It was the meanest tone that I'd heard. . . ."

THE FEBRUARY 11 ARGUMENT between the two men had escalated at one point into a discussion of the Indonesian trip, although not of its substance. In Bobby's recollection, Johnson said, "I did you a favor sending you to the Far East." and Bobby had replied, "A favor! I don't want you to do any more favors for me. Ever." And again, Johnson's own recollection, as he describes the conversation, in the call to Maguire, does not contradict the gist of that recollection: "I told him [Kennedy] that when the situation arose in Indonesia, that I was anxious to demonstrate my confidence in him, and I showed it by sending him out there." The President added a bit of description designed to show Bobby in what Johnson seems to have felt was a less than manly light. "Tears got in his eyes, and he said he's sorry that I sent him to Indonesia only on account of wanting to show confidence in him," Johnson told Maguire. The adding of that note is of a piece with Johnson saying, "But I'm President, and I don't want him," and it bolsters Bobby's analysis of the conversation's tone, and of the word Charles Bartlett, reconstructing it later, used: "so . . . *savage*." (And, of course, Johnson was correct. John Kennedy wasn't President anymore; *he* was. Corbin was fired.)

THE TONE WAS to get meaner. "I'm just like a fox," Lyndon Johnson once boasted. "I can see the jugular in any man and go for it, but I always keep myself in rein. I keep myself on a leash, just like you would an animal." The first phrase in that boast was accurate. Lyndon Johnson had always had a gift for finding a person's "jugular," his most vulnerable spot, the one in which he could most deeply be hurt. The rest of the boast, however, was not. If he kept himself in rein, on a leash, it was a leash that, all through his life, had been frequently unfastened. His ability to hurt had always been combined with a willingness—an eagerness, in fact—to put the ability to use; with a cruelty, a viciousness, a desire to hurt for the sake of hurting.* Now his unerring eye had located, beneath the pale mask of Robert Kennedy's grief, the place in which, because of his brother's assassination, Robert Kennedy was most vulnerable. And the leash came off. Johnson told Pierre Salinger, in a remark he obviously intended to get back to Kennedy, that Jack Kennedy's death might have been "divine retribution" for his "participation" in assassination plots against other heads of state. "Lyndon Johnson said to Pierre Salinger that he wasn't sure but that the assassination of President Kennedy didn't take place in retribution for his participation in the assassinations of Trujillo and President Diem," Robert Kennedy said during an oral history interview in April, 1964. "Divine retribution. He said that. Then he went on and said that when he was growing up, somebody he knew—who had misbehaved—. . . ran into a tree, hit his head, and became cross-eyed. He said that was God's retribution for people who were bad. . . . God put his mark on them. And that this [President Kennedy's assassination] might very well be God's retribution to President Kennedy for his participation in the assassination of these two people."

Although neither of the two assassinations to which Johnson referred had been authorized by the late President, Johnson didn't believe that. Pointing to the picture of President Diem in The Elms the day after Kennedy's funeral, Johnson had told Hubert Humphrey, "We had a hand in killing him. Now it's happening here." In his remark to Salinger, Johnson didn't include the assassination attempts against a third head of state, Fidel Castro, although he was aware that they had occurred, and believed that the Kennedys had had a hand in them as well. A week after the assassination, he was asking J. Edgar Hoover "whether [Oswald] was connected with the Cuban operation [Mongoose]?" His suspicions were soon to harden. By 1965, he was telling an aide, "President Kennedy tried to get Castro, but Castro got Kennedy first." During his retirement, he would tell a journalist that the Kennedys "had been operating a damn Murder, Inc. in the Caribbean." Whether or not his remark to Salinger brought the Castro attempts to Robert Kennedy's mind, the remark was made, as Evan Thomas says, "cruelly and with an unerring instinct for Kennedy's hidden vulnerabilities." And the fact that it struck home is testified to by its target. It was, Kennedy told Arthur Schlesinger, "the worst thing Johnson has said." Kennedy was to tell a friend that the new President "does not know how to use people's talents, to find the very best in them and put the best to work. But more than any other man, he knows how to ferret out and use people's weaknesses."

*For one of many examples, see *The Path to Power,* pp. 191–92.

He had ferreted out one of Kennedy's.

In speaking of Lyndon Johnson, Robert Kennedy had in the past used adjectives like "formidable," "flawed," and "powerful" to describe him. Now a new adjective would be added to the description. Schlesinger, summarizing Kennedy's feelings, writes that "He saw Johnson more than ever as a formidable but flawed man, powerful but dangerous."

25

Hammer Blows

WRITING IN 1964, Theodore H. White would say that "the clash of Robert F. Kennedy and Lyndon Johnson . . . may continue to agitate the Democratic Party for some years to come." That prophecy would prove accurate. Writing in 1997, thirty-three years after White, Russell Baker would recall that the story of the two men, "a story that still makes many an old-timer's blood boil," had "poisoned the Democratic Party for most of the 1960s." With each year, in fact, the passions between the two men would blaze only more fiercely. Even the gunshot in Los Angeles in June, 1968, couldn't extinguish those passions. As Kennedy lay dying the next evening, Johnson, over dinner in the White House, kept asking Joe Califano, "Is he dead? Is he dead yet?" Califano had to make so many calls to the Secret Service or to his assistant Larry Levinson that Levinson finally asked him, "Joe, is this something that he's *wishing* to have happen? Why is he asking it that way?" ("I couldn't tell, because Johnson didn't know, whether he hoped or feared that the answer would be yes or no," Califano was to recall.) After the answer was finally yes, Johnson issued the appropriate public statements, praising Kennedy as "a noble and compassionate leader, a good and faithful servant of the people." "Early the next morning," however, he also made a private telephone call to the Secretary of Defense, Clark Clifford, who had jurisdiction over Arlington National Cemetery. The Kennedy family wanted Robert to be buried in Arlington, and Johnson, Clifford was to relate, "wanted to discuss whether or not Bobby Kennedy had the right to be buried in Arlington." "Stunned" and "dumbfounded" by the call—"one of [my] saddest experiences" in dealing "with [Johnson]"—Clifford told Johnson, he says, that "the regulations were irrelevant, and in any case could be suspended by the Commander in Chief," and "It seemed obvious that Bobby should be buried near his beloved brother." "The politician in Lyndon Johnson understood this," Clifford relates, and Bobby was buried in Arlington, near Jack's grave.

The feud between the two men would, during most of the Sixties, have far-reaching influence—surprising, sometimes, in its impact not merely on their party but on the course of American history. The story of the feud would have a

dozen twists and turns even before the day in March, 1968, on which what Johnson had "feared from the first day of my presidency" came true, and Robert
Kennedy announced that he was running against him for the Democratic nomination, moments in which first one man and then the other could feel for a
moment (and usually only for a moment, for the battle would quickly be
rejoined) the flush of victory over a long-hated foe. But for now, at the end of
these first months after Lyndon Johnson became President, the feud had only one
victor. If the Tom Mann appointment was indeed the "first round," there had also
been during these months the Indonesia and Corbin rounds, and Johnson had
won all three.

In addition, during these months, Johnson had, in his battle with Robert
Kennedy, achieved the overall objective he considered most vital. In order to preserve around his Administration the aura of continuity he considered of overriding importance, it had been necessary to keep Kennedy in it—and, at the end of
those months, Kennedy was still in it. He left later, of course, but for Johnson's
purposes, he had stayed long enough.

AFTER JOHNSON'S RETURN from the ranch, several of the Kennedy men began
leaving.

"Schlesinger declared war, I guess, the day that John F. Kennedy went into
the ground," Ralph Dungan was to say. To Johnson, the historian epitomized the
intellectual unable to deal with the problems of the real world; once, confronted
with a knotty problem in a foreign country, the President, expressing his contempt, asked, "What do you want me to do? Send Arthur Schlesinger to take care
of things?" The President, and Jenkins, who echoed his thoughts, expressed
"mounting irritation" with him. "There was something about [him] which pecu-
liarly roused the Johnsonian ire." And, as is clear from the contemporaneous
entries Schlesinger made in the journal, the feelings were mutual. Despite admo-
nitions to himself in the journal that "I must guard against . . . my dislike of the
current style and corn," the guard was sometimes dropped. The new President's
statement to Schlesinger that he didn't have "the knowledge, the skills, the
understanding" of his predecessor was an assessment with which Schlesinger
thoroughly agreed, in regard to Johnson's personality and brainpower alike.
Although "the new President is a quick study, . . . unlike JFK, he does not retain
what he has been told," he wrote on December 30. "His basic trouble, I imagine,
is that he has never in his political career had to concentrate on substance. . . . Policy for Johnson has always been determined by the balance of
political pressures. Now he must begin to examine the merits of policy *per se,*
and he is not intellectually or psychologically prepared to do this." The historian's enchantment with the former President wasn't fading. Invited to Jackie
Kennedy's Georgetown townhouse that December for a screening of a film on
Jack Kennedy, he "found it almost unbearable to watch that graceful, witty,

incandescent personality." A week later, it snowed in Washington—"almost as deep a snow as the inaugural blizzard. . . . It all began on a fiercely cold day 35 months ago," and that was how it was coming to an end. "The White House is lovely, ghostly and alien. My own depression does not abate." He was soon actively advising Robert Kennedy. "I am . . . more and more persuaded that I am for him whatever he wants," Schlesinger wrote, and at dinner parties the barbs of his very sharp tongue were often aimed at Johnson. He signed a contract to write a history of the Kennedy presidency.

Johnson heard about all this, of course, and "the problem of disengagement" was not, in the event, to prove as "considerable" as Schlesinger had anticipated. By the end of December, the historian was to write, he had been totally "isolated. . . . I have not had a single communication from the President or his staff for the last month—not a request to do anything, or an invitation to a meeting, or an instruction, or a suggestion." In fact, by December, Johnson had begun recruiting his successor: a distinguished historian and author from Princeton, not Harvard: Eric F. Goldman. Goldman's upcoming appointment had been leaked to the press, and Schlesinger was receiving inquiries about it from journalists. On January 27, Schlesinger resubmitted the letter of resignation he had written immediately after the assassination. This time, he was to relate, it was "acccptcd with alacrity."*

WITH SORENSEN, in Johnson's view the sharpest tool, he tried hardest.

"Johnson tried to be very nice to me, and he was very nice," Sorensen was to say. "He was very very nice" not only to him, but "to my sons," he says. Having brought his three little boys to the White House one day in December, Sorensen left them downstairs in the White House Mess while he was in the Oval Office. When Johnson asked after them, Sorensen mentioned they were downstairs. Johnson said, "Let's go down and see them," and "chatted with them very nicely for a while." Since, in their conversations—on the phone and in person—Sorensen unbent not at all, Johnson did the bending. When, in a telephone call before the November 27 speech to Congress, Johnson said that he "rather liked" Galbraith's draft and Sorensen said, "Well, to be frank with you, I *didn't*," Johnson backtracked so fast—"Well, I didn't think it was any ball of *fire*. I thought it's something that you could improve on. . . . I read it in about three minutes. . . . But I think a much better speech could be written. I'm *expecting* you to write a better one"—that Sorensen laughed over the phone. The insulting "cannot fill his shoes" line was simply crossed out; during all the discussions between the two men about the speech, it was never mentioned. In the car riding to Capi-

---

*Schlesinger's opinion of Johnson was to change drastically. By 1978, he would be writing, "For all his towering ego, his devastating instinct for the weaknesses of others, his unlimited capacity for self-pity, he was at the same time a man of brilliant intelligence, authentic social passion, and deep seriousness. . . ."

tol Hill to give that speech, Johnson had tried to tell Sorensen that despite the "corning up" by Fortas and Humphrey, the speech was "90 percent Sorensen." "No sir, that's not accurate," Sorensen replied; "not more than 50 percent Sorensen." "Well, anyway, your 50 percent is the best," Johnson said. Replying "in a more presumptuous fashion than I had ever used with JFK," Sorensen said, "On that point, we agree," and Johnson had simply laughed to break the tension. And when, a few days later, Katharine Graham urged presidential tolerance for the curtness—Sorensen had been "cantankerous" to her, too, she said, but that was what he did "instead of crying. . . . I think he is going to come around . . . if you just give him a little love, and overlook . . ."—Johnson assured her, "I'm going to do it," although, he added, "I've done as much as I can and have any pride and self-respect left." (A few hours later, Johnson asked Sorensen again to stay. Sorensen didn't reply, and finally Johnson had to ask: "Are you with me?" Sorensen's only reply was "I'm still here, Mr. President.") All that December, the flattery continued; Sorensen became accustomed to hearing the President refer to him as "my trusted counselor," even "plugging" a book he had published some years previously. "He was wooing me, in a sense, to stay on," Sorensen knew. At the ranch, as Sorensen was working on his drafts of the State of the Union, Johnson, knowing what he most wanted to hear, found new ways to praise his fallen leader. "Well, your man treated me better than I would have [treated him] if the positions were reversed," he told Sorensen once. But Sorensen's devotion to Jack Kennedy hadn't been ended by the bullets of Dallas. Kennedy "had planned to write . . . a book with me after the presidency," he was to say. "Now that he was gone, I felt some obligation to write it." When he received an offer from the same editor who had published *Profiles in Courage,* he accepted it and handed Johnson a letter of resignation that would take effect on February 29.

Protesting violently, Johnson replayed the theme that had worked before. "You and I know that he is up there looking down on us and wants us to work together, carrying out his ideals, and he would not want you to leave here," he said, and went on, "his speech" growing, in Sorensen's recollection, "only more saccharine"—until he went too far.

Once Sorensen got to know him better, Johnson said, Sorensen "would discover that he treated his staff as if they were his own children."

"Yes, I know," Sorensen replied. That was his only reply, and it was made in a quiet tone, but Johnson evidently understood. He accepted the resignation.

PIERRE SALINGER'S PLUMPNESS, bushy eyebrows, ever-present cigar and good humor (all of which made people forget that he had once been an award-winning crime reporter and a very tough Rackets Committee investigator) had, together with an ability to take a joke, made "Plucky" the butt of a lot of kidding by many of his colleagues in the Kennedy White House. Jack Kennedy's kidding always stopped at a line that left Salinger his dignity, however. With Lyndon Johnson, there was no such line—as became evident over Christmas at the ranch.

First, there was the new President's insistence that Salinger wear that outfit notably unflattering to his portly physique, and then that he mount a horse and trot off on it in front of a battery of photographers despite the fact that he barely knew how to ride, a performance that moved reporters to dub him "Hopalong Salinger." And there followed an incident at the dinner for Ludwig Erhard in the Stonewall gym.

Salinger was vulnerable because in his youth he had been a pianist so proficient that, for a brief time, he had considered a concert career. At Kennedy parties he sometimes played ditties he had composed himself, along with humorous lyrics. Van Cliburn was stepping off the stage after his masterful renditions of Beethoven and Brahms when a startled Salinger heard Johnson say, "Would Mr. Salinger please go to the piano?"

Turning red, Salinger tried to demur. "Do you think it's fair to put me on after Van Cliburn?" he asked. But no demurral was accepted. Trying to make the best of the situation—not that any best was really possible—Salinger, trudging up to the stage, said he would play a piece he had written himself, the "Palm Beach Waltz," so that no one would realize the wrong notes he was hitting. When he finished, there was a reward: a ten-gallon hat, which Johnson presented to him on stage. It was too big; the brim came down over Salinger's eyes.

"Reporters felt sorry for Pierre Salinger that day," one of them was to recall. Those who were his friends felt sorry for him during the entire Texas trip. "For all his striped shirts and big cigars, Salinger is a literate and subtle man, and not disposed toward cornball humor and a folksy approach," one of them says. "When I saw Lyndon having fun with Salinger and putting ten-gallon hats on him and so on, I just had a feeling Salinger wasn't going to wear that hat very long."

Back in Washington, Johnson pushed him further. Soon there was circulating what Schlesinger calls "a terrible story in which Johnson made Salinger eat a plate of bean soup at a White House luncheon out of pure delight in the exercise of authority."

Prior to the ranch trip, during the first month after the assassination, Johnson and Salinger had seemed to have developed a rapport. "Of all the Kennedy people," the easygoing press secretary "seemed to make the transition most easily," Schlesinger was to write. And that, as some longtime Johnson observers understood, was the problem. Having "adopted" Salinger, Johnson "now treated him as if he were one of his veteran deputies," James Wechsler was to write, "and with such men he does not worry about the amenities." After hearing the bean soup story, Schlesinger wrote in his journal that "There is nothing more dangerous, so far as I can see, than being accepted by Johnson as one of his own. I think he has been meticulously polite to those in the White House whom he regards as Kennedy men. But, when he starts regarding them as Johnson men, their day is over. He begins to treat them like Johnson men, which means like servants. That is what happened to Pierre Salinger."

The rapport was gone, as became apparent to the men and women in the

White House press lobby. "Reporters . . . every day saw numerous slight indications that he [Salinger] was not really as happy with the new regime as he said he was," one said. That analysis was correct. "It was impossible for me to stay, and it was just a question of how I figured out how to get out of the White House," Salinger was to recall. And when Johnson noticed the unhappiness, tensions rose on both sides. "The White House press operation . . . deteriorated badly," as the *Los Angeles Times* put it. By February, Salinger was determined to resign. A Senate seat was opening in California, and the deadline for filing nominating petitions was March 20. Early in March, Salinger decided to run—if lawyers could assure him that he was eligible for the seat although he had been living in Virginia. He didn't mention his plans to Johnson—didn't give him any hint of them—even as the deadline approached. The lawyers' definitive answer, that he was indeed eligible, came through on March 19, the very day before the deadline, while he was having lunch at the Sans Souci Restaurant near the White House. And then, needing to be in California the next day to file his petition, he quit—virtually on the spot—in a resignation ("so abrupt as to be rude," one account called it) whose brusqueness made it one of the more startling in White House annals. Walking out of the restaurant (as he passed Ken O'Donnell, sitting at another table, he told him, "I'm on my way to the President's office to resign"; O'Donnell recalls that he "almost fell out of [my] chair" in surprise), Salinger went to the White House, arriving shortly after three o'clock, and went upstairs, where Johnson was having a late lunch with a group of newspaper publishers and reporters in the Family Dining Room. Encountering Jenkins and Moyers outside in the corridor, he told them that he needed to see the President "as quickly as possible," and told the two "startled" men why. Moyers rang Johnson in the dining room. Picking up the phone at the head of a table lined with journalists, the President was told that his press secretary was just outside the door waiting to offer his resignation—which was to take effect that very afternoon.

Johnson's self-possession didn't desert him for an instant. Not one of his luncheon guests, listening to his end of the conversation, had any idea what he was being told. Hanging up the phone, he resumed the lunch as if nothing had happened. And when, after the publishers left, he saw Salinger in the Oval Office at about 3:30, he was all graciousness, telling him he understood perfectly, and that if Salinger would write him a letter of resignation, he would answer it immediately.

Despite the haste with which they were composed, the letters, which were exchanged in the Oval Office at five o'clock, met the requirements of the genre. Salinger's, telling the President "what an honor it has been to serve you," offered his resignation "with sincere regret" and "warm gratitude for your many and repeated kindnesses," and Johnson's accepted the resignation "only with the greatest regret and with a reluctance that bows only to your strong personal desire to return to California. . . . I hate to see you go." Then, in a gesture to reinforce the friendly tone, the President asked Salinger how much the California filing fee would be—$450 was the answer—and, pulling out a roll of bills, paid it (or at least part of it: "He must have heard $250," Salinger was to say), saying, "Here's your first campaign contribution."

"I had given LBJ very little time to consider my successor," Salinger was to write in his memoirs, hardly an overstatement. When Johnson asked the press secretary who should succeed him, Salinger suggested Reedy, because of the "high regard" in which he "was held . . . by the Washington press corps." Johnson told Jenkins to telephone Reedy and "tell him to get over here. He's the new press secretary as of now." The President was therefore able to have an obviously well-qualified successor in place when Salinger, having returned to his office, called in reporters and said he was resigning "effective immediately." And when articles about the "surprise" and "startling" resignation appeared the next day, Johnson made a trip to the press room to assure reporters he was "not disturbed" about it. There was, however, no disguising the basic fact: that the press secretary to the President of the United States had resigned, giving the President less than two hours' notice. Cleaning out his desk, Salinger drove to the airport, catching the seven o'clock flight to San Francisco. With him on the flight was deputy press secretary Andrew Hatcher, who, informed of the impending resignation, had told Salinger to announce his own "at the same time you announce yours. I'm going back to California with you."*

Writing in her diary that evening, Lady Bird was more frank. A "bombshell . . . dropped into our lap late this afternoon," she wrote. "Pierre Salinger walked into Lyndon's office . . . and told him that he was going to resign. . . . Of all the people from the Kennedy Administration, I had felt that Salinger was one of the most professional, most committed to doing a job. Although he is very attached to the Kennedys, I thought we had established a certain simpatico relationship with him. So his sudden departure leaves a big uncertainty in my own thinking."

BUT THAT WAS the last crack in the façade. None of John F. Kennedy's other staff members would resign during 1964. The biggest remaining names on that staff—O'Donnell, O'Brien, Dutton, Dungan—would still be in their White House offices when Lyndon Johnson ran for re-election that year, and when he won the presidency in his own right that November. With the single exception of Robert Kennedy, the faces around the Cabinet table—McNamara, Rusk, Freeman, Udall—would be the same. Key advisers like McGeorge Bundy, Walter Heller and Kermit Gordon would still be at their desks. And even the loss of those three symbolic figures—Sorensen, Salinger and Schlesinger—would not,

---

*Salinger won the Democratic nomination for the California Senate seat, and was appointed to the seat after the incumbent, Clair Engle, died on July 30, 1964, but was defeated in November by the Republican George Murphy.

in the event, have much significance. For in terms of the Johnson presidency, the crucial fact about the three men was that they, like Robert Kennedy, had stayed long enough. Lyndon Johnson had known that after the shock of his predecessor's assassination America needed continuity, and that the key to continuity was that Kennedy men like Sorensen, Salinger and Schlesinger stay in their jobs. And they had stayed—until, for Johnson's purpose, their leaving did little harm. By the time the three men left, short though that time was, the situation had changed. "Continuity"—keeping draped over the new Administration the mantle of its predecessor—was no longer nearly as essential as it had been.

By the time of Salinger's resignation, Washington had been reassured not merely by the continuance in office of members of the old Administration, but by the performance in office of the new Administration—of the new President. Discussing Salinger's resignation in the *New York Times* on March 20, the day after it occurred, James Reston said it did not have the significance it would once have had. While "the nostalgic pretense of the first three months [*sic*] of the Johnson Administration is vanishing" and "The elaborate effort to prove that Boston loves Austin, and vice versa, is less apparent," he wrote, the pretense was no longer necessary because "people here are planning their lives on the assumption that the Johnson Administration is going to be around for quite a while."

The new Administration wasn't going to be the same as the old one, Reston wrote, but that didn't mean that it would be less effective—nor, in fact, that it might not be more effective. "It is not clear who" among the Johnson staffers—Jenkins, Moyers, Valenti or Reedy—will "bring to the White House those useful commodities of vivid language, a sense of history, and, most important, a sense of humor, but Johnson himself will provide many other attributes," Reston wrote. "He is effective precisely because he is so determined, industrious, personal and even humorless, particularly in dealing with Congress." Kennedy, he wrote, "retained an inordinate respect for the . . . elders of the Congress. When they growled, he paused and often retreated," and he had a "detached and even donnish . . . willingness to grant the merit in the other fellow's argument." Johnson, he said, "is not so inclined to retreat," and "grants nothing in an argument, not even equal time. . . . Ask not what you have done for Lyndon Johnson, but what you have done for him *lately*. This may not be the most attractive quality of the new Administration but it works. . . . The lovers of style are not too happy with the new Administration, but the lovers of substance are not complaining."

By March 20, of course, tangible evidence of Johnson's effectiveness was piling up: the passage of the tax cut, foreign aid, education, and appropriations bills, the progress toward passage of the civil rights bill. And beyond these concrete successes was one less tangible but just as impressive: the confidence engendered not just in Washington but in the country as a whole by the aura of competence and determination that emanated from the White House.

The confidence and success were documented in public opinion polls. In March, the country's most respected sampler of such opinion, the Gallup Poll, asked Americans, "Do you approve or disapprove of the way Johnson is handling his job as President?" Seventy-three percent of the respondents said they approved—an overwhelming percentage. In April, the figure would be 77 percent. Even more eloquent was the fact that of the respondents who did not approve—a small enough percentage, in any case—the reason most gave for withholding their approval was not that they disapproved but that they were undecided. In both March and April, months in which over 70 percent of the American people approved of the way Lyndon Johnson was handling the presidency, the percentage that disapproved was 9. The figures for April were 77 percent approval, 9 percent disapproval, 14 percent undecided. Americans of every political persuasion were united in approval. "Two out of three Republicans say that he is doing a good job as President," the poll reported. Seventy-seven percent to 9—disapproval in a single digit. "Every President, of course, enjoys a 'honeymoon' period of high popularity after taking office," Gallup had noted. Still, after the May poll showed similar results, Gallup stated that Johnson's approval ratings "compare favorably with the popularity ratings accorded any of Johnson's predecessors" in a comparable pre-election period since scientific polling techniques were developed.

And the confidence and success were the theme in scores of newspaper columns in addition to Reston's. "In the few short months since last Nov. 22," America has watched "Lyndon B. Johnson making Washington and the government his own," Joseph Alsop wrote. "Acid tests" still lay ahead, he wrote, "but even the Kennedy men whom Mr. Johnson had not quite won over . . . have no doubt that the acid tests will be successfully met when they come." Alsop, Johnson's Washington acquaintance of many years, had always been kindly disposed toward him. Marquis Childs had often, over the years, been extremely critical of him. Now Childs wrote that Lyndon Johnson is "the most energetic and the most ambitious President to occupy the office in a very long time. His ambition . . . is on a heroic scale. It is to unify the country—to resolve the fundamental differences between black and white, capital and labor, rich and poor, North and South." And, Childs said, "he believes he can do just this and his confidence carries with it an added measure of strength. Strength attracts strength, and this is surely one explanation for his extraordinary standing in every indicator of public opinion."

The public persona that had once made him an object of mockery had not disappeared, far from it. He was, at Georgetown dinner parties at least, "the same Lyndon Johnson," Tom Wicker wrote. "Once again he is being referred to as 'ol Cornpone.' " But now, suddenly, the corniness wasn't a drawback, Wicker said. Now "there is usually in the phrase a touch of awe and not infrequently a tone of respect. To paraphrase Lincoln on Grant, a good many people seem to believe it would be wise to find out what brand of corn he uses and send some to the other politicians. . . . Cornpone it may be . . . but so long as Lyndon Johnson's evangelism comes from the heart, the nation is likely to get the message more often than not." Said Roscoe Drummond: "The Johnson Administration is getting more Johnsonian every day. He is just doing what comes naturally. The country likes it. [He] is throwing away most of the old rules about how to be President of the United States—and making his own."

In some of the columns, in fact, there was more than a touch of the awe Wicker mentioned.

"Lyndon Johnson resembles an elemental natural force of some hitherto undiscovered sort—an amiable force, to be sure, not destructive like an earthquake, but still a very powerful force that is only subject to its own natural rules," wrote Alsop. Awe particularly when talking about the new President's legislative accomplishments. Johnson was managing, "in a good deal less than a year, to get through Congress the two most important pieces of domestic legislation to be adopted in a quarter of a century—in a sense, the *only* important pieces of domestic legislation in that long period," Richard Rovere wrote in *The New Yorker.* "It has been an astonishing performance, and one, it seems clear, that was beyond the reach of John F. Kennedy." Part of the explanation for Johnson's legislative success was the momentum generated behind Kennedy's proposals by his assassination, Rovere wrote. "It . . . seems necessary to believe that the gods of history are not above arranging things in such a way that a man may contribute more to the fulfillment of his ideals by being the victim of a senseless murder than by living and working for them." But part was something more, Rovere had to admit, grudging as were the words with which he acknowledged it. "It is hardly possible to believe that a Texas drawl, a strategic display of frugality, and some soft-soaping of Senator Byrd can replace domestic discord with harmony. It seems necessary, though, to believe that such things can—for a time—at least—go quite a long way toward promoting this sort of change, for a change has in fact occurred. The change, Rovere wrote, "is reflected" not only "in the opinion polls" but "in the graciousness and ease with which" Senator Byrd and Representative Smith, the pair of Virginians "who had been thwarting Presidents almost, it seems, since time began," have been "lending themselves to the designs of President Johnson." Awe at the speed with which the accomplishments, accomplishments that went beyond the legislative, had been achieved. Recalling the "people who, in December, were worried that Mr. Johnson would not have time enough before the election to put his own stamp on the country," Eric Sevareid said that the new President had had to accomplish three objectives to put the stamp there. "He had to stamp his own leadership on his predecessor's administration, and this he did in a matter of days; he had to impress and beguile the Congress into a bill-passing frame of mind, and this he did in a matter of weeks; he had to imprint his own personality on the country at large, on a people just getting used to Mr. Kennedy's far different nature, and this Mr. Johnson began to do the moment propriety permitted."

The tone of columnistic comparisons with his predecessor no longer contained even a touch of condescension. In fact, many of them conveyed a journalistic evaluation that the influential Reston put in a single succinct sentence: "President Kennedy's eloquence was designed to make men think; President Johnson's hammer blows are designed to make men act."

THE MAGNITUDE OF the success was apparent also in discussions about politics. By March, 1964, speculation about the identity of the Republican nominee for President—about the merits and chances of Nelson Rockefeller, William Scranton, Richard Nixon and Barry Goldwater—was the hot topic in political circles. By March—by the time Pierre Salinger quit—there was no speculation about the identity of the Democratic nominee. The last of that speculation was over. The Democratic nominee for President would be the man who was now President; there may have been doubts about that in December, but even among Robert Kennedy's most ardent supporters, there was no longer any doubt about that at all.

And the President was going to be a hard man to beat in November's general election. Between March 13 and March 17 Gallup polled Americans about Lyndon Johnson's chances against each of the most likely Republican nominees. "If Barry Goldwater were the Republican candidate and Lyndon Johnson were the Democratic candidate, which would you like to see win?" Gallup asked. Thirteen percent of the respondents said they would like to see Goldwater win. Seventy-eight percent said they would like Lyndon Johnson. (The remaining 9 percent were undecided.) For Goldwater's leading opponent for the nomination, the figures were similar: 16 percent for Nelson Rockefeller and 77 percent for Johnson. Richard Nixon, who had taken himself out of the running, would do better against the President, Gallup found, but not that much better: 24 percent to 68 for Johnson. *Time* magazine said the identity of the Republican nominee didn't really matter. "President Johnson's rising popularity" had made "the whole show academic."

26

Long Enough

LYNDON JOHNSON'S SUCCESSION to the presidency, the transition in which he assumed the power that had once been John Kennedy's, had been so successful, gone so smoothly, that by March, as was apparent from the contemporary journalistic evaluation, it was becoming simply a *fait accompli,* an accepted fact of American political life. And as more time passed, that would turn out to be its fate over a longer term as well.

Some of those who witnessed the succession up close, appreciating the magnitude of his accomplishment, were certain that eventually it would be given the credit it deserved. "History will record the great contribution Lyndon Johnson made in taking us through the transition," Hugh Sidey wrote in 1969.

That has not happened, however. The success, the smoothness of Johnson's succession has come to be viewed—to the extent it is viewed at all—as simply yet another example of the efficacy of the American Constitution's provisions for the orderly transfer of presidential power in a democracy, of the efficacy, as one of the most detailed studies of vice presidential succession puts it, of the "recognized rule which made him President upon the death of the President." The "smooth manner in which presidential power changed hands upon the death of President John Fitzgerald Kennedy was not entirely unlike what had happened on seven other occasions in American history," this study states. "Each time a Vice-President became President and led the country safely through the tragedy and crisis of losing its leader."

Not that history has forgotten the assassination of President Kennedy and the three subsequent days of his funeral ceremonies, of course. The very opposite is the case. Those four days have become enshrined as among the most memorable days in American history. But the achievements of Lyndon Johnson during those four days and the rest of the transition period—the period, forty-seven days, just short of seven weeks, between the moment on November 22, 1963, when Ken O'Donnell said "He's gone" and the State of the Union speech on January 8, 1964—have been afforded so little attention that his succession to the presidency has become, to considerable extent, an episode if not lost to, then overlooked by, history.

There are photographs and moving pictures of the assassination day and the funeral ceremonies whose inherent drama and constant reiteration on television, in movies, in books, in newspapers and magazines—in every form of media, really, in which the reiteration of images is possible—have engraved them so deeply in the American consciousness that they have become iconic images in the nation's history. Jack and Jackie, tanned and radiant, coming off Air Force One in Dallas, pink suit and red roses bright in the sun, and sitting smiling, basking in the cheers, in the back seat of the open car; the President suddenly slumping in Zapruder's lens; Bobby and Jackie, hand in hand in sorrow, coming off the plane, dark blotches on the suit; Jackie coming out of the White House holding her children's hands—black mantilla, little sky-blue coats; the caisson with its six matched grays; prancing Black Jack with boots reversed; Caroline putting her hand under the flag; John-John's salute; Oswald, his mouth open in shock and agony, the Stetsoned Dallas detective aghast as the menacing figure lunges in from the right, revolver in hand; the great procession up Pennsylvania Avenue to the Capitol; the great procession on foot to the cathedral: the three Kennedys, the two brothers and the veiled widow, behind them the world leaders massed and marching.

A single photograph from those four days, and a simple photograph only, in which Lyndon Johnson is prominent has become iconic. It is perhaps the most famous photograph of them all—the picture of the new President taking the oath aboard Air Force One. But although his face is the focus of the camera's eye, it is a face that is only stern and sad and composed, certainly not handsome, and the viewer's eye moves quickly to the face beside his, the very mask of beauty in grief. And that photograph is the only image of Lyndon Johnson during those four days that has become a part of history, although, during those days, he was becoming the most powerful man on earth. When he appears in other photographs, it is not at the center; he is there behind the Kennedy family coming down the steps of the Capitol after the service in the Rotunda, but as the faces of the grieving Kennedys fill the lens, who looks to see who is behind them? What the world saw on television the day of the procession of Kennedys and world leaders following the casket to the cathedral—and what the world has seen over and over during the intervening half century—is, behind the Kennedys, Selassie's medals and towering de Gaulle and Baudouin's sword. Johnson is marching, too, right behind the family and in front of the leaders, marching, windows all along the route, with gunshots from a window fresh in his mind, but, thanks to the vagaries of camera angles, he is barely visible in most photographs of the procession.

But the succession of Lyndon Johnson deserves a better fate in history. For had it not been for his accomplishments during the transition, history might have been different. Because the headlines in that first blizzard of news—PRISONER

LINKED TO CASTRO GROUP; SUSPECT LIVED IN SOVIET UNION—have long been proven false or exaggerated, it has been easy to forget that for several days after the assassination America was reading those headlines, easy to forget the extent of the suspicions that existed during those days not only about a conspiracy but about a conspiracy hatched in Cuba or Russia, two nations with whom, barely a year before, America had been on the brink of nuclear war. If Johnson had not moved as quickly as he did to appoint the Warren Commission and quiet the suspicions, would suspicions have escalated into an international crisis? Perhaps not, and certainly the commission's investigation, which would in its turn be rushed, has been proven inadequate, its report flawed. The answer to that question is not simple, however. International misunderstandings have escalated into war because of folly and illogic before. Guns of August? In weighing the motivations, mixed as always with Johnson, for establishing the Warren Commission, the possibility of November bombs should be allowed at least a small place on the scales.

Nor should other aspects of the transition be passed over as lightly as they have been. Because he moved so swiftly and successfully to create the image of continuity that reassured the nation, it has been easy to overlook how the Kennedy men might simply have resigned. It has been easy to overlook the obstacles—the shock and mystery of the assassination, the mushroom cloud fears, the deep divisions in the country over his predecessor's policies—that stood in the way of unifying America behind his Administration; easy to overlook how difficult to unify even his own party: to rally into line behind his Administration's banner labor leaders, black leaders, liberals, many of whom had, for years, been deeply suspicious of him and who would have needed little excuse to fall irrevocably into line behind another, more familiar banner, the brother's banner, that could so readily have been raised within party ranks; to fall into line behind a leader they knew, and were quickly beginning to love.

AND LYNDON JOHNSON'S ACHIEVEMENTS during those seven weeks went far beyond reassurance and continuity, far beyond even what he accomplished during those weeks for his predecessor's tax cut bill and civil rights. For had he striven only for reassurance and continuity, something much more important would have been lost.

The bullets of Dallas had made John F. Kennedy a martyr—and the martyrdom of a leader lends new power to causes he had championed. Lyndon Johnson knew this. "Everything I had ever learned in the history books taught me that martyrs have to die for causes," he explained to Doris Goodwin. "John Kennedy had died. But his 'cause' was not really clear. That was my job. I had to take the dead man's program and turn it into a martyr's cause." He began to do that when, in that first address to Congress on November 27, he said he was trying to finish what Kennedy had started, "to continue the forward thrust of America that he began." He couched his support of legislation in those terms. "No memorial . . . could more eloquently honor President Kennedy's memory than the earliest possible passage of the civil rights bill for which he fought so long." During the transition he was constantly invoking the late President's memory. And the invocations accomplished their purpose. JFK's martyrdom had galvanized support for the causes with which he had identified himself in his eloquent speeches. "Kennedy's assassination touched many people as they had not been touched before," as an historian has written. "Could the murder of so young and promising a leader be redeemed? Must his life be wasted?" The passage of legislation he had introduced was a way of ensuring it wouldn't be wasted. His death generated behind legislation that had seemed dead in congressional waters a tremendous new momentum.

And Johnson knew something else. Momentum can be lost. "A measure must be sent to the Hill at exactly the right moment," he was to explain. "Timing is essential. Momentum is *not* a mysterious mistress. It is a controllable fact of political life." The time to catch a wave is at its crest. And while the wave of emotion, of affection and adoration, for the martyred young President would roll on for decades—is still rolling on today, almost half a century after Dallas—its crest, the height of the Kennedy tide, came in the weeks immediately following Dallas, in the weeks of Lyndon Johnson's transition. By rushing to push through Kennedy's bills, Johnson caught the crest. The maneuvers by which he made them begin to move through Congress were made easier—in some cases were only made possible—by that wave of emotion. Had he not caught the tide at its absolute height, he might well have lost some of its force, and as the Senate fight of 1964 was to demonstrate, every ounce of that force would be necessary to pass the civil rights bill. By moving as quickly as he did, Johnson caught a tide, seized a moment, that might not have lasted very long.

Caught the tide—and rode the tide, using its force as it rolled forward beyond the transition weeks into the new year of 1964, using it for more than the passage of the civil rights and tax cut bills, or for the yanking of the bit out of Congress's teeth; using the momentum generated by John Kennedy's death for other purposes; using it, in fact, for purposes beyond those Kennedy had enunciated, for the passage of long-dreamed-of liberal legislation whose purposes went far beyond any embodied in Kennedy legislation. Lyndon Johnson used that momentum to launch what he envisioned as (and what, in fact, might have been, had it not been undermined and then destroyed by a war he waged in the jungles of Asia, and by the deceptions he practiced in the name of that war) a vast, revolutionary, transformation of America: a "War on Poverty" that would, in his vision, be the beginning of the transformation of American society into "The Great Society." His declaration that "This administration today, here and now, declares unconditional war on poverty in America" was a prelude to the introduction of legislation that would launch the war on dozens of new fronts.

These seven weeks, the seven weeks between November 22 and January 8, were therefore a period in which there took place in the capital of the greatest republic in the western world a remarkable demonstration of the passage of power, immense power—of its passing, in an instant, from one hand to another, and of its wielding by that new hand, in the first weeks after it closed on that power, with history-changing effectiveness. On one level, the passage was a demonstration of how, in very difficult circumstances (unique circumstances, circumstances for which there existed no precedents to provide guidance), to grasp the reins of a democratic government in a crisis created by the assassination of the head of state and hold the government stable, steady on its course. But this passage was a demonstration of the art of governing on a higher level than reassurance or stability. The higher use Lyndon Johnson made of these seven weeks—the use he made of the crisis: using it, using the transition, as a platform from which to launch a crusade for social justice on a vast new scale—made these weeks not only a dramatic and sorrowful but a pivotal moment in the history of the United States.

FOR LYNDON JOHNSON to have accomplished this, he had had to overcome governmental and political obstacles that had stood in the path of social justice for a century, and that for most of the last quarter of that century—since the last great liberal tide ran out in 1937—had been obstacles that could not be overcome: the congressional resistance and the power of the South that had blocked civil rights and social welfare legislation, for instance. And in addition he had had to overcome another obstacle that had nothing to do with government or politics, but only with himself.

So potent an aspect of his character had the fear of failure been throughout his life, for example, that it had all but paralyzed him in his attempt to reach for the presidency, no matter how deep his yearning for the office. When the office was suddenly thrust upon him, however, when there was suddenly no longer room for doubts or hesitation, when he had to *act*—he acted. If there were fears or doubts, no one saw them.

Gone from Lyndon Johnson during the transition also are the outward manifestations of other aspects of his personality that had been prominent at every other stage of his career. The frenetic, frantic, arm-waving, almost desperate demeanor that had characterized so much of his life was, during this transition period, replaced by a disciplined calmness. As for the alarm clock "inside him" that "told him at least once an hour . . . to go chew somebody out," to "blow his top"—it went off seldom if ever during this period. During these weeks, there was usually, in fact, an underlying note of courtesy when he asked an aide to perform some chore. And, as one aide said, "I've never seen him so composed." "Composed," "calm," "self-possessed," "humility," "self-discipline"—these were the words used to describe him during these weeks. The boastful, gloating quality was gone, even with enemies over whom he now had power. The words he "isn't President anymore. I am": during the transition did those words slip out more than once?—more than the single time he could not resist saying them (or a close

version of them) to Robert Kennedy? Other qualities that had always been prominent in him vanished, not only the bellowing, the jabbing of hands, the waving of
arms and the rushing of words that had invariably alienated audiences and made
his speeches ineffective, but deeper-rooted qualities as well. "Almost at once, the
whining self-pitying caricature of Throttlebottom vanished," George Reedy was
to write. "During this whole period, there was no trace of the ugly arrogance
which had made him so disliked in many quarters. . . . The situation brought out
the finest that was in him."

THE NECESSITY FOR SUBDUING these qualities—for keeping them under
control—may have been obvious to Lyndon Johnson as he assumed the presidency, so clear was it that they would prevent him from accomplishing his goals.
They would, for one thing, have made it more difficult for him in dealing with the
Kennedy Cabinet and White House staffers. A "yielding" nature had not been a
criterion for staff hiring in the Kennedy Administration; most Kennedy men, not
all but most, were, therefore, men who would not be amenable to his methods of
control. Having observed those methods, these men were determined not to submit themselves to them. Wary of signs that he might intend them to do so, they
might leave at the first hint that he would treat them as he treated Jenkins and
Reedy (as indeed the one member of the Kennedy team with whom Lyndon
Johnson *did* slip, Pierre Salinger, left as fast as he could). Other slips could trigger the "mass exodus" he feared. In dealing with the House and Senate, moreover, his usual methods wouldn't help, and might hurt, because a key method had
always been threats, and threats didn't work without power behind them, and
during these first weeks of his presidency, when he was still trying to understand
such fundamentals as the elements of the budget, and was operating against
deadlines—the Christmas recess, the budget-submission deadlines—that made
maneuvering difficult, he still hadn't consolidated his power sufficiently to use it
extensively in his relations with Congress.

Yet, obvious as may have been the necessity for subduing these qualities, for
him to subdue them must have been very difficult. They had not, after all, been
eliminated from his nature. They were still there, powerful as ever—as will be
seen, all too clearly, in the next volume of this work. Lyndon Johnson had grasped
in an instant what needed to be done with Kennedy's men and Kennedy's legislation: his insight into the crisis and the rapidity of his response to it a glimpse of
political genius almost shocking in its acuity and decisiveness. But the genius in
knowing what he needed to do was no more vital in the crisis than the self-
discipline and strength of will that enabled him to do it. Accomplishing what was
needed required him to subdue and to conceal elements of his nature that he had
never before concealed or subdued—elements so basic to his personality that they
had, in fact, governed his behavior during all of his previous life.

Yet he subdued them, overcame them, in a triumph not only of genius but of
will.

•   •   •

As I SAID at the beginning of this book, it is not an examination of Lyndon Johnson's entire presidency, but only of its first phase, and the longer story will be very different in tone. The interruptions in the *Life* and Senate Rules Committee investigations would be brief; Don Reynolds would soon be back in Senator Williams' office; by August *Life* would be running its "net worth" story, and newspapers would be running their own articles. And the tone would be different in other areas as well. The presidency of Lyndon Baines Johnson would be a presidency marked by victories: his great personal victory in the 1964 election, and his great victories for legislation that are the legislative embodiment of the liberal spirit in all its nobility. The Civil Rights Act of 1964. The Voting Rights Act of 1965. Medicare and Medicaid; Head Start; Model Cities. Government's hand to help people caught in "the tentacles of circumstance."

Yet victories would not, as it turned out, be the only hallmarks that would make the presidency of Lyndon Johnson vivid in history. "We Shall Overcome" were not the only words by which it will be remembered. *"Hey! Hey! LBJ! How many kids did you kill today?"* The choruses of the great civil rights hymns were not the only memorable choruses of the Lyndon Johnson years. *"Waist deep in the Big Muddy / And the big fool says to push on."* Fifty-eight thousand dead. Three hundred thousand wounded. The amputations, the blindness, the terrible scars of body and mind. Men looking down at the space where their legs used to be. And fifty-eight thousand and three hundred thousand are the numbers only of the American dead and wounded (not all of them during his presidency—the Vietnam War would continue more than four years after he left office—but virtually all of them after he escalated the war into an American war). The number of Vietnamese—South and North Vietnamese soldiers and civilians—killed and wounded is not in the tens of thousands or hundreds of thousands. It may be (no one has yet made a complete estimate) more than two million: men and women and children killed and maimed and burned alive, some by bombs dropped on villages selected as targets by Johnson himself, dropped by B-52s which flew so high that they were not only invisible but unheard from the ground, so that the people in the villages did not know they were in danger until the bombs hit.

Nor can the losses incurred during the Johnson presidency be measured only in numbers. "It is difficult . . . to remember, much less . . . to understand, the extent to which 'the President,' any President, was revered, respected," before Lyndon Johnson, Tom Wicker was to write shortly after Johnson's presidency ended; difficult to remember so thoroughly had respect and reverence for the institution disappeared during that presidency. It is difficult for most Americans today—more than forty years, two generations, after that presidency ended—to remember, or to understand, such reverence for a President, or for the institution of the presidency, so lasting has been the damage inflicted on it. While much of the damage was inflicted by Richard Nixon, Johnson's successor, it was under Johnson that the damage began.

The story of the presidency of Lyndon Johnson will be different in tone from the story of the transition in part because the elements of his personality absent during the transition were shortly to reappear. Yet for a period of time, a brief but crucial moment in history, he had held these elements in check, had overcome them, had, in a way, conquered himself. And by doing so, by overcoming forces within him that were very difficult to overcome, he not only had held the country steady during a difficult time but had set it on a new course, a course toward social justice. In the life of Lyndon Baines Johnson, this period stands out as different from the rest, as perhaps that life's finest moment, as a moment not only masterful but, in its way, heroic.

If he had held in check these forces within him, had conquered himself, for a while, he wasn't going to be able to do it for very long.

But he had done it long enough.

DEBTS
SOURCES
NOTES
INDEX

Debts

SOMETIMES, despite all my words, words fail me.

They fail me even when trying to acknowledge what my wife, Ina Caro, has done for this book. On all of my previous books she has been the whole team—the only person besides myself who has done research on the four volumes of *The Years of Lyndon Johnson* or on the biography of Robert Moses that preceded them, the only person I would ever trust to do so. During the years I have been working on this fourth volume, Ina wrote a second book of her own, and quite a wonderful one, too. And yet she was still the whole team, finding time not only to write her book but to do for my book the research in archives and libraries that she does so incomparably well. Words fail me in trying to acknowledge this. All I can say to my beloved idealist—in words from my heart—is "thank you."

I FIND MYSELF in a similar quandary when I try to find words to acknowledge what a group of other people have meant to me. Forty-two years ago—in 1970—I brought the half-completed manuscript of *The Power Broker* to the Alfred A. Knopf publishing house. Since that time, my editor—on all five of my books—has been Bob Gottlieb. I have tried before to express my gratitude for the generosity with which he has lavished his time and his talent, a unique editorial intelligence, on these books. He was just as generous with this book, and all I can do is to say, again from the heart, thank you.

With me on that first book was Katherine Hourigan, then a young assistant editor and now Knopf's managing editor. She has played a vital, indispensable role not only in the editing of these books, but in their production. Over the years she has come to be a great friend, a friend to my books and to me. I thank her for being such a friend.

In the room with me so many years ago was the agent who, in 1970, agreed to represent me: Lynn Nesbit. I have said about Lynn that "she has always been there when I need her." I can't find any words more fitting than that to thank her now.

All three of these immensely talented, energetic and dedicated people were there with me forty-two years ago, and they are with me today. That fact alone makes me a very lucky author.

THERE IS A FURTHER REASON that I consider myself lucky. Sonny Mehta, the president of Knopf, came to that publishing house in 1987. So he has been my publisher for only twenty-five years—a mere quarter of a century. In that time, they say, the world of publishing has changed. But, in his dealings with me, Sonny hasn't changed. Not once in twenty-five years has he asked me (or had anyone else ask me) when I am going to be finished with my book. I have literally never once—in forty-two years—heard that question at Knopf. Never once, as I have proposed expanding the number of volumes in *The Years of Lyndon Johnson* from three to four and now to five, has he presided over that expansion with anything other than encouragement, and indeed enthusiasm. Not many people in publishing, it seems to me, would have had the understanding and patience that Sonny has shown with me: an understanding of what I am trying to do with my books, and an understanding also that it might take a long time to do it.

PEOPLE AT KNOPF have meant the world to me. One is Andrew W. Hughes, Knopf's vice president of production and design, who has supervised the production of all four Johnson volumes. He has given me beautiful books, and I thank him for that. In addition, my insistence on rewriting, and rewriting, and rewriting—rewriting with my books in galleys and even in page proofs, even in the last stage of page proofs—has presented everyone at Knopf with daunting problems, and Andy somehow solves them. (As his father, Andrew L. Hughes, solved not only legal but literary problems for me during decades which began when I was a young investigative reporter at *Newsday,* and he was its attorney.) Thank you, Andys, both of you.

The comments Tony Chirico makes about my books are always perceptive, and his support of the whole Johnson project has meant more to me than I can easily express.

Others at Knopf have also been helping my books along for many years: Paul Bogaards, Anne Messitte, Nicholas Latimer, Russell Perreault, Carol Carson. As I walk around the halls of my publishing house, they seem filled with the friends of decades. (And they are filled for me also with the faces of friends no longer there: Bill Loverd and the late Nina Bourne.) For me, *The Years of Lyndon Johnson* has been a great journey, and all of you at Knopf have accompanied me on it. My gratitude also to Maria Massey, who was trapped by my insistence on editing and re-editing myself, and somehow overcame the obstacles I thus placed in her path. And to Lydia Buechler, Cassandra Pappas, Jessica Freeman-Slade and Vimi Santokhi.

ANOTHER COMPANION on every stage of the Johnson journey has been Claudia Wilson Anderson, supervisory archivist at the Lyndon Baines Johnson Library in Austin, Texas. She was at the library when Ina and I first arrived to start our research there in 1976, and her unparalleled knowledge of what is in the vast files there—forty-four million documents at last count—and the helpfulness with which she has always worked with Ina and me to find what we are looking for is a demonstration that, as I have said before, she is an historian in the highest sense of the word.

AT THE JOHNSON LIBRARY also I would like to thank Tina Houston, Linda Seelke, Barbara Cline, Ted Gittinger, Jennifer Cuddeback, Regina Greenwill, Allen Fisher, Bob Tissing, John Wilson, Laura Eggert, Lara Hall, Margaret Harmon, Chris Banks, Will Clements and Eric Cuellar.

ALTHOUGH THE FOCUS of this volume, unlike the last one, is not primarily on the Senate, there is a lot on the Senate in it, so again I must thank Donald A. Ritchie, the Senate historian, for years of help. No one knows the history of the Senate better than he, and he has put that knowledge at my right hand with a generosity that makes me once again deeply indebted to him.

His predecessor, Richard A. Baker, retired during the early stages of this book, but I am grateful to him, too, for his help.

CAROL SHOOKHOFF's tireless typing and retyping and deciphering of my manuscripts was an integral part of this book, as was her perceptive criticism.

JUDE WEBRE's assistance in obtaining newspaper and magazine articles, always quickly and cheerfully, from the Columbia University and other libraries was invaluable to me in doing this book.

Sources

A NOTE ON SOURCES

ANY RESEARCHER ATTEMPTING to re-create the period of Lyndon Johnson's life covered in this book must be very grateful to two of Johnson's staff members.

One is Walter Jenkins. The men closest to Johnson (not that anyone was ever really close to Lyndon Johnson)—his allies in Washington, Texas, New York and across the country—knew that if Johnson was on the Senate floor or otherwise unavailable, the way to get a message to him was by giving it to Jenkins. Jenkins would write it down—often verbatim: he had been a high school speedwriting champion back in Texas—on a yellow legal pad, and then would type up the messages (or have his assistant, Mildred Stegall, type them up) and hand them to Johnson at the first opportunity. These telephone transcript files, kept in the Lyndon Baines Johnson Library in Austin, Texas, in a collection labeled "Office Files of Walter Jenkins, Series 2," therefore furnish an authentic, sometimes almost minute-by-minute, picture of the information coming in to Johnson, and of his activities, in the years 1957 through 1964. In addition, during the years before Johnson routinely taped telephone calls, his method of obtaining a verbatim record of calls he considered important was to have Jenkins listen in on an extension—having first unscrewed the mouthpiece so that the person on the other end of the line couldn't hear him breathing—and take down the conversation. These conversations are in a collection at the Library labeled "Notes and Transcripts of Johnson Conversations." Johnson wanted these notes and transcripts kept indefinitely. When I asked Jenkins why none of them were ever thrown out, he replied that they were kept because "He [Johnson] wanted to remind them"—wanted to be able to recall, and to tell the people he had been talking with, what favors he had done for them, or what they had agreed on, for example. There are three boxes of the "Series 2" and "Notes and Transcripts" papers—or, by the Library's estimate of 800 pages per box—about 2,400 pages. Additional notes and transcripts can be found in other files—for the subjects being discussed—in the Johnson Senate Papers.

The other staff member from the period covered in this book who deserves history's special gratitude is George Reedy, a Lyndon Johnson assistant for fifteen years and, as readers of the last volume will recall, the assistant whom Johnson most relied on for strategic advice during the years of his Senate triumphs. Johnson once complained of Reedy, "When you ask George the time, he tells you how to make a watch," and it is true that his memoranda to Johnson often go into the background of the subject matter before getting to the point, and often make not a single point, but rather lay out all possible options, with analyses of each. Frustrating though this may have been for Reedy's boss, it is wonderful for the historian. The "Vice Presidential Aide's Files of George Reedy," which include not only his memos but the material he was working from and the attachments of such material he gave to Johnson along with the memos, fill forty-six boxes in the Johnson Library. Except for a handful or two of these boxes, they have all been opened to researchers. Other Reedy memos for the periods (before Johnson became Vice President and for the weeks following the assassination) that are also covered in this book—together with attached material—can be found in the Senate Political Files, the Johnson Senate Papers, and the early Presidential Papers, including the Diary Backup Files. While no one (including me) has counted the number of pages that have been opened in all of the Reedy files, the number may be in the area of forty thousand. I don't know how many of these pages I've read, but I've read a lot of them.

Another particularly valuable collection in the Johnson Library, especially for a researcher interested in Johnson's long-running fight with John F. Kennedy for the 1960 Democratic presidential nomination, is the Senate Political Files described below. The "Political Files" contain the office files and memoranda of various Johnson assistants, including not only Jenkins and Reedy but Colonel Kenneth E. BeLieu, Horace Busby, John Connally, Harry McPherson, Gerald Siegel and Warren Woodward. And then there are the various files, individually identified in the chapter notes, of memoranda and letters from such Johnson allies as Thomas G. (Tommy the Cork) Corcoran, Abe Fortas and James Rowe Jr.

Written material comprises only part of the sources for this book. Another part are my interviews with the people involved with Johnson during this period. For example, Walter Jenkins and I spent quite a bit of time together before his death in 1985. As for George Reedy, I describe my interviews with him in the Note on Sources for my previous volume, *Master of the Senate.* Often in my ears as I was writing *The Passage of Power* were the words I heard frequently in Reedy's gruff voice when, in my search for some additional piece of information, I would telephone him in the nursing home in Milwaukee to which he was confined: "I was hoping you would call back. One point I didn't make clear . . ."

Jenkins and Reedy—and so many other Johnson aides and allies—were generous with their time.

John Connally would not even respond to my requests for an interview during the seven years I was researching my first volume—a considerable loss to me, since Connally, in Johnson's estimation "the only man tough enough to handle Bobby Kennedy," was, until 1962, when he began his independent career in elective office by running for governor of Texas, the man who throughout Johnson's career had been the person Johnson turned to for advice and assistance with his most difficult problems. He was, moreover, Johnson's campaign manager in 1960. As I have noted previously, some two years after my first volume was published, "Governor Connally said he had read the book, and now wanted to talk to me at length. He told me that the only way in which he could free the requisite bloc of uninterrupted time would be at his ranch in South Texas. For three days there, we talked, from early in the morning until quite late at night, about his thirty-year association with Lyndon Johnson. Governor Connally had told me that he would answer any question I put to him, without exception. He was true to his word, and discussed with me—as indeed he also did at a subsequent lengthy interview—with considerable, and sometimes startling, frankness, perhaps a score of pivotal events in Lyndon Johnson's life in which he was a key participant. His interviews were especially valuable because, in more than one case, he [was] the only participant in those events still alive. I am all the more grateful to him because his silence about some of these events that he broke in talking to me was a silence that had lasted for decades."

As for Horace Busby, the line in the last letter he wrote to my wife, Ina, from a hospital in Santa Monica a few weeks before he died—"it will be hard on Robert, nobody else can tell him about the vice presidency"—was often in my mind during the time I was writing about those three sad years in Lyndon Johnson's life (even though Buzz *had* in fact talked to me at length about the vice presidency). I describe my interviews with Busby, too—scores of interviews—in the Note on Sources in *Master of the Senate.*

In attempting to learn about and describe Johnson's campaign for the presidency, I also made use of other files kept by Jenkins and other members of Johnson's staff that document what Johnson did with the information that was coming in.

The other basic source for Johnson's campaign for the presidency are my interviews with the people on Johnson's staff during this period: Jenkins himself (in a series of interviews with me before his death in 1985), Reedy, Busby, and Colonel Kenneth E. BeLieu, Yolanda Boozer, Ashton Gonella, Harry McPherson, Mary Rather and Siegel, and with Johnson's Washington allies Corcoran, Fortas and Rowe, and with Johnson's brother, Sam Houston Johnson, and with all the others cited in the chapter notes that follow.

I had not long begun researching the fight between Kennedy and Johnson for the 1960 nomination when I realized that the western and mountain states had been a key battleground, and that two of the key figures in the duel for those states had been, on the Johnson side, Irv Hoff, and on the Kennedy side, the clan's youngest brother, Ted. In 1960, then twenty-eight years old and a relative political novice, Edward M. Kennedy was initially assigned to those states because the Kennedys felt there was little chance of taking them away from Johnson. Luckily for me, both of these men were willing to talk with me at length about what transpired in the West. Senator Kennedy asked me what he could do to be truly help-ful to me. I said that if he really wanted to help, he would have someone find the notes, including notes on individual delegates, that he had been given by Kennedy headquarters and that he took out west with him, and go over them with me, so that I would know in detail what happened there. He did that: During a memorable weekend talking with me in his home in Washington, the senator went over his trip to the West (on which he first proved that, novice or not, he was a possessor of all the Kennedy political magic) state by state and almost delegate by delegate. As it happens, few of the specific incidents the senator recounted have made their way into the book, but the overall understanding he gave me of the battle informs, page after page, what I wrote. It does so because it tallies so perfectly with what the man working those states for the other side—the Johnson side—told me. Irvin Hoff was as generous with his time as Senator Kennedy was with his.

FOR THE ASSASSINATION of John F. Kennedy—the events of that day in Dallas and on Air Force One thereafter—there is, among the seemingly unending tor-rent of books and articles on the subject, also a basic foundational source in the Johnson Library: the reports that the Secret Service agents guarding Kennedy and Johnson typed up and submitted to Secret Service headquarters. Most of them are dated November 29, which meant that they were written within the week following the assassination, and are at least somewhat contemporaneous. Some are even more contemporaneous: for example, that of Special Agent George H. Hickey, which was written on November 22. Others, like that of Spe-cial Agent Glenn Bennett, were written the next day. Herschel Jacks, the driver of Johnson's car, wrote his on November 28. These reports are included in a grey binder labeled "CONFIDENTIAL—Report of the U.S. Secret Service on the Assassination of President Kennedy" that can be found in the "Special Files on the Assassination of President Kennedy" that the Johnson Library has compiled, and that are described below.

FOR THE KENNEDY SIDE of all these events, Theodore Sorensen was endlessly helpful to me. As I said at his Memorial Service,

I live on Central Park West, and Ted lived on Central Park West, and on my walk to and from my office I walked by his apartment.

I was interviewing him for my book, and some of these interviews we would have in the late afternoon. And sometimes I would be writing away at a scene in which he participated—either in the Kennedy White House, because that is part of this book, or during his period working for Johnson, and I would find that I hadn't quite understood something he had told me, or that I needed to ask about some little detail, and I would call him up to ask him, and he would say stop by after work, so again, I would come over in the late afternoon.

We would sit there and Ted would talk. He would be sitting on one sofa in the living room, and I would be on the other sofa facing him. The living room overlooked Central Park. It would be late afternoon. The light would start to fade. I would still have questions. Ted would answer them. The light would be fading, and across from me Ted would be talking—about the Cuban Missile Crisis, about civil rights, about so many things I needed to know about.

I didn't want him to stop, because I felt I was hearing something unique, something irreplaceable. He was not just answering, he was explaining. Because I hadn't been there, in the White House or at the ranch, and he had—and he wanted me to get it right.

When I asked a question, Ted never answered quickly, or glibly. He took his time answering, choosing his words. Sometimes he would say he wanted to think about what I had asked, and I should call him back the next day. Sometimes he himself would call, unsolicited because he wasn't satisfied with what he had said. I realized that he was taking a remarkable amount of time and trouble for me. I felt he was doing it because he believed it was important that he find the precise right words—because it was important that history got it right.

Among the other persons associated with John or Robert Kennedy whom I interviewed, especially helpful were John Culver, Jeff Greenfield, Nicholas deB. Katzenbach, John Seigenthaler, Jean Kennedy Smith and William vanden Heuvel. I must acknowledge that Ted, and probably some of the others, would not agree with everything I have written. But whatever success I have had in recreating accurately the events and persons about which I have written is due in large measure to the effort of these people to help me understand them.

AMONG OTHER INTERVIEWS which proved especially helpful were those with former senators Herman Talmadge of Georgia and Ralph W. Yarborough of Texas. I have described these interviews in the Note on Sources in *Master of the Senate.*

MOST OF JOHNSON'S STAFF MEMBERS have been extremely generous with their time and insights in helping me: BeLieu, Busby, Earl Deathe, Nadine Brammer Eckhardt, Marie Fehmer, Arthur Goldschmidt, Gonella, Richard Goodwin, Harold Pachios, Jenkins, Jim Jones, McPherson, Rather, Reedy, Siegel, Warren Woodward, George Christian; even Jack Valenti, for many years harshly critical of my work, at last decided to contribute to it. Two Johnson aides from the years covered by this book declined to speak with me: Bobby Baker and Bill Moyers. It's unfortunate for me that Moyers declined, because he would have been an important source. For years, he has spoken of writing a book himself about Johnson. Perhaps one day he will, and I can't wait to read it.

• • •

SEVERAL OTHER COLLECTIONS of papers have proved helpful in this volume. The papers of Richard B. Russell ("Russell Papers") at the Russell Library in Athens, Georgia, researched by Ina Caro, were as essential to this volume as they were to the last.

The "Donaghy Papers" refer to interviews conducted by Father Thomas J. Donaghy for his book, *Keystone Democrat: David Lawrence Remembered.* They are included in the Weber Papers, Archives Service Center, University of Pittsburgh.

The "Heinemann Papers" are the original notes of interviews Ronald L. Heinemann conducted and other research he carried out for his biography, *Harry Byrd of Virginia.* They are in Special Collections in the University of Virginia Library in Charlottesville, Virginia.

The "MacNeil Papers" are the notes taken, weekly memos sent to *Time* magazine's New York office, and other raw material of Neil MacNeil, *Time's* long-time congressional correspondent. He made a vast collection of this material available to me at his home.

When a citation refers to an "interview conducted by Katharine Graham," it means one of the interviews that Mrs. Graham conducted for her own book, *Personal History,* sometimes in conjunction with her assistant, Evelyn Small. Transcripts of those interviews were given to the author by Mrs. Graham.

The Theodore H. White Papers at the John F. Kennedy Library contain not only the manuscripts of his books but the notes of his interviews and other materials. It was Ina who researched the White Papers.

The John J. Williams Papers at the University of Delaware Library in Newark, Delaware, contain the original notes of the senator from Delaware's interviews of persons involved with the Bobby Baker investigation, including Don B. Reynolds.

HERE IS a description of the papers in the Johnson Library that form part of the foundation for this fourth volume—and an explanation of how they are identified in the Notes that follow.

Diary Backup: The formal title of these notes on Johnson's activities day by day is "President's Appointments File [Diary Backup]." It was known to his staff as "Diary Backup," and since that is a more accurate description of what it is, that is the title I am using.

Special Files on the Assassination of John F. Kennedy (Special File–Assassination): The file consists of original material and Xerox copies brought together from various White House and Vice Presidential files in 1967 at the time that William Manchester's book *The Death of a President* was published. It includes background material for the trip to Dallas, material on Johnson's activities and meetings after the assassination, statements to the Warren Commission, staff recollections, an analysis of the Manchester book by Jake Jacobsen, the FBI report on the assassination, and other material.

Senate Political Files (SPF): These files cover a time period from 1949 to 1960. They concern the consolidation of Johnson's position in Texas following the 1948 campaign; the 1954 Senate campaign; his 1956 bid for the presidency; and his bid in 1960 for the presidential nomination. They also contain numerous Texas county files that were made into a separate file by the Library staff.

Lyndon Baines Johnson Archives (LBJA): These files were created about 1958, and consist of material taken both from the House of Representatives Papers and from Johnson's Senate Papers. It consists of material considered historically valuable or of correspondence with persons with whom he was closely associated, such as Sam Rayburn, Abe Fortas, James Rowe, George and Herman Brown, Edward Clark, and Alvin Wirtz; or of correspondence with national figures of that era. These files are divided into four main categories:

1. Selected Names (LBJA SN): Correspondence with close associates.
2. Famous Names (LBJA FN): Correspondence with national figures.
3. Congressional File (LBJA CF): Correspondence with fellow congressmen and senators.
4. Subject File (LBJA SF): This contains a Biographic Information File, with material relating to Johnson's year as a schoolteacher in Cotulla and Houston; to his work as a secretary to Congressman Richard M. Kleberg; to his activities with the Little Congress; and to his naval service during World War II.

Pre-Presidential Confidential File (PPCF): This contains material taken from other files because it dealt with potentially sensitive areas.

Pre-Presidential Memo File (PPMF): This file consists of memos taken from the House of Representatives Papers, the Johnson Senate Papers, and the Vice Presidential Papers. While these memos begin in 1939 and continue through 1963, there are relatively few prior to 1946. While most are from the staff, some are from Johnson to the staff. The subject matter of the memos falls in numerous categories, ranging from specific issues, the 1948 Senate campaign, and liberal versus conservative factions in Texas, to phone messages and constituent relations.

White House Famous Names File (WHFN): This includes correspondence with former presidents and their families, including Johnson's correspondence when he was a congressman with Franklin D. Roosevelt.

Statements File of Lyndon B. Johnson (Statements File): A chronologically arranged file of speeches and remarks made by Lyndon B. Johnson throughout his career, together with speech drafts, memoranda, teleprompter texts, note cards, and other backup material, 1927–1972.

Vice Presidential Papers (VPP): The office files, correspondence, reports and other papers kept in Lyndon Johnson's Capitol and Executive Office Building offices between January 20, 1961, and November 22, 1963. This category includes the Office Files of George Reedy (Reedy and Colonel Howard Burris, but not the Office Files of Walter Jenkins, which contained material considered particularly sensitive and were kept separate from the other files by Jenkins and his personal secretary, Mildred Stegall.

Vice Presidential Office Files of George Reedy (Reedy OF).
Office Files of Walter Jenkins (OFWJ).

AUTHOR'S INTERVIEWS

Lola Aiken • David Alpern • Bonnie Angelo • James Anton • Rodney Baines • Richard A. Baker • Ross K. Baker • Inspector Leonard H. Ballard • Jean Douglas Bandler • Milton Barnwell • Robert Barr • Alan Barth • Joseph Bartlett • Robert T. Bartley • Melinda Baskin • Arnold Beichmann • Kenneth E. BeLieu • Merton Bernstein • James Bethke • Roland H. Bibolet • Andrew Biemiller • Rebekah Johnson Bobbitt • Richard Bolling • Paul Bolton • Yolanda Boozer • Bill Bradley • Jim Brady • T. Edward Braswell • Howard Bray • Jack Brooks • George W. Brown • Herbert Brownell • Horace W. Busby • Marcus Burg • Robert Byrd • Joseph Califano • Bob Camfiord • John Carlton • John Carver • James Casey • Louise Casparis • Emanuel Celler • John Chadwick • Brady Chapin • Zara Olds Chapin • Evelyn Chavoor • George Christian • Bethine Church • Blair Clark • Edward A. Clark • Ramsey Clark • Benjamin V. Cohen • Benjamin Cole •

W. Sterling Cole • James P. Coleman • John B. Connally • Nellie Connally • John Sherman Cooper • Thomas J. Corcoran • Ava Johnson Cox • Ohlen Cox • William (Corky) Cox • Anne Fears Crawford • William E. Cresswell • Cynthia Crider Crofts • Margaret Tucker Culhane • John Culver • Carl T. Curtis • Lloyd Cutler • Patrick Dahl • William H. Darden • Willard Deason • Earl Deathe • Harry Dent • John Dollahite • Oliver J. Dompierre • Helen Gahagan Douglas • Allen Drury • Ronnie Dugger • H. G. Dulaney • Lewis T. (Tex) Easley • Nadine Brammer Eckhardt • Julius G. C. Edelstein •Albert Eisele • Gerry Eller • Alan S. Emory • Grover Ensley • Rowland Evans • Creekmore Fath • Truman Fawcett • Marie Fehmer • Bernard J. Fensterwald • Thomas C. Ferguson • John Finney • O. C. Fisher • Gilbert C. Fite • Abe Fortas • Max Frankel • Emil Franks • William J. Fulbright • Barbara Gamarekian • Richard Gardner • David Garth • Jean Gavin • Sim Gideon • Michael L. Gillette • Tom Glazer • Stella Gliddon • Arthur J. Goldberg • Reuben Goldberg • Arthur (Tex) Goldschmidt • John Goldsmith • Glee Gomien • Ashton Gonella • William Goode • Doris Kearns Goodwin • Richard Goodwin • Katharine Graham • Ralph Graves • Kenneth Gray • Jack Greenberg • Robert F. Greene • Bailey Guard • John Gunther • Jack Gwyn • Jeff Gwyn • William Haddad • Arthur Hadley • David Halberstam • Estelle Harbin • D. B. Hardeman • Bryce Harlow • Lou Harris • Richard Helms • Russell Hemenway • Charles Herring • Don Hewitt • Betty Cason Hickman • Irvin Hoff • Robert Hollingsworth • Pat Holt • John Holton • Alice Hopkins • Welly K. Hopkins • Barbara Howar • Phyllis Hower • Ward Hower • Thomas Hughes • Dr. J. Willis Hurst • Patrick B. Hynes • Edouard V. M. Izac • Eliot Janeway • Elizabeth Janeway • Beth Jenkins • Walter Jenkins • Lady Bird Johnson • Sam Houston Johnson • Herman Jones • James Jones • Luther E. Jones • Gwen Jordan • William H. Jordan Jr. • Seth Kantor • Nicholas deB. Katzenbach • Carroll Keach • Chapman Kelly • Murray Kempton • Edward M. Kennedy • Mylton (Babe) Kennedy • Vann M. Kennedy • Eugene J. Keogh • Theodore W. Kheel • Joe M. Kilgore • Robert (Barney) Knispel • Fritz Koeniger • Louis Kohlmeier • Henry Kyle • Joseph Laitin • Brian Lamb • Jessie Lambert • William Lambert • Lansing Lamont • Joseph P. Lash • Trude Lash • Gene Latimer • Kitty Clyde Ross Leonard • Anthony Lewis • Peter Lewis • Evelyn Lincoln • Oliver Lindig • R. J. (Bob) Long • Kathleen Louchheim • Wingate Lucas • Peter Maas • Diana MacArthur • Neil MacNeil • George H. Mahon • Frank Mankiewicz • Gerald C. Mann • Caryl Marsh • Peter Maas • Maury Maverick Jr. • Margaret Mayer • Edward A. McCabe • Eugene J. McCarthy • Sarah McClendon • Richard T. McCulley • Frank C. McCulloch • Daniel J. McGillicuddy • George McGovern • Harry McPherson • Bill McPike • Dale Miller • Powell Moore • Ernest Morgan • Thomas B. Morgan • Robert Morgenthau • Edmund S. Muskie • Jack Newfield • Roger Newman • John Oakes • Patrick O'Connor • Kenneth O'Donnell • John Olds • Dr. Marianne Olds • Frank C. (Posh) Oltorf • Donald Oresman • Harold Pachios • Scott Peek • J. J. (Jake) Pickle • William Proxmire • Edward Puls • Julie Leininger Pycior • Carolina Longoria Quintanilla • Alexander Radin • Richard Rashke • Mary Rather • Joseph L. Rauh Jr. • Elwyn Rayden • Benjamin H. Read

• Cecil Redford • Emmette Redford • George Reedy • Abraham A. Ribicoff • Horace Richards • Floyd Riddick • John E. Rielly • Donald A. Ritchie • William P. Rogers • Jack Rosenthal • Irwin Ross • Elizabeth Rowe • James H. Rowe Jr. • Richard B. Russell III • Russell Sackett • Morley Safer • Darrell St. Claire • Ray Scherer • Arthur M. Schlesinger Jr. • Harry Schnibbe • Daniel Schorr • Budd Schulberg • John Seigenthaler • John Sharnick • Elizabeth A. Shedlick • Emmet Shelton • Norman Sherman • Howard E. Shuman • Hugh Sidey • Gerald L. Siegel • Bill Small • E. Babe Smith • Jean Kennedy Smith • Lon Smith • Carl Solberg • Bernard V. Somers • Theodore C. Sorensen • Natalie Springarn • Jerome Springarn • John Stacks • John L. Steele • Arthur Stehling • Alfred Steinberg • Philip M. Stern • Joe Stewart • John Stewart • Walter J. Stewart • Steve Stibbens • Richard Stolley • Cecil Stoughton • Elizabeth Stranigan • Clayton Stribling • Marsha Suisse • James L. Sundquist • Mimi Swartz • Stuart Symington • Herman Talmadge • George Tames • J. William Theis • Bernard R. Toon • Dr. Janet G. Travell • Marietta Tree • J. Mark Trice • Margaret Truman • Lyon L. Tyler • Stuart Udall • Donald Underwood • Jack Valenti • Frank Van der Linden • Ted van Dyk • Melwood W. Van Scoyoc • James Van Zandt • Cyrus Vance • William vanden Heuvel • Sander Vanocur • William Walton • Delbert C. Ward • Gerald Weatherly • Robert C. Weaver • O. J. Weber • Edwin Weisl Jr. • William Welsh • John Wheeler • Theodore H. White • Vernon Whiteside • Elizabeth Wickenden • Tom Wicker • Claude C. Wild Jr. • Willard Wirtz • Wendy Wolff • Claude E. Wood • Wilton Woods • Warren Woodward • Jim Wright • Ralph W. Yarborough • Harold H. Young • Mary Louise Young • Sam Zagoria • Murray Zweben

ORAL HISTORIES

Lyndon Baines Johnson Library, Austin, Texas

George D. Aiken, Carl B. Albert, Robert S. Allen, Stewart J. Alsop, Clinton P. Anderson, Eugenie M. Anderson, James Anton, Robert G. (Bobby) Baker, Malcolm Bardwell, Kenneth E. BeLieu, Levette J. (Joe) Berry, Roland Bibolet, Sherman Birdwell, Hugo Black, James H. Blundell, Charles K. Boatner, Hale Boggs, Charles E. Bohlen, Richard Bolling, Paul Bolton, T. Edward Braswell, Jack Brooks, Marietta Moody Brooks, Edmund G. Brown, George R. Brown, Richard Brown, Russell M. Brown, Raymond E. Buck, Anthony Buford, Waddy J. Bullion, Cecil E. Burney, Horace W. Busby, Bo Byers, James Cain, Joseph A. Califano, Elizabeth Carpenter, Leslie Carpenter, Clifton C. Carter, Clifford P. Case, John Brooks Casparis, S. Douglass Cater, Emanuel Celler, John Chancellor, Oscar L. Chapman, Warren M. Christopher, James E. Chudars, Frank Church, Ramsey Clark, Tom C. Clark, Earle C. Clements, Clark Clifford, Jacqueline Cochran, W. Sterling Cole, James P. Coleman, John B. Connally, Donald C. Cook, John Sherman Cooper, Thomas G. Corcoran, John J. Corson, Ava Johnson Cox, Ben Crider, Otto Crider, Ernest Cuneo, Carl T. Curtis, Lloyd N. Cutler, Price Daniel, Jonathan Daniels, William H. Darden, Sid Davis, Homer E. Dean, Willard Deason, Marjorie Delafield, Claude J. Desautels, Nancy Dickerson, Ralph Dungan, Dudley T. Dougherty, Helen Gahagan Douglas, Paul H. Douglas, David Dubinsky, Clifford and Virginia Durr, Virginia Durr, Frederick G. Dutton, L. T. (Tex) Easley, James O. Eastland, India Edwards, Louise Casparis Edwards, Allen J. Ellender, Roy Elson, Virginia Wilke English, James Farmer, Truman and Wilma G. Fawcett, Marie Fehmer (Chiarodo), Tom C. Ferguson, Thomas K. Finletter, Elaine Fischesser, Adrian S. Fisher, O. C. Fisher, Sam Fore Jr., Mrs. Sam

Fore Jr., Abe Fortas, Joe B. Frantz, Orville Freeman, Gordon Fulcher, Hector T. Garcia, Reynaldo G. Garza, Eugene B. Germany, Olga Bredt Gideon, W. Sim Gideon, Arthur J. Goldberg, Irving L. Goldberg, Arthur and Elizabeth Goldschmidt, Elizabeth Wickenden Goldschmidt, E. Ernest Goldstein, Ashton Gonella, Callan Graham, Katharine Graham, Josh H. Groce, William Haddad, Walter G. Hall, Estelle Harbin, D. B. Hardeman, Robert Hardesty, Bryce Harlow, Mary Michelson Fish Haselton, Mrs. Jessie Hatcher, Carl Hayden, Walter W. Heller, Richard M. Helms, Charles Herring, Bourke B. Hickenlooper, Betty Cason Hickman, Jack Hight, Lister Hill, Mrs. Oveta Culp Hobby, Luther H. Hodges Sr., John Holton, Welly K. Hopkins, Welly K. and Alice Hopkins, Ardis C. Hopper, Walter Hornaday, Solis Horwitz, Hubert Humphrey, J. Willis Hurst, Henry M. Jackson, Robert M. Jackson, Jake Jacobsen, W. Ervin (Red) James, Leon Jaworski, Walter Jenkins, Alfred T. (Boody) Johnson, Claudia Taylor Johnson, Sam Houston Johnson, Luther E. Jones Jr., Marvin Jones, William H. Jordan Jr., William J. Jorden, Edward Joseph, Nicholas deB. Katzenbach, Carroll Keach, Jesse Kellam, Edward M. Kennedy, Mylton L. Kennedy, Carroll Kilpatrick, Sam Kinch Sr., Robert Kintner, William Knowland, John Fritz Koeniger, Joseph Laitin, Eugenia Boehringer Lasseter, Gene Latimer, Ray Lee, Erich Leinsdorf, Kittie Clyde Leonard, Gould Lincoln, Otto Lindig, C. P. Little, R. J. (Bob) Long, Russell Long, Stuart M. Long, J. C. Looney, Kathleen C. Louchheim, John E. Lyle Jr., Warren Magnuson, George Mahon, Mike Manatos, Frank Mankiewicz, Gerald C. Mann Sr. and Jr., Stanley Marcus, Leonard Marks, Thurgood Marshall, Joe Mashman, Margaret Mayer, Vicky McCammon, Eugene McCarthy, Sarah McClendon, Frank McCulloch, Ernest W. McFarland, Simon McHugh, Marshall McNeil, Harry McPherson, George Meany, Harris Melasky, Dale and Virginia (Scooter) Miller, Newton Minow, Clarence Mitchell, A. S. (Mike) Monroney, Booth Mooney, Powell Moore, A. W. Moursund, Robert W. Murphey, James P. Nash, Dorothy J. Nichols, Lawrence F. O'Brien, Kenneth O'Donnell, Robert Oliver, Frank C. (Posh) Oltorf, Thomas P. (Tip) O'Neill, Hal Pachios, Wright Patman, James Cato Pattillo, Edwin W. Pauley, Harvey O. Payne, Drew Pearson, Arthur C. Perry, Carl L. Phinney, Robert L. Phinney, J. J. (Jake) Pickle, W. Robert Poage, Ella SoRelle Porter, Paul A. Porter, Harry Provence, William Proxmire, Graham Purcell, Daniel J. Quill, Mary Rather, Joseph L. Rauh Jr., Benjamin H. Read, Cecil Redford, Clarence Redford, Emmette S. Redford, George E. Reedy Jr., Horace E. Richards, Chalmers M. Roberts, Charles Roberts, Juanita Roberts, A. Willis Robertson, Fenner Roth, Payne Rountree, Elizabeth Rowe, James M. Rowe, Luis Salas, Leverett Saltonstall, Harold Barefoot Sanders, Josefa Baines Saunders, Norbert A. Schlei, Arthur Schlesinger, Emmett Shelton, Polk and Nell Shelton, Hugh Sidey, Gerald W. Siegel, Ivan Sinclair, George A. Smathers, Bromley K. Smith, Carol Davis Smith, E. Babe Smith, Margaret Chase Smith, Anthony M. Solomon, John Sparkman, Adrian A. Spears, Richard Spinn, Max and Evelyn Starcke, Arthur Stehling, John C. Stennis, Sam V. Stone, Robert Storey, Cecil Stoughton, O. B. Summy, James L. Sundquist, Stuart Symington, Herman E. Talmadge, Hobart Taylor Jr., Willie Day Taylor, J. William Theis, Donald S. Thomas, Homer Thornberry, Strom Thurmond, Bascom N. Timmons, Grace Tully, Stewart L. Udall, Jack Valenti, Mary Margaret Wiley Valenti, Cyrus R. Vance, Carl Vinson, H. Jerry Voorhis, Earl Warren, O. J. Weber, Harfield Weedin, Edwin L. Weisl Jr., Edwin L. Weisl Sr., Wesley West, June White (Mrs. William S. White), William S. White, R. Vernon Whiteside, Gerri Whittington, Tom G. Wicker, Claude C. Wild Sr., James Russell Wiggins, Roger W. Wilkins, Roy Wilkins, Eugene and Helen Williams, Glen and Marie Wilson, Mrs. Alvin J. Wirtz, Wilton Woods, Wilton and Virginia Woods, Warren G. Woodward, Eugene Worley, James C. Wright Jr., Zephyr Wright, Milton R. Young

John F. Kennedy Library, Boston, Massachusetts

Jack Conway, Joseph Dolan, Fred Dutton, Peter Edelman, John English, Myer Feldman, Jeff Greenfield, Edwin Guthman, Milton Gwirtzmann, Louis Harris, Hubert Humphrey, Nicholas deB Katzenbach, Robert F. Kennedy, Marjorie Lawson, Peter Lisagor, Burke Marshall, John Nolan, James Rowe, Pierre Salinger, John Seigenthaler, Theodore Sorenson, Charles Spalding, Joseph Tydings, Adam Walinsky, Bill Walton

United States Senate Oral History Program, Senate Historical Office

Leonard H. Ballard, Roy L. Elson, Grover W. Ensley, Pat M. Holt, Carl M. Marcy, Stewart E. McClure, Jesse R. Nichols, Scott I. Peek, Warren Featherstone Reid, Floyd M. Riddick, Darrell St. Claire, Dorothye G. Scott, Howard E. Shuman, George A. Smathers, George Tames, J. William Theis, Rein J. Vanderzee

Dwight D. Eisenhower Library, Abilene, Kansas

George Aiken, Jack Z. Anderson, John Bricker, Herbert Brownell, Prescott Bush, Ralph Flanders, Barry Goldwater, Andrew J. Goodpaster, Homer Gruenther, Bryce Harlow, Robert C. Hill, Jacob Javits, Kenneth B. Keating, William F. Knowland, Edward A. McCabe, L. Arthur Minnich, Gerald Morgan, E. Frederick Morrow, Maxwell Rabb

Sam Rayburn Library, Bonham, Texas

Carl Albert, Robert S. Allen, Robert T. Bartley, John Brademas, Cecil Dickson, H. G. Dulaney, John Holton, Walter K. Jenkins, Lady Bird Johnson

Richard Brevard Russell Memorial Library, University of Georgia, Athens, Georgia

Harry F. Byrd Jr., Robert Byrd, Lawton Miller Calhoun, John Thomas Carlton, Earl Cocke Jr., George W. Darden, William H. Darden, Robert Mark Dunahoo, James O. Eastland, Allen Ellender, Sam J. Ervin Jr., Luck Coleman Flanders Gambrell, Spenser M. Grayson, Mary Willie Russell Green, Roy Vincent Harris, Roman Lee Hruska, Hubert H. Humphrey, Lady Bird Johnson, Felton Johnston, Wayne P. Kelly Jr., Earl T. Leonard, Russell B. Long, Mike Mansfield, Powell Moore, Richard Nixon, Patience Russell Peterson, William Proxmire, Barboura Raesly, Dean Rusk, Fielding B. Russell, Reverend Henry Edward Russell, Leverett Saltonstall, Carl Sanders, George Smathers, Clara Smith, Jack Spain, Ina Russell Stacy, Betty Talmadge, Strom Thurmond, Robert Troutman Jr., Samuel E. Vandiver Jr., Cash Williams,

BOOKS CITED IN NOTES

Alsop, Joseph W., with Adam Platt. *"I've Seen the Best of It": The Memoirs of Joseph W. Alsop*. New York: W. W. Norton, 1991.

Amrine, Michael. *This Awesome Challenge: The Hundred Days of Lyndon Johnson*. New York: Putnam, 1964.

Ashby, LeRoy, and Rod Gramer. *Fighting the Odds: The Life of Senator Frank Church*. Pullman: Washington State University Press, 1994.

Aune, James Arnt, and Enrique d. Rigsby, eds. *Civil Rights Rhetoric and the American Presidency*. College Station, Tex.: TAMU Press, 2005.

Baker, Bobby, with Larry L. King. *Wheeling and Dealing: Confessions of a Capitol Hill Operator*. New York: W. W. Norton, 1978.

Baker, Leonard. *The Johnson Eclipse: A President's Vice Presidency*. New York: Macmillan Company, 1966.

Baker, Russell. *The Good Times*. New York: William Morrow, 1989.

Beschloss, Michael R., ed. *Taking Charge: The Johnson White House Tapes, 1963–1964*. New York: Simon & Schuster, 1997.

Bird, Kai. *The Color of Truth: McGeorge Bundy and William Bundy; Brothers in Arms*. New York: Simon & Schuster, 1998.

Bishop, Jim. *The Day Kennedy Was Shot*. New York: Funk & Wagnalls, 1968.

Blair, Joan, and Clay Blair Jr. *The Search for JFK*. New York: Berkeley Putnam, 1976.

Bradlee, Benjamin C. *Conversations with Kennedy*. New York: W. W. Norton, 1984.

Bradlee, Ben. *A Good Life: Newspapering and Other Adventures*. New York: Simon & Schuster, 1996.

Branch, Taylor. *Pillar of Fire: America in the King Years 1963–65*. New York: Simon & Schuster, 1998.

Buenger, Walter L., and Joseph A. Pratt. *But also Good Business: Texas Commerce Banks and the Financing of Houston and Texas, 1886–1986*. College Station, Tex.: Texas A&M University, 1986.

Bugliosi, Vincent. *Reclaiming History: The Assassination of President John F. Kennedy*. New York: W. W. Norton, 2007.

Bullion, John L. *In the Boat with LBJ*. Plano, Tex.: Republic of Texas Press, 2001.

Bundy, McGeorge. *Danger and Survival:*

Choices about the Bomb in the First Fifty Years. New York: Random House, 1988.

Burns, James MacGregor. *The Deadlock of Democracy: Four-Party Politics in America.* Englewood Cliffs, N.J.: Prentice-Hall, 1963.

Burns, James MacGregor. *John Kennedy: A Political Profile.* New York: Harcourt, Brace & World, 1961.

Busby, Horace. *The Thirty-first of March: An Intimate Portrait of Lyndon Johnson's Final Days in Office.* New York: Farrar, Straus and Giroux, 2005.

Byrd, Robert C. *The Senate, 1789–1989, Vol. I: Addresses on the History of the United States Senate,* rev. ed. Washington, D.C.: U.S. Government Printing Office, 1989.

Califano, Joseph A. *The Triumph and Tragedy of Lyndon Johnson: The White House Years.* New York: Simon & Schuster, 1991.

Caro, Robert A. *Master of the Senate: The Years of Lyndon Johnson,* Vol. III. New York, Knopf, 2002.

Caro, Robert A. *Means of Ascent: The Years of Lyndon Johnson,* Vol. II. New York: Knopf, 1990.

Caro, Robert A. *The Path to Power: The Years of Lyndon Johnson,* Vol. I. New York: Knopf, 1982.

Chafe, William H. *Private Lives/Public Consequences: Personality and Politics in Modern America.* Cambridge, Mass.: Harvard University Press, 2005.

Chandler, David Leon. *The Natural Superiority of Southern Politicians: A Revisionist History.* Garden City, N.Y.: Doubleday, 1977.

Clifford, Clark, with Richard Holbrooke. *Counsel to the President: A Memoir.* New York: Random House, 1991.

Collier, Peter, and David Horowitz. *The Kennedys: An American Drama.* San Francisco: Encounter Books, 2002.

Connally, John, with Mickey Herskowitz. *In History's Shadow: An American Odyssey.* New York: Hyperion, 1993.

Connally, Nellie, and Mickey Herskowitz. *From Love Field: Our Final Hours with President John F. Kennedy.* New York: Rugged Land, 2003.

Cormier, Frank. LBJ: *The Way He Was—A Personal Memoir of the Man and His Presidency.* Garden City, N.Y.: Doubleday, 1977.

Cotton, Norris. *In the Senate: Amidst the Conflict and the Turmoil.* New York: Dodd, Mead, 1978.

Council of Economic Advisers. *Economic Report of the President, Together with the Annual Report of the Council of Economic Advisers, Transmitted to the Congress, January 1964.* Washington, D.C.: Government Printing Office, 1964.

Dallek, Robert. *An Unfinished Life: John F. Kennedy, 1917–1963.* Boston: Little, Brown, 2003.

Dallek, Robert. *Flawed Giant: Lyndon B. Johnson and His Times, 1961–1973.* New York: Oxford University Press, 1998.

Dallek, Robert. *Lone Star Rising: Lyndon Johnson and His Times, 1908–1960.* New York: Oxford University Press, 1991.

Damore, Leo. *The Cape Cod Years of John Fitzgerald Kennedy.* New York: Four Walls Eight Windows, 1993.

Dickerson, Nancy. *Among Those Present.* New York: Random House, 1976.

Divine, Robert A., ed. *The Johnson Years,* Vol. II: *Vietnam, the Environment, and Science.* Lawrence, Kans.: University Press of Kansas, 1987.

Donaghy, Thomas J. *Keystone Democrat: David Lawrence Remembered.* New York: Vantage Press, 1986.

Donovan, Robert J. *PT-109: John F. Kennedy in World War II.* New York: Fawcett, 1961.

Dorough, C. Dwight. *Mr. Sam.* New York: Random House, 1962.

Douglas, Paul H. *In the Fullness of Time: The Memoirs of Paul H. Douglas.* New York: Harcourt Brace Jovanovich, 1972.

Douglass, James W. *JFK and the Unspeakable: Why He Died and Why It Matters.* Maryknoll, N.Y.: Oebis, 2008.

Dressman, Fran. *Gus Wortham: Portrait of a Leader.* College Station, Tex.: TAMU Press, 1994.

Dugger, Ronnie. *The Politician: The Life and Times of Lyndon Johnson.* New York: Norton, 1982.

Eisele, Albert. *Almost to the Presidency: A Biography of Two American Politicians.* Piper Publishing, 1979.

Evans, Rowland, and Robert Novak. *Lyndon B. Johnson: The Exercise of Power.* New York: New American Library, 1966.

Fay, Paul B., Jr. *The Pleasure of His Company: The Story of a Twenty-One-Year Friendship with John F. Kennedy from His Days in the Pacific through His Years in the White House.* New York: Harper & Row, 1966.

Feerick, John D. *From Failing Hands: The Story of Presidential Succession.* Bronx, N.Y.: Fordham University Press, 1965.

Fite, Gilbert C. *Richard B. Russell, Jr., Senator from Georgia.* Chapel Hill: University of North Carolina Press, 1991.

Freeman, Orville. "A Cabinet Perspective." In Kenneth W. Thompson, ed., *The Johnson Presidency:* Twenty Intimate Perspectives of Lyndon B. Johnson (Portraits of American Periodicals). Lanham, Md.: University Press of America, 1986.

Friedman, Leon, ed. *The Civil Rights Reader:*

Basic Documents of the Civil Rights Movement. New York: Walker and Company, 1968.

Galloway, George B. *The Legislative Process in Congress*. New York: Crowell, 1953.

Garside, Anne. *Camelot at Dawn: Jacqueline and John Kennedy in Georgetown, May 1954*. Baltimore: Johns Hopkins Press, 2001.

Gibbons, William Conrad. *U.S. Government and the Vietnam War: Executive and Legislative Roles and Relationships, Part 2: 1961–1964*. Princeton, N.J.: Princeton University Press, 1986.

Giglio, James N. *The Presidency of John F. Kennedy* (American Presidency Series). Lawrence, Kans.: University Press of Kansas, 1991.

Gilbert, Robert E. *The Mortal Presidency: Illness and Anguish in the White House*. New York: Fordham University Press, 1998.

Gillette, Michael L. *Launching the War on Poverty: An Oral History*, 2nd ed. New York: Oxford University Press, 2010.

Goldfarb, Ronald L. *Perfect Villains, Imperfect Heroes: Robert Kennedy's War Against Organized Crime*. New York: Random House, 1995.

Goldman, Eric F. *The Tragedy of Lyndon Johnson*. New York: Knopf, 1964.

Goldsmith, John A. *Colleagues: Richard Russell and His Apprentice Lyndon B. Johnson*. Santa Ana, Calif.: Seven Locks Press, 1993.

Goodwin, Doris Kearns. *The Fitzgeralds and the Kennedys: An American Saga*. New York: Simon & Schuster, 1987.

Goodwin, Doris Kearns. *Lyndon Johnson and the American Dream*. New York: Harper & Row, 1976.

Goodwin, Doris Kearns. *Team of Rivals: The Political Genius of Abraham Lincoln*. New York: Simon & Schuster, 2005.

Goodwin, Richard. *Remembering America: A Voice from the Sixties*. Boston: Little, Brown, 1998.

Graff, Henry F., ed. *The Presidents: A Reference History*. New York: Scribner Book Company, 1996.

Greenberg, David, and *Cabinet* Magazine. *Presidential Doodles: Two Centuries of Scribbles, Scratches, Squiggles, and Scrawls from the Oval Office*. New York: Basic Books, 2007.

Greenberg, Bradley S., and Edwin B. Parker, eds. *The Kennedy Assassination and the American Public: Social Communication in Crisis*. Stanford, Calif.: Stanford University Press, 1965.

Gunther, John. *Inside U.S.A.* New York: Harper & Bros., 1947.

Guthman, Edwin O. *We Band of Brothers: A Memoir of Robert F. Kennedy*. New York: Harper & Row, 1971.

Guthman, Edwin O., and Jeffrey Shulman, eds. *Robert Kennedy: In His Own Words — The Unpublished Recollections of the Kennedy Years*. New York: Bantam, 1991.

Hamilton, Nigel. *JFK: Reckless Youth*. New York: Random House, 1991.

Hardeman, D. B., and Donald C. Bacon. *Rayburn: A Biography*. Austin: Texas Monthly Press, 1987.

Harrington, Michael. *The Other America: Poverty in the United States*. New York: Macmillan, 1963.

Hatfield, Mark O., and Wendy Wolff, eds. *Vice Presidents of the United States, 1789–1993*. Washington, D.C.: U.S. Government Printing Office, 1997.

Heinemann, Ronald. *Harry Byrd of Virginia*. Charlottesville: University Press of Virginia, 1996.

Heren, Louis. *No Hail, No Farewell*. New York: Harper, 1970.

Hersh, Seymour M. *The Dark Side of Camelot*. Boston: Little, Brown, 1997.

Hoffecker, Carol E. *Honest John Williams: U.S. Senator from Delaware*. Newark, Del.: University of Delaware Press, 2000.

Holland, Max. *The Kennedy Assassination Tapes*. New York: Knopf, 2004.

Humphrey, Hubert. *The Education of a Public Man: My Life and Politics*. Garden City, N.Y.: Doubleday, 1976.

Hurst, J. Willis, and James C. Cain. *LBJ: To Know Him Better*. Austin: LBJ Library, 1995.

Johnson, Lady Bird. *A White House Diary*. New York: Holt Rinehart & Winston, 1970.

Johnson, Lyndon B. *Public Papers of the Presidents of the United States: Lyndon B Johnson (Containing the Public Messages, Speeches, and Statements of the President 1965) in two volumes*. Washington, D.C.: United States Government Printing Office, 1966.

Johnson, Lyndon Baines. *The Vantage Point: Perspectives of the President, 1963–1969*. New York: Holt, Rinehart and Winston, 1971.

Johnson, Sam Houston. *My Brother Lyndon*. New York: Cowles Book Company, 1970.

Kalman, Laura. *Abe Fortas: A Biography*. New Haven: Yale University Press, 1990.

Katzenbach, Nicholas deB. *Some of It Was Fun: Working with RFK and LBJ*. New York: W. W. Norton, 2008.

Kennedy, Robert F. *Thirteen Days: A Memoir of the Cuban Missile Crisis*. New York: W. W. Norton, 1969.

Kotz, Nick. *Judgment Days: Lyndon Baines Johnson, Martin Luther King Jr., and the Laws That Changed America*. Boston: Houghton Mifflin, 2005.

Lasky, Victor. J.F.K.: *The Man and the Myth.* New York: Macmillan, 1963.

Lemann, Nicholas. *The Promised Land: An Account of Sharecropping Families in Their Journey from the Mississippi Delta to Chicago.* New York: Knopf, 1991.

Lincoln, Evelyn. *Kennedy and Johnson.* New York: Holt, Rinehart and Winston, 1968.

Logevall, Fredrik. *Choosing War: The Lost Chance for Peace and the Escalation of War in Vietnam.* Berkeley and Los Angeles: University of California Press, 1999.

Lyons, Louis M. (ed.). *Reporting the News: Selections from Nieman Reports.* Cambridge, Mass.: Belknap Press of Harvard University Press, 1965.

Manchester, William. *The Death of a President: November 1963.* New York: Harper & Row, 1967.

Mann, Robert. *The Walls of Jericho: Lyndon Johnson, Hubert Humphrey, Richard Russell, and the Struggle for Civil Rights.* New York: Harcourt Brace, 1996.

Martin, Ralph G. *A Hero for Our Time: An Intimate Story of the Kennedy Years.* New York: Scribner, 1983.

Matusow, Allen J. *The Unraveling of America: A History of Liberalism in the 1960s.* New York: Harper & Row, 1984.

McCullough, David. *John Adams.* New York: Simon & Schuster, 2001.

McCullough, David G. *Truman.* New York: Simon & Schuster, 1992.

McPherson, Harry. *A Political Education.* Boston: Little, Brown, 1972.

Middleton, Harry. *LBJ: The White House Years.* New York: Harry N. Abrams, 1990.

Miller, Merle. *Lyndon: An Oral Biography.* New York: Putnam, 1980.

Mollenhoff, Clark. *Despoilers of Democracy.* Garden City, N.Y.: Doubleday, 1965.

Mooney, Booth. *LBJ: An Irreverent Chronicle.* New York: Crowell, 1976.

Murphy, Bruce Allen. *Fortas: The Rise and Ruin of a Supreme Court Justice.* New York: Random House, 1991.

MacNeil, Neil. *Dirksen: Portrait of a Public Man.* New York: World Pub. Co., 1970.

Newseum, with Cathy Trost and Susan Bennett. *President Kennedy Has Been Shot.* Naperville, Ill.: Sourcebooks MediaFusion, 2003.

Neustadt, Richard E. *Presidential Power: The Politics of Leadership from F.D.R. to Carter.* New York: John Wiley, 1976.

O'Brien, Lawrence F. *No Final Victories: A Life in Politics from John F. Kennedy to Watergate.* Garden City, N.Y.: Doubleday, 1974.

O'Brien, Michael. *John F. Kennedy: A Biography.* New York: Thomas Dunne Books, 2005.

O'Donnell, Kenneth P. and David F. Powers, with Joe McCarthy. *"Johnny, We Hardly Knew Ye": Memories of John Fitzgerald Kennedy.* Boston: Little, Brown, 1972.

O'Neill, Thomas, and William Novak. *Man of the House: The Life and Political Memoirs of Speaker Tip O'Neill.* New York: Random House, 1987.

Parmet, Herbert S. *Jack: The Struggles of John F. Kennedy.* New York: Dial, 1980.

Patterson, James T. *Grand Expectations: The United States, 1945–1974.* Oxford History of the United States. New York: Oxford University Press, 1996.

Pauley, Garth E. "The Genesis of a Rhetorical Commitment." In James Arnt Aune and Enrique D. Rigsby, eds., *Civil Rights Rhetoric and the America Presidency,* pp. 155–97.

Pauley, Garth E. *LBJ's American Promise: The 1965 Voting Rights Address.* College Station, Tex.: A&M University Press, 2007.

Pearson, Drew, and Jack Anderson. *The Case against Congress: A Compelling Indictment of Corruption on Capitol Hill.* New York: Simon & Schuster, 1968.

The Presidential Recordings: John F. Kennedy—The Great Crises. 3 vols. Edited by Timothy Naftali, Ernest May, and Philip D. Zelikow. New York: W. W. Norton, 2001.

The Presidential Recordings: Lyndon B. Johnson: The Kennedy Assassination and the Transfer of Power: November 1963–January 1964. 3 vols. Edited by the Miller Center, Kent Germany, Max Holland, Robert David Johnson, and David Shreve. New York: W. W. Norton, 2005.

Public Papers of the Presidents: Lyndon B. Johnson, 1963–64. Washington, D.C.: Government Printing Office, 1965.

Reedy, George. *Lyndon B. Johnson: A Memoir.* New York: Andrews & McMeel, 1982.

Reedy, George E. *The U.S. Senate: Paralysis or a Search for Consensus?* New York: Crown, 1986.

Reeves, Richard. *President Kennedy: Profile of Power.* New York: Simon & Schuster, 1993.

Reston, James, Jr. *The Lone Star: The Life of John Connally.* New York: Harper & Row, 1989.

Ripley, Randall B. *Kennedy and Congress.* General Learning Press, 1972.

Roberts, Charles. *The Truth about the Assassination.* New York: Grosset & Dunlap, 1967.

Rowan, Carl T. *Breaking Barriers: A Memoir.* Boston: Little, Brown, 1991.

Rowe, Robert. *The Bobby Baker Story.* Berkeley, Calif.: Parallax Publishing, 1967.

Rubin, Gretchen. *Forty Ways to Look at JFK.* New York: Ballantine Books, 2005.

Russell, Jan Jarboe. *Lady Bird: A Biography of Mrs. Johnson.* New York: Scribner, 1999.

Salinger, Pierre. *P.S.: A Memoir.* New York: St. Martin's Press, 1995.

Salinger, Pierre. *With Kennedy.* Garden City, N.Y.: Doubleday, 1996.

Schaap, Dick. *R.F. K.* New York: New American Library, 1967.

Schlesinger, Arthur M. *A Thousand Days: John F. Kennedy in the White House.* Boston: Houghton Mifflin, 1964.

Schlesinger, Arthur M. *The Cycles of American History.* Boston: Houghton Mifflin, 1986.

Schlesinger, Arthur M., Jr. *Journals: 1952–2000.* New York: Penguin Press, 2007.

Schlesinger, Arthur M., Jr. *Robert Kennedy and His Times.* Boston: Houghton Mifflin, 1978.

Schramm, Wilbur. "Communication in Crisis." In Bradley S. Greenberg and Edwin B. Parker, eds. *The Kennedy Assassination and the American Public: Social Communication in Crisis.* Stanford, Calif.: Stanford University Press, 1965.

Sheatsley, Paul B., and Jacob J. Feldman. "A National Survey on Public Relations and Behavior." In Bradley S. Greenberg, and Edwin B. Parker, eds. *The Kennedy Assassination and the American Public: Social Communication in Crisis,* pp. 149–77. Stanford, Calif.: Stanford University Press, 1965.

Shesol, Jeff. *Mutual Contempt: Lyndon Johnson, Robert Kennedy, and the Feud That Defined a Decade.* New York: W. W. Norton, 1998.

Sidey, Hugh. *A Very Personal Presidency: Lyndon Johnson in the White House.* New York: Atheneum, 1968.

Sidey, Hugh. *John F. Kennedy, President: A Reporter's Inside Story.* New York: Atheneum, 1963.

Smith, Jeffrey K. *Bad Blood: Lyndon B. Johnson, Robert F. Kennedy, and the Tumultuous 1960s.* Bloomington, Ind.: Author House, 2010.

Smith, Sally Bedell. *Grace and Power: The Private World of the Kennedy White House.* New York: Random House, 2004.

Solberg, Carl. *Hubert Humphrey: A Biography.* New York: W. W. Norton, 1984.

Sorensen, Ted. *Counselor: A Life at the Edge of History.* New York: Harper, 2008.

Sorensen, Theodore C. *Kennedy.* New York: Harper & Row, 1965.

Sorensen, Theodore C. *The Kennedy Legacy.* New York: Macmillan, 1993.

Stein, Jean, and George Plimpton. *American Journey: The Times of Robert F. Kennedy.* New York: Harcourt Brace Jovanovich, 1970.

Steinberg, Alfred. *Sam Johnson's Boy: A Close-Up of the President from Texas.* New York: Macmillan Co., 1968.

Steinberg, Alfred. *Sam Rayburn.* New York: Hawthorn Books, 1975.

Texas Almanac, 1961–1962. Dallas: Dallas Morning News.

Thimmesch, Nick, and William Johnson. *Robert Kennedy at Forty.* New York: W. W. Norton, 1965.

Thomas, Evan. *Robert Kennedy: His Life.* New York: Simon & Schuster, 2000.

Travell, Janet. *Office Hours: Day and Night: The Autobiography of Janet Travell, M.D.* New York: NAL/World, 1968.

Harry S., Truman. *Memoirs by Harry S. Truman: Year of Decisions.* Garden City, N.Y.: Doubleday, 1955.

United Press International and American Heritage Magazine. *Four Days: The Historical Record of the Death of President Kennedy.* New York: American Heritage; 1964.

Valenti, Jack. *This Time, This Place: My Life in War, the White House, and Hollywood.* New York: Crown Archetype, 2007.

Valenti, Jack. *A Very Human President: A First-Hand Report.* New York: Norton, 1975.

Valeo, Francis R. *Mike Mansfield, Majority Leader: A Different Kind of Senate, 1961–1976.* Armonk, N.Y.: M. E. Sharpe, 1999.

vanden Heuvel, William, and Milton Gwirtzman. *On His Own: RFK 1964–68.* Garden City, N.Y.: Doubleday, 1970.

Verba, Sidney. "The Kennedy Assassination and the Nature of Political Commitment." In Bradley S. Greenberg and Edwin B. Parker, eds. *The Kennedy Assassination and the American Public: Social Communication in Crisis.* Stanford, Calif.: Stanford University Press, 1965.

Warren, Earl. *The Memoirs of Chief Justice Earl Warren.* Garden City, N.Y.: Doubleday, 1977.

Watson, Denton L. *Lion in the Lobby: Clarence Mitchell Jr.'s Struggle for the Passage of Civil Rights Laws.* New York: William Morrow, 1990.

Weber, Michael P. *Don't Call Me Boss: David Lawrence, Pittsburgh's Renaissance Mayor.* Pittsburgh: University of Pittsburgh Press, 1988.

West, J. B., with Mary Lynn Kotz. *Upstairs at the White House: My Life with the First Ladies.* New York: Coward, McCann & Geoghegan, 1973.

Whalen, Charles, and Barbara Whalen. *The Longest Debate: A Legislative History of the 1964 Civil Rights Act.* Santa Ana, Calif.: Seven Locks Press, 1984.

Whalen, Richard J. *The Founding Father: The Story of Joseph P. Kennedy.* New York: New American Library, 1964.

White, Theodore H. *The Making of the President, 1960.* New York: Atheneum, 1961.

White, Theodore H. *The Making of the President, 1964.* New York: Atheneum, 1965.

Wicker, Tom. *JFK and LBJ: The Influence of Personality upon Politics.* New York: Morrow, 1968.

Wilkins, Roy, with Tom Mathews. *Standing Fast: The Autobiography of Roy Wilkins.* New York: Viking, 1982.

Wilkinson, J. Harvie, III. *Harry Byrd and the Changing Face of Virginia Politics, 1945–1966.* University Press of Virginia, 1984.

Williams, Irving G. *The Rise of the Vice Presidency.* Washington, D.C.: Public Affairs Press, 1956.

Wofford, Harris. *Of Kennedys and Kings: Making Sense of the Sixties.* New York: Farrar, Straus & Giroux, 1981.

WPA. *Texas: A Guide to the Lone Star State.* New York: Hastings House, 1940.

Youngblood, Rufus W. *Twenty Years in the Secret Service: My Life with Five Presidents.* New York: Simon & Schuster, 1973.

Notes

ABBREVIATIONS

AA-S	Austin American-Statesman
BG	Boston Globe
BS	Baltimore Sun
CCCT	Corpus Christi Caller Times
CDN	Chicago Daily News
CSM	Christian Science Monitor
CT	Chicago Tribune
DMN	Dallas Morning News
FWS-T	Fort Worth Star-Telegram
HC	Houston Chronicle
HP	Houston Post
HSTL	Harry S. Truman Library
JFKL	John Fitzgerald Kennedy Library
JSP	Johnson Senate Papers
LAT	Los Angeles Times
LBJA	Lyndon Baines Johnson Archives
LBJA CF	LBJA Congressional File
LBJA FN	LBJA Famous Names File
LBJA SF	LBJA Subject File
LBJA SN	LBJA Selected Names File
LBJL	Lyndon Baines Johnson Library
NYDN	New York Daily News
NYHT	New York Herald Tribune
NYT	New York Times
OFWJ	Office Files of Walter Jenkins
OH	Oral History
PPCF	Pre-Presidential Confidential File
PPMF	Pre-Presidential Memo File
Reedy OF	Vice Presidential Office Files of George Reedy
SAE	San Antonio Express
SEP	Saturday Evening Post
SP	Steele Papers (LBJL)
SPF	Senate Political Files
TPR	The Presidential Recordings: Lyndon B. Johnson
TPR-JFK	The Presidential Recordings: John F. Kennedy
USN&WR	U.S. News & World Report
VPP	Vice Presidential Papers
WHCF	White House Central File
WHCF SF	White House Central File—Subject Files
WHFN	White House Famous Names File

WES   *Washington Evening Star*
WP   *Washington Post*
WS   *Washington Star*
WSJ   *Wall Street Journal*

Introduction

"My future is behind me": Busby interview.
"Go. I'm finished": BeLieu interview.
"I never thought": Clark interview.
"like a shock wave": "The Day Kennedy Died," *Newsweek,* Dec. 2, 1963. **"Lyndon Johnson's ascent"**: Graff, ed., *The Presidents: A Reference History*, p. 595. **"There were times"**: Greenberg and Parker, eds., *The Kennedy Assassination and the American Public,* pp. 3, 4. **"Probably without parallel"**: Sheatsley and Feldman, "A National Survey on Public Relations and Behavior," in Greenberg and Parker, eds., *The Kennedy Assassination,* p. 153. **"Challenge"**: Neustadt, *Presidential Power: The Politics of Leadership from FDR to Carter,* p. 233.
"The thing I feared": Johnson interview with Goodwin, *Lyndon Johnson,* pp. 199, 344. **"Might have incurred"**: Baker with King, *Wheeling and Dealing,* p. 271.
Power always *reveals*: Caro, *Master of the Senate,* p. xxi. **"Well, what the hell's the presidency for:** Fortas, quoted in Miller, *Lyndon,* p. 337; Fortas interview. **"They've got the bit"**: McPherson interview. ***"Murdered"**:* Transcript, "10:10 P.M., to Ted Sorensen, preceded by Bill Moyers and Sorensen," *TPR,* Vol. I, p. 168. **"At that moment"**: Johnson, *The Vantage Point,* p. 40. **"So spontaneous"**: Heller OH I.

1. The Prediction

When he was young: The description of Lyndon Johnson on the road gang is from Caro, *The Path to Power,* pp. 132–34; of him picking cotton, Caro, *Path,* p. 121. For his work in a cotton gin, Caro, *Path,* p. 132.
"From the day": Caro, *Path,* p. 535; Rowe interview. **"By *God"*:** Hopkins interview. **Greenbrier incident:** Caro, *Path,* pp. xiii–xvi.
REA offer: Caro, *Path,* pp. 576–77. **Urged in 1946:** Caro, *Means of Ascent,* p. 120. **"Couldn't stand"**: Harbin, quoted in *Path,* p. 229. **"Detour"; "dead end"**: Caro, *Master of the Senate,* p. 111. ***"Here's where"**:* Connally interview, quoted in Caro, *Means,* p. 120. **"He believed"; "FDR-LBJ"**: Busby interview, quoted in *Means,* pp. 137–39.
"He was"; "Watch": Caro, *Master,* p. 136. **"I never"**: Edward Clark, Corcoran inter-

views, quoted in *Master,* p. 157. **"The right size"**: Jenkins, quoted in *Master,* p. 136.
"Obsolesence": Galloway, *The Legislative Process in Congress,* p. 584. **"Were the happiest"**: Lady Bird Johnson interview, quoted in *Master,* p. 1040.
Johnson at 1956 Convention: Caro, *Master,* pp. 803–27. **"Don't you worry"**: Steele to Johnson, July 8, 1960, SP.
Rayburn's plaque: Steinberg, *Sam Rayburn,* p. 236. **"Consequential action"**: Graham to Johnson, Dec. 20 1956, box 101, LBJA SF, quoted in Caro, *Master,* p. 848. **"If he didn't"**: Corcoran interview, quoted in Caro, *Master,* p. 850. **"If I failed"**: Johnson, quoted in Caro, *Master,* p 850. **"Armageddon"**: "Lyndon Johnson, Civil Rights and 1960," Rowe to Johnson, July 3, 1957, Box 32, LBJA SN, quoted in *Master,* p. 923. **"It opened"**: Reedy, *Lyndon B. Johnson,* p. 120, quoted in *Master,* p. 1003. **"It's just"**: Johnson, quoted in McPherson, *A Political Education,* p. 148, quoted in *Master,* p. 1003.
"We can never": Russell, quoted in *Master,* pp. 853, 1127. By 1957, George Reedy says, "Russell was very determined to elect Lyndon Johnson President of the United States, Reedy OH VIII, p. 100, quoted in *Master,* p. 787
Ranch memo: Herring, Kilgore interviews. **"He was big all right"**: Donald Oresman interview, quoted in *Master,* p. 120. **When they called Connally and Jenkins:** John Connally, Jenkins, Herring, Kilgore interviews.
Washington meeting in 1957: Corcoran, Reedy, Rowe interviews. The meeting is described in *Master,* pp. 948, 949. **"You know"**: Reedy interview. Corcoran was to tell the author also that he told Johnson flatly, "If he didn't pass a civil rights bill, he could just forget [the] 1960 [nomination]." **"It was . . . time"**: Reedy interview. **Explaining:** Rowe interview. During this time, Rowe and Johnson would be discussing the purport of their conversations with, among others, BeLieu, Busby, Connally, Corcoran and Oltorf, and they confirm and supplement Rowe's account. **"An almost mystical"**: Reedy OH IX. **Rowe's memorandum:** McCullough, *Truman,* pp. 590–92; Rowe interview. **"Tend the store"**: *Time,* July 18, 1960; Hardeman and Bacon, *Rayburn,* p. 436. **"Thirty years"**: *Newsweek,* 1958. A **"playboy"**: Douglas, OH, JFKL. **"Sickly"; "He never said a word"**: "Here was a young whip-

persnapper, malaria-ridden and yellah, sickly, sickly," Johnson said. Goodwin, *The Fitzgeralds and the Kennedys,* p. 780.

"I was so anxious": "Telephone Conversation between Abe Fortas and Walter Jenkins," May 21, 1960, "Transcript of Telephone Calls, May 1960," OFWJ, Series 2. **"I'm trying":** Hardeman interview. **"Speculation":** Steele to Williamson, March 4, 1958, SP. **"The Congresional [*sic*]":** *NYT,* June 19, 1960. **"You can cross":** "Telephone Conversation between Secretary Anderson and Walter Jenkins," June 28, 1960, "Transcripts of Telephone Calls—June 1960," OFWJ, Series 2.

"He said he wasn't going to do *anything*": Rowe OH II. **"Endlessly":** Corcoran interview. **"Seen in '56"; "I wrote him a memo":** Rowe interview. **When, in August:** Rowe to Johnson, Aug. 27, 1958; Johnson to Rowe, Sept. 3, 1958, Box 32, LBJA SN. **Just a day; "It won't do you any good":** Rowe interview. **"He wasn't really":** Kilgore interview. **"One so often":** Reedy OH II.

"He's never had": Busby OH, JFKL, Busby interview. **No campaign to manage:** Connally, Jenkins interviews. **As much as "he [Johnson] wanted":** Connally, quoted in Connally with Herskowitz, *In History's Shadow,* p. 160.

"He wanted one thing": Rowe interview. "He started this thing and ran away from it. Because of his insecurity," Rowe said. In an interview with the author, Horace Busby laid Johnson's "hesitancy" to "this combination of self-doubt—that he was rising too high.... 'Don't try for it because you're not going to get it.' " **Jenkins warned Baker; "a fighting record"; "Johnson feared"; "haunted":** Baker, *Wheeling and Dealing,* p. 45. "When counting noses for LBJ ... was often cautioned never to overestimate our strength because Johnson feared losing on the Senate floor." **"Fear of being defeated"; "petrified":** Baker, *Wheeling,* p. 44. Baker also said (*Wheeling,* p. 119), "I think it was Lyndon Johnson's deep fear of defeat that ... led him to declare himself a noncandidate."

Vomiting: Caro, *Master,* p. 211; *Time,* May 21, 1965. **"He had a horror:** L. E. Jones interview.

"Dog run": Described in Caro, *Path,* p. 52, as it was when Sam Ealy and Rebekah moved into it. A second "shed room" was later added behind the house. The Johnsons moved to the ranch in January 1920, and moved off it, back to Johnson City, in September 1922.

People of Johnson City felt: Among the residents of Johnson City who knew Lyndon Johnson as a young man whom the author interviewed were his brother, Sam Houston

Johnson (SHJ); his sister, Rebekah Johnson Bobbitt (RJB); his cousin, Ava Johnson Cox, and Ava's husband, Ohlen Cox, and son, William (Corky) Cox; as well as Milton Barnwell, Louise Casparis, Cynthia Crider Crofts, John Dollahite, Truman Fawcett, Stella Gliddon, Jessie Lambert, Kitty Clyde Ross Leonard, Cecil Redford, Emmette Redford, Clayton Stribling, Mrs. Lex Ward. **Had brought to the dog run:** This account of the Johnsons' time on the ranch, and the rest of Lyndon Johnson's boyhood is from Caro, *Path.* All the quotations can be found in those chapters, and the sources for them are in the notes at the end of *Path.*

"All of a sudden": Anna Itz, quoted in *USN&WR,* Dec. 23, 1963. (See Caro, *Path,* p. 100.) **"The most important":** SHJ interview. **Vacillating in 1948:** Clark, Connally, Oltorf interviews. **" 'Humiliation' ":** Clark interview.

In command: The picture of Johnson running the Senate is from Caro, *Master.* All the quotations except those cited here can be found in that book.

"A splendid": Sidey, *A Very Personal Presidency,* p. 45.

His assistants would hear: This account of Johnson's indecisiveness in his office is from interviews with Busby, Gonella, Jenkins and Reedy, and from Baker, *Wheeling.* **Among the seventeen:** Steele to Williamson, March 4, 1958, SP. **He told Reedy:** Reedy OH, Reedy interview. **$10,000 diversion:** Evans and Novak, *Lyndon B. Johnson,* p. 244. **"Had decided":** Sidey interview. **"This is my home":** Corcoran interview.

"He didn't do anything"; "I finally said": Rowe OH II. **"I think":** Rowe to Johnson, Jan. 17, 1959, Box 32, LBJA SN. The letter refers to "our long phone conversation of last Tuesday night." **"Jim betrayed me":** Corcoran, Rowe interviews.

2. The Rich Man's Son

"Frail, hollow-looking": Van Zandt interview. **"Laddie":** Burns, *John Kennedy,* pp. 71–72. **Dressed like one:** Burns, *John Kennedy,* p. 71; Collier and Horowitz, *The Kennedys,* p. 158; Damore, *The Cape Cod Years of John F. Kennedy;* Paul F. Healy, "The Senate's Gay Young Bachelor, "*SEP,* June 13, 1953. Parmet, *The Struggles of John F. Kennedy,* pp. 149–50. **"Very much"; "a skinny kid":** Davis, quoted in Blair and Blair, *The Search for JFK,* pp. 511–12; Collier and Horowitz, *The Kennedys,* p. 158. **"Oh, Grace":** Grace Burke, quoted in Blair and

Blair, *Search for JFK,* p. 549. **Lyndon Johnson himself:** Caro, *Means of Ascent,* pp. 46–53. **Everyone on Capitol Hill:** Collier and Horowitz, *The Kennedys,* p. 157; Parmet, *Struggles.* **"A Hollywood hotel":** Dallek, *An Unfinished Life,* p. 150. **Told Tierney:** Tierney with Herskowitz, *Self-Portrait,* pp. 147, 153, quoted in Parmet, *Struggles,* p. 131. **In magazines:** For example, Healy, "Gay Young." **"Well, I guess":** Dallek, *An Unfinished Life,* p. 136.

"**He had few**": Burns, *John Kennedy,* p. 98. **"About his only":** O'Brien, *John F. Kennedy,* p. 26. **"He told me":** Smathers, quoted in Blair and Blair, *Search for JFK,* p. 524. **"He never seemed to":** Douglas, quoted in Parmet, *Struggles,* p. 167. **"A good boy":** Hardeman and Bacon, *Rayburn: A Biography,* p. 434. **"Large and fabulous"; "every woman":** Healy, "Gay Young." "In all, a total of 60,000 women decided they could not afford to pass up an opportunity to meet the wife of the former Ambassador to the Court of St. James [*sic*], her three lovely daughters and her unmarried son" (Healy, "Gay Young"). **"Could live":** Whalen, "Evening the Score," quoted in Dallek, *Unfinished,* p. 171. **"No town":** Powers, quoted in Goodwin, *The Fitzgeralds and the Kennedys,* p. 755. **"Boyish":** Ralph M. Blagden, "Cabot Lodge's Toughest Fight," *The Reporter,* Sept. 1952. **"Jack was being":** Healy, "Gay Young." **"Stand back":** Healy, "Gay Young." **St. Lawrence proposal:** Sorensen, *Kennedy,* pp. 58–59.; O'Brien, pp. 272–75. **"Malaria":** Collier and Horowitz, *The Kennedys,* p. 167. **His back, requesting a suite; obtained permission:** Parmet, *The Struggles,* p. 308.

Broke into tears; "looking tanned"; "37th year"; "inspiring": Parmet, *Struggles,* pp. 309–15. **"Young Jack":** *NYHT,* May 25, 1955, quoted in Parmet, *Struggles,* p. 316. **"Applauded":** Parmet, *Struggles,* p. 287. **" 'Old pal' "; "very sharp pain":** Smathers OH.

Effective star turn: O' Brien, *Kennedy,* p. 481; Rubin, *Forty Ways to Look at JFK,* p. 8. **"To *want* to be":** Caro, *Master of the Senate,* pp. 564–64. **"In the terms":** Sorensen interview.

"**Telling me**"; "**I kept picturing**": Johnson, quoted in Goodwin, *The Fitzgeralds,* p. 790. **But the real:** Corcoran, Reedy, Rowe interviews.

"**For the first time**": Schlesinger, *A Thousand Days,* p. 554. *NYT:* Goodwin, *The Fitzgeralds,* p. 790. **"even Democrats":** Douglass, *JFK and the Unspeakable,* p. 8. **Africa subcommittee:** Marcy OH. **Met at least once:**

Senate Historian Donald Ritchie, in Holt OH. **"Not in the top":** Smathers OH.

"**He's smart enough**": Baker, *Wheeling and Dealing,* p. 45. **"Pathetic":** Johnson, "Reminiscences of Lyndon B. Johnson," Aug. 19, 1969, transcript of tape recording, p. 9, LBJL. **"A young whippersnapper":** Johnson, from a conversation with Goodwin, quoted in *The Fitzgeralds,* p. 780. **"weak and pallid":** Johnson, from a conversation with Goodwin, quoted in *Lyndon Johnson,* p. 201.

Jack Kennedy's illnesses, back condition, and overall physical condition are dealt with in many biographies, including Dallek, *An Unfinished Life,* Hamilton, *JFK: Reckless Youth* and Reeves, *President Kennedy.* The discussion of his medical problems in this book is based also on the author's discussions with Dr. Janet G. Travell, who treated the author's own back problems (and to whom his first book, *The Power Broker: Robert Moses and the Fall of New York,* is dedicated). **"Pretty tired":** Hamilton, *Reckless,* p. 87. **"We are still":** Dallek, *Unfinished,* p. 35. **Leukemia; prayers were said:** Hamilton, *Reckless,* p. 104. **"The Goddamnest":** Hamilton, *Reckless,* p. 110. **"Shit!!":** Dallek, *Unfinished,* p. 74. **"They were unable":** Hamilton, *Reckless,* p. 113. **"7,000":** Hamilton, *Reckless,* p. 219. **"Jack's sense":** Hamilton, *Reckless,* p. 104. **"I've never":** Chafe, *Private Lives/Public Consequences,* p. 103. **"Jack Kennedy all during his life":** Billings, quoted in Hamilton, *Reckless,* p. 196.

Tried to enlist; fixed examination: Gilbert, *The Mortal Presidency,* p. 146; Hamilton, *Reckless,* pp. 405–9; Dallek, *Unfinished,* pp. 81–83.

"Bucking bronchos": Frank Henry, "Bucking Bronchos of the Sea," *Science Digest* (condensed from the *Baltimore Sunday Sun,* April 23, 1944). **"Was in pain":** Iles, quoted in Hamilton, *Reckless,* pp. 517–18. **"Jack came home":** quoted in Hamilton, *Reckless,* p. 507.

"**The most confused**": Dallek, *Unfinished,* p. 95. **PT-109 episode:** This account is based on John Hersey, "A Reporter at Large—Survival," *The New Yorker,* June 17, 1944, and on Donovan, *PT-109: John F. Kennedy in World War II.*

"**He wanted to**": Cluster, quoted in Hamilton, *Reckless,* p. 610. **" 'What are you' ":** Maguire, quoted in Hamilton, *Reckless,* p. 610. **"What impressed":** Rhoads, quoted in Hamilton, *Reckless,* p. 610.

Sinking three barges: Hamilton, pp. 621–24. **"A definite":** Dallek, *Unfinished,* pp. 100–102. **Obviously:** Parmet, *Struggles,* p. 116.

"Joe used to": Joseph Kennedy, Sr., quoted

in Goodwin, *The Fitzgeralds*, p. 699. **"A temperament"**: Joseph Kennedy, Sr., quoted in Goodwin, *The Fitzgeralds*, p. 705. **"He looked"**: Lannan, quoted in Hamilton, *Reckless*, p. 680. **"Ill, sad and lonely"**: Ernest W. Rose, Sr., quoted in Travell, *Office Hours*, p. 411. **"Very thin"**; **"My father"**: Goodwin, *The Fitzgeralds*, p. 705. **"I'm just"**: Dallek, *Unfinished*, p. 123. **"We played"**: Blair and Blair, *The Search for JFK*, p. 191. **"He made us"**: Dallek, *Unfinished*, p. 113.

"He was very retiring": Kelly, quoted in Blair and Blair, *Search for JFK*, p. 448. **"He was not the ordinary"**: Dalton, quoted in Parmet, *Struggles*, p. 150. **"Hard"**: Goodwin, *The Fitzgeralds*, p. 646.

Trolley car scene: Parmet, *Struggles*, p. 154. **5,000 to 1:** Joseph Kennedy, quoted in Hamilton, *Reckless*, p. 757.
"The collar": Damore, *Cape Cod*, p. 87. **"Both mediocre"**: Parmet, *Struggles*, p. 149. **Eunice mouthed:** Dallek, *Unfinished*, p. 124. **"A quick"**: Damore, *Cape Cod*, p. 87. **Neville incidents:** O'Donnell, Powers, and McCarthy, *"Johnny, We Hardly Knew Ye,"* p. 69. **Gold Star Mothers speech:** O'Donnell and Powers, *"Johnny, We Hardly Knew Ye,"* p. 54; Powers, quoted in Goodwin, *The Fitzgeralds*, pp. 711–12.

A long day: For example, Dallek, *Unfinished*, p. 123. **"At his best"**: Burns, *John Kennedy*, p. 67. **"It was tough"**: Patsy, quoted in Blair and Blair, *Search for JFK*, pp. 439–40. **"In agony"**: Patsy, quoted in Blair and Blair, *Search for JFK*, p. 440. **"Off we'd go"**: Kelley, quoted in Blair and Blair, *Search for JFK*, p. 438. **"I knew"**: Broderick, quoted in Parmet, *Struggles*, p. 154. **"I feel great"**: Broderick, quoted in Parmet, *Struggles*, p. 154. **"I'd say"**: Sutton, quoted in Blair and Blair, *Search for JFK*, p. 441. **Bunker Hill Day collapse:** Lee, quoted in Hamilton, *Reckless*, pp. 768, 769. See also Parmet, *Struggles*, p. 161.

"That young": Parmet, *Struggles*, p. 191. **"Touch and go"**: Waldrop, quoted in Blair and Blair, *Search for JFK*, p. 565. **Every three months:** Reeves, *President Kennedy*, p. 43. **"A whole new"**: Billings, quoted in Goodwin, *The Fitzgeralds*, p. 745.

"Jack was aiming": Garside, *Camelot at Dawn*, p. 6. **His father's money:** Someone "could live the rest of [their] lives on [his] billboard budget alone," one observer said. "Cabot was simply overwhelmed by money" (Dallek, *Unfinished*, p. 171). **$500,000 loan:** For example, Parmet, *Struggles*, p. 242. "You know, we had to buy that fucking paper," Joe was to say once (Dallek, *Unfinished*, p. 172). **"But . . . then"**: O'Donnell and Powers, *"Johnny, We Hardly,"* p. 79.

"Just made up": Bell, quoted in Parmet, *Struggles*, p. 271. **"Keep"**: *Brooklyn Eagle*, April 26, 1954.
"He could": Billings, quoted in Goodwin, *The Fitzgeralds*, p. 774. **"Even getting"**: Bartels, quoted in Blair and Blair, *Search for JFK*, p. 566. **"A 47-year-old"**: Goodwin, *The Fitzgeralds*, p. 774. **"He told his father"**; **"inconceivable"**: Rose Kennedy, quoted in Goodwin, *The Fitzgeralds*, p. 774. **"Thirty-seven"**: Goodwin, *The Fitzgeralds*, p. 775. **"He told me"**: Krock, quoted in Blair and Blair, *Search for JFK*, p. 571.

Back wouldn't heal; the two operations: Travell interview. **"And the doctors"**: Goodwin, *The Fitzgeralds*, p. 776. "It was a terrible time," Billings was to recall. "He was bitter and low. We came close to losing him. I don't mean losing his life. I mean losing him as a person" (quoted in Goodwin, *The Fitzgeralds*, p. 776). **"Tanned and fit"**: *NYHT*, May 24, 1955. **"Aside from"**: *Boston Post*, May 24, 1955.

"It must have"; **first visit to Travell; Travell treatment:** Travell interview; Travell, *Office Hours*, pp. 5–7. **"Jack had"**: Billings, quoted in Goodwin, *The Fitzgeralds*, p. 776. **"Higher office"**: Garside, Anne, *Camelot at Dawn*, p. 6. **"I'm against vice"**: Alsop with Platt, *"I've Seen the Best of It,"* p. 406. **Map:** Whalen, *The Founding Father*, pp. 446–47. **"Wide incision"**; **"Maybe Jack;"** Travell, *Office Hours*, p. 320. **"Scarcely"**: Travell, *Office Hours*, p. 322. **Travell's Palm Beach visit:** Travell interview, Travell, *Office Hours*, pp. 305–13.

Johnson's first campaign: Caro, *The Path to Power*, pp. 389–436. **"A candidate by El Greco"**: Caro, *Path*, p. 434. **Johnson's collapse:** Caro, *Path*, p. 435.

Johnson's illness during 1948 campaign: Caro, *Means*, pp. 194–208. **"Agonizing"**; **"unbearable"**: Caro, *Means*, p. 195. **"How in the world"**: Dr. William Morgan, quoted in Caro, *Means*, p. 196.

"Learn on the run": Mayer et al., *The Making of the Presidential Candidates*, p. 232; Sorensen interview. **"The Senate"; "No matter"**: *Time*, Dec. 2, 1957. **One reason that:** Burns, *John Kennedy*, p. 189; Parmet, *Struggles*, pp. 380, 381. In 1957, in fact, Minnesota's Democratic-Farmer-Labor party had canceled Kennedy's invitation to be the speaker at its Jefferson-Jackson Day Dinner after he had voted "wrong" on the farm bill (Cabell Philips, "How to Be a Presidential Candidate," *NYT Sunday Magazine*, July 13, 1958). And, *Time* said, "Kennedy's major 1960 problem: he is still in the Senate, and he must vote on highly controversial issues. In his votes last summer on the [1957] civil rights bill, Kennedy managed to please hardly anyone." **"Pieces of power":** White, *Making 1960*; Rowe interview. **"Johnson thinks":** Sorensen interview.

"Just ... jumped at you": Schary, quoted in Parmet, *Struggles*, p. 367. **"Came before":** *NYT*, Aug. 14, 1956. **"And then":** Goodwin, *The Fitzgeralds*, p. 784. **"The dramatic":** Burns, *John Kennedy*, p. 190. **"Jim, do you know?":** Rowe interview. **"The most telegenic":** *BG*, July 22, 1956, quoted in Goodwin, *The Fitzgeralds*, p. 780. **As long as he wore:** Travell, *Office Hours*, p. 320; Travell interview.

"One thing": Davis, quoted in Blair and Blair, *Search for JFK*, p. 512. **"I have never":** Smathers OH. **Magazines:** Laura Bergquist, "Rise of the Brothers Kennedy," *Look*, Aug. 6, 1957. **"The flowering":** Harold H. Martin, "The Amazing Kennedys," *SEP*, Sept. 7, 1957. **Cover stories:** *Time*, Dec. 2, 1957, "The Man Out Front." Phillips, "How to Be"; "Young Man with Tough Questions," *Life*, July 1, 1957; "The Amazing Kennedys," *SEP*, Sept. 7, 1957. *Time, McCall's, Redbook;* **"This man":** William V. Shannon, *NYP*, Nov. 11, 1957.

"His Senate": Dallek, *Unfinished*, p. 226. **"Seldom":** Childs, May 15, 1957, quoted in Goodwin, *The Fitzgeralds*, p. 792.

Applauding at Alsop's: Alsop, with Platt, *I've Seen*, p. 406. **Reversing against Kefauver:** Parmet, *Struggles*, p. 439.

"Enormously successful": Goodwin, *The Fitzgeralds*, p. 794. **"If the convention":** Sorensen, quoted in Shesol, *Mutual Contempt*, p. 25. **"By general agreement"; "Jack Kennedy could":** *Time*, Nov. 24, 1958.

3. Forging Chains

"I still think": Rowe to Johnson, January 17, 1959, Box 32, LBJA SN.

Texas law: *CSM*, May 25, 1960; *HP*, July 13, 1960; *FWS-T*, July 15, 1960; *AA-S*, July 27, 1960; *DMN*, Nov. 9, 1960. **Phone calls to Clark:** Clark interview.

Parr had done so in 1948: Caro, *Means of Ascent*, pp. 308–17. **Same ink in the same handwriting:** Caro, *Means*, pp. 324, 328. **Johnson had assisted:** *Means*, pp. 186, 191.

Needed a lawyer: Clark, Jones interviews. **Another incentive:** Thomas, quoted in Murphy, *Fortas*, p. 105. **"In return":** Murphy, *Fortas*, p. 105. Murphy bases this on his interview with Donald. **Fortas agreed:** "In the Supreme Court of the United States," October Term, 1959, No. 391, "George B. Parr, D. C. Chapa, et al. v. United States of America Respondent,

Petition for a Writ of Certiorari. . . . Abe Fortas, Paul A. Porter, Charles A. Reich . . . Attorneys for the Petitioners." **"Had not asked":** When, in March 1960, Parr's petition for bankruptcy was settled, and, Fortas reported to Johnson, he (Parr) "got about a million out of his bankruptcy proceeding," Fortas told Jenkins, "in view of that I think I will render him a bill for this case and the prior one also. I had not asked for any money, but in view of the recent developments, I think I will . . ." ("Telephone Conversation between Abe Fortas and Walter Jenkins," March 24, 1960, Box 1, Special File Pertaining to Abe Fortas and Homer Thornberry, LBJL). He told Johnson in an earlier letter that he had offered to take the case "without reference to fee," but that Parr's lawyer at the time had declined to have him participate in the case (Fortas to Johnson, April 10, 1959, Box 1, Special File). **"The best break":** "Resume of Telephone Calls on December 7," "Transcripts of Telephone Calls—Dec. 1959," Box 1, Series 2, OFWJ, LBJL. **"We got him off":** Reich, quoted in Kalman, *Abe Fortas*, p. 159. **"Burn your memo up":** Johnson to Jenkins, undated, but attached to "Resume of Telephone Calls—December 7," "Transcripts of Telephone Calls—Dec. 1959," Box 1, Series 2, OFWJ, LBJL. **Monitored:** Murphy, *Fortas*, p. 105; Fortas to Johnson, Dec. 8, 1959. For examples of the reports on the case's progress that Fortas and Porter delivered to Jenkins over the telephone, "Highlights of Conversations on December 4—Paul Porter," "Transcripts of Telephone Calls—Dec. 1959," Box 1, Series 2, OFWJ, LBJL. "Telephone Conversation between Abe Fortas and Walter Jenkins, Dec. 14, 1959. **"He was":** Clark interview.

"It's the politician's task": Johnson interview with Doris Goodwin, quoted in Goodwin, *Lyndon Johnson*, p. 141.

"Democratic Victory Dinner": Steele to Williamson, May 7, 1959, SP. **"You felt":** Steele interview. **"I don't want":** "Conversation with Eddie Higgins, Assistant to Sen. Green (Senator Johnson), Nov. 18, 1959, "Administration, [Administrative], Memoranda, Jenkins, Walter, 1 of 2," Box 633, *JSP.* **Although he had:** Jenkins, McPherson, Reedy interviews, OHs. **"Torn"—"tortured, almost":** Rowe interview. George Reedy also uses the word "torn" to describe Johnson during this period: "I believe he was a man badly torn . . ." (Reedy OH II). A photographer for *Time* magazine got a glimpse of this when he asked him to pose at the gate to his ranch. "Well, all right, but you better take a good one—one I can use in 1960," Johnson said. Reminded by *Time's* reporter John Steele that, as Steele put it, he "had often said that at the end of the present term he wants nothing but retirement, he replied, 'Well, it's nice to know you can run if you want to run' " (Steele to Williamson, Nov. 13, 1958, SP). **Western strategy:** Hoff interview. **Hells Canyon Dam:** Caro, *Master of the Senate,* chapter 38: "Hells Canyon." **"Very sympathetic":** Edward M. Kennedy interview. **"Very fast":** Rowe interview.

"Bobby, you've never": Baker, *Wheeling and Dealing,* p. 43. **"His attitude was"; Jenkins handing out:** Baker, *Wheeling,* p. 43. **Johnson had told him; "I want to ask":** "Transcripts of Telephone Conversations— January 1960," OFWJ, Series 2, Box 1; Dallek, *Lone Star Rising,* p. 564.

First encounter: Busby, Reedy interviews. **Roosevelt tricking Joe Kennedy; "Oh, boy":** Sidey, quoted in Miller, *Lyndon,* pp. 77–78. **"For decades":** Hugh Sidey, "The Presidency: When Ike Wore His Brown Suit," *Time,* Aug. 20, 1979. **"Bobby's a tough one":** Schlesinger, *Robert Kennedy and His Times,* p. 97. **"Did you ever see":** Reedy interview; Reedy, quoted in Collier and Horowitz, *The Kennedys,* p. 534. **"Forget Bobby"; "runt"; "no ambition"; "he was willing":** Thomas, *Robert Kennedy,* pp. 30, 45, 53, 55. "He was not only smaller and slower than his brothers, he *looked* afraid," Thomas writes. "He lacked the jaunty, glowing air of a young Kennedy" (p. 31).

"I wish, Dad": Thomas, *Robert Kennedy,* p. 53. **"Didn't have":** Lasky, *J.F.K.: The Man and the Myth,* p. 63. **"For Christ's sake":** Thomas, *Robert Kennedy,* p. 51. **Breaking his leg:** Thomas, *Robert Kennedy,* p. 51; Schlesinger, *Robert Kennedy,* p. 67. **"Furious":** Thomas, *Robert Kennedy,* p. 51. **Hitting Magnuson; O'Donnell apologizing:** Collier and Horowitz, *The Kennedys,* p. 179. **"I didn't":** Lewis, quoted in Schlesinger, *Robert Kennedy,* p. 66. **"Would have killed him"; "he became":** Thomas, *Robert Kennedy,* pp. 55–56. **"Liked to bite":** Thomas, *Robert Kennedy,* p. 55. **Fierce Dobermans; "terrible time":** Spalding OH, JFKL. **"Ready to punch":** Page, quoted in Thomas, *Robert Kennedy,* p. 55. **Sailing incident:** Thomas, *Robert Kennedy,* p. 56.

He did; "I felt": Thimmesch and Johnson, *Robert Kennedy at Forty,* p. 56. **"At the time":** Maas, quoted in Stein and Plimpton, *American Journey,* p. 50. After a pause, he said, "I was wrong." **When he resigned:** Shesol, *Mutual Contempt,* p. 18; Thimmesch and Johnson, *Robert Kennedy at Forty,* pp. 57–58. **Walking out on Murrow:** Thomas, *Robert Kennedy,* p. 67.

"Black and white hats": Thimmesch and Johnson, *Robert Kennedy,* p. 22. **Giancana exchange:** Thomas, *Robert Kennedy,* p. 83. **Glimco exchange:** Thimmesch and Johnson, *Robert Kennedy,* p. 71. **"Full of shit":** Thomas, *Robert Kennedy,* p. 83. **Gallo exchange:** Thimmesch and Johnson, *Robert Kennedy,* p. 24.

"I wanted": Haddad interview. **"A little keyed up":** Thomas, *Robert Kennedy,* p. 83. **"Bobby hates like me":** "What Makes Bobby Run," *Time,* March 18, 1963. Thomas, *Robert Kennedy,* p. 69. As Thomas notes, he later denied having made the remark. Yet others recall remarks by him in which the wording is similar. Former House Speaker Tip O'Neill writes that Joe Kennedy once told him, "Bobby's my boy. When Bobby hates you, you stay hated" (O'Neill and Novak, *Man of the House,* p. 83). Thimmesch and Johnson quote Joe Kennedy as saying of Bobby, "He's a great kid, he hates the same way I do." (They add "later Joseph Kennedy told a reporter that 'All I ever meant to convey is that he has the capacity to be emotionally involved, to feel things deeply, as compared with Jack and that amazing detachment of his." That is not exactly a denial of the remark. Thimmesch and Johnson, *Robert Kennedy,* pp. 24, 25. And the first full-scale biography of Joseph Kennedy gives the quote almost exactly: "He's a great kid. He hates the same way I do" (Whalen, *The Founding Father,* p. 457). So do early magazine articles about Bobby: for example, *Newsweek,* March 18, 1963. And three journalists who spent time with Kennedy and his staffers— Peter Maas, Jack Newfield, who wrote a book, *Robert Kennedy: A Memoir;* and Robert F. Greene, an investigative reporter who in 1957 was an investigator with Robert Kennedy's Senate Rackets Committee—say that in conversation Robert Kennedy aides and Jack Kennedy aides who had been with the Kennedys a long time repeated the exact remark, "He hates like me" (Greene, Maas, Newfield interviews). Schlesinger writes, "His father was supposed to have said in later years that Robert was more like him than any of the other children because 'he hates like me.' In 1960 he denied to John Seigenthaler that he had ever said this. But . . . to another reporter he said proudly, 'Bobby's as hard as nails' " (Schlesinger, *Robert Kennedy,* p. 97). "Bobby is just as tough as a bootheel," Joseph Kennedy said on another occasion (Schlesinger, *Robert Kennedy,* p. 107).

"Absolute evilness": Thomas, *Robert Kennedy,* p. 81. **Trying to trap Hoffa; would jump; "Frustrated":** Thimmesch and Johnson, *Robert Kennedy,* pp. 73–75. **Use of**

friendly reporters: Greene, Maas interviews. **"The full arsenal":** Thimmesch and Johnson, *Robert Kennedy,* p. 76. **"When Bobby hates you":** O'Neill and Novak, *Man of the House,* p. 83.

"This was the Leader": Barr interview. **"Sonny Boy":** Goldsmith interview. **"A snot-nose":** Baker, *Wheeling,* p. 138. **"If it had someone":** Shesol, *Mutual Contempt,* p. 8.

"Just get one thing": Schlesinger, *Robert Kennedy,* p. 132. **"Bobby and I":** O'Donnell, quoted in Shesol, *Mutual Contempt,* p. 26. **"It really":** Thimmesch and Johnson, *Robert Kennedy,* p. 115.

"Making notes"; "we fell": Schlesinger, *Robert Kennedy,* pp. 133–34.

"Holds his head": Eugene Patterson, *Atlanta Constitution,* Sept. 10, 1960, quoted in Schlesinger, *Robert Kennedy,* p. 218. **DiSalle:** "Di Salle had no alternative," Rep. Wayne Hays reported. "He knew that if he did not come out for Kennedy that Kennedy would come into his state and probably beat him. Kennedy was holding a gun to his head" ("Telephone Conversation between Congressman Hays and Walter Jenkins," Jan. 18, 1960," OFWJ). **"Does not shock":** O'Donnell and Powers, *"Johnny, We Hardly,"* p. 151. **"Stormy"; "fierce"; "real rough":** Lasky, *The Myth,* p.127.

"To get": Mooney, *LBJ,* p. 124. **"Extremely effective":** Reedy OH II. **"We've had":** Rayburn, quoted in Baker, *Wheeling,* p. 119.

Mateos celebration: *Time,* April 25, 1960; *AA-S, DMN,* Oct. 19, 1959. **Six journalists:** *WES, WP,* Jan. 14, 1960.

"Just kidding": "Telephone Call from President Eisenhower to Senator Lyndon B. Johnson, August 4, 1959," "1959," "Notes and Transcripts of Pre-Presidential Conversations of Lyndon B. Johnson," LBJL. **"As usual":** *NYT,* Nov. 26, 1959. **"I didn't think of him":** *NYT,* Dec. 15, 1959.

Brown meeting; "downright angry": "Telephone Conversation between Walter Jenkins and Leonard Marks," Feb. 1, 1960, "Transcripts of Telephone Calls—Feb. 1960," Box 1, Series 2, OFWJ, LBJL. **"Senator Johnson did"; "electable":** Dutton. **Responded on national television:** *NYT,* Jan. 24, 1960; Nov. 1, Nov. 26, 1959. Following the telecast, according to Ed Weisl, Johnson's ally Richard Berlin of Hearst newspapers "had a long talk with Governor Brown in California, and Brown said he was ashamed of himself about what he had said about Lyndon. . . . However, the Governor did not come out and say he would support Lyndon" ("Ed Weisl —," "Transcripts of Telephone Calls—December

1959," Dec. 1959, OFWJ, LBJL. Also see "Resume of Telephone Conversation with Dick Berlin," Dec. 10, 1959.

"Son": Dallek, *Lone Star,* p. 559; Shesol, *Mutual Contempt,* p. 10; Bullion, *In the Boat with LBJ,* p. 111. A. W. Moursund, Johnson's business partner and frequent hunting companion, related the story. Busby, Oltorf, Stehling interviews. Robert Kennedy said only that on the hunting trip, "Johnson took him to an elevated concrete structure from which they awaited in comfort the appearance of deer to be shot. . . . Kennedy was disgusted. 'This isn't hunting. It's slaughter' " (vanden Heuvel and Gwirtzman, *On His Own,* p. 246). **Assuring Bobby:** Evans and Novak, *Lyndon B. Johnson,* p. 246.

"I hear": *CSM,* Nov. 14, 1959. **"I am not":** "Statements of Lyndon Johnson," Jan. 6, 1960, SLBJ, LBJL. **"Spent":** Leslie Carpenter OH.

"The only man": Busby interview. **Jenkins was organizing:** Transcripts of Telephone Calls, January 1960 through April 1960 folders, Box 1, Series 2, Box 1, OFWJ, LBJL. **White said:** Reedy, "Memoranda and Drafts, May 13, 1960, Box 267, Papers of George Reedy, SPF, LBJL. **"What it would take":** Edwards OH. **"I have some":** Jan. 5, 1960, Jenkins's Resume of Telephone Conversations: George Brown—"I have some money that I want to know what to do with. I was wondering if it should be sent to Jake Jacobson or just who should be getting it and I will be collecting more from time to time" ("Transcripts of Telephone Conversations—January 1960," Box 1, Series 2, OFWJ, LBJL). **Envelopes:** Clark, Connally, Wild interviews. And, for example, Gene Chambers: "I gave John some you know what to bring along when he meets Lyndon. . . . It is sizable" (Jan. 20, 1960, "Transcripts of Telephone Calls—January 1960," Box 1, Series 2, OFWJ, LBJL), and "Ed Clark called saying Mr. Hill talked to the Senator and he told him he wanted him to raise some cash. . . . Somebody mentioned it to H. E. Butt and has already sent Clark $1,000. Mr. Butt said this was just a starter" ("Resume of Telephone Conversations—Ed Clark," Jan. 7, 1960, "Transcripts of Telephone Calls—January 1960," Box 1, Series 2, OFWJ, LBJL). Clark said he did not recall this specific contribution, but that most of Butt's contributions were in cash. And see Caro, *Master,* pp. 676, 406–9. **"Twice I personally":** Mooney, *LBJ,* p. 127. He adds that Hunt "said substantial contributions were also being sent to Washington by other oil men and business people in Dallas and Houston."

Convened: "Resume of Telephone Conver-

sations on December 16—Bobby Baker," Dec. 14, 16, 1959, "Transcripts of Telephone Calls—December 1959," Box 1, Series 2, OFWJ, LBJL.
"Wherever": Hoff interview. **"We have no organization":** Jones to Hoff, May 19, 1960. **"Many people do not know"; "Many people":** "Telephone conversation between Irv Hoff and Bobby Baker," Feb. 25, 1960, "Transcripts of Telephone Calls—February 1960," Box 1, Series 2, OFWJ, LBJL.
Wyoming awakening: Reedy OH II.
"They're a": Hoff interview.
"The problem was": Baker, *Wheeling,* p. 44. **" 'We've got to know' ":** Hoff interview.
"If I could": Jan. 25, 1960, "Transcripts of Telephone Calls—February 1960," Box 1, Series 2, OFWJ, LBJL. **Although "Johnson hadn't":** Hoff, "California Situation—as it looked between March 28 and April 5," April 6, 1960; "Johnson for President File, 1959–1960," "Johnson for President—Hoff—California," Box 93, SPF, LBJL. **"The California delegation":** "Irv Hoff from Sacramento," March 30, 1960," "Transcripts of Telephone Calls—March 30, 1960," Box 1, Series 2, OFWJ, LBJL.
"Jesus": Chandler, *The Natural Superiority of Southern Politicians,* p. 265. **"However much":** Caro, *Master,* p. 194. **"Mongrelization":** Caro, *Master,* p. 194. **"Yes, I understand":** Johnson, quoted in Miller, *Lyndon,* p. 226. **The first rupture:** Mann, *The Walls of Jericho,* p. 246. **"A lynching":** Russell, quoted in Mann, *Walls,* p. 249. **"This was the only kind of lynching":** Note on back of Diary page, Feb. 21, 1960, LBJL. **A show:** Fite, *Richard B. Russell,* p. 374. **"A cozy"; "bonhomie":** Rovere, "Letter from Washington," *New Yorker,* March 17, 1960. **Working with Rogers:** Brownell, Rogers interviews. **"A victory":** Javits, quoted in *WP,* April 9, 1960. **"only a pale":** Clark, quoted in *NYT, WP,* April 9, 1960. **"The roles":** *WP,* April 9, 1960. **"Dick, here is":** Clark, quoted in *WP,* April 9, 1960.
Johnson got: *WP,* April 19, 1960. **Gallup Poll:** *WP,* March 16, 1960. **"Lost support":** *NYT,* Jan. 12, 1959. **"Hated":** Rauh OH I. **Douglas went:** Watson, *Lion in the Lobby, p. 425.* JOHNSON REJECTED: *NYDN,* March 11, 1960. **"All the":** Wilkins, quoted in *WP,* May 30, 1960.
Asked Hobart Taylor: *Detroit Sunday Times,* March 27, 1960. **"I talked":** Edwards OH. **Detroit discussion:** David S. Broder, "Johnson Lacks Link with Michigan Party," *WES,* March 28, 1960.
Busch telephoned Fleishman: Fleishman, "Gussie and Lyndon Johnson," *St. Louis Busi-*

ness Journal, Aug. 26–Sept. 1, 1961. **Woods on Convair:** Howard B. Woods, "One Man's Journal" and "Lyndon Talks," *The St. Louis Argus,* April 29, 1960.
"Horace": Busby interview.
Ambassador Hotel fiasco: "Leonard Marks," May 17, 1960, "Transcripts of Telephone Calls—May 1960," Series 2, OFWJ, LBJL. *San Antonio Light,* May 19, 1960; *WP, AA-S, El Paso Times,* May 20, 1960; Gonella interview; *WP,* May 26, 1960; *Denton Record-Chronicle, DT-H,* May 27, 1960.
"Why didn't he?": "Telephone Conversation—E. Janeway Called Walter Jenkins from New York," March 17, 1960, 1:30 P.M. **"We DO":** "Telephone Conversation between Charlie Herring and W. Jenkins," March 23, 1960. Both from Box 1, Series 2, OFWJ, LBJL.
"It was": Clark interview. **"He was always"; "What convinces"; "would quickly"; "had a fantastic":** All from Caro, *Master,* p. 886.
"I was one": Wright interview.
"Just pooh-poohed": Dick Berlin reporting on conversation, March 10, 1960, "Transcripts of Telephone Calls—March 1960," Box 1, Series 2, OFWJ, LBJL. **"Next!":** Baker, *Wheeling,* p.121.
"After some": O'Neill with Novak, pp. 181–82.
"As a"; "would convince": White, *Making 1960,* pp. 94–102. **"Open up":** In their book *Lyndon B. Johnson,* Evans and Novak wrote that "It would create a wide-open convention at LA that just might wind up nominating LJ" (p. 256).
Johnson began helping Humphrey: Evans and Novak, *LBJ,* p. 259.
Kennedy paid a call: "Notes of Conversation, May 3, 1960," p. 3, Notebook 3, Box 1, Krock Papers, "Vice Presidency, 1960, Decision to Run for Vice President," Reference File, LBJL. *HP,* May 8, 1960.
"How the hell" Rowe interview.
A last-minute: White, *Making 1960,* pp. 110–12. "TV is no medium for a poor man," White concluded.
The ambassador; "did not confine": Kearns, *The Fitzgeralds,* p. 799. **The Kennedys had:** Although Schlesinger (*Robert Kennedy,* p. 201) says that after an anonymous Minnesotan sent the material to Lawrence O'Brien, and O'Brien says FDR Jr. brought it up on his own, Schlesinger also quotes FDR Jr. as "blaming its use on Robert Kennedy's determination to win at any cost." He also says that "Roosevelt's memory is that . . . he was under insistent pressure, especially from Robert Kennedy, to bring up Humphrey's war record."

He quotes FDR Jr. as saying, "I don't think that Jack really had anything to do with deciding whether to insist on my going ahead. . . ." He also quotes FDR Jr. as calling this "the biggest political mistake" of his career. FDR Jr.'s quotations are from a "recorded interview by Jean Stein, Dec. 9, 1969, pp. 6–8." The Stein interviews have not been opened by the JFKL. **Although, in fact:** Solberg, *Hubert Humphrey,* pp. 97, 99; Schlesinger, *Robert Kennedy,* p. 201; Thomas, *Robert Kennedy,* p. 95. **"Repeated contacts":** Humphrey, *The Education of a Public Man,* p. 475. **"Any discussion"; "As Kennedy":** Goodwin, *The Fitzgeralds,* p. 799. **"Did not challenge":** Dallek, *Unfinished,* p. 257. **"The biggest":** Schlesinger, *Robert Kennedy,* p. 201.

The tide; Kennedy's telecast; "With a rush": White, *Making 1960,* pp. 107–8. **"I think":** White, *Making 1960,* p. 114.

"Washington heard": *NYT,* May 12, 1960. **"The road":** *NYT,* May 15, 1960.

Johnson press conference: *NYT, WP, AA-S,* May 12, 1960. **Reedy's statement"; "slumped further":** *AA-S,* May 12, 1960. **Cloakroom scene:** *AA-S,* May 12, 1960. **"If you want":** Rowe OH II.

"See those houses"; Indianapolis press conferences: *Amarillo Daily News,* May 29, 1960. **As the plane "thundered":** *Abilene Reporter-News,* May 26, 1960.

Five-day tour: *WS,* May 27, 1960; *DT-H,* May 30, 1960; *Waco News-Tribune,* June 1, 1960.

"Biggest day": *Idaho Falls Post-Register,* May 26, 1960. **Drevlov scene:** *FWS-T,* May 1960. **Pierre scene; "a day that":** *DT-H, HP,* May 30, 1960. **"Hadn't slept":** *Waco News-Tribune,* June 1, 1960.

Kennedy said that he would have: Kennedy had responded to a question as to whether he would "apologize" to the Soviet Union for the U-2 mission by saying, "I certainly would express regret at the timing and give assurances that it would not happen again. I would express regret that the flight did take place." *BS,* May 18, 1960. **"I want"; "It was Mr. Khrushchev":** *NYT, DMN, DT-H,* May 28, 1960. **"At every stop":** *WES,* May 29, 1960. **"I am not prepared":** *NYT,* May 31, 1960. **"Lyndon Johnson alone":** Caro, *The Path to Power,* p. 416.

Swooped across Texas: See "The Flying Windmill" chapter in Caro, *Means.* **Over Hells Canyon itself:** See the "Hells Canyon" chapter in Caro, *Master.* **Strange lines:** *BS,* May 31, 1960. **He told ranchers:** *WES,* May 30, 1960. **"Needs a champion":** *BS,* May 31, 1960.

Theodore White linked: White, *Making 1960,* p. 134.

"He has": *WES,* May 30, 1960. When reporter William H. Blair of the *NYT* asked a person in the audience, Would you vote for a Southerner, he replied, "I didn't think of him that way when he was speaking." *NYT,* Dec. 15, 1959. **Lieutenant governor:** In fact, Drevlov endorsed him. *DT-H,* May 29, 1960. **"There's no":** *DT-H,* May 30, 1960. **"A lion":** Fleeson, *BG,* June 2, 1960.

"And Symington next": "Telephone Conversation between Jim Rowe and Walter Jenkins," June 23, 1960,"Transcripts of Telephone Calls—June 1960, OFWJ, Series 2, Box 1. **Mansfield finally:** Rowe interview. **"Don't come":** Rowe OH II, p. 15; Rowe interview.

A favorite: For Johnson's championing of Church in the Senate, see Caro, *Master,* pp. 859–61, 905–7, 970–75, 988–89. **"To help me":** Caro, *Master,* p. 989. **Kennedy offer:** Ashby and Gramer, *Fighting the Odds,* pp. 124–26. Kennedy's Idaho contact, Robert Wallace, had passed the word to Kennedy that Church "is running for keynoter." **"The little sonofabitch":** Busby OH, JFKL; Busby interview. Church did indeed deliver the keynote address at the Convention.

"Simply couldn't": *HP,* May 29, 1960.

"You and I": "Private Memo," May 26, 1960, Notebook 3, Box 1, Krock Papers, Mudd Library, Princeton University.

31,250: *NYT,* July 3, 1960. **"Successful":** *NYT, WP,* June 5, 1960. **Arizona and Colorado:** *NYT,* June 19, 26, 1960. So completely did Kennedy's forces in Colorado control that state's declaration that Former Senator Ed Johnson was not even allowed to be a member of it.

"Kennedy has got": Rowe OH II. **"Now listen, Adlai":** Morgan interview. **"And how!":** "Private Memo," May 26, 1960, Notebook 3, Box 1, Krock Papers, LBJL, Princeton University.

Some . . . had been promised: *WSJ,* July 1, 1960; Evans and Novak, *LBJ,* p. 263.

"Too raw"; "Sam was just": Bolling interview; Evans and Novak, *LBJ,* p. 265. **Without warning; longtime:** *NYT, WP, BS,* June 30, 1960. **Rayburn's "word"; "The theory":** *NYT,* June 30, 1960. **"Audacious," "blatant":** Evans and Novak, *LBJ,* p. 264.

Had indeed been speculation; "engineered": *NYT,* July 1, 1960. **"The bandwagon":** *El Paso Times,* May 20, 1960.

He had: Hoff interview.

"The boy": "During the entire conversation" in which Johnson tried to persuade Tip O'Neill to support his candidacy, "he never once mentioned Jack Kennedy by name. It was always 'the boy' " (O'Neill with Novak, *Man of the House,* p. 181). In other conversations, it was "Young Jack." Steele to Johnson, July 8,

1960, SP. "Toward Kennedy he is contemptuous," Steele reported. **"Sonny Boy", "Johnny":** *Time,* April 25, 1960; Steinberg, *Sam Rayburn,* p. 522; Dallek, *Lone Star,* p. 569. **"He's a nice":** *DT-H,* May 31, 1960. Or "a fine, attractive young man," as in *WP,* May, 30, 1960. **"Young Jack":** *Time,* July 18, 1960. **"Jack was out":** *Time,* July 18, 1960. Steele to Harry Johnston, July 8, 1960, SP, quoted in Dallek, *Lone Star,* p. 572. "I cannot be absent when public business is at stake. Those who have engaged in active campaigning since January have missed hundreds of votes. This I could not do.... Someone has to tend the store" (*Time,* July 18, 1960). **"Likes to":** *WES,* May 27, 1960. **"Have you heard?":** Judd OH, HSTL. The remark "shocked me," Judd says. "It was one of the most insulting remarks I ever heard. But that was Lyndon's gutsy way. He thought he was going to mow Kennedy down." **"Small cracks":** Sidey, quoted in Miller, *Lyndon,* p. 241. **"All of the enmity":** Lisagor OH, JFKL, quoted in Miller, *Lyndon,* p. 241. In his OH, Lisagor added, "There were a lot of things he said about Kennedy which revealed some basic feelings.... I told Bobby all these things. I don't think I left out a single word, four-letter or otherwise, whereupon Bobby simply turned to the window ... and said, 'I knew he hated Jack, but I didn't know how much.' " **"A 'little scrawny' ":** Lisagor OH. And see Schlesinger, *Robert Kennedy,* p. 205, and Reston Jr., *The Lone Star: The Life of John Connally,* p. 189. **"It is amazing":** Robert G. Spivack, "Watch on the Potomac," *Chicago Daily Defender,* June 27, 1960.

Cook on Investigating Subcommittee: Caro, *Master,* pp. 312–13, and "Out of the Crowd" chapter. **Going to Brough:** "Telephone Conversation between Don Cook and Walter Jenkins," Tuesday, July 5, 1960, 12:40 P.M. **By the next day:** "Arthur C. Perry— Telephone Call of Don Cook from New York," July 6, 1960. Both from "Transcripts of Telephone Conversations—July 1960," Box 1, Series 2, OFWJ, LBJL. **Johnson took a role:** Telephoning Dr. Gerald Labiner in Dallek, *Unfinished,* p. 261. **Johnson decided:** Connally interview. **Connally, Edwards press conference:** *AA-S, BS, NYT, LAT, WES, WPT,* July 5, 6, 1960. **Seizing on the fact:** Burns, *John Kennedy* (p. 159), explains that "While Kennedy's adrenal insufficiency might well be diagnosed by some doctors as a mild case of Addison's disease, it was not diagnosed as the classic type of Addison's disease, which is due to tuberculosis." Travell says this was "a true summary of the facts" (Travell, *Office Hours,* p. 328). **"Does not now":** *BS, NYT, WP,* July 5, 1960. **Sorensen went further:** He said flatly

that "He is not on cortisone." Asked what other drug he might be using, Sorensen replied: "I don't know that he is on anything—any more than you and I are on" (*NYT,* July 5, 1960). **De Sapio ... had:** "Charlie Kress, 10:50 A.M., "Transcripts of Telephone Conversations— July 1960," Box 1, Series 2, OFWJ, LBJL. **"Johnson should disavow":** *BS, NYT, LAT, WES, WPT,* July 7, 1960. Evans and Novak, *LBJ,* p. 272.

"Before the": *WES,* July 6, 1960. **Johnson's announcement:** *NYT, WES, WP,* July 6, 1960. **Voice suddenly broke:** "His voice quavered unexpectedly when he came to the point," McGrory wrote (*WES,* July 6, 1960). **"I had never":** Busby interview. Mooney wrote that "The senator ... I thought seemed slightly ill at ease" (Mooney, *LBJ,* p.129).

Last visit to White House: Mazo OH, Columbia University, quoted in Dallek, *Unfinished,* p. 261. Also see Evans and Novak, *LBJ,* p. 261. **"He got mad":** Herring interview. **"Top-level":** *NYT,* July 9, 1960. **NAACP rally:** *LAT, NYT, WES, WP,* July 11, 1960. **All that weekend:** *BS, LAT, NYHT, NYP, NYT, WES, WP,* July 9–11, 1960. **Prendergast delivered:** *NYT,* July 10, 1960. **Docking and Loveless:** *NYT,* July 10, 1960. **MOVE TO KENNEDY:** *NYT,* July 10, 1960. **JOHNSON SEEMS:** *LAT,* July 9, 1960.

"The single major"; "Everything depends": Joseph Alsop, "Matter of Fact," *WP,* July 8, 1960. On the eve of the Convention, the *NYT* reported that "On one issue, Sen. Kennedy's brother and Sen. Johnson's campaign manager were in agreement. This was that the results of the Pennsylvania caucus on Monday would be significant" (*NYT,* July 7, 1960). **"If we could have":** Connally interview. Johnson himself, in an interview with John Steele, said, "If Dave goes for me, I can make it; if he goes for Kennedy my chances are about washed up" (Steele to Johnson, July 8, 1960, SP). "Telephone Conversation between Bobby Baker and Walter Jenkins," July 6, 1960, in which Baker says, "Will say again, Pennsylvania is the key to the situation"; Special Files–Assassination, Box 1). Chicago Mayor Dick Daley was to say flatly that "Without him [Lawrence], John Kennedy would not have carried the '60 convention" (Donaghy, *Keystone Democrat: David Lawrence Remembered,* p. 136).

"Solely": Weber, *Don't Call Me Boss: David Lawrence, Pittsburgh's Renaissance Mayor,* p. 36. **1958 governorship race:** Thomas McCloskey interview with Donaghy, June 28, 1974, p. 3, Michael P. Weber Papers, Archives Service Center, University of Pittsburgh. **1959 Sunday mass; "just can't":** Donaghy, *Keystone Democrat,* p. 130. **"I figured":**

Weber, *Don't Call Me Boss,* p. 360. **He was afraid:** "Any chance I would have of getting a majority in both houses of the [Pennsylvania] General Assembly would go skimmering if Kennedy was the head of the ticket." Donaghy interviews with David Lawrence, July 16, 1973, p. 5, Thomas McCloskey, June 28, 1974, p. 3, Weber Papers. **"What he wanted":** Hemenway interview. **"I could":** Weber, *Don't Call Me Boss,* p. 360. **"An almost youthful":** Weber, *Don't Call Me Boss,* p. 360. **"Though I don't think":** Donaghy interview with Gerald Lawrence, Part I, July 16, 1973, p. 5, Weber Papers. **"I was very":** Weber, *Don't Call Me Boss,* p. 360.

"Why would you want": Donaghy, *Keystone Democrat,* p. 129. **"We were all":** Rose Kennedy, quoted in Donaghy, *Keystone Democrat,* pp. 370–71. Also: "Joe Kennedy was furious about it. He used to say terrible things because Dave wouldn't do it." (Mathew McCloskey interview with Donaghy, Nov. 2, 1970, p. 3, Weber Papers.)

His ally was; Hopkins had been discussing: Lewis to Kennedy, July 8, 1960, Personal Papers of Welly Hopkins, LBJL. Hopkins interview, OH. Mary to Johnson, July 7, 1960; Mary [Rather] to Johnson, undated, but from the context, that weekend, "Memoranda—DNC—LA, July 11–15, 1960," LBJL.

Daley inviting Lawrence: Weber, *Don't Call Me Boss,* p. 363. **"With the man he had championed":** Weber, *Don't Call Me Boss,* p. 363. **"You'll have eighty-five percent"; "If the party wants me":** Hemenway interview. **"Do what":** Thomas B. Morgan, "Madly for Adlai," *American Heritage,* Aug.–Sept. 1984; Weber, *Don't Call Me Boss,* p. 363; Garth, Hemenway interviews. **"Governor, are you sure":** Wirtz, quoted in Morgan, "Madly," and in Weber, *Don't Call Me Boss,* p. 363. **"Adlai could have said":** Morgan, "Madly"; Weber, *Don't Call Me Boss,* p. 363. **"There was some reason":** Hopkins interview, OH.

Pennsylvania Caucus: *NYT, WP,* July 12, 1960. **"I am not a naïve":** *WP,* July 12, 1960. **4 1/2:** *NYT,* July 12, 1960. **"I don't see how":** Rowe OH II.

Had sent a telegram; Johnson's reply: "Telegrams from Sen. J. F. Kennedy to Sen. LBJ," Box 3, "Special File on Lyndon B. Johnson's Campaigns," Kennedy to Johnson, Johnson to Kennedy, July 12, "July 12, 1960—Transcript of recorded remarks of Debate—Sen. Kennedy and Sen. Johnson, Democratic Convention, Biltmore Hotel," July 12, 1960, Box 39, Statements of Lyndon Baines Johnson, LBJL. **"I want":** Hoff interview. **Connally, Reedy and Busby:** Connally,

Reedy, Busby interviews. **"One major error":** Connally interview; Evans and Novak, *LBJ,* p. 273.

"If it went well": Reedy OH.

Giving an interview: Seigenthaler interview. **"A damned fool":** Seigenthaler OH I, JFKL. **"I know, Daddy"; "You'll see":** Jean Kennedy Smith interview; Seigenthaler OH.

"Tremendous exhilaration": Graham, "Notes on the 1960 Democratic Convention," pp. 4–6.

"I have never found it necessary": *NYDN,* July 13, 1960. **Trying to elevate:** *NYDN, NYHT, WP,* July 13, 1960. **Kennedy finally said:** *San Antonio Light, WP,* July 13, 1960. **Not more than a handful:** *San Antonio Light,* July 13, 1960. **"TV cameras bristled":** *CSM,* July 13, 1960.

Kennedy's leg shaking: Sidey interview. **"Johnson had packed full":** *San Antonio Light,* July 13, 1960. McGrory wrote that there was "a handful" of Massachusetts delegates present (McGrory, *WES,* July 13, 1960). **Description of the debate:** *CT, CSM, HP, LAT, NYD, NYHT, NYT, San Antonio Light, WES, WP.* Scheslinger, Sidey, Wright interviews. **"And when I take":** McGrory, *WES,* July 13, 1960.

"Lyndon sure": Wright interview.

"Johnson felt": Schlesinger interview. **"Big Irish grin":** Wright interview. **"Really, it didn't come off":** Jacobsen, quoted in Miller, *Lyndon,* p. 249. **"He got cured":** Hoff interview.

Last round of infighting: *WP,* July 14, 1960. **Connally won:** *DT-H,* July 14, 1960. **"Flamethrowers":** Schlesinger, *A Thousand Days,* p. 44. **"Chamberlain umbrella man":** Before the Washington State delegation, he said, "I wasn't any Chamberlain umbrella man. I never thought Hitler was right." *CT, NYT, WP,* July 14, 1960. *NYT* quotes Johnson as saying that he had been a " 'fighting liberal' in the Roosevelt administration and a 'working liberal' in the Truman administration." He then declared: "I was never any Chamberlain umbrella policy man. I never thought Hitler was right" (*CT, NYT, WP,* July 14, 1960). **"I was not contributing":** *NYT,* July 14, 1960. "I haven't had anything given to me": Stated before Kentucky and West Virginia delegations, quoted in *NYHT,* July 14, 1960. There are slightly differing versions of his statements in newspaper reports the next day. In the *NYT* and *WP,* Jan. 15, 1960, he is quoted as saying, "I haven't had anything given to me. Whatever I have and whatever I hope to get will be because of whatever energy and talents I have." **"Now this young man":** *HP,* July 14, 1960.

"As one accustomed": Baker, *Wheeling,* p. 114.

Rayburn's speech: *AA-S, DMN, DT-H, NYT,* July 14, 1960. **In the left-hand:** Busby, Rowe interviews. **Connally last-minute maneuver:** "After the commencement of the nominations, he called John Connally . . . to suggest that, if possible, it might be a wise move to get the voting to go over to the next day, to try to get the convention to recess in order to gain some delay. This was not done." Juanita Roberts memorandum dated July 13, 1960, Pre-Presidential Diary unsigned, July 13, 14, 1960; Office of the President Files (OPF) Files, Box 8 (Moyers folders). Also *HP,* July 14, 1960.

"Very, very conservative"; "If it comes down": Edward Kennedy interview. **Rayburn crying:** *Life,* July 28, 1972.

For a western: How close the Johnson strategy came to being successful is shown by remarks such as the one JFK made to Philip Graham (Schlesinger, *A Thousand Days,* pp. 44, 45) on Wednesday. "He added that he might be twenty votes short on the first ballot and asked if there were any chance of getting Johnson votes out of the vice-presidential offer."

For Robert Kennedy's perspective on Johnson's feelings about the first ballot, see Guthman and Shulman, *Robert Kennedy: In His Own Words,* pp. 20, 21. "We were counting votes! We had to win on the first ballot. We only won by fifteen votes. North Dakota had the unit system—I think in North Dakota and South Dakota. We won it [North Dakota] by half a vote. California was falling apart. . . . You know, there were just about thirty-two balls up in the air. . . . There wasn't any place that was stable." Sorensen says, "If the convention ever went into the back rooms, we'd never get out of the back rooms." "On the eve of the convention, John Steele of *Time* magazine told his editors in a confidential memorandum, "The 500 figure Lyndon calls a conservative estimate, and in fact it does not appear to be greatly out of line" (Steele to Johnston, July 8, 1960, SP).

"I want": Busby interview.

4. The Back Stairs

There are four principal written sources for this chapter: two memoranda: "Notes on the 1960 Democratic Convention," dated July 19, 1960, written by Philip Graham and hereafter referred to as "Graham Memo" ("Reference File," LBJL), and a "Private Memorandum," dated Sept. 22, 1960, beginning "I have finally pieced together . . . the events leading up to the

nomination of Lyndon B. Johnson . . . ," by Arthur Krock (Notebook 3, Box 1, Krock Papers, "Reference File," LBJL); and two unusually detailed and thorough articles: Philip Potter: "How LBJ Got the Nomination," *The Reporter,* June 18, 1964, and "Dear Jack Wire, Gained Second Spot for Johnson," by Earl Mazo, *NYHT,* July 16, 1960. But since even these accounts so often conflict, the principal sources also include the author's interviews with John Connally and James Rowe Jr., and with figures in the Johnson camp who, while not as central to Johnson's decisions, were often present in his hotel suite: Horace Busby, Thomas Corcoran, Walter Jenkins, and George Reedy. And, because Sam Rayburn is such a central figure in the episode, the principal sources also include the author's interviews with Rayburn's aides D. B. Hardeman and John Holton.

"Just a minute": Kennedy himself wrote captions for a series of pictures by Jacques Lowe that were published in *Look* magazine (John F. Kennedy, "A Day I'll Remember," *Look* magazine, Sept. 13, 1960): When he called, "Lady Bird answered. She said he was asleep, but she'd wake him. I told Lyndon that I wanted to talk to him, and we agreed to meet in his room in two hours." Johnson is quoted as having said, "The phone rang, and Lady Bird answered it." Moyers says "I remember very distinctly on the morning after the nomination the phone ringing. I was up, and I walked into their bedroom to get them up. As I walked into the darkened bedroom, Mrs. Johnson answered it. She said 'Just a minute,' and she shook Mr. Johnson awake and said, 'Lyndon, it's Senator Kennedy, and he wants to talk to you . . .'" (Moyers, quoted in Miller, *Lyndon,* pp. 255–56.). A secretary who was employed by Johnson from early 1959 to shortly after the Democratic convention, Betty Cason Hickman, says it was she who took Kennedy's call. She also said that she was present in the living room, taking notes, while Kennedy was conferring there with Johnson about the vice presidency. She also says that she composed the telegram Johnson had sent to Kennedy congratulating him on winning the nomination. "Bill Moyers and I, and of course Johnson had his input, too," she says (Hickman OH, LBJL; Hickman interview). These recollections are not supported by the recollections of others, including Busby, Reedy and Rowe; everyone the author interviewed says that there was no one in the room but Kennedy and Johnson.

"Jack Kennedy just called me": Connally interview.

"We had lost"; "Power is": Rowe interview.

"The most insignificant": Schlesinger, *The Cycles of American History*, p 337.

"A bucket": Among the innumerable Texan politicians who corrected the author when he used the word "piss" was Congressman O. C. Fisher, a longtime Garner intimate.

"I wouldn't trade": Schlesinger, *Thousand Days*, p. 47

"Got irritated": Hugh Sidey, "The Presidency," *Time*, July 25, 1988.

Rowe should have been more aware: Rowe interview. **Johnson's 1956 try:** Caro, *Master of the Senate*, pp. 801–25.

Proxmire's challenge: Caro, *Master*, pp. 1015–19. **"Although"**: Evans and Novak, *Lyndon B. Johnson*, p. 290.

Other considerations: Johnson's thinking is from interviews with BeLieu, Busby, Clark, Connally, Corcoran, Goldschmidt, Oltorf, Rather, Reedy, Rowe, and Johnson's brother, Sam Houston Johnson. Also with two of his secretaries. **"To the point"**: Mary Louise Young interview. **Convinced he would die young:** Caro, *Means of Ascent*, pp. 136–38. **"Too long . . . too long"**: Busby, Reedy interviews. **"I don't think anybody from the South"**: MacNeil interview.

He had reconnoitered it: Busby, Jenkins, Oltorf interviews.

Sometime early: Busby, Jenkins, Oltorf interviews. **As a Leader:** McPherson says that he feels that if he continued as Leader, "he would have had to represent the views and objections of the southern committee chairmen to the liberals in the Administration; thus, he would have remained a southern, essentially conservative, figure. It was better to be Vice President . . ." McPherson also says that if Johnson continued as Leader, "his role would have been to put the Kennedy program through Congress. If he had succeeded, the credit would have been Kennedy's. If he had failed, the fault would have been his" (McPherson, *A Political Education*, pp. 178–79).

Johnson was to say: Dugger, *The Politician*, p. 373; *LAT*, July 13, 1960. He also said, "No Texan will be nominated for President in my lifetime" (William V. Shannon, *New York Post*, July 17, 1960). Johnson made numerous other remarks in 1960 to the same effect. For example, on March 12, driving down to New Jersey for a wedding with several friends, in what Evans and Novak describe as a "pensive, introspective, and serious" mood, he said, "A fellow from my part of the country probably couldn't be anything more than another John Garner" (Evans and Novak, *LBJ*, p. 275). **Would still:** Dugger, *The Politician*, pp. 373, 470.

"Clare, I looked it up": Clare Boothe Luce, quoted in Martin, *A Hero for Our Time*, p. 159. **"Lyndon, why in the world?"**: Among the people in Texas to whom Johnson made similar remarks was Robert M. Jackson, editor of the *Corpus Christi Caller-Times*, who was to tell his reporter James M. Rowe that, encountering Johnson at the Corpus Christi airport when Johnson flew back to Texas from Los Angeles, he had asked him, "Lyndon, why in the world did you accept the nomination?," and that Johnson had replied, "Well, six of them didn't have to get elected." Rowe to Caro, May 3, 1983 (in author's possession). **"Well, . . . six of them"**: Kilgore interview. **"You know, seven of them"**: Clark interview.

"Board of Education" scene: Caro, *Means*, pp. 121–22. **"The most insignificant"**: Adams, quoted in Feerick, *From Failing Hands*, p. 67. **"I am"**: Adams, quoted in McCullough, *John Adams*, p. 402. **"Very 'iffy' "**: *Wilmington News*, May 27, 1960; *NYT*, July 4, 1960.

"Maybe": Evans and Novak, *LBJ*, p. 275. **Meeting with Lawrence and McCloskey:** Donaghy, *Keystone Democrat*, pp. 139–140. **"Guaranteed"**: McCloskey interview with Donaghy, Nov. 2, 1970, Michael P. Weber Papers, Archives Service Center, University of Pittsburgh; Donaghy, *Keystone Democrat*, p. 140. **"Well, that is"**: *NYT*, July 4, 1960. **"An opportunity"**: *NYT*, July 6, 1960.

"The labor people"; "the same assurance"; "with [Jack] Kennedy's knowledge": O'Donnell, Powers, and McCarthy, *"Johnny, We Hardly Knew Ye,"* p. 189. **O'Donnell made his promises:** O'Donnell OH I. **When Rauh told Kennedy:** "Katharine Graham Interview Two with Joe Rauh," July 21, 1989, pp. 39, 40 (in author's possession); Rauh interview. **Assurances repeated by Jack Kennedy to other liberals:** He sent word to the Orville Freeman camp "that he was the midwestern liberal he wanted most for a running mate" (Solberg, *Hubert Humphrey*, p. 213). Kennedy went "so far as to designate Humphrey confidant Max Kampelman as a liaison to help plan a joint Kennedy-Humphrey staff session at Hyannisport after the Convention" (Eisele, *Almost to the Presidency*, p. 151). Clark Clifford, as Symington's campaign manager, writes that on the afternoon of the balloting for President, he received from Jack Kennedy "an unequivocal offer" of the vice presidency to Symington, only to have Kennedy tell him the next day, that "I must renege on an offer made in good faith. During the night I have been persuaded that I cannot win without Lyndon on the ticket. I have offered the vice presidency to him—and he has accepted" (Clifford, *Counsel to the President*, pp. 317–19).

"**Pledged to a number**": *WP*, July 17, 1960. A typical response by labor and liberal leaders to the news of Johnson's selection was that given by Reuben G. Soderstrom, head of the Illinois State AFL-CIO. "Labor worked day and night at Los Angeles to get Kennedy so we would be rid of Johnson. And what did they do? They made chumps out of us." George Meany, Soderstrom said, had his "Irish up" over Johnson's selection (*NYT*, July 28, 1960). "**The one name**": Schlesinger, *Robert Kennedy and His Times*, p. 207. "**There was**": Lincoln, *Kennedy and Johnson*, pp. 92–93.

Three men were called: Johnson's discussion with Baker, Connally, and Rowe is based on the author's interviews with Connally and Rowe, and on Baker, *Wheeling and Dealing*, pp. 124–25. In an autobiography Connally "wrote" with Mickey Herskowitz, Connally's description of some of the incidents described in this chapter sometimes varies somewhat—not in any significant aspect—from the way he described them to me, during three days of interviews with me at his ranch in 1985, and during other interviews with him in Austin in 1986. Since I went back and forth over these incidents with him, trying to make him remember all the details he could, I am using the wording he used with me. "**We were not**": Connally interview. "**Your risk**": Connally, Rowe interviews. "**He'll never**": Connally interview. "**Hate your guts**"; "**not a fully committed**"; "**angry and bitter**": Baker, *Wheeling and Dealing*, pp. 125–27. Baker quotes himself as making part of this argument to Senator Kerr a few minutes later, but both Connally and Rowe say Baker used the same phrases in the conversation with Johnson. "**You're going**": Connally interview. "**A strong**": Baker, *Wheeling*, p. 125. "**He would have to carry**"; "**I even expressed**": Connally interviews. "**I don't think**": Baker, *Wheeling*, p. 125. "**Suppose you**"; "**You're totally**": Connally interview.

"**You'll still have the Speaker**": Connally interview.

"**You're a heartbeat away**": Connally interview. "**One heartbeat away**": Baker, *Wheeling*, p. 125. **Rowe couldn't**; "**On balance**"; "**I want**": Rowe interview; Rowe OH II; Senate Daily Diary, July 14, 1960. See also Office of the President Files, Box 8, (Moyers folders), LBJL. "**And that one heartbeat**": Rowe interview.

"**Quiet**": Connally interview. "**Passive**"; "**Well, I'll probably**": Baker, *Wheeling*, p. 125. "**Well, I don't**": Connally interview. "**Oh, you can't**": quoted in Miller, *Lyndon*,

p. 256. "**I was wrong**": Thornberry, quoted in Miller, *Lyndon*, p. 256; Evans and Novak, *LBJ*, p. 279.

Rayburn had seen—Roosevelt Garner feud: Caro, *The Path to Power*, pp. 558–71. "**No man**": Caro, *Means*, p. 558. "**This New Deal**": Garner, quoted in Caro, *Path*, p. 563. "**I saw Jack Garner**": Rayburn, quoted in Krock, Memoranda, July, 1960, p. 1, Arthur Krock Papers, LBJL. "**The first thing**": Eugene Worley OH. "**A premonition**"; "**They are going**": Steinberg, *Sam Johnson's Boy*, p. 528. "**Obvious**": Clements, quoted in Drew Pearson Papers, LBJL.

"**If he were available**": "I asked Lyndon if he were available for the vice presidency. He told me that he was. He then suggested that I discuss the matter with various party leaders while he conferred with his own advisers" (John F. Kennedy, "A Day I'll Remember," *Look*, Sept. 13, 1960). "**There are a couple of problems**": Johnson to Hardeman "and others," July 1960, quoted in Hardeman and Bacon, *Rayburn*, p. 441. They write that in this conversation "Johnson said he was committed not to accept without Rayburn's approval. He had been trying frantically all morning to reach the Speaker." **Couldn't even think**: Krock, Memoranda, July 1960, p. 1, Arthur Krock Papers, "Reference File," LBJL. Lyndon Johnson was to give many different versions of what had occurred. For example, in a tape recording he made for guidance for the ghostwriters of his autobiography, he said "he wanted me on the ticket. I said, 'You want a good Majority Leader to help you pass your program.' I didn't want to be vice president. I didn't want to leave the Senate. . . . I told Kennedy, 'Rayburn is against my state and my state will say I ran out on them.' Kennedy said, 'Well think it over and let's talk about it again at 3:30. . . . The President said, 'Can I talk to Rayburn?' . . . Kennedy talked Rayburn into it . . ." ("Reminiscences of Lyndon B. Johnson, transcript of tape recording, Aug. 19, 1969," OH Collection, LBJL). On another occasion, he said that Kennedy had begun by saying "that he had said many times that he thought I was the best qualified for the presidency by experience, but that as a southerner I could not be nominated. He said he felt that I should be the one who would succeed if anything happened to him" (Schlesinger, "Author's View on How Johnson was Chosen—J.F.K.—'I Held It Out . . . He Grabbed at It," *Life*, July 16, 1965). He gave a similar version to Potter: "He said he hoped I could run with him, that he had said many times . . ."

Kennedy said he had already checked; "**people like**": Jenkins, quoted in Miller, *Lyn-*

don, p. 257. **If Rayburn had anything:** Johnson, quoted in Philip Potter, "How LBJ Got the Nomination," *The Reporter*, June 18, 1964. "Senate Daily Diary," July 14, 1960. This "diary" was kept by Johnson's secretaries. Based of course on what Johnson told them about this meeting, it says, "Senator Kennedy . . . did ask Senator Johnson to be his running mate. Senator Johnson told him he was not interested." **Kennedy said:** Potter, "How LBJ Got." **"With quick nods":** Baker, *Wheeling*, p. 126. **Whatever had been said:** Mazo wrote that the conversation between the two men touched only obliquely on the real purpose of the visit. . . . Nothing was offered in so many words. It wasn't necessary. Nor did Sen. Johnson protest his innocence of any desire for the office. That was not necessary either. The two men understood each other, according to their intimates" (*NYHT*, July 16, 1960). According to Potter, Johnson gave him the following account. "He said he hoped I could run with him. . . . He said he felt that I should be the one who would succeed if anything happened to him. . . . I told him I appreciated his offer but thought I should stay as majority leader. . . . I said I would give it thought, however. . . ." (Potter, "How LBJ Got"). **"We talked mostly":** *LAT*, July 15, 1960. **"You were right":** Connally interview. **"He said":** Jenkins, quoted in Miller, *Lyndon*, p. 257. **"That he had just":** O'Donnell and Powers, *"Johnny, We Hardly,"* p. 190; Miller, *Lyndon*, pp. 257–58. **The Vice President should be:** Jenkins, quoted in Miller, *Lyndon*, p. 257. Hale Boggs recalls that Corcoran and Foley "told me that President Kennedy had offered the vice [presidency] to Johnson, but that Johnson was going to do whatever Mr. Rayburn told him to do" (Boggs OH).

Kerr and Baker: Baker, *Wheeling*, pp. 126–27.

Whether Johnson would mind: Arthur Schlesinger, during interview with Robert Kennedy, Feb. 27, 1965, quoted in Guthman and Shulman, eds., *Robert Kennedy: In His Own Words*, p. 24.

"The idea": Guthman and Shulman, eds., *In His Own Words*, pp. 20, 21. **"You just":** Guthman and Shulman, eds., *In His Own Words*, pp. 24, 25.

A "gesture": Charles Bartlett, "On Choosing a Vice President," *WES*, March 10, 1964. **"I just held it out like this . . . and he grabbed it:"** Schlesinger, *A Thousand Days*, p. 49. In an oral history he gave the LBJL, Bartlett related Kennedy's words this way: "He said, 'I didn't really offer the nomination to Lyndon Johnson. I just held it out to here'— and with his hand he gestured two or three

inches from his pocket." In this oral history, Bartlett says that Jack Kennedy said even more: "He said, 'I hear your editors are upset because you said that Symington was going to be vice president. Well, you can tell them that if you're surprised, so am I." In another oral history, given to the JFKL (p. 49) he quotes Kennedy as having told him, " 'I didn't offer the vice presidency to Lyndon.' He said, 'I just held it out to here . . .' They told him this was a gesture that he had to make, and then he went down and made the gesture, thinking he'd get it over with early in the morning. . . . When he went down there he didn't think there was a reason in the world to believe that Lyndon would accept the thing." **"Shocked" when Johnson "seized":** Robert Kennedy used the word "shocked" when, not long after the Bartlett article appeared, he was interviewed by Philip Potter.

Schlesinger's repeating: His acceptance of Robert Kennedy's version as accurate began in 1965, with his article (an excerpt from his book, *A Thousand Days*, which would be published that year), "Author's View on How Johnson was Chosen—J.F.K.—'I Held It Out . . . He Grabbed at It," *Life*, July 16, 1965. Kennedy, Schlesinger wrote, "decided to do this [offer the vice presidency to Johnson] because he thought it imperative to restore relations with the Senate leader. . . . He was certain that there was practically no chance that Johnson would accept. . . . Kennedy returned to his own suite in a state of considerable bafflement." This view is, of course, also in *Robert Kennedy and His Times*, published in 1978. Contrary views were assailed with his customary vigor. Responding to one by the journalist Tom Morgan in *American Heritage*, he wrote, in a letter to the editor, "In fact, as Robert Kennedy's oral history makes clear, the offer of the vice-presidential nomination was *pro forma;* the Kennedys never dreamed Johnson would accept the offer and when he did, John Kennedy sent Robert Kennedy to do his best to persuade Johnson to change his mind." (Among his other published reiterations of this view is "Correspondence," *American Heritage*, Dec. 1984). Others have repeated it so often that it has been accepted. Hugh Sidey, in *Time*, July 25, 1988, says "Boston-Austin Was an Accident." But there are Jack Kennedy statements that lead to the other view. For example, the columnist Peter Lisagor says that on the Kennedy campaign plane after the convention, "I said to him, 'Boy, that was either the most inspired choice for vice president or the most cynical.' Jack Kennedy said, 'Cynical!' He bristled at the word cynical. He said, 'It's not cynical at all. Democrats have always

done this—an eastern candidate and a Southerner.' He even went to Al Smith, and he said, 'He chose Joe Robinson from Arkansas. So Democrats have always done this. It wasn't cynical at all.' He wanted to win. He said, 'I don't think it was cynical.' And he took great umbrage at the word cynical. It led me to believe that in the continuing controversy over whether he wanted Lyndon Johnson or not . . . I've always felt as a result of that conversation that he had thought it out fairly thoroughly, and maybe he had toyed with some other people, but the idea of winning some southern states prevailed, and he hoped that Lyndon Johnson would take that" (Lisagor OH, JFKL).
Telephoning Bobby: Potter, "How LBJ Got"; O'Donnell and Powers, *"Johnny, We Hardly,"* pp. 191–92; Salinger OH. **"Plus Texas":** Potter, "How LBJ Got." **"How many electoral votes?":** Salinger, quoted in Shesol, *Mutual Contempt,* p. 48; Salinger OH. **"Yes, we are":** Potter, "How LBJ Got." **"Thereupon":** Salinger OH.
Meeting with northern bosses: This account is based on Salinger, *P.S.: A Memoir,* pp. 80–81, Salinger OH; O'Donnell and Powers, *"Johnny, We Hardly,"* pp. 191–92; and Potter, "How LBJ Got." **Had telephoned Lawrence; "I don't want to go"; "authorized":** McCloskey interview with Donaghy, Nov. 2, 1970, p. 3, Archives Service Center, University of Pittsburgh. **The "old pros":** *WP,* July 15, 1960. **"It looked as though"; "All of them"; "I could have belted":** O'Donnell and Powers, *"Johnny, We Hardly,"* p. 192. **"Now Nixon":** O'Donnell and Powers, *"Johnny, We Hardly,"* p. 192. **"Wait a minute":** O'Donnell and Powers, *"Johnny, We Hardly,"* pp. 192–93. **"I'm forty-three":** O'Donnell and Powers, *"Johnny, We Hardly,"* p. 193. **"You get":** O'Donnell OH. **"He wanted":** O'Donnell, quoted in Potter, "How LBJ Got."
"Jack Kennedy had made"; "he was perhaps," etc: O'Brien OH I. O'Brien puts the time of his summons to Kennedy's suite at "6 A.M. or something" like that, but it is clear from his description of what happened when he arrived that it occurred after John Kennedy's meeting with Johnson.
"Sam was in": Patman, quoted in Steinberg, *Sam Johnson's Boy,* p. 530. **"Johnson was going to do":** Boggs OH I. The exact same words were used by Corcoran in one of his interviews with the author. **"Rayburn was adamant":** Clements OH. **Boggs told Corcoran:** Krock, Memoranda, July 1960, p. 1; Hardeman and Bacon, *Rayburn,* p. 442; Boggs OH; Boggs, quoted in Miller, *Lyndon,* p. 256.

"reiterated strongly": Potter, "How LBJ Got." **Poignant:** The closest Rayburn came to giving voice to those feelings was during his conversation with Johnson immediately after Jack Kennedy had left his suite. He said, according to Johnson, that "He would not be happy without me on the Hill" (Potter, How LBJ Got"). **Rayburn said he would; "I think":** Hardeman and Bacon, *Rayburn,* pp. 441, 442.
"John, I've got": Holton interview. Holton gave a slightly different version of these quotes to C. Dwight Dorough, in Dorough's *Mr. Sam,* p. 569. **"I told him":** Hardeman and Bacon, *Rayburn,* pp. 443, 519.
"Positively exuberant:" Boggs, quoted in Miller, *Lyndon,* p. 257. **He told O'Brien and other aides:** Potter, "How LBJ Got." **"Briskly":** *DMN,* July 15, 1960. **"I don't":** Connally interview. **"A wiser man":** Potter, "How LBJ Got." Johnson was to give a longer version of this remark in his "Reminiscences": "Because I'm a sadder and wiser and smarter man this morning than I was last night" ("Reminiscences of President Lyndon Baines Johnson," Aug. 19, 1969, p. 8).
"And then": Connally interview. **"It is a trap":** White, *The Making of the President, 1964,* p. 86.
Number of meetings conflict: Jim Rowe says (OH II), "I finally concluded that where everybody misses what actually happened was that there were three periods of conversation between Johnson and Kennedy, and most people got them down to two. That is why I think all this confusion exists." But it is only part of the reason that confusion exists. **Schlesinger says:** Schlesinger, *Robert Kennedy,* p. 209. **Connally says:** "He [Bobby Kennedy] came not once—he came three times." Transcript, "An American Profile," C-Span, July 1, 1991, p. 11; Connally interview. Johnson was to say, "He came to my room three times to try to get me to say we wouldn't run on the ticket" (Johnson, "Reminiscences," p. 6). Juanita Roberts, in her Pre-Presidential Daily Diary, in effect a log of Johnson's activities, lists only two trips that Robert Kennedy made down to the Johnson suite.
Telephone conversations conflict; Graham says four: They are enumerated in Graham Memo. **Rowe says three:** In his OH II. In his "Private Memorandum, Sept. 22, 1960," p. 2, Arthur Krock says Jack Kennedy "twice sent his brother, Robert F., to Johnson . . ." (Arthur Krock Papers, LBJL). The description of these meetings in this book is based on the author's interviews—repeated interviews, in an attempt to clear up the discrepancies between the various accounts—with

Busby, Connally, Corcoran, Hardeman, Holton, Jenkins, Reedy, and Rowe. The only people alive present that day who refused to talk to the author about it were Bobby Baker and Bill Moyers. Baker's description comes from his book, *Wheeling and Dealing.*

Another principal source for this section is the memorandum, "Notes on the 1960 Democratic Convention," dated July 19, 1960, written by Philip Graham and hereafter referred to as "Graham Memo." Philip Potter interviewed Johnson, both Jack and Robert Kennedy, O'Brien, and O'Donnell, for a detailed account, "How LBJ Got the Nomination," that appeared in the issue of *The Reporter* dated June 18, 1964.

First meeting: The account of this meeting is based on Hardeman and Bacon, *Rayburn,* p. 443, and interviews with Connally. Also *BS,* July 16, which quotes Rayburn as saying to Bobby not "Shit!" but "utter nonsense." The *Sun* said that "Robert was advised that Johnson and his lieutenants were in negotiations with his brother and not with him." The paper said that "Young Kennedy refused tonight to confirm or deny this, asserting that he had no desire to contradict an 'elder statesman of the party.' " **"I don't want":** Connally interview; transcript, "An American Profile," C-Span, July 1, 1991, p. 11. **Were waiting . . . "for the obvious":** Graham Memo, p. 16. **"His hair all hanging down"; "told me":** Rayburn, quoted in Hardeman and Bacon, *Rayburn,* p. 443. **" 'We've got to' ":** Connally interview. **Democratic National Committee offer:** Graham Memo, p. 16. The Rayburn and Connally version of this meeting is supported by Earle Clements, who was in the Johnson suite when Rayburn and Connally emerged from this meeting. Clements says that both Rayburn and Connally told him at that time "that Bobby said there was great opposition from Labor and wouldn't Johnson become chairman of the National Committee . . ." He says that when Rayburn refused that offer, "Bobby said 'Then he'll be the nominee for vice president.' " The uncertainty in the Johnson camp about Jack Kennedy's true feelings is shown by a remark Lady Bird made to Clements a few minutes later: "Do you think they really want him?" (Clements OH). **" 'Shit' ":** Graham Memo, p. 16; Connally interview; on a television program, he cleaned up the quote, saying, "He just kind of spit and used an expletive" (Transcript, "An American Profile," C-Span, July 1, 1991, p. 12).

"Lady Bird intervened"; "felt L.B.J.": Graham Memo, pp. 8, 9. Connally says she said, "Lyndon, I hope you won't do this" (Connally interview).

"Agreeing with her; You don't want it": Graham Memo, p. 9. **" 'All of us were pacing' ";** **And "finally":** Graham Memo, p. 9. **"By which, it soon turned out, Johnson meant":** Connally, Rowe interviews. **Rayburn went back; "Then it's Lyndon":** Rayburn interview with Hardeman, quoted in Hardeman and Bacon, *Rayburn,* p. 444; Connally interview. Juanita Roberts, in her Pre-Presidential Diary, says: "Bob Kennedy said, 'Well, it's Jack and Lyndon.' " **"Suddenly":** *DMN,* July 15, 1960.

"As witness": Graham Memo, p. 9.

"He said something": Graham Memo, p. 9. **"Both agreed"; "Jack was utterly calm":** Graham Memo, p. 10. This account is supported by David Lawrence's son, Gerald, who says that his father was writing the nomination speech (Gerald Lawrence OH, interview with Donaghy, July 16, 1973, Michael P. Weber Papers, Archives Service Center, University of Pittsburgh).

"Come with me!"; "And there was Bobby Kennedy": Busby, Connally interviews. **None of them would ever:** Busby, Connally interviews. Rowe and Holton heard about Rayburn's remark a few minutes later.

Rayburn refused to see him; "It's getting worse": Connally interview. In another version, in Transcript, "An American Profile," C-Span, July 1, 1991, p. 12, Connally says Bobby said, "He's [Johnson's] just got to do it. I said, 'Well, Bobby, he's not going to do that,' so he left. Ten minutes later, he's back . . . had been back down to see Rayburn . . . and had said Jack would phone directly."

Bobby then said; "Roughly, 3:00"; No call came; "was considerably": Graham Memo, p. 11. **"Johnson hasn't heard":** Rowe OH II. **Jack said:** Graham Memo, p. 11. **"Stop vacillating":** Graham in his Memo (p. 11) says that he told Kennedy that "It was too late to be mind-changing" and "that he should remember 'You ain't no Adlai.' " **"Agreed about":** Graham Memo, p. 11. **"Just don't go":** Rowe OH II. **"Johnson took the call";** **"Do you really want me?"** Rowe, quoted in Miller, *Lyndon,* p. 261; Rowe OH II; Rowe interview.

"Everybody": Rowe, quoted in Miller, *Lyndon,* p. 261. **"Whom I had never"; "Graham, my God":** Rowe OH II. Graham Memo, p. 13 says, "Bill Moyers rushed into our room to say Lyndon wanted me at once. 'I'll be along in just a minute.' 'That won't do,' Moyers yelled, and grabbing my arm dragged me down the hall through a solid jam of press people and into the entrance hall of the suite with Rowe and Connally close behind."

"There were just the two of us": Robert Kennedy interview with Arthur Schlesinger, quoted in Guthman and Shulman, eds, *In His Own Words,* pp. 21, 22.

Hawaiian delegates; "LBJ seemed about": Graham Memo, p. 13. **He told them:** Rowe interview. Graham says, "he shouted at me that Bobby Kennedy had just come in and told Rayburn and him that there was much opposition and that Lyndon should withdraw for the sake of the party."

"What am I going to do?"; "I'd never seen him": Rowe interview. **"Phil, call Jack"; " 'Oh, . . . that's all right' "; "You'd better speak to Bobby"; "Well, it's too late now":** Graham Memo, pp. 13, 14. Schlesinger, *A Thousand Days,* p. 56. **"Had just survived":** Graham Memo, p. 15.

"Jim, don't you think?" Rowe OH II. **"My God":** Schlesinger, *Robert Kennedy,* p. 210; Schlesinger, "Author's View—He Grabbed," *Life.*

"As though": *WP,* July 15, 1960.

"I urged"; " 'Bobby's been' "; "I later learned": Graham Memo, pp. 3, 14, 16. **"Did Jack offer":** Graham Memo, p. 16.

"The only people": Robert Kennedy interviews with John Bartlow Martin, in Guthman and Shulman, eds., *In His Own Words,* pp. 304, 22. **"I went"; "flabbergasted"; "Obviously,"** etc.: Guthman and Shulman, eds., *In His Own Words,* p. 22.

Scene in suite: O'Donnell and Powers, *"Johnny, We Hardly,"* p. 194; O'Donnell OH; Miller, *Lyndon,* pp. 258–59. **"Violently":** O'Donnell and Powers, *"Johnny, We Hardly,"* p. 19. **"Joe Rauh, who":** Woodcock, quoted in Miller, *Lyndon,* p.258. **"This is the worst double cross":** *WES,* July 16, 1960. **"Doublecross"; "sell-out":** O'Donnell and Powers, *"Johnny, We Hardly,"* p. 194. **"Savagely":** O'Donnell OH. **Rose shouted; Conway:** O'Donnell and Powers, *"Johnny, We Hardly,"* p. 194. **"I don't think"; "Bobby was shaken":** O'Donnell and Powers, *"Johnny, We Hardly,"* p. 194.

"Do you want me": O'Donnell and Powers, *"Johnny, We Hardly,"* pp. 194–95. **Jack's determination . . . appears never to have wavered; Soapy-Governors confrontation; "sitting in an armchair":** O'Donnell and Powers, *"Johnny, We Hardly,"* p. 195. **"Not to my recollection":** O'Brien OH I. **Lawrence's speechwriters were drafting:** Governor Lawrence, quoted in Donaghy, *Keystone Democrat,* p. 143. Donaghy interview with Gerald Lawrence, Part I, July 16, 1973, p. 3, Michael P. Weber Papers, Archives Service Center, University of Pittsburgh Library System. **"The President wanted":** Guthman and Shulman, eds., *In His Own Words,* p. 22. **"As the years":** O'Brien OH I. **"That was":**

Thomas, *Robert Kennedy,* p. 98. Shesol's conclusion on the same point: "Bobby argued that when he had left the Kennedy suite to meet with Johnson, the two brothers had been in agreement: if Johnson seemed amenable, Bobby should ease him off the ticket. But once plunged into the labyrinth of crowded hallways and snarled communications, Bobby did indeed fall 'out of touch' and was betrayed, however unintentionally, by his own brother. This was, perhaps, too painful to admit, but the alternative was unthinkable" (Shesol, *Mutual Contempt,* p. 56). **"I always":** Dutton, quoted in Thomas, *Robert Kennedy,* p. 98.

"That opened to Johnson": Evans and Novak, *LBJ,* p. 282.

"Bobby was against": Johnson, "Reminiscences." **" 'that little shitass' ":** Baker, *Wheeling,* p. 130. **"I'm not going to":** Connally interview. **Slitting gesture:** Among those who saw it: Herring, Oltorf. Johnson would still be using that gesture in 1968, Evan Thomas relates. In a meeting on April 2 of that year with Eugene McCarthy, shortly after Kennedy had announced his presidential candidacy, "the conversation was 'almost pro forma and casual' . . . until Robert Kennedy's name came up. Johnson said nothing, but drew the side of his hand across his throat." Thomas, *Robert Kennedy,* p. 366. **"I'll cut":** Clark interview.

5. The "LBJ Special"

"Everything's all right now, George": Reedy OH XVI. It was the "first time I ever saw a benevolent smile on Bobby's face," Reedy says.

"Settled": White, *The Making of the President, 1960,* pp. 251, 259.

Gallup Poll: *NYT, WP,* Oct. 5, 12, 1960. **So far behind:** *NYT,* Sept. 7, 1960. **"This boy"; "after that":** Drew Pearson, *WP,* Nov. 5, 1960.

Descriptions of whistle-stop tour: E. Ernest Goldstein, "How LBJ Took the Bull by the Horns," *Amherst,* Winter 1985, pp. 79–81. Reedy, *LBJ,* pp. 129–31; Steinberg, *Sam Johnson's Boy,* pp. 540–43. *Danville Bee,* Oct. 9, 1960; *Richmond Times-Dispatch,* Oct. 9, 1960; *Spartanburg Journal,* Oct. 10, 1960; *WES,* Oct. 10–14, 1960; *Anderson Independent,* Oct. 11, 12, 1960; *Atlanta Journal,* Oct. 11–14, 1960; *Charlotte Observer,* Oct. 11–19, 1960; *Houston Chronicle,* Oct. 11, 1960; *Jacksonville Journal,* Oct. 11, 1960; *Birmingham News,* Oct. 12, 1960; *Greensboro Daily News,* Oct. 12, 1960; *NYT,* Oct. 12, 1960; *Florida Times-Union,* Oct. 13, 1960; *Houston Press,* Oct. 13,

1960; *Jacksonville Journal,* Oct. 13, 1960; *Orlando Sentinel,* Oct. 13, 1960; *CSM,* Oct. 14, 1960; *Meriden Star,* Oct. 14, 1960; *New Orleans States-Item,* Oct. 14, 1960; *Pensacola News,* Oct. 14, 1960; *Tallahassee Democrat,* Oct. 14, 1960; *AA-S,* Oct. 15, 1960; *New Orleans Times-Picayune,* Oct. 15, 1960; *WP,* Nov. 6, 1960; *NYT,* Nov. 6, 1960. **"Potent":** Reedy, *Lyndon B. Johnson,* p. 130.
"The volume would be turned up": Reedy, *LBJ,* p.130. **"The main thing"; "Are we going to sit idly by":** *WES,* Oct. 11, 1960. **"Why, oh why"; "This high-talking, high-spending"; "We just decided":** *NYHT,* Oct. 13, 1960. **Talking about his daddy:** *Anderson Independent,* Oct. 12, 1960; *Corsicana Sun, DT-H,* Oct.12, 1960.
"Nobody asked him": *WES, Oct. 11, 1960; Houston Press,* Oct. 13, 1960; *NYHT,* Oct. 13, 1960. **A deep hush; description of him talking about Joe, Jr.:** *Florida Times-Union, NYHT,* Oct. 13, 1960.
"Good-bye, Culpepper": Reedy, *LBJ,* p. 130; Reedy OH XVII; McPherson, *A Political Education,* p. 181. **"Good-bye, Greer":** *Atlanta Journal and Constitution, NYHT,* Oct. 13, 1960. **"What he was doing":** Eugene Patterson, "Johnson Is the Caboose Man," *Atlanta Constitution,* Oct. 13, 1960.
"The Senator was doing his best work": McGrory, *WES,* Oct. 11; Goldsmith, *Colleagues: Richard Russell and His Apprentice Lyndon B. Johnson.,* pp. 79–80. **"A portable smoke-filled room":** *Birmingham News,* Oct. 12, 1960. **1,247:** *WES,* Oct. 19, 1960.
"Being religioned": Harlow OH, quoted in Dallek, *Lone Star,* p. 586; Harlow interview. **"Two weeks earlier"; "has justified":** McGrory, *Atlanta Constitution,* Oct. 14, 1960. **"Master":** *Chicago Daily News,* Oct. 16, 1960.
"Judas": *Richmond Times-Dispatch,* Oct. 9, 1960. *Orlando Sentinel,* Oct. 13, 1960; Rowe interview. **"Deeply disturbed":** Johnson to Connally, Oct. 18, 1960, JSP, quoted in Dallek, *Lone Star,* p. 586. **"The ever haunting":** Rowe to Humphrey, Nov. 22, 1960, Rowe Papers. **Private polls were showing:** Busby, Rowe interviews; Dallek, *Lone Star,* p. 584; *FW S-T,* Nov. 7, 1960; Busby interview.
Alger was raising: Steinberg, *Sam Johnson's Boy,* p. 543; WES, Nov. 11, 1960. **Spitting at Lady Bird:** *Abilene Reporter-News,* Nov. 6, 1960, WP, Nov. 5, 1960. **Frightened expression:** *WES,* Nov. 5, 1960; Moyers, quoted in Miller, *Lyndon,* p. 271. **"I want you":** Phinney, quoted in Miller, *Lyndon,* p. 271. **Thirty minutes:** *NYT, WP,* Nov. 5, 1960. **"LBJ and Lady Bird":** Hardemann, quoted in Miller, *Lyndon,* p. 271. **"He knew":** Moy-

ers, quoted in Miller, *Lyndon,* p. 271. **"I wanted to find out":** *WES,* Nov. 5, 1960.
Turned the tide in Texas: Harlow, Rowe, Sidey, Sorensen interviews; Evans and Novak, *Lyndon B. Johnson,* pp. 302–4; Miller, *Lyndon,* pp. 271, 272; Goldsmith, *Colleagues,* p. 81. **"A mob in Dallas":** *Abilene Reporter-News,* Nov. 6, 1960. **"We had been told":** Gonella interview, OH.
Vote figures: Unless otherwise indicated, all figures in this chapter are from the *Texas Almanac, 1961–1962,* pp. 460–62.
Making a mockery: For a description of this procedure, see Caro, *The Path to Power,* pp. 721–22. **Texas Republicans charged; new law:** *DMN,* Nov. 10, 1960. Texas Republicans were eventually to say that "at least" 100,000 ballots were illegally disqualified. *NY, HT,* Dec. 4, 5, 1960; *WP,* Dec. 11, 1960; "How to Steal an Election," *Look,* Feb. 14, 1961. "Thousands of Texas voters had their ballots invalidated for failing to mark out minor parties, reports from several cities showed" (*Texas Observer,* Nov. 18, 1960). Also see Steinberg, *Sam Johnson's Boy,* p. 545.
94 precincts, 59,000 invalidated: *SAE,* Nov. 12, 1960; "How to Steal an Election," *Look,* Feb. 14, 1961. **The *Texas Observer* noted:** Nov. 11, 1960. **The factor considered decisive:** Clark, Connally, Jones, Kilgore, Rowe interviews.
12,000, 19,000; "This is a reversal": Paul Kilday to Johnson, Dec. 2, 1960, "1960 Congressional File—K," Box 372, JSP.
Kilday's brother running the West Side: Johnson's long experience with vote-buying on the West Side is in Caro, *Path,* pp 277, 718–23, 736–37; *Means of Ascent,* p 181. **West Side votes; 17,017 to 2,982;** *SAE,* Nov. 10, 1960, and *SAE,* Nov. 7, 1956. **1,324 to 125:** Box 25. In 1956, it voted for Eisenhower, 851 to 523. **Other West Side Boxes:** The figures cited are for Boxes 15 and 17. In Box 12, traditionally a key precinct in the Mexican-American area, the vote was for Kennedy, 523 to 61 (*SAE,* Nov. 10, 1960). John Connally was to say of the West Side, "They [low-income Mexican-Americans] went [to the polls] because the Sheriff told them to go. 'Sheriff Kilday wants you to vote for . . .' " Connally was talking at the time about the 1948 election, but then said the same situation had existed in the 1956 election, and in 1960 (Connally interview).
"Had little to do": Caro, *Master of the Senate,* pp. 745–46. See also Caro, *Path,* pp. 720–23, 732–33; *Means,* pp. 182–83, 189–91, 321. The sources for this description of historic voting patterns in the Valley are given in *Path,* p. 83, and *Means,* pp.458–61. **"You get down":** Clark interview.

Between 1948 and 1960: Clark, Connally interviews, as well as interviews with Luther E. Jones, a one-time Johnson aide who had been, for eight years, Parr's most trusted attorney, and was, in 1960, still close to Parr. In fact, he was one of the attorneys representing him in the early stages of his 1959 court fight; with James. M. Rowe, who covered politics in the valley for the *Corpus Christi Caller-Times* and other newspapers for more than twenty years, and with Joe M. Kilgore, the congressman for the Texas congressional district that adjoined Duval County and included most of the other counties in Parr's sphere of influence. After the 1961 election, the *Chicago Tribune* reported that "the election procedures [in Starr County] are much the same as in George Parr's 'Duchy of Duval.' "

"Slow-motion count": *CCC,* Nov. 9, 1960.

"Pistols were carried": *Texas Observer,* Dec. 2, 1960; *NYHT,* Dec.4, 1960; *CT,* Dec. 12, 1960.

"One charge"; kept a list: Earl Mazo, "Texas Vote 'Irregularities' Listed," *NYHT,* Dec. 4, 1960.

"Strictly L.B.J. Country": Carillo, quoted in Pycior, *LBJ and Mexican Americans,* p. 118. **"The basic core":** Connally, quoted in Pycior, *LBJ and Mexican Americans,* p. 118; Connally interview. **"Our old friends":** Clark interview.

Chancery hearings cut short: Caro, *Means,* pp. 380–84. **"I think Lyndon":** Master in Chancery William Robert Smith, quoted in Caro, *Means,* p. 397.

"Numerous and widespread": *WP,* Dec. 11, 1960.

Three of Johnson's: As Earl Mazo put it, "Texas Republicans . . . have no representation anywhere in the Texas election machinery" (*NYHT,* Dec. 5, 1960). **Steakley said:** *SAE,* Nov. 26, 1960. **Hearings were simply:** *DMN, SAE,* Nov. 12–Dec. 19, 1960; *Texas Observer,* Dec. 2, 1960; *CT,* Dec. 8, 1960; *Kansas City Times,* Dec. 8, 1960. "Time has been a major headache to the Republicans because the Electoral College convenes to vote on Dec. 19—and the Texas results must be overturned before then if it is to affect the outcome."

"Republicans were stunned": Evans and Novak, *LBJ,* p. 302. **Republican strategists:** Harlow interview. **Clinton Anderson was to say:** Miller, *Lyndon,* p. 273. **"Is given much":** "It Was a Johnson Victory, Too," *USN&WR,* Nov. 21, 1960. Sorensen, *Kennedy,* pp. 187–88. **"Could not have been":** Evans and Novak, *LBJ,* p. 302. **"The key":** *USN&WR,* Nov. 21, 1960.

"The maltreatment": Sorensen, *Kennedy,*

p. 215. **"Gambled":** Sorensen, *Kennedy,* p. 222. **"You've got to admit":** O'Donnell, quoted in Philip Potter, "How LBJ Got the Nomination," *The Reporter,* June 18, 1964.

Election night call: Sorensen interview. In his *Kennedy* (p. 211) he says that after Kennedy spoke to Johnson, he joked that "Lyndon says I hear *you're* losing Ohio but *we're* doing fine in Pennsylvania." There are several other similar versions of Kennedy's remark. See White, *Making 1960,* p. 23; Dallek, *Lone Star,* p. 589; Rowe to Humphrey, Nov 22, 1960, Box 32, LBJL. O'Donnell says that "Kennedy hung up the telephone and told us with a smile, "I see we won in Pennsylvania, but what happened to you in Ohio?' " (O'Donnell and Powers, *"Johnny, We Hardly Knew Ye,"* p. 223).

6. "Power Is Where Power Goes"

"I do understand": Johnson, quoted in McPherson, *A Political Education,* p. 450.

"Mix too much": Williams, *The Rise of the Vice Presidency,* p. 19. **"In particular"; "any formal":** Katzenbach, "Memorandum for the Vice President," March 9, 1961, pp. 10, 11, "Vice Presidency—Office Of," LBJL. **"The only":** Schlesinger, "The Future of the Vice Presidency," *The Cycles of American History,* p. 348. **Roosevelt removed:** Williams, *Rise of the Vice Presidency,* pp. 185–98. **Nothing:** Katzenbach, "Memorandum," p. 11. **When Johnson:** Reedy OH. **"The nature":** Katzenbach, "Memorandum," p. 10.

Now Johnson asked: In his biography, *Senator Mansfield,* Don Oberdorfer cites a telephone call Johnson made to Mansfield when Mansfield, despite Johnson's request, was still leaning against taking the job. In that conversation, Johnson assures Mansfield that he would "do anything for you at any time . . . and I will be there every week and I will do everything you want me to do." Oberdorfer cites this as evidence that Johnson "made it plain that he intended to continue to mastermind Senate activity" ("Re: Conversation between Senator Johnson from Austin, Texas and Senator Mansfield in Washington, D.C.," Nov. 11, 1960, Series 22, Box 103, Folder 1, MSS 065, Mike Mansfield Collection, University of Montana Library, cited in Oberdorfer, pp. 154, 155). But in Mansfield's interview with Oberdorfer, quoted in Oberdorfer, *Senator Mansfield,* p. 157, Mansfield said that Johnson "had come to me . . . and asked if I would propose that he be permitted to attend future caucuses . . . and also to preside. In my view this would only constitute an honorary position, and I had no objection." And Mansfield's statement in the caucus that "the proposal was in no way intended to suggest that he was sharing either the responsibility or the authority under the proposal but rather recognition" makes it plain that the November 11th call is no more than Johnson's habitual way of saying whatever he thought would persuade someone to do what he wanted (United States Senate, *Minutes of the U.S. Senate Democratic Conference 1903–1964,* p. 578).

"Owed his prominence": Evans and Novak, *Lyndon B. Johnson,* p. 306. **"No work to do":** Oberdorfer interview with Mansfield, Oct. 8, 1998, Box 2, Folder 3, Oberdorfer Collection, MSS 590, University of Montana Library. **"In my view":** Oberdorfer, *Senator Mansfield,* p. 157; Steinberg, *Sam Johnson's Boy,* p. 547.

"What no other Senate"; he also persuaded: Evans and Novak, *LBJ,* p. 306. **Keeping "Taj Mahal":** Humphrey, *The Education of a Public Man,* p. 243; Evans and Novak, *LBJ,* p. 306. **Bobby Baker would:** "Re: Conversation between Bobby Baker in Miami, Fla. and Senator Mansfield, Wash. D.C.," Nov. 14, 1960, Series 22, Box 103, Folder 1, MSS 065, Mike Mansfield Collection, University of Montana Library. **"I think that":** O'Brien OH. In fact, when Baker broached the subject of resigning, Mansfield replies, "I like things the way they are" ("Re: Conversation between Bobby Baker in Miami, Fla. and Senator Mansfield, Washington, D.C., Nov. 14, 1960," Mansfield Collection).

"Probably hoping"; "He had often"; "had the illusion:" Humphrey, *Education,* p. 243; Humphrey OH. **"Johnson was not":** Humphrey OH I. **"A buoyancy":** Baker, *Wheeling,* p. 133. **Planned to "sit in":** "Conversation between Johnson and Mansfield, Nov. 11, 1960." **"He was going to be":** O'Donnell OH I. O'Brien says (OH VI), "He felt that he would maintain basically the same leadership position with the Senate that he had had as Majority Leader." Humphrey says (OH I) that Johnson "had the illusions that he could be, in a sense, as Vice President, the Majority Leader, and that he could at least be head of the caucus." **"I was both"; "I saw a disaster":** Baker, *Wheeling,* p. 134.

"Like a father": Steele to Williamson, Nov. 12, 1958, SP. **"He thought he *was*":** MacNeil interview.

"He didn't rant and rave": Smathers, quoted in Caro, *Master of the Senate,* p. 562. And see pp. 562–72. **"During his early":** Reedy, *The U.S. Senate,* p. 178. **"Brooding":** Evans and Novak, *LBJ,* p. 306.

January 3 caucus: *Minutes of the U.S. Sen-* ate Democratic Conference, 1903–1964, pp. 577–81. The careful words of the *Minutes* state only "that the suggestion raised questions as to the principle of separation of powers" (p. 578). Baker, *Wheeling,* pp. 135–36; Evans and Novak, *LBJ,* pp. 306–8; Valeo, *Mike Mansfield,* pp. 11–15. **"Can you imagine":** Byrd, *The Senate, 1789–1989,* Vol. I, p. 624. **"Despite":** Shesol, *Mutual Contempt,* p. 63. **"I don't know":** Steinberg, *Sam Johnson's Boy,* p. 547. **Ashen:** Baker, *Wheeling,* p. 135. **"There was":** Baker, *Wheeling,* p. 135. **Mansfield insisted:** Oberdorfer, *Senator Mansfield,* p. 157; Drew Pearson, "The Washington Merry-Go-Round," *WP,* Jan. 18, 1961. **"With each repetition":** Valeo, *Mike Mansfield,* p. 13. Pearson says that Mansfield "assured the meeting that Johnson had not been consulted on the proposition beforehand. This evoked only skeptical Senate laughter" (Pearson, *WP,* Jan. 18, 1961). **"But . . . everyone":** Baker, *Wheeling,* p. 135. **Hardly:** *NYT,* March 19, 1961. **"It was too much":** Humphrey OH I. **After Russell spoke:** Humphrey, *Education,* p. 243. "It was a shock and great disappointment that he could not be Vice President and de facto Majority Leader," Humphrey wrote. **The next day's:** *Minutes of the U.S. Senate Democratic Conference, 1903–1964,* pp. 581–83; Pearson, *WP,* Jan. 18, 1961. **"I now know":** Miller, *Lyndon,* p. 276. **"Those bastards":** Baker, *Wheeling,* p. 135.

Johnson asked Kennedy for an office: Lincoln, *Kennedy and Johnson,* p.153. **"To appoint a staff within":** "TITLE 3—THE PRESIDENT, Executive Order Number ___," "Kennedy, John F.—National Security Council," Box 4, WHFN. **"He told me":** BeLieu interview.

Several persons: Evans and Novak, *LBJ,* p. 308–9; Steinberg, *Sam Johnson's Boy,* p. 551. **After discussing:** Goodwin, *Lyndon Johnson,* p. 165. After discussing the matter with Neustadt, Doris Goodwin wrote that "shortly after the inauguration, he [Johnson] sent an unusual Executive Order to the Oval Office for President Kennedy's signature. Outlining a wide range of issues over which the new Vice President would have 'general supervision,' it put all the departments and agencies on notice that Lyndon Johnson was to receive all reports, information, and policy plans that were generally sent to the President himself." **Would be revised:** Revised draft: "TITLE 3—THE PRESIDENT, Executive Order Number ___," Moyers to Johnson, Jan. 26, 1961, with another version of the Order attached; "Kennedy, John F.—National Security Council," Box 4, WHFN. (Reedy wrote that "He actually proposed that President Kennedy sign

a letter which would virtually turn over the national defense, establishment and exploration of outer space to his vice president" (Reedy, *Lyndon B. Johnson*, p. 133). So confident was Johnson that Kennedy would sign the order that he had a press release prepared to be released when Kennedy had done so: "President Kennedy announced today that he has designated Vice President Lyndon B. Johnson 'to exercise continuing surveillance . . . ,'" undated, "Memos—1961 [1 of 4]," Box 6, Presidential Aides' Files of George Reedy, LBJL. See also Mark O. Hatfield, with the Senate Historical Office, *Vice Presidents of the United States, 1789–1993*, p. 21.
Suggestions incorporated: "Dear Mr. Vice President: Recognizing the need," undated; "Title 3—The President," undated; Moyers to Johnson, Jan. 26, 1961, Box 4, WHFN. **All reports:** Neustadt, quoted in Goodwin, *Lyndon Johnson*, p. 165. **Revised drafts; Busby's comments:** "Title—THE PRESIDENT, Executive Order Number ____," undated, "Kennedy, John F.—National Security Council," Box 4, WHFN.
"Did not like": Reedy, *LBJ*, p. 133. **BeLieu showed:** BeLieu interview. **"A blunder"; "Before I":** Reedy, *LBJ*, p. 133. **"Flabbergasted"; "frankly":** Evans and Novak, *LBJ*, pp. 308, 309.
A new draft was handed to him: Kennedy to Johnson, Jan. 28, 1961, "Kennedy, John F.—1961," Box 6, WHFN. Johnson apparently pleaded for more staff, and Kennedy agreed that sixteen persons could be placed in the Department of Defense "to assist you carrying out the responsibilities outlined in the accompanying letter," but, according to BeLieu, Johnson, realizing that they would be reporting also to McNamara, didn't take advantage of this offer. Kennedy to Johnson, Jan. 28, 1961, "Kennedy, John F.—1961," Box 6, WHFN. "He couldn't hire anyone for the little Joint Chiefs of Staff," BeLieu says. "He didn't have the space (personnel lines) for them" (BeLieu interview). See also Moyers to O'Donnell, Feb. 16, 1961, Box 4, WHFN. **That had disappeared:** Reedy wrote that "I do not believe Lyndon Johnson ever received a verbal acknowledgment" of his proposed order—"let alone anything in writing" (Reedy, *LBJ*, p. 132).
"He understood": Reedy to Johnson, Feb. 9, 1961, "Reedy Memos to LBJ—1961" [1 of 2], Box 6, Presidential Aides' Files of George Reedy.
"A prime minister": Goodwin, *Team of Rivals*, p. 342. **"There were predictions":** Marquis Childs, "Johnson's Role," *WP*, Feb. 17, 1961. **"Had Mr. Lincoln":** Nicolay, quoted in Goodwin, *Team of Rivals*, p. 342.

"The whole thing": Reedy, *LBJ*, p.132. Steinberg quotes Kennedy aides as saying, "Lyndon wants to pull a William Seward" (Steinberg, *Sam Johnson's Boy*, p. 551). O'Donnell says, "He still was going to be majority leader and vice president" (O'Donnell OH I).
"Flabbergasted": Lincoln, *Kennedy and Johnson*, p. 153. **Sixteen posts:** Kennedy to Johnson, Jan. 28, 1961, "Kennedy, John F.—1961," Box 4, WHFN.
"Not one that": Caro, *Master*, pp. 1022–1030. **Kennedy asked; Wiesner:** Divine, ed., *The Johnson Years*, Vol. II, p. 229. **"Wanted to control"; Kennedy "was not about to":** Webb OH. **"Mr. Johnson's hand":** Tom Wicker, "L.B.J. in Search of His New Frontier," *NYT*, March 19, 1961.
"You will become the target": "Reedy to Johnson, July 18, 1961," Box 6, Presidential Aides' Files of George Reedy, LBJL. **Richard Russell . . . had been:** Caro, *Master*, pp. 201–2, 221, 797–98. **"I don't have any budget":** Dallek, *Flawed Giant*, pp. 25, 26. **Committee's powers:** "Reedy to Johnson, July 18, 1961"; Wicker, "L.B.J. in Search"; Kheel, Reedy interviews. **"General supervision":** Kheel, "Report on Government Programs against Discrimination," Aug. 30, 1962, p. 10; Kheel interview. **"Under the way":** "Reedy to Johnson, Aug. 7, 1961," "Memos—1961 [3 of 4]," Box 6, Presidential Aides' Files of George Reedy. **"Administration is in":** "Reedy to Johnson, April 10, 1961," "Memos—1961 [1 of 4]," Box 5, Presidential Aides' Files of George Reedy. **"Jerry Holleman is":** "Reedy to Johnson, May 2, 1961," "Reedy Memos to LBJ—1961 [2 of 2]," Box 6, Presidential Aides' Files of George Reedy. **"It is going to be somewhat":** "Reedy to Johnson, Feb. 8, 1961," "Memos—1961 [1 of 4]," Box 6.
"There was a tribute": Russell Baker, "Feud," *The New York Review of Books*, Oct. 23, 1997. **"Oh, Jack":** Schlesinger, *A Thousand Days*, p. 5.

7. Genuine Warmth

"Liked Johnson personally": Schlesinger, *A Thousand Days*, p. 704. **"Always had"; "He saw":** Schlesinger, *Robert Kennedy and His Times*, p. 621. **"The President and Vice President"; "Their initial":** Sorensen, *Kennedy*, pp. 265–66. As late as 1974, Schlesinger stated flatly: "Kennedy liked Johnson . . . and treated him with great personal consideration" (*The Cycles of American History*, p. 349).
"I can't": O'Donnell OH I, LBJL. **"In charge":** O'Donnell OH. **Permission:** O'Donnell, Powers, and McCarthy, *"Johnny,*

We Hardly Knew Ye," p. 8. **"I want you":** Duke, quoted in Miller, *Lyndon,* p. 278. **Instructed Lee White:** Shesol, *Mutual Contempt,* p. 78. **"Don't":** O'Brien OH, quoted in Shesol, *Mutual Contempt,* p. 78. **"President Kennedy was":** Reedy, quoted in Schlesinger, *Robert Kennedy,* p. 621. **"The President made":** White, *The Making of the President, 1964,* p. 42. **"Had genuine regard":** Dallek, *Flawed Giant,* p. 10.

First leaders breakfast: Lincoln, *Kennedy and Johnson,* pp. 143–45. **"Fiddling":** Lincoln, *Kennedy and Johnson,* p. 145. **Mrs. Lincoln was to calculate:** Lincoln, *Kennedy and Johnson,* p. 161; Schlesinger, *Robert Kennedy,* p. 622. **Breakfasts:** "Favors Granted," Box 26, Office Files of White House Aides—Lawrence O'Brien, LBJL. **Had had more breakfasts with FDR:** Caro, *The Path to Power,* pp. 666–67. **"The smaller"; "did not invite":** Sorensen, *Legacy,* p. 108. **"It didn't take long":** O'Brien OH I.

"Frost is": Dallek, *An Unfinished Life,* p. 323. **"Did not want":** Dallek, *Flawed Giant,* p. 10. **"Was so great":** Feldman, quoted in Shesol, *Mutual Contempt,* p. 99. **"If he had been":** McPherson, quoted in Smith, *Grace and Power,* p. 172. **"If Kennedy had allowed":** Schlesinger, *A Thousand Days,* p. 707. **"Never":** McPherson OH I. **"Tactful and courteous"; Sunday brunches:** Smith, *Grace and Power,* pp. 171, 172.

"So resentful": O'Donnell OH. **Kicking Humphrey in the shin:** Caro, *Master of the Senate,* p. 594. **"Couldn't stand":** Harbin interview, and Caro, *Path,* p. 229. **"The picture":** Caro, *Path,* p. 548. **"The President had":** Mills, quoted in Miller, *Lyndon,* p. 305. **"Those who":** Tom Wicker, "L.B.J. in Search of His New Frontier," *NYT,* March 19, 1961. **Crying to Jim Rowe:** Caro, *Master,* pp. 656, 657.

Now this technique: Evans and Novak, *Lyndon B. Johnson,* p. 313; Baker, *The Johnson Eclipse,* p. 43; Shesol, *Mutual Contempt,* p. 79. **"I'm not competent to advise you on this":** Reeves, *President Kennedy,* p. 732. **"I cannot stand":** Smathers OH.

On Saturday morning: Baker, *Johnson Eclipse,* p. 44, 45. **Flying to Norfolk:** *NYT,* April 16, 1961. **"Systematically excluded":** Dallek, *Flawed Giant,* p. 16. Johnson attended a meeting in January and three meetings in March "at which the Cuba covert program was discussed." The last one he attended was on March 16, so he attended none in the month before the invasion ("Favors Granted," Box 26, Office Files of Larry O'Brien, LBJL). **Had asked:** Baker, *Johnson Eclipse,* p. 45. **Introducing Adenauer:** *WP,* April 17, 1961.

"One of": Dallek, *An Unfinished,* p. 363. **"Those":** Reeves, *President Kennedy,* p. 103. **"There's an old saying":** Schlesinger, *A Thousand Days,* pp. 289, 290. **Salinger found; disheveled:** Reeves, *President Kennedy,* p. 95. **"How could I":** Dallek, *An Unfinished,* p. 367. **Walking into O'Donnell's:** O'Donnell and Powers, *"Johnny, We Hardly,"* p. 274. **"It was":** Cushing, quoted in O'Donnell and Powers, *"Johnny, We Hardly,"* p. 276. **"A general criticism"; "Lyndon, you've got":** Schlesinger, *A Thousand Days,* p. 289.

"Pull a William Seward": Steinberg, *Sam Johnson's Boy,* p. 551. **"White House is unhappy":** Busby to Johnson, Feb. 21, 1961, Box 5, Office of the Vice President, LBJL. **"At least":** Sidey, "The Presidency," *Time,* Jan. 6, 1968. **"Knows every newspaperman":** O'Donnell OH. **"Immediate thought":** Lincoln interview. **"Constant":** Lincoln, *Kennedy and Johnson,* pp. 159, 180. **Walking through Lincoln's office:** Lincoln, *Kennedy and Johnson,* pp. 149–51.

"Kennedy is funny": Bradlee, *Conversations with Kennedy,* p. 194. **"Monstrous":** Alsop OH, quoted in Smith, *Grace and Power,* p. 174.

Busby's visit to Sorensen: "HB to The Vice President, Re: Visit with Ted Sorensen, Feb. 21, 1961," Box 5, Office of the Vice President File, LBJL. **"A liability"; "He couldn't issue":** Gonella interview. **Johnson's feelings:** Fehmer, Gonella interviews. **Simply submitted; planes:** Burris to Jenkins, July 7, 1961, "Chron. File—Burris—April 1961–June 1962 [2 of 2]," Box 6, Vice Presidential Security File. **Not routinely assigned:** For example, Burris to Johnson, Nov. 30, 1962, "Memos to the VP from Col. Burris—July 1962—April, 1963 [1 of 2]," Box 6, Vice Presidential Security File. **"You had to":** Fehmer interview. **Air Force agreed; "Mr. McNamara's office":** Burris to Johnson, March 19, 1962, Box 5, VP Security File. **"The President has reached":** Unaddressed, undated, "Vice President—Office of [2 of 2]," Box 185, VP Security File. **"He just couldn't":** SHJ, *My Brother Lyndon,* p. 108. **"Terrible mistake":** O'Donnell OH. **Sarah Hughes episode:** O'Donnell OH; O'Donnell and Powers, *"Johnny, We Hardly,"* pp. 9, 10; Evans and Novak, *LBJ,* pp. 314–15. **"That bill of yours"; "Sonny, everybody":** O'Donnell OH I; O'Donnell and Powers, *"Johnny, We Hardly,"* p. 9. **Worked out:** O'Donnell and Powers, *"Johnny We Hardly,"* p.8; O'Donnell OH I.

"Don't get me crossways": Walton interview. **He was aware also:** "He wanted no part of a quarrel with Sam Rayburn," O'Donnell says (O'Donnell OH I). **Telephone episode:** O'Donnell and Powers, *"Johnny, We Hardly,"* p. 8; O'Donnell OH I.

Scrounging for a car: "CADILLAC USE FOR LBJ AT RITES REFUSED," unidentified UPI wire copy, clipping from unidentified paper, Aug. 15, 1963, "Colonel Burris [1 of 2]," Box 6, VP Security File.

"Casual banter": Sorensen, *Counselor,* p. 267; Sorensen interview. **"You think":** Walton interview. **"About as low":** Sorensen interview. **"Could not":** Schlesinger, *A Thousand Days,* p. 703.

Rayburn dying: Caro, *Path,* pp. 762–63. **Almost twenty years before:** Caro, *Path,* pp. 757–58. **"Dear Mr. Speaker"; "Dear Bird":** Lady Bird Johnson to Rayburn, Aug. 26, 1961; Rayburn to Lady Bird, Aug. 30, 1961, Box 52, LBJA CF. **"Although the pain was":** Caro, *Path,* pp. 762, 763. **"Was it worse":** Connally interview.

Four Hereford heifers: Johnson to Jacqueline Kennedy, June 5, 1961, "Kennedy, Mrs. John F. 1961," Box 5, WHFN. **A pony:** Johnson to Jacqueline Kennedy, June 5, 1961, "Kennedy, Mrs. John F. 1961," Box 5, WHFN; Adkins to Johnson, Oct. 26, 1961, "Kennedy, John F. 1961," Box 4, WHFN; Lincoln, *Kennedy and Johnson,* pp. 154–57. **"I can see myself":** Jacqueline Kennedy to Johnson, undated, but filed with Roberts to Johnson, Oct. 28, 1962, "Kennedy, Mrs. John F. 1962," Box 5, WHFN. **In the event:** Jacqueline Kennedy to Johnson, May 27, 1963; Carpenter to Johnson, undated, "Kennedy, Mrs. John F. 1961," Box 5, WHFN; "Kennedy, Mrs. John F.—1963," Box WHFN. **"Unbelievable":** Jacqueline to Lady Bird Johnson, Dec. 26, 1961, "Kennedy, Mrs. John F.—1961," Box 5, WHFN. See also Rather to Territo, June 27, 1973, in "Kennedy, John F.—1962," Box 4, WHFN.

Christmas letter: Johnson to Kennedy, Jan. 9, 1962, "Kennedy, John F.—1962," Box 4, WHFN; Reedy interview.

"Three-hour monologue": "LBJ, The Quiet Statesman," Aug. 7, 1961, "Once Confidential Memoranda Prepared by John Steele for the editors of *Time,* Aug. '61—Sept. '68," SP. **No press conferences:** *FWS-T,* Sept. 11, 1963. **He adhered:** Wicker on March 19 writes, "As Leader, LBJ used to see the press often and at length, privately and en masse. The only way to interview him now is by requesting an appointment and waiting to be called—sometimes weeks later. Even then, most of what is said is put off the record and none of it constitutes news." **"In private":** Evans and Novak, *LBJ,* pp. 309, 310. **"Made an appointment with him":** Bartlett OH, LBJL. **"Even in**

his most private harangues":** Shesol, *Mutual Contempt,* pp. 105, 106. **"Either quit":** SHJ, *My Brother Lyndon,* pp. 114, 115. **"Even old":** Evans and Novak, *LBJ,* p. 310. **"There was never":** Bartlett OH, LBJL. **"I always":** Evans and Novak, *LBJ,* p. 312. **"For a man":** Shesol, *Mutual Contempt,* p. 105. **"A triumph":** Sidey interview.

8. "Cut"

"I don't": Caro, *Master of the Senate,* p. 1040; Hynes interview.

"You knew": Busby interview. **"This was":** Reedy, *Lyndon B. Johnson,* p. 134. **"The White House":** Goodwin, *Lyndon Johnson,* p. 182. **"Wandering":** Busby interview. **"Because":** Sam Houston Johnson, *My Brother Lyndon,* p. 109. **"Could no longer":** Mooney, *LBJ: An Irreverent Chronicle,* p. 141. **"He used":** Sidey interview.

"Clapped my back": Baker, *The Good Times,* p. 285; Russell Baker, "Feud," *New York Review of Books,* Oct. 23, 1997. **"I couldn't":** Oltorf interview. **"You know":** Herring interview.

"Yearning": White, quoted in Schlesinger, *A Thousand Days,* p. 1018. **"I don't want":** Schesol, *Mutual Contempt,* p. 102. **"Great":** Rusk, quoted in Miller, *Lyndon,* p. 178. **"He had to":** Wickenden interview.

"Rarely": Goodwin, *Lyndon Johnson,* p. 165.

WHERE'S LYNDON?: Robert W. Richards, Copley News Service, July 24, 1962; *NYHT,* July 8, 1962. **LYNDON JOHNSON GUESSING GAME:** *Des Moines Tribune,* June 26, 1962. **"Now that":** Walter Trohan, "Report from Washington," *CT,* July 28, 1962. **"Chas—Why?":** Scribbled on *DMN,* July 15, 1962, "Memos—July 1962," Box 7, Office Files of George Reedy, LBJL.

"Self-effacement": Schlesinger, *A Thousand Days,* pp. 705, 706; Schlesinger, *Robert Kennedy,* p. 622. **"A man"; "This is a bull":** Moyers, Moynihan, quoted in Schlesinger, *Robert Kennedy,* p. 622. **"Being vice president":** Bolling interview.

"Too worn out": Reed to Johnson, Feb. 21, 1962. **"No":** Scribbled on Willie Day to Johnson, Feb. 26, 1962, both in "Memos—Jan.–Feb. 1962 [5 of 5]," Box 8, Office Files of George Reedy. **"After considering":** Reedy to Johnson, March 7, 8, 9, 1962, "Memos—March, April, May 1962 [1 of 3]," Box 8, Office Files of George Reedy. **Malechek suddenly:** Smith, *Grace and Power,* p. 368. **"Grabbing":** Wright interview. **"Utter":** Goodwin, *Lyndon Johnson,* p. 167.

"The question raised": Reedy to Johnson, "Memos—August 1962," Box 8, Office Files of George Reedy. **"Go":** BeLieu interview. **"Sureness":** Lincoln, *Kennedy and Johnson*, p. 186.

"He has written": Boatner to Johnson, Oct. 1, 1962, "Memos—Oct. 1962," Box 8, Office Files of George Reedy. **Telephoning Louviere:** Baker, *The Johnson Eclipse*, p. 115. **Telephoning Rusk:** Dungan to Kennedy, Oct. 1962, Box 30, POF: LBJ.

As President Kennedy: Bird, *The Color of Truth*, p. 227. **Shocked disbelief:** Robert Kennedy, *Thirteen Days*, p. 27. **In favor of quick action:** Kennedy, *Thirteen Days*, p. 31. **"You have any":** *TPR—John F. Kennedy*, Vol. II, September–October 21, 1962, p. 415. **"The question":** *TPR—JFK*, Vol. II, pp. 415–16.

Joint Chiefs advocated: *TPR—JFK*, Vol. II, p. 428; Kennedy, *Thirteen Days*, p. 36. **"I don't think":** *TPR—JFK*, Vol. II, p. 422. **"We had to be sure":** Sorensen, pp. 675, 676. **"Any premature disclosure":** Sorensen, *Kennedy*, p. 676. **He and the Vice President:** Sorensen, *Kennedy*, p. 686. **"I don't think":** *TPR—JFK*, Vol. II, p. 454. **"The first word":** Darden interview. **"A monumental sense"; Wayne Morse episode:** Caro, *Master*, p. 199. **"I have a Grumman":** *TPR—JFK*, Vol. II, p. 427.

"Blur" of "the crucial meetings": Sorensen interview, Sorensen, *The Kennedy Legacy*, p. 109. **"I now know":** Kennedy, *Thirteen Days*, p. 31. **"Rather impassioned"; "a Pearl Harbor in reverse":** Sorensen, *Kennedy*, p. 684. **"I could not accept":** Kennedy, *Thirteen Days*, p. 37. **"For 175 years":** Leonard C. Meeker, memorandum of Oct. 19, 1962, meeting of [ExComm], quoted in Schlesinger, *Robert Kennedy*, p. 509.

"We spent more": Kennedy, *Thirteen Days*, p. 39. **"very much surprised":** George Ball, quoted in Stein and Plimpton, eds., *American Journey*, p. 135. **"with an intense and quiet":** Douglas Dillon, quoted in Stein and Plimpton, eds., *American Journey*, p. 136. **"Decisive":** Schlesinger, *Robert Kennedy*, p. 510. **Dean Acheson felt; "moved by":** Acheson, quoted in Schlesinger, *Robert Kennedy*, p. 508.

"Inhibited": Kennedy, *Thirteen Days*, p. 33. "During these deliberations, we all spoke as equals," he says (p. 46). "There was no rank, and, in fact, we did not even have a chairman. . . . As a result, the conversations were completely uninhibited and unrestricted. Everyone had an equal opportunity to express himself and to be heard directly. It was a tremendously

advantageous procedure that does not frequently occur within the executive branch of government . . ." **"the most vivid":** Sorensen, *Legacy*, p. 686. **On Saturday; Bobby, sitting on pool edge:** Kennedy, *Thirteen Days*, p. 47.

"In considerable detail": John McCone, "MEMORANDUM FOR THE FILE—Meeting with the Vice President on Oct. 21, 1962," Oct. 22, 1962, quoted in *TPR—JFK*, Vol. III—Oct. 22–28, 1962, p. 7. **"I've been afraid":** *TPR—JFK*, Vol. III—Oct. 22–28, 1962, p. 467.

"That is one launch pad . . .": Arthur Lundall (Assistant Director, Photographic Interpretation, Central Intelligence Agency) in *TPR—JFK*, Vol. III, p. 187. **"It's a very dangerous":** *TPR—JFK*, Vol. III, p. 191. **"This was the moment"; "His hand went up":** Robert Kennedy's handwritten notes, RFK Papers, quoted in Schlesinger, *Robert Kennedy*, p. 514. Schlesinger notes that a "somewhat rewritten and polished" version of this is in Robert Kennedy's *Thirteen Days*, pp. 68–71. **"Inexplicably":** Kennedy, *Thirteen Days*, p. 70. **A messenger:** Kennedy, *Thirteen Days*, p. 71.

Reading Tuchman: Kennedy, *Thirteen Days*, p. 62. **"Check first":** *TPR—JFK*, Vol. III, p. 200. **And in fact:** *TPR—JFK*, Vol. III, p. 191.

"There were"; "After further heated"; "We don't want to push him": Kennedy, *Thirteen Days*, p. 73–76.

A cable clattered; "very personal"; "Mr. President, we and you": *TPR—JFK*, Vol. III, pp. 349–55. **"For the first time":** Kennedy, *Thirteen*, p. 91.

"Frequently": Robert Kennedy memorandum, Nov. 16, 1962, quoted in Schlesinger, *Robert Kennedy*, p. 525. **"Mr. President":** *TPR—JFK*, Vol. III, p. 72. **"I think":** *TPR—JFK*, Vol. III, p. 86. **Every congressional leader; Lyndon Johnson had not said a word:** "5:30–6:30 P.M., Meeting with the Congressional Leadership on the Cuban Missile Crisis," *TPR—JFK*, Vol. III, pp. 58–91. **Kennedy was jolted; "the most difficult":** "he was upset by the time the meeting ended," his brother says. Kennedy, *Thirteen Days*, pp. 53, 55.

"Our hopes"; "raising": Sorensen, *Kennedy*, p. 712.

Since the Jupiters: Kennedy, *Thirteen Days*, p. 94. **"Great injury to NATO":** Schlesinger, *Robert Kennedy*, p. 519.

"The most difficult": Kennedy, *Thirteen Days*, p. 93. **There were indications; The Russian Ilyushin-28 bombers:** *TPR—JFK*, Vol. III, p. 356. Kennedy, *Thirteen Days*, p. 94. **McNamara said:** *TPR—JFK*, Vol. III, p. 357.

The Joint Chiefs delivered: *TPR—JFK,* Vol. III, p. 437. "Well, I'm surprised," Robert Kennedy laughed when he heard the recommendation (p. 438).

The President kept postponing; ignoring the second letter: Sorensen, *Kennedy,* pp. 714–16; *Counselor,* pp. 301–2; Sorensen interview; Schlesinger, *A Thousand Days* pp. 828–29; Schlesinger interview; Kennedy, *Thirteen Days,* pp. 101–4. He left Sorensen drafting: Sorensen interview.

"A U-2"; from all along; "I think tomorrow": *TPR—JFK,* Vol. III, pp. 446–50. "Immediate retaliation"; "The hawks, dreaming": Schlesinger, *Robert Kennedy,* p. 520. "almost unanimous"; "It isn't": Kennedy, *Thirteen Days,* p. 98. When he returned; "Gentlemen": *TPR—JFK,* Vol. III, p. 452.

"Radio and TV reports"; and the exchange with Robert Kennedy: pp. 464–65. "Since then": *TPR—JFK,* Vol. III, pp. 464–65. "I don't say it's a lie": p. 465. "Did we get off": p. 466. Johnson's statements are on *TPR—JFK,* Vol. III, pp. 469–77. Interrupting Rusk: For an example, see p. 466. "I guess": p. 476. "Look, the weakness": p. 470. "He's [Khrushchev] got to get a little blood": p. 474. "I think you're": p. 469. "This ought to start": p. 469. All from *TPR—JFK,* Vol. III.

"A very substantial": p. 478. "It would probably": p. 480. "They've upped": p. 478. "We can't very well": p. 481. Johnson interrupting; "It doesn't mean just": p. 481. "Bite to eat": p. 482. All from *TPR–JFK,* Vol. III.

A quiet word; "Lyndon Johnson was not": Sorensen interview. He had his dinner downstairs: Sorensen, *Kennedy,* p. 716.

"One part"; "The moment Rusk": Bundy, *Danger and Survival,* p. 484. The nine men . . . swore themselves: Sorensen interview. "We agreed without hesitation that no one not in the room was to be informed of this additional message," Bundy says (p. 484). President Kennedy's decision to limit attendance implied to those of us present that it was a move about which the other members of ExComm did not need to know," Sorensen writes (*Counselor,* p. 302). "Their deliberations would remain secret for the next twenty-five years, until McGeorge Bundy described them in his memoir . . . *Danger and Survival,*" Evan Thomas writes (*Robert Kennedy,* p. 227). "The potential": Thomas, *Robert Kennedy,* p. 228.

"I said that": *TPR—JFK,* Vol. III, pp. 486–87. Also see Kennedy, *Thirteen Days,* p. 108, and Schlesinger, *Robert Kennedy,* p. 521–52. "I thought it was my last meal": O'Donnell,

Powers, and McCarthy, *"Johnny, We Hardly Knew Ye,"* p. 394.

"Chilled": Sorensen interview. "The hawks were rising"; " 'All I know' ": Sorensen interview. He has a slightly different version of Johnson's words in *Counselors,* p. 304, and in Shesol, *Mutual Contempt,* p. 97. Johnson's words are not on the tape. Sorensen says that the tape recorder hadn't been turned on because President Kennedy had not entered the room to turn it on. A gap in the tapes, before President Kennedy entered the room, is on *TPR–JFK,* p. 490, of Vol. III.

"Do anything about": p. 490. "If our planes": p. 492. "Let me say, I think": p. 492. "It's just a question": pp. 494–95. "Yes, we can wait": p. 497. All from *TPR–JFK,* Vol. III. "Give them that last chance": President John Fitzgerald Kennedy, on p. 508 of *TPR—JFK,* Vol. III. "But"; "With respect for you, Khrushchev": *TPR–JFK,* Vol. III, p. 517. Everyone stood up: Sorensen, *Kennedy,* p. 717. In a later book he said "everyone stood up and applauded," but when the author took him through the events of that day, he said it as I have written it. "A trace": Sorensen, *Kennedy,* p. 717.

This was the night: Kennedy, *Thirteen Days,* p. 110; Schlesinger, *Robert Kennedy,* p. 525. "With what we were doing": RFK, memorandum, Nov. 15, 1962, quoted in Schlesinger, *Robert Kennedy,* p. 525. "He said after": Bartlett OH, JFKL. "You must know": Jacqueline Kennedy to Sorensen, quoted in *Counselor,* pp. 248–49.

"Together with some": "Memorandum for the Vice President, from the Attorney General," undated. When, however, on December 17th: Winnie to Col. Burris, Dec. 17, 1962. "The happy, joyful": Robert Kennedy to Johnson, Jan. 16, 1963. All from "Kennedy, Robert F. and Family [1957–1964 and undated], Box 6, WHFN.

"After the": Lincoln, *Kennedy and Johnson,* p. 185. "One saw"; "He seemed"; "appeared": Schlesinger, *A Thousand Days,* pp. 1018–19. "I hate": Lincoln, *Kennedy and Johnson,* p. 188. "The vice presidency is filled": Johnson interview with Kearns, *Lyndon Johnson,* p. 164. Finland trip: Rowan, *Breaking Barriers,* pp. 227–29. "Like a fool": McPherson, in Smith, *Grace and Power,* p. 368–69. "It would be a rich treasure": *Miami Herald,* March 17, 1963. WHAT EVER HAPPENED: Ward Just, *The Reporter,* Jan. 17, 1963. " 'Power is' ": *Time,* Feb. 1, 1963. *Candid Camera:* James Presley, "What Is an LBJ?" *Texas Observer,* Oct. 18, 1963.

Never faded; "Johnson projected": Goodwin, *Lyndon Johnson,* p.200. "He came":

Johnson, "Reminiscences of Lyndon B. Johnson," Aug. 19, 1969, transcript of tape recording, OH Collection, LBJL. **"They literally":** Richard Goodwin, Walton interviews. **"Jack Kennedy's":** Baker, *Wheeling and Dealing.* **"He couldn't be":** Gonella interview. **"THE NO. 2":** Paul O'Neill, "The No. 2 Man in Washington," *Life,* Jan. 26, 1962; "Role of Robert Kennedy: No. 2 Man in Washington," *USN&WR,* July 10, 1961; and "What Makes Bobby Run," *Time,* March 18, 1963.

"Every time": Bell, quoted in Miller, *Lyndon,* p. 305. **"Mr. President" and "Johnny":** Thomas, *Robert Kennedy,* p. 169. **"Always talked":** Schlesinger, *Robert Kennedy,* p. 598. **"They hardly":** Isaiah Berlin, quoted in Thomas, *Robert Kennedy,* p. 233. **"Osmosis":** Thimmesch and Johnson, *Robert Kennedy at Forty,* p. 110.

Jenkins call: Seigenthaler interview. **Kitchen scene:** Spalding OH, March 22, 1969, p. 64; Spalding interview with Stein, from Stein Papers, quoted in Schlesinger, *Robert Kennedy,* p. 623; Seigenthaler interview, OH; Shesol, *Mutual Contempt,* p. 9. Bobby gives a summary of it in his OH, Feb. 29, 1965, Guthman and Shulman, eds., *Robert Kennedy: In His Own Words,* p. 26. **Checking with Seigenthaler:** Seigenthaler interview; Seigenthaler OH, Vol. 2 of 4, pp 158–61, JFKL. **"Genuine contempt":** *Life,* Jan. 22, 1962. **"Lies all the time":** Guthman and Shulman, eds., *In His Own Words,* p. 26.

"A bunch"; "simply because": Joseph Kennedy, quoted in Goodwin, *The Fitzgeralds,* p. 473. **"There is":** Joseph Kennedy, quoted in Schlesinger, *Robert Kennedy,* p. 47. **"To write off":** Goodwin, *The Fitzgeralds,* p. 569. **"Came clad":** Goodwin, *Remembering America,* p. 447. **"Horrified":** Rose Kennedy, quoted in Goodwin, *Remembering America,* pp. 446–47.

"A subjugated": Schlesinger, *Robert Kennedy,* pp. 73–74. **"I never saw"; "have become":** Robert Kennedy, quoted in Schlesinger, *Robert Kennedy,* pp. 75–76. **"A maturity":** Schlesinger, *Robert Kennedy,* p. 77.

"Nothing came easy": Jean Kennedy Smith, quoted in Smith, *Bad Blood,* p. 34. **Graduated 56th:** Schlesinger, *Robert Kennedy,* p. 87. **Bunche incident:** Schlesinger, *Robert Kennedy,* pp. 85–87; Thomas, *Robert Kennedy,* pp. 55–56. **"His black and white"; "the madder":** Davison, quoted in Schlesinger, *Robert Kennedy,* p. 86. **"Gutless":** Thomas, *Robert Kennedy,* p. 55. **"An experiencing nature":** Schlesinger, *Robert Kennedy,* p. 602.

"Overloaded": Seigenthaler interview. **As he was:** Interviews with children in TV specials. **"Unlike"; "And please"; "Hush, now":** Thomas, *Robert Kennedy,* p. 187. **As if; "Cannot bear":** Paul O'Neill, "The No. 2 Man." **"There wasn't":** Buchwald, quoted in Schlesinger, *Robert Kennedy,* p. 585. **"Children in"; "Children dissolved":** Schlesinger, *Robert Kennedy,* p. 585. **"Because he":** Robert Kennedy, quoted in Schlesinger, *Robert Kennedy,* p. 589.

"Would fly down": Baldridge, quoted in Thomas, *Robert Kennedy,* p. 190. **"Dad":** Thomas, *Robert Kennedy,* p. 190; Schlesinger, *Robert Kennedy,* p. 589. **"Jack . . . was off":** Thomas, *Robert Kennedy,* p. 91. **"You knew that":** Jacqueline Kennedy, quoted in Thomas, *Robert Kennedy,* p. 91.

Frankfurter incident: Schlesinger, *Robert Kennedy,* p. 379. **"It's pretty easy":** Spalding OH. **"His most tenaciously":** Goodwin, *Remembering America,* p. 444.

Soviet Union trip: Schlesinger, *Robert Kennedy,* pp. 121–26. **"Already Bobby's reputation":** Wofford, *Of Kennedys and Kings,* pp. 32–33. **Meeting frequently:** Thomas, *Robert Kennedy,* pp. 137–38; Schlesinger, *Robert Kennedy,* pp. 499–502.

"The sharpest"; "One immediately"; "Thought he was": Shesol, *Mutual Contempt,* p. 69. **"The most impressive":** Thomas, *Robert Kennedy,* p. 111. **"His willingness"; a quality "he had":** Schlesinger, *Robert Kennedy,* pp. 240–41. **"He had . . . a way":** Thomas, *Robert Kennedy,* p. 246. **"Bob never pauses":** Dolan OH, quoted in Shesol, *Mutual Contempt,* p. 69. **"The band of brothers":** One of them, Ed Guthman, named his book *We Band of Brothers.*

"In the manner"; less [than]: Thomas, *Robert Kennedy,* p. 114. **"It was"; "That was"; "rather precious":** Clark, Morgenthau, Longworth, quoted in Schlesinger, *Robert Kennedy,* pp. 243, 240, 592. **"The strong, stern":** Quoted in Schlesinger, *Robert Kennedy,* p. 190. **"Bullshit":** Goodwin, *Remembering America,* p. 447.

Schulberg episode: Budd Schulberg, "RFK—Harbinger of Hope," *Playboy,* Jan. 1960. **"The worst of times brought":** Thomas, *Robert Kennedy,* p. 210. **"I'm older":** Schlesinger, *Robert Kennedy,* p. 508. **"Very much":** Ball, quoted in Thomas, *Robert Kennedy,* p. 210.

Harriman episode: Shesol, *Mutual Contempt,* p. 71. **Bowles episode:** Sidey, *John F. Kennedy,* p. 125; Reeves, *President Kennedy,* pp. 104–5. **"Became suddenly":** Goodwin, *Remembering America,* p. 187.

"Most obvious fault"; "Why": Pat Anderson, "Robert's Character," *Esquire,* April 1965. "His eyes get steely": Collier and Horowitz, *The Kennedys,* p. 294. Patterson photograph: Pat Anderson, "Robert's Character"; New field interview. "Even approaching": Thimmesch and Johnson, *Robert Kennedy,* p. 28. "I'd like": Paul O'Neill, "No. 2 Man." "Just when": Schaap, *R.F.K.,* p. 47. "From day one": Irwin Ross and Joseph Wershba, "The Kid Brother," *NYP,* March 29, 1964.

"An insult": Collier and Horowitz, *The Kennedys.* "It was almost"; "hysterical," etc.: Thomas, *Robert Kennedy,* pp. 146–49. "The Kennedys made clear": Thomas, *Robert Kennedy,* p. 153. "The truth is unknowable": Thomas, *Robert Kennedy,* p. 154. In April, 1963: Thomas, *Robert Kennedy,* p. 239. "My God": Collier and Horowitz, *The Kennedys,* p. 290.

"Despite": Collier and Horowitz, *The Kennedys,* p. 227. "Walkie-talkies": Schaap, *R.F.K.,* p. 108. Fourteen grand juries; Orchestrated; "It would": Thimmesch and Johnson, *Robert Kennedy,* pp. 262, 78.

"Bobby hates like me": *NYP,* March 29, 1964. And see note, p. 635, Chapter 3. "I'm affected": Guthman and Schulman, eds., *In His Own Words,* pp. 410–17. "They went": Gonella interview. She had resigned from his staff in 1962, but was still a part of the Johnson group socially, and would later return to work for him. Two middle-level: Shesol, *Mutual Contempt,* p. 105.

"No one can outlast"; "I can't stand": Goodwin, *Remembering America,* pp. 72, 415. "He just eats up": Guthman and Shulman, eds., *In His Own Words,* p. 415. "If your brother": Shesol, *Mutual Contempt,* p. 108. "A manipulative": Smith, *Grace and Power,* p. 175. "Makes it very difficult": Guthman and Schulman, eds., *In His Own Words,* pp. 415, 417. "He [Bobby] recoiled": Schlesinger interview. "It was southwestern"; No affection: Schlesinger, *A Thousand Days,* p. 623. "I don't"; "He insisted": Schlesinger, *Robert Kennedy,* p. 205. "Bobby, literally sick": Bradlee, *A Good Life,* p. 210. He couldn't: The day before the balloting, "the count showed 740—21 short of a majority. He concluded crisply: 'We can't miss a trick in the next twenty-four hours. If we don't win tonight, we're dead' " (Schlesinger, *Robert Kennedy,* p. 206). Ted Kennedy interview. Johnson knew: Connally, Corcoran, Reedy interviews. "Ruin": Caro, *Master,* p. 831. "That's Bobby": Corcoran interview. "If it had had": Shesol, *Mutual Contempt,* p. 8.

"Never would": Collier and Horowitz, *The Kennedys,* p. xxx. "Always": Richard Goodwin interview. "Losers' table": Thomas, *Robert Kennedy,* p. 290.

Voodoo doll: Hugh Sidey, "He Made a Truce with a Man He Came Almost to Hate," *Life,* Nov. 18, 1966. "The merriment was overwhelming," Sidey reported. He would pore: Busby interview. "The humane"; "all sorts": Schlesinger, *Robert Kennedy,* p. 592; *A Thousand Days,* p. 696. "They're trying": Busby interview. A storm: Califano, *The Triumph and Tragedy of Lyndon Johnson,* pp. 294–95. "The response": Goldman, *The Tragedy of Lyndon Johnson,* p. 250. "He just": Baker, *Wheeling.*

"Time is": Gore Vidal, "The Best Man—1968," *Esquire,* March 1963. LBJ MAY FACE: *NYHT,* April 6, 1963. "A great many": Gould Lincoln, *WES,* March 7, 1963. "Emphatically not"; "This certainly": *Philadelphia Inquirer,* March 2, 1963. "At this time": *Wichita Falls Record-News,* March 4, 1963. "The Washington press corps": Reedy to Johnson, Jan. 12, 1963, Office Files of George Reedy. "My future": Busby interview.

9. Gestures and Tactics

Received: Fullerwood and Hawthorne to Johnson, Feb. 23, 1963, "Public Activities—Travel [Florida March 11, 1963]," Box 226, Vice Presidential Papers, 1963 Subject File, LBJL. (Unless otherwise specified, all documents in the St. Augustine section are from this file.) "I cannot go": Peek interview. "Nothing to get excited"; would embarrass: Reedy to Johnson, Feb. 28, 1963. Trying to head off the embarrassment, Holland tried—unsuccessfully—to get an appointment with Johnson, and finally sent a message: "I am very anxious to find out what the Vice President's plans are.... The Negroes ... are just trying to make trouble" (Jenkins to Johnson, March 4, 1963).

Reedy learned: Peek interview; Branch, *Pillar of Fire,* p. 37. Exactly 62: Hall to Johnson, March 1, 1963. "St. Augustine does not have"; "if necessary"; "emerge": Reedy to Johnson, Feb. 28, 1963.

How, with barely: Caro, *Master of the Senate,* p. 741. "Squat in the road": Caro, *Master,* p. 889. Johnson told Reedy: Peek interview. Peek found them amenable: Newton to Peek, Feb. 27, 1963, "March 11, 1963, Remarks by Vice President at Dinner Commemorating . . . , Box 77, Statements File; Roberts to Johnson, March 1, 1963. Reedy then persuaded: Reedy interview; Branch, *Pillar of Fire*, p. 38. He didn't want; It wasn't just: Reedy interview. Peek was able to assure: Roberts to Johnson, March 1, 1963. "No event": Johnson to Fullerswood, March 7, 1963, David Colburn Papers, University of Florida, quoted in Branch, *Pillar of Fire*, p. 36.

"Fifty-five": Branch, *Pillar of Fire*, p. 35.

"This was probably"; "good tables"; "a major breakthrough"; "one of the Negroes": "One of the most unusual. . . . ," undated, Reedy to Johnson, "March 1963," Box 8, Vice Presidential Aides' Files of George Reedy.

"He didn't want to have": Peek interview. "I'm *eatin'* with 'em": Peek, quoted in Branch, *Pillar of Fire*, p. 39. "Don't forget us": Robert Hayling, quoted in Branch, *Pillar of Fire*, p. 39.

"Very happy": Peek interview. "Happier than he had been": Reedy interview.

Only a tape recorder: Branch, *Pillar of Fire*, pp. 39–40. Fullerwood and Hawthorne to Kennedy, May 4, "St. Augustine," Box 24, Lee White Papers, JFKL. "They feel that they went even further": undated memo, attached to Hobart Taylor to Walker, Aug. 8, 1963, quoted in Branch, *Pillar of Fire*, p. 40.

"Set up a date": Reedy to Johnson, March 5, "Memos—March 1963," Box 8, Vice Presidential Aides' Files of George Reedy. "LBJ last night": *NYHT*, March 28, 1963.

Inviting Marian Anderson: J. Frank Dobie, "Texas Barbecues: 1903 and 1963," *Congressional Record*, May 17, 1963, pp. A3138–39.

African-American press club scene: Rosemarie Tyler, "LBJ Outstanding at CPC 20-Year Dinner," *Washington Afro-American*, May 25, 1963.

Roberts had: Busby interviews with Garth E. Pauley, in Pauley, *LBJ's American Promise: The 1965 Voting Rights Address*.

A few days before: Busby interview.

Lead story: "JOHNSON SAYS NATION WILL NOT BE FREE TILL ALL ARE BLIND TO COLOR," *WP*, May 31, 1963. So short: Garth Pauley, "The Genesis of a Rhetorical Commitment," in James Arnt Aune and Enrique D. Rigsby, eds., *Civil Rights Rhetoric and the America Presidency*, pp. 155–97. "eloquence": Editorial, "A Voice from the South," *WP*, June 1, 1963. Text of speech: Garth Pauley, "Remarks of Vice President Lyndon B. Johnson, Memorial Day, Gettysburg, Pennsylvania—May 30, 1963," sound recording, Audiovisual Archives, LBJL. See Branch, *Pillar of Fire*, p. 92.

Working himself up; pureness of his

motives: See Caro, *Master*, particularly "The Compassion of Lyndon Johnson" chapter.

Not part of drawing up: White, Lee OHs; McPherson, Reedy, Sorensen interviews. "Fifteen minutes alone": Norbert Schlei to RFK, "Comments of the Vice President on the Civil Rights Legislative Proposals," June 4, 1963; Schlei OH, cited in Schlesinger, *Robert Kennedy*, p. 348; Reedy interview. At 10 a.m.: Daily Diary, June 3, 1963; Reedy interview; Roberts OH. He gave some: "Edison Dictaphone Recording, LBJ-Sorensen, June 3, 1963," OH Collection, LBJL. The next morning: Daily Diary, June 4, 1963. "A Southern preacher": Schlesinger interview. "A very serious": Schlesinger, *A Thousand Days*, p. 971. When at another meeting: *NYHT*, June 5, 1963.

"For a couple of weeks there": Reedy interview. Once: Schlei to Robert Kennedy, June 4, 1963, Box 11, "Attorney General—General Correspondence," Robert Kennedy Papers, JFKL.

"I've got a date": Louis Martin OH, LBJL.

Enlarging CEEO's jurisdiction: "Transcript of Proceedings—Mtg. of July 18, 1963," pp. 96–143, Box 11, OH Collection, LBJL; Reedy to Johnson, June 10, 1963; Reedy to Johnson, undated, "Personal and Confidential," "Memos—June 1963," Box 8, VP Aides' Files—Reedy, LBJL; *NYHT*, June 23, 1963. "I checked": Lee White OH, LBJL; White OH, JFKL; Shesol, *Mutual Contempt*, p. 84.

Conference Room B: Committee on EEO, Minutes of the Seventh Meeting, May 29, 1963, OH Collection, LBJL; Dallek, *Flawed Giant*, pp. 36–37; Lemann, *Promised Land*, p. 138; Schlesinger, *Robert Kennedy*, pp. 335–36. "Within a matter": Conway OH, JFKL, LBJL. "He wanted": Lawson OH.

"In late summer": McPherson OH, interview. "Than I had ever": Busby interview. Grabbing the phone: Wright interview. "Humiliated": For example, "Bobby came in the other day to our Equal Employment Committee, and I was humiliated" (Johnson to Sorensen, Edison Dictaphone recording). Had, in Johnson's mind: Wright, Busby, Reedy, McPherson interviews.

"There have been": *NYT, WP*, May 9, 1963. "Assuming": *NYT, WP*, Nov. 1, 1963. "That's preposterous": Bradlee, *Conversations with Kennedy*, p. 218. "Everybody": O'Donnell OH. "What do you mean": Fay, *The Pleasure of His Company*, p. 259. "There was no": Guthman and Shulman, eds., *Robert Kennedy: In His Own Words*, p. 389. "Reports": Johnson, *The Vantage Point*, p. 2. "The ticket was definitely"; "emphatically": Schlesinger, *Robert Kennedy*, p. 605. "I have never": Frankel, quoted in Miller, *Lyndon*, p. 308. "In

the back room": Thomas, *Dateline: White House,* p. 121. **"Obsessed":** Reedy, *Lyndon B. Johnson,* p. 63. **"His complaints":** Baker with King, *Wheeling and Dealing,* p. 144.

Polls: *AA-S,* Sept. 20, 1963; *WES,* Aug. 25, 1963; *WP,* June 30, 1963. The August 25 poll said Goldwater would beat Kennedy in six southern states if the election were held then. **"I don't know"; "Lyndon never":** *NYHT,* Aug. 27, 1963. **"Said they doubted":** *Philadelphia Inquirer,* July 5, 1963. **"The President":** *Cleveland Plain Dealer,* July 24, 1963. **"If the solid"; "written off":** NYT News Service in *HC,* July 2, 1963. **"New political":** Allen and Scott, "Washington Report," *AA-S,* Oct. 1, 1963.

"The mere mention": *AA-S,* Oct. 2, 1963. About the same: *HC,* July 2, 1963.

With the Texans who mattered: Brown, Clark, Connally, Kilgore, Oltorf, Yarborough interviews. **"Basically":** Brown interview. **"Transcended":** Oltorf interview. **"Lyndon as vice":** "Washington Whispers," *USN&WR,* Jan. 21, 1963. **"He had promised":** Clark interview. *"Loopholes!":* Oltorf interview.

The same Belden Poll: *AA-S, Grand Rapids Press,* Sept. 22, 1963. **"One thing":** Connally interview. **"Still had"; "John controlled"; "almost":** Kilgore interview. **"After":** Connally interview. **"I had frankly":** "Hearings before the Select Committee on the Assassination," 1978, pp. 13, 14. **"The one thing":** Lincoln, *Kennedy and Johnson,* p. 197. **"Did not"; "no desire":** O'Donnell and Powers, *"Johnny, We Hardly Knew Ye,"* pp. 5, 11. **"Well, Lyndon":** "Hearings," p. 14; Connally with Herskowitz, *In History's Shadow,* pp. 170–71; Connally interview.

"John Connally wanted": Hugh Sidey, "Jackie Onassis' Memory Fragments on Tape," *Time,* April 24, 1978. **"That thought":** Connally, *In History's Shadow,* p. 173. **"The last thing":** Yarborough interview. **"Less viable":** Bradlee, *Conversations,* p. 237.

"He'd like": Bartlett, quoted in Miller, *Lyndon,* p. 307. **Reedy went:** Reedy interview. **"Strongly conscious":** Fay, *The Pleasure,* pp. 3, 4.

Connally's trip to Washington: Connally interview; Connally, *In History's Shadow,* pp. 171–73. **"Irritated":** Connally, *In History's Shadow,* p. 173. **"Hurt":** Connally interview. Talking to the ghostwriters of his autobiography during his retirement, Johnson said, "The President got Connally up without telling me about it and got Connally to the White House and they agreed on this November date, and I heard Connally was in town and I . . . asked him what it was all about and he said well he assumed that the President would tell me if he

wanted me told. . . . They had agreed on this date. This was the first I knew about the date" (Transcript, "Tape Recording between Lyndon B. Johnson, Jack Valenti, and Bob Hardesty," March 8, 1969, pp. 7, 8, OH Collection, LBJL. And on another tape recording he made during his retirement, Johnson said, "Kennedy wanted to identify with Connally—Connally's stock was high" (Johnson, "Reminiscences of Lyndon B. Johnson," August 19, 1969, transcript of tape recording, OH Collection, LBJL). Johnson was to say that Kennedy's "poll in Texas showed that only 38% of the people approved of what he was doing as President. And this poll pointed out that if we were to have any chance whatever in the '64 campaign against Goldwater, we had to have the state machinery and the leadership of the state Governor, John Connally, because the Governor is a powerful leader. . . . And he also wanted to have the machinery of the state in back of him in the form of the Governor" (CBS News Special—*LBJ: "Tragedy and Transition,"* May 2, 1970.

10. The Protégé

"There was"; "closed the door"; "You could sense"; "as grim": McDowell OH; Elizabeth A. Shedlick interview. **"The press of business":** *St. Louis Post-Dispatch,* Sept. 14, 1963. **Schedule changes:** *Copenhagen Berlingske Tidende,* Sept.13, 1963. **Canceled:** *WP,* Sept. 14, 1963; *DMN,* Sept. 14, 1963. **"An official guest":** *Copenhagen Aktuelt,* Sept. 15, 1963. **Told the State Department aides:** Sarah McClendon, "Re conversation with Dick Schreiver," undated, p. 5, McClendon Papers.

The call had been: *Des Moines Register,* Sept. 18, 1963; Rowe, *The Bobby Baker Story,* p. 50; "It was reported by friends that the Baker problem was on his mind," (Mollenhoff, *Despoilers of Democracy,* p. 273). **Hill's lawsuit:** G. R. Schreiber, "A Special Report—Onward and Upward with Serve-U," *Vend,* Oct. 1, 1963, pp. 71–74. See also *NYT,* Oct. 8, 1963, which puts it this way: "The company said in the suit that it had retained Mr. Baker to help it obtain placement of vending machines in a government contractor's plants and also alleged that he had interfered to cause cancellation of one of its own contracts. . . ." **"Taken money to":** Murray Kempton, "The Vendor," *The New Republic,* October 19, 1963.

Landau was given a tip: "And recognized immediately the explosive implications of [the] suit" (Laurence Stern and Erwin Knoll, "Washington: Outsiders' Expose," *Columbia Journalism Review,* Spring 1964, pp. 18–23). Other accounts say he was making a routine check of court filings and recognized Baker's name (Rowe, *Bobby Baker Story*, p. 49; Baker with King, *Wheeling and Dealing*, p. 175. **An official of Serv-U assured Landau:** *WP*, Sept. 12, 1963. **"Considerable soul-searching":** Laurence and Knoll, "Washington."

Schreiber had allowed: McClendon interview. **The "protégé":** G. R. Schreiber, "Special Report." **One of its stockholders; business dealings:** The *WP* was to report that Baker and his partners had sold their Carousel Motel to Serv-U for $1,200,000 (*WP*, Oct. 3, 1963).

"He panicked": Reedy OH. **"The way":** Reedy interview. **Fortas suggested:** Reedy OH III. **"Oh my God":** Reedy OH III. **"That was just stupid":** Reedy OH XXI. **Johnson claiming he was not responsible for Baker's election:** Steele, Oct. 28, 1963: "Bobby Baker? He was nominated as Secretary of the Senate by his own senator, Olin Johnston, seconded by Matt Neely; I didn't have anything to do with it and he was here even before I came." "Once Confidential Memoranda Prepared by John Steele for the editors of *Time,* August '61–Sept. '68," LBJL.

Provence call; Jenkins talking to McClendon: "Sarah McClendon to The Secretary, Standing Committee of Correspondents, Senate Press Gallery," April 8, 1964, p. 4 (in author's possession—hereafter identified as "McClendon to Secretary"); McClendon interview, OH. The words she says Jenkins used vary in each of these versions, but the gist is the same. Jenkins was later to recite the details of the McClendon confrontation to, among others, Reedy, Busby, and Margaret Mayer, a reporter for the *Dallas Times-Herald,* who was a friend of Busby's and had once worked for Johnson. In their interviews with me, the gist of the Jenkins-McClendon conversation is the same.

"With a mixture": *Scribner Encyclopedia of American Lives,* Jan. 1, 2007. **"She didn't know":** Andrea Mitchell, quoted in *WP,* Jan. 9, 2003.

McClendon's article: "PROBE DEALS OF LYNDON'S FORMER AIDE" (by Sarah McClendon, North American Newspaper Alliance), *Des Moines Register,* Sept. 18 1963. The Bobby Baker story had been floating around Washington for years. "Possibly no story illustrates the limitations of Senate reporting as it has been done in recent years better than the Bobby Baker story in Washington," wrote James McCartney of the *Chicago Daily News* Washington Bureau. "Gossip about his power and influence as well as about the fortune he has amassed has been common in the Senate

press gallery. Any reporter with eyes could see him wheeling and dealing on the Senate floor. . . . The facts that he own a restaurant franchise in North Carolina and has been the co-owner of a plush motel on the Atlantic Ocean have been common knowledge. . . . Yet Senate press gallery regulars exhibited an astonishing lack of interest in writing about Bobby Baker" (James McCartney, "Vested Interests of the Reporter," originally in Nieman Reports, Dec. 1963; reprinted in Lyons, *Reporting the News*). It wasn't just press gallery regulars who hadn't been reporting it. Drew Pearson had known as far back as April 27, 1960, that, as his associate Jack Anderson reported, "For a couple of years, I have been picking up rumors that my friend, Bobby Baker, has been peddling his influence on Capitol Hill. . . . Yesterday I did a little checking on Bobby. . . . Baker is vice president of an insurance firm, Don Reynolds Associates. . . . Bobby . . . has been a friend and source of mine for years" (Anderson to Pearson, April 27, 1960, Drew Pearson Papers).

Baker: McClendon, "Re conversation with Dick Schreiver," undated.

Jenkins had the editor: "McClendon to Secretary," p. 4. **Jenkins telephoned McClendon:** McClendon ms., McClendon Papers; McClendon OH, interview. **"We have your story":** Indeed he did, she recalls. Jenkins said "he had in his hand a copy of the story I had sent to Texas" (McClendon ms., p. 14). **"I was given the impression":** "McClendon to Secretary," p. 6; McClendon interview. **While "Walter knew":** McClendon ms., pp. 13, 14; McClendon OH I, interview. Jenkins was later to relate these events to, among others, Reedy and Busby. **Only one newspaper:** *Des Moines Register,* Sept. 18, 1963. **Willard Edwards article:** *Chicago Daily Tribune,* Sept. 23, 1963. **"It was":** Laurence Stern and Erwin Knoll, "Washington: Outsiders' Exposé," *Columbia Journalism Review,* spring 1964, p. 19. **And the next Monday:** *Newsweek,* Oct. 7, 1963.

"With plants"; "It is": Murray Kempton, "The Vender," *The New Republic,* Oct. 19, 1963. **"Just trying to sell":** Reedy OH III. **One "horrible":** Reedy interview.

"Bobby": Baker, *Wheeling,* p. 182. **"I knew":** Eleanor Randolph, "BOBBY BAKER BACK, CHIP ON SHOULDER," *Chicago Tribune,* Aug. 21, 1977. **"He's using Lady Bird"; Johnson was petrified":** Baker, *Wheeling,* p. 182. **"Lyndon B. Johnson might":** Baker, *Wheeling,* p. 271. **"He lied":** *Chicago Tribune,* Aug. 21, 1977.

"We spoke": Baker, *Wheeling,* p. 182. **"Very private":** Baker, *Wheeling,* p. 261. **"Is

it going to be": Baker, *Wheeling,* p. 272. **"Put in a kind word"; "I don't want"**: Baker, *Wheeling,* p. 268. **"It became too obvious:** Baker, *Wheeling,* p. 276.
Baker *was*, of course, his protégé: Caro, *Master of the Senate,* pp. 390–94.
$11,025; $1,791,186: U.S. Senate, Committee on Rules and Administration, *Report on Financial or Business Interests of Officers or Employees of the Senate,* Report No. 1175, 88th Cong., 2nd Session, 1964 (referred to hereafter as Senate Rules Committee First Report). **"The man most harmed"**: *WES,* Oct. 10, 1963. **The article:** *WP,* Oct. 6, 1963.
"Friendly lines"; Washington folklore"; Voted to censure: Frederic W. Collins, "Senator Williams—Public Eye," *NYT,* Feb. 9, 1964. **"Something"**: *NYT,* Feb. 9, 1964. **IRS investigation:** Hoffecker, *Honest John Williams: U.S. Senator from Delaware,* pp. 160–61. **None resonated:** McCullough, *Truman,* pp. 742–47, 863. **Add a dimension:** *NYT,* July 21, 1954. **And during:** Hoffecker, *Honest John Williams,* pp. 131–32. **His performance:** *NYT,* Feb. 9, 1964. **"A growing army"**: *WES,* Nov. 1, 1963. **"The conscience"**: *NYT,* Dec. 18, 1970. **"Usually echoed"**: Mollenhoff, *Despoilers of Democracy,* p. 282.
Inviting Ralph Hill: "In the Office of Senator Williams, Sept. 30, 1963, 10:30 a.m–12:30 p.m., Report of Mr. Ralph Lee Hill . . . ," Box 33, Folder 148, John J. Williams Papers, University of Delaware Library; *WP,* Oct. 6, 1963; *SAE, Chicago Sun–Times Special* by Sandy Smith, Oct.6, 1963; Mollenhoff, *Despoilers of Democracy,* pp. 277–78. The discussions between Reynolds and Williams would continue all through October.
Reynolds told Williams that a "political connection": Kempton, "The Vender." **"Because . . . of his social contacts"**: Senate Rules Committee First Report, p. 38. **Johnson had mentioned; "told Senator Johnson"**: Baker, *Wheeling,* p. 83.
Reynolds secured; whose premium would be paid: "Memorandum to: The Files, From: L. P. McClendon and W. Ellis Meehan, Subject: Interview with Walter Jenkins, Re: Life Insurance Sales by Don Reynolds," Dec. 16, 1963, "Hearings before the Committee on Rules and Administration, United States Senate, Jan. 9, 17, 1964, Part I, Testimony of Don B. Reynolds, pp. 33–35, 93–95, 108, 121. Mollenhoff, *Despoilers of Democracy,* p. 299.
Baker brought him; Johnson told him jovially: "Testimony of Don B. Reynolds, accompanied by James F. Fitzgerald, counsel," "Financial or Business Interests of Officers and Employees of the Senate, Hearings before the Committee on Rules and Administration,

United States Senate," Jan. 9, 17, 1964. Reynolds says (p. 108) that he gave Johnson a $50,000 policy, but Baker says there were two policies, each for $100,000 (Baker, *Wheeling,* p. 83). **"Was delighted"**: Baker, *Wheeling,* p. 83. Baker also said, "I knew that if I testified to the total truth, then Lyndon B. Johnson, among others, might suffer severely. Suppose they asked me whether Lyndon Johnson had, indeed, insisted on a kickback from Don Reynolds in the writing of his life insurance policy. A truthful answer would torpedo the Vice President. Suppose they asked me what I knew of campaign funds for Johnson, or, for that matter, President Kennedy" (Baker, *Wheeling,* p. 185).
Jenkins called him in: Eleanor R. Lenhart to Williams, "Memo—Visit from Mr. Reynolds at which time he was talking with the Senator with the knowledge that I was taking notes," Oct. 28. 1963; John J. Williams to files, "Memo—Don Reynolds Insurance Partner," Oct. 28 (but appears to be Oct. 29), 1963, both Box 32, folder 120, John J. Williams Papers, University of Delaware Library. See also Williams to files, Nov. 4, 1963, "The checks are to be furnished tomorrow night"; Williams to files, "Visit from Mr. Don Reynolds today. Mr. Reynolds brought in cancelled check for payment to LBJ's station for $208 and also . . . ," Nov. 18, 1963, both Box 32, folder 120. **"Prodded" him:** Mollenhoff, *Despoilers of Democracy,* p. 298. **Purchasing $1,208 of airtime:** Reynolds, "Testimony," pp. 104–08.
The stereo: "Hearings before the Committee on Rules and Administration, United States Senate, Jan. 9, 17, 1964, Part I, Testimony of Don B. Reynolds," pp. 37–42 (with exhibits of checks and invoices). Mollenhoff, *Despoilers of Democracy,* pp. 297, 298. **Jenkins would later deny, again and again:** For example, in an interview with investigators for the Senate Rules Committee, "Memorandum, Dec. 16, 1963, To: The Files, From L. P. McClendon and W. Ellis Meehan," "Testimony," pp. 93–95. **"He [Johnson] took the stereo"**: Baker, *Wheeling,* p. 196. Baker also says that Reynolds "had originally volunteered to waive his cash commission on the policy and then had reneged," but this in itself would have been illegal. "Testimony," p. 4 (*WES,* March 11, 1964), and Reynolds's own testimony about the circumstances in which he was forced to buy the advertising time and stereo contradicts Baker's statement. Reynolds, "Testimony," pp. 105–08. **"A kickback pure and simple"**: Baker, *Wheeling,* p. 196. **A "shakedown"**: Reynolds, quoted in Mollenhoff, *Despoilers of Democracy,* p. 298. **Proof:** "Reynolds Exhibits 8, 9, 10, 11," pp. 37–41. **$1,000 check:** Reynolds Exhibit 7, "Testimony," p. 36. **$208**

check: Reynolds Exhibit 26, "Testimony," p. 120, also pp. 119–21.

Insurance laws: *WES,* March 11, 1964. **"Precisely my point":** Baker, *Wheeling,* p. 83.

Unfortunate echoes: Senator Williams was to draw the comparison himself: "I see no difference in the acceptance of an expensive stereo than in the acceptance of a mink or vicuña coat, a deep freeze, or an oriental rug" (*NYT,* Jan. 3, 1964).

"He hated that word": Reedy interview. **"He knew":** Busby interview.

There had been speculation: The story of Lyndon Johnson's relationship with the TV stations will be discussed in the next volume, because it was in 1964 that it became a matter of public record and public controversy. The story of his earlier relationship is in Caro, *Means of Ascent* and *Master of the Senate.* For articles that summarize the 1964 revelations, see *WES,* June 9, 1964; *Wall Street Journal,* March 23 and Aug. 11, 1964; *Newsday,* May 27–29, 1964; and *Life,* Aug. 21, 1964. **Five Texas cities:** *Chicago Tribune,* Oct. 25, 1964.

"All that is owned": Johnson, quoted in Caro, *Means,* p. 88. **His denials had omitted:** Caro, *Means,* pp. 105–06. Mollenhoff, who was working very closely with the committee's staff, writes that "Although Vice-President Johnson contended, before and since, that he had no interest and no voice in the L.B.J. Company radio and television enterprises, Reynolds said it was the L.B.J. Company that paid for the insurance policy on the Vice-President's life. The company could not insure Johnson unless he was a person of such value to the firm that he would be regarded as a valuable, key man in the firm's operations, Reynolds suggested" (Mollenhoff, *Despoilers of Democracy,* p. 299). Reedy explains that "At KTBC they had a reason for Johnson wanting to have that kind of a policy. Texas is a community property state. That meant that if he died, half of KTBC would go into the Johnson estate, where it would have to pay inheritance taxes. In order to pay the inheritance taxes they would have had to sell KTBC at a loss. So they wanted a very heavy strong insurance policy on his life" (Reedy OH XXI).

He had been boasting: Caro, *Means,* p. 106. **By 1963, he was not merely a millionaire but a millionaire many times over.** *Life* was to put the net worth of Lyndon and Lady Bird at $14,000,000 (Aug. 21, 1964); the *WSJ* put the estimated market value of the television holdings alone at "around $7,000,000 that year" (March 23, 1964). John Barron of the *WES* put the figure at $9,000,000 (June 9, 1964). Johnson disputed each appraisal, and put the figure at about $4,000,000.

"Trading out"; "lived in fear": Deathe interview. **Reynolds was telling the senator about campaign contributions:** For example, one from North American's Fred Black, who, Reynolds said, handed [Bobby Baker] an envelope containing money and said: "Here's $10,000 for our next President, our boy Lyndon" ("Construction of the District of Columbia Stadium and Matters Relating Thereto—Hearings before the Committee on Rules and Administration," United States Senate, Part 2, Testimony of Don B. Reynolds, Dec. 1, 1964, p. 162).

"The important point": "Statement by U.S. Senator Tom McIntyre (D-N.H.)," Oct. 7, 1963 (in author's possession); Pearson and Anderson, *The Case against Congress,* p. 139. **"The exchange":** *Newsweek,* Oct. 14, 1963. **These funds had been raised and dispensed at Johnson's direction:** Caro, *Master,* pp. 403–13. **Had not been asked:** *WP,* Oct. 5, 7, 1963.

"Bobby's work": *NYHT, NYT, WP,* Oct. 5, 1963. **"Not entirely"; "for once with the united":** Kempton, "The Vender."

"BAKER CALLED": *WP,* Oct. 7, 1963. **"Many senators":** Baker, *Wheeling,* pp. 271–72. **Shortly before:** Sen. Williams was later to tell the Senate that Mansfield had reported to him that "Mr. Baker had tendered his resignation rather than meet with us" (*CR,* May 18, 1965), p. 10,845. **"Baker is a protégé":** *WP,* Oct. 8, 1963. **"Theirs was a close":** *WES,* Oct. 9, 1963.

"Magically disappear": Baker, *Wheeling,* p. 180.

"The integrity": NYT, Oct. 11, 1963. **"Had old Senate hands":** *Newsweek,* Oct. 21, 1963. **"Something of":** Baker, *Wheeling,* p. 184. **"Too soft-hearted"; "He is as hard":** George Dixon, *WP,* Nov. 13, 1963. **"Oh, I went over"; removing autographed picture:** Rowe, *Bobby Baker Story,* p. 61. **Postponing:** *CCC–T,* Oct. 29, 1963. **"The logical":** *Chicago Daily News,* Oct. 29, 1963.

A drumfire: For a summary, *WES,* Oct.25, 1963. **"Near the home":** *Time,* Nov. 8, 1963. **"A Chinese houseboy":** *CDN,* Oct. 29, 1963.

His mistress: "Carole was my lover," Baker said in *Wheeling* (p. 177). **Discovered townhouse:** *Des Moines Register,* Oct. 23, 1963. **"Chain-smoking":** *Time,* Nov. 8, 1963. **"dwell and entertain":** *Life,* Nov. 8, 1963. **"Baker's high-flying":** *Time,* Nov. 8, 1963. **"party house":** *Des Moines Register,* Oct. 23, 1963. It was also termed a "high-style hideaway for the advise-and-consent set" (Ben H. Bagdikian and Don Oberdorfer, "Bobby Was the Boy to See," *SEP,* Dec. 7, 1963).

"Just an ice cube's"; "romantic cau-

cuses": "A Senate Inquiry into Sugar & Spice," *Newsweek,* Nov. 11, 1963. **"Intimate"; "smoky":** *WP,* Oct. 26, 1963. **"Discreet":** *WES,* Oct. 27, 1963. **"The ceiling is red":** *NYT,* Nov. 1, 1963.

"Clad"; had worked at; "associating with": *Des Moines Register,* Oct. 26, 1963; *Time,* Nov. 8, 1963; Smith, *Grace and Power,* p. 410. **"Expelled":** Clark Mollenhoff broke the story in the *Des Moines Register,* Oct. 26, 1963. See also his Oct. 29, 1963, story. "At the direction of the Attorney General, Rometsch was quietly deported to West Germany," Thomas says (*Robert Kennedy,* p. 256).

The official with whom: Thomas, *Robert Kennedy,* p. 255. **"Fueled":** Smith, *Grace and Power,* p. 386. **"Expensive lifestyle":** Smith, *Grace and Power,* p. 386. **"Investigation has not substantiated":** Wannall to Sullivan, July 12, 1963, quoted in Thomas, *Robert Kennedy,* p. 244; *Des Moines Register,* Oct. 31, 1963.

"From the outset": Thomas, *Robert Kennedy,* p. 256.

"Elizabeth Taylor": Thomas, *Robert Kennedy,* p. 255. **"Lesbian prostitute":** Thomas, *Robert Kennedy,* p. 265. **"somewhat nymphomaniacal":** *Newsweek,* Nov. 11, 1963. **"She would do anything":** *Life,* Nov. 22, 1963.

Robert Kennedy asked: Thomas, *Robert Kennedy,* pp. 267, 268. **THE BOBBY BAKER BOMBSHELL:** *Life,* Nov. 8, 1963.

Tom Connally funeral: *NYHT,* Oct. 31, 1963; Oltorf interview. **As a newly elected; never to antagonize:** Caro, *Master,* pp. 132–33, 151.

Baker told McCloskey: "Testimony of Don. B. Reynolds, *Hearings before the Committee on Rules and Administration,* United States Senate, Part I," Jan. 9, 17, 1964, pp. 3–8, 112. Baker himself said flatly that Reynolds "told the truth with respect to . . . the D.C. Stadium deal" (Baker, *Wheeling,* p. 194). **McCloskey won—and selected Reynolds:** "Construction of the District of Columbia Stadium, and Matters Related Thereto," *Hearings before the Committee on Rules and Administration,* United States Senate, Part 2, Testimony of Don B. Reynolds," Dec. 1, 1964, p. 139.

$73,631; $10,000; $4,000: "Testimony of Reynolds," p. 112. "Bobby had indicated that by having produced Senator Johnson, that he had access to top clients for me, that he would introduce me around," Reynolds testified. "And when I met Mr. McCloskey, sir, and I got this performance bond, it was prima facie evidence of his ability to get and produce for me, and it was for services rendered, sir" ("Testimony," p. 115). See also *WES,* Sept. 1, 1964.

"Bag man": "Investigations—Parties & Payments," *Time,* Dec. 11, 1964. **Instructed to deliver:** Mollenhoff, *Despoilers of Democracy,* p. 364. **no more than $5,000:** "Construction of the District of Columbia Stadium," Part 2, p. 145. **Three such deliveries:** "Construction of the District of Columbia Stadium," Part 2, pp. 145, 161.

Violated: *WES,* March 11, 1964. **Reynolds told; Williams obtained a photostat:** "Construction of the District of Columbia Stadium," Part 2, p. 146. **"I was the man"; Reynolds "told the truth":** Baker, *Wheeling,* p. 194.

"An expert": O'Donnell, Powers, and McCarthy, *"Johnny, We Hardly Knew Ye,"* p. 386. **The main topic:** White, *The Making of the President, 1964,* p. 28. White also says, "They discussed television possibilities" for the Convention, "decided that the renomination of Lyndon Johnson would be staged on Wednesday evening. . . ." But the discussants may not have included John Kennedy. "The President, sitting cross-legged on a cushion in his customary place, was more observer than participant." **"Led to":** Schlesinger, *Robert Kennedy and His Times,* p. 604. **"The nonexistence":** Schlesinger, *Robert Kennedy,* p. 605.

"Because everyone": Lincoln, *Kennedy and Johnson,* pp. 199, 200. **"To do this"; "verbatim":** Lincoln, *Kennedy and Johnson,* pp. 204, 205. **"Alerted":** Schlesinger, *Robert Kennedy,* p. 605. **"In eleven"; "unruffled":** Sorensen, *Kennedy,* pp. 55, 263. **"Welcoming":** Schlesinger, *A Thousand Days,* p. 687. **She was described as a rattlebrained woman:** Schlesinger, Sorensen interviews. **"The ammunition":** Lincoln interview.

Young and Burdick called in: Sen. Clark said Baker had announced that Burdick and Young had "withdrawn their candidacies." The *WP* reported Young as saying: "I wanted very much to be on Judiciary. I wrote to everyone on the Steering Committee." Blakley and Long had less seniority. Humphrey said Baker told the Steering Committee that Burdick and Young "weren't interested" in Judiciary Committee seats" (*DMN,* Nov. 15, 1963). Ted Lewis, "Capital Stuff," *NYDN,* Nov. 19, 1963. Yarborough was also to say that Baker kept him off Judiciary: *WP,* Nov. 17, 1963. **"In the peculiar"; "tambourine":** Keith Wheeler, "Scandal Grows and Grows in Washington," *Life,* Nov. 22, 1963. **Paul Douglas; Moss:** *WP,* Nov. 17, 1963.

One word: Reedy interview.

"I began to pick up"; went to Hunt's office: Lambert interview. **"The deeper":** Sackett interview. **No fewer than nine:** In addition to Wheeler, Lambert, and Sackett, they were Mike Durham, Mike Silva, Bill

Wise, Audrey Jewett, Kenneth Reich, and Hal Wingo. **A meeting was scheduled:** Lambert, Sackett interviews.

Reynolds began testifying: "Construction of the District of Columbia Stadium," Part 2, Testimony of Don B. Reynolds, p. 192. Mollenhoff, *Despoilers of Democracy,* p. 295.

Lyndon Johnson had flown: Pre-Presidential Daily Diary, Box 3. **"You two guys":** O'Donnell and Powers, *"Johnny, We Hardly,"* p. 20. **"This was":** Fehmer OH II. **"Much cleaning"; "many telephone":** Carpenter, "Liz Carpenter's Recollections of President Kennedy's Assassination," Box 4, Special Files–Assassination. **Horseflesh influx:** Carpenter, "Recollections." **"Tepid"; hand towels:** "Breakfast . . . in room," "President Kennedy's Trip to Texas," The President's Appointment File [Diary Backup], Box 1, LBJL. **"This is how"; "Will he"; "that was still"; "If you don't":** Abell OH I.

"A real flavor": Carpenter, "Recollections." **"On one"; "The image":** Russell, *Lady Bird,* pp. 215–16.

"In a rage": O'Donnell and Powers, *"Johnny, We Hardly,"* p. 20. **"I'm not surprised":** Reston, *The Lone Star,* p. 264. **"What Connally and Johnson are trying"; Yarborough had been assigned:** Manchester, *The Death of a President,* p. 73; O'Donnell and Powers, *"Johnny, We Hardly,"* p. 21. **When Youngblood:** Manchester, *Death of a President,* p. 73. **"Henry, can I"; "Awkward"; When a reporter; "Well, I told him":** Manchester, *Death of a President,* pp. 73, 74.

"I've bugged him enough": Manchester, *Death of a President,* p. 79.

"There definitely was not": Johnson, quoted in Manchester, *Death of a President,* p. 82. **The waiters heard; "What was that all about?"** Manchester, *Death of a President,* p. 82. **"There was all of this":** Jacqueline Kennedy, quoted in Miller, *Lyndon,* p. 311.

Kennedy had asked Thomas: Manchester, *Death of a President,* p. 78. **"Like a pistol":** Manchester, *Death of a President,* p. 82. **Jones shared with him:** Manchester, *Death of a President,* p. 86.

11. The Cubicle

Moments at the Love Field reception and the motorcade that are not footnoted are from the author's watching of newsreels of the events.

Johnson telephoned: Reedy interview. **"Twice at San Antonio":** *LAT,* Nov. 22, 1963. **"Curt":** *Chicago Tribune,* Nov. 22, 1963. **"Mrs. Kennedy":** Manchester, *Death of a President,* p. 114. **Johnson had had to ask:** Manchester, *The Death of a President,* p. 121–22. The depth of Johnson's pain was hinted at when during his retirement he was reminiscing about the trip. Saying that Yarborough had not ridden with us, he maintained, "I didn't care, but the newspaper boys went wild. It was the biggest ever since de Gaulle farted. There were headlines the next morning and all kinds of queries . . . 'Was it true that Yarborough would not ride with the Vice President?' " (Johnson, "Reminiscences of Lyndon B. Johnson," Aug. 19, 1969, transcript of tape recording, p. 4, LBJL). **Brace and bandage:** Dennis Breo, JFK's dean, and John K. Lattimer, *Lincoln and Kennedy: Medical and Ballistic Comparisons of Their Assassinations.* New York: Harcourt, 1980, quoted in Bugliosi, *Reclaiming History: The Assassination of President John F. Kennedy,* p. 59. Lattimer writes that after Oswald's first shot, the "corset prevented him from crumpling down out of the line of fire, as Governor Connally did. Because the President remained upright, with his head exposed, Oswald was able to draw a careful bead on the back of his head" (Lattimer, *Kennedy and Lincoln,* p. 171, quoted in Bugliosi, *Reclaiming History,* p. 59). **"All right, let's go":** Manchester, *Death of a President,* p. 117.

Don Reynolds walked in; had brought documents with him: No transcript of Don Reynolds's testimony exists in the files of the Senate Rules Committee at the National Archives, and if it exists anywhere else, the author has not been able to find it. After an extensive search of the archives and of Senate records, the Senate Historian Donald A. Ritchie said, "There was less archival control of Senate committee records in those days and some documents of consequence were not preserved." A written summary made of the interview is referred to during the Rules Committee hearings in January 1964 ("I am reading from notes, a summary of testimony—it is called 'Summary of Mr. Reynolds in Executive Session,' " Senator Hugh Scott of Pennsylvania says at one point [p. 103 of the Senate hearings of Jan. 9, 17, 1964]), but that cannot be found, either. The questioning of Reynolds was led by the Rules Committee's minority counsel, Burkett Van Kirk. Both he and Drennan had died before I could interview them, or, to be more accurate, before I knew it was necessary to interview them, but Van Kirk was to recall Reynolds's testimony on November 22, 1963, for a television documentary: "LBJ vs. Kennedy—Chasing Demons," The History Channel, 2003. "Don presented a good case. He could back it up. Everything he had, he had a receipt for. It's hard to argue with a receipt. Or a cancelled check. Or an invoice. It's hard to argue with documentation." Mollenhoff, the Pulitzer Prize–winning investigative reporter for the *Des Moines Register* was, in November 1963, working closely—and on virtually a daily basis—with Senator Williams and the Rules Committee staff. He was to write that "It was a few minutes before 10 A.M. when Reynolds and Fitzgerald were escorted to Room 312, where two committee staff members (Van Kirk and Drennan) waited." Mollenhoff was to report that "in the first two hours, the questioning ranged over the whole scope of Baker's financial operations," including those concerning the District of Columbia Stadium (Mollenhoff, *Despoilers of Democracy*, pp. 295–97).

The journalist Sy Hersh had a series of interviews with Van Kirk, and writes that "at ten o'clock" Reynolds "walked with his lawyer into a small hearing room . . . and began providing . . . Van Kirk . . . with eagerly awaited evidence" (Hersh, *Dark Side of Camelot*, p. 446). Senator Carl Curtis of Nebraska, the ranking Republican member of the Rules Committee, who was told in 1963 about Reynolds's testimony by Van Kirk, confirmed that Reynolds had provided documentation. Also Curtis Files, Curtis Papers; Curtis interview. Mollenhoff, *Despoilers of Democracy*, pp. 295–98; Rowe, *The Bobby Baker Story*, pp. 84–86; Steinberg, *Sam Johnson's Boy*, pp. 602, 611. **The *Life* meeting:** Graves, Lambert, Sackett interviews. **"With every":** Lambert interview.

"I don't care": O'Brien, *No Final Victories*, p. 156. **"If he doesn't:"** O'Donnell and Powers, *"Johnny, We Hardly,"* p. 23. See also Manchester, *Death of a President*, p. 113. **If he valued:** Manchester, *Death of a President*, p. 116. **"Yarborough's going":** O'Brien, *No Final Victories*, p. 157. **Taking Connally:** O'Donnell and Powers, *"Johnny, We Hardly,"* p. 26.

"Kennedy weather": Manchester, *Death of a President*, p.122. **"There is Mrs.":** Bugliosi, *Reclaiming History*, p. 27. **"There never":** Robert J. Donovan, quoted in Bugliosi, *Reclaiming History*, p. 27. **O'Brien made sure:** O'Brien, *No Final Victories*, pp. 156–57.

Senate hearings: In "Construction of the District of Columbia Stadium, Part II," "Testimony of Don B. Reynolds," p. 192," Reynolds says he testified from "about 10 to 1," but the committee's counsel says, "You were interviewed practically the whole day," and Mollenhoff, who was working closely, on a daily basis, with the committee's staff, writes that "It was almost time for the usual noon luncheon break when the insurance man got started on

his story of how he had been pressured into taking advertising time on the L.B.J. television station . . . and about the gift stereo. . . . It was about 12:30 P.M., Washington time—11:30 A.M. in Dallas, Texas—when Van Kirk and Drennan suggested they send a girl for sandwiches and milk, rather than interrupt Reynolds's testimony by going out to eat. The questioning and the discussion of the L.B.J. Company's affairs, as Reynolds knew them, went on" (Mollenhoff, *Despoilers of Democracy*, pp. 295–97). Also see Rowe, *Bobby Baker Story*, pp. 84, 85; Steinberg, *Sam Johnson's Boy*, pp. 602, 611; Curtis interview. **"Mr. President":** Nellie Connally, *From Love Field*, p. 7.

In Washington, at about the same time, Reynolds was showing: Between 1:30 and 2:30, "he [Reynolds] produced records to substantiate his story" (Mollenhoff, *Despoilers of Democracy*, p.297). The invoices and checks are Exhibits 7 (p. 36), 8–11 (pp. 38–41), 12 (p. 43) in of "Reynolds Testimony," Part 1, Jan. 9, 17, 1964, which is when they were introduced into the public record at open hearings of the committee. On page 97, the committee's counsel notes "they are in the examination of Don B. Reynolds. They are in the original."

In New York, *Life* editors: Lambert, Sackett interviews.

"Startled"; "report or explosion": "Statement of the President, Lyndon Baines Johnson, concerning the events of Nov. 22, 1963," attached to Johnson to Warren, July 10, 1964, p. 2 (hereafter referred to as "Johnson Statement.") **Connally knew:** Connally interview.

"Not normal": Youngblood, *Twenty Years in the Secret Service: My Life with Five Presidents*," p. 113. In his typed report to Chief of the Secret Service James J. Rowley, he describes the movements as "very abnormal." Youngblood to Chief, Subject: "Statement of Rufus W. Youngblood, Vice Presidential Detail (office 1–22) concerning details of events occurring in Dallas, Texas, on Nov. 22, 1963." Youngblood, "Secret Service Reports," Box 3, SP-ASS (hereafter referred to as Youngblood to Chief). **"Voice I had never":** "Notes taken during interview with Mrs. Johnson, June 15, 1964," p. 2 (hereafter cited as "Mrs. Johnson's Notes").

Grabbing Johnson's shoulder: "I turned in my seat and with my left arm grasped and shoved the Vice President, at his right shoulder, down and toward Mrs. Johnson and Sen. Yarborough. At the same time I shouted, 'Get down!' I believe I said this more than once. . . . I quickly looked all around again and could see nothing to shoot at, so I stepped over into the back seat and sat on top of the Vice President. . . ."

(Youngblood to Chief, p. 3). In his memoir, Youngblood wrote, "I turned instinctively in my seat and with my left hand I grasped Johnson's right shoulder and . . . forced him downward. 'Get down,' I shouted, 'get down.' (p. 113). I swung across the back seat and sat on top of him" (Youngblood, *Twenty Years,* p. 562). See also "Transcript from Mrs. Johnson's tapes relating to November 22, 1963," p. I (hereafter referred to as "Mrs. Johnson's Transcript"). The day after the assassination, Johnson wrote Rowley: "Upon hearing the first shot, Mr. Youngblood instantly vaulted across the front seat of my car, pushed me to the floor and shielded my body with own body, ready to sacrifice his life for mine" (Johnson to Rowley, Diary Backup, Box 1, Nov. 23, "November 23"). **"His knees":** Transcript, CBS News Special, "LBJ: Tragedy and Transition," May 2, 1970, p. 5.

"Close it up": Testimony of Rufus Wayne Youngblood, Special Agent, Secret Service," *Hearings Before the President's Commission on the Assassination of President Kennedy, Washington, 1964,* Vol. II, p. 149 (hereafter referred to as Youngblood Testimony).

He knew he would have: "Statement of Herschel Jacks, Texas Highway Patrolman, Made on Nov. 28, 1963," Commission Exhibit 1024, "Hearings," Vol. XVIII, p. 801.

"Terrifically fast": "Transcript from Mrs. Johnson's tapes relating to November 22, 1963" (hereafter referred to as "Lady Bird Transcript"), p. 1. **"Zoomed":** Johnson, "Reminiscences," p. 11. **"Stay with them—keep close":** Youngblood, *Twenty Years,* p. 113; "To: Chief James J. Rowley, From: ATSAIC Emory Roberts, The White House Detail, SUBJECT: Schedule of events prior to and after the assassination of President John F. Kennedy in Dallas, Texas, on Friday, November 22, 1963," p. 3, *Report of the U.S. Secret Service* (hereafter referred to as "Roberts Report"), "Secret Service Reports," Box 3, Special Files, Assassination, LBJL.

Shortwave radio: Youngblood to Chief, pp. 1, 2. See also "Statement by Jerry D. Kivett concerning the events of Nov. 22, 1963," *Report of the U.S. Secret Service on the Assassination of President Kennedy,* U.S. Treasury Department, p. 2, Box 3, Special Files, Assassination, LBJL ("Kivett Statement"), and Kivett Testimony, *Hearings before the President's Commission on the Assassination of President Kennedy, Washington, 1964* (these hearings, commonly referred to as the Warren Commission, will hereafter be referred to as "Hearings"), p. 1. **Now Johnson heard:** Transcript, CBS News Special, "LBJ: Tragedy and Transition," May 2, 1970, p. 4. **"I am switching":**

Manchester, *Death of a President,* p. 166. **"He's hit!"** "Kivett Statement," p. 1. **"Let's get out of here":** "Lady Bird Transcript," p. 1; Johnson, Transcript, CBS News Special, p. 4. **"Hospital":** Bugliosi, *Reclaiming History,* p. 41; Youngblood, *Twenty Years,* p. 114. **What Youngblood was seeing:** Youngblood, *Twenty Years,* p. 113. **Thumbs-down:** Bugliosi, *Reclaiming History,* p. 44.

"Hospital": "Johnson Statement," p. 562; "To: Chief; From: SA Jerry D. Kivett—Vice Presidential Detail; Statement regarding events in Dallas, Texas, on Friday, November 22, 1963," *Report of the U.S. Secret Service on the Assassination of President Kennedy,* U.S. Treasury Department, p. 1, Box 3, Special Files, Assassination, LBJL (hereafter referred to as "Kivett Report"). **"Tight-lipped and cool":** Youngblood, *Twenty Years,* p. 114.

Lying quietly: Youngblood to Chief, p. 3; Youngblood, *Twenty Years,* p. 114; "Johnson Statement," p. 562. **"An absolute physical coward":** Vernon Whiteside, quoted in Caro, *The Path to Power,* p. 156. **World War II episode:** Caro, *Means of Ascent,* Chapters 2 and 3. **Heart attack episode:** Caro, *Master of the Senate,* Chapter 27, "Go Ahead with the Blue."

"A good man": Lady Bird Johnson, *A White House Diary,* p. 7.

"All right, Rufus": Youngblood, *Twenty Years,* p. 114. **A single word:** Fletcher Knebel, "Lyndon Johnson, Trained for Power," *Look,* Dec. 31, 1963. **Told Johnson:** "Johnson Statement," p. 562; Johnson, "Reminiscences," p. 12; Johnson, *The Vantage Point,* p. 9. **"Okay, pardner":** Youngblood, *Twenty Years,* p. 114.

"I wondered if": "Lady Bird Transcript," p. 2. **Slammed back:** Youngblood, *Twenty Years,* p. 115. **Hands were grabbing:** Johnson, "Reminiscences," p. 12.

His left shoulder hurt: Travell interview. **Hustled:** Johnson, "Reminiscences," p. 12. **"One last look":** "Lady Bird Transcript," p. 2. **Small white room:** Youngblood, *Twenty Years,* p. 116. **Stationing men:** G. D'Andelot Belin (General Counsel, U.S. Secret Service) to Rowley, "Secret Service Report on the Assassination of President Kennedy," March 19, 1964, "Secret Service Reports," Box 3, Special Files, Assassination, LBJL; "Youngblood Testimony," pp. 149, 152.

"Look here, I'm not leaving": "Mrs. Johnson's Notes." **Remembering:** In her transcript Lady Bird says, "I even remember one little thing he said in that hospital room, 'Tell the children to get a Secret Service man with them' " ("Lady Bird Transcript, p. 5). William Manchester interviewed Youngblood on November 17, 1964. In his book, *The Death of a Presi-*

dent, he says (p. 232) that Youngblood told him that Johnson "said to Bird, 'I want you to give me the current whereabouts of Lynda and Lucy,' " and that it was after she gave Johnson that information that Youngblood told the agent, Jerry Kivett, to "put the girls under protection."

The notes of Manchester's interview with Youngblood are among the papers at Wesleyan University that the university has refused to open to researchers, including this author, so Manchester's notes have not been read. But Manchester's account, and that of the many Johnson biographers who have accepted that account, does not square with statements Youngblood made, a week after the assassination, in a typed report to the chief of the White House Secret Service detail, Gerald A. Behn, or in his sworn testimony before the Warren Commission. In his typed report to Behn, dated November 29, 1963, Youngblood says of his time in the cubicle, "During this time, many things occurred and I don't recall now the exact order. I talked to Mrs. Johnson and obtained information about Lynda and Lucy, and told SA [Special Agent] Kivett to make the necessary calls to have them placed under Secret Service protection" (Youngblood to Chief, p. 4). In his testimony before the Warren Commission, Youngblood did not mention Johnson's daughters in his initial statement. Asked by Arlen Specter, the commission's assistant counsel, to "describe briefly what security arrangements if any were instituted . . . for the Vice President's daughters," he said, "While we were in the hospital . . . I asked Mrs. Johnson—I knew generally where Luci and Lynda were, but I wanted get the very latest from her, since sometimes these girls might visit a friend or a relative. . . . So I confirmed the locations with Mrs. Johnson and then told Agent Kivett . . . to make the necessary calls to have Secret Service protection placed around Lynda and Luci." "Youngblood Testimony." In his memoir, *Twenty Years in the Secret Service,* Youngblood wrote (p. 117), "While their father was Vice President, the Johnson daughters did not receive Secret Service protection. . . . We needed to assign men to them as quickly as possible. I asked Mrs. Johnson for their precise whereabouts and then told Jerry Kivett to inform headquarters and arrange protection for them at once." In none of his accounts about the time following the assassination does Youngblood mention Johnson asking about his daughters at all.

In her notes (June 15, 1964), Mrs. Johnson says that at The Elms that night, "I think I remember Lyndon having Secret Service protection for Lynda and Lucy. I think I called

Lynda when I got home. She had gone to stay with the Connally children. It may have been the next morning when I called" ("Mrs. Johnson's Notes").

Asked Youngblood to have them found: "Kivett Statement," p. 2.

Cliff Carter: "Kivett Report," p. 2. **"We didn't know":** Thornberry OH; Brooks interview.

Asked Youngblood to send an agent: Johns to Rowley, "Statement regarding events in Dallas, Texas, on Nov. 22, 1963 (hereafter identified as "Johns Report"), p. 2, Special Files, Assassination, LBJL.

"Mr. Johnson asked me": Kellerman Statement, March 9, 1964, "Hearings," Vol. II, Commission Exhibit 1024, pp. 725–27; "Kellerman Report," pp. 2, 3.

"Lyndon and I didn't speak": "Through it all, Lyndon was remarkably calm and quiet" "Lady Bird Transcript," p. 2.

"All through": Thornberry OH. **"I did not think":** Emory Roberts to Rowley, Subject: Schedule of Events prior to and after the assassination of President John F. Kennedy in Dallas, Texas, on Friday Nov. 22, 1963, p. 1, "Report of the U.S. Secret Service," "Secret Service Reports," Box 3, Special Files, Assassination, LBJL. **The Secret Service wanted:** Carter OH IV; "Youngblood Testimony," p. 158; Youngblood, *Twenty Years,* pp. 116–17.

Johnson did not agree: "Roberts Report," p. 5; "Affidavit of Clifton G. Carter," May 20, 1964, "Hearings," Vol. III, p. 475. **"Well, we want":** Brooks OH I. **He wouldn't leave:** "Youngblood Testimony," pp. 152, 153; Emory Roberts Testimony, "Hearings," Vol. XVIII, pp. 4, 5.

"Every face"; "Always there was Rufe": "Lady Bird Transcript," p. 2. She was to recall that later, on the plane, he said that "The Service had never lost a President," and "I felt so sorry for the way they felt" ("Mrs. Johnson's Notes, p. 2).

"Face of Kenny": "Lady Bird Transcript," p. 2.

Then, at 1:20; "He's gone": "Statement of President Lyndon B. Johnson," July 10, 1964, Vol. V, p. 563, "Hearings." "It was Ken O'Donnell, who, at about 1:20 p.m., told us that the President had died," Johnson said. In transcript, CBS News Special, "LBJ: Tragedy and Transition," May 2, 1970, p. 5; when Cronkite asks, "Who brought that word ['He's gone'] to you?," Johnson replies, "Kenneth O'Donnell." Secret Service Agent Johns says he heard O'Donnell "inform Vice President Johnson that President Kennedy had died" (TO: Chief FROM ASAIC Thomas L. Johns, Vice Presidential Detail, SUBJECT "Statement regarding events in Dallas, Texas, on Friday, Nov. 22, 1963," p. 3, "Secret Service Reports, Box 3, Special Files, Assassination, LBJL). Emory Roberts says he informed Johnson of Kennedy's death at 1:13, "Roberts Report," p. 5. And Carter Affidavit, "Hearings," Vol. III, p. 475.

"That Kennedy had been shot": Sackett interview. **One decision:** Lambert, Sackett interviews. **"I told him":** Lambert, Graves interviews.

No one thought to notify; secretary "burst into"; Reynolds said, "You won't need these": Mollenhoff, *Despoilers of Democracy*, p. 299; Rowe, *Bobby Baker Story*, p. 86. In 2003, Van Kirk said that he had been called out of the hearing room while Reynolds was testifying "to be told that Jack Kennedy had been killed. . . . I knew that if I went back in and told Don Reynolds that Lyndon Johnson was the new President, he'd clam up, so I just went back in and said nothing and we continued the questioning for another two or three hours and I tried to get every bit of information out of him I could." But that was forty years after the event, and Mollenhoff, who was working closely with him and with Senator Williams in November 1963, said in a book published in 1965 that no one in the room knew about the assassination until "shortly after 2:30 P.M., Washington time, "a woman secretary burst into the room, sobbing almost hysterically. As Reynolds and the interrogators looked at her in surprise, she cried: 'President Kennedy has been killed!' At first they thought it was a joke—a bad joke." Curtis said that that was his understanding of what had occurred. Sy Hersh, after his interviews with Van Kirk, wrote that Reynolds was still being questioned at 2:30 P.M. when a secretary burst into the hearing room with the news from Dallas." (He also quotes Van Kirk as telling him in an interview with Hersh, "There's no doubt in my mind that Reynolds' testimony would have gotten Johnson out of the vice presidency" [Hersh, *Dark Side*, p. 446]).

Baker releasing Fortas: Baker, *Wheeling*, p. 160.

12. Taking Charge

"And right then"; "very little passed": Thornberry OH. **"Quiet":** Rather interview.

Change in demeanor: Brooks interview, OH; Thornberry OH; "Transcript from Mrs. Johnson's tapes relating to November 22, 1963," Special Files, Assassination, LBJL (hereafter referred to as "Lady Bird Transcript"). **"Set":** Brooks interview. **"Almost a**

graven": "Notes taken during interview with Mrs. Johnson," June 15, 1964, p. 4, LBJL (hereafter cited as "Mrs. Johnson's Notes").

Still urging: "To: Chief; From: SAIC Youngblood—Vice Presidential Detail; Subject: Statement of SAIC Rufus W. Youngblood, Vice Presidential Detail (office 1–22), concerning details of events occurring in Dallas, Texas, on November 22, 1963," Nov. 29, 1963 (hereafter referred to as Youngblood to Chief; "Emory Roberts to Rowley, Subject: Schedule of Events prior to and after the assassination of President John F. Kennedy in Dallas, Texas, on Friday, Nov. 22, 1963," p. 1, U.S. Treasury Department (hereafter referred to as "Roberts Report"), "Secret Service Reports," both Box 3, Special Files, Assassination, LBJL; Carter OH IV; "Testimony of Rufus Wayne Youngblood, Special Agent, Secret Service," *Hearings Before the President's Commission on the Assassination of President Kennedy, Washington, 1964*, Vol. II (hereafter referred to as "Youngblood Testimony"), p.158; Youngblood, *Twenty Years*, pp. 116–17. **"We've got":** Manchester, *The Death of a President*, p. 233; Roberts Report, pp. 3, 4.

Was "disturbed": Holland, *The Kennedy Assassination Tapes*, p. 14.

"Part of a far-ranging": Youngblood, *Twenty Years*, p. 123. **"A fear that":** Charles Roberts OH I. **"Sir, . . . we *must*":** Youngblood, *Twenty Years*, p. 118. **"That in my opinion":** "Testimony of Kenneth P. O'Donnell," *Hearings*, Vol. VII, p. 451. **"We've got":** Manchester, *Death of a President*, p. 233.

Johnson reached: Johnson, *The Vantage Point*, p. 9; Carter, quoted in Miller, *Lyndon*, p. 314; Brooks OH, interview. **Announced it as quickly:** "Emory and I were in complete agreement on this point, but Lyndon Johnson was shaking his head even before I finished speaking," Youngblood recalls (Youngblood, *Twenty Years*, pp. 116–20). Brooks recalls him saying, "Well, we want to get the official report on that [Kennedy's condition] rather than some individual" (Brooks interview). **When O'Donnell said:** Youngblood, *Twenty Years*, p. 118. **"Adamant":** Youngblood, *Twenty Years*, p. 117.

"mentioned . . . the attempt": *NYHT*, Dec. 24, 1963; Kilduff, in his OH, JFKL, says "Johnson's reaction was going back to Lincoln, too."

He and Youngblood agreed: Youngblood Report, p. 5.

"Quick plans": "Lady Bird Transcript," p. 3. **"The most decisive":** "Mrs. Johnson's Notes," p. 4.

To ask Johnson's permission; "Mr. President"; "He reacted"; "No": David Wise,

"Revealed—Johnson's Delay of Death News," *NYHT,* Dec. 24, 1963; "Awful Interval," *Newsweek,* Jan. 6, 1964; Youngblood, *Twenty Years,* p. 119; "Lady Bird Transcript," p. 3; Manchester, *Death of a President,* p. 221. Youngblood's *Twenty Years* (p. 119) has "He was the first to address him by the title." **Delay in announcement:** Youngblood, *Twenty Years,* p. 119, and Kilduff account in *Newsweek,* Jan. 6, 1964. **"By now":** After Johnson left Parkland, Kilduff went to the press room and made the official announcement of Kennedy's death. But when asked about Johnson's whereabouts, he told the reporters that "out of 'considerations of security,' he couldn't say" (*Newsweek,* Jan. 6, 1964).

Making his dispositions: Brooks OH I; Jesse Curry OH; Valenti OH II.

"Homer, you go": Brooks interview.

In a rush: Stoughton interview; Richard B. Trask, "The Day Kennedy Was Shot," *American Heritage,* Nov. 1988. **"Getting out":** "Lady Bird Transcript," p. 3. **Pierpoint caught:** Newseum, with Trost and Bennett, *President Kennedy Has Been Shot,* p. 96. **"We weren't thinking":** Charles Roberts OH. **Suspecting:** Stoughton interview.

Seating arrangements in car: Thornberry OH; Youngblood to Chief, p. 5; "Youngblood Testimony," p. 153; Youngblood, *Twenty Years,* p. 122. **"Let's don't have":** Thornberry OH I. **"The swiftest":** "Lady Bird Transcript," p. 3. **"Suddenly there before us":** Youngblood, *Twenty Years,* p. 121. **"Practically ran up":** Youngblood to Chief, p. 6.

"I want this kept": Youngblood, *Twenty Years,* p. 123. Kivett says, "At first the Vice President was put in the bedroom; however he said this was in bad taste and he moved up to the sitting room." "Statement by Jerry D. Kivett concerning the events of Nov. 22, 1963," *Report of the U.S. Secret Service on the Assassination of President Kennedy,* U.S. Treasury Department, p. 3, Box 3, Special Files, Assassination, LBJL (hereafter referred to as "Kivett Statement"). **"Very real indeed":** Youngblood, *Twenty Years,* p. 123.

Thornberry argued for Washington, Thomas and Brooks for Dallas: Brooks interview, OH I; Manchester, *Death of a President,* p. 269. **"Suppose":** Youngblood, *Twenty Years,* p. 125. **"I took the oath":** Goodwin, *Lyndon Johnson,* p. 170. **"Very much in command"; "I agree":** Manchester, *Death of a President,* p. 267.

He wanted privacy: Fehmer OH, interview; Youngblood, *Twenty Years,* p. 123. When Johnson, during his retirement, was giving direction to the ghostwriters of his memoir, he told them: "I was in the President's bedroom. Hell, I was President. . . . I don't see any difference in the bedroom and the sitting room. He wasn't going to sleep in the bed and I was trying to talk to [Robert] Kennedy and take pills and locate the Judge and do all these things I had to do. . . . I don't think I would be apologetic about it" (Johnson, "Reminiscences of Lyndon B. Johnson," August 19, 1969, transcript of tape recording, pp. 4, 5, OH Collection, LBJL).

"For millions": Johnson interview with Doris Goodwin, *Lyndon Johnson,* p. 170; "Statement of President Lyndon B. Johnson," July 10, 1964, Vol. V, p. 563, *Hearings* (hereafter referred to as "Johnson Statement").

Hickory Hill scene: Schlesinger, *Robert Kennedy and His Times,* pp. 607–8; Manchester, *Death of a President,* pp. 256–59; Morgenthau interview. **Johnson-Bobby calls:** Youngblood to Chief, p. 6; "Youngblood Testimony," p. 154. Fehmer, Katzenbach interviews.

"I wanted to say something": "Johnson Statement," p. 563. See also Johnson, *Vantage Point,* p. 13. **"In spite of his shock and sorrow":** Johnson, *Vantage Point,* p. 13. Johnson said Bobby was "very businesslike, although I guess he must have been suffering more than almost anyone except Mrs. Kennedy" (Johnson, recorded interview by Walter Cronkite, CBS News Special, May 6, 1970, quoted in Shesol, *Mutual Contempt,* p. 115).

Kennedy's accounts; "a lot of people": O'Donnell, Powers, and McCarthy, *"Johnny, We Hardly Knew Ye,"* pp. 35–36. **"Do you have any objection":** Manchester, *Death of a President,* p. 269. **"I was too surprised":** O'Donnell and Powers, *"Johnny, We Hardly,"* p. 37. **"I was sort of taken aback":** Quoted in Schlesinger, *Robert Kennedy,* p. 609. **"They want"; "No, not necessary"; "anyone who can":** Katzenbach, *Some of It Was Fun,* p. 130. **"Absolutely stunned"; "He could have"; "he may have wanted"; "Calling Bobby":** Katzenbach interview. **"Frankly appalled":** Katzenbach, *Some of It,* p. 131.

"The facts are unclear": Manchester, *Death of a President,* p. 271. **Johnson was to say:** Johnson, *Vantage Point,* p. 13. **"They're going":** Katzenbach interview.

"Bobby started it": Fehmer OH. **"I was":** Fehmer interview.

"As much as": Holland, *Kennedy Assassination Tapes,* p. 24. **"Get Sarah Hughes":** Manchester, *Death of a President,* p. 272. **"I was all right":** Fehmer interview. **"Some of us did feel":** O'Donnell and Powers, *"Johnny, We Hardly,"* p. 37.

Hammering began: Fehmer OH II. **"Reclining":** Manchester, *Death of a President,* p. 310. **"In an effort":** Fehmer OH II.

"Something that left me stunned": O'Donnell and Powers, *"Johnny, We Hardly,"* p. 34. "She was entering": Fehmer OH II.

"It was a very, very hard thing to do": Mrs. Johnson's Diary, Box 1, "November 22," pp. 6, 7; Holland, *Kennedy Assassination Tapes,* p. 23. "Well": Manchester, *Death of a President,* pp. 316, 317. "She understood": Manchester, *Death of a President,* p. 322.

"It was suffocating"; "kept looking out": O'Donnell and Powers, *"Johnny, We Hardly,"* pp. 34, 36. McHugh, Kilduff episode: O'Donnell and Powers, *"Johnny, We Hardly,"* p. 34. Manchester makes this a vivid episode, but as Roberts writes, "There is a paucity of evidence that this conflict of plans generated the blazing controversy that Manchester later perceived" (Roberts, *The Truth about the Assassination,* p. 108). "In a highly desperate": "Testimony of Kenneth P. O'Donnell," *Hearings,* Vol. VII, p. 454; Roberts, *The Truth,* p. 108.

"The huge figure": Jack Valenti, *WP,* Nov. 22, 1993. "Even in": Valenti OH II. "In a strange way": Valenti, *A Very Human President,* p. 45. "You see": Busby interview. "When I walked in": Johnson, *Vantage Point,* p. 13. "We are ready": Transcript, "Tape recording between Lyndon B. Johnson, Jack Valenti, and Bob Hardesty," March 8, 1969, p. 2, OH Collection, LBJL. "Put the pool": "Liz Carpenter Recollections," p. 19, Box 4, Special Files, Assassination, LBJL. "I want you on my staff": Valenti, *WP,* Nov. 22, 1993. "We can't leave here"; "You must remember Sarah Hughes": O'Donnell and Powers, *"Johnny, We Hardly,"* p. 35. "I could not imagine"; "Bobby gave me": O'Donnell and Powers, *"Johnny, We Hardly,"* p. 35.

"Almost whispering": Charles Roberts, "Pool Report—Dallas to Washington," Nov. 22, 1963, p. 1, Special Files, Assassination, LBJL. "Johnson was adamant": O'Brien OH VI. "Thank God"; "standing tall"; "taking command"; "as many": Stoughton interview. Witnesses whose presence: "Liz Carpenter Recollections," p. 20.

"In itself": Youngblood, *Twenty Years,* p. 129. "Shoulder to shoulder": "Testimony of Lawrence O'Brien," *Hearings,* Vol. VII, p. 470. "We can talk": O'Brien OH VI. "Noncommittal": O'Donnell OH.

Reporters' wild ride: Sid Davis OH; Roberts, *The Truth,* p. 109. "They don't know": Davis OH. "We've got the press here": Charles Roberts OH.

"Now we're going to have": Charles Roberts OH.

"In they came"; "Johnson particularly": Judge Sarah Hughes, as told to Michael Drury,

"The Woman Who Swore in President Johnson Recalls What Happened Aboard Air Force One, 2:38 p.m., Dallas, Nov. 22, 1963," Box 2, Special Files, Assassination, LBJL. He made sure: Stoughton interview.

"Mrs. Kennedy wanted": Hughes to Drury. "Do you want?": Davis OH I. Stoughton describes Johnson as "upset that Jackie wasn't" making her appearance "faster than she was" (Stoughton interview). "She said": O'Donnell and Powers, *"Johnny, We Hardly,"* p. 36. "Your mind": "Liz Carpenter's Recollections," pp. 23, 18. "Had not known this man": Sid Davis OH. "Big. *Big*": Stoughton interview.

"Now": Charles Roberts OH, p. 17. "Johnson particularly"; "Mrs. Kennedy wanted": Sarah Hughes, as told to Drury.

"Something larger": Valenti interview. "I think I ought": O'Donnell and Powers, *"Johnny, We Hardly,"* p. 36. "A hush": Charles Roberts OH. "Cast down": Sarah Hughes, as told to Drury. "Absolutely steady": Valenti, *This Time, This Place,* p. 28.

"Now let's get airborne": Charles Roberts, "Pool Report"; Sid Davis, "My Brush with History," *American Heritage,* Nov.–Dec. 2003; Charles Roberts OH.

13. Aboard Air Force One

"Legitimated": Neustadt, *Presidential Power,* p. 237. "Illustrate how": Verba, "The Kennedy Assassination and the Nature of Political Commitment," in Greenberg and Parker, eds., *The Kennedy Assassination and the American Public,* p. 351. "Only two uniforms": Truman, *Memoirs by Harry S. Truman: Years of Decisions,* p. 7.

"Violence was missing": Schramm, "Communication in Crisis," from Greenberg and Parker, eds., *The Kennedy Assassination,* p. 3. Oswald arrested; "He also is being questioned"; "a definite": ABC News, Newseum, *President Kennedy Has Been Shot,* pp. 127, 129.

The first detailed study: Sheatsley and Feldman, "A National Survey on Public Relations and Behavior," in Greenberg and Parker, eds., *The Kennedy Assassination,* pp. 149–77. The study was carried out by a division of the National Opinion Research Center, and hereafter it will be identified as "NORC Study." Four out of five: SRS-350 Codebook: *Kennedy Assassination Study,* November, 1963, p. 6, NORC Library, University of Chicago.

"Like a shock wave": "The Day Kennedy Died," *Newsweek,* Dec. 2, 1963. 92 percent: Sheatsley and Feldman, "A National Survey,"

p. 152. A Gallup poll in Greece, reported on Dec. 15, found that "just 24 hours after the assassination, 99 per cent of Athenians were found to be aware of the tragic occurrence" (Sheatsley and Feldman, "A National Survey," p. 153). **166 million; 31.6:** A. C. Nielsen Co, "TV Responses to the Death of the President," quoted in Schramm, "Communication in Crisis," p. 14. **"Probably without parallel":** Greenberg and Parker, eds., *The Kennedy Assassination,* p. 153. **"The first loss":** Schramm, "Communication in Crisis," p. 3. **"For all practical":** Schramm, "Communication in Crisis," p. 4. **Only 88 percent:** Sheatsley and Feldman, "A National Survey," p. 159. **"When President Franklin":** *NYT,* Nov. 24, 1963. **NORC survey timetable:** Sheatsley and Feldman, "A National Survey," p. 151–51.

"Terrible responsibility: Jonathan Schell, "The Time of Illusion: VI—Credibility," *The New Yorker,* July 7, 1965, quoted in Neustadt, *Presidential Power,* pp. 230–31. **"Lyndon Johnson's ascent":** Graff, ed., *The Presidents: A Reference History,* p. 595. **"Some":** Evans and Novak, *Lyndon B. Johnson,* p. 338. **"We came":** Manatos OH, LBJL. **"I always felt sorry":** Moyers, quoted in Miller, *Lyndon,* p. 336. On another occasion, Johnson said, "I came into office by assassination—knowing that I was living under that burden" (Johnson, "Reminiscences of Lyndon B. Johnson," August 19, 1969, transcript of tape recording, OH Collection, LBJL, p. 26). **"A Texas murder":** Manchester, *The Death of a President,* p. 228.

"I wish our leader": "The Senate: A Crisis in Leadership," *Newsweek,* Nov. 18, 1963. **And now the other bills were being held up:** As the Kennedy administration may have been starting to realize. Speaking to Wilbur Mills of Arkansas, chairman of the House Ways and Means Committee, about why the tax-cut bill wasn't making more progress through Mills's committee, Kennedy asked him what would induce a committee member from the South who might otherwise favor the bill to oppose it? Mills replied that opponents would "get him"—get his vote to oppose the tax bill—by saying that in return they would oppose release of the civil rights bill from the House Rules Committee. "Let's take a fellow . . . who was prone to vote for the tax bill. . . . How would they get him?" Kennedy asked Mills. "I mean, what, would be the offer on civil rights that would get him?"

"Block it in the Rules Committee," Mills replies (Reeves, *President Kennedy,* p. 623).

In his last press conference before his assassination, Kennedy was asked, why, in addition

to the tax-cut bill and the civil rights bill, the foreign aid bill had suffered its "worst attack . . . since its inception," and "several appropriation bills are still hung up in Congress for the first time in history this late. What's happened on Capitol Hill?"

"Well, they're all interrelated," Kennedy replied. "I think there is some delay because of civil rights—that's had an effect upon the passage of appropriation bills. There isn't any question." *WP,* Nov. 15.

The legislative situation at the time of Kennedy's assassination is summarized in Giglio, *The Presidency of John F. Kennedy,* p. 286; Dallek, *An Unfinished Life,* pp. 707–8. Tom Wicker, at the time of the assassination the White House correspondent for *The New York Times* and later head of its Washington Bureau, was to write that "while it will never be known to a certainty whether the Kennedy tax and civil rights bills . . . have been approved in Congress had Kennedy not been murdered . . . these bills were widely believed to be bogged down and stalled on the day of his death. . . . In the time allotted him, Kennedy never was able to lead Congress effectively" (Wicker, *JFK and LBJ,* p. 147).

"The first priority": *NYHT, NYT, WP,* Jan. 26, 1963. **The pace of the hearings:** The Kennedy Administration had been pressing for a vote in the Finance Committee to speed up the pace of the hearings, a vote to, in effect, repudiate Byrd's tactics. The vote was held on November 15th. Exactly two members of the 17-member committee voted for it. There were twelve votes against it, and three members weren't present (Reeves, *President Kennedy,* p. 658).

In an issue that hit the newsstands the week he died, *Newsweek* said "his legislative program was bogged down in the least productive Congress in memory" (*Newsweek,* Nov. 25, 1963).

"We are at the critical stage": Burns, *The Deadlock of Democracy,* p. 2. The last section of his book is titled "Leadership: The Art of the Impossible?" **"This Congress has gone further":** Lippmann, quoted in Johnson, *Vantage Point,* p. 34. **"Sat longer":** "The Lethargic 88th vs. L.B.J.," *Life,* Dec. 13, 1963. **"It has seemed impossible":** Childs. **"there was no assurance"; Kennedy's final press conference:** *WP,* Nov. 15, 1963. **"Is, here and now":** Evans and Novak, *NYHT,* Nov. 24, 1963. **"A man who wore":** "Lyndon Johnson: His Life, His Family, His Ways," *NYP,* Nov. 27–Dec. 2, 1963. **"trying":** Rauh interview. **"Mr. Johnson needs":** *LAT,* Nov. 24, 1963. **"As the first southerner":** Shannon, *NYP.*

"The eleven weeks": Neustadt, *Presiden-*

tial Power, p. 240. **"If I am elected"**: Schlesinger, *A Thousand Days,* p. 121. **"Faced the unprecedented"**: Neustadt, *Presidential Power,* p. 258.

During the very next week: Cameron to Bermingham, "Johnson-Economy (Advisory-Biz)," Nov. 25, 1963, White Papers, Box 322, JFKL.

Even Truman's: Neustadt, *Presidential Power,* p. 258.

"Illegitimate"; "the bigots and the dividers": Johnson interview with Goodwin, quoted in Goodwin, *Lyndon Johnson,* p. 170. **"I simply"**: Goodwin, *Lyndon Johnson,* pp. 174, 175. **"And one"**: Sidey, *A Very Personal Presidency,* p. 86. **"I'm not sure"**: Sidey interview; Sidey, *Very Personal Presidency,* p. 86. **"He felt"**: Jenkins OH, Nov. 12, 1980. **"A lot"**: Goldman, *The Tragedy of Lyndon Johnson,* p. 24. **Busby found himself:** Busby OH VII, pp. 25–26. **And the key word:** Busby interview. **Among the "things he envied":** Jones interview. **"Our pool"**: Lady Bird's Diary, Box 1, Saturday, Dec. 21, 1963. **"Immobilized," "paralyzed":** For example, "I would think, what if I had a stroke like my Grandma did, and she couldn't even move her hands. . . . That was constant, with me all the time. . . . I always had horrible memories of my grandmother in a wheelchair all my childhood" (Johnson, "Reminiscences," pp. 24, 25).

"Everything": Johnson interview with Goodwin, quoted in Goodwin, *Lyndon Johnson,* p. 172. **"I was"**: Johnson, *The Vantage Point,* p. 12. **"I knew I could not allow:** Johnson, *Vantage Point,* pp. 12, 18, 21.

"Almost vertical": "I'm assuming he did that because he may have been afraid there could have been somebody on the ground who would try to shoot at it," Davis says (Newseum, *President Kennedy Has Been Shot,* p. 121). **At every Air Force base:** Manchester, *Death of a President,* p. 352. **"Who knew"**: Wicker, *JFK and LBJ,* p. 162. **Border:** Manchester, *Death of a President,* p. 353.

In Los Angeles: *Newsweek,* Dec. 2, 1963. **In New York:** *NYT,* Nov. 23, 1963. **First bulletins:** Newseum, *President Kennedy Has Been Shot,* p. 33. **"The last thunderbolt"**: Manchester, *Death of a President,* p. 362.

1:36; "Mr. Johnson": *NYT,* Nov. 23, 1936. This time is also a matter of dispute, with various accounts putting the time of Kilduff's announcement between 1:33 and 1:37. **"Vice President Johnson"; "We began"**: Newseum, *President Kennedy Has Been Shot,* p. 87. **"There has been"; "we have learned"**: "JOHN F. KENNEDY: ASSASSINATION 1 #2 (RADIO) (Nov. 22, 1963). "It appeared"; "We now"**: *Ibid, # 1.* **Two heads:** Greenberg and Parker, eds, *The Ken-*

nedy Assassination, p. 11; Manchester, *Death of a President,* pp. 352, 353. **"People"**: Wicker, *JFK and LBJ,* p. 159. **"It could"**: *Chicago Tribune,* Nov. 22, 1963. **"The German alert"**: Manchester, *Death of a President,* pp. 352, 353.

"Like going back"; "sobbing"; "his eyes were brimming": Charles Roberts OH I.

"That long, long"; "my first"; "You make"; "No"; "He's my": Manchester, *Death of a President,* pp. 347–350. **They decided to drink:** Talking to the ghostwriters of his autobiography during his retirement, Johnson said, "I wouldn't want to say this in the book, but I thought they were just wineheads. They were just drinkers, just one drink after another coming to them trying to drown out their sorrow and we weren't drinking of course. . . ." (Transcript, "Tape Recording between Lyndon B. Johnson, Jack Valenti and Bob Hardesty," March 8, 1969, pp. 7, 8, OH Collection, LBJL).

Pulled a pad: "Aboard Air Force One," "Diary Backup," Box 4, Special Files, Assassination, LBJL. **"Duplex, Duplex"**: Transcript, "3:13–3:24 P.M., CST, Andrews AFB, AF-1 (Chester Clifton), and the White House (Jerry Behn)," pp. 42–45, *The Presidential Recordings of Lyndon B. Johnson,* Vol. I. **"I needed"**: Goodwin, *Lyndon Johnson,* p. 177. **"Noncommittal"; "Bill, I don't"**: O'Donnell OH. **Cabinet meeting postponed:** Transcript, "3:13–3:24 P.M. CST, AF-1 (Malcolm Kilduff, Chester Clifton), Andrews AFB, and the White House (McGeorge Bundy), *TPR,* Vol. I, pp. 56–58.

"None of us": O'Brien OH, LBJL. **Van Buren quote:** Schlesinger, *Robert Kennedy and His Times,* p. 609.

"It's the Kremlin": Charles W. Bailey, "Memorandum to the President," undated, Box 4, Special Files, Assassination, LBJL.

Orders began: Transcript, "3:13–3:24 P.M., CST, Andrews AFB, AF-1 (Chester Clifton), and the White House (Jerry Behn)," *The Presidential Recordings,* Vol. I, pp. 43, 44. **"Winner, Winner"**: Transcript, "3:13–3:24 P.M., CST, Andrews AFB, AF-1 (Malcolm Kilduff) and the White House (Andrew Hatcher)," Vol. I, p. 54. **"According to plan"**: Valenti, *This Time, This Place,* p. 29. **"I want his friends"**: Manchester, *Death of a President,* p. 386. **"I want my staff"**: "Liz Carpenter's Recollections of President Kennedy's Assassination," p. 24, Box 4, Special Files, Assassination, LBJL. **"I want you"**: Valenti, *This Time,* p. 28.

Drafting, improving the: "Nov. 22, 1963—Remarks of President upon Arrival at Andrews Air Force Base," Box 89, Statements of Lyndon Baines Johnson; Fehmer interview; "Tape Recording between Lyndon B. Johnson,

Jack Valenti, and Bob Hardesty," p. 4. Valenti, *This Time,* p. 29; *A Very Human President,* pp. 50, 51.

"Tell the Vice President": Transcript, "3:13–3:24 P.M., AF-1 (Malcolm Kilduff, Chester Clifton), Andrews AFB, and the White House (McGeorge Bundy), *TPR,* Vol. I, p. 60. **Youngblood was sent:** Transcript, "3:13–3:24 P.M. CST, The White House (Jerry Behn) and AF-1 (Rufus Youngblood)," *TPR,* Vol. I, pp. 51, 52. **"Shaky":** Bird, *The Color of Truth,* p. 266. **Putting his hand over the phone:** Manchester, *Death of a President,* p. 371. **To Rose Kennedy:** Transcript, "3:15 P.M. CST, "AF-1 (President Johnson, Lady Bird Johnson, and . . . the White House, and Rose Kennedy," *TPR,* Vol. I, pp. 63–65.

"Masterful": Roberts OH. **"As calm":** Thornberry OH I. **"Let's get":** Fehmer OH II. **Until he was stopped:** Valenti, *Very Human President,* p. 55.

Bobby had walked; "There's so much"; Ethel handing him glasses: Schlesinger, *Robert Kennedy,* p. 609. **"He had the most wonderful":** Thomas, *Robert Kennedy,* p. 277.

Arriving at Andrews: Thomas, *Robert Kennedy,* p. 277; Schlesinger, *Robert Kennedy,* p. 610; Manchester, *Death of a President,* p. 387. **Ran up the stairs:** Nancy Dickerson, quoted in Newseum, *President Kennedy Has Been Shot,* p. 142; Manchester, *Death of a President,* p. 387. **"Where's Jackie?":** Carpenter, "Recollections," p. 24; Thomas, *Robert Kennedy,* p. 277. **Pushed his way; "didn't look":** Carpenter, "Recollections," p. 24; Valenti, *This Time,* p. 29; Valenti, *Very Human President,* p. 55. **Valenti felt:** Valenti, *WP,* Nov. 22, 1993. **"Everyone":** Manchester, *Death of a President,* p. 386. **"Trapped":** Valenti, *Very Human President,* p. 56; *This Time,* p. 29. **"Hi, Jackie":** Manchester, *Death of a President,* p. 387.

"A fallen chieftain": Manchester, *Death of a President,* p. 389. **"Yearned for a cry":** Theodore White, quoted in Manchester, *Death of a President,* p. 388. **"He [Johnson] said:** Manchester, *Death of a President,* p. 387. **Couldn't recall it; "I would not have felt"; "I just observed":** CBS News Special—LBJ: 'Tragedy and Transition,' " May 2, 1970. **"A deliberate snub":** Bishop, *The Day Kennedy Was Shot,* p. 406.

"The scene": Mary McGrory, "The Return," *NYP,* Nov. 24, 1963.

"He was very reassuring"; "Because of the noise": Robert Asman, Harry Reasoner, quoted in Newseum, *President Kennedy Has Been Shot,* p. 145. **He assigned:** Manchester, *Death of a President,* p. 402. **"Get in the second":** Valenti, *Very Human President,* p. 3. **"Any important matters"; Kennedy did something":** "File: Transition / State," Box 167, White Papers, JFKL; Manchester, *Death of a President,* p. 402.

"No other words": Bird, *Color of Truth,* p. 266. **"Surprisingly stable"; moving:** Manchester, *Death of a President,* p. 402. **"Like an invisible":** Amrine, *This Awesome Challenge,* p. 10.

"Stay with Lady Bird"; "It's a terrible thing"; "Don't think": Carpenter, "Recollections," p. 26. **"Don't you want to go in?":** Moyers, quoted in Miller, *Lyndon,* p. 323.

Scene in office: Fehmer, Jenkins, Reedy interviews; Nelson, Juanita Roberts OHs. **"He had to":** Nelson OH. **"Reassuring pat"; "Walter, let's have Marie":** Roberts OH III. **"Nothing worked":** Nelson OH. **Fehmer went home:** Fehmer interview, OH. **"I didn't know him":** Roberts OH III. **"Much chaos":** Fehmer interview. **"Total command":** Nelson OH. **"Almost a different person":** Fehmer interview. **"No lost motion"; Bundy:** Roberts OH III. **"I have needed you":** Transcript, Telephone call, "7:10 P.M. EST, To Dwight D. Eisenhower," *TPR,* Vol. I, pp. 78–79. **Hoover call:** Reedy interview. **Herbert Hoover call:** From notes taken by Johnson staff, pp. 79, 80. **J. Edgar Hoover call:** Manchester, *Death of a President,* p. 405. **Maguire call:** Transcript, "9:10 P.M. EST, To Richard Maguire, *TPR,* pp. 84, 85. **Goldberg call:** Transcript, "9:06 PM, EST, To Arthur Goldberg and Dorothy Goldberg. All from *TPR,* Vol. I.

"Especially Sorensen": Moyers, cited in Sorensen, *Counselor,* p. 364. **"White-faced":** McGrory, *NYP,* Nov. 24, 1963. **"Kindly, strongly":** Sorensen, *Counselor,* p. 364. No transcript of this call exists. **Congressional leaders:** White to Parker, Nov. 22, 1963, "Johnson Cover II and Narrative—Nation, Time files, White Papers; Reedy." **"That perhaps":** Sidey, *Very Personal Presidency,* pp. 41, 42.

Letters to John and Caroline: "Kennedy, Mrs. John F. 1963," Box 7, WHFN. **"He would never":** Manchester, *Death of a President,* p. 406. **"I'm going":** Busby interview.

"Drive home": Valenti, *A Very Human President,* p. 6. **Surprisingly small:** Sidey, Steele interviews. **Scene at house:** Busby, Hurst, Valenti interviews. **"The aura":** Busby, *The Thirty-first of March,* pp. 151–2. **"Hello, Mr. Sam":** Peggy Starke to Busby, undated, "This is rough and without continuity as I transcribed it as you told it" (in author's possession). In his book, Busby says (p. 152) that he said, "How I wish you were here." **Travell had called:** Travell, *Office Hours,* p. 429. **Hurst was waiting:** Hurst and Cain, *LBJ: To Know Him Better,* p. 7. **"More controlled":** Busby, *Thirty-first of March,* p. 152. **"Composure":** Busby interview. **"I guess"; "I don't":** Busby, quoted in Miller, *Lyndon,* p. 324. **"That's the last":** Valenti interview. **"I want you"; "Take care":** Busby, *Thirty-first of March,* p. 153. **"Almost to"; "You know":** Busby interview.

"I want to think out": Valenti interview. **"A sounding board":** Carter OH; Jack Valenti, "Achilles in the White House: A Discussion with Harry McPherson and Jack Valenti," *Wilson Quarterly,* Spring 2000.

Johnson talking: Valenti interview; Carter OH; Valenti OH II. Valenti, "Achilles in the White House"; Valenti interview. **"We sat"; "Everything":** Carter OH. **"By God":** Valenti interview. **"That whole night":** Moyers, quoted in Miller, *Lyndon,* p. 325. **"Do you realize":** Valenti interview. **"He told Moyers":** Carter OH.

Until three: "President's Diary–Nov. 22, 1963," Box 2, Special Files, Assassination, LBJL. **"Well, good night":** Valenti interview. When he went to his bedroom, Moyers says, "I looked down and could see shadowy figures moving through the grounds. The Secret Service had on a heavy guard."

14. Three Encounters

"As it did"; "Her face": Goodwin, *Remembering America,* pp. 228, 230. **A decision:** Schlesinger, *Robert Kennedy and His Times,* p. 610; Manchester, *The Death of a President,* pp. 435, 442–43. **"For a moment":** Schlesinger, *Journals,* pp. 204, 205. **"Close it":** Manchester, *Death of a President,* p. 443. **"Why, God?":** Spaulding in recorded interview, Jan. 22, 1970, quoted in Schlesinger, *Robert Kennedy,* p. 611.

Bundy had told Johnson Friday evening: Stegall to Johnson, 8:05 a.m., Nov. 23, "Manchester File," Box 1, Special Files, Assassination, LBJL. **Johnson didn't get:** unaddressed, unsigned, yellow notepaper. "Mac comes in early Sat. & saw Bobby & Mrs. Lincoln said he hoped they didn't (have to) move quickly—But [evidently Bundy] failed to tell & Pres. went into little office. . . . Finally an amicable basic agreement that office would be occupied after funeral—"Current," Box 4, Special Files, Assassination, LBJL. **"I have an appointment":** Manchester, *Death of a President,* p. 453. Manchester quotes Secret Service Agent John J. O'Leary, who Manchester says was

standing by Evelyn's desk, as saying that there was "anxiety on his [Johnson's] part to get in. In his book *Lyndon,* Merle Miller says (p. 601) that Moyers was present at this encounter, and that Moyers "said that Lyndon was not at all rude, but on the contrary, told Mrs. Lincoln when he saw her packing up things, 'You don't have to do that—you just take your time.' " Miller also says that "in *Robert Kennedy and His Times,* Arthur M. Schlesinger, Jr., mentions no such encounter." But in fact Schlesinger does indeed mention it, on page 627, in an account that is fundamentally the same as Manchester's, and that Schlesinger says is based not only on an interview Kennedy gave to Manchester, but on an account Lincoln gave to him, Schlesinger, as recorded in his journals on March 25, 1964. Lincoln gave a similar account to me in my interview with her in 1993. And in a recorded interview with John Bartlow Martin, Robert Kennedy says, "He came to the White House on Saturday and started moving all my brother's things out Saturday morning at nine o'clock. I went over and asked him to wait, at least until Sunday or Monday" (Guthman and Shulman, eds., *Robert Kennedy: In His Own Words,* p. 406). Johnson did, in fact, have an appointment scheduled for 9:30, with Dean Rusk ("The President's Appointments, Sat., Nov. 23, Box 1, Diary Backup, LBJL). The author couldn't reconcile Moyers's statement with those of Lincoln and Robert Kennedy, because of Moyers's refusal to be interviewed. **"A mix-up":** Bundy, quoted by Kennedy, in Schlesinger, *Robert Kennedy,* p. 627.

"Ran so": Schlesinger, *Robert Kennedy,* p. 626. **"During":** Johnson interview by William J. Jordan, Aug. 12, 1969, OH Collection, LBJL.

"Very short": Bundy to Johnson, Nov. 23, Special Files. **"No pictures":** Bundy, Nov. 23, "[President Johnson's Statements and Schedule, Nov. '63–Jan. '64]," Box 3, Special Files. Assassination, LBJL. **"I was upset":** Schlesinger, *Robert Kennedy,* p. 627. **"Bobby was late":** Bundy, quoted in Manchester, *Death of a President,* p. 476. **"Quite clear":** Shesol, *Mutual Contempt,* p. 120. **"Awful"; "We won't":** Freeman Diary, quoted in Manchester, *Death of a President,* p. 477. **"There was real":** Manchester, *Death of a President,* p. 478. **"Kennedy expressed":** Schlesinger, *Robert Kennedy,* p. 627.

"I'll make it": Transcript, "3:54 P.M. to John McCormack," *TPR,* Vol. I, pp. 115–16. **"The Kennedy aura":** Transcript, "2:10 P.M. to George Smathers, *TPR,* p. 109. **"Might be resented":** Manchester, *Death of a President,* p. 478. **"I didn't like that":** Schlesinger, *Robert Kennedy,* pp. 627–28; Manchester,

Death of a President, p. 480. **"It will"**: Manchester, *Death of a President*, p. 480.

15. The Drums

"Block by block": Manchester, *Death of a President*, p. 537. **"All you"; "the drums"**: Major General Philip Wehle Clifton, quoted in Manchester, *Death of a President*, p. 538. **"A sea of faces"**: Lady Bird Johnson, *A White House Diary*, pp. 8, 9.

"Can I have" Manchester, *Death of a President*, p. 541. **"There was"**: UPI and American Heritage, *Four Days*, p. 84. *If Jackie:* Manchester, *Death of a President*, p. 540. **"Her behavior"**: Lady Bird Johnson, *A White House Diary*, pp. 8, 10. **"You just kiss"; Joint Chiefs**: Manchester, *Death of a President*, p. 542.

"The juxtaposition"; "A new dimension": *NYT*, Nov. 24. **"Marked . . . the first time"**: *NYT*, Nov. 25, 1963. **"Clustered"**: Heren, *No Hail, No Farewell*, pp.4, 9.

"The mighty": *WP*, Nov. 24, 1963. **"A strange counterpoint"**: Johnson, *The Vantage Point*, p. 33.

"The drama": Sidey, *A Very Personal Presidency*, p. 43.

"I would to God": Russell, *Lady Bird*, p. 231. **Surprisingly small**: McNeil, Sidey, Steele interviews.

16. EOB 274

All dates 1963 unless otherwise noted.

The atmosphere in 274 comes from interviews with Fehmer, Jenkins, Reedy, Sidey, Steele; from oral histories by Carter, Fehmer, Juanita Roberts, Nelson; from the memos sent back to *Time* magazine in New York by Washington bureau chief John L. Steele and correspondents Lansing Lamont and Loye Miller.

Some of the items: All from "November 23, 1963, "Diary Backup," Box 1. **"It was . . . almost"**: Goodwin, *Lyndon Johnson*, p. 201. **"With which"**: John McCone, "Memorandum for the Record," Nov. 25, 1963, "Meetings with the President—23 Nov. 1963–27 Dec. 1963," Box 1, John McCone Memoranda, LBJL.

"There will be": Transcript, "5:52 P.M. to McGeorge Bundy," Nov. 23, *TPR*, Vol. I, p. 123.

Had turned to Smathers before: Caro, *Master of the Senate*, pp. 658, 855. **He telephoned him**: Transcript, "2:10 P.M. to George Smathers," Nov. 23, *TPR*, Vol. I, pp. 107–12.

"We stand": Gordon to Johnson, Nov. 23,

1963, "FI 4 Budget—Appropriations Nov. 22, 1963–Jan. 31, 1964," Box 21, WHCF—FI (Gen). **"I told him"; "Now I want to say"**: Walter Heller, "HIGHLY CONFIDENTIAL–"Notes on Meeting with President Johnson, 7:40 P.M., Saturday, Nov. 23, 1963," Papers of Gardner Ackley, microfilm Reel #2, LBJL. **Anderson told him**: Transcript, "1:55 P.M. to Robert Anderson and Ollie Mae Anderson," Nov. 23, *TPR*, Vol. I, pp. 102–4. **Udall, Wirtz and Freeman had urged:** For example, "Secretary Freeman called and said as follows . . . ," "Jenkins to Johnson, Nov. 23," November 23, "Diary Backup," Box 1.

"Indefensible": Evans and Novak, *Lyndon B. Johnson*, pp. 365–66; *WP*, Nov. 16, 21, 23, 6. **"Just the moment"**: Reedy interview. **"They've got the bit"**: Reedy interview. **"We could not afford"**: Johnson, *The Vantage Point*, p. 39. **The two leaders**: Humphrey, *The Education of a Public Man*, p. 264; Amrine, *This Awesome Challenge*, pp. 54, 55. **"They don't know"**: McPherson interview. **"They told me"**: Transcript, "3:30 P.M. from John McCormack and Hale Boggs," *TPR*, Nov. 26, Vol. I, p. 182. Humphrey himself recounts that Johnson asked him, "How many votes do you have?," and he replied, "I'm not sure." Johnson, Humphrey says, said, "That's the trouble with that place up there. You fellows don't count votes" (Humphrey, *Education*, p. 264). **When Johnson tried to reach O'Brien:** Reedy interview.

"Grief and disbelief; "the details": Sorensen, *Counselor*, pp. 367, 380–81; Sorensen interview.

"Gov. [George] Romney": All from "Diary Backup—November 23, 1963," Box 1, Diary Backup. **"Harry Provence"**: Jenkins to Johnson, Nov. 23, "Diary Backup—November 23, 1963," Box 1, Diary Backup. **McCone closed**: Steele interview. **"The President"**: Jenkins to Johnson, Nov. 23. **"You're wonderful"**: Transcript, "1:44 P.M., from Ralph Yarborough," Nov. 23, *TPR*, Vol. I, p. 101. **"One call after"**: Reedy interview. **"Apparently"**: Reedy to Johnson, Nov. 23. All from "Diary Backup—November 23," Box 1, Diary Backup.

"The President and Mrs. Johnson": "Draft—Program at Rotunda, Attachment # 1, November 24, 1963," Box 1, Diary Backup. **An usher**: Manchester, *Death of a President*, p. 518.

"I think we ought": "7:01 P.M. to J. William Fulbright," Dec. 2, *TPR*, Vol. II, p. 80. **"Talked little"**: Valenti, *A Very Human President*, p. 152. **Lodge, who**: Gibbons, *U.S. Government and the Vietnam War*, pp. 203, 209. **McCone said**: Johnson, *Vantage Point*, p. 43.

"Net result": Johnson, *Vantage Point,* p. 44. **It was decided:** Gibbons, *U.S. Government,* pp. 209–11; Johnson, *Vantage Point,* p. 45. The preliminary plan, NSAM 273, would be approved by Johnson on Nov. 26. **"Only South Vietnam":** Johnson, *Vantage Point,* p. 22.

"It was so": Logevall, *Choosing War,* p. 108. **"Firm":** Wicker, *JFK and LBJ,* p. 205. **"We had spent":** Johnson, *Vantage Point,* p. 44. **"The main objective":** Johnson, *Vantage Point,* p. 44; Dallek, *Flawed Giant,* p. 99. **"I am not going"; "I don't think":** Wicker, *JFK and LBJ,* p. 205; Wicker interview. Wicker says Moyers told him after the meeting that Johnson had said this.

On Oct. 2, McNamara and Taylor: *NYT, WP,* Oct. 3. **"We need a way":** Dallek, *Unfinished,* p. 680. **Salinger announcement; "their judgment":** Dallek, *Unfinished,* p. 680. **"Reaffirmed":** *NYT,* Nov 25. **"White House sources said":** *WP,* Nov. 25. **NSAM 273:** Gibbons, *U.S. Government,* pp. 209–10.

"Days filled"; "Sometimes he": Juanita Roberts OH. **"A changed man":** Fehmer interview. **"I've never":** Moyers, quoted in Miller to Parker, Nov. 28, p. 5, *Time* files, Box 321, "LBJL of 22," White Papers, JFKL. **"Direct":** Steele to Parker, "Johnson Cover & Kennedy Narrative XVII," Nov. 23, White Papers. **"There were":** Sidey interview. **"Seems to be":** Miller to Parker, Nov. 23, "Johnson Cover—VIII—Nation," *Time* files. **"He was thinking":** Busby interview.

"I knew": Johnson, *Vantage Point,* p. 29.

"George": Transcript, "10:17 A.M. to George Meany," Nov. 23, *TPR,* Vol. I, pp. 93–94.

Telephoned each of them: Transcripts, "4:20 P.M. to Walter Reuther," Nov. 23, *TPR,* Vol. I, p. 120; "4:15 P.M. to Dave McDonald; President Johnson joined by Arthur Goldberg," Nov. 23, *TPR,* Vol. I, pp. 116–19." **"Liked":** Goodwin, *Lyndon Johnson,* p. 181. **"Should be told":** Reedy to Johnson, "Diary Backup—November 23, 1963," Box 1, Diary Backup, Nov. 23.

"It's just": Transcript, "9:20 P.M. to Martin Luther King, Jr.," *TPR,* Vol. I, pp. 161–62. **"Sort of":** "5:55 P.M. to Whitney Young" and "6:23 P.M. from Whitney Young," *TPR,* Vol. I, pp. 137–42.

Albert, Weisl, Kappel, Bundy, Brown, Reynolds and Rolvaag transcripts: *TPR,* Vol. I, pp. 94–95, 101–2, 97–100, 95–99, 121–23, 132–34, 157–58.

Johnson woke: Salinger, *With Kennedy,* p. 331. In this book, he says simply, "I told him I would stay," but Shannon, his friend, wrote on the day of President Kennedy's funeral that

Salinger told him he would resign the next day. Shannon, *NYP,* Nov. 25.

Schlesinger's lunch: Heren, *No Hail, No Farewell,* p. 16; Shesol, *Mutual Contempt,* p. 143.

"Almost all": Goldman, *The Tragedy of Lyndon Johnson,* p. 17. **"I keep supposing":** Schlesinger, *Journals,* p. 206. **"We came":** Walton interview.

"I'd like": Sorensen, *Counselor,* p. 368. **"George, I wish":** Reedy OH III. **"Johnson really":** Dungan OH, LBJL.

Comparing notes: Wechsler column, *NYP,* Dec. 4. **Johnson reminded him:** Galbraith, quoted in Miller, *Lyndon,* p. 337; Sorensen interview. See also Schlesinger, *Journals,* p. 206: "A telephone call from Ken reported that he had seen Johnson, and that Johnson had asked him to work with Sorensen on the message. Ken seemed in high spirits. . . . He is a realist." **"I just want":** Schlesinger, *Journals,* p. 209. **With Stevenson; "I know, and you know":** Evans and Novak, *LBJ,* p. 342; Schlesinger, *Journals,* p. 211. **"Don't expect me":** Nicholas Lemann, "The Unfinished War," *The Atlantic Monthly,* Dec. 1988. Also see Evans and Novak, *LBJ,* p. 340. **"I'm afraid to":** Sorensen, *Counselor,* p. 382. **"He did not have":** Walter Heller, "HIGHLY CONFIDENTIAL—Notes on Meeting with President Johnson, 7:40 p.m., Saturday, Nov. 23, 1963," Papers of Gardner Ackley, microfilm Reel #2, LBJL. **"I don't know":** Dungan OH. **"Please stay":** White, *The Making of the President, 1964,* pp. 44, 45. **"In these"; "Never once"; "restraint":** Goodwin, *Lyndon Johnson,* p. 175. **"In [these] first":** Evans and Novak, *LBJ,* pp. 339–40.

Bundy entered: McPherson, *A Political Education,* p. 216. **"Magnificent":** Evans and Novak, *LBJ,* p. 340.

"Associates": *NYP,* Nov. 25. **"With swollen":** Heren, *No Hail,* p. 17. **"Talk the same":** Schlesinger, *Journals,* p. 211. **"If you act":** Schlesinger, *Journals,* p. 209. **"To me"; "I know"; "I want you":** Sorensen, *Counselor,* pp. 378–80.

"By remaining": Johnson, *Vantage Point,* p. 19. **"Intensity":** Evans and Novak, *LBJ,* p. 339.

"The end of the service": Manchester, *Death of a President,* p. 603. **Telephoning O'Brien:** Transcript, "4:04 P.M. to Larry O'Brien," Nov. 25, *TPR,* Vol. I, p. 158; Busby interview. **O'Brien went to work:** Johnson, *Vantage Point,* p. 39.

"Abrupt, urgent": White, *Making 1964,* p. 48. **"President Johnson":** *NYT, WP,* Nov. 26. **"Hoping":** Box 1, Diary Backup.

"Electricity"; "Unprecedented": *WES,*

Nov. 26. **"Take the measure"**: Duke, quoted in Miller, *Lyndon*, p. 334. **"Had never worked out"**: Read interview. **"The President had had"**: Read, quoted in Miller, *Lyndon*, p. 334. **Prince Kantol**: "Meeting with Prince Kantol, Prime Minister of Cambodia," Box 1, President's Appointment File [Diary Backup], Nov. 26. **"Grasping the essence"**: Read, quoted in Miller, *Lyndon*, p. 334. **"The average dignitary"**: Nov. 26. **"Understood"**: Duke, quoted in Miller, *Lyndon*, p. 334. **"The shrewdest man"**: White, *Making 1964*, p. 45. **"Without smiles"**: *NYT*, Nov. 26.

And then came: "Memorandum for the President, Subject: Revised Recommended Schedule for Your Meetings with Visiting Chiefs of State . . . ," Nov. 25, Box 1, President's Appointment File [Diary Backup], Nov. 25. **De Gaulle had lectured**: Frankel reported in the *NYT* (Nov. 26) that at their previous meeting, "de Gaulle showed scant deference to the then Vice President. 'What have you come to learn?' he asked Mr. Johnson coldly that day." **Unpleasantness had been rekindled**: Johnson, *Vantage Point*, p. 23. **"Does that"**: Transcript, "4:00 P.M. from McGeorge Bundy," Nov. 25, *TPR*, Vol. I, p. 157. **When de Gaulle now asserted**: Johnson, *Vantage Point*, p. 23. **With "the real"**: Read interview; Read, quoted in Miller, *Lyndon*, p. 334.

As he had been walking: White, *Making 1964*, p. 45. **He had realized**: Reedy interview. **Scranton was waiting**: White, *Making 1964*, p. 45. **Talking points**: "For the President: Agenda for the Meeting with the Governors," Nov. 25, "Agenda for the Governors' Meeting," Box 1, President's Appointment File [Diary Backup], Nov. 25. **Johnson's talk to the Governors**: "(*NOT TO BE RELEASED*)—OFF THE RECORD REMARKS OF PRESIDENT JOHNSON TO A GROUP OF GOVERNORS OF THE UNITED STATES PRESENT IN WASHINGTON TO ATTEND THE FUNERAL OF JOHN F. KENNEDY, HELD IN THE EXECUTIVE OFFICE BUILDING, 8:30 pm., Monday, Nov. 25, 1963," Box 1, President's Appointment File [Diary Backup], Nov. 25. **"He just"; Reedy was**: Valenti, Reedy interviews. **They . . . applauded**: McGeorge Bundy was to say later that evening that "I heard their outburst, and I thought that was very touching—and good." Transcript, "9:29 P.M. from McGeorge Bundy," Nov. 25, *TPR*, Vol. I, p. 164. **"Astounded"**: *NYT*, Nov. 26; Reedy interview. Evans and Novak, who spoke to some of the Governors after Johnson's talk, were to write that "The Governors . . . were strangely comforted. . . . There was an atmosphere of confidence, a *presidential* atmosphere of

latent power and decision" (italics in original) (Evans and Novak, *LBJ*, p. 348).

"The President showed"; "The most impressive"; "What about your tax bill?": "HIGHLY CONFIDENTIAL—Troika Meeting with President Johnson, Monday, Nov. 25, 1963. Notes by Gardner Ackley, Box 1, Appointment File [Diary Backup]; Heller OH II. **"Tell them to lay off"**: Heller OH II. **"I can defend"; "you won't pee"**: Heller OH II.

Dillon and others had believed: Dillon to Johnson, Nov. 25, p. 3, "Ex FI 11–4, Nov. 22, 1963—Jan. 22, 1965, Box 59, WHCF SF, LBJL. That attitude is shown when Moyers, in a conversation with Sorensen, says that the President feels that if he can get the budget down in the one hundred billion dollar range, "then he'll . . . talk to [Byrd]. Sorensen replies, "I think you can get the tax bill—I *know* you can get the tax bill without doing that . . . I think that a budget of 101.5 [billion] dollars can be described in such a way—and accurately so—that it's very clear that it's an economy-type budget." A lower figure is not necessary, he says. "The tax bill has the majority of votes on the Finance Committee and has a majority of votes on the Senate floor." Shortly thereafter, Johnson comes on the phone and tries to explain, saying, "They're not going to give [us] the tax bill unless we get our budget down to 100 billion [dollars]," and therefore "it's a question of" either cutting the budget to Byrd's figure, or losing the tax bill. To which Sorensen replies, "I don't think that really is the choice." The president again tries to explain: "Byrd's just not going to . . . report any bill, unless somebody gives him assurance it's not going to be over 100 billion. . . . I don't think that 100 billion with the tax bill is as bad as 102 billion without one." "I'm not sure that *is* the choice, yet," Sorensen replies. (Transcript, "10:10 P.M. to Ted Sorensen; preceded by Bill Moyers and Sorensen," Nov. 25, *TPR*, Vol. I, pp. 154–71). **"The President indicating"; "We won't have the votes"; "It was as simple"**: Ackley notes.

To get the budget down: Ackley notes, pp. 2, 3. **Dillon, Heller agreed**: Ackley notes, p. 3. **They had felt**: Gordon OH. **"Even now"**: Sidey, *A Very Personal Presidency*, pp. 40–41.

Telephoning not only: Evans and Novak, *NYP*, Dec. 4. **"All of us"**: Johnson, *Vantage Point*, p. 39. **"Murdered"**: Transcript, "10:10 P.M. to Ted Sorensen, preceded by Bill Moyers and Sorensen," *TPR*, Vol. I, p. 168.

"Charming": *Newsweek*, Dec. 2. The *NYHT* commented (Nov. 28) that in the past "he has mumbled or sped through his speeches." **"Overshadowing"; "He knew"**: Miller, Loye to Parker, "PREX WEEK—11

(NATION)," *Time* files, in White Papers, Box 321, "LBJL of 22." **"If it failed":** Miller, *Lyndon,* p. 337.

Kilgore telephoned: Evans and Novak, *LBJ,* p. 419; Kilgore interview. **Telling Busby:** Busby interview; Evans and Novak, *LBJ ,* p. 349. **On a notepad:** His full scribble on this point was: "Yesterday product of hate—get rid of object—desire—Hate—International—Justice—Poverty Equality." Box 1, President's Appointment's File [Diary Backup], Nov. 23. **"Commit LBJ":** Sorensen, *Counselor,* p. 381. **Short shrift except for Busby:** Sorensen says (*Counselor,* p. 381) that after he had "reviewed all these drafts," he "decided to start fresh." And Hubert Humphrey tries to take credit (Miller, *Lyndon,* p. 338) for the crucial line, but in fact the three-paragraph segment is on page 3 of Busby's draft ("DRAFT: MESSAGE, JOINT SESSION," p. 3) attached to "The speech as drafted is 1900 words," "Busby to Johnson, Nov. 26," Box 89, folders 1 and 2, "Nov. 27, 1963, Remarks of the President before a Joint Session of Congress, House Chamber—Capitol," Statements File. **"I who cannot":** "TCS—Nov. 26, 1963, Mr. Speaker . . . ," Box 89, folder 1, "Nov. 27, 1963, Remarks of the President before a Joint Session of Congress," Statements File, LBJL. "At the time I resented the deletion, but now acknowledge that this and other changes were wise," Sorensen says (*Counselor,* p. 382).

"A little corning up": Evans and Novak, *LBJ,* p. 348, has "I corned it up a little," and Murphy that he "added some corn pone" (*Fortas,* p. 119). **"Well, what the hell's the presidency for?":** Fortas, quoted in Miller, *Lyndon,* p. 337. **"Never":** To: Parker, From: Miller, "PREX WEEK—11 (NATION)," Nov. 29, White Papers. **His edits:** On "Mr. Speaker . . ." Also on "TCS—Nov. 26, 1963," Box 89, Folder 1, Statements File, LBJL. **The text:** "FOR IMMEDIATE RELEASE—OFFICE OF THE WHITE HOUSE PRESS SECRETARY . . . (AS ACTUALLY DELIVERED), Nov. 27, 1963.

Later he would explain; "I never thought": Goodwin, *Remembering America,* p. 335. **"He'd be with them forever"; "he was with us"; "master and slave":** Caro, *Master,* p. 866. **"Not then, no":** Talmadge interview. **Had asked Russell:** Margaret Shannon, *Atlanta Journal and Constitution,* Nov. 24, 1963; Gilbert C. Fite, *Richard B. Russell, Jr.: Senator from Georgia,* p. 404. **Something that had to do:** Caro, *Master,* "We of the South" chapter. **"Everywhere you looked":** Sidey interview.

"In the most important": Evans and Novak, *LBJ,* p. 349. **"It was"; "his only"; "Most striking":** *NYT, WP,* Nov. 28. **"Grandeur":**

Amrine, *Awesome,* p. 182. **Johnson emerges:** *NYT,* Nov. 28. **"It would have been":** James Reston, "The Office and the Man," *NYT,* Nov. 28. **"Hardly believe":** Kilgore interview. **"No one doubted":** Mary McGrory, "Johnson's Path"; Doris Fleeson, "LBJ and Congress," *NYP,* Nov. 29. **"It was like":** Caro, *Master,* p. 583. **"Across":** *Newsweek,* Dec. 9. **"Something different":** Reston, "Office and the Man." **Johnson's speech:** David Lawrence, *NYHT,* Nov. 28. **"Established himself":** *WP,* Nov. 28. **"For the tradition":** *Time,* Dec. 6. **"Not a fluke of history":** *NYHT,* Nov. 28.

17. The Warren Commission

All dates 1963 unless otherwise noted.
"The atmosphere"; "Russia was not": Johnson, *The Vantage Point,* p. 26. **Very dangerous":** Transcript, Nov. 29, "To Mike Mansfield; President Johnson joined by Dean Rusk," *The Presidential Recordings,* Vol. I, pp. 241–42. **"With that single":** Johnson, *Vantage Point,* pp. 25–26.

Congress was circling: *BS,* Nov. 26, 27; *WP,* Nov. 26. **Eastland would say:** Caro, *Master,* p. 867.

His first suggestion: Holland, *The Kennedy Assassination Tapes,* pp. 90, 91; Max Holland, "The Key to the Warren Report," *American Heritage,* Nov. 1995; *WP,* Nov. 26; Murphy, *Fortas,* p. 116. **Fortas was later:** Jenkins to Johnson, Nov. 25, p. 2, "Ex FG 1—Nov. 23, 1963–Jan. 10, 1964," Ex FG 1, LBJL; Murphy, *Fortas,* p. 117. **A "ghastly":** Murphy, *Fortas,* p. 116. **"Texas justice":** *TPR,* Vol. I, p. 148.

He quietly gave: Carr, in announcing there would be a state Court of Inquiry, said "he had not discussed" the Court with the President, and technically that may have been accurate. But he had discussed it with Cliff Carter, who, after conferring with Johnson, told him, "Good idea, but purely a state matter. Can't say president asked for it" (Carter to Johnson, Nov. 24, 1963, Special File, Assassination, LBJL).

Learning that: Murphy, *Fortas,* p. 117. **He himself made:** Transcripts, "10:40 A.M., to Joseph Alsop," pp. 149–56; "10:30 A.M., to J. Edgar Hoover," pp. 145–47; both Nov. 25, *TPR,* Vol. I. As Holland points out in *TPR* (Vol. I, p. 148), "there is no record of a phone call from Johnson to Graham," but McCone, after talking to Johnson on November 26th, wrote that "The President personally intervened, but failed with Mr. Al Friendly and finally 'killed' the editorial with Mrs. Graham" (John McCone, "Memorandum for the Record," Nov. 26, 1963, "Meetings with the

President—23 Nov 1963–23 Dec 1963," Box 1, John McCone Memoranda, LBJL. *Post* editorial: Nov. 26.
Executive Order: "EXECUTIVE ORDER No. 11130—"Appointing a Commission to Report upon the Assassination of John F. Kennedy," Nov. 30, 1963," *Public Papers of the Presidents: Lyndon B. Johnson, 1963–64* (Washington, D.C.: GPO, 1965), 1:14.
"Men ... known to be": Johnson, *Vantage Point*, p. 26. **Robert Kennedy suggested:** Johnson, "Reminiscences of Lyndon B. Johnson," Aug. 19, 1969, p. 17.
"Whose judicial ability"; "We had never"; "to me": Johnson, *Vantage Point*, p. 26. **Richard Russell personified:** Caro, *Master*, "A Russell of the Russells of Georgia," pp. 164–202. **"As close to"; "that did not prevent them"; "firmness"; "things were more complicated"; "a demonstration":** Caro, *Master*, pp. 372–81. **"Oh, I would too:"** Transcript, "1:15 P.M. to Abe Fortas," Nov. 29, *TPR*, Vol. I, p. 261. **Nor were these:** Reedy interview.
"Extrajudicial bodies"; "The service of five justices": Warren, *The Memoirs of Earl Warren*, pp. 356–57. **Tarnished the Court's:** Evans and Novak, *Lyndon B. Johnson*, p. 337. **"I was sure"; "Would have been chaos"; "told them"; "I considered":** Warren, *Memoirs*, pp. 355–56.
Russell's reasons: Fite, *Richard B. Russell, Jr.*, pp. 405–6; Goldsmith, *Colleagues*, p. 101; William Jordan, Reedy interviews. **"Oh, no, no":** Transcript, "4:05 P.M. to Richard Russell," Nov. 29, Vol. I, pp. 291–300.
"Only the two of us": Warren, *Memoirs*, p. 357. **"And you'd go fight":** Transcripts, "8:30 P.M. to Thomas Kuchel," Nov. 29, *TPR*, Vol. I, pp. 354–55; "8:55 P.M. to Richard Russell; President Johnson joined by Albert Moursund," Nov. 29, *TPR*, p. 367. In his "Reminiscences," Johnson has a slightly different version (p. 16): "I said, 'I know what you're going to tell me, but there is one thing no one else has said to you. In World War I, when your country was threatened—not as much as now—you put that rifle butt on your shoulder. I don't care who sends me a message. When this country is threatened with division, and the President of the United States says you are the only man who can save it, you won't say no, will you?' He said, 'No, Sir.'" **Tears came:** Transcript, "8:30 P.M. to Thomas Kuchel," Nov. 29, *TPR*, Vol. I, p. 355. **"Mr. President":** Warren, *Memoirs*, p. 358.
"He didn't want": Transcript, "5:10 P.M. to Everett Dirksen," *TPR*, Vol. I, p 313. **The 1952 breakfast:** Caro, *Master*, pp. 475–76.
WARREN HEADS: *NYHT*, Nov. 30.
The country felt: Max Holland, "The

Key"; Holland, *Kennedy Assassination Tapes*, pp. xvii–xxi; Bugliosi, *Reclaiming History*. **By 1983; 2003 poll:** Gallup News Service, "Americans: Kennedy Assassination a Conspiracy," Nov. 21, 2003.
"Brought us through": Johnson, *Vantage Point*, p. 27. Johnson said in his "Reminiscences" (p. 17), "I shudder to think what churches I would have burned and what little babies I would have eaten if I hadn't appointed the Warren Commission."

18. The Southern Strategy

The stalemate: Caro, *Master of the Senate*, pp. 63 ff. **"In a way":** Byrd, *The Senate 1789–1989, Vol. I: Addresses on the History of the United States Senate*, p. 477. **"As when":** Douglas, quoted in Byrd, *The Senate*, p. 597.
Did not carry over: See notes for Chapter 12, "Taking Charge." Also Giglio, *The Presidency of John F. Kennedy*, pp. 286–87.
Never, however, had so many: "Dates Appropriations Bills Have Been Cleared for the President, 1951–1963," *Congressional Quarterly*, Dec. 6, 1963, p. 2135. **Four had:** "Committee and Floor Action on Appropriations, 1961–63," *Congressional Quarterly*, Dec. 6, 1963, p. 2134; *Cong. Record*, p. 22620. "More than ever before, the appropriations process in 1963 was characterized by delay," the *Congressional Quarterly Almanac* said (p. 132). **"The longer these bills":** Cannon, *Congressional Quarterly*, Dec. 6, 1963, p. 2133. The showdown in the appropriations process was called "unprecedented" by the *Congressional Quarterly Weekly*, Dec. 6, 1963, p. 2131. **"This Congress has gone further":** Lippmann, quoted in Johnson, *The Vantage Point*, p. 34. **"A scandal":** *Life*, Dec. 13, 1963. **"Least productive":** Shannon, *NYP*, Dec. 1963. **"Logjam":** Then Majority Leader Scott Lucas and Russell both use that term in 1949 in referring to it. Caro, *Master*, pp. 216–17.
"Archaic": Kuchel in *NYP*, Jan. 8, 1964. **1949 civil rights fight:** Caro, *Master*, pp. 215–18. **Johnson had been one:** *Master*, pp. 218–22.
His battlefield: The southern strategy was explained to the author by, among others, Senator Talmadge, Thurmond's aide Harry Dent, and Richard Russell aides William H. Darden, Gwen and William H. Jordan and Powell Moore, and journalists Neil MacNeil and John Goldsmith. And it was explained in detail by Senator Joseph S. Clark of Pennsylvania in a speech to the Senate on Nov. 21 (*Cong. Record*, pp. 22618–22). It also becomes quite clear during the conversations Johnson had

with senators, as when, on November 30, George Smathers says that the southerners were hiding "behind the tax bill—and hiding behind a lot of other bills, just on the pretense of being against them when the real fact is they're against the civil rights bill" (*TPR,* Vol. I, p. 386). **"No one had had to":** Dent interview. **Filibuster and time limit:** Caro, *Master,* p. 216.

Even while; One of the eight: *Cong. Record* Nov. 21 1963, pp. 22621–22. *Congressional Quarterly Weekly,* p. 2132; Kenneth Crawford, "What's Wrong Here?" *Newsweek,* Dec. 23. 1963. **"Unzip":** Califano, *The Triumph and Tragedy of Lyndon Johnson,* p. 126. **"Everybody":** Crawford, "What's Wrong." **Clark introduced:** S. RES. 227, Nov. 21, 1963. **"Unprecedented":** *Congressional Quarterly,* Dec. 6, 1963, p. 2131. **"Already too much money":** *Congressional Quarterly,* Dec. 6, p. 2133. **Russell's own:** *Congressional Quarterly,* p. 2133.

"Assembled": Caro, *Master,* p. 845. **"Mongrel race":** Caro, *Master,* p. 194. **"Massive resistance":** Caro, *Master,* p. 845. **"The new civil rights legislation":** *Richmond Times-Dispatch,* June 11, 1963.

McCormack and Smith; "He won't give you a hearing": Transcript, "4:17 P.M. to A. Philip Randolph"; Transcript, "12:04 P.M. to John McCormack and Leslie Arends," both Nov. 29, 1963, *TPR,* Vol. I, pp. 252–53, 300. **Trying to bargain:** *NYT,* Dec. 5. **"No plans":** *WP,* Nov. 1963. **"He [Smith] won't do one":** Transcript, "1:30 P.M. to Robert Anderson," Nov. 30, *TPR,* Vol. I, p. 381. **"We're going to have to":** Transcript, "11:10 A.M. to Katharine Graham," Dec. 2, 1963, *TPR,* Vol. II, p. 46. **"If we don't"; "a miracle":** Transcript, "2:05 P.M. to George Smathers," Nov. 30, 1963, *TPR,* Vol. I, p. 386. **"I couldn't move":** Transcript, "Telephone Interview with Senator Russell Long, Aug. 23, 1989," 14726, Room 109, shelf 1–5a, Heinemann Papers, Special Collections, University of Virginia Library. **"It was stalled":** Gordon OH. **"Two Virginians":** Richard Rovere, "Letter from Washington," *The New Yorker,* Feb. 15, 1964. **"He'll pass them":** Goldsmith, *Colleagues: Richard Russell and His Apprentice Lyndon B. Johnson,* p. 103. **He said that":** Orville Freeman, "A Cabinet Perspective," in *The Johnson Presidency,* ed., Kenneth W. Thompson, p. 143.

19. "Old Harry"

"Almost archaically elaborate": Forrest Davis, "The Fourth Term's Hair Shirt," *SEP,* April 8, 1944. **"Apple-cheeked apple-**grower":** William S. White, "Meet the Honorable Harry (The Rare) Byrd," *Reader's Digest,* April, 1963; see also Benjamin Muse, "The Durability of Harry Flood Byrd," *The Reporter,* Oct. 3, 1957; and Wilkinson, *Harry Byrd,* p. 307. He is "the apple-cheeked archconservative" in Mooney, *LBJ,* p. 49.

"There they are": Caro, *Master of the Senate,* pp. 939–40. **"His extreme obsessive hatred":** Gunther, *Inside U.S.A.,* p. 707. **"The name Byrd":** White, "Meet the Honorable." **"The Byrd machine is genteel":** Muse, "The Durability." **"Virginia breeds"; "runs the commonwealth":** Gunther, *U.S.A.,* pp. 705, 708. **Only 17 percent:** "The Squire of Rosemont," *Time,* Oct. 28, 1966. **"Surmounts":** White, "Meet the Honorable." **"The apparent invincibility":** Muse, "The Durability."

"He hated": Douglas, *In the Fullness of Time,* p. 228. Douglas described him as "The world's largest apple grower, with cheeks as ruddy as his pippins" (p. 228). **"He had a habit":** Cotton, *In the Senate,* p. 165. **"Blind to charts"; "if you":** Long interview with Heinemann, Aug. 23, 1989, 14726, Room 109, Shelf 1–5a, Heinemann Papers, Special Collections, University of Virginia Library.

"When you have to hunt": Heinemann, *Harry Bird of Virginia,* p. 7.

"Debt had robbed him": Gerald W. Johnson, "Senator Byrd of Virginia," *Life,* Aug. 7, 1944; "The Congress: Giving Them Fits," *Time,* Aug. 17, 1962. **"Improvident political promises"; "The American dollar is the only thing"; "Once the American dollar goes down":** James R. Sweeney, "Harry Byrd: Vanished Policies and Enduring Principles," *The Virginia Quarterly Review,* Autumn 1976, pp. 602, 603.

"Almost a sacred duty": MacNeil interview. **"Would have no truck":** Dillon to Heinemann, July 18, 1989, 14726, Room 109, Shelf 1–a, Heinemann Papers. **Franklin Roosevelt; "then this fellow"; "I am the only":** "The Congress: Giving Them Fits," *Time,* Aug. 17, 1962; David Lawrence, "The Lesson of Sen. Harry Byrd," *WES,* Nov. 15, 1965.

"Misleading . . . mythology"; "new words, new phrases"; "Illusions": Heinemann, *Harry Byrd of Virginia,* pp. 394, 395. **"The civilian employment":** *Time,* Aug. 17, 1962. **"Measured his success as a senator":** Long OH, LBJL. **Powers as a chairman:** Caro, *Master,* pp. 82–83. **"Senator Byrd was a gentleman of the old school":** Dillon to Heinemann, July 18, 1989, Heinemann Papers, Special Collections, University of Virginia Library. **"The old man won't begin":** Heinemann, *Harry Byrd,* p. 386. **The chairman had let it be known:** MacNeil interviews; Transcript, "10:20 A.M. from Robert Anderson," Dec. 2, 1963, *TPR*, Vol. II, p. 34. **"He couldn't get a quorum":** transcript, "2:10 P.M. to George Smathers," Nov. 23, 1963, *TPR*, Vol. I, p. 111. **"Pillow fight in the dark":** Greenberg, *Presidential Doodles.* **"Absolute"; "nothing could be done"; "did not oppose":** Dillon to Heinemann, Heinemann Papers. **"A sweet dear guy—loved him":** Long interview with Heinemann, Heinemann Papers. **Douglas was informed:** Steinberg, *Sam Johnson's Boy,* p. 407.

FDR's attempt: "The Gentleman from Virginia," *Time,* Aug. 17, 1962; "The Squire of Rosemont," *Time,* Oct. 28, 1966. **"Actually helped me":** Heinemann, *Harry Byrd,* p. 399. **Trying to create an alliance with Kerr:** Goldsmith, MacNeil interviews; Long interview with Heinemann, Heinemann Papers. **"Always recognized":** Dillon to Heinemann, July 18, 1989, 14726, Room 109, Shelf 1–5a, Heinemann Papers. And see Heinemann, *Harry Byrd,* p. 397.

"Probably" Byrd "has never been more powerful": *WP,* Nov. 17, 1963. **"You *couldn't* go around Harry Byrd":** Busby interview. One of the most powerful Democratic members of the Finance Committee was Clinton Anderson of New Mexico, one of the senators Johnson referred to as the "whales" of the Senate. But, as Johnson said after talking to him, "he, out of deference to Harry Byrd, wouldn't dare do it" (take it up outside of regular committee procedures) (*TPR,* Vol. II, p. 35). **Johnson had spent a lot of time:** See *Master,* pp. 148–49, 338, 413, 562, 629, 865, 901. **Not offhand:** "$100 billion" was "a sum he viewed as a psychological barrier," wrote John Goldsmith (*Colleagues,* p. 104).

"Harry Byrd *always*": Transcript, "10:31 A.M. to Clinton Anderson," Nov. 27, 1963, *TPR,* Vol. I, p. 194. **"It would look a lot better":** Transcript, "10:20 A.M. from Robert Anderson," *TPR,* Vol. II, p. 36. **Mansfield phone call:** Transcript, "10:50 A.M. from Mike Mansfield," *TPR,* Vol. II, p. 96. **Johnson telephoning Byrd:** "The Full Treatment," *Time,* Dec. 13, 1963; MacNeil interview.

Planning went into that visit; "had gotten a commitment": Valenti OH II; Valenti, *A Very Human President,* p. 196. **Not only:** Transcript, "2:14 P.M. to Robert Anderson, President Johnson joined by Harry Byrd," Dec. 5, 1963; *TPR,* Vol. II, p. 159; MacNeil interview. **"They [the Finance Committee] are going to":** Transcript, "3:30 from Willard Wirtz," *TPR,* Vol. II, p. 192. **"If you don't mind":** *Time,* Dec. 13, 1963. **"I told the President you simply can't":** *WP,* Dec. 11, 1963.

"Kermit"; "He had to get that tax cut": Valenti OH, interview. **"The committee . . . knows how":** "HIGHLY CONFIDENTIAL—Troika Meeting with President Johnson, Monday, Nov. 25, 1963," p. 3, Notes by Gardner Ackley, Box 1, Appointment File [Diary Backup].

"The talk": Lady Bird Johnson, *A White House Diary,* p. 17. **"He went back":** "Mrs. Johnson's Diary," Dec. 20, Box 1, LBJL. **"I worked as hard":** Johnson, *The Vantage Point,* p. 36. **"Then":** Valenti OH II.

"Abundantly clear": Kermit Gordon, "Memorandum to Heads of Departments and Agencies," Box 14, Kermit Gordon Papers, JFKL, quoted in *TPR,* Vol. II, p. 347. **"Is anyone going up on you?":** Transcript, "9:40 A.M. to Kermit Gordon," Dec. 12, 1963, *TPR,* Vol. II, p. 347. **"He's the only guy":** Transcript, "2:14 P.M. to Robert Anderson, President Johnson joined by Harry Byrd," Dec. 5, 1963; *TPR,* Vol. II, p. 162. **Announced:** *NYT,* Dec. 8, 1963.

"Obviously": Freeman Diary, Dec. 11, 1963, quoted in *TPR,* pp. 327–28. **"Orville Freeman's":** Transcript, "9:40 A.M. to Kermit Gordon, Dec. 12, 1963, *TPR,* Vol. II, pp. 344–49.

"We haven't"; "General": Transcript, "12:15 P.M. to John Gronouski," Dec. 23, 1963, *TPR,* Vol. II, pp. 703–08. **Ten days later, Gronouski announced:** *NYT,* Jan. 3, 1964. **"If I am":** Manatos to O'Brien, Jan. 7, 1964, "Tax Bill 1963–1965 [1 of 2]," Box 9 [2 of 2], Office Files of Mike Manatos, JFKL.

The Long amendment: Transcript, "4:50 P.M. from C. Douglas Dillon, "Dec. 12, 1963," *TPR,* Vol. II, pp. 369–73.

"I'm working in"; "Right": Transcript, "11:33 A.M. from Harry Byrd," Dec. 13, 1963, *TPR,* Vol. II, pp. 383, 384. **"You can tell":** Heinemann, *Harry Byrd,* p. 400; Goodwin, *Remembering America,* pp. 261–62. **Russell Long watched:** Long interview with Heinemann, Heinemann Papers.

20. "The Johnsons in Johnson City"

"I think": Henry Wilson to O'Brien, Jan. 10, 1964, "Wilson: Presidential," Box 5, Ex LE/HU, LBJL. **"They tell me":** Transcript, "10:15 P.M., to Andy Hatcher," Dec. 23, 1963, *TPR,* Vol. II, p. 774.

Every time: For example, *NYT,* Dec. 5, 1963. In *NYT,* Dec. 5, "McCormack said Smith would not agree to the plan. He said there was therefore no choice but discharge." **The only thing":** "Notes on the First Congressional Leadership Breakfast Held by the President on

Dec. 3, 1963," Presidential Appointments File [Diary Backup], p. 2, LBJL. **Had, in fact:** *NYT,* Dec. 5, 1963. **"Indignity":** *NYT,* Dec. 8, 1963. **"Given signature":** O'Brien to Johnson, Nov. 29, 1963, "Office Files of the White House Aides—Henry Hall Wilson, Jr.," 1963–1967, LBJL. **"I've never":** *NYP,* Dec. 4, 1963. **Telephoning Bolling:** "6:56 P/M., to Richard Bolling," Dec. 2, *TPR,* Vol. II, pp. 70–74. **"I was always reluctant":** Dec. 3, 1963.

Had asked for a group: *WP,* Dec. 3, 1963. **"What about one meeting a day?"** Roberts to Johnson, "Lee White asks for times . . . ," undated, "December 1963," Box 2, Diary Backup, LBJL.

"With Johnson": Wilkins with Matthews, *Standing Fast,* pp. 243–44, 294–96; Wilkins OH I. **"Some of":** Farmer OH. **Kennedy "believed":** Wilkins, *Standing Fast,* pp. 294, 296. **Johnson took the call:** Transcript, "9:51 A.M., from G. Mennen Williams," *TPR,* Vol. II, pp. 28–30. **Not merely explaining to King:** Kotz, *Judgment Days,* p. 66. **"A magnolia":** Whalen and Whalen, *The Longest Debate,* p. 81. **"I left":** Wilkins, *Standing Fast,* p. 296. **"There has been":** *NYT,* Dec. 3, 1963. **"As a southerner":** *WP,* Dec.4, 1963. **Showing King the list; "LBJ is a man":** Kotz, *Judgment Days,* pp. 66, 67. **"Almost by a Negro ghost-writer":** Wilkins, quoted in "White to Mitchell," Feb. 4, 1964, LE/HU 2, Jan. 30, 1964–Feb. 19, 1964, LBJL. **"Still signing mail":** Transcript, "10:30 P.M. to Roy Wilkins, *TPR,* Vol. II, pp. 777–81.

And they came: "The labor and Negro leaders are streaming in," Doris Fleeson reported (*WP,* Dec. 5, 1963). "Congressional mail is reported heavy in favor of action now" (*WP,* Dec. 5, 1963).

"Republicans have": Wilson to O'Brien, Dec. 2, "Office Files of the White House Aides—Henry Hall Wilson, Jr.," 1963–1967, LBJL.

Bringing Meany: Amrine, *This Awesome Challenge,* p. 123; " 'This Is Lyndon'—And It Is," *Newsweek,* Dec. 16, 1963; Biemiller interview. **"This cemented":** Biemiller OH, interview.

Leadership breakfast; "Where do you get": "Notes on the First Congressional Leadership Breakfast Held by the President on Dec. 3, 1963," Presidential Appointments File [Diary Backup]. **"Definite word":** Transcript, "12:10 P.M. to David McDonald; President Johnson joined by Martin Luther King, Jr.," Dec. 3, 1963, p. 98. **McCormack had been wondering:** Transcript, "12:10 P.M. to David McDonald; President Johnson joined by Martin Luther King, Jr.," Dec. 3, 1963, *TPR,* Vol. II, p. 98. **"Can we make":** Transcript, "3:00

P.M. to Carl Albert," Dec. 3, 1963, *TPR,* Vol. II, pp. 101–08. **"We're going":** Transcript, "1:29 P.M. to Dave McDonald," *TPR,* Vol. I, pp. 263–65. **Vote counting:** Transcript, "6:00 P.M. to Carl Albert," Dec. 4, 1963, *TPR,* Vol. II, pp. 143–44.

"Your judgment": Transcript, "11:11 A.M. to Albert Thomas," Dec. 5, 1963, *TPR,* Vol. II, pp. 153–55. **"Told him":** Transcript, "3:22 P.M., from Homer Thornberrry," Dec. 3, 1963, *TPR,* Vol. II, pp. 108–12.

"President Johnson": *NYT,* Dec. 4, 1963. **"This move"; "The consensus":** *NYT,* Dec. 5, 1963. **Business Advisory Council meeting:** *WP,* Dec. 5, 1963. **"I talked to both of them":** Transcript, "6:00 P.M. to Carl Albert," Dec. 4, 1963, *TPR,* Vol. II, pp. 143–44. **"I am the only President":** *NYP,* Dec. 5, 1963. **"That they either":** Transcript, "6:00 P.M. to Carl Albert," Dec. 4, 1963, *TPR,* Vol. II, p. 144. **"Labor meeting:** *BS,* Dec. 5, 1963.

"Guys with": Shuman interview; Watson, *Lion in the Lobby,* p. 580. **Meany explained; Wilkins "repeated":** *BS, NYP, NYT, WP, WES,* Dec. 5, 6, 1963.

Johnson and O'Brien knew: Reedy interview; Whalen and Whalen, *Longest Debate,* p. 80. **Contacting the priests:** *NYT,* Dec. 5, 1963. **"Negro and labor":** *WP,* Dec. 4, 1963. **"Heavy in favor:** *WP,* Dec. 5, 1963. **"We've just got":** Transcript, "6:08 P.M. from Larry O'Brien," Dec. 4, 1963, *TPR,* Vol. II, p. 146.

A quiet meeting: Watson, *Lion in the Lobby,* p. 581; MacNeil interview.

"reasonably soon": *Richmond Times-Dispatch,* Dec. 5, 1963; *NYHT, NYP, NYT, WP,* Dec. 5, 6, 1963. **Brown explained:** *NYP, NYT,* Dec. 6, 1963. **A firm date had been set:** *WP,* Dec. 4, 1963. **"It was a compromise"; "spared himself":** *NYT,* Dec. 8, 1963. **"But by then":** "Despite 'Frugality,' the Budget Rises," *Newsweek,* Dec. 16, 1963.

Actually filed not by: *NYT, WP,* Dec. 9, 1963; *NYP, WES,* Dec. 9, 10, 1963. **"Larry? Larry?"** Transcript, "3:35 P.M. from Larry O'Brien," Dec. 9, 1963, *TPR,* Vol. II, pp. 257–58. **Put Jenkins:** Reedy interview. **"They'll sign it"; Smith confessed:** Transcript, "7:06 P.M. to Carl Albert," Dec. 9, 1963, *TPR,* Vol. II, p. 280. **Headlines of triumph:** *WP, NYT,* Dec. 6.

"TEXAN SITS TALL"; Steele article: John L. Steele, "The Political Virtuoso Gathers the Forces to Take on the Job," *Life,* Dec. 13, 1963. **"There was nothing tentative":** West with Kotz, *Upstairs at the White House,* pp. 283–87. **"I think we'll probably":** West, *Upstairs,* p. 288. **"I had our favorite":** Lady Bird Johnson, *A White House Diary,* p. 14. **"Does this telephone"** West, *Upstairs,* p. 290. **"Mr. West":** West, *Upstairs,* pp. 290–91.

"Congress seemed"; "demanding of": Evans and Novak, *Lyndon B. Johnson*, pp. 366–67. On Dec. 21: *NYT, WP*, Dec. 20–25, 1963. "Perhaps": Amrine, *This Awesome Challenge*, p. 125. "At that moment": Johnson, *The Vantage Point*, p. 40. "Had dodged": Amrine, *This Awesome Challenge*, p. 126.

21. Serenity

In this chapter, all December quotes are from December 1963 and all January quotes from January 1964 unless otherwise noted.

Much of the description of these two weeks on the ranch comes from the many hours of newsreel footage, including outtakes, taken at these events. "Sere and bleak"; "whisked off": Cormier, *LBJ: The Way He Was*, p. 19. "So empty": Wicker interview. "Island town": Gliddon, quoted in Caro, *The Path to Power*, p. 57.

Photo session: "The Presidency: Whatever You Say, Honey," *Time*, Jan. 3, 1964; "Sparerib Summit," *Newsweek*, Jan. 6, 1964; Betty Beale, "Johnson's House Tells of His Life," *Life*, Nov. 15, 1964; *BS*, Dec. 26, 1963. Lynda's red shift; to prove: *Newsweek*, Jan. 6, 1964. *BS*, Dec. 26, 1963: "It's marimaki. It's not what you think it is," he told reporters. "She blushed, and so did some of us," Cormier says (*LBJ*, p. 23). "Overflowing": Cormier, *LBJ*, p. 23. "That's where": *LAT*, Dec. 29, 1963; *Newsweek*, Jan. 6, 1964. "I've got": Cormier, *LBJ*, pp. 24, 25.

Erhard visit: Wray Weddell, Jr., "Talk of the Towns," *AA-S*, Dec. 27–Dec. 31, 1963, Jan. 2, 1964; *Fredericksburg Standard*, Dec. 30, 1963; *NYHT*, Dec. 30, 1963; *San Antonio Light*, Dec. 27, 1963; *Time*, "The Presidency: Waging Peace," Jan. 10, 1964. "Alert and": *NYHT*, Dec. 29, 1963. "*Nothing* remotely": *NYT*, Dec. 28, 1963. "Diplomatic staffers": *Newsweek*, Jan, 6, 1964.

"A rare bit of Nuremberg": WPA, *Texas: A Guide to the Lone Star State*, p. 639. Visited the Pioneer Memorial: *A-AS, BS, DMN, NYT*, Dec. 30. State dinner: *AA-S, Fredericksburg Standard, Home Democrat, Midland Reporter*, Dec. 27, 1963; *NYT, NYHT*, Jan. 1, 1964. "No one": Cormier, *LBJ*, p. 29. "The leaders of two": *DMN*, Dec. 30, 1963. "The George Jessell": *LAT*, Dec.29, 1963.

"The fact that": Unidentified official, quoted in *DMN*, Dec. 31, 1963. "The homelike": Erhard, quoted in *NYT*, Dec. 30, 1963. Felt that: For example, "What seemed to please both sides most was the rapport developed by Mr. Johnson and Dr. Erhard and the extreme good feeling that now seems to prevail

between the two governments. That was not always the case when Dr. Adenauer and President Kennedy were at the head of their governments" (*NYT*, Dec. 30, 1963).

"The same moral views"; looked at the world": *NYT*, Dec. 30, 1963. "All these questions"; "Enchanted": *Time*, Jan. 10, 1964. "That I think": *NYT*, Dec. 31, 1963. "Stetson Statesmanship"; "Sparerib Summit": *Newsweek*, Jan. 6, 1964. "Somehow": Cormier, *LBJ*, p. 28.

"The Kennedys transported": *NYHT*, Jan. 1, 1964.

"I've got to be thinking": Elizbeth Wickenden, quoted in Dallek, *Flawed Giant*, p. 61; Goldschmidt, Wickenden interviews.

"The [military] situation": John McCone, "Memorandum for the Record," Dec. 29, 1963, p. 28, "Meetings with the President— 23 Nov 1963—27 Dec. 1963," Box 1, John McCone Memoranda, LBJL.

"undermined": Sorensen, *Counselor.* "We spent": Stephen Sorensen interview.

Full press corps tour: *DMN*, Dec. 29, 1963. "There go the winter oats": DMN, Dec. 29, 1963. Bundy: *NYT*, Dec. 28. Newspapermen; "in vain": *DMN*, Dec. 29, 1963. "With a view": *NYT*, Dec. 28, 1963.

Salinger was aware; "I gave": *BS*, Dec. 28, 1963. Salinger on horse: *Newsweek*, Jan. 6, 1964; *DMN*, Dec. 29, 1963. "Rode off into": *NYT*, Dec. 28, 1963. "It is not": *BS*, Dec. 28, 1963. "Members of the press": *NYT*, Dec. 28.

"Entertainment arouses": Tom Wicker, "LBJ Down on the Farm," *Esquire*, Oct. 1964.

Boating excursion: "At the LBJ," *BS*, Jan. 6, 1964.

"A good man": Cormier, *LBJ*, p. 19. Giving them gifts; Calling Potter's editor: *Time*, Jan. 17, 1964; Wicker interview.

Oreole visits: *BS, NYT*, Jan. 6, 1964; Cormier, *LBJ*, pp. 31–32. "It is an experience": Wicker, "LBJ Down on the Farm."

Joint Chiefs: *NYT*, Dec. 31, 1963.

A "highly-sophisticated"; "Cornball": *LAT*, Jan. 5, 1964. "A notable lack": Peter Lisagor, "On the LBJ Ranch," *NYP*, Dec. 27, 1963. Driving back to Austin: *NYHT*, Jan. 1, 1964. "His own brand"; "A Johnson we had never seen": Cormier, *LBJ*, p. 19. "Politics has been"; "He seems a casual king": Wicker, *NYT*, Jan. 6, 1964. "Unaffected," "old-shoe": Lisagor, "On the LBJ Ranch." "Relaxed": *LAT*, Dec. 29, 1963. "Presidential home life": *BS*, Jan. 6, 1964. "Washington's canniest": Russell Baker, *NYT*, Jan. 9, 1964. "The one": Wicker, "LBJ Down on the Farm." "Perfect": "The Press: Down on the Ranch," *Time*, Jan. 17, 1964.

"The Bunton strain": See chapter with that title in Caro, *Path*. **Showing a house he wasn't really born in:** *DMN*, Dec. 29, 1963. He told reporters he was born "right in that room there, pointing to the corner" (*NYT*, January 6, 1964; *BS*, Dec. 26, 1963). He told reporters, "Don't miss the old house a half mile down the road where I was born." "No, you weren't, corrected his aunt Jessie Hatcher." "Well, it was in the same place, it wasn't the same house," he amended." **"There used":** Robert Semple, "The White House on the Pedernales, *NYT*, Oct. 3, 1965. **His father's last stand:** Caro, *Path*, pp. 87–88. **"The most important thing":** SHJ interview.

Behind those doors: Fehmer, Gonella, Jenkins, Rather interviews. **Might have seemed:** The description of Johnson making phone calls in which he was determined to get the person on the other end to do something comes from the descriptions of, among others, Busby, Jenkins, SHJ, Rather, Reedy, Valenti.

"I had," she was to say, questions: Mayer interview. **"Margaret always":** Busby interview. **Johnson telephoned:** Transcript, "8:45 P.M. to Albert Jackson," *TPR*, Vol. III, pp. 144–51. **Jackson . . . continually trying to cultivate:** Busby, Reedy interviews. For example, in 1959 Jenkins reported to Johnson that "Albert Jackson called and said that he had not been satisfied with some of the columns that Bob Hollingsworth and Margaret Mayer had written, and he told them so—that is in connection with the slant they give their articles about Senator Johnson. He says he has been keeping as close check as possible, but that you can't always control the articles. . . . What I would like for you to do when you have something you want brought out in an article, get in touch with me and I will see that it is brought out. . . . Ask George [Reedy] to call me and tell me what is wanted and I will see that it is done" ("Resume of Telephone Conversations by Long Distance . . . Albert Jackson,") Nov. 7, 1959, "Master File Index 1959—Jenkins, Walter [2 of 2], Box 96, JSP. **In the morning:** Transcript, "11:00 A.M. from Albert Jackson," *TPR*, Vol. III, pp. 157–58.

Bank mergers: *NYT*, July 17, 1963. **Had not been:** *WSJ*, Oct. 17, Dec. 23, 1963. **"A strongly adverse":** Buenger and Pratt, *But Also Good Business*, p. 201. **Justice Dept. opposed":** *NYT*, *WSJ*, Oct. 14, 1964; "Conversation between Dick Maguire and the President—Dec. 27 [1963]—Time: Approximately 12:15 P.M. (This call was not recorded.) **"Would set a precedent":** "Houston Bank Merger . . . Reasons against . . . as dictated by Dick Maguire," both from "Ex Be 2–4, Nov. 22, 1963—July 8, 1965," WHCF SF, Box 4.

"A very serious": "From: Walter Jenkins to" Pres US." **High stakes:** Fran Dressman, *Gus Wortham: Portrait of a Leader*, p. 171; *NYT*, March 20, 1965; Clark, Oltorf interviews. **The President had:** Transcript, "1:55 P.M. to Jack Valenti, et al.," Dec. 25, 1963, *TPR*, Vol. II, pp. 808–10. **Wortham had been; "twisted":** Caro, *Means*, p. 102. **120,000:** *NYT*, March 20, 1968. **"I told Gus":** Transcript, "11:55 A.M. from George Brown," *TPR*, Jan. 2, 1964, Vol. III, pp. 69–78. **"I have been":** *NYT*, Sept. 4, 1965. **"I was under":** *CT*, Oct. 29, 1968. **The letter:** Jones to Johnson, Jan. 3, 1964. **Satisfied Johnson:** On Jan. 7 he wrote Wortham: "Our friend whom you had visit with me at the ranch sent me a very gracious letter in exactly the fashion that you would have him do it" (Johnson to Wortham, Jan. 7, 1964). Johnson was satisfied perhaps also because of a memorandum he had received from Valenti following a talk Valenti had with the *Chronicle*'s editor, Bill Steven, which told Johnson that "Steven says he and Jones are excited over the role of the *Chronicle* as your voice in Texas," and that "Collier's job [in Washington] will be . . . to serve as a vehicle for answering any unfavorable stories that may be printed by other newspapers" (Valenti to Johnson, Dec. 30, 1963). Jones's letter, Johnson's letter, and Valenti's memo are all from "Ex BE 2–4, Nov. 22, 1963—July 8, 1965," Box 4, WHCF SF, LBJL.

Telephoned Brown and Jones: Transcripts, "11:20 A.M. to George Brown," "11:04 A.M. to John Jones," both Jan. 8, 1964, *TPR*, Vol. III, pp. 280–81, 265. **Saxon announced:** "Decision of Comptroller of the Currency James J. Saxon on the Application to Consolidate . . . , —Statement," Jan. 13, 1964; *NYT*, *WSJ*, Jan. 14, 1964. **"Is the *Chronicle?*":** Transcript, 9:05 P.M., Jan. 20, 1964, *TPR*, Vol. III, p. 678. **"A paragraph":** Transcript, "8:45 P.M. to Jack Valenti and Mary Margaret Valenti," *TPR*, Vol. IV, p. 394. **Bank:** The JFKL says that the Saxon Papers cannot be seen by researchers because they have not been processed, and that there are no plans at present to process them. In 1968, Gus Wortham's American General Co. increased its investment in the bank from 120,000 to 925,000 shares (*NYT*, March 20, 1968).

"What do we need": Transcript, "8:45 P.M. to Albert Jackson," Jan. 4, 1963, *TPR*, Vol. II, pp. 150–51.

Christmas Day . . . call: Transcript, "8:39 P.M. to Amon Carter, Jr., President joined by Lady Bird Johnson," Dec. 25, 1963, *TPR*, Vol. II, pp 826–32. **Close depot:** *NYT*, Dec. 13, 1963. **Retiring Timmons:** By Jan. 19, 1964, the byline of the *Star-Telegram's* new Washington reporter, Robert Hilburn, had begun appearing in the paper. Easley, Mayer, Hollingsworth, *Record* interviews. **"During his"**: Timmons OH, LBJL. **"White House business"**: McCammon OH. **"To see to it"**: *WSJ*, Aug. 11, 1964. **"With Moursund"**: McCammon OH. **"Mr. Johnson"**: Fehmer interview. **"Linked"**: *WSJ*, Aug. 11, 1964. **"The same thing"**: McCammon OH. **Sometimes**: Clark, Shapiro interviews.

"Wasn't labeled": Ferguson interview. **Other lines**: Clark, Deathe interviews. **"I want"**: Transcript, "Time Unknown, before 12:45 A.M., Office conversation with Walter Jenkins," Jan.13, 1964, *TPR*, pp. 491–92.

"Deteriorating"; "The past thirty days": Johnson, *Vantage Point*, pp. 62–63. **"wishful thinking"**: *Vantage Point*, p. 63. **"quite a lecture"**: Dallek, *Flawed Giant*, p. 103. **"The situation is very"; "a little less"**: Gibbons, *The U.S. Government and the Vietnam War, Part II: 1961–1964*, pp. 211–12.

Mansfield's memo: Gibbons, *U.S. Government*, pp. 215–216. **Johnson's response**: Transcript, "9:55 P.M. to Frank Valeo, Dec. 23, 1963," *TPR*, Vol. II, pp. 757–75.

"The stakes": Dallek, *Flawed Giant*, p. 103. **Rusk arrived**: Logevall, *Choosing War*, p. 91. **Approving more advisers and a committee**: Gibbons, *U.S. Government*, p. 212.

Krulak committee's report; "progressively escalating": Beschloss, *Taking Charge*, p. 200. **"There's one"**: Transcript, "5:45 P.M. to John Knight," Feb. 3, 1964, *TPR*, Vol. IV, p. 98. **"No President"**: Dallek, *Flawed Giant*, p. 101.

"It was clear"; "juggling": Gibbons, *U.S. Government*, p. 213. The *Pentagon Papers* call it "an accounting exercise" (p. 191). **"In the last"**: *Pentagon Papers*, pp. 303–06. **"We have called back"**: *Public Papers of the Presidents: Lyndon B. Johnson, 1963–1964*, p. 211.

Johnson approves Krulak report; no such memorandum: Gibbons, *U.S. Government*, pp. 213–14. **"We're going to try to launch some counterattacks ourselves. . . . We're going to try to touch them up a little bit in the days to come,"** Johnson told a friendly newspaper executive on January 31 (Transcript, "1:32 P.M. to Walker Stone," Jan. 31, 1964, *TPR*, Vol. III, p. 1044).

"Above all else": Logevall, *Choosing War*, p. 108. **"What is your own internal thinking?"** Transcript, "12:35 P.M. from McGeorge Bundy," March 2, 1964, *TPR*, Vol. IV, p. 847.

Whittington incident: E. Ernest Goldstein, "How LBJ Took the Bull by the Horns," *Amherst*, Winter 1985; Goldstein OH, LBJL; *DT-H*, Jan. 5, 1964; Busby, Fehmer interviews.

Had its beginning under Kennedy: Lemann, *The Promised Land*, pp. 129–45; Goldman, *The Tragedy of Lyndon Johnson*, pp. 37–38; Reeves, *President Kennedy*, p. 656; Sorensen, *Kennedy*, p. 753; Giglio, *The Presidency of John F. Kennedy*, pp. 117–18; Harrington, *The Other America;* Douglas Cater, "The Politics of Poverty," *The Reporter*, Feb. 13, 1964; Newfield, Schlesinger, Sorensen, interviews.

Harrington and Macdonald: "It is part of John Kennedy's legend that *The Other America* spurred him into action against poverty . . . but the consensus among Kennedy aides is that he read MacDonald's review, not the book itself," Lemann writes (*Promised Land*, pp. 130–31). **"Social Security"**: Cater, "Politics of Poverty." **"Future economic growth alone"**: Council of Economic Advisers, *Economic Report of the President, Together with the Annual Report of the Council of Economic Advisers, Transmitted to the Congress, January 1964*, pp. 2, 72. **Articles by Bigart stirred Kennedy**: Gordon OH IV, LBJL. **"In the air"**: Goldman, *The Tragedy*, p. 38

"A quiet investigation": Gordon OH IV. **Kennedy gave him; "to come up"; "Perhaps"**: Capron, quoted in Gillette, *Launching the War on Poverty*, pp. 11, 12. **"The agencies weren't"; "Go back"**: Cannon, quoted in Gillette, *Launching*, p. 13. **"Keep at it"**: Heller, quoted in Gillette, *Launching*, p. 14.

Scammon . . . told: Reeves, *President Kennedy*, p. 656. **"I then heard"; "Come back to me"**: Heller OH I, LBJL. **"Current"**: Thomas, *Robert Kennedy*, p. 305. **"I am still very much"**: Heller OH I, quoted in Gillette, *Launching*, p. 14. Lemann (*Promised Land*, p. 135) writes that "Everyone close to Kennedy agrees that he certainly did not have any kind of major effort in mind." And he adds (p.141), "In the weeks following the assassination . . . , John F. Kennedy, as his associates went to work burnishing his reputation, began to become more liberal—in particular, more liberal than Lyndon Johnson. Caution and pragmatism do not make an easy foundation on which to build an argument for historical greatness, and they were not stressed in the memorialization of Kennedy." One of the early examples of such "memorialization" in regard to a poverty program came very soon after the assassination. Writing in the *SEP*, Schlesinger stated that "in one of the last talks I had with him, he was musing about the legislative program for next January and said, 'The time has come to organize a national assault on the causes of poverty, a comprehensive program, across the board'" (Schlesinger, "A Eulogy for J.F.K.," *SEP*, Dec. 14, 1963).

"Gordon's schedule": Capron, quoted in Gillette, *Launching the War on Poverty,* p. 18. **"Public awareness":** Evans and Novak, *Lyndon B. Johnson,* p. 434.

"That's my kind of program": Heller OH I, LBJL. **"So spontaneous":** Heller OH I. **"Point blank":** Heller, quoted in Lemann, *The Promised Land,* p. 141. In his "Notes on Meeting with President Johnson, 7:40 P.M., Saturday, Nov. 23, 1963" (Gardner Ackley Microfilm, Reel 2, LBJL), Heller wrote that he "strongly urged me to move ahead on the poverty theme in the hope that we can make it an important part of the 1964 program.... In answer to a point-blank question, [He] said we should push ahead full-tilt on the project." Gordon says (OH IV, LBJL), "He [Johnson] immediately seized on the idea as an important one, one that was compatible with and consistent with his own purposes in the presidency, and encouraged us to go on."

The emphasis; "we started out"; "it was": Capron, quoted in Gillette, *Launching,* p. 21. **December 20 meeting:** Sundquist, quoted in Gillette, *Launching,* p. 22.

Johnson had reserved: "We are asking for new obligational authority of $500 million," he told John Kenneth Galbraith on Jan. 29. "We thought that's as much as we could get by with to start it off" (Gillette, *Launching,* p. 23). In Johnson's memoirs he explains that he searched "for ways to reduce spending, mainly in Defense but in other departments as well, so that money could be used to start the poverty programs. A poverty bill that would increase the budget at the outset would have little chance of success" (Johnson, *Vantage Point,* p. 71). **"Gordon and Heller had been thinking":** Johnson, *Vantage Point,* pp. 73–74.

"How are you going to spend?": Evans and Novak, *LBJ,* p. 428. Their account "was a word-for-word account, without quotes, from my memo on the affair," Heller was to say (Heller OH I, LBJL).

"Extremely": Heller, quoted in Gillette, *Launching the War on Poverty,* p. 29. **"'Look'":** Heller OH I. **"He wanted":** Heller OH I. **"The challenge":** Johnson, *Vantage Point,* p. 74.

"All of us": *NYP,* Jan. 5, 1964.

The ranch . . . was an appropriate setting: For the psychological impact that being on the ranch had on Johnson, see Caro, *Master of the Senate,* the "Memories" chapter. For a fuller description, see Caro, *The Path to Power,* the chapters entitled "The Best Man I Ever Knew" and "The Bottom of the Heap."

"I've always been an early riser": Cormier, *LBJ,* p. 18. **Calling E. Babe**: E. Babe Smith interview. **"We always get up":** Stehling interview. Writing in her diary about

this vacation on the Ranch, and the War on Poverty, Lady Bird Johnson said, "It was the right setting to discuss it. It was on that ranch that he had been born, and there were memories. The day he got back, talking with a friend [Mrs. Johnson does not identify him], he said, 'I waked up at 6:30. All my life I waked . . . I waked up on a road gang. 'You get up early, don't you? You had to . . . You can't tell me you ever made the big leagues not getting up early. It takes us a little longer [to achieve success] than some other folks.' " **"We always talked":** Cox interview. **"Hated poverty":** Hurst interview; Hurst and Cain, *LBJ: To Know Him Better,* p. 12. **"Rags" incident:** Hurst and Cain, *LBJ,* p. 5.

"Hounded": Evans and Novak, *LBJ,* p. 428.

"Just a few feet"; "it struck me": Johnson, *Vantage Point,* p. 73.

Hackett's committee had been urging: Lemann, *Promised Land,* pp. 128–33. **According to Busby:** Busby interview. **"I realized":** Johnson, *Vantage Point,* p. 75. Also see Matusow, *The Unraveling of America,* p. 123; Lemann, *Promised Land,* pp. 143–44. **Instead, there were orders:** For example, Capron to Heller, Jan. 4, 1964. **"Your preliminary":** Gordon and Heller, "Memorandum for Secretary of Agriculture, Secretary of Commerce . . . , Jan. 6, 1964," "Ex We9 Poverty Program, Nov. 22, 1963–Feb. 28, 1964," Box 25, WHCF, LBJL.

"State of the Union"; secretary was driven up: Sorensen interview; *NYT,* Jan. 9, 1964. **First draft contained:** TCS, "1964 State of the Union—First Draft, Desired Length: 2,500 words, length of this draft: 2,783 words, Jan. 1, 1964," "Jan. 8, 1964, 1964 State of the Union—Folder II," Box 92, Statements of Lyndon Baines Johnson, LBJL. **Those sentences remained unchanged:** All the drafts can be found in various folders in Box 92, Statements of Lyndon Baines Johnson, LBJL. Busby, Sorensen, Valenti interviews. **"It doesn't sound":** Sorensen interview. **Kennedy had said it:** Schlesinger, *A Thousand Days,* p. 1005; Lemann, *Promised Land,* p. 145.

"The whole idea": Wickenden interview.

"Under the budget": "Texts of Johnson's State of the Union Message and His Earlier Press Briefing," *NYT,* Jan. 9, 1964. **Johnson had added":** "For the President . . . 3,007 words," Box 92, Statements of Lyndon Baines Johnson, LBJL.

"The tumultous [sic]": Marquis Childs, "Johnson's Program," *NYP,* Jan. 9, 1964. **"persistent reports":** *NYT,* Jan. 9, 1964. **"Almost"; "promises":** *NYT,* Jan. 9, 1964. **"Republicans": *WP,* Jan. 9, 1964. **"remarkable":** Krock column, *NYT.* **"President Johnson's first":** *NYT, Time.* **"Reinforced":** *NYP,* Jan. 9, 1964.

"The stunner": "A Bold Gamble by the President," *Newsweek,* Jan. 20, 1964. **"a near miraculous":** *WP,* Jan. 9, 1964.

"No one": *NYT,* Jan. 9, 1964. **"At least one":** Cater, "Politics of Poverty." **"In launching":** Walter Lippmann, "Today and Tomorrow," *WP,* Jan. 9, 1964. **"Once before":** "A Bold Gamble by the President," *Newsweek,* Jan. 20, 1964. **Where, as a small boy:** Caro, *Path,* p. 69.

22. "Old Harry" II

"Searching for Harry Byrd": Johnson, Lady Bird, *A White House Diary,* p. 35.

"Locked up": Transcript, "8:21 P.M. to Kermit Gordon," Jan. 6, 1964, *TPR,* Vol. III, pp. 208–09. **"I've got a surprise":** Heinemann, *Harry Byrd of Virginia,* p. 400. **"I congratulate":** *Statesville Record & Landmark,* Jan. 9, 1964. **"I appreciate"; "that was":** Transcript, "3:25 P.M. to Harry Byrd," Jan. 8, 1964, *TPR,* Vol. III, p. 292. **"Speed–up":** *NYT,* Jan. 10, 1964. **"High gear":** *WP,* Jan. 15, 1964. **"footrace":** WP, Jan. 17, 1964.

"Harry started": MacNeil interview. **"Secret ally":** Evans and Novak, *Lyndon B. Johnson,* p. 375. **"Stunned":** *TPR,* Vol. III, p. 728. **"In a panicky":** Transcript, "12:34 P.M. from George Smathers," Jan. 23, 1964, *TPR,* pp. 737–41. **His solution would require; Anderson, Ribicoff, Hartke telephone calls:** Transcripts, "1:05 P.M. to Clinton Anderson," "1:11 P.M. to Vance Hartke," "1:14 P.M. to Abraham Ribicoff," all Jan. 23, *TPR,* Vol. III, pp. 741–47. The call to Anderson lasted 33 seconds, the call to Hartke, one minute and 47 seconds, the call to Ribicoff, three minutes and 31 seconds, a total of five minutes and 51 seconds (Online Finding Aid for Description of Recordings and Transcripts of Johnson Telephone Conversations, *http://www.lbjlib.utexas .edu/johnson/archives.hom/dictabelt.hom/dic-tahist.asp*). **"I hope"; "Well, I want to tell you"; "That Harry Byrd"; "You make them":** Transcripts, "1:17 P.M. to Harry Byrd," "Late afternoon from Harry Byrd to White House operator," "5:40 P.M. to Harry Byrd," *TPR,* Vol. III, pp. 748–50, 768–70.

"The clock is ticking": *WP,* Jan. 10, 1964. **"Startled officials":** Evans and Novak, *LBJ,* p. 375. **"Record time":** *WP,* Jan. 29, 1964. **Passed:** *NYHT, NYT, WP,* Feb. 8, 1964.

The reductions ... were a key: This will be analyzed in volume V of this work.

23. In the Books of Law

"The undercurrent"; But Celler: UPI in *Redlands* (Calif.) *Daily Facts.* **Smith slowing down the hearings; "going over":** *NYT,* Jan. 23, 1964. "Under the leadership of ... Smith ... and Colmer the Rules Committee is now cross-examining members of the Judiciary Committee, obviously for the purpose of deciding for itself whether it likes this measure," the *Times* had editorialized on Jan. 18th. **"after seven days":** *NYT,* Jan. 23, 1964.

Johnson told; Only 178: Transcript, "11:50 A.M., to Larry O'Brien," Jan. 18, 1964, *TPR,* Vol. III, p. 618.

Republican leaders; "reluctant to take it away": *NYT,* Jan. 23, 1964. **"I said, 'If I were you, Charlie'":** Transcript, "Time Unknown—Office Conversation," Jan. 25, 1964, *TPR,* Vol. III, p. 879. **"He wants to know":** Transcript, "12:55 P.M. to James Webb," Jan. 18, 1964, *TPR,* Vol. III, pp. 622–23. **"I showed him":** Transcript, "3:30 P.M. from James Webb," Jan. 21, 1964, *TPR,* Vol. III, p. 694.

The following day; "All during": *NYT,* Jan. 23, 24, 1964. **"I have been here":** *NYT,* Jan. 24, 1964. **"Very happy":** *NYT,* Jan. 26, 1964. **"Congress ... is moving":** Childs, *WP,* Feb. 10, 1964.

"They can filibuster": Dallek, *Flawed Giant,* p. 169. **McCullough had; "we ... not give away":** Katzenbach, *Some of It Was Fun,* p. 139. **One tenet:** Katzenbach, *Some of It,* p. 120. **Robert Kennedy had:** Katzenbach, *Some of It,* pp. 121, 122; Katzenbach interview. **Dirksen had promised; "he obviously"; "expected President Johnson":** Katzenbach, *Some of It,* pp. 129, 141, 143; Katzenbach interview. **"This bill will":** Katzenbach OH II, JFKL. In an interview, Katzenbach said that in 1964, "I'm sure that Everett Dirksen" agreed to go along with the bill "because he was sure that Johnson was going to give things up [agree to amendments and compromises that would weaken the bill]— after all, he knew what Johnson had done in the past. Well [this time] Johnson wasn't going to give anything up. And Dirksen got himself committed on that bill before he realized Johnson wasn't going to give anything up." And Katzenbach also said, "Dirksen did the job. He had to do it. He had come out so publicly for civil rights. Because he thought Johnson would water it down" (Katzenbach interview). **And now "he obviously wanted":** "Civil Rights: Debate in the Senate," *Time,* April 10, 1964; "The Congress: A Falling-Off among Friends," *Time,* April 17, 1964; "Civil Rights: At Last, a Vote," *Time,* May 15, 1964; MacNeil, *Dirksen,* pp. 233–34; Solberg, *Hubert Humphrey: A*

Biography, pp. 223, 225; MacNeil interview; Katzenbach, *Some of It,* p. 131. **"under [President] Kennedy":** Evans and Novak, *Lyndon B. Johnson,* p. 378. **Dirksen was confident; "expected President Johnson":** See Katzenbach interview above.

Compromises had always been a key element: See Caro, *Master of the Senate,* passim. **"We knew":** Talmadge, quoted in Mann, *The Walls of Jericho,* p. 400; Talmadge, Dent interviews. **"I am in favor":** Solberg, *Hubert Humphrey,* p. 223. **"No wheels":** Dallek, *Flawed Giant,* p. 117. **"I knew":** Johnson interview with Goodwin, *Lyndon Johnson,* p. 191. **"No compromises":** Goodwin, *Remembering America,* pp. 257–58.

"I'll do": Guthman and Shulman, eds., *Robert Kennedy: In His Own Words,* pp. 211–12; Katzenbach interview. **Counting:** For example, Manatos to O'Brien, Feb. 27; April 13, Office Files of Mike Manatos, JFKL.

"You have this great opportunity now": Humphrey, quoted in Miller, *Lyndon,* p. 368. **"I would have been":** Humphrey, *The Education of a Public Man,* p. 274. **Russell "knew all":** Humphrey, *Education,* p. 274. **"Sized me":** Humphrey OH III, LBJL. **Now, however (he learned the rules):** "Cracking the Whip for Civil Rights," *Newsweek,* April 13, 1964; Mann, *Walls of Jericho,* pp. 396–98.

A series of Russell maneuvers: Territo to Jenkins, Feb. 26, 1964, LE / HU 2, Nov. 22, 1963–June 18, 1964, Box 65, "EX LE/HU," LBJL. **Quorum calls had always:** Caro, *Master,* passim; Watson, *Lion in the Lobby,* p. 608; Mann, *Walls of Jericho,* p. 397. **Only once:** Humphrey, *Education,* p. 279. **"a veritable":** Humphrey, *Education,* pp. 275, 279. **"Now you know":** Humphrey OH III. **"He had a sense":** Humphrey, *Education,* p. 276. **"He is a man":** Humphrey on *Meet the Press,* March 8, 1964, quoted in Mann, *Walls of Jericho,* p. 395; Humphrey OH III.

"Of the greatest importance": Humphrey, *Education,* p. 273.

Protection: Calvin Trillin, "Letter from Jackson," *The New Yorker,* Aug. 29, 1964. **A Cleveland rabbi:** Friedman, ed., *The Civil Rights Reader,* p. 203. **"The officers forced me":** Bessie Turner, quoted in Friedman, ed., *Civil Rights Reader,* p. 200. **"A mob might form":** Trillin, "Letter from Jackson."

"You couldn't"; "This was"; "Just wait"; "I hope": All from Mann, *Walls of Jericho,* pp. 412–13. **He went in:** Mann, *Walls of Jericho,* p. 417. O'Brien had reported to the President that Humphrey felt Katzenbach and Humphrey, among others, have been negotiating over the language of amendments that Dirksen has proposed, and that "Dirksen feels that that [his

meeting with Johnson] would present him an opportunity to discuss this directly with you" (Transcript, "5:50 P.M. to Larry O'Brien," April 28, 1964, *TPR,* Vol. VI, pp. 281–82). But Johnson, shortly before Dirksen arrives, tells Mansfield, "I'm going to tell him [Dirksen] that I support a strong civil rights bill. . . . I'm going to say, 'Now, these details can't be decided down here in the White House . . ." (Transcript, "11:32 A.M. to Mike Mansfield," April 29, 1964, *TPR,* Vol. VI, pp. 325–26). **"You say";** **Dirksen going in:** *NYHT,* April 29, 30, 1964. Mann, *Walls of Jericho,* p. 417. **To reporters' questions:** Mann, *Walls of Jericho,* p. 417. As the Whalens put it (*The Longest Debate,* p. 173), "Having learned . . . that the President was not going to make any deals, Dirksen decided it was time to talk with Humphrey and company." **"He made it clear to everybody that . . . he wouldn't substitute anything for it; that if they filibustered, they could filibuster, but he didn't want *any other* bill"** (Rauh, quoted in Miller, *Lyndon,* p. 369). The *NYT* reported that Johnson and Dirksen did discuss the civil rights bill. **"All I know":** Whalen and Whalen, *Longest Debate,* p. 169. **In reality:** Mann, *Walls of Jericho,* p. 431. **"Battlefield briefings":** Whalen and Whalen, *Longest Debate,* p. 170.

Johnson took: Explaining that passing a civil rights bill in the Senate required, as Watson puts it, "a force the Senate would respect," NAACP Lobbyist Clarence Mitchell said, "The President supplied that force" (Watson, *Lion in the Lobby,* p. 596). "Humphrey was Mitchell's liaison with the President," Watson writes. "But Johnson still maintained regular contact with Mitchell by calling him at his home . . . to . . . issue marching orders" (Watson, *Lion in the Lobby,* p. 600). Watson reports that Russell was to say that Johnson "put so much pressure on everybody there wasn't any doubt about this bill getting through" (Watson, *Lion in the Lobby,* p. 626).

"I couldn't argue"; Exceptions began: Whalen and Whalen, *Longest Debate,* pp. 178, 202. **Johnson and Hayden:** Udall to Johnson, May 7, 1964, "LE/HU 2—Interior," LBJL. And see all "LE/NR 7–1, Central Arizona Project." "The Historic Vote: 71 to 29," *Newsweek,* June 22, 1964; Mann, *Walls of Jericho,* p. 427.

"Mike, these people": Transcript, "1:50 P.M. to Mike Mansfield," April 1, 1964, *TPR,* Vol. V, pp. 623–24. **Gruening and Bartlett:** *NYT, WP,* March 31, April 7, Aug. 21, 1964. **"I am prepared":** *NYT,* May 14, 1964.

"The daily sessions"; "Having learned": Whalen and Whalen, *Longest Debate,* pp. 157, 171. **"We are carving"; after all; "he wasn't":** Mann, *Walls of Jericho,* pp. 409–10.

"**Going to be against**": Transcript, "12:11 P.M. to Hubert Humphrey," April 30, 1964, *TPR*, Vol. VI, p. 360. **When Johnson telephoned Dirksen:** Transcript, "4:30 P.M. to Everett Dirksen," May 13, 1964, *TPR*, Vol. VI, pp. 661, 662.

"**An idea**": Mann, *Walls of Jericho*, p. 442; Whalen and Whalen, *Longest Debate*, p. 185. **He still didn't:** Whalen and Whalen, *Longest Debate*, p. 189. **Russell suddenly began pressing for amendments:** *Newsweek*, June 22, 1964; Whalen and Whalen, *Longest Debate*, pp. 166–67. "**We need more time**": Whalen and Whalen, *Longest Debate*, p. 190. **The cloture motion passed, 71–29:** "The Historic Vote: 71 to 29," *Newsweek*, June 22, 1964. **73–27:** "The Congress: The Final Vote," *Time*, June 26, 1964. **Overriding the judge:** *LAT, NYHT, NYT, WP, NYT, WP,* July 1, 2, 3, 1964. **Voting Rights Act:** Caro, *Means of Ascent*, pp. xiii–xxi; *Master*, pp. 715–16.

24: Defeating Despair

"**Defeats Despair**": *NYT*, Jan. 9, 1964. "**Controlled**": Schlesinger, *Robert Kennedy and His Times*, p. 611. "**Painful**": Guthman, *We Band of Brothers*, p. 244. "**As if**": Seigenthaler interview. "**It was**": Guthman, *We Band*, p. 246. "**At Hobe Sound**": Salinger, quoted in Shesol, *Mutual Contempt*, p. 140. "**In the middle**": vanden Heuvel and Gwirtzman, *On His Own*, p. 2. **Agents . . . would see:** Collier and Horowitz, *The Kennedys*, p. 315. "**He was wearing**": Seigenthaler interview. "**I don't**": vanden Heuvel inteview. "**So complete**": vanden Heuvel and Gwirtzman, *On His Own*, p. 3. "**Smiling, relaxed**"; "**as energetic**": "Bobby's Back," *Newsweek*, Jan. 20, 1964; *NYT*, Jan. 12, 1964; *WS*, Jan. 12, 1964. "He looks tanned, healthy and more relaxed," the *WS* said (Jan. 9, 1964). "**Through the election**"; "**STAYING ON**": *WS*, Jan. 9, 1964.

"**The suffering**": vanden Heuvel and Gwirtzman, *On His Own*, p. 24. "**I didn't have**": Seigenthaler interview, OH. "**A little too large**": Murray Kempton, "Pure Irish," *The New Republic*, Feb. 15, 1964. "**How do?**" "**You're young**": Collier and Horowitz, *The Kennedys*, pp. 314–15. "**When did he**": Jean Kennedy Smith interview.

"**Now he is alone**"; "**What is different**": Kempton, "Pure Irish." "**It was almost as if a part of** *him* **had died**": Newfield interview.

"**Sensed**": Thomas, *Robert Kennedy*, p. 283. "**Understandable**": Thomas, *Robert Kennedy*, p. 283. "**in a way**": Shesol, *Mutual*

Contempt, p. 130; Thomas, *Robert Kennedy*, p. 277. "**Began**": Thomas, *Robert Kennedy*, p. 283. "**Perhaps**": Schlesinger, *Journals*, p. 214. "**Obviously**": Bradlee, *Conversations with Kennedy*, p. 131. "**So do I**": Collier and Horowitz, *The Kennedys*, p. 317. "**Worried**"; "**restless**": Thomas, *Robert Kennedy*, pp. 283–84. "**Quieted**": Thomas, *Robert Kennedy*, p. 284. "**Never really wanted**": Schlesinger, *Robert Kennedy*, p. 614. "**Wondered how long he could continue**": Schlesinger, *Journals*, p. 616. "**I cannot say what his essential feeling**": Schlesinger, *Robert Kennedy*, p. 616.

"**He changed**": For example, Newfield, vanden Heuvel interviews. Of course, as Seigenthaler says, "I don't think you could go through what he went through and not change" (Seigenthaler interview). Anthony Lewis says, "Most people acquire certainties as they grow older; he *lost* his. He changed—he grew—more than anyone I have known" (Schlesinger, *Robert Kennedy*, p. 593).

"**It's an impressive**": Penn Kimball, "Robert Kennedy," *Life* magazine, 1966. **Cuban fishing boats:** Schlesinger, *Robert Kennedy*, p. 636. "**There was**": vanden Heuvel interview.

Orphanage party: Maas, quoted in Stein and Plimpton, *American Journey*, pp. 146–47; Maas interview; *WS*, Jan. 12, 1964. "The child's innocent cry knifed to the hearts of all who heard it," the *WS* said. **Home for the aged:** Bradlee, *A Good Life*, p. 295; Thomas, *Robert Kennedy*, p. 293.

"**I have**": Collier and Horowitz, *The Kennedys*, p. 321. "**There's nothing**"; "**Unhappy**"; "**He didn't like**": Novello, Kempton, Hundley, all quoted in Schlesinger, *Robert Kennedy*, p. 637. "**How's Jimmy doing?**": Seigenthaler interview. "**otherwise**": Schlesinger, *Robert Kennedy*, p. 637. "**I saw him**": Morgenthau, quoted in Thomas, *Robert Kennedy*, p. 283. "**to go where**": Thomas, *Robert Kennedy*, p. 284.

"**I'm tired**": Thimmesch and Johnson, *Robert Kennedy at Forty*, p. 146.

"**What's important**": Schlesinger, *Robert Kennedy*, p. 631. And see Goodwin, *Remembering America*, p. 246. "**I had**": Bradlee, *A Good Life*, p. 295. "**Anybody**": Kimball, *Life* magazine, 1966. **Bobby Kennedy was always** "**a work in progress**": Newfield interview; Newfield, quoted in Goldfarb, *Perfect Villains*, p. 312. "**Before that**": vanden Heuvel interview. "**Knew how to hate**": Kempton, "Pure Irish," *The New Republic*, Feb. 15, 1964.

Never called him "The President": Newfield interview; Thomas, *Robert Kennedy*, p. 291. "**What does he know?**"; "**All those**": Goodwin, *Remembering America*, pp. 244, 250.

"There were"; "An awful"; "Said to Jackie"; "He was against": Guthman and Shulman, eds., *Robert Kennedy: In His Own Words*, pp. 405–11. "I just": Guthman and Shulman, eds., *In His Own Words*, p. 344. "They're all scared"; "Ralph Dungan was"; "Our President": Guthman and Shulman, eds., *In His Own Words*, pp. 411–12, 417.

"The thing I feared": Johnson interview with Doris Goodwin, *Lyndon Johnson and the American Dream*, pp. 199, 344. "Royal family": Reedy interview. "If": Schlesinger, *Robert Kennedy*, p. 647.

Appoints Mann: *NYT, WP,* Dec. 15, 1963. "a colonialist": Goodwin, *Remembering America*, p. 245. "Our power"; "Johnson has"; "Staff people": Schlesinger, *Robert Kennedy*, pp. 630–33. Proposal was leaked: Guthman, *We Band*, p. 247; Shesol, *Mutual Contempt*, p. 151. The article is in *WP,* Jan. 13, 1964. "Where did the *Post* get its story on Bobby?" he demanded of Bundy. (Transcript, "1:05 P.M. to McGeorge Bundy," Jan. 13, 1964, *TPR,* p. 462.) "I'm going to send": Transcript, "1:25 P.M. to Richard Russell," *TPR,* pp. 400–04. During the conversation with Russell, the subject of the 1960 convention—and of Bobby's failure to force Johnson off the ticket—came up, with the two men sneering at the failure. When Johnson tells Russell that he's sending Bobby to Indonesia, Russell says, "Tell him to be tough, too . . . like he was in Los Angeles," and laughs.

Waseda speech; "Tears"; "to remain"; "less than private"; "Never discussed"; "bitter": Guthman, *We Band*, pp. 248–53; *NYHT, NYT,* Jan. 18, 19, 1964. "We are of": *NYT,* Jan. 29, 1964. The photograph of Kennedy not looking at Johnson as they shook hands is in the *NYT,* Jan. 29, 1964. "Used": White, *The Making of the President 1964,* p. 261.

"A gutsy": Guthman, *We Band*, p. 254. Summoning Kennedy: Johnson's version of the confrontation is in Transcript, "5:21 P.M. to Cliff Carter; followed by Richard 'Dick' Maguire and Ken O'Donnell," Feb. 11, 1964, *TPR,* Vol. IV, pp. 472–76. Kennedy's version is in Guthman and Shulman, eds., *His Own Words,* pp. 406–07. Kennedy talked to Seigenthaler and Goodwin about the confrontation at the time. Seigenthaler OH, JFKL. Hadn't even known: Guthman and Shulman, eds., *In His Own Words,* p. 406. "If he's such": O'Donnell OH. "I know": Seigenthaler OH.

"I suggested": Guthman and Shulman, eds., *In His Own Words,* pp. 406, 407. "Do it": Goodwin, *Remembering America,* p. 248. Johnson . . . recalling it": Transcript, "5:21 P.M. to Cliff Carter, followed by Richard

'Dick' Maguire and Ken O'Donnell," Feb. 11, 1964, *TPR,* Vol. IV, p. 475. "A bitter, mean": Guthman and Shulman, eds., *In His Own Words,* p. 406. "I did you a favor": Goodwin, *Remembering America,* p. 248. "I told him"; "tears got": Transcript, "5:21 P.M.," pp. 474–75. "So savage": Bartlett OH, JFKL.

"I'm just like a fox": Caro, *Master,* p. xxi, quoting Dickerson, *Among Those Present,* pp. 154–55. "Divine retribution" for his "participation": Guthman and Shulman, eds., *In His Own Words,* pp. 326–27. Neither of the two: For example, Thomas, *Robert Kennedy,* p. 392. "We had a hand": Shesol, *Mutual Contempt,* p. 131. "Whether": Transcript, "1:40 P.M., from J. Edgar Hoover," Nov. 29, 1963, *TPR,* Vol. I, p. 275. "President Kennedy": Califano, *The Triumph and Tragedy of Lyndon Johnson,* p. 295. "Murder, Inc.": Leo Janos, "The Last Days of the President," *Atlantic Monthly,* July 1973. "Cruelly": Thomas, *Robert Kennedy,* p. 292. "The worst": Schlesinger, *Robert Kennedy,* p. 649. "Does not": Prettyman, Barrett, quoted in Schlesinger, *Robert Kennedy,* p. 687. "He saw": Schlesinger, *Robert Kennedy,* p. 687.

25. Hammer Blows

Telephone call to Clifford: Clifford, Clark, *Counsel to the President,* pp. 545–46. The fact that Johnson made an "early . . . morning" call to Clifford—at 5:41 A.M., June 5th—is recorded in the President's Appointments File [Daily Diary]—June 5th. Historian Jeff Shesol asked Clifford about his conversation with Johnson during an interview, and, Shesol reports, Clifford said, "That was a very delicate situation, and I wondered whether I should even mention it [in the book]." He also said, "I don't want to go on any further than I did in the book." The Johnson Library says that no recording of the call exists, and there is no recording of it in the library's "Recordings and Transcripts of Conversations and Meetings" file. Whether Johnson continued to press Clifford on whether Robert Kennedy had the right to be buried at Arlington is unknown, but on June 6 Clifford telephoned to tell him the specific authority that gave Robert Kennedy that right. On that date, Johnson aide Jim Jones reported in a memo to Johnson: "Secretary Clifford reports that a three-acre plot was set aside for President Kennedy at Arlington Cemetery. At the time, Secretary McNamara enunciated that this plot would be available for burial of members of the Kennedy family. . . . Clifford

just wanted you to know there is authority for the senator to be buried in the Kennedy plot" (Shesol, *Mutual Contempt*, p. 553; Jim Jones to Johnson, June 6, 1968, "June 5–6, 1968, Action Memos after Kennedy Assassination Report," Box 102, President's Appointment File [Diary Backup]).
"Schlesinger declared": Dungan OH. **"What do you want":** Goldman, *The Tragedy of Lyndon Johnson*, p. 134. **"I must guard":** Schlesinger, *Journals*, p. 223. **"The new President; "found it"; "almost":** Schlesinger, *Journals*, pp. 216–19. **Johnson had begun:** Goldman, pp. 3–34. **"Accepted":** Schlesinger, *Journals*, p. 224. **Schlesinger's opinion:** Schlesinger, *Robert Kennedy*, p. 626.
"Johnson tried": Sorensen interview. **"He was very very nice" to sons:** Sorensen recalled the scene in the White House Mess during one of his interviews with the author. He also recalled that after Johnson had gotten up and left the table, "one of the three [boys] turned to me, and said, 'He's not very much like a President.'" After he repeated this remark to the author, Sorensen paused for a quite a long time. Then he said, "I think maybe I shared that feeling. Out of the mouths of babes."
"Rather liked" Galbraith's draft: Transcript, "10:10 P.M. to Ted Sorensen; preceded by Bill Moyers and Sorensen," *TPR*, Vol. I, pp. 164–71. **Simply crossed out:** Sorensen interview. Sorensen writes in *Counselor* that "He [Johnson] understandably deleted" that line— one of Sorensen's characteristic understatements (p. 382). **"Ninety percent":** Sorensen, *Counselor*, p. 383. **Katharine Graham call:** Transcript, "11:10 A.M. to Katharine Graham," Dec. 2, 1963, *TPR*, Vol. II, p. 41. **"Are you?":** Sorensen interview; Sorensen, *Counselor*, p. 385. **Sorensen became accustomed:** Sorensen, *Counselor*, pp. 383, 385. **"Well, your man":** Sorensen interview. **"Had planned"; "You and I":** Sorensen, *Counselor*, pp. 388–89.
"Hopalong": For example, *Abilene Reporter-News*, undated. **"Do you think?":** *WP*, Dec. 31, 1963; AP story, *Big Spring Herald*, Dec. 30, 1963; Steinberg, *Sam Johnson's Boy*, p. 648; slightly different version in *NYT*, Dec. 30. **"Reporters felt":** Steinberg, *Sam Johnson's Boy*, p. 648. **"For all":** Amrine, *This Awesome Challenge*, p. 105. **"A terrible"; "There is":** Schlesinger, *Journals*, p. 225. **"Adopted":** James Wechsler, "LBJ & Pierre," *NYP*, March 24, 1964.
Rapport was gone: Salinger was to say that Johnson had at first been "accessible to me, but that dried up around February or March." Salinger OH, JFKL. **Reporters:** Amrine, *Awe-*

some, p. 103. **"It was impossible":** Salinger OH, JFKL. **"The White House press":** *LAT*, March 22, 1964. For example, *WP*, March 15, 1964: "No one would be surprised to see him leave later in the year. Reporters recently were surprised when Valenti started monitoring Salinger's press conferences." Also see *WP*, March 20, 1964. **Salinger was determined:** Salinger, *With Kennedy*, pp. 343–45; Guthman and Shulman, eds., *Robert Kennedy: In His Own Words*, pp. 412–13.
"So abrupt": Amrine, *Awesome*, p. 105. **Walking out of the restaurant; encountering:** Salinger, *With Kennedy*, p. 346. **"Almost fell out":** Salinger, *With Kennedy*, p. 346. **Went to the White House:** "Democrats: Senator Salinger," *Time*, March 27, 1964; *NYT*, *WP*, March 22. **"As quickly"; "Startled":** Salinger, *With Kennedy*, p. 346.
Johnson's self-possession; When he saw Salinger: Salinger was to give this account of what happened. "I said, 'Mr. President, goodbye. I'm leaving.' He said, 'Where are you going?' 'I'm going to California.' 'What are you going to do there?' 'I'm going to run for senator.'" Booknotes, Nov. 12, 1995. Salinger, *With Kennedy*, p. 346. **"The letters":** *WES*, March 20, 1964. **"He must have heard":** Salinger, *With Kennedy*, p. 347.
"I had given LBJ very little time": Salinger, *With Kennedy*, p. 347. **"effective immediately":** *Newsweek*, March 30, 1964. **"Surprise" and "startling" resignation:** "Surprise" is *WES*, March 20, 1964. *WP*, *WES*, March 22, 1964.
"Not disturbed": *NYT*, *WES*, March 22, 1964.
"At the same": Salinger, *With Kennedy*, p. 346; *WP*, March 20, 1964.
A "bombshell": Lady Bird Johnson, *A White House Diary*, p. 96.
"The nostalgic pretense": James Reston, *NYT*, March 20, 1964. **"Do you approve?":** *WP*, March 11, 1964. **March and April:** *WP*, May 15, 1964. **"Two out of three":** *LAT*, May 15, 1964. **"Every President":** *WP*, July 1, 1945. **"Compare favorably":** *WP*, May 15, 1964. **"In the few":** Joseph Alsop, *WP*, April 20, 1964. **"The most energetic":** Marquis Childs, *WP*, May 27, 1964. **"The same":** *NYT*, May 3, 1964. **"The Johnson Administration":** Roscoe Drummond, *LAT*, May 14, 1964. **"In a good deal less":** Richard Rovere, "Letter from Washington," *The New Yorker*, Feb. 15, 1964.
A hard man to beat: Gallup Poll, March 1964, *"Poll Data Bank,"* The Roper Center for Public Opinion Research. **"President Johnson's":** "Republicans: The Man to Beat," *Time*, May 8, 1964.

26. Long Enough

"History will record": Sidey, quoted in Middleton, *LBJ: The White House Years,* p. 13. **"recognized rule":** Feerick, *From Failing Hands,* p. 20. **"Everything I had ever learned":** Goodwin, *Lyndon Johnson,* p.178. **"Kennedy's assassination touched":** Patterson, *Grand Expectations,* p. 531.

"A measure must be sent": Goodwin, *Lyndon Johnson,* pp. 226–27. Johnson also said: "In some ways Congress is like a dangerous animal that you're trying to make work for you. You push him a little bit and he may go just as you want but you push him too much and he may balk and turn on you. You've got to sense just how much he'll take and what kind of a mood he's in every day. For if you don't have a feel for him, he's liable to turn around and go wild. And it all depends on your sense of timing."

"Almost at once": Reedy, *Lyndon B. Johnson,* p. 137. **"It is difficult":** Tom Wicker, "Hey, Hey, LBJ . . . ," *Esquire,* Dec. 1983.

Index

ABC, 255, 356
Abell, Bess, 299–300
Abilene Reporter-News, 150
Acheson, Dean, 211, 516
Ackley, Gardner, 421–2, 423
Adams, John, 110, 113, 116, 537
Adams, Sherman, 283, 285
ADA World, 78
Adenauer, Konrad, 183
AFL-CIO, 98, 136, 142, 174, 492, 495
Agriculture Department, U.S., 162, 188, 513
    in 1965 budget debate, 478–9, 480
Air Force, U.S., 186–7, 265
Air Force One, 184, 186, 317, 329, 356, 386,
    502, 599
    in flight from Dallas to Washington, D.C.,
    ix, x–xi, 341–2, 354–5, 357–63
    in flight to Dallas, 309–10
Air Force Two, 329–30, 567
Alaska, 567
Albert, Carl, 178, 408, 485, 493
Alexander, Birge, 307–8
Alexander, Lucia Johnson, 307–8
Alger, Bruce, 149
Algeria, 32
Allen, Robert S., 267
Alliance for Progress, 454, 581
Alsop, Joseph, 53, 99, 185, 442, 595–6
American Association for the United
    Nations, 24

American Civil Liberties Union, 66, 242
American General Insurance Company, 524
American Jewish Congress, 78
American Power Company, 96
Americans for Democratic Action, 77
American Telephone and Telegraph, 408
Anderson, Clinton, 14, 155, 168, 554–5, 567
Anderson, Marian, 255
Anderson, Robert B., 69, 92, 397, 408, 464,
    475, 478, 482
anti-Semitism, 230–1
appropriations bill, 419, 455–6, 460–1, 499,
    501, 561, 594
Area Redevelopment Program, 455
Arends, Leslie C., 548
Arizona, 59, 93, 567
Arkansas, 66, 266
Arlington National Cemetery, 342, 385–6,
    414, 415, 572, 587
Army Corps of Engineers, U.S., 529
Arthur, Chester A., 114, 350
Arvey, Jake, 125
Associated Press, 194, 254, 275, 288, 357,
    504
Atlanta Constitution, 147
Atomic Energy Commission, 343

Bailey, John, 13, 14, 68, 125, 294
Bailey, Oreole, 505, 516–17, 519, 543

Baines, Huffman, 505, 519
Baker, Dorothy, 281
Baker, Robert G. "Bobby," xiii, 6, 17, 22, 33,
    60–1, 66, 68, 72, 74, 75, 81, 116, 134,
    139, 164, 166, 168–9, 199, 227, 243,
    249, 266, 310, 312, 473, 476, 499
  RFK's confrontation with, 106
  scandal of, *see* Baker scandal
  vice-presidency offer to LBJ as viewed by,
    118–20, 121
Baker, Russell, 174–5, 201, 519, 587
Baker scandal
  Baker's business transactions and, 289–90
  Baker's resignation in, 288–9
  campaign funds and, 297
  conviction in, 281
  D.C. stadium deal and, 292–4
  Fortas and, 318
  Johnson business holdings and, 308–9
  Johnson business kickbacks and, 284–5
  Lady Bird's "soft soap" in, 280–1
  LBJ Company and, 284–5
  LBJ's wealth and, 298
  Life's coverage of, 291–2, 296–9, 308, 313,
    521, 604
  media and, 278–80, 289–91
  Reynolds's revelations in, 283–7, 292–4,
    299, 308–10, 312–13
  RFK and, 291
  Senate reaction to, 288–9
  Serv-U Corp. lawsuit and, 276–8, 280
  sex in, 289–90, 296–7
  White House connection to, 290–1
  Williams's investigation of, 282–9, 292–4
Baldrige, Tish, 234
Ball, George, 211, 239, 365, 401
Baltimore Sun, 516, 518
Barksdale Air Force Base, 528
Barnes, Ben, 115
Barnett, Ross, 108, 207
Barr, Joe, 100
Bartlett, Charles, 124, 138, 142, 195–6, 224,
    272, 584
Bartlett, Edward L., 567
Battle, John S., 145
Baudouin, King of the Belgians, 385, 599
Bay of Pigs invasion, 182–7, 228, 240–2
Beaverbrook, Lord, 230–1
Beer, Sam, 409
Behn, Gerald, 358, 360
BeLieu, Kenneth E., 169, 207
Bell, Jack, 44–5, 194, 254
Ben-Gurion, David, 81–2
Berlin, Isaiah, 248
Berlin, Richard, 83
Bickel, Alexander, 236–7
Biemiller, Andrew, 492
Bigart, Homer, 538
Billings, Lem, 34–5, 45–6
Bissell, Richard, 242

Black, Fred, 278–9
Black, Hugo, 154
Black Jack (horse), 382, 385, 386, 599
Black Stars social club, 247
Blakley, William A., 296
Boatner, Charles, 204, 207
Boggs, Hale, 127–8, 257–8, 443, 493
Bohlen, Charles E. "Chip," 512
Boise, Tom, 74, 88
Bolling, Richard, 94, 485–6, 492, 498, 558,
    569–70
Bolshakov, Georgy, 236
Boozer, Yolanda, 505
Boston Herald, 433
Boston Post, 29, 231
Bowles, Chester, 235, 240–1, 243
Bradlee, Ben, 185, 197, 245, 265, 272, 374,
    574, 576, 578
Brinkley, David, 378–9, 380
Broder, David S., 78–9, 95
Broderick, Tom, 43
Brooklyn Eagle, 45
Brooks, Jack, 316–17, 319, 321–2, 324, 332
Brotherhood of Sleeping Car Porters, 488
Brough, Frank, 96
Brown, Clarence, 496–7, 498, 569
Brown, George R., 4–5, 6, 8, 72, 268, 524–7
Brown, Herman, 70, 160, 524
Brown, Pat, 70–1, 74, 100, 267, 409, 421
Brown & Root, 4, 8, 55, 70, 85, 160, 269,
    494, 524–5
Brown vs. Board of Education, 76, 445, 462
Bruce, David, 512
Bryan, William Jennings, 90
Bucharest, 214
Budget and Accounting Act of 1921, 350
Budget Bureau, 170, 263, 395, 421, 480, 544,
    552
  Agriculture Department and, 478–9, 480
  base-closing issue and, 513–14, 528
  Byrd and, 422–3, 474–8, 481–2, 484, 499,
    512–13, 540, 545, 552
  in State of the Union address, 512–13, 545,
    549
budget of 1965, 395–6, 397, 421–3, 516, 553
Bunche, Ralph, 231–2
Bundy, McGeorge, 224, 242, 248, 329, 358,
    361, 368, 374, 375–6, 377, 392, 400,
    409, 412, 414, 417, 424, 580, 582, 593
  in Cuban Missile Crisis, 208, 217–18, 220,
    221
  in JFK-LBJ transition, 365–6, 413
  in Johnson Ranch visit, 512–13
  Vietnam conflict and, 401–3, 535
Bundy, William P., 532
Burdick, Quentin N., 296–7
Burke, Vincent J., 349
Burkley, George G., 358
Burns, George, 482n
Burns, James MacGregor, 27, 347

Burris, Howard L., 186–7, 200
Busby, Horace, 71, 81, 92, 97, 103, 108, 112,
 131, 200, 250, 252, 256, 264, 286, 370,
 371, 427, 472, 521, 536, 544
 in bedtime episode, 405
 on LBJ moniker, 5–6
 at LBJ-RFK first meeting, 61–3
 LBJ's demeanor described by, 319, 332
 LBJ's reprimand of, 352
 LBJ's vice-presidential role and, 184,
 185–6
Busch, August, 79–80
Business Advisory Council, 408, 495
Byrd, Harry, 393–5, 397, 422–3, 431, 453,
 455, 458, 596
 background of, 467–9
 economic philosophy of, 468–9, 474–5
 LBJ's relationship with, 472–6, 553–4
 1965 budget debate and, 422–3, 474–8,
 481–2, 484, 499, 512–13, 540, 545, 552
 racism of, 468
 Roosevelt and, 471
 Senate power of, 466, 469–72
 tax bill and, 346, 347, 393–4, 395, 397,
 455, 464–5, 484, 498–9, 552, 555–7
Byrd, Harry Flood, Jr., 474
Byrd, Robert C., 13, 85, 168
Byrd, Westwood, 472
Byrd, William, 467

Califano, Joseph, 82, 249, 587
California, 59, 71, 74–5, 83, 140, 267, 592–3
Cambodia, 416
Camelot, 197–8
Candid Camera (TV show), 226, 344
Cannon, Clarence, 143, 456, 567
Capron, William M., 538, 540
Carlton, John "Jake," 472
Carousel Motel, 279, 289–90
Carpenter, Leslie, 71
Carpenter, Liz, 196, 299–300, 322, 331, 335,
 358, 360–2, 366, 427
Carr, Waggoner, 441
Carroll Arms, "Quorum Club" at, 290
Carswell Air Force Base, 529–30
Carter, Amon, Jr., 528–9
Carter, Amon, Sr., 529
Carter, Cliff, 316, 322, 331, 360, 367, 370–2,
 403, 414, 441
Castro, Fidel, 183, 240, 241–2, 440, 446, 447,
 574, 585
CBS News, 140, 141, 322–3, 356
Celler, Emanuel, 498, 558–9
Central Arizona Water Project, 567
Central Intelligence Agency (CIA), 170, 212,
 392, 400, 402, 450, 574
 in Bay of Pigs invasion, 183, 184
 Operation Mongoose of, 242, 574, 585
Chambers, James F., Jr., 522–3

Chaney, James, 565
Chapman, Oscar, 72, 98
Charleston (South Carolina) Courier, 280
Chavchavadze, Helen, 197
Chavez, Dennis, 14, 92
Chicago Daily News, 96, 289
Chicago Tribune, 203, 280, 307, 549
Childs, Marquis, 53, 171, 347, 393, 547, 560,
 595
China, People's Republic of, 402, 534
Choosing War (Logevall), 535
Christian Science Monitor, 71
Church, Frank, 92
Churchill, Pamela, 43
civil rights, xiv–xv, xix, 113, 348
 in Birmingham crisis, 257, 263
 clergymen's role in, 565–6
 congressional stalemate on, *see* Civil
 Rights Act of 1964
 Forty Acres incident and, 536–7
 LBJ's early voting record on, 8–9
 in Meredith crisis, 207–8, 239, 252
 Mississippi violence and, 565
 in presidential transition, 348–50
 in St. Augustine dinner episode, 251–5,
 406
 in State of the Union address, 547
Civil Rights Act of 1957, xiv, 9–10, 12, 57–8,
 75–8, 348, 431, 454, 491, 561
 Part III of, 76–7
Civil Rights Act of 1960, 57–8, 76, 98, 144,
 348, 431, 491, 561
Civil Rights Act of 1964, xv, 430–1, 482,
 538, 540, 554, 557, 558–64, 594, 601,
 604
 civil rights leaders and, 488–92
 cloture motions in, 564, 567, 568–9
 congressional deadlock on, xiv, 345–8,
 393–5, 452–60, 462–4
 discharge petition in, 485–8, 490, 492–6,
 498, 559–60
 filibuster on, 553–4, 567
 House passage of, 560, 569
 JFK and, 345–6, 462, 560–1
 LBJ's advice to JFK on, 345–6, 462
 LBJ's signing of, 569
 Leadership Conference and, 77, 496
 1964 election and, 345–8
 organized labor and, 492, 495–6
 RFK and, 562–3
 Senate passage of, 568–9
 southern attempts at compromise on,
 561–2, 566
Civil Rights Commission, 491
Civil War, U.S., 8
Clark, Edward A., 6, 21, 47, 54–5, 56, 82–3,
 87, 93, 115, 140, 151–3, 193, 257, 269,
 531–2
Clark, Joseph, 76–7, 101, 168, 457, 460–1
Clark, Ramsey, 237–8

Clark, Thomas, Harris, Denius & Winters, 531
Clark, Tom, 202, 237
Clements, Earle, 121, 127
Cleveland, Grover, 114n
Cleveland Plain Dealer, 267
Cliburn, Van, 509, 517, 591
Clifford, Clark, 587
Clifton, Ted, 272, 331, 333, 358, 360, 361, 382
Cloth Hat, Cap and Millinery Workers International Union, 136
cloture vote, 258–60, 564, 567, 568–9
Coates, Winnie, 224
Cohen, Ben, 15
Cohn, Roy, 64
Cold War, 95, 450
Collier, Everett, 525, 527
Collins, Chairman, 143
Collins, LeRoy, 107
Colmer, William M., 558
Colorado, 59, 93
Commerce Department, U.S., 460–1
Committee on Equal Employment Opportunity (CEEO), 172, 173–4, 196–7, 226, 243, 325
changed mandate of, 262–4
community action concept, 546
Congress, U.S., xv, xvi, 202, 238, 398, 530, 539
appropriations bills in, 455–6, 460–1, 499, 501, 561, 594
civil rights bill deadlocked in, 345–8, 393–5, 452–60, 462–4
court-packing scheme and, 452–3
LBJ's joint address to, 425–36
1948 election and, 457
southern coalition in, xiv, 453–5, 457–9
Warren Commission and, 440–1, 450–1
see also House of Representatives, U.S.; Senate, U.S.
Congressional Quarterly, 461
Congressional Record, 31
Congress of Racial Equality (CORE), 488
Connally, Ben, 55
Connally, John, 5, 8, 12, 16–17, 21, 55, 71, 81, 93, 97, 99, 103, 105, 106, 107, 108, 109, 139, 149, 151, 153, 190–1, 207, 228, 303, 506
JFK assassination and, 311, 313, 420–1
JFK's meeting with, 273–4
political rise of, 269–74
and vice-presidency offer to LBJ, 118–20, 121, 122, 123, 129–34, 137
Yarborough's feud with, 272, 301, 307, 309
Connally, Nellie, 190, 301, 311, 361, 371
Connally, Tom, 292
Connor, Bull, 257
Constitution, U.S., 161, 164, 239, 329, 456, 598
Article II of, 162, 328
Article I of, 161–2

separation of powers in, 161
Twelfth Amendment of, 161n
Twentieth Amendment of, 349
Twenty-fifth Amendment of, 161n
vice-presidential powers in, 161–3
Constitutional Convention of 1787, 161
Conway, Jack, 136, 140, 263–4
Cook, Donald, 96–7
Coolidge, Calvin, 114, 350
Cooper, John Sherman, 443
Corallo, Anthony "Tony Ducks," 65
Corbin, Paul, 583–4
Corcoran, Thomas G., 6, 7–8, 15, 25, 93, 111, 127–8, 181–2, 246
Corcoran & Rowe, 12
Cormier, Frank, 504–5, 507–8
Coronado, Thomas, 257, 492
Corpus Christi Caller-Times, 115
Cotton, Norris, 468
Council of Economic Advisers, 396, 421, 538
Cox, Archibald, 236–7, 444
Cox, Ava Johnson, 247, 520, 543
Crider, Ben, 3
Cronkite, Walter, 143, 323, 355–6
Cuba, xi, 182–3, 211–12, 240–1, 343, 440, 450, 512, 574, 600
Cuban Exile Brigade, 183
Cuban Missile Crisis, xi, xii, xiii, 208–24, 343, 375, 454, 575
blockade in, 211–14, 215
congressional meeting on, 215–16
ExComm meetings on, 208–9, 210, 211, 215, 216
JFK's television address and, 212
LBJ's bellicosity in, 211–12, 215, 216, 218–19, 222
onset of, 208
Oval Office conference on, 220–1
RFK in, 210–11, 213–15, 217, 220–3, 230, 239
Turkey-missiles trade in, 216–17, 219–22
U-2 shootdown in, 217, 219–20
war hawks in, 208–9, 215–16, 219–20, 222
Cushing, Richard Cardinal, 184
Cyprus, 512

Daley, Richard, 13, 14, 99, 100, 101, 125, 154
Dallas Junior Leaguers, 149
Dallas Morning News, 69, 129, 130, 307
Dallas Times-Herald, 521–2
Dallek, Robert, 52, 177, 183
Daniel, Price, 69, 154
Darden, William H., 209
Davis, James, 299
Davis, Mary, 28, 51
Davis, Sid, 334–5, 354, 356
Deadlock of Democracy, The (Burns), 347
Deathe, Earl, 287, 531–2

Defense Department, U.S., 170, 172, 264, 439, 460, 480, 540
  base closing issue and, 513–14
Defense Ministry, German, 291
de Gaulle, Charles, 194, 385, 388, 392–3, 415–18, 421, 512, 599
Delaware, 105, 246
Democratic Congressional Campaign Committee, 160
Democratic Midwest Conference, 79
Democratic National Committee, 72, 130, 133, 135–6, 262, 266, 368, 372, 583–4
Democratic National Convention of 1956, 7, 31–2, 49, 66–7, 111
Democratic National Convention of 1960, xii, 8, 98, 101, 229–30, 245–6
  floor fight threat in, 131–2, 140–2
  LBJ-JFK debate in, 102–5
  nominations in, 143
  opening of, 144–5
  vice-presidency issue in, 140–3
  voting in, 107–8
Democratic National Convention of 1964, 349, 350, 535–6
Democratic Party, Kansas, 83
Democratic Party, Texas, 303
Democratic Party, U.S., xiii, 49, 58, 70, 240, 395, 408, 527
  civil rights bill and, 486–7
Democratic Senatorial Campaign Committee, 24, 297
Denmark, 275, 278
Dent, Harry, 459
De Sapio, Carmine, 13, 14, 15, 97, 98–9, 100, 122, 125
Des Moines Register, 279–80, 283, 290
De Valera, Eamon, 388
Dewey, Thomas, 14
Dillon, Douglas, 211–12, 219–20, 222, 224, 248, 320, 394, 409, 421–3, 469–70, 481–2, 571
Dirksen, Everett, 288, 291, 408, 446, 547–8, 554, 561–2, 564–6, 568
  tax bill amendment of, 554–6
DiSalle, Mike, 13, 14, 67–8, 100, 125
Dobrynin, Anatoly, 220, 221–2, 378, 417
Docking, George, 59, 99
Dodd, Thomas J., 345, 457
Dolan, Joseph, 237
Douglas, Helen Gahagan, 180
Douglas, Paul, 77–8, 167, 168, 297, 453, 457, 468, 471
Douglas, William O., 29, 231, 235
Douglas-Home, Alec, 392–3
Downs, Bill, 141
Draper, Theodore, 183
Drennan, Lorin, 308, 310, 318
Drevlow, William E., 88
Drummond, Roscoe, 250, 596
Dubinsky, David, 142, 407

Duke, Angier Biddle, 177, 193, 197, 415, 417
Dulles, Allen, 442–3, 445, 449
Dungan, Ralph, 186–7, 207, 410, 491, 580, 588, 593
Duong Van (Big) Minh, 401
DuPont, 282
Dutton, Fred, 70–1, 138, 593

Eastland, James, 431, 440, 448, 471, 561
Economic Defense Board, 162
education bill, 499, 594
Edwards, India, 72, 78, 97, 189–90
Edwards, Willard, 280
82nd Airborne Division, U.S., 257
Eisenhower, Dwight D., 10–11, 15, 55, 69, 89, 98, 115–16, 118, 128, 144, 149, 151, 155, 172, 212, 268, 371, 378, 391, 392, 400, 408, 409, 419, 423, 435, 439, 454
Eisenhower Administration, 48, 188, 283
election of 1960, ix, x, 9, 21–2, 32, 266–7, 288, 295, 406, 418, 523, 538
  Adolphus Hotel incident in, 149–50
  age issue in, 95
  alleged fraud in, 154, 156
  black anti-Johnson sentiment in, 78–80, 98
  civil rights issue in, 57–8, 75–80, 98, 144, 348
  Democratic Convention in, *see* Democratic National Convention of 1960
  Democratic field in, 10, 14, 53
  health issue in, 96–7
  Indiana primary in, 87
  LBJ-Pat Brown meeting in, 70–1
  LBJ's central headquarters in, 71–2
  LBJ's criticism of JFK in, 95–6
  LBJ's southern campaign in, 144–50
  LBJ's strategy in, 11–16, 23–6, 54–5, 58–61, 87–91, 97–8
  LBJ's western tour in, 88–93
  LBJ-Woods meeting in, 79–80
  Mexican-American vote in, 151–5
  organized labor and, 98, 101
  Parr problem in, 55–6
  Parr's vote getting in, 150–5
  Pennsylvania delegate vote and, 100–2
  religious issue in, 84–6, 100
  southern vote in, 155–6
  televised debates in, 155
  Texas laws and, 54–5
  Texas vote in, 150–5
  U-2 incident and, 89
  western states in, 59–60, 72–5, 79, 83, 90–3, 107–8
  West Virginia primary in, 84–6, 87, 144
  Wisconsin primary in, 84
election of 1964, ix, xix, 112, 115, 264–7, 270–2, 294–6, 368, 395, 406, 408, 410, 413, 437, 511, 515–16, 526, 527, 539, 542, 578, 581, 604

election of 1964 *(continued)*
   civil rights bill and, 345–8
   drop Johnson rumors in, 264–70, 294–5, 307
   New Hampshire primary in, 351, 583
   RFK and, 410, 413, 536
   Texas and, 265–6, 268–73
elections
   of 1848, 8*n*, 113
   of 1876, 444
   of 1926, 467
   of 1928, 14
   of 1932, 99, 120
   of 1934, 471
   of 1937, 5, 11, 47
   of 1938, 423
   of 1940, 62, 160
   of 1941, 11
   of 1946, 5, 29, 40–43, 282
   of 1948, 5–6, 11, 13–14, 21, 47, 55, 56, 94,
      153–4, 227–8, 292, 453, 457
   of 1952, 15, 29, 32, 53, 100, 448, 471
   of 1954, 11, 54, 153
   of 1956, 7–8, 31–2, 49–50, 53, 55, 67, 100,
      151, 474
   of 1958, 23, 48, 99–100, 112, 115, 297
   of 1960, *see* election of 1960
   of 1961, 467
   of 1962, 151, 209, 210, 269
   of 1964, *see* election of 1964
   of 1968, 112, 115, 249–50, 265, 580, 588
   of 1972, 250
   of 2008, 527*n*
Ellender, Allen, 471
Ellington, Buford, 72, 145
Ely, Walter, 74, 75
Enemy Within, The (Robert Kennedy), 67, 238
Engle, Clair, 593*n*
Enterprise, USS, 378
Erhard, Ludwig, 388, 392, 506–10, 511, 517,
   591
Esquire, 249
Essex, USS, 213–14
Evans, Roland, 85, 94, 112, 139, 155, 164,
   167, 171, 187, 194, 195, 240, 255, 344,
   348, 394*n*, 412, 414, 424, 433, 448, 501,
   539, 554, 562
ExComm, xii, 208–13, 215–17, 220, 222, 223
Executive Order No. 11130, 442
Exercise of Power, The (Evans and Novak),
   412
Export-Import Bank, 397

Face the Nation, 71
Fairchild Stratos Corporation, 251–3
Fair Deal, 453, 537
Fair Employment Practices Commission
   (FEPC), 173, 174
Farley, Jim, 140
Farmer, James, 487–8, 491, 569

Faubus, Orval, 66
Fawcett, Truman, 19
Fay, Paul B. "Red," 265, 272
Federal Bureau of Investigation (FBI), 66,
   242, 290, 451
   JFK assassination investigation and, 392,
      441–2
Federal Communications Commission (FCC),
   286, 522
Federal Reserve, 409, 524
Feeney, Father, 231
Fehmer, Marie, 81, 187, 299, 322, 324, 326,
   328–30, 331, 336, 360–1, 367–8, 403–4,
   505, 530, 531–2
Feild, John G., 174
Feldman, Myer, 179, 181
Ferguson, Thomas C., 531–2
Fifth Marine Expeditionary Brigade, U.S.,
   223
Fillmore, Millard, 114, 350
financial aid bill, 397–8, 499, 501
Fine Arts Commission, 188–9
Finland, 225
Fish, Mary, 195
Fitzgerald, "Honey Fitz," 36
Fitzgerald, James F., 308
Fleeson, Doris, 91, 142, 282, 283, 434, 496
Fleishman, Alfred, 80
Florida, 107, 108, 145, 155
Ford, Gerald R., 443, 449, 495
foreign aid bill, 397–9, 414, 424–5, 501–2
Fortas, Abe, 15, 56, 82, 154, 174, 277–8, 279,
   318, 405, 427–8, 441, 443, 590
Fort Worth Star-Telegram, 528–9
Forty Acres Club, 536–7
Fowler, Henry H., 421, 478
France, 32
Frankel, Max, 266, 416–17
Frankfurter, Felix, 234
Fredericksburg Standard, 510
Frederika, Queen of Greece, 385, 388, 415
Freeman, Orville L., 118, 140, 142–3, 344,
   363, 376, 397, 422, 465, 478–9, 512,
   513, 593
Fritchey, Clayton, 205
Frost, Robert, 179
Fulbright, J. William, 215–16, 367, 368, 401
Fullerwood, Fannie, 251–3

Galbraith, John Kenneth, 141, 197, 397, 409,
   411, 427, 589
Gallagher, Mary, 333, 360
Gallo, "Crazy Joey," 65
Galloway, George B., 7
Garfield, James, 114
Garner, John Nance, 110, 120–1, 141
Garrison, Jim, 574
Gatov, Elizabeth, 198
General Accounting Office, 308

George Burns and Gracie Allen Show, 482n
Georgia, 265
Germany, Federal Republic of (West Germany), 262, 357, 506
Gettysburg Address, 255–6
Giancana, Momo "Sam," 65
Gibbons, William C., 534
Gilpatric, Roswell L., 220, 517
Glass, Carter, 471
Glimco, Joey, 65
Glynn (LBJ's valet), 331
Goldberg, Arthur, 142, 174, 368, 400, 407
Goldfine, Bernard, 283
Goldman, Eric F., 249, 410, 589
Gold Star Mothers, 41–2, 51
Goldstein, E. Ernest, 536–7
Goldwater, Barry, 250, 267, 268, 515, 567, 568, 597
Gonella, Ashton, 81, 150, 186, 198, 228, 243
Gonzalez, Henry, 301–2
Goodman, Andrew, 565
Goodwin, Doris Kearns, 45, 85–6, 170, 203, 206, 227, 411–12, 473, 562, 600
Goodwin, Richard, 203, 227, 235, 240, 244, 246, 249, 373, 409, 562, 577, 579, 581
Gordon, Kermit, 352, 395–6, 421–2, 465, 477–8, 479, 512, 539, 540–1, 543–4, 552, 593
Gore, Albert, 167, 168, 471
Gould, Jack, 50, 342–3, 386–7
Government Accounting Office, 282
Government Printing Office, 557
Graff, Henry, xi, 344
Graham, Katharine, 442, 464, 590
Graham, Philip, 9, 77, 103–4
   and vice-presidency offer to LBJ, 129–37, 138n
Grant, Ulysses S., 458–9, 595
Graves, Ralph, 318
Great Britain, 240
   Profumo Affair of, 290–1
Greater Houston Ministerial Association, 144
Great Society, xviii, 601
Greenland, 275
Gronouski, John, 479–80
Grozny, 217–18, 222–3
Gruening, Ernest, 567
Gugler, Eric, 437
Gulf of Tonkin, 534–5
Guns of August, The (Tuchman), 213
Gunther, John, 467
Guthman, Ed, 362, 571, 582–3

Hackett, David, 544
Haddad, William, 65
Haganah, 231
Haile Selassie, Emperor of Ethiopia, 385, 388, 415, 599

Halleck, Charles, 485–6, 490, 497, 499, 558, 559–60, 561
Hamilton, James, 566
Harbin, Estelle, 180
Hardeman, D. B., 15, 128, 150
Harding, Warren G., 48, 114
Harding Administration, 542
Harlow, Bryce, 148
Harper, Reverend, 391
Harriman, W. Averell, 240, 367, 368, 500, 582
Harrington, Michael, 538
Harris, Charles, 37
Hartke, Vance, 87, 471, 554–6
Hartson (NASA aide), 263–4
Hatcher, Andrew, 360, 485, 593
Hatcher, Jessie, 505
Hayden, Carl, 14, 93, 378, 461, 471, 567
Hayes, Rutherford B., 444
Head Start, xix, 604
Hearst, William Randolph, Jr., 30–1
Heller, Walter W., 352, 394n, 396–7, 409, 411, 421, 423, 478, 512, 593
   War on Poverty and, 538–41, 543
Hell's Canyon Dam, 59, 74, 90
Helms, Richard, 242
Henry V (Shakespeare), 237
Heren, Louis, 387
Herring, Charles, 11–12, 82, 98, 202
Herseth, Ralph, 88–9, 90, 91
Hersey, John, 37–8
Hickey, George, 316
Hill, Clint, 314, 381
Hill, Lister, 471
Hill, Ralph, 276–7, 283
Him and Her (Johnson family beagles), 500
Ho Chi Minh Trail, 534
Hoff, Irvin, 72–5, 93, 102, 105
Hoffa, Jimmy, 65–6, 233, 242, 577, 579
Hoffman, Frank Nordhoff "Nordy," 493
Holland, Spessard L., 251, 460
Holleman, Jerry R., 174
Holton, John, 128
Hoover, Allen, 368
Hoover, Herbert, 368
Hoover, J. Edgar, 291, 368, 392, 400, 441–2, 577, 585
Hopkins, Welly, 4, 101
House of Representatives, Texas, 4, 18, 503
House of Representatives, U.S., 5, 39, 43, 190, 258, 371, 383, 407, 418, 453, 459, 460, 482, 490, 603
   Appropriations Committee of, 72, 456
   Civil Rights Act of 1964 passed by, 560, 569
   in Constitution, 161
   discharge petition and, 485–8, 490, 492–6, 498, 559–60
   District of Columbia Committee of, 293
   Finance Committee of, 346

House of Representatives, U.S. *(continued)*
  Housing Committee of, 29
  JFK assassination inquiry in, 450
  Judiciary Committee of, 187, 346, 463,
    495, 498
  Rules Committee of, 260, 346, 463, 467,
    485–6, 493–4, 495, 497, 554, 558, 559,
    560, 569
  Un-American Activities Committee of, 440
  U.S.-Soviet wheat deal and, 501–2
  Ways and Means Committee of, 181, 455
  see also Congress, U.S.; Senate, U.S.
Houston, Sam, 505
Houston Chronicle, 207, 303, 523–7
Houston Endowment, 524
Hughes, Sarah T., 187–8, 328–9, 331–6, 356
Humphrey, Hubert, 96, 117, 178, 180, 288,
    407, 410, 428, 585, 590
  civil rights bill and, 260, 457, 563–9
  foreign aid bill and, 397, 398–9
  LBJ's power grab and, 164–5, 168
  in 1960 election campaign, 10, 14, 25–6,
    53, 54, 59, 70, 79, 83, 84–6, 87, 98, 107,
    246
Hunt, George P., 298, 308, 318
Hunt, H. L., 72
Hurst, J. Willis, 370–1, 543
Hurxthal, Lewis, 96

Iceland, 276, 279
Idaho, 59, 72, 74, 92
Ikeda, Hayato, 417
Illinois, 154, 156, 471, 568
Indiana, 13, 57, 87–8
Indonesia, 582, 584
Inside U.S.A. (Gunther), 467
Interior Department, U.S., 162, 480, 567
Internal Revenue Service, 66, 242, 282, 522
International Brotherhood of Teamsters, 65,
    66
International Ladies' Garment Workers
    Union, 142, 407
Iowa, 88, 99
Iran, 225, 543
Ireland, 293
isolationism, 64
Israel, 231
Itz, Anna, 21

Jacks, Herschel, 310, 313–14
Jackson, Albert, 521–3, 528
Jackson, Henry M. "Scoop," 118
Jackson, Robert M., 115
Jacobsen, Jake, 105
Janeway, Eliot, 82
Japan, 439
Javits, Jacob, 76
Jaworski, Leon, 55

Jefferson, Thomas, 113, 537
Jenkins, Walter, 6, 17, 23, 56, 96, 122, 123,
    131, 187, 189, 275, 284, 329, 332, 352,
    360, 361, 367, 369, 410, 498, 531, 588,
    592, 593, 594, 603
  Baker scandal and, 277–9, 281
  Lady Bird and, 192–3
  1960 campaign and, 12, 61, 68, 71, 72,
    74–5, 82, 83, 91–2
Jetton, Walter, 508
Jews, 230–1
John F. Kennedy Library, 170, 579
Johnson, Andrew, 8*n,* 114, 350
Johnson, Edwin "Big Ed," 93
Johnson, Eliza Bunton, 18
Johnson, Lady Bird, x, 7, 74, 80, 88, 106,
    109, 112, 121, 123, 130, 134, 141, 143,
    177, 185, 190–1, 197, 246–7, 248, 263,
    275, 319, 330, 352, 358, 360, 371, 429,
    437, 474, 477, 489, 516, 536, 552
  in Adolphus Hotel incident, 149–50
  Baker's phone conversation with, 280–1
  business holdings of, 284, 286
  Jenkins and, 192–3
  JFK assassination and, 310, 313–17,
    321–2, 323, 335, 361–3, 365–6
  in JFK funeral procession, 380–4, 400–1
  JFK's ranch visit and, 299
  Johnson Ranch Christmas vacation and,
    505–9, 513, 515, 520
  in move into White House, 388, 500–1
  in 1960 southern tour, 148, 149–50
  on Salinger's resignation, 593
Johnson, Lucia, 520
Johnson, Lucy Baines, 80, 141, 195, 316,
    437, 500–1, 505, 507
Johnson, Lynda Bird, 182, 195, 316, 437,
    500, 505–7, 513
Johnson, Lyndon B.
  "Bunton strain" legacy of, 519–20
  business interests of, 521–7, 530–2
  as champion of rights, 569–70
  childhood of, 3–4, 20, 204
  childhood poverty of, 542–3, 546–7, 550–1
  college years of, 159–60, 351–2
  compassion of, 484, 486, 536–7
  cruelty of, 584–5
  deception and secrecy of, 530–2, 536
  education of, 159–60, 351–2
  elected to House, 5
  elected to Senate, 6–7
  failure and humiliation feared by, 17, 21,
    74, 82, 193, 203, 353, 602
  family background of, 17–21
  first national political experience of, 160
  Gettysburg speech of, 255–7
  handshake technique of, 416–17
  heart attack of, 112, 181, 314–15, 474
  iconic swearing-in photograph of, 599
  illness of, 47–8

JFK misread by, 26–7, 32–3, 47–8
JFK's 1960 debate with, 102–5
JFK's vice-presidency offer to, 109–15,
    118–23, 132
Kennedy staff's contempt for, 187, 198,
    200–3, 225, 243, 325, 406, 410–11
LBJ moniker of, 5–6
in 1960 southern campaign, 144–50
personal image of, 536–7
physical descriptions of, 11, 20, 57, 204,
    225, 319, 331–2, 404, 430, 434–5,
    499–500, 504, 514–15, 520–1, 550
political genius of, 603–4
political pressure applied by, 521–9
popularity of, 594–5, 597
presidential ambition of, 3–5, 11–12, 16,
    21, 95, 348, 484
private phone lines of, 530–2
RFK's feud with, *see* Johnson–R. F.
    Kennedy feud
ruthlessness of, 521, 536
"sales pitch" of, 11–12
as Senate Majority Leader, 7, 15, 22–3,
    111–12, 160–1, 166–7, 245–6, 454
sense of conviction of, 82–4
southernness as liability of, 8–9, 114–15
speechmaking style of, 89–90, 145–6,
    255–7
vote-counting skill of, 245–6
wealth of, 298, 313
World War II experience of, 314
see also presidential transition of 1963
Johnson, Lyndon B., vice presidency of
    Agriculture Department appointment and,
        188–9
    Baker scandal and, *see* Baker scandal
    Bay of Pigs fiasco and, 182–7
    Camelot aura and, 197–8
    CEEO mandate change and, 262–4
    Cuban Missile Crisis and, *see* Cuban
        Missile Crisis
    "dump Johnson" rumor and, 264–70,
        294–5, 296, 307
    Finland visit and, 225
    foreign trips in, 193–4, 225
    formal dinner invitations sought by, 197–8
    at formal meetings, 202–3
    former Senate colleagues of, 180–1
    Gettysburg speech in, 348, 406
    Hughes appointment and, 187–8
    JFK-Connally meeting and, 273–4
    JFK's editing of LBJ's speech in, 272–3
    Kennedy Administration's civil rights bill
        and, 258–61
    Kennedy Administration's exclusion of,
        176–80, 183–6, 196–8, 200–2, 204–5,
        207, 224–6, 294–5
    LBJ's attempts to see JFK and, 195–6
    LBJ's demeanor and, 181–2, 195, 202–3,
        206–7

LBJ's gift giving and, 191–3
LBJ's Senate power grab and, 163–9
LBJ's waning influence in, 268–71
loyalty pledge and, 193, 195
media and, 193–4, 201, 203–5, 226
Meredith crisis and, 207–8
office issue and, 169, 172, 199–200
presidential succession matter and, 189
proposed executive order and, 169–72
psychological and physical toll of, 225–6
remembrance plaque episode and, 224
St. Augustine episode in, 251–5, 406
Senate sessions and, 199
Seward episode and, 184–5, 193
transportation issue and, 184–7, 243
White House dinners and, 180–1
Johnson, Magnus, 515
Johnson, Rebekah, 17, 18, 19, 520
Johnson, Sam Ealy, Jr., 17–21, 112, 486–7,
    515, 519, 520, 543
Johnson, Sam Ealy, Sr., 18
Johnson, Sam Houston, 17, 21, 187, 200
Johnson, Tom, 18
Johnson, U. Alexis, 211
Johnson Administration, 398, 530, 542
    Cuban fishing boats incident and, 575
    Kennedy team retained by, 596–7
    Kennedy team's departure from, 588–9
    1965 budget and, 478–9
Johnson Ranch, 17–18, 55, 543
    JFK's and Jacqueline's visit to, 299–300
    private phone system of, 530–1
    RFK's visit to, 71
Johnson Ranch Christmas vacation (1963),
    503–21
    business of state in, 512
    Erhard state visit and, 506–11, 517
    family photo session in, 504–5
    Joint Chiefs at, 512
    LBJ's image creation in, 511, 514–15,
        519–20
    media criticism of, 517–19
    1964 election and, 515–16
    outings in, 515–17
    press conferences in, 512–14
    press tour in, 505–6
    Stonewall state dinner in, 507–11
Johnson–R. F. Kennedy feud
    Corbin dispute and, 583–4
    first face-to-face encounter and, xii, 61–3
    Hughes appointment and, 187–8
    impact of, 587–8
    Indonesia mission and, 582, 584
    JFK and, 242–3
    and LBJ's public humiliation in meetings,
        263–5
    Mann appointment and, 581–2, 588
    mutual hatred in, 244–5
    remembrance plaque incident and, 224
    RFK on, 587

Johnson–R. F. Kennedy feud *(continued)*
  RFK's vulnerability and, 584–5
  social class and, 248–9
  and vice-presidency offer to LBJ, 139–40, 227–30
  White House misunderstood confrontation and, 374–7
Joint Chiefs of Staff, U.S., 183, 208–9, 213, 217, 381, 384, 402, 429, 439, 512, 517
Jones, James, 352
Jones, John T., Jr., 303, 523–4, 525–7
Jones, Larry, 72
Jones, Luther "L. E.," 17
Jones, Winnie, 303
Jordan, B. Everett, 289
Judd, Walter, 95
Just, Ward, 226
Justice Department, U.S., 187, 221, 228, 233, 243, 460, 461, 527, 571–2, 574
  Anti-Trust Division of, 524, 526
  "get Hoffa" squad of, 66, 242, 577
  RFK's staff at, 236–8

Kansas, 99
  Democratic Party of, 83
Kantol, Prince of Cambodia, 416
Kappel, Frederick, 408–9
Katzenbach, Nicholas deBelleville, 163, 174, 236, 325–6, 327, 328, 441, 444, 561–2, 564
Kefauver, Estes, 10, 26, 32, 48, 49–50, 53, 66, 67, 167
Kellam, Jesse, 520, 521–3, 531
Kellerman, Roy, 317, 357
Kempton, Murray, 280, 288, 572–3, 577, 579, 583
Kennedy, Caroline, 52, 191–2, 369, 379, 381, 383–4, 386, 388, 599
Kennedy, Dorothy, 106
Kennedy, Edward "Ted," 59–60, 61, 68, 91, 107, 234, 379, 385, 572
  in Chappaquiddick incident, 246
Kennedy, Ethel, 65, 232, 235, 247, 248, 571–2
Kennedy, Eunice, 41, 379
Kennedy, Jacqueline, x–xi, 30, 52, 191–2, 224, 234, 324, 364, 366, 380, 388, 437, 500, 571, 588–9
  in funeral procession, 381, 383–5
  JFK assassination and, 307, 311, 320–1, 329, 357–8, 362–3, 579, 599
  in Johnson Ranch visit, 299–300, 301, 302
  LBJ's gifts to, 191–3
Kennedy, John, Jr., 369, 379, 381, 383, 386, 599
Kennedy, John F., ix, x, xv, xvi, xvii, xviii, 10, 67, 70, 72, 79, 102, 124–5, 137, 141–2, 145, 163, 165, 201, 207, 234, 236, 271, 290, 292, 349, 434, 435, 452, 469, 470, 526, 546, 550, 564, 590, 594

Addison's disease diagnosis of, 43–4, 96–7
assassination of, *see* Kennedy, John F., assassination of
back ailment of, 30–1, 36–9, 42–3, 45–6, 51
Bay of Pigs fiasco and, 182–4
Big Steel crisis and, 205
celebrity of, 52–3
charm and charisma of, 34–5, 155
in Cuban Missile Crisis, 208–14, 216, 220, 222–4
descriptions of, 27–8, 51–2
funeral of, 381–6
Gold Star Mothers speech of, 41–2
illnesses of, 29–30, 33–5, 39–40, 43–4
inaugural speech of, 175, 427
in Johnson Ranch visit, 302–3
LBJ as treated by, 176–80, 184
LBJ's 1960 debate with, 102–5
LBJ's executive order request and, 169–72
LBJ's misreading of, 26–7, 32–3, 47–8, 174–5
LBJ's office request and, 169, 172
LBJ's Senate power grab and, 174–5
LBJ's vice-presidency talks with, 122–3, 132
marriage of, 30
as martyr, 600–1
McCarthy censure vote of, 48–9
in 1946 campaign, 40–3
in 1952 senatorial campaign, 29–30
in 1956 election, 31–2, 46, 49–51
in 1960 election, 56–7, 59, 61, 68, 71, 83, 84–7, 91, 92, 93, 94, 95–100, 101, 102–7
1964 Civil Rights Act and, 345–6, 462, 540–1
presidential succession concern of, 189
PT-109 saga of, 37–8
religion issue and, 84–5, 86, 100, 146–7
RFK's relationship with, 138, 228–9, 312, 573–4
Senate career of, 29–33, 44–5, 49, 52
shyness of, 29, 40
speechmaking style of, 51–2, 83
television medium and, 49–50
vice-presidency offer to LBJ by, 109–15, 118–23, 132, 138–9
women and, 28–30, 34–5
World War II service of, 28, 37–8
Kennedy, John F., assassination of
additional inquiries into, 450
Air Force One's flight to Washington, D.C. and, ix, x–xi, 354–5, 357–64
autopsy and, 373
conspiracy fears and, 320–1, 343, 354, 356–7, 401, 440–1, 574, 600
FBI and, 392, 441–2
JFK's death announced, 323
LBJ-RFK phone conversations and, 324–8, 332–3

LBJ's composed demeanor in, 314, 319–
    20, 324, 331–2, 365
LBJ's experience of, 313–15, 317–20, 324
LBJ's hospital vigil and, 317–18
LBJ's trip to back Air Force One after,
    321–2
prelude to, 300, 307–10
presidential motorcade and, 311–12
public reaction to, xi–xii, 354–5
race to Parkland Hospital and, 315
and RFK's grief and personality change,
    575–6
rumors and, 356–7
sound of gunshots and, 313–14
swearing-in ceremony and, 335–6, 356,
    599
swearing-in debate and, 322–9, 330, 331,
    332–3
television coverage of, xi–xii, 341–3
time of death dispute and, 355–6
see also presidential transition of 1963;
    Warren Commission
Kennedy, Joseph P., Jr., 36, 39, 40, 64
Kennedy, Joseph P., Sr., 27, 29, 30, 32, 34, 40,
    42, 46, 48, 62, 64, 65, 84, 85, 100, 103,
    105, 106, 141, 230, 232, 233–4
Kennedy, Kathleen (John Kennedy's sister),
    43, 232
Kennedy, Kathleen (Robert Kennedy's
    daughter), 232–3
Kennedy, Pat, 384
Kennedy, Robert F., xi, 29, 35, 85, 92, 97,
    103, 105, 107, 117, 122, 127, 141–2,
    144, 195, 196, 258, 262, 295, 312, 381,
    383, 385, 400, 561, 568, 603
anticommunism of, 235
anti-Semitism opposed by, 230–1
Baker scandal and, 291
Baker's confrontation with, 106
black-and-white outlook of, 235, 575
closed coffin decision of, 373–4
compassion and gentleness of, 234–5,
    576–7
Cuban Missile Crisis and, 210–11, 213,
    214–15, 220–3, 239, 242
death of, 578, 588
on dumping LBJ from 1960 ticket, 265–6
as father, 232–3
"get Castro" obsession of, 241–2
grief and personality change of, 571–9
Hoffa obsession of, 65–6, 242, 577
Hughes appointment and, 187–8
as instrument of JFK, 240–1, 243
JFK assassination crisis and, 324–8, 362–4,
    373–4
JFK's legacy and, 577–8
JFK's relationship with, 138, 228–9, 312,
    573–4
Joseph Kennedy's stroke and, 233–4
Justice Department staff of, 236–8

LBJ assessed by, 579–80
LBJ's feud with, see Johnson–R. F.
    Kennedy feud
LBJ's first encounter with, xii, 61–3
LBJ's transportation requests and, 243
on McCarthy Committee, 64–5
on McClellan Committee, 66–7
at 1956 Democratic Convention, 66–7
1960 campaign and, 67–8
1964 Civil Rights Act and, 562–3
1964 election and, 410, 413, 536
presidential ambition of, xii–xiii
reading habit of, 238
rudeness of, 240–1
ruthless streak of, 63–5, 68, 230, 232, 239,
    575–6, 578
speechmaking of, 65
temper of, 231–2, 240–1
underdogs favored by, 231–2, 233
University of Virginia incident and, 231–2
vice-presidency offer to LBJ opposed by,
    122–5, 129–38
Vidal on, 249–50
in visit to Johnson Ranch, 71
vote counting by, 245
Warren Commission appointments of,
    442–3, 445
Warren Commission report doubted by,
    574–5
Kennedy, Rose, 34, 45, 100, 231, 234, 361
Kennedy, Tom, 101
Kennedy Administration, xvii, 398, 457, 475,
    481, 603
Camelot aura of, 197
LBJ's exclusion from, 176–80, 183–6,
    196–8, 200–2, 204–5, 207, 224–6, 294–5
proposed civil rights legislation of, 258–61,
    489–90
southern conservative coalition and, 454–5
vice-presidency offer debate and, 116–18,
    126–7, 133–4, 344–5
Kennedy and Johnson (Lincoln), 295
Kentucky, 59, 106, 108, 267
Kerr, Robert, 123, 164–5, 280, 471–2
Keynes, John Maynard, 469
Khmer Serei, 416
Khrushchev, Nikita, 89, 95, 211, 213–14,
    216–20, 221, 223, 236, 359, 393, 440,
    446–7, 512, 548
Kiker, Douglas, 511, 518
Kilday, Owen, 151
Kilday, Paul, 151, 154
Kilduff, Malcolm, 321, 323, 331–3, 335,
    355–6, 357, 360, 367–8
Kilgore, Joe, 11–12, 16, 115, 270, 427, 433–4
Kimovsk, 214
King, Martin Luther, Jr., xviii, 155, 257, 407–
    8, 488, 490, 491, 493, 565, 569
Kirwan, Mike, 72
Knight, John, 534

Knowland, William, 10–11
Korean War, 283
Krock, Arthur, 45, 93, 548–9
Krulak, Victor H. "Brute," 533–4
KTBC-TV, 284, 285n, 286–8, 308, 312, 520, 531
Kuchel, Thomas, 564
Ku Klux Klan, 565

Labor Department, U.S., 199
Lambert, William, 298, 308, 318
Landau, Jack, 276, 282
Lanin, Lester, 197
Laos, 236
Lawrence, David L., 13, 14, 57–8, 99–102, 116, 117, 122, 125, 131, 143, 400, 429, 435
Lawrence, W. H., 15, 87
Lawson, Marjorie, 263–4
LBJ Company, 187, 308
LBJ Ranch, *see* Johnson Ranch
Leadership Conference on Civil Rights, 77, 496, 565
League of Nations, 542
Lee, Robert E., 458–9, 467
Legislative Process in Congress, The (Galloway), 7
Lehman, Herbert, 167
Lehman, Robert, 409
Lend-Lease, 240
Levinson, Larry, 587
Lewis, Anthony, 64, 494, 497
Lewis, John L., 101
Life, xiii, 52, 228, 230, 242, 309, 318, 347, 443, 456, 499
    Baker scandal covered by, 291–2, 296–9, 308, 313, 521, 604
Lincoln, Abraham, 8n, 114, 171–2, 192, 223, 320–1, 340, 373, 379, 542, 560, 568, 569–70, 595
    Gettysburg Address of, 255–6
Lincoln, Evelyn, 45, 118, 172, 178, 184–5, 191–2, 196, 197–8, 207, 224–5, 271, 295–6, 335, 357, 360, 374
Lincoln, Gould, 250
Linton, Ron, 243
Lippmann, Walter, 347, 456, 550
Lisagor, Peter, 96, 518
Liston, Sonny, 241
"Little Congress," 160
Lloyd, Bill, 392
Lodge, Henry Cabot, Jr., 29, 44, 144, 401–2, 532
Loftus, Joseph, 98
Logevall, Fredrik, 535
Long, Edward V., 296
Long, Huey, 467
Long, Russell, 425n, 465, 469, 470, 474, 481, 483

Longworth, Alice Roosevelt, 238
Look, 52, 71
López Mateos, Adolfo, 69
Lord, Thorn, 93
Los Angeles Times, 123, 307, 349, 517–18, 592
Louisiana, 155, 156, 266
Louviere, Vernon, 207
Loveless, Herschel C., 24, 88, 94, 99
Lübke, Heinrich, 385
Lucas, Scott, 458
Luce, Clare Boothe, 115
Luce, Henry R., 115
Lyndon B. Johnson Library, 170, 353

Maas, Peter, 576
Macapagal, Diosdado, 385, 388
MacArthur, Douglas, 443
Macdonald, Dwight, 538
Macdonald, Torbert, 35
Macmillan, Harold, 216, 290–1
MacNeil, Neil, 166, 475, 553
Mafia, 450, 460, 577
Magnavox Company, 285, 312
Magnuson, John, 63–4
Magnuson, Warren, 72, 472
Maguire, Richard, 294, 368, 584
Making of the President, 1960, The (White), 156
Malaysia, Federation of, 582–3
Malechek, Dale, 205, 507, 513
Malechek, Jewel, 507
Manatos, Mike, 344, 481
Manchester, William, 302, 328, 330, 363, 369, 376
Mankiewicz, Frank, 574
Mann, Thomas C., 581, 588
Mansfield, Mike, 14, 91, 92, 125–6, 178, 180, 288, 291, 383–4, 393–4, 397, 475, 533, 547, 557, 563, 566–7, 568
    Dodd's criticism of, 345
    LBJ's power grab and, 164–5, 167–9
    Mundt amendment and, 398–9, 415
Marks, Leonard, 75, 81
Marsh, Charles, 4–5, 25
Marshall, Burke, 236, 263, 561
Martin, John Bartlow, 135, 242, 579
Martin, Louis, 262
Martin, William McChesney, 409
Maryland, 86, 285
Massachusetts, 344
Mayer, Margaret, 521–3, 528
Mazo, Earl, 153
McCall's, 52
McCammon, Vicky, 505, 530–1
McCarthy, Eugene, 102
McCarthy, Joseph, 28, 48, 61–2, 64, 97, 105, 131, 230, 231, 235, 282
McClellan, John, 66, 289, 460, 471

McClellan Committee, 66–7, 233
McClendon, Sarah, 81, 87, 278–9
McCloskey, Matthew, 116, 125, 293, 308
McCloskey & Company, 293–4
McCloy, John J., 442–3, 445, 449
McCone, John, 212–13, 375, 392, 400, 401, 402, 512, 574
McCormack, John W., 31, 84, 143, 178, 376–7, 378, 383, 463, 485, 492–3, 501, 513
McCracken, Tracy, 107, 108
McCulloch, William M., 486, 495, 561, 568, 569
McDonald, Admiral, 517
McDonald, David, 142, 407, 493
McDowell, Bart, 275–6
McFarland, Ernest, 448
McGrory, Mary, 89, 91, 97, 147, 148–9, 288, 364, 368, 434, 573
McHugh, Godfrey, 331, 333, 357–8, 360
McIntyre, Thomas J., 287, 425n
McKinley, William, 114
McKinnon, Clinton D., 74–5
McMahon, Pat "Pappy," 37–8
McNamara, Robert, 173, 228, 242, 248, 380, 387, 391, 400, 424, 478, 512, 517, 535, 549, 580, 593
  bases closings issue and, 513–14
  Cuban Missile Crisis and, 213–14, 217, 220, 222–4
  JFK assassination and, 357, 365–6, 373
  LBJ's transportation issue and, 187, 210
  Vietnam conflict and, 401–2, 532, 536
McPherson, Harry, 179–80, 226, 244, 264, 412
Means, Marianne, 203
Meany, George, 98, 136, 142, 492, 493, 496
  LBJ's telephone conversation with, 406–7
Medicaid, xix, 604
Medicare, xix, 455, 604
Meet the Press, 564
Meredith, James, 207–8, 239, 252
Mesta, Perle, 195
Metcalf, Lee, 93
Meyner, Robert, 53, 59, 105
Miami Herald, 226
Michigan, 79, 137, 140
Mid-Atlantic Stainless Co. Inc., 285n
Mikoyan, Anastas, 388, 392–3, 415, 417, 421
Miles, Marvin, 123
Military Air Transport Service (MATS), 186–7, 210, 243, 253
Miller, Fishbait, 429
Miller, Loye, 404–5, 426
Miller, Merle, 426
Miller, Ray, 68
Mills, Wilbur, 181
minimum wage, 454, 538
Minnesota, 59, 78, 92
Mississippi, 108, 155, 156
  civil rights violence in, 565
  Meredith crisis in, 207–8, 239, 252

Missouri, 59, 155
Mitchell, Andrea, 278
Mitchell, Clarence, 466, 491, 565
Model Cities, 604
Mohole (ocean drilling project), 494
Mollenhoff, Clark, 283, 290
Mongoose, Operation, 242, 574, 585
Monroney, Mike, 102, 567
Montana, 59, 72, 91–2, 93
Mooney, Booth, 68, 72, 201
Morgenthau, Robert, 238, 577
Morse, Wayne, 209–10, 288
Moss, Frank Edward, 297
Moursund, A. W., 504, 516, 530–2
Moursund & Ferguson, 531
Moyers, Bill, 133, 150, 204, 331, 359, 360–1, 366, 367, 370–2, 408, 426, 428, 445, 543, 592, 594
  Forty Acres Club incident and, 536–7
  on LBJ's transformed demeanor, 404–5
Moynihan, Daniel Patrick, 204
Mundt, Karl E., 397–9, 414, 424–5, 461, 501–2, 566
Murphy, Bruce, 56
Murphy, George, 593n
Murrow, Edward R., 64, 140, 143
Mutual Contempt (Shesol), 244

Nashville Tennessean, 230
Nathan, Robert, 140
National Aeronautics and Space Administration (NASA), 173, 559–60
National Aeronautics and Space Council, 163, 172–3, 199, 205, 226, 280
National Association for the Advancement of Colored People (NAACP), 57, 98, 466, 488, 491, 496, 566
  St. Augustine dinner episode and, 251–4
National Bank of Commerce (Houston), 523–4
National Broadcasting Company, xi
National Council of Churches, 496, 566
National Guard, Alabama, 257
National Guard, Mississippi, 207
National Interreligious Convocation, 565
National Opinion Research Center, 342–3
National Press Club, 278, 528
National Science Foundation, 494
National Security Action Memorandum (NSAM), 273, 403, 532
National Security Council, 163, 172–3, 177, 179, 199, 202, 226, 227, 240, 359, 575
National Urban League, 407, 488
National Youth Administration (NYA), 541, 546
Navy, U.S., 36
NBC, 386
Nelson, Richard H., 367–8
Neustadt, Richard, xiii, 170, 340, 343, 349–51

Nevada, 59
Neville, Mike, 41
New Deal, 5, 268, 411, 452–3, 537, 550
New Frontier, 198, 248, 271, 434
New Hampshire, 351, 583–4
New Jersey, 105
New Mexico, 59, 92–3, 155
New Republic, 280
Newsweek, xi, 14, 142, 280, 287, 289, 320,
    322, 334, 341, 345, 357–8, 425, 435,
    497, 549–50, 596
New York Daily News, 291, 296, 549
New Yorker, 28, 37, 538, 596
New York Herald Tribune, 31, 142, 153, 250,
    436, 449, 511, 518, 549
New York Post, 52, 348, 349, 549
New York State, 86, 136, 140, 240
New York Times, xi, 15, 32, 49, 70, 86, 93, 94,
    98, 117, 135, 173, 174, 181, 201, 230,
    258, 267, 283, 343, 355, 356, 380, 385,
    388, 393, 403, 416, 433–4, 485, 491,
    494, 497, 514, 517, 518, 529, 538, 547,
    549, 553, 558, 559, 560, 571, 594
Ngo Dinh Diem, 401, 585
Ngo Dinh Nhu, 401
Nixon, Richard M., xix, 10–11, 54, 78, 116,
    142, 144, 147, 148, 150, 155, 156, 163,
    516, 523, 597, 604
Nokes, George, 104
North American Aviation, 276, 279
North American Newspaper Alliance, 278–9
North Atlantic Treaty Organization (NATO),
    216, 218, 417
North Carolina, 266
North Dakota, 105, 246
Novak, Robert, 85, 94, 112, 139, 155, 164,
    167, 171, 187, 194, 195, 255, 344, 348,
    394*n,* 412, 414, 424, 433, 448, 501, 539,
    554, 562
NSAM, 273, 403, 532
Nuclear Test Ban Treaty, xiii

Obama, Barack, 527*n,* 569
O'Brien, Elva, 180
O'Brien, Lawrence F., 126–7, 137, 138,
    140–1, 164, 179, 180, 181, 294, 332,
    333–5, 357, 359, 360, 373, 399, 429, 481
    discharge petition and, 485, 487, 493,
        496–7, 498, 559
    in JFK-LBJ transition, 344–5, 409, 593
    U.S.-Soviet wheat deal and, 414–15, 424
O'Donnell, Kenneth, x, 63, 67, 68, 178, 180,
    183, 189, 195–6, 197, 213, 258, 271,
    272, 294, 360, 373, 435, 550, 577, 581,
    592, 598
    Hughes appointment and, 187–8
    in JFK-LBJ transition, 344–5, 409, 593
    JFK's assassination and, 309, 311, 317–21,
        327, 329, 330–6, 354, 357, 359, 550

and JFK's instructions on treatment of LBJ,
    176–7, 186
    JFK's ranch visit and, 299–300, 302
    and vice-presidency offer to LBJ, 117,
        123–5, 136–7, 138, 140, 165
Office of Civil and Defense Mobilization, 170
Of Thee I Sing (Gershwin), 110
Ohio, 67–8, 156, 267
Oklahoma, 59, 96, 108, 267
Oltorf, Frank C. "Posh," 269, 292, 314–15
Omnibus, 50
O'Neill, Thomas P., Jr. "Tip," 83–4
On the Waterfront (film), 238
Operation Mongoose, 242, 574, 585
Operations Plan 34-A-64 (OPLAN 34-A),
    403, 533
Oregon, 59, 90
organized labor, 492, 495–6
    1960 election and, 98, 101
    presidential transition and, 406–7
    vice-presidency offer to LBJ opposed by,
        136–7, 140–2
O'Sullivan, Ulrick, 357
Oswald, Lee Harvey, xi, 341–2, 356, 359,
    380, 392, 400, 440, 450, 574, 585
    murder of, 386–7, 388, 401
Other America, The (Harrington), 538
Oval Office, 437–40, 479
    Cuban Missile Crisis conference in, 220–1
    iconic aura of, 439
    LBJ in, 439–40
    origin of, 437
    size and shape of, 435

Pace, Frank, 169
Park Chung Hee, 385
Parr, George Berham, 55–6, 150–5
Patman, Wright, 20, 127
Patterson, Eugene, 147
Patterson, Floyd, 241
Peace Corps, xiii, 204, 331, 372, 430, 454,
    536
Pearl Harbor attack, 210, 417, 444
Pearson, Drew, 69, 92, 145
Pearson, Lester, 417
Peek, Scott, 251–3
Pennsylvania, 58, 99–102, 156
Pentagon Papers, 535
People's Party, U.S., 90
Perry, Arthur, 96
Petroleum Club, 269
Philadelphia Inquirer, 267
Philip, Duke of Edinburgh, 385
Phinney, Carl L., 149
Pierpoint, Robert, 322
Poland, 273
poll tax, 467
Porter, Paul, 56
Post Office Department, U.S., 479–80

Potter, Phil, 516, 518–19
poverty, 538–9, 542–3
  in LBJ's childhood, 546–7, 550–1
  in State of the Union address, 546–7, 549
  see also War on Poverty
Powers, Dave, 41–2, 44, 222, 299, 311, 344,
  357–8
Prendergast, Mike, 13, 14, 15, 99
Prendergast, Tom, 467
presidential transition of 1963
  achievement of, 600–1
  anxiety and, 343–4
  assessment of, 598–9
  Cabinet meetings in, 371, 374–7, 400
  civil rights leadership and, 407–8
  congressional address in, 376–7
  congressional leadership and, 358, 361,
    369, 400
  continuity theme of, 345, 351, 365–7,
    376–7, 399, 402, 408–9, 511, 538, 544,
    581, 588, 594, 597, 600
  economic team meeting in, 421–4
  foreign policy in, 368–9, 392
  JFK's funeral in, 385–6
  JFK's martyrdom and, 600–2
  joint session of Congress in, 425–36
  Kennedy Administration's legislation and,
    345–8, 419
  Kennedy staff in, 344–5, 351, 358–61,
    365–6, 368, 406, 409–14
  labor union leadership in, 406–7
  LBJ's in-command demeanor in, 368, 371,
    404–5, 421–2, 602–3
  LBJ's letter to JFK's children and, 369
  LBJ's sense of inferiority and insecurity in,
    351–3
  lying in state period in, 378–85
  machinery of government in, 349–51
  media coverage of, 378–80, 386
  memorial service in, 391–2
  national day of mourning in, 380, 400
  in previous administrations, 114, 340–1, 350
  state governors conference in, 418–21
  success of, 598
  television medium in, 341–3
  time constraint factor in, 349–51
  of Truman, 340–1
  viewing of JFK's coffin in, 384–5
  world leaders and, 392–3, 415–18
President's Committee on Juvenile
  Delinquency and Youth Crime, 544
Profiles in Courage (John F. Kennedy), 590
Profumo, John, 291
Provence, Harry, 278–9, 400
Proxmire, William, 111, 168
Pryor, "Cactus," 509, 511
PT-59, 39, 410
PT-109, 37–8, 39
Purdue University, 559–60
Pursuit of Happiness, The (film), 49

Queen Elizabeth, 43
Queen Mary, 231
Quorum Club, 290, 296

Randolph, A. Philip, 488, 491
Rather, Mary, 319
Rauh, Joseph L., Jr., 77, 117, 136, 142, 348,
  565–6
Rayburn, Sam, 8, 14, 15, 25, 29, 31, 50, 68–9,
  72, 81, 94, 97–8, 104, 106–7, 110, 120,
  129, 130, 133, 135, 178, 204–5, 328,
  433, 473, 485–6, 500
  decline and death of, 190–1
  Hughes appointment and, 187–8
  vice-presidency offer to LBJ opposed by,
    111, 116–17, 119, 121–2, 126–9, 131–2,
    134, 137, 143
Read, Benjamin H., 415–18
Reardon, Ted, 410
Redbook, 52
Reedy, George, 80, 108, 118, 174, 177, 184,
  200, 250, 257, 261, 268, 272, 273, 275,
  285, 307, 332, 352, 360, 367, 368–9,
  377, 399, 400, 407, 410, 421, 473, 511,
  532, 593, 594, 603
  Baker scandal and, 277–80, 298
  on Johnson-Kennedy feud, 63, 244
  on LBJ, 16, 82–3, 163, 167, 170–1
  on 1957 civil rights bill, 10, 13
  1960 campaign and, 24, 58, 68, 73, 87,
    103, 107, 112, 144
  St. Augustine incident and, 251–4
  vice president's role memo of, 206
  on wheat deal, 398
Reich, Charles, 56
Rembert, Clyde, 522
Reporter, The, 226, 467, 549–50
Republican National Convention of 1964,
  567, 569
Republican Party, U.S., 150–1, 152, 155, 156,
  432, 486–7, 494–7
Reston, James, 70, 77, 86–7, 94, 351, 393,
  433, 435, 580, 594–5, 597
Reuther, Walter, 122, 136, 140, 142, 263, 407
Reynolds, Don B., 282–7, 289, 299, 310, 318,
  499, 604
  Senate testimony of, 308–9, 312–13
Reynolds, John, 409
Riata Club, 269
Ribicoff, Abe, 125, 142, 471, 554–5
Richardson, Sid, 12, 71, 270
Richmond Times-Dispatch, 462
Riley, John J., 243
Roberts, Chalmers, 436, 472
Roberts, Charles, 320, 334, 336, 357–8, 362
Roberts, Emory, 317, 320, 322
Roberts, Juanita, 255–6, 367–8, 391–2, 400,
  403–4, 437, 488, 555
Roberts, Owen, 444

Robertson, A. Willis, 471
Rockefeller, Nelson, 597
Rogers, William P., 76
Rolvaag, Karl, 409
Rometsch, Ellen, 290–2, 296–7
Romney, George, 400
Roncalio, Teno, 73, 107
Roosevelt, Eleanor, 24, 70
Roosevelt, Franklin D., xii, 4, 5, 27, 45, 49,
    58, 62, 85, 99, 114, 115, 140, 141, 162,
    173, 179, 268, 314, 324, 340, 376, 423,
    469, 537, 550
  Byrd and, 471
  court-packing scheme of, 452–3
  death of, 341–3
  Harry Byrd and, 471
  Oval Office and, 437, 438–9
Roosevelt, Franklin D., Jr., 85–6, 246
Roosevelt, Theodore, 114, 350
Rose, Alex, 136, 142, 407
Ross, E. P., 247
Ross, Kitty Clyde, 247
Rotary Club, 41
Rovere, Richard, 465, 596
Rowan, Carl, 225
Rowe, Elizabeth, 182
Rowe, James H., Jr., 4, 7, 9, 15–16, 17, 50,
    60, 85, 93, 102, 129, 131, 136, 149, 171,
    173, 181–2, 412
  Armageddon memo of, 13–14
  LBJ's relationship with, 25
  1960 election and, 54, 59, 87, 91–2
  and vice-presidency offer LBJ, 109–11,
    118, 120–1, 123, 132–4
Rowe, James M., 115
Rowley, James J., 371
Royal Highland Regiment, 385
Ruby, Jack, 386, 440
Runyon, John W., 522
Rural Electrification Administration (REA), 5
Rusk, Dean, 173, 196, 202, 207, 219–21, 320,
    376, 380, 387, 391, 400, 401, 409, 413,
    415–16, 424, 478, 507, 510, 512, 513,
    533, 593
Russell, Jan Jarboe, 300
Russell, Richard Brevard, xiv, 111, 173, 461,
    465, 467, 471, 566, 582
  civil rights issues and, 8–9, 10, 76–7, 258,
    260, 347, 423, 431, 457–9, 462, 464,
    497, 563, 567, 568
  Cuban Missile Crisis and, 209–10, 215–16
  LBJ and, 8–9, 348, 431
  LBJ's power grab and, 164, 169
  Warren Commission appointment of,
    443–9
Russell, Robert E. Lee, Jr., 447

Sackett, Russell, 298
St. Augustine dinner, 251–5, 406
St. John, George, 34

St. Lawrence Seaway project, 30, 44–5
St. Louis Argus, 79
Salinger, Pierre, 124, 136, 183, 225–6, 320,
    321, 402, 409, 413, 429, 446, 553,
    571–2, 585, 593–4, 597, 603
  LBJ's treatment of, 514, 590–3
  resignation of, 590–3
Saltonstall, Leverett, 30
Samuelson, Paul, 409
Sanders, Governor, 429
Sanford, Terry, 255, 295
Saturday Evening Post, 29–30, 52, 468
Saxon, James J., 524, 527
Sayre, Francis B., 263
Scammon, Richard, 294, 539
Schary, Dore, 49
Schell, Jonathan, 343–4
Schlesinger, Arthur M., Jr., 32, 104, 118, 124,
    129, 135, 196–7, 204, 217, 223, 231,
    232, 233, 248, 261, 266, 374, 376, 397,
    413, 429, 574–5, 577, 581–2, 585–6,
    591, 593–4
  on "dump Johnson" plans, 294–5, 296
  in JFK-LBJ transition, 344, 409–10, 411
  on JFK-RFK relationship, 228–9
  on LBJ-RFK relationship, 176, 177,
    179–80, 244–5
  resignation of, 588–9
  RFK's friendship with, 67
Schreiber, G. R., 277
Schroeder, Gerhard, 507
Schulberg, Budd, 238–9
Schwerner, Michael, 565
Scott, Paul, 267
Scranton, William, 418, 597
Seaborg, Glenn T., 173
Second Bomb Wing, U.S., 528
Second Infantry Division, U.S., 257
Securities and Exchange Commission
    (SEC), 27
Seigenthaler, John, 103, 229–30, 232,
    572–3
Senate, U.S., x, xv, 48, 172, 344, 371, 383,
    395, 418, 431, 444, 456, 482, 603
  Agriculture Committee of, 471
  Appropriations Committee of, 259–60,
    460–1, 471
  Armed Services Committee of, 209, 461,
    471
  Baker scandal reaction in, 288–9
  Banking Committee of, 471
  civil rights bill in, 558, 560–9
  cloture vote in, 258–60
  in Constitution, 161
  court-packing proposal and, 452–3
  Democratic Campaign Committee of, 94,
    393–4
  Democratic Steering Committee of, 111,
    165, 167, 296, 471
  filibuster rule of, 75, 111, 258–60, 452–3,
    459–60

Finance Committee of, 282, 346, 393–4, 397, 422, 423, 455, 462, 466–72, 474, 476–7, 481, 552, 553–4, 555
Foreign Relations Committee of, 32, 92, 106, 292, 367, 401
Government Operations Committee of, 471
Judiciary Committee of, 76, 296, 440, 471, 561
Labor Committee of, 471
LBJ as Majority Leader of, 7, 15, 22–3, 111–12, 160–1, 166–7, 245–6, 454
LBJ's power grab in, 163–9
Naval Affairs Committee of, 36
1958 election and, 75
quorum call tactic of, 563–4
Rackets Committee of, 65, 233, 242, 244
Reynolds's testimony to, 308–9, 312–13
Rules Committee of, 289, 291, 296, 299, 308–9, 310, 318, 604
tax bill passed by, 556–7
U.S.-Soviet wheat deal in, 398–9, 424–5, 499, 561
vice president's constitutional powers and, 161–3
see also Congress, U.S.; House of Representatives, U.S.
Serv-U Corporation, 276–80, 282, 288, 296
Sevareid, Eric, 596
Seventh Heavy Bomb Wing, U.S., 530
Seward, William H., 171–2, 184, 321
Shakespeare, William, 237, 238, 351
Shannon, William V., 52, 349, 409, 456, 541–2
Shesol, Jeff, 138*n*, 195, 197
Shoup, David M., 517
Shreveport Journal, 528
Shreveport Times, 528
Shriver, Sargent, 204, 368, 377, 407
Sidey, Hugh, 23, 24, 62, 96, 110, 184, 201, 247, 352, 369, 388, 405, 424, 433, 598
Siegel, Gerry, 473
Sihanouk, Prince, 416
Sinclair, Ivan, 367
Smathers, George, 24, 29, 31, 33, 52, 108, 164, 167, 178, 182, 234, 251, 265, 393, 394–5, 397, 398, 465, 472, 477, 554–5
Smith, Alfred E., 14, 99
Smith, E. Babe, 542–3
Smith, Howard J., 260, 346, 463–4, 465, 467, 485–6, 488, 492, 495, 496–7, 498, 499, 558–60, 569, 596
Smith, Jean Kennedy, 103, 383, 573
Smith, Merriman, 334, 357–8
Smith, Stephen, 266, 294–5
Social Science Research Council, 342
Social Security, 454–5, 538
So Relle, Ella, 247
Sorensen, Stephen, 512
Sorensen, Theodore, 49, 53, 97, 116, 156, 179, 182, 185, 258, 261, 294, 295, 352, 358, 375, 398, 410, 429, 484, 545, 561, 593–4

Cuban Missile Crisis and, 209–11, 213, 215–18, 220–4
Edwards episode and, 189–90
on JFK-LBJ relationship, 176
in JFK-LBJ transition, 344, 399–400, 409, 413
LBJ's joint session speech and, 399–400
1964 State of the Union address and, 512, 544, 546, 550
resignation of, 589–90
in War on Poverty, 539–40, 544
South Carolina, 266
South Dakota, 88–9
Southern Caucus, xiv, 9, 444, 465, 561
Southern Christian Leadership Conference, 488
Southern Newspaper Publishers Association, 528
Soviet Union, xi, xvi, 219, 235–6, 343, 365, 440, 450, 600
Sputnik launched by, 66, 177
U-2 incident and, 89
U.S.'s wheat deal with, 397–9, 424–5, 501–2
Spalding, Charles, 229, 235, 374, 571
Spivack, Robert G., 96
Springer, Elizabeth B., 481, 557
Sputnik, 66, 172, 246
Staats, Elmer, 421
Standard-Times, 31
State Department, U.S., 170, 183, 195, 214, 240, 263, 276, 392, 402, 417, 424, 439, 480, 507, 583
appropriations bill and, 460–1
U.S.-Soviet wheat deal and, 414–16
State of the Union address of 1964, 491, 544, 545–51, 552, 598
budget in, 512–13, 545, 549
civil rights in, 547
community action concept in, 546
foreign policy in, 548
LBJ's childhood poverty and, 546–7, 550–1
media reaction to, 548–50
poverty theme of, 546–7, 549
precedents of, 537–8
Republican reaction to, 548
RFK and, 571
Vietnam conflict in, 548
Steakly, Zollie, 154
Steele, John L., 15, 57–8, 193–4, 405
LBJ described by, 499–500
Stegall, Mildred, 367, 374, 403
Stehling, Arthur, 543
Steven, William P., 527
Stevenson, Adlai E., 7–8, 10, 14, 26, 31, 53, 59, 67, 70, 93, 100, 101–2, 107, 111, 117, 205, 376, 410, 413, 414
Stevenson, Coke, 55
stock market crash of 1929, 27
Stokes, Thomas L., 457

Stone, Harlan, 324
Stoughton, Cecil, 322, 333, 334–5
Strategic Air Command, 223, 439, 528–9
Students Speak for Civil Rights, 565
Sukarno, Achmed, 582–3
Supreme Court, U.S., 56, 98, 153–4, 443, 444
   Roosevelt's court-packing scheme and,
    120–1, 452–3
Sutton, Billy, 43
Swindal, Jim, 323, 331, 354, 360, 361, 386
Symington, Stuart, 10, 14, 26, 53, 59, 70, 79,
   84, 92, 93, 95, 96, 102, 107, 118, 122,
   131, 135

Taft, Robert A., 15, 453
Taft, William Howard, 437
Taft-Hartley Act, 29
Talmadge, Herman, 431, 562, 568
tax cut bill, 422–3, 432, 460, 538, 540, 545–6,
   561, 594
   amendments to, 482–3, 553–6
   Byrd and, 346, 347, 393–4, 395, 397, 455,
    464–5, 484, 498–9, 552, 555–7
   Majority Report on, 556–7
   Senate passage of, 556–7
   stalemate on, 462, 465, 475–6, 478, 480–3
Taylor, Antonio, 263
Taylor, Hobart, 78, 263–4
Taylor, Maxwell, 212, 402
Taylor, Zachary, 8n, 113
television, 49, 378–80
   JFK assassination on, xi–xii, 341–3
   JFK's funeral on, 386
   LBJ's joint session address on, 425–6
   Oswald's death covered by, 386–7
Tennessee, 155
Territo, Dorothy, 367
Texas, 126, 207, 400, 440–1
   Democratic Party of, 303
   discharge petition votes of, 493–4
   Kennedy staff's hatred of, 410
   in LBJ's southern campaign tour, 149–50
   LBJ's waning influence in, 268–71
   1960 vote in, 150–5
   1964 election and, 265–6, 268–73
   two-office problem of, 54–5
Texas Broadcasting Company, 521
Texas Cattle Kingdom, 17
Texas National Bank, 524
Texas Observer, 151
Texas State Board of Insurance, 531
Thimmesch, Nick, 66, 242
Thomas, Albert, 302, 303, 322–3, 324, 332,
   494, 498, 524–7
Thomas, Donald, 56, 531
Thomas, Evan, 234, 236, 239, 242, 291, 374,
   574, 585
Thomas, George, 189, 331
Thompson, Llewellyn, 219–20

Thornberry, Homer, 120, 127, 316–17, 319,
   321–2, 323, 332, 362, 405, 494
Thurmond, Strom, 431, 459
Tierney, Gene, 28
Tilden, Samuel J., 444
Time, 15, 23, 24, 52, 53, 54, 57, 71, 115, 184,
   193, 201, 226, 228, 404–5, 424, 426,
   436, 475, 505, 510, 518, 519, 549, 597
Times (London), 387
Timmons, Bascom, 528–30
Tippit, J. D., 356, 391
Tippit, Marie, 392
Today, 205
Tower, John, 268
Travell, Janet, 46–7, 51, 370
Treasury Department, U.S., 480, 554
Trinity River Navigation Project, 529–30
Trujillo, Rafael, 585
Truman, Bess, 283
Truman, Harry S., 16, 49, 69, 94, 114, 115,
   285, 292, 323, 345, 350, 351, 368,
   371–2, 376, 378, 391, 397, 400, 408,
   435, 438–9, 457, 471
   Fair Deal program of, 453, 537
   presidential transition of, 340–1
   Rowe's Armageddon memo to, 13–14
   southern conservative coalition and, 453–4
   swearing-in of, 340–1
   Vaughan scandal and, 282–3
Tuchman, Barbara, 213
Turkey, 216–20
Turner, Bessie, 565
Turnure, Pamela, 333, 357
TVA, 469
Twelfth Amendment, 161n
Twentieth Amendment, 349
Twenty-fifth Amendment, 161n
Tyler, Carole, 289–90, 291, 297
Tyler, John, 114, 350

U-2 shootdown incident, 89
Udall, Stewart, 344, 397, 567, 593
United Automobile Workers (UAW), 77, 136,
   140, 263, 407, 496
United Mine Workers, 101
United Nations, 231, 413, 414
United Press International, 268, 334, 558–9
United States Steel Corporation, 205
United Steelworkers of America, 142, 407,
   493, 496
Unruh, Jesse, 415
Urban Affairs Department, U.S., 455
USIA, 402
U.S. News & World Report, 155, 228, 269
Utah, 59, 297

Valenti, Jack, 322, 391, 392, 401, 418, 478,
   520, 524–5, 527, 543, 594

JFK assassination and, 360–3, 365, 367, 370, 371
LBJ-Byrd meeting described by, 476–7
LBJ's demeanor described by, 331–2, 336, 362–3
at state governors conference, 420–1
Valeo, Francis R., 533
Van Buren, Martin, 113, 359
vanden Heuvel, William, 244, 572, 575–6, 579
Vanderbilt, Jeanne Murray, 226
Van Kirk, Burkett, 308, 310, 318
Vantage Point, The (Johnson), 477
Vatican, 231
Vaughan, Harry, 282–3
Vend, 277, 280
Vidal, Gore, 249–50
Viet Cong, 401, 403, 534
Vietnam, Democratic Republic of (North Vietnam), 401, 403, 533
Vietnam, Republic of (South Vietnam), 402, 533
Vietnam War, xix, 604–5
    Krulak commission report on, 533–4, 535
    LBJ's hardening view of, 532–3
    1964 election and, 535–6
    OPLAN 34–A and, 403, 533
    in State of the Union address, 548
    troop replacement policy for, 534–5
    U.S. aims in, 401–3
Virginia, 145–6, 155, 462, 467, 474
"Viva Kennedy" committees, 151, 153
Voting Rights Act of 1965, 569, 604

Waco News-Tribune, 278
Wagner, Robert F., 86, 99, 100, 125
Wagner Act of 1935, 469
Waldron, Bob, 106
Wallace, George, 266
Wallace, Henry A., 162
Wall Street Journal, 94, 530
Walsh, David, 36–7
Walton, William, 188–9, 409–10
War on Poverty, xix, 538–45, 601
    announcement of, xvii–xviii
    budget issue in, 540–1
    Heller's role in, 538–41, 543
    LBJ's childhood poverty and, 542–3
    NYA model for, 541, 546
    provenance of, 544–5
    in State of the Union address, 546–7
Warren, Earl, 323, 378, 383, 443–6, 451
Warren, Nina Elisbeth Palmquist, 378
Warren Commission, 440–51
    Congress and, 440–1, 450–1
    creation of, 442, 450–1
    FBI and, 392, 441–2
    fear of conspiracy and, 440–1, 446
    media reaction to, 449–50

members of, 442–3, 445–9
purpose of, 442
report of, 450, 574–5, 600
Washington, George, 202, 467, 537
Washington Afro-American, 255
Washington Evening Star, 78–9, 147
Washington Monument, 439
Washington National Cathedral, 263
Washington Post, 9, 56, 77, 117, 135, 256, 276–7, 282, 288, 291, 380, 388, 403, 433, 436, 441–2, 461, 463, 472, 496, 548, 549, 553, 557, 582
Washington Star, 56, 142, 495
Washington State, 59, 105, 107
Washington State Democratic Convention of 1960, 89
Webb, James E., 173, 205, 263–4, 559–60
Wechsler, James, 591
Weisl, Edwin, 81, 82, 408, 409
West, J. B., 500–1
West, Wesley, 299
Westinghouse Broadcasting, 334
West Virginia, 13, 57, 84–6, 107, 116, 144
Wheeler, Keith, 296–7, 308–9, 318
White, Byron "Whizzer," 236–7
White, Lee, 177, 181, 262–3
White, Theodore H., 49, 71–2, 84–5, 86, 90–1, 129, 144, 156, 177, 363, 415, 583, 587
White Stars club, 159
Whittington, Gerri, 491, 505, 536–7
Why England Slept (Kennedy), 36
Wickenden, Elizabeth, 202, 545
Wicker, Tom, 181, 343, 354, 357, 402, 433, 515, 516–19, 595–6, 604
Wiesner, Jerome B., 173
Wiley, Mary Margaret, 80, 106
Wilkins, Roy, 78, 466, 487–91
Williams, G. Mennen "Soapy," 53, 79, 122, 137, 142, 490
Williams, John J., 282–9, 292–4, 476–7, 552, 604
Williamson, Hugh, 161
Willkie, Wendell, 62
Wilson, Henry, 484, 486
Wilson, Will, 154
Wilson, Woodrow, 435, 537, 542
Wirtz, Willard, 101, 376, 397, 400, 422, 512
Wisconsin, 59, 84, 107, 140
Wofford, Harris, 235–6
Wolfe, Herbert E., 251–2
Woodcock, Leonard, 136
Woods, Howard B., 79–80, 491
World War I, 213, 445
World War II, 85, 453
    JFK in, 28, 37–8
    LBJ in, 314
Worley, Ann, 121
Worley, Gene, 121

Wortham, Gus, 524–7
Wright, James C., 83, 104–5, 206
Wright, Sammy, 429
Wright, Zephyr, 429, 489
Wyoming, 59, 73, 83, 93, 107, 246

Yale Law Journal, 236
Yalta Conference (1945), 240
Yarborough, Ralph W., 310, 313, 400
    Connally's feud with, 272, 301, 307, 309

    Kennedy's LBJ ranch visit and,
      299–303, 307
Young, Stephen M., 296
Young, Whitney, 407–8, 488, 490–1
Youngblood, Rufus W., 301, 310,
    313–17, 320–4, 326, 361, 365–6,
    370, 371
Youth Conservation Corps, 455

Zapruder, Abraham, 599

A Note About the Author

For his biographies of Robert Moses and Lyndon Johnson, Robert A. Caro has twice won the Pulitzer Prize for Biography, has twice won the National Book Critics Circle Award for Best nonfiction book of the year, and has also won virtually every other major literary honor, including the National Book Award, the Gold Medal in Biography from the American Academy of Arts and Letters, and the Francis Parkman Prize, awarded by the Society of American Historians to the book that best "exemplifies the union of the historian and the artist." In 2010, he received the National Humanities Medal from President Obama.

To create his first book, *The Power Broker: Robert Moses and the Fall of New York,* Caro spent seven years tracing and talking with hundreds of men and women who worked with, for, or against Robert Moses, including a score of his top aides. He examined mountains of files never opened to the public. Everywhere acclaimed as a modern classic, *The Power Broker* was chosen by the Modern Library as one of the hundred greatest nonfiction books of the twentieth century. It is, according to David Halberstam, "Surely the greatest book ever written about a city." And *The New York Times Book Review* said: "In the future, the scholar who writes the history of American cities in the twentieth century will doubtless begin with this extraordinary effort."

To research *The Years of Lyndon Johnson,* Caro and his wife, Ina, moved from his native New York City to the Texas Hill Country and then to Washington, D.C., to live in the locales in which Johnson grew up and in which he built, while still young, his first political machine. Caro has spent years examining documents at the Johnson Library in Austin and interviewing men and women connected with Johnson's life, many of whom had never before been interviewed. The first volume of *The Years of Lyndon Johnson, The Path to Power,* was cited by *The Washington Post* as "proof that we live in a great age of biography . . . [a book] of radiant excellence . . . Caro's evocation of the Texas Hill Country, his elaboration of Johnson's unsleeping ambition, his understanding of how politics actually work, are—let it be said flat-out—at the summit of American historical writing." Professor Henry F. Graff of Columbia University called the second volume, *Means of Ascent,* "brilliant. No brief review does justice to the drama of the story Caro is telling, which is nothing less than how present-day politics was born." And the London *Times* hailed volume three, *Master of the Senate,* as "a masterpiece . . . Robert Caro has written one of the truly great political biographies of the modern age."

"Caro has a unique place among American political biographers," according to *The Boston Globe.* "He has become, in many ways, the standard by which his fellows are measured." And Nicholas von Hoffman wrote: "Caro has changed the art of political biography."

Caro graduated from Princeton University and later became a Nieman Fellow at Harvard University. He lives in New York City with his wife, Ina, an historian and writer.

A Note on the Type

The text of this book was set in a typeface called Times New Roman designed by Stanley Morison for *The Times* (London), and introduced by that newspaper in 1932.

Among typographers and designers of the twentieth century, Stanley Morison was a strong forming influence, as typographical adviser to the Monotype Corporation of London, as a director of two distinguished English publishing houses, and as a writer of sensibility, erudition, and keen practical sense.

In 1930 Morison wrote: "Type design moves at the pace of the most conservative reader. The good type-designer therefore realizes that, for a new fount to be successful, it has to be so good that only very few recognize its novelty. If readers do not notice the consummate reticence and rare discipline of a new type, it is probably a good letter." It is now generally recognized that in the creation of Times Roman, Morison successfully met the qualifications of his theoretical doctrine.

Composed by North Market Street Graphics, Lancaster, Pennsylvania
Printed and bound by Berryville Graphics, Berryville, Virginia
Typography and binding design by Virginia Tan and Cassandra Pappas

PHOTOGRAPHIC CREDITS

Insert I follows page 202; Insert II follows page 426

Associated Press: I 5 bottom, II 2 bottom far left, II 8
© Bettmann/Corbis: II 12
©John Bryson/Sygma/Corbis: I 5 top
Hulton Archive/Getty Images: II 6 bottom
Lyndon Baines Johnson Library and Museum: I 4 top; I 8 bottom; I 9; II 1 bottom; II 3 bottom; II 4 top; Bill Berger, *Hondo Anvil Herald,* I 8 top; Jeff Broody, I 1 top; *Dallas Times-Herald,* I 11; Lawrence Krebs, I 1 bottom; R. L. Knudsen, I 14 top; Dan Lewis, II 4 bottom; Frank Muto, I 10, I 13 bottom; Yoichi Okamoto II 9, II 13, II 14, II 16; Abbie Rowe, I 14 bottom; Cecil Stoughton, II 1 top, II 5, II 6 top, II 10 and 11, II 15; U.S. Army I 12, I 13 top
John F. Kennedy Presidential Library and Museum, Boston: I 2; © *Look/* Douglas Jones, I 3 bottom; Abbie Rowe, White House, II 7; Cecil Stoughton, White House, I 16, II 3 top; © John Vachon, *Look* magazine, I 3 top
Jacques Lowe: I 4 bottom, I 6 and 7, I 15